NEW TESTAMENT EPISTLES

ROMANS

A CRITICAL AND EXEGETICAL COMMENTARY

_____ *by* _____

GARETH L. REESE

HEAD OF NEW TESTAMENT DEPARTMENT
CENTRAL CHRISTIAN COLLEGE OF THE BIBLE
MOBERLY, MISSOURI

Scripture Exposition Books, LLC
803 McKINSEY PLACE
MOBERLY, MISSOURI
65270

Acknowledgments

A list of the authors and publishers who have given permission for their works to be quoted is found at the end of this volume immediately following the pages of "Selected Bibliography."

The Scripture quotations contained herein, unless otherwise noted, are from the New American Standard Bible, copyrighted 1960, 1962, 1963, 1971, 1972, 1975, 1977, 1995 by the Lockman Foundation. Used by permission.

Suggested Cataloging Data

Reese, Gareth L., 1932-
    New Testament Epistles : Romans. A critical and exegetical commentary on Paul's epistle / by Gareth L. Reese.

    [vi], lxxxii, 828 p. : 27 cm.
    Spine Title: Romans.
    Bibliography: p. [771]-791.
    Includes index.
    ISBN 0-971-765200

    1. Bible. N.T. Romans - Commentaries. I. Title. II. Title: Romans.

BS2665.3.R42 1996   89-133036

PREFACE

What? Another commentary on Romans? What need is there to restate ideas that have appeared in print for 300 years or more? How will Christian unity be encouraged or fostered by a book that simply parrots the peculiar party emphases often heard in the religious circle in which the author moves?

The first question implies that there has been a sufficient number of commentaries on Romans already written, so that surely there is nothing new or refreshing to be gleaned from Paul's letter by any modern exegete.

The second question reflects the well-known fact that for many years most Protestant commentaries on Romans have re-expressed either Luther's or Calvin's ideas. However, in the past few decades, several scholars have observed that the old "faith" vs. "meritorious works" explanations offered for many verses since the time of the Reformers may in fact be a faulty way of presenting what Paul actually wrote. During these same recent decades, a lively debate has been carried on concerning the nature of 1st century "Judaism" and especially concerning Paul's relationship with the Judaism of his day.

The third question rightly recognizes that attempting to make what the Bible says match and teach peculiar party dogmas has been and continues to be one of the greatest hindrances to Christian unity. It also assumes that the old cliche, "That is just *your* way of interpreting it!" *is* true. After all, we tend to think everyone indulges in private interpretations at least *some* of the time.

Perhaps the need for another commentary on Romans can be appreciated when consideration is given to the following matters. For over a hundred years, Moses Lard's *Commentary on Paul's Letter to the Romans* has been about the only scholarly work on the letter produced in the Restoration Movement (though several have been written on a level intended for use by Sunday School teachers). Lard was attempting to address the problems his generation faced as they struggled with Calvinism; also, he was writing for people whose grammar school education normally included a study of Latin, as well as Greek and Hebrew in the colleges, so his work makes abundant use of words in these languages. These two things cause his book to be most difficult for present-day readers to understand. Our generation still faces a huge task of evaluating certain favorite and oft-propagated Calvinistic themes; these still need to be scrutinized in the light of what Romans says. In addition, certain new theologies (such as Neo-orthodoxy and Neo-liberalism) with their corresponding new ways of interpreting Scripture are faced by the modern Bible student who works his way through current commentaries. Not only does the student need to be enabled to recognize these theologies when he meets them, he needs to be informed where, in several instances, these are shown to be false by Romans. Certainly, the correctives found in Romans need to be brought to bear to aid the direction theology goes in the 21st century, or the next generation may find itself without any clear word from the Lord.

A brief explanation needs be given regarding the format followed by this commentary. The comments are based on the New American Standard Bible. This version has been chosen since it is the version used in most of the colleges and seminaries.

Experience with the first printing of this commentary has shown it to be used not only as a college textbook, but also by laymen who are seeking a helpful commentary. It is difficult to write for these two very different audiences at the same time. In an effort to meet the needs of both, a particular plan has been followed. To keep the overall length of the book within reasonable limits, every effort has been made to limit comments to one page per verse.

Those *comments* offered on the phrases of Romans on the upper portion of each page are intended to be a rather brief and succinct explanation of what Paul wrote; these are aimed at the needs of both leader and layman alike. In order to get an idea of the message of Romans, it is suggested that the reader have an open Bible handy, and read from it the paragraph or chapter about to be studied before reading the comments found on the upper portion of these pages.

The *Introductory Studies* contain necessary information for both the scholar and the Sunday School student/teacher; it is therefore suggested that these be thoughtfully studied twice, once before reading any of the comments offered for the verses Paul wrote, and again after all the comments on the whole epistle have been finished.

It is in the *footnotes* and *Special Studies* where matters of special interest to those wanting a detailed and thorough treatment are addressed. The reader may take one of two approaches to these footnotes: they may be read at the same time the comments are read, or they may be saved for a second, in-depth journey through the book. The *Special Studies*, each one of which takes up a topic vitally related to the overall understanding, not only of the message of Romans, but of New Testament theology as a whole, may be studied independently, or in conjunction with the in-depth journey through the book.

A few aids requested by students have also been included. (1) Students who have worked through the footnotes have found it difficult to locate those sources that are indicated by *op. cit.* and *ibid.* To make the sources of quotations easier to find, we have given the full bibliographic information the first time any work is quoted, whether in the Introductory Studies, or in comments on the text, or in the Special Studies. Thereafter when the same work is quoted, enough of the title is given so that if need be, it may be quickly located by referring to the relevant bibliography, whether it be the one included at the end of the Special Study, or the one found at the close of the book. (2) There are times the student wishes to examine the possible meaning of but one verse. To aid quick location of comments on any verse, the upper right-hand corner of each page tells which verse is covered on that page. (3) An exhaustive index has been provided at the end of the book. References to comments are given by page number; references to information in footnotes are given by page number followed by the letter "n" (e.g., 24n means the topic is found in a footnote on page 24). To facilitate locating information to which the index points, the upper left-hand corner of each page includes the page number.

Preface, continued

As with any book written by men, so, too, it should be with this one: the careful Bible student filters everything he hears or reads through the Word of God. If it matches the Word, then it may be accepted. If it does not match what God has said in the written Word, then it is to be rejected. This commentator encourages his readers to interact with what is herein presented. Where the reader finds what seem to be obvious mistakes, he/she is encouraged to communicate with the author so that later editions may be corrected. Working together in this way, we can offer to the next generation a tool that will help them appreciate the lasting value of the epistle to the Romans.

Preface to the 2012 Printing

Earlier printings of this commentary were produced before the publication of the contents of the Dead Sea Scroll known as 4QMMT. The sigla 4Q means the manuscript fragments were found in cave 4 and Qumran. MMT is the scholarly abbreviation of the Hebrew words assigned as a title to the scroll; this title that may be translated "some significant works of Law." The publication of the contents of this scroll has illumined for us the expression "works of the Law" found in Romans 3:20,28 and also in Galatians 2:16 and 3:2. The Dead Sea Scroll shows the expression signified man-made religious rules based on passages in the Law. Such rules are similar to those condemned by Jesus when He spoke of the "traditions of the elders" which, when observed, said He, led people to violate the Law of Moses (Matthew 15:3-9; Mark 7:1-9). In the light of this new information from the Scrolls, the comments offered on certain verses – especially those in Romans where "works" are contrasted with the faith that saves – have been rewritten to reflect the now obvious fact that "works of the Law" refer to such religious rules as long have been known as the traditions of the elders, and not to obedience to anything God has commanded. The result of this is that it is easy to see that faith is to be defined as habitually doing what God commands.

TABLE OF CONTENTS

INTRODUCTORY STUDIES

COMMENTARY ON THE EPISTLE TO THE ROMANS

SPECIAL STUDIES

INTRODUCTORY STUDIES TO ROMANS

Romans – what a beautiful and influential letter! It, letters like it, and the four Gospels were read aloud in the public worship service beginning shortly after they were written; this was one way Christians could continue steadfastly in the apostles' doctrine, and the practice continued for several hundred years in all the churches. Early in the history of the canon, when collections of such New Testament writings began to be included in single volumes (something made possible for the first time by the invention of the codex style of book binding), Paul's letter to the Romans was considered to be so important it was given first place in the volume that contained a collection of his letters. For example, in the Chester Beatty Papyri (a 3rd century AD collection of manuscripts, which includes a three-volume edition of New Testament Scriptures[1]), Romans stands at the head of the Pauline Epistles. Since it was not the first to be written, its position may be taken as testimony of a growing awareness in the churches of its cardinal importance.

No book or section of Scripture has played a more important part in the history of the church and in the lives of some of its most notable leaders than Paul's epistle to the Romans. Augustine,[2] Luther,[3] Wesley,[4] Bunyan,[5] and Barth,[6] are just some of the names that come immediately to mind. No Christian can read it for the first time without feeling

---

[1] Altogether there are eleven papyrus codices in the Chester Beatty collection. They contain parts of nine Old Testament books, fifteen New Testament books, and two non-canonical books. P[45] has portions of the four Gospels and Acts. P[46] is a remarkable collection of Paul's letters to churches – Romans, Hebrews, 1 and 2 Corinthians, Ephesians, Galatians, Philippians, Colossians, 1 and 2 Thessalonians. P[47] consists of ten leaves from the middle section of Revelation. P[46] has in recent times been given a late 1st or early 2nd century date. Y.K. Kim, "Palaeographical Dating of P[46] to the Later First Century," *Biblica* 69:2 [1988], p.248-257.

[2] In AD 386, in Milan, Italy, it was an almost chance reading of Romans 13:13,14 that led Augustine to decide to break with his immoral and un-Godly past way of life. He embraced Christianity, and then became such an influential leader and thinker that his writings would significantly impact church history and doctrine for over 1000 years (through the medium of the Roman Catholic Church, in which much of what Augustine taught became dogma).

[3] In AD 1515, Martin Luther, professor of theology at the University of Wittenberg, began to teach a course on Romans to his students. As he prepared his lectures, he became more and more aware of the Epistle's emphasis on the doctrine of justification by faith. The doctrine he found in Romans was different from the dogma he had learned in the Roman Church. His new discovery opened the meaning of other Scripture passages, whose import he had never seen before. Before long, he broke with Rome and started the Protestant Reformation. For nearly 500 years, church history and doctrinal studies have felt again and again the effect of the influence of the Epistle to the Romans on one man's life.

[4] In 1738, John Wesley, back in England after a trip to America (during which he had an opportunity to witness firsthand the assurance of salvation that Moravian Brethren professed), still unsure of how a man comes to a right relationship with God, one that will inspire assurance and confidence, heard a man reading from the Preface of Luther's Commentary on Romans. He tells us that he felt his heart "strangely warmed"; he had come to understand what faith in Christ can mean in a man's life. It was this hearing of Romans that launched the Evangelical Revival of the 18th Century, and, among others, resulted in the beginnings of the Methodist Church.

that he has been introduced to heights and depths he never knew before.

> There is no telling what may happen when people begin to study the Epistle to the Romans. What happened to Augustine, Luther, Wesley, and Barth launched great spiritual movements which have left their mark in world history. But similar things have happened, much more frequently, to very ordinary people as the words of this Epistle came home to them with power. So, let those who have read thus far be prepared for the consequences of reading further: you have been warned![7]

We are dealing with profound topics in Romans, so the reader must be prepared to do some deep thinking. Some of the hardest questions that thinking men ask are, "Who am I? Where did I come from? Why am I here? Where am I going?" It is questions like these, the answers to which help mold and define a man's world view, that one finds expounded in the pages of Romans. With deftness and sureness, Paul covers such things as the result of Adam's sin on the rest of God's creation, the providence of God, the predestination of men and things, the place of the Jews, and the matter of how God saves men. All of these are high and profound subjects. What a boon to the man who, because of a careful study of Romans, comes to think God's thoughts after Him.

The Need and Place of Special Introductory Studies

In the years since the dawn of the age of reason, those matters usually designated as "Introductory Studies"[8] have received an increasing amount of time and effort. The use of

---

[5] It was a reading of Romans that led to the conversion of John Bunyan (1628-1688). Before his conversion he served an apprenticeship as a tinker (i.e., a mender of pots and pans), spent time in the military during the English Civil War, and married a Puritan wife. About 1653, he joined the Puritan movement and became one of its leaders. In Bedford, Bunyan began to preach, and soon was one of the most popular preachers of the area. After the Restoration (the re-establishment of the Monarchy in England under Charles II and James II), it was unlawful to conduct worship services except in accordance with the Established Church. Bunyan continued his preaching for the Puritans, and was imprisoned in the Bedford county jail for a period of 12 years. During his imprisonment, his library consisted of the Bible and Foxes' *Book of Martyrs*. It was during his imprisonment that he wrote *Grace Abounding to the Chief of Sinners* (1666). Imprisoned a second time in 1675, he wrote *The Pilgrim's Progress*.

[6] Religious, or theological, liberalism had gained a near stranglehold on theology as the 20th century dawned. In 1918, Karl Barth, a Swiss preacher, published a brief commentary on the Epistle to the Romans. In the preface of that book, he admitted that his study of Romans had been a joyful discovery. Much of what he had learned from liberal theologians did not match what he experienced as he read Romans. His brief commentary proved to be the death of old liberalism, and the beginnings of a theological movement known today as Neo-orthodoxy. While it rightly has been said that Barth's theology was neither "new" nor was it "orthodox," it is still a fact of history that a study of Romans led this man to make an impact on the world, the extent of which has not yet been fully felt in the churches and seminaries.

[7] F.F. Bruce, *The Epistle of Paul to the Romans* (Grand Rapids: Wm. B. Eerdmans Publishing Co., 1963), p.60.

[8] It has become rather accepted among Bible students to categorize introductory studies under two headings: (1) general introduction, which deals with canon, text, inspiration, and versions; and (2) spe-

reason and the scientific method as tools by which men can expand their knowledge and understanding of any given subject is not to be deplored. Still, in the early days of such investigation, not every Bible student was ready to permit the same methods (i.e., textual criticism, historical criticism, etc.) to be used in the study of the Scriptures as were used in the study of other literature. However, men who hold the Bible dear have nothing to fear from the use of those tools even when it comes to the study of the Bible, unless the user of the tools starts from an a priori conviction[9] of what will be the result of the investigation, or unless the user attempts to alter or doctor the evidence to make it fit or "prove" his predetermined understanding of the material he is investigating. It probably can be said that there was no need to spend a great amount of time on introductory studies concerning Romans until some scholars came along who did exactly what was just objected to as an improper use or application of the scientific method.[10] Once some faulty or questionable conclusions about Romans had been published in the name of scholarship, it became necessary for others to "run similar experiments" in order to correct what was deemed to be faulty or incorrect in the earlier studies. As a result, the number of pages spent in introductory studies (at least in the commentaries aimed at scholarly audiences) has tended to increase significantly.[11]

In accordance with the stated aims of this present work on Romans, it has seemed best simply to call attention to some of the earlier studies and their conclusions, in order that the reader may have a beginning awareness of some of what is at issue. It does not seem needful to repeat all the detailed arguments that proponents and opponents of various hypotheses have marshaled. Readers whose interest is sufficiently stirred can easily enough avail themselves of the scholars' own works.

---

cial introduction, which deals with authorship, date of writing, place of writing, destination, occasion, and purpose of writing.

[9] An example of such an a priori conviction would be the belief that there is no supernatural, or the assumption that we live in a purely mechanistic universe. Such presuppositions will lead to ignoring any evidence (should there be any found) that might suggest the contrary. Using the scientific method, one might take either of these suppositions as a hypothesis, and then examine the evidence for or against it. But to assume such a position as a given, as an absolute, is sure to prejudice the findings of any subsequent 'investigation.'

[10] Some scholars had begun with naturalistic presuppositions, used only the evidence that would tend to prove their starting point, and then published 'assured conclusions' that were inimical to the faith once for all delivered to the saints. Other scholars took the philosophy that was currently popular as their starting point, and tried to alter or doctor the Bible 'evidence' to show that the Bible was in agreement with the prevailing philosophy. This was done usually with good intentions – namely, to save some of the Bible's 'enduring values' for the present generation. But over time, the results of such doctoring of the evidence has led to less faith rather than to an abiding or growing faith.

[11] The subscription found in the KJV ("Written to the Romans from Corinth, and sent by Phoebe, servant of the church at Cenchrea") probably represents an early attempt at giving a brief introduction to this letter. How different from the twelve to over ninety page (in small type) treatments of these matters in 19th and 20th century works on Romans.

One of the time-honored scientific methods of Bible study is called the grammatical-historical method. Its fundamental premise is this: if one pays careful attention to the words of Scripture themselves, and if one can reconstruct the historical situation out of which and to which the particular Scripture is addressed, he has gone a long way both toward being able to understand what God has said and also toward being able to make intelligent and relevant applications of what he finds in Scripture.

Paying careful attention to the topics covered in the introductory studies we are about to undertake will prove helpful, especially when it comes to an attempt to reconstruct the historical situation. To illustrate what we must do as we attempt to reconstruct the historical background, one might compare the reading of the letter to the Romans with listening to one side of a telephone conversation. From past personal experience or through information learned from others, you may know a little about the person on the other end of the line. You cannot hear what the person on the other end of the line is saying, but you can arrive at a pretty close approximation by listening carefully to what you can hear at this end. Likewise, from sources outside of Romans we may learn a little about the people addressed, but it is mainly from the letter we are studying that we must attempt to deduce the situation which prompted the letter and to which it was addressed.

Historical Allusions

We determine such things as author, time, and place of writing, the ones to whom the letter is addressed, and the reason for the letter, mainly by "listening" very carefully to what the letter itself says, and then secondarily, by comparing what is learned from the letter itself with the historical record found in the Book of Acts.

As they write letters to friends and loved ones, people often include references to what they have been doing or thinking, or what is happening around them, or what their immediate plans for the future are. Such historical allusions are exactly what we must look for in Romans. Since it was the custom of the ancients to bunch most such historical allusions either at the beginning of their letters and/or at the close, we shall pay special attention to these portions of Romans to see what can be learned.

As we begin reading at Romans 1:1, we find the name "Paul," and the words "apostle" and "Gentiles" connected with it. These are marks which help identify the writer of this letter. We find the name "Christ Jesus," whom we are told was "born of a descendant of David according to the flesh" and who also has been "declared *to be* the Son of God ... by the resurrection from the dead." These statements might be looked on as time notes, helping us to locate approximately what time in history this letter was written. Romans 1:5 tells what the writer has been doing recently: he has been trying to "bring about the obedience of faith among all the Gentiles." Verses 6-7 tell us something about the potential readers of this letter: they are "saints" (verse 7) living in the Gentile world (verse 5) at Rome (verses 7, 15). A comparison with other letters from the 1st century after the incarnation and resurrection of Jesus shows us that the introduction to Romans, which is seven verses long, is much more detailed than most introductions were. We wonder why. A comparison between the present letter and some others written by "Paul" indicate another remarkable difference: all the other letters[12] were addressed to "churches" in this or that city or province; we wonder what, if any, is the significance of the absence of the word "church" in this address.

Beginning at Romans 1:8, following the customary 1st century letter style, is a statement of thanksgiving to deity. In these thanksgivings there was usually specified (if possible) something the writer thought praiseworthy about the readers. In this letter, the one thing the writer thanks God for is that the "faith" of the readers was "being proclaimed throughout the whole world." We ponder over the possible reason why this particular feature should be emphasized. Then the writer tells us about one of the petitions that is regularly included in his own prayer life: it involves a long-standing desire to visit the readers (a desire that has heretofore been hindered from being realized) in order that he may preach the gospel to them "also who are in Rome." Included, too, is a desire to impart to them "some spiritual gift" so that they "may be established." Just what does this tell us about the readers? What is a "spiritual gift"? In what sense were they not already "established"? The reason the writer makes all this a matter of prayer is that he is aware that his travels to preach are ordered by "the will of God." The reason why he wants to preach the gospel is that "it is the power of God for salvation to everyone who believes"; in it is revealed the righteousness of God.

Examining the first seventeen verses of chapter 1, we find the word "gospel" used four times; "Gentile" (or "Greeks") used four times; "faith" (or "belief") used seven times; and "Jesus Christ" (or "Son") used eight times. Does such an emphasis already prepare us for the theme that is uppermost in the writer's mind, and about which he intends to expand?

Moving to the closing paragraphs of the letter, we continue our search for further clues to help us determine all we can about the author, date, destination, purpose, and occasion which led to the writing of this letter. In Romans 15:14-21, we learn that some of the major ideas included in the letter are already known to the readers; in these matters, this letter is just a reminder, but a reminder perfectly in harmony with the writer's commission to be a minister to the Gentiles. Verses 19-20 tell us about the writer's own recently completed activities: in the areas between Jerusalem and Illyricum he has fully preached the gospel, making it his aim especially to see to it that those areas unevangelized by others have an opportunity to hear and obey the gospel. This new-area evangelism is the reason he has been hindered from visiting the readers of this letter earlier (verse 22; cp. Romans 1:13); but now the needs for his special services in these eastern Mediterranean

---

[12] Cp. 1 Thessalonians 1:1; 2 Thessalonians 1:1; 2 Corinthians 1:2; 2 Corinthians 1:1; Galatians 1:2.

areas have been fulfilled and he is anticipating an evangelistic campaign in Spain (verse 24). His immediate plans therefore are to go to Jerusalem with an offering for the poor (verses 25-26), and then to stop and visit the readers during his trip from the east to Spain (verse 28). In fact, he hopes to be helped on his way to Spain by the readers (verse 24). Now that he has shared his plans and dreams, he asks for the prayers of the readers for both his visit to Judea and his coming visit to Rome (verses 30-32). He closes chapter 15 with a prayer (some have called it a benediction) for the readers, "Now the God of peace be with you all. Amen." Was this, at some time in the past, the end of the letter? If it was, from whence is our chapter 16? If it was not the original ending, how does one explain this "benediction" before the actual end of the letter?

Chapter 16 opens with an introduction of a Christian woman named Phoebe, and includes a request that the readers do what they can to assist her while she is present in their midst. Then in verses 3-15 we encounter an unexpectedly long list of people (some twenty-six named people, some Jewish and some Gentile), plus two additional "households" and also some "house-churches," to whom the writer sends personal greetings. How is it to be explained that a person who has never before been to a place (and 15:22-24 indicates the writer has not before visited where the readers live) would know that many people there? The mention of "all the churches of Christ" in 16:16, and the fact that a "report" of the obedience of the readers is common knowledge to all (verse 19), may help explain one of the reasons why this letter was written. Did the writer hope to prevent the readers from deviating from their past consistent course of obedience to Christ, because he feared that any such deviation could have disastrous consequences not only for the readers but for all the churches? Whether or not this is the reason for the warning, just who are the tendentious teachers whose negative influence might turn the readers away from obedience, and about whom Paul therefore warns the readers (verses 17-20)?

As we come toward the close of chapter 16, we observe that some English Bibles have the benediction ("The grace of our Lord Jesus be with you") only as a part of verse 20; others have it twice, at verses 20 and 24. Having observed in some of Paul's other letters that such a benediction is the last thing he writes, we wonder if Romans at one time ended either at verse 20 or 24.

Verses 21-23 tell us some things that we have not learned earlier in this search for historical allusions: where the writer is (he is staying with Gaius); who is with him (Timothy, Lucius, Jason, Sosipater, Erastus, and Quartus); and who (Tertius) has been privileged to do the actual writing as the letter was being dictated. Verses 25-27 form a closing doxology, but as we read it, we see it becomes rather long and involved, and in fact (the way it is translated in the NASB) seems to end without ever completing the thought. Is this not a surprising, and perhaps even disturbing, way for such a grand letter to come to a close?

From these few brief notes, one must attempt to reconstruct the historical background out of which and to which this letter was written. Most of the points that follow are conclusions drawn from the above allusions, plus other relevant material from Scripture and early Christian literature.

Authorship and Attestation

The question of authorship is of vital importance. If this letter was written by an apostle of Jesus Christ (and we remember that apostles were promised a special endowment of the Holy Spirit so that they would be guided into all the truth, John 16:13), then there is every likelihood that Romans is no less than an inspired word from God, and is therefore something that men may ignore only at their own risk and peril. On the other hand, if it is not a letter whose ultimate source can be traced to the revelation and inspiration of God Himself, then the letter perhaps can be safely ignored.

Authorship has to do with who wrote the letter. *Attestation* has to do with the evidence that can be appealed to in order to establish authorship. Such evidence can be both internal (within the letter itself) or external (anything outside the letter, whether elsewhere in the other books of the Bible, or in early Christian literature). In fact, the evidence found in early Christian literature is of different kinds: there are brief references to the letter (which show it was recognized as an authoritative word from God, but which do not identify who wrote it), and there are quotations from the letter (which actually name the human author of the quoted words).

From the letter itself to the Romans, we learn that the writer calls himself Paul (1:1), the apostle who has been commissioned by Jesus Christ to go to the Gentiles (1:1,5; 11:13; 15:15-20). In Acts 13-21, we have a record of Paul's evangelistic activities in the region between Jerusalem and Illyricum, so the statement in Romans 15:19 is in agreement with what we know about Paul from other sources. From Acts 24:17 we learn that on his last recorded trip to Jerusalem he came "to bring alms to my nation"; therefore, the statement about taking an offering to Jerusalem in Romans 15:25,26 is also in perfect harmony with what we know about Paul. There is nothing in the statements the writer makes about himself that would cause the slightest suspicion that it was anyone other than Paul who dictated the letter while Tertius wrote, and thus we can say that internal evidence points to Paul as the author of this letter.

The external evidence is in complete agreement with the internal. Clement of Rome (AD 96), Ignatius (AD 115), Polycarp (AD 115), and Justin Martyr (AD 150) each have six or more passages in his writings which are taken from Romans,[13] thereby showing the letter already existed, was familiar to the churches, and was valued as an authoritative

---

[13] I Clement 25 reads, "Casting off from us all unrighteousness and iniquity, covetousness, debates, malignities, deceits, whisperings, backbitings, hatred of God, pride, boasting, and vain-glory and ambition. For they that do such things are hateful to God: and not only they that do them, but they also who have pleasure in them." These words certainly are taken from Romans 1:29ff. Polycarp's letter to the Philippians has "and must all stand before the judgment seat of Christ, and everyone give an account of himself," which strongly suggests he alludes to Romans 14:10. Nine such passages reflecting Romans

word.[14]   Marcion (AD 140) is the oldest known reference where Paul is specifically called the author of Romans.[15]   After this date, the literature is full of passages where Romans is attributed to Paul.[16]

The evidence for the Pauline authorship of Romans is so strong that not even the hypercritical skeptics of the Tubingen school in Germany during the past century have questioned the authenticity and genuineness of Romans.[17]   When anyone picks up a copy of Romans, he can be confident he holds in his hands a genuine composition of the apostle Paul.

Place and Date of Writing

Three references in chapter 16 imply that Paul is in Corinth when he writes this letter to Rome.[18]   First, Cenchrea, the hometown of Phoebe, was the eastern seaport of Corinth. If it is assumed that Paul is in Corinth when he writes, then it would help explain how he knows about Phoebe and her intended visit to Rome. Second, Romans 16:23 indicates Paul is the guest of a man named Gaius; 1 Corinthians 1:14 shows that a man named Gaius, one of Paul's early converts in Achaia, called Corinth home.   If it is proper to affirm that

---

can be found in Clement, twelve in Ignatius, six in Polycarp, and seven in Justin Martyr, we are told by A.T. Robertson, "Romans, Epistle to the," in *A Dictionary of the Bible,* edited by James Hastings (New York: Charles Scribner's Sons, 1909), Vol.4, p.295.

[14] Three of the ancient heretical sects – Ebionites, Encratites, and Cerinthians – rejected the book, not because they denied Paul's authorship, but because they could not make its doctrines harmonize with their own peculiar teachings.

[15] See Tertullian, *Against Marcion*, V.15.

[16] A few examples will suffice. Irenaeus (AD 180), who quotes Romans over fifty times, in one place quotes Romans 1:1-4 after introducing the passage with these words, "This same thing Paul has explained, writing to the Romans ..." (*Against Heresies*, III.58). In *Instructor* I.6 and I.8, Clement of Alexandria (AD 190) writes "the apostle in the Epistle to the Romans ... says, 'I would have you wise toward good, but simple towards evil' [see Romans 16:19]", and "Behold therefore, saith Paul, the goodness and severity of God [cp. Romans 11:22]." In his *Miscellanies* III.12 is a statement taken from Romans 6:2, "In like manner writes Paul in the Epistle to the Romans, 'How shall we who have died to sin live any longer in it?'" Tertullian, *Against Praxeus*, 13, wrote, "But I will call Christ alone God as the same apostle [Paul] does; of whom Christ came, who is, he says, God over all, blessed forever." This can only come from Romans 9:5.

[17] It will be a matter of study in subsequent notes whether or not the letter as we now have it is substantially in the same form as originally dictated by Paul, or whether a few words here and there, or even a chapter or two, may not be original. Nevertheless, the Pauline authorship is granted to the overwhelming majority of the letter, even by those who question a few small parts.

[18] At a later time in these introductory studies, attention will be directed to the question of the integrity of chapter 16. If chapter 16 is not original to the epistle, then there is very little indication of the place of writing.

both verses refer to the same Gaius, then Corinth is the place of writing. Third, if the Erastus who joins in sending greetings to Paul's readers (Romans 16:23) may be identified with the Erastus who at a later date is connected with Corinth (2 Timothy 4:20), then we would have another bit of evidence pointing to Corinth as the place of writing.

At the time he writes the letter, Paul tells his readers (15:25,26) that he is about to depart for Jerusalem to deliver to the saints there the offering that was being collected and sent by the churches in Macedonia, Achaia, Asia, and Galatia. This offering was initiated and completed during Paul's third missionary journey. Each congregation selected men whom they trusted to carry their portion of the offering. Some of the men selected to serve in this capacity are named in Acts 20:4. A comparison of the names found in Romans 16:21 with those in Acts 20:4 suggests that, at the time Paul writes, the couriers already are beginning to assemble with Paul preparatory to their journey together to Jerusalem. The rather generally accepted chronology of the life of Paul dates the third missionary journey from AD 54-58. Remembering that it was in Greece, whose capital was Corinth, where Paul spent the three months immediately preceding this visit to Jerusalem (Acts 20:2,3), it is not unreasonable to deduce that his letter to Rome was composed during that three-month period. What "three months" these were can be determined within rather close limits. The Mediterranean was closed to sailing during the fall and winter on account of the prevailing stormy weather during those seasons. When Paul left Corinth, the winter was past, for he purposed to go by sea (Acts 20:3). Yet spring could not have been far advanced, for he hoped to be in Jerusalem by Pentecost (Acts 20:16). Putting all these bits of information together, we may conclude that the letter to Rome was written during the winter of AD 58.

Destination

The titles now given to the books of the New Testament are not part of the original text, but were first written on little tags that were attached to the scrolls by the churches which made collections of all the scrolls. These titles were already being added sometime before the middle of the 2nd century AD. The superscription "To the Romans" is not something Paul wrote, but rather reflects the understanding of the people who first attached these title tags. It is not possible, at this point in time, to determine whether those people relied on Romans 1:7,15 or whether they relied on tradition when the first title tag was composed and added.

There is a very weak bit of manuscript evidence, also reflected in one or two church fathers, that the words "in Rome" were at some time, by some one, omitted at both verses 7 and 15. Codex Boernerianus (G), a 9th century bilingual manuscript (Greek with inter-linear Latin), instead of "in Rome" reads "in love" at verse 7, while it has no words at all in verse 15 where other manuscripts have "in Rome." One cursive manuscript (47) has a marginal note that "some one" (apparently an ancient commentator) "makes no mention of the words 'in Rome' either in the interpretation or in the text." Minuscule manuscripts 1739 (10th century) and 1908 (11th century) have marginal readings that omit "in Rome" at verse 7, but not at verse 15. Manuscripts that lacked "in Rome" are much older than the 9th century, however. The Latin in Codex G is a copy of the old Latin version (2nd century). Origen (c. AD 250) also knew of the letter with "in Rome" missing. Ambrosiaster (4th century) worked with manuscripts that did not have "in Rome" in them. In the text he made, he just left a blank space here, apparently intending to fill the words in later, but for some reason never did.[19]

An Ephesian (rather than Roman) destination for at least a portion of what we call Romans has been proposed by T.W. Manson.[20] One very old manuscript, the Chester Beatty Papyrus (P[46]), has no chapter 16, but does have the doxology (16:25-27) at the close of chapter 15. This feature, plus the absence of the words "in Rome" in the few sources noted above, led Manson to this hypothesis: Romans as it appears in the Chester Beatty Papyrus reflects the letter as Paul originally wrote it to Rome. Manson then conjectures that Paul, at a later time, sent a copy of the letter, minus the words "in Rome" but with the addition of the greetings in chapter 16, to the church at Ephesus. This would mean that the people greeted in chapter 16 lived in Ephesus rather than in Rome. Not many scholars have followed Manson's lead. Even if we were to deny the integrity[21] of chapter 16, we would still have chapters 1-15 destined for the saints in Rome.

Christians in Rome

To know as much as we can learn about the recipients of this letter will contribute toward a better understanding of what Paul says to them. Paul's language in Romans 1:7,8, 12:5, and 16:19 suggests the readers are already Christians. Not only that, but they are meeting regularly for worship in several different congregations (16:5-15). When, then, was Christianity first introduced to Rome? Who was responsible? From what ethnic backgrounds had the converts come? Did they have elders and deacons in the churches?

---

[19] This evidence is slight, but it is barely likely that it arose through a transcriptional error. If this omission occurred in only one place, the conjecture of a transcriptional error might be sufficient. If it occurred only in one manuscript, we might ascribe it to the delinquencies of a single scribe. As it is, we must accept it as an existing variation supported by slight evidence, but evidence sufficiently good to demand an explanation. Such explanation will be offered in the course of these notes. In the meantime, let it be well-remembered that the manuscript evidence strongly favors the inclusion of "in Rome" in the text, and all modern textual authorities include the words at both verses 7 and 15.

[20] T.W. Manson, *Studies in the Gospels and Epistles* (Philadelphia: Westminster Press, 1962), p.225-241.

[21] Later in these introductory studies, special attention is given to the matter of integrity.

1.   The Beginnings of Christianity in Rome

Three prominent views have been proposed and defended with reference to the origin of the church in Rome: it was started by Peter; it was started by Jews who were present in Jerusalem for Peter's Pentecost sermon (AD 30) and who returned to their hometown; it was started by Christians (converted elsewhere) who subsequently moved to Rome and who then converted others and planted churches.

One large segment of Christendom has taught for a long time that the church at Rome can be traced to the work of Peter after he arrived in Rome as early as AD 42, who (they would teach) also became the first pope.   The evidence to support this belief is traditional. Dionysius of Corinth (AD 170) and Irenaeus (AD 180) both say that Peter and Paul *founded* the churches at Corinth and then at Rome.[22]   Eusebius (AD 325) and Jerome (AD 400) have Peter in Rome for 25 years.[23]   Isidore of Spain (c. AD 636) puts the different tradi-

---

[22] The Clementine Homilies, composed at the close of the 2nd century at Rome (?), represent Peter as one who came to the west early to preach the gospel (*Epistle of Clement to James*, c.1).   According to Dionysius of Corinth, in his epistle to the Corinthians, as reported by Eusebius (*Church History*, II.25.8), Peter and Paul having founded the church at Corinth went thence into Italy, where they founded the Roman church, and suffered martyrdom at the same time.   Irenaeus, as given by Eusebius (*Church History*, V.8.2), testifies that both Peter and Paul preached at Rome, and founded (Greek, *themeliounton*) the church there at the time Matthew wrote his Gospel.   (The verb "founded" may mean either to lay the foundation of something, or to strengthen something already begun [Arndt-Gingrich, *Lexicon*, p.356]. Which meaning does it have in these passages about "founding" the church?   It may be true that Peter worked in Corinth after Paul first preached the gospel in that city [cp. 1 Corinthians 1:12 and 4:14,15], but it is unlikely that "founded" means that they jointly planted the church there.   Neither Paul nor Peter was the first to preach the gospel in Rome.   "Founded" [as used by Dionysius and Irenaeus] must mean "grounded or strengthened" rather than "planted," for there was a congregation in Rome before Paul ever came to Rome, as this Roman epistle shows; and Peter did not get to Rome [as far as what Scriptural evidence would show] until after Paul did.)

[23] Eusebius (*Church History*, II.14.6) says Peter went to Rome in the reign of Claudius (AD 41-54) to encounter Simon Magus, and thus brought the light of the gospel from the east to those in the west.   In his *Chronicon*, Eusebius gives the second year of Claudius (i.e., AD 42) as the date, and writes, "Peter, the head, having founded the first church in Antioch, set out for Rome preaching the gospel; and besides the church in Antioch, he was the first president of that at Rome also, until his death."   Jerome repeated the tradition that Peter, after having been bishop of Antioch, governed the Roman church for the space of 25 years.   Jerome wrote, "Simon Peter ... after having been bishop of Antioch ... pushed on to Rome in the second year of Claudius to overthrow Simon Magus, and held the sacerdotal chair there for 25 years until the last, that is, the fourteenth year of Nero" (*Lives of Illustrious Men*, ch.1).

The assumption that Peter took up his residence in Rome during the early years of the reign of Claudius contradicts all we know about Peter's later life from the New Testament.   Although we may accept it as certain that Peter did ultimately visit Rome and met his death there, it is not so certain that he arrived as early as the time of Claudius.

- The tradition that Peter was for 25 years bishop of Rome undoubtedly took its rise from the statement of Justin Martyr [*Apology*, I.26] that Simon Magus came to Rome during the reign of Claudius.   After the confrontation of Peter and Simon in Samaria as recorded in Acts 8, it would not be unexpected that their names should be connected at a later time.
- In the time of Eusebius, tradition commonly spoke of visits to Rome by both Simon Magus and Peter. Consequently Eusebius, accepting the earlier date for Simon's arrival in Rome, quite naturally assumed also the same early date for Peter's arrival there, although Justin himself does not mention Peter in connection with Simon Magus in the passage which Eusebius quotes.
- Jerome then simply repeated what Eusebius wrote, and since Jerome's time this tradition has been almost universally accepted in the Roman Catholic Church, though in recent years many more candid scholars of that communion acknowledge that so long an episcopate there is a fiction.

tions together in the following manner: "After [Peter] had founded the church at Antioch, he went to Rome in the reign of Claudius Caesar to meet Simon Magus and preached the gospel for 25 years, holding the pontificate."[24]   These few statements of the early writers are the basis of the theory that Peter is the one who first planted the church in Rome.

Protestants have been nearly unanimous in denying to Peter the distinction of being the first to bring the gospel to Rome.   As a basis for making this denial, rather than relying on the tradition on which the Roman Church bases its claims, they have pointed to the indications in Scripture regarding the travels of Peter.   Acts 1-11 has Peter in Jerusalem, Judea and Samaria in the years between Pentecost (AD 30) and his need to defend his actions in the matter of Cornelius to the brethren in Jerusalem (c. AD 42).   At least until his angelic release from prison, Acts 12 has Peter still located in Jerusalem (AD 44).[25] Acts 15 and the parallel passage in Galatians 2:1-10 have Peter in Jerusalem for the conference on circumcision, which was held in AD 51.   Next, we find Peter in Antioch (Galatians 2:11).   After this, we know little for certain about the next 10 or 15 years of Peter's life and travels.   1 Corinthians 9:5 tells us that Peter has been on evangelistic journeys, and the presence of the "Cephas party" there (1 Corinthians 1:12) indicates he likely had visited Corinth sometime after Paul planted the church (but before Paul wrote 1 Corinthians to them in AD 57).   Romans 15:20 has been used by some to prove that Peter had not been to Rome before Paul wrote his epistle to Rome.[26]   Nor is it likely that Peter is there in Rome at the time Paul writes, for Peter's name is not included among those greeted by Paul.   It is clear from 1 Peter 1:1 that Peter also worked in Asia Minor – Pontus, Galatia, Cappadocia, Asia, and Bithynia – sometime before he wrote to them (c. AD 65). Acts 28:30 tells about Paul's two-year-long first Roman imprisonment (AD 61-63).[27] During this two-year period, he wrote the Prison Epistles (Ephesians, Colossians, Philemon, and Philippians), in which Paul names his fellow-workers in the gospel in Rome. Peter is not in Rome at this time, for after naming several of his friends at Rome, Paul concludes the list by saying, "These are the only fellow-workers in the kingdom of God" (Colossians 4:11).   Released from his first Roman imprisonment, Paul visited the churches in the east again,[28] until he was arrested and brought to Rome a second time.   From this

---

[24] *The Life and Death of Peter* (quoted by Samuel Davidson, *An Introduction to the New Testament* [London: Samuel Bagster and Sons, 1849], Vol.2, p.159).

[25] Chapter 12 also records the death of Herod Agrippa I, which may be dated in AD 44. See the author's "New Testament Chronology," in his *New Testament History: Acts* (Moberly, MO: Scripture Exposition Books, 2002), p.x-xxi.

[26] The most confident statement one should make, based on Romans 15:20, is that it *possibly* indicates no apostle has been to Rome before Paul writes to them in AD 58. But it is far from certain that the passage demonstrates such as a fact. (See comments below at Romans 15:20, especially footnote #48.)

[27] To judge from what we read in Acts 28:17-22, when Paul arrived at Rome it had been unvisited by Peter. If Peter (the apostle to the Jews) had been laboring there before Paul came, we might expect the Jewish population there to have a greater knowledge of Christianity than is apparent in Acts 28:22.

[28] See further notes at Romans 15:24 for details on Paul's travels after his first visit to Rome.

second imprisonment, he wrote 2 Timothy; Peter was not in Rome at the time Paul wrote that letter, if we may judge what Christian leaders are in the city from 2 Timothy 4:11, where Paul says "Only Luke is with me." Peter may well have arrived in Rome late in his life, and may even been martyred there as early Christian literature seems to substantiate,[29] but that his was the privilege to be the first to preach the gospel in Rome, and thus to plant the church there, seems hardly defensible.

If it was not Peter, is it possible that the beginnings of the church in Rome may be traced to the evangelistic work done by people present in Jerusalem at the Pentecost birthday of the church (Acts 2)? Mention is made in Acts 2:10 of Roman visitors, some Jews by birth, others converted to the Jewish religion, who were present at Pentecost. Is it not likely that some of them were converted as a result of Peter's sermon,[30] and then took the gospel home to Rome[31] when they returned from the feast? In countless towns the synagogue furnished a cradle for the birth of the church. Jews who had become Christians would enter the synagogues at Rome and teach the assembled Jews the gospel story.[32] So, it is supposed, the gospel came to Rome shortly after Pentecost (AD 30).[33]

---

[29] See the Special Study "Was Peter Ever in Rome?" in the author's *New Testament History: Acts*, p.447-452.

[30] Some have conjectured that there is a kernel of truth behind the legend that Peter planted the church at Rome – not that he was there personally, but that people who heard his Pentecost sermon and were baptized then took the gospel to Rome. In this way, the church at Rome is indirectly traced to Peter.

[31] Some have objected that new converts would have difficulty knowing enough about Christianity to organize a church in Rome. It would take more than what they absorbed on the day of Pentecost, it is urged, to lay the foundations of a church in Rome. (*Reply*: This objection seems to overlook what we are told in Acts 2:42 about the new converts continuing steadfastly with the apostles for a period of time. It is not difficult to imagine the visitors staying longer than they had originally planned, delaying their return home just so they could hear more of the good news, even staying long enough, perhaps, to help cause the need for a community of goods shared with the visitors by the local residents [2:44-47].)

[32] While it can be demonstrated in Acts that apostles like Paul and Barnabas used the synagogues as ready-made audiences for the gospel, it is rather hard to demonstrate that pilgrims to Pentecost went home and did likewise. Godet asks, "How comes it that no circumstance analogous to that which on the above hypothesis gave rise to the Roman church, can be proved in any of the other great cities of the empire? There were Jewish colonies elsewhere than at Rome. There were such at Ephesus, Corinth, and Thessalonica. Whence comes it that, when Paul arrived in these cities, and preached in their synagogues for the first time, the gospel appeared as a thing entirely new? Is there any reason for holding that the Christianity of Palestine exercised a more direct and prompt influence on the synagogue of Rome than on that of the other cities of the empire?" *Commentary on the Epistle to the Romans* (Grand Rapids: Zondervan Publishing House, 1956), p.38.

[33] Lenski and others have appealed to Acts 28:17-29 to disprove the hypothesis that the origin of the Roman church can be traced to worshipers present at that first Pentecost after the resurrection of Jesus. They ask why the synagogue leaders should come to Paul desiring information about Christianity if for years the synagogue at Rome had been the scene of gospel preaching? (A possible rebuttal to Lenski's argument would be that the banishment of the Jews by Claudius, about 10 years before Paul arrived in Rome, could well have led to a complete rupture between the synagogue and the Jewish Christians. When the Jews were allowed to return after the death of Claudius in AD 54, there was little communion between the Christians and the Jews.)

Is there any extra-Biblical evidence to support this supposition? The earliest hint that the gospel is known in Rome comes from the time of Tiberius, who died in AD 37.[34] Then there is the possibility that the coming of Christianity to Rome had something to do with the edict of Claudius against the Jews (AD 51), which led to Aquila and Priscilla's being in Corinth at the time Paul first came to that city (Acts 18:2). This deduction is based partly on the reason for the decree,[35] and partly on the opinion that Aquila and Priscilla were Christians before they met Paul (i.e., they were Christians before they were banished from Rome).[36] The first really solid evidence of Christianity in Rome is Tacitus' account of the spread of Christianity to the city of Rome before the time of Nero, who began to rule in AD 54.[37] And, of course, Paul's epistle to the Romans indicates Christians have been in Rome "for many years" (Romans 15:23) before AD 58; in fact, they have been there long enough for their existence to be known, and for reports about them to have

---

[34] The traditions said to prove that the gospel had come to Rome before the death of Tiberius are weak. "First, we are told in the Clementine Homilies that in the reign of Tiberius tidings came to Rome 'that a certain one in Judea, beginning in the spring season, was preaching to the Jews the kingdom of the invisible God,' and working many wonderful miracles and signs' (*Homilies*, l.c.6). 'In the same year in the autumn season a certain one standing in a public place cried and said, "Men of Rome, hearken. The Son of God is come in Judea, proclaiming eternal life to all who will, if they shall live according to the counsel of the Father, who hath sent him"' (*Homilies*, l.c.7). Tertullian (*Apologeticus*, c.5) records, 'Tiberius, accordingly, in whose days the Christian name made its entry into the world, having himself received intelligence from Palestine of events which had clearly shown the truth of Christ's divinity, brought the matter before the Senate, with his own decision in favor of Christ. The Senate, because it had not given the approval itself, rejected the proposal'." E.H. Gifford, "Romans," in *The Bible Commentary*, edited by F.C. Cook (New York: Charles Scribner's Sons, 1886), Vol. 3, p.4. After each quotation Gifford gives his opinion that each is fictitious, untrue, or that its writer was deceived.

[35] Suetonius (*Life of Claudius*, ch.25) tells us the Jews in Rome were constantly engaged in tumults over one "Chrestus," a name many think is a reference to "Christus" (i.e., Jesus Christ). Elsewhere in the empire, when the gospel came to town, the unbelieving Jews created disturbances. Perhaps this also happened at Rome, and led directly to Claudius' decree banishing all Jews (he made no distinction between Christian and non-Christian) from Rome.

[36] If they were not already Christians when Paul began working and living with this couple in Corinth, we would expect them to be among his first converts there. The fact that no mention is made of this has been interpreted to mean that they were Christians before they came to Corinth. (Nor should Romans 15:20 be used as proof that Aquila and Priscilla were *not* Christians when Paul got to Corinth. Paul's efforts to plant a church in Corinth, even if Priscilla and Aquila preceded him there and were Christians before he arrived in Corinth, would not be contrary to Paul's stated practice [Romans 15:20,21 and 2 Corinthians 10:16] of evangelizing where Christ was not named. There is a difference between but one or two folk already converted, and a whole congregation of converts. It is where the latter was true that Paul would not stay long. He must be on his way to tell those men the good news who had no one else to tell them.)

[37] "The name (Christians) was derived from Christ, who in the reign of Tiberius suffered under Pontius Pilate, the procurator of Judea. By that event the sect of which he was the founder received a blow which for a time checked the growth of a dangerous superstition; but it revived soon after, and spread with recruited vigor not only in Judea, the soil which gave it birth, but even in the city of Rome, the common sink into which everything infamous and abominable flows like a torrent from all quarters of the world." Tacitus, *Annals*, XV.44.

circulated among the churches out in the Roman Empire (Romans 1:8,16:19).[38]   The fact that it is nearly twenty years after Pentecost (AD 30) before there is solid evidence of a church in Rome causes us to be hesitant about attributing its origin to the pilgrims from Rome who heard Peter's first gospel sermon.

A third suggestion concerning the origin of the church in Rome is that it was planted by travelers who went to Rome after becoming Christians while living in the provinces.[39] The conditions of travel in the Roman Empire were exceptionally advantageous.   From Antioch, Corinth, Ephesus, and other cities, a great deal of traffic went to Rome; and it was in those cities that Paul had done much of his evangelistic work.   From many of these cities came young men who traveled with Paul, studying for the ministry.   It would be strange if none of his converts ever got to Rome.   Now, remember all the people to whom Paul sends his greetings in Romans 16:3-15.   Suppose these people are some of these very converts who have, since their conversion within the past ten years or so, come to Rome. They would certainly preach and teach (cf. "the church that is in their house"). Furthermore, some members of the Christian community in Rome are endowed with spiritual gifts (Romans 12:6-8).   Since such gifts were passed on by the laying on of an apostle's hands (Acts 8:17,18), it is not beyond belief to suppose some of the gifted people in Rome have had hands laid on them by none other than Paul himself, before they moved on to Rome.

What conclusions may we draw about the beginnings of Christianity in Rome?   We know nothing from direct evidence; we can only surmise.   Someone evidently was responsible for the conversion of Aquila and Priscilla before they (along with all Jews) were banished from Rome by Claudius in AD 51, but we do not know who evangelized them.   When the edict expired, many of those Jews would return.   How many, we wonder, were (like Aquila and Priscilla) Christians, who took their new faith with them when they left Rome, and brought it with them when they returned, so that very shortly after their return from exile there was a "church ... in their house"?   Many of the names in chapter 16 have also been found in inscriptions linked with the imperial household.   If this is not just coincidence, we wonder how these converts eventually came to be involved with the imperial household.   Whether or not the people greeted in chapter 16 were the "saints in Caesar's household" (Philippians 4:22), their coming to Rome was sure to nurture the Christianity that was already there.   Their coming would also be the stimulus for the beginning of more new congregations in the city.

---

[38] Such reports about Rome do not, by themselves, necessarily imply the church already has a long history.   It did not take long for such reports to circulate.   Paul can make a similar statement about the church at Thessalonica (1 Thessalonians 1:8), and that perhaps less than six months after the gospel was first preached in Thessalonica.   But taken together with his statement about his desire "for many years" to visit the brethren in Rome, the circulation of news about the church there does imply an existence of some years' duration.

[39] Hans Leitzmann, *The Beginnings of the Christian Church* (New York: Charles Scribner's Sons, 1952), p.111,133,199, has suggested that just as Paul and Barnabas went out from Antioch of Pisidia (Acts 13), so other missionaries from Antioch went to Rome and were responsible for the preaching of the gospel there that led to the founding of a church in the city.

2. Composition of the Church at Rome

Whereas the question of who planted the church in Rome may have a bearing on the interpretation of one verse, and also perhaps on the question of the historical basis of the papacy, it is different with the question of the ethnic backgrounds of the persons who were members of the church when this letter was written to them. The scholars have long debated the relative strength of the Jewish and Gentile elements in the church, and the conclusions reached by the debaters have been the basis on which interpretations of the whole book have been made to depend.[40]

Lenski's suggestion[41] that the relative proportion of Jews and Gentiles in the church was about 50:50 is hardly acceptable. He first of all asserts that the whole of the church is composed of the people named in Romans 16; then having studied the names, he decides that about half are Jewish names, and about half are Gentile. Such an ethnic mix, he believes, would explain how Paul can sometimes address them as though they were Gentile, and at other times (cf. Romans 4:1, 7:1) write as if they were very familiar with the Law of Moses. It is this commentator's conviction that it is hard to sustain Lenski's suggestion that there were only two dozen members in the church at Rome; see the times that "the saints who are with them" and "the church that is in their house" occurs right alongside the people called by name in chapter 16.[42]

Some scholars have argued that the majority of the Roman church was of Jewish background.[43]   F.C. Baur (1792-1860) introduced the theory that the epistle[44] is primarily

---

[40] For the different views and advocates, see Donald Guthrie, *New Testament Introduction* (Chicago, IL: Inter-Varsity Press, 1963), Vol. 2, p.23,24.

[41] R.C.H. Lenski, *The Interpretation of St. Paul's Epistle to the Romans* (Columbus, OH: Wartburg Press, 1945). p.19.

[42] Having missed the ethnic composition of the church and its numerical size, Lenski (we believe) also misses the purpose for which Paul addressed this letter to the Romans. Lenski uses the suggested ethnic composition as a proof that Paul is coming to Rome to do Jewish mission work in that city (*ibid.*). That there were more than two dozen members in the church at Rome seems implied from what we know about the church in later history. Philippians will be written from Rome about five years after Romans, and chapter 1 of that letter indicates significant numbers of church members. Some six years after the writing of Romans, the Roman church was very large. At the outbreak of the Neronian persecutions in AD 64, the historian Tacitus speaks of the Christians in Rome as "an immense multitude." (Tacitus, *Annals,* XV.44. See also I Clement VI.1.)

[43] James Denney, "St. Paul's Epistle to the Romans" in *The Expositor's Greek Testament* (Grand Rapids: Wm. B. Eerdmans Publishing Co., 1967), Vol.2, p.563-567, presents and evaluates six of the usual arguments given to prove the Jewish-Christian character of the church. Theodor Zahn, *Introduction to the New Testament* (Grand Rapids: Kregel Publications, 1953), Vol.1, p.421ff, has no question in his mind but that the constituent members of the Roman church were basically Jewish.

[44] The reader will have observed that Paul's composition to Rome has interchangeably been called "a letter" and "an epistle." Tertius himself, who was Paul's penman in the writing of Romans, calls this an *epistolē* ("letter") in Romans 16:22; the word is translated "letter" and "epistle" with almost equal frequency in the KJV and ASV. There is a slight difference in the connotations of the English words: "letter" has reference to a spontaneous, intimate, friendly, personal message from one person or group to another per-

addressed to Jewish Christians and was intended to expose the weakness of their reliance on formal obedience to the Mosaic Law.   He felt that when the epistle is closely examined, there is a large element in it which is essentially only of Jewish interest – the validity of the Law, the nature of redemption, the standards by which a man may be righteous in God's sight, the choice and rejection of Israel.   Baur asserted that the main portion of the epistle is to be found in chapters 9 to 11, and only to Jewish people would the information contained therein be particularly relevant.[45] He also pointed to such statements as Romans 4:1 ("Abraham our forefather according to the flesh") and 7:1 ("I am speaking to those who know the law") as corroboration of the opinion that the congregation was primarily of Jewish background.   Plausible as all this may sound, it cannot be accepted, for it ignores what Paul himself says about the nature of the Roman church.[46]

Probably the prevailing opinion about the composition of the church at Rome is that Gentile Christians formed the greater proportion of the membership at the time when the Roman letter was written.[47]   Paul numbers the church at Rome among the Gentile churches (Romans 1:5-7); he includes them among the Greeks and barbarians to whom he is obliga-

---

son or group; "epistle" has reference to more formal writing that is intended for general circulation.   Ever since G. Adolph Deissmann (*Bible Studies* [Winona Lake, IN: Alpha Publications, 1979 reprint of the 1901 English edition], p.3-12,42-49) called attention to the sharp distinction between a genuine letter and a literary epistle, and asserted that Paul's writings were more properly classified as private, personal letters rather than epistles, argument has ensued over whether Romans is rightly called a letter or an epistle.   If Paul intended it (ultimately) for more than just the immediate audience to whom it was addressed, and there is evidence that he was aware of who he was (an apostle) and of the importance of the Roman church on the future of church history, then technically it should be called an "epistle."   But in common usage, "letter" and "epistle" are now used as though they were synonymous terms, and there need be no misunderstanding when sometimes we call Paul's writings "letters" and sometimes "epistles."

[45] Baur's own students criticized him for his exaggerated and one-sided emphasis on the importance of chapters 9 to 11.   It can be demonstrated that Baur's attempt to classify the books of the New Testament into Petrine and Pauline and "peacemaker" documents (see this explained in the author's *New Testament History: Acts*, p.xxii-xxiii) was the result of an a priori assumption of the validity of Hegel's philosophy (thesis, synthesis, antithesis), followed by an attempt to make the Bible match that prevailing philosophy of Baur's day.   While not any longer attempting to make the Bible fit Hegelian philosophy, William Manson, *Epistle to the Hebrews* (London: Hodder and Stoughton, 1951), p.172-184, has urged that the major portion of the church at Rome was Jewish on the grounds that the argument of the epistle throughout is more applicable to Jews than to Gentiles.

[46] James Denney urges that not even chapters 9 to 11 will support the structure Baur tried to build from it.   Instead of being addressed to Jewish Christians, Denny asserts "it is precisely and unambiguously to the Gentiles that all this section is addressed.   In 9:1ff, 10:1ff, Paul speaks of the Jews in the third person (my prayer to God for *them*, etc.).   He calls them *my* kinsmen, not *yours* or *ours*.   He quotes himself, but not his readers (11:1), as proof that God has not cast off His people, which he would hardly have done had they also been Christian Jews [however, see note on this verse, GLR].   He uses the fate of the Jews, the natural branches, to warn his readers, grafted into the tree of life contrary to nature, against contempt, pride, and unbelief.   Whatever the motive of these chapters may have been, it cannot have been that the bulk of the Romish Church was Jewish in origin, or strongly Jewish in sympathy.   The apostle's own application of their teaching in 11:17-24 proves exactly the reverse." *Romans*, p.566,567.

[47] Denney, *Romans*, p.562,563, summarizes five arguments most often alluded to as proof of this conclusion.

ted to preach (1:13-15). He definitely addresses them as Gentiles (11:13), and he implies the Romans are among the Gentiles whom he, as a priest, is offering up to God (15:14-16).[48] There were Jewish Christians in the congregation, but Gentile Christians seem to have outnumbered them, though it is conceivable that the influence and power of the Jewish Christians was greater than the proportion of their numbers.[49]

3. Organization of the Church

While it has already been demonstrated that several congregations made up the church at Rome, it might be well to ask about the organization of the church.[50] When this letter was written, was it as well organized as the churches in Galatia, or Asia, or in Corinth[51] – with duly selected and ordained elders and deacons?

One opinion, often expressed, is that the Roman church was not well organized. Several strands of evidence are connected to show this conclusion is correct. It is stressed that Romans is not addressed to "*the church* at Rome" as are other letters of Paul to cities where there was an organized church.[52] Romans 1:11 is interpreted to mean that the church

---

[48] Romans 7:1 ("I am speaking to those who know the law") is explained in this fashion by those who believe the Gentile Christians made up the majority of the membership of the church in Rome. When we recollect that in the apostolic age, for at least the first twenty years, the Old Testament (especially the passages that dealt with Messiah) was one of the sources of Christian preaching; when we add to this the possibility that the Law and Prophets were read during the public worship in the early churches (cp. comments on Galatians 4:21) just as they had been in the synagogues; when we add to this the fact that in most congregations the earliest converts were of Jewish background, which would tend to grant them influential status among newer converts from among the Gentiles, even where there was no Judaizing influence; then it is not surprising that *any* Christian in those young churches would soon know the Old Testament Scriptures as well as the teaching of Jesus and the apostles. Romans 4:1 ("Abraham our forefather ...") no more proves the Roman readers were all of Jewish background than 1 Corinthians 10:1 proves that the church members at Corinth were all Jewish.

[49] C.H. Dodd, *Romans* in the Moffatt Commentary Series (New York: Harper and Row, 1966), p.xxviii, thinks the Jewish influence at Rome was stronger than it would have been if Paul had founded it. It is difficult to know whether such a comment reflects the old and discredited higher critical views of the Tubingen school of a Pauline v. Petrine conflict in the apostolic church, or whether it reflects the suspicions about Gentile Christians which the work of the Judaizers tended to engender and about which one reads in the New Testament.

[50] This question is of special interest to those who would find Biblical warrant for a hierarchical form of church government, with the laying on of hands before new leaders are officially qualified to govern and to 'administer the sacraments.' Some defenders of such government (and of apostolic succession) suggest that one reason for Paul's intended visit was to officially organize the church.

[51] The churches of Galatia functioned for a year or two after they were planted at the beginning of Paul's first missionary journey before the missionaries returned and led the selection of elders for each congregation (Acts 14:23). The churches in Asia (for example, Ephesus per Acts 20:17 and Philippi per Philippians 1:1) had duly appointed elders and deacons. The church at Corinth also had leaders to whom the church members were expected to be in submission (1 Corinthians 16:15,16; see also 1 Corinthians 12:28, where certain spiritual gifts are named, some of which would be leadership gifts).

[52] "The church ... in their house" is mentioned in the greetings contained in chapter 16. If the presence or absence of the word "church" is a criterion by which one may decide whether or not a group of believers is "organized" or not, the evidence would be that those congregations at Rome were organized.

is not organized yet, but the organizing is something Paul will attend to when he arrives in the city.[53]   It is also affirmed that elders and deacons are not mentioned by name in Romans precisely because there were none yet ordained in that city.[54]   Still others appeal to the statements in early Christian literature that "Peter and Paul founded (*themeliounton*, Grk., "established") the church at Rome" as evidence the church there was unorganized until the apostles themselves could arrive on the scene.[55]

Those commentators on Romans who write from within the perspective of a non-hierarchical type of church government have been satisfied to affirm that the church at Rome was organized.   Merely because Paul does not mention elders and deacons is no argument that there were none; Paul's usual custom in his letters is to specify such things only when there was need for correction.   And while it surely is untenable to affirm, "All Jewish Christians and all proselytes knew how to organize; namely, after the pattern of the synagogues,"[56] remember that there were some spiritually gifted people at Rome already, and some of these gifts could well make leaders.   Furthermore, would not some of Paul's fellow-workers who are now in Rome, to whom greetings are sent in chapter 16, be the very kinds of men who would provide leadership to the congregations?   Just as strong a case can be made that the churches at Rome were organized as can be made that they were not.

Actually, while personally believing the congregations at Rome already would have elders and deacons, we admit that we do not have enough evidence to be absolutely dogmatic, one way or the other, concerning the organization of the Roman church in AD 58.   While this is true, we certainly are not confined or limited to the hierarchical opinion as to the reason for Paul's planned visit.

---

[53] That Paul would impart to them some spiritual gift, that they "may be established," must be balanced with the statement in chapter 12:6-8, which indicates some members in Rome already had spiritual gifts. If the presence or absence of such gifts (given by the laying on of an apostle's hands) is the criterion by which it is determined whether or not a congregation is organized, the evidence of Romans 12 would be in favor of the church there being organized.

[54] That the actual words "elder" and "deacon" do not appear in Romans is not necessarily evidence that no leaders have been duly selected before the time Paul writes this letter.   There were elders among the churches of Galatia (Acts 14:23), yet nothing is said about the elders and deacons in Galatia in Paul's epistle to the Galatians.

[55] See footnotes #22 and #23 on page xi (*supra*) where these quotations were introduced and explained. *Themelioō* may refer to being strengthened in personal faith.   See, for example, Ephesians 3:17 and Colossians 1:23 where the verb is used, and by no stretch of interpretation does it have anything to do with 'ordaining leaders so that the church may be officially organized.'

[56] Lenski, *Romans*, p.21.

Special Problems

Each person who comes to a study of Romans brings with him a certain set of understandings which are the result of that person's previous interaction with both the Word of God and with the mindset he finds (and must deal with) in the everyday world.   Instead of uncritically assuming those understandings are true, it is better if the student questions his assumptions in the light of what is found in the Scriptures.   There are several critical areas where the questioning of (or failure to question) previous assumptions has a significant bearing on what the student will "hear" or "learn" during his study of Romans.

1.   The Integrity of the Epistle

"Integrity" is a technical word in introductory studies, dealing with 'the wholesome preservation of the text in substantially the same form as it proceeded from the hand of the writer.'   The student need not be acquainted with the Greek text, but simply with several different English translations, and he soon will see that there is a problem with some verses, for the verses are in whole or in part omitted.[57]   A little diligent study of the critical apparatus in one of the modern Greek Testaments will soon show more divergent readings that require some explanation.   The chapters about which there is the most question are chapters 15 and 16.

Evidence that must be satisfactorily explained.   There is the testimony of the early Christian writers, evidence (in some cases) that is older than any existing manuscript of Romans.   Gifford has gathered the evidence into a conveniently read summary:

> Clement of Alexandria [AD 190] quotes passages from both chapters 15 and 16 frequently, and describes them as belonging to the Epistle to the Romans, without the least apparent consciousness that this could be doubted.[58]

> Tertullian, writing AD 207-210 against Marcion's "*Antitheses,*" or Contradictions between the Old and New Testaments, says (*Adv. Marc.* v.13) "What great gaps Marcion made especially in this Epistle [to the Romans] by expunging whatever he would, will be clear from the unmutilated text of our own copy.   Some passages however, which ought according to his plan to have been expunged, he overlooked: and it is enough for my purpose to accept these as instances of his negligence and blindness."   In his subsequent argument Tertullian quotes no passage from chapters xv-xvi, and refers to xiv.10-13 as being [at] the close of the Epistle ("*in clausula*") ....[59]

---

[57] A comparison of the KJV and the NASB will immediately show some problem with Romans 16:24. An "Amen" is also included at the close of 16:20 in the KJV that is not included in the NASB.   The least these observed differences should do is arouse curiosity as to why there are such differences.

[58] Gifford, *Romans*, p.21.

[59] Gifford, *Romans,* p.20,21.   It is true that Tertullian, Irenaeus, and Cyprian, who quote largely from Romans, have no references to chapters 15 and 16.   It may be observed, however, that mere omission to

Origen [AD 210] ... after quoting the Doxology (xvi:25-27) in its usual place at the end of the Epistle ... proceeds: "Marcion, who tampered with the writings of the Evangelists and Apostles, entirely took away [*abstulit*] this paragraph; and not this only, but also from that place where it is written, *Whatsoever is not of faith is sin* (xiv:23), right on to the end he cut away all [*cuncta dissecuit*]. But in other copies, that is, in those which have not been corrupted by Marcion, we find this very paragraph differently placed. For in some manuscripts after the passage above mentioned, *Whatsoever is not of faith is sin*, there follows in immediate connection (*statim cohaerens*), *Now unto him that is of power to establish you*: but other manuscripts have it at the end, as it is now placed."[60]

In addition to the evidence from the early church fathers, there is evidence found in the various manuscripts. (1) The weakly supported omission of "in Rome" at Romans 1:7, 15 has already been alluded to in the above treatment of the destination of this letter.[61] (2) The doxology (16:25-27) is found in several different places in the manuscripts.[62] (3) The

---

quote is not in itself conclusive, for neither do they quote 1 Corinthians 16, and such omission to quote 1 Corinthians 16 has not been taken as evidence that they were aware 1 Corinthians 16 lacked integrity.

[60] Gifford, *Romans*, p.21. (Gifford is quoting Rufinus' Latin version of Origen's works.) Origen speaks of a diversity of *location* for the doxology before his time, a diversity independent of Marcion's mutilated copies, but he gives no evidence of *omission* either of the doxology or of chapters 15 and 16 before Marcion's time, i.e., about AD 140. Origen's use of the word *dissecuit* to describe Marcion's treatment of the text most naturally means that Marcion himself cut off the last two chapters, though some recent scholars have urged that it means Marcion simply used an older text from which the two chapters were missing. (A.H. McNeile, *Introduction to the Study of the New Testament*, revised by C.S.C. Williams [Oxford: At the Clarendon Press, 1953], p.156, states that *dissecuit* "may mean either the same as *abstulit*, or 'separated off,' i.e., treated as not belonging to the epistle.") But Origen's use of the word *dissecuit* most naturally means that Marcion himself cut off the last two chapters. (There is a manuscript variation in the Latin translations of Origen, and F.J.A. Hort's reconstruction of the Latin text, along with the slightly different meaning it gives [i.e., Marcion omitted only the doxology, not the last two chapters], is explained in Denney, *Romans*, p.577.) "The passage from Origen does not prove, as some have inferred, that Marcion regarded the Doxology in particular as spurious, nor that he appealed to earlier MSS. as omitting it, nor that Origen found it *omitted* in any other MSS. besides those which had been mutilated by Marcion. It does prove that Origen knew of copies corrupted by Marcion, which omitted all after the last verse of ch. xiv. It implies that, *as far as Origen knew*, ... no *other* MSS. *omitted* the Doxology, but some placed it between xiv. and xv." Gifford, *Romans*, p.21.

[61] Page ix-x *supra* and footnote #19. Codex G, which omits "in Rome," is also is one of the Graeco-Latin manuscripts which has the doxology missing.

[62] "1. The best MSS, both Alexandrian and Western, place it at the end of chapter xvi (Sinaiticus, B, C, D, Latin, Peshitta Syriac, Boharic and Ethiopic versions). Origen in his Greek texts knew the doxology in this position. [Because of Erasmus' respect for the Vulgate, the doxology is at the end of chapter 16 in the Textus Receptus.] 2. Many less important MSS place it at the end of chapter xiv. Among the more weighty of these are Codex L [Codex Angelicus], many minuscules [as, e.g., the minuscule 66, which after the "Amen" of 16:24 puts *telos* ("end") to mark the end of the epistle, but then adds the doxology, and has this note in the margin, "In ancient copies, the end of the epistle is here (i.e., 16:24), but the rest (i.e., the Doxology) is found at the end of chapter 14."], some codices used by Origen (according to the Latin translation), [many Byzantine lectionaries] and the Harklean Syriac. [See also: Chrysostom, Theodoret, Damascenus, Theophilus of Antioch, Oecumenius, and other Greek writers]. 3. A few late authorities place it after both chapter xiv and chapter xvi (Codices A and P, minuscules 5, [17], 33, [and the Armenian version]). 4. The Chester Beatty papyrus (P[46]) places it after chapter xv. [In fact, the Chester Beatty Pa-

benediction ("The grace of our Lord Jesus be with you," 15:24) is found in several locations.[63]   (4) Chapters 15 and 16 are not omitted in any known manuscript of Romans.[64] (5) The capitulations ("section headings") found in some Latin manuscripts suggest that whoever added those section headings was working with a manuscript that had chapters 15 and 16 missing.[65]

A third line of evidence that must be considered comes from within the letter itself. Some have proposed, for various reasons, that chapter 16 could hardly have been addressed to Rome.[66]   Others have debated, from stylistic and linguistic grounds, the authorship of

---

pyrus has 15:33 at the end of chapter 14, as well as the doxology at the end of chapter 15.]   5. The Graeco-Latin MS Gg, supported by Marcion, omits it altogether.   In Gg, however, a space is left [between chapters 14 and 15] that is large enough to accommodate the doxology.   The doxology is omitted in D[3] (or rather marked for erasure by the corrector), in Ff[gr], and in some manuscripts spoken of by Jerome.   It should be noted that in F a blank space is left after 16:24, and the corresponding space in the Latin (f) is occupied by the doxology.]"   Guthrie, *New Testament Introduction*, Vol.2, p.33.   (Comments enclosed in brackets [ ] added by GLR.)

[63] See footnote #123 at chapter 16, where the locations and evidence for each is presented.

[64] We are here speaking of "unmutilated manuscripts," with "mutilated" being defined as "pages missing at the beginning or end."

[65] "In many manuscripts of the Latin Bible, especially codex Amiatinus and Fuldensis [the two best manuscript copies of the Latin Vulgate], both of the 6th century, there is a division into sections (*capitulatio*) marked by numbers in the text, and a prefixed table of contents with corresponding numbers, in which the subject of each section is briefly described.   The 50th section in the Codex Amiatinus 'On the peril of one who grieves his brother by his meat,' corresponds with xiv.15-23:   But the next and last section, 'On the mystery of the Lord kept secret before His passion, but after His passion revealed,' answers to nothing else in the remainder of the Epistle except the Doxology.   It is therefore a natural conclusion that this capitulation was first adapted to a Latin MS. in which the Doxology was placed immediately after xiv.23, and [that] xv. and xvi. [were] omitted."   Gifford, *Romans*, p.22.   The evidence of Codex Amiatinus is particularly important, as the headings in it can be traced to a text earlier than Jerome.

[66] The alleged reasons why chapter 16, either all or in part, was once not part of Paul's letter to Rome, but was instead addressed to Ephesus, include: (1) It is unlikely that Paul would know so many people in a town where he has never been as are greeted in chapter 16.   (2) In all the other New Testament references to them from the same decade during which Romans was written, Priscilla and Aquila are living either in Ephesus or Corinth.   (3) Epaenetus (Romans 16:5) is connected with Asia, and Ephesus was the capital of the Roman province of Asia.   (4) Sailing from Cenchrea, Phoebe would be more likely to be going east toward Ephesus, than west toward Rome.   (5) The tone of the warning in 16:17-19 would better match Ephesus (remember what Paul said to the Ephesian elders, Acts 20:28-35) than it would the tone of the rest of the letter to Rome.   (6) Chapter 15 ends with words that sound like the conclusion of a letter. (Until the discovery and publication of the Chester Beatty Papyri, critics could assail the integrity of chapter 16 only on purely internal grounds.   After its discovery, they quickly pointed to the location of the doxology in P[46] as "striking support from external evidence" of their view.)

While most of these alleged reasons are dealt with either in comments at the appropriate place in the text or later in these introductory studies, it does seem worthwhile to comment on (4) at this place. Romans nowhere says that Phoebe is sailing from Cenchrea.   It simply states that Cenchrea is her place of service.   On the supposition she was going to Rome, what would be more natural than a stop in Corinth on her way from Cenchrea to Lechaeum, the western port of Corinth, where she would board her ship for a voyage to Rome?

the doxology.[67]

Explanations offered to account for the evidence.   The complicated set of facts has not yet been clearly explained, and perhaps cannot be.   Four different theories have been suggested to explain the textual variants and the contents of chapter 16.   Within these four explanations there is a further variation, for some hold that both chapters 15 and 16 were not part of the original letter; others hold that just chapter 16 does not enjoy integrity.

1. *Paul wrote short, and someone else lengthened it.*   The usual scenario is that Paul wrote short (chapters 1-15 to Rome, chapter 16 to Ephesus[68]), and whoever collected Paul's letters at Ephesus was responsible not only for putting the two parts together,   but also for

---

[67] A rather sizable number of modern writers reject the Pauline authorship of the doxology.   Harnack's suggestion about the authorship of the doxology is set forth in footnote #160 on chapter 16.   C.K. Barrett, *The Epistle to the Romans* (New York: Harper and Brothers, 1957), p.11,12, denies the Pauline authorship of the doxology, and urges that the wording of it as it now stands is an orthodox attempt to counteract the Marcionite character of a once shorter doxology (p.287).   Karl Barth, *The Epistle to the Romans* (London: Oxford University Press, 1933), p.522,523, denied the Pauline authorship on the grounds of style.   Robert Scott, *The Pauline Epistles*, p.204, attributed the doxology to Luke because of the stylistic and linguistic similarities to the pastoral epistles, which he also attributed to Luke.   Kirsopp Lake and Silva Lake, *Introduction to the New Testament* (London: Christophers, 1938), p.98, reject the Pauline authorship of the doxology, and attribute it instead to the collector of the Pauline letters.   John Knox, "Romans," in *The Interpreter's Bible* (Nashville: Abingdon Press, 1951), Vol.9, p.364, writes, "There is all but universal agreement among students of this letter that these verses were not originally part of it. The style is not Paul's and the content, while not un-Pauline, is not adapted to the closing argument of this particular epistle."   He thinks it was composed in the 2nd century as a suitable conclusion to a collection of Paul's letters, in which Romans stood last.   He writes, "It is also clear that this doxology, so long and elaborate, may well have been designed to bring, not only Romans, but the entire [Pauline] corpus, to an impressive end" (p.368).

On the other hand, Gifford, *Romans*, p.25ff, defends the Pauline authorship of the doxology against a number of these "arbitrary hypotheses."   Guthrie, *New Testament Introduction*, p.35, has reminded us it is "notoriously difficult to establish any conclusive tests of style" and thereby either affirm or deny Pauline authorship.   F.J.A. Hort, "On the End of the Epistle to the Romans," in *Biblical Essays*, compiled by J.B. Lightfoot (London: Macmillan Co., 1893), p.324-329, carefully compared the phrases of the doxology in Romans with the phrases in Paul's earlier and later epistles and found a remarkable number of similarities. While neither denied the Pauline authorship of the doxology, both Lightfoot and Alford thought the doxology was not part of Paul's original letter to Rome.   "Probably," writes Alford, "on reperusing his work either at the time, or as the altered style seems to import, in after years at Rome, he subjoins the fervid and characteristic doxology with which it closes."   Henry Alford, *Greek Testament* (London: Rivingtons, 1871), Vol.3, p.80,81 and Sanday and Headlam, "A Critical and Exegetical Commentary on The Epistle to the Romans," in *The International Critical Commentary* (Edinburgh: T&T Clark, 1895), p.xcv,xcvi, also defend the Pauline authorship of the doxology.

[68] Ernest Renan's solution (*Saint Paul*, [New York: G.W. Dillingham, 1887], p.xxvii-xxx) differs just slightly.   He suggested the original letter was a circular addressed to four different churches: Rome, Macedonia, Thessalonica, and Ephesus.   Each copy included chapters 1-11 plus those parts of chapters 12-16 that were specially suited to each individual church addressed.   The letter to Rome was made up of chapters 1-11 and 15;   the one to Ephesus comprised 1-14 plus 16:1-20;   the one to Thessalonica was 1-14 plus 16:21-24;   the one to Macedonia was 1-14 plus 16:25-27.   Someone later assembled all the parts into one, and this is the ancestor from which our present copies of the letter have descended.   J.B. Lightfoot (*Biblical Essays*, p.287ff) strongly opposed Renan's views.   At the least, there would have to be some modifications in chapter 1, too, before that chapter would be general enough to be addressed to anywhere but Rome.

composing the doxology to serve as a suitable conclusion for the whole collection.[69]   Then when the materials were adapted for use in the public worship services, "in Rome" was omitted from chapter 1, and chapters 15 and 16 also were deleted.   Objections to this first attempted explanation include: no definite evidence[70] of the independent circulation of chapters 1-15 exists; and if either the doxology is shown to be original, or if chapter 16 was addressed to Rome,[71] then the theory has been proved faulty.

   2. *Paul wrote short, and lengthened it himself.*   One variation of this theme is that chapters 1-14 were originally a circular letter intended for churches Paul had not yet visited, and written perhaps about the same time as Galatians.   Later, when he had opportunity to write to Rome, specific reference to Rome was added to chapter 1, and chapters 15[72] and 16 were added as a covering letter.[73]   A second variation on this theme is that 16:3-20 belonged originally to a second letter addressed by Paul to the Roman church, but written after his release from his first Roman imprisonment.[74]   A third variation of this theme is that two copies of the same letter (differing only slightly) were written and sent by Paul at the same time: the shorter form of the letter consisted of chapters 1-15 sent to Rome; the longer form of the letter (chapters 1-16, minus "in Rome" in chapter 1) was sent to Ephesus. Marcion shortened the copy sent to Rome, which influenced Western textual tradition. The statement by Origen about Marcion's expunging *two* chapters is based on the Alexandrian textual tradition which reflected the longer copy sent to Ephesus.   The Chester Beatty Papyrus is a copy of the letter sent to Rome (with the doxology at the end); the fact that it also included chapter 16 means that this scribe was aware of the text known

---

[69] James Moffatt, *Introduction to the Literature of the New Testament* (Edinburgh: T&T Clark, 1961 reprint), p.139-142.

[70] While the doxology appears at the close of chapter 15 in the Chester Beatty Papyrus, it is not absolute proof that Romans ever circulated minus chapter 16, for even P[46] carries chapter 16.   Yet one wonders what led someone to locate the doxology here when other manuscripts have it either at the end of chapter 14, or at the end of chapter 16.

[71] Both of these topics will be covered in notes on chapter 16.   There it will be demonstrated that ample evidence exists for connecting chapter 16 with Rome, and for the doxology's being a suitable summary of what has been taught in Romans.

[72] Kirsopp Lake, *The Earlier Epistles of St. Paul* (London: Rivington's, 1911), p.362, attempted to explain the fact that 15:1-13 continues the argument of chapter 14 by suggesting that Aquila had told him such a continuation would be desirable.   F.C. Burkitt, *Christian Beginnings* (London: University of London Press, 1924), p.126,127, suggested that 15:1-13 was deliberately composed to serve as a weld to join the existing epistle with the additional material Paul wished to add.

[73] Lake, *ibid.*, p.362.   In a later work, the earlier letter is no longer thought to be a circular, but rather was addressed to "some other church."   Lake and Lake, *Introduction to the New Testament*, p.108.

[74] This is Gifford's suggestion, *Romans*, p.29,30.   He thinks this suggestion will relieve most of the difficulties felt if those verses were written before Paul had ever been to Rome.   It does not appear in Gifford's presentation who was responsible, or how the two letters came to be combined into our present form.

as the Alexandrian text.[75]   Objections to this second attempted explanation include: it does not account for the personal allusions in 1:7-15; it does not offer any explanation of the effect of Marcion's mutilation of the text; the first two variations do not explain how the second letter ever came to be attached to the first; the theory that the doxology was originally written by Paul at the close of chapter 14, and then later transferred to its present position at the end of chapter 16, does not account for the strong textual tradition still evinced in the family of manuscripts headed by codices Vaticanus and Sinaiticus.

3. *Paul wrote long, and shortened it himself.*   Lightfoot suggested Paul's original letter to Rome contained our entire present epistle except the doxology, and that at a later time, perhaps during his first Roman imprisonment, Paul turned Romans into an encyclical letter. He made it a circular by cutting out "in Rome" in chapter 1, by omitting chapters 15 and 16, and by adding the newly created doxology to what was left to give the encyclical a fitting conclusion.[76]   Objections voiced to this third attempted explanation include: it is difficult to explain why Paul should make a break at 14:23 when nothing in 15:1-13 is unfit for general circulation; all of Paul's other letters circulated from place to place and the personal references in them did not detract from their usefulness; the theory is unnecessary and unsupported.[77]

4. *Paul wrote long, and someone else shortened it.*   As has already been noted, there is considerable testimony to the fact that Marcion excised chapters 15 and 16.   Examining 15:1-13, hardly any other course was possible for Marcion if he held the anti-Jewish opinions ascribed to him.   Verse 4 says Christians can gain instruction from the Jewish Scriptures.   Verse 8 describes Christ as "a servant to the circumcision."   Verses 9-12 have Old Testament quotations that may have contributed to his dislike of these verses.   The doxology makes reference to the value of "the Scriptures of the prophets," and if Marcion understood this to be a reference to the Old Testament prophets, that too would have to be cut out.   Marcion's truncated text did in fact influence textual history in the West, and this influence might explain why some manuscripts of the Vulgate have "section headings" that

---

[75] This third view is that of T.W. Manson, given in the *Bulletin of the John Rylands Library*, XXXI (1948), p.237-240, and later included in *Studies in the Gospels and Epistles* (Philadelphia: Westminster Press, 1962), p.225-241.   The scribe who copied P[46] has, after the doxology, made a slash diagonal mark to indicate a break, and then has copied chapter 16.   Knox, *Romans*, p.365, thinks this is incontrovertible evidence, from a very early period, that some copies of Romans ended with chapter 15.   Both Manson and Knox have accepted the critical opinion that chapter 16 was not originally sent to Rome.   Knox also affirms that the doxology was not written by Paul, but was added years later by whoever made a collection of Paul's letters.

[76] J.B. Lightfoot, *Journal of Philology*, 1871, No.6.

[77] If the epistle were abbreviated by Paul himself, and the doxology added to it, and this at Rome, as Lightfoot suggests, it is strange and almost unaccountable that no copy of this genuine abbreviated recension has been preserved, and that no known Latin Codex contains the doxology after 14:23 (though one Vulgate manuscript does have a blank space at that place).

seem to indicate chapters 15 and 16 were missing from some copies of Romans.[78] It might also help explain how copies of Romans came to be in existence (cf. Origen[79]) that had the doxology after chapter 14 – they would be copies made of Marcion's text after he removed everything from 14:23 on, but with the doxology attached. Marcion's influence would also explain, as no other theory has done, why the break came after chapter 14, instead of the middle of or after chapter 15. Those who object to this fourth attempt to explain the diverse evidence urge that it does not account for the (alleged[80]) omission before Marcion's time of chapters 15 and 16 from some copies of Romans; that it does not account for the eventual inclusion of the doxology at chapter 14[81]; that it does not easily explain the absence of "in Rome" in chapter 1[82]; and that it does not explain why the benediction (15:24)

---

[78] It might also explain why no trace whatever of such an abbreviated Latin codex (or Greek, for that matter) still exists. Any church in possession of a mutilated copy of Romans which was known to have resulted from the work of a heretic like Marcion would feel no real reason for preserving it. But would any church possessing an abbreviated copy of Romans, known to be a genuine work of the apostle Paul, have allowed it to disappear, so that not even one copy exists among the hundreds of manuscripts of Romans still extant?

[79] Origen's statement has been quoted on page xxi. Gifford, *Romans*, p.21,22, interprets Origen's statement to mean that the copies of Romans that in his day did not reflect any of Marcion's corrupting influence were of two kinds: (1) those that had sixteen chapters with the doxology after chapter 14; and (2) those that had 16 chapters with the doxology at the end of 16. We wonder if another interpretation of Origen's statement is possible: namely, that fifty years after Marcion's mutilation of the text, Origen knew of some copies of Romans that consisted of only 14 chapters plus the doxology which, though cut off by Marcion, had since been restored by someone else other than Marcion or his followers.

[80] Whether or not there is real evidence of the existence of any manuscripts with chapters 15 and 16 missing before Marcion tampered with the text, as we have seen, depends on the precise meaning of the one Latin word (*dissecuit*) in Rufinus' Latin translation of Origen. This is hardly sufficient evidence to affirm there were copies of Romans circulating before AD 140 with the last two chapters missing.

[81] As noted earlier (see footnotes #60, #62, and #79), the usual explanation offered is that the doxology found after chapter 14 was due to someone attempting to supply a satisfactory conclusion to Marcion's shortened text. The genuine Pauline doxology (some have affirmed that interpolations were added) was returned, but for some reason the rest of chapters 15 and 16 were not. The position of the doxology after 15:33 in P[46] is attributed to a later scribal attempt to harmonize a text that descended from Marcion's mutilated copy, with a text that was descended from a copy of Romans that still had all 16 chapters intact. After all, Paul never elsewhere ends a letter with a doxology, so it might seem out of place appended to chapter 16.

[82] Gifford, *Romans*, p.24, expresses his opinion that Marcion would have been more likely than Paul to be the one who removed "in Rome," but he suggests no reason why Marcion should have done so. Even if we could come up with a plausible reason why Marcion removed "in Rome," it would not cover up the original destination of the letter, for in his canon it still had the title "To the Romans." Why remove it from the text, only to leave it conspicuously in the title? H.A.W. Meyer, *Critical and Exegetical Handbook to the Epistle to the Romans* (Winona Lake, IN: Alpha Publications, 1979 reprint), p.28, suggested, "Perhaps some church, which received a copy of the epistle from the Romans for public reading, may have *for their own particular church-use*, deleted the extraneous designation of place, and thus individual codices may have passed into circulation without it." In reply to Meyer, it might be asked if he could demonstrate where such a thing was done to the person and place references of any other letter used for public worship. Knox, *Romans*, p.356-358, offers an interesting suggestion to explain the absence of "in Rome." First of all, he appeals to the order of books in Marcion's canon – Galatians, 1 and 2 Corinthians, Romans, 1 and 2 Thessalonians, Ephesians, Colossians, Philemon, Philippians. He then reminds us that when Paul's letters were first collected, they were still written on scrolls. 1 & 2 Corinthians preceded by a shorter letter (e.g., Marcion used Galatians) would take one roll; Romans and the others would take another roll. His

is moved and changed.[83]

Where, then, does the question of integrity stand?   These statements seem to be true: (1) In the three hundred or more manuscripts still extant and which are unmutilated, Romans appears just as we have it in our English Bibles – that is, with *sixteen* chapters and *with* the doxology (though the location of the doxology varies).   (2) The earliest evidence of a text with less than what is included in our sixteen chapters is Marcion, and the removal of the last two chapters is attributed to Marcion himself, who objected to their contents on doctrinal grounds.   (3) Though there is still not a satisfactory explanation for all the evidence (e.g., "in Rome" is missing; the location of the doxology), the result of the best textual criticism is represented in the text found in the Nestle/UBS Greek texts: it treats chapters 15 and 16 as being in the original, and it treats the doxology as being part of the original, rather than an addition some writer invented and added later.

When one examines the whole field of investigation, nothing is found that conclusively throws any doubt on the genuineness or integrity of the closing chapters.   On the contrary, as one hypothesis after another is refuted, more and more proof accumulates for the genuineness and integrity of what the critics question.   We would affirm that the entire letter "To the Romans" as found in our Bibles is essentially the same as the autographed copy Paul originally sent.

2. Philosophy, Dogma, and Hermeneutics

It has not been easy through the centuries, as a study of the history of interpretation makes clear, to find just the right method by which to explain the Scriptures to people unfamiliar with them.   Several terms have been used to refer to this effort.   *Exegesis* seeks to determine what meaning the text had for its author and its original readers. *Interpretation* (or exposition) has to do with making application of the meaning to today's readers.   *Hermeneutics* is the term applied to the rules and methodology by which exegesis

---

final suggestion is that before Marcion's time, Ephesians (it has "in Ephesus" missing in some manuscripts) stood first in "Volume I" along with the Corinthian correspondence; while Romans (with "in Rome" removed, so that it too serves as a sort of cover letter for the collection) stood first in "Volume II" (with Galatians where Ephesians was in Marcion's canon). (*Note*: There are assumptions made by Knox that are not easy to accept: [1] that whoever collected the books felt free to add to or subtract from the text at will; [2] that whoever collected the Pauline books rejected the Pastoral Epistles as being Paul's, there thus being no need to find a place in "volume 1" or "2" or "3" to include these.)

[83] While an appeal to the influence of Marcion's mutilation does not seem to account for all the evidence, neither does the idea that some Roman opponents of Paul deliberately suppressed and withheld the concluding chapters of the letter from the public; that then in the 2nd century several attempts were made to supply a fitting conclusion – in the Eastern church the doxology was added to 14:23, while in the Western Church it was 15:1-32 and 16:3-20 that were added; then, at a still later date, these two additions were combined with a third known reading (15:33-16:2 and 16:21-24); and that somewhere in all this conglomeration the genuine conclusion is accurately preserved.

is first done and then by which interpretation is made.[84]   "Hermeneutics is the science and art of Biblical interpretation.   It is a science because it is guided by rules within a system; and it is an art because the application of the rules is by skill, and not by mechanical imitation."[85]   The material found in the Bible, written between 2000 and 3500 years ago in Aramaic, Hebrew, and Greek, poses some special problems for the modern exegete/interpreter, who must not only be able to work in those languages, but who must also be acquainted with cultures and environments both ancient and modern (for the modern ones differ considerably from those that prevailed in the ancient world).   And there are other limitations to this science that must be recognized.

> Not every meaning in an author's mind can be conveyed by language. Matters concerning his unique individuality that draw on a complex of private experiences in his past cannot be shared.   Certain experiences, such as the taste of apricots, also cannot be represented by words.   Likewise, the visual images that often accompany the matters we wish to transmit cannot be represented verbally.[86]

Yet even with all these limitations, it is still possible to closely approximate what the author intended, simply because God has chosen to convey His message to men in human language.[87]   "The language of the Bible is human language and, as such, is subject to the same principles and laws that govern the interpretation of any other book or writing other

---

[84] Little agreement is found as to the terms by which the different disciplines have been designated. For example, some use 'interpretation' to mean what we have styled as 'exegesis,' namely, "an explanation of what is not immediately plain in the Bible"; they then use 'exposition' to designate what we have called 'interpretation,' or the applying of the text and its meaning to men and women today.

[85] Bernard Ramm, *Protestant Biblical Interpretation*, 3rd rev. ed. (Grand Rapids: Baker Book House, 1970), p.1.   The observation that hermeneutics is both an art and a science is well taken.   The reader of this definition should be careful, however, lest he get the idea from the words "*Biblical* interpretation" that this is a tool that is needed or useful only to those who would interpret the Bible.   In fact, the same methods are used to interpret any literature.

[86] Daniel P. Fuller, "Interpretation, History of," in *International Standard Bible Encyclopedia*, edited by Geoffrey Bromiley (Grand Rapids: Wm. B. Eerdmans Publishing Co., 1982), Vol.2, p.863.

[87] "The chance that an interpreter will succeed in grasping an author's verbal meaning is greatly enhanced by the limitations of possible meanings that have been imposed upon words by cultural norms and conventions ... Nevertheless, the interpreter always has to guess at the meaning of a communication he wants to grasp.   He tries out several possible meanings which certain crucial words or phrases can have until coherency with all such crucial terms and the text as a whole is reached.   Virtually absolute certainty that one person has understood another can be achieved when the two are in direct conversation with each other, for then it is possible to ask questions to see if the meanings guessed at were correct. But in construing a text whose author cannot be consulted, a claim to validity in interpretation can never have more than a high probability."   Fuller, *Interpretation, History of*, p.863,864.

than the Bible."[88]

The significance of this whole topic will become obvious with but a moment's reflection. If a person is to accept the New Testament as his rule of faith and practice in matters of religion, it is evident that he must know rather precisely what the New Testament is saying, for if its real meaning is missed the authority of Scripture is nullified.[89] Again, if hermeneutics is ignored, there is a real danger of confusing authorities – that of Scripture and that of the individual interpretation of it. Or worse, if hermeneutics is ignored, there is the very real danger that currently popular philosophy or dogma will control the explanation offered for any given passage, rather than letting the original author's actual message come through.

It is the thesis of this introductory study that when men permit currently popular philosophy or theological dogma to control what they see in any ancient text, they have forfeited any claim to exegesis. This thesis will be demonstrated by an appeal to the history of interpretation (with special emphasis on how Romans has been explained) where it can be clearly seen what happens when the "interpreter" reads the Biblical text through colored glasses. This brief history of interpretation is also offered in order that the contemporary student will be enabled to appreciate and evaluate what he may read in other commentaries on Romans and other Bible books.

Pre-Christian Interpretation

In the time of Ezra (450 BC) we have one of the earliest recorded efforts to interpret the Scriptures. During the exile in Babylon, the language spoken by the people of Israel changed from the Hebrew language in which the Law of Moses had been written to Aramaic. So, when they returned to the land of Israel and assembled to hear a reading of the Law by Ezra, it became necessary for the reading to be accompanied by an explanation or translation into Aramaic (Nehemiah 8:7,8).[90] This translation model is a particularly

---

[88] H.L. Drumright, "Interpretation," in *Zondervan Pictorial Encyclopedia of the Bible*, edited by Merrill C. Tenney (Grand Rapids: Zondervan Publishing House, 1975), Vol.3, p.297.

[89] Such a statement presumes that Scripture should judge the beliefs and actions of the church, rather than the church sitting in judgment of the Scriptures. This also assumes (because of a lack of any real evidence to the contrary) that the New Testament writings are what they claim to be, the inspired word of God. (Of course, even the evidence for and against has been and may be submitted to critical study, to ascertain its validity.) If God has spoken, and the evidence is that He has, then His word must be made the norm and criteria by which all men's actions are finally judged.

[90] In Nehemiah 8:7, the KJV reads "caused to understand" where the NASB reads "explained;" both are attempts to render the hiphil form of the verb *bin*. In verse 8, the KJV has "distinctly" where the NASB reads "translating;" in this case, the Hebrew verb is *parash*, which means "to be explained." The use of the two terms helps us to see what was being done: Ezra was speaking Hebrew, and his helpers were translating into Aramaic the Hebrew terms Ezra was reading so they could easily be understood by the audience.

apt illustration of what exegesis should be today – the exegete makes the Scriptures clear and understandable by transmitting them into the language spoken by his audience, and then adding only such further explanation as is needed for clarity's sake.

Another method of "interpretation" arose during the captivities. There were things commanded in the Law that could not be carried out while the people were in bondage – for example, going to the tabernacle/temple to worship at Passover, Pentecost, and Tabernacles. Rather than ignore these commands, they were given a new "meaning" under the pretext that the intent behind the command was being obeyed, even though they were not literally doing what the command required.[91] After the captivities were ended, a few returned to the holy land, but the majority did not. Thus, by the time of Christ, there were five or more Jews outside the land for every Jew in the land. Many of those outside were influenced in their thinking by the Greek customs bequeathed to the world as a result of Alexander the Great's conquests, while many of those inside the land tried to observe the Law of Moses as carefully as they could.[92] There seems to have grown up two different ways of explaining the Law – one that might be styled Palestinian Judaism, and one that might be styled Hellenistic Judaism.[93] In addition, some of the Old Testament commands were of a rather general nature ("you shall not do any work" on the seventh day). Jewish teachers therefore felt obliged to add flesh to these bones: they made up specific applications of the general commandments and proceeded to hand these down from one generation to another by word of mouth. Before long, Jewish interpretation was more interested in making Scripture fit culture or tradition than in making culture and tradi-

---

[91] Samuel Sandmel, *Judaism and Christian Beginnings* (New York: Oxford University Press, 1978), p.9ff.

[92] The tension over how to interpret the Law for the contemporary situation is well illustrated by the schools of Hillel and Shammai in the 1st century BC. Hillel, born in Babylon, emigrated to Jerusalem when he was about 40 years of age. There eventually became head of the Sanhedrin, and was known to be very sympathetic to modifications of the letter of the Law in order to make it fit the modern cultural and social developments. Shammai, on the other hand, who was vice-president of the Sanhedrin under Hillel, was a very strict legalist when it came to applying the Law's commands. "It has been told that his formalism led him to starve his infant grandson nearly to death in an attempt to make him fast on the Great Day of Atonement. At the Feast of Tabernacles, he insisted that the booth required at the season be built over the bed of his daughter who was in the agony of childbirth." Drumwright, *Interpretation*, p.298.

[93] Donald A. Hagner, "Paul in Modern Jewish Thought," in *Pauline Studies*, edited by Donald Hagner and Murray T. Harris (Grand Rapids: Wm. B. Eerdmans Publishing Co., 1980), p.143-165. While not all modern scholars would agree about a discernible difference between Palestinian and Hellenistic Judaism, it certainly can be agreed that one of the major points of difference between Pharisees and Sadducees was over the degree to which Hellenistic culture could be accepted by Jewish people, with the Pharisees insisting on the old ways, and the Sadducees being willing to accommodate themselves to the new culture.

tion submissive to Scripture.   A whole new method of interpretation that emphasized the 'hidden meaning' of the passage had grown up.[94]

Jesus' Interpretation of the Old Testament

Jesus was familiar both with the methods and content of the interpretations current among the Jewish leaders of His day.   He was aware, for example, how they had explained away the Mosaic rule about divorce (Luke 16:18; Matthew 19:3-9).   He was aware of their added rules that tried to specify what was work on the Sabbath, and these were the occasion for several confrontations between Jesus and the religious leaders (Luke 6:1-11, 13:10-17, 14:1-6).   On one occasion, Jesus flatly stated that their elevation of tradition above Moses (He used as illustration their "hidden meaning" about Corban, i.e., an offering to God) had resulted in actual transgression of what God had commanded (Matthew 15:1-9).   On another occasion, Jesus showed that there was a clear distinction between what Moses commanded and what the scribes and Pharisees taught.   In light of this truth, He told His audience that they were expected to observe what Moses taught, but should avoid the man-made rules and practices of the religious leaders (Matthew 23:1-33).

Jesus accepted as historical facts the creation of Adam and Eve (Matthew 19:4); the Mosaic authorship of Deuteronomy (Mark 10:3-5) and Exodus (Luke 20:37); the inspiration of David (Matthew 13:35, 22:43), Zechariah (Matthew 21:4), Jeremiah (Matthew 2:17), and Isaiah (Matthew 15:7); the Old Testament record of Jonah (Matthew 12:40); the destruction of Sodom and Gomorrah (Matthew 10:15, 11:23,24; Luke 17:28,29); the Flood in the time of Noah (Luke 17:26,27); and the predictive nature of Daniel's prophecy (Matthew 24:15).   Jesus nowhere raised a doubt about the historical facticity of any recorded Old Testament event, but assumed the truth of every Old Testament reference to which He called attention.

Though He accepted the Law, Prophets, and Psalms as authoritative Scripture, Jesus did not accept either of the ways that Scriptures were interpreted by His contemporaries.

---

[94] "Qumran. – The Habakkuk Commentary from Qumran best illustrates the use of the term *psr* as applied to scriptural texts in that community.   In a thoroughgoing attempt to apply the prophet's words to contemporary history, the Qumran interpreter of Habakkuk relentlessly quotes verse by verse, and in each instance applies the exposition with the formula *psrw 'l*, 'its (hidden) interpretation is thus ....'   This example is illustrative of the origin of the literary form of the pesher.   It incorporates not only interpretation, but also application and commentary, and endeavors to elucidate hidden meanings in the words of the prophet, the import of which are known only in the inner circle of the chosen ...."   D.G. Burke, "Interpretation," in *International Standard Bible Encyclopedia*, edited by Geoffrey Bromiley (Grand Rapids: Wm. B. Eerdmans Publishing Co., 1982), Vol.2, p.862.

"In traditional Jewish exegesis of the Hebrew Scriptures, the Prophets and the Writings were treated largely as commentaries on the Torah.   Alongside the surface meaning of the text, the *pesat*, was the more extended application, the *deras*, which might appear farfetched at times ... Leading rabbis set forth certain rules to be followed in scriptural interpretation: Hillel (ca. 10 BC) propounded seven, Ishmael (ca. AD 100) thirteen, and Eliezer ben Yose (ca. AD 150) thirty-two.   These remained normative into medieval times."   F.F. Bruce, "Interpretation of the Bible," in *Evangelical Dictionary of Theology*, edited by Walter A. Elwell (Grand Rapids: Baker Book House, 1984), p.566.

Instead of the traditions of the scribes, Jesus offered His own authoritative explanation (Mark 1:22, "He was teaching them as one having authority, and not as the scribes"). He treated the Mosaic Covenant and its Scriptures as temporary ("You have heard it was said, but I say to you," Matthew 5:27-28, implies that Jesus' words were to be accepted as authority rather than Moses), yet He explained that Moses was intended to be authoritative until it was all fulfilled (Matthew 5:18). He objected to the religious leaders' attempts to twist the Law and Prophets to suit themselves, just as He objected to their attempts to "force" the Kingdom of God that had been preached since John the Baptist (Luke 16:16). From the very first of His ministry, Jesus introduced His explanation of the relation between the Old Testament and the New – it was the relationship of promise to fulfillment.[95] He placed Himself in the focus of all the rays of Old Testament prophecy (John 5:46; Luke 4:17-19). After His resurrection, when His suffering for the sins of the world was a thing of the past, He could direct their attention to Moses and the prophets and explain "to them the things concerning Himself in all the Scriptures" (Luke 24:27), showing how they anticipated His suffering and the glory to follow. Now it could be clearly seen that no distinction need be made between a text and its true meaning as the Jews had been doing. Instead, it could be seen that there was a planned relationship between what had been written long before in the text and the historical facts of Jesus' ministry, death, resurrection, and entrance into glory.[96]

Apostles' Interpretation of the Old Testament

We affirm that the apostles perfectly reflected the teachings they learned from Jesus when it came to interpreting the Old Testament (cf. Acts 3:18-21). They repeated Jesus' interpretation of the Old Testament messianic types and prophecies: the tabernacle was a "copy and shadow of heavenly things" (Hebrews 8:5) and the Law was only a "shadow of the good things to come" (Hebrews 10:1); Matthew appeals to over 40 Old Testament passages that were "fulfilled" in Christ; Paul affirms that the gospel was "promised beforehand through His prophets in the holy Scriptures" (Romans 1:2).[97]   The apostles accepted with-

---

[95] This summary statement should not be interpreted to mean that every verse and event in the Old Testament is somehow a prediction or type of the life and ministry of Jesus.   But it does harmonize with what is said in Romans about how God's plans were once hidden, a mystery which has, since Jesus' incarnation, been more fully revealed.   "The messianic interpretation of the Old Testament, cherished and developed in the early New Testament church, is here founded by Jesus Himself. This interpretation understands the Old Testament in terms of promise and fulfillment, a pattern of divine preparation and deeds that reach their climax in the life, death, and resurrection of the Christ (cf. e.g., the handling of the Suffering Servant of Isa. 53 in Acts 8:32f. and Lk. 22:37; cf. also Mk 14:27; *et al.*)." Burke, *Interpretation*, p.862.

[96] "So for all Christians, the Old Testament would never be the same.   From that point on, it would always be seen as a document bearing witness to Christ.   And Christ's own teachings would take on an authoritative role in its proper interpretation." Wayne G. McCown, "Hermeneutics," in *A Contemporary Wesleyan Theology*, edited by Charles W. Carter (Grand Rapids: Francis Asbury Press, 1983), Vol.2, p.741.

[97] Some current studies have emphasized the use of the Old Testament by the New Testament writers. Liberal scholarship has particularly called attention to a few passages in such a way as to discredit the doctrine of inspiration.   One hears the charge that some New Testament writers are guilty of practicing "rabbinic exegesis."   Since Paul studied in the Rabbi's schools, it is not unusual to read the charge that he

out question the inspiration of the Old Testament (2 Timothy 3:16; 2 Peter 1:20,21). The apostle John accepts the unity of Isaiah, attributing chapters 6 and 53 to the same Isaiah (John 12:38-40), and Matthew attributes chapters 6,9,40,42, and 53 all to the prophet Isaiah (Matthew 3:3, 4:14, 8:17, 12:17, 13:14). Hebrews 1:1,2 reflect the idea of progressive revelation everywhere assumed in the New Testament – the revelation made of old to the fathers by the prophets has given way to His perfect and final revelation in Christ. The apostles often affirm that the Old Testament contained precision predictive prophecy: for example, on Pentecost Peter said that what was happening that day was a fulfillment of Joel's prediction (Acts 2:16), and later said that "all the prophets who have spoken, from Samuel and his successors onward, also announced these days" (Acts 3:24).

Up to this point, the topic has been the interpretation of the *Old* Testament. When it comes to the interpretation of certain *New* Testament statements, Peter offers some interesting observations (2 Peter 3). He shows that prophecies about the second advent of Jesus are to be taken literally; that what looks to men like unreasonable delay in the execution of God's announced purposes is not delay at all, but rather has a gracious reason behind it, giving even Christians time to come to repentance, lest they perish. Peter also notes that there are some things in Paul's writings that are hard to understand, and which some distort (i.e., explain them in an improper way). Peter closes with a *caveat emptor* to his readers lest they be eternally ruined by these erroneous interpretations. There is, then, a right and a wrong way to understand the Scriptures, and the whole matter we are studying can and does have eternal significance.

We have seen previously that Hellenistic culture and philosophy, when allowed by the Jews to control their interpretation, got them into problems that earned the rebuke of Jesus. After the close of the apostolic age, it is sad to see how often philosophy and dogma have been permitted to control the interpretation of the Bible.

Platonic and Stoic Philosophy Influenced Exegesis

The philosophies of Greece tended to emphasize a mind-body dualism, and before the 1st century these Greek ideas had been embraced by some in the Jewish community in Alexandria. Though not the first to make an attempt to harmonize explanations of the Old Testament with philosophy, Philo (30 BC to AD 50) is the best-known representative of the Jewish Alexandrian allegorical method of interpretation. Philo was influenced by both Stoicism and Neoplatonism. "He learned his hermeneutical principle from Stoicism, which proposed to move beyond the literal to the 'higher' allegorical truths of Greek literature."[98]

---

especially at times adopted their methods. He is accused of reckless disregard of the context and historical background at Romans 9:25; he is accused of interpreting like Hillel at Galatians 3:16, and of displaying a rather flagrant example of allegorical interpretation at Galatians 4:21-31. Romans 3:10-19, 9:14-18, and Hebrews 2:12-13 are pointed to as examples of stringing passages together like the rabbis were wont to do, without any regard to the passage's original setting or intent. Matthew 2:15, where Matthew applies a passage in Hosea to the sojourn of the infant Jesus in Egypt, is called one of Matthew's rather flagrant examples of finding a meaning in an Old Testament passage that certainly was not intended

He taught that all Scripture contained a twofold meaning – literal and allegorical, which corresponded to the body and soul of man. As the soul was judged to be more important than the body, so the allegorical meaning of Scripture was more important than its obvious meaning. By way of example, in his commentary on Genesis 2:10-14, Philo made the four rivers of Eden stand for virtues: prudence, temperance, courage, justice. Likewise, the main source from which the four rivers branched represented goodness, which was judged to be the basic virtue. Philo occupied himself almost exclusively with the Pentateuch.[99]

Many of the same allegorical methods introduced by Philo to Jewish interpretation can be observed in the later Christian writers in the school at Alexandria.[100] Clement of Alexandria and Origen are two of the better-known representatives of this school. "To them, much in the Bible that was intellectually incredible or morally objectionable if under-

---

by its original writer.

The affirmation that conservative scholarship has simply denied or ignored the problems raised by these passages cannot be substantiated. One simply needs to consult the host of conservative commentaries published in the last quarter century. Furthermore, we would affirm that the Old Testament record, in places at least, was deliberately written as it was so that it might serve as a "preview" of coming attractions. Consider that the record of Melchizedek in Genesis was deliberately written as it was so that he might serve as a type of Christ (see Hebrews 7:3, "made like the Son of God"). And consider that Ephesians 5:31,32 show that the record in Genesis 2:24 was written so that men would have an illustration of the unity God intends with reference to Christ and the church. We would affirm that it is a precarious practice to charge the writers of these verses with practicing peculiar hermeneutics. How much better to simply respect and reflect the explanations they have given to us of those Old Testament verses. That would be thinking God's thoughts after Him, we affirm.

[98] McCown, *ibid*. Greeks considered a poet like Homer to be inspired (an "inspiration" different from the inspiration attributed to Biblical writers). "If a poet like Homer was inspired, then what he said about the gods could be acceptable to thoughtful pagans only if it were taken to be a veiled allegorical presentation of truths otherwise attained by philosophical reasoning." Bruce, *Interpretation*, p.566.

[99] Drumwright, *Interpretation*, p.299. "His treatment of Genesis 28:11 illustrates the measure of ingenuity involved. The text (simply) says, 'Taking one of the stones of the place [Jacob] put it under his head and lay down in that place to sleep' (RSV). The explanation of the text, according to Philo, is both literal and allegorical. The literal teaching is that the true disciple of the Word eschews the luxuries of soft living and is willing to suffer hardship in order to gain virtue. The deeper truth is that Jacob chose one of the spiritual intelligences of that holy place, and placing it close to his mind, rested in that intelligence, laying his life upon it." McCown, *Hermeneutics*, p.741.

[100] The Epistle of Barnabas (c. AD 130), which circulated among the churches of Egypt for a while, is one of the first examples of 'Christian' literature written from an allegorical standpoint. It uses the "hidden meanings" of the Old Testament to demonstrate the superiority of the Christian religion to the Jewish. "The point made by the Epistle of Barnabas was that the Old Testament had meaning only when it was understood in terms of the gospel. This author was given to an extreme typology. History was meaningless; God's covenant had always been made with Christians. In fact, his attitude toward the Old Testament was not far from that of the Gnostics. In everything he had to find Christ, so that typology was the basic principle of interpretation. The celebrated example of Abraham's 318 servants serves to illustrate his methodology. By combining two separate passages, he arrived at the number of Abraham's servants as 318, which was represented by the numerical value of the letters TIH. He said the 'T' stood for the cross, and the 'IH' for Jesus (the two letters being the same two letters found in the beginning of the name Jesus in the Greek). This was the mystery that Abraham meant to communicate by the number of his servants." Drumwright, *Interpretation*, p.301.

stood literally could be made intelligible and congenial if it was allegorized."[101]   Origen attempted to justify his use of Platonic philosophy by an appeal to Proverbs 22:20.

> On the basis of a Greek translation of Proverbs 22:20, Origen proposed that Scripture has meaning on three different levels, corresponding to the body, soul, and spirit. The bodily sense, said Origen, is the literal meaning: it is useful merely for the instruction of the simple. It was the deeper and hidden soul and spirit levels of meaning that truly interested Origen: these required a "mystical" interpretation to bring them to light. In his view, "Scripture wove into the narrative, for the sake of more mystical truths, things that never have occurred – sometimes things that would never have occurred."[102]

Bruce thus summarizes the results of the Alexandrian allegorical method:

> By allegorization, it was believed, the intention of the Spirit who spoke through the prophets and apostles could be penetrated. But this approach was largely arbitrary, because the approved interpretation depended so largely on the interpreter's personal preference, and in practice it violated the original intention of the Scriptures and almost obliterated the historical relatedness of the revelation they recorded.[103]

Aristotle's Philosophy Influenced Exegesis

The exegetical school at Antioch followed principles of interpretation that were directly opposed to those of its rival at Alexandria. Antioch insisted on emphasizing the very elements – the literal and historical meaning of the text – that Alexandria disparaged.

> The school at Antioch was noted for its literal and grammatical interpretation of the Bible. The earliest representative of it whom we know is Theophilus, bishop of Antioch about AD 180, whose second and third books dedicated to a certain Autolycus are full of literal exegesis of the Old Testament. Later Antiochians were expert in the study of Hebrew or of the Greek text of the Old Testament. Their exegesis, under the influence of the prominent Jewish community of the city, was ordinarily soberly literal.[104]

---

[101] Bruce, *Interpretation*, p.566.

[102] McCown, *Hermeneutics*, p.742,743.   Origen's three-fold meaning included the literal, the moral, and the spiritual senses, suitable for the simple stage, the more mature, and the fully mature. "Application is made to the will in the second stage and to Christ and the church (typology) in the third, though in practice Origen often reverses the two. Thus, Noah's ark refers historically to the Flood, then typologically to Christ's provision of an ark of salvation (the church), and finally, devotionally, to the individual preparation of an ark of conversion." Geoffrey W. Bromiley, "The Interpretation of the Bible," in *Expositor's Bible Commentary*, edited by Frank E. Gaebelein (Grand Rapids: Zondervan Publishing House, 1979), Vol.1, p.67,68.

[103] Bruce, *Interpretation,* p.566.

[104] Robert M. Grant, "History of the Interpretation of the Bible: Ancient Period," in *The Interpreter's Bible*, edited by George A. Buttrick (Nashville: Abingdon Press, 1952), Vol.1, p.110.

Theodore of Mopsuestia (AD 350-428), perhaps the greatest exegete of the early church, and John Chrysostom (AD 354-407), the greatest preacher of the early church, are two of the better known Antiochians. Two influences that lie behind the hermeneutical method used at Antioch are Aristotle's philosophy[105] and the Semitic background[106] of many of the early members of this school. While they consciously opposed the extreme allegorical methods of Alexandria, they did allow that the Bible contained figurative language.

> The School of Antioch did accept and practice typological interpretation so long as it was not allowed to overshadow or substitute for the original, literal meaning of the text. They referred to the allegories of the Alexandrians and their kin, however, perhaps somewhat disdainfully, as mere "theories." In this area, they proffered a helpful distinction – between allegory and metaphor. Although they eschewed allegory altogether, they embraced metaphor within their understanding of the literal meaning of Scripture, as an intentional use of figurative language in the original text.[107]

Tragically, in this commentator's view, the influence of the Antiochian school on Biblical interpretation was cut short. At the council of Ephesus in AD 431, the school at Antioch was included in the anathema on Nestorius, and the writings of its best authors were declared heretical (not so much because of the method they used, but because of the position they took in the Christological controversy). When the Eastern and Roman churches separated from each other, the influence of Antioch was reduced even further as far as Western thought was concerned. Consequently, some form of Origen's allegorical method prevailed in the Western church for the next thousand years.

Church Dogma Influenced Interpretation

Before Augustine (AD 354-430) learned the allegorical method of interpretation from Ambrose of Milan, he believed there were many philosophical difficulties in the Old Testament.[108] Using the allegorical method he was able to explain away these difficulties and embrace the Christian faith. If there remained any unresolved problems, the interpret-

---

[105] Grant, *History*, p.109.

[106] Fuller, *Interpretation*, p.865.

[107] McCown, *Hermeneutics*, p.743.

[108] "Augustine's entire early career may be regarded as a search for a tenable exegetical method. Only when he discovered and accepted allegorization ... was he able to enter into traditional Christianity. Before that time he was a halfhearted Manichaean. Like Marcion, his Manichaean teachers insisted on a literal interpretation of the Old Testament in order to prove its absurdity. They emphasized anthropomorphic expressions in order to ask ironically whether God has hair and nails. They criticized the morality of the patriarchs. As for the New Testament, they again followed Marcion in their claim that the text had been interpolated by Judaizers. Augustine began to suspect their veracity when they proved unable to provide a copy of the original, genuine text. But Old Testament problems continued to disturb. Only the sermons of Ambrose of Milan were able to bring him to a fresh view of the Old Testament." Grant, *History of Interpretation*, p.112.

er must be guided by what the church (i.e., Catholic Church) dogma says. "When Gregory the Great established papal supremacy in AD 590, the authority of tradition as interpreter of scripture became an institution."[109]

Monastic exegesis (AD 650-1200) had one purpose, to promulgate and support the dogmas of the Roman church. "The task of the interpreter changed. Instead of trying to get at the true sense, he now had to substantiate the imposed interpretation, or indeed, to provide the texts that might seem to support what was agreed in advance to be the authentic dogmatic meaning."[110] Generally speaking, the allegorical method of interpretation dominated medieval hermeneutics. Origen's threefold sense soon developed into the fourfold sense (literal, allegorical, moral, and anagogical), as stated and illustrated by Guibert of Nogent (d.1124).[111] For example, for Guibert, the Jerusalem in the Bible was literally the earthly city, allegorically the church, morally the individual Christian, and anagogically the new Jerusalem. Every time an interpreter came to the word, all these senses had to be understood, or the point of the passage was missed. Or again, a reference to water could denote on different levels literal water, moral purity, the practice and doctrine of baptism, and eternal life in the heavenly Jerusalem.

> This method served more to illumine the position of the expositor and the church than to interpret the original intentions of the text. A passage could be interpreted to mean several things at once, and of course only a priest (or the pope) could tell which was true and which heretical.[112]

Scholastic exegesis (AD 1200-1500) begins to reflect growing uneasiness with the dogmatic interpretations in the light of the intellectual awakening that would result in the Renaissance. First one, then another, of the fourfold meanings would be emphasized as the Scholastics tried to reconcile interpretation with newly rediscovered knowledge.

Not all of the medieval scholars cultivated the fourfold sense of Scripture. Many emphasized, instead, the literal interpretation; this often went hand in hand with the study

---

[109] McCown, *Hermeneutics*, p.744.

[110] Bromiley, *Interpretation*, p.70. Following the collapse of the Roman Empire, "Latin ceased to be a spoken language in Europe, except among the clergy, very few of whom could read Greek or knew any Hebrew. Thus, for the ordinary Christian, the Scriptures took on the dull, secondhand flavor of its monkish interpreters." McCown, *Hermeneutics*, p.744. It became popular to formulate Catenae, or chains, of Scripture verses and sayings of the church fathers, as a guide to interpretation.

[111] "A sixteenth-century poem explains these levels as follows: 'The *letter* shows us what God and our fathers did. The *allegory* shows us where our faith is hid. The *moral* meaning gives us rules of daily life. The *analogy* shows us where we end our strife'." McCown, *Hermeneutics*, p.744.

[112] McCown, *Hermeneutics*, p.744. Allegorical interpretations were used to prove papal supremacy. Innocent III (AD 1160-1216) based papal supremacy on the two great lights of Genesis 1:16-18, the sun representing the spiritual power (the papacy), and the smaller one, the moon, which takes its light from the sun, representing the temporal power (secular government). Thus the state takes its orders from the church.

of the Hebrew language, knowledge of which could be gained from Jewish rabbis who now populated Europe in some numbers. One eminent rabbi was Rashi (Solomon ben Isaac, d.1105), who influenced the teachers of the Abbey of Saint Victor at Paris to seek the meaning in the Old Testament books that their writers had in mind when they wrote. He also influenced Nicholas of Lyra (d.1340), whose fifty-volume commentary on the whole Bible (*Postillae Perpetuae in Vetus et Novum Testamentum*) reflects on almost every page the opinions of Rashi. Sometimes he rejects the interpretation of Rashi and goes to the Targums for the nuances of a Hebrew word or for some Bible custom; often he prefers Rashi to Jerome or some other Christian authority. Nicholas' writings, in turn, had influence on the Waldenses and the Reformers.[113]

Humanism Influenced Exegesis

"Humanism" refers to "the principles or culture of the scholars of the Renaissance who pursued and spread the study, and a truer understanding of the literature, ideas, etc., of ancient Rome and Greece."[114] The Renaissance called attention to the necessity of going back to the original. John Colet influenced Erasmus.[115] Erasmus (d.1536) and other humanists, by their Greek and Hebrew studies, laid the foundation for a return to a philological understanding of the Scriptures.[116] Martin Luther, for example, was influenced by Erasmus, and frequently expresses a preference for the grammatical-historical interpretation.[117] But like the Roman church before him, Luther also erred when he tried to make interpretation subservient to a particular doctrine. "Luther never explained why his understanding of justification by faith alone was the 'doctrine of faith'

---

[113] John T. McNeill, "History of the Interpretation of the Bible: Medieval and Reformation Period," in *The Interpreter's Bible*, edited by George A. Buttrick (Nashville: Abingdon Press, 1952), Vol.1, p.122. Luther's enemies composed the jingle *Si Lyra non lyrasset, Lutherus non saltasset* ("If Nicholas had not played on his lyre, Luther would not have danced"). This jingle may oversimplify the matter, for Nicholas of Lyra was indebted to others besides Rashi, and Luther to others besides Nicholas. McNeill adds, "Many sixteenth-century commentators besides Luther, humanist, Roman Catholic, and Protestant, used the *Postillae* with appreciation." p.123.

[114] Clarence L. Barnhart, ed., *Thorndike-Barnhart Comprehensive Desk Dictionary* (Garden City, NY: Doubleday & Co., 1953), p.386.

[115] "The English scholar John Colet caused a sensation when he returned to Oxford from the Continent in 1496 and, in a course of lectures on the Pauline Epistles, expounded them in the light of their historical setting, according to the plain meaning of the text. His methods of exegesis influenced Erasmus." Bruce, *Interpretation*, p.567.

[116] "Whereas Romanism had considered the Bible to be so abstruse that it could be properly interpreted only by the clergy, who with the help of allegory kept the Scriptures submissive to church tradition, the Reformation advanced the principle of the Bible's perspicuity. This did not deny its inexhaustible profundity, but rather asserted that the Bible was understandable to all insofar as it was interpreted historically and grammatically. Thus the Reformers stressed both the study of the Bible in the original languages and the translation of it into the language of the people." Fuller, *Interpretation*, p.865.

[117] McNeill, *History of Interpretation*, p.123.

by which all the Bible should be interpreted.   Some parts of Scripture fared badly as Luther applied his rule to them."[118]

Calvin also urged the use of the grammatical-historical method of interpretation.[119] In the preface to his commentary on Romans, Calvin wrote, "It is the first business of an interpreter to let the author say what he does, instead of attributing to him what we think he ought to say."[120]   But Calvin did not always follow this rule.   He never wrote a commentary on Revelation, and is reported to have said he was totally unable to find its meaning.[121]   His insistence on the absolute sovereignty of God as his chief rule led him to elevate this doctrine above Scripture, and to interpret in its light; this is hardly permitting "the author to say what he does, instead of attributing to him what we think he ought to say."

Dogma Again Influenced Interpretation

In the Catholic world, the counter-reformation had an impact on interpretation within the sphere of that church's influence.   Roman Catholicism became more strident about the need to interpret in the light of church tradition.   "At the fourth session of the Council of Trent (April 8, 1546), it decreed, 'No one shall presume to interpret the said sacred Scripture contrary to that sense which the holy mother Church hath held and doth hold'."[122]

The Protestants did little better.   They, too, subordinated interpretation to dogma. Various Protestant groups began to develop theological creedal formulas as the authoritative statements of their faith, and then these groups severely persecuted any who dared interpret Scripture in a way contrary to what the creeds set forth.   "True exegesis became impossible, for the creeds were regarded as the authoritative interpretation of Scripture. Thus, once again, biblical interpretation became handmaid to the dogmas of orthodoxy and often degenerated into a search for proof texts to support its exalted doctrines."[123]

---

[118] Fuller, *Interpretation*, p.865.

[119] "John Calvin was a systematic exegete of the grammatical-historical school; his first exercise in this field was a commentary on a treatise of the Roman philosopher Seneca."   Bruce, *Interpretation,* p.567.

[120] Louis Berkhof, *Principles of Biblical Interpretation* (Grand Rapids: Baker Book House, 1958), p.27. "Calvin, as a biblical scholar, was committed to expounding the unique message of each biblical author, as reflected in the words and grammar of the written text, which he interpreted against the background of its original historical setting.   He did accept and employ typology in a limited sense, as did Luther, but not as a substitute for the literal meaning.   He recognized and explained, for instance, the typology of the messianic references in the Psalms, but only after he had commented on them historically, as referring originally to David."   McCown, *Hermeneutics*, p.745.

[121] McNeill, *History of Interpretation*, p.124.

[122] Fuller, *Interpretation*, p.866.

[123] McCown, *Hermeneutics*, p.745.

Rationalism Influenced Interpretation

In the 17th and 18th centuries, the philosophy now called rationalism was the popular philosophy.[124]   Three developments led rationalists to reject the then-current methods of Biblical interpretation.   First, Bible interpreters had been accustomed to teaching the Ptolemaic concept that the universe was geocentric, and this was shown to be false by Copernicus, Kepler, Galileo, and others, even though the pope condemned Copernicus' heliocentric ideas as contrary to Scripture.   The natural scientists, accepting what the Pope said the Bible teaches, turned away from Scripture as well as away from Ptolemaic cosmogony.   Second, the earlier humanist practice of investigating the text and authorship of ancient documents, plus the epistemological reflections of Bacon[125] and Descartes,[126] and the use of the experimental method, began to influence the way the Bible was interpreted.   Third, the dogmatism in both Catholic and Protestant interpretation resulted in a reaction away from those methods; but as is often the case in controversy, the pendulum of reaction swung too far the other way.   According to rationalist reasoning, if the Bible supposedly bolstered the dogmatic interpretations, as the theologians asserted it did, then obviously the Bible could not be the word of God!   So if the Bible is not the inspired word of God, then what is it?   The rationalists then subjected the Bible to a more rigorous scientific investigation than ever before.   And before long, the method of interpretation called the historical-critical method had been accepted as the proper way to explain the text of Scripture.[127]

---

[124] "Rationalism.   1. In philosophy, the belief that truth may be attained through human reason. Rationalism exalts the supremacy of reason and emphasizes deductive logic.   2. In religion, the subordination of experience and revelation to human reason.   Religious rationalism is usually antisupernatural, opposing equally the claims of churches, clergy, creeds, scriptures, and mystics – except as such claims square with rationalistic conclusions."   Donald T. Kauffman, *The Dictionary of Religious Terms* (Westwood, NJ: Fleming H. Revell Co., 1967), p.368.

[125] Francis Bacon (1561-1626) substituted the inductive approach of modern science for the a priori methods of scholastic philosophy.

[126] Rene Descartes (1596-1650), the "father of modern philosophy," based his philosophy on the proposition "I think, therefore I am."   His emphasis on an intellectual basis for philosophy marked a break with the supernaturalism of the Middle Ages.

[127] It is not easy to find a written definition or description of the "historical-critical method."   What must be done is to call attention to each of its components.   "Method" implies that this is an application of scientific principles, as in the scientific method.   "Critical" is related to the discipline known as "higher criticism" which investigates the circumstances of composition, including such matters as date, place, authorship, unity, purpose, style, and influence a writing may have had.   "Critical" is not captious faultfinding but is instead an investigation conducted in a reasonable manner in order to pass judgment upon the qualities or merits of a thing.   "Historical" does not carry the same meaning in this connection that it does when one speaks of the "grammatical-historical method."   In many theological works, one finds the term "historicism" used instead of the longer title "historical-critical method;" this is because the views styled "historicism" are assumed by the users of the historical-critical method.   ("Historicism" is a name given to that view which regards any person, event, culture, institution, or philosophy as capable of being explained solely in terms of its historical antecedents.)

R.N. Soulen, *Handbook of Biblical Criticism* (Atlanta: John Knox, 1976), p.78, offered this explanation: "The term Historical Critical Method refers to that principle of historical reasoning ... that reality is uniform and universal, that it is accessible to human reason and investigation, that all events historical and natural occurring within it are in principle comparable by analogy, and that man's contemporary experience

Modern criticism began in the eighteenth century with the appearance of Deism in England and the Enlightenment (*Aufklarung*) in Germany, both of which reflected a rationalistic philosophy which assumed that the Bible, like all other literature, must be interpreted in terms of universal laws of human reason. The religious values in the Bible were not to be found in any divine self-revelation breaking into history but only in the timeless truths contained in the Bible; and these universal truths were to be determined by human reason. From this rationalistic perspective, miracles are simply impossible; neither could Jesus be the divine Son of God. A proper "historical" approach had to penetrate behind the Gospel portrait of Jesus as a divine being – the incarnate Son of God – to reconstruct a purely "historical" portrait, that is, a naturalistic, non-supernatural picture of Jesus of Nazareth.

One of the first of these rationalistic interpretations of Jesus ... distinguished sharply between the real Jesus and the quite unhistorical portrait in the Gospels. Jesus, who can be reconstructed only from faint traces remaining in the Gospels, was only a Jew who proclaimed the imminent end of the world in a thoroughly Jewish sense. After Jesus' death, when this event had not occurred, His disciples conceived of Him as a suffering redeemer for all mankind. They stole His body from the tomb and began to proclaim His resurrection from the dead. The picture of a divine Christ in the Gospels is the product of the disciples' interpretation of Jesus as a dying Saviour and is quite unhistorical. It represents Christian faith, not historical fact.[128]

---

of reality can provide the objective criteria by which what could or could not have happened in the past is to be determined."

Two other attempts at explaining the method follow. "The Historico-critical method developed out of the interest of German scholars in objectively validated conclusions about the Bible. It is governed by three principles: (1) *autonomy* – the research scholar makes up his own mind in the light of the evidence; (2) *analogy* – the credibility of a past event rested in the light of its similarity to the modern experience; (3) *causality* – the conclusion or datum is part of a cause-effect series." George A. Kelley, *The New Biblical Theorists* (Ann Arbor, MI: Servant Books, 1983), p.21. Kant's philosophy has greatly influenced this method of interpretation. The historical-critical method "means the abandonment of the doctrine of verbal inspiration. The deistic concept of nature and God which was part of the spawning process of the Enlightenment found no place for a divine intervention of God into creation through any supernatural, revelatory manner ... It also means the introduction of distinction and discontinuity between the Word of God on the one hand and the Bible on the other. And coupled with this is the methodological presumption that there are errors in the Bible. As the proper object of historical method, the Bible is to be treated like any other set of documents from the past. And like any other document, it is subject to the intrusion of error." Harvie M. Conn, *Contemporary World Theology* (Nutley, NJ: Presbyterian and Reformed Publishing Co., 1973), p.6,7.

[128] George E. Ladd, *The New Testament and Criticism* (Grand Rapids: Wm. B. Eerdmans Publishing Co., 1967), p.41,42. To show that the method of the critic is not materially different, when dealing with accounts of Jesus, than when dealing with, say, Socrates, it may be noted that the historian finds very different pictures of Socrates in Plato's *Dialogues,* Xenophon's *Memorabilia*, and in Aristotle. Finding these conflicting accounts, he must make some choice between them, or combine them in some plausible manner. He will use his historical skill and perception built up over the years to arrive at a picture of Socrates which seems to fit all the evidence (after he has accepted some evidence outright, rejected other evidence, and harmonized accounts where possible). Now the scholar, using the historical critical method, proposes to do the same with the Gospel accounts of Jesus.

Making the Bible match the currently popular philosophy certainly changes what one thinks the text says.   It can hardly be styled "exegesis."   In stark contrast to the humanist, dogma-driven, and rationalist approaches, there were men in the 18th century who pointed the way to how exegetes should work, including J.A. Bengel[129] and J.A. Turretini.[130]

Hegel's Philosophy Influenced the Historical-Critical Method

Hegel's philosophy included a dialectic where there was a tension between one position (thesis) and a second position (antithesis), from whose interaction a third position (synthesis) emerged.   He applied this view to history, which he also conceived as being an evolutionary process.   In religion, he thought the dialectic process caused movement from nature religions through religions of spiritual individuality to Christianity, which was viewed as the highest form of religion.   Under the influence of Hegelian philosophy the Graf-Wellhausen documentary hypothesis[131] arose, as well as a theory about the priority of

---

[129] "In his early years [Bengel] was troubled by the textual variations in the few Greek MSS of the New Testament that were available to him ... [H]e outlined the strategy for his life work: first, to determine as nearly as possible from all available MSS the New Testament author's original wording, and then to write a commentary based on this text.   He appealed to others to send him New Testament MSS.   The readings selected for his Greek New Testament published nine years later were based on the division of MSS into 'families' and on the principle that ever since has been employed in textual criticism: 'The more difficult reading is to be preferred' ... As planned, his New Testament commentary *Gnomon* appeared eight years later (1742).   The hermeneutical ideal toward which Bengel strove ... is summed up in the preface to his commentary on Revelation (1740), where he says, 'I desire to transmit to others nothing of myself, but simply what is found in the Scriptures ... An interpreter is to be compared with a fountain builder.   He may not pour any water into the spring, but may work only to cause the fountain to run freely, sufficiently, and without impurity'."   Fuller, *Interpretation,* p.866.

[130] "Turretini, a Reformed theologian from Geneva, set forth in *De Sacrae Scripturae interpretandae methodo* (1728) the basic hermeneutic that should control the literary, and especially the historical, interpretation of the Bible ... This hermeneutic can be summarized in four propositions.   (1) Since the God who gave revelation in the Bible also endowed people with the rational faculty necessary for receiving communication, the Bible's communication is to be grasped in the same way as other communications. (2) Since the Bible presumes the validity of the law of contradiction, which states that a thing cannot be both true and not true at the same time, no biblical interpretation can be accepted as true that clashes with what is already known to be true.   Otherwise we could not live in relation to the world about us (for if yes could be no, how could we be sure of any fact?)   (3) Since it is a historical book, the Bible must be understood from the vantage point of its own writers as they lived in their own times and places, rather than from any modern vantage point.   (4) Since the Bible is to speak for itself like any other book, the mind, subject to the law of contradiction, must come to the Bible as a *tabula rasa*, emptied of all cherished concepts derived from our modern view of life."   Fuller, *Interpretation,* p.867.

[131] Wellhausen believed he could discern evidence of four separate documents (J, E, D, and P) underneath our present Pentateuch.   "He declared that first (ca. 800 B.C.) there was the preprophetic religion (JE), in which God was regarded as a local tribal deity countenancing revenge on enemies and ritual sacrifice.   In antithesis to this arose (ca. 623 B.C.) the prophetic religion (D), whose God exemplifies love and which considers a high ethical life to be more important than sacrifice.   The synthesis came (ca. 500 B.C.) in the priestly religion (P), with its codification of laws and ritual."   Fuller, *Interpretation,* p.867. The documentary theory operates under the theory that the Prophets were the real founders of Israelite monotheism, which the Pentateuch, as we have it, fraudulently attributes to Moses.

Mark's Gospel.[132]   Hegel's philosophy also had a direct effect on how Paul's writings were understood.

> Under the influence of Hegelian philosophy, F.C. Baur abandoned the rationalistic effort to find timeless truths in the New Testament and instead found in the historical movements of the early church the unfolding of wisdom and spirit. Jesus' teachings, expressing His religious consciousness, formed the point of departure. Theological reflection began over the question of the place of the law in the church; and the history of the apostolic age was interpreted in terms of the conflict over this question. Paul, the first Christian theologian, took the position that the Christian was freed from the law (thesis). Jewish Christianity, represented by James and Peter, took the opposite position that the law was binding upon Christians (antithesis). Out of the conflict between Pauline and Jewish Christianity emerged a synthesis in the old catholic church of the second century, which effected a successful harmonization of the two contradictory positions.

> Baur solved the problems of the date and authenticity of the various New Testament books in terms of their *Tendenz*. Books which clearly reflect either Pauline or Jewish theology were thought to be early; books reflecting the synthesis were late. This critical principle led Baur to conclude that only four epistles [Romans, Galatians, 1 and 2 Corinthians] were authentically Pauline.[133]

Evolutionary Theory Modified the Historical-Critical Method

When Darwin's theory of the origin of species was transferred from the realm of nature to that of history, it at once introduced a new element into the historical-critical methodology. This new element has been dubbed the "history-of-religions school" (*Religionsgeschichte*). The working assumption of the comparative religions method is that Judaism and Christianity were no different from any other religion in the world, and a comparative study of religions in the 1st century world would show the influences of contemporary ideas on the early Christian texts. In this way each ancient religion could be assigned its place on the evolutionary ladder. This approach views the Bible not as a record of God's revelation to mankind, but as a record of man's religious experience; it em-

---

[132] In spite of early Christian literature which affirms that the Gospels that contain the genealogies were written first, Mark was affirmed to be the earliest Gospel to be written, and then it and another document, now lost, called Q (from the German *Quelle*, 'source, fountain') were allegedly used by the men who compiled the books called Matthew and Luke. "In these two oldest literary sources, scholars of this 'old liberal' school believed they had recovered the true historical Jesus, freed from all dogmatic theological interpretations. Jesus was seen as a great religious personality who taught an ideal ethical religion, which had universal validity apart from its particular historical setting. Jesus' pure ethical religion was, however, radically modified after His death by diverse theological interpretations so that the gentle prophet who preached God's love and goodness was deified and exalted, thus becoming the object of Christian faith and preaching. This precipitated the 'Jesus of history – Christ of faith' controversy which stood at the heart of the old liberal theology." Ladd, *The New Testament and Criticism*, p.44.

[133] Ladd, *The New Testament and Criticism*, p.43.

phasized the history of the time rather than any message from God.   What was of special interest was the significance of certain similarities that exist between the vocabulary and religious practices found in the Biblical religions and in the non-Biblical religions.

> Under this movement may be grouped the Hellenistic school, the Gnostic school, and the Mysteries school, all of which appeal to parallels to show that the New Testament in many of its parts has been influenced by these pagan streams of thought.   Such books as the Gospel of John and the Epistle to the Hebrews have been seen as products of a Hellenizing of Christianity.   Some scholars consider Gnosticism to have been part of the background of Paul's Epistles, while the mystery religions are supposed to have contributed some of the ideas of early Christian thought.[134]

When the practitioners of this method were finished, the New Testament had ceased to be an authoritative source of Christian doctrine and practice, but had become instead just another part of the total picture of 1st century religions.   Jesus was identified as another of the Jewish apocalyptic teachers, while Paul was identified as another teacher of Hellenistic thought.[135]

It has now been shown that the proponents of the *religionsgeschicte* method at times played rather loosely with the evidence as they attempted to show purely natural sources for the New Testament materials.   It is rather difficult to find evidence of a well-developed Gnostic religion in the 1st century, so 2nd century Gnosticism was used, and then attempts were made to show that parts of the New Testament (e.g., Colossians and the Pastoral Epis-

---

[134] Donald Guthrie, "The Historical and Literary Criticism of the New Testament," in *Expositor's Bible Commentary*, edited by Frank E. Gaebelein (Grand Rapids: Zondervan Publishing House, 1979), Vol.1, p.442.

[135] "Schweitzer's 'historical Jesus' was, therefore, according to Schweitzer's [Albert Schweitzer, *The Quest for the Historical Jesus*] own assertion, a stranger to the modern man, whose views of history and the universe no longer allow him to believe that the world will come to its end by the appearance of a heavenly Son of Man to inaugurate the perfected Kingdom of God.   According to Schweitzer, Jesus died in disillusionment; and Schweitzer's historical Jesus is disillusioning for modern religion and can no longer provide a historical basis for Christian faith.   Historically, Jesus belongs to first-century Judaism and has no relevance for the modern man.

"As the comparative religions school interpreted Jesus in terms of Jewish apocalyptic, it often interpreted Paul in terms of the Hellenistic religions prevalent in the Graeco-Roman world.   The ancient Mediterranean world was full of cultic 'mystery' religions which worshiped various ancient nature deities as heavenly 'lords.'   By the performance of certain cultic acts, such as ablutions or sacred meals, the worshiper believed himself to be personally identified with the deity and thus assured of personal immortality.   W. Bousset made classic the view that the Palestinian church was thoroughly Jewish in outlook, worshiping Jesus as a man who had been exalted to God's right hand as the heavenly Son of Man who was to come to earth in glory.   Only when the church took root in the Hellenistic world, in Syrian Antioch (Acts 11:20ff), was Jesus for the first time worshiped as a present heavenly divine being, Lord.   In Christian faith, the Jewish Son of Man was interpreted against a pagan background and became the Hellenistic divine Lord.   Paul was interpreted as more of a Greek than a Jew.   The center of Paul's belief in Christ was the heavenly Lord patterned after the pagan cults, and Pauline sacraments, baptism and the Lord's Supper, were understood as adaptations of the cultic rites of the mystery religions by which the worshiper was identified with the Lord in his death and resurrection and was thus made partaker of his life." Ladd, *The New Testament and Criticism*, p.45-47.

tles) came from the 2nd century.   Another of the problems this method never did explain is why, if Christianity is simply a clone of one of the pagan religions, it was able to survive while the others did not.

> If Christianity from the beginning had been nothing more than such a syncretistic religious structure of an ecstatic, magical, ascetic sort, it would not have been worth outliving those sects of the Ophites, etc.   And in accordance with the brazen laws of history, it would have had to perish instead of finally emerging as victor ... in the gigantic struggle with all the powers of the ancient world.   There must have been something in Christianity which was different from that religiosity, a power that raised it above all those formations.   This distinctive element is the Gospel and the impression it conveyed of the person of Jesus Christ.[136]

The passing of time has also shown another flaw in the *religionsgeschicte* method: the failure to examine the validity of the evolutionary basis for scientific and historical studies.

> After World War I, as the idea of unilinear evolution began to lose ground, and as material accumulated, comparative religion split into specialist fields – the history of religion, the psychology of religion, the sociology of religion, and the phenomenology of religion among them – and the synthetic approach was less and less cultivated.[137]

Existentialism (Kierkegaard) Modified the Historical-Critical Method

Modify the historical-critical method so that it matches existential philosophy, emphasize a method of interpretation called the dialectical approach, and you have Neo-orthodoxy as taught by Karl Barth.   Existentialism is a term that embraces a variety of philosophies and attitudes which attempt to view one's world from the standpoint of the actor and his own personal experiences rather than (as in many past schemes of philosophy) from that of a detached spectator.   Its origins may be traced to the nineteenth century philosophers Kierkegaard, Nietzsche, and Dostoevski.   Kierkegaard's philosophy[138] began as an attack on Hegel's idealism, yet included a dialectical element similar to Hegel's thesis, antithesis, synthesis, (save Kierkegaard called his synthesis "paradox"[139]).   From Kant is

---

[136] Ernest von Dobschutz, quoted by Fuller, *Interpretation,* p.867.

[137] E.J. Sharpe, "Comparative Religion," in *New International Dictionary of the Christian Church*, edited by J.D. Douglas (Grand Rapids: Zondervan Publishing House, 1974), p.248.

[138] Some of the major ideas emphasized by Kierkegaard include: "Eternity is more important than time;   sin is worse than suffering;   man is an egotist and must experience despair;   God is beyond reason and man;   Christianity stands opposed to this world and time and to man's reason;   paradoxes are the inevitable result of man's reflections;   Christian ethics are realizable only in eternity."   Dagobert Runes, ed., *Dictionary of Philosophy* (Patterson, NJ: Littlefield, Adams & Co., 1963), p.160.

[139] Unlike Hegel, Neo-orthodox theologians start with two incompatible principles.   First you take up

borrowed the distinction between "noumenon" and "phenomenon"[140] and it is applied to history so that a distinction must be made between *historie* (the event that actually happened) and *geschichte* (man's interpretation or understanding of the event).[141]

The Neo-orthodox view of revelation would certainly influence the explanation offered for a passage such as Romans 1:16,17. "Revelation," as Barth used the term, is not limited to the written Word of God which we call the Bible, nor even to God's revelation of Himself in the incarnate Son. Revelation is an experience of men. When men have an "encounter" with God in a "crisis" in their lives, and they are subjectively sure that it was God speaking to them – that was a "revelation" from God to them. To the Neo-orthodox thinker, the Bible *becomes* the Word of God only when the passage "comes through" to the reader (i.e., only when the passage has a special force or meaning to the reader).[142] According to Neo-orthodox thinking, God's speaking to men is not limited to the Word; any crisis (e.g., a narrowly missed auto accident, the sight of a police car, a critical illness, etc.) can be an occasion when God speaks to the man. One wonders how all this is to be harmonized with Paul's statement that the gospel is the place where God exercises His power to save men? Since, in Neo-orthodox thinking, the Bible does not have to be free from human mistakes and errors,[143] is this another error in the Bible?   And how shall we

---

one side of the problem and pursue it to its logical conclusion. Then you take up the other side of the problem and pursue it to its logical conclusion. Once this is done, you will find it hard to come to a synthesis, because the two sides were incompatible in the first place. Yet you are supposed to accept both sides of the problem as truth (the lack of synthesis is called "paradox"). Barth's commentary on Romans introduced the dialectical method of explaining theology: all theological assertions are paradoxical in character; no synthesis is possible; man must retain both elements in his thinking.

[140] "Phenomenon" refers to the thing as it exists, the thing in itself; "noumenon" refers to man's apprehension of it in his mind.

[141] Many critics – evangelical and non-evangelical scholars included – think Barth's handling of the historicity of the resurrection of Jesus is evasive. They contend that his writings do not really defend the resurrection as an objective historical fact independent of subjective faith. And the contention is apparently correct, for Barth speaks of the crucifixion as *historie*, but categorizes the resurrection as *geschichte* rather than *historie*.

[142] Extreme care must be taken when reading Neo-orthodox works, for Biblical terms are given different meanings than what most conservative Protestants are used to. Thus, one must be aware that to the Neo-orthodox there is a difference between the "word" and the "Word" of God. The former is merely a vehicle in which the latter (the real message from God) is carried. The vehicle may be Jesus as the Word made flesh; it may be the Scripture which points to the Word made flesh; it may be the sermon which is the vehicle for the proclamation of the Word made flesh. To the Neo-orthodox, for one to receive a message from God as he reads or hears about Jesus, it is not necessary to be concerned about the historical Jesus; what is of concern is the Christ of faith as proclaimed by the apostles and the early church. Nor is there any need to make the written words in our Bible somehow synonymous with the Word of God; although they may be the words of men, they may still be used as a vehicle by which a reader may hear the Word of God. Sermons, songs, or other events may likewise, in Neo-Orthodox thinking, be vehicles through which the Word of God comes home to men.

[143] Existential theology denies that faith is based on historical events or on a series of propositional truths. Instead, it asserts faith is concerned instead with crisis or encounter. Consequently, it is a matter of indifference what higher and lower criticism may declare.   "... all Neo-orthodox theologians ... reject the Bible as the Word of God *written*. For them the Bible is a fallible, human group of documents, containing many errors of both history and doctrine. For them the Bible is a human 'witness' to a revelation received

harmonize all this with Paul's statement that faith comes by hearing the word of Christ (Romans 10:17)? Neo-orthodox writers also have difficulty explaining what "sin"[144] is, and also what the atonement had to do with the sins of the world.[145] Nor is it surprising that we still hear echoes of the old "Jesus of history vs. the Christ of faith" debate repeated in Neo-orthodox writings.[146] Neo-orthodoxy has often been castigated as being irrational when it requires its adherents (who likely hold to a correspondence theory of truth) to retain both elements of the paradox in their thinking. This retention of contradictory statements is designated as a "leap of faith," and such "faith" is designated as man's highest emotion, since it is something not dependent on reason or evidence. One wonders how this idea of faith can be harmonized with "faith" as it is used by Paul in the book of Romans.

In later years Barth came to renounce some of the existentialist presuppositions that had controlled his thinking when he wrote his *Christliche Dogmatik* (1927). In the preface to his *Church Dogmatics*, Barth observes that his presuppositions led him to dethrone God by making Him conformable to our prior knowledge of existence. It is helpful that Barth recognized the pitfalls in attempting to make the Bible agree with current philosophical

---

by the prophets and the apostles. Their point of view is that it makes little difference whether the alleged errors in the Bible are real errors or not, for they say that God could give His revelation through erroneous documents as well as through documents that were without error. In other words, God's revelation was really independent of the Bible text. The Bible thus might be a collection of myths and unreliable sagas and still be used by God as the occasion of giving a revelation of Himself as Lord to the reader who hears the Bible proclaimed. Some parts of the Bible might be the Word of God to one man, and not to another. Other parts might be God's Word to the second man and not to the first, who is left cold and unresponsive since he did not have an 'encounter' with God while reading or hearing it. The *whole* Bible is not the Word of God *written*, in the view of these thinkers, but any part of it might *become* the Word of God to different individuals." Floyd Hamilton, *The Basis of the Christian Faith*, revised edition (New York: Harper and Row, Publishers, 1964), p.264,265.

[144] "Adam had no existence on the plane of history" and "the entrance of sin into the world through Adam is in no strict sense an historical happening." Barth, *The Epistle to the Romans*, p. 171. It is little short of amazing that in expounding the fifth chapter of Romans, Barth can explicitly deny what is taught therein (Romans 5:12,16,17,18,19). Of course, that he can do so is a result of his understanding of "symbolical language."

[145] "The atonement is not history. The atonement, the expiation of human guilt, the covering of sin through His sacrifice, is not anything which can be conceived from the point of view of history. This event does not belong to the historical plane ... It would be absurd to say: in the year 30 the atonement of the world took place." Emil Brunner, *The Mediator* (Philadelphia: Westminster Press, 1934), p.504,505.

[146] "The Word of God in the Scriptures is as little to be identified with the words of the Scriptures as the Christ according to the flesh is to be identified with the Christ according to the spirit ... He who identifies the letters and the words of the Scriptures with the Word of God has never understood the Word of God ... The historical appearance of Jesus is not, as such, revelation ... the so-called historical Jesus is not as such the Christ." Emil Brunner, *The Theology of Crisis* (New York: Charles Scribner's Sons, 1929), p.19,36. "The assumption that Jesus is the Christ is, in the strictest sense of the word, an assumption, void of any content that can be comprehended by us." Barth, *Romans,* p.36.

theory.   Would that he had also renounced some of the Reformed dogma that continued to control his thoughts about what the Bible says.

Dissatisfaction with the results which Neo-orthodox methods achieved led some American and European scholars to embark on what is now called the Biblical Theology Movement, or "canonical exegesis."[147]   For decades, Bible scholarship had been primarily about historical matters (i.e., literary sources, comparative religions, forms and redactors) while theology languished.   The Biblical Theology Movement attempted to emphasize the unity behind it all by methodological reflection upon the content of the entire biblical canon.   Whereas the old liberalism had emphasized the differences between Pauline, Johannine, and Petrine theology, the newer discipline tried to emphasize the similarities. But the presuppositions on which canonical exegesis and subsequent interpretation for modern minds rested were to doom it to failure, just as they had led to the decline of Neo-orthodoxy.

> ... the biblical theology movement was made up of biblical scholars in North America and Europe who shared liberal, critical assumptions and methods in an attempt to do theology in relation to biblical studies. This new way of doing theology was most fundamentally concerned to do justice to the theological dimension of the Bible, which previous generations of liberal scholars had almost completely neglected. Accordingly, the movement reflected an interest of European neo-orthodox theologians of the 1920's and beyond. Neo-orthodoxy and the biblical theology movement shared the common concern to understand the Bible as a fully human book to be investigated with the fully immanent historical-critical method and yet to see the Bible as a vehicle or witness of the divine Word. This meant a meshing of the modern naturalistic evolutionary world view as developed by natural science, modern philosophy, and critical history with the biblical view of a God who gives meaning and coherence to this world in his personal acts in history.[148]

Like its Neo-orthodox ancestry, the biblical theology movement was a reaction against the old classic religious liberalism.   However, while rejecting some of the extremes to which the historical-critical method of Bible study led, the movement continued to embrace the presuppositions and procedures of the historical-critical method.   Just as Neo-orthodoxy

---

[147] Care must be exercised in the use of names to designate this movement that flourished in the mid-20th century. A much older, and much more conservative, method of Bible study had also been designated as "Biblical theology" (as contrasted, for example, with "systematic theology"). The older discipline was an emphasis on what the Scriptures themselves say on theological topics, rather than emphasizing dogmatic theology at the expense of the clear meaning of Biblical verses. There is little relationship between the older "Biblical theology" and the modern method that is also called "canonical exegesis." A good introduction to "canonical exegesis" is found in Brevard S. Childs, *Biblical Theology in Crisis* (Philadelphia: Westminster Press, 1970).

[148] Gerhard F. Hasel, "Biblical Theology Movement," in *Evangelical Dictionary of Theology*, p.149.

rejected the idea that all Scripture had its origin rooted in God's inspiration of the human writers, the biblical theology movement did likewise, espousing the Neo-orthodox views of revelation and inspiration.   Both viewed revelation essentially as God revealing Himself in Christ, and the Scriptures are simply a witness to this revelation.   Both viewed the Bible, not as the word of God, but only one of many things that may become the word of God if in an existential moment its reader hears God speaking to him.   Both held to the view that God continues to reveal Himself in history, with the result that present history and personal experience are of more value than Scripture when it comes to a vehicle through which God reveals Himself to man.

> One of the major tenets of the biblical theology movement was the concept of divine revelation in history ... The emphasis on revelation in history was used to attack both the conservative position, which holds that the Bible contains eternal truths and serves as a deposit of right doctrine, and the liberal position, which claims that the Bible contains a process of evolving religious discovery or simply progressive revelation.   The emphasis on revelation stressed the divine self-disclosure and shifted the content away from propositional revelation and doctrine to the neo-orthodox concept of encounter without propositional content.   The corresponding emphasis on history meant that the revelational encounter in history provided the bridge of the gap between past and present in that Israel's history became the church's history and subsequently our modern history.[149]

After a generation or so during which it flourished, by the mid-1960's the movement began to lose its appeal.   Neither the "Biblical" nor the "theological" emphases of the movement proved satisfactory even to members sympathetic to the movement.   As for the Bible, the historical-critical method continued to prove inadequate as a means of understanding what the Scriptures themselves meant to their writers and original audiences.   On the other end, the theological interpretations offered by which the Biblical text was still supposed to be meaningful to modern man were too wedded to the present moment, and too subject to change as new philosophies came along, to give any permanent ground on which to build a solid lifestyle or world view.[150]   In addition to these weaknesses, the lack of agreement within the movement of what divine revelation is, or where it takes place, plus the elevation of history above the Scriptures, proved to be too much of a hindrance for the movement to find general acceptance.

Existentialism (Heidegger) Modified the Historical-Critical Method.

As soon as interest in Kierkegaard's system began to wane and interest in Heidegger

---

[149] Hasel, *Biblical Theology Movement*, p.150.

[150] It soon became evident that each theologian was giving his own interpretation as he tried to apply the text to modern man.   Disdainfully it was often said, "There are as many biblical theologies as there are biblical theologians."   How this disintegration of theology was to be overcome, if indeed it could be, became a challenge that existentially oriented theologians could not answer.

began to grow, it was necessary for those critics who try to match Scripture to the prevailing philosophy to modify their method again. Modify the historical-critical method so that it matches Heidegger's existential philosophy, add the new features of interpretation called form criticism and demythologization, and you have the Neo-liberalism of Rudolf Bultmann.[151] One of the emphases of Heidegger was his distinction between authentic and inauthentic man. Heidegger affirmed that the ability to make decisions is the thing that makes man utterly different from any other being in the world. Now if decision-making is man's essence, then only the man who is not afraid to make decisions is an "authentic man." The man who tries to avoid making decisions (he lives instead by old traditions, or lets legalistic ethical systems make his decisions for him, or identifies himself by reference to his social roles toward other people) is not being himself; that is, he is an "inauthentic man." Bultmann took this distinction between authentic and inauthentic man as his key to understanding, and went to work to reinterpret the mythological language of the Bible.[152] He, too, took advantage of the distinction between the two German words for history, *historie* and *geschichte*, and in 1921 introduced the method called form criticism to New Testament study.[153] A fresh turning point in New

---

[151] Bultmann's whole aim was to make the Christian message relevant for his contemporaries: those contemporaries, as he saw it, held a scientific world view which cannot accept the mythological world views found in the Bible. "In Bultmann's view the most pressing task facing theologians in the 20th century was to discover a 'conceptuality' in terms of which the New Testament could be made understandable to modern man, and then to work out the details of this interpretation. Bultmann believed that he had found such a conceptuality in the existentialist philosophy of Martin Heidegger, and spent virtually his entire career reading the New Testament as a Heideggerian document and using historical-critical methods to eliminate from the text elements resistive to existentialism." R.C. Roberts, "Bultmann, Rudolf," in *Evangelical Dictionary of Theology*, p.180. A full discussion of the relationship between Heidegger and Bultmann can be found in John Macquarrie, *An Existentialist Theology* (London, SCM Press, 1955).

[152] For Bultmann, "myth" had reference to the use of language symbols or images of this world and this life to conceptualize the divine or otherworldly. "Demythologization" did not mean eliminating the imaginary person or thing (as the English word might suggest), but to *reinterpret* the idea contained in the story in modern language so as to provide self-understanding for the 20th century scientific mind.

[153] Form criticism (*formgeschichte*, German) is an attempt to study the forms the *geschichte* (interpretations) took in the religious community before they became fixed in their present scriptural sequence. A fundamental presupposition behind form criticism is that the New Testament books are mainly products of the editing work of the early church, just like much of the already-circulating materials of non-Biblical ancient literature was simply collected, arranged, and edited by the ancient "writer." Form criticism is a special method of analysis and interpretation of the sources that have come to be collected and arranged. By means of form criticism, when applied to Biblical studies, the critic is supposed to be able to learn what actually happened, as distinguished from the editorial modifications of the historical events by the church as they collected these previously-existing materials. Special emphasis must be given to the "life setting" (the *Sitz im Leben*, German) which led the men who were telling about the events to put them in the particular forms (legends, parables, miracle stories, sayings, passion story, etc.) in which we now find them embedded. Some practitioners even affirmed they could determine the probable historical validity of any event by determining which "form" it is encased in (e.g., myths or legends are the least historical, while the passion story is the most historical).

While some attention must be paid to the "life setting," the form critics have allowed their imagination and presuppositions to influence their conclusion. For example: (a) Form critics suppose the "life setting" will explain why certain features are included in the Gospel records. (E.g., the mission charge in Matthew 10 supposedly reflects the methods used by Jewish Christians to evangelize Palestine between AD 30 and 66. Or again, the inclusion of some authoritative pronouncement by Jesus is believed to reflect some need in the life of the early church – for example, Matthew 5:19 allegedly reflects an attack by strict Jewish Christians on Paul.) But if such "life setting" events determined the content of the Gospel records, why do

Testament studies began in 1941 when Bultmann introduced demythologization. The center of this program is Bultmann's contention that he finds two things in the New Testament: 1) the Christian gospel (*kerygma*); and 2) the 1st century world view, mythological in character (*didache*).[154] He used form criticism as one means by which he stripped away the *didache* so that he was left with the *kerygma*.[155] Once he found the meaning of any

---

we not find such a practice for events which we know were real? The circumcision question was a live debate for a quarter of a century in the early church, so why has it not left a more distinct mark on the Gospels? (b) While a "life-setting" in the early church may explain why certain incidents and sayings were preserved and *recorded*, such a setting does not account for the *origin* of the saying. Its historical *origin* must be sought in the life and ministry of Jesus.

[154] The gospel essence, what Bultmann called the *kerygma* (a transliteration of the Greek word meaning "the content of what is preached"), is the irreducible core with which our modern age must be confronted and which we must believe. However, modern man, he insisted, cannot accept the mythical framework in which the gospel essence is wrapped. So, "theology must undertake the task of stripping away the mythical framework from the *kerygma*." According to Bultmann, this mythical framework is not specifically Christian, anyway. As examples of such a 1st century mythical world view, he cites the belief in a three-storied universe (heaven above, earth in the middle, hell below the earth – a view Bultmann contended the Bible presents); the supernatural intervention in this world of either God or Satan; demon possession and divine guidance of human life; atonement through the vicarious effects of Christ's death; the pre-existence of Christ; the virgin birth; and the bodily resurrection of Christ.

[155] It is hardly a use of the "scientific method" when one attempts to doctor the evidence to fit a preconceived theory. Yet we affirm that this is exactly what Barth and Bultmann have done, even though they have tried to clothe their actions in scientific garb. "Despite their differences, Bultmann and Barth both proposed a theory of interpretation that regarded *die Sache* ('the subject matter') about which a text spoke as the basis for understanding its statements. Barth's method of interpretation in the 20th century was very similar to that of Luther and Calvin, who in their application of the rule of faith forced the Bible to be interpreted by a subjectively chosen subject matter. Nevertheless, J.M. Robinson has attached to Barth's method of interpretation the name 'New Hermeneutic.' [Cf. *The New Hermeneutic, New Frontiers in Theology*, edited by James M. Robinson and John B. Cobb (New York: Harper and Row, 1964).] Robinson climaxed his essay 'Hermeneutic Since Barth' by referring to the hermeneutic advocated by ... Hans-George Gadamer in his *Truth and Method* (Eng. tr., 2nd ed. [1975]). Like Barth, Gadamer regards 'the subject matter' *(die Sache)* as the key for understanding what another human mind has sought to express. He says, e.g., '... The hermeneutical problem is not one of the correct mastery of language, but of the proper understanding of that which takes place [*der rechten Verstandigung uber die Sache*] through the medium of language' (Eng. tr., pp.346ff). For Gadamer, 'that which takes place [*die Sache*]' is the force which grips an interpreter when the horizon of the text (the author's intended meaning modified by subsequent history) fuses with the horizon of the interpreter – a horizon that is shaped by his individuality as it carries on a friendly conversation with the text under consideration." Fuller, *Interpretation*, p.869.

The change of terminology from "hermeneutics" to "hermeneutic" is intended to convey the truth that a fundamental change has taken place in methodology. "Traditionally, hermeneutics dealt with the rules to be observed in Biblical exegesis. Today it enjoys a wider reference. Hermeneutics is a fundamental inquiry into the conditions which must obtain in the understanding of history or historical documents. Thus, it embraces both the methodological rules to be applied in exegesis as well as the epistemological presuppositions of historical understanding ... The enlargement of the scope of hermeneutics from regulative principles of analysis to the art of interpreting historical documents to disclose their meaning to us today is often traced back to Schleiermacher ... Schleiermacher rightly saw that the hermeneutical problem of bridging the horizontal gap between what the text has to say and our life today cannot be solved by the critical-historical method alone ... Wilhelm Dilthey further developed Schleiermacher's psychological hermeneutics ... Rudolf Bultmann's grasp of the hermeneutical problem retains continuity with Schleiermacher and Dilthey." Carl E. Braaten, "History and Hermeneutics," Vol.2 of *New Directions in Theology Today,* edited by William Hordern (Philadelphia: Westminster Press. 1966), p.130ff. Under all this verbiage is hidden the fact that what the New Hermeneutic does is put the interpreter's ideas onto the text, rather than hearing the intention of the author who wrote it.

event, he could reinterpret it in modern terms. Thus, he supposed that when the book of Romans speaks of man as a "sinner" and as under the control of a power called "death," it has reference to inauthenticity. Likewise, "salvation" was being willing to be open to the options of the future, and being willing to make decisions. "Faith" became almost synonymous with "'authentic existence', in which a person, freed from all regrets for the past, fears of the future, fixed systems of thought, and dependence on things of the world, takes full responsibility for his actions and lives fully in the moment."[156] The 'Fall of Adam' was basically a statement of human sinfulness and finitude. "The cross becomes to him a continuing challenge for humanity to undergo crucifixion with Christ. As such the once-for-allness and sacrificial nature of Jesus' death are regarded as untenable. The resurrection as a fact of history is to Bultmann utterly inconceivable."[157]

Certain objections have been raised, and properly so, against the form critical method of interpreting Scripture. Harvie M. Conn has given a very understandable summary of these, and we begin with his second one:

> 2) Form criticism does injustice to the writers of the Gospel records. Matthew, Mark, and Luke are reduced to mere editors of documents, and the Gospels to self-contradictory records. All this does radical injustice to the basic unity of the Gospel record ....

> 3) Form criticism separates Christianity from Christ. The great assumption of this method of study is that the Christian community, not Christ, exercised the major creative role in the production of the Gospels. However, the message of the New Testament is centered, not in the community, but in Christ (2 Corinthians 4: 5). The church, like Paul and his fellow apostles, was witness, not creator (1 Corinthians 4:1,2). Its major responsibility was not creation of new traditions, but the preservation of old ones.

> 4) Form criticism separates Christianity from the apostles. Bultmann and others completely discount the presence of the apostles as guardians of the accurate tradition of the early church concerning Jesus. The apostles were an authoritative source of information about the facts and doctrines of Christianity and of Christ. Acts 1:21,22 underlines this strategic control the apostles exercised over the spread of the gospel in the years of oral transmission. Their presence was intended to prevent the occurrence of precisely the situation described by form criticism. The apostles were God's guarantee of the continuity and integrity of the historic Christian faith.

> 5) Form criticism seems oblivious to the small time lag separating the historical facts and the written documents. [Matthew's Gospel was written

---

[156] Fuller, *Interpretation*, p.868.

[157] G.L. Borchert, "Demythologization" in *Evangelical Dictionary of Theology*, p.309.

in the 50's. Mark's and Luke's in the 60's.] Paul received his account of the tradition in the mid-30's (Galatians 1:18). Many of the apostles and eye-witnesses of Jesus lived throughout the entire period in which the Gospels were written. Where is the time for the collection, creation, and circulation of these community "sagas" and "myths"? The events of Jesus' life were not hidden from public view (Acts 26:26). There were witnesses both for the defense and the attack on Christianity. The gospel exploded into life in the midst of well-attested history. Form criticism cannot explain this at all.[158]

Dissatisfaction with the results produced by Barth and Bultmann has led some of their students to attempt to modify their work so that it produces an interpretation more in harmony with the observed phenomena in the New Testament. Three of these newer approaches are *Heilsgeschichte*, Structuralism,[159] and Redaction criticism.[160] Some comment is needed on the first of these.

Heilsgeschichte is a German word variously translated as "salvation history," "holy

---

[158] Harvie M. Conn, *Contemporary World Theology: A Layman's Guidebook* (Philadelphia: Presbyterian and Reformed Publishing Co., 1973), p.31,32.

[159] Structuralism, or structural analysis, is a modification of form criticism, wherein the form of the writing as a whole is subjected to careful scrutiny. "An impetus to this approach was given by Paul Schubert in his *Form and Function of the Pauline Thanksgiving* (1939). Until this work appeared, it was widely supposed that, apart from the conventional salutation and thanksgiving at the beginning and the greetings at the end, Paul's letters were unstructured for the most part; study since then has brought to light fairly well-defined structures in the main body of the letters." F.F. Bruce, "Criticism," in *New International Standard Bible Encyclopedia*, edited by Geoffrey W. Bromiley (Grand Rapids: Wm. B. Eerdmans, 1979), Vol.1, p. 824. Structuralists will find parallel structures in the Old or New Testaments and plot the similarities on specially devised grids. Once the form has been recognized, anything that does not fit the structure is either removed as being unauthentic, or given some special explanation. J.D. Crossan, "From Moses to Jesus: Parallel Themes," in *Bible Review* 2/2 (Summer, 1986), p.18-27, affirms he has found such a parallel structure in the infancy narratives of Matthew and the story of Moses' infancy. Crossan suggests the reason Matthew tells us the Sermon on the Mount was delivered on a mountain (whereas Luke has it delivered on a plain, Luke 6:17) is because of the conscious effort to continue this deliberate comparison between Moses (remember Mt. Sinai) and Jesus. "... [T]he structuralist approach ... abandons all concern to keep the plenary sense in line with the primary sense. It may ignore all questions about the historical background of a text, its original life setting, and the course of its transmission; it may even be quite uninterested in the author's intention, since its concern is with the final form of the text as an independent linguistic phenomenon." Bruce, *Interpretation*, p.568.

[160] Redaction criticism is another modification of form criticism. It attempts to answer some of the questions that form criticism left unanswered. While form criticism emphasized the fragments that were put together to form our present Bible books, redaction criticism attempts to divine the aims and purposes of the redactors or editors who put the fragments together. When applied to the synoptic Gospels, what the scholars do is emphasize the differences in order to find some indication of the redactor's perspective or motivation that caused him to modify and edit the tradition that came to him until it reached its present form. (Bornkamm, Marxsen, Conzlemann, and Haenchen have produced books on Matthew, Mark, Luke, and Acts, respectively, in which the Bible books are subjected to redaction criticism.) Such an approach is destructive to any view of apostolic authorship for the New Testament books, and is also opposed to any idea of inspiration as the ultimate source of the Biblical materials. It also throws much doubt on any historical note in the materials while emphasizing the theological viewpoints.

history," "history of redemption," or "salvation in history."   The term seems to have first been used by J.A. Bengel (1687-1752).[161]   His working thesis was that one can understand the history recorded in the books of the Bible only as he sees God's eternal purpose of redemption gradually unfolded in them.   The historical events narrated in the Bible not only follow a chronological principle, but also a teleological principle.   In many cases, the historical events are recorded because at those special times in history God was progressively revealing His redemptive purpose.   God was moving all of history toward the goal that Daniel and Revelation particularly predict.[162]   J.J. Beck of Tubingen (1804-1878) and J. Christian K. von Hofmann (1810-1877), a Lutheran theologian, both added some modifications to the idea.   Beck tried combining Hegel's philosophy with *Heilsge-schichte*, and insisted that a teleological view of history required a connection between the various stages of history.   *Heilsgeschichte* might be likened to a tree or some other organism, where all the stages of the process are equally important, because they become part of the organism.   Hofmann, influenced by the modern approach to history as taught by Leopold von Ranke,[163] took a position against Beck, noting that in a teleological view of history in which revelation was progressive, the earlier elements could not serve the same function as the later ones.   Over against some liberal theologians who were his contemporaries, and who wanted to dispense altogether with the Old Testament because they believed they could find the whole truth in the New, Hofmann insisted that the historical records in the Old Testament are not to be ignored or rejected.   Instead, he maintained that the superiority of the New Testament is lost when it is studied in isolation, for it is only when we see in Jesus and in the New Testament the fulfillment of the Old Testament prophecies that we have the right to say that in the New we have the completion of God's redemptive purposes.   "In his principal writing, *Der Schriftbeweis*, Hofmann asserted that the Bible was not to be treated as a textbook in theology, morals, or philosophy

---

[161] See footnote #129 for more about Bengel's method of exegesis.   "... [I]t is interesting that Bengel's contemporary in New England, Jonathan Edwards, also conceived of presenting a 'rational divinity' along these very lines, as his posthumously published *History of Redemption* may be considered as the first work of the American *Heilsgeschichte* school.   His interest was apparently spontaneous since there is no evidence that Edwards knew of the work of Bengel.   If we remember further that John Wesley was influenced by the work of Bengel, we can see the significant fact that German, English, and American pietism showed a simultaneous concern for our subject."   J.H. Gerstner, "Heilsgeschichte," in *Evangelical Dictionary of Theology*, p.505.   Gerstner goes on to show that the idea of "redemption" being the unifying theme running all through the Bible had its advocates as early as Irenaeus, and suggests that pietism may have come back to it as a result of the debate with the Roman Church over tradition and dogma being elevated above the authority of Scripture.   (It surely is worth observing that the book of Romans will talk about God's eternal purpose of redemption in Christ.)

[162] In the 19th century, W.N. Darby took Bengel's views and modified them.   Darby was followed by Scofield, whose annotated Reference Bible did much to popularize those views, and *Heilsgeschichte* became Dispensationalism.

[163] His modern method of historical research relied upon original sources rather than tradition or legend for its material, and stresses scientific objectivity in historical writing.

of religion, but as the story of God's redeeming acts in particular historical events."[164]   He was able to show that the coming of Jesus was the outcome of God's dealings with His chosen people Israel; that the life and teachings of Jesus as recorded in the New Testament formed the basis of the church; and, over against a purely sociological view of the church then prominent among Protestants, that the church is the place where God, through the work of the Holy Spirit, is still at work in His world, working out His redemptive purpose.

According to *Heilsgeschichte* advocates, the major events in salvation history are the calling of Abraham, the exodus from Egypt, the exile, and the incarnation, death, and resurrection of Jesus Christ.[165]

> ... [I]n history God has made a progressive revelation of his nature as redemptive.   The biblical understanding of history is that the God of creation has involved himself in the affairs of his creation and that in a specific chain of events in earthly, human affairs, God has prepared salvation for his creation.   This salvation is redemption from the totality of sin.   The very core of the Scriptures is the history of this step-by-step process of salvation.   Thus, as an interpretive principle, this is an approach to the Scriptures from the viewpoint of how they view themselves.   The Bible presents the successive unfolding of steps in the divine plan for man's salvation from sin as a part of history itself.

> God is at work in historical events.   Genesis 1-11 shows man's involvement in sin so that he needs salvation.   The history of God's provision of this salvation begins in Genesis 12 with God's call of Abraham, and it continues in his raising up Abraham's descendants to the status of a people through the Exodus and subsequent events for God's redemptive purpose. Through this people God would bring his Redeemer-Savior into the world and establish his kingdom, his spiritual rule among men.

---

[164] Willard H. Taylor, "Heilsgeschichte," in *Beacon Dictionary of Theology*, edited by Richard S. Taylor (Kansas City: Beacon Hill Press, 1983), p.252. Hofmann made this last statement at a time when the majority of Protestant theologians were treating the Bible as a textbook of theology (remember the attempts to make the Bible match the creeds), or, if they disliked the traditional theology, they treated the Bible as a textbook on morals or on the philosophy of religion.   When a similar statement is made by 20th century *Heilsgeschichte* devotees, it has another meaning altogether.   To the modern student who feels a need to attempt to reconcile Biblical statements with the developing and constantly changing conclusions of the sciences, it has come to be used to mean that the Bible may very well have human mistakes in it with reference to science or history or astronomy or geology, since, after all, it is only interested in salvation.   It is not uncommon, in the 20th century, to hear the statement, "The Bible is authoritative in matters of faith and practice." As spoken by *Heilsgeschichte* advocates, the statement conceals the widely held belief that the Scriptures are *not* authoritative or trustworthy in matters of science or history.   We affirm that such a statement by modern *Heilsgeschichte* theologians is a serious departure from the Bible's own affirmations about itself.   Jesus Himself said "Thy word is truth" (John 17:17) – nothing but pure, holy truth!   Some Roman Catholic theologians have charged the contemporary *Heilsgeschichte* proponents of abandoning the doctrine of the verbal inspiration of the Bible if they teach that it is authoritative only with respect to faith and morals.

[165] See E.C. Rust, *The Christian Understanding of History* (London: Lutterworth Press, 1947); Otto A. Piper, *God In History* (New York: Macmillan Co., 1939); Erick Sauer, *The Dawn of World Redemption and the Triumph of the Crucified* (London: Paternoster Press, 1951).

In Jesus of Nazareth this redemptive purpose is brought to its realization. His presence in the world inaugurated the kingdom of God among men. By the once-for-all sacrifice of himself he brought to glorious climax the long, full sweep of the mighty redemptive acts of God in history. The Synoptic Gospels report that as life ebbed away from Jesus on the cross he 'uttered a shrieking cry' and yielded up his spirit to the Father ... John reports that that cry was one word in Greek, *tetelestai*. In English this is rendered, 'It is finished' (John 19:30). The Latin versions rendered it *consummatum est*; i.e., 'It is brought to a consummation.' All that God, in the call of Abraham, set in motion to re-create his lost creation was brought to a glorious reality in the historic event of the incarnation, crucifixion, and resurrection of Jesus, God's redeemer.

In Romans 8:21-23, Paul viewed this as having such long reach that the total effect of sin, even in the material cosmos, would be effaced in relation to the anticipated release of man from sin in the resurrection. In Ephesians and Colossians, Paul viewed all this salvation-history as God's orderly administration of the affairs of his household so as to bring all of them once again and forever under one 'captain', Jesus Christ.[166]

If the above summary were the whole picture of 20th century *Heilsgeschichte,* it could be accepted without much reservation. However, "more recently, the idea of *Heilsgeschichte* has served to help theologians out of the corner into which historicism had forced them."[167] Oscar Cullmann, a Swiss theologian, has had a telling influence in the modification and acceptance of this method of interpreting Scripture, and Cullmann is indebted to both Barth and Bultmann for some of his major ideas.

From Karl Barth, Cullmann's *Heilsgeschichte* concept has borrowed many basic ideas for a new approach to history. From Barth also has come an emphasis on the indispensability of a Christocentric understanding of the New Testament and the concept of the definitive role of faith in divine revelation. From Rudolf Bultmann, Cullmann has borrowed the exegetical methods of form criticism in his reconstruction of the history of New Testament Christianity. Because of this relationship, there is much wisdom in referring to Cullmann's insights as neo-orthodox in direction.[168]

---

[166] Ray Summers, "Contemporary Approaches in New Testament Study," in *The Broadman Bible Commentary*, edited by Cliffton J. Allen (Nashville: Broadman Press, 1969), Vol.8, p.55,56.

[167] Watson E. Mills, "Heilsgeschichte," in *The New International Dictionary of the Christian Church*, edited by J.D. Douglas (Grand Rapids: Zondervan Publishing House, 1974), p.457. When the principles and methods of the historical-critical method are applied to the Bible, it is reduced to a purely human work sharing the relativism of all the rest of history. Yet the principal reason people study the Bible is the conviction that it is the Word of God. How are these two opposing viewpoints to be reconciled? The Neo-orthodox and Neo-liberal theologians have tended to disclaim any interest in the historical contents of the Bible, and treat the historical narratives either as witness to, or as symbols of, timeless truths.

[168] Conn, *Contemporary World Theology*, p.39,40. "In his early years Cullmann became disenchanted with liberalism and then with dialectical theology because he saw how both tried to make the facts of Scripture fit a modern philosophical point of view. Then he espoused the methodology of form criticism

Although Cullmann is critical of the skeptical results of Bultmann's form criticism, and although he himself feels these methods "help us draw nearer to the historical Jesus," he also concedes that the technique of form criticism "establishes the deviation of the early Christian community from Jesus as its object" [*Scottish Journal of Theology* XIV/3 (Sep. 1961), p.233]. In short, form criticism discloses the Bible as the product of the early Christian community and not a totally reliable account of the life and teaching of Jesus. Regardless of Cullmann's own criticism of Bultmann's use of form criticism, ultimately his use also often makes a separation between the Bible and the Word of God. So, for example, he calls the biblical accounts of creation and the second coming "myths." He is not completely willing to admit the reality of revelation as inscripturated, infallible truth.[169]

Major criticisms of the modern *Heilsgeschichte* method are related to its concept of revelation, to its relatively low view of Scripture, and to its strong dependence on a subjectivism similar to that found in Neo-orthodoxy.

The great emphasis of *Heilsgeschichte* is on history and the revelation of God in history ... However, this underlining of history as a vehicle for revelation is said to mean that Scripture is not the ultimate datum of the Christian religion. The ultimate datum is holy history. Scripture is understood as merely the record of that more ultimate datum, not the reality itself. As George Ernest Wright, an Old Testament scholar belonging to this same school, has said, revelation is given in historical deeds, not words [*God Who Acts*, p.11ff]. The New Testament is to be understood as a testimony to God's acts of deed-revelation.[170]

An interpreter is said to know this [sacred] history only as he identifies himself with it. It is especially here that the salvation-history school shows its neo-orthodox presuppositions. History remains history and not revelation, if the student does not participate in this history by faith. In spite of a strong emphasis on biblical history, these men still "hesitate to regard the meaning of salvation as objectively given and accessible. Instead they continue to speak of religious experience or decision as a fulcrum of revelation" [Carl F. H. Henry, *Frontiers in Modern Theology*, p.44,45] ... In connection with Cullmann's views on revelation, we should also note that he is still strongly

---

as the best way to rediscover the faith of the early Church." Fuller, *Interpretation*, p.871. "Cullmann insists that faith is a 'decision to align my existence with that concrete [redemptive] history revealed to me, with that sequence of events (*Salvation in History*, p.69)." Fuller, *ibid.*

[169] Conn, *Contemporary World Theology*, p.43. The idea that the New Testament is made up more of *geschichte* than of *historie*, that is, what we read is not actually what happened but is the early church's modification of the traditions received from Jesus and the apostles, is often expressed popularly as "It was the faith of the early church ...." To an audience accustomed to identifying the teachings of Jesus, the apostles, and the early church as being the same, such a statement can be very misleading, for the audience will "hear" something other than what its speaker really means or believes.

[170] Conn, *Contemporary World Theology*, p.41. This concept of God's revelation in deeds, not words, is popularly stated in this dictum: "Our faith is in Jesus, not in the Bible!"

dependent on the subjectivism of neo-orthodoxy ... The *Heilsgeschichte* scholar believes that, unless man understands, it is not even revelation.[171]

Dogma Still Controls Interpretation

By the late 19th century, the "assured results of higher criticism" had reflected negatively on certain truths contained in the Scriptures, and subscribed to by both Jesus and the apostles. The higher critics were confident that the Bible is a record of man's religious experience (not a revelation from God). Their naturalistic world view ruled out anything like a virgin birth, an incarnation, a bodily resurrection from the grave, or a literal second coming. Further, the higher critics maintained that the first five books of the Old Testament were not written by Moses but were the products of many hands; that the book of Isaiah was not one book, but was a compilation of two or more works; that the book of Daniel was to be dated several hundred years later than the time it describes, for its details reflect a history written after the fact, not precision predictive prophecy; that the Fourth Gospel differs so radically from the first three Gospels that its contents cannot be confided in, nor can the book provide a dependable framework for the life and teaching of Jesus; that the editors or compilers of Matthew and Luke probably copied the work of Mark; that it is impossible to reconstruct a history of Jesus' ministry, since so little is actually known of the "historical Jesus"; and that Paul probably did not write several of the letters attributed to him. No wonder Pope Pius X condemned "modernism" in his 1907 encyclical letter *Pascendi gregis.*

But the historical-critical method could not be decreed into oblivion. Its use by Catholic theologians was as popular as among liberal Protestants. On September 30, 1943, Pope Pius XII issued his encyclical *Divino afflante Spiritu* which ended the church's official opposition to "modernism" and gave tribute to textual criticism and restored "true freedom" to Catholic exegetes. Then in Vatican Council II (1962-1965), the general aims of the Biblical Theology Movement were endorsed,[172] and so was the form critical method

---

[171] Conn, *Contemporary World Theology*, p.42,43. "*Heilsgeschichte* offers a new view of the Bible. It is not a book that the Holy Spirit dictated to various authors; but it is not, either, merely a collection of subjective views on religion. Rather, God has used human beings, notwithstanding the limitations of their persons and their age, to become aware of what He was doing for the salvation of mankind, and obediently to record it as they understood it. The interpreter, in turn, will grasp the truth of the Bible only when, in addition to his scholarly studies, he is himself a living participant in God's dealing with history in and through the Church." Otto A. Piper, "Heilsgeschichte," in *A Handbook of Christian Theology*, edited by A.C. Cohen and M. Halverson (Nashville: Abingdon Press, 1958), p.159.

[172] Just as the four-fold method of interpretation used in the Middle Ages helped the Roman Church to justify her dogma, so we think the Biblical Theology method is going to be used in the 20th century. "In the past two decades there has been a spate of literature, mostly by Roman Catholics, on the *sensus plenior* of Scripture, defined by R.E. Brown as 'the deeper meaning, intended by God but not clearly intend-

for the study of the Scriptures.[173] We should not be surprised if the future history of interpretation shows that this authoritative pronouncement has had a negative influence on Biblical exegesis, just as have attempts to force Scripture to match dogma in the past.

Summary and Endorsement

This review of the history of interpretation should have warned each Bible student to beware of placing either dogma or the currently popular philosophy above Scripture, and then of trying to make Scripture harmonize with or support it.

> One cannot review the history of biblical interpretation without observing that exegetes have been too often influenced in their work by epistemological presuppositions of which they themselves were more or less unaware. "Historical" exegesis, for example, which vehemently claimed to have reached the highest possible degree of objectivity, was chiefly dominated by philosophical premises of a naturalistic type. Not only have the allegorical or "spiritual," and, to a lesser extent, typological interpreters practiced eisegesis rather than exegesis, but also many self-styled "exegetes" have done so: for instance, the "liberal" students who spiritualized the eschatological element in the teaching of Jesus or the "neo-orthodox" theologians who dismissed the "mythological frame" as alien to the New Testament.[174]

---

ed by the human author, that is seen to exist in the words of Scripture when they are studied in the light of further revelation or of development in the understanding of revelation.' [R.E. Brown, "Hermeneutics," in *The Jerome Bible Commentary* (Englewood Cliffs, NJ: Prentice-Hall, 1968), p.616.] Most evangelicals have avoided the term *sensus plenior*, since the concept of 'development in the understanding of revelation' seems to leave the door open for the magisterium to define 'God's intentions;' nonetheless, evangelicals use such terms as 'secondary sense' to function in the same way as *sensus plenior*. The problem has to do with both the legitimacy of *sensus plenior* and, allowing its legitimacy, finding the principles for determining deeper meanings." Gordon D. Fee, "Hermeneutics and Common Sense: An Exploratory Essay on the Hermeneutics of the Epistles," in *Inerrancy and Common Sense*, edited by Roger R. Nicole and J. Ramsey Michaels (Grand Rapids: Baker Book House, 1980), p.164,165.

Brown appeals to the New Testament, which on a number of occasions gives a deeper meaning to an Old Testament passage, as proof that all Scripture has a literal meaning as well as a *sensus plenior*. We would reply that we can trust an apostle to give us such a deeper meaning, but where are there any apostles today? (Brown would answer, "Even after the end of the biblical era and the close of the public revelation ... God guides the Church and Christians in the understanding of revelation," and "The surest guide to [the fuller interpretation] is an authoritative interpretation of the words of Scripture in a more-than-literal way – authoritative in the sense that it comes from one of the guides to revelation, e.g., the New Testament, the Church Fathers, Church Pronouncements, etc. ... If there are real meanings of Scripture ... that are of importance to the divine plan for man's salvation, the most likely matrix for their emergence to clarity and acceptance is the context of Church life." Brown, *ibid.*)

[173] See "Criticism, Biblical," in *The Catholic Encyclopedia*, edited by Robert C. Broderick (Nashville: Thomas Nelson Inc., 1976), p.143, and "Form Criticism," p.224,225. See also, C.P. Ceroke, "Biblical Theology," in *The New Catholic Encyclopedia* (Washington, DC: Catholic University of America, 1979), Vol.17, p.40-42. In that same encyclopedia, the article on "Hermeneutics" by G. Woods, Vol.2, p.507-512 is a presentation and apology for the form critical method of exegesis.

[174] Samuel Terrien, "History of the Interpretation of the Bible: III. Modern Period," in *The Interpreter's Bible*, edited by G.A. Buttrick (Nashville: Abingdon Press, 1953-1956), Vol.1, p.140.

Two hundred years of experimentation with the historical-critical method should be enough to show it is an unsatisfactory approach to Bible interpretation.[175]

But what method of exegesis shall we use in order that we may arrive at the message the writer intended and deliver it to the 21st century reader? The method to be used is an ancient one that has been called the grammatical-historical method.[176] If the method has demonstrated any weakness, it is at the point of application to the modern reader. Yet the weakness is not inherent in the method, but rather in the student using the method. We would call attention to a recent article by Lewis A. Foster entitled *Realgeschichte: Old and New in Interpretation*. It is to be hoped that his writing will call the scholarly world back to the time-proven method of exegesis. After a brief overview of the history of interpretation, he offers *Realgeschichte* as a better alternative. Having explained his choice of the German word *real*, he writes about the methodology to be used.

> Is this term *Realgeschichte* indicative of the starting point, the goal, or the methodology of the interpretation? Truly, all three match the concept of *real*. Our primary interest is what was actually said and done. Important to understanding this is the factual nature of the record and the plan and purpose of the writers. The significance of all this to the life and involvement of the reader must become real also. *Realgeschichte* looks for the actual in the happening, the factual in the recording, and the compelling in the application.[177]

Gordon D. Fee has made an apologetic for the same method of interpretation in his "Hermeneutics and Common Sense."

> Sound hermeneutics with regard to the Epistles, therefore, seems to require the following three steps:
>
> 1. *Understand as much as possible of the original setting.* The interpreter, if you will, must remove his twentieth-century bifocals, shedding the filter of twentieth-century mentality, and put himself back into the first century. For the Epistles this has a double focus: (a) The interpreter must try as best he can to reconstruct the situation of the recipients. That is, he must ask, how is this letter, or this section of the letter, an answer to their problems or a response to their needs? In every case, a primary concern of interpretation is to try to hear what <u>they</u> would have heard. (b) He must try to live with the author and understand his mentality and his context. Above everything else the interpreter must try to understand what the author *intended* the recipients to hear. A maxim of hermeneutics for the Epistles is: *The correct meaning*

[175] See Gerhard Maier, *The End of the Historical-Critical Method* (St. Louis: Concordia, 1974), and the chapter titled "The Historical-Critical Method: The Bible's Deadly Enemy," in Harold Lindsell, *The Bible in the Balance* (Grand Rapids: Zondervan Publishing House, 1979), p.275-302.

[176] Drumwright, *Interpretation*, p.304,305, gives a brief summary of the principles and procedure embraced in the grammatical-historical method.

[177] Lewis A. Foster, "*Realgeschichte*: Old and New in Interpretation," in *Journal of the Evangelical Theological Society* 28/2 (June 1985), p.153-168.

of a passage must be something the author intended and his readers would have understood. ....

2. Hear the Word of God that is addressed to that situation. ... The point here is not that some parts of the Epistles are inspired and others are not, but rather that the recipients' context often reflects a problem which needs correcting or a lack of understanding that needs enlightening. Our task is to discover (or "hear") the Word of God that was addressed to that situation, the Word that called for the recipient's obedience or brought them to understanding.

3. Hear the same Word as it is addressed to our situation. [We must learn to identify similar settings and similar situations as those to which the Scriptures were first addressed, and then we can be assured that the Word that God spoke to them in such a situation is the same Word He would speak to us in the twentieth-century in a similar situation.][178]

As we set out to explain what Romans meant to its original readers, and as we would hear its message for our day, we must exercise every caution lest, as have others before us, we be influenced in our understanding either by dogma or philosophy. Of course, it will not be easy to come to Romans without all the baggage of the centuries. Nevertheless, our study will profit us only if we let God speak to us through this Roman epistle, and that, not what we want to hear, but what He intends for us to hear.

3. Paul and Judaism

The relationship between Christianity and Judaism is a vast theme whose importance is momentous and whose ramifications are far reaching. Attitudes in both camps toward each other have been significantly affected by such historical events as the incarnation of Jesus and His rejection by many of the leading Jews of His day; the persecution of the early church by Jewish antagonists; the Jewish-Roman war and the destruction of Jerusalem in AD 70; the rise of rabbinic Judaism; the persecution of the Jewish community by the established church during the middle ages in Europe; and the rise of Zionism and its support or rejection by whole "Christian" groups on the basis of some dispensational scheme of eschatology.

Defenders of Judaism have tended to blame Paul for the deterioration in the relationship between the two great religions, while the apologists for Christianity have pointed to alleged serious departures from what God revealed through Moses as the reason for the disaffection with Judaism on the part of Christianity. In the course of the debate through the centuries since Calvary, there have been times that the actual position held by

---

[178] Fee, *op. cit.*, in Nicole and Michaels, *Inerrancy and Common Sense*, p.168-176.

the other side has been misrepresented, both by Christian and by Jewish protagonists. In recent years a whole new study of the topic has occupied the efforts of scholars on both sides. Both have made a fresh attempt honestly to understand the other (though at times dogma and current philosophy have clouded such understanding) and to explain what actually separates the two religions. In the course of the 20th century, several fresh hypotheses have been offered by Jews and Christians alike, each attempting to explain what 1st century Judaism actually was, what Paul (and Jesus) actually taught, and why the two religions which came from the same roots should have come to a parting of the ways.

Because the conclusions reached in this whole area of study have such far-reaching ramifications, not only in New Testament studies and New Testament theology, but also with reference to relationships between Roman Catholicism and Protestantism, as well as relationships between Protestant bodies, and between Christian and Jew, it is very important that students of Paul's Roman letter be conversant with the whole current debate about Paul's treatment of the Law of Moses and his apparent rejection of Moses and Judaism as a viable religion now that Christ has come. Jewish writers on these matters, as well as Christian writers, must be given a hearing if the reader would attempt to avoid the errors and misrepresentations of the past as he attempts to form his own world view in the light of Scripture.

We begin our study with the statement of the conviction that Jesus and Paul are in agreement, and that their presentation of the Judaism in their day is a correct representation of how things actually were. Implied in this conviction is the idea that if there is a difference between Christianity and Judaism, that difference results from the teaching of Jesus, a teaching which Paul in turn faithfully reflected. Flatly rejected is any notion that Paul modified or deliberately changed what he received from Jesus so that it is Paul who is responsible for Christianity's differences from Judaism. How many times do we hear Paul affirm that he was simply repeating what had been delivered to him by Christ Himself (cf. 1 Corinthians 11:23 and 15:3, along with Galatians 1:11,12).

Using information gathered from the words of Jesus Himself, we can ascertain that in some matters the Judaism Jesus encountered was different from that which Moses had originally taught. While Jesus expected men to submit to the Law of Moses as long as it was in force[179] (and it was until Calvary), He did not require of Jewish people that they submit to the traditions of the elders (especially when those traditions differed from and

---

[179] That Jesus expected His Jewish contemporaries to obey Moses' Law can be seen in His instructions to the lepers to go show themselves to the priests (Matthew 8:1-4; Luke 5:12-14, 17:14), a thing required by the Law itself (Leviticus 14:1-32). His expectation that Moses' revelation be binding on the Jews as a rule of faith and practice can also be seen in Jesus' opening words in His denunciation of the scribes and Pharisees (Matthew 23:1-33). On that occasion, Jesus made reference to the fact that those religious leaders "sit in Moses' seat," and therefore all that they tell men to do and observe (all, that is, which is in harmony with Moses), men are still expected to observe and keep. In this we suppose that Jesus was simply reflecting God's own attitude toward obedience to Moses' Law, for we remember that Jesus spoke only what God sent Him to say (John 12:49).

tended to nullify what God had clearly expressed through His servant Moses). Mark 7:1-13 is but one passage where Jesus clearly shows that many of the contemporary religious traditions and practices of men were not at all in agreement with the commandments of God given long ago through Moses. What becomes rather evident in all this is the fact that Judaism as practiced by 1st century religious leaders had changed in many areas so that it differed from what was actually taught in Moses. It is usually affirmed that those changes began to be rather pronounced at the time of the captivity (500+ years before Christ), when men were no longer able to visit the temple (tabernacle) for certain yearly feasts, nor no longer able to offer the prescribed sacrifices at that place. In captivity, they accommodated their practices to what their captors would permit. Upon their return from the captivity, Ezra tried to call the people back to the old ways, but was not wholly successful. A century or so later, during the intertestamental period, we find the rise of the Pharisees and Sadducees and their corresponding abhorrence of or espousal of the Hellenistic culture introduced since Alexander the Great had conquered the ancient world. The changes and departures from what God had commanded through Moses thus became even more pronounced with the introduction of Greek ideas into Jewish practices. At the time when Jesus came into the world, the Sadducees were in control of the Jewish religious system; with the fall of Jerusalem, the influence of the Sadducees also was ended, and Pharisaism (Talmudic Judaism) became normative Judaism.[180] Through the centuries since, Judaism has continued to develop and change.[181]

---

[180] We have tended to agree with present-day scholarship (cf. Howard Marshall, "Palestinian and Hellenistic Christianity: Some Critical Comments" in *New Testament Studies* 19:3 [April, 1973], p.274) when we have refused to make any great distinction between Palestinian (rabbinic or Pharisaic) Judaism and Hellenistic (Diaspora) Judaism, a distinction that once played a major factor when men attempted to explain the difference between Palestinian Judaism and the Judaism that it was thought Paul was attacking and rejecting in his epistles. An excellent overview of this whole matter can be found in Donald Hagner, "Paul in Modern Jewish Thought," in *Pauline Studies*, edited by Donald Hagner and Murray Harris (Grand Rapids: Wm. B. Eerdmans Publishing Co., 1980), p.143-165. A more in-depth presentation is E.P Sanders, *Paul and Palestinian Judaism* (Philadelphia: Fortress Press, 1977). He shows that many of the standard works about Judaism that were relied on by Christian theologians were flawed in their presentation of what Palestinian Judaism actually taught and practiced.

[181] "Hebrew religion began to give rise to Judaism after the destruction of the temple and the exile of Judah in 586 BC ... The Jewish religion of the biblical period evolved through such historical stages as the inter-testamental, rabbinic, and medieval to the modern period of the nineteenth century with Orthodox, Conservative, and Reform Judaism ... The Babylonian exile brought certain modifications in Jewish religious life ... Scribes became the priestly interpreters of the Torah, setting forth their own authoritative teachings. By the second century BC, the Pharisees taught that the oral law carried the same authority as the law of Moses ... The destruction of the temple in AD 70 and the scattering of thousands of Jews from the land brought a sudden demise to the priesthood. Johanan ben Zakkai, a Pharisee, was soon permitted by the Romans to open an academy at Jabneh. He took it upon himself to install rabbis as the keepers and legislators of Torah. By word of mouth the rabbis passed their teachings from generation to generation until the oral law (Mishnah) was written down about AD 200, Rabbi Judah ha-Nasi its chief editor. By AD 500 the Talmud was completed with the issuing of the Gemara, a rabbinical commentary on the Mishnah." M.R. Wilson, "Judaism," in *Evangelical Dictionary of Theology* (Grand Rapids: Baker Book House, 1984), p.588ff. For greater detail than Wilson, the student would want to consult the article by R.K. Harrison on "Judaism" in *Zondervan Pictorial Encyclopedia of the Bible*, Vol.3 (Grand Rapids: Zondervan Publishing House, 1975), p.727-730; Kaufmann Kohler's article on "Judaism" in *The Jewish Encyclopedia*, Vol.7 (New York: KTAV Publishing Co., 1901), p.359-368; and J.M. Oesterreicher's article on "Judaism" in the *New Catholic Encyclopedia*, Vol. 8 (Washington, DC: Catholic University of America, 1967), p.3-13.

We affirm that Paul's objection to the Judaism of the 1st century was not the result of pagan or Hellenistic or Gnostic influences upon his thinking, though each of these ideas has been advocated by some influential writer in the past century. We affirm that the source of Paul's theology, as Paul himself asserted on more than one occasion, is to be found in the incarnation and teaching of Jesus, and the revelation and inspiration of the Holy Spirit, rather than in naturalistic sources.

Indeed, there were several areas of contention between Christianity and 1st century Judaism, precisely because in those areas Judaism had its doctrine or practice wrong.

(1) *Judaism had a monistic view of God.*   That is, they held to the idea that there was only one person in the Godhead. On the great day of questions (Matthew 22:34-46), Jesus tried to correct this view, but His listeners would not listen to His instruction. Jesus, and the New Testament writers in harmony with Him, teaches the pluralistic unity of the Godhead, with Father, Son, and Holy Spirit alike given the name and attributes of deity. Of course, as long as Judaism rejects the deity of Jesus, there will be a rejection of His message and religion also.[182]

(2) Kohler writes of *Judaism's attitude about eternal punishment* in these words: "Notwithstanding its unmitigated severity against heathenism with its folly and vice, and against every mode of compromise therewith, Judaism does not, like other creeds, consign the non-believer to eternal doom."[183]   In this it certainly is at odds with Jesus,

---

[182] "Jews and Jesus. Ever since Jabne [i.e., Jamnia, AD 70, and the academy opened by the Pharisee Johanan ben Zakkai, in which Pharisaic Judaism became normative Judaism], Judaism has precluded belief in Jesus as the Redeemer. Although some later Jewish teaching developed with Christianity in mind, the Talmudic sages avoided direct discussion of the gospel. The few hostile passages in the Talmud that, according to the opinion of competent scholars, refer to Jesus, do so without naming Him. Moreover, in speaking of Gentiles, rabbinic literature hardly distinguishes between Christians, worshipers of the one, true God, and pagans, worshipers of idols. Maimonides seems to have been the first to hold a mildly positive view of Christ's work. Maimonides (*Mishneh Torah, Hilkhot Melakhim* 11:4) held that Jesus' teaching, like Mohammed's, 'only served to clear the way for the King Messiah to prepare the whole world to worship God with one accord' (cf. So 3:9) ... But not till Reform Judaism made its voice heard did Jesus and Christianity – topics shunned till then by most Jews and even today by some of them – become a matter of investigation.   Not until then were such words spoken as those of Sigismund Stern, a German Jewish school teacher of the middle of the 19th century: 'Judaism and Christianity must hold out a brotherly hand to each other, for the sake of their common work for mankind ... [The Jewish believers] must love their Christian fellow men, not merely as fellow human beings, but feel related to them in faith and bound to them with special ties.' Since then, a new appreciation of the person of Jesus – not to be mistaken, however, for faith in Him as the Christ – has set in. Even a scholar as steeped in tradition as Joseph Klausner (1874-1958) called Jesus a great moral teacher. Claude J.G. Montefiore (1859-1939), the founder of Liberal Judaism in England, saw in Him a new type of prophet. Rabbi Leo Baeck (1874-1956) – the distinguished head of German Jewry at the time of Hitler and one-time president of the World Union for Progressive Judaism – acclaimed Him as the manifestation 'of what is pure and good in Judaism.' The Conservative theologian Rabbi Milton Steinberg (1903-1950) spoke of Him as 'an extra-ordinarily beautiful and noble spirit, aglow with love and pity for men.' And the existential thinker Martin Buber (1878-1965) regarded Him as 'my great brother.' Of the several statements made by American rabbis on this theme, the most interesting are those of Maurice Eisendrath, president of the Union of American Hebrew Congregations ... In 1963 he called on Jews to reappraise their 'oftentimes jaundiced view of him in whose name Christianity was established,' and in 1965 he asked that Jesus, 'this Jewish hero,' be incorporated 'into our never too overcrowded company of saintly spirits'."   J.M. Oesterreicher, "Judaism," p.12.

[183] Kohler, "Judaism," p.366.

who warned about the danger of being cast into hell, where the worm dies not and the fire is not quenched.   Could it be that Romans 1-3 are intended to refute the erroneous ideas of Judaism about the certainty of final judgment and the fate of the heathen?

(3) *Judaism's beliefs about the world to come* seem to have included the view that the life to come was but a mere reproduction of this present life with all its relations and conditions restored and made permanent.   That is one reason the Pharisees had trouble answering the Sadducees' extreme case about the woman who had seven different men as husband (Luke 20:27-38).   Jesus responded to this "reproduction of the present life" presupposition by appealing to the power of God as capable of producing another kind of life.   In harmony with this Paul writes of the deliverance of creation from the bondage of corruption (Romans 8:21) and of future resurrection (Romans 8:11).

(4) Judaism also seems to have held *the belief that Jewish people are acceptable to God as they are*, that they did not need the gospel.[184]   In response to this mistaken belief, Paul constantly emphasizes that according to God's plan the gospel is "to the Jew first"; he insists (Romans 10) Israel had failed to attain to the righteousness of God because they had not responded to the gospel in faith; and he holds out the promise that unbelieving Israel can be grafted back in if they quit their unbelief (Romans 11:23).

(5) On the topic of *the possibility and actuality of sinless perfection as actually achieved by many Jewish saints*, Kohler wrote, "... rabbinical Judaism denies that sin is inherited from parents, pointing to Abraham the son of Terah, Hezekiah the son of Ahaz, and others as instances to the contrary ... and insists on the possibility of sinlessness as manifested by various saints (Shab. 55b; Yoma 22b; Eccl. R. i.8, iii.2)."[185]   Such assertions regarding the possibility of sinlessness are contrary to the plain statements by John ("If we say we have no sin, we are deceiving ourselves ... if we say we have not sinned, we make Him a liar, and His word is not in us") and Paul ("there is none righteous, not even one" and "all have sinned and fall short of the glory of God").

(6) *Judaism does not allow for a "power of evil" infecting creation*,[186] as Paul seems to teach in Romans 5:12 and 7:8-11 ("the sin") and 8:20 ("subjected to futility/vanity").

(7) *Judaism's idea of what sin is, and the seriousness of sin*,[187]   seems at variance with the

---

[184] See Pinchas Lapide and Peter Stuhlmacher, *Paul: Rabbi and Apostle* (Minneapolis: Augusburg, 1984), which reflects the debate between a Jewish scholar and a Christian scholar, in which the former attempts to show from the New Testament that Paul meant the gospel only for the Gentiles, and not for Israel.

[185] Kohler, "Judaism," p.362.

[186] See Kohler, "Judaism," p.361.   "Judaism knows of no 'law of sin in the body' of which Paul speaks (Romans 7:23-25)."   Kohler, p.362.   Paul's presentation of 'slavery to sin' (Romans 6) resulting from a man's own personal acquiescence to the devil's temptations would also be an idea foreign to Judaism.

[187] "Sin, according to Jewish teaching, is simply erring from the right path, owing chiefly to the weakness of human nature [his body makes man cherish sensual desires; Judaism does not hold a doctrine of mankind's depravity inherited from Adam] (Numbers 15:26; 1 Kings 8:46; Psalms 19:13, 78:38, 102:14; Job 4:17-21); only in the really wicked is it insolent rebellion against God and his order ('pesha' or 'resha'; Isaiah 57:20; Psalms 1:4-6, 36:2 ...).   And there is no sin too great to be atoned for by repentance and reparation (Ezekiel 18:23; Yer. Peah 1:126b; Kid. 40b)."   Kohler, "Judaism," p.362.
   Because of the Christian use of many Old Testament passages to demonstrate that Jesus is indeed the promised Messiah, many of the passages once admitted by Jews to be Messianic are no longer so in-

revelation (even in type and prophecy in the Old Testament) of the necessity of Calvary to atone for sin (cp. Romans 3:21-26, 5:6-11 and 8:3), and with the assertions found in the New Testament about what "sin" is and how exceeding sinful and heinous sin actually is (cp. Romans 5:20 and 7:13).

(8) The idea of *the permanence of the Law* was an idea that gradually took hold in Judaism.[188] "Because the prophets had insisted that the punishment of the Exile was the result of a breach of covenant law, the repatriates were encouraged to take its observance far more seriously in the future. Its permanence and stability could not be questioned, since it alone had survived when cult and nation alike had been destroyed by the Exile."[189] In opposition to Judaism's views, Paul has much to say about the temporary nature of the Mosaic Law, not only in Romans but also in Galatians, 1 and 2 Corinthians, Colossians, and 1 Timothy 1:6- 11.[190]

(9) Israel was conscious of being *God's "chosen people,"* with a mission to be a priest and teacher of the nations.[191] This was conceived as a permanent commission.[192] Is this

---

terpreted. "The famous 53rd chapter of Isaiah was formerly taken as the authority for a belief in vicarious atonement. The special Christological interpretation has always been repudiated by [Talmudic and later] Judaism ... (see S.R. Driver and A.D. Neubauer, *The Fifty-Third Chapter of Isaiah According to the Jewish Interpreters*, Oxford, 1877). Thus Ibn Ezra (q.v.; 1167) refers the expression 'my servant' to all those God-fearing Jews who were in exile; Sa'adya (q.v., 892-942) to the prophet Jeremiah. Both of these commentators reflect traditional exegesis: their views do not merely represent contemporary opinion. The suffering of the Servant was regarded by the nations as an expiation for their sin; but this opinion, put into the mouths of the Gentile kings, was erroneous, and the outcome of their amazement at the persistence of the Servant under such unparalleled persecution. The impossibility of a vicarious atonement is clearly stated by the refusal of God to allow Moses to become a substitute for the sins of Israel. 'Whosoever hath sinned against me, him will I blot out of my book' (Exodus 32:31ff)." Herbert Loewe, "Judaism," in *Hastings Encyclopedia of Religion and Ethics* edited by James Hastings (New York: Charles Scribner's Sons, 1915), Vol.7, p.583,584.

[188] "Though not revealed till Sinai, the Law was considered a living being, identical with the wisdom that existed before time (Proverbs 8.22-31). Like wisdom, the Torah [whole body of law] was the craftsman at God's side; it served Him as the plan according to which he created the world (*Ab.* 3.14; *Gen. Rabbah* 1.1). The Law was perfect and immutable; yet it had to be interpreted, supplemented, and adapted to the exigencies of time." J.M. Oesterreicher, "Judaism," p.5.

[189] R.K. Harrison, "Judaism," p.729. "While the immutability of the Torah, that is, the law of Moses, both the written and the oral Law, is declared by Maimonides to be one of the cardinal doctrines of Judaism, there are views expressed in the Talmud that the commandments will be abrogated in the world to come (Nid. 61b). It is especially the dietary laws that will, it is said, be no longer in force in the Messianic time (Midr. Teh. on Ps. cxlvi.4)." Kohler, "Judaism," p.367.

[190] Some recent writers have attempted to show that Paul's opposition to the abiding validity of the Law mellowed as the years passed. Especially objectionable among these is the suggestion offered by Hans Hubner (*Law in Paul's Thought* [Edinburgh: T&T Clark, 1984]) that Paul's views changed between the writing of Galatians (where he is rather harsh on Judaism) and the writing of Romans (where he is supposed to be more understanding and tolerant). The reason such a reconstruction is objectionable is that Paul's doctrine is not (as Hubner supposes) something he himself developed by a trial-and-error method until he found something that the average man would accept. Both E.P. Sanders, *Paul, the Law, and the Jewish People* (Philadelphia: Fortress Press, 1983), and Heikki Raisanen, *Paul and the Law* (Tubingen: Mohr, 1983) have written important critiques of Hubner's book, which first appeared in German in 1978.

[191] "Israel, then, has been chosen, like Israel's ancestor Abraham ... to be a blessing to all nations on earth (Genesis 12:3, 19:18); and the name by which the Lord calls him at the Exodus (Exodus 4:22), 'My

the suppressed thought in the background that Paul refutes as he writes about how Israel was chosen to be the channel through which Messiah came into the world, and how, because of unbelief, most had been rejected as tools in God's hands (Romans 9:11)?

(10) The function of Israel as a "chosen people" is to be the heirs and custodians of the Torah, *in order to keep the great ideals of the Torah before the eyes of the world*.[193] All men will one day be brought near to the Kingdom of Heaven by observance of the Torah, which in the meantime has been guarded and passed on to new generations by Israel as she fulfills the mission God put her in the world to accomplish. When that future day dawns when all men will embrace the revelation of God as given in the Torah, then the sacrifices Israel had to make and the suffering she had to endure[194] to keep the ideals of the Torah alive will be seen to have been worth it all. Paul's affirmation that *Messiah* came through Israel, and that Israel's devotion and allegiance should be to Him (rather than to the Torah), now seem more pointed and relevant.

---

first-born son,' betokens in the language of the time his mission to be that of the priest and teacher in the household of the nations, leading the rest by his precept and example to the worship of the Only One (Exodus 19:6; Isaiah 61:6). 'A people dwelling in solitude and not counted among the nations' (Numbers 23:9; Deuteronomy 7:7), but watched over by divine providence with especial care (Deuteronomy 27:18-19, 32:8-12), the standard-bearer of incomparable laws of wisdom and righteousness in the sight of the nations (Deuteronomy 4:5-8), Israel has been created to declare God's praise to the world, to be 'His witnesses' (LXX, 'martyrs') testifying to His unity, 'the light of the nations,' and the 'covenant of the people to establish the earth' (Isaiah 43:10,21; 49:6-8). 'To Israel's house of God the nations shall flock to be taught of His ways and to learn to walk in His paths.' This is to bring humanity back to its normal condition, peace and bliss on earth, because righteousness will then prevail everywhere and the whole 'earth shall be full of the knowledge of the Lord' (Isaiah 2:2-4, 9:6, 11:4-9, 65:25; Micah 4:1-4)." Kohler, "Judaism," p.363.

[192] "Both in Babylon and after the Return the Jews held tenaciously to the belief in their divine election. Countless texts and teachings reminded them of the fact that God had chosen them to be His people, His witnesses, a kingdom of priests, a beacon of light and truth to the nations of the earth. However much they might have fallen short of their duty, however much they might have neglected not only to teach others, but even themselves to remain faithful to their sacred tasks, God had not deposed them forever from the office to which he had appointed them and their ancestors ... [T]hey never felt themselves to have been superseded. Their mission was not taken from them." Loewe, "Judaism," p.584.

[193] Contrast this Judaistic view of Israel's mission with Paul's statements in Romans 9-11, that Israel was chosen to be the channel through whom Messiah came into the world, and He was the One who would bring all men of faith to the Kingdom of God.

[194] The problem of the suffering of the righteous and the seeming prosperity of the wicked has always proven a difficult question to answer satisfactorily. A rather standard view is that Jewish people must be prepared to defend their mission at the cost of their lives and to sacrifice their material prosperity (which may be harder than to suffer martyrdom) in order to be a part of the "remnant" God is using to keep the ideals of the Torah before the eyes of the world. "Few maxims ... are more revelatory of the genius of this sturdy religion than the word of the wise man: 'Whom the Lord loveth he chasteneth, and scourgeth every son whom he receiveth' (Hebrews 12:6; cf. Proverbs 3:12). That was a lesson which, it seemed, the whole history of the nation had taught. Through the fires of adversity God was perfecting his chosen people, was burning away their dross, was subjecting them to constant and bitter punishment, but with the purpose of fitting them for their glorious destiny. Through sin they had fallen short – hence slavery to one heathen overlord after another; hence also the misfortune of being scattered over the face of the earth, far from the Promised Land ... In the future, when the time of testing and trial was over, when Israel had truly repented of her many sins, and as obedient sons and daughters performed the Father's will, once again the age of gold would dawn." Morton S. Enslin, "Palestine" in *The Interpreter's Bible* edited by George A. Buttrick (Nashville: Abingdon Press, 1951), Vol.7, p.112.

(11) Judaism also had certain rather definite views about the Jews as a separate people, and about what might be called *"identity markers"*[195] by which this separateness was to be maintained.[196]   It must be remembered that this separateness is not so much racial as it is religious – the separation was originally to be maintained to insure the purity of the religion more than the purity of the race.   We should not be surprised by Paul's statements about certain dietary rules and certain ceremonies (e.g., circumcision) being intended to be reflect negatively on this whole Jewish concept of how such separateness is to be achieved.

More could be said in this vein, but enough has been set forth to enable the reader to grasp the general idea of the real reason for the rejection of Judaism in favor of Christianity by the followers of Jesus Messiah.   Even though the Jew should have been in a better position to be in a right standing before God because of the privileges God had granted to the seed of Abraham, Paul is doing them a great favor by pointing out their need to obey the gospel in order that God might reckon them as righteous in His sight.   Indeed, he has done both Jew and Gentile a great favor by emphasizing the need for "the obedience of faith" to the gospel which is grounded on the atoning death and resurrection of Christ.   The covenant made with Abraham, not the Law which came 400 years later, is the basis according to which some from all nations will be blessed now that the Seed (Christ) has come.   This has always been God's plan, and it is this eternal purpose which Paul explicates in such grand detail as he writes his epistle to the Romans.

Occasion And Purpose For Writing

"When beginning a study of any New Testament epistle, the question must be asked,

---

[195] There is a kernel of truth in Dunn's presentation of the sociological "identity and boundary markers" one would expect to find in Judaism.   James D.G. Dunn, "The New Perspective on Paul," in *Bulletin of the John Rylands University Library* 65 (1983), p.95-122.

[196] "The Sinaitic covenant which rendered Israel 'a kingdom of priests and a holy nation' (Exodus 19:6) became, the Rabbis say, 'a source of hatred to the nations' (Shab. 89a: a play upon words, 'Sinai' – 'Sin'ah'), because it separated it from them by statues and ordinances, such as the dietary and the Levitical purity laws and others intended to prevent idolatrous practices.   Like the priest in the Temple, whose garments and mode of life distinguished him from the rest in order to invest him with the spirit of greater sanctity and purity (1 Chronicles 23:13), so Israel was for all time to be impressed with its priestly mission by all those ceremonies which form so prominent a feature in its religious life ... Particularly the Mosaic and, later on, the Pharisaic laws had for their object the separation of the Jewish people from all those influences prevalent in heathendom which led to idolatry and impurity; wherefore not only intermarriage, but also participation in any meal or other festive gathering which could possibly be connected with idol-worship was prohibited ...."   Kohler, "Judaism," p.365.

"Some of these [613 commandments] are understood to be divine marks of distinction to separate Israel from the other nations – statutes ('*hukkot*') which are designated as unreasonable by the heathen world, such as laws concerning diet, dress, and the like (Sifra, Ahare Mot. xiii).   Others are called 'testimony' ('*eduyot*'), in view of their having been given to make Israel testify to God's miraculous guidance, such as the festive seasons of the year; while still others are 'signs' ('*ot*'), being tokens of the covenant between God and Israel, such as circumcision, the Sabbath (Genesis 17:11; Exodus 31:13), the Passover (Exodus 12:13, 13:9), and, according to the rabbinical interpretation, the tefillin (Deuteronomy 6:8, 11:18)." Kohler, *op. cit.*, p.367.

'What was the occasion which prompted the author to write?' Every New Testament letter was called forth by some specific historic circumstances and needs."[197] By "occasion" is meant what prompted the writer to write at the point in time that he did. Through the years, most scholars have agreed that the most obvious reason for writing when he did was that Phoebe's planned trip to Rome (Romans 16:1,2) would provide Paul with just the opportunity he needed to get this letter delivered.[198]

While there is rather general agreement as to the occasion, it is another matter when it comes to determining the purpose Paul had in mind for writing. In the apparent absence of any specific purpose statement (as e.g., Luke 1:1-4 explains the purpose of Luke's Gospel, or John 20:30-31 explains the purpose for writing John's Gospel), the best we can do is try to deduce the purpose from all that is written in the letter to the Romans. This has led scholars, in the past, to suggest a number of proposals as to Paul's purpose. One suggestion is that Romans is a *personal apologetic*. For some time now, Paul has desired to come to Rome, and now he writes to inform them he is coming. Romans, according to this theory, was written to gain for himself and his work the sympathy of the Roman church. Chapters 1-8 are written to make them understand his doctrine, and chapters 9-11 are given to explain to them his mission. As with many of the scholars' suggestions, this one may express part of Paul's purpose, but it overlooks much in the letter. For instance, it overlooks the fact that many of the Romans (see the names of his friends and acquaintances in chapter 16) were already in sympathy with Paul and his work. And what of chapters 12-15, which are not included in the above explanation of purpose? Not only does this first suggestion overlook portions of the letter, it presupposes that the Roman church was predominantly Jewish, and that the Jewish-Christians felt they had a priority on Christ, and were opposed to the Gentiles coming into the church. Such a presupposition is simply more than we can know from the meager evidence we have.

A second suggestion regarding Paul's purpose for writing is that Romans was intended to be *didactic* or *dogmatic*, a *systematic formal treatise on Christian doctrine*. This

---

[197] F. Sherwood Smith, *Thirteen Lessons on Romans* (Joplin, MO: College Press, 1979), p.8. Critics differ much as to Paul's aim or purpose in writing this letter. Since Baur's time, the "purpose for writing Romans" has become one of the most controverted in the whole range of New Testament criticism. "The question stands thus: If we assign a special practical aim to the epistle, we put ourselves, as it seems, in contradiction to the very general and quasi-systematic character of its contents. If, on the contrary, we ascribe to it a didactic and wholly general aim, that makes Romans differ from the other letters of Paul, all of which spring from some particular occasion, and have a definite aim" (Godet, *Romans*, p.47). Another circumstance which lends difficulty to the question of determining purpose is the fact that "Paul had not yet been at Rome, and consequently we have none of those lifelike pictures and graphic strokes which set so vividly before our eyes the inner life of those Churches to which his earlier Epistles were addressed, Thessalonica, Corinth, and Galatia. In such circumstances speculation has free scope, and theories are more easily formed than refuted. By exaggerating some features and disregarding others, it is easy to give an air of plausibility to very different views of the prevailing tendencies of thought and practice in the Christian Community at Rome, and of the corresponding purpose of the Epistle" (Gifford, *Romans*, p.11).

[198] In the 20th century, we are so used to writing a letter, putting it into an envelope, licking a stamp, affixing it to the envelope, and then letting the postal service deliver it, that we have a hard time realizing how different it was for an ordinary citizen to send a letter in the ancient world. Not only did you have to find someone going to the place where you wished to send a letter, but he had to be someone you could trust to make the extra effort to find the addressee and deliver the letter.

was the opinion that was specially in vogue at the time of the Reformation. Luther called Romans "the absolute epitome of the Gospel" and Melanchthon called it a "compendium of Christian doctrine." In ancient times, it was a regular thing in scholarly circles to set forth one's magnum opus in the form of a letter.[199] According to this theory, Romans is just such a scholarly work. Why would Paul write his greatest treatise on Christianity to Rome? Because Rome was the greatest city in the world, the capital of the greatest empire the world had ever seen, and there was no doubt in Paul's mind that what happened in Rome was of tremendous import to the future of Christianity. Therefore, it was needful for the church in that city to have an orderly and comprehensive statement of the Christian faith. The church there had never had an apostolic witness, and at best their grasp of Christianity was secondhand. Paul himself, though he had long desired to visit Rome, had never been there, and he did not know if he would ever get there. Just in case his present journey to Jerusalem should end his travels and opportunities to have a part in the direction the Roman church should take, Paul writes this letter, a sort of "theological last will and testament," in which he distills the very essence of the last word about his faith and message. If he never personally is allowed to visit Rome, at least the church there will have his written word to guide them as they in turn influence the future.[200] While much of this second suggestion is true,[201] it also seems to fail to take into account all the pertinent verses in Romans,[202] and it also fails to note that there are many facets of the gospel that are not developed at all in Romans.[203] If they are not developed, how can Romans be called a "compendium of Paul's theology," or a "formal treatise on Christian doctrine"?

---

[199] Romans has the form of a letter or an epistle. "It is worthy of notice that while the Old Testament does not contain one entire book, but at the most a few verses in an epistolary form, yet of the two hundred and fifty-six chapters in the New Testament, one hundred and seventeen are in that form. Of these Paul wrote eighty-seven chapters ... Various reasons are assigned for the abounding of epistles in the New Testament ... The state of literature throughout the world about the time of the first propagation of the gospel greatly favored this style of communication. Long treatises were written in the *epistles* of learned men. We might cite those of Cicero, Seneca, Symmachus and Pliny, the Younger. In fact both ancients and moderns have in this way handled a great variety of topics, friendship, art, science, politics, literature and religion." W.S. Plumer, *Commentary on Romans* (Grand Rapids: Kregel Publications, 1971), p.2,3.

[200] G.G. Findlay, *The Epistles of Paul* (New York: Wilbur B. Ketcham, 1892), p.137, called the epistle "a formal manifesto."

[201] This hesitancy to accept "a systematic formal treatise" as the purpose for which Paul wrote Romans is not intended to imply that there is nothing orderly or systematic in the way the letter is written, and the ideas therein presented. There is nothing comparable in any other of his epistles (unless it is Hebrews) to the connected train of thought which runs from 1:16 to 11:36.

[202] In chapters 12-15, there is much that is specially pertinent to the church in Rome. In these chapters the reader of Romans is made quite aware of a particular community with particular needs. The "systematic formal treatise" theory rather ignores what is included in these chapters.

[203] The resurrection is not developed in Romans as it is in 1 Corinthians 15. The Lord's Supper is not developed as it is in 1 Corinthians 11. Church polity is not developed as it is in the letters to Timothy and Titus. The return of the Lord is not developed as it is in Thessalonians. The New Covenant is not developed as it is in 2 Corinthians 3, Galatians 3, and Hebrews 8-10. Christology is not developed as it is in Colossians 1.

A third attempt at identifying Paul's purpose in writing is to call Romans an *irenic*, or a *conciliatory letter*. The theory is that the Jewish and Gentile elements in the church, or in Rome, needed to be unified. Some scholars who have espoused this opinion believe that the Roman Christians were divided into two congregations (one Jewish, the other Gentile) which were antagonistic to each other, or at least disturbed by numerous points of friction.[204] Some scholars suggest that when Paul wrote, he was extremely anxious about the breaking down of racial barriers between Jew and Gentile the world over. In fact, his journey to Jerusalem with the offering was an attempt to win over the Christians in Judea to a positive attitude about their brethren from among the Gentiles in Asia and Greece. Gentile Christians in Rome, likewise, it is supposed, needed help with their anti-Jewish feelings, and this is why Romans was written to them. Other scholars suggest that after the Jews, who had been banished from Rome by the edict of Claudius, returned, a new treaty of peace became necessary between the Christians of Gentile and the Christians of Jewish backgrounds. Romans, this theory suggests, was this treaty, for Romans emphasizes that Jews and Gentiles are equal before God; their rights and weaknesses are similar; and if any advantage existed in favor of one group, it was abolished in Christ, who united all in one universal religion. Objections to this attempt at identifying Paul's purpose for writing have included: though there were people from both Jewish and Gentile backgrounds in the church at Rome, there is no evidence they were not getting along with each other; this "irenic" theory emphasizes Romans 14-15, but does not satisfactorily account for the first ten chapters of Romans; while chapters 14-15 do suggest some points of friction, there is little to limit these points to Jewish versus non-Jewish points.

Still another group of scholars has taken the opposite position, and instead of seeing Paul's purpose as irenic, they suggest that Romans is a *polemic*. The theory begins with the assumption that the church at Rome was not only Jewish, but Jewish in the "Petrine sense," i.e., heavily legalistic. Paul's epistle is then viewed as a grand effort to transform this Petrine congregation into a Pauline type of Christianity.[205] Perhaps the most telling objection to this theory is that it has never been shown that Peter and Paul preached such a different type of Christianity. And if it were true that the Roman Church was "Petrine" in thinking, it would not be easy to understand how Paul could have congratulated his readers on the "form of teaching" (as he does at 6:17) if his intention had been to substitute a new concept of the gospel for the one they had.

A fifth suggestion as to the purpose of Romans is less objectionable – it treats Romans as a *warning against possible false doctrine*. According to this theory, Paul wishes to warn the Romans about the Judaizers, who either already are at Rome, or, as is more probable, who Paul is fearful will come to Rome and start their devilish work there. After he has seen the devastation and division these men caused in Galatia and Antioch, he is anxious to prevent any such disruption among the brethren in Rome. So he carefully sets

---

[204] Such an attempted reconstruction sounds vaguely familiar. Is it not based on the presuppositions of Baur and the Tubingen school of a previous century?

[205] F.C. Baur, *Paul, the Apostle of Jesus Christ* (London: Williams and Norgate, 1876), Vol.1, p.308ff.

out the place and value of the Law, and the method by which God counts men as righteous and sanctifies them (chapters 1-8). One of the hardest questions many Judaizers could ask ('If the gospel Paul preaches is true, how is it that so many of God's chosen people have rejected it?') is answered (chapters 9-11). The whole presentation throughout is thought to be conducted with reference to such attacks as Judaizers (whether within or outside of the church) would make upon Paul's gospel presentation. 16:17-20 is thus understood to be the statement of Paul's intent all along, a statement which he reserved until the very end of the letter. Those who question whether this suggestion rightly represents Paul's real purpose urge that it does not completely explain all the phenomena of Romans,[206] nor does it take into account that 16:17-20 looks almost like an afterthought, rather than being a primary statement of purpose.

Such then are some of the older attempts to discern the purpose for which Romans was written.[207] It probably can be said that none of these older attempts to explain the purpose for the writing of Romans has proven to be entirely satisfactory, nor has any gained a general acceptance by the majority of students of Romans. Since 1960, as a result of scholars' attempts to interpret Romans through historical-critical methodology, a number of newer and often competing hypotheses as to the purpose for writing have been advanced. The historical-critical method has as one of its starting points the view that all New Testament documents were written out of a specific historical situation and addressed to a specific audience who had concrete concerns and problems. What has led these new critics to advance so many competing hypotheses as to the purpose of Romans is the difficulty in determining the specific historical situation (the *Sitz im Leben*, the critic sometimes calls it) behind Romans. Although there is much variety of emphasis between various writers' positions, there are basically two opposing viewpoints: (1) some suppose the letter reflects the writer's situation and interests more than the readers' situation; (2) others suppose the letter reflects the reader's situation (whether in Rome or elsewhere) more than the writer's.

Recent representatives of the first viewpoint would include Leenhardt,[208] who argues that Paul's wish to express to the Romans what his missionary work to Spain could mean

---

[206] In Paul's letters, where specific adversaries (and their teachings) are being refuted, we are told that "some" teach so-and-so, but it is in error. In Romans, there are not many places where specific adversaries are named. 2:1-5 and 3:1-8 are about the only places in the doctrinal section where it is hinted that actual adversaries are in mind. It may be more in harmony with the overall view of Romans to say Paul was conscious of the usual arguments that men everywhere regularly used in an effort to refute the gospel, and that he simply anticipates these, and answers them before they can be personally raised by whomever the opponent might be. At times these opponents will be Jewish; at times they will be Gentile.

[207] Many older commentaries will present one or more of these ideas in detail. See, for example, Gifford, *Romans*, p.9-20, wherein the view is defended that Paul's purpose was to teach Christian doctrine, and reasons for rejecting Baur's irenic or conciliatory view are presented at length; Godet, *Romans*, p.47-58, which presents the pros and cons of the apologetic, the polemic, and the didactic aims of the letter; and Denney, *Romans*, p.568-575, in which the dogmatic, controversial, and conciliatory views are offered as possible purposes.

[208] Franz Leenhardt, *The Epistle to the Romans: A Commentary* (London: Lutterworth, 1961), p.12-23.

for the unity of the church was the occasion; Martin,[209] who proposes that Paul wished to teach the church at Rome and elsewhere about the worldwide missionary mandate found in the gospel; Bornkamm,[210] who viewed Romans as Paul's "last will and testament" – a summary of his theology in light of the impending danger in Jerusalem; Jervell,[211] who supposes Romans is a draft of the address Paul will give when he arrives at Jerusalem with the offering, so that his collection and he himself will not be rejected; Karris,[212] who urges that Romans sums up Paul's missionary theology and paraenesis; and Wuellner[213] (who calls for the use of the method of New Testament study called rhetorical criticism, rather than the older method called literary criticism which tried to identify what genre of literature Romans is, i.e., Bultmann's identification of Romans as a form of diatribe, or Stierwalt's identification of Romans as a letter-essay), who affirms that the argumentation (the rhetoric) in Romans emphasizes two themes – Paul as an agent of the gospel for the *nations*, and Paul as an agent of the gospel to the church(es) at Rome – both of which relate to his claim for support and for authoritative teaching.

Typical of the contemporary writers who espouse the second viewpoint would be Klein,[214] who affirms that Romans 15:20 is the key to the purpose of the letter, and that a comparison of Romans 1:15 and 15:20 shows that "Paul can consider an apostolic effort in Rome because he does not regard the local Christian community there as having an apostolic foundation" which, in Klein's view, they certainly needed; Marxsen,[215] who supposes Paul wrote to settle the conflict between Jewish and Gentile Christians which arose when the Jewish Christians (who had been expelled from Rome by the decree of Claudius, cp. Acts 18:2) returned to Rome after Claudius' death in AD 54, not only to find a church there but a church greatly different from the one they knew, because it was predominantly Gentile in membership and lifestyle and worship; Minear,[216] who proposes that Romans is written to deal with the conflict between "the 'weak in faith' who condemned

---

[209] James P. Martin, "The Kerygma of Romans," *Interpretation* 25 (1971), p.303-328. It is perhaps a fatal flaw in this article that it does not attempt to explain how the exhortations to the "weak" and "strong" brothers of Romans 14:1-15:13 fit into this larger overall theme of the universal faith and mission of the church.

[210] Gunther Bornkamm, *Paul* (New York: Harper and Row, 1971), p.88-96.

[211] Jacob Jervell, "The Letter to Jerusalem," in *The Romans Debate* edited by Karl P. Donfried (Minneapolis: Augsburg Publishing House, 1977), p.61-74.

[212] Robert J. Karris, "Romans 14:1-15:13 and the Occasion of Romans," in *The Romans Debate*, p.75-99.

[213] Wilhelm Wuellner, "Paul's Rhetoric of Argumentation in Romans: An Alternative to the Donfried-Karris Debate over Romans," in *The Romans Debate*, p.152-174.

[214] Gunter Klein, "Paul's Purpose in Writing the Epistle to the Romans," in *The Romans Debate*, p.32-49.

[215] Willi Marxsen, *Introduction to the New Testament* (Philadelphia: Fortress Press, 1968), p.92-109.

[216] Paul S. Minear, *The Obedience of Faith* (London: SCM, 1971). Minear speculates that the Roman Christians were not involved in a unified congregation, but were members of various cells and competing house churches, and that Romans was written to help achieve unity among the believers in Rome.

the 'strong in faith'" (i.e., the Jewish and Gentile Christians, respectively) and "the 'strong in faith' who scorned and despised the 'weak in faith'"; and Wiefel,[217] who suggests that as Claudius' edict was being rescinded, a continued ban was imposed on formal synagogue meetings, a development which contributed directly to the formation of the many house churches we read about in Romans 16. Wiefel further supposes that most of these house churches were dominated by a Gentile Christian theology and ideology, and that the anti-Semitic attitudes found in contemporary Rome also were reflected by the Gentile majority during the meetings in the house churches. It is precisely this lack of unity among the Roman believers that Paul writes to correct. Brinsmead[218] has combined several of these views, along with an affirmation that "justification" involves justice toward the weak and oppressed, as he makes his presentation of the purpose for which Paul wrote Romans, namely that any man (be he Jew or Gentile) who understands and appreciates God's "justification" will certainly welcome into hearty fellowship anyone who shares in that justification, irrespective of whether he observes the Law or disregards the Law; in fact, if he himself has experienced "justice," he will be actively involved in seeing that justice is done toward all.

Having rejected the historical-critical method of interpretation, and having opted for the grammatical-historical method, we would propose that both Paul's purposes and the readers' needs should be taken into account as one attempts to define Paul's purpose in writing. The expression we would use to summarize the purpose, as we perceive it, is that Romans is what might be called an *historic didactic*. It is "historic" because the epistle is historically grounded. Certain historical circumstances, some in the church at Rome, some in the fulfillment of the need to take the gospel to the Gentiles, and some in Paul's own life, called it forth. It was also "didactic" because in it Paul explained, especially for the benefit of those in Rome who did not know him, the gospel he had been preaching.[219] Considering both the carefully structured doctrinal portion that forms the bulk of the letter and the historical allusions included in the epistle (i.e., in the first part of chapter 1 and in

---

[217] Wolfgang Wiefel, "The Jewish Community in Ancient Rome and the Origins of Roman Christianity," in *The Romans Debate*, p.100-119.

[218] Robert D. Brinsmead, "Notes on Justification in Romans," in *The Christian Verdict*, Essay 9 (1983), p.16. Gunter Klein, "Paul's Purpose in Writing the Epistle to the Romans," p.40-42, gives five reasons why this theory will not hold up under critical investigation. Key among these is the fact that there is still no convincing proof that the contention between the strong and weak brothers dealt with in 14:1-15:13 arose out of a Jewish vs. Gentile milieu. Not less important is the matter of outlining Romans: shall we regard Romans 1-11 as the theological foundation of the intended peace settlement? If so, how shall we link Romans 12 and 13 to such a theme?

[219] One notable point, often ignored in discussions of the purpose behind the writing of Romans, is Paul's own theme statement in Romans 1:16,17. He tells us that the gospel reveals God's way of saving man, a way that has always been conditioned on faithfulness. An exposition of this theme would require a careful statement of the temporary place of the Law of Moses, and the historic election of Israel to a special function (the channel through which Messiah comes into the world). Such an exposition, rightly understood, would supply a more satisfactory and comprehensive explanation (than does the alleged "polemic" purpose for Romans) for all the tacit references to Judaism (see above, "Paul and Judaism"), as well as for the concluding warning about "Judaizers" (16:17-20).

the verses following 15:14 and continuing through chapter 16), it becomes evident that *both* Paul's purposes and also the needs of the readers must be taken into account in any statement of the purpose for which Romans was written.

1. Paul's Purposes

If we were to concentrate on Paul's motives as they can be discerned from the contents of the letter, perhaps it is most correct to state that they were all vitally related to his apostleship (Romans 1:1, 1:5, 11:13, 15:15,16). Jesus had commissioned him to be an apostle, and he was going to be obedient to the "heavenly vision" (Acts 26:19,20). Such a commission included both the message to be delivered and the audience to whom it was to be delivered. As was true of all the apostles of Jesus, the message to be delivered is the gospel (the "good news" of what God has been and is doing in His world). In the case of Paul, the particular audience to whom he was specially sent was the Gentiles. Because he was an apostle to the Gentiles, and because many of the people in Rome were Gentiles (Romans 1:5), it appears Paul intends by means of this letter to introduce himself and the heart of his message to the Roman Christians who do not know him personally, and thereby further carry out his commission as an apostle of Jesus Christ. Several emphases can be distinguished:

1) Paul intends by means of this letter to inform them of his plans (15:22-25) and his desire for them to share with him in prayer (15:30-32) and in his mission work to unevangelized areas (15:20-24).

2) Paul wishes to make it possible for the beliefs and lifestyles of the Roman Christians to be in harmony with the gospel message. Romans 1:18 through 11:36 form a closely reasoned presentation of God's eternal plan (8:28) to have a family who would love Him, and an exposition of how God carried out that plan in time (9:1-11:36). It is possible for men, once the slavery to sin is broken (6:1ff), to demonstrate God's perfect will in their everyday behavior (12:1ff).

3) He wishes to press the exclusive claims of Christianity – that God's way of saving men is found in the gospel, and only in the gospel! Of all the religions to which men give allegiance, only one other (Judaism) is of divine origin. The Gentiles, too, once had a divinely-revealed worship, but long ago they had departed from their original pristine knowledge of the Creator and His will, and had degenerated in their worship to idolatry (1:18ff) and to loss of community in their lifestyles. Of course, such idolatry is not valid, but then neither (since Calvary) is Judaism, whether that Judaism is the pure religion as given through Moses, or the contemporary form of Judaism with its changes and departures from what was originally given to Moses. The major doctrines that are found in all of Judaism (e.g., the basis of the Judgment, physical descent from Abraham gains for a man right standing in God's sight, the Law is intended to be a permanently valid religious guide, there is no such thing as slavery to sin, the reason why God selected Israel to be His "chosen people"), whatever sect or party one may appeal to, need to be corrected in light of the gospel message. The new covenant has taken the

place of the temporary Mosaic covenant.

4) Paul wishes to answer the standard objections he has heard over and over as he has pressed the exclusive claims of Christianity. The objectors' arguments seem to be reflected at 3:1-8, 6:1,15, and 9-11.

5) Paul may even have been aware that he was writing for a circle larger than just the Roman believers to whom this letter was originally addressed. 16:26 may well imply that the New Testament "prophets" knew they were writing letters that would become "Scriptures" for God's new covenant people.

2. Reader's Needs

Just as Paul himself had certain reasons for writing, so it may be affirmed that the letter is addressed to certain historical needs the readers themselves had. Among the historical needs that can be ascertained from the contents of the letter are these:

1) There was the need for the Roman believers to be aware of the influence on others that they, in their strategic position in the ancient world, would exert. Twice Paul mentions their "reputation" and how anxious he is that their reputation continue to exert a positive influence (1:8, 16:19).

2) There was therefore a need that they "be established" (1:11) by an apostolic letter now and by an apostolic visit later. Not that the Roman Catholic doctrine of apostolic succession is correct, or that some ecclesiastical official must be present to ordain leaders before any group of believers can rightly be called a "church," but any group of believers (even those churches originally planted by apostles, as Acts 14:22 shows) constantly needs to be called to compare their beliefs and practices with the gospel of Christ, and to bring their doctrine and life into harmony with that gospel. Some prophets and teachers may already be in Rome (12:6,7), but these men's work could only be helped and multiplied by the visit of an apostle. (All the "gifts" – apostles as well as prophets, evangelists, and pastoring teachers – which Jesus gave to the church were needed if the saints were to be equipped for service so that the body of Christ is built up, Ephesians 4:11-16.)

3) There was the need for the Roman believers to be involved in the worldwide mission of spreading the gospel (1:12,13, 15:24), and thereby fulfill one of the purposes for which they had become part of the "Israel of God" – a people chosen by Him to carry out an historic function of making God known to those who have not heard. Their behavior toward fellow Christians (12:3-8), their behavior toward those not yet won to Christ (12:14-21), and their cooperation with local and national civil authorities (13:1-7) would all contribute to the furtherance of the gospel.

4) There was a need for the Roman Christians to be vitally and personally involved in bringing about the community of all believers. Not only could this be accomplished by their prayers for the saints at Jerusalem, that the offering Paul was taking to Jerusalem would prove acceptable to them (15:30-31), but also by their prayer that God would allow Paul to carry out his own plans for evangelizing new areas (15:32), of course, with their cooperation. In addition, their own efforts to accept and welcome strong and weak brothers so that all would feel they belonged (14:1-15:13) would help foster this feeling of community on the local level.[220]

5) There was need for the Roman church to be on the lookout for any teachers who might come and by their teaching (contrary to apostolic gospel) cause dissension and stumbling into sin and perdition (16:17-20). This would negate all the good that God and His Son and His apostle(s) and His gospel have accomplished up to the moment.

6) There was even opportunity for those few in Rome (16:3-15) who knew Paul personally to vouch for him and his message, and help prepare the others in the community for his coming visit.

Relevance of Romans

Modern readers of Romans can identify with their 1st century brethren in Rome. Today's readers have not had the privilege of knowing Paul personally, yet (as much as did the Romans) they need his apostolic ministry in order to be "established" or strengthened. Unless they have the revelation of God's plans and purposes that is available only in the message of the apostles, they will have no way to know what the God who created expects of His creatures. Only by hearing the gospel as the apostles presented it, and only by embracing it and demonstrating it in life-situations, will they be what God wants them to be. Just like the Romans, today's believers need to be presented with weighty opportunities to be involved in sharing the message (the gospel) with Jews and Gentiles who have not yet heard and obeyed. Christianity is still the only valid religion in the world, the only way by which men will come to have right standing in God's sight. Is not part of God's purpose still this: He would have "vessels" who serve an honorable purpose? Does He not want those people who comprise the "Israel of God" today to be involved as His tools and vessels, serving the honorable use of sharing the message, and thus leading all nations to the obedience of faith?

For nearly 2000 years, a study of Romans has provided the impulse in at least a few

---

[220] To attempt to make chapters 14 and 15 the whole purpose for which the whole letter was written is surely asking too much of those two chapters. But neither are the chapters an optional extra, just tacked onto the close of the letter. That Paul should include such a long paragraph of instructions about how to treat your brother if he is a weak brother, or how to treat him if he is a strong brother, surely indicates how important the peace and unity of the Christian community in Rome was, and that Paul was anxious that each individual Christian do what he could to see that "the unity of the Spirit in the bond of peace" continued uninterrupted.

men's lives that has led them to affect the history of the church and of the world in a significant fashion for centuries. Perhaps, in God's dispensation of history, a modern student of Romans will be so changed that he, too, will become a special tool in God's hands, calling lost men back to the worship and service of their Maker, thus influencing history for generations or centuries.

Outline of the Epistle

The outline now presented is intended to give a more detailed overview of the contents of Romans than the outline given in the table of contents. Even greater detail can be found in the summary paragraph which (with few exceptions) immediately precedes the comments offered for each of subpoints of the outline listed below.

INTRODUCTION: THE FUNDAMENTAL THEME. 1:1-17
    A. The Apostolic Greeting. 1:1-7
    B. Thanksgiving. 1:8-15
    C. Statement of the Fundamental Theme of Romans. 1:16,17

I. THE UNIVERSAL NEED OF THE SALVATION OFFERED IN THE GOSPEL. 1:18-3:20

    A. Righteousness (Salvation) is Needed by Gentiles. 1:18-32

    B. Righteousness (Salvation) is Needed by Jews. 2:1-3:8
       1. God's Judgment Against Sin. 2:1-16
       2. Direct Reference to the Jews Showing They Have Failed to Keep the Law. 2:17-24
       3. Direct Reference to the Jews Showing that Circumcision Will Not Save. 2:25-29
       4. Answers to Jewish Objections to the Proof of Their Guilt. 3:1-8

    C. Righteousness (Salvation) is Therefore Needed by All. 3:9-20
       1. Proof from Scripture that All are Sinners. 3:9-18
       2. Conclusion to the First Section of Romans. 3:19,20

II. THE UNIVERSALLY NEEDED SALVATION (OFFERED IN THE GOSPEL) HAS BEEN PROVIDED BY GOD FOR BELIEVERS THROUGH THE REDEMPTION THAT IS IN JESUS CHRIST. 3:21-4:25

    A. God's Plan of Salvation (Justification) Explained. 3:21-31
       1. Its Nature. 3:21-24
       2. Its Ground. 3:25
       3. Its Object. 3:26
       4. Its Result. 3:27-31

B. The Same Plan of Salvation was Taught in the Old Testament.   4:1-22
   1. Abraham was Justified by Faith.   4:1-5
   2. David Taught Justification by Faith.   4:6-8
   3. This Plan of Salvation is Universal, not Being Limited by the Presence or Absence of Circumcision.   4:9-12
   4. This Plan of Salvation Does not Require Obedience to the Law of Moses. 4:13-22

C. God's Purpose for Recording Abraham's Justification by Faith.   4:23-25

III. THE UNIVERSALLY NEEDED SALVATION (OFFERED IN THE GOSPEL) HAS THE MOST BLESSED EFFECTS – PEACE WITH GOD, COMPLETE DELIVERANCE THROUGH CHRIST FROM DEATH AND SIN, THE HELP OF THE HOLY SPIRIT, ALL CULMINATING IN ULTIMATE GLORIFICATION.   5:1-8:39

A. God's Plan of Salvation Involves Blessed Effects on Believers.   5:1-11

B. God's Plan of Salvation Involves Blessed Effects on the Whole Human Race. 5:12-21

C. God's Plan of Salvation Involves Blessed Effects on Slaves of Sin.   6:1-23

D. God's Plan of Salvation Involves Blessed Effects on Those Who Struggled to Meet the Law's Demands.   7:1-25

E. God's Plan of Salvation Involves Blessed Effects on Those in Whom the Holy Spirit Now Indwells.   8:1-30

F. God's Plan of Salvation Involves Blessed Effects on Those Who are God's Elect, and Thus They are Objects of His Love.   8:31-39

IV. GOD'S ETERNAL PURPOSE TO PROVIDE THE UNIVERSALLY NEEDED SALVATION TO ALL MEN EXPLAINS HIS DEALINGS WITH ISRAEL IN THE PAST, PRESENT, AND FUTURE.   9:1-11:36

A. Paul's Concern Because of the Jews' Tragic Rejection of Christ.   9:1-5

B. God's Dealings with Israel *in the Past* are Just as God Revealed they Would Be – It has Always been the "Remnant."   9:6-29

C. God's Dealings with Israel *in the Present* are in Harmony with the Doctrine of Justification by Faith.   9:30 - 11:10

D. God's Dealings with Israel *in the Future* Will be in Harmony with the Doctrine of Justification by Faith.   11:11-32

E. A Hymn of Praise to God.   11:33-36

V. EXHORTATIONS AND PRACTICAL INSTRUCTIONS BASED ON THE FOREGOING DOCTRINAL EXPOSITIONS.   12:1-15:13

A. Concerning the Christian's Relation to God.   12:1,2

B. Concerning the Christian's Relation to the Church.   12:3-16

C. Concerning the Christian's Relation to Those Outside the Church. 12:17-21

D. Concerning the Christian's Relation to Civil Authority.   13:1-7

E. Concerning the Christian's Relation (Love) to All Men.   13:8-14

F. Concerning the Christian Relationship Between Strong and Weak Brothers.   14:1-15:13

VI. CONCLUSION OF THE EPISTLE WITH PERSONAL ALLUSIONS AND CHRISTIAN SALUTATIONS.   15:14-16:27

A. Apology for Admonitions.   15:14-21

B. Announcement of the Apostle's Future Plans.   15:22-33

C. Commendation of Phoebe.   16:1,2

D. Salutations Addressed to Personal Friends in Rome.   16:3-16

E. Warning Against all who Cause Division and Offenses.   16:17-20

F. Salutations from Paul's Fellow-laborers to the Christians at Rome.   16:21-23

G. Concluding Doxology.   16:25-27

COMMENTS ON PAUL'S
EPISTLE TO THE ROMANS

INTRODUCTION: THE FUNDAMENTAL THEME. 1:1-17

A. The Apostolic Greeting. 1:1-7

Summary: Verses 1 & 7 – Paul, a divinely chosen and accredited apostle, gives Christian greeting to the Roman Christians, themselves also divinely called.

Verses 2-6 – I preach, in harmony with what the Jewish Scriptures teach, Jesus the son of David and the Son of God, whose commission I bear.

1:1 – *Paul, a bond-servant of Christ Jesus, called as an apostle, set apart for the gospel of God,*

Paul. It was the practice in the ancient world to begin a letter with three things: signature, address, and greeting. Ancient writing materials were scrolls, and since they had no letterheads, it was only prudent to include these three vital bits of information at the beginning. Following 1st century convention, Paul signs the letter right at the first. Since there were many men named Paul, in the rest of verse one he identifies which Paul is writing this letter. "A bond-servant of Christ Jesus ..." is the Paul who writes.

A bond-servant of Christ Jesus. The designation "bond-servant" may be something that is true of all Christians,[1] but we prefer to think that Paul uses the term in its special sense. In the Old Testament, the word "servant" was a title used to designate the prophets,[2] and we picture Paul here emphasizing his official dignity as he introduces himself to his readers. If he uses the term in its official sense, notice how quietly Paul steps into the place of the prophets, and how he claims to be a mouthpiece for God in this New Testament age. And also notice how he uses the name of "Christ Jesus" in a connection hitherto reserved for Jehovah, *i.e.*, "servant of Jehovah." Paul recognizes Christ Jesus as his master, in whose behalf he speaks, and on whose behalf he acts.

Called *as* an apostle. This explains how Paul has come to be a "bondservant." He has been called to this position! Remember what happened on the Damascus Road, and what Jesus said to Paul on that memorable occasion: "I have appeared to you, to appoint you a

---

[1] "Bond-servant" (*doulos*) is a term Jesus directed His disciples to use (Matthew 10:25, 20:27; Mark 10:44), and it is a term Christians customarily used (Galatians 1:10; Colossians 4:12). As the word is thus used, all Christians are "servants of Christ" in the sense that they are in submission to Him as their Lord and Master.

[2] Isaiah 20:3; Jeremiah 7:25; Amos 3:7; and "My servants the prophets" in Jeremiah 44:4.

minister and a witness ... (to) the Gentiles, to whom I am sending you."[3]   Paul was as much an apostle of Christ as were any of the original twelve, who also had been called and sent by Jesus.[4] The rather emphatic expression "*called* as an apostle" may imply that Paul's apostleship has been disparaged by someone; and lest that "someone" get to Rome and do his insidious work there, so that the people doubt his message, Paul drives home the fact that he is a *called* apostle.

Set apart for the gospel of God.   "Apostle" was a word that meant 'one sent on a mission.' The mission on which a man might be sent differed with his particular commission, so Paul here specifically defines what he has been commissioned to do.   Paul had been "set apart" both by God (Galatians 1:15-16) and by the church at Antioch (Acts 13:2) to preach the gospel.   "Gospel" means 'good news,' and the whole phrase might mean 'the good news of which God is the author,' or 'the good news about God.'[5]   It is good news that a Savior has gone to Calvary, to set a world of sinners free!

1:2 – *which He promised beforehand through His prophets in the holy Scriptures,*

Which He promised beforehand.   Here begins a concise summary of the gospel that Paul has been commissioned to preach.   It is not usual in a 1st century letter to have so much extra information in addition to "signature, destination, and greeting," but since so many of the readers do not know Paul personally, it is necessary for him to carefully define every term he uses.   This concise summary of the "gospel of God" continues through verse 6. The 'good news' was promised for centuries "beforehand."   That is, before it actually occurred in history, God had been predicting what it would be like.   The gospel was not a new invention, never before heard of.   Rather, it was promised in the Old Testament. Beginning at Genesis 3:15 in the Garden of Eden, one can then see the promise repeated over and over, but prominent is the promise to Abraham (Galatians 3:8).

Through His prophets.   When we read David in Psalms 22-24, 110, 118, Isaiah 53 and 55, and Zechariah 12 and 13, it sometimes seems as if we are reading one of the Gospels. Both Jesus and the apostles often affirmed that their teaching was in complete harmony with what the prophets had predicted.[6]   Their Jewish audiences especially needed this assurance, since the gospel was placed in the stead of the Law of Moses.[7]

---

[3] Acts 26:16,17.

[4] Matthew 10:1; Mark 1:17, 2:14; Luke 6:13; John 15:16,19.

[5] It depends on whether the construction is construed as a subjective genitive or an objective genitive. Most commentators tend to understand the former sense.

[6] John 1:45, 5:46, 8:56, 12:16;   Luke 24:27,44;   Acts 3:21-24, 10:43.

[7] That the Law and the gospel are different, see John 1:17, Romans 6:14, and the statements in Hebrews 7:12, 18; 8:7-13, and 9:6-10.   The New Covenant has taken the place of the Mosaic Covenant. The Mosaic was temporary, and has no further validity since Calvary (Galatians 3:23ff; Colossians 2:13,14).

In the holy Scriptures. 48 out of the 50 times the word "Scriptures" appears in the New Testament, the reference is to the Holy Spirit-inspired writings we call the Old Testament. In fact, it may be that the Jews gave the term "writings" (i.e., Scriptures) only to those special books that were inspired of God.[8] But non-Jews also had their sacred writings, so Paul indicates he has in mind those "writings" that are "holy" (i.e., those writings that have that special "holy" characteristic about them) – that is where the words of the prophets about the coming good news are to be found. The gospel Paul preached, he wants them to know, is the fulfillment of what God had promised during all the ages before Jesus' coming.

1:3 – *concerning His Son, who was born of a descendant of David according to the flesh,*

Concerning His Son.[9] The subject of the gospel Paul has been commissioned to preach is God's "Son." Verses 3 and 4 will emphasize two important facts about this Son: His humanity and His deity.

Who was born of a descendant of David according to the flesh. The Old Testament prophets indicated that the coming Messiah was to be a direct lineal descendant of David (Psalm 89:29,36; Jeremiah 23:5). Paul here affirms that such descent was true in the case of Jesus. The Greek word translated "born" (*ginomai*) is not the usual word for "born" (which is *gennaō*). Paul uses the same unusual word at Galatians 4:4, and the phrase there could be rendered "Christ *became* of a woman." Both passages which use *ginomai* are in harmony with the idea that Paul had knowledge of the virgin birth.[10] The term expresses a transition from one state or mode of existence to another – from His pre-existent state to His incarnate state. Since only Mary was a fleshly parent of Jesus, it is implied here that Mary (as well as Joseph, as the Gospel of Matthew tells us) was of the lineage of David.[11]

---

[8] To see the special Jewish use of the word *graphē* (i.e., Scripture, writing), take a concordance and run the references where it occurs, and it can be seen that it is reserved for the 22 sacred books of the Law, Prophets, and Holy Writings. Other Jewish writings, even if they were included in what we now call the Apocrypha or Pseudepigrapha, were not called *graphē*.

[9] Paul often refers to Jesus as the "Son." This term has several different senses or emphases. Sometimes it is used in its *official* sense. That is, there is emphasis on the fact that Jesus was Messiah, that He was deity, co-equal with the Father. The word "Son" is used all through the book of Hebrews in this official sense. Sometimes, the word "Son" is used in what is called its *ethical* sense. This means Jesus held the same views and ideas as did the Father. There was a perfect union, absolute intimacy, and a mutual knowledge between the Father and the Son. Perhaps Matthew 11:27 is an example of this ethical use of the designation "Son." Again, the word "Son" is at times used in its *metaphysical* sense. When this emphasis seems intended, there is reference to Jesus' incarnation. We do not call Jesus "Son" because God the Father had a "baby" back in eternity before creation, nor does the term "Son" indicate Jesus is less than co-eternal with the Father. Which of the three senses is intended here in Romans is not a matter of question, because the context plainly shows we are talking of Jesus' humanity – i.e., "Son" is used in its metaphysical sense.

[10] See Matthew 1:18-25 and Luke 1:26-38 for the actual statement of Jesus' virgin birth. Both use *parthenos*, a word which means only "virgin," not simply a "young woman."

[11] This information about Mary's lineage is in harmony with the hypothesis that Matthew's genealogy is that of Joseph, while Luke's genealogy is that of Mary, thus explaining the puzzling differences in the two lists. It could thus be said that Jesus was of the lineage of David in two senses: *legally*, through Joseph,

"According to the flesh" has already prepared us for the suggestion that there was another side to Jesus besides His perfect humanity.[12]

1:4 – *who was declared with power* to be *the Son of God by the resurrection from the dead, according to the Spirit of holiness, Jesus Christ our Lord,*

Who was declared with power *to be* **the Son of God ... according to the Spirit of holiness.** This is the affirmation that there was another side to Jesus, other than His perfect humanity. He was also deity. It should be observed that there is a parallelism in verses 3 and 4 that can be pictured in this manner:

> "Concerning His Son,
>> Who was born [son of man in weakness]
>>> from the seed of David,
>>>> according to the flesh,
>
>> Who was shown to be the Son of God in power
>>> from the resurrection of the dead,
>>>> according to the spirit of holiness."[13]

In order to fulfill that which had been predicted in the Old Testament concerning Him, the Eternal Son must both become the son of man, and be manifested as the Son of God. Perhaps Paul is expressing here an idea similar to one Jesus tried to present to the Jews on the Great Day of Questions. According to Matthew 22:41-46, Jesus asked the religious leaders about their understanding of the Old Testament prophecies concerning the coming Messiah. "Whose son is He?", Jesus asked. They rightly responded, "The son of David," because the prophets had indicated Messiah would be of David's lineage. Then Jesus tried to show them that the Old Testament said more, that Messiah also was to be David's "Lord!" The only way both predictions about Messiah could be true is if He was God in-

---

who would have been recognized in Jewish circles as the legal representative of the family, and *actually,* through Mary, from whom Jesus inherited His fleshly body.

[12] That "flesh" (*sarx*) here speaks of Jesus' humanity is evident. Even the NIV (which so often uses "sinful nature" where the Greek has *sarx*) renders this phrase "according to His human nature." The word *sarx* is used with several different connotations in Scripture. The Arndt-Gingrich *Lexicon*, p.750-752 lists these different meanings: (1) the material that covers the bones of a body, (2) the whole body, (3) a man (flesh and blood), (4) human or mortal nature, earthly descent, (5) corporeality, physical limitations, life here on earth, (6) external or outward standard of life – human standards, (7) the instrument of sin (Romans 8:4) *, and (8) the flesh as the source of the sexual urge. [* We question #7 because it seems to reflect the doctrine of total depravity as a result to the race inherited from Adam after his Fall. This whole matter of whether man has an inherited "sinful nature" will be dealt with in detail in the notes over chapter 5:12ff, which see.]

[13] The careful reader will have observed that whereas the NASB capitalizes "Spirit," thus leading the reader to think "Spirit of holiness" is one of the names for the Holy Spirit that we find in the Bible, we have used lower case "s" on "spirit," thus causing the reader to observe that we are speaking of Jesus as He was by nature when not incarnate. If "flesh" denoted all that was human in Jesus, then "spirit of holiness" denotes all that was Divine in Jesus. One reason for choosing small "s" is that to make it a reference to the Holy Spirit destroys the parallelism that seems to be in the mind of the writer.

carnate. Those who fail to see in Jesus one infinitely more transcendent and greater than David will miss who He really is!

"Declared with power" has a marginal reading, "[declared] in an act of power," and might just as satisfactorily be translated "powerfully shown to be" "the Son of God."[14] The resurrection is what proved Jesus was Who He claimed to be.

By the resurrection from the dead.   This expression presents several inherent difficulties. The word translated "by" is *ex*, which is not the usual way of writing "by means of," and the word "dead" is plural in the Greek. The NASB margin gives "as a result of" as an alternative way of translating *ex*. This would be in harmony with their translating "Spirit of holiness" as though it were speaking of the Holy Spirit, and would affirm that *after* Jesus' resurrection the Holy Spirit demonstrated effectively that Jesus indeed was the divine Son of God. Objections to this have been stated on this fashion: It does not appear to be the object of Paul to state the *time* when the thing was done, but only to declare the *fact*, and the evidence of the fact. Since "after" is not the usual and natural meaning of *ex*, it seems best to understand that it was *by* the resurrection that Jesus was proven to be the Son of God.[15]   When it comes to satisfactorily explaining the plural "dead [ones]," many different solutions have been proposed. One writer points back to the dead bodies that Jesus raised during His earthly ministry.[16] Some see a reference to the saints who rose from the dead after Jesus' resurrection (Matthew 27:52,53), and who thereupon entered the city of Jerusalem. Perhaps a better suggestion to explain the plural is that the resurrection of Jesus involves or includes the resurrection of others – both their rising to walk in newness of life, and their bodily resurrection at the end of the age.[17]

Jesus Christ our Lord.   These words seem to be a further identification of the "Son"

---

[14] "Son of God" here is used in its *official* sense. (See footnote #9.) We are speaking here of His deity. There is a problem with the word order in the original. Instead of taking "with power" as modifying the verb "declared," it is possible to read it "declared to be the Son of God with power." If we read it this way, then we are thinking of Jesus, after His resurrection, when He was enthroned on the throne of David (Acts 2:30-33), now invested with power and authority, as Lord of the universe.

[15] It must be admitted that the preposition *ex* sometimes does express "time – of the time when something begins from" [see William Arndt and F. Wilbur Gingrich, *A Greek-English Lexicon of the New Testament* (Chicago: University of Chicago Press, 1957), p.235, meaning #5 for *ek*], but it is more often used to denote origin, cause, motive, reason. Still a rather pleasing explanation can be given once we have rendered it "after." 'The expression does not refer to the divine nature, but to the dispensation of the Spirit after His resurrection, whose descent on the Day of Pentecost terminated the controversy whether He [Jesus] was the Son of God,' would be one way of expressing it.

[16] Moses E. Lard, *Commentary on Paul's Letter to Romans* (Des Moines, IA: Eugene S. Smith, 1875), p.29.

[17] The same expression used here in Romans 1:4 also appears at Acts 26:23, where the emphasis is on Jesus' resurrection in particular. Yet the plural expression also appears elsewhere with the emphasis that many will rise (Acts 23:6, 24:21; 1 Corinthians 15:12-21; Philippians 3:11). Romans 6:4ff and 8:11 show that it is possible Paul already is introducing the ideas of rising in newness of life, and rising from the grave at the last day, as he appeals to His resurrection as proof of what the Son of God can do.

about whom Paul is speaking.[18]   The Son of God is none other than the One who was born a babe in Bethlehem town, and was named "Jesus" just as the angel instructed Mary to do (Luke 1:31).   That same One was none other than the promised "Messiah" (Christ).[19] And not only is He "the salvation of Jehovah" and the Messiah, but He is also the enthroned "Lord" by the time Paul writes Romans.[20]   "Lord" means that Jesus is sitting on the throne of the universe, actively controlling what happens, until God's goals for history are all completely carried out.[21]

1:5 – *through whom we have received grace and apostleship to bring about* **the** *obedience of faith among all the Gentiles, for His name's sake,*

Through whom we have received grace and apostleship.   It is the "Lord" who has bestowed "grace" and "apostleship."   Paul's position and task are by this much holy and exalted.   If the Son of God, the Savior, the Messiah, the ascended and enthroned Lord bestowed them, then they are of infinite import.   "We" likely speaks of "we apostles."[22] "Grace" is a harder word to explain with any certainty.   Is Paul saying he received two things, grace and apostleship, or is he saying he received one thing, "apostolic grace" (or "the grace of apostleship")?[23]   If we opt for two things, how does "grace" differ from "apostleship"?   Does "grace" here refer to his conversion, since men are saved by grace (Ephesians 2:8)?[24]   When the person studying Romans consults the commentaries and translations, he will find both options presented.   If we think Paul is telling us that two things were bestowed on him (as the NASB translates it), then he is saying Jesus is the reason men can be saved ("grace"), and that it was Jesus who called him to be an apostle, just as much as it was Jesus who called the original twelve.

---

[18] The words are in the genitive case, and perhaps they agree in case and number with "Son," and are a further explanation of that word.   But since there was no punctuation in the original, it is also possible that the words describe the "dead" who are raised as belonging to Jesus Christ, i.e., 'the dead ones of Jesus Christ our Lord.'   Here we tend to agree with the ASV translators who took it as being in apposition to "Son," and translated "*even* Jesus Christ our Lord."

[19] "Messiah" is the Hebrew, "Christ" is the Greek, and both mean "anointed one."

[20] On the Day of Pentecost following Jesus' death and resurrection, Peter is able to announce that God has "made Him both Lord and Christ – this Jesus whom you crucified" (Acts 2:36).

[21] In the Septuagint version of the Old Testament, "Lord" (*kurios*) was used to translate the Hebrew words "Jehovah" and "Adonai," the former expressing the self-existent, independent, eternal and unchangeable I AM; and the latter expressing His authority and sovereignty over us.   It should not escape our notice that here Paul applies to Jesus a title that in the Old Testament was used for God – another of the evidences of Jesus' deity.

[22] "We" probably does not mean "we Christians generally," for it could not be said of all of them that they had received the office of "apostleship."   It is therefore better to understand that Paul is associating himself with the other apostles of Jesus.

[23] In Romans 15:15,16, it appears that "grace" is used to refer to Paul's ministry, so it would not be unheard of if "grace" here referred to his apostolic office.

[24] See the extended notes on the subject of "grace" included at verse 7 of this chapter.

To bring about *the* obedience of faith among all the Gentiles. Elsewhere, Paul calls himself "the apostle to the Gentiles,"[25] and we would see this phrase in Romans 1:5 as expressing the purpose why the grace and apostleship were bestowed on Paul.

Now we are immediately plunged into one of the problems in this epistle, namely, the nature of "faith." Does the expression "obedience of faith" denote one thing (we might call it an "obedient faith"), or does it denote two things (we might speak of "faith and obedience")?[26] It probably is true that any commentator on Romans will write his notes of "explanation" here so that they agree with what he understands the Bible to say elsewhere with reference to the conditions of salvation. It probably also is true that one's comments here will reflect whether it is the initial salvation of the Gentiles, or their whole Christian life, that is thought to be in Paul's view. If it is their initial salvation, then we would want to speak of an "obedient faith." If it is their whole Christian life, then their initial response is followed by a life of obedience.[27]

For His name's sake. The name stands for the person, so this phrase expresses the idea that the conversion of the Gentiles would bring glory and praise to Jesus.[28] The delight we feel when men are converted is so great, we almost forget that there is joy in heaven, both among the angels and in the heart of Jesus.

1:6 – *among whom you also are the called of Jesus Christ;*

Among whom you also are. The church at Rome was made up, partly at least, of Gentiles. Paul was the apostle to the Gentiles (verse 5 told us), and now this truth is applied to the readers. They are Gentiles, so he is perfectly within his commission to address them, teach them, exhort them.

---

[25] Romans 11:13; 1 Timothy 2:7. "Gentiles" is a translation of the Greek *ethnē*, a word that can also be translated "nations." This being true, not only non-Jews, but also Jews are sometimes included in the term "nations." Only when it is evident there is particular reference to non-Jews is the word rendered "Gentiles."

[26] The particular doctrine involved in this whole question is inextricably related to the conditions required of a man for salvation. Shall we agree with those who emphasize God's part in the salvation of a man, and say that when he receives the gift of "faith" he is instantaneously saved, and that without any response on his part? Or shall we agree with those who emphasize *both* God's and man's part in salvation, and teach that "an obedient faith" is the condition on which God is pleased to grant salvation (or, in the language of later verses in Romans, "impute justification")?

[27] See Gareth L. Reese, *New Testament History: Acts* (Moberly, MO: Scripture Exposition Books, 1996), p.598ff, for the Special Study titled, "The Faith that Saves," where it is affirmed that the "faith" in "justification by faith" is an obedient faith, that it comes by hearing the gospel (rather than being something just given by God), and that it includes knowledge, assent, confidence, and obedience. In addition to the information given there, Romans 1:8, 16:19, and 16:25 also have a bearing on the matter. Those passages would tend to show that the faith in Paul's view is something that expresses itself in actions that others can see. In Romans 3:28ff and in chapter 4:1ff, this whole subject will be discussed in greater detail.

[28] The antecedent of "His" is "Jesus Christ our Lord" in verse 4. The idea of glory being received by Jesus is the further purpose why Paul received "grace and apostleship." The nearer purpose was the obedience of faith among the Gentiles.

The called by Jesus Christ. In verse 7, we shall study the concept of "call" in detail. Whether this expression (literally, "called ones of Jesus Christ") means called *by* Jesus or called *to belong to* Jesus is debated in the commentaries.[29] The Roman readers had become obedient to the faith because they had responded to a "call."

At this point we have finished the long explanation about Paul's commission to be an apostle (begun in verse 1), and we return to the usual items included in the beginning of a 1st century letter, now taking up the destination and greeting.

1:7 – *to all who are beloved of God in Rome, called* as *saints: Grace to you and peace from God our Father and the Lord Jesus Christ.*

To all who are beloved of God in Rome. This shows to whom the letter was written. It was not to the whole city's population indiscriminately, but to those who were Christians in the empire's capital city.[30] There is no real reason to suggest that "beloved" is meant to designate Christians of *Jewish* background, whereas "called to be saints" designates Christians of *Gentile* descent. Nor is there any real reason to follow those Calvinistic commentators who speak not only of God *now* loving the believers, but also of the fact that He loved them from all eternity, and never would stop loving them.[31] It simply is a term of endearment, as Wycliffe understood when he rendered it "darlings of God."

Called *as* saints. All Christians are saints, not just some who were eminently holy during their lifetimes, and since have been canonized. The word "saint" is regularly given in the New Testament to Christians living in this world. The connotation in the term is that the Christians are a *separated* people, *set apart* to the service of God. The Christians came to be "saints" because they were "called" to this holy position, and called (invited) through the gospel, as 2 Thessalonians 2:14 plainly shows.[32] In light of the fact that, later in Romans, Paul talks about "holiness" (sanctification) as something to be progressively developed in the life of each individual believer (Romans 6:12-19, 8:1-17), it is not beyond reason that "saint" here might also carry the idea of that freedom from blemish, spot, and stain to which God expects the Christian more and more to attain.

---

[29] Albert Barnes, "Romans" in *Notes on the New Testament* (Grand Rapids: Baker Book House, 1953), p.27, writes, "Those whom Jesus has called to be His followers."   In objection to Barnes' explanation, it is usually noted that "calling" to salvation is invariably ascribed by Paul to God (Romans 8:30, 9:24;   1 Corinthians 1:9; etc.), and so it is believed this phrase should be explained, not as "called *by* Christ," but "called (by God) *to belong to* Jesus."

[30] In the Introductory Studies, p.viii, ix, xxiii, we have noticed that some few manuscripts omit "in Rome," but that the weight of the evidence is in favor of retaining these words.

[31] William Hendriksen, *New Testament Commentary: Romans* (Grand Rapids: Baker Book House, 1981), p.46, is an example of how Calvinistic comments on this expression run.   It reflects the ideas of unconditional election, and of the unconditional perseverance of the saints – two topics we shall have to study in the course of our exegesis of Romans.

[32] Consult Special Study #1 at the close of comments on chapter 1 for further details on both "Call" and "Grace."

Grace to you and peace. "Grace to you" was the common greeting in 1st century Greek-world letters. "Peace to you" (*shalom*) was the common greeting among Hebrew speaking people. Perhaps Paul combines these two greetings in most of his letters because in Christ and in the church there has come to be a unity between Jew and Gentile. But there undoubtedly is also a spiritual significance inherent in these words of greeting. A word study of "grace" shows that this is a significant word in the Bible, and includes both God's favorable attitude toward the man He had created and the actions God takes to benefit that man.[33] We suppose Paul is here praying that all that God does to help a man live the Christian life will be made available to the readers as he prays for "grace" to be granted to them. Then when Paul prays that they may enjoy "peace," he has in mind, we suppose, both peace with God and peace with man. Further, it is likely that even the word order is significant: a man must have "grace" before he can have "peace."

From God our Father and the Lord Jesus Christ. These two are the providers of the grace and peace that Paul prays his readers will enjoy. The association of both the Father and the Son as Paul does here and elsewhere in his letters is a strong affirmation of the deity of Jesus. God and Jesus are associated as though they were equal sources of the blessings for which Paul prays.[34]

As we conclude our comments on this paragraph of apostolic greeting, it would be well to summarize some of the theological points that have been introduced. (1) There is a complete set of ideas about the commission and authority of an apostle. (2) There is implied the status in the eyes of God of the Christian community ("beloved"). (3) Something has been said about the proper relation of the Old and New Testaments (what was but a promise in the Old has come to pass in the gospel). (4) There has been teaching about the person of Christ, which includes His deity. (5) The idea of a distinction between the persons of the Godhead has been introduced. (6) The suggestion that there is a divine plan that ranges over and through history is also in the background, as well as the fact of God's providence which is moving history toward the goal the Godhead had in mind when all this was created.

B. Thanksgiving.   1:8-15

Summary: As he gives thanks to God, Paul expresses his thanks for them again, as has been his habit for some time, and informs them of his long-standing request to God that he himself may be permitted to visit Rome and preach there also, something he has been eager to do.

---

[33] Consult Special Study #1 on "Call and Grace" at the close of chapter 1, where it is shown "grace" includes what Jesus did at Calvary, it includes the sending of the preacher to help the lost man know God's way of salvation, it includes the "convicting" work of the Holy Spirit as He helps a man respond to the gospel preaching, and it includes the help the indwelling Spirit gives a Christian to live the Christian life.

[34] Much more will be said about the deity of Jesus in our study of Romans. See especially the comments at Romans 9:5. The first chapter of Hebrews also should be consulted, for it unequivocally attributes deity to Jesus (see 1:3, and 1:8,9).

1:8 – *First, I thank my God through Jesus Christ for you all, because your faith is being proclaimed throughout the whole world.*

First. "First" suggests there will be a 'second, third, etc.,' but what was to follow, Paul apparently never says.[35]   Perhaps no more is intended than "before proceeding to the main part of this letter."

I thank my God. It was the usual custom in 1st century letters to follow the signature, address, and greeting with a word of thanksgiving.   Greeks usually thanked the "gods" and then spoke of the recipient's health and welfare.   Following the usual form for letters, Paul includes a thanksgiving in all his letters except Galatians.[36]   In these thanksgivings he expresses thanks either for something the readers are doing for the cause of Christ, or (as in 1 Corinthians) he thanks God for what He Himself is doing among the readers.   "*My* God" may reflect that Paul's knowledge of God was living and personal, rather than merely abstract and speculative.

Through Jesus Christ. Christians in the 20th and 21st centuries are accustomed to close their prayers with the words "In Jesus' name we pray."   Perhaps this custom reflects not only what Paul says here, but also what is enjoined in Ephesians 5:20 and Hebrews 13:15. But how is it that thanks may be given to God "through Jesus Christ"?   The mediatorial activity of Jesus, our great High Priest, must be in mind.   "As it is through Christ that God's grace is conveyed to men (verse 5), so it is through Christ that men's gratitude is conveyed to God.   The mediatorship of Christ is exercised both Godward and manward."[37]

For you all. Students of Paul have noted that his thanksgivings often have intimations of coming themes already included in them.   Since there is a hint of dissension between strong and weak brothers in chapters 14 and 15, perhaps the "all" is significant, suggesting the unity and harmony that Paul would see prevail among *all* his readers.

Because your faith is being proclaimed throughout the whole world.   "Faith" is practically equivalent to saying "your Christianity."   At Romans 1:5, we have already observed that the "faith" that is a topic in this letter is something that expresses itself in actions which others can see.   The changed lives evident among those who have responded to the gospel at Rome,   the continual Christian service that daily characterized their lives,

---

[35] Some have found the "next thought" in verse 10.   Still others have supposed that the next thing on Paul's mind is expressed in verse 13.   James Denney has explained the broken Greek grammar in this way, "Paul's mind unconsciously leaves the track on which it started, at least as far as the linguistic following out of it is concerned."   "Romans" in *Expositor's Greek Testament* edited by W. Robertson Nicoll (Grand Rapids: Wm. B. Eerdmans Publishing Co., 1967), Vol.2, p.587.

[36] We suppose the distressing news so recently learned about the situation among the Galatian churches so filled Paul with emotion that he is anxious to get to the point he wished to express as he wrote to the Galatians.   He certainly cannot thank God for what the Galatians are about to do (i.e., revert to Judaism at the instigation of the Judaizers).

[37] F.F. Bruce, *The Epistle of Paul to the Romans* in The Tyndale New Testament Commentary Series (Grand Rapids: Wm. B. Eerdmans Publishing Co., 1963), p.76.

these things were topics of conversation elsewhere throughout the empire.[38] Rome was the capital of the world, and her influence extended everywhere. Likewise, Christians living elsewhere in the empire would know about the spread of the gospel to Rome; how the church in Rome thrived (or not) would affect Christianity elsewhere in the empire.[39]

1:9 – *For God, whom I serve in my spirit in the* **preaching of the** *gospel of His Son, is my witness* **as** to *how unceasingly I make mention of you,*

For. Whenever a verse begins with "for," it either gives a reason for something just said, or it gives a further explanation of something just said. In verse 8, Paul introduced to his readers the fact that they were part of his prayers. Here he explains how much he prays for them and why.

God ... is my witness. God, who hears Paul's prayers and knows their frequency and content, can testify to the truthfulness of the claim Paul has just made. He does pray for them. He does petition God that he may be allowed to visit Rome. Paul is taking a solemn oath, as indeed he does elsewhere in his writings,[40] and he is not disobeying Jesus' admonition to "swear not at all" (Matthew 5:33-35), for what Jesus prohibited was frivolous use of God's name to cover up a character defect which results in not being true to one's promises.[41]

Whom I serve in my spirit in the *preaching of the* **gospel of His Son.** The word translated "serve" (*latreuo*) can also be translated "worship," and pictures a life devoted to God. After a person has become a Christian, his "spirit" is alive (Romans 8:10) and is able to give directions to the soul and body, so that the whole man is controlled.[42] This is

---

[38] It would appear that the term "world" is here limited to the Roman Empire, a sense elsewhere often found when *kosmos* is used in the New Testament (see Arndt-Gingrich, *Lexicon*, p.447, 4.a).

[39] In our Introductory Studies, p.ix-xiv, we examined the question of the origin of the church at Rome. The language of this verse probably cannot be used as an argument either for or against a recent date for the beginning of the church in the capital, for 1 Thessalonians 1:8 has a similar expression about the church in Thessalonica, and this was written (likely) within six months after that congregation was established. The Roman church could be six months, or six years, or more, old, as far as this expression is concerned.

[40] Compare 2 Corinthians 1:23, 11:31; Galatians 1:20; Philippians 1:8; 1 Thessalonians 2:5,10.

[41] It is this commentator's conviction that in order to understand what the Bible says on any subject, one must take all the passages on the subject, and put their teachings together (a method Jesus Himself used, Mark 10:2-9 [where Jesus shows the religious leaders that the Old Testament says more on the subject of marriage and divorce than just the one verse the religious leaders quoted from Deuteronomy 24:1-5], and Matthew 22:41-46 [where Jesus shows that the Old Testament said more about the coming Messiah than that He was to be a descendant of David]). Since we doubt Paul is disobeying Jesus, we must find a way to harmonize the apparent discrepancy between what Jesus said about not swearing and His devoted followers taking oaths on occasion. The suggestion in the comments above, where Jesus is understood *not* to be prohibiting *all* oaths, but only the careless use of God's name, is, in this commentator's opinion, the best way to harmonize the passages.

[42] It seems certain the Bible teaches a trichotomy when it comes to man's constituent parts. Man thus is made up of body, soul, and spirit (see 1 Thessalonians 5:23 and Hebrews 4:12 where there seems to be a distinction between soul and spirit). When a man commits his first sin, we would understand that he

how Paul can say that by the direction of his "spirit" he is able to serve God.   In verse 1, Paul spoke of the "gospel of God."   Now he uses the expression "gospel of His Son."   If verse 1 meant that God is the *author of* the gospel, then verse 9 means that the gospel is *about* His Son.   Jesus, the Son, since He was incarnate, is the visible evidence of good news that God has been making.[43]

***As to* how unceasingly I make mention of you.**   Paul's prayer life must have been amazing, and is worthy of a special study.   He prayed for his friends and family, and he prayed for people he'd never seen, and for communities where he had never been.

1:10 – *always in my prayers making request, if perhaps now at last by the will of God I may succeed in coming to you.*

Always in my prayers making request.   The NASB is an improvement over the KJV in that it clearly shows that "always" belongs with the thought of verse 10, rather than the thought of verse 9.   There was a request that Paul had been making to God for some time.[44]

If perhaps now at last ... I may succeed in coming to you.   Paul had tried to visit Rome before, but had been hindered (verse 13).   "If perhaps at length on some occasion," is how Meyer rendered the Greek.[45]   "The *pote*, which can hardly be conveyed in English, marks an indefiniteness which even yet attaches in the writer's mind to the fulfillment of this hope."[46]   Perhaps even yet, if God wills, such a journey can be completed.

By the will of God.   James 4:14,15 contain instructions to the Christian to include divine

---

dies spiritually; that is, the spirit part is no longer able to function as God intended, namely, in the giving of directions to the soul which in turn animates the body. With the spirit part 'out of order,' man is then a slave to sin (i.e., the devil), and lives in a body of sin, as Romans 6 will show. When conversion occurs, the part of man that is affected most is his spirit ("that which is born of the Spirit is spirit," Jesus told Nicodemus, John 3:6). Once a man's spirit is alive again, he can again practice self-control, with the help of the indwelling Holy Spirit, and he can live a life dedicated to God, because the old slavery to sin is broken. Many of these ideas will become clearer as we work our way through Romans.

[43] The NASB translators added some words ("preaching of the") in italics to show the English readers that the words are not in the Greek, but are a possible interpretation of what the original actually says. When he writes "I serve ... in the gospel of His Son," Paul either means that his service consists in making the gospel known (i.e., by preaching), or that he serves according to the rules and requirements contained in the gospel.

[44] Here is a verse to take into account when one studies the matter of persistence in prayer, versus "vain repetition," which was condemned by Jesus (Matthew 6:5-8). There is a large difference between persistence (an example of which can be seen in Luke 18:1-8) in prayer, and vain repetition.

[45] H.A.W. Meyer, *Critical and Exegetical Hand-book to the Epistle to the Romans* (Winona Lake, IN: Alpha Publications, 1979), p.43.

[46] Denney, *Romans*, p.588. The translation "now at last" in both the ASV and NASB, actually omits any attempt at translating *pote*, one of two Greek words in this place that mark the indefiniteness of time.

providence when making plans about the future.[47]   When in God's own good time it was right for Paul to go to Rome, *then* (he was confident) God would so rule and arrange it that the long-awaited journey would become a reality.

1:11 – *For I long to see you in order that I may impart some spiritual gift to you, that you may be established;*

For I long to see you.   The word translated "long" (*epipotheō*) is elsewhere rendered "earnestly desire, greatly desire."[48]

In order that I may impart some spiritual gift to you.   What this "spiritual gift" was, commentators are not agreed.   Some suppose Paul uses *charisma* here to designate what the Roman brethren would receive as a result of Paul's instruction or teaching while in Rome.[49]   Others, noting that "spiritual gifts" were regularly passed on by the laying on of an apostle's hands (Acts 8:17,18; 2 Timothy 1:6), have affirmed that it was such miraculous gifts Paul wished to impart to the Roman brethren.[50]   Without hesitation this commentator would opt for the second interpretation, were it not for the fact that Paul uses the word "spiritual gift" in the singular.   Still, we might affirm that had he written, "in order that I may impart some spiritual gifts (plural) to you," it would have implied that they had *no* gifts at all, and this was not entirely true (Romans 12:6-8).   Still, having weighed the evidence pro and con, this commentator tends to accept the second interpretation as the correct one.

That you may be established.   "You" is plural in the Greek.   The impartation of the *charisma* was to be for the benefit of all.[51]   This was one way they would be "established,"

---

[47] Consult Special Study #2, "The Providence of God," which is included at the close of chapter 1.   We shall see that such a thing as divine influence and intervention in human history is an idea implied a number of times in Romans, not only in chapter 1, but all through the book.

[48] 2 Corinthians 5:2;   2 Timothy 1:4.

[49] This is the meaning suggested in the Arndt-Gingrich *Lexicon*, p.887, meaning #1, when it is explained as being some "spiritual possession."   Some commentators also affirm the context rather requires this first interpretation, since it also speaks of Paul's receiving something of like kind back from them.   However, be aware that after asserting that this first meaning is correct, some theologians insist this verse is evidence that "grace" (*charis*, the root of *charisma*) is mediated only by ordained ministers.   Even were we to accept this first explanation of what Paul wished to impart to the Romans, it would not be absolute proof that one must have an ordained minister present before the ordinances of Christ can be properly administered.

[50] The word *charisma* does indeed sometimes refer to miraculous gifts; see meaning #2 in Arndt-Gingrich *Lexicon*, p.887.   See also 1 Corinthians 12-14 and Romans 12:3-8.   One question often raised at this point is how some of the brethren at Rome could already have spiritual gifts, as Romans 12 indicates they did, if no apostle has yet been to Rome (as Romans 15:20 implies), since the gifts were given by the laying on of an apostle's hands.   The simplest answer to this seeming objection is that the brethren who have the gifts received them from an apostle before they moved to Rome and became members of the congregation there.   [Thus we have rejected Bengel's affirmation that this verse proves that neither Peter nor any other apostle has been to Rome, because the Romans were "inferior" in respect to spiritual gifts. John Albert Bengel, *Gnomon of the New Testament* (Edinburgh: T&T Clark, 1860), Vol.3, p.11.]

[51] In this commentator's opinion, one of the errors of the modern charismatic movement is that they

confirmed in the truth. It would result in a wider knowledge of God's New Covenant expectations for them than was possible where there were but few divinely inspired preachers present. Also at this time, few books of the New Testament Scriptures had yet been written,[52] so the Roman Christians were dependent on apostles or spiritually gifted men for their knowledge of the faith. Thus, we see that Paul's interest for them was spiritual. They could grow in grace and knowledge if they just had the fuller information that spiritual gifts would make available, and this growth would result in stability in their lives.

1:12 – *that is, that I may be encouraged together with you* **while** *among you, each of us by the other's faith, both yours and mine.*

That is. As Paul speaks about his desire to impart a spiritual gift so that they may be established, he realizes that these words could be interpreted as implying criticism of a deficiency in the church at Rome. He quickly seeks to allay any misunderstanding and prevent any hurt feelings by pointing out that the benefits of his coming visit to Rome would not be one-sided. He and his missionary work would be enriched by his association with the Roman Christians.

That I may be encouraged together with you *while* **among you**. When saints spend time together, it can prove to be a time of encouragement. To see other Christians, at work and happy in Christ, proves a stimulus to renewed fervor in serving Christ.

Each of us by the other's faith, both yours and mine. Here is one of the places in Scripture where the idea of 'mutual ministry' is set forth. Like the different parts of the body, which receive nourishment from one member and pass it on to the next (cp. Ephesians 4:16), so the different members in a local congregation feed and nourish each other for the benefit of the whole body. Paul also had a practical motivation in mind. He shortly will introduce the fact that he hopes the Roman brethren will provide the financial means for a proposed evangelistic tour of Spain (Romans 15:24). It must be carefully observed also that a common "faith" was the uniting factor in this anticipated fellowship. It would seem to imply that the modern attempt to use 'fellowship' as a means of producing a 'common faith' is an inversion of the divine order of things.[53]

---

have wrongly suggested that the spiritual gifts (at least the gift of tongues) are for the edification of the person who receives the gift, and they sometimes appeal to 1 Corinthians 14:4 as proof. In refutation of this, 1 Corinthians 12-14 repeatedly affirms that the spiritual gifts are for the profit of the whole body (the whole congregation). See 1 Corinthians 12:7, 13:1-13 (the gifts are to be exercised in a loving rather than a selfish way), 14:4,5 (the church will be edified if the "more excellent way" is followed), and especially 14:12. Even Romans 1:11 with its plural "you" shows that the spiritual gifts were for the benefit of all, not just the recipient.

[52] According to the traditional dates given for the writing of the New Testament books, the only ones written before Romans were Matthew (AD 50), 1 and 2 Thessalonians (AD 51), 1 and 2 Corinthians (AD 57), and Galatians (AD 57).

[53] What is intended in this last note is a criticism of many of the attempts of the ecumenical movement to produce a 'union' of disparate 'faiths.' There is no intention of discouraging efforts to "preserve the unity of the Spirit in the bond of peace" among brethren who may differ on this or that matter of opinion.

1:13 – *And I do not want you to be unaware, brethren, that often I have planned to come to you (and have been prevented thus far) in order that I might obtain some fruit among you also, even as among the rest of the Gentiles.*

And I do not want you to be unaware, brethren. This expression is one of Paul's characteristic ways of emphasizing what he is about to say.[54] In the previous verses, Paul has been speaking of his *desire*; now he is going to tell them about his *plan* or *purpose*, which is a step nearer realization than is desire.

That often I have planned to come to you. "Planned" is a verb expressive of 'settled determination.' How many times he had purposed to come to visit them, we have no means of determining. We know of at least one instance when this long-cherished intention had been publicly expressed before this. That was the time at Ephesus, a few months earlier, when he said, "After I have been there (Macedonia and Achaia and Jerusalem), I must also see Rome" (Acts 19:21).[55]

(And have been prevented thus far). Just what had hindered his anticipated trip to Rome can be ascertained, at least in part, from Romans 15:20-22. Paul had a burden to evangelize where men had not yet heard the gospel, and in order that the men in Asia Minor and Greece might hear, Paul had to stay there and preach. One might also infer from the context in Romans that divine providence had something to do with the delay, since Paul had been ordering his travel plans in harmony with God's will (verse 10).[56]

In order that I might obtain some fruit among you also. "Fruit" has often been explained as meaning people won to Christ.[57] While such an 'evangelistic' interpretation may be suggested by 1:14,15, it also may be that Romans 15:20 is against it. "Fruit" in Romans 15:28 (and in Philippians 4:17) has reference to a missionary/benevolent offering. If the Roman Christians participate in a missionary offering that helps Paul on his way to Spain, both he and they will obtain "fruit" – Paul as he benefits from their generosity, and the Roman Christians as they share in the reward God gives to those who have helped support missionaries.

---

[54] See also Romans 11:25; 1 Corinthians 10:1, 12:1; 2 Corinthians 1:8; 1 Thessalonians 4:13.

[55] As indicated in the Introductory Studies, p.vii,viii, we have Romans written from Greece, during the three months Paul spent there, about which we are told in Acts 20:2,3.

[56] Some have also appealed to Acts 16:6-8, where we learn that Paul's evangelistic itinerary was determined by the Holy Spirit. Others, with less likelihood (in our opinion) of giving the real reason, appeal to 1 Thessalonians 2:18, where the enemies of the gospel put up obstructions in Paul's way.

[57] The 'evangelistic' interpretation would explain "among you" as equivalent to "in your city." Inherent in such an explanation is this further thought: Paul wanted to have the opportunity to preach the gospel there, and he wanted to see men respond to the invitation. Seeing responses to the invitation encourages a "preacher;" it makes him want to preach the gospel all the more. If, instead, we should understand the words to mean, "among you who are already Christians," then "fruit" must be given a different explanation. If "fruit" is a benefit they are to receive, then it might consist of helping to further their Christian lives (a meaning sometimes given to "fruit" in John 15:5,16). Or if "fruit" is something Paul is to receive, then the "missionary/benevolent offering" explanation (offered in the comments) would be the better one.

Even as among the rest of the Gentiles.   Paul was the apostle to the Gentiles, and since Rome was a Gentile city, it was within the purview of his commission.   It was in the Mediterranean world east of Italy where Paul had evangelized among the 'other' ("rest of") Gentiles he here speaks about.[58]

1:14 – *I am under obligation both to Greeks and to barbarians, both to the wise and to the foolish.*

I am under obligation both to Greeks and to barbarians.   The older translations read, "I am debtor," but this English word "debtor" now has the connotation of 'owing money to,' and such is not the idea here.   What Paul is expressing is his feeling of obligation to preach the gospel to as many men as he could.   His feeling of such an obligation no doubt stemmed from the fact that the risen Jesus had appeared to him personally, on the Damascus Road, and told him this is what He wanted Paul to do.   With such a mandate, it would be difficult to ever feel that one was 'off duty.'   In this phrase, Paul divides the human race according to language; the term "Greeks" includes all who spoke the Greek language, while "barbarian" was anyone who did not speak the Greek language.[59]

Both to the wise and to the foolish.   If Paul now divides the human race according to culture, "wise" speaks of the men of culture, art, or aristocracy, while "foolish" designates the uneducated, the uncultured, the non-aristocrat.   Wherever men lived, whatever their social standing, Paul felt an obligation to take the gospel to them, for he was aware that it was relevant to all men, whatever their language or culture or social standing.   He recognized the basic truth that underneath all human classifications there lies but one distinction that has eternal import, namely, whether a man is saved or lost!   If lost, he needs the salvation offered in the gospel, and Paul will do what he can to get the gospel to him.

1:15 – *Thus, for my part, I am eager to preach the gospel to you also who are in Rome.*

Thus, for my part.   "As far as he was concerned, he was willing to preach in Rome; but whether he should do so or not, rested not with him, but with God."[60]

I am eager to preach the gospel to you also who are in Rome.   Paul's readiness to preach in Rome was no more or less than the obligation he felt to preach to all men.[61]   "You also

---

[58] If "among you" in the previous clause meant "among you Roman Christians," then this expression would be evidence that the congregation at Rome was predominantly Gentile in character.

[59] Arndt-Gingrich *Lexicon,* p.251 and p.132,133.   The reader who wishes to study these terms in detail may find C.E.B. Cranfield, *A Critical and Exegetical Commentary on the Epistle to the Romans* in the International Critical Commentary on the New Testament, edited by J.A. Emerton and C.E.B. Cranfield (Edinburgh: T&T Clark, 1975), p.83, a helpful beginning as he lists five different explanations of the terms Paul here uses.

[60] Charles Hodge, as quoted by Geoffrey B. Wilson, *Romans: A Digest of Reformed Comment* (London: Banner of Truth Trust, 1969), p.22.

[61] At Romans 1:1 there is a rather elementary definition of "gospel."   Now it seems appropriate to look

who are in Rome" means more than just 'you Christians.'   It speaks of all the inhabitants of Rome, of whom the Christians were a portion.[62]

C. A Statement of the Fundamental Theme of the Epistle.   1:16,17

> *Summary*:   God works through the gospel to save men.   In it, God's way of salvation for all men is explained, and it is conditional.   The condition is faith, just as the Old Testament had affirmed.

1:16 – *For I am not ashamed of the gospel, for it is the power of God for salvation to everyone who believes, to the Jew first and also to the Greek.*

---

into the contents of the gospel in greater detail.   When one studies the passages where *kerussō* ("preach") and *euangelizō* [or *euangelion*] ("preach the gospel") appear, as well as Peter's and Paul's sermons in Acts, and then assembles the information learned in the context of each passage, it is possible to outline the truths called "gospel" in this fashion:

FACTS TO BE BELIEVED
1) The Law of Moses does not save.   1 Timothy 1:3-11; Galatians 2:16, 3:2-8
2) Facts concerning Jesus Christ
   a) He fulfills Old Testament prophecies.   Romans 16:25; Luke 1:67-79; Acts 13:32-33; Galatians 3:8; Hebrews 8:8-13
   b) His birth, of the seed of David.   Luke 2:10-14
   c) His ministry.   Acts 10:36-43
   d) His crucifixion.   1 Corinthians 15:1-11
   e) His burial.   1 Corinthians 15:1-11
   f) His resurrection.   1 Corinthians 15:1-11
   g) His post-resurrection appearances.   1 Corinthians 15:1-11
   h) His ascension and exaltation.   2 Corinthians 4:5; Acts 9:20

COMMANDS TO BE OBEYED
1) Emphasis on obedience.   Romans 16:25,26; 1 Peter 1:1-3,9,22-23
2) Some of the commands in the gospel
   a) Belief.   Mark 16:15,16; Acts 16:31
   b) Repentance.   Luke 24:47; Acts 2:38, 3:19, 17:30,31
   c) Baptism.   Mark 16:15,16; Acts 2:38, 8:35-38, 10:48; 1 Corinthians 1:17
   d) Faithfulness.   Romans 1:17; Colossians 1:23
3) People who do not obey, perish!   2 Corinthians 4:3; 2 Thessalonians 1:8

PROMISES TO BE ENJOYED
1) For all nations.   Matthew 24:14; Mark 13:10, 16:15; Luke 24:47; Colossians 1:6,23
2) Remission of sins – salvation.   Luke 24:47; 1 Corinthians 1:21, 15:1,2
3) New life – new creation.   1 Peter 4:6
4) Seasons of refreshing.   Acts 3:19,20, 2:38 ["gift of the Holy Spirit"]
5) Kingdom of God.   Acts 20:25, 28:31
6) Peace.   Ephesians 6:15
7) Return of Christ.   Acts 3:19-21
8) Judgment.   Acts 10:42
9) Heaven.   Colossians 1:5; 2 Thessalonians 2:10; 2 Timothy 1:10

This is the "gospel" that is the "power of God for salvation" (Romans 1:16,17; 1 Corinthians 1:18,24), and is a presentation that is simple and suitable to all, just as Paul has implied in Romans 1:13-15.

---

[62] We had a similar expression in verse 13, and treated it also as though the Roman Christians were representative of the whole Gentile community.   (See footnote #57, above.)

For. He has just stated that he is eager to preach to those who are in Rome. Here in verses 16 and 17 he explains why he is so eager for them to have the gospel.

I am not ashamed of the gospel.[63] "I am not ashamed" is perhaps an instance of the figure of speech called litotes, a deliberate understatement to emphasize the opposite. Paul means that he is *proud* of the gospel, and counts it a special honor to proclaim it. This is a revealing statement when we stop to recall all Paul has had to suffer and contend with, just for the privilege of preaching it. He recently had been chased out of Thessalonica,[64] smuggled out of Berea,[65] laughed at in Athens.[66] He had suffered the loss of all things for the sake of the excellency of the knowledge of Christ Jesus.[67] He was regarded by many men as but little better than sewage.[68] Still, he was proud of the gospel. To be proud of something and to stand up and contend for it – when it seemed no one else would or was interested – is not easy. Yet this is exactly what Paul was doing. There is a "shame" that is far more blameworthy, and that would be the shame that would motivate a man to *fail* to speak for Jesus, just as Jesus Himself warned.[69]

For it is the power of God for salvation. This is why ("for") Paul is not ashamed of the gospel. Notice the verb tense: Paul says "*is* the power," not "was." "The Gospel is not simply the content of the early Christians' sermons, for God is *still at work* through the preaching of the cross. The action of God initiated in the cross continues through the proclamation of this saving event."[70] The gospel is not just a retelling of some 2000-year old history of what God did once-upon-a-time. As the gospel is preached, God Himself, *right then*, goes to work, exerting His power in an attempt to woo and win the listener to Himself. The gospel is the lever, as it were, by which God would move the world. The doctrine implied here is no different from what is presented elsewhere in the New Testament – God works through the Word to convert and save men.[71] "Salvation" includes

---

[63] The "gospel" has already been explained in comments and notes at verses 1 and 15. The KJV reads "gospel of Christ," but there is insufficient manuscript authority to include the words "of Christ."

[64] Acts 17:1-10.

[65] Acts 17:11-15.

[66] Acts 17:32.

[67] Philippians 3:8.

[68] 1 Corinthians 4:13.

[69] Mark 10:38; Luke 9:26.

[70] Richard A. Batey, *The Letter of Paul to the Romans*, in The Living Word Commentary (Austin, TX: R. B. Sweet Co., 1969), p.24. [Emphasis mine, GLR.]

[71] Because God works through the Word, it is a good idea to saturate every sermon and lesson with Scripture, thus allowing the results of the message to be dependent on the power of God, rather than on the wisdom of men.

deliverance of body and soul from the power and penalty of sin and death. This salvation is something that has both a present and a future dimension, as the rest of the book of Romans will show. There is forgiveness and reconciliation and deliverance from a life of slavery to sin in the present, and a resurrection body and the glories of heaven in the future.

To everyone who believes. This salvation that God provides is not bestowed on all men indiscriminately. It is imputed or reckoned by God to those who "believe."[72] Belief is here presented as the condition with which a person must comply before God counts him as 'saved.' And there is no limitation as to who may meet the condition. 'Anyone' may believe. No longer is God working specially with certain families (the patriarchs) or with a certain people (the Jews). This salvation is available to anyone, whether Jew or Gentile.[73]

To the Jew first and also to the Greek. Earlier, in verse 14, Paul had classified men by language and culture. Now he classifies men by religion. Because God had been working with the Jews for 1500 years, they were the better prospects in each community; 1st century preachers regularly started their evangelistic efforts in the synagogue with the Jews first.[74] It should not be overlooked that this verse implies that the gospel was adapted to all – in fact, it can be affirmed that Christianity is the only religion in the world that is adapted to all times and places. This universal nature of the gospel is one of the evidences

---

[72] The verb form translated "believes" is a present participle, which implies *continuing action.* See notes at Romans 1:5 on "obedience of faith," and also consult the extended study (in the author's Acts commentary) of the "faith" that God requires as the condition on which He grants salvation. Suffice it to observe here that faith is not a one-time thing, but a *continuing thing.* The verb tense reads "who (continues to) believe."

[73] In an earlier time, Restoration preachers were much more apt to emphasize the distinction between the Old and New Covenants than are (perhaps) their 20th and 21st century counterparts. Not that the struggle with one-covenant theology is all in the past, or that all church people are clear in their minds about the distinction between the Mosaic (temporary until Christ) and the New Covenants (lasting until the second advent). But perhaps present-day expositors are saving their comments about the Law versus the Gospel for passages where it clearly is the topic. Still, the old-time need to instruct their hearers perhaps explains why I.B. Grubbs, *An Exegetical and Analytical Commentary on Paul's Epistle to the Romans* (Cincinnati: F.L. Rowe, 1946), p.33ff, contrasts each expression in this verse with what a person under the Law would think. His explanatory chart follows:

THE GOSPEL		THE LAW
(1) The Power	vs.	(1) Legal Weakness (8:3,4)
(2) Of God	vs.	(2) Human Righteousness (10:1-2; Philippians 3:9)
(3) Unto Salvation	vs.	(3) Legal Condemnation (7:9,10; 2 Corinthians 3:6-9)
(4) To Every One	vs.	(4) Jewish Exclusiveness (3:21-23, 10:11-3)
(5) That Believeth	vs.	(5) Legal Works (9:30-32, 10:3-5)

It is possible that Grubbs' presentation is exactly what is needed at this place, especially if the doctrines of the Judaizers are foremost in Paul's mind as he writes.

[74] "Not that the gospel was any more adapted to Jews than to others; but to them had been committed the oracles of God; the Messiah had come through them; they had the law, the temple, and the service of God, and it was natural that the gospel should be proclaimed to them before it was to the Gentiles." Barnes, *Romans*, p.34.

of its divine origin, for (could it not be said) only an all-knowing God could design such a universal gospel.

1:17 – *For in it* **the** *righteousness of God is revealed from faith to faith; as it is written, "BUT* **THE RIGHTEOUS man** *SHALL LIVE BY FAITH."*

For. Either we are about to be given a reason why Paul is not ashamed of the gospel, or we are being given an explanation of how the gospel is "the power of God for salvation to everyone who believes," or we are being told why it is suitable to everyone.

In it. In the gospel (such as Paul was commissioned to preach) is where we read about the "righteousness of God."

The **righteousness of God is revealed.** Some would explain "righteousness" as if it were one of God's attributes,[75] and then go on to show how it is the purpose of the gospel to reveal or make known this attribute of God. Others would affirm that *dikaiosunē* here is something God does, i.e., it speaks of "right doing."[76] It is likely this disagreement about 'attribute' or 'action' that leads to the long discussions found in the commentaries concerning the proper way to translate the word here, with some in favor of "justification" and others in favor of "righteousness."[77] Still others take a mediating position, urging that the two above views are not mutually exclusive; appealing to Romans 3:21-26, where this expression is explained in some detail, they find both ideas present.

This discussion about the subtle connotations of English words may be something brand new to many Bible readers, but it is absolutely necessary if one would grasp the content Paul is trying to convey, for words communicate ideas. Perhaps at this place we could substitute "God's way of saving men" as a simple explanation of *dikaiosunē.* God

---

[75] Warren Wiersbe, *Be Right* (Wheaton, IL: Victor Books, 1977), p.17, is an example of those who explain "righteousness" as being one of God's attributes, as he writes, "The word 'righteousness' is used in one way or another over sixty times in this letter (righteous, just, and justified). God's righteousness is revealed in the gospel; for in the death of Christ, God revealed His righteousness by punishing sin; and in the resurrection of Christ, He revealed His righteousness by making salvation available to the believing sinner. The problem 'How can a holy God ever forgive sinners and still be holy?' is answered in the gospel. Through the death and resurrection of Christ, God is seen to be 'both just and justifier' (Romans 3:26)."

[76] Nouns that are formed by adding the *-sune* suffix regularly express *a quality.* (See Clarence W. Gleason, *A Greek Primer* [New York: American Book Co., 1931], p.226.) While this might seem to fortify the argument that one of God's attributes is in view here in verse 17, it could also be thought of as a 'quality' God sees or attributes to man, similar to the quality of 'holiness' (*hagiosune*), spoken of in 2 Corinthians 7:1. We might also admit that "righteousness" in Romans 3:5 is indeed an attribute of God, without having to insist on the same meaning here in verse 17.

[77] Lard, *Romans*, p.39-44, labors long to demonstrate that "justification" would be the proper way to translate here, since the ideas of right and wrong among the Hebrews were forensic ideas (i.e., words connected to the law courts, and verdicts of "guilty" or "not guilty" as determined before a judge). George Mark Elliott, in a class on Romans at The Cincinnati Bible Seminary, opted for "righteousness" as a satisfactory translation, since the thing being talked about (he believed) includes a propitiation for sin, a concept that goes far beyond the judicial term "justification."

is the source of it; it is something He bestows or imputes to man.[78] "Revealed" suggests that before the time when the gospel was preached, i.e., before the cross and the resurrection and Pentecost, God's way of saving man was not as clearly delineated as it now is.   In fact, in Romans 16:25, we are told that God's way of saving man was a "mystery ... kept secret for long ages past." "Mystery" means that it was taught in the Old Testament, but not as clearly as it is in the gospel.

Before continuing the explanation of this theme passage, it would be well to summarize what has been learned thus far.   The gospel proclaimed unleashes God's power to save.   It does this by revealing the plan or process designed by Him by which men may be counted (judged) as "just" or "righteous" (not guilty) in His sight.   This is what we understand Paul to mean when he affirms that God's way of saving men is revealed in the gospel.

From faith to faith.   It is because of this phrase that we believe *dikaiosunē* in the previous phrase is something God does for man (who meets this condition), rather than simply being an attribute of God.   "Faith" is the condition man must meet before God imputes salvation to him.[79]   The previous verse spoke of "belief" while this one uses the word "faith."   Both words come from the same root, and therefore deal with the same topic.

Still, once it has been proposed that "from faith" speaks of the conditional element in salvation, what idea are we to understand that the words "to faith" convey?   Various interpretations have been advanced, each seeking to win the reader's confidence for being the right one.[80]   In view of what is set forth in later chapters in Romans, we would opt for

---

[78] In later comments, we will be introduced to the whole matter of "imputed" or "infused" righteousness. The comments in the text reflect the conclusion there reached, that salvation is something God (acting as a judge) attributes or considers or imputes to certain men.   The careful reader will also have observed that whether the genitive case is considered to be *objective* (something God does) or *subjective* (something God is) depends on how *dikaiosunē* is explained (is it an "attribute" or an "action").   Since we have tended to explain "righteousness" as being "God's way of saving man," we have understood the genitive case ("of God") to be objective, to mean "provided by God."

[79] See notes at Romans 1:5 where this topic of faith being the condition on which God imputes righteousness was introduced.

[80] (1) Perhaps least satisfactory is the interpretation thrust at us in some 20th century translations, such as TEV's original rendering "by faith alone." [Later editions of TEV read "by faith from first to last."] (2) William Sanday and Arthur C. Headlam, *The Epistle to the Romans* in International Critical Commentary (Edinburgh: T&T Clark, 1895), p.28, proposed that it speaks of a smaller quantity of faith (in an individual) producing a larger quantity (as in a whole society), and they appeal to Psalm 84:7 and 2 Corinthians 2:16 where they believe similar expressions speak of a spread from an individual to the world at large.   (3) Not all commentators are wont to take "from faith to faith" as modifying "righteousness."   Some have proposed that the phrase should rather be seen as related to the verb "revealed." (See John Murray, *The Epistle to the Romans* in The New International Commentary on the New Testament [Grand Rapids: Wm. B. Eerdmans Publishing Co., 1965], p.32.)   But is the revelation to be understood as being *dependent* on whether or not a man has faith?   We think not.   The revelation is made in the gospel, whether or not a man believes it.   (4) Still another attempt to explain satisfactorily this rather enigmatic phrase is the one that suggests the first "faith" signifies belief in the Old Testament times, while "unto faith" signifies belief in the New Testament age. (See J. Peter Lange, *The Epistle of Paul to the Romans* [Grand Rapids: Zondervan Publishing House, nd], p.76, where this view is attributed to Origen, Chrysostom, and Theodor-

the explanation which takes "to faith" (*eis pistin*) as being a goal, an end toward which one is moving. Romans encourages the readers to understand that "faith," not law-keeping, is the way to salvation. That whole idea, we believe, is here introduced. God's way of saving man is conditioned on faith (not law-keeping, or some other equally difficult or impossible condition) *in order to encourage men to believe.* If the conditions God held out to men were beyond any possibility of being met, few men would be interested. But when the lost man understands that God's way requires faith, he will be more likely to attempt to do God's will. God chose the condition He did so men will be encouraged, or induced, to believe.

As it is written. The verse about to be quoted is Habakkuk 2:4, a verse that is quoted two other times in the New Testament (Galatians 3:11; Hebrews 10:38). The background of the passage is this: Habakkuk is perplexed by the seeming ease of the wicked, as though wicked men in Judea were getting away with their wickedness, and he asks God about this. God replies that the Chaldeans are coming as God's means of punishing the wicked Jews. Now the prophet wants to know why God will allow the wicked Chaldeans to punish the Jews, since in his view the Jews were more righteous than the foreigners. God's answer is that all sinners, whether Jew or Chaldean, will be punished; it is only the ones who are righteous by faith who shall live.

"BUT THE RIGHTEOUS *man* SHALL LIVE BY FAITH."[81] This quotation from Habakkuk tends to corroborate the interpretation given above for the phrase "righteousness of God." It is something objective, a righteousness bestowed on the believer.[82] The LXX reads, "The righteous *one* shall live by my faith." This could give a different slant to the passage – "Because I am faithful (God is speaking), the righteous man shall live" or "the righteous man shall live in accordance with the faith I (God speaking) prescribe." Paul, by inspiration, is giving a Divine explanation of the Old Testament passage, and at the same time is making it perfectly clear that "faith" has always been the condition upon which "living" is predicated. F.F. Bruce has pointed out that "life" (especially in the sense of eternal life) and "salvation" were practically synonymous terms, since Aramaic-speaking

---

et.) (5) One other alternative suggestion is that of H.C.G. Moule, *The Epistle of Paul the Apostle to the Romans* in The Cambridge Bible for Schools and Colleges (Cambridge: At the University Press, 1952), p.58, who proposes that "from faith" speaks of "the initial step, the entrance to justification," and that "unto faith" speaks of "the life of the justified [as being] maintained by faith."

[81] The KJV reads "The just shall live by faith," a variation that obscures from the English reader that the Habakkuk 2:4 passage is speaking about the same "righteousness" that Paul has been saying is revealed in the gospel. On the other hand, the rendering "just" certainly introduces the idea of a verdict from a judge, which is a prominent idea in the Bible doctrine of justification (or righteousness).

[82] Once again it is necessary to consider whether "by faith" is connected with "righteousness" or with "live" (or "revealed" in the previous instance). The student who wishes to pursue this technical matter will find the arguments well summarized in William Hendriksen, *Romans*, p.64-65 [who urges connecting "by faith" to the verb "live"], and in Cranfield, *Romans*, p.101-102 [who urges connecting "by faith" to the word "righteous"].

Jews used the same word (*hayye*) for both "life" and "salvation."[83]   Perhaps, too, it should be pointed out that "faithfulness" is a perfectly proper translation of the Greek word *pistis*; in fact, that is the word used by the NASB at Matthew 23:23 to translate *pistis*.[84]

I. THE UNIVERSAL NEED OF THE SALVATION OFFERED IN THE GOSPEL. 1:18-3:20

A. Righteousness (Justification, Salvation) is Needed by Gentiles. 1:18-32

Summary: The Gentiles once had a correct knowledge of God, but as time passed, they deliberately ignored it.   Therefore God 'gave them up' and their sins became more aggravated.   Now they not only are sinning, but they have no sorrow for their sins. Sinners are in desperate need of the "righteousness" that is revealed in the gospel.

1:18 – *For the wrath of God is revealed from heaven against all ungodliness and unrighteousness of men, who suppress the truth in unrighteousness,*

For the wrath of God is revealed from heaven.   Beginning at 3:21, Paul will elaborate 'God's way of saving men.'   Before that, beginning here in 1:18, he explains why such a salvation is so urgently needed.   All men, be they Gentile or Jew, have sinned, and sinners (unless forgiven) are in danger of suffering God's wrath.   "For" suggests we are being given a reason for what was just set forth in the theme sentence.   If men are to be saved, the condition will have to be 'faith,' for all have sinned.   There is a great need for the good news that proclaims a righteousness by faith, for no one is perfectly righteous in his own actions and thoughts.

The "wrath of God" is an expression the Bible reader frequently encounters, including in the New Testament, where it occurs some 30 times.[85]   When found in men, anger or wrath is usually condemned as being sinful.[86]   It is clear, since God does not sin,

---

[83] Bruce, *Romans*, p.81.

[84] Bruce has pointed out that Habakkuk 2:4 is quoted at Hebrews 10:38 in a context where "faithfulness" is the thing being encouraged.   He reminds us that the Hebrew word *'emunah*, translated "faith" in Habakkuk 2:4 (the LXX uses *pistis*), means "steadfastness" or "fidelity."   It is not just a one-time thing, a one-time belief, on which God bestows "righteousness."   The condition God looks for is one of steadfastness, fidelity, faithfulness.   *Romans*, p.80.

[85] It should be observed that the dictum of liberal theologians that the God of the Old Testament is a God of wrath, whereas the God of the New Testament is a God of love, is not quite in harmony with what one finds on the pages of the New Testament.   The Bible everywhere presents a uniform picture of the nature of God.   It is a serious error to assert a kind of evolutionary progress in the doctrine of God from the early pages of the Old Testament to the closing pages of the New Testament.

[86] See Galatians 5:20 and James 1:19,20.

His "wrath" must be somewhat unlike men's wrath. Men's wrath is sometimes triggered by unholy thoughts of revenge, or long-nursed memories of ancient hurts unfairly suffered. God's wrath is His settled displeasure against sin, and it grows out of His very nature (which is holiness). There is nothing selfish or momentarily out of character in God's wrath.[87]

Paul says that the wrath of God "is revealed." Where does one look to find this revelation? Does one look to the message of the gospel, where (we have already been informed) God's righteousness is revealed? While it may be true that there are New Testament warnings about the wrath of God on the ungodly, such an explanation does not seem to fit the context following. Shall we instead look in the Old Testament for this revelation of God's wrath? Possibly, in part, but the present tense verb ("*is* revealed") seems to point to some revelation being made even as Paul writes, rather than to some past revelation, as the Old Testament was. If not in the Old Testament, where shall we look to see God's wrath in action? "Wrath" seems to suggest punishment. Was there any punishment being felt by the Gentiles, even while they continued to live in this world? Indeed, as the following verses show, every time God 'gave them up,' a new 'hurt' was felt by the sinning Gentiles. It is precisely in these temporal punishments for sin that one can see God's wrath at work.[88] We live in a moral universe, and retribution does operate in such a moral universe. Just as the "righteousness of God" is something that can be experienced in the sphere of human life, so the "wrath of God" (as just explained) is also something that can be experienced in the sphere of human life.[89]

> Verse 18 begins a terrifying indictment of human sin. Paul turns first to the sins of those who are without the light of a [written] revelation ... It may seem strange to some that Paul devotes nearly three chapters to an exhaustive examination of the problem of sin. However, slight views of sin never lead to a fervent appreciation of grace. Man is ever ready to excuse himself. He wears his sins lightly, and tends to dismiss them as mere peccadilloes. In his view they offer no barrier to blessing. After all, forgiveness is God's business! (Heine) ... Paul must therefore insist that the gravity of sin must be measured by the strength of the Divine reaction it provokes. God is not indifferent to sin. It continually calls forth His holy abhorrence. Sin is an affront to the holiness of God, it is a direct assault upon His majesty, and the

---

[87] Even among men, not all anger or wrath is sinful. Do we not speak of a 'righteous anger'? So God's wrath can be in perfect harmony with His righteous character, His holiness, and His love.

[88] Some might hesitate to speak of 'Gentiles' as we comment on these verses in chapter 1, since the word 'Gentiles' does not specifically appear. It might even be urged that Jews can commit all the sins listed in chapter 1. True, but in Romans 3:9, Paul will summarize his own writing up to that point, and will say he has demonstrated before that both Jews and Gentiles (Greeks, NASB) are guilty of sin – and so some of the verses preceding chapter 3 must deal with Gentiles. Therefore, we conclude that chapter 1 shows the guilt of the Gentiles, and their need for the salvation offered in the gospel.

[89] The explanation that emphasizes a temporal punishment for sin does not by any means rule out the possibility of future punishment, too. We would affirm that a temporal experience of God's wrath is but a preview of the 'wrath to come' at the end-time (1 Thessalonians 1:10). It might well be viewed as a gracious warning from God that men ought to quit sinning before punishment becomes more acute and onerous.

"wrath of God" is an expression which indicates the righteous outflow of Divine disfavor upon the sinner. This wrath is not an automatic judgment upon sin by an anonymous cosmic computer ... Rather, the phrase "the wrath *of God*" points to the most intense, personal response to sin within the Divine being ....[90]

"Heaven" can refer to God's residence, God's throne room. The word "heaven" can also speak of the atmosphere around earth (as in the expression "birds of the heaven"). And the word "heaven" is also used to refer to the expanse of space where the stars and planets are hung. This being true, the expression "from heaven" has received a number of different explanations. One commentator thinks it means that the heavenly bodies are proofs of God's wrath against sin. But it does not say "heavenly bodies;" it says "from heaven." Another thinks the reference is to Christ, who will come from heaven as the ultimate executioner of God's wrath. But it does not read "will be revealed" (future); it reads "is revealed" (present). Barnes, it seems, is on the right track when he writes,

... this expression ... means simply that the divine displeasure against sin is made known by a divine appointment; by an arrangement of events which evince that they have had their origin in heaven and are divine.[91]

Against all ungodliness and unrighteousness of men. "Ungodliness" is a failure in one's duties to God. It is a lack of reverence, a neglect of worship due Him, even a giving of homage to idols instead of to Him. "Unrighteousness" is a failure in one's duties to his fellow man. It shows itself in such acts as murder, theft, adultery, retaliation. The two words together encompass the violation of all the commands of God. The order is also important. When a man's relationship to God is wrong, it leads regularly to derangement of his relationships with his fellow man.

Who suppress the truth in unrighteousness. The word translated "suppress" is *katechō*, a word that can be rendered: 1) "hold fast, keep, maintain, observe;" or, 2) "hold down, keep back, restrain, hinder."[92] Both meanings have been tried by commentators. If we take the first meaning, then the verse says the Gentiles do hold some truth, but they do it in a wicked way ("in unrighteousness"). The wicked way would be that though they have the truth, there is no corresponding practice in life; rather, there is just the opposite. They know what God expects, and yet they go on and sin anyway. If we take the second meaning, then the passage affirms that the Gentiles keep God's truth from pervading society by their continual, deliberate practice of unrighteousness. The truth was there, and was available for man, but wicked men ignored it themselves and kept it from others.

What is the "truth"? Certainly not the truth contained in the gospel. It appears that

---

[90] Geoffrey Wilson, *Romans*, p.23,24.

[91] Albert Barnes, *Romans*, p.39.

[92] Arndt-Gingrich, *Lexicon*, p.423,424.

Paul is speaking of a people who have not yet heard the gospel. The "truth" in this context seems to be limited to the truth about God and His requirements that can be learned from nature (verses 19,20, and 25) and from such revelations as men received during the Patriarchal Age (verse 32). The truth revealed in the Law of Moses seems to be excluded by the context.

> From whence had this truth been derived? Originally from God Himself. From Him it had come either immediately, as in the case of Adam, or mediately through angels, or inspired men, as in subsequent ages [*i.e.*, the age of Moses and the prophets]. Some, therefore, had it in the form of an original revelation; others in the form of an [oral] tradition. But whether in this form or that, it was the truth, and the only truth the world had prior to the [Mosaic Age and the] gospel.[93]

The reader should be sure to observe that chapter 1 will affirm that all men have some revelation from God, by which they are expected by God to live. They may not have Moses or the gospel, but they have some truth.

1:19 – *because that which is known about God is evident within them; for God made it evident to them.*

Because that which is known about God is evident within them. Meyer suggests this verse gives a reason why the wrath of God comes to such men (*dioti* means "because").[94] There was a time when the Gentiles had a knowledge of God, and a right knowledge at that! It was a failure to act upon that knowledge that resulted in wrath. The marginal reading "among them" is probably to be preferred to the reading of the text ("within them"), for it does not seem likely this is talking about an *innate* knowledge of God. What was "known" about God is specified in the next verse, and so is how it came to be known (i.e., by observation and contemplation). "Evident" says the revelation from God was understood clearly. Paul asserts that the Gentiles knew enough to be responsible for their own sins. Being therefore culpable, they needed the salvation offered in the gospel.

For God made it evident to them. God had endowed men with minds and an ability to reason. Men were capable of seeing and investigating His works, and of coming to the right conclusion.[95] The next verse will explain this all in more detail.

---

[93] Lard, *Romans*, p.48.

[94] "They keep down the truth through immorality; if they did so out of ignorance, they would be excusable: but they did not do so out of ignorance, and therefore God's wrath is manifested against them." Meyer, *Romans*, p.56.

[95] It would seem that certain Calvinistic theologians have missed the import of what Paul says here in chapter 1 about the Gentiles. Some Calvinists insist on 'total depravity' and 'total inability' since the Fall, so that sinful men cannot even think right or reason right until they have a first work of grace. Does not this passage (and indeed Paul's sermon on Mar's Hill, Acts 17) indicate that even fallen men still can get some things right? Does it not affirm that their understanding functions enough to allow them to come to a proper knowledge and grasp of the truth? We shall have more to say on this topic when we come to chapters 5 and 7.

1:20 – *For since the creation of the world His invisible attributes, His eternal power and divine nature, have been clearly seen, being understood through what has been made, so that they are without excuse.*

For since the creation of the world.   The New Testament is everywhere in harmony with the doctrine set forth in Genesis that in the beginning God created.   One discards much more of the Bible than a few chapters of Genesis when he decides to reject the idea of an original creation.   Ever since God finished His work of creation (Genesis 2:1,2), men have been able to look at the finished product and from it to get some idea of the nature of the Creator.

His invisible attributes, His eternal power and divine nature, have been clearly seen. God's "invisible attributes" are those things which cannot be perceived by one of the five senses.   These traits may be known, but are not such as are discoverable simply by the eye or the touch.   There is a contemplation necessary, and an observation.   Exactly which "invisible attributes" Paul has in mind are immediately specified – namely, God's "eternal power" and God's "divine nature."

God had to have a great deal of power to create this universe.   One current theory of matter is that all matter is a form of energy.   Think how much "power" is contained in (and can be unleashed from) one tiny atom.   Note, too, that it speaks of God's "eternal" power.   How do we obtain from the things created the idea of God's *eternal* power?   The very fact that God created this universe implies that He must have existed before the creation, and also had a 'never-failing omnipotence' even back then before creation.   From observation of the things created, we should become aware of God's power, a power that far surpasses any other creature, a power that elevates Him above all others.

"Divine nature" (*theiotēs*) is a word that occurs only here in the New Testament.[96] On this word, Trench wrote,

> ... It is not to be doubted that St. Paul uses this vaguer, more abstract, and less personal word, just because he would affirm that men may know God's power and majesty ... from His works; but would *not* imply that they may know Himself from these, or from anything short of the revelation of his Eternal Word.[97]

The difference between *theotēs* and *theiotēs* has been expressed beautifully by E.K. Simpson:

---

[96] Words with a similar root are found elsewhere in the New Testament.   *Theotēs*, found in Colossians 2:9 means "deity."   *Theios*, found at Acts 17:29, means "divine qualities."   If a single characteristic of God is denoted by *theiotēs* (some commentators hold it is a word that summarizes all the attributes of deity – an opinion which Lard, *Romans*, p.52,53 refutes), then it is the supremacy of Jehovah to all other gods that seems to be the thing intended.

[97] R.C. Trench, *Synonyms of the New Testament* (Grand Rapids: Wm. B. Eerdmans Publishing Co., 1966), p.8.

The **hand** of omnipotence may be traced in the countless orbs that bespangle the heavens, and in the marvelous co-adjustments of our comparatively tiny globe (that's *theiotēs*); but in the Son we behold the **face** of God unveiled, the express image and transcript of his very being.[98]

"Clearly seen" means 'are surveyed, contemplated, are under observation.' The created world has always, from the time of its creation, taught lessons about its Maker. "The heavens declare the glory of God, and the firmament shows His handiwork" (Psalm 19:1, NKJV). The two verbs, "being understood" (*nooumena*, from *nous*, "mind") and "clearly seen" (*kathoratai*, from *horaō*, to "see") – the one speaking of intelligence, and the other of physical sight – "describe how, on contemplating God's works, man can grasp enough of His nature to prevent him from the error of identifying any of the created things with the Creator, thus enabling him to keep his conception of the Deity free from idolatry."[99]

Being understood through what has been made. Just as the previous expression did not indicate all knowledge of God is innate, neither does this expression indicate all knowledge of God that men originally had came from a study of nature. Adam lived 930 years. He certainly talked to his sons and told them the instructions God had given to him. Noah lived 950 years, and he certainly talked to his sons and shared God's instructions with them. God did give revelations to these patriarchs, and those men by oral tradition would pass that revelation on. Verse 32 will speak of a knowledge about right and wrong that could come only by revelation, and which was then passed on (we presume) by oral tradition. Paul is saying that all nations (Gentiles) had some light, some knowledge of God. At one time the Gentiles had a proper concept of God. And even after this concept had been lost as the years passed, still the very creation left them without excuse for leaving the one true and living God. There has never been a time or place where the knowledge of God was completely extinguished.[100]

In passing, it should be observed that Paul's presentation of God and His creation is opposed to all ideas of pantheism. Instead of God's being in all the things made, Paul shows that there is no identity between the two. Rather, God has a transcendent though (at times) immanent relationship to the creation.

---

[98] E.K. Simpson, *Words Worth Weighing in the Greek New Testament*, quoted by William Hendriksen, *Exposition of Colossians and Philemon* (Grand Rapids: Baker Book House, 1964), p.111.

[99] Bruce, *Romans*, p.84.

[100] Even we who have a written revelation also need the help of the evidence offered by the creation to strengthen our faith. (Remember, faith is doing what God says in His word because the sufficiency of the evidence shows that word is true.) In the study of apologetics, there is a valuable place for the theistic arguments. The bird singing, the grass growing, the worm in the ground, the shape of snowflakes – you cannot account for these apart from God. But this evidence has limitations. Even though from a study of nature you can reason to a First Cause, you cannot know Him personally, at least not as He can be known from the pages of Scripture. You cannot learn John 3:16 by studying nature. You cannot know that Jesus died on the cross and rose from the dead by looking at a flower. That said, Paul is clearly affirming here that certain traits or characteristics of the Creator can be known by a careful observation of the things created.

So that they are without excuse. "So that" seems to express result,[101] especially in view of the following verse which begins with "because." Implied in this presentation is the idea that knowledge involves duties. When men have a certain knowledge, God expects them to live by that knowledge. If they do not live in harmony with their knowledge, that is sin, and the sin brings condemnation. God has given the Gentiles so clear an evidence of His "eternal power and divine nature" that the Gentiles have no excuse for being idolaters. They have traditions respecting His perfections, so they have no excuse for hindering the truth by their iniquity.[102] Involved also in this presentation is the idea that sin implies a knowledge of good and evil.

1:21 – *For even though they knew God, they did not honor Him as God, or give thanks; but they became futile in their speculations, and their foolish heart was darkened.*

For even though they knew God. Gentiles cannot plead a lack of knowledge! Instead, what really happened is that the Gentiles deliberately ignored the knowledge God had given them. "For" represents *dioti* ("because") and assigns a reason for the conclusion just given in verse 20 about the Gentiles' being without excuse. It has already been established (verses 18-20) that the Gentiles knew God. Now verses 21-23 will document the wrong course taken by humanity.

They did not honor Him as God. They did not worship God as they should have. The following verses will show that such failure to honor God soon results in an appalling condition in man's relation to man. This failure to honor God did not just happen. It was deliberate. They knew God, but they closed their minds. They refused to honor God.

Or give thanks. What must be wrong in the heart of a man who will not thank the Creator of all for His blessings! Ingratitude is sin (2 Timothy 3: 2, "unthankful," ASV). Lack of gratitude to God is not simply a small breach of etiquette (like when a child doesn't say "Thank you!" but has to be prompted) – it is basically heathenish. Paul will go on to show that this unwillingness to render gratitude to God for His mercies is one of the causes why the Gentiles subsequently went into idolatry.

---

[101] Some have urged that in this verse, "so that" indicates *purpose* rather than *result*. At first sight it may seem like a small difference, but underneath lies the whole subject of predestination as taught by Calvin. If the 'evidence' was put in creation by God with this *purpose* in mind, namely, that certain men would be without excuse, then predestination to damnation would be taught. If, on the other hand, as Luther taught, this verse speaks of a *result,* then individual predestination to damnation would not be taught. (W.E. Vine, *The Epistle to the Romans* [Grand Rapids: Zondervan Publishing House, 1948], p.19, has given a different emphasis when he writes, "... the meaning is that it was the purpose of God to remove from man all possible excuse for ignorance of Himself.")

[102] In passing, it might be of value to note that the entire drift of Romans 1 is against the view that the condemnation of mankind is due simply to Adam's sin being imputed to the whole race. Chapter 5 will indicate that something was passed on to the race from Adam, but here in chapter 1 men are represented as being personally responsible for their guilt, in that they have sinned against the light (knowledge of God) they might have followed. We shall have to be careful that our explanation of either chapter does not contradict what is taught in the other.

But they became futile in their speculations. The verb translated "became futile" (and its corresponding noun) often are used in the LXX to refer to idolatrous tendencies and practices.[103] A man who refuses to honor or thank God misses one of the great purposes for which he was made. "*Became* futile" suggests the futility was not something inherited from Adam. *Dialogismos* ("speculations") might be translated "thoughts, opinions, reasonings, disputes, arguments."[104] Being unwilling to worship God as they ought, they commenced to think idolatrous thoughts. They were using their minds for a purpose other than that for which God had given them minds.

And their foolish heart was darkened. The word "heart" has a number of connotations in Scripture. Hendriksen has summarized it this way,

> Of course, the word's exact meaning in each case depends on the context. Sometimes, in Paul, when the word *heart(s)* is used, the emphasis is on the emotions or feelings (Romans 1:24, 9:2); sometimes on the intellect (Romans 10:6-9); and sometimes on the will (Romans 2:5).[105]

Here the idea seems to be that the intellectual knowledge they had gradually became lost. They once had right knowledge, but through the centuries, the truth faded.[106] Once again it should be observed that the verse does not say men's "reason" and "heart" were darkened as a result of Adam's sin. It was for men's own sins that such a penalty was exacted – a part of the wrath of God.

1:22 – *Professing to be wise, they became fools,*

Professing to be wise. "When men are reasoning God out of their souls, they usually make

---

[103] Trench, *Synonyms*, p.180-183, shows that "futile" (*mataios*) carries the idea of "not fulfilling the purpose for which it was made," whereas a synonym *kenos* (also translated "vain, futile") simply means "empty, hollow, producing no return." "Futile" is used of idolatrous thoughts and practices at Jeremiah 2:5; 2 Kings 17:15; Acts 14:15; 1 Corinthians 3:20, etc.

[104] Arndt-Gingrich, *Lexicon*, p.185

[105] Hendriksen, *Romans*, p.72.

[106] The truth that faded was 'spiritual truth,' knowledge about God and His will. It is doubtful that 'secular knowledge' is involved, as Calvin and his followers imply. In some systems of apologetics, this verse is used to prove that man's reasoning abilities are so depraved by sin that one cannot start with empirical evidence and reason out 'proofs for God.' (It is asserted that Aristotelian trust in the reasoning ability of natural man is foreign to Paul.) This commentator doubts that the verse affirms so much about the sinner's ability to reason. The verse more likely says only that sinning man no longer seeks the truth with intellectual honesty and integrity, but uses his reason to rationalize his desires and conduct. [This whole topic can be pursued in Cornelius Van Til's *The Defense of the Faith* (Philadelphia: Presbyterian and Reformed Publishing Co., 1955), where it is held that no sinner's reasoning is right without divine assistance; and in Floyd Hamilton's *The Basis of Christian Faith*, revised edition (New York: Harper and Row, 1964), in the paragraph about "presuppositionalism" (p.34), where the idea that man's reasoning ability is so impaired that theistic arguments are useless, is rejected.]

large pretensions to wisdom."[107]   Josephus (*Ant.* I.4) tells about the people's pretense to great wisdom in the time of Nimrod and the tower of Babel.

They became fools.   It was in their conduct, about to be detailed in the following verses, that they showed their foolishness.   Men like Socrates and Seneca decried the folly of idolatry, yet did not have the courage to dissuade men altogether from worshiping the gods with which they found fault.

1:23 – *and exchanged the glory of the incorruptible God for an image in the form of corruptible man and of birds and four-footed animals and crawling creatures.*

And exchanged the glory of the incorruptible God for an image.   Scripture everywhere presents the truth that man's knowledge of God, in the beginning, was monotheistic, and that polytheism developed later.   It is not possible to square with Scripture the evolutionary theory of the development of religion from a beginning in animism and polytheism to an eventual intelligent concept of monotheism.   It is not an *evolution* the Bible pictures; it is a *devolution*.   Instead of an advance by stages into a better knowledge of God, it went the other way.

It is difficult to define "glory" as it is here used of God.   Since the term is contrasted with "image" in the next phrase, it seems to be used of the 'shape' or 'form' or 'body' that God has.[108]   One is reminded of the description of God on His throne, found in Revelation 4:2-3, where one of the first things John sees as he looks at the throne is an emerald sphere of dazzling light.   Perhaps this sphere of light is none other than the "glory" of God, the Shekinah of the Old Testament.   If, indeed, the ancients had some idea of God's shape or form, it is a bit more understandable why they wanted an image (an idol, a shape, a form) to worship when they foolishly went away from the original, true knowledge of God.

God is here described as being "incorruptible."   The word means "not liable to decay, imperishable."[109]   God is exempt from wear and waste and final perishing.

"Image" is from *eikon*, a word that presumes a prototype that the "image" resembles. "Thus, the monarch's head on the coin is *eikon* (Matthew 22:20); the reflection of the sun in the water is *eikon* (Plato, *Phaedo*, 99d); the statue in stone or other material is *eikon* (Revelation 13:14) ...."[110]   It should not escape our notice that 'images' as objects of worship are the product of men who have gone away from the true God.   Verses like this

---

[107] Lard, *Romans*, p.55.

[108] Franz Delitzsch, *A System of Biblical Psychology* (Grand Rapids: Baker Book House, 1966), p.60-62.   Scripture speaks of God's body of light, His form of light (Numbers 12:8; Psalm 17:15); of His "form" (*eidos* in John 5:37; *morphē* in Philippians 2:6).

[109] Joseph Henry Thayer, *A Greek-English Lexicon of the New Testament* (New York: American Book Company, 1889), p.88.

[110] Trench, *Synonyms*, p.50.

should reinforce our abhorrence of such objects of worship. Men ought to make, instead of images of creatures, the glory of the incorruptible God the object of their adoration.

In the form of corruptible man. What folly to worship something that wastes away, when one could be worshiping the *incorruptible* God! Many of the images or idols that archaeologists have unearthed are in the forms of men or women. Think of Jupiter, Hercules, Romulus, and the Greek gods and goddesses. "It was proof of great degradation that they thus adored *men* with like passions as themselves and attempted to displace the true God from the throne, and to substitute in His place an idol in the likeness of men."[111]

And of birds. The Egyptians had "gods" in the shape of the ibis and the hawk. After reminding his readers that man was made in the image of God, Lard has this explanation:

> In making an idol to represent God, their first thought would be to make one as nearly like Him as possible. They would, therefore, make it like man, feeling that thereby they were making it like God. But as they sunk in grossness, they would make their idols to resemble those beasts and fowls from which they derived most benefit, or those animals and creeping things they most feared. Those [that benefitted] they would worship; these [that they feared] they would seek to propitiate.[112]

And four-footed animals. In Egypt, four different divine bulls were worshiped. Worship was offered to cattle, lions, cats, dogs, weasels, and otters. Sheep were worshiped in Sais (ancient capital of lower Egypt) and in Thebes, but were sacrificed and eaten in Lycopolis (an ancient city of upper Egypt). The hippopotamus and crocodile too were objects of worship.

> Calf worship was part of the religious worship of almost all ancient Semitic peoples. At least as early as the Exodus, living bulls were worshiped in Egypt. The Babylonians looked upon the bull as the symbol of their greatest gods. The bull was a sacred animal in Phoenicia and Syria. Among the Semitic Canaanites the bull was a symbol of Baal.[113]

To this day, two of the most sacred objects of worship in India are the cow and the monkey.

And crawling creatures. Reptiles, snakes, lizards. Who hasn't seen a picture of Egyptians with an amulet in the form of a snake on the upper arm or as a 'crown' on the top of the head? If Lard (quoted above) is correct, then one can discern how far away from the true God a people have fallen by observing the objects of their worship. If we have here an order of objects suggestive of progressive degradation, then the worshiper of crawling

---

[111] Barnes, *Romans*, p.46.

[112] Lard, *Romans*, p.56.

[113] Merrill C. Tenney, ed., *The Zondervan Pictorial Bible Dictionary* (Grand Rapids: Zondervan Publishing Co, 1963), p.141.

creatures is much farther away from the true knowledge of God than the worshiper whose "idol" is one of the other forms listed.[114]   Now we have come to the verses where we see God's wrath being revealed!   The Gentiles had a knowledge of God.   They deliberately ignored that knowledge, so "God gave them up" (KJV).

1:24 – *Therefore God gave them over in the lusts of their hearts to impurity, that their bodies might be dishonored among them.*

Therefore God gave them over.   Because they did not glorify Him as God, because they were unthankful, because they became polytheists and idolaters, God's wrath was displayed.   Note the same words, "God gave them over," in verses 26 and 28, also. *Paradidōmi* ("gave then over") means to "hand over to the power of another."   Several writers suggest a three-fold involvement in the word – a permissive, a privative, and a judicial element.

- By *permissive* is meant that God permits or allows wicked men to have their own way, like the father in the parable of the prodigal son permitted the younger son to go to the far land.   God permitted the wicked men to fall into uncleanness and impurity, and did not summon them to all everywhere repent, as He does now through the gospel (Acts 14:15,16 and 17:30, and perhaps Romans 3:25).   The permissive aspect does not exhaust this term "God gave them over."

- By *privative* is meant that God withdraws His gracious aid.   When these Gentiles plunged into sin, God did not work with them as He did with His chosen people.   God worked with the chosen people by sending them the Law, the Prophets, warnings, and chastisements, by which He tried to restrain or recall His chosen people from idolatry and impurity.   Some have illustrated this privative idea by picturing a drifting boat – the restraining hand is removed, and the drifting boat is on its own.   The privative aspect does not exhaust this term "God gave them over."

- By *judicial* is meant that the appropriate punishment for their sin came into effect. There seems to be a temporal punishment for every sin.   Over-indulgence results in a headache or a hangover.   Some sins result in addiction.   When the Gentiles turned away from God, shutting Him out of their thoughts and hearts, and giving His honor to senseless idols, the appropriate punishments for such sins automatically were experienced by the wicked men.   Not only is there an appropriate punishment, but there is the 'hardening effect of sin.'   Sin cuts the optic nerve of the soul.   "Experience as well as Revelation says that the most terrible and just penalty of sin is the hardening

---

[114] Wilson, *Romans*, p.29, has this reminder (which is similar to one found in many Protestant writers): "It needs to be noted that idolaters do not commonly think of themselves as idol worshipers.   They invoke their deities by means of the image (they say); they do not bow down to the image itself.   This sophistry is still favored by Rome in her vain attempt to justify her willful departure from the Word of God, and yet this is the very thing which the Bible condemns root and branch.   Aaron made a golden calf, but he did not have the slightest intention of leading the people to worship this image.   He said, 'Tomorrow is a feast *to the Lord*' (Exodus 32:5).   The calf was simply an aid to devotion, but God's judgment of the matter was very different.   'They have made a calf in Horeb, and *worshiped a molten image*.   Thus they exchanged their glory for the likeness of an ox that eateth grass' (Psalm 106:19,20)."

of the sinning heart."[115]   "... who steels his heart against the truth shall find his heart hardened" (Johnson).   "That the Lord, having constituted as the righteous law of his moral government, that sin should produce darkness of heart and moral instability, declared that he would allow the law in their case to take its full course" (Trench).[116]

None of these three ideas – privative, permissive, or judicial – should be looked upon as impinging on the freedom of the will in man.   "Just as man, while his fidelity is rewarded by God through growth in virtue, remains withal free and does not become a virtuous machine; so also he retains his freedom, while God accomplishes the development of His arrangement, in accordance with which sin is born of sin."[117]   Just as the saved man can, while being saved, rebel and become lost – so the lost man can come to repentance and get out of the "given up" condition.[118]

A concept called the providence of God is understood as being involved in the background of most of these verses in Romans 1.   It is not that God just created the universe and man, put certain divine laws into operation, and then went off somewhere to let it run its course.   The Bible everywhere pictures God as active in His world, moving it to the goal He has always had in mind.   Part of His involvement in the world is His active "giving them over," as verses 24,26, and 28 tell us.   He not only put certain laws into operation, He continually sees that they work![119]

In the lusts of their hearts to impurity.   The term translated "lusts" is *epithumia*, a neutral word meaning "desire."   The context must determine if the desire is good or evil.[120] 1 Peter 1:14 uses the same word to describe the motive behind unconverted men's behavior. Such behavior is 'desire centered;' they did it just because they wanted to, because they were hungry for it.   God did not cause these desires all of a sudden to flare up.   Nor did

---

[115] Moule, *Romans*, p.62.

[116] Both the quotation from Johnson and the one from Trench come from *A Syllabus on Romans*, by George Mark Elliott.

[117] Meyer, *Romans*, p.63.   An impressive modern statement of this principle of divine retribution for sin is provided by C.S. Lewis in *The Problem of Pain* (New York: Macmillan Co., 1965), p.115ff.   The lost, Lewis says, "enjoy forever the horrible freedom they have demanded, and are therefore self-enslaved."

[118] The reader who wishes a more detailed study of the permissive, privative, and judicial aspects of this expression, "God gave them over," will want especially to consult E.H. Gifford, "Romans" in the *Bible Commentary*, edited by F.C. Cook (New York: Charles Scribner's Sons, 1886), and Meyer, *Romans*, comments on verse 24.   An extreme position, too, ought to be avoided, namely, that immediately when these sins (idolatry and immorality) started to appear, God *immediately* "gave them up" and, as it were, said, "Let them perish!"   It was not the case that they were hurled immediately into everlasting punishment. Even Jezebel, who appears to have committed all the sins named in the present context, was given time and opportunity to repent (cp. Revelation 2:20).   In the days of Noah, people had 120 years to repent while the ark was being prepared (1 Peter 3:20).   But in the meantime, while final punishment was awaiting, they suffered the appropriate temporal punishments.

[119] See Special Study #2 on "The Providence of God" at the close of notes on chapter 1.

[120] Arndt-Gingrich, *Lexicon*, p.293.

God cause the impurity that resulted.   He did give them up to the natural consequences of the desires already working in them.   Unrestrained by reverence for and a sense of accountability to God, they had nothing to control their behavior except the desires of their hearts.   "Impurity" (*akatharsia*) is a word that has moral overtones.   It speaks of sexual sins, immorality, unnatural vices.[121]   Idolatry is often the source of immorality, as the immoral acts are thought of as being part of the worship of the gods and goddesses.[122]

That their bodies might be dishonored among them.   "That" is an articular infinitive in the Greek, a construction that often expresses purpose, sometimes result.[123]   Perhaps here the idea is result – dishonor was the result of doing what their desires suggested.   Verses 26 and 27 will specify some of the ways the Gentiles dishonored their own physical bodies.   As to the fact that God's Word teaches that sexual sins dishonor the body, see 1 Corinthians 6:18.   In their immoral and unnatural acts "among them(selves)," i.e., with one another, they dishonored each other's bodies.

1:25 – *For they exchanged the truth of God for a lie, and worshiped and served the creature rather than the Creator, who is blessed forever. Amen.*

For they exchanged the truth of God for a lie.   We have had the verb "exchanged" at verse 23, and verse 25 closely resembles that previous verse.[124]   The "truth of God" that they gave up is primarily the truth respecting the worship due to God, as the context shows.   The "lie" is the idea that the idol is a real god, and that worship of such is an acceptable practice.[125]   This verse begins with "for," which means it is a reason for something just said.   Perhaps it is a further reason why God gave them up.   Perhaps it gives the reason for the moral degradation.   If the latter is correct, then it would be Paul's actual statement of what has been earlier stated in these comments, that idolatry leads to immorality.

---

[121] Arndt-Gingrich, *Lexicon*, p.28.

[122] "Here is noticed a further stage of judicial degradation; the *mataiotēs* ['futile in speculations,' verse 21] of idolatry, itself judicial, had its further judicial consequences in the *akartharsia* ['uncleanness, impurity'] of abominable sensuality.   Similarly, in Ephesians 4, the *ergasian akatharsias pasēs en pleonexia* ['working of uncleanness in greediness'] prevalent among the nations, is traced to their *mataiotēs*, in that they had become 'alienated from God.'   It is notorious that idolatrous worship was not uncommonly accompanied by debauchery; notably that of the Phoenician Astarte, and of Aphrodite and Dionysus (see Livy, xxxix.8, for an account of the Dionysia at one time in Rome; and Athen., xiii pp.574,579, and xiv. p.659, for the Aphrodisia at Athens and Corinth); cf. Numbers 25, etc., 'The people joined themselves unto Baal-peor,' and the allusion to it, 1 Corinthians 10:8.   On that occasion no more is intimated than promiscuous intercourse between the two sexes ...." J. Barmby, "Romans" in the *Pulpit Commentary* (Grand Rapids: Wm. B. Eerdmans Publishing Co., 1962), p.12.

[123] H.E. Dana and Julius R. Mantey, *A Manual Grammar of the Greek New Testament* (New York: MacMillan Company, 1927), p.213.

[124] The same root, *allassō*, is used, though in in verses 25 and 26 Paul employs the compound form *metallassō*.   It means to give up one thing in order to receive another.

[125] Vine, *Romans*, p.23, reminds us that "Isaiah speaks of the idolater as failing to perceive that there is 'a lie in his right hand,' Isaiah 44:20; Jeremiah calls the molten image falsehood, Jeremiah 10:14; 13:25; cp.16:19, 20; so 'their lies,' Amos 2:4."

And worshiped and served the creature rather than the Creator.   "Worship" generally denotes that part of one's duty to God which is internal.   Worship is the surrender of your will to the One you reverence.   "Service," on the other hand, generally denotes that part of one's duty to God which is external, such as sacrifices, rites, services.[126]   "Rather than" implies that they worshiped the creature only, and the Creator not at all.[127]   The progressive character of religious error is well caught by David Brown's observation on this verse.   "Professing to worship the Creator *by means of* the creature, they soon came to lose sight of the Creator *in* the creature."[128]   The kinds of "creatures" that became gods to these men have been suggested in verse 23.

> **The creature ... the Creator.** – The difference between the two is immeasurable.   The Creator is self-existent, unconditioned and unlimited in power and knowledge.   To the Creator the creature not only owes its existence, but by Him it is conditioned; from Him it received its power and its knowledge, and those limitations by reason of which it enjoys the blessing of dependence on its Creator.   To substitute the worship of the creature for that of the Creator is therefore the very height of perverseness and folly, meriting the retribution mentioned in the passage.[129]

Who is blessed forever.   Readers of Scripture often find these added doxologies, or ascriptions of praise to God, when His name is mentioned.   The idea may be that no matter how much the Gentiles may dishonor God, His glory has not been diminished or impaired.   He is still the supreme, one, true, and living God!   Men therefore owe to Him, and Him alone, their praise and adoration "forever."

Amen.   This is a Hebrew word transliterated first into Greek, then into English.   When men speak it, it is a strong affirmation, meaning "So be it!" or "So let it be!"[130]   Why does "Amen" appear so often through the Scriptures?   First, it implies that the human writer gives his solemn assent to what the Holy Spirit has just said through him.   Second, it sometimes marks the place where the congregation would respond "Amen" as the letter was read aloud in the public worship service.

1:26 – *For this reason God gave them over to degrading passions; for their women exchanged the natural function for that which is unnatural,*

---

[126] See notes on Romans 1:9 for additional comments on the word "serve."

[127] The preposition could be rendered "more than," implying that they did worship the Creator a little, but we agree with the ASV/NASB which read "rather than," which implies they worshiped the Creator not at all.

[128] Quoted by Wilson, *Romans*, p.31.

[129] Vine, *Romans*, p.23-24.

[130] "Amen" is sometimes spoken by God, and in such instances it means "It is and shall be so!"   In Isaiah 65:16 it is used to describe the character of God as one who is faithful to His word.   Likewise, in Revelation 3:14, when used of Christ, it seems to guarantee the truth of what He says.

For this reason. Because they "worshiped the creature rather than the Creator." After pausing to express his own reverence for the Creator, Paul resumes his explanation of the penalty that came upon man when God gave them up. The "impurity" spoken of in verse 24 is now specified.

God gave them over to degrading passions. Literally, "passions of dishonor" (cp. comments at verse 24).[131] These "degrading passions" include the unnatural lusts which women came to cherish for other women, and which men came to cherish for other men. "God gave them over" implies a descent from a lofty position to a lower one.

> The graded descent of the Gentiles is here worthy of note. They knew God – this is the plane from which they took their downward course. But they did not honor Him as God; they became foolish in their reasonings; their heart, failing in the perception of spiritual things, became darkened; they played the fool; lost the true notion of God; ended in worshiping and serving the creature. At this point God abandoned them; and again they began to descend – this time into moral and physical corruption. Down they went, and still down, until they touched the bottom of human degradation. How sublime the height from which they fell; how low was the depth they reached![132]

Paul is about to catalog the moral degeneracy of the ancient world. The sexual vices he speaks of, the pagan religions did not restrain, but rather promoted.

> Today, the increasing prevalence of those sexual perversions, which are regarded by the avant-garde as "interesting variants," is a dreadful mark of God's wrath upon a civilization that glories in its "post-Christian" character.[133]

For their women exchanged the natural function for that which is unnatural. Evidence of lesbianism (homosexual relations between females) is abundant in the Greek and Roman writers.[134] Be sure to let it register that the Holy Spirit here calls lesbianism "unnatural" (literally, 'against nature'). "The expressions 'women' (*thēleiai*) and 'men' (*arsenes*), literally their 'females' and their 'males' (not *gunaikes* [wives] and *andres* [husbands]), are chosen because the predominant point of view is simply that of sex."[135]

---

[131] The word translated "degrading" or "dishonor" is *atimios*. For the use of *timē* and *timios* to denote what is seemly or honorable indulgence of sexual desires, see 1 Thessalonians 4:4 and Hebrews 13:4.

[132] Lard, *Romans*, p.60.

[133] Wilson, *Romans*, p.31.

[134] Lard, *Romans*, p.60,61, gives numerous references, both ancient and modern.

[135] Meyer, *Romans*, p.66. Not all commentators are agreed that "lesbianism" is a proper explanation of the vice with which Paul here charges the women. Batey believes Paul had "prostitution" in mind. *Romans*, p.30. David Lipscomb and J.W. Shepherd, "Romans" in *A Commentary on the New Testament Epistles* (Nashville: Gospel Advocate Company, 1943), p.40, suggest, by a reference to Leviticus 18:22,23, that it was beastiality.

1:27 – *and in the same way also the men abandoned the natural function of the woman and burned in their desire toward one another, men with men committing indecent acts and receiving in their own persons the due penalty of their error.*

And in the same way also. It is because of the way this verse is introduced that we tend to think the previous verse spoke of homosexuality. Verse 27 speaks of the same sin, only between males.

The men abandoned the natural function of the woman. Just as the Holy Spirit gave God's verdict on homosexuality, that it was unnatural, so here He gives God's verdict on heterosexuality, that it is "the natural" way. The present-day effort to legalize homosexuality is not new, nor is it any more to be condoned today than before.[136]

And burned in their desire toward one another. Barnes (pages 48,49) gives a long list of cases where men of the ancient world not only practiced such debauchery, but even publicly defended it, and even made laws urging such practices. A Biblical example of this degrading perversion of the natural and proper ways of gratification of sexual desires on the part of men is seen in the case of the men of Sodom (Genesis 19:4-8).

Men with men committing indecent acts. Literally, "males on males performed *the*[137] unseemliness." Meyer uses the term *paederastia* (sodomy with a boy) to describe what Paul here speaks of. "And vice did not stop with the crude and unnatural vices. Society from top to bottom was riddled with unnatural vice. Fourteen out of the first fifteen Roman Emperors were homosexuals."[138]

And receiving in their own persons the due penalty of their error. The margin reads "upon themselves," and suggests that the appropriate temporal penalty for their sin (see notes on verse 24 for the judicial aspect of "God gave them over") was experienced. The NEB reads, "the fitting wage of such perversion."[139] Some think the "due penalty" refers to some disease or debilitating physical problem often found to result from such deviant

---

[136] Men and women who find themselves submerged in this vice are not just to be condemned and avoided. Rather, as Romans will go on to show, such individuals need the salvation offered in the gospel to help them out of their life of sin. Places of service in the church surely are not to be offered to practicing homosexuals, though they indeed may be to individuals whose slavery to sin has been broken, whose sins are forgiven, and who demonstrate they have risen to walk in newness of life.

[137] The article "the" is present in the Greek. It is likely an article of previous reference (pointing back to verse 26) and suggests "the well-known unseemliness."

[138] Barclay, *Romans*, p.25.

[139] Bruce, *Romans*, p.85, suggests that "error" is too weak a word in modern English to translate *planē* in a context like this. Both Bruce and the translators of the NEB have interpreted the *planē* to be the homosexuality, rather than the earlier turning from God to idols. If they are correct, then "perversion" would be the better English word. Bruce appeals to Jude 11, "where the 'error (*planē*) of Balaam' is the idolatry and fornication of Baal-Peor into which the Israelites were seduced by his counsel (Numbers 25:1ff; 31:16)."

behavior.[140]   Others think that because the next verse contains that fearsome expression, "God gave them over," that a further penalty from Him (beyond the "giving up" of verses 24 and 26) is the "due penalty" of which this verse speaks.

1:28 – *And just as they did not see fit to acknowledge God any longer, God gave them over to a depraved mind, to do those things which are not proper,*

And just as they did not see fit to acknowledge God any longer.   "Just as" is "not equivalent to 'because,' but means rather 'just in like proportion as.'   The degree of God's punishment corresponded exactly to the degree of man's deflection from God."[141]   Earlier in chapter 1, Paul introduced the subject of mankind's deliberately rejecting God's revelation of Himself.   Now the effects to mankind of this deliberate refusal are further developed.   "Did not see fit" suggests the idea of a self-willed choice after deliberate consideration of the matter.[142]   "Acknowledge God," as the marginal note shows, literally is "to have God in knowledge."   The word for knowledge (*epignōsis*) means an exact, advanced, thorough knowledge.   The original knowledge of God, derived from revelation and nature, was a correct knowledge.   But men refused to cultivate this knowledge so that it would grow and increase; as a result, God "gave them over to a depraved mind," and shortly they became "the Gentiles who do not know God" (1 Thessalonians 4:5).

God gave them over to a depraved mind.   There is a play on words in the original that is difficult to reproduce in English.   "Just as they didn't see fit to keep God in their minds, so God gave them up to a mind that wouldn't 'see fit' (i.e., would not function as a mind should)."   *Adokimos* ("depraved"), the adjective form of the word in the previous clause translated "did not see fit" (*adokimazō*), is not an easy word to translate.   The ASV used "reprobate," a word that means "unprincipled, morally abandoned."   Both "depraved" and "perverted" have a connotation in English of sexual error, but the following verses list sins other than sexual ones, so these English words are not quite right to use to render the Greek. When God gave them over, their minds no longer were able "to see fit," i.e., to examine and judge and scrutinize.   Their minds were "void of judgment."   (Verse 32 will indicate that these men still have an awareness of God's requirements, but their minds no longer controlled the men in a behavior pattern in harmony with His requirements.)   There seem to be three levels of descent in verses 24 to 28.   First God gave them over to "impurity"; then He gave them over to "degrading passions"; and thirdly, He gave them over to a "depraved mind."

---

[140] Some believe a recent such "due penalty" could be AIDS (Acquired Immuno-Deficiency Syndrome), which has come to plague the gay community.   See "Being Gay is a Real Hazard," in *The Saturday Evening Post*, October 1982, p.26ff.

[141] W. Sanday, *The Epistle to the Romans*, in the "Laymen's Handy Commentary" Series, edited by Charles John Ellicott (Grand Rapids: Zondervan Publishing House, 1957), p.31.

[142] The verb *dokimazō* can mean to put to the test, to assay (as with metals), to discern, to examine.   It can also mean "to approve after testing."   (See Arndt-Gingrich, *Lexicon,* p.201, and Thayer, *Lexicon*, p.154).   Thus, the translation of the NASB, "they did not see fit," takes this second meaning of *dokimazō*, and we are told that it was not that they *could not* keep God in their knowledge, but rather that they deliberately *chose* not to.

To do those things which are not proper.   The sins are specified in the following verses. Such influences as might restrain men from such sins have been withdrawn.   The word translated "proper" (*kathēkon*) speaks of what is fitting conduct or what is a duty when one is aware of his responsibility toward his Creator.

1:29 – *being filled with all unrighteousness, wickedness, greed, evil; full of envy, murder, strife, deceit, malice;* **they are** *gossips,*

Being filled with all unrighteousness.   The evil men were already filled with unrighteousness at the time God gave them over (verse 28).[143]   "Unrighteousness" has already been treated at verse 18, where we were told that God directs His wrath against all "unrighteousness."   The NASB outlines the following list of vices into three groups – one group of four introduced by "being filled with," a second group of five introduced by "full of," and a third group of twelve introduced by "*they are*."[144]   Similar catalogs of sins are found in Paul's other epistles, as at 2 Corinthians 12:20, Galatians 5:19-21, and 1 Timothy 1:9,10.

> Unrighteousness is the opposite of "justice."   The Greeks defined "justice" as *giving to God and to men their due*.   The "unrighteous" man is the man who robs both man and God of their rights.   He has so erected an altar to himself in the center of things that he worships himself to the exclusion of God and man.[145]

God's "wrath" (the appropriate punishment for sin) is expressed in the loss of community, when each individual lives only for his own benefit and has no concern for others.   Note that the following sins are sins against 'the neighbor,' resulting when men turn on one another and exploit one another.

Wickedness.[146]   *Ponēria* denotes "delighting to injure others, doing evil to others, dangerous, destructive."[147]

---

[143] "Being filled" is a perfect participle in the Greek.   A perfect tense participle indicates a state simultaneous with the main verb ("God gave them up," in this case), but which has resulted from an action prior to the action of the main verb.   See J. Gresham Machen, *New Testament Greek for Beginners* (New York: Macmillan Company, 1923), p.187,188.

[144] Barnes, *Romans*, p.50, suggests that "unrighteousness" is a general word, and "the particular specifications of the inquiry follow."   Hendriksen, Cranfield, Murray, and A.T. Robertson (*Word Pictures in the New Testament* [Nashville: Broadman Press, 1931], Vol.4, p.332) all opt for the same division or classification found in the NASB.

[145] William Barclay, *The Letter to the Romans* in the Daily Study Bible Series (Philadelphia: Westminster Press, 1957), p.26.

[146] In the KJV, the second word in Paul's list is "fornication."   However, the Greek text behind the ASV and NASB does not have this word in it.   Sexual sins have already been dealt with in a previous verse and we would not expect this "specific" sin to be included in this general listing.

[147] George Ricker Berry, "New Testament Synonyms" in *A New Greek-English Lexicon to the New*

The Greeks defined *ponēra* as *the desire of doing harm.* When the Greeks described a woman as *ponēra*, they meant that she deliberately seduced the innocent from their innocence. In Greek one of the commonest titles for Satan is *ho ponēros, the evil one,* the one who deliberately assaults, attacks, and aims to destroy the innocence and goodness of men. *Ponēros* describes the man who is not only bad, but who wants to make everyone as bad as himself, the man who wishes to drag others down to his own level. It is destructive badness.[148]

Greed. *Pleonexia* is a "desire for more." This desire often leads a man to use unlawful and violent means to obtain the object desired. If it operates in the material sphere, it means grasping at money or things, whether or not it costs the greedy man his honor and honesty. If it operates in the ethical sphere, it means the ambition which tramples on others to gain something one does not have.

Evil. *Kakia* describes "vice, wickedness, ill-will, malignity."[149] "*Kakia* is the most general Greek word for badness. It describes the case of a man who is destitute of every quality which would make him good ... It has been described as the forerunner of all other sins. It is the degeneracy out of which all sins grow and in which all sins flourish."[150] As was noted above in comments on the perfect participle "being filled," these first four terms characterize a man's mental and moral state before and after the third time God gives him up. They speak of attitudes held after "impurity" and "degrading passions" have become a way of life.

Full of envy. Once a man's thinking is 'unrighteous, wicked, greedy, and evil,' he will demonstrate what is in his heart by some of the following actions. "Envy" is a neutral term – one can be jealous for what is right, or jealous for what is evil – so the context must determine. Here it is something evil. It is discontent with the knowledge or sight of another person's possessions or success or advantage. It "... is essentially a grudging thing. It looks at a fine person, and is not so much moved to aspire to that fineness, as to resent that the other person is fine. It is the most warped and twisted of human emotions."[151]

Murder. This is the unlawful killing of a human being with malice and aforethought, often called premeditated killing. Assassinations, execution of slaves, the deaths of the gladiators in the amphitheaters, the exposure of unwanted children, were well-known examples of such killings.

Testament (Chicago: Wilcox & Follett Co., 1948), p.126. Berry informs us that another word translated "evil" (*kakos*) means evil in itself. *Ponēros* is a more active word. A *kakos* man is content to be evil by himself. A *ponēros* man wants to get others to be evil, too!

[148] Barclay, *Romans*, p.27.

[149] Arndt-Gingrich, *Lexicon*, p.397. Compare notes in footnote #147.

[150] Vine, *Romans*, p.27,28.

[151] Vine, *Romans*, p.28.

Strife. "Strife is angry contention, hostile struggling, fighting, conflict, the disposition to be quarrelsome and contentious."[152]   Strife is born of envy and ambition and the desire for prestige.

Deceit.   The word is akin to lying.   The word sometimes was used for the "bait" like that employed to trick fish into biting.   It is the practice of misleading another into believing what is false.   It is an action done with an ulterior motive; it is the use of devious and underhanded methods in order to get one's own way.

Malice.   The state of mind which leads its possessor to misinterpret the words and actions of others, putting the worst construction on the other person's conduct, ascribing to even the best deed the worst of motives.   The possessor's own motives are often evil; he cannot but think that other people are motivated in the same way.[153]

***They are* gossips.**   The evil here described is that of secretly conveying information, in a sly manner via hints and innuendoes, that is detrimental to the name and character and welfare of others.   *Psithuristēs* is almost onomatopoetic as it means "whisper" (compare the interjection "psst!" used to attract the attention of one with whom you wish to secretly communicate).   The "gossip" will often enjoin the listener not to mention the matter just shared with another soul.

1:30 – *slanderers, haters of God, insolent, arrogant, boastful, inventors of evil, disobedient to parents,*

Slanderers.   The word *katalalos* literally means "to speak down," or "to speak evil of another."   This evil differs from the preceding word in that the slanderer does not whisper the accusations in the ear; this word means he quite openly makes his accusations.

Haters of God.   Note the margin, "hated by God."   There is a question whether this word is to be taken as active (they hate God) or passive (God hates them).   Since the context is speaking of "sins" these Gentiles commit, it seems the active sense is better.[154]   "This word describes the man who hates God because he knows that he is defying God.   [To him], God is a barrier between him and his pleasure ... He would gladly eliminate God if he could ..."[155] and then there would be no barrier to any behavior he might wish to pursue.

Insolent.   A "bully" behaves with insulting and humiliating arrogance toward those who are not powerful enough to retaliate.   "Persons are insolent when in their haughtiness they

---

[152] Lipscomb and Shepherd, *Romans*, p.43.

[153] Trench, *Synonyms*, p.40.   Observe that the Greek word *kakoētheia* here translated "malice" is a different word than appeared earlier in this same verse, also translated "malice" in original edition of the NASB, and "evil" in the updated version.

[154] Meyer, *Romans*, p.69, argues for the passive sense.

[155] Vine, *Romans*, p.29,30.

look down upon others with contempt, and so treat them and speak to them as to mortify them and wound their feelings."[156]   It is not so much that they hurt for the sake of revenge, but simply because they get pleasure from hurting others.

Arrogant.   "Proud" is the word used in many English translations.[157]   It is an inordinate self-esteem, an unreasonable conceit about the superiority of one's talents or beauty or wealth or accomplishments.   It is a contempt for everyone else except one's self.

Boastful.   In present-day terms, this is the "con man" ("con" is short for confidence).   It is almost synonymous with swindler.   Think of the wandering quack doctor who sold his "snake-oil" cures, promising they would cure scores of ailments.   Think of the "pigeon drops," where unsuspecting people are conned out of their life's savings.   Think of the fraudulent land sale schemes, and the appeals for charities that do not exist.   Think of the cheap products that are sold at prices only quality goods should command.

Inventors of evil.   That is, they invent new ways to do evil.   A new invention comes along, and inspired by the powers of darkness, they devise a way to use that new invention for their own selfish ends.   For example, when the computer was invented, it wasn't long till some "hackers" were using it to commit crimes against banks and corporations.   Or an old scheme has been declared illegal by government statute, so the inventor of evil devises a new scheme that is just outside the law, and he continues to pamper his own appetites at the expense of others.

Disobedient to parents.   At first sight, to see this common attitude included in this list of sins is surprising.   Looked at from a human standpoint, it seems incongruous.   But men seldom see things as God sees them, especially if they have gone away from God as these Gentiles had.   When children do not show their parents honor and respect, when they do not listen to their parents ("disobey" is *apeithēs*, a "stubborn refusal to be persuaded"), when they do not provide for their parents in their old age, a society is in real trouble. Perhaps no other sin included in this list indicates more clearly the great depth to which the Gentiles had sunk, and how completely their humanity had been wrecked, all because they refused to honor God and give Him thanks.

1:31 – *without understanding, untrustworthy, unloving, unmerciful;*

Without understanding.   TEV translates it, "They are immoral."   What they do and leave undone is not determined by their *sunesis* (the faculty of intelligence, insight, critical discernment).[158]   The word does at times have a religious and ethical significance, and this

---

[156] Lard, *Romans*, p.65.

[157] "Proud" is the word that is used three times in Scripture when it is said that "God resists the proud" (James 4:6; 1 Peter 5:5; Proverbs 3:34).

[158] The word translated "without understanding" is *asunetos*, which is made up of an alpha privative [which negates what the rest of the word says] and *sunetos*. Thayer, *Lexicon*, p.582, explains the difference between *sunesis* and *phronesis* as being applications of wisdom [*sophia*] to details: *sunesis* is

is the idea the TEV translators have tried to express.

Untrustworthy.   "They do not keep their promises" is the way the TEV reads, while the ASV reads "covenant breakers."   Men make contracts and bargains; then if it benefits their self-interests, they unscrupulously ignore the promises they made.   The word also tends to shade off into the areas we label as graft and corruption.   Men are entrusted with certain responsibilities of public trust; when they think no one is looking, they subvert to their own use what really belongs to another.

Unloving.   Of the several Greek words for love, *storge* is the one reserved for family affection, that special relationship between members of the same family.   Child abuse and spouse abuse are the direct result of the lack of such love, as is the abandonment of a wife and children by the husband.   Most commentaries also point out the practice of exposure of unwanted children by their parents as being an example of such an "unloving" attitude.[159]

Unmerciful.[160]   One who is unmerciful shows no pity toward others, even though they are poor, crippled, handicapped, or helpless.   Human life is considered cheap, and those who are unfortunate, or are "too old to contribute to society" are shown no pity or care.   That Gentiles are "unmerciful" can be seen from the fact that only where the gospel (that power of salvation that these Gentiles so desperately needed) has gone, are the hearts of men open to appeals for sufferers of hunger, plague, epidemics, and natural calamities.

1:32 – *and, although they know the ordinance of God, that those who practice such things are worthy of death, they not only do the same, but also give hearty approval to those who practice them.*

And, although they know the ordinance of God.   In this verse, the main point of the whole argument which began at verse 19 is repeated, namely, that the Gentiles were sinning in spite of better knowledge.   In fact, Paul uses the word for "full knowledge" (*epignōskō*). An "ordinance" (*dikaiōma*) "is that which God as Lawgiver and Judge has ordained; what He has determined, and demands, as right."[161]   How did the Gentiles know about the de-

---

critical, apprehending the bearing of things, while *phronesis* is practical, suggesting lines of action.

[159] As this word is pondered, and applications and illustrations of it are sought, one wonders if the attitude of 70% of a group of parents recently questioned, who said if they had it to do over again, they would not have any children, is not an example of "unloving."   And if exposure of infants after birth because they were unwanted was "unloving," could not abortion also be classified as an example of "unloving" before birth?

[160] "Implacable," which is the next word in the KJV, does not appear in the older manuscripts which are behind the Greek text translated by the ASV/NASB.

[161] Meyer, *Romans*, p.71.   The KJV uses the word "judgment" to translate *dikaiōma*, whereas the ASV/NASB uses "ordinance," so the reader will not think the final judgment is the thing talked about.   The word *dikaiōma* is used with different connotations in Romans.   Sometimes it speaks of a declaration that a thing is "right" – as in Romans 8:4 – hence, an "ordinance." (Cp. Luke 1:6; Romans 2:26; Hebrews 9:1,10.)   Other times it speaks of a declaration that a person is "righteous" – as in Romans 5:16 – a verdict, a judgment, given by a judge, of not guilty, a verdict of acquittal.   (The KJV sometimes uses the word

cree God had given? At creation, in the Garden of Eden, God spoke to man face to face. After the expulsion from the garden, there were revelations given by God from time to time, and there was oral tradition by which this information was passed along to the race. If men were to know the ordinance of God, God would, of course, have had to reveal His will to men, for "no one knows the thoughts of God except the Spirit of God."[162] The New Testament is full of references to things that were revealed to men in Old Testament times, but about which there is no specific word recorded in the Old Testament.[163] Likewise, the "ordinance of God," here spoken of as being common knowledge among the Gentiles, implies just such an original revelation from God Himself. Romans 1 has therefore spoken of two kinds of revelation available to the Gentiles – the one that comes from observing the things made, and the one that is a special revelation made to man by God Himself. And Romans 1 also shows how men deliberately rejected and ignored both to their own detriment.

That those who practice such things are worthy of death. This phrase expresses part of the content of the ordinance of God that the Gentiles knew perfectly well. Not only did the Gentiles know the ordinances, they knew the penalties threatened to those who did not keep the ordinances. "Practice" (the Greek verb *prassō*, as distinguished from *poieō*, "to do") expresses not the occasional sin, but the habitual practice of life. The "death" threatened may be spiritual death, physical death, or ultimately eternal death (punishment) – and whichever is intended (and all could be), the Gentiles understood that it was a divine penalty for their life of sin.

"righteousness" to translate *dikaiōma*, and the English reader has no way of knowing the Greek word is not *dikaiosunē*, which is also rendered "righteousness," a fact that hinders doing a careful word study based solely on the English translation.)

[162] 1 Corinthians 2:11.

[163] Several examples of such things that God revealed, but about which there is no specific word recorded in the Old Testament, are these: (i) Abel. "By faith Abel offered a more acceptable sacrifice" (Hebrews 11:4, ASV). Now "faith" is doing what God says. That such sacrifice was an act revealed to Abel, Cain, and others, is implied. Yet the Old Testament record has no mention of this revelation about sacrifice. (ii) Abraham, we would affirm, was a man of faith before he was called from Ur of the Chaldees. That implies a revelation of what God expected of him, and no such revelation is actually recorded in the Old Testament. (iii) Melchizedek was a contemporary of Abraham. He knew enough to be a priest of the Most High God (Hebrews 7:1-3). That implies a revelation about priesthood and the functions of a priest, yet the Old Testament contains no such record. In the light of these examples (and more could be given), we affirm that when the New Testament says that the Gentiles knew the "ordinance" of God, it means more than simply what they could learn by observing the things He created. It speaks of revelations made to them (or to their parents and handed down by oral tradition) by God by word of mouth.

That the same kind of information about God and His 'ordinances' was available to Gentiles down through the ages can be seen by an appeal to the 'wisemen' who came to Bethlehem shortly after Jesus' birth to worship Him. They knew about the coming Messiah (ever since Genesis 3:15), and they knew who God was when He spoke to them in a dream. That implies a knowledge that would result from a revelation, rather than simply knowledge learned by observing the creation.

One additional evidence can be adduced about the knowledge the Gentiles have. Missionaries to lands where the gospel has never been testify that one of the things that gives them a point of contact is that the natives are aware there is a God, and that their sins have offended Him. In years gone by, someone has kept alive in these distant cultures the knowledge of God and His ordinances, though in many cases the knowledge is greatly defective, just as we would expect it to be after centuries of living in a 'given over' ("God gave them over") condition.

They not only do the same, but also give hearty approval to those who practice them. Here is the aggravation of their sin against better knowledge. Here is a man who knows the fatal consequences of his actions, yet goes ahead and sins.[164] But not only that, he is absolutely callous to the moral ruin of others. He does not raise his voice in protest or indignation or warning. So what if they are lost too? Nothing so encourages a man to sin as to show him we think the better of him for it.

Indeed, the man who has been 'given over to a depraved mind' (verse 28) is in sorry shape, and is in desperate need of the salvation offered in the gospel![165]

---

[164] Here we have the present tense of *poieō*, which expresses a series of repeated acts.

[165] Several lines of thought need to be pursued as a result of this study about the condition of the Gentiles.

a) These terrifying conditions are general the world over; they are not just the picture of 1st century Rome. Consult M'ilvane, *Christian Evidences*, pages 362-404.

b) This whole section is a strong polemic against the theory of evolution. The picture here is of devolution (going down) rather than evolution (rising higher). It teaches creation, rather than the eternality, of matter. It teaches that monotheism came first, and polytheism came later. "Human history is not the story of a beast that worshiped idols, and then evolved into a man worshiping one God. Human history is just the opposite." Wiersbe, *Be Right*, p.22.

c) It should be seen, too, that a man's worship has a bearing on his character. Worship of idols is basically degrading, whereas worship of the living God is uplifting. Idolatry and licentiousness go together, for through idolatry, men can get religious sanction for the sins they want to commit. Worship of the living God, on the other hand, carries with it a moral persuasion toward righteousness.

d) This chapter has a certain bearing on the doctrine of total depravity. The people who commit these sins are regarded as still knowing what is right and wrong, and what is the penalty for the wrong. They can distinguish between right and wrong. They are not totally bad.

e) "The Transforming Power of the Gospel," by J.V. Coombs is a good chapter in *The Indiana Pulpit*, edited by W.H. Book (Cincinnati: Standard Publishing Co., 1912). All the fruitage of sin, all the degrading consequences of being 'given over' by God, are remedied and rectified, just as Romans will go on to demonstrate.

Special Study #1

"CALL" AND "GRACE"
IN THE BIBLE AND IN THEOLOGY

In harmony with one of the stated purposes of this commentary on Romans, it is necessary to enter into a rather detailed study of two often used Biblical words. Commentaries written from certain theological viewpoints, whether the viewpoint be Roman Catholic, Reformed, Arminian, Neo-orthodox, Evangelical, or Conservative, will regularly use terminology intended to sustain and propagate the particular viewpoint, even when it has to be read into the verse(s) being commented upon. Certain key Biblical words are especially susceptible to such treatment. Two such words have already been used in Romans, "call" and "grace." It therefore seems appropriate at this point to help the reader not only to understand what certain theological language he encounters in the average commentary means, but also to help the reader begin to assemble Biblical verses that should be included in his own viewpoint, so that it matches, as closely as is humanly possible, what God has revealed in His Word, rather than what some theologian has said.

Reformed, or Calvinistic, theology has had an extensive influence in Europe and America for several hundred years, and in evangelical circles enjoyed a revival of influence in the last half of the 20th century. When one considers that Neo-orthodoxy also is related to, and is a descendant of Reformed theology, it can easily be understood why, it seems, a majority of books recently published reflect Reformed thinking. It may seem that comments in this Special Study (as well as in the commentary on Romans as a whole) are unnecessarily anti-Calvinistic. However, just as early in the Restoration Movement the teachers and preachers had to attempt to provide a balance against Reformed theology, so it falls to their heirs a century later to attempt to provide the balance again.

I. CALL, CALLING, CALLED

When it is remembered that John Calvin "found" some of his special emphases while studying Romans and 1 Corinthians (and then read them into the other books of the New Testament), it is to be expected that a study of these books will also involve an interaction with some of his peculiar conclusions. It also should be remembered that for Calvin, God's absolute sovereignty was the beginning point of all other doctrines, and no other doctrine dared impinge on that sovereignty. Thus God's "call" is such that it will be answered and that it will be effective (at least for the "elect" as he viewed some men to be from all eternity). After all, when God speaks, "It is so!" (Genesis 1:3; Isaiah 55:10-11;

Hebrews 11:3). So, a rather a common expression used to explain "call" in the commentaries is the language "effectually called." In turn, this implies that some men get a different kind of call from God, one that is not effective. There is no response to the call, and therefore (in Reformed thinking) the call was not accompanied by that working of the Holy Spirit that regularly accompanies the call extended to the elect, and to which, of course, there is a response. The elect respond because their call was effectual; that is, it was accompanied by that working of the Spirit which guarantees a proper response.

With this overview in mind, it now seems proper to look at the Biblical doctrine of "calling" – both the calling to become a Christian, and the calling to become a "minister." Both of these topics were introduced in Romans 1 – the call to be a Christian is suggested in Romans 1:6 ("called by Jesus Christ") and in Romans 1:7 ("called to be saints," KJV); and the call to the ministry being suggested in Romans 1:1 ("called to be an apostle," KJV).

In the Old and New Testaments together, the words "call" or "calling" (in their noun, verb, and adjective forms) are used some 700 times. The Hebrew word regularly so translated is *qara*, and the Greek word is *kaleō*. Five main ideas may be conveyed by either of these words. (1) "To call" means 'to summon or invite.' (2) The verb can have the sense of "calling on God," i.e., to summon His help or protection. (3) "To call" can be the equivalent of "to name," e.g., God called the light day, and the darkness night, or where the angel instructed, "You shall call His name Jesus!" (4) "To call" can express the idea "to designate" (or "to salute someone else by name"), as in the prohibition "Do not call anyone on earth your father ...." (5) "Calling" may be synonymous with "vocation" as in 1 Corinthians 7:20 (KJV), "Let each man remain in that calling (vocation) in which he was called (invited by the gospel to be a Christian)."[1]

A. Call to the Ministry

Many of God's leaders received their call to service directly from God in a dramatic way. Think of God speaking to Moses in a burning bush. Think of how God arrested Paul during his trip to Damascus. Because of this, there are those who believe no man should enter God's service (in a specialized ministry) unless he has received a divine summons as miraculous and dramatic as Moses' or Paul's. Some commentaries on Romans 1:1 speak of Paul's call to be an apostle as being an "effectual call."[2] What is implied is that the invitation or summons to Paul given by Jesus was accompanied by the enabling work of the Holy Spirit, whereas the call to, for example, Judas Iscariot was not

---

[1] See J.H. Thayer, *A Greek-English Lexicon of the New Testament* (New York: American Book Company, 1889), p.323 [*kaleō*] and p. 349,350 [*klēsis*, and *klētos*]. See also E.M. Blaiklock, "Call, Calling," in *The New International Standard Bible Encyclopedia*, edited by G.W. Bromiley (Grand Rapids: Wm. B. Eerdmans Publishing Co., 1979), Vol.1, p.580,581.

[2] William Hendriksen, *New Testament Commentary: Romans* (Grand Rapids: Baker Book House, 1981), p.40.

– thus explaining how one actually became an apostle, and the other did not. It is rather assumed that whether or not one became an apostle rested wholly on God's action, and that man's response or failure to respond has no bearing on the ultimate result of the "call."

The matter of man's response (or co-operation with God's call) will be examined subsequently. The matter of a dramatic call being necessary needs some attention at this place. Not all of God's leaders are summoned by a dramatic call by God Himself; for example, there are Biblical examples of the "call" being extended by another man. Consider the calling of Timothy (Acts 161-3). When Paul was looking for an assistant, he chose Timothy, and the passage indicates Paul made this choice partly because of Timothy's good character (the result of Bible training received from his mother and grandmother, 2 Timothy 1:5; 3:15). In his turn, Timothy was instructed to seek out "faithful men" to whom he could entrust the gospel, who would then teach others (2 Timothy 2:2). Even though a prophecy (1 Timothy 4:14) had been made about Timothy's being a minister-evangelist, and some might be inclined therefore to affirm even his call was dramatic and spectacular, it would be difficult to show that all the "faithful men" Timothy was instructed to send into the ministry experienced a similar prophecy about their future.

We would summarize the "call to ministry" topic by saying it may be spectacular (some in the Bible were), or it may be ordinary (some in the Bible were), given by one who already is a special servant of God.[3] Further, there is precious little in Scripture to substantiate the view that the dramatic calls (assuming God still so calls some to service) are of two kinds, with only one of the two being "effectual." Rather, we read of men who (like Demas, 2 Timothy 4:10) quit the ministry of their own choice.

B. Call to be a Christian

A call to salvation and a call to become a Christian are synonymous terms. Many men are called, but not all respond to the call ("many are called, but few are chosen," Jesus said, Matthew 22:14). How shall this failure to respond be explained?

Reformed theology postulates several kinds of "call" to explain why some respond and others do not. (1) There is *vocatio realis*, the "general call."

> God calls every normal human being. He does this through the *vocatio realis*
> – *realis* because this general call comes not through words but through *res*
> (things), namely, nature, history (of individuals and nations), and conscience.
> (Cf. Romans 1:20, 2:14,15; Job 34:24, 38:1-42:6; Psalms 8:2,4, 19:1-4, 46:11;
> 104.) However great and important the influence of this *vocatio realis* is, no

---

[3] Practical application of this bit of information would lead the present generation of church leaders to be on the lookout for promising potential leaders, and to be regular in extending to them words of exhortation and invitation into the ministry. Without such constant attention to recruitment, leadership in the church will be greatly diminished from what it could be.

one can ever come to a saving knowledge of the triune God through this general, external call. Through the *vocatio realis* man is rendered without excuse (Romans 1:20) if he does not worship and obey Him Whose majesty, eternal power, and divinity speak to all through his mighty works in nature, in history, and in human life and conscience. But the *vocatio realis* does not proclaim the good tidings of great joy (Luke 2:10) for all who believe in Jesus Christ as the Son of God and as the divine Savior.[4]

(2) A second kind of "call" is the *vocatio verbalis*, the "invitation." Geldenhuys explains,

> For the salvation of sinners there is an urgent need for much more than the *vocatio realis* can offer. And now it is the glory of the Christian faith that it unequivocally proclaims that Almighty God, who through the *vocatio realis* has called and is continually calling all to a realization of His divine majesty and omnipotence, through His Word calls sinners to repentance and to salvation. This calling to a saving faith in Jesus Christ, the Lord, through the authoritative Word of God is designated the *vocatio verbalis*. This external calling through the Gospel is to be proclaimed to all nations (Matthew 28:19, 24:14; Mark 16:15) as an earnest invitation and urgent summons that everyone should repent and believe in Him Who is the all-sufficient Saviour.[5]

(3) A third type of call is the *vocatio efficax*, the "effectual calling." Once more letting Geldenhuys present Reformed theology, we read that it takes more than simply an "invitation" to get men to respond. He writes,

> But to have practical effect in the life of men, the *vocatio verbalis* must, as it were, break through into the mind, will and heart – the innermost being – of man. For this is needed the "effectual calling," *vocatio efficax*.[6]

Or in the words of the *Westminster Shorter Catechism*,

> By "effectual call" is meant not just an invitation through the Word and the work of the Holy Spirit to become a Christian, but the language means "the work of God's Spirit, whereby, convincing us of our sin and misery, enlightening our minds in the knowledge of Christ, and renewing our wills, He doth persuade and enable us to embrace Jesus Christ ...."[7]

---

[4] J. Norval Geldenhuys, "Effectual Calling," in *Basic Christian Doctrines*, edited by Carl F.H. Henry (New York: Holt, Rinehart and Winston, 1962), p.178.

[5] Geldenhuys, *Effectual Calling*, p.179.

[6] Geldenhuys, *Effectual Calling*, p.179.

[7] Questions 29-31, quoted by J. Oliver Buswell, *A Systematic Theology of the Christian Religion* (Grand Rapids: Zondervan Publishing House, 1962), Vol.2, p.157ff. Reformed theologians justify this distinction

Briefly, that is the Reformed view of the different kinds of calls.   These key verses of Scripture are used within Reformed doctrine to justify the distinctions made.

- *Matthew 22:14*, "Many are called, but few are chosen" is explained to mean "Many are invited (*vocatio verbalis*), but few are effectually called."[8]
- *2 Timothy 1:8,9*, "... the gospel according to the power of God; who has saved us, and called us with a holy calling, not according to our works, but according to His own purpose and grace which was granted us in Christ Jesus from all eternity ...," is affirmed to teach that it is "through the sovereign and omnipotent power and grace of God that we are effectually called to become the inheritors of the salvation wrought by God through Jesus Christ."[9]
- *1 Corinthians 1:26-30* is used to show that men did not deserve to be called, so the calling must be all of God.
- *1 Corinthians 1:9*, "God is faithful, through whom you were called into fellowship with His Son, Jesus Christ our Lord," is used to show the divine act involved in the calling, even after sin had broken the fellowship between the sinner and God.
- *Ephesians 1:18*, "I pray that the eyes of your heart may be enlightened, so that you may know what is the hope of His calling ...," is used to show that through the effectual calling, God enlightens men's minds to see and accept the truth of the gospel, and changes men's defiled hearts so that they can come to him in sincere repentance.[10]
- *1 Peter 2:9,10*, "... that you may proclaim the excellencies of Him who has called you out of darkness into His marvelous light ...," is said to show that the call was so effectual it not only produces a changed life, but also produces an evangelistic fervor that spreads abroad the news of the wonderful things God does.

A summary paragraph or two should suffice in this effort to help us understand the Reformed doctrine of "call."

We cannot know how or when God calls us in such an effectual way, nor can we exactly define the connection between the *vocatio verbalis* and this *vocatio*

---

between different kinds of calls partially by appealing to the different meanings for *qara* and *kaleō*. Of the different possible connotations, the "effectual call" emphasizes the meaning of "call" which signifies "to designate" rather than "to summon."   In the action of calling men to be His children, Reformed writers are wont to ask, Is it not the case that the action of calling them implies "cause to become"? They are "designated" to be "His children" – i.e., "caused to become" His children; thus, it is evident the call produced results, the Reformed argument continues.

[8] Readers should be aware that Jesus used two different, though related, words. "Many are called (*klētoi*), but few are chosen (*eklēktoi*)." *Eklēktoi* is the regular word used for "elect" or "chosen," and it is not one of the words regularly translated "call." A logical question to ask, then, is why do Reformed theologians use a different word when they want to make "call" mean "effectual call"?

[9] Geldenhuys, *Effectual Calling*, p.180.

[10] To be clear, this passage speaks of people who are *already* Christians being enlightened, not of how one *becomes* a Christian in the first place!   Reformed theologians must do better than this to justify the idea of an "effectual call."

efficax, or the relationship between effectual calling and regeneration, but the New Testament leaves no doubt as to the fact that God is in no way, regarding the effectual calling, dependent on the merits, preparedness, or worthiness of man or of any human instrument. God "called us by his own glory and virtue" (2 Peter 1:3). The triune God himself is the sole cause of and instrument of this calling.[11]

The effectual calling of God is not an afterthought of the Almighty, but is grounded in His eternal purpose (Romans 8:28-30) ... That the effectual, irresistible calling of God, however, does not annul or abrogate the personal responsibility of believers is clearly and consistently taught by the Word of God. Thus, Paul writes to Timothy: "Fight the good fight of faith, lay hold on eternal life, whereunto thou wast called ..." (1 Timothy 6:12). And Jesus said, "Enter ye in by the narrow gate" (Matthew 7:13) ... Christians are earnestly called upon to "walk worthy of the calling wherewith ye were called" (Ephesians 4:1; cf. 2 Peter 1:10,11).[12]

Non-Reformed theology, on the other hand, makes no such distinction between an effectual call and a general call or an invitation. Instead, appeal is made to 2 Thessalonians 2:14 to show that the same call is given to all men when the gospel is preached. It reads, "And it was for this (salvation through sanctification by the Spirit and faith in the truth) He called you through our gospel, that you may gain the glory of our Lord Jesus Christ." Whether or not the call produces results depends not on the kind of call given, but upon the kind of soil (heart) the seed falls upon (Matthew 13:18-23).[13]

II. GRACE

Various religious groups have favorite verses they memorize and quote. One such verse is Ephesians 2:8, "For by grace you have been saved through faith; and that not of yourselves, it is the gift of God." The hymn books have numerous songs about the grace of God: "Saved by Grace," "Amazing Grace," "Marvelous Grace of Our Loving Lord," "Wonderful Grace of Jesus," and "Victory Through Grace." It can be a quirk of human nature that when a good thing is habitually misused, well-meaning people often avoid that good thing altogether. So it is, in the Restoration Movement, that one seldom hears sermons on the grace of God. There is the little memorized definition, "Grace is unmerited favor," but other than that, why is it that so little is said about grace? And just what is involved and implied in that little memorized definition?

---

[11] Geldenhuys, *Effectual Calling*, p.182.

[12] Geldenhuys, *Effectual Calling*, p.183.

[13] Faith comes by hearing the Word of Christ (Romans 10:17). The "seed" in the parable (Matthew 13:4) is explained later (Matthew 13:19) to be the "word of the kingdom," i.e., the gospel of Christ. The gospel Paul preached (through which God called men to salvation) and the "seed" sown in men's hearts are the same thing.

The word "grace" appears over 170 times in the English Bible. The Greek word translated "grace" is *charis*, and the LXX used this word to translate the Hebrew word *hen*, even though the Greek and Hebrew words had slightly different connotations. Actually, there are several other Hebrew words that are very close to the ideas that can be conveyed by *charis*. The Hebrew word *no'am*, often translated 'favor' or 'kindness,' is one. The word *hesed*, translated 'lovingkindness' or 'mercy' (*eleos*), is another. It is regularly affirmed that *charis* is one of those ordinary Greek words that the Bible writers adapted, pouring new content into it, and thus using it to convey a spiritual idea not ordinarily found in the word outside of New Testament and early Christian writers. In fact, Paul is the one to whom is attributed the honor of giving this special meaning to *charis*.[14]

"Grace" (both the Hebrew and the Greek words) can be either an attitude or an action. Of the several connotations found for the words, these are the ones usually delineated in the word studies: (1) At times, "grace" is an *appearance* which charms or delights another. (2) At times, "grace" is the *attitude* that leads to gracious actions. (This is the meaning being emphasized in the memorized definition, "Grace is unmerited favor.") (3) At times, "grace" is the *action* by which the favor is bestowed. (This is the meaning regularly being emphasized in the songs about grace.) (4) Finally, there is the *gratitude* felt by the receiver of the favor, that is expressed by "grace."[15]

Theologians have tried to narrow the meaning of "grace" down to just one special sense, and this has proven to be problematic. The essential cause of the trouble is the attempt to define the exact relationship between the divine action and the human response in the work of redemption of individual souls. Is the redemption all of God, is it all by man's actions, or is it the result of a combination of both God's "grace" and man's response?

A. "Grace" in Roman Catholic Theology

Before we can understand Roman Catholic thinking in regard to what "grace" is supposed to be and what grace is supposed to do for a man, we must first consider what Catholic doctrine affirms happened to man at the Fall. That is, according to Catholic doctrine, what was it that man lost at the Fall? Grace can then be explained as the restoration of what was lost.

> The Roman Catholic concept of Grace is based on the conviction that salva-
> tion is nothing less than the divinization of the soul, the enjoyment throughout

---

[14] See this affirmed in L.B. Smedes article on "Grace" in the *New International Standard Bible Encyclopedia*, Vol.2, p.548; and in H.D. McDonald's article on "Grace" in *Zondervan Pictorial Encyclopedia of the Bible*, edited by Merrill C. Tenney (Grand Rapids: Zondervan Publishing House, 1975), Vol.2, p.801. What is usually affirmed is that the Hebrew word *hen* had no special implication of "redemptive grace" like the word does when Paul is finished with it, and the Greek word *eleos* (pity, favor) in the New Testament denoted God's relation to human misery rather than to human sin.

[15] Wm. F. Arndt and F.W. Gingrich, *A Greek-English Lexicon of the New Testament* (Chicago: University of Chicago Press, 1956), p.885,856, and Thayer, *Lexicon*, p.665,666.

eternity of the beatitude God himself enjoys. To achieve this end, it is
necessary that the soul be elevated to a higher order of being. An infusion of
supernatural powers and virtues is required, the exercise of which will merit
for man the splendor of the final beatific vision; sanctifying grace is that
elevating, supernatural power. Adam and Eve possessed it before the Fall
but lost it with that aboriginal calamity, although they did not lose their natural
powers of reason and will (see Sin, Original). Redemption is the restoration
of that supernatural power and the virtues it infuses, and is made possible by
the satisfaction made to God's justice by Jesus Christ and the participation of
the believer in his mystical body the church, through which the lost
sanctifying grace is once more given.[16]

Roman Catholics make a distinction between the natural powers which were not lost at the
Fall, and the supernatural powers and virtues which were. Roman Catholics also believe
that "sanctifying grace" is something God does to the man, as He *infuses* into his soul these
lost powers. It can also be implied from the expression "*sanctifying* grace" that there are
other kinds of grace in the Roman Catholic scheme of things.

Over the centuries, Roman Catholic theologians have created a host of fine
theological distinctions to deal with the questions and issues that naturally
arose concerning this scheme.[17] Is the first movement of the will toward faith
an effect of grace or simply a free, autonomous human act? If it is an effect
of grace, then are those that are not so prompted by grace abandoned
intentionally by God? If they are abandoned, in what sense are they
responsible for not being saved? Actual grace and sanctifying grace,
prevenient grace and subsequent grace, sufficient grace and efficacious grace
– these and numerous other concepts, which many Protestant theologians
seem unaware of, enabled the Roman Catholic to order and defend his beliefs
with great subtlety.[18]

---

[16] Van A. Harvey, *A Handbook of Theological Terms* (New York: Macmillan Co., 1964), p.108,109.
The reader will note that this paragraph is full of expressions that have a particular connotation in Catholic
theology: infusion, merit, beatific vision, satisfaction, justice.

[17] Some background information will help us understand what Harvey is writing here. Theologians tend
to take some currently popular emphasis and try to make the Bible fit it. In the age of the Apologists an
emphasis on freedom of the will led to reduced emphasis on the role of grace. Augustine, during his
debate with Pelagius, changed his doctrine from belief in the freedom of man to choose to accept or reject
the offer of divine grace, to a position where man's freedom was a culpable ability to choose only that which
is evil. Then the introduction of Aristotelian metaphysics and psychology in the 13th century led to a
comprehensive rethinking of the doctrine of grace. After the Reformation and the introduction of non-
Catholic ideas about grace, the Council of Trent set forth the position held in the Roman church until Vatican
II.

[18] In Roman Catholic theology, the following definitions seem to hold true: *Actual* grace is a passing
or temporary help or power given by God to enable the soul to perform some particular act. It is usually
contrasted with sanctifying or habitual grace. *Co-operating* grace is that by which God concurs or
cooperates with a man already converted, in order to strengthen him in faith. *Efficacious* grace is that
grace that is inevitably followed by the effect for which it is intended. This is one form of actual grace, and

These distinctions, however, all rest on the view that grace is a supernatural power that, without destroying the freedom of the will, infuses the supernatural virtues of faith, hope, and charity into the soul, virtues that are rewarded with the final vision for which life is destined. It follows also that grace may be given and received in degrees, and that the successful use of what one has merits an increase in grace.[19]

The key idea in Roman Catholic theology is that grace is an infusion into the soul of certain supernatural powers and virtues. One might almost affirm that "grace" has been narrowed to one special sense, an *act*.

B. Grace in Lutheran Theology

Grace in Luther's theology is primarily "favor," an *attitude* on the part of God toward sinners, primarily the forgiveness of sins. Luther only gradually realized that his doctrine of justification as being something God "imputed" to man (rather than being something "infused" into man as Rome taught) was irreconcilable to the basic Roman doctrine. In order to understand Luther's doctrine, it will be necessary to consider several other topics, including what happened to the race as a result of Adam's sin. Harvey's summary of Luther's doctrine shows these topics:

> Protestant theologians commonly say that the difference between Luther and Rome was that grace, for the latter, was an impersonal substance or medicine while, for the former, it was the attribute of God, his graciousness. This is somewhat misleading. It would be better to say that grace, for Luther, is what God is. It is God resolving to be for man, to be present to him despite his rebelliousness. Grace is not [just] a divine attitude that could be easily replaced by another, like wrath. It is, rather, God acting out of his deepest being.[20]

There was considerable difference between Luther and Rome when it came to the result of the Fall. Here we must become acquainted with the "image of God" (*imago Dei*,

---

is usually contrasted with sufficient grace. *Irresistible* grace is that grace that cannot be resisted by the will of man. *Prevenient* grace is that supernatural power that quickens and assists the will to have faith. *Sanctifying* or *habitual* grace is a supernatural but permanent quality infused into the soul that imparts to the soul the power of performing actions that are supernatural in character. The three infused powers, or virtues, or habits, are faith, hope, and love. *Sufficient* grace is a form of actual grace, which, though sufficient to do what it is intended for, is not efficacious because of the resistance of the recipient. According to some Roman Catholic teaching, all men have sufficient grace to lead them to faith. (Taken from Harvey, *Handbook of Theological Terms*, p.111,112.)

[19] Harvey, *Handbook of Theological Terms*, p.109.

[20] Harvey, *Handbook of Theological Terms*, p.110.

Latin) and the "likeness of God" (*similitudo Dei*, Latin).

> *Similitudo Dei* means the "likeness of God" and is, according to some Roman
> Catholic teaching, to be distinguished from the "Image of God," which Adam
> also possessed before the Fall.   The "likeness of God" refers to those
> supernatural graces Adam possessed and of which he was deprived when he
> sinned, while the "image of God" refers to his natural endowments of reason
> and free will that remained intact even after the Fall.   The Protestant
> Reformers rejected this distinction because they believed it was based on a
> misinterpretation of what is merely poetic parallelism in Genesis 1:26.   They
> insisted that the "image of God" designates man's original righteousness that
> was lost in the Fall.   This loss [Protestants go on to affirm] consequently
> distorts the entire being of man [total depravity].[21]

> "Image of God" (*imago Dei*) is the likeness to God in which, according to
> Genesis 1:26ff, God originally created man.   It has been suggested by some
> Old Testament scholars that these verses express a primitive belief that man's
> likeness to God consists in his bodily form and not in his possession of spirit,
> as in modern thought, because elsewhere in the Old Testament God is
> regarded not as a spirit but as one who can be seen (Numbers 12:8).   However
> that may be, since the 1st century BC, the "image of God" has been taken to
> refer to an original spiritual possession of some sort that was lost in the Fall,
> and this meaning, albeit in various forms, has persisted in the history of
> Christian thought ... The concept [of the "image of God"] has played an
> important role in Roman Catholic and Protestant discussions concerning the
> nature and extent of original sin.   Roman Catholic theology makes a
> distinction between certain supernatural gifts given to Adam in addition to his
> natural human ones and those gifts truly essential to his existence as man.
> The former are composed of the supernatural endowments of sanctifying
> grace, which gives justice [a technical term used to refer to the integrity or
> righteousness which man lost by virtue of his sin], and the preternatural gifts
> of immortality and integrity.   The preternatural gifts do not belong to man by
> nature, yet they do not, like grace, put man in the supernatural order of being.
> When Adam fell, according to Roman Catholic teaching, he lost his
> supernatural endowments (the *similitudo Dei*) and his preternatural gifts, but
> his human nature (*imago Dei*) remained intact.   To be sure, his human nature
> was "wounded," since man was left vulnerable to concupiscence (any desire
> or appetite of the lower faculties of human nature not brought under the
> dominion and control of the rational faculties), but the wound was not so deep
> as to permit one to say that man's essential powers of reason and free will (his
> "image of God") were destroyed ... Luther argued that man had lost the "image
> of God" in everything but name only, and this loss involved the loss of
> freedom of the will.[22]

---

[21] Harvey, *Handbook of Theological Terms*, p.220.

[22] Harvey, *Handbook of Theological Terms*, p.125,126.

This may seem like a long digression in our study of grace, but it seems warranted to introduce this material at this place – not only so we understand "grace," but so that we will understand comments made in later chapters of Romans, when Paul himself takes up the discussion of the Fall and its consequences.

Luther rejected the Roman Catholic distinction between the natural and supernatural endowments of man and argued, therefore, that man (in the Fall) even destroyed his free will. This conclusion led Luther in turn to an inevitable acceptance of predestination. All this has a bearing on Luther's doctrine of grace. A further comment or two from Harvey will help us to see this:

> The philosophical problem of freedom [of the will] is further complicated in theology by the ideas of God's providence, omniscience, and omnipotence, as well as the ideas of sin and grace. The idea of God's providence, especially when joined with the ideas of foreknowledge and predestination, raises acute questions concerning the independence of the will. If all human events can be foreseen [by God] ... in what sense is human decision really free? Or if, since the Fall of Adam, it is impossible for man to will [to do] the good, in what sense is [man's] choice real and significant?
>
> Augustine (AD 354-430) had ... argued that, although Adam possessed both the ability not to sin (*posse non peccare*) and the ability to sin (*posse peccare*) before his Fall, he lost the former by exercising the latter. This original freedom of man, he believed, could only be restored by an act of divine grace. This, however, raises the question whether man has the ability to accept or reject grace, and with that question the problem of freedom returns. Augustine quite consistently argued that grace is irresistible and prevenient, that is, that an act of God is itself required to enable the will to accept grace and that this grace is irresistible to those whom God wills to give it.[23]

Luther's doctrine at this point is not greatly different than Augustine's. Augustine's doctrine has been summarized as (1) all men since Adam are utterly lost in sin. (2) Only grace can enable the human will to have faith. (3) God's grace is irresistible. (4) It is given only to a limited number of men, the others perishing. Lutheran doctrine agrees with the first two points, and seems to reject the last two. Rather than grace being irresistible, Lutheran doctrine says, "Men, then, do possess the power to thwart the operation of the divine grace whereby God intended to produce faith in them (*gratia resistibilis*)."[24] Rather than being limited, Lutheran doctrine teaches "universal grace"

---

[23] Harvey, *Handbook of Theological Terms*, p.102.

[24] Francis Pieper, *Christian Dogmatics* (St. Louis: Concordia Publishing House, 1950-1957), Vol.2, p.29. This is the standard work in English on Lutheran doctrine. Men who hold that grace is irresistible sometimes ask, "Can man resist the almighty power of God?" Luther would have responded, in the affirmative, with this axiom, "When God works through means, He can be resisted; when God operates without means, in His uncovered majesty, He cannot be resisted." Pieper, after paraphrasing Luther's own words, goes on (p.30) to offer this further explanation: "When God deals with men through His Word and says to them, 'Come unto Me' (Matthew 11:28), resistance is possible; so Christ reports: 'Ye would

(*gratia universalis*). "God's gracious disposition in Christ is not limited to a part of mankind, but extends over all men without exception."[25]   Wherever the gospel is preached, it is 'serious and efficacious grace' that is extended.

> In spite of the fact that the grace of God does not attain its purpose in all men, it is still serious and efficacious (*gratia seria et efficax*). God's gracious will in Christ is not some sort of *laissez-faire* attitude, which does not go beyond a halfhearted, idle wish (*otiosa complacentia, nuda velleitas*), but God has set His heart on the conversion of all men and puts His full power into the means of grace to effect His purpose.[26]

If all of this seems to lead us to a conclusion about "grace" and "faith" that seems to be contradictory, we *are* understanding Luther aright!   Lutherans themselves admit they teach two ideas that are irreconcilable by human reason.

> In teaching, with Scripture, both *gratia universalis, seria, et efficax*, and the *sola gratia* [by grace alone, without human merit or cooperation], we are confronted with a difficulty, the question which at times has constituted the *crux theologorum*: Why, then, are not all men converted and saved? Both the Calvinists and the synergists ... are ready with an answer. The Calvinists answer by denying the *universalis gratia*, the synergists by denying the *sola gratia*. But both of these solutions are contrary to Scripture. The Lutheran Church refuses to answer the question. It recognizes at this point a mystery which cannot be solved in this life and teaches that both the *universalis gratia* and *sola gratia* must be maintained side by side, without any rationalistic compromise. The Lutheran Church teaches that in this question all our thoughts must remain within these limits: Whoever is saved, is saved by grace alone, and not because of a lesser guilt or a better conduct over against grace; whoever is lost, is lost through his own fault, and not through a lack of the grace of God or of the gracious operation of God. The various attempts to solve this problem reveal theological immaturity. No mature theologian will indulge in such speculation. Universal grace is and will remain an article of faith.[27]

In summary, then, "grace" in Lutheran theology is God's gracious attitude or disposition, whereby He cherishes man, and for Christ's sake forgives them. Whereas the

---

not' (Matthew 23:37). But when Christ will appear on Judgment Day in His uncovered majesty ('in all His glory'), all resistance is excluded, for 'before Him shall be gathered all nations,' etc., (Matthew 25:31-32)."

[25] Pieper, *Christian Dogmatics*, p.21.

[26] Pieper, *Christian Dogmatics*, p.28.

[27] Pieper, *Christian Dogmatics*, p.32,33.

Roman church had emphasized one sense of *charis*, namely, an *action*, Lutherans emphasize one other sense of *charis*, namely, an *attitude*. Furthermore, for Luther, there were no degrees of grace, for if grace denotes God's forgiveness, a man is either forgiven or he isn't. He saw no reason to speak of grace for special occasions (actual grace). And to Luther, the expression "prevenient grace" leading to justification, implied that there could be a grace that did not lead to justification, and this was unacceptable to him.[28]

C. Grace in Reformed Theology

Instead of grace being limited to an attitude as in Lutheran theology, the followers of John Calvin presented grace as being something God does, an action performed on man by God through the Holy Spirit. At first sight, there is little difference from grace in Roman Catholic theology (indeed Calvin studied for the priesthood), but there are a few areas where he and his followers modified what Rome taught. Calvin also rejected Luther's views about the irresistibility and universality of efficacious grace.

Reformed theology teaches, first of all, that it is important to make a distinction between common grace and special grace, if the relationship between God's grace and the human situation is to be understood.

Common grace is something God does for all men; its benefits are experienced by all mankind. It is not unusual to find Reformed theologians speaking of God's sustaining of creation, of His divine government and control of human society so that sin is restrained and culture[29] and civil righteousness are promoted (i.e., in the language of Romans 1, God is still in the process of 'giving men over' only when men's sins warrant – otherwise man retains within himself a fear that restrains sin), and of His continuing care for creation, namely, the sending of rain and fruitful seasons, food and gladness, and other blessings that help men to live together in a generally orderly and co-operative society.[30]

Special grace is something God bestows only on the "elect," and it is the means by which He redeems, sanctifies, and glorifies His people. Much like the Roman church has a host of fine theological distinctions, so does Reformed theology. Following are some of these customary distinctions. *Prevenient* grace is necessary to help sinful man (who is totally depraved and totally unable, and dead in trespasses and sins) even want to respond

---

[28] Harvey, *Handbook of Theological Terms*, p.110.

[29] Common grace does not lessen the Reformed theologian's understanding of human depravity. The art, learning, philosophy, culture, and statesmanship in the unregenerate does not obviate their continuing, desperate need for the special grace of God.

[30] See M. Eugene Osterhaven, "Common Grace," p.172-175, in *Basic Christian Doctrines*, edited by Carl F.H. Henry.

to God's initiative. After He does this first work of grace, Reformed theologians then picture God as giving the "gift of faith" to the elect person, and at this point the elect is instantaneously saved. *Efficacious* grace is grace that accomplishes the purpose for which it was given. If God bestows it, of course it could not fail to perform what He intended; otherwise He would not be God. This grace that saves the sinner is said to be indefectible; that is, it will continue without fail until the sinner is finally at home in eternal glory. *Irresistible* grace means that God's efforts to save the sinner cannot be resisted. When God wishes to regenerate a sinner, that regeneration will come to pass through His all-powerful word and will. This does not mean that the sinner may not try to struggle against God, at first, but the struggle eventually will be seen to be futile, for what man can overcome God? *Sufficient* grace is grace that is adequate for the saving of the believer. If a man fails to respond to God's call, it does not mean there was something lacking on God's part, or that He failed to exercise sufficient power to do the job. The fault is said to rest entirely with the man, and the man will be condemned for his unbelief.[31]

In the light of this brief presentation, it becomes easier to understand what many religious people think when they quote Ephesians 2:8, "For by grace you have been saved, through faith ...." The "grace" that precedes "faith" in this passage is understood to be prevenient grace that enables a sinner to believe. When the language *sola gratia* is used, it expresses the idea that salvation from first to last is an action God does upon the sinner. All ideas of co-operation or synergism are rejected by Calvinistic theologians. When the expression "saved by grace" is used, it is almost synonymous with the activity of the Holy Spirit whereby He convicts a man of his sin, regenerates him, sanctifies him, and ultimately glorifies him. "Grace" is thought of as being 'power' exerted in the soul and life of the elect.

Bible students outside the Reformed tradition have regularly raised several weighty objections to this presentation. One is that it seems to make God a respecter of persons when He calls some effectually, and only 'invites' others; yet the Bible presents God as not being a respecter of persons (Acts 10:34). A second objection is that the Bible seems to present two sides to salvation, God's part (Romans 3:24-26, 8:1-4) and man's part (Philippians 3:12-14; Ephesians 4:1; Hebrews 3:1,2). If this is true, then it would be in harmony with Scripture to affirm that God's call and grace can be resisted (2 Thessalonians 1:9,10; 2 Peter 1:10). A third objection involves the whole matter of 'freedom of the will' or 'freedom of choice.' More will be said on this topic later (see Special Study #7 on the perseverance of the saints, p.348ff below). Suffice it here to suggest that Reformed theology's denial of any freedom of choice or will for the wicked (who are slaves of sin) or

---

[31] This last point is one that has caused no little difficulty for Calvinistic theologians. How can the lost be predestined not to be one of the elect, and at the same time held responsible for his failure to respond to 'irresistible, efficacious, sufficient grace'? As the Lutherans simply require belief in seeming contradictory positions, so the Calvinists admit that the conclusion to which their doctrine brings them is not 'comprehensible.' "It is important always to remember that the operation of God's grace is a deep mystery that is far beyond our limited human comprehension." Philip E. Hughes, "Grace," in *The Evangelical Dictionary of Theology*, edited by Walter L. Elwell (Grand Rapids: Baker Book House, 1984), p.482.

for the righteous (who are slaves of Christ) is a hard doctrine to accept in the light of the constant invitation in Scripture, "Whosoever will ...."

D. Grace in 20th Century Religious Liberalism and Neo-Orthodoxy[32]

In liberalism, grace has become a generous attitude or action by one human being toward another.   Liberal Protestantism gave up the ideas that Adam and Eve, or the Fall, were historical events, or that a penalty had been passed on to the race because of Adam's sin, or even that the death of Jesus was a vicarious atonement for mankind.   So there actually was no such thing as a forgiveness of sins to be granted by a God in heaven.   There was no reason to speak of grace as something God feels or bestows on man, nor was there any reason to think 'grace' had to be exclusively linked to something Jesus did at Calvary. So the liberal Protestant came to interpret Jesus as the highest example of how a man could be gracious and generous toward other human beings.[33]

Neo-orthodoxy, as found in Barth, Brunner, and Tillich, reacted against the theology of religious liberalism.[34]   Beginning with the assured conclusions of higher criticism of the Bible, the Neo-orthodox also rejected the historicity of Adam and the Fall; but they did teach that the 'myth' of original sin was closer to the truth than the old liberal idea of the inevitable progress and inherent goodness of man.   As a result of their view of man's 'fallenness' ("Adam" was sort of a religious every-man), there was also room in Neo-orthodoxy for 'grace.'   Just what grace's place was, Neo-orthodox theologians argued. Some reserved the word "grace" for the few times God has actually been present in certain

---

[32] This commentator has rejected the conclusions and the methodology of both religious liberalism and Neo-orthodoxy for studied and weighty reasons.   Chester A. Tulga, *The Case Against Modernism* (Chicago: Conservative Baptist Fellowship, 1949) and a second volume by the same writer, *The Case Against Modernism in Foreign Missions* (Chicago: Conservative Baptist Fellowship, 1950), and Robert Lightner, *Neo-Liberalism* (Chicago: Regular Baptist Press, 1959), are good sources for an introduction to the objections to modern religious liberalism.   For similar indictments of Neo-orthodoxy, see Charles C. Ryrie, *Neo-Orthodoxy: What it is and What it Does* (Chicago: Moody Press, 1956), and Chester A. Tulga, *The Case Against Neo-Orthodoxy* (Chicago: Conservative Baptist Fellowship, 1951).   But for the sake of being current, it seems proper to include a brief discussion of how "grace" is explained in these disciplines.

[33] Harvey, *Handbook of Theological Terms*, p.110,111.

[34] "Liberalism" is a designation given to the system of theology that emphasized the use of reason, the conclusions of modern science, and the application of modern philosophy as tools of Bible interpretation. "Liberal" means "free," and the liberal claimed to be free of 17 centuries of conservative interpretation of the Bible.   Religious liberalism often emphasized human goodness and progress, and proclaimed the "fatherhood of God and the brotherhood of man."   It originated in Europe in the 19th century and flourished in America in the decades before World War II.   When two world wars had caused men to lose hope in the inherent goodness of man, and liberalism lost favor with the theologians, two new movements sprang up out of the ashes of the old – Neo-orthodoxy and Neo-liberalism.   The conclusions and methods of both these theologies are inimical to the Christian faith.

historical events (of which the Bible is a record).[35]   Others tended to limit grace to that power that preserves all being from nothingness (i.e., what some call 'providence').[36]   All the Neo-orthodox rejected the Catholic doctrine of "infused grace."

Neo-liberalism, as propounded by Bultmann and Bonhoeffer, Moltmann (theology of hope), and Gutierrez (theology of liberation), has again changed the emphasis being made when grace is the topic.   In the past, when 'justification' and 'sanctification' were topics of the hour, theologians tried to relate them to grace, and emphasized either God's attitude or action on behalf of men.   In the present, when certain social and political ideologies and the philosophy of existentialism are clamoring for men's attention, it has become fashionable to define grace as it relates to these current issues of concern. Bonhoeffer's (1906-1945) call to imitate Christ and his stress on God's "costly grace" as opposed to "cheap grace" has caused a renewed emphasis on the ethical implications of grace.   Since man is a citizen of a political society, and a member of a socio-economic class, and a bearer of a particular culture in a particular stage of development, all these must be taken into account if we are to understand how grace is communicated to and expressed in human beings.

In many of these 20th century emphases there is a kernel of truth, for the "grace" taught in the Bible has many aspects.   But when one reads these 20th century theologies, he comes away feeling empty and hungry and disappointed.   If the theologians are right, and there is no favor or bounty to be had from God on high, then man's condition is most likely hopeless.   What does the Bible itself have to say on the subject?

E. Grace in Biblical Theology

As Paul made his farewell address to the Ephesian elders, he summarized in a brief expression the message he had been preaching.   He called it "the gospel of the grace of God" (Acts 20:24).   Perhaps some similar summary of the New Covenant message is what Luke meant when he characterized Jesus' own preaching as being "words of grace" (Luke 4:22, ASV).   Several writers have collected and organized the references to grace in various New Testament books.

> The book of Acts uses "grace" in both its special Christian sense and in a weaker, more general sense.   *Charis* points to the salvation that appeared in Jesus Christ (Acts 15:11).   The gospel is the word of grace (14:3).   Miracles accompany the preaching of grace, perhaps demonstrating its power (6:8; 14:3).   Grace enables Apollos to help believers (18:28).   Paul commends the elders of Ephesus to the "word of His grace that has power to build you up ..."

---

[35] Arthur C. Piepkorn, "Grace," in *The Encyclopedia of the Lutheran Church*, edited by Julius Bodensieck (Minneapolis: Augsburg Publishing House, 1965), Vol.2, p.955, writes, "In twentieth century Reformed Theology, Karl Barth (b.1886) has strongly emphasized God's free grace."

[36] This was Paul Tillich's view of grace.   See Harvey, *Handbook of Theological Terms*, p.112.

(20:32), and the church [at Antioch] commended Paul and Barnabas to the grace of God for the work they were to accomplish (14:26). The presence of grace marked the new believing community ... (4:33; 11:23; 13:43; 15:40). But *charis* is also used to say that someone had favor in another's eyes: the early Church found *charis* with "all the people" (2:47). Stephen recalls that Joseph found favor with Pharaoh (7:10), and David with God (7:46). The other places speak of someone doing another person a favor (24:27; 25:3,9).[37]

Naturally, the various meanings of the word were simply taken over from the ordinary language by the New Testament writers ... The very elasticity of the word enabled it to receive still another – new and technically Christian – meaning. This seems to have originated in part by fusing together two of the ordinary significances. In the first place ... *charis* may mean "a gift." In 1 Corinthians 16:3; 2 Corinthians 8:19, it is the money given by the Corinthians to Jerusalem. In 2 Corinthians 9:8 it is the increase of worldly goods that God grants for charitable purposes. In 2 Corinthians 1:15 it is the benefit received by the Corinthians from a visit by St. Paul. In a more spiritual sense *charis* is the endowment for an office in the church (Ephesians 4:7), more particularly for the apostolate (Romans 1:5; 12:3; 15:15; 1 Corinthians 3:10; Ephesians 3:2,7). So in 1 Corinthians 1:4-7, *charis* is expanded into "word and all knowledge," endowments with which the Corinthians were especially favored. In 1 Peter 1:13, *charis* is the future heavenly blessedness that Christians are to receive. In the second place, *charis* is the word for God's *favor* ... But God's favor differs from man's in that it cannot be conceived of as inactive. A favorable "thought" of God's about a man involves of necessity the reception of some blessing by that man, and "to look with favor" is one of the commonest Biblical paraphrases for "bestow a blessing." Between "God's favor" and "God's favors" there exists a relation of active power, and as *charis* denoted both the favor and the favors, it was the natural word for the power that connected them. This is very clear in 1 Corinthians 15:10, where St. Paul says, "not I, but the grace of God which was with me" labored more abundantly than they all: grace is something that *labors*. So in 2 Corinthians 12:9, "My grace is sufficient for thee; for my power is made perfect in weakness"; cf. 2 Timothy 2:1, "strengthened in the grace," and 1 Peter 4:10, "stewards of the manifold grace." Evidently in this sense "grace" is almost a synonym for the Spirit ... and there is little real difference between "full of the Holy Spirit" and "full of grace and power" in Acts 6:5,8, while there is a very striking parallel between Ephesians 4:7-13 and 1 Corinthians 12:4-11, with "gifts of grace" in the one passage, and "gifts of the Spirit" in the other. And this connection between grace and the Spirit is found definitely in the formula "Spirit of grace" in Hebrew 10:29 ....[38]

---

[37] L.B. Smedes, *Grace,* p.552.

[38] Burton Scott Easton, "Grace" in *International Standard Bible Encyclopedia,* edited by James Orr (Grand Rapids: Wm. B. Eerdmans Publishing Co., 1949), Vol.2, p.1290,1291.

In Hebrews we are told that Jesus became a man "so that by the grace of God He might taste of death for everyone" (2:9, ASV). Perhaps this means that because God looked on man with favor, Jesus was sent to be the atoning sacrifice for those lost men. In Romans 6:12-14, "grace" seems to be synonymous with help to live the Christian life by controlling and mastering the desires the devil stirs up as he tempts men to sin. In 1 Peter 5:12, Peter urges his readers to "stand firm" in the "true grace of God." In this passage, grace is but a synonym for the Christian religion. In Christianity is where a man experiences the grace of God; do not quit Christianity in the face of persecution, Peter exhorts.

> So *charis*, "grace," becomes almost an equivalent for "Christianity," viewed as the religion of dependence on God through Christ. As one may think of entering Christianity, abiding in it, or falling from it, so one may speak of entering into (Romans 5:2), abiding in (Acts 13:43), or falling from (Galatians 5:4) grace; cf. 1 Peter 5:12.[39]

With these verses in view, it now seems appropriate to attempt a definition of grace, one that will include both attitude and action. It seems apparent that more is needed than simply "unmerited favor." Stewart has suggested that grace is "a kind and merciful disposition, manifesting itself in acts of unmerited goodness, especially towards the sinful and erring."[40] Another possible definition of grace is *'all that a loving God feels and does to save men.'* That "all" would include the fact that God is not willing that any should perish, the preparation of the world for the coming of Jesus, the incarnation and ministry of Jesus, His death on the cross and subsequent resurrection, the sending of preachers with the good news that forgiveness is now available to believers, the help of the Holy Spirit as He convicts men of sin through the Word, the help the Holy Spirit gives the Christian to live the Christian life, and ultimately their glorification in heaven.

CONCLUSION

During the course of this study of God's "call" and God's "grace," one thing has become rather obvious: the definition given to either of these words may be seriously altered or affected by current theological debate. Still, it seems proper to attempt to let the Scriptures themselves determine the content and meaning that each word is used to express.

Concerning God's "call" to salvation, or to specialized ministry: in the former it would appear that "call" is rather synonymous with 'invitation' or 'summons,' and that this invitation is offered to men as the gospel is preached in their hearing. It would also appear true that men have the power either to accept or reject the invitation. Concerning the latter, it would appear that God's "call" sometimes is given in a dramatic way, and sometimes

---

[39] Easton, *ibid.*

[40] A. Stewart, "Grace" in *Hastings Dictionary of the Bible*, edited by James Hastings (New York: Charles Scribner's Sons, 1902), Vol.2, p.254.

simply through men encouraging others to give their whole lives to some specialized ministry. This call, too, is one men have the power either to accept or reject.

As for "grace," it must be noted that its use in Scripture is such that it sometimes is an attitude and sometimes an action. When speaking of God, it seems best to try to define it thus: *Grace is all that a loving God feels and does to save a man.* The word is also used at times of men's favorable attitudes and actions toward other men. To try to explain it (in any of its particular occurrences in Scripture) as being in this instance efficacious, or in another as being universal, or in still another as being irresistible, is to attempt to attach to the basic definition of the word "grace" an idea that the word itself does not imply.

SELECTED BIBLIOGRAPHY

Ahane, C. M., "Grace, Controversies on," in *New Catholic Encyclopedia.* Washington, DC: Catholic University of America, 1974. Vol.6, p.670-678.

Blaiklock, E.M., "Call; Calling," in *The New International Standard Bible Encyclopedia*, edited by Geoffrey W. Bromiley. Grand Rapids: Eerdmans Publishing Co., 1979. Vol.1, p.580,581.

Colborn, F., "Grace, Theology of," in *New Catholic Encyclopedia.* Vol.16, p.196,197.

Easton, Burton Scott, "Grace" in *The International Standard Bible Encyclopedia*, edited by James Orr. Grand Rapids: Eerdmans Publishing Co., 1949. Vol.2, p.1290-1292.

Esser, H.H., "Grace, Spiritual Gifts," in *The New International Dictionary of New Testament Theology,* edited by Colin Brown. Vol.2, p.115-124.

Geldenhuys, J. Norval, "Effectual Calling," in *Basic Christian Doctrines*, edited by Carl F.H. Henry. New York: Holt, Rinehart and Winston, 1962. p.178-184.

Hughes, Philip E., *But For the Grace of God.* Philadelphia: Westminster Press, 1964.

Klein, William W., "Paul's Use of *Kalein*: A Proposal," *Journal of the Evangelical Theological Society*, 27:1 (March 1984), p.53-64.

McDonald, H.D., "Grace" in *The Zondervan Pictorial Encyclopedia of the Bible*, edited by Merril C. Tenney. Grand Rapids: Zondervan Publishing House. 1975. Vol.2, p.799-804.

Pieper, Francis, *Christian Dogmatics.* St. Louis: Concordia Publishing Co., 1953. Vol.2, p.3-34.

Piepkorn, Arthur C., "Grace" in *The Encyclopedia of the Lutheran Church*, edited by Julius Bodensieck. Minneapolis: Augsburg Publishing House, 1965. Vol.2, p.947-958.

Smedes, L.B., "Grace" in *The New International Standard Bible Encyclopedia.* Vol.2, p.547-552.

Stewart, A., "Grace" in *Hastings Dictionary of the Bible*, edited by James Hastings. New York: Charles Scribner's Sons, 1902. Vol.2, p.254-257.

Special Study #2

THE PROVIDENCE OF GOD

"Providence" is one of the words not specifically used of God in our English Bibles, but which expresses an idea which is everywhere assumed in Scripture.[1]   Providence has reference to that care, and preservation, and government which God exercises over all things that He has created, so that they will accomplish the purposes for which they were created.   The Old Testament tells us that God "rested" (Genesis 2:3) when He finished the work of creation, but it was not a rest of inactivity, for Jesus said, "My Father is working still, and I am working" (John 5:17).   Scripture also affirms that Deity "upholds all things by the word of His power" (Hebrews 1:3; Colossians 1:17).

As indicated in the comments on chapter 1, man originally started out monotheistic in his beliefs.   Only where there is monotheism can there be any idea of God's providence. A multitude of gods would be at cross-purposes with each other, and this would rule out any consistent care (conservation), or preservation, or government in our world.   But One God could very well be expected to exercise such general supervision of His creation as the Bible everywhere presents God as doing.   Various expressions in both Old and New Testaments assume and assert God's involvement in His creation.

I. PROVIDENCE IN THE OLD TESTAMENT

Genesis 2:7ff presents God as preparing a garden, putting man in it, and giving instructions to the man what is expected of him.   Job 33:4 reads "the Spirit of God made me; the Spirit of the Almighty gave me life."[2]   Whether Elihu is thinking of God's part in the actual conception of Elihu, or simply that the Spirit had a part in the continuation of the

---

[1] "Providence" comes from the Latin *providentia*, which means "foresight, to be concerned about something, to make provision for something." The Greek word translated "providence" is *pronoia*, and is used of *men's* foresight or care at Acts 24:2 and Romans 13:14. The word is used in classical Greek for forethought, both human and divine. It is used in inter-Testamental books (Wisdom 14:3, 17:2) of *God's* providence. There are Hebrew and Greek words that express a corresponding idea, such as *ra'ah*, "provide" (Genesis 22:8; 1 Samuel 16:1 ["select," NASB]) and *problepō*, "provide" (Hebrews 11:40).

There is a dispute about exactly what Acts 2:23 means when it speaks of God's *prognōsis* (translated "foreknowledge" in the NASB). The Rhemish translators chided Theodore Beza for using "God's providence" to translate this passage. James Hastings, "Providence" in *Hastings Dictionary of the Bible*, edited by James Hastings (New York: Charles Scribner's Sons, 1909), Vol.4, p.143.

[2] Some English versions read "the breath of the Almighty gave me life" in the second member of this parallelism, but it is perfectly proper to translate *ru'ah* by "Spirit" in both members. In fact, the TEV so renders it.

race since Adam, it rather strongly presupposes something like "providence." Isaiah 34:16 tells us that prophecy will be matched by fulfillment: "the Spirit of the Lord will perform this."[3] This too requires a "government" over creation exercised by God. Isaiah 63:14 tells us that the cattle coming down out of the hills into the valleys are guided by the Spirit of God. When considered in its context (i.e., 63:11ff), this is an illustration of God's providential care for Israel. Psalm 104 shows that God works in nature for the benefit of all His creatures. After God created the sun, moon, and stars (Genesis 1:14ff), we are told in Jeremiah 31:35 and 33:20 that God continues to cause these to shine. Numerous passages could be pointed out wherein is (1) declared God's preserving power; (2) asserted God's control of the regular operations of nature; (3) declared God's sovereignty over birth, life, disease, death, afflictions, and prosperity; (4) affirmed that such things as accidents and chance are not overruled;[4] (5) taught that God uses harmful or poisonous creatures for purposes of His government; (6) affirmed that retributions come from God to wicked men; (7) deliverance is ascribed to God; (8) declared His supreme authority over men; and (9) affirmed His dominion over national prosperity and adversity.[5] Lobstein has this summary paragraph about providence in the Old Testament:

> Atmospheric phenomena are regarded as due to the immediate activity of God (Job 36:27-28, 37:2-6,10-13, 38:25ff; Psalm 29:3ff), all this ultimately being for the benefit of man. He draws man from the womb and guards him throughout the life to which He Himself appoints the limit (Psalm 22:10ff; Job 14:5). The divine protection rests especially upon His chosen people Israel (Psalm 105; Hosea 11:1ff), keeping them from peril and nourishing them (Exodus 13-16; Numbers 11; Psalm 91; 105-107). While in punishment He hardens the heart and sends evil thoughts (Exodus 7:3; 2 Samuel 24:1), He can render evil intents futile and turn them to good (Genesis 50:20; Psalm 2); and fertility and drought are instruments of blessing and of punishment in His hand (Deuteronomy 28:12-23).[6]

---

[3] The Hebrew Scriptures are not always easy to translate. Some of the modern versions read as if the animals that the previous context in Isaiah have been speaking of will all assemble just as God arranges for them to do. But the passage is really speaking about God's threatenings against the ungodly, and Isaiah here reminds the people of these, and also promises that all the curses against disobedience will take effect. God had so commanded, and the Spirit would see to it that it came true!

[4] While not stopping to list verses for the other points, this one is important, so some verses will be given. See Exodus 21:12-13; Deuteronomy 19:4-5; 1 Kings 22:34,38, compared with 21:19; Proverbs 16:33. These verses seem to imply that "providence" does not demand that we believe that God causes everything that happens, simply because we say He exercises care and government over His creation.

[5] "Over five hundred passages [might be] cited," to confirm what is here outlined, S.H. Platt suggests, after he lists nearly a whole page full of references by which these evidences of providence are shown to be assumed and asserted in the Old Testament. See his article on "Providence," in *Cyclopedia of Biblical, Theological, and Ecclesiastical Literature*, edited by John McClintock and James Strong (Grand Rapids: Baker Book House, 1969), Vol.8, p.708.

[6] P. Lobstein, "Providence" in *The New Schaff-Herzog Encyclopedia of Religious Knowledge*, edited by Samuel Macauley Jackson (Grand Rapids: Baker Book House, 1949), Vol.9, p.307.

All through the Old Testament, even though God is pictured as exercising a care and government over His creation, man's power of choice and voluntary action are also presupposed. Appeals are made for obedience, and warnings are given that disobedience will be punished.

II. PROVIDENCE IN THE NEW TESTAMENT

In the Sermon on the Mount, Jesus strikes the keynote of God's providence. He speaks of "the heavenly Father" who feeds the birds and who clothes the lilies of the field (Matthew 6:26-30). Earlier in that same Sermon, as Jesus was teaching the Model Prayer, one phrase is of vital importance to our subject. When Jesus taught them to pray, "Thy will be done on earth as it is in heaven," it is clearly implied that much will go on, on earth, that is not in harmony with the Father's will. We therefore do not expect "providence" to mean that all that happens on earth is predestined by God to happen, or that creation is like an unthinking robot that simply does what it is programmed to do. On another occasion (Matthew 10:29-31) He affirmed that the Father is aware of every sparrow that falls and the number of hairs on a man's head. Jesus' high priestly prayer (John 17) is addressed to a Father who is requested to care for the bodies and souls of all His children. Not only prayer itself, but answered prayer, requires that God have providential control over His creation.

In Romans 9-11, Paul will give us a glimpse of his philosophy of history. To Paul history is an arena where God is playing out His purposes with men and nations, bringing them all to the goal He had in mind when He created. 1 Corinthians 15:20-28 add some thoughts to this, showing how all was subjected to vanity because of Adam's sin, and how all will be restored to its pristine condition at the second advent of Jesus. This all requires a personal involvement by the Creator in His creation. The teaching in 1 Peter 1 and Hebrews 12 on suffering as chastisement and discipline from the Father is another concept that requires a providential control over our world. The succession of covenants that Galatians 3 and Hebrews 8-10 speak about, and the restraint (forbearance) that God exercises according to 2 Peter 3, also require that there be such a thing as the providence of God.

Just as the Old Testament asserted both the providence of God and the fact of human freedom, so does the New. Notice the passages in Acts where both God's foreordination and human freedom are plainly stated. "There were gathered together against Thy holy servant Jesus, whom Thou didst anoint, both Herod and Pontius Pilate, with the Gentiles and the peoples of Israel, to do whatever Thy hand and Thy purpose had predestined to occur" (Acts 4:27,28). And Peter says in another place that Jesus "was delivered up according to the predetermined plan and foreknowledge of God," yet he accuses the people of guilt in their actions when he says, "you by the hand of lawless men did crucify and slay" (Acts 2:23, ASV).

Having shown how both Testaments assume and assert the providence of God, it will be helpful to emphasize some details, and to answer some standard objections.

III. GENERAL AND SPECIAL PROVIDENCE

In many studies of providence, one finds a distinction between "general providence" (what God does for all men generally) and "special providence" (what God does specially for the believers).   It will be helpful to note each of these briefly.

A. General Providence

Matthew 5:45 tells us that He makes the rain to fall on the just and the unjust.

Deuteronomy 32:8 and Acts 17:26 tell us that God determines when nations rise and fall, and how far their boundaries will spread.   After its beginning with one (Adam), He had a hand in the spread of the human race from the Mesopotamian valley all over the world.   "He has made of one every nation that dwells on the face of the world."   Daniel 2:21 informs us God changes times and seasons, and that He removes kings and puts kings into office.

Such are examples of the kinds of involvement God has in His world as He cares for it, preserves it, and governs it.   They are "general" things He does for all men alike, whether they are saint or sinner.

B. Special Providence

Matthew 6:33 tells us God provides food, shelter, and clothing to those who put the kingdom of God first.   That's something done specially for the believer.

Romans 8:28 tells us God causes all things to work together for good to those who love Him, and who are called according to His purpose.   That's special providence.

Answered prayer is an example of God's special providence.   Matthew 7:7-11; James 1:5, 5:16; and 1 Peter 3:12,13 all assume that the One to whom prayer is addressed will do something in His world in answer to the prayer.   Unless one believes in "providence," he has no reason to pray!   Jesus taught us to pray, "Give us this day our daily bread" (Matthew 6:11).   That implies providence.   When believers make their plans for the future with the prayer "If the Lord wills" on their lips (James 4:13-15; Jeremiah 10:23), it means that the believer recognizes that future hours and days on earth are clearly dependent on God's will and activity in the world.

God gives believers help right at the moment they are tempted so they can withstand the temptation.   1 Corinthians 10:12-13 tell us that He knows how much each Christian is able to bear (and that varies with the individual), and will not permit the devil to tempt beyond each Christian's capacity to resist.   And not only that, right when the temptation comes, God also plants a thought in the believer's mind about how to escape the temptation.   That's an active participation on behalf of the believer that would not be available if there were no providence.

It is the teaching of the New Testament that God's providence means that God is near the believer, over him, and about him constantly. As Peter worded it in the letter he wrote to believers, promising them special providence, "It matters to Him about you!" (1 Peter 5:7). What an empty promise, unless indeed there is such a thing as God's special providence.

We must resist the temptation to think about general and special providence independently of Jesus. Just as God the Father and the Holy Spirit have been shown to have something to do with the care, preservation, and government of creation, so does the exalted Jesus. When He is called "Lord," nothing less is implied than that Jesus is sitting at the right hand of the Father on the throne of the universe, actively controlling what is happening. In fact, the two verses from Hebrews and Colossians referred to in the first paragraph of this Special Study specifically refer to Jesus as the one who "upholds all things."

IV. PROBLEMS AND OBJECTIONS

Through the centuries, certain standard objections have been raised by skeptics who question the fact of providence. Often these objections resulted from the fact that the current definition and explanation of providence reflected a contemporary (and sometimes even temporal) doctrinal or philosophical emphasis. It is not surprising that men's views of providence were colored by pressing interests of the moment, for the same thing is true of other theological beliefs and statements.[7] However, there are some objections that seem to intrude themselves whatever the age or the peculiar interest of the age.

(1) The problem of evil in the world is one of these difficult objections to answer. If God is really in control, why are there natural calamities that claim hundreds and thousands of lives? Why is there pain and suffering? Why do the wicked seem to prosper more than the righteous? Does it not seem one of these is true: either that God is not all powerful (if He were, He would stop the evil), or He does not love (and the Bible affirms that He does love), or else the doctrine of providence is not in harmony with the observed facts?

Through the centuries, men have struggled to reconcile their understanding of God's involvement in and government over creation with the presence of evil. "Occasionalism"[8]

---

[7] See Special Study #1, on "Call" and "Grace," for a reminder of how current issues clouded the debate on these topics.

[8] "Occasionalism" represented God as the sole actor, and the creature only gave God an occasion to act, the creature being merely an instrument by which God absolutely and irresistibly accomplished His design. This was the view that resulted when Nicholas Malebranche (1638-1715) attempted to harmonize the new principles of Descarte with the theology of Augustine. Evil was thus explained as being the result of Adam's sin on the race (man is left only with an ability to sin), and any good is the result of God acting on a man since man was incapable of producing the good by himself. This pre-understanding allowed the theologians to believe in the providence of God and at the same time explain the presence of evil.

and "concurrence"[9] were two such attempts, both of which proved to be inadequate.

Of the numerous passages in the Bible where the inspired writers provide God's answer to this seeming contradiction, perhaps James 1 is the most helpful. First, read James 1 and observe where God's providence is assumed: God will give wisdom in answer to prayer; God can use trials to perfect and complete the believer; good and perfect gifts come from the Father; etc. Next, read the same chapter, noting what it says about "evil." The readers have been "dispersed" (verse 1). Was it by persecution, similar to Acts 8:1-4? This dispersion resulted in "various trials" that the Christians would need "wisdom" to know how to handle. Was it a similar dispersion that led to some who used to be rich now being poor (James 1:10), their property having been confiscated; and the "poor" now being in even more humble circumstances (verse 9)? In all of this there would be a temptation to quit the faith (verse 12). Yet in spite of all the trials, in spite of all the evil, God still loved those hurting people. He was not the cause of the evil. The devil was! The devil is the one who placed the temptations before the Christians as he "carried them away" and stirred up their "desires" (verse 14). After being tempted, it was men (not God!) who nursed the idea and let it grow to action. God had a purpose in permitting the evil. James' readers were a "first-fruits." There were going to be other Christians in the future who would be helped to see their way through trials by the triumphant way the readers of this letter handled the evil that came into their lives. And at the close of a life of overcoming, God would be there to bestow the "crown of life" on the ones who have been tested and approved (verse 12).

A third reading of James 1 will add several additional truths. God did not keep the trials[10] from happening, but He implies that He is perfectly willing and ready to help the believer through the trials. The universe that God created is a moral universe, and this implies that there must be temptations and trials that will give men an opportunity to exercise their freedom. Even though God is practicing a general supervision over His creation,[11] the devil is given permission to do his work.[12] Observe, too, (James 1:2) that

---

[9] "Concurrence" (sometimes spelled "concursus") is the idea that God and man together produce men's actions. There are two causes for all effects: God is the first cause, and man is the second. Now the moral quality of an evil act can be blamed on the creature, while the effectual cause of the act is attributed to God. God excites men to act, but they act in accord with their nature. This is very often the way present-day Bible dictionaries will attempt to harmonize the doctrine of Divine Providence with the presence of evil in the world.

[10] The word *peirasmos* can be translated either "trial" or "temptation," per William Arndt and F.W. Gingrich, *A Greek-English Lexicon of the New Testament* (Chicago: University of Chicago Press, 1956), p.646. If it speaks of an "enticement to sin," then "temptation" is the proper English word. If the word speaks of a "test" (and even an enticement to sin can also be a test), then "trial" or "test" is the proper English word.

[11] "General supervision" appears to be a better expression than just simply 'oversight' or 'supervision.' The latter words suggest that everything that happens in the world, however minute, is somehow the result of God's direct and willful action. This seems not to be so, in the light of the wording of the Model Prayer ("Let your will be done") and similar passages (be sure to include Genesis 1:28-31 and 2:15-17, where God delegated some oversight of the creation to man). There are things He does not approve of happen-

men "encounter" (NASB) or "fall into" (ASV) these various trials – they are not forced or coerced into them because God inexorably wills each particular trial.   Instead, God's grace has gone to work to counteract what the devil was permitted to do.   James reminds his readers how God, "in the exercise of His will ... brought [them] forth[13] by the word of truth," so that they could together blunt and eventually overcome the evil and its effects in the lives of men.

Romans 8 will give more help with the problem of evil in the world, but enough has already been learned from James to see that the presence of evil is not a sufficient problem to lead us to question or deny the truth of the doctrine of God's care, preservation, and government of His creation.

(2) A second problem faced by one who would understand God's providence is the matter of the difference between providence and miracle.[14] Isn't everything God does a miracle?   What need is there to speak about providence?   C.S. Lewis has defined miracle this way: "The divine art of miracle is not the art of suspending the pattern to which events conform, but of feeding new events into that pattern."[15]   The difference between providence and miracle is this – providence is God's everyday care and preservation and government of His creation, whereas "miracle" is something that does not happen every day.   Both speak of God's activity in His world, but "miracle" is something new being fed into the pattern.   In the Bible, miracle didn't happen every day.   In fact, after creation, there are only four or so brief periods of time when miracles were concentrated – at the Flood, at the Exodus, during the life-and- death struggle with Baalism during Elijah and Elisha's time, and at the fullness of time when Jesus became incarnate and Christianity was

---

ing in His world, but He permits it, all within the scope of His "general superintendence" over creation.   But certainly, Scripture does not permit us to credit God with causing or deliberately willing or irresistibly predetermining each individual happening (remember, for example, "God does not tempt any one," James 1:13).

[12] When James tells us there is "deception" involved (verse 16), that implies that the devil has been at work.

[13] The reference is evidently to the new birth, or to their conversion to Christianity, though it is not the regular word (the one used in John 3:3,5,6 and Titus 3:5) used for the new birth.

[14] At an earlier time, when skeptics were denying the possibility of miracle, some attempted to base their denials on the so-called laws of nature.   Providence was appealed to by the theologians as being the reason why all nature moved according to fixed and consistent rules.   The skeptics replied that the laws of nature are simply based on men's observation; if something unusual is observed (things folk tended to call 'miracle'), it did not prove a miracle had occurred.   It simply gave evidence that the original observation was not comprehensive enough before men drew up their conclusions which they then called natural laws.   By means of this simple argument, 'miracle' was denied, and even the idea of 'providence' was called into question, and doubt cast on it.   C.S. Lewis has written a delightful book in which he addresses this whole attempt at the denial of miracle.   It is titled *Miracles: A Preliminary Study*, and was originally published in New York by the Macmillan Company, 1948, but has been reprinted many times.

[15] C.S. Lewis, *Miracles*, p.72.

introduced and credentialed.[16]   The Bible suggests that we live in an open universe, rather than a closed one.   God has stepped in before, and He can do it again.   But in the meantime, as we await the second advent, God continues to move all of creation toward the goal through the exercise of His providence.

(3) A third matter that for some creates a difficulty for the idea of God's providential control is the vastness and complexity of the universe.   Man lives on a little planet that rotates around one of the lesser stars in a cluster of stars located near the edge of a rotating galaxy approximately 150,000 light years across and 25,000 to 40,000 light years thick in its central area.   This galaxy is but one of countless nebulae extending in all directions from us on an average of 2,000,000 light years apart, and receding from each other at incredible speeds which increase with distance.[17]   In addition, the second law of thermodynamics seems to indicate that our universe is slowly running out of energy and will end in total disorganization of energy at some future date.   How is all of this to be harmonized with the idea of providence?   Simply this: if man's idea of God's omnipotence is so limited that He could not handle an immense universe, then "your God is too small!"   The Bible specifically tells us that the creation was subjected to "futility" when Adam sinned (Romans 8:20); so, within God's general supervision, indeed it could very well be running down, and except for His personal intervention at the second advent, it very well could end in total disorganization.

(4) A fourth factor that has caused a change in how the providence of God is presented is the shift from an emphasis on God's transcendence to an emphasis on God's immanence.   "Transcendence" does not have a precise significance either in philosophy or theology, but as the term is used here, it signifies that God is a being who stands above or beyond or against all finite beings.   He transcends the creation in the sense that His being is not identical with or His power not exhausted by the realm of finite being.   This concept of God's transcendence is implied when God is characterized as being "holy."   On the other hand, "immanence" suggests God dwells within the creation (including man),[18] and His sustaining and preserving creation is generally limited to His energizing the wills and souls of believers.   Those theologies that emphasize God's transcendence also talk of His providence, while those who emphasize His immanence tend to downplay His providence, or ignore the idea all together.   Neo-orthodoxy returned to a transcendent God after

---

[16] There were also miracles in the case of Jonah, two during Isaiah's time (2 Kings 19:35, 20:9-11), and two or three in Daniel's time.   Still, it can be said that there are only four or so epochs in all recorded history when God was stepping in to work "miracles."

[17] Whether it will continue to expand, or whether the universe expands and contracts, is a matter of debate among the scientists.

[18] *Webster's New International Dictionary of the English Language*, 2nd edition Unabridged (Springfield, MA: G&C Merriam Co., Publishers, 1948), p.1245, explains immanence as taught by pantheism and theism in these words: "In Pantheism, immanence is thought of as uniform, God being present in the impersonal and the personal, in the good and the evil.   According to theism, God is immanent in various degrees, being more fully present in the personal than the impersonal, in the good than in the evil."

religious liberalism had opted for immanence. Neo-liberalism also tends to speak for immanence rather than transcendence. All of these theologies were (and are) struggling to be relevant, to have a bearing on and to answer the contemporary critical issues and problems.

> Radical theology ... seeks to grapple with root issues in times of crises. The crisis it addresses has several facets, at once cultural, ethical, ecclesiastical, political, historical, and religious. The root problem is that modern man lives in an environment where many human beings experience a profound sense of the absence of God. Where religion flourishes it seems to have little cultural relevance. The historians have declared this the "Post-Christian Era." There is a cultural sense of the loss of transcendence. Modern men and women feel trapped within the closed walls of "this-sidedness." There seems to be no access to the eternal or the transcendent. Nature has been demythologized. History has been de-supernaturalized; ethics have been de-absolutized.

> The church faces a serious crisis of *relevance*. If, for example, we discover that the traditional categories of Christian religion are no longer credible, what is left for the church to do? If the Incarnation is a myth and the crucifixion of Christ merely a Roman tragedy, what do we do with billions of dollars of church property, thousands of professionally trained clergy, and millions of church members? Do we quietly close the doors of the churches, give pink slips to the clergy, turn over our assets to the United Fund, and apologize to our members, saying, "Sorry, we were wrong. There is no God and the biblical Jesus is a myth"?[19]

This was the problem faced by 19th century liberal theology, and, in the 20th century, by the Death of God Theology, the Theology of Hope, and Liberation Theology in the third world. Instead of God's being over all, in control, and through regenerated people bringing changes for the better into society, it almost seems as though man by himself must bring these changes; and (in 20th century liberal theology's opinion) unless modern man is actively involved in such social programs, his theology (may we say, his Christianity) is not relevant.[20]

To this commentator, it seems that what is sorely needed is a return to doctrinal affirmations that are shaped by Scriptural statements, rather than trusting dogmas that have been shaped by the exigencies of the moment. Only in this way will we have access to the

---

[19] R.C. Sproul, "Twenty Years After the Death of God Movement," in *Christianity Today*, 29:9 (June 14, 1985), p.18,19.

[20] Liberation theology has two major themes. First, it proclaims the need for liberation from various forms of oppressions: political, economic, social, sexual, racial, and religious. Second, it has the conviction that theology must grow out of the indigenous basic Christian communities. Unless church people are involved in this "liberation" effort, their religion is irrelevant. And since Latin America, Africa, and most parts of Asia are vastly different in their forms of "oppression," the theology that arises in each area will display considerable variety.

truth of God that will stand for the ages.   Then, when redeemed men begin to live out that truth in their lives, their religion will be eternally relevant, and the providence of the Holy God will be experienced and appreciated.

CONCLUSION

The idea that God exercises a care, preservation, and government over the things He created, so that they will accomplish the purposes for which they were created, is eminently Scriptural.   This doctrine does not require that everything that happens in the world, including evil, is somehow to be attributed to God's active involvement in His world as He exercises His providence.   This doctrine is opposed to pantheism, which confuses God *with* the world; to deism, which separates God *apart* from the world; to fatalism, which has an impersonal God *over* the world; and to naturalism, which excludes God *from* the world.

SELECTED BIBLIOGRAPHY

Buswell, James O., "Providence" in *The Zondervan Pictorial Bible Dictionary*, edited by Merrill C. Tenney.   Grand Rapids: Zondervan Publishing House, 1963.   p.692,693.

Davison, W.T., "Providence" in *Hastings Encyclopedia of Religion and Ethics*, edited by James Hastings.   New York: Charles Scribner's Sons, 1919.   Vol.1, p.415-420.

Henry, Carl F.H., "God Who Stays: Divine Providence," in *God, Revelation, and Authority* (Waco, TX: Word, 1983), Vol.6, p.455-484.   A supplementary note, "Auschwitz As a Suspension of Providence," follows on p.485-491.
   He laments the decline in men's awareness of the doctrine of providence.   Shows how one's views of God's personal involvement in His creation affects the disciplines of history, economics (e.g., Marxism vs. capitalism – where neither system works well when men forget God's rule), sociology (e.g., behavior is predictable by computerizing present-day attitudes – a danger when God's influence and control are disregarded), education, and science (e.g., genetic engineering).   Henry shows that the "New Age" world view – i.e., that all is God – is untenable with the Biblical view that God's creation and God's providence are separate acts.   He shows how a loss of belief in God's providence among Jewish people has been accelerated by the holocaust; but not much less devastating among Gentiles has been their seeming inability to harmonize the problem of evil with the idea of providence.   Unless God's providential government of His creation is recognized, then there can be no such thing as temporal (and perhaps even eternal) punishment for sin.   Even one's viewpoint about the value and efficacy of prayer depends on the providence of God.   (Unless there is a God who providentially rules His creation, and is moving it toward a goal, all prayer does is change one's own attitudes; it could do nothing to change things.)   While many beneficent consequences of God's providence are forfeited by unbelievers, Romans 8 shows God's providence is a real blessing, at least for the redeemed.   Calls for a recovery of the Biblical emphasis on Divine Providence.   Thought-provoking and timely reading.

Lobstein, P., "Providence" in *The New Schaff-Herzog Encyclopedia of Religious Knowledge*, edited by Samuel Macauley Jackson.   Grand Rapids: Baker Book House, 1957.   Vol.9, p.306-311.

Platt, S.H., "Providence" in *Cyclopedia of Biblical, Theological, and Ecclesiastical Literature*, edited by John McClintock and James Strong.   Grand Rapids: Baker Book House, 1968-70.   Vol.8, p.707-711.

B. Righteousness (Justification, Salvation) is Needed by Jews. 2:1-3:8

1. God's Judgment Against Sin. 2:1-16

Summary: At the final judgment, when God passes sentence and punishes sin, He will do so without partiality. Future judgment is to be based on "deeds," not on such privileges as whether one was Jew or Gentile. Included in this paragraph are the standards God will use in the judgment, standards that are applicable to all men. This is preparatory to the special reference to the Jew found in the next paragraph.[1]

2:1 – *Therefore you are without excuse, every man of you who passes judgment, for in that you judge another, you condemn yourself; for you who judge practice the same things.*

Therefore. The theme running all through the condemnation of the Gentiles (1:18-32) is that they have sinned in spite of better knowledge. The same thing is now said to be true of the Jews. They too sinned, and that in spite of better knowledge.[2] A man who knows God's ordinances, and willfully rejects them, is in danger whether he is Gentile or Jew.

You are without excuse. To be "without excuse" is to be without any defense that can be offered to justify behavior. A man cannot say he did not know God's will. He cannot say he could not help himself. There is no defense he can offer that will sound plausible. The same expression was used of the Gentiles in 1:20.

Every man *of you* who passes judgment. Just as Paul in 1:18 designated the people who were the topic of his writing by the general term "men," and only in the course of the presentation made it clear that it was "Gentiles" whom he had in mind, so here he says "every man," and only later makes it clear that the principles he sets forth apply to the Jews as much as to anyone. Writers have called this a "Nathan-like parable" (2 Samuel 12:1-4), with several verses intervening before we get to "Thou art the man!" Batey uses a different Old Testament illustration. "The apostle uses an approach similar to that of Amos, who disarmed his audience by first delivering his oracles against the surrounding

---

[1] The reader who compares commentaries on Romans will observe that there is no agreement among commentators concerning the way to outline Romans 2:1-16. Some authors have suggested that while 1:18-32 spoke of the "sinful Gentile," it is the "good Gentile" (the moral Gentile) who is in Paul's mind as he writes 2:1-16. To see this theme followed, with appropriate comments on the verses, see Bruce, *Romans*, p.86-92, or Barmby, *Romans*, p.50-55. Since Paul speaks of "Jews" by name as early as verse 9, this commentator sees no real value in putting off (in our outline) the idea that Jews are being discussed until verse 17.

[2] The force of *dio*, "therefore," has been the subject of much debate. Usually the word introduces a conclusion based on some preceding facts (i.e., 'such and such is true; *therefore,* you must do such and such'). However, the fact in the preceding chapter on which the argument in chapter 2 is based is not easily discovered. Instead of gathering up the whole current of Paul's teaching respecting the Gentiles, some writers point to this or that single verse in 1:18-32.

nations before condemning Judah and Israel for their sins (Amos 1:1-2:16)."[3]   All this supposes that if Paul, earlier, had openly named the Jews as he does in 2:17, their opposition to what he had to say would have been aroused, and they would have closed their ears to something they needed to hear.   Further, the fact that Jews are not specifically named causes any reader to apply the argument to himself.   These are the standards any and all readers will be judged by in the final judgment.   "Passes judgment" is a translation of *krinō*, a word that in this context seems to mean "criticize, find fault with, condemn."[4] The behavior pictured is in contrast to the hearty approval some Gentiles gave their fellow sinners.   While Romans 1:32 implied that hearty disapproval of those who practice sin is expected by God, Paul now shows that it is possible for a man to "find fault with" another's sinful behavior, and still stand condemned for his own sins in the final judgment.

For in that you judge another, you condemn yourself.   A man must be careful when he passes condemnatory judgment on another, that he is not blind to his own sins.   To condemn another man for his sin is to admit that there are divine standards by which men (critic and criticized alike) are expected to abide.   In his agreement with those divine standards, the critic has implicitly acknowledged the correctness of his own coming condemnation at the hands of God.[5]

For you who judge practice the same things.   The Jews were guilty of many of the same sins as were being committed by the Gentiles (and cataloged in Romans 1:18-32), and all those sins were sins against the light.   They knew better, and refused to obey God's direct and specific revelations.[6]   "Practice" is the same word (*prassō*) used in 1:32, and indicates a habit pattern of life.

---

[3] Batey, *Romans*, p.32.

[4] Arndt-Gingrich, *Lexicon*, p.453.   The word often has a legal connotation, and is used of both human courts and God's final judgment.   The word, too, can have the idea of "passing judgment" or "making a decision" about something, and the decision need not always be an unfavorable one.   Rather, in each case, the context determines if it is favorable or unfavorable.

There is much teaching in the Scriptures on the topic of judging.   There is some judging that Christians are expected to do: they will have to 'discern' if men they meet are prospects for salvation and need to hear the gospel (cp. Philip's meeting with the Ethiopian, Acts 8:30-40); they will have to 'examine' teachings, to determine whether or not they are false (2 John 9-11; 1 Corinthians 10:15); they are to "decide" cases of dispute between brethren (1 Corinthians 6:4,5).   There is also some judging that is outside the Christian's right to do: hypocritical, condemnatory judging (Matthew 7:1-5); and 'deciding' a man's eternal destiny (1 Corinthians 4:5), something that is the prerogative of Almighty God.

What Paul's readers had been doing as they passed judgment on others was similar to what Jesus spoke against in the Sermon on the Mount (Matthew 7:1-5).   Men are prone to condemn in others the very sins they permit themselves to commit.

[5] "Condemn" in the second half of this clause represents *katakrinō*, a compound form of *krinō*, which regularly means "to pass an adverse sentence."   Thayer, *Lexicon*, p.332,333.

[6] There is a sense in which it can be said the Jews did not practice the same kind of idolatry as the Gentiles, for such use of actual idols had been pretty much eradicated from amongst the Jewish people during the Babylonian captivity.   However, there are numerous statements in the Gospels that show the

2:2 – *And we know that the judgment of God rightly falls upon those who practice such things.*

And we know.[7]   Men can know about the "judgment of God" only by external testimony,[8] and such testimony God Himself had given on numerous occasions.   Everywhere in the Old Testament, through the voices of Moses and the prophets, God taught the Jew about the coming judgment and the standards to be applied.   And before there was a Mosaic covenant and revelation, God had already spoken to the earliest men, in some detail, about the coming judgment (see Jude 14,15).

That the judgment of God.   The judgment Paul has in mind here seems to be the final judgment at the end of the age, especially since verses 5-16 go on to give greater detail about this final judgment.[9]   In order to understand all that is said in the following verses about this final judgment, it seems appropriate to summarize what the Bible says elsewhere about this judgment.   The Bible everywhere teaches that in the final judgment, God's Word will be compared to men's lives.   If the comparison is favorable, God will say, "Well done, good and faithful servant ...!"   If the comparison is unfavorable because men have refused and rebelled, then the sentence will be, "Depart from me, ye that work iniquity!"   This passage in Romans 2 defines and identifies in some detail what the particular "Word" is that will be used in individual men's cases.[10]

Rightly falls upon those who practice such things.   For "rightly falls," there is a marginal note, "the judgment of God is according to truth against those ...."   The word in the Greek is a noun (*alētheian*), not an adverb (*alēthos*), and we therefore hesitate to agree with the English versions that treat it as though it were an adverb, as the NASB and TEV do.   The NASB margin is more likely correct, and this verse is then understood as giving a *standard* in accordance with which the judgment of God is pronounced.   The "truth" that God revealed (see "ordinances" in 1:32, and "that which is known" in 1:19, and what is im-

---

conduct of the Jews to be as Paul here asserts (see Matthew 3:7, 12:39, 23:1-36).   Josephus also says his countrymen committed all kinds of wickedness, omitting none that were known to men.

[7] The KJV reads "*But* we know" (the Greek word is *de*).   There is some difficulty for the translators as to whether verse 2 is a contrast to what is said in verse 1, or whether verse 2 is a continuation of the thought of verse 1.   "And" or "besides" is how the idea of continuation is expressed by translators.

[8] "Know" represents the Greek word *oida*, a word which means "to know for a fact, by external testimony."   It has a synonym, *ginōskō*, which means "to know by personal experience."   Sanday and Headlam, *Romans*, p.55.

[9] Besides the final judgment, there is a judgment that God passes every day as He watches over His creation.   1 Peter 1:17 speaks of how God impartially "judges" (present tense, continuing action) each man's work during that man's life here on earth.   The context here in Romans 2 requires this passage to be explained as having reference to the Great Judgment Day at the close of the age.

[10] Verses that suggest such a comparison between men's lives and the Word of God are Revelation 20:12 ("the dead were judged from the things written in the books [books of Scripture?] according to their deeds"), and John 12:48 ("The word I spoke [My message] will judge him at the last day," said Jesus).

plied in "know" in 2:2) is the standard He will use as He judges.[11] "Those who practice such things" means "every man," no matter of what age or what nation.

> The Apostle adroitly couches his argument in general terms so as surely to embrace the Jew without as yet naming him. He is thus craftily preparing his mind for the tremendous conclusion – a conclusion which will cut him loose from Abraham, from circumcision, from the Law, and send him in despair to Christ.[12]

For an explanation of "such things" see the comments on "same things" in verse 1.

2:3 – *And do you suppose this, O man, when you pass judgment upon those who practice such things and do the same* **yourself,** *that you will escape the judgment of God?*

And do you suppose this, O man. God is going to judge! That much has been revealed again and again.[13] Does Paul's reader ("you" is singular) think he is the only exception to the rule – the one man whose judgment will be by some other standard than "according to truth" (verse 2)?

When you pass judgment upon those who practice such things and do the same *yourself.* This repeats what was explained in verse 1.

---

[11] Another explanation is sometimes found for this expression.   It is that God will judge those who are guilty of such things, not according to appearances, but according to the merits of the case. His judgment is not concerned with what race a man belongs to, but whether or not that man's life is in harmony with the revelation He had given.   Not a few writers note that Jews thought they would be given exemption from the judgment, or at least highly preferential treatment over other races. Barclay, *Romans*, p.34,35, gives several enlightening examples.   "God loves Israel alone of all the nations of the earth." "God will judge the Gentiles with one measure and the Jews with another."   "All Israelites will have part in the world to come."   "Abraham sits beside the gates of hell and does not permit any wicked Israelite to go through."

[12] Lard, *Romans*, p.73.

[13] Using different parables and ways of illustrating what it will be like, the Bible seems to present the idea of one general judgment of all at the end of time.   The Judgment of the Wheat and the Tares (Matthew 13:24-30 and 36-43) closes with the consummation of the age, the wicked in torment, and the righteous in heaven.   The Judgment of the Sheep and Goats (Matthew 25:31-46) immediately precedes a sentence to either heaven or hell.   The "coming" (*parousia*) of Jesus is closely connected with the judgment seat of Christ (2 Corinthians 5:1-10 and its discussion of a new [resurrection] body should be compared with 1 Corinthians 15:20-28 which show how that new body is given "at His coming"); with the transformation [into resurrection bodies] of those who are still alive on earth at the time of His coming (1 Thessalonians 4:15); with the destruction of the Man of Lawlessness (2 Thessalonians 2:8); and with the renovation of the universe (2 Peter 3:4 and context).   Since all of this is true of what happens at the time of the *parousia*, it is difficult to agree with those eschatological schemes which have a thousand years or more of time, and several more judgments, after the *parousia*.   The Great White Throne judgment seems to be but another way of presenting this same final judgment, for both righteous ("the sea [cp. Revelation 15:2] gave up the dead which were in it," Revelation 20:13) and wicked ("Hades gave up the dead in it," Revelation 20:13) are present at this judgment, too.   Furthermore, it is followed by eternity in the lake of fire for the wicked – just as was the Sheep and Goat judgment.   Then when one adds to this all the Old Testament passages about the "day of the Lord" (which 2 Peter 3:10 identifies as the final judgment), there is nothing in any of these passages that would necessitate the idea that there are two or three different judgments at the end of the church age (and later).   The Bible, we repeat, seems to present the idea of one general judgment which is followed either by eternity in heaven, or eternity in hell.

That you will escape the judgment of God? "You" is emphatic in the Greek, and such an emphatic construction implies a contrast with someone else. "Do *you*, of all people, suppose you will escape?" 'If you know enough of God's will to know He disapproves of the sins you condemn in others, then you also know about how His final judgment will be "according to truth." Yet you still think you are an exception to the rule? How strange!' Of all men, the Jew, so distinguished by the special revelation given to him, should least have fallen into such error.[14]

2:4 – Or do you think lightly of the riches of His kindness and forbearance and patience, not knowing that the kindness of God leads you to repentance?

Or do you think lightly. This verse goes together with verse 3, and together they give the two possible mental attitudes a man must have if he thinks he can continue to practice sins and yet escape condemnation in the judgment. Either he thinks he is exempt, or he must despise all that God has been doing to try to save him! "Think lightly" means to "look on with a feeling of contempt."[15] Because some penalties and punishments for sin seem so long coming, men are apt to think they never will be punished. So instead of turning from their sin, they look with contempt on God's efforts to save them, as though such efforts were not needed in their case.

Of the riches of His kindness and forbearance and patience. "Riches" (a word that expresses abundance) likely modifies all three attributes which follow. It says God's kindness is abundant, His forbearance is exceeding, and His patience is full and long. "Kindness" is an attitude towards others that expresses itself by trying to do good to those others. Included in God's goodness would seem to be the provision He made for the forgiveness of sins. For the Jew (or anyone, for that matter) to suppose he could get away with his sin without suffering any punishment is tantamount to despising the Lord's provision for forgiveness. "Forbearance" speaks of delay of deserved punishment. This delay is but a temporary thing, and after a certain lapse of time, unless other conditions intervene (e.g., repentance, in this context), the punishment will fall.[16] "Patience" is the word that expresses "putting up with people."[17] Chrysostom defined the word "patience" as the "characteristic of the man who has it in his power to avenge himself, and who deliberately does not use it. It is the spirit of the man who could wipe out the man who hurts and

---

[14] Perhaps it can be affirmed that the Jew is "the servant who knew His Lord's will," and whose judgment will therefore be more rigorous if that will is neglected (Luke 12:47,48). As noted in footnote #11 above, some Jews did have the notion they would be exempt from the judgment (or at least from any condemnation). They trusted their descent from Abraham (Matthew 3:8,9; John 8:33); in their circumcision (Galatians 5:1ff; Romans 4:9ff); and in the fact that God had entrusted the Law to them, as evidence they would get preferential treatment.

[15] See the meanings given for *kataphroneō* in Arndt-Gingrich, *Lexicon*, p.421.

[16] Trench, *Synonyms*, p.196-200.

[17] Two Greek words express "patience." *Makrothumia*, used here, means "patience under provocation, referring to *persons*." *Hupomonē* is the word used when "patience under trials, referring to *things*" is the

insults him, but who in patient mercy stays his hand."[18]   God does not have a short, quick temper – instead He waits long before He actively interposes punishment.   When a man sins and is not immediately hurled into Hell, he owes his continued life on earth, with its opportunity to repent, to the patience of God!

Not knowing that the kindness of God leads you to repentance?   The refusal to acknowledge the reason for the delay in deserved punishment is likely deliberate.   Men knew about God's characteristics, and about the coming judgment, but they willfully went on practicing their sins as though there were no danger.   "Repentance" is a change of mind and a change of action, resulting from a Godly sorrow for sin, and including restitution where possible.[19]   "Leads" likely expresses effort, or attempt to lead.[20]   While punishment is temporarily withheld, God is at work, tenderly and kindly, trying to lead sinners to repentance, lest they perish!   His special work among the Jewish nation was not just a privileged position for the Jew to bask in all the while lovingly content with his lot – it should have been viewed for what it was (an opportunity to change) and quickly grasped. "To miscalculate the significance of the time which God grants for repentance and mistake God's longsuffering for approval will be disastrous (2 Peter 3:9)."[21]

2:5 – *But because of your stubbornness and unrepentant heart you are storing up wrath for yourself in the day of wrath and revelation of the righteous judgment of God,*

But because of your stubbornness and unrepentant heart.   The margin reads, "In accordance with your stubbornness ...," and the expression suggests the norm according to which (or in conformity to which) a judgment is rendered, or rewards and punishments are given.[22]   In passing, let it be observed that this "good man" (this moral Jew) needs to repent, and that is evidence he too is a sinner, just like the man described in chapter 1. "Stubborn" (*sklēroteta*) means "insensible, unimpressionable (no impression is made by contact, as when a man touches a stone)."[23]   God's goodness was in operation, trying to

---

topic.   George Ricker Berry, *A New Greek-English Lexicon to the New Testament* (Chicago: Wilcox & Follett Co., 1948), p.10.

[18] Alluded to by Barclay, *Romans*, p.36.

[19] See the Special Study on "Repentance" in the author's commentary on *Acts*, p.145-149.

[20] Sanday and Headlam, *Romans*, p.56, speak of "leads" as being a conative present, which would put emphasis on the effort or attempt to lead.   Dana and Mantey, *Manual Grammar*, p.186, use the expression "tendential present" of action which is purposed or attempted or intended to occur.

[21] Batey, *Romans*, p.34.   The careful reader will note that the verse about the longsuffering of God leading to repentance in Romans is addressed to a different audience than is the passage in Peter. Romans is addressed to unconverted Jews, whereas Peter is addressed to readers who are already Christian.   It is significant that God's "goodness" is needed by both classes.

[22] Arndt-Gingrich, *Lexicon*, p.408.

[23] "Stubbornness" is not an adjective, and so does not modify "heart," as though Paul were writing here

lead the man to repentance, but it made no impression on the man. It was just as if his will was petrified as a result of long sinning. "Heart" here is what modern man calls his "mind," and it is in the mind that repentance takes place – as the definition given above had it, "a change of *mind* ...." The unrepentant in heart continues to make moral decisions with no regard for what God would wish the man to do.

You are storing up wrath for yourself. Not only are there temporal punishments for sin (about which Romans 1:21 speaks), but there is also an eternal punishment for sin, about which this context speaks. "Store up" can also be translated "treasure up," as when a man continues to add to his hoard of wealth which he has secreted away in a secure place. "This purposely chosen word glances back at 'riches,' and heightens the tragic nature of the foolish conduct that redounds to one's own destruction."[24] By persisting in sin, a man is adding to the "wrath" that will be inflicted on the last day. Degrees of punishment for the wicked is a Biblical doctrine. Impenitent Jews will *themselves* suffer wrath. It is not at all like some Jews thought, that only *others* (e.g., the Gentiles) would get back what they had "stored up."

In the day of wrath and revelation of the righteous judgment of God. The "day of wrath" is the day of final judgment, the day when God executes His wrath against sinners. Chapter 1 has shown that the present age has its tokens of God's wrath and righteous judgment, yet the final manifestation of His wrath is reserved until the "day of wrath."[25] As He passes final sentence, all will see the fairness and equity of His judgments. The decision He renders will be the one that is right, the one that ought to be rendered. The Bible never did teach that the purpose of the final judgment is to determine for the first time what each man's destiny shall be; that destiny is something already known in this life (John 3:36). (Furthermore, when physical death occurs, a man is either in blessedness or torment immediately; see The Rich Man and Lazarus in Luke 16:19ff, and study the references on Paradise and Hades. A man knows his destiny before he ever stands before God in the Final Judgment). Instead, it could much more suitably be said that the final judgment is a final vindication of God for the rewards and punishments already in part bestowed. He will be shown to have been perfectly "right" in what He does with men.

2:6 – who WILL RENDER TO EVERY MAN ACCORDING TO HIS DEEDS:

Who WILL RENDER TO EVERY MAN ACCORDING TO HIS DEEDS. As is the format of the NASB, words printed in all caps indicate a quotation from the Old Testament, in this case from Psalm 62:12. Paul is saying, 'Here is a verse in the Bible that says all

---

of a "stubborn (hard) heart." Stubbornness is a quality of the will.

[24] Meyer, *Romans*, p.84.

[25] All through the Old Testament, the Bible reader finds the expression "the day of the Lord." It is a day of judgment in the future, sometimes referring to a day in history; but ultimately it is a prediction of the great and terrible day of the Lord, which Peter tells us is the final judgment (2 Peter 3:1-10, especially verse 10). It is a day when God executes His wrath against sinners per Revelation 6:17; 1 Thessalonians 1:10; John 3:36; and Ephesians 5:6. Though the last two Scripture references could speak of this life, the first two plainly show that God's wrath is *not* exhausted in this life.

men will stand in the judgment. What I am saying is not some new doctrine just recently introduced to the world.' "Every man," the Psalmist said. Some 20th century Bible teachers have affirmed that the righteous will not be judged, but only stand at the judgment seat of Christ to be rewarded. But note the context following here in Romans. It speaks of wrath for some, and blessing for others – all of whom went through the judgment.[26] Every man who ever lived will have his personal turn before the Judge of the universe. The Judge will then "render" (i.e., give back, recompense) to each just what he deserves. As the man acted towards God, so God will act towards the man.

Verse 2 stated that His judgment will be "according to truth." "According to his deeds" gives another norm, or standard, which God will take into account as He passes judgment. What is pictured as happening at the final judgment is that a man's life ("his deeds") will be compared to the Word of God ("truth"), just as was explained in verse 2. The kind of "deeds" to be taken into account is specified in verses 7-10 following: perseverance in doing good, on the one hand; disobedience to truth and obedience to unrighteousness, on the other.[27] Paul teaches, with definiteness and precision, that "deeds" – what a man has done, the tenor of his life – are one of the things that will be taken into account on the judgment day.[28] At the judgment, when a man's "deeds" are assessed, the thing God

---

[26] True, according to the explanation previously set forth, the context of Romans 2:6 is "Jewish;" Paul is establishing the fact that a Jew cannot escape the Judgment merely because he is a Jew. Because a true principle of interpretation of Scripture is to pay attention to whom it is spoken, some attempt to show (in spite of 2:6) that *not* all men will stand in the judgment; they affirm the Christian is exempt. The topic of the final judgment will be introduced later in Romans (chapters 14,15) where the people who are "giving an account to God" *are* Christians. In addition, we have also maintained that Romans 2:1-16 presents a picture that is true of all men, and so is especially true of the Jew. It *does* teach that *all* men will be judged.

[27] The careful reader who has worked through several commentaries on Romans will have observed that most commentators spend much effort and time on this phrase. The problem that besets these writers is that they think they must explain away an apparent contradiction between "saved by *faith*" (as Romans teaches) and "judged by *works*" (as Romans also teaches). The solutions offered to the problem are ingenious and varied: (1) Paul speaks here only hypothetically of how the destiny of men would be determined if there were no gospel (Melanchthon, Alford, Hodge, Batey). (2) Paul is inconsistent in his presentation, confusing his old Jewish beliefs [judgment according to works] and his new Christian beliefs [justification by faith] (Fritzsche, Sanday [in part]). (3) Justification by faith has to do with the entrance into salvation, whereas "judgment according to works" speaks of the conclusion of the Christian life (Godet, Sanday and Headlam). (4) A saving "faith" is something that grows and is completed or perfected as the result of previous "works" (Luthardt, and the Roman Catholic Church generally).

This commentator would affirm that the apparent contradiction is not in what Paul says, but in the explanation that the commentators have put on Paul's words. Those commentators who find themselves in difficulty have defined "faith" as "trust," and thus have left no room in their definition of faith for "acts of obedience." Instead, if we identify the faith that saves as an "obedient faith" – a faith that does what God says – this verse about one's works being a condition of judgment is not embarrassing at all. (See Special Study #16, "The Faith that Saves," in the author's commentary on *Acts*, p.598-610.)

One other positive result of defining the faith that saves as an "obedient faith" is the delightful way Paul and James then complement each other. James writes that a "man is justified by deeds" (James 2:24) and uses Genesis 15:6 to prove it (see James 2:23), while Paul writes that a "man is justified by faith" (Romans 3:28) and also uses Genesis 15:6 to prove it (Romans 4:3). The faith that saves must be a faith that acts (could we say "faithfulness" over a period of time), not just a one-time mental assent.

[28] This is consistent with Scripture generally. The Jew would likely have remembered these Old Testament passages (in addition to Psalms 62:12) which teach judgment on the basis of deeds: Job 34:11;

will be looking for is the tenor of life, the total impact of his character and conduct – toward which way (obedience or disobedience?) do his actions consistently lean? Sinless perfection has never been required by God for salvation; instead, He looks to see if repentance has resulted when His goodness tried to lead the sinner to repentance. The tenor of life being "right" is what God looks for as He compares men's lives ("deeds") to the Word He has given them to live by.[29] If a man receives according to his deeds, there can be no cause of complaint about God's sentence. If Jew or Gentile, pagan or Christian, be finally rejected, it will be for his own personal sins followed by a stubbornness and refusal to repent.

2:7 – *to those who by perseverance in doing good seek for glory and honor and immortality, eternal life;*

To those. In verses 7-10 we have an example of inverted parallelism, to give special prominence to the universality of the retribution. Verses 7 and 10 go together and describe the way the righteous man lives and his destiny, while verses 8 and 9 together describe the way the stubborn and unrepentant man lives and what will be his ultimate destiny. One other technical note is needed, and that is the observation that there is no main verb in verses 7-10. The NASB added some words in italics in verse 9 to make up this deficiency. What a person reading the original would do is go to the context and borrow a verb that has already been used. We shall go to verse 6 and borrow the verb "will render," so now verse 7 reads "to those who by perseverance in doing good seek for glory and honor and immortality, *He will render* eternal life." Likewise, we will repeat the same borrowed verb in verse 8, which then reads, "*He will render* wrath and indignation ...."

Verses 7-10 state in detail what Paul understands Psalm 62:12 to mean when it says "God *will render* to every man according to his *deeds*." Paul divides the human family into two classes, just as Jesus Himself did – saved and lost (Matthew 7:24-29, 13:41-43, 25:31ff). To the first class, having compared their deeds to "truth," God will render everlasting life. To the second, after a similar comparison, He will render wrath and indignation, tribulation and distress.

Who by perseverance in doing good. The word translated "perseverance" is *hupomonē*, which speaks of "patience under trial, putting up with things" (see footnote #17 above). Implied is the idea that "doing good" will take effort; it will require the acquiescence of the will to accomplish something which otherwise might not be done. The singular "good" (the same word was plural, "deeds," in verse 6) looks at one's whole life – it was steadfastness in well-doing. Those who continue doing good works are the ones who will be rewarded with eternal life (Matthew 10:22; Hebrews 10:38,39; Revelation 2:10).

Proverbs 24:12; Jeremiah 17:10, 32:19. New Testament verses also assert the same fact: Matthew 7:16, 16:27, 25:31ff; 1 Corinthians 3:8; 2 Corinthians 5:10; Galatians 6:7ff; Ephesians 6:8; Colossians 3:24; Revelation 2:23, 20:12, 22:12.

[29] Great care has been exercised during the writing of the comments on this phrase lest an erroneous idea intrude – namely, that the "deeds" are meritorious, that is, that the doing of the deeds somehow helps earn salvation. The uniform message in the Bible is that man can do nothing to earn his salvation. See Romans 3:24 where this topic is explained by Paul.

Seek for glory and honor and immortality.   "Glory," "honor," and "immortality" are qualities of the heavenly life with God, to be enjoyed by the righteous after the judgment. That these are sought for suggests that the man was willing to forsake his sins, was willing to respond to God's goodness by repenting, was willing to submit to God and obey His laws, because he was aware of the blessings God was offering in heaven.   We are reminded of Abraham, who because he wanted to be a resident of the "city that has the foundations, whose builder and maker is God," obeyed when God called.   The desire to share in the future blessings is the thing that motivated men to persevere in doing the good in the meantime.   Exactly what "glory" means in this passage is hard to define.   Perhaps it is the same "glory" spoken of in Romans 3:23.   Perhaps there is some reference to the "glory" that lights all of heaven (Revelation 21:11,23), by which the nations of the redeemed will walk (Revelation 21:24).   Perhaps it is simply a synonym for praise from God, like "Well done, good and faithful servant!"   "Honor" denotes the esteem in which the redeemed will be held by God.   "Immortality" would better be translated "incorruption" for the Greek word *aphtharsia* suggests "no decay."[30]   A man who lives in a world subjected to vanity and corruption and disintegration can indeed appreciate and anticipate a world where all these are no more.   Not only will his resurrection body be perfect, but the heavenly world will be too.

Eternal life.   As noted above, we add the verb "He will render" to complete the sense. To those, whoever they be, whose lives are characterized by doing the good that God revealed pleases Him, He will grant "eternal life."   Eternal life here is more than simply endless existence, for even the wicked have that (Matthew 25:46; Revelation 14:11).   In this context it must speak of the blessedness of heaven, a quality of life which is characterized by intimate communion with God, and the other qualities (glory, honor, immortality) this verse has specified.[31]

2:8 – *but to those who are selfishly ambitious and do not obey the truth, but obey unrighteousness, wrath and indignation.*

But.   As noted above, verses 8 and 9 go together, and describe the life and destiny of the wicked.

To those who are selfishly ambitious.   The Greek word *eritheia* is not of certain translation here.   It used to be supposed that the word was related to *eris*, a word denoting "strife," where two parties oppose each other.   Now the lexicographers are not so sure of this derivation.[32]   More recently it is understood to express the desire to put oneself forward even at the expense of others (maybe even taking advantage of others).   In this sense it would well describe the man who refused to listen to God, because he was more interested in his own personal ambitions than in God's ambitions for him.   The picture is

---

[30] Another Greek word, *athanasia*, is the one that means "no death" or "immortality."

[31] The Bible reader must be careful when he comes to the expression "eternal life."   In some passages, eternal life is spoken of not as a future gift, but as a present possession for the believer (John 3:16,36).

[32] See Arndt-Gingrich, *Lexicon*, p.309.

of the man who uses all his faculties, even stooping to unscrupulous acts, to evade the commands of God which he knows he ought to obey.

And do not obey the truth, but obey unrighteousness. The "truth" here is the same as in verse 2, namely, God's revealed will. "Do not obey" (*apeithō*) is a stubborn refusal to be persuaded, a willful refusal to do what God requires.[33] It is the behavior of a man who has a knowledge of God and deliberately ignores it. As would be expected, "obey" in both clauses is present tense, signifying a habitual course of conduct. "Unrighteousness" (everything God has forbidden) is personified as a master who gives the orders these wicked men carry out. Chapter 7 will indicate that the real evil master is the devil, who is stirring up men's desires for what God has forbidden. Cp. also Romans 6:13,16,17,19.

Wrath and indignation. Again it will be remembered that we must supply the verb "He will render," with the "wrath and indignation ..." being the things the wicked will receive. "Wrath" was explained at Romans 1:18 as being God's settled anger against sin. It is the attitude felt within. "Indignation" is the action that expresses wrath externally. Indignation, too, may express that turbulent, boiling anger that is the beginning of the expression of wrath.[34] Wrath is the longer lasting of the two kinds of anger.

2:9 – There will be *tribulation and distress for every soul of man who does evil, of the Jew first and also of the Greek,*

There will be **tribulation and distress.** The two previous expressions looked at eternal punishment from God's standpoint. These two look at it from the sufferer's standpoint. He will feel "tribulation and distress." "Tribulation" is suffering that results from pressure. "As applied to future punishment, it denotes the pressure of the calamities that will come upon the soul as the just reward of sin."[35] "Distress" translates *stenochōria*, to be confined in a narrow place. It is the hopelessness one feels when he is shut up without any possibility of escape, the anguish felt when he is suffering and there is no place to turn for relief.

For every soul of man who does evil. Does this mean that the soul in particular is the subject of future punishment?[36] Or is this a Hebraism where the soul stands for the whole person (as in Acts 2:41,43 and 27:37)? "Does" is the compound form *katergazomai* (the simple form *ergazomai* occurs in the next verse), and suggests a perseverance in doing evil. "Evil" is one of the synonyms used in Scripture for "sin,"[37] and especially characterizes the

---

[33] In John 3:36, "belief" (*pisteuō*) is contrasted with "disobedience" (*apeithō*). This contrast is possible only if "belief" includes "obedience." Also see notes at Romans 11:30.

[34] Trench, *Synonyms*, p.130-134.

[35] Barnes, *Romans*, p.64.

[36] Some writers have ventured the suggestion that, after the judgment, the wicked lose their resurrection bodies (that is why it is called the "second death" in Revelation 20:14) and only the soul is punished. See Sanday, *Romans*, p.38; Meyer, *Romans*, p.88; Barnes, *Romans*, p.64.

[37] See Thayer, *Lexicon*, p.320. Also compare comments on the word "evil" at Romans 1:30.

acts as being contrary to law, either divine or human.   In verse 8, this "evil" was explained as "not obey[ing] the truth, but obey[ing] unrighteousness."   What Paul means by "*every soul*" is spelled out in the next phrase.   It is a universal punishment of evil men.

Of the Jew first and also of the Greek.   When we had this expression at Romans 1:16, it was explained as meaning "priority."   The Jews had been privileged with divine favor far above the Gentiles in the centuries before Christ came (Romans 3:1,2; 9:4,5), and greater privilege carries with it a corresponding greater responsibility (Luke 12:47-48; Psalm 50:3-8; 1 Peter 4:17).   Surely in the background is the matter of degrees of punishment.   Both Jewish and Gentile doers of evil will be punished, but the punishment of the former will be more severe because their opportunities and privileges were greater.

2:10 – *but glory and honor and peace to every man who does good, to the Jew first and also to the Greek.*

But glory and honor and peace.   With verse 10, the parallelism returns to the subject of verse 7, the destiny of the saved.   God will render to them glory and honor and peace. "Peace" is an additional characteristic of the life of the redeemed.[38]   It may be the opposite of "tribulation and distress" threatened on the wicked in verse 9.   It may speak of the absence of any wrath or indignation on God's part toward them.   There is a tranquility and a happiness that results from being accepted by God.

To every man who does good.   Perhaps the change to the simple verb (see notes on verse 9) here reflects the grace and mercy of God.   In the case of the wicked man, it was persistence in evil doing that was punished.   In the case of the righteous, it is perseverance (verse 7) in the simple effort to accomplish the good that is rewarded.   Of course, there is no way that the doing of the good merits salvation either here or hereafter.

To the Jew first and also to the Greek.   Just as there was a priority assigned to the Jew with respect to punishment, so there is one assigned with respect to reward.   If the phrase in verse 9 suggested degrees of punishment, the same phrase in verse 10 suggests degrees of reward.[39]   Salvation is "also to the Greek."   The clear doctrine of the New Testament is that the Jews had no monopoly on divine favor with respect to salvation.   Yet there still is the fact that God had favored them in Old Testament times.   The covenants were made with them, Christ (according to the flesh) came through them, and Gentiles were as a wild olive branch grafted in among believing Jews.   The doctrine Paul sets forth here is that the Jews who responded to the responsibility God gave them will be rewarded accordingly.[40]   In the final judgment, the topic of this paragraph, God will judge all men in the same way

---

[38] Some note the three terms, "glory and honor and incorruption," in verse 7, and have supposed that "peace" simply is substituted for "incorruption."   Vine, *Romans*, p.34, suggests the change means that the reward exceeds the aim and effort.   They aimed for "incorruption" and not only got it, but got "peace" too.

[39] The Scriptures do seem to teach "degrees of reward" in 1 Corinthians 3:12-15, where a man can lose "reward" and still be saved, and in Matthew 5:12 where Jesus says "Your reward in heaven is *great*."

[40] See Romans 9-11 where the "favorable treatment" of the Jews is explained in detail by Paul.

– He will compare their lives with the "truth" they had.   He will also take into account the opportunities and responsibilities they had.   Then He will reward or punish accordingly.

2:11 – *For there is no partiality with God.*

For there is no partiality with God.   This seems to be the third principle of judgment Paul lists.   In verse 2, he showed that it is "according to truth."   In verse 6, it is "according to deeds."   Now it is "without partiality," or according to available light.[41]   To show partiality is to play favorites, to show favoritism to some by treating them differently from how others are treated.   The ones who are favored get a "break;" they get some benefit others were equally eligible for, but were omitted simply on the whim of the benefactor.   It will not be like this with God.   His judgment is "righteous" (verse 5).   He will judge each man alike, on the basis of available light (i.e., on the basis of how much "truth" he had).

2:12 – *For all who have sinned without the Law will also perish without the Law; and all who have sinned under the Law will be judged by the Law;*

For.   Verse 12 appears to be an explanation of the expression "no partiality" as it explicitly states on what principles God judges men.   All men have some "truth," whether they live in the Patriarchal, Mosaic, or New Testament age.   If God expected one of the Patriarchs to obey the gospel or be damned, it could be said that God was not being fair.   But if God requires of the Patriarchs that their lives conform favorably to patriarchal "truth" they had available, there is nothing unfair or partial about that!   It might even appear that the expression "to the Jew first" (in verses 9 and 10) does imply that God plays favorites.   Not so!   Even if they were specially favored in this life, they are not granted immunity from the standards by which God will judge all men.

All who have sinned without the Law.   If any man is sent to perdition, it will not be due to transgression of some "truth" he did not have, but because of sin against such light as he did have.   "While it is true that there is no respect of *persons* with God, it is also true that he has respect to the different situations in which men are placed in reference to the knowledge of His law."[42]   "Sinned" should be explained by what has been already said in the

---

[41] As we come to Romans 2:11-16, we are into one of those paragraphs over which every commentator seems to struggle – trying to fathom what it says, and struggling to make it harmonize with what the Bible says elsewhere.   As will be noted in due course, even the translators of the New Testament get into the act (whether or not to put verses 14-15, or verses 13-15, in a parenthesis; and whether or not to use a capital "L" on "law") as they try to make the train of Paul's presentation meaningful to English readers.

One of the first problems that must be addressed is to note and attempt to explain the relationship of all the verses (11,12,13,14) that begin with "for."   Maybe if we could determine what "reason" or "explanation" each verse is, we would have made considerable progress toward understanding this passage.   Is verse 11 an explanation of verse 10 ("to the Jew first and also to the Greek" – *for* there is no partiality with God)?   If so, then our note about a third principle of judgment should have been saved until verse 12.   Is verse 12 connected with verse 11, explaining what "no partiality" means?   Or is verse 12 connected to verse 2, explaining what revelation the man was expected to obey?   And do verses 13 and 14 explain verse 12, or do they go back to the idea of verse 6 (explaining the works necessary if a man's tenor of life is to be right)?   Each of these questions must be addressed in due time as the verses are handled.

[42] Murray, *Romans*, p.69.

context. It is looking back on a man's life from the standpoint of the judgment, and what is seen is a habit pattern of sin and disobedience.[43]

Now we have come to the expression "without the Law," which in the margin is given as "without law." The NASB capitalizes the word when (in the opinion of the translators) it has reference to the Law of Moses, and uses small "l" when it is "law in general" (of which the Law of Moses would be but one example).[44] Likely the decision of the translators to use a capital "L" is correct in this verse (where anarthrous *nomos* appears in the Greek). It does seem to have reference to Gentiles who did not come under the rules God set forth in the Law of Moses. As learned in chapter 1, those Gentiles did have rules given by God to direct and order their conduct, but it was not the Law of Moses. It was only to a certain nation (Israel) that the Law of Moses was given. All other peoples, save the Jews, would be included in the expression "all who ... without the Law."[45]

Will also perish without the Law. The word "perish" is regularly used in the New Testament for the eternal punishment of the wicked (Matthew 10:28, 18:14; John 3:16 where "perish" is contrasted to "eternal life").[46] They perish because their life as a whole was one that could be classified as 'they sinned.' Though they did not have the privilege

---

[43] The verb "sinned" is in the aorist tense, and it is true that the aorist sometimes speaks of a single act. But it can hardly be affirmed that such is the meaning here in a context that has been dealing with the tenor, or direction, of a man's whole life. So this is likely an example of what Dana and Mantey (*Grammar*, p.196) call a "constative aorist," where an action that happened over a long duration of time is viewed in its entirety.

[44] The NASB, in this matter of capitalization of certain words such as "Law," represents a departure from the practice found in the KJV and ASV. The translators of those older versions preferred to allow the reader to decide if "law" was a reference to Moses' Law or not, rather than thrusting an interpretation at the reader. It certainly is not always easy to decide exactly what was in the Bible writers' minds. Sometimes they wrote "the law" (*ho nomos*) and sometimes they wrote "law" (anarthrous *nomos* [the word "law" with no "the" in front of it]). Whenever we find the first of these two different constructions, the reference is usually to the Law of Moses. It is the second usage that can baffle the reader. Sometimes it has reference to the Law of Moses, sometimes it does not, and sometimes you cannot tell. Not only is there the matter of ambiguity, but there are times the decision one makes about the meaning of anarthrous *nomos* in a certain verse will affect the explanation of a whole passage of Scripture.

[45] Some writers try to defend the proposition that "the law" (*ho nomos*) always has reference to the Law of Moses, while "law" (anarthrous *nomos*) always refers to law in general. Lard, Sanday, and Lipscomb are examples of writers who attempt this. The attempt to keep this distinction causes Romans 2:12 to say that there were people who had no law at all. But if we make Romans 2:12 say the Gentiles had no "law" of any kind, we have contradicted what was taught in chapter 1:19,32. It just will not do to try to say the people "without law" had no immediate or direct revelation from God, for we have already been told that God had given ordinances to these people. They had a declaration of God's will concerning man's conduct! To guard against making 2:12 contradict chapter 1, we are required to conclude that "law" (anarthrous *nomos*) here *is* a reference to the Law of Moses.

[46] Some teachers have used the word "perish" to prove the doctrine of the future annihilation of the wicked. That "perish" (*apollumi*) does not mean annihilate can be seen from a study of 2 Peter 3:6 ("the world at that time was destroyed [*apollumi*]"). If "world" in that verse means the globe we live on, the earth, it was not annihilated in the Flood in Noah's time. If "world" speaks of the wicked people who inhabited the world, they were not annihilated either. Though their physical lives were taken from the earth,

of knowing what God set forth in the Law of Moses, they did have divinely given "truth" to live by; it was this truth that they habitually disregarded, and it was this truth by which they are found guilty and are sentenced to perish.

And all who have sinned under the Law will be judged by the Law. Here the doctrine is that men are judged according to the principle of available light.[47] Jews, who had the Law of Moses, will have their lives compared to the precepts and prohibitions of the Law they had. Again, "sinned" is looking back on a whole lifetime from the vantage point of the future judgment. The life was one that was characterized by sin. "Judged" might well be rendered "condemned" in this verse. Of the Gentiles it was said they would "perish"; but of the Jews it is said they will be "judged" (*krithēsontai*). This is not to be understood as affirming that the disobedient Jew was going to receive less punishment than the sinful

---

Peter tells us they were still in existence over two thousand years later when Jesus visited them in prison (1 Peter 3:18-20). "Perish" signifies the loss of well-being, not the loss of being.

[47] Judgment on the basis of available light is an idea whose content has been hard to grasp by many Bible students. There are several Scriptures where it is affirmed that in the judgment a man will be held responsible for living according to the light he had or could have had. See Matthew 11:21,22, 10:15; Luke 12:47,48; James 3:1; John 9:39-41, 15:23,24; and Romans 2:12. Men who sin "without Law" will perish. Sin is transgression of God's law (1 John 3:4). Therefore, even the Gentiles in the Patriarchal Age did have a law from God to live by, though it was not in written form as was the Mosaic Law. When these Gentiles sinned, it was a disregard of the law God had given them, and they will find in the judgment that the truth they ignored and broke will be the standard by which they are judged. The fact that the Gentiles did not have the greater light of the Law of Moses does not mean they were not responsible to abide by the light they did have. The perdition of the Gentiles, if it ensues, will not be due to a transgression of a code they did not have, but due to sin against such light as they had. If without knowledge of the Law of Moses they sinned, then without reference to the Law of Moses their doom will be.

Now it is not unusual for students in America, unfamiliar with "Gentile" cultures, to think the poor Gentiles are benighted – in great ignorance of what God expects – and that somehow this statement about their being 'condemned for not living up to the light they had' is an unfair thing. Well, folk who have lived among the "Gentiles," even in the present century, state that they do have a knowledge. The Gentiles are not as benighted as we may think. Max Ward Randall, who has done missionary work all over the world, has stated (in a lecture at Central Christian College, Moberly, MO) that no matter where he has gone, he has found 4 things in every culture that serve as a point of contact for preaching the gospel: (1) a sense that there is a deity somewhere they have offended; (2) a sense of personal guilt; (3) the idea that a sacrifice is necessary to placate the offended deity; and (4) the idea of a go-between (a mediator between man and the offended deity) being needed. Warren Wiersbe agrees (*Be Right*, p.28). "You find among all cultures a sense of sin, a fear of judgment, and an attempt to atone for sins and appease whatever gods are feared."

One further thought needs to be expressed. Just because a Gentile has not been privileged to have access to the greater revelation that was embodied in Moses' Law does not mean all was hopeless. Many Gentiles did get things right. The tenor of their lives was in harmony with the limited revelation they had. Think of Abel, Seth, Enoch, Noah, Abraham, and Melchizedek. But how much more favorable would have been those men's chances of pleasing God had they had greater light, and even had it in a written form (like Moses' Law was) so they did not have to depend on the fickle memories of their fathers and grandfathers who were responsible to pass on God's truth by word of mouth. (By parity of reasoning, how much better will be the chances of Gentiles today to please God, if we who have it will take the gospel to them – which is exactly the point Paul is laboring to make in these early chapters in Romans.)

Gentile. On the contrary, the greater the privilege, the greater the corresponding responsibility, and the greater the punishment. If anything, *krithēsontai* is a stronger word than *apollumi* in the previous phrase.

2:13 – *For not the hearers of the Law are just before God, but the doers of the Law will be justified.*

For. The train of thought in verses 13-16 is hard to follow. The ASV puts verses 14 and 15 in parentheses, while in the KJV it is verses 13 to 15 that are so treated. The NASB uses no parentheses at all.[48] Since this verse begins with "for," it likely is an explanation of how it is possible for God to judge on the bases that verses 2, 6, and 11 say He will (namely, according to truth, according to deeds, and without partiality). Verse 13 explains how it is possible for the Jew to be "judged" (perish) even though he had the Law. Verses 14 and 15 then show how the same basis of judgment (whether or not he was a 'doer of the Law') could be applied to the Gentile's case.

Not the hearers of the Law are just before God. As this commentator understands it, verse 13 says nothing different from what has been the idea of the whole paragraph thus far. Earlier, it was explained that what God looks for is the tenor of a man's life – does it compare with the revelation he had? Now Paul says that what God looks for are not just hearers, but "doers." If verse 13 speaks of Jewish hearers, then the capital "L" ("Law") is correct, even though we have another case of anarthrous *nomos* (cp. verse 12). "Just" or "righteous" is one of the technical words in Romans, and is related to the same root from which "righteousness" (1:17) comes. In this context it is contrasted to "perish" and "judged" (verse 12). "Before God" seems to mean "in God's sight." When God passes judgment (according to "deeds," as well as "according to truth"), He will look for more than just "hearing the Law" before he pronounces men "just," and in consequence of the pronouncement grants eternal life (verse 7) to them.

But the doers of the Law will be justified. "Doers" requires no more by way of explanation than a reminder of what was stated in verse 7 about "perseverance in doing good." It is not sinless perfection that is envisioned, but that the direction of a man's life was positive. Jewish people who had the Law of Moses as their guide were expected to

---

[48] Of course, there were no punctuation marks in the original manuscript copies of the Bible. All such aids are added by men. Sometimes they help, and sometimes they hinder, the reader as he tries to understand what the Holy Spirit wrote.

If we follow the reading of the ASV, it would seem that verse 13 gives reason why men perish (as verse 12 asserted) – that reason being a general truth that only "doers of law" (anarthrous *nomos*) shall be justified – and this is true whether he be a Jewish "doer of Law" or a Gentile "doer" of such "law" as they had. It is then taken for granted that Paul's readers would admit the Jews had a "Law" they were expected "to do." With this fact tacitly understood, by putting verses 14-15 in parentheses, they are seen to be a verification of the fact that the Gentiles too did indeed have a "law" by which they could be judged (though it was not the Law of Moses).

This commentator frankly admits to having more than ordinary difficulty trying to follow Paul's train of thought as presented in the NASB. He has therefore opted, in the notes of explanation, to follow the lead of the KJV which puts verse 13 inside the parentheses, too.

consistently abide by that Law.[49]   As God judges, He will look for whether or not the Jew's "deeds" were 'in accordance to truth.' If the comparison is favorable, God will "justify" the Jew.

This is the first use of the word 'justify' in Romans, a word about which much will be written in later chapters.   As later in Romans, it here has a legal connotation, of a judge pronouncing a verdict of acquittal.[50]

> It does not follow, because one people are favored with a Divine revelation (the Law of Moses), that therefore *they* shall be *saved*; while others who have not had that revelation shall finally perish: this is not God's procedure; where he has given a *law* – a *divine revelation* – he requires *obedience* to that law; and only those who have been *doers of that law* – who have lived according to the light and privileges granted in that revelation, *shall be justified* – shall be finally acknowledged to be such as are fit for the kingdom of God.[51]

2:14 – *For when Gentiles who do not have the Law do instinctively the things of the Law, these, not having the Law, are a law to themselves,*

For.   Verses 14 and 15 will explain how the same standard (whether or not a man is a 'doer of law') can be applied to the Gentiles: they had a "law" from God, albeit not the Law of Moses.   What "law" the Gentile did have, to which his "deeds" can be compared to in the judgment, is explained in these two verses, especially in the phrases "do instinctively the things of the Law," "are a law unto themselves," and "the work of the Law written in their hearts" (though there is little agreement as to the exact meaning of each of these phrases).

---

[49] Each method (KJV, ASV, or NASB) of treating verses 13-15 has its problems – places it seems to contradict Scripture elsewhere.   Following the lead suggested by the KJV, this is the problem we come up against: there seems to be a contradiction between Romans 2:13 ("doers of the Law will be justified") and Romans 3:20 ("By the works of the Law no flesh will be justified").   One attempt at alleviating this apparent contradiction is this: the context of both verses shows that two different topics are being discussed.   In 2:13, "doers of the Law" (a present tense, continuous action) speaks of the tenor, or direction, of a man's life being right when compared with the Word of God (the Law in the Jew's case) at the judgment.   In 3:20, Paul is affirming that no one has been sinless perfect (has without exception always done the "works" of the Law), so as to earn salvation.   In other words, the apparent difficulty has been solved by giving two different definitions to the word "doer."   Henry Alford (*Alford's Greek Testament* [London: Rivingtons, 1871], Vol.2, p.332) will attempt to solve the apparent difficulty by modifying the meaning of the word "justified."   He explains that verse 13 is only hypothetical – no one ever really was "justified" by 'doing' the works of the Law.   It is only by "faith" that a man is really justified, will be his argument.   Alford's attempt is similar to all those commentators who might roughly be classified as "faith-only."   When Paul plainly asserts that "works" do in some sense play a part in whether or not a man is "justified," the "faith-only" people (who rule out any "works" at all as being a part of "faith") must put forth an explanation that is plausible, if they are to continue to hold to their "faith-only" doctrine.

[50] Paul will show, later in his presentation, that the reason God can 'justify' sinners (none have perfectly lived by the revelation granted to them), while remaining perfectly consistent with His own holiness and righteousness, is because of Calvary.   Though none, at the judgment, will be seen to be sinless perfect, many will be seen to have been on the whole consistently in accord with the available light they had.

[51] Adam Clarke, *Clarke's Commentary on the Holy Bible* (New York: Methodist Book Concern, nd), Vol.6, p.49.

When Gentiles who do not have the Law. Though it is another example of anarthrous *nomos*, again it would appear the NASB translators have interpreted rightly, as the next phrase will show. The Law was intended for the Jews, as a sort of constitution for their nation (Exodus 19,20). All non-Jews continued under the 'truth' revealed during the Patriarchal age.[52] "When" (*hotan*) suggests the supposed case could take place at any time, and could frequently occur.[53] "Gentiles" has no article in the Greek, so it does not speak of all the Gentiles collectively, but rather of individual Gentiles here and there among whom the supposed case occurs.[54]

Do instinctively the things of the Law. Such commands as those dealing with stealing, committing adultery, coveting, respect for parents, truth, justice, honesty, chastity, are "the things of the Law." Here the Greek does read "*the* Law," and this is the context that shows "law" (anarthrous *nomos*) in the previous phrase really speaks of the Law of Moses. Paul is saying that individual Gentiles, at times, did some of the very things the Law of Moses commanded, and they had never seen the Law of Moses. They did it "by nature" (ASV). The NASB reads "instinctively;" this is a translator's interpretation and opinion, and the word choice may not be right![55] The usual way of determining what any expression in Scripture means is to see how it is used elsewhere in the Bible. At Romans 2:27, "by nature" is contrasted with the "letter (written Law of Moses) and circumcision."[56] That is, "by nature" suggests Gentiles were without something the Jews had, a written revelation. At Ephesians 2:3, the same expression occurs again, and we learn that "by nature" means "something that by long usage becomes a habit pattern of life."[57] The Gentiles did not have any documentary law like the Jews had, but they did have special divine revelations

---

[52] Available light is defined as being the revelation a man has the opportunity of knowing. When God gave the Law of Moses to the descendants of Abraham, those who did not have it had no change made in their status. They were still under the rules of the Patriarchal Age. And when they stand in the judgment, they will be judged as to whether or not they lived up to the Patriarchal rules. As to what the Patriarchal rules were, see the comments on "ordinances, knew God, truth," in previous verses. In addition, not a few would appeal to the Noachide Commandments. Concerning these commandments, see notes at Acts 15:29 in the author's commentary on *Acts*, or W. Carl Ketcherside, "Covenants of God," in the *Mission Messenger*, Vol.22:4 (April, 1960), p.3,4.

[53] Meyer, *Romans*, p.91.

[54] The absence of the article before the noun places emphasis on the characteristic expressed in the noun; i.e., people whose characteristic is "Gentile." Dana and Mantey, *Manual Grammar*, p.149.

[55] Meyer, *Romans*, p.92, thinks the term "by nature" speaks of "the original constitution given with existence, and not moulded by an extraneous training, culture, or other influence beyond the endowments of nature and their natural development," and he compares Ephesians 2:3. But it is doubtful that in either passage "by nature" simply means "doing what comes naturally." It must also be admitted that Arndt-Gingrich, *Lexicon*, p.877, give "instinctively" as a possible translation for *phusis*.

[56] Beware! In the NASB, it is hard to see that the same expression translated "by nature" in the ASV occurs both at 2:14 and at 2:27 – for the same Greek word is rendered "instinctively" at 2:14 and "physically" at 2:27.

[57] Thayer, *Lexicon*, p.660.

whose contents had been spread abroad by oral tradition. Those revelations contained some instructions similar to those later given to Moses. These God-given instructions had then been followed through generations until they had become almost a habit for many. Thus, Paul says, 'the Gentiles were by nature doing the things of the Law.'[58]

These, not having the Law, are a law to themselves. Again, though it is anarthrous *nomos*, it is the Law of Moses that the Gentiles did not have. As has been sufficiently documented earlier in this study of Romans, the Gentiles did have truth from God to direct their paths, so "they are a law to themselves" hardly means they just made their own rules. It rather says that they are not accountable to any other law and are not to be judged by any dispensation different from that under which they live.[59] It may also be a clear recognition that not every generation of Gentiles had an equal opportunity to know what God had revealed, since some deliberately changed it before they passed it on to their children, while others just failed in their duty to pass it on. In spite of all these difficulties, as the next verse explains, it still is possible for God to hold them accountable for the light they had opportunity to know.

2:15 – *in that they show the work of the Law written in their hearts, their conscience bearing witness, and their thoughts alternately accusing or else defending them,*

In that they show the work of the Law written in their hearts. Verse 15 is an explanation of the previous expression, "these are a law unto themselves." The "work of the Law" is likely the same as "things of the Law" (verse 14). The Law of Moses was given to help men guide their behavior in a manner that God would approve. Even though the Gentiles were without that written guide, Paul still affirms it was possible for the Gentiles to have

---

[58] The phrase that says "Gentiles do by nature the things of the Law" has some bearing on the doctrine of total depravity. Paul is here saying that there is a sense in which it is perfectly proper to say that the unregenerate can do good. God's image in man has not been completely effaced by Adam's sin, or our own! (Karl Barth favored the theory that "Gentiles" here in 2:14 is a reference to Gentile Christians, rather than as we have suggested, unregenerate Gentiles. In this, Barth follows Augustine, but few have agreed with them. The whole context has yet to bring "Christians" into view. It is still speaking of lost men's need for the salvation offered in the gospel.)

[59] Not every religion in the world is simply "cultural." If all were simply cultural, then each religion would be just fine for the people who have it. But if any religion has been divinely revealed (and the Patriarchal, Mosaic, and Christian religions have been), it would be out of harmony with what Scripture says to do what the Ecumenical Movement has done – i.e., Bangkok '73 – namely, to call for a "moratorium on missions" on the grounds that all religions are simply cultural.

In a similar vein, why take the gospel to unreached peoples if they can be saved by living up to the light they have? Will not they have a better chance in the judgment if all they have to answer for is the little light they already have? Are we not doing them a disservice by giving them opportunity for more light? The answer is "No!" Even if a few Gentiles here and there do live up to the light they have, all Gentiles would have a much more favorable opportunity for salvation if they have the gospel and the help of the indwelling Holy Spirit.

(at times) the same correct behavior which was envisioned in the Law.[60]   "Written in their hearts" seems to be a contrast to what was done in the Law's case, namely, "written on two stone tablets."   Observe carefully that it does not affirm that the "Law" was written in their hearts, but that the "*work* of the Law" was written there.   What this likely means is that the Gentiles had memorized the content of the oral traditions they heard from their ancestors.[61]

---

[60] Beneath the surface of the presentation here is the idea that God has required certain things in every dispensation.   For example, stealing is still wrong in the Christian era, not because it was forbidden in the Ten Commandments, but because the prohibition against stealing is repeated in the New Covenant Scriptures (e.g., Ephesians 4:28).   Similarly, we would expect God to have given some rules in the Patriarchal Age that are repeated in the Mosaic Code.   When the Gentile's behavior was in harmony with his Patriarchal rules, he also would be 'showing (doing) the same things the Law required.'

[61] In the comments we have been careful not to identify "by nature" and "written in their hearts."   Were we to make this identification, then Romans would teach that certain ideas of right and wrong are innate. While the Bible may teach that men are born with a certain sense of "oughtness," this commentator doubts there is an innate sense of what is right or wrong.   "Right" and "wrong" are things, he believes, that must be learned.

Romans 2:14,15 have considerable impact on one's world view.   Do men have an innate knowledge of God, and of His view of what is right and wrong?   If so, this might be a way to explain why there are similarities between God's revealed religion (Moses and the Prophets, for example) and paganism.   How shall we explain the fact that the Code of Hammurabi (who was roughly a contemporary of Abraham) has many of the same rules that 500 years later are found in the Law of Moses?   How do we explain other similarities between certain forms of paganism and God's divinely revealed religion?

The answer one gives to this question has certain far-reaching ramifications.   It even relates to the method a man decides to use for interpreting Scripture.   Perhaps one of the most potentially influential topics that modern Bible scholars are debating is this very matter of method.   In the Restoration Movement (and indeed for centuries in Christianity) the method used has been called the "grammatical-historical method."   (D.R. Dungan's *Hermeneutics* [Cincinnati: Standard Publishing Co., nd], and J.S. Lamar's *Organon of Scripture* [Philadelphia: J.B. Lippencott & Co., 1860], two volumes long-studied in the Restoration Movement, both taught the grammatical-historical method – a method that begins with the assumption that the Holy Spirit-inspired Scriptures are true and infallible, and then requires careful attention to historical background and to the grammar of the text in order to understand what the Holy Spirit intended to communicate.)   Since the rise of 19th century religious liberalism, this method has been widely rejected in favor of some other method, whether it is the "historical-critical method," or "form criticism" or "redaction criticism" (see the explanation of these terms in the Introductory Studies).   A number of young scholars in the Restoration Movement, having studied under Krister Stendahl, are using some of these newer methods.   They presume to sit in judgment over the Scriptures because they have an innate sense of what is right and wrong.   Using the problems in the field of textual criticism, they attack the inspiration of the Bible.   Using the Mari tablets, they affirm that "the Mari prophets form part of the pre-history of Biblical prophecy" (i.e., the uniqueness of the Biblical revelation is questioned; the use of "prophets" to proclaim a message from a deity was nothing new or unheard of).   Using Ugaritic texts, they find a parallel for the Old Testament Psalms (e.g., there are lines exactly like Psalm 68:4, except where Psalms reads "Lord" the Ugaritic material has "Baal").   (All of this is documented in the periodicals *Mission* and *Restoration Quarterly*.)   Such a use of the historical-critical method, if it becomes accepted in the Restoration Movement, will spell the death of the Movement.   A movement that is based on "Where the Scriptures speak, we speak" has no foundation left, indeed, has no reason left for its existence, if the critics who use "innate knowledge of right and wrong" to adjudge the Scriptures as faulty or mistaken should finally prevail.

Once again, let it be asked, "How shall we explain the similarities?"   And do men have an innate knowledge of right and wrong that allows them to sit in judgment over the Scriptures?   This commentator explains the similarities on the basis that there were revelations given by oral tradition to the Gentiles that were similar to those later given in written form to Moses.   And since it is difficult to find the idea of innate knowledge of right and wrong taught in the Bible, he refuses to sit in judgment over the Scriptures, as if by human intuition he were wiser than the Holy Spirit who gave the Scriptures in the first place (as the

Their conscience bearing witness.   The conscience is an innate faculty which prompts a man to do what his mind thinks is right, and criticizes him when he does what his mind thinks is wrong.

> The conscience [in Paul's writings] is a natural faculty which belongs to all men alike (Romans 2:15), and pronounces upon the character of actions, both their own (2 Corinthians 1:12) and those of others (2 Corinthians 4:2; 5:11). It can be over-scrupulous (1 Corinthians 10:25); and is blunted or "seared" by neglect of its warnings (1 Timothy 4:3).[62]

The conscience of the Gentile passed its judgments ("This is right!"   "This is wrong!") in accordance with the way the mind had been trained and instructed by the oral traditions (see "written in their hearts" above).

And their thoughts alternately accusing or else defending themselves.   This phrase has been explained in two different ways.   Some have understood it to picture the Gentiles as reasoning among themselves on questions of right and wrong, and thus arriving at "laws" by which their society was to be governed (laws that God would also take into account when He judges men's deeds).   Clarke is one writer who presents the passage as though Paul were explaining that the Gentiles did have "laws" (they made their own) by which they lived, and which could be used as God decides whether or not they were "doers of law."   He writes,

> ... that they have a law and act according to it, is further proved from their conduct in *civil* affairs; and from that correct sense which they have of *natural justice* in their *debates*, either in their *courts of law* or in their *treatises on morality*.   All these are ample proofs that God has not left them without light; and that, seeing they have such correct notions of *right* and *wrong*, they are accountable to God for their conduct in reference to these notions and principles.[63]

The second way of explaining this phrase about "thoughts" (or 'reasonings') is that it shows how the conscience operates.   It approves what a man thinks is right, and criticizes what a man thinks is wrong.[64]   That the Gentile has a conscience that "works" is proof that there also was a standard of right and wrong impressed on his mind.   The presence of such a standard is evidence that there was a "law" to which God could compare a Gentile's life to, when he came to stand in the judgment.

Scriptures themselves everywhere assert).

[62] Sanday and Headlam, *Romans*, p.61.

[63] Clarke, *Commentary on the Whole Bible*, Vol.6, p.49.

[64] From the word order, "accusing" and "defending," some have conjectured that the accusing was the rule, and the defending the exception to the general order of events.   See Lard, Sanday and Headlam, and Vine, *in loc.*

Thus, in verses 13-15, Paul has shown all men have some law, some truth, by which they can be judged. Some have the Law of Moses; some have oral tradition that began with God revealing His will; but all have some "law."

2:16 – *on the day when, according to my gospel, God will judge the secrets of men through Christ Jesus.*

On the day when. In comments on verse 11, we addressed the problem of how to trace Paul's train of thought through these verses. Having chosen to follow the lead of the KJV translators (who put verses 13-16 in parentheses), we connect what is said in verse 16 with what was said in verse 12. Verse 16 tells us on what day both the Gentile world and the Jewish world would be arraigned, namely, the day when Jesus acts as judge of all men, the Great Judgment Day. Connecting the verses together we have this flow of thought: "The Gentiles will be judged without the Law, and the Jews will be judged by the Law ... on the day when God judges all men."[65]

According to my gospel. "Just as I have been preaching" is what this phrase means. Paul had regularly included in his gospel message the idea that there was a day coming when God would judge the world.[66] It does not say all men were going to be judged on the basis of whether or not they had obeyed the gospel, for such an idea would contradict what already has been clearly said about judgment on the basis of available light (verse 12ff).[67]

God will judge the secrets of men through Christ Jesus. Some passages read as though God Himself will be the Judge (Deuteronomy 32:36; Psalms 50:4; 1 Samuel 2:10; Ecclesiastes 3:17; Romans 3:6; Hebrews 13:4), while others read in such a way that Jesus is presented as the Judge (Matthew 25:31ff; John 5:22,27; 2 Corinthians 5:10). It appears

---

[65] If we follow the suggestion of the ASV, which put verses 14 and 15 in parentheses, then we must connect verse 16 with verse 13, and so connected, verse 16 tells about the day when the "doer of law" shall be justified. It was Origen who first noted the difficulty of connecting verse 16 to verse 15. The "thoughts of men accusing and condemning" are not conceived of as rising up at the judgment, but rather during the times before the judgment. In other words, verse 15 is talking about the present life, whereas verse 16 is talking about the final judgment; therefore verse 16 must be connected with something earlier in the passage.

[66] Examples of Paul's presentation of the final judgment as part of his gospel proclamation are Acts 13:40,41 and 17:30,31. See also Romans 14:10; 1 Corinthians 4:5; 2 Corinthians 5:10; 1 Thessalonians 3:13, 4:13-18, 5:1-11; 2 Thessalonians 1:5-10; Hebrews 13:17.

[67] Paul's expression "my gospel" should not be interpreted to mean that his message was different from, say, James' or Peter's or Jesus' message, in spite of some modern attempts to so use the expression. On the contrary, numerous expressions in Paul show his message had the same content as that of Jesus and the twelve – see 1 Corinthians 15:11, and the "extension of the right hand of fellowship" at that private meeting between Paul and Peter during the Jerusalem Conference (Galatians 2:6-9). In addition, the letter sent from Jerusalem at the close of that Conference specifically stated the harmony between the leaders of the Jerusalem church and Paul (Acts 15:23-29). A second use sometimes made of this expression "my gospel" should also be rejected. Though early Christian literature does report that Luke's Gospel reflected the preaching of Paul, this verse in Romans should not be used to prove that the Third Gospel was written under the direct supervision of Paul. The inspiration of Luke's Gospel would better be attributed to Luke's being a prophet than that Paul dictated the Gospel while Luke merely penned it.

from this verse that God has appointed Jesus to do the judging in His behalf – the same thought that was expressed in Acts 17:31. "The secrets of men" are the hidden desires, passions, and inner motives that led to men's actions. So not only the actions ("deeds") are to be brought out into the open at the judgment, but also the inner thoughts and motives that produced the actions will be made evident. And this is true for "men" in general, whether they are Jew or Gentile, unbeliever or Christian.

2. Direct Reference to the Jews Showing They Have Failed to Keep the Law. 2:17-24

> *Summary*: Jewish opponents of the gospel made appeal to the fact that God had given into their care His special revelation of the Law, and this was evidence (the Jew asserted) that God would give the Jews preferential treatment. Paul answers that they have sinned grievously by not keeping the Law God gave them.

2:17 – *But if you bear the name "Jew," and rely upon the Law, and boast in God,*

2:17 – But. Verse 17 introduces a long supposition, the reply to which begins in verse 21.[68] In the next few clauses, Paul will list the areas where the Jew prided himself as being superior to the Gentile, and therefore eligible for preferential treatment. Paul will admit that God had indeed given the Jews some wonderful privileges, but Paul will also insist that the Jew has abused those privileges. As verse 13 stated, not just hearers, but *doers* of the Law shall be justified.

If you bear the name "Jew." To many people in the 20th century, "Jew" is a word with a negative connotation; it is spoken with a slur in the voice. But it was not always that way. The word was first used nearly synonymously with 'Judeans' about 750 BC (2 Kings 16:6); and then about 100 years later with the same meaning, i.e., designating people from the tribe of Judah (and perhaps also Benjamin, Jeremiah 34:6-9). In the book of Esther, where the term is often used, since most of the captives came from Judah, "Jews" still seems to have its ancient meaning. Later, the use of the term was extended so that it was used of anyone of the Hebrew race. As early as Hezekiah's time (king of Judah from c.724-695 BC), the language of Judah was called Jewish (2 Kings 18:26,28; Nehemiah 13:24; Isaiah 36:11,13). By the time we come to the New Testament, the term "Jews" (meaning Israelites, Hebrews) is often contrasted with "Gentiles,"[69] and "Jews" and "Israel"

---

[68] The first word of verse 17 in the KJV is "behold" (some more recent manuscripts read *ide*, "behold," instead of the older reading *ei de*, "but if"), and this obscures the supposition-answer construction that is obvious in the older Greek manuscripts. The corruption of the text is a rather easy one to explain. Originally the letters all ran together with no spaces between words as we are used to, and the omission of one letter was an easy mistake for a copyist to make.

[69] Mark 7:3; John 2:6; Acts 10:28; Galatians 2:14,15. This is not the place for a long discourse on "Israel" and "Judah," as though the two terms have always been mutually exclusive, the former referring to the ten northern tribes and the latter referring to the two southern tribes. The doctrine of some that the 10

appear to be used interchangeably.[70]   When Paul wrote, "Jew" was an honorable name, indicative that a man was a member of the "chosen people" of God.

> Although the Jews were uniquely privileged, enjoying privileges above all others, they did not seem to realize that these blessings implied obligations. Many of these people, instead of using their superior endowments to help those in need, merely bragged about their prerogatives.[71]

The Jew was wont to boast about his special position, and "I am a *Jew*" was one of the ways he expressed his boastfulness.   See an illustration of this exclusive attitude in the parable of the Pharisee and the Publican (Luke 18:9-14).   Other similarly-used expressions follow.

And rely upon the Law.   There is a sense in which it is right to rest on God's Law.   It is a divinely revealed standard of right and wrong.   And a Jew, in the midst of an argument about morality or ethics, could rightly say, "I know my position is right, because the Law says so!"   But if the Jew himself did not, like the Psalmist, allow the "light" to guide his steps in the path of obedience (Psalm 119:105), his boast about having the Law was rather empty.   To be proud of the mere fact of having the Law, as though possession proved that its possessor was a special favorite of God above all others, was a serious flaw in the Jew's thinking.   It is a wonderful thing to have a Bible in the home, but surely no one believes he is going to be saved just because he owns a Bible.

And boast in God.   Perhaps the sense can be expressed this way: 'We worship *God*, not lifeless and dumb idols like you do!'   To be proud of God, the creator and ruler of heaven and earth, the one who is Rock, Refuge, Governor, and Savior, is surely a laudable thing. Laudable, that is, unless the boast arises from bigotry and conceit, in which case the boast is a sham on which God frowns.

---

tribes are lost, that they never came home from the captivity, is a fiction, shown to be such by Paul's statement about "twelve tribes" in Acts 26:7; by the fact that the New Covenant was to include both the house of Israel and the house of Judah (Jeremiah 31:31-34; Hebrews 8:6-13); by the fact that people from all 12 tribes returned after the Babylonian Captivity (1 Chronicles 9:3; Ezra 2; Ezekiel 33-48); and by the readers addressed in James 1:1.   This whole matter is of some significance in light of the violently anti-Jewish programs of some 20th century white supremacists who claim to have Scriptural backing for their position and practices, and in light of the popularity of British-Israelism (or Anglo-Israelism) in some religious circles.

[70] At the birth of Jesus we find these two statements: "Where is He who has been born king of the Jews" (Matthew 2:2), and He "will shepherd My people Israel" (Matthew 2:6).   In Acts 2:5 we are told that the people at Jerusalem were "Jews ... from every nation under heaven," yet Peter refers to these same people as "Men of Israel" (2:22) and as "all the house of Israel" (2:36).   In Antioch of Pisidia, Paul addressed the men in the synagogue with these words, "Men of Israel" (Acts 13:16), yet when the service was over, it was "Jews" who departed from the place of worship (13:43).   And Paul could speak of himself as being "a Jew by nature" (Galatians 2:15) and at the same time as being "of the nation of Israel" (Philippians 3:5).

[71] Hendriksen, *Romans*, p.100.

2:18 – *and know* His *will, and approve the things that are essential, being instructed out of the Law,*

And know *His* will. Literally, it reads "the will," that is, the supreme will. It is a commendable thing to know God's will, and it is culpable not to know it when there is opportunity. The Jews had many means of knowing God's perfect will. They had the living oracles, prophets sent by God, synagogue services every Saturday during which the Law and the Prophets were read to them, and parents who were instructed to teach their children day and night. But mere knowledge of God's will is not of itself a mark of superiority. Mere *knowing* does not make one better, but *doing*.

And approve the things that are essential. Note the marginal reading, "distinguish between the things which differ." Both Greek words (*dokimazō* and *diapherō*) are capable of different meanings: the former can be "distinguish" or "approve,"[72] while the latter can be either "differ" or "essential (surpass, excel)."[73] Probably the marginal reading is the better of the two, for a man reading it would be reminded of the distinctions between clean and unclean, of days and seasons that were especially holy to the Jew, and of rites and customs prescribed by the Law, of which the whole Gentile world had been left in ignorance. The Jew claimed that he, better than the Gentile, could understand and judge what was best. Again, there was an attitude problem that resulted in empty boasts, for God had intended the Jew to use his privileges to help and serve his not-so-fortunate neighbors.

Being instructed out of the Law. It was because they had been instructed[74] out of the Law of Moses since childhood that the Jew claimed to be able to better judge what was right and what was important.

2:19 – *and are confident that you yourself are a guide to the blind, a light to those who are in darkness,*

And are confident that you yourself are a guide to the blind. There is an untranslatable particle (*te*) in the Greek which accords to this boast a self-assurance that allowed no question of the fact. The Jew was persuaded (and rightly so, in his own opinion) that the people around him were debased and ignorant, but that he could tell them a thing or two (yea, many things) of great importance. The Jew had no doubt that he was superior. However, we should not read into this verse the idea that the Jews were evangelistic for their religion. God had intended that others would come to know Him through the instrumentality of the Jews (Exodus 19:6, they were to be a "kingdom of priests"), but they

---

[72] See chapter 1, footnote #142, where this same word was explained either as the test or the results of the test.

[73] Arndt-Gingrich, *Lexicon*, p.189. Exactly the same expression occurs in Philippians 1:10 (where the NASB had "excellent"), with the same uncertainty of meaning.

[74] *Katēcheō* (compare our word "catechize") means to instruct, and primarily it speaks of oral instruction. It could have been by parents in the home, or by religious leaders on the Sabbath, or by teachers in the Rabbinical schools, that Jewish people heard Scriptures explained.

made little effort to tell others about Jehovah.[75] "Blind" is one of several terms found in the context that the Jew applied to the Gentile. All Gentiles were spiritually blind, in darkness, foolish, babes, the Jew thought. And in each of these areas where the Gentile was deficient, the Jew was confident he could supply just what was needed. "Guide" speaks of someone who knows the way, and can lead others to their destination. Figuratively, the word was used for an "instructor" or "teacher" (Matthew 15:14, 23:16).

A light to those who are in darkness. "Light" is another figurative expression, here meaning teacher. "Darkness" speaks of the spiritual ignorance found in the Gentile world (cp. Isaiah 42:7, 49:6, 60:2,3). Where did the Jew get an idea like this? God intended for Israel to be missionary-minded. The Old Testament is a missionary book, from beginning to end.[76] To a certain extent, the Jews understood this. During the captivity and after, they vigorously defended their monotheism. They translated the Scriptures into languages which the Gentiles could understand. But they failed, too, and because of their failure, the God of heaven was blasphemed by the Gentiles, as we shall hear from Paul in a moment.

2:20 – *a corrector of the foolish, a teacher of the immature, having in the Law the embodiment of knowledge and of the truth,*

A corrector of the foolish. A "corrector" is a "trainer," one who by instruction, or correction, or discipline, helps the unskilled or untaught to reach a new level of competence. The word "foolish" is used in two senses in the Scriptures: (1) to denote those who are void of sense, reason, or intelligence; and (2) to denote those who act rashly or wickedly. In the Jew's estimation, both senses were true of the Gentiles in things moral and religious.

A teacher of the immature. "Immature" (infants) was another term used by the Jews to denote the Gentiles. 'Infants' or 'babes' was a term also applied to the very recent proselyte from heathenism to Judaism, and reflecting the fact that the new convert is almost totally untaught and unskilled in the new religion. The Jew pictured himself not only as a mature adult, but as sufficiently skilled (whether he had any formal courses on how to teach) as to be able to teach any of those new converts.

Having in the Law the embodiment of knowledge and of the truth. A similar phrase in verse 18 was given, as is this one here, as the reason why the Jew could instruct the "backward" Gentiles. "The Law" again is a reference to the Law of Moses (or perhaps all the Old Testament Scriptures). "Embodiment" is an attempt to express the idea in the Greek word *morphōsis*, which means "form" or "shape." A study of Greek synonyms may be helpful here. Another word (*schēma*) is also translated "form" or "shape," but the difference between the two is this: the latter tends to express the outward (and often acci-

---

[75] It is widely accepted that the Jews made little effort to proselytize the Gentiles to Judaism. Matthew 23:15 speaks of partisan proselytizing – of Jews to the beliefs of the Pharisees – rather than of Gentiles to Judaism.

[76] Genesis 22:18; Isaiah 9:2, 56:6,7; Malachi 1:11; plus the passages referred to in the text above out of Exodus and Isaiah. See the author's manuscript, "The Missionary Message of the Old Testament," delivered at the *North American Christian Convention*, Kansas City, MO, 1982.

dental) form, while the former expresses inner (intrinsic and essential) essence.[77] The Jew, rather pompously, affirmed that he had the essential, intrinsic, concrete form of truth. What a surprise to find out the Law of Moses, good as it was (Romans 7:12), was itself only an "example and shadow of heavenly things," and "a shadow of the good things to come" (the New Covenant revelation), as the writer of Hebrews explains in 8:5 and 10:1. Vine suggests that "knowledge" is put first, before "truth," because the Jew was inclined to attach more importance to knowledge.[78]

2:21 – *you, therefore, who teach another, do you not teach yourself? You who preach that one should not steal, do you steal?*

You therefore who teach another, do you not teach yourself?   Now we have come to the series of five rhetorical questions designed to confront the Jew with the wide gap between his profession and his actual practice.   These questions are the answer to the supposition that began in verse 17.   Here is the "Thou art the man!" we have been expecting since verse 1.   When we read the verse, we should stress the word "teach" since "you" is not emphatic in the Greek.   "Let not many of you become teachers," James 3:1 says, because the teacher will incur stricter judgment.   Paul is expressing the same idea to these Jews who presumed they were teachers of others.   'You more than any need the very lesson you seek to give to others, for if you *teachers* don't heed it, not only is your guilt greater, but your punishment also will be greater!'

You who preach that one should not steal, do you steal?   "Preach" (or 'proclaim') meant to herald something publicly, whether in the synagogue, or on the street.[79]   The Jews were only too happy for any opportunity to tell the Gentiles that God disapproves of stealing. But the sad thing is, the Jew himself often was guilty of thievery.[80]   If stealing includes such things as covetousness, false weights and measures, extortion, exorbitant interest, bribery, oppression, cheating, embezzling, holding back wages fairly earned, and such like, all of which were clear violations of the 8th commandment, there is abundant evidence in the Minor Prophets that such sins were all too prevalent in the Jewish community.   And in New Testament times, Jesus accuses the religious leaders of "devour[ing] widows' houses" (Matthew 23:14).

2:22 – *You who say that one should not commit adultery, do you commit adultery? You who abhor idols, do you rob temples?*

---

[77] Thayer, *Lexicon*, p.418.

[78] Vine, *Romans*, p.40.

[79] The Greek word is *kērussō*.   A "herald" is one who delivers a message from an authority, and delivers the message exactly as the authority gave it.   The "town crier" in old New England would have fulfilled a similar function.

[80] Henriksen, *Romans*, p.105, makes reference to Strack and Billerbeck's *Commentary on the New Testament from the Talmud and Midrash*, p.107-115, for examples of the very sins which Paul accuses his contemporaries of being guilty of.

You who say that one should not commit adultery, do you commit adultery? This sin, too, was common among the Jews, as Matthew 12:39, Luke 16:18, and John 8:1-11 document. "The Talmud accuses some of the most celebrated of their rabbis, by name, of this vice. Josephus also gives the same account of the nation."[81] Matthew 19:8,9 indicate Moses had allowed the Jews, because of the hardness of their hearts, to divorce their wives and take others if they so desired. While this may not have been adultery in the eyes of the Law of Moses, yet it surely was in the sight of God, whose original intention for marriage was one man and one woman united to each other for life. And dare we exclude the hidden sins of the heart (Matthew 5:28) from the thing here charged against the Jews?

You who abhor idols, do you rob temples? *Bdelussomai*, translated "abhor," means to turn away from something because of the stench.[82] It is an expression of physical disgust. We have noted earlier (in notes at 2:1) that the severe treatment the Jews received during the Captivity (itself a punishment for being involved in idolatry) is the thing that taught the Jews this abhorrence of idols. The KJV reads "Dost thou commit sacrilege?" instead of "Do you rob temples?" This phrase has given expositors no little trouble. Since the Captivity, Paul cannot accuse them of being actual idolaters, but perhaps the spirit of idolatry still persisted, a spirit of "sacrilege." "Sacrilege is the crime of violating or profaning sacred things; of appropriating to common purposes that which has been devoted and consecrated to the service of God."[83] "Covetousness" ("Greed," NASB) is idolatry (Colossians 3:5 KJV); perhaps the spirit that would withhold from the true God that which was His due, and bestow affections due to Him on something else, is the sin the Jews were committing, or at least so thought the KJV translators when they used "sacrilege" to translate *hierosuleō*.[84] The other meaning, "rob temples," suggests that while the Jews were repulsed by the idol worship, they were not so repulsed by the gold and jewels that one might find in such a shrine. In fact, if opportunity presented itself, their greed would allow them to plunder the pagan temples. Nor is there any doubt that Jews were guilty of plundering the heathen temples, and they did it in spite of God's clear prohibition of such actions (Deuteronomy 7:5,25,26). Theophylact wrote, "For if they did abhor the idols, yet nevertheless, dominated by covetousness, they touched the idol-offerings for filthy lucre's sake."[85] Furthermore, the defense of the Christians by the Ephesian town clerk, declaring that they were *not* "temple robbers" (Acts 19:37) may well reflect the reputation of the Jews in that place. If they were actually plundering pagan temples, their abhorrence of idols was not as great as they pretended it to be. And their acts of avarice and greed were in direct disobedience to the Law they professed to revere.

---

[81] Barnes, *Romans,* p.74.

[82] Thayer, *Lexicon*, p.99.

[83] Barnes, *Romans*, p.74.

[84] On the tendency of the Jews to profane sacred things, see Nehemiah 13:10-12; Malachi 1:13,14, 3:8,9; and Matthew 21:12,13. Josephus also tells how some Jews appropriated to their own use some valuable gifts that Fulva, the donor, had intended go to the temple at Jerusalem (*Ant.* XVIII.3.5).

[85] Quoted by Barmby, *Romans*, p.56, and by Meyer, *Romans*, p.100.

2:23 – *You who boast in the Law, through your breaking the Law, do you dishonor God?*

You who boast in the Law. See what was said about "rely upon the Law" in verse 17. The following phrase shows that anarthrous *nomos* here is actually a reference to the Law of Moses.

Through your breaking the Law, do you dishonor God? "Breaking the Law" translates *parabainō*, a word that means to 'cross over the line.' God had drawn some lines about what was right and wrong, and had specifically warned the Jews, but they did not listen. They deliberately transgressed. There is an interesting contrast between Paul's presentation of the sins of the Gentiles (chapter 1) and his presentation of the sins of the Jews (chapter 2). The order in chapter 1 was sins against God, against themselves, and then against others. The order in chapter 2 is sins against neighbors, sins against self, and then sins against God. The laws they had been breaking, as implied in the rhetorical questions just asked, were some of the very ones included in the Ten Commandments. The NEB translates the last phrase as a statement, "You are dishonoring God!" The Greek would allow it to be translated either as a statement or as a question.[86] A question is often a forceful way of driving home a point. It is the whole life and conduct, not just the profession of the lips, that does real honor to God. "God is dishonored by the transgressions of His people, in a manner in which He is not dishonored by the same transgressions of the wicked, who make no profession of being His (Haldane)."[87]

2:24 – *For "THE NAME OF GOD IS BLASPHEMED AMONG THE GENTILES BECAUSE OF YOU," just as it is written.*

For "THE NAME OF GOD IS BLASPHEMED AMONG THE GENTILES BECAUSE OF YOU," just as it is written. There are two possible sources in the Old Testament for this quotation to which Paul alludes to prove his point about God being dishonored. Perhaps it is taken from Isaiah 52:5, or perhaps from Ezekiel 36:20-23. In the Isaiah passage, the conquerors of Israel think lightly of Israel's God because He was not able (they supposed) to help His people. Actually, the sins of the people brought on their sad plight, so it could be said that because of the Jews' behavior God was blasphemed. In the Ezekiel passage, too, the conduct of the Jews is the thing that caused the nations to blaspheme God. Men have regularly judged a man's religion by his life. So too, the Gentiles, who had a concept of many gods, judged a man's god by his conduct. Good man – good god; bad man – bad god, was their theory. How tragic that the very people whom God called to be the means of making His name known to the Gentiles instead were the cause of the Gentiles speaking evil of and dishonoring Him. The dishonor done to God arose from their greed for gain, their deceit, and their hypocrisy, all of which were fully

---

[86] Those who would translate it as a statement note that the next verse begins with "for," as though it were giving a reason for something just said. (See this method of translating defended in Cranfield, *Romans*, p.170.) Those who favor translating it as a question appeal to the context which has been a series of questions about teaching, stealing, committing adultery, and robbing temples. (See this method of translating defended in Hendriksen, *Romans*, p.105.)

[87] Quoted by Wilson, *Romans*, p.45.

known to the Gentiles among whom they lived. Far from the Gentiles having a monopoly on sin, Paul affirms that Scripture ("just as it is written") has characterized the Jews as likewise being guilty of sin, and an aggravated sin at that. Israel had failed at being what (according to Romans 2:19) they pretended to be: "a light for those who are in darkness."

3. Direct Reference to the Jews Showing that Circumcision Will Not Save. 2:25-29

> *Summary*: Having pointed out that the mere possession of the Law did not guarantee preferential treatment of the Jew in the judgment, now Paul goes on to deal with the matter of circumcision in the same way.

2:25 – *For indeed circumcision is of value, if you practice the Law; but if you are a transgressor of the Law, your circumcision has become uncircumcision.*

For indeed circumcision is of value. Just as the Jew somehow thought possession of the Law exempted him from punishment for his sins, so he viewed the mark of circumcision as another reason he should be given preferential treatment at the judgment. Paul will show that in spite of his privileges, the Jew was still guilty of personal acts of sin, and therefore needed the salvation offered in the gospel. It is almost as though Paul can hear another of the standard Jewish objections to the presentation in the earlier verses about the standards God will apply in the judgment. "For," with which this verse begins, perhaps is Paul's reply to a suppressed Jewish argument. The Jew would argue, 'Ah, but what about the covenant of circumcision? Is there no value in that mark of special covenant relationship?' Paul's reply is this: There is a value in circumcision (seen in its Old Testament context) only if the spiritual reality it is supposed to represent is present (Deuteronomy 10:16; Jeremiah 9:26; Ezekiel 44:9). Note, too, that Paul uses the word "value" or 'profits;' he does not say 'justify.' The position of the circumcised Jew was more advantageous (for knowing God's will) than that of the uncircumcised Gentile, Paul will show in Romans 3:1-18. Later in Romans, Paul will show that circumcision was never intended to be more than a temporary thing (see Romans 4:9-13). After Abraham's time, circumcision was preserved in the Jewish community as a token of their covenant relationship with God,[88] but it could not replace the faithfulness the Law required. Circumcision was of value only as a sign of obedience to the Law. As with Paul's comments concerning the Law, so is his argument regarding circumcision: its possession does not substitute for obedience.

If you practice the Law. The same thing was said earlier (verse 13) when Paul wrote about being "doers of the Law." It is talking, not of sinless perfection, but of habitual, consistent practice. Such habitual practice was just the thing Paul is suggesting that was absent from the lives of the Jews.

---

[88] "When *Jew* had come to be the peculiar designation of the children of the covenant, persons were said to become *Jews* by circumcision. Thus Esther 8:17 ... in the LXX has, 'And many of the Gentiles having been circumcised also became Jews' ... [T]he known fact of other races as well as the Jews having practised, and still practising, circumcision is not subversive of the scriptural view of its being a peculiarly Jewish rite. For the Jew alone it had peculiar significance." Barmby, *Romans*, p.57.

But if you are a transgressor of the Law. "This language must not be taken as signifying a single transgression only; it must be taken as denoting habitual transgression – a life of sin."[89]

Your circumcision has become uncircumcision. The perfect tense verb signifies 'has become and remains.' The Jew, even though a descendant of Abraham, who rebelled and sinned against God became like the heathen in character, and in God's estimation of him. This whole matter of God's estimation of him is explained in the following verses.

2:26 – If therefore the uncircumcised man keeps the requirements of the Law, will not his uncircumcision be regarded as circumcision?

If therefore the uncircumcised man keeps the requirements of the Law. "If therefore" indicates that this verse is a legitimate deduction from the two "if-clauses" in verse 25. Once again, as in verse 11ff, Paul is distinctly declaring the impartiality of God's dealings. "Uncircumcised man" was a Jewish term to designate "Gentile."[90] "Keeps" comes from *phulassō*, a word which implies careful attention to, like the attention required of one who would guard a treasure lest something happen to it. It also is a present tense verb, which implies habitual, continued action. See verse 14 for the sense in which it could be said that a Gentile could "do (or keep) the things of the Law." If before the time of Abraham there were men the tenor of whose lives was right, and they were (on the basis of Calvary) acceptable to God, then should we not expect also that during the Mosaic Age some, outside the Jewish nation, would get things right too?[91] The word translated "requirements" here was translated "ordinances" in Romans 1:32.

Will not his uncircumcision be regarded as circumcision? The implied answer is, "It certainly will be!" The argument about the value in God's sight of physical circumcision follows the same line as Paul's argument about hearers of the Law (verses 12-16). Without obedience, neither is of any value when it comes to being justified in God's sight. The Gentile, on the other hand, who is obedient to the revelation he has, will be accepted by God, even though he never was circumcised. "Regarded" is the same word in the Greek that will be translated "reckoned" in Romans 4:3. The Greek is a future tense, passive voice verb. God is the implied agent who does the "regarding," and the time of the reckon-

---

[89] Lard, *Romans*, p.97.

[90] Some writers appeal to Cornelius (Acts 10) as an example of men who, though uncircumcised, kept many of the requirements of the Law. Luke's term for these "proselytes of the gate" is "devout." "The reference to *proselytes of the gate* (Philippi) is not only arbitrary, but also incorrect, because the text has in view the pure contrast between circumcision and uncircumcision, without any hint of an intermediate stage or anything analogous thereto." Meyer, *Romans*, p.102. While we agree with Meyer about the identification of the uncircumcised, still it must be admitted that what is said here about God's estimate of man would be just as true of the devout man as of the uncircumcised.

[91] Batey's comment, in this commentator's opinion, misses the point of Paul's presentation. Batey writes, "Here, it should probably be pointed out that the possibility of a Gentile living free from sin is only suggested theoretically by Paul for the sake of showing that circumcision alone is no talisman (cf. 3:23)." *Romans*, p.42. So far, none of the verses about being "doers of the Law" have implied either impossibility or sinless perfection.

ing is likely the final judgment.[92]   The whole point is that the standards to be applied in the final judgment are "according to truth" and "according to works."   The man who consistently does according to the light he has will be approved, whether he is Jew or Gentile.   For God to reckon uncircumcision as circumcision is to say that its presence or absence makes no real difference in God's acceptance of a man.[93]

2:27 – *And will not he who is physically uncircumcised, if he keeps the Law, will he not judge you who though having the letter* of the Law *and circumcision are a transgressor of the Law?*

And will not he who is physically uncircumcised, if he keeps the Law.   "Physically" is used to translate the same Greek word that was translated "by nature" in verse 14 (ASV). As it did there, so here it means "without any written revelation," in this case, a revelation that requires circumcision.   The persons in question are uncircumcised by virtue of long practice among their Gentile ancestors, not because of a wrong attitude of heart toward God (which effectively caused the Jews to be regarded as uncircumcised in God's sight). Compare what was said in verses 14 and 26 on keeping the Law.

Will he not judge you.   Verse 27 is regarded by most modern expositors as a continuation of the question begun in verse 26, and so they read "not" before "judge," even though there is no *ouchi* present in the Greek.[94]   The verb "judge" is neutral, and may mean either acquit or condemn.   Each time the word appears in the Greek, the translator must decide from the context which meaning is intended.   "'Condemn as guilty,' is the idea here.   Compare Matthew 12:41,42, 'The men of Nineveh will rise in judgment with this generation and shall condemn it, etc.'   The idea is that of 'putting to shame by contrast.'"[95]   That the Gentile would judge the Jew was just the opposite of what the Jew expected.   The Jew expected that, because of his position, he would judge the Gentiles.   Instead, the Gentile's consistent behavior in view of limited revelation would condemn the inconsistent behavior of the Jew who had much greater opportunities.[96]

---

[92] It would be possible to say the future tense pictures anytime in the future, whenever God passed judgment on a man's life.   God does pass judgment every day on the quality of a man's life (see notes in chapter 4).   However, there is also a final judgment to be faced in the future, too, even after the daily scrutinizing by God.

[93] The reader must be careful here.   When God commands something (and He did command circumcision of the Jews), it is likely not possible to be justified while deliberately refusing to do as commanded. On the other hand, a one-time obedience to something commanded is of no value either, when God has told us He is looking for a lifetime characterized by faithfulness (a consistent doing of His requirements).

[94] The modern expositors apparently have done it right.   If the "not" is omitted, then verse 27 must be understood to be an answer to the question asked in verse 26, and that in turn makes it most difficult to follow the line of thought in the passage.

[95] Sanday, *Romans*, p.43.

[96] There are several enigmatic verses about redeemed men helping somehow in the final judgment.   1 Corinthians 6:3 tells about judging angels.   The "overcomer" will "rule (judge?) the nations" along with Christ (Revelation 2:26,27, 19:15).   Whether the actual work of passing judgment is meant, or simply condemn by example, or both, is not easy to decide.

Who though having the letter *of the Law* **and circumcision are a transgressor of the Law?**[97]   The point of this expression is to show that the Jews' transgression was all the more culpable.   "Letter" refers to the *written* Law of Moses (perhaps the whole Old Testament) in contrast to the oral tradition which was all the Gentile who would know God's will had access to.   As noted earlier, "circumcision" was the seal of the Old Covenant, and it too implies greater privileges than the Gentile outside that covenant had.   The preposition "though" (*dia*) marks the condition or circumstance under which the transgression was done.   It might be paraphrased, 'With all the advantages of the written Law and of the covenant of which circumcision was the seal, you still consistently transgress?   That just aggravates your guilt!'   In all this section, which begins with "if" (verse 26), we must not overlook the fact that such a thing as here contemplated is a distinct possibility.   Not all Jews are referred to, nor all Gentiles.   But there are some of both groups who were children of God because they were "doers" of the revelation granted to them.

2:28 – *For he is not a Jew who is one outwardly; neither is circumcision that which is outward in the flesh.*

For he is not a Jew who is one outwardly.   This verse, beginning with "for," seems to be explanatory of something just said.   Verses 28 and 29 explain what the Jew, and all of us, are to see in the condemnation of the Jew by the Gentile (verse 27).   "When Paul says, he is not a Jew, he does not mean that he is a Jew in no sense.   He means that he is not the sort of Jew who will stand approved in the last day with God,"[98] even though he was a member of the Jewish race.   The man who was a Jew only outwardly did not possess the true character, nor manifest the true spirit, which God had contemplated when He had called the Jewish people to be a "holy nation."

Neither is circumcision that which is outward in the flesh.   "Circumcision it certainly was, but not the circumcision which aids in saving.   Circumcision was of service only when the Law was kept."[99]   Without a corresponding attitude of heart, the mere outward circumcision was nothing, as the next verse will explain.

2:29 – *But he is a Jew who is one inwardly; and circumcision is that which is of the heart, by the Spirit, not by the letter; and his praise is not from men, but from God.*

But he is a Jew who is one inwardly.   In a final parting word to the Jew, Paul stresses that it is not in externals but rather in the inward condition of the heart that a man is a true Jew, i.e., a child of God.

> Paul's opponents among the Jews were building their hope for eternity on the
> mere fact they were Jews, and therefore, as they thought, God's chosen people.
> This reminds us of the days of John the Baptist, when those people were simi-

---

[97] For an explanation of "transgressor of the Law," see notes at Romans 2:25.

[98] Lard, *Romans*, p.98.

[99] *Ibid.*

larly resting their case on the parallel circumstance that they were "Abraham's seed" (Matthew 3:9; John 8:38,39). Paul, on the other hand, draws a sharp distinction between Jew and Jew: (a) the person who is a Jew outwardly only; that is, a Jew by virtue of physical or biological descent, nothing more; and (b) the individual who is a Jew not only outwardly but also inwardly; that is, a Jew to the eyes of the One before whom the secrets of men's hearts and lives are an open book ....[100]

Paul will show in chapter 11 that there was an Israel within Israel, a remnant who tried to do right when all those around were going into apostasy and bringing reproach on the Lord, a true spiritual Israel as contrasted to literal, physical Israel.

And circumcision is that which is of the heart. When God instituted the ordinance of circumcision, he distinctly taught that more was involved than simply the outward cutting of the flesh (see Deuteronomy 10:16, for example). He intended that men's lives be holy, cut off from sin. He wanted a life of consistent behavior prompted by thoughts submissive to His revealed will.

By the Spirit, not by the letter. Here is another place the translator must make a decision before he translates – is it "spirit" (man's inner nature or attitude), or is it "Spirit" (the Holy Spirit)? The KJV and ASV opted for the former while the NASB chooses the latter. A considerable difference of doctrine is involved.[101]

- One thing that is involved is the work of the Holy Spirit in the Old Testament. If we read "Spirit," then the verse implies that it was the Holy Spirit who made it possible for an Old Testament Jew to have a heart circumcision, and that in true Judaism the Holy Spirit is the active principle. Now this seems to contradict John 7:37-39 (which shows the indwelling of the Holy Spirit was not available before the death, resurrection, and ascension of Jesus) and Galatians 3:1-14 (which shows the Holy Spirit was not active in the Old Testament like He is in the New).
- If we translate it "spirit," then we are thrust into the area that Delitzsch has designated as "Biblical Psychology." The verse would have direct bearing on the makeup of a man (his body, soul, and spirit), and would seem to say that there is something synonymous in the terms "heart" and "spirit."[102]

---

[100] Hendriksen, *Romans*, p.108.

[101] Grubbs, *Romans*, p.52, contends that the distinction here "is not between a good Jew and a bad Jew, but between a Jew and a Christian. Under the dispensation of grace, outward Judaism amounts to nothing; we must be Christians, 'for we are the circumcision, who worship by the Spirit of God, and glory in Christ Jesus, and have no confidence in the flesh' (Philippians 3:3)." While he is correct that Judaism is no longer a viable religion, at least where men have heard the gospel (see the argument of the book of Hebrews), Romans 2 is not the passage to prove it. Grubbs' mistake was to assume that every time there is a mention of "letter and spirit" that the topic is the relation of the Law to the gospel. If one were to try to read Romans 2:25ff, substituting "Jew" for "circumcision," and "Christian" for "uncircumcision," he would get into insuperable difficulties.

[102] Those who would capitalize "Spirit" do so on the basis that the idea that genuine circumcision was something that was within has already been expressed in the word "heart." (See Cranfield, *Romans*, p.175, who appeals to Deuteronomy 30:6 as proof that "circumcision of the heart" is something God Himself

In comments above, we have spoken about a submissive attitude, and that is what "spirit" would be if there is any difference in it from the "heart."[103]   What God wanted was a life whose outward actions resulted from a submissive spirit, not just from the fact that God had written down the rules for behavior somewhere.   "Letter" here probably has reference in particular to the command concerning circumcision.

And his praise is not from men, but from God.   There is a play on words here.   "Judah" (from which the word "Jew" comes) means "praise" (Genesis 29:35, 49:8).   One of the characteristics of the Jews who were Paul's contemporaries was their desire to secure the praise of men (Matthew 23:5,27; Luke 16:15).   Such praise is of little value compared to having praise from God.   The "praise" from God that finally matters are the words, "Well done, good and faithful servant; enter thou into the joy of your Lord!"   Thus we have returned to the topic of the final judgment, and the sentence God will pass, as being the one all-important matter.   The praise of God can be bestowed only on those who conform *really*, not just externally, to His revealed requirements.

For the great majority of Jews, Paul's astonishing conclusion was the exact opposite of the Jew's own estimate of himself.   Paul insists that "Jewishness" (having "praise" from God) was more than physical descent from Abraham, or possessing the Living Oracles, or having the seal of circumcision.   Instead, it was a matter of the heart, which demonstrated itself in consistent conduct in harmony with God's revelation.   This was so revolutionary that any Jew would raise what he thought were conclusive objections against such a heretical doctrine.   To these standard objections Paul now turns his attention.

Perhaps a summary of Romans thus far would be valuable before we proceed to chapter 3.   Since Romans 1:18, Paul has been showing that the whole world is guilty before God.   *Gentiles are* – they had a knowledge of God, they sinned against that knowledge, God punished them even in this life, and still they refused to repent.   *Jews too are* – for they do the same things they condemn in the Gentiles, they did not meet the standards that God has revealed He will use in the judgment.   Five rhetorical questions (expecting a positive answer) show the Jews' sin, and Jewish objections to the "guilty" verdict are readily answered.   The objection based on "circumcision" is answered by saying that circumcision means something only if it is evidence of an inward reality.   Three other objections are about to be answered in chapter 3.

---

accomplishes.)   It has also been remarked that the other two places Paul uses "letter" and "spirit" (Romans 7:6 and 2 Corinthians 3:6) that the reference is to the Holy Spirit.

[103] A brief presentation of trichotomy (body, soul, and spirit) seems in order.   That there is a difference between "soul" and "spirit" seems to be taught in Hebrews 4:12 and 1 Thessalonians 5:23.   The *body* is the house the soul and spirit are housed in, and is made of flesh, blood, and bone.   The *soul* is the thing that animates the body.   And in the man who is not a slave to sin, God intended that the *spirit* give directions to the soul, which in turn would animate the body.   We might compare this to a man driving a General Motors automobile.   The man would be like the "spirit" – giving directions to the engine and drive train (the "soul") – which in turn are both housed in a "body by Fisher."   The "body" moves as the "engine and drive train" cause it to move, all at the will and direction of the "spirit" (the driver).

4. Answers to Jewish Objections to the Proof of their Guilt.   3:1-8

Summary: Three objections are answered: 1. What advantage is there to being a Jew? 2. Is God going to be unfaithful to His promises to the Jew? 3. If my sin gives God an opportunity to look good as He forgives, why should He punish my sin?

3:1 – *Then what advantage has the Jew?   Or what is the benefit of circumcision?*

Then.   We would expect the Jew to fight back against Paul's presentation; at least he could be expected to try to salvage something out of the Jew's special status.   It might seem as though Paul has proved too much in chapter 2, and the Jewish objector jumps at the opportunity to point out that Paul's conclusion is inconsistent with certain known truths. Each of the following questions (verses 1,3,5) is best explained as though it were a question asked by the Jewish objector.   Paul answers each objection by showing that his doctrine is not as inconsistent as the Jew imagined.

What advantage has the Jew?   Or what is the benefit of circumcision?   It is almost (the Jewish objector suggests) as though Paul's presentation accused God of doing something absolutely useless when He instituted the Jewish nation and religion and circumcision.   If the Jew is no different in God's sight from the Gentile, why should God go to all the trouble?   The reply the Jew anticipated was "None!   There is no advantage." But this is not the answer Paul gives.

3:2 – *Great in every respect.   First of all, that they were entrusted with the oracles of God.*

Great in every respect.   Though there is no advantage in being a Jew outwardly, yet there is great advantage in having his opportunities.   Though there is no advantage in the mere outward mark of circumcision, there was much advantage in the covenant relationship to which it related.

First of all.   Some have translated it "chiefly, mainly," since there is only one advantage listed here.   The idea would then be that there is nothing so advantageous as having a written revelation.[1]   Others have insisted that "chiefly" is not a good translation of *proton*. The proper translation is "first," they argue, and in the midst of dictation either Paul forgets that he had started a list and so never says "secondly" or "thirdly," or else it is affirmed that other advantages are enumerated at Romans 9:4,5.[2]

That they were entrusted with the oracles of God.   It is a mark of high privilege, and a sober responsibility, to be the special depository of a revelation from God.   An "oracle" (*logia*) is a message from a deity, a divine communication.[3]   "Living Oracles" (Acts 7:38)

---

[1] Wilson, *Romans*, p.49; Vine, *Romans*, p.44.

[2] Barmby, *Romans*, p.80.

[3] *Logia* was used by the Greeks for the answers (usually short sayings) from the gods to questions

is likely a parallel expression. "The name 'oracles' is applied in the New Testament only to revelations made to Moses (Acts 7:38), and to the Divine utterances generally (Hebrews 5:12; 1 Peter 4:11)."[4]   There seems to be little reason to limit the expression to anything less than the whole body of Old Testament Scriptures.[5]   Plumer tries to help us appreciate all that is involved:

> Think of how much is here included – the history of creation, of the Fall, of the deluge, of the dispersion, of the call and trials of Abraham, of the history of his descendants, of the exodus from Egypt; the law; the records of kings good and bad; the proverbs; the sublimest songs; predictions respecting the course of events to the end of the world; and all these abounding in precepts, promises, warnings and encouragements of the most weighty character.[6]

Still there is more to be learned from this statement.   It implies that it is as *written* Scripture that these "oracles" were entrusted to the Jews.   Anything simply oral would be susceptible to getting lost in the telling as time passed, rather than be like a treasure that could be stored or committed or confided into someone's keeping.   Further, there is implied a confidence on God's part in the Jews, that they would "guard" the treasure.   "This confidence was not misplaced, for no people ever guarded a sacred trust or deposit with more fidelity, than the Jews did the sacred scriptures."[7]   Once more, that the "Scriptures" should be called the "oracles of God" involves the whole matter of the inspiration of the Old Testament. Scripture is God's "speech" written.   No wonder Paul begins his list of advantages of being a Jew by appealing to God's depositing with them the divine oracles!

3:3 – *What then?   If some did not believe, their unbelief will not nullify the faithfulness of God, will it?*

What, then?   This is to be regarded as the second of the current series the Jew puts forth in objection to Paul's presentation about how it will be in the judgment, for Jews as well as Gentiles.   The Greek reads *ti gar.*   The *gar* concedes the preceding statement about advantages in having the oracles of God, while *ti* suggests a difficulty implied in it.

If some did not believe.   Alford and others translate *ēpistēsan* "were unfaithful," taking it in the sense of being "unfaithful to the covenant, the very condition of which was to walk in the ways of the Lord and observe His statutes."[8]   Again, there seems to be a word play

---

asked by their worshipers.   Philo used the expression with reference to the Ten Commandments in a treatise he wrote, *On the Life Of Moses*, chap. xxii.

[4] Gifford, *Romans*, p.82.

[5] Meyer, *Romans*, p.112, urges the expression should be limited to the revealed promises of the coming Redeemer.   Others would follow Philo's lead and limit it to the Decalog.

[6] William S. Plumer, *Commentary on Romans* (Grand Rapids: Kregel Publications, 1971), p.110.

[7] Barnes, *Romans*, p.78.

[8] Alford, *Romans*, p.337.

in the Greek, for "entrusted" (*episteuthēsan*) and "did not believe" (*ēpistēsan*) sound very similar, thus guiding us to what it was that was not believed.[9]

Their unbelief will not nullify the faithfulness of God, will it? God had made certain promises to Israel. One of God's characteristics is "faithfulness;" He always keeps His promises![10] The Jew supposes he has found a fatal flaw in Paul's presentation. 'If what you say about the Jew's unfaithfulness is true, then does it not follow that God must of necessity be unfaithful to His promises?' is how the Jew was objecting. 'If a Jew should be lost, it seems to me that God has not kept His promises to the Jew,' is another way of wording the objection. What the Jew has omitted from his presupposition about the promises of God is that God's promises were always conditional.[11]

3:4 – *May it never be! Rather, let God be found true, though every man* **be found** *a liar, as it is written, "THAT THOU MIGHTEST BE JUSTIFIED IN THY WORDS, AND MIGHTEST PREVAIL WHEN THOU ART JUDGED."*

May it never be! Here begins Paul's reply to the second objection. The KJV reads "God forbid!" which is a way to express, in English, the rather forceful and indignant repudiation the Greek construction involves, though there is no word for "God" in the Greek.[12]

Rather, let God be found true. Paraphrased, 'Never think anything other than that God always keeps His promises!' It is impossible for God to lie (Hebrews 6:18; Titus 1:2; Numbers 23:19). "Found" suggests the idea that God is being dragged into court, where His truthfulness will be judged. When the trial is finished, it will be supremely evident that God's words are in perfect accordance with the facts.

Though every man *be found* **a liar.** If God's methods seem to be contradictory to men's expectations, it is man who has misunderstood what God was promising. God's promises

---

[9] A number of writers insist that the "faith" that the Jews lacked, in this passage, is none other than belief that the Old Testament promises of Messiah have been fulfilled in Jesus. (So say Meyer, Gifford, Godet, Sanday and Headlam.) The basis of the insistence is that, elsewhere in the New Testament, the word "unbelief" is regularly used of exactly such lack of faith in Jesus (Matthew 13:58; Acts 28:24; 1 Timothy 1:13). However, note that faith in Jesus as Messiah has not yet come into Paul's presentation; rather, the context is dealing with faithfulness (or the lack of it) to God's Old Covenant revelation.

[10] "Faithfulness" is the same word translated "faith" in Romans 1:17, and this fact should help us when we try to define what "faith" is as we study chapter 4.

[11] Jesse Wilson Hodges, *Christ's Coming and Kingdom* (Grand Rapids: Wm. B. Eerdmans Publishing Co., 1957), p.73-107, shows the presence of the conditional element, even when it was not specifically stated. For example, Jonah came preaching, "Forty days and Nineveh shall be destroyed!" Yet when Nineveh repented, the destruction was avoided. "Unless you repent" was implied in the warning.

[12] The construction *mē genoito* is one of the few examples of the optative mood found in the New Testament. It expresses a wish. "The phrase *mē genoito* is an optative of wishing which strongly deprecates something suggested by a previous question or assertion. Fourteen of the fifteen New Testament instances [of this construction] are in Paul's writings, and in twelve of these it expresses the apostle's abhorrence of an inference he fears may be (falsely) drawn from his argument." Dana and Mantey, *Manual Grammar*, p.174.

to Israel will come to pass even if every Israelite proved to be unfaithful. It is man, not God, who would be untrue! Also remember that not only were God's promises conditional, but God's promises included "cursing" as well as "blessing."

As it is written. The verse about to be quoted comes from Psalm 51:4, and is used to vindicate the character of God. It was spoken by David, and David's attitude is elemental – elemental to anyone who wants to have his life and thoughts in harmony with God.

> Nathan had convicted David of gross sin in the matter of Uriah, and foretold the punishment that was to come to David. In this Psalm (51:4), [as he utters these words in a state of deep repentance for past sins], David sees that his sin was so heinous and directly against God that the sentence of condemnation pronounced against him was right and he confessed that God might be seen and declared to be righteous, and in this sense be justified by those who heard the sentence upon him ... The passage is quoted to show that what Paul has just deduced from the character of God accords with the oracles of God, which the Jews so jealously guarded.[13]

"THAT THOU MIGHTEST BE JUSTIFIED IN THY WORDS, AND MIGHTEST PREVAIL WHEN THOU ART JUDGED." The quotation is from the LXX, which gives a little different angle than the Hebrew does.[14] David is saying that not only he, but anyone who heard about it, could recognize that God's dealings have been right. It was David, not God, who had done wrong! This passage is not saying David sinned in order that God might have opportunity to forgive. That is not the reason any man sins! Nor is the passage to be interpreted to mean God takes evil and makes good to come from it. It is true that God sometimes uses evil men to accomplish His purposes, but that is not what is taught here. "When thou art judged" pictures God being put on trial, and when the trial is over, God has stood the test; He prevailed in the case brought against Him. Though someone accused Him of injustice, He was acquitted. ("Prevail" means "winning a case in court." [15])

3:5 – *But if our unrighteousness demonstrates the righteousness of God, what shall we say? The God who inflicts wrath is not unrighteous, is He? (I am speaking in human terms.)*

But. This is to be regarded as the third in the current series of objections which a Jew

---

[13] Lipscomb and Shepherd, *Romans*, p.65.

[14] The Hebrew reads "that thou mightest be pure" (i.e., be esteemed pure). The LXX has "mightest prevail."

[15] Arndt-Gingrich, *Lexicon*, p.561. God is often judged, i.e., arraigned in human thought, because of His dealings with men. God is judged when men blame Him for creating man with the ability to sin. God is judged when men blame Him for decreeing that the consequences of Adam's sin should be passed on to the whole race. God is judged when men blame Him for requiring of men that they be holy in character, even in the midst of trials. (God often appoints what is hard, but never what is wrong.) God is judged when men blame Him for some calamity that has intruded into their lives. God is judged when men censure Him for not revealing more about the future. Yet God is right in what He does and in the judgments He pronounces. A man must keep this in mind if his attitude is to be in harmony with what Scripture says.

might raise as he attempted to show Paul's presentation of how judgment will be was in error.   This objection was suggested by Paul's reply (in verse 4) to the previous objection.

If our unrighteousness demonstrates the righteousness of God, what shall we say? "Unrighteousness," one of the New Testament synonyms for sin, has been explained at Romans 1:18.   In this context it speaks of the sins of the Jews that resulted because of unfaithfulness to the written revelation from God.   "Righteousness" here likely denotes one of God's attributes, His just and holy character.[16]   Included too would be mercy and faithfulness.   "What shall we say?" means "what inference can we draw?"   Paraphrased, the Jew's question reads, 'If my sin gives God an opportunity to publicly and conspicuously demonstrate His holy mercy, where does that leave your argument about God's condemnation of sinners when He judges?   Doesn't it prove your doctrine is wrong?' Worded another way, 'If my sin brings into greater prominence the character of God, why is He angry?   Instead of judging and condemning me, you'd think He'd be happy.'

The God who inflicts wrath is not unrighteous, is He?   The question expects a negative answer.   To the Jewish objector, Paul's teaching led logically to the conclusion God was being inconsistent and unfair.   "Inflicts wrath" is the same thing as punishing the sinner.[17] 'How can God consistently punish when at the same time He benefits by having His righteousness stand out in greater prominence?   You are not teaching God is unfair, are you?'

(I am speaking in human terms.)   Here Paul tells us he has been using the language of others as he raises these three questions in the opening verses of chapter 3.   These words should not be interpreted to mean that this part of Romans is uninspired.   Rather, it amounts almost to an apology for arguing whether God is right or wrong in His actions.

3:6 – *May it never be!   For otherwise how will God judge the world?*

May it never be!   Just as in verse 4, Paul begins his reply with an indignant negation. God is never being unfair or unjust when He punishes the sinner.

> The Jew should have remembered that God is the author of two classes of promises.   In the one, He proposes to bless Israel, provided they keep His statutes.   In the other, He threatens to punish if they do not.   Fidelity to His word requires that He should remember the threats no less than the promises.[18]

For otherwise how will God judge the world?   This is the first answer to the objection raised in verse 5.   Both Paul and his readers alike held it as axiomatic that God was going to judge the world.   What has been said earlier in chapter 2 about the fact of a coming judgment would not be questioned.   The third objection just proposed by the Jew was in-

---

[16] Consult the comments at Romans 1:17 to review what was said about the different ways the word "righteousness" is used in Romans.

[17] "Wrath" has been explained at Romans 1:18 and 2:8.

[18] Lard, *Romans*, p.104.

consistent with belief in a final judgment; therefore, the objection is in error.   That God is going to judge "the world" (all mankind) is the same idea concerning a general judgment as was expressed earlier (see notes at 2:3-16).   The same thing will be affirmed again in Romans 3:19.   If on that day God could not condemn a sinner because his sin had been an occasion for God to display His righteousness, that would wreck the moral universe.

3:7 – *But if through my lie the truth of God abounded to His glory, why am I also still being judged as a sinner?*

But if through my lie the truth of God abounded to His glory.   This is the second answer to the objection in verse 5.   Paul is drawing an illustration from his own personal life to show that the reasoning behind the objection was false.   From the orthodox Jewish standpoint, Paul's conversion and message about Jesus was a big lie.   It was false; there could be no truth to it.   The "truth of God" stands for His truthfulness (as in verse 4) and His righteousness (as in verse 5).   "Abounded to His glory" is another way of saying "demonstrates the righteousness of God" (verse 5).   Again, men do not sin just to give God an opportunity to show what a marvelous God He is.   By this allusion to his own example, Paul is showing he knows the objector does not really think so either.

Why am I still being judged as a sinner?   From the Jewish standpoint, Paul the Christian was an apostate from the religion of the fathers; consequently, the Jews condemned him as a sinner.   'If you say a man who sins won't be judged, if his sin gives God an opportunity to display His glory, then why are you still condemning and persecuting me?' Paul asks.   'Why don't you Jews treat me as you want God to treat you?'   Paul's reply to the Jewish objection is telling.   Not many Jews would have said Paul's apostasy was an occasion for the display of God's righteousness and glory (though it really resulted in just that).

3:8 – *And why not* say *(as we are slanderously reported and as some affirm that we say),* *"Let us do evil that good may come"?*   *Their condemnation is just.*

And why not *say*.   This is the third answer to the objection the Jew offered in verse 5.[19]   Paul uses the same argument against the objector that the objector has been using against Christianity.   He turns it right back on them, saying that, 'The same thing you say we wickedly teach, you yourselves must hold if your objection is to have any validity.'

(As we are slanderously reported and as some affirm that we say).   Paul (like the other apostles) was charged by his Jewish adversaries of encouraging people to sin.   Evidently, the Jew who heard the gospel thought that "grace" tended to remove all restraints against sinning, restraints erected by the "Law".   If the restraints were removed, men would plunge more into sin.[20]   The Greek translated "slanderously reported" is "we are blasphemed;" it

---

[19] Some versions translate the particle *mē* ("not") that begins verse 8, and some do not.   Those who do not think it is simply a sign that an interrogative statement (that expects a negative answer) follows.   The line of thought is easier to follow if this particle is translated (as the NASB does), and verse 8 is assumed to be a further reply to the Jewish objector.

[20] We might learn from these objections, raised by a Jew, that once a man has heard the gospel but

means to be spoken of in a reproachful manner. Paul was hounded at every step by the enemies of the gospel. Sometimes those enemies simply misrepresented what Paul said; at other times they deliberately perverted his doctrine. His use of the strong term 'blasphemed' ("slanderously") seems to suggest deliberate perversion in this topic's case.

"Let us do evil that good may come"? Perhaps the Jewish detractors of Paul had heard something similar to Romans 5:20, "Where sin increased, grace abounded all the more." Paul has now used three terms to designate the same idea: "good" (in this verse), "glory" (in verse 7), and "the righteousness of God" (in verse 5). Now we see how Paul has turned the Jewish argument back against them. Leaving out the parenthetical phrase, the verse says this: 'If the glory of God can be promoted by my sin, and if because of that fact I will not be condemned or held guilty for my sin, then why not carry the doctrine out to its logical conclusion? Why not make it a principle of conduct? Why not, all of us, do *all the evil we can* in order to promote God's glory?'

Their condemnation is just. The very idea that men can sin so as to promote the glory of God is absurd! There is something perverse in the man who can take the gospel truth and twist it so it appears to teach what these slanderers said it did. Such slanderous men are under a damnatory sentence of God, and Paul here concurs with God's verdict.

> Paul ... is a stranger to that all-pervasive moral anemia which nowadays is euphemistically described as "Christian tolerance." "The admission must be squarely and honestly made, that the inspired men of both Testaments felt and expressed moral indignation against wrong-doers, and a desire for their proper retribution at the hand of God ... Sympathy with the right implies reprobation of the wrong" (Dabney).[21]

Paul has now answered the standard Jewish objections to the Christian understanding of the doctrine of the final judgment. He has tried to help the Jew see what the Jew's own oracles from God actually taught. He is now ready to clinch his presentation of the guilt of all men by appealing to a series of Old Testament passages that plainly show this truth.

C. Righteousness (Justification, Salvation) is Therefore Needed by All. 3:9-20

1. Proof from Scripture that All are Sinners. 3:9-18

> *Summary*: A thoughtful question based on the advantage of having the oracles of God is now answered. Verse after verse in those oracles spoke of the sin of all men. Instead of resulting in the possessor's justification, the Law only served to increase men's awareness that they were sinners.

---

does not want to obey it, he can display an amazing ingenuity in justifying his own sin and refusal to obey.

[21] Wilson, *Romans*, p.53.

3:9 – *What then?   Are we better than they?   Not at all; for we have already charged that both Jews and Greeks are all under sin;*

What then?   This seems to be a continuation of the "what then?" the objector asked in 3:3, though this interpretation is by no means certain.   If it is not the objector asking another question, then the question asked in 3:9 is Paul's way of getting the reader to contemplate where the whole argument since 1:18 has led.   The reason for the hesitation at this place will become obvious as further phrases are commented upon.

Are we better than they?   The reader will observe that the margin reads, "Are we worse than they?"   Not only do we have the problem of who is speaking, but also the problem of how to translate *proechometha* ("better" or "worse"?).   *Proechometha* can be either a middle voice or a passive voice verb in the Greek.   "The main question is as to the sense of this verb, which occurs only here in the New Testament, and has, therefore, to be interpreted from consideration of the sense of which the verb is capable, and the probable drift of the argument."[22]   At least three different attempts at explanation have been made.

(1) The marginal reading represents an attempt to translate it as a passive voice: 'Are we surpassed?   Are we bettered by the Gentiles?   Are we worse than they?   Do the privileges we Jews have bring us into greater condemnation than the Gentiles will suffer?' This is the way Lightfoot, Vine, and the ERV incline to translate it, but there are several objections to this rendering.   Paul will immediately answer the question with a strong negative, and a denial of "greater condemnation because of greater privilege" would contradict all that was said in chapter 2.   Further, there has been nothing in the passage to suggest any idea of superiority of the Gentile over the Jew.   Therefore, to attempt to translate the verb as though it were passive seems unsustainable.   However, there are still two possible explanations of the phrase if we opt for the middle voice.[23]

(2) Some suggest the translation, 'Do we put forward (anything) in our own defense?'   Or as the ERV marginal note reads, 'Do we excuse ourselves?'   If this translation is adopted, then the speaker likely is Paul rather than the objector, and this might be urged as the ordinary meaning of the middle voice.   However, the translators have had to insert an object ("anything") which is not in the Greek, and this may not be defensible.

(3) Most scholars, ancient and modern, and most English translations express the idea as the NASB has, "Are we better than they?"   Though this would be one of the few places in all Greek literature where the middle voice is so translated, it seems to fit what the context requires.[24]   If it is correct, it is the Jewish objector who is asking another question of Paul: 'You have admitted there is an advantage in belonging to the Cho-

---

[22] Barmby, *Romans*, p.81.

[23] The Greek has three voices for its verbs, whereas English has but two.   Like the English active voice, the Greek active voice signifies the subject of the verb is doing the acting.   Like the English passive voice, the Greek passive voice signifies the subject is being acted upon.   The English has no equivalent of the Greek middle voice, which usually signifies that the subject is acting upon itself (often for its own benefit).

[24] "This rendering, though it gives essentially the same sense as if *proechomen* [an active voice form] ... had been written, is commended by its suitableness to the course of the argument, and the middle voice may, perhaps, be accounted for as denoting the Jews' supposed claim of superiority for themselves." Barmby, *Romans*, p.82.

sen People (verse 2).   Isn't it then true that we Jews are better off than the Gentiles?   Isn't it true that we Jews will be treated differently in the judgment?'

Not at all.[25]   Here begins Paul's answer to the Jew's last question.   God's method of judging is still affirmed to be a comparison of a man's life with the revelation he had.   And when this is done, the Jew cannot claim any advantage over the Gentile in the matter of justification before God.   Instead of singling out Jews (or Gentiles) as being superior, it uses inclusive language to indict all men of sin.

For we have already charged that both Jews and Greeks are all under sin.   Here is a reason for the negative answer Paul just gave to the objector's question.   To "charge" is to prove, or accuse, or convict.   That Greeks were guilty of sin was shown in Romans 1:18-32.   That Jews are guilty of sin has been shown in chapter 2.   "Sin" here is *hamartia*, to "miss the mark."   "When applied to moral things the idea is similar, it is missing the true end of life, and so it is used as a general term for *sin*."[26]   When Paul says that all men are "under" sin, it means either that they are guilty of sinning, or are under condemnation for sin, or that sin is a power that controls man, and all men who sin become slaves of sin (an idea that will be developed later in Romans).

3:10 – *as it is written, "THERE IS NONE RIGHTEOUS, NOT EVEN ONE;*

As it is written.   This phrase, which occurs about 90 times in the New Testament, is the common way quotations from the Old Testament are introduced.   Verses 10-18 are passages taken from various parts of the Old Testament,[27] and are quoted to prove the charge about the universal guilt of man.[28]

"THERE IS NONE RIGHTEOUS, NOT EVEN ONE.   This comes either from Psalm 14:1 or Psalm 53:3, quoting neither the LXX nor the Hebrew verbatim, but giving the sense of the passage.[29]   God is pictured as looking down from heaven on the children of men at

---

[25] Those translations that preferred the passive voice for the verb in the question, translate this phrase "not in every respect."   That is, in some respects the Jews were worse off, but "not in every respect."

[26] Berry, *Synonyms*, p.117.   The same root word was used at 2:12 and 3:7.

[27] "The verses are a striking instance of the way in which the apostle weaves together passages taken from different sources.   It also affords an example of the way the text of the Old Testament was corrupted [by post New Testament Scribes].   The whole passage as it stands here is found in some manuscripts of the LXX, as part of Psalm 14, whence it has been copied not only into the Vulgate, but also into our own Prayer Book, which will be seen to differ from the Bible version."   Sanday, *Romans*, p.47.

[28] Some have tried to interpret these verses as though they were intended to prove merely the guilt of the Jews, on the basis of the fact that only to Jews would the Scriptures be of any force by way of argument.   This commentator finds it hard to limit the application of these passages to Jews alone (though they certainly are included, too, as verse 19 plainly demonstrates).   Verse 9, which introduces this series of quotations, affirms "*Both* Jews and Greeks are *all* under sin," so we would expect the verses to prove *universal* guilt, especially after they are introduced by a phrase like "as it is written."

[29] For example, in the Hebrew the verse reads simply, "There is none that doeth good."   The phrase "not even one" is not in the Hebrew, but is in the LXX.   Sometimes the New Testament writers cite the

large (not just the Jewish people only), to see if there were any who did understand and seek after God. After giving careful scrutiny, God declares the result of His search, "There is *none* righteous, *none* that doeth good, no, not one." "Righteous" here means totally free from sin, never having committed one single sin.[30]

3:11 – *THERE IS NONE WHO UNDERSTANDS, THERE IS NONE WHO SEEKS FOR GOD;*

THERE IS NONE WHO UNDERSTANDS. Paul's language is taken from Psalm 14:2 or 53:2. In the Hebrew it is not said verbatim that "there is none who understands," but it is strongly implied that none were found when God made His investigation. To "understand" God's will and man's duty and obligations to Him is the idea.[31]

THERE IS NONE WHO SEEKS FOR GOD. None "endeavors to know and do His will, and to be acquainted with His character."[32] "None who seek Him perfectly, or without a failure."[33]

3:12 – *ALL HAVE TURNED ASIDE, TOGETHER THEY HAVE BECOME USELESS; THERE IS NONE WHO DOES GOOD, THERE IS NOT EVEN ONE."*

ALL HAVE TURNED ASIDE. This is still part of the quotation, and is from Psalm 14:3 or 53:3. Because their understandings were darkened, they turned aside from the way leading to God, the way pleasing to God. They once were on the right way, but no longer.

Hebrew, sometimes the LXX, and sometimes (as here) neither one exactly (they just give the sense of the passage). The way the New Testament writers quote the Old Testament is a very strong argument for the inspiration of the New Testament writers.

[30] In Luke 1:6, both Elizabeth and Zacharias are called "righteous," and in Matthew 1:19, Joseph is called "righteous." It is therefore evident that the word in Luke and Matthew has a sense different from its meaning here in Romans 3:10. Zacharias, Elizabeth, and Joseph were "righteous" in the sense that the tenor of their lives was right, but they were not "sinless perfect," which is the meaning of the word here in Romans. Throughout chapter 3, Paul is talking of the righteousness (wholly free from sin) that would be necessary if a man is not to be condemned under the Law.

[31] In many commentaries, Calvinistic interpreters are wont to emphasize what they call "total depravity" as they comment on these verses. If "total depravity" meant no more than the truth that every man has sinned, there would be little objection to the term, for Romans surely teaches that "all have sinned and fall short of the glory of God." But Calvinistic theologians mean more than "all have sinned." "TOTAL DEPRAVITY. Theological term for man's condition following Adam's Fall. This, according to orthodox Christian doctrine, imparted to all men a bent toward evil and an inability to do good apart from divine grace. Calvinism holds to a thoroughgoing total depravity which makes election and predestination necessities for salvation." Donald T. Kauffman, *The Dictionary of Religious Terms* (Westwood, NJ: Fleming H. Revell, 1967), p.415. To comment upon Romans 3 as though it demonstrated the truth of "total depravity" in the Calvinistic sense is eisegesis (i.e., reading personal notions into the text). It would be better to provide exegesis of the text.

[32] Barnes, *Romans*, p.86.

[33] Lard, *Romans*, p.109.

TOGETHER THEY HAVE BECOME USELESS. "Together" says that one and all, the whole mass of mankind is involved. There was a time they were useful to God; He could have worked through them to save others, or He could have been praised by them, but not now (unless they repent). The Hebrew word translated "useless" "means to become putrid and offensive, like fruit that is spoiled. In Arabic, it is applied to milk that has become sour."[34]

THERE IS NONE WHO DOES GOOD. When Paul says "there is none who does good" we must understand it the same way as "there is none righteous" (verse 10). There is none who do good wholly and without exception – none who never sin.

THERE IS NOT EVEN ONE." The only way Jews could be better than Gentiles (verse 9) is for the Jew to be sinless perfect. If there were someone who was sinless perfect, that one could expect preferential treatment in the judgment. The problem is that the existence of such a sinless perfect person is contrary to what the Jews' own Scriptures teach. Consequently, for a Jew to plead he should get preferential treatment, he would have to deny his own Scriptures, for they say "there is not even one" who has never sinned.[35]

3:13 – *"THEIR THROAT IS AN OPEN GRAVE, WITH THEIR TONGUES THEY KEEP DECEIVING," "THE POISON OF ASPS IS UNDER THEIR LIPS"*;

"THEIR THROAT IS AN OPEN GRAVE. This part of verse 13 comes from Psalm 5:9 and is taken verbatim from the LXX.[36] Commentators have made several suggestions as they attempt to explain how sinners' speech is like an open grave. One is that where there is death, the peace and happiness of the deceased's survivors is swallowed up; i.e., the slanderer ruins the peace and happiness of the objects of his slander. Another idea is that as dead bodies soon bloat and give off a foul and noxious odor, so likewise the words of sinners poison the atmosphere. The speech of sinners is corrupt and corrupting.

WITH THEIR TONGUES THEY KEPT DECEIVING." This also comes from Psalm 5:9, verbatim from the LXX; the Hebrew reads "they make smooth their tongue." "In their conversation and their promises, they have been false, treacherous, and untruthful."[37] The Greek verb is an imperfect tense, which signifies continuous action in the past time.

"THE POISON OF ASPS IS UNDER THEIR LIPS." This phrase is from the LXX of Psalm 140:3. "The asp [LXX], or adder [Hebrew], is a species of serpent whose poison is of such active operation that it kills almost instantly, and that without remedy. It is small,

---

[34] Barnes, *Romans*, p.86.

[35] When the Psalmist pictures God as looking down at men, it was before the incarnation of Jesus. Jesus did live a sinless life (Hebrews asserts this numerous times, as do other New Testament Scriptures), so Jesus must be understood to be the one exception to this statement that no man was sinless perfect.

[36] Verse and chapter numbers in the LXX are different from the numbering in the Hebrew of Psalms. This is verse 10 in the Hebrew.

[37] Barnes, *Romans*, p.86.

and commonly lies concealed, often in the sand of the road, and strikes the traveler before he sees it."[38]   Actually the poison is contained in a small sac at the base of each fang, and the fangs are concealed by the lips. The point of the comparison seems to be this: "What such lips say is to reputations as the poison of the asp is in the blood."[39]

3:14 – *"WHOSE MOUTH IS FULL OF CURSING AND BITTERNESS";*

"WHOSE MOUTH IS FULL OF CURSING AND BITTERNESS."   Paul has taken this phrase from the LXX of Psalm 10:7, but not quite exactly, for the LXX adds the word "deceit."   The Hebrew reads "deceit and oppression."   In this Psalm, David is describing his enemies.   The word "full of" (*gemō*) is a word that conveys the impression of being heavily loaded.   *Pleroō* is a synonym, but it means simply to be 'filled to the top.'   The wicked are seen to be, not just full of cursing, but "overloaded" with sin.   When a man curses another, he is expressing a prayer in which he calls for God to harm or damn the object of his malediction.   Such opprobrious language is grievous to God, who created the mouth to bless and honor Him instead of uttering blasphemies, malignities, and execrations against men.   "By 'bitterness' is meant those wounding, stinging words which the wicked utter"[40] when they wish to hurt another's feelings.

3:15 – *"THEIR FEET ARE SWIFT TO SHED BLOOD,*

"THEIR FEET ARE SWIFT TO SHED BLOOD.   This verse, and the next two, are abridged or condensed from Isaiah 59:7,8, where the Hebrew and LXX agree.   The passages Paul selected come from the midst of a long description of the character of the nation in the time of Isaiah.   The same thing could be seen in Paul's time, and in our own. To "shed blood" is to commit murder, and God through Isaiah charges the nation with being eager to commit murder on the slightest provocation.   "They frequently and without compunction committed murder and did violence.   They rushed fiercely on their victims to gratify their malice or to satisfy their vengeance."[41]   And often, the slights for which men will kill others are trivial.

3:16 – *DESTRUCTION AND MISERY ARE IN THEIR PATHS,*

DESTRUCTION AND MISERY ARE IN THEIR PATHS.   "Misery" is distress, wretchedness, affliction.   "Destruction" represents *suntrimma*, which means "that which is broken, fractured, shattered; then calamity, ruin, destruction."[42]   We might call to mind the broken and shattered lives that drunken drivers leave behind; often too, it was innocent

---

[38] *Ibid.*

[39] Lard, *Romans*, p.109.

[40] Lipscomb and Shepherd, *Romans*, p.70.

[41] *Ibid.*

[42] Thayer, *Lexicon*, p.607.

people who were the ones caused to suffer by the sin of others.   It is almost as if he says, 'Wherever these sinners go, you can trace them by the ruin and misery they leave behind.'

3:17 – *AND THE PATH OF PEACE HAVE THEY NOT KNOWN."*

AND THE PATH OF PEACE HAVE THEY NOT KNOWN."   "They lived in contention themselves and involved others in like quarrels and disquiet."[43]   These wicked men's actions were not productive of happiness, either for themselves or for others.   Restless themselves because of guilt, they seek to destroy the peace of everyone else.   Think of the numberless ways in which men injure their fellow men – terrorism, bombings, hostages, abuse of mates and children, torture, crime sprees, genocide, whole peoples forced to become refugees; it is evident the charges of sin made years ago are still true today.

3:18 – *"THERE IS NO FEAR OF GOD BEFORE THEIR EYES."*

"THERE IS NO FEAR OF GOD BEFORE THEIR EYES."   This is taken from the LXX of Psalm 36:1.   "God, whose very presence should inspire men with the fear of doing wrong, is entirely disregarded.   They are destitute of any sense of His presence, let alone any regard for Him."[44]   "Where God is not feared, nothing else is; and when this last barrier to vice is destroyed, sin comes in like a flood."[45]   Three things have been noted by Paul in this series of quotations from the Old Testament.   (1) The fact that *all* were sinners, verses 10-12.   (2) The kinds of sins men do – sins of the tongue, verses 13,14; and sins of deed, verses 15-17.   (3) The real reason for the sin, the thing that is beneath all that precedes, is an absence of any reverence for God, verse 18.   While not all Jews nor all Gentiles were guilty of all the sins enumerated, still all are guilty of some.

2.   Conclusion to the First Section of Romans.   3:19,20

> *Summary*:   This is an application specifically to the Jews of the universal indictment of men, finally and unequivocally driving the Jew from any ideas of preferential treatment in the judgment.

3:19 – *Now we know that whatever the Law says, it speaks to those who are under the Law, that every mouth may be closed, and all the world may become accountable to God;*

Now we know.   "Know" is *oida*, to know by external testimony.[46]   The testimony of Scripture is that God gave the Law of Moses specially to the Jews; thus, Paul has in mind here particularly the Jew.   The Jew would admit that the Gentile was under condemnation,

---

[43] Plumer, *Romans*, p.117.

[44] Vine, *Romans*, p.50.

[45] Lipscomb and Shepherd, *Romans*, p.71.

[46] On the meaning of the different synonyms for "know," see notes at 1:32 and 2:2.

but the Jew should recognize that the same Scripture that condemned the Gentile was even more applicable to the Jew, for the Law of Moses really was Jewish law.

That whatever the Law says. It is difficult to confine "Law" to the Pentateuch. The above quotations (verses 10-18) were drawn from the Psalms and Isaiah, not the Pentateuch, and yet Paul here classes those quotes as "Law." The word "Law" elsewhere is used to cover the whole range of Old Testament revelation from Moses onward.[47]

It speaks to those who are under the Law. Paul makes this statement in order to prevent the Jew from evading the force of his argument. The Jew might try to argue the passages quoted had reference to the Gentiles, not to the Jews. Indeed they may have reference to the Gentiles, but that is not all. Jews, too, the ones who were specially "under the Law," were certainly included in the group who had sinned habitually. Paul uses two different Greek words here for "say" or "speak." "Says" (previous clause) represents *legō*, while "speaks" is a translation of *laleō*. The difference in the two words is that *laleō* emphasizes the act of speaking, as opposed to silence, while *legō* emphasizes the content or substance of what was said.[48] God has not been silent; He has spoken to the Jews in the Law.

That every mouth may be closed. Paul wants no more pleading by the Jew that he will have special consideration at the judgment. The argument has been conclusive for any opponent. There are no loopholes; there are no more possible replies. The only proper thing for the objector is to be silent on the topic he has been contending about.

And all the world may become accountable to God. "All the world" includes the Jew as well as the Gentile. "Accountable" is a translation of *hupodikos*, a word that could be translated "guilty." It is a courtroom word meaning "one who has lost his suit, and is therefore liable to punishment."[49] The defendant tried to defend himself, but failed; the charges against him were found to be true. Implicit in this language is the idea that every man in the world is an object of God's scrutiny during this life; every man, too, is answerable to Him in the final judgment.

3:20 – *because by the works of the Law no flesh will be justified in His sight; for through the Law* **comes** *the knowledge of sin.*

Because. The first word of verse 20 indicates that a reason is now to be given for what has just been said.[50] The whole world is guilty of sin before God because (though all have

---

[47] In 1 Corinthians 14:21, the term "Law" is used, yet Isaiah is quoted. In John 10:34 and 15:25, we find the word "Law," yet a Psalm has been quoted. How much is included in "Law" will prove important in discussions concerning the relation of the Law and the gospel, where it is said the "Law" was temporary. The determination of just what is "Law" will also prove to be important in discussions with certain 20th century religious groups whose doctrine requires that "Law" be limited to the Ten Commandments, or whose doctrine insists there is a difference between the "Law of God" and the "Law of Moses."

[48] Berry, *Greek-English Lexicon*, p.59.

[49] Thayer, *Lexicon*, p.643.

[50] "Therefore" in the KJV improperly translates *dioti*, and this tends to change the meaning of the whole

"law" to live by) "by the works of the Law no flesh will be justified"; therefore, even the Jew should be silent, having ceased his objections.

By the works of the Law. This is another example of anarthrous *nomos*.[51] In this case it seems the NASB (with a capital "L" on "Law") was correct in treating it as a reference to the Law of Moses. Just what does Paul mean by this expression "works of the Law," which he has not used before in Romans, but will be using several times in the verses following? Have there been any clues in the foregoing chapters of Romans that would give us a hint as to the meaning of this new expression?

- At Romans 2:13 we had the affirmation that "doers of the Law will be justified." That verse spoke of a habitual pattern of obedience to what God has commanded.
- Since Paul here at 3:20 wrote that "works of the Law" do not justify, it is obvious the two expressions ("doers of the Law" and "works of the Law") are *not* synonymous expressions; if they were, 2:13 and 3:20 would contradict.[52]
- The Dead Sea scroll 4QMMT has thrown light on the expression "works of the Law." That document speaks about "some significant works of the Law" and goes on to list nearly two dozen man-made rules based on one or another verse found in the Law.[53]
- Just as did the authors of the 4QMMT scroll, so the Pharisees also had numerous such man-made rules (Hebrew *halakhot*, 'how to walk'). On the basis of those rules they criticized Jesus' disciples for picking the heads of grain and eating them (Matthew 12:1), for eating with unwashed hands (Matthew 15:2), and for eating with tax-gatherers and sinners (Matthew 9:11). Such rules are called "the traditions of the elders" at Matthew 15:2. In Jesus' reply to the Pharisees (Matthew 15:3, "why do you transgress the commandment of God for the sake of your tradition"), it again is obvious that "works of the Law" were not the same as observing the Law of Moses.

No flesh will be justified in His sight. Perhaps Paul has quoted this phrase from Psalm 143:2, both here and in Galatians 2:16. If so, it would be another example of an appeal to the Old Testament to show it taught the same doctrine he was teaching, even when it comes to the matter of the way a man is "justified."[54] Paul substitutes "all flesh" (*pasa sarx*) for

---

passage for the English reader. If we begin verse 20 with "therefore," then it is thought to be the grand conclusion to which Paul has been building since 1:18. In the thesis, he had stated that in the gospel was to be found a means whereby man could be declared just before God. Then several chapters were spent demonstrating that such "declared justification" was needed by all – the Gentile needed it, and so did the Jew (though he often fancied within himself that he really did not) because all had sinned. Verse 20 was then interpreted as though it were the conclusion to this whole first argument. (The outline of the first three chapters of Romans presented in these notes in fact tends to follow the lead of the KJV; however, the "summary statement" for verses 19,20 is based on the paragraphing of the NASB.)

[51] The expression "anarthrous *nomos*" has been explained at Romans 2:12.

[52] The NIV, which reads "by observing the Law," a dynamic equivalent rendering of "works of the Law," has erred at this place, as well as at Romans 3:28 and Galatians 3:2,10. The NIV translation thus makes Romans 3:20 contradict Romans 2:13. This is unacceptable.

[53] Abegg, M., "Paul, 'Works of the Law' and 4QMMT." *Biblical Archaeology Review* 20:6 (Nov-Dec. 1994), p.52ff.

[54] Such appeals to Old Testament Scriptures have been made already at Romans 1:2, 1:17, 2:6, 2:24,

the Old Testament reading of "every man living" (*pas zōn*).   Whether Paul's use of "no flesh" means anything more than "no human being" (whether from among Gentiles or Jews) is debated.[55]   Some suppose he uses the word here to denote the idea of universal frailty and weakness in the creature.   "Justified" was explained in comments on Romans 2:13; it is a word from the law courts, a sentence of "not guilty" pronounced by a judge. "In His sight" pictures God as the Judge in this court, and even the Old Testament indicated that His verdict of "not guilty" was based on men's faithfulness to His revelation.

For through the Law *comes* **the knowledge of sin.**   "For" tells us we are being given a reason why "by works of the Law no flesh will be justified."   One effect of the Law God gave was to increase men's knowledge (*epignōsis*, 'full knowledge') of sin.   "Had God never given a law touching sin, or revealed to us what it is, the concept of sin would never have been in our minds."[56]   Paul will write in Romans 7:7, "I would not have come to know sin except through the Law."   The Pharisaic "works of the Law" did not help men to know what God calls sin.   Paul here introduces a topic he will explain in greater detail later.   (Paul's explanation of the real purpose of the Law is in Romans 5:20 and 7:7-12.)

II. THE UNIVERSALLY NEEDED SALVATION (OFFERED IN THE GOSPEL) HAS BEEN PROVIDED BY GOD FOR BELIEVERS THROUGH THE REDEMPTION THAT IS IN JESUS CHRIST.   3:21-4:25

A. God's Plan of Salvation (Justification, Righteousness) Explained. 3:21-31

1. Its Nature.   3:21-24

> *Summary*:   The way of salvation God has provided is apart from Law; it is for all who believe; it is a free justification; it is possible because of the "redemption" in Jesus.

3:21 – *But now apart from the Law* **the** *righteousness of God has been manifested, being witnessed by the Law and the Prophets,*

But now.   "But" suggests a contrast to what was just presented in previous verses.   Those verses presented a dismal picture of man's situation.   They are all sinners; they are all accountable to God.   With "but" there comes a ray of hope.   Perhaps some of those who were "doers of the Law" yet have reason for optimism that not all is lost.   "Now" may be either temporal (at this present time) or logical (as things stand).   If we take it as *temporal*,

---

3:4, and 3:10-18.

[55] See the comments about "flesh" (*sarx*) at Romans 1:3, especially footnote #12.

[56] Lard, *Romans*, p.112.

the idea is "in this Christian age, as distinct from the Patriarchal and Jewish dispensations," and we can appeal to verse 26 ("at the present time") for corroboration of this interpretation. It would be a reminder that God's way of saving man came at a very strategic moment in the world's history – in Galatians 4:4 it is called "the fullness of time." If we take it as *logical*, there is a reference to the word "justified" in verse 20. While no human being will ever be justified "by works of the Law" (3:20) there is a way to be justified – a way provided by God Himself, a way that has always been available to mankind, a way made plainer in the gospel than it ever was revealed before. It is in light of this last statement that it becomes plainer; it is evident that Romans 3:21-28 is one of the most important passages in the whole Roman letter. Here, as in few other passages, the mind of God concerning salvation is explained, and the man who would understand how God views this subject will need to pay careful attention to what is here set forth.

Apart from the Law. At this phrase, the commentaries take any one of several definite directions. As the margin indicates, it may be translated "Law" or "law." (1) Translating it as "Law," some think it means "apart from the Law of Moses," and this is a key verse in the debate about the relation of the Law and the gospel. Since Paul has stated in 1:16,17 that God's way of salvation is revealed in the gospel, and since this verse says it is "apart from the Law," that shows there is no relation or connection between the dispensations of the Law and the gospel, other than that the first pointed to the second. "The righteousness of God is imparted to the believer without the Law of Moses helping him thereto."[57] Scripture is clear elsewhere that the Law of Moses was temporary; it was nailed to the cross; it was abrogated.[58] Not only do "works of the Law" not justify, the very Law itself has been set aside and a new covenant has come in its place. Christians are under the law of Christ (1 Corinthians 9:21). This option is likely the meaning intended by Paul. However, we would call attention to two other options found in the commentaries. (2) Since "the Law" here follows closely upon "works of the Law" in the previous verse, not a few writers, having erroneously interpreted "works of the Law" to be obedience to the Law, go on to insist that what Paul means is that a man cannot earn his salvation by meritorious works.[59] (3) Before the Dead Sea Scrolls helped us to know what "works of the Law" meant in the 1st century, it was common to hear that "apart from the Law" means "without perfect obedience to any law."[60] While it is true that God never did require perfect obedi-

---

[57] Meyer, *Romans*, p.129 shows that Augustine so explained the passage and his interpretation has been followed by some others.

[58] Hebrews 7:12 (where the word translated "change" means "abrogated"), 8:6-13, 9:8,9, and 10:9.

[59] While it may be urged that "as a gift by His grace" (verse 24) teaches that justification cannot be earned or merited, it seems premature to read this idea back into verse 20's expression "works of the Law." Nothing in the verses before 20 prepares the reader for the comment about "meritorious works" here in verse 21. This explanation centered around 'meritorious works' is part of a larger system of doctrine that, in this commentator's opinion, makes the Bible contradict itself by suggesting that it is less than an *obedient* faith that God requires for salvation. (Perhaps if the idea of 'meritorious works' could be divorced from being part and parcel of the faith-only doctrine, it might be more acceptable.)

[60] Interpreters who suppose that "works of the Law" (3:20) means perfect obedience to the Law find support for this view in the fact that not even saved men have to be sinless perfect (faithful, yes; sinless perfect, no), and in the fact that such an explanation seemed to fit all the places the phrases "not by works"

ence, but rather looks at the tenor or direction of a man's life (Romans 2:6-10), that may not be the point here.

***The* righteousness of God has been manifested.** It has been observed at 1:17 that, in Romans, the word "righteousness" is not used always with the same sense. It is also evident that the meaning assigned to the word in the theme paragraph (1:16,17) is the one to be assigned here; what we are talking about is "God's way of saving men." "Of God" also has a meaning similar to what was found at 1:17; namely, provided by God, or bestowed by God, or worked out by God. "Manifested" (*phaneroō*) means to make visible or known what has been hidden or unknown, or to make something thoroughly understood.[61] The word is often used to express what happened at the Incarnation, when Jesus became visible to human eyes in a way He had not before been visible. The verb is perfect tense in the Greek, which signifies past completed action with present continuing results.[62] What God had in mind concerning His way of saving men was dimly previewed and foreshadowed in the Old Testament times, but it is made very clear when we come to the New Testament. "The initial moment of the manifestation was the appearance of Christ on earth."[63] Ever since Calvary, how God was going to save men is clearly understood.

Being witnessed by the Law and the Prophets. "The Law and the Prophets" was a Bible-times designation for what we call "the Old Testament Scriptures."[64] In this old designation, "Law" stood for the Pentateuch and "Prophets" covered not only the former and latter prophets, but the Psalms as well. Rather than being something brand new, the way of salvation that Paul was preaching had been predicted in the Old Testament. In Romans 4, Paul will give the example of Abraham from the Law, and of David from the Prophets, to show that "the righteousness of God by faith" was taught in the Old Testament.

> The law of Moses and the prophets of the Old Testament foretold the coming of Jesus Christ and the salvation that should be brought to light through Him ... In (Christ's) springing "out of Judah," in His being "made under the law," and that He "died for our sins according to the scriptures; and that He was buried; and that He hath been raised on the third day according to the scriptures" (1 Corinthians 15:3,4), they have become a powerful and ever-living witness to Him. How the ceremonies of the law pointed to Christ is

---

or "apart from law" are used elsewhere in the New Testament (Romans 3:28, 4:6-8; Galatians 2:16,21, 3:10,13; Ephesians 2:9; Philippians 3:9; 2 Timothy 1:9; Titus 3:5).

[61] Thayer, *Lexicon*, p.648.

[62] Dana and Mantey, *Grammar*, p.200.

[63] Sanday, *Romans*, p.49.

[64] In the absence of what we might call a universally accepted name (like "Old Testament" has become for us) a number of different expressions were used to designate the Old Covenant writings: The Law (Matthew 11:13; John 10:34); The Prophets (Acts 10:43, 13:27; Romans 16:26); Moses and the Prophets (Luke 16:29, 24:27); the Law and the Prophets (Matthew 5:17, 7:12); The Law, the Prophets, and the Psalms (Luke 24:44).

elaborately unfolded in the book of Hebrews.   The tabernacle, the priesthood, the lavings, and the sacrifices, all pointed to Christ.   The prophets bore direct testimony to the Messiah that He would come just as He did come.[65]

God's "righteousness through faith," a salvation that is conditioned on faithfulness to what God has revealed, was depicted in such passages as Habakkuk 2:4; Genesis 15:6; Psalm 32:1,2; and Isaiah 53.   The manifestation of this righteousness, though "apart from the Law," is not in any way opposed to the teaching of the Law and the Prophets, being, in fact, anticipated by them.

3:22 – *even* **the** *righteousness of God through faith in Jesus Christ for all those who believe; for there is no distinction;*

Even *the* **righteousness of God through faith in Jesus Christ.**   It can be observed that in verses 21 and 22, the theme proposition given in 1:17 is repeated, only with some elaborations.   "Even" tells us this is an explanation of the phrase "righteousness of God" mentioned in the previous verse.[66]   This explanation makes it plain that "righteousness of God" does not (in this context) refer to one of His attributes, but to His plan for reckoning men righteous (saving them).[67]   This explanation (verse 22) goes on to point out that the righteousness spoken about is a righteousness which is co-extensive with faith.   As our title for this section says, "Salvation has been provided *for believers* ...."   Again, it is stated that God had to provide this salvation.

> The Roman poet Horace, laying down some lines of guidance for writers of tragedies in his day, criticizes those who resort too readily to the device of a *deus ex machina* to solve the knotty problems which have developed in the course of the plot.   "Do not bring a god on to the stage," he says, "unless the problem is one that deserves a god to solve it."   (Horace, *Ars Poetica*, 191f).[68]

Indeed, how to forgive sins has been called "a problem fit for God."

> There is no problem in the world so difficult as that of forgiveness!   How to remit punishment without cheapening sin!   How to pardon a wrong and yet

---

[65] Lipscomb and Shepherd, *Romans*, p.74.

[66] The Greek particle is *de*, and could be translated "and, but, also, even."   Some have tried to use "but," making verse 22 adversative to something said in verse 21, but that creates all kinds of difficulties. "Even" is the word that makes the most sense here.

[67] Some object to thus reducing the phrase "righteousness of God" in this phrase to either God's attribute of justice or to His plan of saving men.   One writes, "Why may we not understand it of the righteousness which Jehovah devised, Jesus executed, and the Spirit applies, and which is therefore justly denominated the righteousness of God?" (Robert Frew, in an editor's note added to *Barnes' Notes on Romans*, p.91.) Another tells us that God's justice and God's plan of justifying men are so interwoven that it is not proper to separate them. (Barmby, *Romans*, p.xi.)   Such argument may be technically correct, but for the sake of clearer understanding of the subject at hand, we shall continue to point out which of the alternatives seems to be in the forefront in each of the individual passages.

[68] Bruce, *Romans*, p.101.

to vindicate the right!   How to restore the guilty and yet to teach the offender to hate his offense!   It has been called "a problem fit for God." (Chavassee)[69]

Though repeating the theme of the letter, Paul now adds the object of faith ("faith" being the condition on which righteousness is reckoned by God) – it is faith *in Jesus Christ!*[70]   It is a righteousness conditioned on faith, not faith in God merely, nor in the general truths of the Christian religion, but faith in Jesus Christ![71]   Neither is it a righteousness by *fiat* (God just declaring men redeemed).   Man must put himself in a place to receive God's forgiveness, by exercising his faith (by responding to the gospel and becoming a believer).

For all those who believe. That is, God's justification apart from Law is bestowed on all who are believers.   "Those who believe" is a present tense verb which pictures continuous action, but not sinless perfection.   God looks for the tenor of a man's life.   God's way of saving man has been manifested, and even before that it was witnessed to in the Law and the Prophets.   But not all will profit, because not all will accept it and become believers. It will profit only those who continually believe.[72]

For there is no distinction.   Our version has included this phrase as part of verse 22, but you cannot tell in the original if it goes with what precedes or with what follows.   If we read it with verse 22, then it tells us that there is no distinction among men as to the way they will be justified.   All men will be saved, if at all, upon the condition of faith, and that without any distinction between Jew and Gentile.   If we read it with verse 23, then it tells us that there is no distinction among men as to who needs this justification.   All men have sinned and come short of the glory of God.   Therefore, if any man is saved, he will have to

---

[69] Quoted by George Mark Elliott, *Biblical Theology Notes* (Cincinnati: The Cincinnati Bible Seminary, 1954), p.57.

[70] "Jesus Christ" is in the genitive case in the Greek, and a genitive case can have several possible interpretations.   (1) In verse 22 some have affirmed it is a genitive of *source*, meaning "the faith which Jesus Christ has enjoined."   (2) Most writers opt either for the *subjective* genitive ("the faith *of* Jesus Christ," as the KJV did it), or the *objective* genitive ("faith *in* Jesus Christ," as the ASV and NASB did it). A defense for the subjective genitive might take this form: "Dr. Hausleiter contends that the genitive is subjective not objective, that like the 'faith of Abraham' in ch.iv.16, it denotes the faith (in God) which Christ Himself maintained even through the ordeal of the Crucifixion [and Hebrews 12:2 does hold out the example of Jesus as a pattern for faith], that this faith is here put forward as the central feature of the Atonement, and that it is to be grasped or appropriated by the Christian in a similar manner ... [as the next phrase says, "unto all them that believe"].   If this view held good, a number of other passages (notably 1:17) would be affected by it."   After summarizing this defense of the subjective genitive, Sanday and Headlam, *Romans*, p.84, then reject it because an attempt to apply it to all those other passages results in what they call a forced interpretation for many of them.

[71] "He mentions 'Jesus Christ' five times in the opening verses of Romans (1:1-8) but has only made one other reference to Him up to the present passage (2:16).   Now his attention focuses on the place of Jesus Christ in God's saving action.   'God was in Christ reconciling the world to himself, not counting their trespasses against them, and entrusting to us the message of reconciliation' (2 Corinthians 5:19).   The offense of the gospel for many people lies in its affirmation that in one historical person God has acted decisively to save all mankind."   Batey, *Romans*, p.50.

[72] See notes at Romans 1:16 on the phrase "every one who believes" to find an explanation of the similar expression here in verse 22.   Murray, *Romans*, p.110, suggests that "through faith in Jesus unto all who believe" is similar to "from faith to faith" in 1:17.

be "justified" on the condition of faith. Both the conditionality and universality of the righteousness of God may be expressed. There is no distinction as to how (conditionality) this righteousness is received; there is no distinction as to who (universality) needs it.

3:23 – *for all have sinned and fall short of the glory of God,*

For all have sinned. Since it begins with "for," this verse either gives a reason for something just said, or a further explanation. From 1:18 to 3:20, Paul has demonstrated no one is sinless perfect. All (at least all above the age of accountability) have missed the mark[73] that God's laws have prescribed. Therefore, there was a need for God's way of saving man, a justification conditioned on faithfulness to His revelation.

And fall short of the glory of God. "Fall short" (*hustereō*) is a present tense, middle (or passive) voice verb. The present tense indicates present continuous action; since they have sinned in the past, as a consequence they continue to fall short of the glory of God. The middle voice[74] would imply subjective reflection; the sinners themselves are aware something is wrong.[75] Numerous attempts have been made to explain just what "the glory of God" is.[76] Some of the more notable ideas are: (1) Man was created in the *image* (glory) of God, and when he sins he falls short of that image.[77] (2) Man falls short of the *praise* he might offer to God if he had not sinned (compare Isaiah 43:7 KJV, "I have created him for my glory"). (3) Man does not live up to the *moral standards* inherent in God's personal character. (4) Man has forfeited *future glory* (heaven).[78] (5) The one that appears to come closest to meeting what this context has been discussing is "Man falls short of the *approval of God* he would have had if he hadn't sinned."[79] A similar meaning

---

[73] In comments on 2:12, where an aorist tense was used in the original, yet translated "have sinned" in the English, it was noted that at times the aorist tense sometimes is constative (see footnote #43 on chapter 2). Some similar explanation likely is in order for the aorist tense that lies behind the translation here at 3:23. On the word "sin," here meaning "miss the mark," see notes at Romans 3:7.

[74] See footnote #23 above, for an explanation of the different voices a Greek verb may have. In the present tense, there is no difference in spelling between a middle and a passive form. Context will often help the reader decide which voice the verb form is.

[75] Two other verses where the middle voice may imply a subjective reflection are 1 Corinthians 5:7 ("unleavened") and Luke 15:14 ("he began to be in need").

[76] The reader is reminded that a discussion of "glory" was included at Romans 1:23, and that a discussion of the "image of God" was included in Special Study #1 on "Call" and "Grace."

[77] Murray, *Romans*, p.113, opts for this explanation, suggesting that when man sins, he fails to reflect the glory of God as he should. It would thus involve an idea similar to what was taught in 2:24, how men's sins cause others to blaspheme rather than praise Him.

[78] The present tense verb "fall short" seems to speak of a "glory" here and now that the sinner misses, rather than some future glory.

[79] Such, essentially, is the explanation of "glory" favored by Meyer, Alford, Barnes, and others. A slight variation of this same idea is found in E.F. Harrison, "Romans" in *The Expositor's Bible Commentary*, edited by F.E. Gaebelein (Grand Rapids: Zondervan Publishing House, 1976), Vol.10, p.41, where he speaks of how man lost the privilege of enjoying direct communion with God as he had originally in Paradise.

for "glory" (i.e., praise or approval from someone) is likely the idea at John 5:41,44; 7:18, 8:50,54; and 12:43.

3:24 – *being justified as a gift by His grace through the redemption which is in Christ Jesus;*

Being justified as a gift by His grace. The subject of the participle "justified" (i.e., the ones to whom this "justification" is granted) is found in the word "all" in verse 23.[80] There is no proof of universalism here (as though it says like "all have sinned … all are justified [saved]"), because 1:16,17 and 3:22 have already insisted on the condition of *faith* before a man is counted as "just" by God. The tense of the participle (present) indicates continuous action. It seems that "justification" is not a one-time thing, but something that God does for a man over and over again.[81] It is well to remember, too, that the words "righteousness" and "justified" come from the same root – though one is a noun and the other is a verb. "Justified" therefore is continuing the same idea found in "righteousness of God" – namely, God's way of saving men!

"As a gift" means that justification cannot be earned, purchased, or merited by man.[82] Justification is a gift given by God. It is gratis. It is free. But it is not cheap! It cost God plenty! Man does not earn it, but it is conditional. Since it is a gift and cannot be purchased by man, no man is so rich that he can buy salvation; and no man is so poor that he cannot obtain it. Whether rich or poor, slave or free, male or female, Jew or Greek, any who hear the gospel can meet the condition of belief in Jesus.

"By His grace" tells why God provided the needed justification to men who had become sinners.[83] Back in eternity, God looked with favor on the man He was about to create (Ephesians 1:4-14), and out of that favor comes whatever is necessary to efface the effects of sin.[84] Let it be said again, in this context, "grace" is the reason why salvation is provided; it does not say that man's response was caused by a first work of grace.

---

[80] "Justified" is a nominative plural participle, and the only thing nominative plural in the context with which it can agree is "all" in "all have sinned."

[81] While it is possible the present tense pictures a continuing stream of individuals, one at a time, being justified as the ages pass, it is also true that Romans 4 seems to suggest that justification was something that happened in Abraham's life on several different occasions. What was true of Abraham, the father of the faithful, is also true of the Christian. The statement found in many commentaries that "justification is an *act*, not a process," reflects denominational dogma, rather than the present tense verb form found here.

[82] The use of the same word "freely" (*dōrean*) elsewhere helps us to understand its meaning. For example, in 2 Thessalonians 3:8, this word is translated "without paying for it." In John 15:25, this same word is translated "without a cause." So men who are justified "freely" are justified "without paying for it," without doing anything to deserve it.

[83] Calvinistic theologians spend time here discussing whether God's grace, which is the thing that prompted God to provide the atonement (the propitiation in Christ's blood), preceded His decision to let man sin (supralapsarianism), or followed His decision to let man sin (infralapsarianism). We see little to be gained by entering into this abstruse theological question.

[84] See Special Study #1 on "Grace" at the close of chapter 1, where it was demonstrated that "grace" involves both an attitude and an action on God's part.

Through the redemption which is in Christ Jesus. "Through" represents *dia*, which means "on account of, because of." Now we know how God can justify us freely. Now we know how much it cost God to provide the possibility of justification for sinners. It is because of the atoning death of Christ that God is able to redeem lost man. There are two words translated "redeem" in the New Testament: *agorazō*, meaning "to purchase, to acquire at the market place;" and *lutroō*, meaning "to deliver, to ransom, to set free, to rescue."[85] It is a form of the latter word which Paul uses here to explain how it is possible for God to justify sinners. "Redemption" is a word taken from the world of slavery.[86] It usually implies the triple idea of bondage, a payment of a ransom, and deliverance from the bondage. Theologians have no difficulty with the idea of bondage to sin being broken by what Jesus did at Calvary, but they have real difficulty trying to explain to whom the ransom price was paid.[87] Perhaps the simplest solution to this difficult problem is to say

---

[85] See Arndt-Gingrich, *Lexicon*, pages 12 and 484. There are strengthened forms of these words, made by adding a preposition to the verb stem – thus we have *exagorazō* and *apolutrosis*. Vine, *Romans*, p.55, distinguishes between the two words in this manner: "*Exagorazō*, to redeem, lays stress upon the price paid. *Apolutrosis* lays stress upon the actual deliverance."

[86] In the ancient world, a slave's freedom from bondage could be purchased. The sum of money that represented the slave's worth was deposited in a certain temple, under the pretense that it really was the god worshiped in that temple who was purchasing the slave from his human owner. The priests in the temple then gave the sum of money to the human owner, and the slave was transferred into the ownership of the god. Once this transaction was done, the slave was a *freedman*, though formally he remained the property of the god. Once this ancient custom is known, it can be seen how *apolutrosis* came to have the connotation 'deliverance from slavery.'

[87] Commentators have argued at length whether or not the word *lutroō* (and its cognate *apolutrosis*) always implies or includes the idea of the price paid to ransom or to redeem. The correct answer to this problem seems to be – there are times when it does, and times when it does not. In the Old Testament, there are times when "redeem" is used that the idea of price seems to be included. In ancient Israel, both property and life could be redeemed by making the appropriate payment (Leviticus 25:25-27; Ruth 4:1-12). Since the first-born was spared in the last plague which God visited on Egypt, He had a special claim on these, so that the first-born thereafter had to be redeemed by a money payment (Exodus 13:13-15). The probable meaning of Isaiah 43:3 is that Cyrus was promised a domain in Africa as a compensation for giving up captive Judah – and the lands in Africa are therefore called a "ransom" for Judah. On the other hand, there are times when the word "redeem" is used in the Old Testament that there seems to be no idea of the "price" included. God's deliverance of His people from Egypt is spoken of as a redemption (Exodus 6:6, 15:13), and He is Israel's redeemer (Psalm 78:35); yet it seems evident that no price was paid to Egypt for Israel's redemption from captivity. Once again, God's people are found in captivity (Babylon), and again the language of redemption is used in connection with their release (Jeremiah 31:11, 50:33,34). In the New Testament, there are times that "price" is included in the idea of ransom (redemption). See 1 Peter 1:18,19, where we are told that the ransom price is the shed blood of Christ. See also Titus 2:14; Ephesians 1:7; 1 Corinthians 6:20; and Revelation 5:9.

The fact that in many of these passages a "price" is involved has led theologians to tackle another problem. The chief difficulty that arises when we think of the word "redeem" as including the "price" of the redemption is the question, 'Who receives the ransom payment?' The question is not directly answered in Scripture, but theologians have been wont to make suggestions anyway. (1) Some argue that the ransom was paid to the devil. Irenaeus and Origen, for example, so taught, after suggesting that when a man sins, he becomes a slave of the devil. Following the example of the 1st century deliverance from slavery where the price was paid to the original owner, they reasoned the price must be paid to the devil. Most modern writers are not ready to affirm that God owes the devil anything in exchange for the men He delivers from the devil's bondage. (2) Others suggest that the ransom was paid to God to satisfy His holy justice. But who paid it? Did Jesus (as some understand Galatians 3:13 to say)? Did God pay it to Himself? Since none of the answers proposed to the question appears to be satisfactory, perhaps it is a topic

that "redeem" does not always include compensation; so that all speculations as to the person to whom the ransom was paid, and the reason why it was indispensable, have led only to centuries of useless guessing.

But the meaning and nature of the act of redemption, *as regards man*, is our deliverance from the bondage of sin. In Ephesians 1:7 KJV, "redemption" is explained as being equal to "the forgiveness of sins."

> One prominent feature of Paul's usage of the word "redemption" is the double reference in the word: (a) with a present application to the forgiveness of sins based on the ransom price of the shed blood of Christ (Ephesians 1:7; 1 Peter 1:18,19); and (b) a future application to the deliverance of the body from its present debility and liability to corruption (Romans 8:23). This latter event is associated with the day of redemption (Ephesians 4:30), not in the sense that redemption will then be operative for the first time, but that the redemption secured by Christ and applied to the soul's forgiveness is then extended to the body as well, so that salvation is brought to its intended consummation.[88]

"In Christ Jesus" tells us that the redemption has been effected by Him. He is the author and perfecter of redemption.[89] The reading "Christ Jesus" (it is not "Jesus Christ") likely suggests that the glorified Christ (as contrasted to the human Jesus) is in view.[90] Hebrews 2:17,18; 4:14-16; and 7:25, tell of the ministry of the exalted Christ in heaven, how He offered His blood on the mercy seat in the antitypical Holy of Holies, how He now gives grace to those who need it, how He functions as high priest on behalf of believers, and how He has yet to come a second time for salvation to those who eagerly await Him. Likely all these ideas are implied in the expression "in Christ Jesus."

---

theologians ought not spend time speculating upon.

We may not be able to solve the problem about the "price" and to whom it may have been paid, but we can understand that Christ has been the cause of the believer's being freely justified. He has freed believers from the bondage of sin and delivered them from the penalty of sin, and done this through the shedding of His blood.

[88] E.F. Harrison, "Redemption," in *Baker's Dictionary of Theology* (Grand Rapids: Baker, 1960), p.439.

[89] Hendriksen, *Romans*, p.131, defends the translation "*in* Christ Jesus." "This redemption was accomplished *in*, probably meaning 'in connection with,' Christ Jesus, the Anointed Savior. Most translators have adopted this or a very similar translation, namely, '*in* Christ Jesus.' Some, however, prefer '*by* Christ Jesus.' The Greek allows either. In favor of 'in' or 'in connection with' is the fact that in v.23,24, 'God' is clearly mentioned as the Author of the believer's redemption. Not to Jesus alone, but to God Triune should be accorded the praise and glory for man's deliverance from sin and its consequences. It was accomplished or brought about in and through Christ Jesus; that is, by means of his voluntary suffering and death on the cross."

[90] Sanday and Headlam, *Romans*, p.87, have pointed out that the variant reading "Christ Jesus" uniformly has reference to the glorified Christ, as opposed to Jesus' earthly ministry.

2. Its Ground.   3:25

Summary: The underlying basis or foundation on which God's way of saving man rests is the atoning, propitiatory death of Christ.   Faith is again emphasized as the condition on which God reckons justification.

3:25 – *whom God displayed publicly as a propitiation in His blood through faith.*   **This was** *to demonstrate His righteousness, because in the forbearance of God He passed over the sins previously committed;*

Whom God displayed publicly. Christ Jesus is the One whom God displayed. "Displayed publicly" is an attempt to convey the meaning of *protithēmi*.   The lexicons give at least two possible meanings for the word.[91]   The verb sometimes has the meaning "to plan previously, or to purpose beforehand," and is so translated at Ephesians 1:9.   The Peshitto Syriac opts for this meaning in the present passage, and so does Hendriksen, who urges that Paul here intends "the divine eternal counsel ... that Jesus was to be the One through whom the plan of salvation would be realized."[92]   Some writers assert that "set forth" (KJV, ASV) is equal to "a substitute, given in our place."   Though it is true that Christ's death was substitutionary and vicarious, it is doubtful that *protithēmi* is one of the words or expressions used to teach this truth.   The other meaning offered in the lexicons is "to place in public view," or "to exhibit in a conspicuous place, as goods are exhibited or exposed for sale, or as premiums or rewards of victory were exhibited to public view in the games of the Greeks."[93]   The word is also used of the "showbread" that was *exhibited* on the table in the tabernacle.   So this phrase tells us that Jesus was placed out before the world as an object to be looked upon and taken notice of.   "The public exhibition was made by his being offered on the cross, in the face of men and angels.   His crucifixion was not concealed; it was done openly.   He was put to an open shame."[94]   The verb also is in the middle voice, indicating God's personal concern in the public display and propitiation provided thereby.

As a propitiation.   While the word "redemption" conveys the idea of release from bondage, "propitiation" conveys the idea of the removal of the liability to God's wrath.[95]

---

[91] Arndt-Gingrich, *Lexicon*, p.729.

[92] Hendriksen, *Romans*, p.131,132.   Paul has used *protithēmi* once before in Romans, at 1:13, where it spoke of his "purpose" to visit Rome.

[93] Barnes, *Romans*, p.93.

[94] *Ibid.*

[95] The word in the original is *hilastērion* (from *hilaskomai*), an important word that requires careful attention.   First, a look at the lexicons reveals that in classical Greek, the word meant to "placate" or "appease" an angry god.   (Certainly, this meaning does not fit Biblical usage.   Paul can hardly be thought of as saying that in Jesus' death man provided a sacrifice that placated an angry God.   The Bible nowhere presents the death of Christ as though it were a sort of rain dance that would please an angry god, who in turn would make it rain.   Nor is there anything of appeasing a god by human sacrifice, like throwing a babe

"The words of the *hilaskomai* group do not denote simple forgiveness or cancellation of sin, but that forgiveness or cancellation of sin which includes the turning away of God's

---

into the Ganges River, or into a sacred well pit as the Inca Indians did in Mexico. To arrive at such a conclusion, one would have to ignore the evidence in the Old and New Testaments, and accept only the scattered and infrequent use of the word in pagan and non-Biblical writings as normative for the meaning of the word.) Paul insists that God, not man, has provided the "propitiation;" this fact alone does not fit the idea of "appeasing an angry God." In the LXX, the translators used *hilastērion* for the Hebrew *kipper* ("make atonement") and cognate words, among which is *kapporeth*, ("mercy seat," or "place where sins are atoned for or wiped out"). Because of this usage by the LXX, the word took on a new meaning in addition to the one it had in classical Greek. Once we come to the New Testament, we find *hilastērion* used twice, at Romans 3:25 and Hebrews 9:5. New Testament scholars now have to discern what its meaning is, and then how to translate it into English so the modern reader will understand the concept being taught.

As to the meaning of the Greek word in the New Testament, scholars are divided between those who believe it is a noun and those who believe it is an adjective. Those who insist it is an adjective will supply the noun *thuma* ("sacrifice, victim") so that it now means "propitiatory sacrifice." According to this, the sense of the whole passage is, "God set forth Christ in the sight of the intelligent universe as the victim of propitiation for the sins of the world." (Lard, Meyer, Murray, Lightfoot, Hendriksen, Sanday, Cranfield, etc., opt for this meaning.) Objections given against it are: [a] the passages alleged to show *hilastērion* is an adjective do not show it – *hilastērion* is a noun – and [b] the words "in his blood" which soon follow in Romans 3:25 convey the idea of "sacrifice" or "victim," so it would be doubtful that *hilastērion* also meant victim. Thus, the most widely accepted interpretation of the meaning of the word in the New Testament is that it is a noun, and somehow has reference to the "mercy seat" and to all that was involved therewith, as is nicely explained in Hebrews 9:24-28. According to this explanation, the idea conveyed about Christ being a "propitiation" (the antitypical mercy seat) is as follows: The mercy seat was the lid or cover on the Ark of the Covenant. It was made of gold, and shadowing it with their outstretched wings were the Cherubim. In the chest, below this cover, were the tables of stone on which were written the Ten Commandments which Israel had violated, and for which violation they were liable to suffer the wrath of God. Before the Ark of the Covenant, once a year, on the Day of Atonement, stood the high priest representing the people. He had taken blood from the altar of burnt offering, and as he came into the Holy of Holies, he sprinkled the blood on the mercy seat, in order to cover the sins of the people (Leviticus 16:14,15). It was from this mercy seat that God pronounced pardon; it was by this means that the people were reconciled to God (Leviticus 16:2; Exodus 25:22). When the sacrificial blood was sprinkled on this cover, it ceased to be a place of judgment and wrath, and became instead a place of mercy. The blood came between the violated law and the violators, the people. In a similar fashion, the blood of Jesus turns away the wrath that God holds toward the man who had sinned. (Several arguments have been advanced against this conclusion that Christ is pictured as the antitypical mercy seat. [a] Lard rejects it because *hilastērion* is anarthrous, whereas in the Old Testament, the article is always there if it refers to the mercy seat. However, Gifford, *Romans*, p.97, and Lange, *Romans*, p.133, both show that the anarthrous construction is exactly proper if the reference is to the mercy seat. [b] This would be the only place in the Bible where Christ is called "the mercy seat." However, only once are we told that Christ is the antitype of the brazen serpent (John 3:14), and only once are we told He is the curse-offering (Galatians 3:13). If inspired writers say a thing once, that should be sufficient to establish it. [c] This interpretation makes Christ to be the victim whose blood is sprinkled and at the same time the place on which it is sprinkled. However, this is no more unsuitable or unusual than the double reference that occurs at Hebrews 9:11,12, where Christ is at one and the same time both the victim whose blood is shed and the high priest by whom it is offered.)

The final problem to be faced is finding an English word or phrase that satisfactorily conveys this idea to readers of the English Bible, because there is no English word that is completely suitable. In days gone by, the word "propitiation" meant no more than "placate" or "appease" (like the classical meaning of *hilastērion*), and because of this, the use of it in our English versions has been objectionable to some. Instead, many have urged the use of "expiation," and this might be a good word, were it not that it has been redefined and misused in the past half century. Originally, "expiation" meant the cancellation or removal of sins. The difference in meaning between "propitiation" and "expiation," in English, if we assign-

wrath. This is not a process of celestial bribery, for the removal of the wrath is in the last

---

ed to each word its actual significance, has been explained by Arthur Pink (*The Satisfaction of Christ* [Swengel, PA: Bible Truth Depot, 1955], p.105). "'Propitiation' defines the bearing which Christ's sacrifice had *Godwards*; it placated Him. 'Expiation' has reference to the bearing which Christ's sacrifice had *manwards*; it removed the sins of His people." Worded another way, propitiation speaks of appeasing the anger God feels, while expiation is the removal of the weight of guilt the man feels. There is no doubt that Christ's death removed men's sins and burden of guilt, but is that all that is involved in *hilastērion*?

As for the modern misuse of the English word "expiation," this needs to be said. As early as 1903, Adolf Deissmann urged it should be translated "expiation." C.H. Dodd, in 1935, in *The Bible and the Greeks* (Naperville, IL: Alec R. Allenson, 2nd edition, nd), p.82-95, urged it should be translated "expiation" or "remedy," and then assigned a special meaning to these words. According to the thinking of these men, there is nothing of the idea of turning away the wrath of God in the word *hilastērion*. There is said to be nothing more in the death of Christ than a persuasive inducement offered to man by God. Further, it is argued that the "wrath of God" means no more than a process of cause and effect whereby disaster (physical, natural, temporal) inevitably follows sin. Suffice it to say here that this view is considerably less than the Scriptures teach. (For a development of the criticisms and objections to Dodd's theory, see Roger Nicole, *Westminster Theological Journal*, 17:2, p.117-154; and Leon Morris, *The Apostolic Preaching of the Cross*, p.125-185.) Now the student should be aware that this less-than-Biblical view (i.e., that Christ's death was no more than an "expiation" or "remedy") is written into the Revised Standard Version ("expiation" is used to translate Romans 3:25; 1 John 2:2, 4:10; and Hebrews 2:17), and also into the New English Bible (remember that C.H. Dodd was the "moving spirit" behind that translation) where instead of "propitiation" we find "remedy" (1 John 2:22, 4:10) and "expiate" (Romans 3:25; Hebrews 2:17). Probably the average reader of these (and other) versions is unaware that this change in wording involves a basic divergence in the concept of God and the problem of sin and its forgiveness. (That the RSV translators followed this less-than-Biblical line of thought in their translation, see Joseph Bayly, *Sunday School Times*, June 4, 1946, p.194.) To translate *hilastērion* by "expiate" (and mean what the translators of the RSV and NEB meant) is to violate both the lexicography and the hermeneutics of the passage. (See the significance of nouns ending in *-tērion* in A.T. Robertson, *A Grammar of the Greek New Testament in the Light of Historical Research* [Nashville: Broadman Press, 1934], p.154-157.) Even without this misuse, the English word "expiation" has no connotation of wrath being removed, and therefore is not quite adequate to translate *hilastērion* as it was used in the Bible.

In all this debate about how to translate *hilastērion*, what does not appear on the surface is that behind the scenes is a debate about the wrath of God. Modern scholars have been wont to say that the Old Testament presents God as a God of wrath, whereas the New Testament presents Him as a God of universal love and mercy. If indeed there is no wrath to be averted, then to translate *hilastērion* with some English word that implies the removal of wrath is gratuitous. But then when some such word as "expiation" is chosen, there still is the question of what is involved. "If one reduces the language of Scripture from 'propitiation' to 'expiation' in all instances, he still must answer the question, 'Why should sins even be expiated?' What would happen if no expiation were provided? Can one deny that, according to the teaching of the Scripture, men will die in their sins? The logical implication of the denial of propitiation as unworthy of God [leads to] the teaching that God will ultimately manifest His forgiving love to everyone, regardless of how one is related to Christ – a point of view that is increasingly the vogue, but one that is contrary to Scripture." (P.K. Jewett, "Propitiation," in *Zondervan Pictorial Encyclopedia of the Bible*, Vol.4, p.904-5.) "Though it is being consistently denied, there is indeed such a thing as the WRATH OF GOD that rests on the sinner, and must be removed if he is to be saved" (Hendriksen, *Romans*, p.132), and such removal of wrath is exactly what *hilastērion* implies, however (whether noun or adjective) we may choose to translate it. Perhaps we must do what the translators of the LXX did – take an existing word (in our case, "propitiation") and redefine it. No longer does it mean that a man brings a sacrifice to appease the wrath of his god, but it now means God Himself has provided the sacrifice that turns away His wrath from sinning men. As Paul penned it, "God publicly displayed Christ as this kind of *hilastērion*."

resort due to God Himself."[96]   God's wrath is not a figurative way of describing some impersonal law operative in the universe.   Rather it is God's personal, active, holy displeasure against sin, directed at the sinner (as we learned in Romans 1:18-31).   In the first part of Romans, Paul has shown that the wrath of God is directed against Gentiles as well as Jews.   Now, when he turns to the subject of salvation, he tells us that God deliberately and publicly has shown to the whole world how that wrath is to be removed. That is what Christ as the *hilastērion* (propitiation) means.

In His blood. The blood of Christ is the means of propitiation.   Jesus became the means of turning away God's wrath when He shed His blood.[97]

> The fundamental principle on which God deals with sinners is expressed in the words "apart from shedding of blood," i.e., unless a death takes place, "there is no remission" of sins (Hebrews 9:22).   But whereas the essential of the type lay in the fact that blood was shed, the essential of the antitype lies in this, that the blood shed was the blood of Christ.   Hence, in connection with the Jewish sacrifices, "the blood" is mentioned without reference to the victim from which it flowed, but in connection with the great antitypical sacrifice of the New Testament the words "the blood" never stand alone; the One who shed the blood is invariably specified, for it is the Person that gives value to the work; the saving efficacy of the Death depends entirely on the fact that He who dies was the Son of God.[98]

Through faith.   This expression limits the benefits of the propitiation to believers.   That a way of turning away God's wrath has been provided by God has been trumpeted to the

---

[96] Leon Morris, "Propitiation," *Baker's Dictionary of Theology*, p.425.

[97] "The Scriptures often speak of the blood of Christ in a way that ought not to be forgotten.   In instituting the Lord's supper our Savior says, 'This is My blood of the new testament;' or, 'This is the new testament in My blood,' Matthew 26:28; Mark 14:24; Luke 22:20 ... In Acts 20:28 we are informed that the flock of God was purchased with His own blood.   In Romans 5:9 saints are said to be justified by His blood.   In 1 Corinthians 10:16 the Lord's supper is called the communion of the blood of Christ.   In Ephesians 1:7 we are said to have redemption through His blood.   In Ephesians 2:13 it is said we are made nigh by the blood of Christ.   In Colossians 1:14 we are said to have redemption through His blood.   In Colossians 1:20 we are said to have peace through His blood.   In Hebrews 9:14 the blood of Christ is said to purge the conscience from dead works to serve the living God, and it is said to do this *much more* than the blood of bulls and goats fitted men of old to be public worshipers.   In Hebrews 10:14 saints are said to enter the holiest by the blood of Jesus.   In Hebrews 10:29 Christ's blood is called the blood of the covenant.   In Hebrews 12:24 it is called the blood of sprinkling.   In Hebrews 13:12 Christ is said to sanctify the people with His own blood.   In Hebrews 13:20 His blood is called the blood of the everlasting covenant.   In 1 John 1:7 it is said the blood of Jesus Christ God's Son cleanses us from all sin.   In Revelation 1:5 it is said He hath washed us from our sins by His own blood.   In Revelation 5:9 the saints in glory say to Him, 'Thou hast redeemed us unto God by Thy blood.'   In Revelation 7:14 the saved are said to have washed their robes and made them white in the blood of the Lamb.   In Revelation 12:11 it is said the conquerors overcame by the blood of the Lamb."   Plumer, *Romans*, p.134.

[98] Vine, *Romans*, p.56.   It is a quotation from Hogg and Vine, *Notes on Thessalonians*, p.168.

whole world ("publicly displayed"), but only where there is faith will it be applied.[99]   The "faith" here is likely the same as verse 22 where the expression "through faith in Jesus Christ" was used.

***This was* to demonstrate His righteousness.**   Now we are given two purposes (one here in verse 25, and the other in verse 26) why God set forth Jesus as a propitiation. *Endeiknumi,* translated "demonstrate" here, was translated "show" in 2:15.   It implies giving proof (of something) to someone.   What God did at Calvary is evidence, proof, of His "righteousness."   The majority of commentators have explained "righteousness" in this instance as being an attribute of God.[100]   The same word appears again in verse 26, along with the qualifying statement, "that *He may be just,* while justifying the one who believes in Jesus."   Thus, the word "righteousness" suggests that God did not do something wrong or inconsistent with Himself when He treated sinners as He did in the ages before the cross.   God must be perfectly consistent with Himself.   He cannot break His own law or violate His own nature and still be righteous.   God is love – and a God of love wants to forgive sinners.   But God is a God of wrath; a consuming fire.   Sin must be punished. God is holy – and holiness must uphold His righteous requirements.   How can God be consistent and not punish sinners at the same time?   The answer is Calvary.

Because in the forbearance of God.   It was observed in notes at Romans 2:4 that "forbearance" means a temporary delay of deserved punishment.   God deliberately held back; He temporarily suspended the execution of His vengeance, even though the sinners deserved punishment.

He passed over the sins previously committed.   'Committed previous to the time when God set forth Christ as the propitiation,' is the idea.   "The pre-Christian sins are not those of individuals prior to their conversion, but the sum of the sins of the world before Christ."[101]   The word *paresis* ("passed over") is translated "remission"[102] in the KJV; but it is not the usual word for "forgiveness" which is *aphesis.*   It is hard to find a good word

---

[99] Actually, because of the Greek word order (*hilastērion dia pisteōs en tō auto haimati*) two different explanations have been offered.   Some read "by faith in His blood" while some read "by faith, in His blood" (or as the NASB has it, "in His blood through faith").   The first way says a man must have faith in Christ's blood if he would be saved (i.e., the phrase "in His blood" is connected to "faith").   The second way, as explained in the comments above, takes "in His blood" with "propitiation."   Perhaps the Greek construction is purposely ambiguous, just because Paul wished to emphasize both ideas.   On the other hand, those who reject the first option give the following apology for their choice: "Faith is never said [in the Bible] to be in the blood.   Faith is imposed in a living Person.   Faith is the means of making the pardon ours; the blood is the means of its effect [of making the pardon being available]."   Vine, *Romans*, p.55.

[100] Each time *dikaiosunē* appears, it must be decided whether it is something God is (one of His attributes) or something God does (His way of saving men).   This has already been pointed out in notes at 1:17.

[101] Meyer, *Romans*, p.139.

[102] The English word usually has the meaning "forgiveness, pardon, letting the punishment go."

to express the meaning of *paresis*, which denotes something about halfway between pardon and punishment.[103] The "passing over" of sins differs in two ways from forgiveness: (1) The passing over was but temporary – it was provisional. (2) The passing over was something done "in the forbearance of God." The people whose sins were thus "passed over" seem limited, by the context, to the faithful in the pre-Christian eras.[104] In all those ages since man first sinned, here was God 'saving'[105] sinners (who believed) without any atonement for their sins having yet been offered. His wrath against all ungodliness had been revealed from heaven, yet here was God bestowing mercy without any propitiation having yet been provided. The seeming lack of proper punishment might look, to the casual observer, as though God's "righteousness" (His attribute of "righteousness") were slumbering. Instead, God was looking forward to Calvary where redemption would be purchased and propitiation provided; then God's justice would be seen to be intact, and His moral government maintained.[106] There was a need to "demonstrate" (*endeixis*) His righteousness, and this He did at Calvary. No one can accuse God of evil for the way He handled the sin problem, either in Old Testament or in New Testament times!

3. Its Object. 3:26

> *Summary*: The object of God's plan of justification, His way of saving man, is a vindication of His justice.

3:26 – *for the demonstration,* **I say,** *of His righteousness at the present time, that He might be just and the justifier of the one who has faith in Jesus.*

For the demonstration, *I say.* In comments on the word "demonstrate" in verse 25, it was noted that there were *two* purposes God had in mind when He set forth Christ as "pro-

---

[103] This is the only place *paresis* occurs in the New Testament, but the idea seems to be alluded to in Acts 17:30, where Paul says God "looked beyond" or "overlooked" men's sins in the ages before the coming of Jesus.

[104] The preceding context has spoken of "through faith," and the following context about one who "has faith in Jesus."

[105] For a discussion of the controversy over whether or not Old Testament people's sins were "forgiven" or "passed over," see Trench, *Synonyms*, p.114, and Lightfoot, *Notes on the Epistles of Paul* (Grand Rapids: Zondervan Publishing House, 1967), p.273. See Hebrews 9:13-15 and 10:1-4 for another statement of what God "did" with people's sins in the ages before Calvary.

[106] The thoughtful reader often questions, at this point, what would have happened even to the faithful if Jesus had not gone to Calvary. The answer seems to be that they would have been lost in spite of their faithfulness. They had not been sinless perfect; their sins would need to be punished if God was to be true to Himself. One other thing might be considered in this matter. It appears from the New Testament that until Jesus died, even the faithful from the Old Testament times did not enter heaven, but were assigned to "Paradise." Once Jesus, of His own free will, went to Calvary, then God could move the souls in Paradise to heaven because their sins had been atoned for. (See this possible explanation of "Where were the dead?" presented in some detail in a Special Study "Hades and the Intermediate State of the Dead," in the author's *New Testament History: Acts*, p.135ff.)

pitiation." We have now come to the second of these.[107]

Of His righteousness at the present time. "Righteousness" has the same meaning it has had for several phrases, namely, God's attribute of righteousness. "The present time" is the time since Calvary, the gospel dispensation.[108]

That He might be just and the justifier. Here Paul seems to define what he meant when he spoke about "God's righteousness" in the immediate context. "Just" expresses the character of God (His "righteousness"), while "justifier" expresses God's action as He imputes righteousness to faithful men (pronounces faithful men "not guilty"). His action is perfectly consistent with His character.

> God had retained the integrity of His character as a moral governor. He showed due regard to His law and to the penalty of the law, by His plan of salvation. Should He forgive sinners without an atonement, justice would be sacrificed and abandoned, and the law would cease to have any terrors for the guilty ... He showed that He had a great regard for [His law], that He would not pardon *one sinner* without an atonement ... no principle of justice has been abandoned; no threatening has been modified; no claim of His law has been let down; no disposition has been evinced to do injustice to the universe by suffering the guilty to escape. [God has shown that] He is, in all this great transaction, a just moral governor, as *just* to His law, to Himself, to His Son, to the universe, when He *pardons*, as He is when He sends the incorrigible sinner down to hell.[109]

Without the death of Jesus, God would be inconsistent with His own character were He to justify the guilty (even the "faithful" guilty).

Of the one who has faith in Jesus. Literally, "of the one who is of the faith of Jesus," as the NASB margin shows. This phrase is connected to the word "justifier" so that it says God is justifier of the one who believes in Jesus. "The redemption that was provided in Jesus was only for those who believe in Christ. No provision was made to justify any out

---

[107] In verse 25b, the Greek was *eis endeixin*, while here in verse 26, it is *pros tēn endeixin*. There is a change of preposition, and an added article in this second phrase. *Eis* indicated the immediate purpose of the propitiation (i.e., the vindication of God's righteousness with respect to His handling of sin in the past). *Pros* indicates a further purpose God had in mind for the propitiation (i.e., a way to justify believers in the Church Age without impinging on His righteousness). The article is likely an article of previous reference; it takes us back to the previous *endeixis*. Each of these technical features is already included in the comments made on the phrases.

[108] Before and after Calvary is the way "previously" (verse 25) and "at the present time" (verse 26) have been explained. Calvary is picked as the dividing point because there is where God publicly exhibited the propitiation.

[109] Barnes, *Romans*, p.97.

of Christ, or one who refuses to believe on him."[110] "In *Jesus* ... must mean the Jesus of history, the One who was born in Bethlehem, was crucified, rose again, and ascended to heaven. The claim that it is possible to believe in a Christ who is not the Jesus of history to which Scripture bears testimony, is false."[111]

We have now completed three parts of this long presentation of what is involved in God's way of saving men: its nature, its ground, and its purpose.[112]

4. Its Result. 3:27-31

> *Summary*: Three things result from God's method of justification. (1) It gives glory, not to man, but to God, verses 27,28. (2) It includes Jew and Gentile in one universal method of salvation, verses 29,30. (3) It establishes the Law on its true basis, verse 31.

3:27 – *Where then is boasting? It is excluded. By what kind of law? Of works? No, but by a law of faith.*

Where then is boasting? Boasting is the result of pride over something one has (or supposes he has) done. Salvation does not fall into this category, for it is not something man has done, but is something God has provided.[113] Boasting also has a connotation of an inordinate feeling of self-importance. The Greek word here is *kauchēsis*, so that it is the boasting itself (not the object of boasting, which would be *kauchēma*) which is excluded. The Greek also reads "*the* boasting," and there is a strong likelihood it is an article of previous reference – the same boasting earlier alluded to, namely, something the Jews especially were doing.[114]

---

[110] Lipscomb and Shepherd, *Romans*, p.77.

[111] Hendriksen, *Romans*, p.134.

[112] "In the explanation of the method of justification for all who have sinned, we find: (a) the gratuitous character of justification ("freely"); (b) the origin of it ("through his grace"); (c) the objective means ("through the redemption"); (d) the subjective means ("through faith"); (e) the relation to it of Christ's sacrifice ("God set Him forth as a propitiation in His blood"); (f) the reason for the sacrifice ("to show His righteousness because of the passing over of sins done aforetime"); (g) the final purpose ("to show His righteousness at this present time")." Meyer, *Romans*, p.149.

[113] The Greek particle *oun* with which this verse begins shows this verse is connected with the preceding presentation (verses 21-26). Thus we have spoken of how salvation is not something man can boast he has accomplished.

[114] The word "boast" was used twice before, at Romans 2:17 and 2:23. "It is true that all human glorying (boasting) is equally excluded, but the question has special reference (as the article shows) to the boasting before mentioned (2:17,23), namely that of the Jew, which [Paul] has been combating throughout the whole section (2:17 to 3:20). It is this sense of conflict brought to a victorious end, that gives so triumphant a tone to the Apostle's question, the tone of a conqueror looking round for an adversary who has already disappeared." Gifford, *Romans*, p.94.

It is excluded. The passive voice implies God as the agent – it is God who has excluded all boasting. The aorist tense points to an act in the past, and probably matches the aorist tense "displayed publicly" in verse 25. When God publicly exhibited Jesus on Calvary's tree, He decisively shut out all possibility of boasting by men, at least as far as how salvation is accomplished.

By what kind of law? Here we have come to a third use of the word "law" in Romans.[115] In this instance it means "a rule that governs actions, a norm, an arrangement, a system, a principle of procedure."[116] Some kind of arrangement excludes boasting. What is that arrangement, Paul asks.

Of works? The sense is, "Is the arrangement that gets rid of boasting one that calls for works?" Our explanation of "works" should be governed by what has been said in the preceding context about works (where it has been proposed that "works of the Law" means man-made rules like the traditions of the elders which purportedly were based on this or that verse in the Law of Moses). God's system for saving men is one that is conditioned on faithfulness to His laws, not on doing actions men have legislated. If men could make the rules on which salvation is conditioned, then they might be able to boast.

No, but by a law of faith. "No!" is Paul's response to the question about works. Well, then, what arrangement does get rid of boasting? One that calls for "faith" does.[117] "If a man is saved not as a righteous person, but as a pardoned criminal, where is there room for boastfulness? There is none at all; it is excluded."[118]

3:28 – *For we maintain that a man is justified by faith apart from works of the Law.*

For. Some older English versions read "therefore," and the difference in English readings reflects a difference in the Greek manuscripts. The best manuscripts are about equally divided between "for" (*gar*) and "therefore" (*oun*).[119] If we accept the reading "therefore,"

---

[115] In comments on Romans 2:12, we learned that *nomos* sometimes means "law" and sometimes "Law."

[116] *Nomos* with this same meaning is also found at Romans 7:21 and 8:2, and at James 1:25, 2:8,9,12.

[117] Some have supposed that "law of faith" is another name for the gospel (for example, such is the opinion expressed in both Thayer and Arndt-Gingrich as they give meanings for *nomos*). Instead of limiting the expression to the gospel, this commentator prefers to view the expression as referring to God's eternal arrangement whereby men have always been justified by faith, as Romans 4 indeed will demonstrate.

[118] J.W. McGarvey and Philip Y. Pendleton, *Thessalonians, Corinthians, Galatians and Romans* (Cincinnati: Standard Publishing Co., 1916), p.322.

[119] Codices Sinaiticus, Alexandrinus, and Beza, have "for"; while Vaticanus and Ephraemi have "therefore." Bengel suggested that *oun* was accidentally copied here by a scribe whose eyes inadvertently picked up the *oun* in the previous verse. *Romans*, p.52.

verse 28 is a summary of all that has been said since verse 21.[120]   If we adopt the reading "for," verse 28 gives a reason for the assertion in the close of verse 27.   Boasting is excluded by "a law of faith," *for* the "law of faith" is an arrangement whereby *sinners* are justified – not one where man-made religious practices are specially rewarded.   If we follow the NASB's "for," then this verse looks forward also to the presentation about to be made in chapters 4 and 5.

We maintain.   The English words "reckon" and "conclude," found in some translations, have too much of a connotation of an inference being drawn.   The word *logizomai* instead suggests "taking something into account, to think, to be of an opinion."[121]   Instead of this being an inference, Paul is making an assertion.   'We hold,' or 'We declare it to be true,' is the idea.

That a man is justified by faith.[122]   "A man" is any man, Jew or Gentile, male or female, bond or free.   The same way of salvation is applied by God to one and all, if they are men of faith.   All that was said about the noun "righteousness" in Romans 1:17 could be repeated here when we take up the verb "justify," since both come from the same root. "Justify" is a present tense, continuous action verb form, and likely suggests that rather than being a one-time thing, justification is something God accounts to a man over and over again during his life of faith.[123]   "Faithfulness"[124] is the thing God looks for as He,

---

[120] One point in favor of "therefore" being the original reading is the fact that the word translated "maintain" is the regular word for a "conclusion" to which one has arrived. See the KJV, "We conclude therefore."

[121] Arndt-Gingrich, *Lexicon,* p.476-77. The same Greek word was translated "suppose" in Romans 2:3.

[122] "It was over this passage that Luther made his famous translation, 'we are justified by faith *only*,' a daring act which gave rise to that [faith-only] doctrine." Lard, *Romans*, p.123. Lard's statement is true as far as modern Protestant Christianity is concerned, but Lenski, *Romans*, p.272,273, shows that others had added it before Luther's time.

So that Luther is not unjustly criticized, it should be pointed out that the cause for which Luther was contending was correct. He was denying the then-current Roman Catholic definition of faith, and its system of salvation by works ("satisfactions" which were a part of penance). In the Scriptures, "faith" includes knowledge, assent, confidence, and obedience. Rome had given her own definition to "faith," canceling out all the elements except "assent," and then teaching that it was not "assent to Christ" but "blanket assent to whatever Rome says." Further, mere assent was not enough. To the Roman Catholic, mere assent was just "unformed faith" (*fides informata*). Something else was needed to give this "faith" (assent) a "form." What was it that gave faith its form? Works of love, Rome taught, appealing to Galatians 5:6 (but, in this commentator's view, misinterpreting the passage). Thus, Rome taught, God justifies a man after the man does the good works (works of love) that Rome prescribed (that is, when the man demonstrated *fides forma*, a faith that has shape or form). When Luther insisted that "*only*" should be read at Romans 3:28, he was denying the idea that *Rome* could determine which works were required as a condition of salvation.   It is very doubtful that it can be shown (as some of Luther's theological children now teach) that Luther's definition of the faith that saves would rule out "works" (obedience) that *God* might require. Luther was right in denying the Roman doctrine, but he was wrong to add a word to the text to prove his point.

[123] Compare comments at Romans 3:24 where another present tense verb ("being justified") was used.

in love, counts men as "not guilty."[125]   Do not forget that both Jew and Gentile are justified by faith (verse 30 will say).   Faithfulness to what He had commanded was the thing God looked for in the Patriarchal and Mosaic Ages, and the thing He looks for in the New Testament Age.[126]

Apart from works of the Law.   Paul repeats what he said in verses 20 and 21, that this justification is "apart from works of Law."   All the different explanations suggested for those verses are also found in the commentaries at this place.[127]   "Without having to obey rules like the Pharisees and Essenes drew up" is still the idea.   That being true, it can readily be seen that Paul did not mean to teach that no works or actions are to be performed, or that no obedience is expected by God as a condition of justification.   There are certain things that men are required to do if they are to be men of faith (James 2:14-26, "faith without works is dead," because it is faith only).   Nor are acts of obedience to God's commands the grounds of men's justification.   Conditions on which God grants justifica-

---

[124] That *pistis* can be translated "faithfulness" has already been demonstrated at Romans 3:3. We will deal with what Paul means when he writes "justified by faith" in comments on chapter 4:3. Suffice it to say here, that this commentator objects to the doctrine which affirms that the "faith" that saves is a belief without any actions being included. It is here being affirmed that it is an erroneous interpretation of the last phrase in Romans 3:28 that has led to the modern faith-only explanation that the faith that saves excludes all "works" of any kind. Most of the religious teachers who are "faith-only" also teach that no one can be forgiven without repentance also being expected, too. If "faith" and "repentance" are not the same things, how can it consistently be taught that "justification is by faith *only*," when repentance is also expected?

[125] What all is involved in God's "justification" will be set forth at Romans 4:3.

[126] "Faithfulness to what?" has now been answered again. In Old Testament times, it was faithfulness to what God said. Abraham and David are examples, chapter 4 will show. Yes, they were sinners on occasion. But God saw they were habitually "faithful;" the direction of their lives was right. In New Testament times, faithfulness to what Jesus says (Romans 3:26 has spoken about Jesus as the object of our faith) is what God looks for. No matter which revelation from God a man has, faithfulness to it is what God expects before He justifies.

[127] As before, three different explanations are set forth. (1) The reference is to works which the Law of Moses required. A good case can be made for this interpretation. (a) Since 2:17, Paul has been driving the Jew from his boasting in the Law. 3:27 even repeated the idea that this boasting is excluded. (b) 3:29 asks if God is the "God of Jews only," from which it might be inferred that "law" just spoken of was the Jews' Law. In this light, consider McGarvey's comment: "If only those who kept the Law of Moses could be justified, then only could Jews be justified, for they alone possessed this law, and it was addressed only to them. But this state of affairs would belie the character of God [who is also interested in Gentiles]." McGarvey and Pendleton, *Romans*, p.323. (J.W. McGarvey, in "Justification by Faith," printed in the January 1866 issue of *Lard's Quarterly* affirmed that the explanation of "works of law" as meaning "works of Jewish Law" is only a couple of centuries old, going back to Bishop Bull of the Church of England, and first published in 1685.) (2) Those who used "meritorious works" to explain the earlier verses, use the same explanation here at 3:28. Its advocates appeal to 4:4 (works that demand a payment) to defend their interpretation that 3:28 speaks of meritorious works. (Perhaps as it became a popular proof text against the Roman Catholic emphasis on meritorious works, in the midst of the furious controversy against Rome, all other possible interpretations of the passage were relegated to the background.) (3) A third group of interpreters, who understand the expression to mean "without perfect obedience to any law," deliberately reject any specific reference to the Law of Moses, because in verse 21 "apart from law (anarthrous *nomos*)" was clearly distinguished from the Law of Moses ("being witnessed in the Law and the Prophets"). (4) With 4QMMT helping us understand what "works of the Law" actually were, none of the above explanations needs any longer to be defended.

tion or salvation, yes; but not the basis that makes it possible for Him to grant it – that basis is Calvary![128]

3:29 – *Or is God* the God *of Jews only?* *Is He not* the God *of Gentiles also?* *Yes, of Gentiles also,*

Or is God *the God* of Jews only? Now begins the second result of God's plan of salvation. Not only does it result in glory to God, but it includes Jew and Gentile in one universal method of salvation. Commentaries differ about how "or" relates to the previous verse. (1) Some have supposed it is related to the phrase "apart from works of the Law." This requires us to understand the previous phrase to refer to the Law of Moses, and then verses 29 and 30 are supposed to be further argument to prove Paul's point. Just in case the Jew, because of his belief in the permanently abiding validity of the Law, still doubted what Paul has affirmed about justification by faith, Paul shows that the Jew could be right only if God is interested in saving none but the Jews.[129] (2) Others have supposed that "or" is related to the expression "a man (any man, we have explained it) is justified" in the first part of verse 28. If the Jewish objector says that "man" in that phrase must be limited to Jews only, he must be asserting that God saves Jews only, because only Jews have "works of the Law." That God is interested in saving Jews only is a conclusion manifestly shown to be false by the Old Testament record itself. If faithfulness to what God has spoken is the condition of salvation, then surely there is an opportunity for the Gentiles, too, to be justified. The opportunity for Gentiles is as sure as it is that God is the God of all men, not just of the Jews. This second way of explaining this passage seems to be the

---

[128] "The meritorious cause of our justification is the *atoning blood of Christ*, and by faith, repentance, baptism, etc., we appropriate the blood of Christ. These acts, on our part, do not make us *worthy* of justification, but they are the *conditions* fixed by Christ, on compliance with which He invests us with the benefits of His blood; i.e., justifies us." McGarvey and Pendleton, *Romans*, p.323. James 2:14-26 connects good works with faith as its essential fruits, the evidence that faith is not dead. These works justify (James 2:24); justification is not "faith only" (i.e., devoid of these works). Paul says essentially the same thing in Galatians 5:6, when he writes about "faith working through love" (i.e., a faith which evidences its existence by love to God and benevolence to man). So, while men are justified by faith, apart from works of law, the faith is not alone; "faith" is not simply knowledge, assent, and confidence (trust). The faith God looks for as He would justify men is a faith that includes knowledge, assent, confidence, and obedience. Indeed, some of the "works" Paul expects of the Roman Christians will be set out in detail in chapters 11-15, but this belongs to a later stage of the argument. At present, the important thing to emphasize is that justification is by faith, and that does not require a man to observe the man-made "works of the Law."

[129] *Bible Commentary* is an example of such an interpretation. "Man must be justified by faith without works of law, or else the justification which God has provided depends on a condition, which none can fulfill but they which are under the Law. God would thus show that He cared for none but Jews, and belonged to them only." Gifford, *Romans*, p.95. This commentator has rejected the explanation that "or" is related back to the phrase "apart from works of the Law" (if, that is, "law" is understood to refer exclusively to the Law of Moses). The reason he has rejected this method of interpretation is that it does not seem to be possible to follow it all the way through the next phrases and chapters in Romans without getting into contradictions in our doctrinal system. Such an interpretation, applied to verse 30, would require us to teach that for the Jew, justification was possible without his having to be faithful to the revelation he had, a conclusion patently out of harmony with what was taught in chapter 2 ("according to truth" and "according to works," and "without partiality").

better way.[130]

Is He not *the God* of Gentiles also?   With a few brief, lively questions, Paul destroys the possibility of believing God's way of saving man was something good only for the Jews.

Yes, of Gentiles also - The updated NASB no longer has a dash here and another one following the first clause of verse 30.   The dashes were an attempt to help readers see that the flow of thought begun with "Yes, of the Gentiles also" continues on through verse 30. Verse 30 gives Paul's proof that God's care and provision of salvation is for all men, not just of the Jews.   He is the God of the Gentiles as truly as He is of the Jews.   His reckoning of men as saved or lost is the only reckoning that counts.   When it comes to justification, men are all justified by faith, or they are not justified at all.

3:30 – *since indeed God who will justify the circumcised by faith and the uncircumcised through faith is one.*

Since indeed God ... is one – To remind the Jew that he himself believed that God was God of the Gentiles, as well as of the Jews, Paul calls to the Jew's attention that familiar Old Testament passage that all Jews had memorized, "Hear, O Israel, the Lord our God, the Lord is one."[131]   There was not one god for the Gentiles and another for the Jews.   The Lord is the only Lord there is.

> The argument is strictly logical.   If there is to be any distinction between Jews and Gentiles as to how they will be saved, this can only be upon the assumption either that there are more gods than one by whom they will be justified, or that they will be justified ... in some different way.   That neither of these is the case Paul shows [as he continues his presentation].[132]

> No one will think of questioning the absolutely fundamental fact that God is one.   Who created the Gentiles?   The same God who created the Jews.   To whom do they belong?   To the same God to whom the Jews belong.   Here there is a use of Deuteronomy 6:4, "Hear, O Israel, the Lord our God is *one* Lord."   God's very oneness makes Gentiles His as much as Jews.[133]

Who will justify the circumcised by faith.   "The circumcised" are the Jews.   Paul is

---

[130] The careful reader will have noted that whichever way verse 29 is connected to verse 28, the interpreter must assume a suppressed thought which then must be supplied in order to make the sense clear.   It is much easier, in this commentator's opinion, to find the suppressed thought for the second option – in the emphasis that "works of the Law" are not what God looks for – rather than to find the suppressed thought in the Jews' belief in the idea of the abiding validity of the Law of Moses.

[131] In the Hebrew, "Hear, O Israel, Jehovah our Elohim is the only Jehovah."   While allowing for the pluralistic unity of the Godhead ("Elohim" is plural), it still affirms that outside the Godhead there is no other self-existent deity or deities.

[132] Sanday, *Romans*, p.54.

[133] Lenski, *Romans,* p.274.

showing that the one God does not have two ways of saving men, one for the Jews and another for the Gentiles.   The future tense, "will justify," likely does not look forward only to the final judgment.   It rather expresses the unalterable principle on which God always acts toward faithful men.[134]

And the uncircumcised through faith.   The "uncircumcised" are the Gentiles. Actually, there is no article in the Greek before either of the designations, and the omission of the article is vital.   If it read "*the* circumcision," or "*the* uncircumcision," it would imply that *all* of both groups would be justified.   That, of course, is not true, so the article is omitted.   Just *some* Jews and *some* Gentiles are justified; only those in either group who are "faithful" are reckoned as just by God.   On the other hand, there is an article before "faith" in this second phrase, likely the article of previous reference.   The "faith" that will save the Gentiles is the very same faith (so the force of the article) as that on which the Jew will be saved.   The other thing to observe is the change in prepositions: "*by* (*ek*) faith" and "*through* (*dia*) faith."   Just what Paul intended in the change of prepositions is not easy to discern.[135]   Perhaps it reflects the more difficult time the Gentile had in his attempt to be faithful, given the fewer privileges and blessings he had as compared to the Jew with his Law.   As we see it, Paul has said there is but one God, and but one way of justification, namely, God declares men (Jew or Gentile) righteous on the condition of faith.

3:31 – *Do we then nullify the Law through faith?   May it never be!   On the contrary, we establish the Law.*

Do we then nullify the Law through faith?   This brief statement gives the third of the results of God's way of saving man.[136]   As it has been through this whole context, "Law" here refers to the Law of Moses.[137]   Paul is anticipating another Jewish objection; there-

---

[134] Compare what was said at Romans 3:28, where we had a present tense verb.   God's reckoning of faithful men as "righteous" is not something limited only to the final judgment, but rather is something God does all the time as He looks over His world to see how they are living.

[135] The usual distinction between *ek* and *dia* is this: *ek* denotes the origin, source, or cause out of which something comes, or on which something depends; whereas *dia* suggests the means or instrument by which something is done.   Thus, it is sometimes said the Jew must keep on believing the revelations he had which pointed him to Christ, i.e., justification came "out of the faith" he already had; whereas the Gentile who did not have the revelation the Jew had, must come to faith in Jesus, i.e., justification will come "through the faith" in the gospel now being revealed to him.   While such an explanation may do justice to the literal meaning of the prepositions, it is doubtful that the conclusion matches what has already been clearly taught in Romans about judgment on the basis of available light.   (Would not the explanation about the Gentile needing to have faith in the gospel negate what was said earlier about men who never heard the gospel before they died?)

[136] In the commentaries, the reader will find discussed the question of the relation of verse 31 to the rest of the argument – is it the conclusion of the preceding train of thought, or the introduction to a new train of thought that continues through chapter 4?   Some even suggest that 3:31 should really be 4:1, thus showing its vital relation to what follows.   The notes in this commentary treat the whole of 3:27-31 as transitional.

[137] A few verses back, at verse 27, we had the third use of *nomos* ("arrangement").   Some have tried to explain verse 31 as if *nomos* here meant the same as it did in verse 27.   Paul is then understood here in verse 31 to be saying, "We establish this arrangement (law) which requires faith for salvation."   This

fore *nomos*, though anarthrous, is really a reference to the Law of Moses (see the word capitalized in the NASB). The Jewish objector is presented as thinking that Paul's doctrine of justification by faith actually relegates the Law to a place of relative unimportance. To the objector, Jews for centuries had fought and died to protect the Old Testament Scriptures; so no Christian teacher should ever leave an inference that he thinks the Law is unimportant! Thus, in this verse, Paul hastens to show he is not one to say the Law was unimportant; rather, he is simply demonstrating its real purpose. "Through faith" is shorthand for the affirmation made in verse 28, that justification is by faith apart from works of the Law. Paul's statement here is that he, unlike those who advocated those man-made works of the Law, is the one who is giving the Law its proper respect.

May it never be! As in verse 4, Paul uses this expression of horror lest a false inference be drawn from his presentation.

On the contrary, we establish the Law. "Establish" is not a translation of *didōmi* (to give) or of *tithēmi* (to set up), but of *histēmi* (to confirm or make valid). Just as Jesus accused the Pharisees of making the Law of Moses void by their traditions (Matthew 15:3,6), so behind Paul's words here is the same idea. Emphasis on works of the Law does not establish the Law of Moses; it does not give the Law its proper place. The Law was a codification of God's will to the children of Israel. When "works of the Law" led those very Israelites to ignore or set aside what God had said, then God's intentions for giving the Law were circumvented. There is no way a Jewish person could be faithful to God's revelation and at the same time set aside the very revelation God had given to them. There is no way that a man may ignore the revelation God has given him and at the same time still be found to have "faith" so as to be justified. What Paul here teaches helps give the Law its proper authority and respect.[138]

In this closing paragraph of chapter 3, Paul has given a threefold result that accrues from God's way of saving man. Each of the ideas here introduced are worked out in detail in the following chapter: (1) That justification is by faith and apart from works of Law will be explained in 4:1-8. Neither Abraham nor David had works of the Law, yet both were justified. (2) That this justification is available to any man, Jew or Gentile, is worked out in 4:9-12. Abraham was justified before he was circumcised, so it cannot be said that whether or not a man is circumcised has anything to do with his justification. (3) That this doctrine helps establish the Law in its proper place is worked out in 4:13-23.

---

commentator concludes it is better to think of Paul as answering another Jewish objection to his teaching.

[138] Paul's statement about "establishing law" is not contradictory to what he elsewhere says about the abrogation of the Law of Moses, which took place when Jesus died on Calvary (Romans 10:4; 2 Corinthians 3:7; Hebrews 8-10; cp. footnote #58 at Romans 3:21). Furthermore, the explanation offered for verse 31 is in harmony with the idea that the "faith" that saves is an obedient faith – an idea everywhere set forth in Holy Scripture. It is also in harmony with what has been said earlier about God's judgment being "according to truth" and "according to deeds." God looks for "deeds" that are in harmony with the "truth" He has vouchsafed to man. That truth, in the case of the children of Israel, was the Law of Moses.

Perhaps a word of encouragement is needed here to the honest mind that would like to ascertain the teaching of Scripture. Much of the preceding presentation has been very technical, and it is not at all easy to work one's way through what must seem at times a maze of possible interpretations.

- For example, why does "Law" or "law" or "arrangement" matter? Will not a pursuit of such technical matters discourage the average Bible reader? We pray not. Paul himself uses *nomos* in two different senses in Romans 3:21 and 27, and unless the reader is careful to "catch" the different connotations, he will completely miss the train of thought Paul is presenting.
- Or take a second example. Why does it matter whether justification is something God does once or several times during a man's life? Well, the underlying dispute is this – does the Bible teach once saved, always saved? That is, once a man is justified initially, is that justification thereafter irrevocable? Many commentators defend the doctrine of unconditional eternal security as they comment on the verses that speak about justification. Therefore, great care is needed to say just what Paul himself says here, no more and no less, and then let our beliefs about eternal security be influenced by the Scriptures themselves.
- Or take a third example. What does it matter how we understand "works of the Law," whether or not it is synonymous with "obedience to the Law"? After all, we in the 21st century do not have the same problems with "works of the Law" that readers of the 1st century did. This last statement betrays a fundamental lack of understanding of much of the contemporary soteriological debate. The denominational world, which teaches *sola fide* (i.e., that salvation is by faith only, without any works, yea, even without any works of faith), bases their approach to doctrine on Romans 3. They read "apart from works of the Law" to mean '*No Works*, no matter what commandment or law prescribed them.' As other passages are explained, those passages are made to be subservient to this "No Works!" dogma. And so we are told that "doers of the Law will be justified" (2:13) is merely hypothetical; James 2:14-26 speaks of final justification as being by works, whereas initial justification (as supposedly everyone knows from Paul!) is by faith only; and baptism is relegated to being merely an outward sign of an inward grace (for to make anything more of it would be to make it a "work" – something we cannot do in the light of Paul's teaching in Romans 3). It is precisely because of the popularity of *sola fide* that this commentator has taken such pains to be certain exactly what Paul is saying when he uses the expression "apart from works of the Law." Popular as 'faith alone' is, it is hard to harmonize that dogma with what Paul actually says here in Romans, or what the Bible says elsewhere about the faith that saves.

So let us not be discouraged by the necessity of doing some careful study and thinking on these matters, for if we would be heralds of Christ Jesus' blessings, we must first understand precisely the message we are to proclaim. And let us be aware that many "interpretations" of certain passages are the result of opposition to an error that was the subject of great debate at the time the interpreter lived, rather than an actual exposition of what the passage itself says. Often, while the original 'error' was indeed wrong, the verses used to prove it wrong were mishandled, too – and then these misinterpretations have come down to us as being "what the Bible says." All these misinterpretations have to be sorted through, and discarded, before we arrive at the thoughts the Scriptures themselves teach.

B. The Same Plan of Salvation (Justification by Faith) was Taught in the Old Testament. 4:1-22

1. Abraham was Justified by Faith. 4:1-5

Summary: Paul confirms what he maintained about justification by faith (3:28) by appealing to Abraham, an example from the Patriarchal Age of justification by faith.

4:1 – *What then shall we say that Abraham, our forefather according to the flesh, has found?*

What then shall we say. "Then" (*oun*, "accordingly") suggests a close connection between 4:1 and what was just said in chapter 3. Paul has maintained that men have always been justified by faith, never by "works of the Law." To this, someone replies by asking how Paul's doctrine matches what happened in the case of Abraham.[1] 'Paul, if your doctrine of how God saves men is right, it surely ought to be demonstrated in the case of Abraham, for if anyone ever was right before God, he was.'

That Abraham, our forefather according to the flesh, has found? The ASV has a different word order and punctuation: it reads, "that Abraham, our forefather, hath found according to the flesh." These two ways of translating quickly point up the problems one faces in this verse. Abraham is designated as *our* forefather. Who is included in "our"? Paul and his Roman readers?[2] The Jewish objector and all his Jewish brothers? The word translated "found" (*heuriskō*) is also translated "obtained" in Hebrews 9:12. In this context, it has to do with finding or obtaining justification before God. If "Abraham" is the object of the infinitive "found," the idea is "By what means do we find Abraham was justified?" If "Abraham" is the subject of the infinitive, the idea is, "By what means did Abraham obtain (find) justification?" The meaning assigned to "according to the flesh" depends on its position in the sentence.[3] If we follow the lead of the ASV, then "according to the flesh" would be the sphere where "works" are done. 'What salvation did Abraham ever accomplish for himself?' Paul's answer will be, 'None!' If we follow the lead of the NASB, then

---

[1] There are some technical difficulties in the opening verses of chapter 4. First, is "Abraham" the subject or the object of the infinitive "to find"? Second, who asks the question of verse 1? Is it Paul asking a rhetorical question, or is it a Jew raising an objection? If it is a rhetorical question, then likely "Abraham" is the object of the infinitive: "What do we find when we examine Abraham's case? How was he justified?" (Lenski is one who defends this way of translating the verse.) If it is a Jewish objector's question, then "Abraham" is likely the subject of the infinitive; "How does your doctrine of justification agree with how Abraham was justified? How did Abraham find (obtain) his justification?" (The ASV and NASB so understand verse 1, and this is the way we shall explain it in our notes.)

[2] This description of Abraham as "our forefather" has been used by those who would affirm that the majority of the Roman church were of Jewish background. But it is not necessarily proof of such nationality for the readers, since in the same chapter (4:11,12) Paul will speak of Abraham as being the forefather of all who are believers, whether of Jewish or Gentile backgrounds.

[3] This is another of the verses where the word "flesh" appears (see 1:3, 2:28, 3:20), a word that will be the subject of a detailed study later. Some commentators try to make "flesh" mean "our old sinful nature." Indeed, one of this commentator's objections to the original NIV is that it regularly translates "flesh" as "sinful nature" – for example, see Romans 7:5. At this place, the NIV leaves the word completely untrans-

physical descent from Abraham is the thing stressed.[4] 'How was our forefather saved?' It is partially because of this expression that it seems more than likely that it is a Jewish objector who is asking about Abraham's justification.

4:2 – *For if Abraham was justified by works, he has something to boast about; but not before God.*

For if Abraham was justified by works, he has something to boast about. It will be remembered that 3:27 said something about boasting, and how any boasting was excluded by the arrangement that made faith the condition of justification. Now the Jewish objector is saying, 'Abraham could boast about being justified by works. Paul, your doctrine is wrong!'[5] "Justified by works" in this context likely is synonymous with "justified by works of the Law." A reminder also seems to be in order. "Justify" is a word from the court room to signify the sentence passed by the judge. It means to declare just or righteous. On what condition was righteousness reckoned to Abraham? To be "justified by works" is the same thing as being declared just because of keeping man-made religious rules ("works of the Law"). Now that is the exact position Paul's opponents took when they insisted that "works of the Law" were necessary to be saved. Using their own Law to refute their position, Paul appeals to the example of Abraham. The condition on which God reckoned Abraham righteous[6] was not that of observing "works of the Law."[7] That being so, Abraham had no right to boast; he had no right to be proud.

---

lated, unless it is included in the words "in this matter." A textual commentary which explained why the NIV translators made the choices they did would likely be revealing.

[4] According to the better manuscripts, at least as far as word order is concerned, "according to the flesh" is joined to "our forefather," rather than to "has found."

[5] Actually, this first phrase in verse 2 may be thought of as either part of the question asked by the objector, or as the beginning of Paul's answer to the objection. It would be rather unusual for Paul's answer to begin with "for," but it would not be unusual for the objector to use "for" to give a reason for a statement he had just made.

[6] When Paul writes that "Abraham was justified," it is evidently in *God's* sight that Abraham was thought to be considered just. There is no valid reason to suppose that it is in *men's* sight that Abraham was justified (even though verse 2 may speak about boasting before men).

[7] Before the discovery of 4QMMT, the explanation that "justified by works" refers to perfect obedience, i.e., Abraham was sinless perfect, was the interpretation often read in the commentaries. It was alleged that Jews regularly insisted that Abraham was sinless perfect. In order to appreciate what was the Jewish attitude it is helpful to quote some of their own writings. "Therefore thou, O Lord, God of the righteous, has not appointed repentance for the righteous, for Abraham, Isaac, and Jacob, *who did not sin against thee*, but thou hast appointed repentance for me, who am a sinner" (*Prayer of Manasseh*, verse 8. Emphasis mine, GLR.) *The Book of Jubilees*, probably dating from the 2nd century BC, minimizes the weaknesses of the patriarchs, and contains this statement, "Abraham was perfect in all his deeds with the Lord, and well-pleasing in righteousness all the days of his life (23:10)" (quoted in Hendriksen, *Romans*, p.145). In addition, some have affirmed that the Jews even used Genesis 15:6 (a verse Paul is about to quote to the contrary) to prove it (see Sanday and Headlam, *Romans*, p.100,101). The Talmud, too, has passages (Kiddusch f.82.1; Joma f.28.2; Beresch. rabba f.57.4) where it is inferred from Genesis 26:5 that Abraham kept the whole Law of Moses. (This infers Abraham had a sort of intuitive knowledge of the Mosaic Law, long before the Law was actually given at Sinai.) In light of Romans 3:23, it is difficult to accept the idea that Abraham was sinless perfect.

But not before God. This is certainly to be understood as part of Paul's answer to the objector. Abraham did not go about making his own religious rules, and then boasting about observing them. Abraham's acceptance before God was not based on obedience to any man-made religious rules. God did declare him righteous, and the Genesis record of his life plainly shows that it was his "faith" (i.e., habitual obedience to what God commanded) that God took into account when He pardoned Abraham.

4:3 – For what does the Scripture say? "AND ABRAHAM BELIEVED GOD, AND IT WAS RECKONED TO HIM AS RIGHTEOUSNESS."

For what does the Scripture say? In all theological controversies, it is well to see what the Scriptures say. Paul turns to Genesis 15:6 to substantiate his claim about how Abraham was justified. When one reads the following quotation, the emphasis should be placed on the words "believed" and "reckoned." The Old Testament expressly states that Abraham was "reckoned as righteous" (which implies he really was not sinless perfect), and it was his "faith" (faithfulness, not sinless perfection) that was the condition upon which God declared him as righteous.

"AND ABRAHAM BELIEVED GOD. "Believed" is first in the Greek word order, showing there is emphasis on the word. *Belief* (faith, doing what God said), not "works of the Law," was counted to Abraham as righteousness. The nature of Abraham's belief is explained in verses 17-22, and note especially that it was not a one-time thing, not just a single act of faith.[8] Genesis 15:6 is not the first time in Abraham's life that he believed God. Hebrews 11:8 indicates Abraham was a man of faith even before he left Ur of Chaldees for the land God would lead him to, as recorded in Genesis 12; so Abraham has been a man of faith for a long time before his 86th year, events from which are recorded at Genesis 15:6. Verses 17-22 will go on to show Abraham continued to be a man of faith after the events of Genesis 15:6.

The historical background of Genesis 15:6 is important to understanding what Paul is here teaching. Called out of his tent at night, Abraham is invited by God to contemplate the heavens, and to count, if he can, the myriads of stars. Then God promises, "So numerous shall your descendants be."[9] The next verse in the Genesis record is verse 6, and it is a comment by Moses explaining what Abraham's response was and what God did in return. The reader of the Genesis account immediately is moved to ask, 'How could Moses detect that Abraham believed? And how did Moses know that God counted his belief as righteousness?' As far as the second question is concerned, what God was thinking can only be known if He reveals it to men. Moses would have known about the reckoning of

---

[8] The Hebrew word translated "believed" is *'aman*, which means "to be firm, to be constant, to be faithful, to be permanent, durable, to remain steadfast, to trust, to believe." Gesenius' *Hebrew-English Lexicon to the Old Testament*, translated by S.P. Tregelles (Grand Rapids: Wm. B. Eerdmans Publishing Co., 1952), p.58,59. While the Greek verb form is an aorist tense (often signifying one act in the past), the Hebrew form used in Genesis 15:6 is unusual, and indicates that Abraham proved constant in his faith. If we think of this as another example of the constative aorist (Dana and Mantey, *Grammar*, p.196), thus indicating a faith that covered a considerable period of time, then it does nicely represent the Hebrew verb tense.

[9] Galatians 3:29 tells us God had spiritual descendants in mind more than physical.

faith as righteousness only by the help of the Holy Spirit.   Concerning the first question, that too may have been a matter of revelation and inspiration, for Moses himself was not there to personally see Abraham's response to God's promise.   Such revelations are never made in the abstract; they grow out of situations that clearly demonstrate them.   Moses would have had the past record of Abraham's life before him.   In it he could have seen the tenor of Abraham's life; whenever God spoke, Abraham proved constant.[10]

AND IT WAS RECKONED TO HIM AS RIGHTEOUSNESS."   The expressions "reckoned as righteousness" and "justified" deal with the same topic.   The "it" refers to Abraham's steadfast faith, his obedient faith, his continuing faith.   God took that faith into account and declared Abraham "righteous."

"Reckoned" is an important word.   It occurs nine more times in this chapter of Romans,   so it is evident that if Paul's argument is to be understood,   this word's meaning

---

[10] In the comments on this passage, the words "faith" and "belief" have been used as if they were synonymous, though in English the two words have a slightly different connotation. Because of the fact that the English noun "faith" has no corresponding verb (like "belief" is the noun, while "believe" is the corresponding verb), translators have been forced to use both of the English words to translate one Greek root (*pist-*, found in *pistis*, the noun, and *pisteuō*, the verb). At Romans 3:3 it has already been shown that "faithfulness" is a possible and proper way to translate *pistis*. At Romans 3:28, much has already been set forth on the topic of "faith" – whether it is composed of three elements (knowledge, assent, and trust) and thus might be designated as "faith-only"; or whether it is composed of four elements (knowledge, assent, confidence, and obedience) and thus might be designated as an "obedient faith." Certainly, as previous comments have demonstrated, when the Bible says "apart from works," it does not exclude the works of faith. Paul opens and closes Romans with the expression, "obedience of faith" (1:5, 16:26). Again, it should be pointed out that James also quotes Genesis 15:6 (the same passage Paul alludes to here in Romans 4:3), and used it to show that "works of faith" are of necessity included in the "faith" that God reckons for righteousness – or it is a dead faith, because it is alone. (The reader needs to be careful here. James does *not* say the faith is dead because it failed to result in justification; he says it is dead when and if no "works" are involved.) In addition, let it be taken into account that Paul and James are not in contradiction to each other as they both quote Genesis 15:6. When Paul says "justified by faith, without works of the Law," the "works" he is talking about are man-made Jewish *halakah*. When James says, "justified by faith, not without works," the "works" he is talking about are "works of faith," i.e., the consistent obedience to the revelation a man has. Paul himself shows that, for him, the faith that saves is "faithfulness." In Romans 4:12, we will be told that Abraham was the father of them who "walk in the steps of the faith of Abraham" (ASV). That is not just one-time mental assent! In Romans 4:17-25, we are told of the quality of Abraham's faith, namely, that it was something that was steadfast over a period of years. In light of Galatians 5:6, written just a few weeks before Romans, "faith" to Paul is not just "faith-only" (knowledge, assent, and trust). He there shows that "faith" is something that demonstrates its presence through works of active benevolence. And in Galatians 3:26,27, Paul tells us that baptism is included in the "faith" that justifies. Just after he writes "sons of God by faith," he uses "for" and goes on to explain that baptism into Christ is part of the "faith" by which men become sons of God. Assuming, also, that Paul is the writer of Hebrews, chapter 11 shows over and over how faith is doing what God says, as he records how "because they were faithful" the heroes did great things for God and were enshrined forever on the pages of Holy Scripture. The faith that saves, in the Bible, is never contrasted to the "works of faith."

All of this is of vital importance, for Romans will go on to present the truth that men today are saved just as was Abraham. The reason God could declare Abraham just is because of the blood of Christ; the condition God looked for was obedient faith (faithfulness). The same is still true for us. The blood of Christ is the basis, or the ground, of our salvation; what God looks for is faithfulness. (Since many people deny, for example, the importance of baptism by using what Paul has written in Romans about "apart from works," it is of vital importance to have a clear concept of what the Bible says about "faith," both for our own response to God's revelation and for what we shall say as we would lead others to salvation.)

must be carefully studied.[11] "The word (*logizomai* in Greek; *hashab* in Hebrew) occurs frequently in the Scriptures, and is translated variously by, 'to think, to intend, to purpose, to imagine, invent, devise, to reckon, account, esteem, impute, etc."[12] For example, 1Samuel 1:13, "Eli *thought* she was drunk."[13] It is a word used in the world of record keeping. Like the Latin *imputare*, the Greek *logizomai* means "to put down (something) on an account (whether it is a debt or credit the context decides)."[14] God took Abraham's faith and put it on His record book, so that the record read that Abraham was "righteous." When God justifies a sinner, He *imputes* or reckons righteousness to the sinner.[15] "The righteousness attributed to Abraham is not an actual righteousness, but something else (faith) that is considered and treated as if it were equivalent to such righteousness. It is so treated by God acting as the judge of men."[16] So the Genesis record shows that Abraham was not himself "righteous" (sinless perfect); instead, his faith was counted as righteousness.[17]

---

[11] Verses 4,5,6,8,9,11,22,23,24. The KJV used three different words, "count, reckon, and impute" to translate the same Greek word, and thus obscures the clearness and force of Paul's argument for the English reader.

[12] Barnes, *Romans*, p.102.

[13] See also Genesis 38:15; Psalm 32:2; 2 Corinthians 5:19; 2 Timothy 4:16; Philemon 18,19; Galatians 3:6; and James 2:23.

[14] "The metaphor in the word 'imputed' is commercial, from the balancing of accounts. Strictly speaking, in order for a man's account to stand right before God, there ought to be placed to his credit 'righteousness,' or a complete fulfillment of the divine law. But, in the case of the believer, his faith is taken *in lieu of* righteousness. It is treated as an equivalent to it, and has the same effect of setting the account right before God." Sanday, *Romans*, p.183.

[15] Note, it is *imputed* righteousness, not *infused* righteousness. Roman Catholic theologians have regularly taught an *infused* righteousness. The KJV, which uses *imputed* to translate this word at 4:22, is a deliberately anti-Catholic translation, and rightly so, for the Catholic dogma is wrong. "It is not meant that the righteousness of Christ is *transferred* to them, so as to become personally theirs – for moral character cannot be transferred – nor that it is *infused* into them [implanted into their souls], making them personally meritorious – for then they could not be spoken of as ungodly [verse 5]; but that Christ died in their stead, to atone for their sins; and the results or benefits of His death are so reckoned or imputed [credited to their account] to believers as to make it proper for God to regard and treat them as if they had themselves obeyed the law; that is, as righteous in His sight." Barnes, *Romans*, p. 105. Barnes' note here is on the whole in the right direction, but it would be better to say (with Paul) that God credits faith to their account, and so treats them as though they had not sinned, and He can do this consistent with Himself because of Christ's death in their stead.

[16] Sanday, *Romans*, p.56. Because of its "forensic" connotation, some do not like to use "impute" as a translation of *logizomai* in Romans 4. But we see nothing out of place in this idea. After all, "justify" pictures a judge passing a sentence, and that is a forensic act. It is also true that "impute" used to be associated with a certain theory of justification, and this led the opponents of that theory to dispute its suitableness as a translation in Romans 4. In spite of this association, "impute" is still a good word.

[17] The reader here must keep his thinking sharp. Since James quotes Genesis 15:6 to prove that Abraham indeed did "works" (an active faith), it must be that James uses "works" in a different sense than Paul. For Paul, when he affirms Abraham did not have works, means (as the context in Romans shows) that Abraham did not have the kind of works (perfect obedience) that would permit him to boast. Abraham was faithful, but he was not sinless perfect. And, of course, no one would read James' statement to mean that he, like many of his Jewish contemporaries, thought Abraham was sinless perfect. Faithful, yes.

"Righteousness" here has the same meaning it did at 1:17 and 3:21 – it is God's way of saving man.   Abraham's faith was taken into account by God in order to reckon his justification (his being counted as "not guilty," or "righteous").[18]   The preposition *eis* (translated "*as* righteousness" in the NASB) should be taken in its usual signification, "toward" or "in order to."[19]   God took his faith into account *in order that* He might acquit him from guilt.   Worded another way, faith was the condition of his being pardoned by God.

Because of the need to pause and comment in detail on almost every word that Paul has quoted from Genesis 15:6, it is possible to forget the point he was making.   The whole phrase taken from Genesis, the apostle has affirmed, is proof that Abraham was not justified by "works of the Law."   Rather, his justification was something granted by the Judge on the condition of faithfulness.

4:4 – *Now to the one who works, his wage is not reckoned as a favor, but as what is due.*

Now to the one who works.   To reinforce what has been affirmed in the passage taken from Genesis, Paul takes an illustration from everyday life.[20]   The man who puts in a full day's work can claim his wages as a right.   And when the employer gives the workman his

---

Sinless perfect, hardly.

In the course of these comments, several times the harmony between Paul and James on the topic of justification has been introduced.   A summary may be in order at this place.   There are three key words that appear in both men's writings – justify, faith, and works.   If both men give the same definition to all three words, then there indeed is a contradiction between Paul and James.   But if one of the words has a different meaning as each man uses it, then there is no contradiction.   Is the ambiguity, then, to be found in faith?   It has been shown that for both, the faith that saves is an obedient faith.   Is the ambiguity, then, to be found in the word justify?   This question has not been specifically addressed, but the answer is "No!"   Some have tried to show that for Paul, justification is initial justification, something done for the sinner at the time of a man's conversion; whereas for James, justification is something done for the saint, long after conversion.   Now, in James, it might be argued that in the case of Abraham, it is justification of the saint (interpreted to mean something akin to "approval"), for the sacrifice of Isaac was long after Genesis 15:6 (if indeed that was Abraham's initial justification).   But it will hardly do to say that James' second illustration, of Rahab the harlot, is an example of justification of a saint.   No, both Paul and James are using "justify" in the same sense – of the act of the judge passing sentence, something he does over and over in a man's life.   So, we have determined that the ambiguity is to be located in the different meanings for the word "works," just as explained in the first paragraph of this footnote, and also in footnote #10.

[18] "Righteousness" speaks of how God *thinks* of Abraham, not of what Abraham was in his own person.   God's reckoning Abraham as righteous did not change Abraham (he still continued on in his faithfulness); but it did affect his status with God.   Abraham still sinned from time to time, but God counted him as "not guilty" nevertheless.   (What this note has done, in effect, is to deny the Roman Catholic doctrine of infused righteousness, the idea that God made a change in Abraham's person.)

[19] The preposition *eis* does not mean "instead of."   To so translate it would tend to make faith a meritorious thing, for if "faith" is substituted for "righteousness," then there would be no real difference between "justified by works (righteousness)" and "justified by faith."   Such a conclusion would be out of harmony with the verses immediately following where Paul shows that God's way of saving is not something a man earns.

[20] Paul has already emphatically denied that any man can boast of justification because of his works (3:27).   So it is clear that 4:4 is not to be interpreted to mean that there were some who had so worked (never sinned) as to be able to merit justification.

paycheck, it is not a gift; it is a debt, something the employer owes the workman.   Again, care must be taken in applying the illustration to the case at hand.   "Works" must be understood to be synonymous with "works of the Law," the kind of works (Jewish *halakah*) that would allow the performer of the works to boast.[21]

His wage is not reckoned as a favor but as what is due.   "Wage" is probably a better choice, in this context, to translate *misthos* than the KJV "reward."   A wage "that is due" is one that would be fair compensation for the work done.   Having done the work, the worker has a claim on the wage.   "Favor" translates the same word (*charis*) that was translated "grace" in 3:24.   In the next verse, when he makes application of the illustration, Paul will show that justification was not something earned, but something given as a favor. In the background, Paul has been assuming that the language of Genesis 15:6 implies that what was done in Abraham's case (and indeed in the case of all who are justified) was a matter of favor, a matter of grace.   Now he is about to emphasize openly what before had been only implied.

4:5 – *But to the one who does not work, but believes in Him who justifies the ungodly, his faith is reckoned as righteousness,*

But to the one who does not work.   Here begins Paul's application of the illustration from verse 4.   When God justifies, it is "ungodly" men who are justified.   These men have not "worked," have not done "works of the Law," have not merited their justification.[22]

But believes in Him who justifies the ungodly.   "Believes" is present tense, continuous action.   It is that obedient faith (or faithfulness) that God looks for as a condition on which He may justify.   Where such faithfulness is not present, the ungodly man remains unjustified, and still liable to the wrath of God.   "Him who justifies" is evidently a reference to God, who in the context has been spoken of as the One who justified Abraham (Genesis 15:6).   The strong word "ungodly" (*asebēs*) is likewise understood as applying to Abraham in particular (though what is said of him is true of all men who are justified). Abraham, Paul says, was a sinner; he was "ungodly."[23]   In fact, if God is going to justify

---

[21] To use this verse to prove that "faith" is opposed to all works, even the works of faith, is possible only if it is wrenched from its context.   Rather than simply giving his own definition to the words, the exegete must be careful to allow the original writer to explain with what meaning he is using words.

[22] Christianity is the only religion in the world based on "grace."   All the other major religions and systems in the world are based on merit.   In school, earn so many points and get a superior grade; that is merit.   At work, put in so many hours, and get your pay, and keep your job; that is merit.   In Scouts, earn so many merit badges, and be advanced to Life or Eagle Scout; that is merit.   Even the Jews, who argued that Abraham never sinned, and so earned his own salvation, were emphasizing merit.   But God's way of saving men has never been based on merit.

[23] The same word, in its noun form, was used at Romans 1:18.   Some have understood *asebēs* to mean that at one time in his life, Abraham was an idolater.   Though that is certainly a possibility, the word itself does not absolutely require such a meaning.   "The word *asebēs*, which does not occur in the Gospels or in Acts, is frequent in the LXX, and is not limited to its strict etymological sense, 'one who does not worship the true God,' but is also used in the general sense, 'irreligious, ungodly, wicked,' being quite as common as *adikos* or *anomos*, and far more common than *hamartolos*.   The word has been admirably

anybody, it will have to be ungodly people, for that is all there are (all have sinned).

> The description of God as one "that justifieth the ungodly" is so paradoxical as to be startling – not to say shocking. In the Old Testament, the acquittal of the guilty and the condemnation of the innocent are alike repeatedly denounced as the acts of unjust judges [e.g., Deuteronomy 25:1]. [When Solomon dedicated the temple, he asked God to condemn the wicked and justify the righteous, 1 Kings 8:31,32.] Indeed, for the better guidance of judges in the administration of justice, the God of Israel offers Himself as their example. "I will not justify the wicked," He says in Exodus 23:7; in the LXX version the same Greek words are used to convey what God forbids in the law as Paul here uses to declare what God in fact does in the Gospel. No wonder that he thought it necessary above to maintain that God, in justifying sinners, nevertheless preserves His own character untarnished. [Romans 3:26 has told us that God is *just* – not a crooked judge – when He justifies the ungodly.][24]

His faith is reckoned as righteousness. With this repetition of the language of Genesis 15:6 (see verse 3), Paul concludes his appeal to Abraham for proof that God has always justified men by faith. Abraham's justification was not one of "debt" for Abraham was one of those men who could be classified as "ungodly." His obedience had not been perfect. On the contrary, his justification was a matter of favor. Here again we see the nature of the faith that is reckoned as righteousness. It is a faithfulness that at the same time recognizes the presence of sin in the life. Faithfulness, yes; perfect obedience, no. So justification is not merited; it is a matter of grace.[25]

2. David Taught Justification by Faith.   4:6-8

Summary: By quoting David's own words, Paul further confirms his affirmation about justification by faith (3:28), this time drawing his example from the Mosaic Age.

4:6 – *just as David also speaks of the blessing upon the man to whom God reckons righteousness apart from works:*

Just as David also.   David is introduced as a witness whose testimony agrees with Paul's

---

explained ... as describing 'whatever is offensive to God's person, contrary to His nature, injurious to His name, or unbecoming of His honor and majesty in the world' ... The strong word is chosen, as in verse 6, to heighten the contrast between the unworthiness of man and the mercy of God in justifying man." Gifford, *Romans*, p.101.

[24] Bruce, *Romans,* p.115.

[25] In a nutshell, here is Paul's doctrine of justification by faith. God treats as "not guilty" the man who is persistent in his faith. Such persistence, such faithfulness, is the first and sole condition. To a Jew, such a doctrine was a scandal of no mean proportions. To them, it amounted to asserting that God was in

assertion that men have always been justified by faith.   Whether we think of verses 6-8 as being proof of Paul's interpretation of Genesis 15:6, or whether the verses give a second example from the Old Testament of God's way of justification, matters little.   Either way, it is affirmed that Abraham's justification by faith was not an isolated example, laboriously culled from the pages of the Old Testament.   What was true about God's way of saving men in the Patriarchal Age was true in the Mosaic Age, too, even after the Law of Moses had been ordained and in force for years.   David, almost as much as Abraham, was a hero to the Jewish mind.   What God did in his case was surely similar to what God would do in the case of any Jew (yea, any man, for that matter).

Speaks of the blessing upon the man to whom God reckons righteousness apart from works.   This introduction of the testimony from David, about how God reckons righteousness, serves to show that under the Law, too, faithfulness continued to be the way God saves men.   "Blessing" translates *makarismos*, a word that does not simply mean a feeling of being happy; instead, it signifies that a declaration of blessedness has been bestowed by God.   As explained earlier, "reckon righteousness" and "justify by faith" are interchangeable terms.   And as earlier, "apart from works" here means without "works of the Law" (*halakah*).   The man to whom God credits righteousness has been faithful to God's requirements for forgiveness.

4:7 – *"BLESSED ARE THOSE WHOSE LAWLESS DEEDS HAVE BEEN FORGIVEN, AND WHOSE SINS HAVE BEEN COVERED.*

"BLESSED ARE THOSE WHOSE LAWLESS DEEDS HAVE BEEN FORGIVEN. The passage quoted is Psalm 32:1,2.   David's sad fall into sin is commemorated in two penitential Psalms, 32 and 51.   As he speaks Psalm 32, David is aware he has been forgiven for his sin.   But such blessing is not limited to David.   See how he includes all "those" whose sins are forgiven.[26]   This Psalm, as explained by Paul, throws additional

---

the business of acquitting the guilty, godless man. But they were rejecting Jesus as the Messiah, and therefore they disregarded the redemptive transaction at Calvary. Without that, God could not be just as He justifies the ungodly. Include Calvary, and the scandal is gone! Furthermore, a man who is faithful to God is no longer in the category of the habitual sinner. He rather is a person who has committed himself to all that God is, to all that God has done, and to all that God will do. On this basis, God may think of him as not guilty, even though at times he does sin and is guilty. In this doctrine there is hope for us all. No man need worry that he has forfeited his salvation because he sinned once, or occasionally. He may rejoice in God his Savior, as he repents of his sin, and continues on in his faithfulness to God.

[26] Because modern critics have difficulty seeing the same doctrine in an Old Testament passage that Paul presents, it has become popular to excuse Paul's "clumsy handling" of the Old Testament passage by calling what Paul does an example of Rabbinic exegesis. All that was needed for the rabbis (and remember Paul had studied under Gamaliel) was to find one similar word in each of two separate passages, and they would build a theological house on that similar word. In this case, supposedly, the word is "reckoned," found in Genesis 15:6 and in Psalm 32:2. Instead of casting doubt on the accuracy of what Paul does with the passage from Psalms, how much better to suggest that this is another example of how the Holy Spirit helped men to understand the depth and meaning of the Old Testament passages. Compare Jesus opening the minds of the apostles so they might understand the Scriptures (Luke 24:45). Also compare what Peter did on Pentecost (Acts 2), as he explained the prophecy about the Holy One not undergoing decay. It has been the constant practice of the church to recognize that the apostles could

light on what justification involves.   The person to whom God counts righteousness is the person whose sins have been forgiven.   "Lawless deeds" is a better translation of *anomia* (a word for sin not used before in Romans) than the KJV's "iniquity," for the Greek word literally means "no law."   The deeds that were forgiven were those that were "not in conformity to law."[27]   "Forgiven" is a translation of *aphiēmi*, the same word that appears in the Model Prayer ("Forgive us our sins").   It means "to send away, to cancel, remit, pardon, forgive."[28]

AND WHOSE SINS HAVE BEEN COVERED.   The word for "sins" here is from the same root that was used in 2:12 and 3:7.[29]   It means to miss the mark.   "Covered" is the translation of *epikaluptō*, a strengthened form of *kaluptō*, "to hide."   In 3:25 we have learned that the blood of Christ is the "covering" (propitiation) that averts the wrath of God from the sinner.   The justified man (justified in God's sight) is the man "whose sins are not abolished, but forgiven; not annihilated, but covered up, removed from sight, propitiated."[30]   By appealing to these words, Paul has shown us that for him, justification is nothing else but the pardon of sin.

4:8 – *BLESSED IS THE MAN WHOSE SIN THE LORD WILL NOT TAKE INTO ACCOUNT."*

BLESSED IS THE MAN WHOSE SIN THE LORD WILL NOT TAKE INTO ACCOUNT."   This is from Psalm 32:2.   Not all of the verse is quoted, but as much of it as is pertinent to Paul's argument.   This is the negative way of expressing what God does when He reckons faith as righteousness.   Paul has used the same word for "sin" here that he used in the previous phrase, though the Hebrew has a third word here, *'avon*, which means "to turn aside" (a deliberate act).   The marginal note in the NASB reminds us that "take into account" is a translation of the same word earlier translated "reckoned" (verse 3).   Now it is evident how the quotation from David helps substantiate the case Paul is making for justification by faith, apart from works of law.   David lived while the Law of Moses (one example of "law" given by God to man) was in force, yet he did not believe or teach that a man was reckoned as righteous because of innocence from all sin.

---

give infallible explanations of Old Testament Scriptures.

[27] The Hebrew word behind "lawless deeds" (*phesha'* from the verb *phasha'*) occurs frequently in the Old Testament, and when applied to political affairs, signifies revolt or rebellion.

[28] Arndt-Gingrich, *Lexicon*, p.125.   The Hebrew word rendered "forgiven" in Psalm 32:1 means "lifted up," as when a cloud is raised, or "borne away," or as when the scape goat "bore away" the sins of the people into a land uninhabited.

[29] David used *chat'ah*, a Hebrew word that means "to miss the mark," just as the Greek word does.   It is not just an accidental missing the mark that one has tried to hit; it is a deliberate action where one aims for a mark different from the one God set up, one that pleases the sinner better.

[30] Sanday, *Romans*, p.57.

3. This Plan of Salvation (Justification by Faith) is Universal, not Being Limited by the Presence or Absence of Circumcision. 4:9-12

Summary: The assertion that God justified all men, Gentiles as well as Jews, by faith (3:29,30), is now demonstrated by an appeal to the Old Testament.

4:9 – Is this blessing then upon the circumcised, or upon the uncircumcised also? For we say, "FAITH WAS RECKONED TO ABRAHAM AS RIGHTEOUSNESS."

Is this blessing then upon the circumcised, or upon the uncircumcised also? "Then" shows this question is closely related to the point just made. It was all introduced by the words "Abraham *our forefather*," so that all Abraham's children are included in the blessing of justification by faith. David spoke of "those" whose sins are forgiven. Is "those" limited just to those who were Abraham's physical descendants, Jews who were circumcised, as Abraham and David both were? By asking this natural question, Paul has reintroduced the second of the points asserted in the closing verses of chapter 3. His point is this: the Old Testament itself shows that God justified uncircumcised men, and if He did it back then, He can do it now. Justification by faith is not limited to the physical descendants of Abraham. The constant effort of 1st century Judaizers to get the church to require circumcision of all Gentile converts shows the high regard the Jews had for this rite.[31] When Paul lists the chief elements of his pre-Christian self-righteousness, circumcision is given the honor of heading the list (Philippians 3:5). In the Jewish mind, there was a close and vital relationship (almost cause and effect) between circumcision and justification. One gets the impression that circumcision was viewed as being proof of a man's right standing with God. It would not be easy for a Jew to accept what Paul now says, that there is no relationship at all.

For we say, "FAITH WAS RECKONED TO ABRAHAM AS RIGHTEOUSNESS." By this repetition of Genesis 15:6, Paul explains what he means by "blessing" in his previous question. Moses, the great lawgiver and prophet, has unequivocally stated that Abraham was justified by faith. This is now a conceded point, but what inference can be drawn from it?

4:10 – How then was it reckoned? While he was circumcised, or uncircumcised? Not while circumcised, but while uncircumcised;

How then was it reckoned? What were Abraham's circumstances (circumcised or uncircumcised?) at the time his faith was reckoned for righteousness?

While he was circumcised, or uncircumcised? If Abraham were circumcised before he

---

[31] This frenzied effort of the Judaizers is alluded to in Acts 15:1,5; Galatians 2:3,4, and 5:1-6. If Wilson, *Romans,* p.69, is correct when he says that circumcision was "the first meritorious act of obedience to the Law" that a Jewish boy observed, then the effort of the Judaizers, and Paul's rejection of it as having in no way merited justification, is even more understandable.

was justified, then the Jew might argue that justification is only for Jews. But if Abraham was uncircumcised at the time he was justified, then other uncircumcised people (i.e., the Gentiles), too, might be justified. Thus, Paul's assertion that Gentiles are eligible for God's gracious justification would stand.

Not while circumcised, but while uncircumcised. This is Paul's answer to his own question. A comparison of Genesis 15:6 and 17:10 will show this is the correct and only possible answer to the question. He was circumcised in his 99th year (Genesis 17:24), at which time Ishmael was 13 years old (Genesis 17:25). Now when one considers that Abraham was justified (Genesis 15:6) even before Ishmael was born, it soon becomes evident what the answer to the question is.

> The history of Abraham is conclusive on this point. "And he believed God, and He reckoned it to him for righteousness" (Genesis 15:6). After this, Ishmael was born; and when thirteen years old (Genesis 17:25), he and Abraham were circumcised on the same day. This was a fearful blow to those who claimed that there could be no salvation (Acts 15:1) without circumcision, for the father of the Israelites was justified 13 years or more before he was circumcised.[32]

Quite plainly, circumcision was not required of Abraham in order to be reckoned as righteous. This is quite sufficient to show that the blessing of justification is not limited to Jews (circumcised people) only. All that remains is to remind the objector what the Old Testament itself says about the nature and value of circumcision.

4:11 – *and he received the sign of circumcision, a seal of the righteousness of the faith which he had while uncircumcised, that he might be the father of all who believe without being circumcised, that righteousness might be reckoned to them,*

And he received the sign of circumcision. The complete thought is this: Thirteen or more years after he was justified, he received the sign of circumcision.[33] When God instituted circumcision (Genesis 17:11), He said, "And you shall be circumcised ... and it shall be the sign of the covenant between Me and you." Other covenants too had their visible sign of confirmation – for example, the rainbow (Genesis 9:12,13,17) and the burning lamp (Genesis 15:17,18). In the case of Abraham, circumcision showed there was a covenant between God and Abraham.[34]

---

[32] Lipscomb and Shepherd, *Romans,* p.84.

[33] Circumcision itself was the sign. This is a genitive of apposition.

[34] Perhaps it can be said that circumcision was intended to be more than an external sign that there was a covenant between God and Abraham. It may be that circumcision signified that God expected a change of heart in the men under the covenant. Moses himself so explained it, when he said, "Circumcise therefore the foreskin of your heart, and be no more stiff-necked" (Deuteronomy 10:16, ASV). Compare also Deuteronomy 30:6; Jeremiah 4:4; Romans 2:28,29; Philippians 3:3.

A seal of the righteousness of the faith which he had while uncircumcised. A "sign" and a "seal" are two different concepts. Circumcision was both a "sign" and a "seal"; a sign of the covenant, and a seal of the righteousness by faith. *One* of the purposes which circumcision served was that it sealed Abraham's justification. "A *seal* is the mark of wax or other substance, which is attached to deeds and official letters, to confirm, ratify, or make them binding. To affix the seal was to confirm the contract or the engagement."[35] Circumcision was given to Abraham, like a seal affixed to a document, to authenticate a state of things already existing (viz., the righteousness based on faith which was his for years before he was circumcised).[36] *Another* of the purposes which circumcision served is found in the Old Testament record of its institution. At the time God appointed circumcision, there was a covenant made with Abraham (some words from which Paul will allude to in verse 17), and circumcision was also the sign of that covenant.[37] "*The* faith" refers us back to what was said in 3:30, 4:3, and 4:5. Circumcision neither contributed to Abraham's justification nor to the promise made to him by God.[38]

---

[35] Barnes, *Romans*, p.107.

[36] In passing, it should be recalled that whereas circumcision was the seal of a covenant made with Abraham, the indwelling Holy Spirit (not baptism) is the seal of the New Covenant (Ephesians 1:13). Some Protestant teachers attempt to prove that baptism is something that follows a man's initial justification (which they allege is conditioned on faith-only). One argument advanced to demonstrate this is that baptism takes the place of circumcision as the "sign and seal" of the covenant. Proof that baptism takes the place of circumcision is supposedly found in Colossians 2:11,12. So, in their system, baptism is only a "sign and seal" to a salvation which had already been received before baptism, which also changes baptism's purpose from being "unto the remission of sins" (Acts 2:38 ASV). The facts in the case, however, are that baptism of a penitent believer is analogous to the Jewish physical birth (see John 3:3-5), while the true analogy of circumcision – the sign and seal of the New Covenant – is the gift of the Holy Spirit (Ephesians 1:13, 4:30; 2 Corinthians 1:22). True, the gift of the Holy Spirit is timed chronologically close to baptism, since it is actually given at baptism, whereas fleshly circumcision to the Jewish infant was normally given eight days after birth. Logically, though, it is easy to distinguish between birth and the seal. A Gentile proselyte to Judaism (a choosing adult) was required to be circumcised before acceptance into the community, and normally the Jewish child would be cast out unless circumcised (Genesis 17:14). Likewise, the New Testament does not recognize as a Christian one who does not have the Spirit dwelling in him (Romans 8:9; Acts 19:1-5). The Spirit, then, and not baptism, is the Christian's "sign and seal."

(There is a considerable difference between emphasis on an inner obedience [which Colossians 2:11,12 does speak of], and saying that Colossians shows that circumcision and baptism are both simply outward signs [and optional at that] of an inward grace. B.W. Johnson, *People's New Testament* [Delight, AR: Gospel Light Publishing Co., nd], Vol 2, p.230, has these comments on Colossians 2:11,12. "IN WHOM YE ARE CIRCUMCISED. Are there those who say that you ought to be circumcised? In Him is the true circumcision, not done by hands, not the cutting off of a little flesh, but the putting off of the entire body of the sins of the flesh ... This putting off of the body of sins of the flesh (verse 11) is associated with baptism (verse 13)." Taken in its context, Colossians says nothing about baptism taking the place of circumcision as the sign and seal of the covenant.)

[37] Paul's presentation of God's dealings with Abraham (see Romans 4:17,18) indicates that there was some relationship between Genesis 15:5,6 and Genesis 17:5. On the earlier occasion, God had said "So shall your descendants be" (i.e., as numerable as the stars in the heavens). On the later occasion, God says Abraham is to be "the father of a multitude." In other words, the covenant made at the later occasion (the one that was sealed with circumcision) repeated and explained in more detail what had been promised earlier. That circumcision was also the "seal of the righteousness of the faith" indicates that over the years God had approved of Abraham's faithfulness.

[38] "The apostle here puts forth his view of the real import of circumcision. It was not (as so many of his contemporaries supposed) the cause or condition of Israel's privileges, so much as the sign or ratification

That he might be the father. Paul here reveals one of the purposes God had in mind when He justified Abraham, and then on a much later occasion gave him the seal of the covenant.[39]   God pronounced Abraham righteous on the condition of faith, so that Abraham could be the father of all believers.   "The word 'father' here is used evidently in a spiritual sense, as denoting that Abraham was the ancestor of all true believers; that he was their model and example."[40]   That it is possible for Gentiles as well as Jews to be his spiritual children is now set forth.

Of all who believe without being circumcised, that righteousness might be reckoned to them. Here we are told that Gentiles may follow Abraham's example by being a believer, and the result will be that God will reckon righteousness to them.[41]   In passing, observe that "believe" is a present tense, continuous action verb form.   As has been affirmed earlier, it pictures a continuing faithfulness, rather than a one-time thing; faithfulness, but not perfect obedience to any law.   What is done for believing Gentiles, when righteousness is reckoned to them, is the same thing done for Abraham (Romans 4:3).

4:12 – and the father of circumcision to those who not only are of the circumcision, but who also follow in the steps of the faith of our father Abraham which he had while uncircumcised.

And the father of circumcision.   Here we are told that Jews, Abraham's physical descendants, may also follow his example – be a believer, and be justified.   If Jews follow merely the example of circumcision, and omit the example of faith, they will miss having righteousness reckoned to them.

To those who not only are of the circumcision.   Mere circumcision would not avail. The mere performance of the rite was no guarantee of justification, unless it was attended with a faith like Abraham's.   "Spiritual kinship and not physical descent is the determining factor.   It is only those who share Abraham's faith who are accounted his spiritual heirs."[42]

---

of them.   It ratified a state of things already existing when it was instituted."   Sanday, *Romans*, p.58.

[39] *Eis* ("that") and the infinitive have the same meaning here as was explained at 3:26 (footnote #107). It denotes purpose.

[40] Barnes, *Romans*, p.107.

[41] We have, because the context seems to so require, used "uncircumcised" and "Gentile" as though the terms were interchangeable.   We are aware that "other nations also observed the ceremony, such as the Egyptians and Phoenicians, but not the Philistines, Babylonians, Greeks, or Romans.   It is still observed, not only by Mohammedan nations who claim to be descended from Abraham, but by the Abyssinian, Egyptian, Polynesian and other peoples.   Among these latter the rite is generally performed about the age of ten or twelve years, as a preliminary to marriage, and as admitting to full civil and religious tribal privileges.   With the Hebrews circumcision had a special significance.   They regarded it as a sign of the covenant between God and His people, and they alone of all nations circumcised their infants, thereby devoting them from their birth to Jehovah."   J.R. Dummelow, editor, *A Commentary on the Holy Bible* (New York: Macmillan Co, 1927), p.26.

[42] Wilson, *Romans*, p.70.

But who also follow in the steps of the faith of our father Abraham. While all of Abraham's descendants were circumcised, he was not equally the father of them all. It was only to such of those who had his faith that he was a spiritual father. Compare John 8:39-44, where Jesus denied that the unbelieving Jews were the children of Abraham, or of God either, but asserted that they were of their father the devil. "Follow" is a translation of *stoicheō*, a well-known military term, meaning to 'march in file.' It compares the conduct of one person to another. It is a continual following, or a continual walking in harmony with Abraham's example.[43] The expression "the steps of Abraham's faith" (ASV) is a key passage to help us understand that the faith that saved Abraham was not 'faith-only.' It is something that continued over the years, at least since Genesis 12:1, if not before that. As the next phrase indicates, Paul is referring to all those years before Abraham was circumcised, an event which took place when Abraham was 99 years old (see notes above at Romans 4:10).

Which he had while uncircumcised. In Abraham's case, the righteousness that was imputed was not imputed by God at the first glimmer of faith on Abraham's part. It was imputed after Abraham demonstrated his faith in some actions, over a period of time.[44] All this is important, for men today who become Abraham's children do so by following his example of a lifestyle of faithfulness.

4. This Plan of Salvation (Justification by Faith) does not Require Obedience to the Law of Moses. 4:13-22.

> *Summary*: In 3:31, Paul affirmed that his presentation of justification by faith established "the Law." In this paragraph he will put the Law in its proper perspective.

4:13 – *For the promise to Abraham or to his descendants that he would be heir of the world was not through the Law, but through the righteousness of faith.*

For the promise to Abraham or to his descendants. Paul now takes up the third of the "assertions" made in the closing verses of chapter 3.[45] He repeats the ideas introduced in

---

[43] The KJV translates this phrase "who also walk in the steps ...." "Walk" is used metaphorically to describe the activities and conduct of life.

[44] "The blessing promised to Abraham included from the first 'all families of the earth' (Genesis 12:2,3), and the same universality is seen in each renewed promise, that his seed shall be as the dust of the earth (Genesis 13:16), and as the stars of heaven (15:5). Abraham's faith in the promise was seen in his conduct on each occasion, and on the last it was expressly recorded and 'counted to him for righteousness'." (Gifford, *Romans*, p.102,103.)· Over and over and over again, through the passing years, when God came to examine Abraham, He found the patriarch to be continuing in his faithfulness. The command from God (who calls himself El Shaddai) to Abraham, to "Walk before Me and be blameless," is not commanding something new from Abraham, but a continuation of the surrendered life that had already been demonstrated by Abraham.

[45] The verse begins with "for" which shows that a reason (or explanation) for something just said is about to be introduced. Some would connect verse 13 with verse 12, and understand that verse 13 is giving a reason why Abraham can be a "father of us *all*," the reason being that the Law of Moses did not

3:21-28 ("apart from works of law"), and then develops his proposition to show that he is actually establishing law rather than nullifying it. The "promise" will be further explained in the next phrase, "that he would be heir of the world." "Descendants" is likely a better translation than "seed" in the KJV, even though *spermati* is singular in the Greek. This does not appear to be limited to Christ (like a similar passage in Galatians 3:16-18), but is an alternate way of designating the Jews (who earlier were called "the circumcision").[46]

That he would be heir of the world. To what promise made to Abraham does this refer, for there is none in these exact words in the Old Testament? "Heir" suggests a gift to be obtained, and "world" is capable of several meanings, so the explanations offered for this expression are various. (1) Some see reference to God's promise to Abraham and his descendants about possession of the land of Canaan (Genesis 17:8). Those who reject this explanation do so on the basis of the context in Romans, wherein no mention has been made of the land of Canaan. (2) Some have urged that "heir of the world" is another way of saying "a father of many nations have I made you" (Genesis 17:5, KJV). Those who reject this explanation do so on the basis that the Genesis 17 passage is not the main passage in Paul's mind; Genesis 15:5-6 is.[47] (3) Those who accept the reading found in the KJV, "to his seed, that he should be heir of the world," understand it is Christ, not Abraham, who is here called "heir of the world." The promise that the coming Messiah would become heir of the world will be fulfilled when "the kingdom of the world has become the kingdom of our Lord, and of His Christ" (Revelation 11:15). Those who reject this explanation do so on the basis that it introduces into the discussion a new element (a promise made to Messiah that He would be heir of the world) for which we have not been prepared by earlier portions of Paul's argument. (4) Another explanation is based on the meaning of "world" as being every nation, every land. The special doctrine of this passage is that believers in "every nation" are to be justified by faith and thus become, as a gift to him, part of Abraham's "seed." (5) A rather satisfying explanation is that "heir of the world" is Paul's interpretation of the spiritual meaning of the promises made to Abraham (Genesis 12:3, 15:5,6, 18:18, and 22:18). In its final application it would refer to the new heavens and new earth (Romans 8:18; 2 Peter 3:13; Revelation 21:9-22:5). According to Hebrews 11:10, Abraham was looking for the city that has the foundations, whose builder and maker is God. Surely "heir of the world" involves not only the condition of entrance (justification by faith) into the heavenly city, but also the possession of the inheritance too.

Was not through the Law. As the marginal reading shows, this is another example of anarthrous *nomos*.[48] In the context of the present discussion, the expression is an abbrevi-

---

limit justification to the Jews any more than circumcision did.

[46] "With regard to the Greek words *hē tō spermati autou* ["or to your seed/descendants"], it has been suggested that Paul may perhaps be thinking of Christ as the true seed of Abraham (cf. Galatians 3:16). But in view of verses 16 and 17, this is not likely. And in the case of Christ, *dia dikaiosunēs pisteōs* ["through the righteousness of faith"] would hardly be appropriate." Cranfield, *Romans*, p.239.

[47] It might be easier to show that "heir of the world" is another way to say "so shall your descendants be" (Genesis 15:5) if indeed Paul himself had actually referred to that verse.

[48] See this expression, and the problem involved in it, explained at Romans 2:12. A question that has

ated form of "not through works of the Law" found at 3:20. The promise to Abraham and his descendants that they should inherit the world was conditioned on faithfulness to what God had commanded, not on the observance of man-made religious rules such as "works of the Law."

But through the righteousness of faith. Paul is merely repeating what he had already worked out in detail in 4:2,3. The promise to Abraham and his descendants was made in connection with their faithfulness; God always looks for the tenor of a man's life (Romans 2:6-10). Because he was a justified man in God's sight, justified by faith, God also made some promises to Abraham about being heir of the world. The same conditional promise holds good for Abraham's spiritual descendants.

4:14 – *For if those who are of the Law are heirs, faith is made void and the promise is nullified;*

For if those who are of the Law are heirs. "For" shows that we are being given a reason for the thought that has just been stated in verse 13. The argument is not conducted historically (as was the argument about whether or not justification depended on circumcision in any way), but dogmatically. Paul is basing his argument on the wide difference between "works of the Law" and "faithfulness" (consistent obedience). "Heirs" has been explained in notes on "heir of the world" in verse 13; so has anarthrous *nomos* ("of law").

Faith is made void. If a man's justification depended on his observance of "works of the Law," then the other possibility for being justified (i.e., sins pardoned) is completely ruled out. Faithfulness and "works of the Law" cannot coexist as equal conditions of justification, and ultimately of inheritance.

And the promise is nullified. The man who depends on "works of the Law" for his justification cannot at the same time depend on participating in any promise made to Abraham or his descendants. The reason is this: all the promise ever talked about, by way of conditions, was faith.

4:15 – *for the Law brings about wrath, but where there is no law, neither is there violation.*

For the Law brings about wrath. "For" seems to say that verse 15 is a second reason for the thought stated in verse 13. Not only are "works of the Law" and "faithfulness" separate and distinct concepts (verse 14), but making void the Law by observing the traditions of the elders results in wrath rather than justification (verse 15). Here, for the first time in this whole section, the word "Law" is preceded by an article in the Greek, so the NASB rightly reads "the Law."[49]   The Law of Moses produces or brings about wrath because it

---

been examined several times since 3:21 is whether (when we have an anarthrous *nomos*) it is "law" of any kind, or the "Law of Moses" in particular, that is the point Paul is arguing. In many instances we have agreed with the NASB and used "Law" to translate the anarthrous construction. In this paragraph, especially in verses 15 and 16, there is reference to "*the* Law."

[49] If we understand that verse 15 has reference to the Law of Moses producing wrath, it would be wrath for Jews. Of course, Gentiles, too, face wrath. It would be understood from chapter 1 that Gentiles have

sets forth God's standard for conduct. Men who disregard this standard and act as they please place themselves directly under God's wrath. Law inevitably imposes penalties for failure to keep it. Divine law also involves divine wrath (punishment).[50]

But where there is no law, neither is there violation. *Nomos*, here, has no article in the Greek, so the NASB rightly renders it "law," a term inclusive of the Law of Moses, and/or any of God's laws, whether given in pre-Mosaic times or since Calvary. Paul's meaning seems to be this: violation or transgression[51] of God's laws carries with it a corresponding penalty. It is not possible for anyone to claim he has not transgressed God's laws, for only when no law at all is present is there no transgression.[52] Since no one from Adam's time onward has ever lived in a state where there were no laws from God to which he was answerable, no one can claim exemption from God's wrath.

4:16 – *For this reason* **it is** *by faith, that* **it** **might be** *in accordance with grace, in order that the promise may be certain to all the descendants, not only to those who are of the Law, but also to those who are of the faith of Abraham, who is the father of us all,*

For this reason. 'Because law produces wrath, because all have sinned.' It is doubtful that verse 16 introduces a new thought. Rather, it appears to be a summing up and a giving of an application to what has already been set forth.

It is **by faith.** Several things have been said to be by faith: justification is by faith (3:28); faith is reckoned as righteousness (4:3); the blessedness of being forgiven (4:7,8); the promise of being heir of the world (4:13). If one must choose one of these, then the last one, the promise, would be the topic still under discussion.

That *it might be* **in accordance with grace.**[53] In 3:24, as Paul was giving detailed information about God's way of saving man, he stated that it was "by His grace." If man were justified by works of Law, his innocence would make it impossible for God to be gracious. Only when sinners are to be justified by faith is there any room for God's favorable attitude and action on the sinner's behalf.[54]

Patriarchal laws, disobedience to which did the same thing for them – that is, it resulted in God's wrath.

[50] Later in Romans (at 7:8,11), it will be shown that the presence of a law from God gives the devil an opportunity to tempt man. At the same time, law gives no help to the man to keep the commands, and provides no atonement for those who do not obey God but follow the allurements of the devil instead.

[51] Lard, *Romans*, p.143. "Violation" in the NASB represents *parabasis*, a word translated "breaking the Law" in 2:23, and "transgression" in 2:27.

[52] This is another way of saying "all have sinned" (Romans 3:23).

[53] The words in italics show that there is no similar word in the Greek. This is a terse sentence even in the Greek. Paul gives a few bold strokes, and allows the reader to fill in the ideas from the context.

[54] See notes on "grace" at 3:24, and in Special Study #1 at the close of chapter 1.

In order that the promise may be certain to all the descendants. This is the reason God made the condition "faith." If He had made it "works of the Law," there would be few (the only ones who have such *halakah* are Jews) who could inherit the promise. "Certain" is *bebaios*, which means "firm, reliable, dependable."[55] The descendants (Abraham's spiritual children)[56] can depend on the promise coming true for them. God so planned it that way.

Not only to those who are of the Law. Jews are the people meant by this phrase. Just as Paul used "law" in two different senses in 3:21, so he uses it in two different senses in this context (verses 15 and 16). "*The* law" here is a reference to the Law of Moses, and the people who were subject to it were Jews.[57]

But also to those who are of the faith of Abraham. This evidently is a reference to Gentiles, who exercise the same kind of faith as uncircumcised Abraham exercised.[58] Believing Jews and believing Gentiles are thus both included in "all the descendants." "The faith of Abraham" is reintroduced here in connection with the type of faith a man must have to please God. Abraham's faith in all its beauty and strength is then described in verses 17-22.

Who is the father of us all. "Us all" means all us believers, whatever ethnic background we may be (see verse 11). "Here first St. Paul seems distinctly to turn from his Jewish opponents to his co-believers, Jewish and Gentile. Henceforth [save for the closing chapters] there is little if any anti-Jewish reasoning."[59]

4:17 – *(as it is written, "A FATHER OF MANY NATIONS HAVE I MADE YOU") in the sight of Him whom he believed,* **even** *God, who gives life to the dead and calls into being that which does not exist.*

(as it is written, "A FATHER OF MANY NATIONS HAVE I MADE YOU"). This quotation, taken from Genesis 17:5, is used to support the extended sense in which "descendants" has been used in verse 16. It also verifies the preceding statement that Abraham is the "father of us all." God made this promise to Abraham when he was an old

---

[55] Arndt-Gingrich, *Lexicon*, p.137.

[56] The word "descendants" (*spermati*) likely refers to the same people to whom it did in verse 13. There is an element of universality in this term, as the rest of the verse goes on to indicate.

[57] In verse 14, the expression "of the Law" was interpreted as shorthand for "works of the Law" because that meaning seems to be demanded by the context. Here in verse 16, "of the Law" has been explained as referring to the Law of Moses, again because that is the meaning the context seems to demand.

[58] Hendriksen, *Romans*, p.157, attempts to show that only one group of people are in mind here in verse 16 – those who are not only of the Law (i.e., Jews), but who are also believing Jews ("of the faith of Abraham"). In the light of the following expressions which have a universal tone to them, we take it that two groups are in Paul's mind.

[59] Moule, *Romans*, p.95. "Wonderful the triumph of the Gospel, which made it not only possible but profoundly *natural* for former Pharisees and former idolaters to unite as 'we' and 'us' in Christ." *ibid.*

man, and a year or so before the birth of Isaac. Yet God says, "I have already done it." In His mind or purpose, God had granted that Abraham would be the father of many nations.[60] The patriarch's name was changed from Abram to Abraham ("father of a multitude") on this same occasion. All of this would demonstrate that what God purposes is as good as accomplished![61]

In the sight of Him whom he believed, *even* God. When the parenthetical phrase about Abraham's being the father of many nations is taken into account, it can be seen that this phrase is connected to verse 16. Thus 'Abraham is the father of us all in the sight of God.' The words "he believed" picture Abraham as standing before God at different times in his life, at Genesis 15, at Genesis 17, and at Genesis 22 (a passage about to be alluded to by Paul), all the while full of faith and the works of faith. The same faithfulness that Abraham exercised as recorded in Genesis 15 determined his attitude and actions in the circumstances recorded in Genesis 17 and 22. The rest of Romans 4:17 and the verses following seem to be introduced to show how Abraham's faith was, in essence, the same as the justifying faith of New Testament times.

Who gives life to the dead. Some suppose this expression anticipates verses 19 and 20, where Abraham and Sarah are "dead" as far as reproducing any children is concerned, yet God gave "life" and Isaac was born. Some suppose the expression anticipates verses 24 and 25, and that Paul is comparing the rescue of Isaac (whom Abraham fully intended to sacrifice, believing that God would raise him from the dead, Hebrews 11:19) and the resurrection of Jesus. Still others urge that "who gives life to the dead" is an attribute of God.[62] The present tense verb form indicates this is something God regularly does.

And calls into being that which does not exist. It is likely that this phrase reflects God's power to create. There is an uncompleted sentence in the Greek, as the marginal reading shows, and it might be translated "God calls into being what does not exist as (easily as He calls) that which does exist." No mortal can comprehend the divine creative power. The bringing of animate and inanimate objects into existence and their maintenance is God's activity. Again, the present tense verb form indicates this is something God does continually.

---

[60] "Nations" is the same word (*ethnē*) translated "Gentiles." It is *goyim* in the Hebrew. And the Hebrew translated "have made" (*nathan*) is "give, grant, set, or constitute." Gesenius, *Lexicon*, p.572-3.

[61] Paul's use of Genesis 17 is another place that the modern critics have wondered about his explanation. It is argued that no such prophetic meaning as Paul gives it would have been understood by Abraham or Moses. Moule responded to such criticisms in this manner: "Compare the remarkable phrase of Galatians 3:8, where Scripture is, as it were, identified with its Inspirer, and the words of Genesis are distinctly claimed as a prophecy of the gospel. It is a shallow criticism that objects that *Moses* probably had no such design. Whether so or not, the Apostle, like his brethren (1 Peter 1:11) and his Lord (Matthew 22:43), claims that behind the knowledge, thought, and words of the prophets, lies everywhere the thought and purpose of Him 'who spake by them.' And if indeed Jesus is the Eternal Son, is such a preparation for Him *out of proportion*?" Moule, *Romans,* p.95.

[62] Meyer, *Romans*, p.167, cites 1 Samuel 2:6; Wisdom 16:13; Tobit 13:2; Deuteronomy 32:9; John 5:21; 2 Corinthians 1:9; and 1 Timothy 6:13 as other examples where this same attribute of God is alluded to.

As with the previous phrase, so with this one – its relation to the context is somewhat uncertain. Perhaps the phrase is suggested by verse 17, where God has called Abraham the father of many nations when as yet he had no children. Perhaps the language anticipates verse 21, where what God promises He is able to perform.[63] The reference, ultimately, is to the "many nations" which were to spring from Abraham. Not only had they yet no existence at the time when God was speaking to Abraham, but since Abraham and Sarah had now entered a childless old age, nothing seemed less likely than that they should ever exist.[64]

4:18 – *In hope against hope he believed, in order that he might become a father of many nations, according to that which had been spoken, "SO SHALL YOUR DESCENDANTS BE."*

In hope against hope he believed. Because Abraham knew Him to be such a God, namely, One who constantly gives life to the dead and who has creative power, he was able, contrary to all human expectations, in hope to believe.[65] The word order in the Greek is "who against hope in hope believed."[66] "Against hope" means contrary to, or beyond, human expectations. "In hope" (literally "upon hope") means that Abraham grounded his faith upon hope – hope in the *God* he knew, the God who on that memorable occasion recorded in Genesis 17 called Himself El Shaddai, which means "the all-powerful One, who can do whatever needs to be done." Abraham had no hope in what man can do, but hoped instead in what God could do.

In order that he might become a father of many nations. Paul seems to be telling us what was in Abraham's mind as he continued to believe. God had said he would be the father of many nations, and Abraham himself wanted to be such a father.[67] Paul has already explained "father of many nations" in 4:13-17 as denoting spiritual children from all over the world.

---

[63] "Calls" raises some of the same theological problems here as its use did in chapter 1. Is its sense here simply "to name, to speak of, to describe" non-existent things as though they existed? Or does the word "calls" actually mean "to summon, to command" non-existent things to come to pass? (Calvinistic writers are accustomed to use the language "effectual call" to explain this verse.) Or does the word mean "to call into being, to create, to bring into existence" things that before were non-existent? The latter is the way the NASB translators understood it.

[64] Bruce, *Romans*, p.118.

[65] It must be noted that the relative pronoun "who," with which this verse begins in the Greek, refers to Abraham, whereas in the previous verse the relative pronoun "who" referred to God.

[66] The wording of the KJV, "who against hope believed in hope," suggests the untenable idea that hope is the object of his belief. What we are being told is that Abraham believed in that which God had promised, and for which he therefore hoped.

[67] It is contrary to Paul's emphasis ever since 3:27 to make this verse say Abraham "believed" in order to be worthy enough to earn the right to be the father of many nations. To say that hope of heaven (Hebrews 11:10), or a desire to be a father of many nations, motivated him is something different from saying Abraham thought of his belief as being meritorious.

According to that which had been spoken, "SO SHALL YOUR DESCENDANTS BE."   The reference is again to Genesis 15:5, where God promised that Abraham's descendants would be as numerous as the stars of the heaven.   Paul has said "he believed," and then quotes language from events that were years apart.   Abraham's faith was a continuous thing.[68]   The same faith exhibited in Genesis 15, he continued to walk by in Genesis 17.

4:19 – *And without becoming weak in faith he contemplated his own body, now as good as dead since he was about a hundred years old, and the deadness of Sarah's womb;*

And without becoming weak in faith he contemplated his own body.   Verse 19 seems to be an explanation of "against hope" (verse 18), while verses 20 and 21 will set forth the meaning of "in hope" (verse 18).   Abraham considered the difficulties,[69] but such consideration does not indicate his faith has grown weaker.   "Contemplated" comes from *katanoeō*, which means to "look at with reflection, to consider carefully."[70]   Faith is not synonymous with credulity.   Faith is based on evidence, and the mind can weigh or consider the evidence.   In Abraham's case, he weighed the physical improbabilities versus the promise of God.   Such consideration does not mean his faith had weakened.

Now as good as dead since he was about a hundred years old.   This is one of the things Abraham took into consideration.   Abraham was at an age when it was highly improbable from a merely physical standpoint that he would father any children.   His body was dead as far as procreative activities were concerned – yet that was no obstacle to the fulfillment of the promise God made to him.

And the deadness of Sarah's womb.   This is another adverse circumstance which Abra-

---

[68] Paul does use an aorist tense when he writes "he believed," but in the light of the context it must be another example of what Dana and Mantey have called the "constative aorist," where an action is contemplated in its entirety, regardless of the extent of its duration.   (Dana and Mantey, *Grammar*, p.196.)

[69] The KJV reading, "he considered *not* his own body," represents a manuscript variation at this place. The better manuscripts (Sinaiticus, A, B, C, etc.) omit the "not," and the presence or absence of the "not" makes this difference in interpretation.   (1) According to the reading of the KJV, Paul is thinking of the time recorded in Genesis 15:1-6 (he has just quoted verse 5 in Romans 4:18), when he says Abraham did *not* consider the difficulties.   On that occasion, Abram took no heed at all to the difficulties attending the promise.   He did not fix his mind upon the fact that his own body was already deadened – he being about 86 years old – nor upon the deadness of Sarah's womb.   Rather, he just embraced the promise.   Romans 4:22 would then be a repetition of what Paul had earlier said using Genesis 15:6, namely, that Abraham was justified by faith that night when God called him out to count the stars.   (2) According to the reading of the NASB, Paul is thinking of the time recorded in Genesis 17:15ff, from which some of Paul's language is plainly borrowed.   On that occasion, Abraham *did* consider the difficulties attending the promise about him and Sarah.   He is 99 years old (Genesis 17:1), and Sarah is sterile, but still he continued to believe. Following this line of reasoning, Romans 4:22 is an assertion by Paul that the justification by faith that was imputed at Genesis 15:6 (Romans 4:3) was renewed or extended on the later occasion (Genesis 17) when the triumph of Abraham's faith was even more conspicuous.

All this has considerable bearing on the subject of justification by faith – whether justification is a one-time thing, or whether it is something that happens over and over again in a believer's life.   James 2:23 should also be taken into account, for that passage deals with Genesis 22 (the sacrifice of Isaac), and says that at that time justification was extended or renewed again.   (Cp. what was said at Romans 3:24,28.)

[70] Arndt-Gingrich, *Lexicon*, p.416.

ham fully contemplated as he considered the evidence. Two different words are used in this passage for "dead, deadness." The word used of Abraham is a perfect tense participle, the tense indicating that Abraham had once had the power of reproduction, but had lost it (he thought).[71] The word used of Sarah states a simple fact: she had never had the power of conceiving; she was sterile, barren. When he thought about it, Abraham found that to be no obstacle, either, to the fulfillment of God's promise.

4:20 – *yet, with respect to the promise of God, he did not waver in unbelief, but grew strong in faith, giving glory to God,*

Yet, with respect to the promise of God, he did not waver in unbelief. A third thing Abraham considered was the promise, and Who it was Who had made it. The "promise of God" is the one about numerous descendants (verse 18), about being the father of many nations (verse 17). Abraham did not ignore the difficulties. He considered the whole situation, and did not doubt. "Waver" translates *diakrinō*, which means "to take issue, dispute with someone, be at odds with oneself, doubt, waver."[72] It is that mental struggle (and corresponding paralysis of behavior) into which a man may enter when there are conflicting facts available to his attention. "In the midst of these violently conflicting facts, he had to make up his own mind (*diakrinō*). He had to decide whether to believe God against nature, or believe nature against God."[73] He kept right on walking by faith.

But grew strong in faith. Two questions face the reader here: how shall we translate the aorist passive verb, and how shall we understand the dative case ("in faith")? The verb may have its actual passive meaning, "was strengthened, was confirmed." If so, then God is the agent who by His continuing revelations to Abraham provided the continuing evidence his faith needed. On the other hand, many Bible students, including the NASB translators, think the passive form here (like a deponent verb) has an active meaning.[74] The dative case may be a dative of means. If so, it would be translated "his faith gave him strength" (TCNT), or "he waxed strong through faith" (ASV). His faith gave him strength to meet the obstacles.[75] Or perhaps the dative case may be a dative of sphere. If so, it

---

[71] Compare Hebrews 11:12 on Abraham's condition at 100. Some have urged from the fact that Abraham fathered children by Keturah after Sarah's death (since the record of this marriage occurs in Genesis 25:1-4, after the record of the death of Sarah in Genesis 23) that he was not as "dead" as he supposed at age 100; Sarah did not die till Abraham was 120. However, just because the record of the marriage does not occur until Genesis 25 is not proof that the marriage to Keturah was subsequent to Sarah's death. The fact is, though this commentator supposes that Abraham did in fact marry Keturah *after* Sarah died, we just do not know at what time in his life Abraham married Keturah.

[72] Arndt-Gingrich, *Lexicon*, p.184. The KJV uses "staggered," a picturesque word derived from Tyndale, who substituted it for Wycliffe's more-exact and simple "doubted."

[73] Lard, *Romans*, p.148.

[74] Arndt-Gingrich, *Lexicon*, p.263, give an active translation to the passive form of *endunamoō*.

[75] The dative of means is regularly explained that his faith gave him the power to continue to attempt to conceive a son, in spite of his "deadness" and Sarah's "barrenness." Hebrews 11:11 is appealed to in order to show this interpretation is right, for that passage says that "by faith [Abraham], together with Sarah,

would be translated "he was strong in faith" (KJV) or "he grew strong in faith" (NASB). This latter explanation has a certain appeal, as it tells us Abraham has grown in faith since those early days of his walk with God. Though years have passed since the promise was first made (Genesis 15), he has not begun to see the fulfillment of the promise. Yet he still continued to walk by faith. Then God repeated the promise to him in his advanced age (Genesis 17). Abraham immediately obeyed the command God gave at that time that all male members of his household be circumcised (Genesis 17:9-14, 23-26). His faith had grown stronger through the years; he was more consistent than before in his behavior, more consistent in matching his lifestyle to the revelation God had given to him. The following two clauses express some of the effects this growing faith produced.

Giving glory to God. Perhaps "glory" here means "honor." A man honors God when he submits to God's authority and obeys all He says. "This phrase does not necessarily refer to a verbal ascription of praise, but may be used of anything which tends to God's glory, whether in thought, word, or deed (cp. Joshua 7:19; Ezra 10:11; Jeremiah 12:16; Luke 17:18; John 8:24; Acts 12:23)."[76]

4:21 – *and being fully assured that what He had promised, He was able also to perform.*

And being fully assured. This apparently is a second effect of Abraham's growing faith. Hebrews 11:1 likewise says that "faith [produces] a conviction of things not seen." *Plērophoreō* literally means to "fill completely," then "to fill one with any thought, conviction, or inclination," then to be "persuaded, fully convinced, or assured."[77] It apparently says that over the years, Abraham's conviction about what God can do grew till it became complete assurance.

That what He had promised, He was able also to perform. This is the content of Abraham's assurance. As Genesis 18:14 records God as saying, "Is anything too difficult for the Lord? At the appointed time I will return to you, at this time next year, and Sarah shall have a son."

4:22 – *Therefore also IT WAS RECKONED TO HIM AS RIGHTEOUSNESS.*

Therefore also. Verse 21 explains the consequence of the kind of faith described in verses 17-20. There is a manuscript variation on "also" (*kai*). Some good manuscripts carry it; other good ones omit it. If we retain it and translate it "and," then verse 22 tells

---

received power to beget a child." (See F.F. Bruce, *The Epistle to the Hebrews* in The New International Commentary on the New Testament [Grand Rapids: Wm. B. Eerdmans Publishing Co, 1964], p.299.)

Murray, *Romans*, p.151, gives two reasons this interpretation should not be adopted. "(1) There is no evidence Paul has in view simply the later period in Abraham's life of faith when he actually begat Isaac. The promises quoted in this chapter have reference to an earlier period (cf. v. 22). (2) The idea that the strength by which Abraham begat Isaac is in the forefront here does not so well accord with the phrases that follow."

[76] Sanday, *Romans*, p.61.

[77] Thayer, *Lexicon*, p.517.

us that the faith that Abraham had at the later time (Genesis 17) in his life did not differ significantly from the faith he had at the earlier time (Genesis 15) when his faith was reckoned for righteousness.   Thus, the emphasis of the verse would be on Abraham's *faith*, and we are back to where we started in 3:28, that *faith* is the important thing when it comes to conditions on which God grants justification.   If we retain it and translate it "also," then verse 22 tells us that Abraham was justified again by God, about the time of the birth of Isaac.   The same thing that was done, and specifically recorded at Genesis 15:6, was done by God for Abraham again, though it is not specifically recorded in the Old Testament. And *faith*, the kind just described in the previous verses, was the condition!

IT WAS RECKONED TO HIM AS RIGHTEOUSNESS.   See notes at Romans 4:3, where the import of this expression was explained.   Abraham's faithfulness, his growing faith, was the thing God took into account in order to reckon his justification, while his sins (he was "ungodly", verse 5) were covered by Christ's propitiatory sacrifice at Calvary.[78]

C. God's Purpose for Recording Abraham's Justification by Faith. 4:23-25

> *Summary*:   Paul tells us what God had in mind when He caused the record of Abraham's justification to be written.   God intended it to benefit future generations, so they could understand His way of saving man and share in the same kind of justification themselves.

4:23 – *Now not for his sake only was it written, that it was reckoned to him,*

Now not for his sake only was it written.   Verses 23-25 are an application of what was learned from the study of Abraham's life of faith, and the means of his salvation.   It is certainly an honor to have a record of your life immortalized in Scripture if your life was one that was pleasing to God.   Abraham could have believed, had righteousness imputed to him over and over again, then died and gone to glory, and no man living after him would have known anything about it.   But God did not make his a case of record via the Genesis account just for his honor alone.   God intended that future generations also benefit from a

---

[78] For many verses now, the distinction between "faith" (faithfulness) and "works of the Law" has been emphasized.   We have alluded to a popular interpretation of "works of the Law" before 4QMMT became known, namely, that the expression was synonymous with sinless perfection.   Some readers of such comments have certainly wondered whether anyone in the ancient world would think of himself as innocent of all sin.   Romans 3:9-20 has been an argument against the idea that some are sinless, and if it cannot be demonstrated that some entertained the idea of sinless perfection, then the whole explanation of "works of the Law" as meaning perfect obedience is hard to accept.   (1) See footnote #7 at Romans 4:2 concerning Jewish thinking about the sinlessness of Abraham.   (2) Then there were the piercing questions at the beginning of chapter 2 aimed at shattering Jewish complacency about not having broken any law. (3) Years after the writing of Romans, someone at Ephesus was saying, "I have no sin!" (see 1 John 1:8). So it appears that not everyone in the 1st century was convinced about the universality of sin.   However, we judge that Jewish pleas of sinless perfection were refuted at Romans 2:1-3:18.   In fact, if Abraham had righteousness reckoned to him, he was not (in and of himself) righteous.   Again, given the better understanding of "works of the Law" learned from 4QMMT, we doubt that we should any longer attempt to explain the phrase as being synonymous with perfect obedience.

study of the Old Testament Scriptures,[79] that from the record of Abraham future generations should learn the way in which men may be regarded as "saved" by God.

That "IT WAS RECKONED TO HIM."   That is, that Abraham's faith was reckoned to him as righteousness; his faith was the condition on which God granted justification. Remember Romans 1:17 (ASV), "from faith unto faith," which has been explained to mean "on the basis of faith in order to encourage others to believe."   Verse 23 has said the same thing.   Abraham's faith (and consequent justification) is an example to encourage others to believe (and be justified).   There is a similarity between Abraham's faith and the faith of the redeemed in the New Testament age.

> Abraham put faith in a God who "giveth life to the dead."   And in like manner the [one who would become a] Christian must put faith in God as the Author of a scheme of salvation attested by the resurrection of Christ.   The death of Christ was the ground of that scheme, the resurrection of Christ was its proof, without which it would [not be possible for God to justify man].[80]

4:24 – *but for our sake also, to whom it will be reckoned, as those who believe in Him who raised Jesus our Lord from the dead,*

But for our sake also.   God's intent when He inscripturated the record of Abraham's justification by faith was to assure men this side of Calvary that righteousness shall be imputed to them in a like manner.

To whom it will be reckoned.   Observe that (in the Greek) the verb is present tense.   It expresses a general and constantly recurring fact.   Just as righteousness was reckoned to Abraham over and over in his life (see notes at Romans 4:19), so it is reckoned in the New Testament believer's life.   It does not look forward to one day in the future (say at the final judgment), as the NASB "will be reckoned" might tend to lead the reader to think.   It is something God does for all believers (past, present, and future) all the time.

As those who believe in Him.   This relative clause defines the class to which we must belong if that which was reckoned in the case of Abraham is to be reckoned to us.   It is just as universal as 3:28,29 maintain.   It includes all who believe, and excludes all who do not.   "Believe in Him" is the same Greek that we had at Romans 4:5, literally "believes *upon (epi)* Him."   It emphasizes the need of reliance upon God, rather than reliance on ourselves.   The present tense verb signifies continual believing, a habit pattern of life.

Who raised Jesus our Lord from the dead.   God is the One who raised Jesus from the dead.[81]   "It is not enough to believe on God simply.   We must believe on Him as *raiser of*

---

[79] There are many other Scriptures that affirm the value to the Christian of a study of the Old Testament. See, for example, Romans 15:4; 1 Corinthians 10:11; and 2 Timothy 3:15-17.

[80] Sanday, *Romans*, p.61.

[81] Hendriksen, *Romans*, p.160, gives a long list of references which show that the apostles often

Jesus from the dead. If not, our faith is void; it will not be counted."[82] Just like Abraham's faith included an assurance that God could give life to the dead, it is absolutely necessary to believe in the bodily resurrection of Jesus Christ. The reason for this is obvious. Unless our faith includes this assurance, our faith is not like the faith of Abraham. Worded another way, "To reject Christ's resurrection is to reject Him; and to reject Him is to reject the sole basis of redemption."[83]

4:25 – Him who was delivered up because of our transgressions, and was raised because of our justification.

Him who was delivered up because of our transgressions. "Delivered" is *paradidōmi*, the same word translated "gave up" in Romans 1:24,26,28 (ASV). It is also used in the New Testament of what Jesus Himself did as He submitted to death (Galatians 2:20; Ephesians 5:2,25); of what wicked men did as they delivered Him over to His crucifiers (Luke 24:20; Acts 3:13); and of what God Himself did (Romans 4:25 and 8:32). Perhaps the LXX of Isaiah 53:12, "his soul was delivered to death," is behind Paul's language here. "Because of" is an attempt to translate the preposition *dia* and the accusative case.[84] Such a construction expresses a causal relationship; that is, it traces an effect to a cause. If the emphasis is on the cause, it is translated "because." If the emphasis is thought to be on the effect, it is translated "in order that."[85] What all this means is this: Perhaps verse 25 says Christ died *because* of our transgressions (emphasis on cause); our sins made His death necessary if God was to redeem us. Or perhaps it says Christ died *in order to* atone for our transgressions (emphasis on effect). "Transgressions" translates *paraptōma*, a synonym for sin not used before in Romans. It is a word that has several senses. In its milder sense it denotes an error, a mistake, a fault; in its stronger sense, it means trespass, a willful sin.[86] Romans 3:9-23 has already detailed what some of these "trespasses" are.

And was raised because of our justification. "Raised" is a passive voice verb – God

---

asserted the fact that Jesus had risen from the dead, and also that God had raised Him. In the face of 21st century denials of the bodily resurrection of Jesus, it is important to hear this uniform testimony of witnesses who were in a place to know what happened. In this regard, special attention given to 1 Corinthians 15:1-11 is instructive.

[82] Lard, *Romans,* p.150.

[83] Lard, *Romans,* p.151.

[84] The Greek language varies the spelling at the end of nouns and adjectives to indicate the word's function in its sentence, whether it is the subject (nominative case), or shows possession or separation from (genitive case), or is the indirect object of the verb (dative case), or is the direct object (accusative case). In addition, the Greek language did not originally have prepositions. The prepositions were invented to help the different cases (genitive, dative, and accusative) specifically express the ideas that were already inherent in them. Some prepositions can be followed by more than one case, and in these instances the meaning of the preposition changes dramatically.

[85] Gifford, *Romans,* p.109 has an extended note on *dia* followed by the accusative case.

[86] Berry, *Synonyms,* p.118.

raised Him. "Because of" is the same construction as in the first part of the verse.[87] "Justification" here represents a different Greek word than was translated "justification" or "righteousness" before in this letter. Before, the word sometimes was *dikaiosunē*,[88] and sometimes *dikaioma*.[89] Now the word is *dikaiōsis*. Many writers comment here as though the new word were completely synonymous with the previous ones. Lard, for example, writes concerning how Jesus was raised "in order to complete the provisions for justification," and then he goes on to explain how Jesus' blood had to be offered in the antetypical Holy of Holies in heaven (Hebrews 10:11-18) following His resurrection.[90] On the other hand, it may be that *dikaiōsis* is deliberately used in Romans 5:18 to refer to the resurrection of the body. Perhaps Paul is here introducing the topic that will be explained fully later, how Jesus' resurrection guarantees the resurrection of all men from the dead by negating what Adam's sin did to the race, thus broadening our concept of what all is involved in "God's way of saving man."

III. THE UNIVERSALLY NEEDED SALVATION (OFFER-ED IN THE GOSPEL) HAS THE MOST BLESSED EFFECTS – PEACE WITH GOD, COMPLETE DELIV-ERANCE THROUGH CHRIST FROM DEATH AND SIN, THE HELP OF THE HOLY SPIRIT, ALL CULMI-NATING IN ULTIMATE GLORIFICATION. 5:1-8:39

A. God's Plan of Salvation (Justification by Faith) Involves Blessed Effects on Believers. 5:1-11.

> *Summary*: Because of the death and resurrection of Jesus, the results to the believer include both nearer consequences – peace, access, hope, courage; and more remote consequences – final salvation and the glories of heaven.

5:1 – *Therefore having been justified by faith, we have peace with God through our Lord Jesus Christ,*

Therefore. What follows is a conclusion drawn from the undeniable assertion about justification by faith (3:28) just presented and documented in the second major portion of

---

[87] Some insist that both *dia* clauses be treated the same way; either both should be translated "because," or both should be translated "in order to." Others (e.g., Westcott, Hendriksen) take the first one as emphasizing cause, and the second one as emphasizing the effect.

[88] See notes at Romans 1:17 under the word "righteousness."

[89] See footnote #160, at Romans 1:32.

[90] Lard, *Romans*, p.151.

Romans (3:21-4:25). Or perhaps it could be said that Paul now elaborates in some detail several of the marvelous features included in God's way of saving man – features inherent in what was asserted in 4:25 (ASV), how Jesus was "delivered up for our transgressions and was raised for our justification." Another suggestion as to the connection with the preceding is this: in the thesis of Romans, Paul has quoted from Habakkuk that the "just *shall live* by faith" (KJV). Perhaps chapters 5 to 8 are Paul's description of the "life" that results from God's way of saving man.

Having been justified by faith. The aorist tense participle points to a definite time in the past when Paul and other believers were justified.[1] The passive voice points to God as the agent who did the justifying, just as we learned in 3:26. The participle is plural, agreeing with the subject of the sentence: it includes Paul and other believers. "Justified *by faith*" sets forth the same condition that Paul has asserted all the way through Romans.[2]

We have peace with God. As the marginal note shows, there is a manuscript variation here. The preponderance of manuscripts read "Let us have peace" rather than "we have peace."[3] What Paul urges in this exhortation is that the readers will be conscious of and enjoy the blessings that result from God's way of saving man. "Let us appreciate and realize the peace with God we have as a result of being justified by faith!"[4]

"Peace" is the "tranquil state of a soul assured of its salvation through Christ, and so

---

[1] What "justified" means has been explained in notes at 2:13, 3:20, and 3:26.

[2] See notes at Romans 1:8,12,17, and 4:3,5,16. "No one who believes the Bible doubts that a man is justified by faith. The question at issue is, whether he is justified by faith before it leads to obedience, or whether by a faith that manifests itself in obedience. Paul tells us exactly how faith does make children of God: 'For ye are all sons of God, through faith, in Christ Jesus. For as many of you as were baptized into Christ did put on Christ' (Gal.3:26,27). Faith, then, saves one by leading him to accept salvation from sin in God's appointed institutions, leading him to the obedience of faith; he becomes the child of God by being led by faith to be baptized into Christ, so putting on Christ, and in Christ he is saved." Lipscomb and Shepherd, *Romans*, p.92.

[3] There is one letter's difference, in the Greek, between the subjunctive "let us have," and the indicative "we have." The subjunctive *echōmen* is spelled with an omega [long "o"], whereas the indicative *echomen* is spelled with an omicron [short "o"]. Westcott and Hort give the subjunctive form in their text, and do not even have a footnote giving the alternate indicative reading. The second edition of the United Bible Society Greek Text adopts the indicative reading, giving it a "C" rating (indicating a considerable degree of doubt that it is the correct reading). Critics have set forth several arguments to justify the indicative reading. One suggestion is that some scribe, making a copy of Romans as someone read it aloud, accidentally substituted an omega in the word where the reader had pronounced it as though it contained an omicron. Another contention is that an exhortation (such as the subjunctive would be) is out of place in this particular part of Romans, since what is said both before this place and after is didactic. Both these defenses for the indicative can be answered satisfactorily. It could just as easily be affirmed that the scribe wrote the indicative (omicron) where the reader had pronounced the subjunctive (omega) word that Paul originally wrote. And why would an exhortation be out of place as Paul begins this section about the blessings resulting from God's way of saving man? An exhortation to appreciate and enjoy these blessings is entirely in order.

[4] These comments merely are an attempt to express the idea of the verb *echō* in a way similar to what Thayer's *Lexicon*, p.267, suggests. He writes, "i. *echein ti* is said of opportunities, benefits, advantages, conveniences, which one enjoys or can make use of ... Rom.5:1."

fearing nothing from God and content with its earthly lot, of whatever sort that is."[5]   The peace spoken of is the same peace spoken of in Romans 1:7.   On the basis of Romans 5:10,11 as compared with 5:1, Hendriksen suggests that "the basic meaning of peace is *reconciliation* with God through the death of His Son.   This implies the removal of divine wrath from the sinner, and the latter's reconciliation to divine favor."[6]   The "we" who are encouraged to enjoy this peace are the spiritual seed of Abraham (Romans 4:23-25).

Through our Lord Jesus Christ.   This expression might be called the keynote of chapter 5, since it appears several times in the chapter.   "Through" makes Jesus the mediator[7] of all this peace that justified believers are to enjoy.   He can function as mediator because He is both "Lord" and "Christ."[8]

5:2 – *through whom also we have obtained our introduction by faith into this grace in which we stand; and we exult in hope of the glory of God.*

Through whom also.   "Also" reminds the reader that other blessings have already been enumerated that are through Jesus.   Through Jesus we have justification (3:21-28); through Him we have peace (5:1); also through Him we have access into grace.

We have obtained our introduction by faith into this grace in which we stand. "We have obtained" is a perfect tense in the Greek; it speaks of past completed action with present continuing results.   The past "action" must be a reference to the process of conversion culminating at one's baptism into Christ (as chapter 6 will show).[9]   Ever since then, "we"[10] have access into grace.   When used of persons, *prosagōgē* ("introduction") signifies an approach to their presence; when used of a state, as here, it speaks of an introduction or entrance into it.[11]   *Prosagōgē* often denotes the privilege of approaching or being introduced to someone in higher station; one who would see a king needed the right to enter the king's presence, and someone to introduce him to the king.   Likewise, one

---

[5] Charles L. Feinberg, "Peace," in *Baker's Dictionary of Theology*, p.399.

[6] Hendriksen, *Romans,* p.169.   That a man whose sin remains unforgiven is in a state of enmity with God is made clear in such passages as John 15:18,24, 17:14; Romans 1:30 and 8:7; Ephesians 2:16; James 4:4.

[7] The Greek construction is *dia* and the genitive case, a construction regularly explained as expressing "intermediate agent" or the "instrument" by which something is done.   See Thayer, *Lexicon*, p.133.

[8] See notes at Romans 1:4 on "Christ" and "Lord."

[9] Conversion is spoken of as a "process" rather than a single, instantaneous act, because it has been shown in previous studies that the faith that saves includes obedience as well as knowledge, assent, and confidence.   In harmony with this, the perfect tense implies an action in the past that occurred over a space of time.

[10] As in 5:1, the plural points to Abraham's spiritual seed: included would be Paul, the Roman Christians, Christians through the ages, and we, too, who are Christians.

[11] Lard, *Romans*, p.154.   See also Thayer, *Lexicon*, p.544.

who would enter into "grace" needs Jesus to "introduce" him to it. Jesus opened the way for men to obtain the favor of God. As often before in Romans, "faith" is held out as the condition on which God grants this introduction to grace.[12] The commentaries differ markedly on the meaning of "grace" in this place.[13] Some suppose it is synonymous with the favor of reconciliation. Some suppose it stands for the state of peace that Christians are to enjoy. Some advocate that it speaks of "the gracious covenant" in which believers stand. Still others propose that "grace" is here a reference to continual justification that the believer experiences.[14] A slightly different, but related, explanation is that "grace" here speaks of the help the indwelling Holy Spirit gives so the Christian may live a victorious life.[15] "In which we stand" also is a perfect tense verb in the Greek. We took our stand in the past, and we continue to stand by faith.[16]

And we exult in hope of the glory of God. The same debate encountered concerning the word "have" in verse 1 continues on when we come to the word "exult." Is it indicative or subjunctive; a statement or an exhortation?[17] Just as it seemed that exhortation was the appropriate idea for verse 1, so it seems that verse 2 should be rendered "Let us rejoice ...," for the justification and the access into grace granted to the believer are incentives for rejoicing. The word translated "exult" comes from the same root as the word "boasting"

---

[12] "Faith" has been explained in numerous places in Romans 1-4, but see 1:17 and 4:3. Several modern versions note that a manuscript variation occurs at this place, with some manuscripts (Vaticanus, and the family called Byzantine Text) omitting the words "by faith." Since Sinaiticus, Alexandrinus, and others among the majuscules, plus several ancient versions and fathers, include the reading, we tend to agree with the NASB and include it in the text. "Even if not expressed, it is implied (cf. 11:20)." Bruce, *Romans*, p.123.

[13] See notes on "grace" at Romans 1:5, 1:7, 3:24, and 4:16.

[14] At Romans 3:24 and 4:5, the tense of the verb "justify" has suggested that "justification" is something that God does over and over again in the life of the believer. If "grace" here stands for this continual justification, then we are told that each time God justifies a believer, it is a matter of grace.

[15] The reader who has pondered what has been said earlier about "grace" in Special Study #1 will take note that "grace" in Romans 5:2 is something that follows conversion. It just is not possible (as some interpreters are wont to do) to explain "grace" as the mysterious operation of the Holy Spirit on the heart of sinful man by which the man's depraved nature is overcome, and the man is thereby enabled to become a believer. "Grace" in this verse does not precede conversion; it is something into which conversion (justification by faith) provides access.

[16] Here is introduced a topic that will be a source of continuing study – namely, the doctrine of eternal security, or, as it is sometimes called, the perseverance of the saints. Is that security conditional or unconditional? Does the Bible teach once saved, always saved? Or is it possible for a man once saved to lose his salvation? It would seem that in Romans 5:2, the 'standing' in grace is something conditioned on faith, just as was the initial access into grace. But more evidence than this must be studied before a firm conclusion can be reached.

[17] There is no manuscript difference in spelling in the case of "exult" as there is in the case of "have" in verse 1, where there are both indicative and subjunctive readings. Instead, whatever decision was reached for "have" in verse 1 will likely be continued on when the interpreter comes to "exult." If he took the first as indicative, so he will treat the second. If he decided for the subjunctive for "have," he likely will decide that verse 2 is also an exhortation.

at Romans 3:27.[18]   The Christian does have his "boasting" (something to rejoice over), but it is not something based on his own works or merits.   The thing the Christian rejoices about is his hope of glory, a glory provided by God.   "Peace" and "access" spoke of the past and the present.   But what about the future?   There is a "glory" awaiting the believer, even the glory of heaven.[19]   "Glory" looks forward to the ultimate salvation when the redeemed receive their glorified bodies, and are illuminated by the Divine Glory that bathes the New Jerusalem.[20]

> More about this coming glory will come into view when we reach the eighth chapter.   But the glory of God is the end for which He created man, and it is through the redemptive work of Christ that this end will be achieved.   So long as His people remain in mortal body, it remains a *hope*, but it is a sure hope, one that is certain of fulfillment, because those who cherish it have already received a guarantee of its realization in the gift of the Holy Spirit, who fills their hearts with the love of God.[21]

This "glory" just described is the object of the believer's hope.[22]   Paul urges the Romans to let their minds dwell on the "glory of God," and then exhorts them to exult or jubilate over the prospect.

5:3 – *And not only this, but we also exult in our tribulations, knowing that tribulation brings about perseverance;*

And not only this.   Paul has spoken about the day his readers became Christians (*i.e.*, were justified by faith).   He has spoken about the glories of the last day (i.e., hope of the

---

[18] The word translated "exult" is *kauchōmetha*, a word that is regularly translated "glory" in our English versions.   The reason the translators depart from their usual practice here, and use "exult" rather than "glory," is because another word for "glory" (*doxēs*) occurs immediately following, and to translate both words as "glory" would cause confusion for the reader.

[19] In His high priestly prayer, Jesus prayed that He might be glorified with the glory that He ever had with the Father before the earth was (John 17:5), and in verse 24 of that same chapter is a prayer that believers might be able to behold that glory of Christ.   See also 2 Thessalonians 2:14, which speaks of believers gaining "the glory of our Lord Jesus Christ."

[20] Revelation 21:23,24 speak of the glory of God that illumines New Jerusalem.   Romans 8:30 speaks more about this future glory the Christian hopes for, and 8:23 speaks about the new body the redeemed will receive at the second coming of Jesus.   "Glory" is a word that has a variety of meanings, depending on the passage where it appears.   Compare what was learned at Romans 1:23, 2:10, 3:23, 3:27 (boasting), and 4:10.   Cranfield attempts to provide a comprehensive definition of "glory" that covers all the passages: "By the *doxa tou theou* is meant here (cf. 3:23; 8:17,18,21,20; 9:23) that illumination of man's whole being by the radiance of the divine glory which is man's true destiny but which was lost through sin, as it will be restored (not just as it was, but immeasurably enriched through God's own personal participation in man's humanity in Jesus Christ – cf. 8:17), when man's redemption is finally consummated at the *parousia* of Jesus Christ."   *Romans*, p.260.

[21] Bruce, *Romans*, p.120.

[22] "Hope is a complex emotion made up of a *desire* for an object, and an *expectation* of obtaining it. Where either of these is lacking, it is no longer hope, but just wishing."   Barnes, *Romans,* p.119.

glory of God).   But what about the time intervening between the two?

> The Christian's rejoicing is not confined to the future; it embraces the present
> as well.   It extends even to what would naturally be supposed to be the very
> opposite of a ground of rejoicing – to the persecutions that we have to undergo
> as Christians.[23]

But we also exult in our tribulations.   As in verse 2, "exult" should be read as an
exhortation: "Let us exult in our tribulations!"   The present tense urges continuous action
– "Let us go on rejoicing in our tribulations!"   The Greek reads "*the* tribulations," that is,
the afflictions that every Christian knows about in this life.[24]

> It was hard to be a Christian at Rome ... The word Paul uses for trouble is
> *thlipsis*, and *thlipsis* literally means *pressure*.   All kinds of things may press
> in upon the Christian – the pressure of want and need, the straitened
> circumstances, the pressure of sorrow, the pressure of persecution, the
> pressure of unpopularity and loneliness.[25]

Paul can promise no exemption from tribulations, for he knows that "through many tribulations we must enter the kingdom of God."[26]   Tribulations are the appointed portion of
the faithful, just as our Lord told His disciples, "In the world you have tribulation."[27]

> Glorying [rejoicing, exulting] in tribulation is not the natural effect of
> tribulation – which, as we see, provokes a great part of mankind to murmur
> against God, and even to curse Him.   It is only the knowledge that these
> tribulations are the appointment of his heavenly Father, which enables the
> Christian to rejoice in them, for in themselves they are evil, grievous and not
> joyous.   Hebrews 12:6; Revelation 3:19.   There is no shortcut to glory.   The
> believer must follow the path marked out for him by his Savior, for the cross
> always precedes the crown.   Philippians 1:29,30.[28]

Paul's encouragement to rejoice in tribulations is not greatly different from what Jesus Him-

---

[23] Sanday, *Romans*, p.64.

[24] "In Romans 2:9 the singular 'tribulation' is used with reference to the penalty awaiting the wicked.
Here the plural is used with reference to the 'pressures' that come to Christ's believers through the hatred
of the world (John 15:18, 16:20, etc.)."   Lenski, *Romans*, p.337.   "The *thlipsis* are the physical hardships
and sufferings that Paul regards as the inevitable portion of the Christian; cf. Romans 8:35ff; 1 Corinthians
4:11-13, 7:26-32, 15:30-32; 2 Corinthians 1:3-10; 11:23-27."   Sanday and Headlam, *Romans*, p.125.

[25] Barclay, *Romans*, p.72.

[26] Acts 14:22.

[27] John 16:33.

[28] Wilson, *Romans*, p.82.

self said about rejoicing when persecuted for righteousness' sake.[29]

> Christ rejoiced that He could suffer to redeem man (Hebrews 12:3). He looked beyond the suffering to the redemption for man, and in that rejoiced. True faith in Christ imparts the same spirit to man. As we partake of this spirit, we rejoice that we can endure affliction, suffering, persecution, and self-denial to honor God and help man. [Cp. Acts 5:18,40,41; 16:25; 2 Timothy 2:11,12].[30]

Knowing that tribulation brings about perseverance. The participle "knowing" is probably to be taken as causal, "because we know."[31] This then is a reason why Christians can be exhorted to rejoice in tribulations, because they know what tribulations can produce. "Step by step tribulation carries us upward to the great hope that does not put to shame."[32] This phrase suggests the first step. Tribulation keeps producing perseverance. The word translated "perseverance" is also translated "patience," "endurance," "fortitude," and "steadfastness."[33]

> *Hupomonē* means more than [passive] endurance; it means the spirit which can overcome the world; it means the spirit which does not passively endure but which actively overcomes and conquers the trials and tribulations of life ... *Hupomonē* is not the spirit which lies down and lets the floods go over it; it is the spirit which meets things breastforward and overcomes them.[34]

As each tribulation comes along, the Christian is pictured as bravely, courageously going on, without faltering or complaining. The tribulation is looked on as an opportunity for growing, so the Christian sets about to come through the hard times victoriously.

5:4 – *and perseverance, proven character; and proven character, hope;*

And perseverance, proven character. This is the second step. When the Christian has persevered, he finds that his Christian character has been built up or strengthened. "Proven character" is an attempt to translate *dokimē*. The word sometimes has an active sense, as when it is used of a "test" or "ordeal" as in 2 Corinthians 8:2. Sometimes, the

---

[29] Matthew 5:11,12.

[30] Lipscomb and Shepherd, *Romans*, p.94.

[31] See footnote #8 at Romans 2:2 for the meaning of *oida*, here translated "knowing."

[32] Lenski, *Romans*, p.337.

[33] Arndt-Gingrich, *Lexicon*, p.854. See footnote #17 at Romans 2:4 where the meaning of this word *hupomonē* is distinguished from its synonym *makrothumia*.

[34] Barclay, *Romans*, p.72.

word is used with the meaning "approved, because the test was passed."[35]

> *Dokimē* is used of metal which has been passed through the fire so that everything base has been purged out of it. [The English use the word 'sterling' of coinage that has been passed through the fire.] It describes something out of which every alloy of baseness has been eliminated. When affliction [tribulation] is met with fortitude, out of the battle a man emerges stronger, and purer, and better and nearer God.[36]

The "approval" may be God's approval of the man's character; God permits the tribulations to come to test and purify our faith; and when we persevere, God approves.[37]

And proven character, hope. This is the third step in the series that tribulation is said to produce. Perseverance produces proven character, and proven character in turn produces hope. See the progressive nature of all this: first comes justification (along with peace and access into grace); then come tribulations; for the one who faces tribulation in the right spirit there comes perseverance; perseverance produces approval; and an awareness of God's approval in turn results in the subjective, personal assurance concerning all the blessed future that God has promised to His children. How can a man know he is saved? Once he has been justified, if he patiently and triumphantly endures the tribulations God appoints, and emerges from them approved, he may well indulge in the hope of final acceptance. His faithfulness now virtually guarantees the end.[38]

5:5 – *and hope does not disappoint, because the love of God has been poured out within our hearts through the Holy Spirit who was given to us.*

And hope does not disappoint. The hope the Christian has of the glory of God (5:2) will not prove illusory. When one fails to receive the thing for which he has long hoped, he is greatly disappointed. If one has been telling others of his hope, when others learn his hope was deceptive, he may even feel shame because he is aware they know his hoped-for boon

---

[35] Arndt-Gingrich, *Lexicon*, p.201.

[36] Barclay, *Romans*, p.73.

[37] It is hard to exhaust what Paul teaches in verses 3-5. God does not tempt any man to sin (James 1:13), but He may appoint and permit what is hard. These things that are hard are occasions for Christian character development. 2 Corinthians 12:10 reads, "When I am weak, then I am [made] strong." The worst thing that can happen to a man may be the best thing that could happen, if the man does not let it get the best of him, and if he (at his extremity) lets the power of God go to work. At the same time, a man must be careful. His trials and tribulations may be the result of his own foolishness; if this is the case, the tribulations may *not* result in proven character at all! George Mark Elliott used to caution: "Don't fool yourself! Sometimes when a man thinks he is wearing a martyr's crown, he really is wearing a fool's cap!"

[38] The comments on "hope" have assumed that the expression in 5:2, "in hope of the glory of God," governs the meaning of "hope" all through this context. Thus, it would seem that those commentators who write as though "hope of better things in this life than the present tribulations" (even if such hope would help a man to face his present crisis) have missed the point of this passage. The reader may wish to become more acquainted with the Theology of Hope, which will be explained and evaluated in the comments on Romans 8:24,25.

will not be obtained.[39]   Those who have been justified by faith, and who, step-by-step, have come to their hope of glory, will not be disappointed.   They shall certainly obtain what is hoped for.   The Christian hope is such that it will be fulfilled.

Because the love of God has been poured out within our hearts.   Perhaps "because" connects this idea to the exhortation to "exult in tribulations."   Perhaps "because" gives a reason why Christians can be certain their hope of glory will not be disappointed. Precisely because "God loves us!" is the reason.[40]   "Whom the Lord loves, He disciplines" (Hebrews 12:6).   In fact, the whole thought in Hebrews 12:4-13 should be carefully correlated to Romans 5:3-5.   The justified believer understands that it is because God *loves* that He permits such tribulations for the benefit of the believer.   God is only doing what any loving father would do for his child; thus, he can rejoice in the tribulations.   God plans something better for His children; His disciplinary care over them is evidence He has great plans for them in the future.   "Poured out" is a perfect tense verb, indicating a past act with present continuing results.   The verb also implies an abundance in God's provision.   The word picture in the verb is that of a fountain "pouring forth" its refreshment.[41]   Paul names the "heart"[42] as the place or faculty in man where man becomes aware of God's love, as the Holy Spirit "pours out" the love of God.

Through the Holy Spirit.   This apparently is the first reference to the Holy Spirit in this Roman letter,[43] and introduces the theme of the Holy Spirit's work on behalf of the redeemed that will be fully developed by Paul in chapter 8.   One question that regularly is addressed in comments on this passage is whether Paul is saying the Holy Spirit has immediate access to the hearts of redeemed men, or whether (as is true of His work as He leads a man to become a Christian) He works through the Word.[44]   Though it has regularly

---

[39] This feeling of shame, the ASV translators thought, is the point of the verse, for they rendered it, "and hope putteth not to shame."

[40] It is admitted that the Greek is ambiguous, and could mean "God's love for us" or "our love for God." It would appear that the context (verse 8) points us to the former as the meaning in this place.

[41] "The idea of spiritual refreshment and encouragement is usually conveyed in the East through the metaphor of 'watering.'   Paul seems to have had in his mind Isaiah 44:3, 'I will pour water upon him that is thirsty, and streams upon dry ground; I will pour My Spirit upon thy seed,' etc."   Sanday and Headlam, *Romans*, p.125.   See the same word used at Acts 2:17,35, 10:45.

[42] See notes at Romans 1:21 and 2:5 where the Biblical "heart" has been explained.   As before, so here, what today is called the "mind" or "intellect" seems to be the thing intended.

[43] Romans 1:4, 1:9, and 2:29 are disputed passages, but, as comments in each place indicate, apparently are not references to the third person of the Godhead.

[44] Before any answer can be given to the question, the reader would surely want to run the Biblical references on the indwelling Christ, the indwelling Word of God, and the indwelling Spirit.   It soon becomes rather evident that one is not complete without the other two.

   Some have supposed it is a complete misunderstanding of what this verse affirms to even raise the question.   The reason they assert misunderstanding is because these interpreters have supposed that all the passage affirms is that the *presence* of the Holy Spirit (which can be possible only if God gives Him as a gift) is in itself proof that God loves us.   To them, His *presence* is proof enough; no further testimony by

been taught in the Restoration Movement that the Holy Spirit works only through the Word of God, both in conversion and after, this commentator is not ready to affirm that the Spirit works *only* through the Word *after* conversion.[45]   Thus, Paul has here assured his readers that the fact that God loves them is the precious thought that will sustain them through tribulations, and this awareness of God's continuing love is something the Holy Spirit produces as He works to apply the benefits of redemption to those who are justified by faith.

Who was given to us.   The aorist tense verb looks back to the time when the recipient was justified (verse 1) as being the time when the Holy Spirit was given.   Other passages also point to the time of conversion as the time when the indwelling gift of the Holy Spirit is given.   For example, in Acts 2:38, the gift of the Holy Spirit is promised to those penitents who are immersed; and in Ephesians 1:13,14, the Holy Spirit is given to those who believe.   In agreement with these passages are those verses that speak of the Holy Spirit dwelling in the bodies of believers, such as 1 Corinthians 6:19 and Romans 8:9-11.   The proof given in this verse that the believer's hope will not be disappointed is thus very similar to the argument in Ephesians 1:13,14, where Paul tells us that the indwelling Holy Spirit is given as a "pledge" (a promise, a down payment) of the future redemption (resurrection) of the body.   Likewise here, Paul tells us that the indwelling Holy Spirit produces an awareness of God's continuing love, and that is a proof or pledge that God will invest us with what we hope for.[46]   It is because God loves us that our hope will not be disappointed.

5:6 – *For while we were still helpless, at the right time Christ died for the ungodly.*

For while we were still helpless.   "For"[47] tells us we are being given a reason for something

---

the Spirit to the man's heart is needed.   However, this seems short of what verse 5 teaches.   Just as Romans 8:16 may speak of a testimony borne by the Spirit to man's spirit, so this verse seems to say that it is the Holy Spirit who actively keeps refreshing our hearts with the precious truth that God loves us.

[45] In the midst of a controversy, as they are trying to win an argument, antagonists can often be forced into an extreme position they did not hold or espouse at the beginning of the debate.   Perhaps in the heat of debate with Calvinism, the Restoration Movement defenders went to an opposite extreme.   While trying to show that "faith comes by hearing ... the Word of Christ," rather than by an immediate action on the heart of the alien sinner, it may be that the heat of the controversy led the Reformers to insist that God *always* works through the Word as He appeals to the hearts of men, whereas a more Scripturally defensible position would have been that *in conversion*, the Holy Spirit works through the Word to lead men to conviction and repentance.   Such a presentation would have left open the possibility that the indwelling Holy Spirit, a gift from God at conversion, can speak directly to the redeemed man's heart (always, of course, in harmony with what is written in the Word).

[46] Modern charismatics give a considerably different explanation to these verses.   In charismatic theology, it is taught that all Christians are to have an experience that follows conversion, and in recent years an attempt has been made to show that this experience is the same as the "baptism of the Holy Spirit" that one reads about in the New Testament.   They then attempt to explain this Romans passage as though it teaches that one result of receiving the baptism of the Holy Spirit is that it fills the heart with love for others and for God.   In this commentator's judgment, such an explanation misses the point of the context in Romans 5 which is *God's* love for us rather than *our* love for God.

[47] The reader of the Greek text will note there is a manuscript variation at this place.   Some read *eti*

just said, but specifically what that something is is a matter of interpretation. Some believe verses 6-10 give a second proof that the justified man's hope will not be disappointed.[48] Others believe Paul is giving his readers a reason why they can believe that God loves them, even though they are permitted by Him to be in the midst of "tribulations" (verse 3). In the light of the following context, perhaps there is truth in both explanations. Not only does God love the redeemed as much or more (see "much more then" in verse 9) than He loved them when they were still unforgiven sinners, but the hope that is based on what God has promised to justified men cannot fail (verses 9,10). Not only is there the inner, subjective awareness of God's love (verse 5); there is also (verses 6-8) this objective, actual proof of His great love! If God's love resulted in Calvary for men who were sinners, then it surely can be expected that His love will result in heaven (rather than wrath) for those who are redeemed and reconciled to Him. "Helpless" is the first of four words[49] Paul uses in verses 6-10 to describe the state, not of the Gentiles only, but of all men who have sinned, before the benefits of Calvary have been applied to their lives. "Helpless" means too feeble, too weak, too powerless to save themselves. Perhaps the repetition of the word "still" emphasizes the truth taught in 3:19-4:25, that while some thought they could save themselves, in reality they were *still* helpless to save themselves.[50]

At the right time. The ASV margin reads "according to the time," or "according to season." "The phrase ... has been variously explained as (1) a time appointed by the Father, or (2) foretold by the prophets, or (3) opportune for Paul and his readers ... [or]

---

gar, some read *eide*, some read *ei ge*, some read *eiper*, and some read *ei gar*. The last four, all beginning with *ei* ("if"), express a condition: *ei ge* would imply the fact that there was no doubt that the condition expressed (Christ's death for the ungodly) had actually happened; the other three "if" clauses do not imply any such certainty. The NASB follows the reading *eti gar*, and translates it "for while," and no condition at all is expressed. Nestle's 21st edition of the Greek text carried the reading *ei ge*. The second edition of the United Bible Society's Greek text gives this reading a "D" classification, indicating the least possible degree of certainty that it is the correct reading. B.F. Westcott and F.J.A. Hort, *The New Testament in the Original Greek* (New York: Macmillan Co., 1929), in an appendix on page 586, explain that the reading they accepted (*ei ge*) was likely a primitive error for the reading they supposed to be original, namely, *eiper*. This uncertainty about the original text makes it even more difficult to be certain exactly what was Paul's train of thought here. The comments on the text assume that the NASB translators have made the right decision about this textual variant.

[48] Barnes, *Romans*, p.116, and Lard, *Romans*, p.157, are examples of this way of explaining the connection of verse 6 to the rest of the passage. Not only does the Holy Spirit make us aware that God loves us, but a simple look at Calvary, where God did so much for His *enemies*, should convince any man that there must be a heaven for those who through justification have become God's friends. If there were no heaven (like that for which the redeemed hope), why would God send Jesus to a Calvary?

[49] The others, in the following phrases, are "ungodly," "sinners," and "enemies."

[50] In footnote #47, the problem of the original Greek text of this verse has been partially explained. The textual reading that the NASB follows has two words (*eti*) just alike in the first clause, "For while (*eti*) we were still (*eti*) sinners ...." This is the repetition upon which the comments about "still" are based. It is common knowledge among Greek scholars that such duplication was one method regularly used by Greek writers for emphasis. Perhaps a lack of understanding of this Greek idiom is what led some copyists to deliberately leave one of the two words out of this first clause of verse 6, as they were making their copies of Romans. Theirs was a sincere effort (they thought) to correct a mistake believed to have crept into the manuscripts at the hands of an earlier copyist.

(4) the general state of the world was opportune for God's purpose."[51]   The idea is that it was a time divinely appointed as the opportune moment for God to demonstrate His love. "At the exact time fixed by the Father, and therefore precisely when it would do the world the largest measure of good"[52] is when Christ died.   "Now or never was the time for saving the ungodly; now or never was the acceptable time (2 Corinthians 6:2); and God's love did not suffer the right time for their salvation to elapse, but sent Christ to die for them the sacrificial death of atonement."[53]

Christ died for the ungodly.   The word order in the Greek shows there is stress on both "Christ" and "died."[54]   It was *Christ* who died.   It was Christ who *died*!   Both items are important.   What was explained in detail in 3:21-26, and briefly suggested in 4:24,25, is here simply alluded to.   The fact of Christ's death, and the benefits to believers from His death, are expressed in various ways in the New Testament.   There is no article before "ungodly" in the original; thus the idea is that it was people who had this quality for whom Christ died.[55]   Lenski's comment, which shows that "ungodliness" was a characteristic of all men since Adam, is not to be dismissed or overlooked.   Nor is his presentation of the great truth that "*for* the ungodly" expresses precisely the idea of the vicarious, substitutionary nature of Christ's death.   The preposition is *huper*, and prominent among its secondary meanings is "instead of" or "in place of."

> This secondary meaning is so evident in such a volume of instances in the papyri that the attempt at this date to eliminate this meaning from the allied New Testament passages needs no refutation.   Consider only the plain statements of the papyri: a man who is unable to write gets another to write for him.   The latter signs his name with *huper*, "in place of" the one for whom he writes.   Scores of examples have the meaning "in behalf of," and only mean

---

[51] Gifford, *Romans*, p.112.   "There was a due season for Christ to come.   There was a long providential preparation, a remarkable concurrence of many conditions, before the 'fulness of time' [Galatians 4:4] for God to send forth His Son had come.   A select nation must be prepared by centuries of discipline.   Time must be allowed for the human race to grow into the historic age so that the proofs of the facts connected with the advent of the Son of God could be adequately established.   A language more copious and precise than any earlier one must be developed; a world government, wider and stronger than the world had before seen, must be consolidated, to favor unwittingly, even while it wickedly opposed, the dissemination of the gospel.   And then, when this wonderful preparation was completed, in due season, Christ died." Lipscomb and Shepherd, *Romans*, p.96.

[52] Lard, *Romans*, p.157.

[53] Meyer, *Romans*, p.186.

[54] In English, word order is significant, helping the reader to know what is subject, verb, object, etc.   In Greek, where the spelling is varied to show these functions, it was possible to emphasize certain words by placing them either first or last in the sentence.   The order here is, "Christ, we being still helpless, at the right time, for ungodly ones, died."

[55] The word rendered "ungodly" is *asebēs*, which was explained in comments at Romans 4:5.   It is active and positive irreligion, a deliberate withholding from God of His dues of prayer and of service; a standing, so to speak, in battle array against Him (Trench, p.242).

that this behalf or benefit is "instead of." Christ died in our stead, *huper*, [Romans 5:6]; *anti* (Matthew 20:28) and *peri* (Matthew 26:28) state this same fact from only a slightly different standpoint. Aside from all the other evidences, *huper* taken by itself forever establishes the fact that Christ's death was vicarious; he died as our substitute, *instead of* the ungodly, in their place.[56]

This description of the purpose of the death of Christ, and of the quality or character of those for whom He died, serves to bring out vividly the nature or character of God's love.

5:7 – *For one will hardly die for a righteous man; though perhaps for the good man someone would dare even to die.*

For. This "for" appears to continue the thought of verse 6, that Christ's dying for ungodly people is proof that God's love goes far beyond what is common among men. Taking an illustration from the known conduct of men, Paul says, scarcely can any be found who love a good man enough to die for him, let alone, as God did, love enough to die for sinners and ungodly men.

One will hardly die for a righteous man. The general idea of this and the next phrase is obvious, namely, to set forth in bold light how Christ's death for ungodly men transcends most all human instances of self-sacrificing love for others. However, the exact meaning of several of the terms is doubtful. "Hardly" says that this is an event that one cannot expect to occur often. But just what is the import of "righteous" in this passage?[57]

Though perhaps for the good man someone would dare even to die. This clause seems to present an exception to what was just said in the first half of the verse. "Though" represents the Greek word *gar*, which is usually translated "for."[58] "Perhaps" or "possibly" is a good rendering of *tacha*; it reflects the fact that "hardly" (*molis*) differs slightly in meaning from "perhaps." Who is this "good man" for whom some might dare to die? Three answers have been given to this question in the commentaries. (1) There are those

---

[56] Lenski, *Romans*, p.345. It has seemed appropriate to emphasize this point about the substitutionary nature of Christ's death precisely because some 20th century theologians have doubted or denied it altogether. The "slightly different standpoint" of *anti* (which *does* mean "in place of") and *huper* has been well stated in Lange's commentary, p.164. "*Huper, for, for the good of*, [in the interests of]. It is a fuller conception than the idea *instead of, anti*."

[57] The word translated "righteous" was used at Romans 1:17, and will appear again at Romans 5:19. It seems to have a different meaning here in 5:7 than in those other two places. Here, it seems to describe the man who does right according to human standards. More will be said about this in the comments on "good man" in the next phrase.

[58] As indicated in notes at Romans 1:9, "for" either provides an explanation of, or gives a reason for, something just said. The reader of the Greek text will have noted that the word *gar* appears three times in rather close succession in this passage: the first word in verse 6, the first word in verse 7, and now at the beginning of this second clause in verse 7. If this third instance were also translated "for," this clause being discussed would be understood as giving a reason for saying "hardly" in the previous clause. Paul cannot affirm that such self-sacrificial acts never occur, but they are not frequent, he can affirm.

who affirm that "good man" is a synonymous term for the "righteous man" in the previous clause.[59]   (2) There are those who have affirmed that "righteous" and "good" are neuter words, meaning a "righteous cause" or a "good cause," but the context (which speaks of the kind of *men*, rather than the *cause*, for which Christ died) appears to be against this. (3) The most commonly presented view is that the "good man" is one who is more attractive (he inspires attachment and devotion because of being a benefactor) than the "righteous" man who is merely just.   Typical of the attempts to explain the alleged distinction between the synonyms is this:

> The distinction between *dikaios* [righteous] and *agathos* [good] ... corresponds to our distinction between *just* and *kind* ... The righteous man, who does all that the law or justice requires, commands our respect and admiration; the good man, the benefactor, who is governed by love, inspires us with love and gratitude.   Then we would have the following sense: "It is hardly to be expected that anyone would die for a righteous man, though for a good man (i.e., for a kind benefactor or intimate friend), this self-denial might possibly be exercised and does occasionally occur."[60]

When Paul says someone might "dare" (*tolma*, "have the courage to") to die, he is taking note of the fact that such self-sacrifices are usually made headlong and heroically in a moment of sympathetic generosity.

5:8 – *But God demonstrates His own love toward us, in that while we were yet sinners, Christ died for us.*

But God demonstrates His own love toward us.   Now comes the point of the illustration, and the contrast between what men "hardly" do and what God does.   "Demonstrates" (or "commends") means to place in favorable light in order to win full acceptance.[61]   "Love"

---

[59] Matthew 5:45; Luke 23:50; and Romans 7:12 are appealed to as showing the words "righteous" and "good" are nearly synonymous.   While indeed in those passages they may be synonymous, the question remains, are they synonymous here in chapter 5?   If the words are taken as being synonymous, then this second phrase is explained simply as being Paul's admission that there are a few known cases in history (Jonathan and David; Damon and Pythias) where a man has loved another enough to die for him.

[60] Lange, *Romans*, p.165.   While favoring the view that the two words are not synonymous in this passage, Lange also expresses the fact that this interpretation is not completely satisfactory.   Vine, on the other hand expresses confidence about the distinction, indeed about the whole passage, in these words: "Justice is the empowering motive of the righteous man; love is that which inspires the good man.   The former meets with respect; the latter meets with affection.   Bearing this in mind, and with regard to the 'for' before 'peradventure' [i.e., 'perhaps'] at the beginning of this second statement, the meaning may be set forth somewhat as follows: – 'To die for a righteous man is difficult – perhaps the idea may be considered improbable in any case – and yet I would not say this, for peradventure for the good man some one would even dare to die.'   This meaning has regard to the differences between the righteous and the good, as well as the fact that both sentences begin with 'for.'   In the Greek there is no definite article before 'righteous,' but there is before 'good,' and this serves to bring out the distinction as in the explanation." Vine, *Romans*, p.76.

[61] The word was used previously at Romans 3:5.   Comments on both passages should reflect that the

here translates *agapē*, the Greek word for "love" which expresses more than just the emotion of the heart. *Agapē* has to do with the mind and the will; it speaks of doing what is spiritually best for another because the one doing the loving sees something of value in that other person.[62]   "God goes far beyond all that man would do or conceive and commends His love to us as deeper, stronger, and purer than human hearts can know."[63] It should also be observed that the will of the Father has something to do with the death of Christ, as indeed with the whole "scheme of redemption."[64]

In that while we were yet sinners.   This is explanatory of the way God demonstrated His love.   The word translated "sinners" is *hamartōlos*, and means "to miss the mark."   It pictures men who missed the mark of honoring God with their lives.   This third in a series of words Paul uses to describe the state of men before being redeemed by Calvary helps to emphasize the surpassing nature of God's love.   It was "sinners," not "good men," whom God loved and for whom Christ died.   "Yet" may repeat the idea emphasized in verse 6 (see footnote #50), or it may imply that for Paul and his readers a change has taken place. Now that they are in Christ they can no longer be classified as "sinners;" their lives now are bringing honor to God!

Christ died for us.   This is the fourth time in three verses that we have had the preposition *huper* ("for").   It means "in our stead, to save us from death.   He took our place; and by dying Himself on the cross, saved us from dying eternally in Hell."[65]

5:9 – *Much more then, having now been justified by His blood, we shall be saved from the wrath of God through Him.*

Much more then.   Paul uses a simple argument *a fortiori*, from the greater to the lesser.

---

word does not so much mean "prove" or "show" or "exhibit" as it does "commend."

[62] "*Agapē*, the Greek word for the greatest of the Christian virtues, is a largely untranslatable word. The real meaning is unconquerable benevolence.   If a man has *agapē*, no matter what other people do to him or say of him, no matter how other people treat him, he will seek nothing but their good.   He will never be bitter, never resentful, never vengeful; he will never allow himself to hate; he will never refuse to forgive. No matter what his fellow men are like in themselves, and no matter what they do to him, he will seek only their good." Barclay, *1 Timothy*, p.114.   Within the limits that God's holiness and justice permit, all the above statements could be said of God's love, too.

[63] Lipscomb and Shepherd, *Romans*, p.97.

[64] "It is not (as represented by some schools of theologians) that the Son, considered apart from the Father, offered himself to appease God's wrath ... but rather that the Divine love itself purposed from eternity and provided the atonement, all the Persons of the holy and undivided Godhead concurring to effect it (cf. Romans 3:24, 8:32; Ephesians 2:4; 2 Thessalonians 2:16; John 3:16; 1 John 4:10)." Barmby, *Romans*, p.124.

[65] Barnes, *Romans*, p.118.   See notes at verse 6 and at Romans 15:3.   Admitting that *huper* has meanings shading all the way from "about" (*peri*) to "in place of" (*anti*), it still is affirmed that this is one of the Biblical expressions used to convey the idea of a substitutionary atonement.   In the two instances *huper* is used in verse 7 it certainly meant "in stead of" or "in the place of."   It can mean no less when used of Christ's death *for* others!

If God's love operated when men were sinners so as to provide a means of forgiveness, certainly He can do what is lesser and preserve those redeemed from future wrath. Justified men will not be disappointed in their hope.   If men who are now Christians were justified by the death of Christ when they were lost in sin, how much more shall they be saved from wrath now that they are restored to God's favor.

Having now been justified by His blood.   Instead of just saying Christ "died" for us, Paul now writes "His blood."[66]   This is sacrificial language.   As Hebrews 9:22 asserts, without the shedding of blood there is no remission of sins.   "The blood of Christ is the great antecedent reason which enables God to be just while justifying the unjust.   In other words, it procures justification.   Belief is a mere condition, not a cause or reason."[67]

We shall be saved from the wrath *of God* through Him.   This is the first use of the word "save" in this epistle.   Note that Paul here distinguishes between initial justification (or the pronouncing of sinners as "not guilty" in the past) and their final salvation from the future wrath of God.[68]   "Wrath" here is the same future wrath threatened in 2:5,8.   Salvation from wrath "through Him" is more than just what was done at Calvary; it is explained in the next verse as being something further guaranteed by the operation of the living, exalted Christ.

5:10 – *For if while we were enemies, we were reconciled to God through the death of His Son, much more, having been reconciled, we shall be saved by His life.*

For if while we were enemies.   "For" indicates we have a reason for, or an explanation of, the statement just made about being saved from wrath.   "Enemies" is the fourth in a series of terms Paul has used since verse 6 to characterize men's condition before redemption.   It is not clear whether it expresses mutual enmity, or whether it speaks of how God regarded sinning men, or whether it simply expresses an alienation from God that men felt because of their sin.[69]   Whatever the meaning, it anticipates the opposite idea about to be introduced, viz., reconciliation.

We were reconciled to God through the death of His Son.   This is the first use of the word "reconciliation" in Romans.   Originally the word meant to "exchange" – like a money changer who exchanged equivalent values.   From there it came to mean "to adjust a difference, to reconcile, to restore to favor."[70]   When a husband and wife have a dispute

---

[66] See notes at 3:25 for the phrase "in His blood."   See notes at 3:24 for "justified."

[67] Lard, *Romans*, p.159.

[68] Salvation is viewed from different aspects in the Scriptures.   Sometimes it is viewed as a past event (2 Timothy 1:9; Titus 3:5).   Sometimes salvation is viewed as a present process for the Christian (see 1 Corinthians 1:18, 15:2; and 2 Corinthians 2:15, where the *present* passive is used).   Sometimes, salvation is viewed as something yet future (1 Peter 1:5; 1 Corinthians 5:5; 1 Thessalonians 5:8).

[69] When men harbor a feeling of "enmity," it has a sinful connotation to it.   We cannot attribute enmity (in this sense) to God, for there is nothing sinful or wrong in His attitudes toward man.   If it speaks of His hostility toward man, it reflects the fact that sinners are objects of His displeasure.

[70] Thayer, *Lexicon*, p.333.

and separate, there is a feeling of hostility and alienation. When they make up, we call it a reconciliation, and the hostility and alienation are gone. So it is with redemption of sinners. Sin caused men to be separated from a holy God. Hostility and enmity ensued. But a reconciliation has been made possible by Jesus going to Calvary. In the case of those who are justified by faith, the separation is over. The alienation is past. A reconciliation has taken place.[71]

> By our enmity, our sin, our ungodliness, we had gotten ourselves into the desperate status that deserved nothing from God but wrath, penalty, damnation; and unless God did something to change this our status, it would compel him to treat us thus. By means of Christ's death God changed this into an utterly different status, one that despite our enmity, etc., enabled him to go on commending to us His love – this very love that changed our status, this love that impelled Christ to die for us hostile enemies of God.[72]

---

[71] A continuing dispute centers around the question of who is reconciled to whom? Some have urged that God is reconciled to man. Others have insisted that it is man who is reconciled to God. The answer hinges in part on the previous expression "enemies" (who was it who had feelings of hostility toward the other?), and partly on what the Scripture teaches elsewhere on this subject.

- Those interpreters who think of man as wholly passive in salvation tend to teach that it was God whose hostility is gone, that it is God who is reconciled to man. For example: "In verse 10 the apostle speaks of reconciliation in terms of its objective accomplishment. *God is reconciled* by the death of His son. 'On man's part nothing has happened; no internal change, no step towards God; all this follows as a consequence of the reconciliation here spoken of.' (Ruckert, as quoted by Hodge). It is to this consequence that Paul now turns in the phrases that follow. The knowledge that God is a reconciled Father in Jesus Christ suffuses the believing heart with exultant joy [verse 11]. Moreover, as God was reconciled by the death of the Mediator, even so believers receive this reconciliation through the mediation of the risen, exalted Christ." Wilson, *Romans*, p.87.

- On the other hand, those interpreters who teach that there is both God's part and man's part in salvation tend to teach that it was man who is reconciled to God. A typical comment on this passage would be: "God has always loved the world (John 3:16). It was this love which dated from all eternity that caused Him to give his Son into death for the ungodly world (Romans 5:8). God needed no reconciliation, nothing to change Him, for God is love – why should HE change? The whole trouble was with US, with what we had made ourselves (enemies), with the state into which we had placed ourselves (sin, godlessness)." Lenski, *Romans*, p.352. Lard, *Romans*, p.159, worded it this way: "The whole doctrine of reconciliation, as in operation, is here stated in one brief sentence. We are reconciled to God, *not God to us*. Reconciliation implies a change, a change from enmity to love, and from disobedience to obedience. But this change takes place wholly in us, and in no part in God. God is unchangeable; with Him there is not even the semblance of turning. ... Every effort to make it appear that in reconciliation there is a mutual change, a change in God from enmity to love, as well as in us, but dishonors Him, as it seems to me, and perverts his truth."

- Sanday and Headlam, *Romans*, p.129,130, give the most cogent argument for a *mutual* reconciliation – since the anger of God toward sinners (Romans 1:18) ceases at the time of reconciliation. Readers pursuing this topic will want to include 2 Corinthians 5:19; Ephesians 2:16; Colossians 1:20,21; and Romans 11:15 in their study.

Murray, *Romans*, p.172, is an excellent source for the argument that "enemies" should be understood passively, not actively. That is, it does not refer to man's enmity toward God, but rather God's holy hostility toward sinners. He further asserts that the point of Romans 5:9-11 is that God Himself provided the means for the removal of His hostility towards sinners.

[72] R.C.H. Lenski, *The Interpretation of St. Paul's Epistle to the Romans* (Columbus, Ohio: Wartburg Press, 1945), p.351. "Death" here is viewed as all along in this passage, as a propitiation, with a view to justification. See Romans 3:24,25.

What God did at Calvary is made known to men through "the ministry of reconciliation" and the "word of reconciliation" that invites men to "be reconciled to God" (2 Corinthians 5:18-21). In this passage, Paul will say more about this part of reconciliation as he says, "we have now received the reconciliation" (verse 11).

Much more, having been reconciled. Again we have an argument from the greater to the lesser. If a *dying* Savior could effect the reconciliation of *enemies*, it surely is to be expected that a *living* Redeemer would continue to do all that is required to complete the deliverance of His *friends*. The reconciliation was accomplished objectively at Calvary; it is experienced subjectively at the time a man is initially justified.

We shall be saved by His life. "Saved" likely has the same meaning it did in verse 9. Possibly included is our present preservation, and certainly included is our future deliverance, and all this is dependent on the living Lord.[73] What is explained in Romans 8:23, 8:34 and 1 Corinthians 15:22ff, is also implied. Paul has emphasized the love of God, the blood of Christ, the reconciliation of enemies, the justification of sinners, and the activity of the living Redeemer as real reasons the Christian can be confident his hope of glory will not be disappointed. Perhaps it is true that this all is but Paul's expansion of Jesus' own affirmation, "Because I live, you shall live also" (John 14:19).

5:11 – *And not only this, but we also exult in God through our Lord Jesus Christ, through whom we have now received the reconciliation.*

And not only this. Something more than being reconciled and saved by His life, is the idea. While we are being saved by the living Lord, we shall continue to boast in God.

But we also exult in God through our Lord Jesus Christ. "Exult" is a present participle,[74] agreeing with the "we" in "we shall be saved." The idea thus presented is that, while we are being saved, we shall continue to boast in God. The word translated "exult" was translated "boast" at Romans 2:17 and 23. Perhaps the NASB translators chose a different English word in this passage because there is a boasting that is bad (like the Jews of chapter 2 were doing), and a boasting (exulting) that brings honor to God (like this verse suggests). Christians boast in God – not in themselves, nor in their ancestry; they exult in who God is and what He has been doing in history, and this kind of boasting praises Him.

---

[73] Some suppose that "by His life" is a reference to living the Christian life. "We are saved by entering into Christ and living His life, reproducing the life of Christ in our lives." Lipscomb and Shepherd, *Romans*, p.99. A more likely suggestion is that in "by His life" there is a contrast between the death of Christ, and His living state subsequent to His death. "In His life-state, or living state, subsequent to His death, Christ consummates all the provisions of salvation [see Hebrews 9:24-26], and in person superintends the work. In this way He brings it to a successful end, and so saves us by His life, or by being alive." Lard, *Romans*, p.160.

[74] A few manuscripts read the same way verse 3 reads, a form that could be either indicative or subjunctive. If this reading were correct, then verse 11 would give a third thing the readers were exhorted to boast about – hope of the glory of God (verse 2), tribulations (verse 3), and God Himself (verse 11). The alternate reading is so weakly attested that the United Bible Society's Greek Text does not even list it in its apparatus.

How one can "boast in God" and do it "*through* our Lord Jesus" is not easy to explain. Wycliffe Commentary suggests that "boasting" here means to "express devotion to," and it is only through a relationship with Jesus that a man can express his devotion to God.[75]

Through whom we have now received the reconciliation. Since this language is the most difficult in this whole passage to harmonize with the idea that it is man's hostility to God that is removed when reconciliation takes place, some have used this phrase to show that in the Pauline doctrine of reconciliation, it was God's attitude toward men that changed from hostility to favor; reconciliation was something men have received.[76] Others have explained that men individually receive the reconciliation when they appropriate it "by faith" (5:2). That it takes a rather lengthy presentation to arrive at this conclusion can be seen from the following typical comment on this phrase:

> To receive the reconciliation is to receive that which effects it. We are reconciled to God by the death of his Son. Hence, to receive the reconciliation is to receive Christ's death; and to receive his death is to believe in it and accept it as an atoning sacrifice for our sins.[77]

Even though such an explanation seems at first cumbersome, it may be on the right track, for it gathers together many of the ideas that are presented in the context. "Through whom" very likely expresses the mediation of Christ in this matter of reconciliation, just as the mediation of Christ was emphasized in verses 1 and 2 in relationship to peace with God and access *by faith* into grace. The "faith" that was there specifically stated is surely implied here in verse 11. "Now" tells us that the reconciliation is something already enjoyed; one does not have to wait until the last day to be reconciled. When a man is justified by faith is the time when he receives the reconciliation.[78]

---

[75] A Berkeley Mickelsen, "Romans," in *The Wycliffe Bible Commentary*, edited by Charles Pfeiffer and Everett F. Harrison (Chicago: Moody Press, 1962), p.1197.

[76] See footnote #71, above. Arndt-Gingrich, *Lexicon*, p.415, explain that it reads "*receive* the reconciliation" because men are passive (i.e., they are acted upon by God) in the matter of salvation.

[77] Lard, *Romans*, p.160. "'The reconciliation' ... which is effective for the whole world of sinners by changing their status from unredeemed to redeemed men does not save any of them until it is bestowed individually and received individually. Unbelief rejects the reconciliation and thus perishes despite it. The reconciliation is there, but unbelief turns from it and thus is not justified on the basis of it but causes the blood of Christ to be shed in vain. This is tragedy, indeed. But we who by faith clasped this reconciliation to our hearts were justified because of it, sing praises to God, and all our exultation is made possible 'through our Lord Jesus Christ,' through whom God reconciled us to himself." Lenski, *Romans*, p.356.

[78] The KJV reads "by whom we now have received the atonement." 300 years ago, this translation was entirely satisfactory, but the word "atonement" has changed meanings since, so that it now gives the English reader a wrong idea. Originally, it meant to make at one [reconcile] those who were before estranged. In the 20th century, "atonement" means "that which constitutes the cause that makes reconciliation possible." Since the same root word is used in verse 11 as was used in verse 10, and since we are not talking about the *cause* but the actual removal of feelings of alienation, it seems best to use the same English word to translate both verses. The only other places in the New Testament where the word is used are Romans 11:15 and 2 Corinthians 5:18-20.

B. God's Plan of Salvation (Justification by Faith) Involves Blessed Effects on the Whole Human Race.   5:12-21

Summary: Verses 12-19 present a comparison of the effects of the Fall of Adam and the redemptive act of Christ.   What we lost in Adam (*viz.*, physical life) through no act of our own, we regained in Christ through no act of our own (*viz.*, when Jesus returns, all men will be raised from the dead).   Further, the death of Christ does much more than just give us back our physical life.   It makes provision for the forgiveness of our personal sins – something the Law of Moses was never intended to do, verses 20 and 21.

5:12 – *Therefore, just as through one man sin entered into the world, and death through sin, and so death spread to all men, because all sinned –*

Therefore.   The premise to which verse 12 is connected is not easy to determine with certainty.   Perhaps it is connected with the general thought in the whole preceding paragraph.   Perhaps, as 5:1 was one conclusion drawn from the assertion about justification by faith (3:28), so 5:12-21 is a second conclusion drawn from that undeniable assertion.   God's way of saving men has numerous blessings flowing out from it – blessings to believers, blessings to the whole race.

This paragraph into which we are now entering has often been called one of the most difficult parts of the New Testament to understand and explain.   There are several things which make the passage difficult: (1) There is a broken sentence, as indicated by the dash at the close of verse 12 in the NASB.   Verse 12 is the first member of a comparison, but where is the second member?   Is it suppressed, or is it finally introduced when we get to verse 18?[79]   (2) In this passage, Paul uses terminology that was perfectly familiar to his 1st century readers, but which are not such everyday familiar terms to 21st century readers.   (3) Adding to our difficulty, these verses were the ones in which Augustine discovered his doctrine of original sin – namely, that as a result of Adam's sin, a fallen nature, an old sinful nature, is automatically passed on to each baby that is conceived and born into the world.   Thus, anyone studying Romans is almost forced into a study of the effects of Adam's sin to the race.[80]   (4) Lastly, in the course of this paragraph there are Greek words (roots) that

---

[79] The KJV translators put verses 13 to 17 inside parentheses to indicate their opinion that verse 18 is the second member of the comparison.   This is the explanation this commentator has determined is most likely correct (reasons for its acceptance will be given from time to time in the comments), but the reader should also be aware not all agree with this conclusion.   Lenski, for example, denies the idea that verses 13-17 form a parenthetical statement.   So does J. Barmby in "Romans" in *The Pulpit Commentary*, edited by H.D.M. Spence and J.S. Exell (Grand Rapids: Wm. B. Eerdmans Publishing Co., 1962), Vol.18, p.125.

[80] Many Bible students will be offended and horrified that anyone would question, let alone reject, the doctrine of original sin, as taught by Augustine, and later by Calvin.   Let it be observed that this commentator has no wish to say anything other than what God's Word says on the subject.   If it teaches that I as a man inherit concupiscence (a desire to do evil, and only the ability to sin) from Adam simply by virtue of my physical birth, then I wish to believe it, admit it, and teach it.   If the Bible does not teach original sin as Augustine and Calvin believed it does, then this commentator does not wish to believe or teach what they did.   Does the Bible teach an inherited sinful nature or not – that is all the discussion is about in the

have slightly different suffixes attached – which thereby change the meaning greatly – but which are very difficult for the translator to express.[81]

Just as through one man. "Just as" obviously indicates a comparison or parallel, but where is the second part of the comparison?[82] It would seem that verse 18, which begins with "so" is the second half of the comparison. Putting the two verses together, we have "*just as* sin and death entered the world because of one man's sin and so spread to all men, ... *so* the free gift of 'justification of life' comes to all men because of one Man's 'act of righteousness'." The "one man" is explained in verse 14 to be Adam. As Paul writes on in this passage, it quickly becomes evident that he regarded the account of Genesis 3 as being an authentic, historical account.[83] His whole argument turns on this important fact that the whole human race has come from Adam: he regarded Adam as the first man, whose disobedience to God's commandment had far-reaching consequences for the whole human race.[84]

Sin entered into the world. "Sin" here is a translation of *hamartia*, the word that means

---

notes following. There is no wish or attempt to reject what God actually says is man's condition since the Fall. Our only wish is to understand what He actually says our nature or condition is since Adam's transgression and the passing on to the race of the penalty for that transgression.

[81] For example, see *dikaiōsis*, *dikaiosunē*, and *dikaiōma*, all of which are translated by the same word in some English versions. In the verses that follow, the comments will explain the difference in meaning where these different words appear.

[82] Charles Hodge, *Commentary on the Epistle to the Romans* (Grand Rapids: Wm. B. Eerdmans Publishing Co, 1953), p.145. Likewise interpret W.J. Conybeare and J.S. Howson, *The Life and Epistles of St. Paul* (Hartford, CT: S.S. Scranton Co., 1910), p.555,556.

[83] Readers who are cognizant of Neo-liberal and Neo-orthodox theologies in the 20th century will also be aware that both, having first accepted the historical-critical method of interpretation, have been wont to affirm that there was no such individual as Adam, but rather that "Adam" is a sort of religious "everyman." That is, what is told about that non-historical character is a valid truth of what happens to all men. Genesis 1-11 are explained away as being mythological or poetical language, rather than an actual historical account. Behind the readiness to accept the historical-critical method is a desire to adapt the Bible's teaching so that it matches the "assured results" of modern philosophy or modern science, in hopes that the resulting position will be easier to defend against the attacks of unbelief. However, J.G. Vos has pointed out the consequences of such a capitulation to the prevailing climate of skepticism: "This argument of Paul in Romans 5 depends absolutely for its validity on the fact that as Jesus was a historical person, so Adam was a historical person. There cannot be a proper parallel between a mythical Adam and an historical Christ. Adam is as essential to the Christian system of theology as Jesus Christ is. Christ is, indeed, called in Scripture 'the second Adam' or 'the last Adam.' Any theory which tends, as the common form of evolution does, to eliminate Adam as a real historical person, is destructive of Christianity. Yet this very thing is done by the common form of evolutionary theory. It has no more room for a real Adam than it has for a real fall of mankind into sin. And if Christ as the second Adam came to undo the harm done by the first Adam, then we must needs continue to believe in the reality of the first Adam." "Surrender to Evolution: Inevitable or Inexcusable?" *Torch and Trumpet* 16:2 (February, 1966), p.20.

[84] Paul's imprimatur on the Genesis account also flatly contradicts the "Secret Doctrine" taught by New Age Movement that originally there were *seven* races that originated on Atlantis – the races being the Aryan master race, plus the Toltecs, Rmoahals, Tlavatli, Turanians, Akkadians, and Mongols. The New Testament plainly asserts that all the nations that dwell on the face of the earth came from "one" (i.e., Adam). See Acts 17:26, Romans 5:12, and 1 Corinthians 15:22.

to miss the mark.[85]   "World" here evidently stands for the human race, for the context goes on to speak about "all men."[86]   The verb "entered" implies that "sin" already existed elsewhere before it came into the world.   Indeed, the Bible speaks of the origin of evil in heaven (Revelation 12:7-9),[87] and of the activities of the devil on earth before Adam sinned (2 Corinthians 11:3; 1 Timothy 2:14), but the first act of sin *in the world* (and that brought consequences for all Adam's descendants) was when Adam transgressed God's command about not eating of the tree of the knowledge of good and evil.[88]

And death through sin.   Adam was responsible for bringing two evils into the world – "sin" and "death."   Death was introduced into the world because Adam sinned.   "If, after his first sin, Adam had never committed another, nor had any other man ever sinned, still

---

[85] See notes at Romans 2:12 and 3:7 where the root meaning of this word was explained. Meyer's note deserves study: "Sin. 1. Not sinfulness, *habitus peccandi* – for the word never is so used in the Bible. 2. Not original sin. 3. Not merely actual sin in abstract. 4. But what sin is according to its idea and essence, consequently the determination of the conduct in antagonism to God, conceived however as a force, as a real power working and manifesting itself – exercising its dominion – in all cases of concrete sin (cp. v.21, 6:12,14, 7:8,9,17, al.)." Meyer, *Romans*, p.195. Compare with this Gifford's explanation: "*Sin* is here viewed as a whole, and St. Paul points to the source from which all human sin has flowed; any distinction therefore between the propensity, the act, or the habit, would here be out of place." *Romans*, p.116. Arndt-Gingrich, *Lexicon*, p.42,43 after listing "the action (*hamartēsis*), as well as its result (*hamartēma*), of every departure from the way of righteousness" and "a condition or characteristic quality" as explanations for "sin," then go on to explain how in Paul "sin" is often personified as a "ruling power" which men serve, and from which men can be freed. They also indicate their opinion that "sin as a ruling power" is what is intended in Romans 5:12.

[86] "World" is used with several meanings in Romans. At 1:8, the sense seems to be "earth, this terrestrial ball on which we live." At Romans 3:6,19, it evidently is limited to "mankind, the human race." The decision about the meaning of "world" (in 5:12) has far-reaching implications when it comes to understanding what is the Biblical worldview. In a moment, Paul will say that "death" also entered the world when Adam sinned. If "world" is not limited just to the human race, then this verse would teach that there was no death (neither in animals nor plants) in the world before Adam sinned. If "world" is limited to the "human race," then one could have animals not only living on earth before Adam (as Genesis shows is true), but one could also hold that the animals were dying before man was created. Romans 8:20 will show that creation was subjected to futility at some time in the past: was the time when Adam sinned? Is there some relation between "death entered the world" (5:12) and "futility" (8:20) becoming a universal curse on all creation?

[87] How it was possible for the devil himself to sin in the beginning (after all, doesn't one need a "temptation" and a "tempter" to induce him to sin?) is nowhere explained in Scripture. That sin could exist at all in a universe where God is, is one of those questions that has long baffled human reason. One can only surmise that God's determination to create a moral universe where man could make a choice of necessity required that some means be temporarily permitted that would offer him the wrong choice.

[88] It is true that Eve had something to do with the introduction of sin into the world, for the Bible elsewhere indicates she was first in the transgression (Genesis 3:6; 1 Timothy 2:14). Several suggestions have been proposed to explain the apparent contradiction between how it is that Eve could sin first, while Paul here attributes to Adam the introduction of sin into the world. (1) The name "Adam" was given to the *created pair*. Genesis 5:1,2 (ASV) says, "In the day when God created man ... male and female created He them ... and *called their name Adam*." (2) Another suggests that the sin of the woman was not complete in its effects without the concurrence of the man. Thus, even though Eve committed the first sin, it was not until Adam sinned that the effects of sin entered the world.

death for the whole human race would still have followed. It followed not from his second sin, nor third, nor from all. It followed from his first only."[89] "Death" speaks of physical death, the death of the body, as indicated in verse 14.[90] The relation between sin and death is not so much cause and effect, as it is crime and penalty. God had decreed beforehand that if Adam sinned, mortality would be the penalty.[91]

And so death spread to all men. "And so" equals "in this manner, in consequence of which." Beginning with this phrase, the rest of verse 12 and the verses following explain in great detail exactly what was meant in the first part of verse 12, namely, what "sin and death entered the world" meant. Adam's sin resulted in a penalty of physical death to the whole race. The reason all Adam's descendants die physically is because Adam sinned. From the moment a man is born, his body begins to die. Sooner or later, each man experiences the return to dust that Adam's body suffered. The decreed penalty pervades the whole race.[92]

---

[89] Lard, *Romans*, p.165.

[90] Two evidences are regularly appealed to in order to show that the "death" Paul had in mind is physical death. Not only is an appeal made to the context, verses 13-17, where physical death is the topic, but most students of the Bible also recognize that behind Paul's expression is what is said in Genesis 2:17 and 3:19. In Genesis 2:17, God threatened, "in the day that you eat from it you shall surely die (Hebrew, "dying, you shall die")." In 3:19, after man had eaten, that threatened penalty was put in force. We read, "By the sweat of your face you shall eat bread, till you return to the ground, because from it you were taken; for you are dust, and to dust you shall return." It would be hard to believe that Adam understood this language of anything but physical death. We admit that Adam was finally 930 years old when he died, but this delay in the infliction of the penalty is no proof that "you shall surely die" meant something else (e.g., punishment in hell) other than physical death. When Adam sinned, he began to die. Before Adam sinned, he was a perfect physical specimen, not susceptible to sickness and death. After the Fall, he is susceptible – and this slow process of dying is the physical make-up that all men have inherited from Adam by virtue of physical descent.

[91] Adam suffered more penalties than physical death (there were other temporal punishments for his sin – e.g., expulsion from the presence of God and the garden, and even the earth was cursed on his account, Genesis 3:14-19), but physical death was what was passed on to the whole human race. There are verses in the Bible that teach that there is a spiritual death that results when a man commits his own first sin (Ezekiel 18:4; Romans 6:23; James 1:15; Romans 7:9-11), and no doubt this happened in Adam's case, too. But such "spiritual death" is hardly the topic in Romans 5. If it is true that "physical death" and not "spiritual death" is the topic in chapter 5, then those who believe chapter 5 teaches original sin and total depravity inherited from Adam are in error. (See Special Study #4 on this whole, difficult theological problem at the close of comments on chapter 5.) This phrase also may have a bearing on the question of how man's body was created – mortal or immortal. It might be affirmed that if because of sin, man's physical body became mortal, then it follows that he was created immortal – or at least would have become immortal through eating of the tree of life in the midst of the Paradise of God (Genesis 3:22). (The nature of man's *soul* [is it an immortal thing?] is another topic altogether.)

[92] "Now, assuming death to be, as to our present state, no more than an adequate penalty of a *single sin*, the nature of sin becomes a little more real to us. One sin is an enormously terrible thing. At this rate (the death of every single human being), what would be an adequate penalty for the sins of a single life lasting a period of 50 years? The question is perfectly bewildering!" Lard, *Romans*, p.167.

Because all sinned – .   "Because"[93] gives a reason why "death spread to all men."   Paul says that, when Adam sinned, all of Adam's physical descendants "sinned" too.[94]   How can this be?   "All sinned" when Adam did because the whole race of mankind has come from Adam.[95]   Not that they sinned *personally*; rather, they sinned *representatively*. Adam stood for and represented the whole of his posterity.[96]   Our connection with Adam is a connection of physical descent, down through generation after generation.   What happened to Adam's body when he sinned, we inherit by virtue of that physical relationship.[97]

---

[93] "Because" is just one possible translation of the Greek, *eph' hō*.   The Latin Vulgate translators thought *hō* was a masculine pronoun whose antecedent was "one man."   They translated "*in whom* all have sinned."   This in turn aided the development of the doctrine of an inherited sinful nature from Adam. A second way to translate is to understand that *hō* is a masculine pronoun whose antecedent is "death." "In the death penalty imposed on Adam is inherently included the idea that all men sin."   This, too, hearkens of the doctrine of original sin.   A third way to explain the Greek is to say that *eph' hō* (being the abbreviated way of writing *epi touto hoti*) is a conjunction meaning "because."

[94] The KJV here could be misleading.   It reads "all *have* sinned," which might lead the reader to believe that Paul is talking about each person personally having committed acts of sin, which have resulted in "death" for them too, just as the Fall did for Adam.   The use of the helper "have" is not warranted since the Greek verb is an aorist tense, not a perfect tense.   Further, the introduction of the idea that all men die physically because *they* have each personally sinned (rather than because *Adam* sinned) is completely foreign to the context, and to what Scripture presents elsewhere.   Against the interpretation that men die physically because of their own personal sins is the fact that infants, who have never personally and actually sinned, sometimes die.   Death, in the case of these sinless ones, must result from some other cause than that it is a penalty for their own sins.   Instead, it is because of Adam's sin that all men (including infants) die physically.

[95] The expression "all sinned" cannot be so explained as to become evidence for the doctrine of original sin.   To explain "all sinned" as is done by many, as though it means "original sin" or *habent peccatum* (i.e., only the ability to sin remains in mankind after the Fall) is to disregard linguistic usage.   The word *hēmarton* means "they sinned," and nothing more.   To confirm this, consult the lexicons on the meaning of the word.

[96] This is one of those "1st century expressions" that make this passage difficult for 21st century readers to understand.   Jewish readers would immediately understand this language.   "In Hebrews 7:9,10, we have a parallel case, which may shed some light on the statement here in Romans.   It is there said of Levi that, before he was born and while he was still 'in the loins' of his ancestor Abraham, he 'paid tithes' to Melchizedek.   Now if Levi, while still in the loins of Abraham, could and did pay tithes, with equal certainty could the whole posterity of Adam, while still in him, sin."   Lipscomb and Shepherd, *Romans*, p.102. Another verse from Paul also shows that it must have been "representatively" that all sinned in Adam.   1 Corinthians 15:22 reads, "In Adam all die."   The language admits of but one interpretation, namely, that all die as a consequence of the sin Adam committed; that is, 'all die in him.'   Again, the verb "sinned" is an aorist tense, just as were "entered" and "spread."   All three are historical aorists, and point to what happened at one time in the past.   It will not do to attempt to say that "all sinned" at a different time than Adam did.   Therefore, since they were not even born yet, the "all" must be represented by their common ancestor.

[97] It should be emphasized that the only penalty contemplated for this "sin" that is attributed to *all* representatively, is that of physical death.   It is for actual, *personal* sins (not the sins of someone else) that the Scriptures threaten punishment in hell.   Hence, no one of Adam's posterity will ever, after dying physically, be punished further for what Adam did.   If any of his descendants suffer in the next life, it will be because of their own unforgiven personal sins.

There is this penalty of physical death due to our physical relationship with Adam because God so decreed it.[98]   And Paul's argument will be that there is a relationship, too, between what Christ did and the whole race, precisely because God so decreed it.

5:13 – *for until the Law sin was in the world; but sin is not imputed when there is no law.*

For until the Law.   "For" indicates that verse 13 is a continuation of the explanation of verse 12a that was begun in verse 12b.[99]   Verse 12b has said that "death spread to all because all sinned".   This is the statement that is now illustrated and explained.   It was Adam's sin that really did bring physical "death" to the whole race.   The word "law" here denotes the Law of Moses,[100] and the word "until" covers all the time between Adam and Moses, as verse 14 specifically reads.

Sin was in the world.   "Sin" is a translation of *hamartia*, the same word used in verse 12, though the Greek in verse 12 is "*the* sin" while in verse 13 there is no article.   Lenski explains the significance of the absence of the article in this way: "There is no article, 'sin' as such, all kinds of sin.   After '*the* sin' as a deadly power came in through Adam's transgression, its presence appeared everywhere: 'sin (of all kinds) was in the world,' everywhere."[101]   The point being made is this – it was not from personal individual acts of sin that the physical deaths of the sinners resulted.   Physical death was the result of Adam's sin.

But sin is not imputed when there is no law.   To "impute" sin to a person is to credit or

---

While we suffer no other *punishment* than physical death, it is possible that Adam's descendants suffer some *consequences* because of what he did.   To illustrate: A man may commit murder, and be sentenced to be executed for the crime.   There is also the distinct possibility that the man will suffer punishment in the next life too, if he is found guilty (unforgiven) in the final judgment.   After he pays the death penalty, his wife and family suffer humiliation and hardship because the father and breadwinner is no longer able to fulfill his responsibilities to them.   They suffer the consequences, but they are not guilty of committing the murder, nor do they have to pay the penalty for committing the crime.   In a similar way, *in this life*, Adam's descendants live in a world that still suffers from the curse pronounced on it at the Fall. For Adam's descendants, neither the consequences nor the penalty for the guilt extend to *the next life*.

[98] Some will object to taking "all sinned" as being "representatively" on the grounds that it explains the expression "all sinned" in 5:12 in a way that is different from how the same expression was explained in 3:23.   It can be shown, however, that in both cases the explanation given is only what the context seems to demand.   The best evidence that 5:12 means that it was "representatively" that all sinned in Adam is Romans 5:19, which speaks of what God 'constituted' men because of Adam's sin.   'Constituted' is the reason why the notes can speak of what God decreed would result to the race if Adam sinned.   Something that a man himself does personally cannot also be "constituted" of him.   "Constituted" is possible only where the "sin" in "all sinned" was representative, instead of something done actually and personally.

[99] Footnote #79 above explains the parenthesis that was used by the KJV translators to enclose verses 13-17.

[100] Though *nomos* is anarthrous in verse 13a, it refers to the Law of Moses, as the context clearly shows. (See notes at Romans 2:12 for more details about anarthrous *nomos* in Romans.)

[101] Lenski, *Romans*, p.363.

debit his account,[102] to hold him responsible for it, to hold him liable to punishment. In the context, it is "sin that results in physical death" that is or is not being "imputed." But how shall we understand "when there is no law"? It says that "until the Law (from Adam to Moses) ... there was no law." Surely this cannot be taken strictly since it has already been taught in Romans that people before Moses' time had "laws" (revelations from God) to live by.[103] Though the Mosaic Law did not yet exist, there were "laws" in the world – the law of sacrifice (consider Cain and Abel), a law against murder (Genesis 9:6), and also other laws of right and wrong (Genesis 26:5). Had that been a period when men had no laws whatsoever given to them by God, there could have been no personal acts of sin, for sin is transgression of God's laws. Thus, "when there is no law" cannot mean "those pre-Mosaic generations had no laws given to them by God," for Paul has already told us here in verse 13 that "sin (all kinds of sin) was in the world." We therefore conclude that the meaning of this language is that 'there was no law, the violation of which resulted in physical death, given to men by God.'

5:14 – *Nevertheless death reigned from Adam until Moses, even over those who had not sinned in the likeness of the offense of Adam, who is a type of Him who was to come.*

Nevertheless death reigned from Adam until Moses. "Nevertheless" introduces a bold contrast to the preceding verse. A condition was there stated (there was no law like the one given to Adam, with a penalty like 'in the day that you eat from it you shall surely die' attached to it), yet (in contrast to what might be expected) death reigned. People died. Why? The only explanation is that death was passed on to the race because Adam sinned. Physical death is here personified as a tyrant who dominated over all,[104] and that tyrant gained access to those men who lived before the Law of Moses was given (and, indeed, he has access to all of Adam's physical descendants) because Adam sinned.

Even over those who had not sinned in the likeness of Adam's offense. Included in

---

[102] Arndt-Gingrich, *Lexicon*, p.251, inform us that *ellogeō* is a commercial technical term, meaning to "charge (something) to someone's account."

[103] See Romans 1:18,32 and 2:14,15.

[104] Though there were a few scattered exceptions to this statement about death reigning (Enoch, and later Elijah), they do not contradict the point being made. Bible students also sometimes raise the objection that some sins did have a death penalty attached to them in the ages between Adam and Moses – an example being that whoever commits murder is to be executed by society (Genesis 9:6). We may admit that for some sins a man might be put to death at the hands of society, but such a death was not a natural result of that sin as is death resulting from Adam's sin. Again, the deaths of those who died in the Flood is sometimes introduced to prove there must have been laws given to men before the Flood that had the death penalty attached. Instead of the deaths of those people who perished in the Flood being proof against what Paul here affirms, they go to confirm it. Were it not for a penalty to the race that made physical death possible, how would the rising waters have been able to hurt the people in Noah's day? Students also recall that Lot's wife was turned into a pillar of salt because she disobeyed, and the students sometimes think they have found another proof that the explanation offered for these verses is faulty. We reply that she would have died anyway – a natural death because of Adam's sin, were it not for her act that brought a premature death. Her act of looking back merely hastened the day.

"those who had not sinned" would be the whole human family from Adam to Moses.[105] Paul does not say they had not sinned at all, for that they had all sinned (all kinds of sin) has already been affirmed (verse 13a). Paul does say there was one way they had not sinned, namely, "in the likeness of the offense of Adam." "Offense" translates *parabasis*, a deliberate transgression of a distinct commandment.[106] To sin "in the likeness of the offense of Adam" means to break a commandment like the one he broke – one that had a threat like "dying you shall die" (Hebrew) attached to it as a penalty for breaking it.[107]

Who is a type of Him who was to come. That is, Adam was a type of Christ, the One whose coming was promised and anticipated from the time of Adam on.[108] A "type" is a resemblance, a similarity to, or a preview of coming attractions.[109] A type may resemble its antetype in various ways, in single points or in many. In the present illustration, Paul will show some similarities between Adam and Christ; he will also point out some dissimilarities.

> The resemblance between Adam and Christ was their acts and the consequences of their acts. The one act affected the whole human family; that of Christ did likewise. The act of Adam brought death to all men; the obedience of Christ brings all men out of the grave (1 Corinthians 15:22; Acts 24:15).[110]

---

[105] Some suppose that the only members of the human family in view (when it says in this verse that they have not sinned in the likeness of Adam's transgression) are *infants*. Infants, it is argued, before the age of accountability, could not be guilty of personal, deliberate, voluntary sin, as Adam was. The interpretation follows this line: in those days before Moses, many infants perished – in the deluge, and at Sodom and Gomorrah. Not being guilty of personal sin so as to deserve death, they must be suffering because of a penalty put on the race because Adam sinned. While, at first sight, this may be an attractive view, it is rather difficult to see how infants could sin "in the likeness of Adam's transgression." He was an adult, a rational being, who used his will and power of choice to sin. Infants are not capable of sinning like that. Therefore, nothing is gained by trying to limit the phrase being explained to infants.

[106] See *parabasis* explained in notes at Romans 2:23 and 4:15.

[107] Perhaps it should be reiterated that Paul carefully shows there are several differences between Adam's sin and the sins of others. In verse 12 we have seen that Adam sinned personally, while the rest of us sinned representatively in him. Now in verse 14 we see that the penalty attached to the sins (that of Adam, and those of Adam's posterity) is different.

[108] The Greek participle that closes verse 14 could be translated "who *is* to come" or "who *was* to come." If the former translation is correct, the coming was future to the time when Paul wrote; in other words, it is a reference to Christ's second coming. If the ASV/NASB translation ("was") is correct, then the coming was future from the time of Adam; in other words, the reference was to Christ's first coming into the world. It appears that the latter interpretation is correct, since Paul evidently has in mind the death of Christ and His resurrection (as the following verses show), which took place at Christ's first coming into the world.

[109] The Greek word *tupos* is sometimes translated "type," sometimes "figure," and sometimes "pattern." *Tupos* is used of the "mark" made by the nails in Jesus' hands (John 20:25); of the little images pagans made of their gods (Acts 7:43); of the "pattern" or model followed when building the tabernacle (Acts 7:44); and of the "example" to be imitated or followed (1 Corinthians 10:6,7).

[110] Lipscomb and Shepherd, *Romans*, p.104. The dissimilarities are about to be emphasized in verses 15-17.

5:15 – *But the free gift is not like the transgression.   For if by the transgression of the one the many died, much more did the grace of God and the gift by the grace of the one Man, Jesus Christ, abound to the many.*

But the free gift is not like the transgression. Here Paul introduces the first of the dissimilarities in the comparison between Adam and Christ.   In fact, several dissimilarities will be introduced; in each case, Paul begins with a reference to Adam's sin, and then makes reference to Christ's redemptive act, showing how (though both affect the race) the one differs from the other, especially as to its consequences.[111]   The word (*charisma*) translated "free gift," ending in -*ma*, emphasizes the result of Christ's redemptive act.[112] The word (*paraptōma*) translated "transgression," also ending in -*ma*, emphasizes the result of Adam's sin.[113]   Thus, the first point of the contrast between Adam (the type) and Christ (the antitype) is that the *result* of each one's act is diametrically opposite.   Exactly what the result in each case is, Paul now goes on to explain.

For if by the transgression of the one the many died.   The "one" here is Adam, and the "transgression" is his first sin (the "Fall" that has been the topic since verse 12).   The "many" here stands for the whole human race (verses 12 and 18 both read "all men").[114]

---

[111] Earlier in comments on this paragraph, it was noted that one of the things that makes this paragraph difficult to explain is the fact that it is hard even to translate because of the series of Greek words with slightly different suffixes.   Not only must the commentator explain what the verse means, he must also make an effort to translate it first.   There is a series of Greek nouns ending in -*ma*, each of which emphasizes the result of an action (nouns ending in -*sis* simply emphasize the action itself).   How then, when translating into English, can the translator show the distinction between *hē dōrea* (verse 15) and *to dōrēma* (verse 16)?   And how shall he show the distinction between *parabasis* (verse 14) and *paraptōma* (verse 15)?   Further, the verses at hand are exceedingly elliptical.   As we go, we shall have to supply the missing nouns and verbs – and at times it is disputed which noun and which verb should be supplied from the context.

[112] It is from verse 10 that we draw the conclusion that the "death of His Son" is what is here called the "free gift."

[113] *Paraptōma* is a deviation from the path of truth and righteousness, a fault.   Hendriksen, *Romans*, p.180 argues that it sometimes is a mild term (as perhaps Galatians 6:1), and sometimes is a very serious thing (as in Romans 11:11).   Lenski, on the other hand, writes, "The term is not a mild term.   It excludes all excuse, and brings out the full gravity of the act that constitutes 'the Fall.' ... [When this is not recognized] a false contrast is here introduced, namely that 'the Fall' was a mild, inadvertent slip on Adam's part, while Christ's act was a deliberate, purposeful proceeding.   The opposite is true; so grave was the inexcusable Fall of Adam that it killed all men ... Whatever the mild sense of the 'Fall' as found in the papyri and elsewhere may be, only the gravest sense applies in the New Testament." *Romans*, p.366.

[114] "Many" may be another of the Jewish expressions found in this context.   In the light of Isaiah 53:12, where Christ as the one is contrasted to mankind as the many, when this verse in Romans says "the many died," a man familiar with the Old Testament would think of "mankind" as the "many" who died.   The KJV ignores the article "the" before "many," reading "if through the offence of one many be dead," and this translation reflects a Calvinistic bias toward partial or limited atonement.   How difficult it is to make a translation that does not reflect the biases of the translator, and yet how helpful such an unbiased translation is to those who would know just what God says!

By the decree of God, Adam's transgression (the same word used in the previous phrase) resulted in a sentence of physical death to the race.[115]

Much more. Here appear these words again (see verses 9,10). There is a greater degree of certainty about how Christ's death affects the race than how Adam's sin affected the race!

Did the grace of God. See "grace" explained in notes at Romans 1:7 and 3:24. It was because of God's attitude of grace – because, back in eternity, He looked with favor on the man He was about to create – that provision was made for the redemption of man, redemption of both body and soul. "Grace" (God's grace in this phrase, Christ's grace in the next phrase) is the reason why redemption is provided.

And the gift by the grace of the one Man, Jesus Christ. "Gift" here is *dōrea*, a different word from the one (*charisma*) used earlier in verse 15.[116] Here in verse 15b, one thing that results (see the -*ma* ending in *charisma*) from Christ's redemptive act (verse 15a) is

---

[115] "Died" in verse 15 is to be explained in the same way "death" in verse 12 was explained. However, because the verb is an aorist tense, some urge that "died" in verse 15 expresses something more than did "death" in verse 12. So, let it be asked again, In what sense did men *die* when Adam sinned? Some would urge that men died spiritually at the instant Adam sinned, and they die physically in the end. Does the tense of the verb "died" justify such a conclusion that all men die both physically *and spiritually* because of the sin of Adam? It seems not. "That all died physically when Adam sinned is conceded – not died actually and physically at the moment, for then would the race have become extinct; but sentence was then pronounced, provision was then completed, and only a brief respite stayed the end. So sure were all to die, that the event is spoken of as if it had already taken place. But did men also die spiritually in Adam? That Adam, both in body and spirit, was, so soon as he sinned, cut off from vital union with God seems certain, and that, but for the redemption which is in Christ, he would then have died and been forever lost is equally true. But what of his posterity? We deny that Adam's sin ever touched or in any way affected the spirit of his posterity. We deny for lack of proof. The sin of Adam cleaves to his posterity up to the point where body and spirit separate; beyond this point, in this writer's opinion, the spirit is as free from its influence as though the sin had never been committed. But the instant one of Adam's posterity commits a personal sin, his spirit becomes involved; and he now stands where Adam stood when he first sinned. Adam's sin has corrupted our bodies; our own sin [and only our own sin] corrupts our spirits. For Adam's sin we die physically; for our own sin alone can we be lost eternally." Lard, *Romans*, p.177,178. It can be seen from this paragraph that Romans 5:15, as well as 5:12, has a bearing on the doctrine of original sin. If the "death" decreed by God for the race is spiritual death – if the guilt of Adam's sin is passed on to his posterity *spiritually* – then the Bible teaches original sin. But if Adam's descendants are under the penalty of *physical* death (and nothing more) because of Adam's sin, then the Augustinian doctrine of original sin inherited by the race is not taught in the Bible.

[116] Here is another place where the translator has difficulty. Even if he wished to indicate to English readers that the two words for "gift" are different, how would he do it? Sanday and Headlam suggest that *dōrea* could be translated 'boon,' i.e., the highest and best of gifts. *Romans*, p.140.

called a gift (*dōrea*).[117]   Verse 17 will explain that *dōrea* is a reference to "righteousness" (justification, God's way of saving man).   All of a sudden, Paul is talking about salvation from sins, instead of simply physical death and resurrection.   But this should not be surprising.   He warned us in the beginning of the verse about "dissimilarities."   One dissimilarity is that Christ's redemptive act involved more than simple removal of the sentence to physical death.   In the preposition "by" ("the gift *by* the grace ...") Jesus Christ is declared to be the channel by means of which this *dōrea* (salvation) comes to mankind. In the phrase "the grace ... of Jesus," Paul tells us the reason why this *dōrea* is provided. Back in eternity, not only did the Father look with favor on the man about to be created, but so did Jesus.   How Jesus became this channel is here called "the grace of the one Man." That Jesus is here called "Man" immediately reminds us of the incarnation.[118]   The incarnation is one thing involved in the 'how' by which Jesus became the channel.   The context also has spoken of His death, and that too is included in the 'how.'   Even the article "the" before "one Man," though omitted in the KJV, is important, for by it Paul alludes to his presentation of Christ as the antitype of Adam: one man, Adam, affected the race; *the* one Man, Christ, likewise affected the race.   In the *results* to the race there is a similarity; but there is also a dissimilarity, as we shall soon learn, in that Christ's redemptive act potentially has results much more far reaching.

Abound to the many.   Both verbs, "many died" and "[did] abound," are historical.   The former refers to the time when Adam fell; the latter to the time when Christ shed His blood on the cross.   At first sight, "the many" at the close of verse 15 seems to be identical with "the many" in the first part of verse 15.   Now if the expressions are identical, then we have verse 15 teaching universal salvation, for "the many" who died would be the same "many" to whom the gift of righteousness abounds.   Such a doctrine (universal salvation) is surely contrary to what the Bible everywhere teaches, so any explanation of verse 15 that would make it teach universal salvation cannot be right.[119]   Paul himself (verses 16,17) goes on to explain that he did *not* mean to teach universal salvation.   He did teach that everyone

---

[117] Not only does the paragraph say that the sentence of physical death (that was passed on to the race because of Adam's sin) is removed in the redemptive act of Christ, but in addition, Christ's act provided forgiveness of sins to those who will receive it.   Thus, the notes read "*one thing* that results from Christ's redemptive act is here in verse 15b called a gift."

[118] In verse 10, this "man" has been called "His Son."   In the incarnation, God's Son became flesh.

[119] Other expedients are found in the commentaries, as writers try to avoid making Paul contradict what the Bible says elsewhere.   Some have supposed that Adam represented *the whole* of the human race, and Christ represented only a part, and that "the many" in the two members of this verse, when added together, would make up the *whole* of the race.   Such an attempt to explain the passage is to introduce into it a theological doctrine (limited atonement, and reprobation from all eternity of part of mankind) that has been invented by men, rather than one that God Himself has taught in His Word.   Others try to take the first "the many" in an unlimited sense meaning the whole race, and then try to limit the second "the many" to only the redeemed.   While this could be defended in this context, the obvious idea that occurs to most readers of verse 15 is that the two terms are co-extensive.   The explanation given in the notes takes "the many" as co-extensive, but explains that salvation from sins (as distinguished from the resurrection of the body) is only potential for "the many;" whoever participates in this boon does so conditionally, rather than automatically (as is the case with bodily resurrection from the dead).

will be raised from the dead, but he did not teach that all would also be saved from eternal punishment.

5:16 – *And the gift is not like* **that which came** *through the one who sinned; for on the one hand the judgment* **arose** *from one* **transgression** *resulting in condemnation, but on the other hand the free gift* **arose** *from many transgressions resulting in justification.*

And the gift is not like *that which came* **through the one who sinned.** The parallel way verses 15 and 16 begin should tell us that the explanation of the contrast between Christ and His type Adam is being continued.[120] "Gift" here is *dōrēma*, and the *-ma* suffix emphasizes the result or effect of the "gift." As noted earlier, "gift" (*dōrea*) is explained in verse 17 as being "righteousness," i.e., justification, God's way of saving man. The 'unlikeness' of the gift (salvation) is that it must be received (it is conditional), whereas the physical death and resurrection (resulting from Adam's and Christ's act) are not conditional.[121] Or some have worded it that the second contrast (the first contrast dealing with *result* was stated in verse 15) deals with the *quantity* of sins involved. The careful reader will observe that the NASB has a number of words in italics in verse 16, indicating that in the Greek this verse is very elliptical – a number of words that are needed to complete the thought are not specifically written, though the omitted words are implied. In such cases it is perfectly permissible to supply the words that the context demands should be supplied. "That which came" likely repeats the idea found in the verb "entered" used in verse 12. "The one who sinned" refers to Adam's first act of sin.

For on the one hand. Adam's sin and its result is here explained again.

The judgment *arose* **from one** *transgression* **resulting in condemnation.** *Krima* is the word translated "judgment," and the *-ma* ending emphasizes result – thus a good translation would be "sentence" (the sentence a judge pronounces at the close of a trial). When the one (Adam) sinned, God passed sentence on the guilty, and that sentence resulted in "condemnation" (physical death to Adam and his posterity).[122] The word translated "one" can be either masculine or neuter; because the contrast presented in the remainder of the verse deals with "transgressions, the NASB translators took it as neuter and supplied "transgression."

---

[120] The *New English Bible*'s rendering at this place catches the idea: "The gift of God is not to be compared in effect with the one man's sin ...."

[121] This note about 'unlikeness' is based on the fact that in the phrases following, the contrast is between "one transgression" (Adam's) and "many transgressions" (Adam's posterity, except Christ who was sinless). For a moment, Paul drops the Adam-Christ typology, and is contrasting (not one act of Adam and one act of Christ) but the sin of Adam and the sins of his descendants.

[122] As the marginal note shows, the Greek literally reads "the sentence (was) to condemnation." This is no harder to understand than is the modern expression, "he was sentenced to prison." "Condemnation" is the punishment meted out when the one found guilty of sin was sentenced by God. Verse 12 has told us that Adam's sin implicated the whole race in this same condemnation to physical death.

But on the other hand.   Christ's redemptive act and its result is here in view.

The free gift *arose* from many transgressions resulting in justification.   "Free gift" is the way the NASB translators have tried to help English readers see that there are two words for "gift" in this context.   The NASB uses "free gift" when the Greek has *charisma*, and "gift" when the Greek is *dōrea*.   As in verse 15, "free gift" speaks of the results of Christ's redemptive act.   "Many transgressions" tells us that not only Adam's sin, but the personal sins of all of Adam's entire posterity, are covered by the redemptive act of Christ.

"Justification" here is *dikaiōma*, the sentence of a judge acquitting the innocent.[123] A moment's reflection will show that the "justification" here in verse 16 cannot mean (as this English word has sometimes been used in Romans to mean) "reckoned (by God) as righteous or saved."   The "justification" (*dikaiōma*) in verse 16 is something given to all men unconditionally, whereas "salvation" (at times, also, designated as "justification" [*dikaiosunē*]) is conditional (as Romans 1:17 and 3:28 have so forcefully stated).   The "justification" (*dikaiosunē*) of 1:17 and 3:28 is not something given to all men; it is only granted to the faithful.   Therefore, the "justification" (*dikaiōma*) here in verse 16 must not be the same "justification" of 1:17 and 3:28.   In verse 18, the NASB translators will render this same word *dikaiōma* as "righteousness."

5:17 – *For if by the transgression of the one, death reigned through the one, much more those who receive the abundance of grace and of the gift of righteousness will reign in life through the One, Jesus Christ.*

For if.   This seems intended to explain the latter part of verse 16, and shows that the 'verdict of acquittal' indeed is conditional, and is not as extensive as the 'verdict of condemnation' that resulted from Adam's sin.

By the transgression of the one, death reigned through the one.   "The death" (Grk.) that reigned over the whole race was physical death, and it permeated the race because Adam sinned.[124]   One has but to read Genesis 5, the "book of the generations of Adam," and note the solemn repetition of the phrase "and he died," to see that death was reigning.

Much more.   This is the fourth time these words have appeared in chapter 5.   In these words "much more" is the hope of the believer.   Suppose the redemptive act of Christ took care of only the effects of Adam's sin.   Suppose that what we lost in Adam (through no act

---

[123] Paul uses three different Greek words in verses 16-18, all of which are built off the same root, *dikaio*-. In verse 16, it is *dikaiōma*, which the NASB translates "justification."   In verse 17, the word is *dikaiosunē* (the NASB renders it "righteousness"), which has been explained at Romans 1:17 as meaning pardon, or the forgiveness, the salvation that God provides for the believer.   In verse 18, the word is *dikaiōsis*, which seems to speak of no more than being restored to life at the final resurrection, yet the NASB renders it "justification" just as they translated *dikaiōma* in verse 17.   It is certainly understandable if the English reader has difficulty following the thread of thought in verses 16-18 when the translation gives little help, not even distinguishing between different words (though they are from the same root).

[124] See verse 12 on death permeating the race, and see verse 14 on death "reigning."

of our own) is regained in Christ (through no act of our own), and no more.   Where would there be any forgiveness, any possibility of a verdict of acquittal for sinners?   If the life we lost in Adam is returned in Christ, and no more, then Adam's descendants are all lost – condemned for their own personal sins.   But Christ's act does much more!   Not only is the cross a cancelling of the effects of the sin of Adam, but in it there is also atonement for sins for those descendants of Adam who are believers.

Those who receive the abundance of grace and of the gift of righteousness. "Abundance" picks up the word "abound" that was used in verse 15, and enlarges on the idea introduced there.   The root word in "abound" expresses superabundance, overflowing riches.   Jesus' redemptive act greatly exceeds the effects of Adam's sin.   Men "receive" the "grace ... and gift of righteousness" when they obey the gospel.   At that point they are justified by faith.   Here in the word "receive" is where we see that the "much more" is conditional.   There is emphasis on the word "receive;" not everyone is saved and reigns in life as a result of Calvary, like everyone dies as a result of Adam's sin.   "Grace" here is the same as in verse 15; God has expressed His "grace" toward man in an abounding way. The "gift of righteousness" is also abundantly made available; that is, God's way of saving man (*dikaiosunē*) is a gift from God, and it is lavishly given.[125]   The forgiveness of our sins is not something God owes to sinners.   It is not a debt.   It is a gift from God.   Such is the meaning of this phrase, "*gift* of righteousness."

Will reign in life through the One, Jesus Christ.   Earlier, Paul has written "death reigned," and we might have expected "life will reign," but the contrast involves "much more" than this.[126]   It is not just that 'life reigns over us' like death reigned over us. Instead, those who receive the gift of righteousness will themselves "reign in life."   The receiving of the grace and the gift was but a means to an end.   The "life" likely conveys the same idea of abundant life, both in this life and the next, that Jesus spoke about resulting from the new birth.   ("An hour is coming and now is, when the dead shall hear the voice of the Son of God; and those who hear shall *live*," John 5:25.)   In fellowship with the risen Lord, the Christian participates in an exciting way to live now, and after His second advent, the reigning in life continues (2 Timothy 2:12; Revelation 22:5).   Romans 5:21 will explain how the "reigning" ultimately leads to "eternal life" (heaven).   "Through the One, Jesus Christ" reaffirms the idea that Jesus is the mediator of this life.   With His own blood, He redeemed us and made it possible for men to receive the gift of righteousness.   Perhaps also implied is the idea that the resurrected, living Lord has something to do with making it certain the Christian "will reign in life."   That is, part of His mediatorial work is to aid and assist the Christian on his pilgrimage through this life to the next.

5:18 – *So then as through one transgression there resulted condemnation to all men, even so through one act of righteousness there resulted justification of life to all men.*

---

[125] "Gift" is *dōrea*, and this expression "the gift of righteousness" is the one that has helped us understand what Paul had in mind when he used *dōrea* and its cognates in this context.

[126] "Here again is the 'much more:'   death reigned – one king;   all believers shall reign – many kings." Lenski, *Romans*, p.376.

So then. Now that Paul has very carefully explained what he wrote in 5:12, the way is clear to resume and complete the comparison that was introduced in verse 12.[127] The first part of verse 18 repeats (with certain modifications of expression) what verse 12 said; the last part of verse 18 (beginning with "even so") is the completion of the comparison begun in verse 12.

As through one transgression there resulted condemnation to all men. Paul writes "one transgression" here, whereas in verse 12 he had said "one man."[128] He uses "condemnation" here instead of "death" that he used in verse 12, because he has explained (verse 16) that physical death was something God decreed ('sentenced') for the whole race who descended from Adam.[129] The "condemnation" to which all men were sentenced is physical death. If one were to attempt to explain that the condemnation is spiritual death and therefore universal condemnation to hell because Adam sinned, by parity of reasoning he would be forced to admit that Paul taught universal salvation in the second part of this comparison (verse 18b). Since such a conclusion would be contrary to other clear passages of Scripture, we are therefore limited to the explanation that the "condemnation" resulting from Adam's sin has reference to physical death, and to no further effect beyond the grave.

Even so. Here begins the second half of the comparison between the one act of Adam, and the redemptive act of Christ.

Through one act of righteousness. The word translated "righteousness" is *dikaiōma*, the same word just translated "justification" (verdict of acquittal) in verse 16. Since, in the preceding context, Paul has no less than three times referred to Christ's death (verses 6,8,10), and no less than two times in the parenthetical explanation (verses 13-17) specifically named Jesus, and since in the verse 19 he again refers to Christ's death in the word "obedience," there is little doubt what the "one act of righteousness" refers to. God's 'verdict of acquittal' and the redeeming act of Christ are so inseparable that they may be spoken of as though they were interchangeable terms.

There resulted justification of life to all men. The very expression "justification of life," which sounds unusual to our ears, ought to alert us that it is some other "justification" than

---

[127] See footnote #79 and the comments on the first phrase of 5:13, where the thread of thought of this whole paragraph is explained, including the KJV use of parentheses around verses 13-17.

[128] In verse 15 Paul already had substituted "the transgression" for the longer expression he used in verse 12, "through one man sin entered into the world." The whole context has been talking about the Fall of Adam into sin when he committed his first transgression.

[129] Some translations (e.g., ASV) add some words from the context to verse 18a, so that it reads "As through one trespass *the judgment came* unto all men to condemnation." This helps the reader more easily to see that the phrase about a "sentence (judgment) to condemnation (physical death)" in verse 16 is just another way of saying what was already written about 'death entering the world because all sinned (representatively)' in verse 12. In both parts of verse 18, the reader of the Greek text recognizes that he must add both a noun and a verb to complete the sense, and he simply picks up a noun from the previous explanation and adds the verb *ginomai*, which was often omitted in such constructions. Thus he reads that "the judgment came" and, later, "the free gift came."

the justification we met in Romans 1:17 and 5:17 ("gift of righteousness"), i.e., something other than God's way of saving those men who are believers.[130] The Greek word here translated as "justification" is *dikaiōsis*, the same word met at Romans 4:25, and which, it was suggested, had particular reference to the resurrection of the body. "Justification of life" is evidently the opposite of the "death" to which all men were condemned when Adam sinned. What Paul has told us about the blessed effects to the whole race that result from God's way of saving man is this – the penalty of physical death to which God sentenced the race when Adam sinned is removed by sentence of God through the redeeming act of Christ. There is a "justification of life," a "justification" that results in "life." Though all die because Adam sinned, everyone will be raised from the dead because Christ arose.

In other words, this whole paragraph has been Paul's expansion of what he says succinctly in 1 Corinthians 15:22, "As in Adam all die, so also in Christ all shall be made alive." As far as the matter of physical death is concerned, the effects of Christ's death are co-extensive with the effects of Adam's sin. What we lost in Adam through no act of our own, we regained in Christ through no act of our own. But in addition to removing the penalty of physical death, God's way of saving men also provides for "much more." However, the "much more," which also includes the forgiveness of personal sins, is conditional on whether or not the man becomes a believer.

5:19 – *For as through the one man's disobedience the many were made sinners, even so through the obedience of the One the many will be made righteous.*

For as through the one man's disobedience the many were made sinners. So important is all of this, that Paul explains it ("for") one more time. The "one man" was, as we have learned in verse 12, Adam. The "disobedience" (*parakoē*, an unwillingness to hear, active disobedience because he failed to listen[131]) was Adam's first sin. "The many" is synonymous with "all men," as verse 18 has just said. "The verb *kathistēmi* [translated "made"] is a very significant word; indeed, it is the key that unlocks the meaning of the verse. It signifies 'to set down, place, make, appoint, ordain, constitute'."[132] The verb is passive; God is the implied agent. God *constituted* the many sinners. Notice carefully that they were not personally guilty of the act of sinning, but that (on account of Adam's disobedience) they were counted (by God) as "sinners." Before Adam's disobedience, they were not constituted; after Adam's sin, they were. A person is not 'constituted' or 'declared' to be a sinner who is one by his own act.   If he is a sinner by his own act, he is

---

[130] Some interpreters have indeed supposed that "justification" here has reference to God's way of saving man by forgiving their sins. "Such an interpretation involves one in no small trouble, though. Especially does Hodge seem perplexed. If, he reasons in effect, the phrase *all men*, in the latter part of the verse, denotes really the whole human race, then since justification signifies release from personal sins, and life means eternal life; how can we escape the conclusion of universal salvation? Indeed, according to his interpretation there is no escape from it. But his remedy lay in correcting his premises, not in seeking to escape from a correct conclusion from false premises." Lard, *Romans*, p.186,87. We must conclude that "justification of life" has reference to something other than forgiveness of personal sins.

[131] Trench, *Synonyms*, p.243.

[132] Lard, *Romans*, p.187.

so independently of all acts of declaration. It now becomes rather obvious what verse 12 means when it says "all sinned." It means that God "made them sinners," or God 'decreed that they were sinners,' but not that they were personally guilty of sinning in Adam's act.

Even so through the obedience of the One the many will be made righteous. "As it is by the imputation of Adam's disobedience that many are 'constituted sinners,' so it is through the imputation of Christ's obedience that the many are 'constituted righteous'."[133] Christ is the "One" and His death on Calvary is evidently what is here called "obedience."[134] "The many," as earlier in this verse, includes the whole race, all the posterity of Adam. It is as extensive as the "many" who were constituted sinners. "Will be made" (future tense form of *kathistēmi*) perhaps looks forward to the second advent when all of Adam's race will be raised from the dead. "Righteous" is a translation of *dikaioi*, a different word than used anywhere else in this context.[135] This word, different from the one usually used for forgiveness (*dikaiosunē*), evidently means 'righteous for the sole purpose of being raised from the dead.' God, again, is the implied agent. He is the one who determined the whole race would be subjected to the penalty of physical death; He is the one who has determined that the whole race will be raised from the dead. Because of the obedience of Jesus, God can remove the penalty of physical death, and at the same time still be true to Himself. Of course, how it goes with each man spiritually, after the resurrection, will depend on whether or not he has "received the gift of righteousness" (verse 17).

5:20 – *And the Law came in that the transgression might increase; but where sin increased, grace abounded all the more,*

And the Law came in. The ASV reads, "And the Law came in besides,"[136] showing there is a connection to what was said in verse 12. When Adam sinned, "the sin" entered the world, and "death" entered the world. And so, in God's administration of mankind's welfare, it became necessary for the Law of Moses to be introduced into the world for the benefit of the race.[137] Just how it was intended to benefit the race is explained in the next phrase.[138]

---

[133] Wilson, *Romans*, p.94.

[134] Philippians 2:8 tells us about this obedience, when it says "He humbled Himself, by becoming *obedient* to the point of death, even death on a cross." Hebrews 5:8 speaks of the "obedience" Christ learned as He went to Calvary.

[135] See footnote #123 above.

[136] "Besides" does not appear in the NASB, which takes no note of the preposition *para-* in *pareisēlthen*.

[137] As the marginal note shows, this is another example of anarthrous *nomos* (see notes at 2:12). In verse 20 the context seems to demand a reference not just to law in general, but specifically to the Law of Moses.

[138] Barnes makes an interesting conjecture to explain what at first seems to be a break in the line of thought. Paul has been talking about the entrance and removal of the physical death penalty to all mankind, and then all of a sudden he starts talking again about the Law of Moses. Why? "What is said in verses 20,21 seems designed to meet the Jew, who might pretend that the Law of Moses was intended

That the transgression might increase.   Here is the reason why, in God's plan, it became necessary for the Law to enter the world.   We say 'in God's plan' because the Law did not actually enter the world at the time Adam sinned (there was a long time between Adam and Moses, verse 14).   Because *paraptōma* ("transgression") has been used in the preceding verses (15,17) to emphasize the result of Adam's transgression, many would affirm that the emphasis here is also on the result.   As the result of Adam's transgression, "the sin" (verse 12) was in the world, and people needed to be made aware of how much each individual had surrendered to sin's dominion.[139]

How is it that the Law makes transgression increase?   Clearly, the Law does not make men sin (a fact plainly affirmed in chapter 7), but its presence does give "sin" an opportunity to try to extend its dominion.   So one explanation for how the transgression increased is that there would be more acts of sin.   In chapter 7, Paul will give a second possible explanation about how the transgression increased, when he explains that the presence of Law helped men to be more aware of exactly what things God calls "sin." That is, men's self-awareness of the sins they have committed is the thing that increases. A third possible explanation is that men needed to become aware of how bad a thing sin really is, and the presence of the Law helped men's understanding of the heinousness of sin (see 7:13).

But where sin increased.   "Sin" (literally "the sin" in the Greek, the same expression as in verse 12) speaks of personal acts of sin where men fail to listen to God's laws, and surrender instead to the dominion of sin.[140]   The circle of sin keeps widening, as man after man falls to Satan's deception, just as did Adam.

Grace abounded all the more.   "However much the circle of sin widened, the circle of grace still stretched far beyond it; and however great the height that sin attained, grace still mounted above it."[141]   God's love abounds where men recognize and acknowledge their sin.[142]   The devil has never been able to out-perform God.   The Bible everywhere presents God as greatly superior to the devil.   Whatever the devil may do to ruin man (and this is

---

to meet the evils of sin introduced by Adam, and therefore that the scheme defended by the Apostle was unnecessary." *Romans*, p.144.

The NEB reads, "The Law intruded into this process," because the Greek word *pareisēlthen* sometimes signifies to enter secretly or stealthily.   But it hardly fits here to say that the entrance of the Law of Moses into the world was somehow out of place (that it was an "intrusion" where it did not belong).

[139] This paraphrase of "transgression might increase" is justified both by the fact that *hamartia* in the next phrase is clearly a synonym for what happened when 'the result of the transgression' increased, and on the basis that 'increased in men's consciousness' or some similar explanation is likely what is intended.

[140] How "sin" (the devil) tempts a man after the man becomes aware of God's law will be explained in detail in chapter 7.   What is there explained is assumed in the comments here on this phrase.

[141] Lard, *Romans*, p.192.

[142] On "grace," see notes at Romans 3:24, 4:16, and 5:15.   Again, it includes both attitude and action. In verses 20 and 21, "grace" is the opposite of "sin."   If sin is intended by the devil to ruin man, then "grace" is all that God thinks and does to save the man.

something that increases), God's provision for man's forgiveness and reclamation always greatly surpasses it.[143]

5:21 – *that, as sin reigned in death, even so grace might reign through righteousness to eternal life through Jesus Christ our Lord.*

That. This *hina* clause ("that") apparently expresses God's purpose for making His grace to far surpass the increase of sin. It was God's purpose that the benefits of redemption to the whole race should infinitely transcend the hurt and penalty that resulted from sin.

As sin reigned in death. Again, it is "the sin" that is personified and represented as reigning like a tyrant. "Death" should likely be understood in the same sense here as in verses 12 and 14, namely, physical death. It is hard to decide whether the Greek construction for "in death" is a dative of sphere (death was the sphere wherein the sin exercised its dominion), or a dative of agent (death was the agent or means by which the sin established its dominion).[144]

Even so grace might reign through righteousness to eternal life through Jesus Christ our Lord. Grace is also personified, and is pictured as a benign king whose reign is established by means of Christ's atoning death, and whose reign will ultimately issue in eternal life in heaven. While grace reigns, "righteousness" is one thing made available to man.[145] "Righteousness" (*dikaiosunē*) is God's way of saving a man, conditioned on faith, and grounded on the atoning death of Christ, as in 1:16,17 and 3:21-26. Grace's reign also sees to it that righteousness leads to eternal life. "Eternal life" is evidently something more (remember "super abounded" in the previous verse) than merely the opposite of physical death; thus we think of eternal life in heaven. "Through Jesus Christ our Lord" tells us that grace's reign is also intimately related to the mediatorial work of the living Lord.[146]

---

[143] The Greek for "abounded" is *huperperisseuō*, "super abounded."

[144] The KJV reads "sin hath reigned *unto* death," as though "death" were the goal to which sin led. Such a translation might be defended by the context, both verse 12 and the phrase following in verse 21, which does read "*unto* [*eis*] eternal life."

[145] Perhaps in the background of this whole paragraph was a conscious effort on Paul's part to help his readers see that the Law of Moses had nothing to do with the taking away of the penalty passed on to the race because of Adam's sin, nor did it have anything to do with taking away personal sins. But it was God's gracious intention that the Law prepare men to appreciate the redemption that is in Christ – and this was done as the Law helped men to become more aware of what sin is, and of their desperate need for redemption and the righteousness of God. This preparatory value of the Law of Moses is set forth at length in Galatians 3:19-26 and Romans 7.

[146] "The human name 'Jesus' may suffice to describe or emphasize the humiliation of the Incarnate life, but the undimmed glory of His resurrection life demands the full title, 'Jesus Christ our Lord'." Wilson, *Romans*, p.96.

SPECIAL STUDY #3

THE DOCTRINE OF SIN IN THE BIBLE

In order to appreciate what Romans teaches about sin and salvation, and in order to have a background and understanding against which to study and compare the whole question of "original sin," it will be beneficial to survey the key verses in the Scriptures (and also the Apocrypha) that deal with the topic of "sin."

It has been said that there are three classes, or kinds, of sin in the Hebrew Old Testament. (1) The lightest infractions are those that are called *chet, chata, chatta'ah,* or *chattath*, a fault, a shortcoming, a misstep, to sin, err, miss the mark. (2) Of a more serious nature are the sins described by *'avon, 'avah,* or *'aven*, a breaking of a commandment, iniquity. (3) The most serious sins are those called *pesha'* (transgression) and *resha'* (wickedness). There is the idea of rebellion involved in *pesha'*, and of what has become a habit or state in *resha'*. Psalm 106:6 mentions all three words, "We have sinned (*chata*) like our fathers, we have committed iniquity (*avah*), we have behaved wickedly (*resha'*)." A similar threefold list is found in Exodus 34:7, "Who forgives iniquity (*'avon*), transgression (*pesha'*), and sin (*chatta'ah*)."

An even greater number of words are employed for "sin" in the New Testament. (1) There is the *hamartanō* group, including *hamartia* and *hamartēma*, meaning to miss the mark.[1] (2) There is the *parabaino* group, including *parabasis* and *paraptōma*, meaning to transgress [some rule or law], cross over the line.[2] (3) *Anomia* is iniquity, disregard for God's law.[3] (4) *Asebia* is ungodliness, disregard for God's person.[4] (5) *Adikia* is injustice, wrongs done to our neighbor.[5] (6) *Opheilēma* is the word translated "debts" (sins of omission, things we ought to have done) in the Model Prayer, Matthew 6:12. (7) *Ponēria* is the desire to hurt others.[6] (8) *Parakoē* is a failure to listen, resulting in disobedience.[7] (9) Some other words appear but once or twice, such as *agnoēma*, a sin

---

[1] See notes at Romans 2:12, 3:7, and 5:12. The word may mean a single act, a habit, a state, even a power that exercises dominion (as in Romans 5).

[2] See notes at Romans 2:23,27.

[3] See notes at Romans 4:7.

[4] See notes at Romans 1:18.

[5] See notes at Romans 1:18.

[6] See notes at Romans 1:29.

[7] See notes at Romans 5:10.

done in ignorance (Hebrews 9:7), and *hēttēma*, which means being defeated, a failure to render in full measure (1 Corinthians 6:7).

As one studies the various portions of Scripture, it would be best not to try to read back into an Old Testament narrative a New Testament definition or understanding of sin or its consequences, any more than we would read back into the New Testament a modern definition or understanding. Every effort will be made to let each passage speak for itself.

I. SIN IN THE OLD TESTAMENT

A rather standard subdivision of the Old Testament books is to break them up into Law, Prophets, and Holy Writings.[8]

A. The Law

Genesis 3 is the record of the Fall, the sin by Adam and Eve. God gave a command to be obeyed, the devil came and questioned the truthfulness of what God said, and the humans exercised free will in deciding whether or not to eat. The penalty for disobedience was enforced by God, and in addition mankind was driven from the Garden of Eden.[9] Adam still had personal, face-to-face communications with God even after the Fall.

Genesis 4 records Cain's reaction to God's rejection of his sacrifice, and God's kindly discussion with Cain. "If you do well, will not your countenance be lifted up? And if you do not do well, sin is crouching at the door; and its desire is for you, but you must master it," God said. Sin here is personified, and is pictured as waiting for an opportunity to take over in Cain's life. It all depends on Cain's choice – will he continue to disregard God's will, or will he change for the better? Will he "do well," or not? Also, notice that man is not left to himself before or after sinning; there are voices of God that warn, promise, and condemn.

Genesis 6 brings us to the record of the Flood. God sees that the "wickedness (*ra*, Heb., evil, displeasing to God or man) of man was great on the earth, and that every intent

---

[8] This commentator is indebted to E.R. Bernard's excellent article on "Sin" found in the *Hastings Encyclopedia of Religion and Ethics* (New York: Charles Scribner's Sons, 1921), Vol.11, p.528ff, for the general outline of this Special Study and also for some of the key comments.

[9] What was man's "nature" before the Fall? Did it differ after the Fall? For example, was there an "evil nature" that Adam was created with, or did he, after his sin, come to have an "evil nature" (*yetser hara* in the Hebrew)? Genesis 3 just does not say. Let it be observed that the Old Testament does not anywhere teach a corruption of human nature derived or inherited from Adam. All it teaches is that all of Adam's descendants also sinned just like Adam; that is, they all broke God's commands at the instigation of the devil. It has even been said to be remarkable that there is an absence of any further reference to the Fall in the Old Testament (the "Fall" is not itself mentioned even in Job 31:33, Hosea 6:7, or Isaiah 43:27).

(*yetser*, Heb.) of the thoughts of his heart was only evil (*ra*, Heb.) continually" (6:5).[10] The implication in the word "wickedness" is that God had something in mind for the people that they were failing to do, even though He had made known His will to the antediluvians. God's "seeing" the failure suggests the idea that He keeps a record, an account, of men's lives. Also, notice that thoughts as well as actions can be sin. Genesis 6:11,12 read, "Now the earth was corrupt (*shachath*, Heb., harmed, destroyed, ruined) in the sight of God, and the earth was filled with violence (*chamas*, Heb., to oppress, to injure). And God looked on the earth, and behold, it was corrupt; for all flesh had corrupted their way upon the earth." Evil thoughts in the heart soon bear fruit, and the result hurts other men and the environment, too. When sin has become great, God sends punishment, in this case, the Flood. "But Noah found favor in the eyes of the Lord" (6:8). It was possible to live a life pleasing to the Lord. Genesis 6:9 tells us that Noah was "righteous," living in conformity with God's revealed will.[11]

After God began making covenants with Abraham and his descendants, there are times that those outside the covenant relationship still had things right. Abimelech (Genesis 20) is living by Patriarchal law, and in some respects is more righteous than Abraham, who tried lying about Sarah.[12] A special revelation to Israel does not leave all others with no knowledge of sin; they still have divine rules to live by.

In time, Israel receives the Law at Sinai (Exodus 20-24, and developed in Exodus, Leviticus, Numbers and Deuteronomy). The written revelation of God's will should make it comparatively easier for future generations to know God's will than what oral tradition had provided previously. The sacrifices that were offered continually for each breach of the Law would increase men's awareness of the need for something better than bulls and goats to take away sins. The distinction between "clean" and "unclean" should have sharpened men's consciousness of the need to judge all their actions in the light of what God has revealed is pleasing to Him. The physical death penalty that was exacted for many sins should have been an encouragement to stamp sin out of their lives, if possible. A life in harmony with God's commands not only pleases Him, but also results in man's good (Deuteronomy 6:24, 10:13). Toward the close of the 40 years in the wilderness, when Moses had finished giving the Law to a new generation, he spoke about how he had set before them life and death, blessing and cursing. Therefore they were to *choose* life so that they might live (Deuteronomy 30:19).

---

[10] The reader will note that the two words in the expression *yetser hara*, which plays an important part in later Jewish theology, come from the language in Genesis 6:5.

[11] It is likely that "walked with God" (Genesis 5:24) is another way of expressing the same idea. It is not sinless perfection, but it is submission to God. Sin would be the opposite – a self-assertion, a disobedience, a departure from God.

[12] As was the case of Melchizedek alluded to earlier, Amos 1 is a further example of people in the Gentile world who had things revealed to them by God by which they were expected to live.

B. The Prophets

The former prophets teach that the essence of sin is departure from God, and they chronicle Israel's idolatry and punishment for such departure. In Judges, over and over again, departure from God is the cause of sufferings. In the books of the Kings, the standard by which men's reigns are measured is whether they permitted or repressed idolatry in the land. When the Northern Kingdom was taken into captivity, surely men learned (albeit, the hard way) that departure from God carries with it severe penalties from God.

Several lessons are learned from the record of David's sin with Bathsheba. (1) Sins are hard to cover up, yet men foolishly try. (2) There is the possibility of immediate forgiveness when the sinner repents. (3) Punishment after forgiveness may be long and severe. (4) A parent's sins may result in consequences that hurt and bring suffering to the children for several generations. The sin of David when he numbered the people (2 Samuel 24) contains some difficult truths. Somehow, Jehovah Himself "caused" this sin, much the same way the evil spirit[13] which came upon Saul is described as "from God."[14] This fact causes readers to reflect on the interaction of divine control and human freedom.

The later prophets (such as Amos, Hosea, Isaiah, and Micah) helped men see the moral character and moral requirements of God with a clarity not before available to men. Repentance was something people both inside and outside of Israel (cf. Jonah) needed. Jeremiah and Ezekiel show that individual men are personally responsible for their sins; the guilt of the father's sins is not something that hereditarily can be passed on to the children (Ezekiel 18:4,20).

C. The Holy Writings

In the Psalms we find sensitive men confessing sin. Their deep sense of sin arises out of the pressure of suffering in some form. It is not so much the fear of future punishment (though that was a known doctrine), but the pressure of present affliction that led to the confession. Their sins have broken their happy relationship with God, and this relationship the confessor desires to have restored. Psalm 51 is David's confession after his sin with Bathsheba. A verse oft-quoted in almost any discussion of the doctrine of sin is Psalm 51:5, "Behold, I was brought forth in iniquity, and in sin my mother conceived me," and after quoting it, it is not unusual to hear comments about how this verse proves the doctrine of an inherited sinful nature.

---

[13] The Old Testament warns persistently against people being involved in the occult, where evil spirits can have opportunity to extend the dominion of darkness to an extent not otherwise possible to them. In most cases, men's involvement with, and control by, the evil spirits results from their own wickedness opening the way for the evil to come in and take over. But there are also mediumistic tendencies that are passed on to the third and fourth generations, and this seems to be a hereditary consequence that children and grandchildren of evil men must contend with.

[14] See 2 Samuel 24:1. 1 Samuel 16:15-23 and Judges 9:23 are similar. Yet James 1:13-16 will teach that God personally tempts no man. How can it be said God "caused" these evils in the Old Testament?

In Proverbs, man's horizontal relationships with other men is the topic. Thus, righteousness (right relations with other men) is wisdom; sin (wrong relations with fellow men) is folly.

The book of Job shows us the high moral awareness possible for a man without the Law. (Job was likely a contemporary of Abraham, and so was living before the Mosaic Law was given.) That Job is a righteous man is significant. It says something about the possibility of living a life in harmony with God's will, even generations after Adam. Also significant are the devil's activities as he makes accusation against the righteous in the courts of heaven. God places limitations on the devil as the devil is given permission to "test" Job. These limitations are instructive of the relative power or authority of the devil and God; they are not co-equal. The universality of sin is acknowledged (Job 4:17, 14:4, and 15:14-15).[15] Job 31 is a kind of list of things that Job knows are sin; the items included involve much more than a casual reading of Old Testament history, before Job's time, would suggest that God had clearly revealed. Even certain thoughts and desires are enumerated in this list of sins. Job also brings up again the relationship between sin and suffering. What is learned here is that sin does not always bring immediate suffering, and suffering does not always imply sin has been committed.

Ecclesiastes emphasizes the universality of sin in 7:20, "Indeed, there is not a righteous man on earth who *continually* does good and who never sins." So all have sinned (both omission and commissions), and "righteous" does not mean sinless perfect.

Daniel's book is also included in the Holy Writings in the Hebrew Bible. In chapter 9:5-19 is recorded Daniel's confession of the sins of the people that had resulted in their captivity in a foreign land. There is also an approximate date given for the coming of the promised Messiah who would make atonement for the sins of the world. Chapter 12 speaks of everlasting life for the righteous and everlasting disgrace and contempt for the unrighteous. The Old Testament elsewhere had spoken of rewards and punishments beyond this life, as, for example, Isaiah 65,66. The penalties for breaking God's law are not limited just to this side of the grave.

II. BELIEFS ABOUT SIN AS REFLECTED IN THE APOCRYPHA AND PSEUDEPIGRAPHA

That references from the Old Testament Apocrypha are included in this study should not be construed as implying that this commentator holds that the apocryphal books are to be considered as canonical. He does not. Nevertheless, what is there written can surely be helpful in a historical study, for we can see *when* some new expressions and ideas about sin were recorded for the first time.

---

[15] Some writers appeal to these three passages to prove that sin is inherent in human nature.

A. Ecclesiasticus (The Wisdom of Jesus the Son of Sirach)

This work is usually dated about 180 BC, and says much about the righteous versus the wicked. Joshua ben Sira (his name in Hebrew) had a school in Jerusalem, and his book offers advice on practical and Godly living. In language that reminds one of Genesis 4:7, Joshua denies to sinners the excuse that they cannot help themselves, 27:10. He asserts the fact of human freedom and responsibility in very clear terms, 15:11-20. Death to the race is a penalty for Eve's sin, 25: 24.[16] Joshua accounts for physical evils in the world as a necessary complement to moral evil in man, and designed for its punishment, 39:28-31, 40:8-11.

B. The Wisdom of Solomon

A 1st century BC composition, perhaps written in Alexandria, this pseudepigraph shows an indebtedness to Greek ethics and rhetoric.[17] The passages in Wisdom which point out the folly of image worship are similar to those on the same theme in Psalms and Isaiah. It should be noted that Wisdom 12:10ff, which appears to teach a doctrine of hereditary sin, applies it only to the Canaanites, and not to mankind at large.[18]

C. The Prayer of Manasseh

According to 2 Chronicles 33:11ff, when the wicked king Manasseh had been carried into captivity, he repented. This prayer of 15 verses is supposed to be his prayer of repentance, but more likely was composed (by a Jewish author in Palestine?) between the 2nd century BC and the 1st century AD. In this confession of sin, we encounter for the first time an unqualified statement of the later Jewish belief that some of the patriarchs were completely sinless. ("You therefore, Lord God of the upright, have not ordained repentance for the upright, for Abraham, Isaac, and Jacob, which have not sinned against you," verse 4.)

D. 2 Esdras

This book, written late in the 1st century AD, shows that at the time it was written, there was in Judaism a doctrine of inborn, inherited sin.   2 Esdras 4:30,31 read, "For a

---

[16] "Sin began with a woman, and because of her we all die." According to Sirach, Eve's sin was the cause of death, but only the beginning of sin. This language, while teaching the inheritance of death from Eve, does not necessarily imply a doctrine of inherited sin.

[17] "The influence of Greek philosophy is evidenced by the dependence on *logos* speculations in the treatment of personified Wisdom and by the acceptance of various pagan teachings: the creation of the world out of pre-existent matter; the pre-existence of souls; the impedimentary character of the body; perhaps too, the doctrine of emanation." M.G. Kline, "Apocrypha," in *Zondervan Pictorial Dictionary of the Bible*, edited by Merrill C. Tenney (Grand Rapids: Zondervan Publishing House, 1963), p.51.

[18] "The idea of the derivation of a universal taint [inherited] from Adam's transgression is altogether wanting." Bernard, "Sin," *Hastings Encyclopedia of Religion and Ethics*, Vol.11, p.532.

grain of evil seed was sown from the beginning in the heart of Adam, and how much ungodliness it has produced up to this time and will produce before the judgment comes. Estimate for yourself how great a crop of ungodliness a grain of evil seed has produced."[19] 3:21,22 word it this way, "For the first Adam, burdened with a wicked heart, transgressed and was overcome, as were also all who were descended from him. So weakness became permanent, and the Law was in the heart of the people with the evil root; and what was good departed, and what was evil remained." 7:48 reads, "For an evil heart has grown up in us, which has alienated us from these commands, and has led us off to corruption and the ways of death, and shown us the paths of perdition and removed us far from life, and that, not just a few, but almost all who have been created." Such inborn "evil" does not preclude the continued exercise of free will. See 2 Esdras 8:59,60 and especially 9:11, which reads, "And as many as disdained my Law, while they still had freedom, and while an opportunity to repent was still open to them, did not understand but scorned it."[20] A most difficult question to answer concerns the source of this "inherent evil heart" idea – did it come from Roman or from Greek philosophy? It should be noted that, according to Esdras, the "evil heart" was in Adam *before* he committed his first sin, evidently placed there by God at creation, and that it can be resisted (if only by the greatest of efforts).

E. The Book of Enoch

Dated between the 2nd century BC and the 1st century AD, this pseudepigraphical work purports to record revelations given to Enoch and Noah. In this work the origin of sin is due to fallen angels and demons, 9:4, 15:11.[21]

---

[19] We are using Protestant terminology when we call this work 2 Esdras. In the Latin Vulgate, it appears as IV Esdras. Chapters 3-14 present seven visions, allegedly given to Ezra while he was in Exile. To this original Jewish portion of the book, some Christian authors added the other chapters in the now extant work. The Jewish original was an attempt to answer the problem of evil befalling the Jews that was acutely posed by the fall of Jerusalem in AD 70. The Christian addition "predicts" the casting off of Israel in favor of the church.

[20] The Apocalypse of Baruch, which bears a close relationship to 2 Esdras, also bears witness to the belief in the freedom of choice, 54:15,19. Sanday and Headlam, *Romans*, p.137-39, have a short study on "The Effects of Adam's Fall in Jewish Theology." It is concluded that, (1) the Fall of Adam brought death not only to Adam himself but to his descendants; (2) the Fall of Adam also brought sin and the tendency to sin; (3) yet in spite of this the individual does not lose his [personal] responsibility. The writers also note that the second point is disputed by other Jewish scholars, such as Edersheim and Weber.

[21] As the Jews struggled with the question of the origin of evil, it was attributed to Eve, to Adam, to the evil spirits, and to God who created man with an evil heart.

[PHARISAIC, SADDUCAIC, AND RABBINIC JUDAISM'S VIEW OF SIN. For many, "sin" largely consisted of neglecting or breaking external laws, and with matters of mere ritual. *Abhoth*, v.10f, names the seven main transgressions as (i) neglect in the matter of tithes, of the offering of the dough-cake, and of the seventh-year fruits; (ii) corrupt administration of justice; (iii) profanation of the NAME; (iv) idolatry; (v) incest; (vi) murder; and (vii) failure to observe the Sabbatical year. For those Jews whose idea of sin was more ethical than ritual, the origin and cause of sin was variously explained. According to Josephus (*Wars*, II.viii.14), the Sadducees emphasized man's control over his actions: "God is not concerned in our

III. SIN IN THE NEW TESTAMENT

A. The Gospels

In the four Gospels we have the testimony of Jesus about sin. Men's stubborn resistance to the leadership God would exercise in their lives, whether through the heaven-sent messengers or through the revealed truth contained in Scriptures, is something that deserves punishment. John's Gospel continually warns against the sin of unbelief. It has even been said that the sin of unbelief in Jesus as the Christ, the Son of God, holds in the New Testament much the same position which idolatry holds in the Old Testament. Jesus' testimony assumes that sin is universal, else what would be the value of calling all men everywhere to repent?[22] The universality of sin among men is also behind the affirmation that "no one is good except God alone" (Mark 10:18). He implies that the world is a moral place, and perhaps even that the world is under the dominion of sin, when He teaches that stumbling-blocks are unavoidable (Matthew 18:7-9). He certainly taught that the devil has a kingdom he rules over (Matthew 12:25-26). The devil's subjects in that kingdom are in bondage (John 8:31; Matthew 6:24). When the devil offered to give Jesus all the kingdoms of the world (Matthew 4:8,9), it just may be that his dominion is such that the kingdoms were his to give. Certainly, in the parable of the tares the devil's power is such that even while the Son of Man is sowing good seed ("the sons of the kingdom") in the world, so too is the devil sowing seed ("the sons of the evil one", Matthew 13:37-39). In some cases, the reason men remain in the devil's kingdom is that, because they do not understand the word of the kingdom when it is preached to them, the devil comes and snatches away the truth from their hearts (Matthew 13:19). Turning to another aspect of sin as taught by Jesus, He emphasizes that it is possible for attitudes and motives, as well as the acts, to be sinful (Matthew 5:21-25, 15:9); in fact, these attitudes and actions can become a persistent habit pattern (Matthew 7:16-20, 12:35). Men's responsibility and degree of guilt may vary (Luke 10:12-16), and so correspondingly will their punishment (Luke 12:47,48). Jesus recognizes men's freedom of will to accept or reject an invitation (Matthew 23:37). Jesus Himself had power to cast out evil spirits, and He at times delegated the same power to others, with the ultimate result that the devil (the evil spirits'

---

doing or not doing what is evil ... to act what is good or evil is at men's own choice." The Essenes, on the other end of the discussion of the relation of "free will" and "divine sovereignty," asserted that "fate governs all things" (*Antiquities*, XIII.v.9), or that "all things are best ascribed to God" (*Antiquities*, XVIII.i.5). The Pharisees occupied a sort of middle ground, thus, "when they determine that all things are done by fate, they do not take away the freedom from men of acting as they think fit; since their notion is, that it hath pleased God to make a temperament (*krasis*, 'combination'?) whereby what He wills is done, but so that the will of man can act virtuously or viciously" (*Antiquities*, XVIII.i.3). There has been a tendency in Judaism to lay some of the responsibility for human sin upon God. Sin is partly due to the *yetser hara*, the evil impulse, that was implanted in man by God when He created (*Bereshith rabbah*, c.27).]

[22] Matthew 4:17; Luke 13:3.

master) also suffered a defeat (Luke 10:17,18). The temptations suggested by the devil have something to do with leading a man into sin (Matthew 4:1-11; Luke 22:40), though in Jesus' case, the devil was unsuccessful. When Peter tries to hold Jesus back from going to the cross, Jesus rebukes him by calling him "Satan" (Matthew 16:23), evidently suggesting that Peter's ideas were prompted by Satan, and his words were a temptation. Jesus also spoke about the source of sin being an evil heart (Matthew 15:10,19) in some cases, and the offenses of other sinners being a source of temptation in other cases (Matthew 18:7). He also put His imprimatur on the idea that some temporal evils and sicknesses are the result of sin (Matthew 9:2-6). That God judges and punishes unforgiven sin lies at the root of Jesus' teaching. He came emphasizing the need men have to be forgiven, since there is no salvation without forgiveness (Matthew 6:12, 18:23-35). He also warned about a sin for which there was no forgiveness.[23] As a result of His death and resurrection, Jesus instructed that "repentance and remission of sins should be preached in His name to all the nations" (Luke 24:47, ASV). As the gospel was being preached, the Holy Spirit would convict the world of sin, righteousness, and the judgment (John 16:7-11). He spoke of a coming final judgment at which men's lives will be compared to God's righteous requirements (Matthew 25:31-46).

B. The Book of Acts

What Judas did in betraying Jesus is called "iniquity" (*adikia*) and "transgression" (*parabainō*) in Acts 1:18,25 (KJV). Even though men deliberately crucified Jesus, their act was done "in ignorance" (Acts 3:17); that is, it was a sin that was forgivable. Conditions men are expected to meet in order to have their sins forgiven are set forth in Acts 2:38, 3:19, and elsewhere, such as 10:43. The salvation and new covenant relationship provided by Jesus are intended to turn men "from their wicked ways" (Acts 3:25,26). The interaction between the devil's temptations and men's willingness to listen and act as the devil prompts is clearly seen in chapter 5. The devil planted the idea in the minds of Ananias and Sapphira (5:3), but they also contemplated the matter by nourishing it in their minds (5:4). In this case, the sin resulted in quick temporal punishment, and likely, too, eternal. When Stephen closed his defense before the Jewish religious leaders, he certainly implied that they were free to choose some other course than the sinful course they were pursuing (7:51-53). Philip alluded to the bondage that sin can get a man into, as well as the fact that the "intention of the heart" may be in need of being forgiven (8:22,23). Paul, speaking to Elymas, alluded to the fact that people involved in the occult are "sons of the devil" and their actions are opposed to "righteousness" and to the "straight ways of the Lord" (13:8-10), but he also graciously offered the sinner a way out of his sin.

---

[23] Matthew 12:31-32; Mark 3:28,29; Luke 12:10. In the context, the religious leaders have been attributing to evil spirits the work of the Holy Spirit in the actions and words of Christ. This persistent denial of the real source of Jesus' person and message, despite some measure of felt truth, is evidently what Jesus was identifying as a sin for which there was no forgiveness. It is the condition of the heart, more than the words that come from the heart, that Jesus calls "blasphemy" and says is unpardonable.

C. Paul

Perhaps Paul's doctrine of sin can be understood by taking note of what he wrote on some of the same topics already introduced in earlier portions of this study. The universality of sin is clearly taught both by experience and in the Scriptures (Romans 1-3). He rejects the rabbinic doctrine of the sinlessness of the patriarchs (Romans 3-4). Paul also speaks about the bondage of sin, and about how a man can be a slave to sin (Romans 6). He shows how men are sinless at the beginning of their lives; then how, when men become aware of God's laws, sin (personification, read "devil") sprang into operation and tempted the man; and when the man sinned, he died (chapter 7). He writes about how men's hearts can be darkened by their own acts of sin (Romans 1:21), and how this sin then destroys men's vertical relationship with God (Ephesians 4:18; Romans 8:7), and their horizontal relationships with men (Romans 1:28-31). When it comes to the matter of what can be inherited from parents, Paul emphasizes that consequences can be hereditary, such as physical death to the whole race because Adam sinned (Romans 5:12-19; 1 Corinthians 15:22). But it is doubtful that Paul ever intended to imply that men inherit a "sinful nature." Paul's presentation of the sin of Adam is not so much that thereby human nature was infected in itself, but rather that thereby "the sin" (an alien power) got a footing in the world, and then, one by one, involved all men in their own actual, personal acts of sin.[24] Paul often uses the expression "the flesh" when he speaks of what prompts men to act in opposition to God. We would affirm that when "the flesh" so acts contrary to God, it is because the devil has moved in and stirred up the desires of the flesh, rather than that the flesh is hereditarily tainted from birth. "Neither the flesh in the material sense, nor human nature on the whole, are in themselves evil; for the body may be brought into subjection (1 Corinthians 9:27), may become a temple of the Holy Ghost (1 Corinthians 6:19), and its members may be 'servants to righteousness unto sanctification' (Romans 6:19)."[25] Though for the justified man the old bondage to sin is broken (Romans 6), it does not mean the justified man no longer faces the devil's temptations. He does, but he is no longer a slave to the devil. In God's providence, when the devil offers one of his temptations, God provides the way of escape (1 Corinthians 10:13), and the justified man can exercise self-control, if he but will (see, 'stop letting sin reign in your mortal body!' at Romans 6:12); if not, he can submit to the devil and sin. Such continued sin is out of harmony with God's perfect will, and if persisted in, will result in the man's being lost (Romans 6:16-23, 8:6-8; Galatians 5:19-21).

D. John's Epistles

In 1 John 3:4, John shares his understanding of the essence of sin, as he writes, "Sin is the transgression of the law" (KJV), or "Sin is lawlessness" (NASB). Like Paul, John

---

[24] "This is very far short of the Augustinian doctrine of Original Sin, which appears to be a development of 2 Esdras 3:21 [and] 4:30, rather than of anything to be found in the NT." Bernard, "Sin," *Hastings Encyclopedia of Religion and Ethics*, Vol. 11, p.535.

[25] *Ibid.*

teaches that Christians do sin (1 John 1:8-10),[26] but their sin is not to be a habitual thing (1 John 3:6,9 and 5:16). What John adds to what has been stated before is that the Christian has help to master the devil's temptations, a help that the non-Christian does not have (1 John 5:18).[27] The devil's activity that lies behind human sin is clearly enunciated in 1 John 3:8-12 and 5:18,19.[28] John also writes about a "sin leading to death" and a "sin not leading to death" (1 John 5:16,17), and various are the speculations that attempt to identify exactly what is the "sin leading to death." Perhaps the most satisfying suggestion is that John has in mind the same thing Hebrews talks about when Hebrews speaks of willful apostasy from Christ (as in Hebrews 6:4-6 and 10:26-29).[29] When it comes to the dominion that the devil temporarily exercises, John writes, "we know ... the whole world lies in *the power of* the evil one" (1 John 5:19).

E. James

James 1:14-16 indicates that the fact a man sins should not be blamed on God, as though God were the ultimate cause of temptation. Instead, James explains how the tempting process works. The Greek reads 'Each man being drawn away and enticed is tempted by his own lusts.' First he is tempted by an unnamed agent (the devil). Then the desires ("lusts") thus excited begin to cry out to be satisfied. The man then begins to think about what he has been tempted to do (James says the lust has "conceived"), then he carries it out, only to find out that in the end what he has done brings "death." James does not indicate that the source of the temptation is the man's "own desires." Men experience temptations when the devil is at work in them.[30] James, like John, demonstrates that sin is transgression of God's law (James 2:8-11). Earlier, it has been noted that sometimes there is a relationship between sins and sickness; James seems to suggest that in such cases

---

[26] Some writers, noting that "sin" is singular in verse 8, whereas it is plural in verse 9, have supposed that verse 8 is speaking of the "old sinful nature" while verse 9 speaks of acts of sin produced by that old nature. While it is true that "sin" in verse 8 is *hamartia*, the same word Paul uses in Romans 5:12, it would be hard to show that John and Paul are speaking of the same thing. In fact, it is better to understand that the singular and plural in verses 8 and 9 are pointing to the same thing. Not only can the Christian not say he has *never* sinned; the fact is, he would best be confessing his *sins*!

[27] Romans 8 also presents the help the indwelling Spirit gives to the Christian to help him live the Christian life.

[28] John is likely merely repeating what he had heard Jesus Himself say about the devil's agency that lies behind human sin, John 8:44.

[29] A careful reading of the warning passages in Hebrews (2:1-4, 3:7-4:13, 5:11-6:20, 10:19-31, 12:18-29), where people who sin are threatened with everlasting punishment, will show that the writer does not have in mind ordinary sins after baptism which all Christians are liable to commit (as 1 John 1:8 shows), but a willful repudiation of Christ, a quitting of the Christian religion, i.e., apostasy from Christ.

[30] The explanation of how temptation works found in James is not greatly different from what was presented in Acts 5 or Romans 7. Involved are these things: (1) the person about to be tempted must be aware of God's law; (2) the activity of the tempter, who plants thoughts and stirs up the desires of the body; (3) acquiescence of the person's will which results in the performance of what was suggested in the temptation.

there is also a relationship between the forgiveness of sins and healing (James 5:14, 15).[31]

F. Hebrews

Sin is presented as a besetting, impeding power, causing men to be ensnared (12:1), and resulting in an inner awareness or consciousness of guilt that cries to be removed (9:9,14). One prominent aspect of the doctrine of sin in Hebrews is the fact that sin separates a man from God.[32] The separated man needs the functions of a priest to help him get back into perfect relationship with God. Now Jesus is a much better high priest than the Aaronic priesthood ever was, for He offers a better sacrifice (His own blood), serves in a better tabernacle (heaven itself), and inaugurates a better covenant (better than the Mosaic covenant). By His death, Jesus rendered the devil powerless (though the devil once had the power of death, Hebrews 2:14,15). Hebrews 10:19-31 summarizes the whole presentation up to that point, and encourages men to keep on being faithful to Jesus, for apostasy from Him, even if to go back to Judaism, has terrifying consequences. Hebrews 4:15 may have some bearing on the doctrine of an inherited sinful nature, for it affirms that Jesus was "tempted in all points like as *we are, yet* without sin" (ASV). How can Hebrews affirm His perfect sinlessness if the very body He lived in was inherently sinful?[33] Hebrews 3:12 (ASV) also is a help in this matter of an inborn sinful nature, for it speaks of "an evil heart of unbelief." It says that *unbelief* is what makes the heart "evil," not that it was born that way. Finally, what does Hebrews say about the relationship between sin and suffering? Instead of suffering's being a consequence of personal sin, Hebrews gives another suggestion as to why people may suffer when it explains that sometimes God permits suffering as a means to the Christian's perfection (Hebrews 2:10,11; 12:5-11).

G. Revelation

Revelation 12:7-9 tells about a time when there was war in heaven.[34] The devil and

---

[31] The case of the healing of the paralytic by Jesus (Matthew 9:2-6) would be a similar instance of the relationship between forgiveness and healing.

[32] The Hebrews writer often uses the word "perfection" when he would affirm that the reason for separation is gone, and therefore so is the separation itself. See 7:11,19; 10:1,14.

[33] In Romans 8:3, we are told that God sent "His own Son in the likeness of sinful flesh and as an offering for sin." Now the expression "likeness of flesh of sin" does not mean that Jesus' body was tainted by a defect inherited from Adam (though, indeed, some have gone so far as to offer the farfetched suggestion that the reason Jesus had to be born of a virgin was so that He could avoid a sinful nature such as is passed on by the father at the time of conception). Rather, Romans 8:3 tells us that Jesus' body was capable of offering to Him the same temptations that any human body can, once it has been "carried away" and "enticed" by the activity of the devil. It is not a sin to be tempted, but it is a sin to submit to the temptation.

[34] A commentator's explanation of exactly when this war took place, or will take place, likely is dependent on his eschatological views. The futurist, who views Revelation 4-19 as not happening until the time of the future Great Tribulation, thinks the war has not yet happened. The continuous-historical interpreter thinks the war took place just after Jesus' earthly ministry, when He returned in triumph to heaven. The spiritual-allegorical interpreter and the historical cycle interpreter are likely to view these verses as being a

his angels (likely to be identified with the evil spirits, or demons, one meets elsewhere in Scripture) lost, and were "thrown down to the earth."[35] The devil and his angels are not as powerful ("they were not strong enough") as the powers of God that are opposed to them. Revelation 12:10-12 announce the cosmic significance of the results of the war in heaven: God will bring His salvation into the world, and Satan (the accuser of the brethren) will find his accusations are fruitless in the case of those who are under the blood of the Lamb. Still, it will be a time of "woe" to earth and sea, to the "woman" (the nation of Israel?) who gave birth to the Christ (the male child), and to the "rest of her offspring" (spiritual Israel?). The time is coming when God will put a complete end to the devil's ability to tempt and deceive, for at the second advent of Christ, the devil and all his angels and all his followers will be cast into the lake of fire (Revelation 20:10-15, 19:20; Matthew 8:29).

SUMMARY AND CONCLUSION

On the major ideas about sin traced through Scripture, these conclusions can be expressed:

(1) God created the universe as a moral universe, thus allowing for the possibility there would be sin. The devil exercised his freedom of choice, persuaded other angels to join with him in rebellion, and eventually lost the war in heaven. Being cast down to earth, these forces of evil are still trying to thwart what God is doing in His world.

(2) In an effort to extend his dominion over the earth, the devil set about to tempt Adam and Eve, and proved to be successful. Adam's sin was the occasion for the power of sin to gain a foothold among the human race. God, Who is over all, decreed a penalty of physical death to the race because Adam sinned.

(3) Since Adam's time, the devil has been using the same technique on Adam's descendants. His success rate is nothing less than universal, for all have sinned and come short of the glory of God. Sin is transgression of God's law, and it brings separation from God.

(4) The process the devil follows when tempting a man includes these steps: the man must be aware of God's law; the devil proposes something contrary to what the man knows to be right; the man allows his mind to meditate on the proposed sin; if the man then

---

parenthetical explanation of the origin of evil, back before Adam sinned.

[35] Jude 6 has also spoken of a rebellion by angels, and how those rebellious angels are kept in bondage until the judgment day. Not a few interpreters also are reminded of Revelation 9:1-11, where a hellish swarm of "locusts" are permitted to go forth from the abyss to do their harm on men, and whose leader is the devil (called Abaddon or Apollyon in verse 11).

wills to do it, his action is sin.

(5) As the devil makes his "proposal," he has the ability to plant thoughts in men's minds, and also to stir up the desires of men's bodies. In fact, it would appear that each and every act of sin that men commit is a result of yielding to a personal temptation instigated by the devil. It is exceedingly doubtful that the Bible presents the idea that men's bodies or hearts are able to prompt a man to sin without first being tempted by the devil. Or, wording it another way, it is difficult to find, in the pages of Scripture, either the doctrine of an inborn sinful nature inherent in the flesh, or an inborn evil heart that of itself prompts men to sin.

(6) When a man commits his first sin, he becomes what the Bible calls a "slave of sin," and he lives in a "body of sin." This seems to suggest some limitation on the man's freedom of will, but such freedom of choice is not wholly lost, either in Adam, or in the man's own submission to the devil's temptation.

(7) Man's personal acts of sin can result in both temporal and eternal punishments to the sinner himself, and in hard *consequences* to his family and neighbors in time, but an eternal *penalty* for the man's guilt is not experienced by family or neighbors.

(8) Lest someone accuse God of being responsible for the sin in the world because He made it a moral universe in the first place, it should be observed that God's grace has always exceeded what the devil and his dominion are able to do. That is, God has always been at least one step ahead of the devil, providing help to each man to get out of the slavery to sin, that the man's own sin got him into. The incarnation of Jesus, His propitiatory death on Calvary, and His mediatorial work in heaven are all part of God's continuing provision to help men to get out of the consequences of wrong choices.

SELECTED BIBLIOGRAPHY

Bennett, W.H., "Sin (Hebrew and Jewish)," *Hastings Encyclopedia of Religion and Ethics*. New York: Charles Scribner's Sons, 1921. Vol.11, p.556-560.

Bernard, E.R., "Sin," *Hastings Encyclopedia of Religion and Ethics*. New York: Charles Scribner's Sons, 1921. Vol.11, p.528-536.

Berkouwer, G.C., *Sin* (Studies in Theology Series). Grand Rapids: Wm. B. Eerdmans Publishing Co., 1971.

Buswell, J. Oliver, "The Nature of Sin," *Christian Faith and Modern Theology*, edited by Carl F.H. Henry. New York: Channel Press, 1964. p.175-189.
    (This is an excellent summary of how "sin" is treated in Neo-orthodox and Neo-liberal theologies, and is useful for one who would compare what Scripture says and what modern theologians say.)

Carder, Muriel M., "The Biblical Concept of Sin in Translation," *Indian Journal of Theology*, 20/1,2 (1971), p.43-56.

Carter, Charles W., "Hamartiology: Evil, the Marrer of God's Creative Purpose and Work," in Volume 1 of *A Contemporary Wesleyan Theology*, edited by Charles W. Carter and others. Grand Rapids: Francis Asbury Press, 1983. p.235-280.

Dye, T. Wayne, "Toward a Cross-Cultural Definition of Sin," *Missiology*, 4/1 (1976), p.27-41.

Eisenstein, Judah David, "Sin," *The Jewish Encyclopedia*. New York: KTAV Publishing House, 1901. Vol.11, p.376-379.

Harrison, William K., "The Origin of Sin," *Bibliotheca Sacra*, 130 (1978), p.58-61.

Kirn, O., "Sin," *The New Schaff-Herzog Encyclopedia of Religious Knowledge*. Grand Rapids: Baker Book House, 1957. Vol.10, p.432-439.

Kromminga, Carl G., "Sin," *Baker Dictionary of Theology*, edited by Everett F. Harrison. Grand Rapids: Baker Book House, 1960. p.486-489.

Mackintosh, H.R., "Sin (Christian)," *Hastings Encyclopedia of Religion and Ethics*. New York: Charles Scribner's Sons, 1921. Vol.11, p.538-544.

Milne, Bruce A., "The Idea of Sin in Twentieth-Century Theology," *Tyndale Bulletin*, 26 (1976), p.3-33.

Pittenger, Norman, "An Interpretation of Sin," *Religion in Life*, 44/4 (1975), p.428-431.

Ryrie, Charles C., and Killen, R. Allen, "Sin," in *Wycliffe Bible Encyclopedia*, edited by Charles F. Pfeiffer. Chicago: Moody Press, 1975. Vol.2, p.1593-1595.

Scott, Otto J., "The Definition of Sin," *Chalcedon Report*, 218 (Sept.1983), p.1,2.

Slack, Kenneth, "Recent Thinking on Christian Beliefs: VII. Sin and Salvation," *Expository Times*, 88/8 (1977), p.228-232.

Swadling, Harry C., "Sin and Sinlessness in 1 John," *Scottish Journal of Theology*, 35/3 (1982), p.205-211.

SPECIAL STUDY #4

THE DOCTRINE OF ORIGINAL SIN

In comments on Romans 5:12, "original sin" was defined as the doctrine that as a result of Adam's sin, a fallen nature, often called an old sinful nature, is automatically passed on to each baby that is conceived and born into the world.[1] The whole paragraph (Romans 5:12-21) is often explained as though that old sinful nature is the "sin and death" that is passed on to the whole race. A brief study of this doctrine, the verses said to support it, and its history, will be helpful as the Bible student attempts to understand himself as he is portrayed in the Scriptures.

I. PASSAGES ALLEGED TO TEACH THE DOCTRINE OF A HEREDITARY SINFUL NATURE

There are a few verses that are regularly quoted by defenders of the doctrine of original sin. "Behold I was brought forth in iniquity; and in sin my mother conceived me," wrote David at Psalm 51:5 as he confessed his sin with Bathsheba. Psalm 14:2,3, "The Lord has looked down from heaven upon the sons of men, to see if there are any who understand, who seek after God. They have all turned aside; together they have become corrupt; there is no one who does good, not even one." How does one explain this universality of sin, it is asked, unless there is something inherent about it? Paul not only wrote Romans 5:12-21, but also Ephesians 2:3, which reads in part, we "were by nature children of wrath." Doesn't "by nature" indicate that liability to wrath is hereditary?

In addition to these favorite passages, there are certain words or expressions that are said to teach the doctrine also. "Flesh," as used in Paul's writings, for example, where it is often opposed to "spirit," certainly indicates something inborn in all of us that is opposed to God's will, it is affirmed. In addition, there are certain verses where the word "evil" is predicated of men's hearts or imaginations or thoughts. This 'evil bent,' it is believed, is something inborn in all, rather than acquired by personal sins.

II. HISTORY OF THE DOCTRINE IN THE CHURCH

In Special Study #3, it has been shown that no doctrine of a hereditary sinful nature

---

[1] The reader must be careful in his definition of terms when this topic is studied. Some use the expression "original sin," and mean no more than the idea that the first, the original sin, in the world was the Fall of Adam. Others use the expression "original sin" when they wish to express nothing more than the universality of sin, that is, that sin is something of which every living man is guilty. A third group uses the expression "original sin" when they want to express the idea that, as a result of Adam's sin, God imputed "death" to all the race. There is nothing hereditary in this – just something God reckons. Again, others, during the long history of the controversy, have used the expression "original sin" to express the idea that something is passed on to the whole race through heredity, though there has not always been agreement as to exactly what (whether concupiscence, as Catholics teach, or depravity, as Calvinists teach) it is that is inherited. It is particularly with this latter usage of the term that this Special Study is concerned.

is found in Judaism until late in the 1st century AD. It was not something taught in the Old Testament Scriptures, but was likely something imported into Judaism from Greek philosophy, which posited that while spirit is good, matter (including a man's body) is evil. It would be an almost expected step for any Hellenistically-influenced Jew to try to find the doctrine taught in Scripture.[2]

It is almost universally admitted that just as there was no doctrine of inborn evil in Judaism until late, so there was no doctrine of inborn evil in the early church – neither during the apostolic times nor the sub-apostolic. For example, a Roman Catholic authority admits, "... it is true that Paul does not explicitly say all that will be said by the Council of Trent."[3] The same source further admits that the Catholic Church's definition of doctrine on this point is only hinted at in the Bible, and asserts that the Church was perfectly within her rights to proceed beyond the clear statements of Scripture as the present-day doctrine was formulated.[4] A Protestant authority words it this way, "The church doctrine [of sin] is a continuation of the development of the Biblical doctrine [of sin] only to a very limited extent."[5] Another writes,

> ... when we pass on to consider the writings of the Fathers of the early church, we find that they did not directly adopt St. Paul's teaching as the basis of their doctrine, nor borrow that presented in Jewish literature. They started afresh to elaborate a doctrine of original sin.[6]

It seems that it was not until the church's controversy with Gnosticism that one begins to read in early Christian writers a real emphasis on the original state of man and on the consequences of the Fall.[7]   Irenaeus (c.130-c.202), who wrote *Against Heresies* and *The*

---

[2] Non-Christian Jews would not appeal to the Christian Scriptures for their proof, so it is not usually affirmed that the writer of 2 Esdras took his idea of inborn sin from Paul.

[3] I. Hunt, "Original Sin – In the Bible," in *The New Catholic Encyclopedia* (Washington, DC: Catholic University of America, 1967 [reprinted 1981]). Vol.8, p.777.

[4] C.J. Peter, "Original Sin – In Catholic Faith and Theology," *The New Catholic Encyclopedia*, Vol.8, p.777. The writer goes on to affirm that the Catholic leaders had divine inspiration when they formulated the current doctrinal statement. He writes, "... the Church relied on the Spirit of truth who guides its faith throughout the ages."

[5] O. Kirn, "Sin," *The New Schaff-Herzog Encyclopedia of Religious Knowledge* (Grand Rapids: Baker Book House, 1957). Vol.10, p.435.

[6] F.R. Tennant, "Original Sin," *Hastings Encyclopedia of Religion and Ethics* (New York: Charles Scribner's Sons, 1921). Vol.9, p.560.

[7] "Gnosticism. A syncretistic philosophico-religious movement which in pre-Christian times had fused into one system such widely different elements as Babylonian astral mythology, cabalistic Judaism, Persian dualism, and Greek philosophy. Its main purpose was ethical, its chief doctrine that emancipation came through knowledge, *gnosis*, the possession of which saved the initiates from the clutch of matter." *Webster's International Dictionary*, 2nd edition (Springfield, MA: G&C Merriam Co., Publishers, 1948), p.1070. Many of the movement's eastern religious ideas were carried back to the Mediterranean world by Alexander the Great's soldiers, and by exiles who returned to their homelands from those eastern areas. The dualism involved taught that matter is evil, while spirit is good. This resulted in a real problem when

Demonstration of the Apostolic Preaching, did not appeal to Romans 5 as proof for his doctrine of sin (and it must be remembered that Romans has already been accepted as canonical and authoritative by Irenaeus' time), but rather based it on his own "recapitulation" theory. According to this theory, Jesus' life recapitulated the career of Adam, but in reverse, removing by His perfect obedience the curse Adam had brought on mankind. "On original sin as an inherent disease, or as the source of concupiscence, [Irenaeus] is quite silent."[8] In *Apostolic Preaching* occurs an idea of inherited sin, but it is inherited from Cain, and is true only of the descendants of Cain. "God's curse on Cain is spoken of as handed down by natural heredity to his posterity."[9]

Origen (c.185-c.254) changed his views in his later years. Earlier in his life, he taught that all souls lived in a previous, celestial existence, before coming to earth to live in a body. The "Fall" in the Genesis account is an allegory describing how these souls, by exercising freedom of the will, came to sin during that pre-existence.[10] Origen was banished from Alexandria, and upon coming to Caesarea came in contact with the practice of infant baptism.[11] Since, in the early church, baptism was connected with forgiveness of sins, it became necessary to "find" some sin an infant could be guilty of, for which he would need to be baptized in order to have forgiveness. Since it was not possible for the infant to have personally committed any acts of sin, it must be some inherited guilt for which infants were being baptized, Origen decided. He borrowed the idea of seminal existence from Hebrews 7:9,10 (where Levi paid tithes to Melchizedek while still in the loins

---

it came to explaining creation. How could a good God (Who is spirit) create an evil world (which is matter). One solution to this thorny problem is a series of emanations from God. God created an aeon, who created another aeon, and so on, until one eventually created Jesus, who created the devil, who in turn created the world. In this way, God could not be blamed for creating an evil world. Another necessary doctrine is that Jesus never did become the God-man (a denial of the incarnation), for a good God could not inhabit an evil body. It was also taught that Jesus did not die to give man salvation, but to give him knowledge. When it came to ethics, some Gnostics were ascetics, trying to crush evil matter; others were libertarians, believing it made no difference to one's spirit what the body did. As the incipient forms of this doctrine began to enter the churches, some of the books of the New Testament were written to refute it – such as John's Gospel and Epistles, Jude (which records the arrival of the false teachers predicted in 2 Peter), and perhaps Colossians and 2 Timothy. Two influential Gnostic teachers who tried to rewrite Christian doctrine in Gnostic terms were Valentinus (fl. 138-158) and Basilides (fl. 130-140). It was the effort to refute these two men's teachings that we encounter when we read the anti-Gnostic writings in the early church fathers.

[8] Tennant, "Sin," *Hastings Encyclopedia of Religion and Ethics*, p.560.

[9] *Ibid*. Tennant also posits that Irenaeus got this idea from Alexandrian Judaism, which Tennant says tended to "emphasize the gravity of Cain's sin, and the sin of his descendants." He also makes this critical point: "This work of Irenaeus serves further to show that in his time the idea of inherited sinfulness was not as yet definitely coupled with that of Adam's Fall."

[10] What is objectionable about this is that it is a denial that all humans are descendants of Adam. It is polygenism rather than monogenism, and polygenism is something that cannot be harmonized with the Bible, as has been shown at Romans 5:12 (and the related footnotes #83 and #84).

[11] At this early time, the "baptism" was by immersion, as indeed it still is in the Greek Orthodox Church.

of Abraham), applied it to the whole race, and now (having changed from his earlier views) taught that all men descended from Adam. It was from the Old Testament ceremony of purification (compare what was done for Mary and Jesus when Jesus was 40 days old, Luke 2:22-24) that Origen also developed his idea of an inborn 'uncleanness.' All that remained was to put the two ideas together (seminal existence of the race in Adam, and 'uncleanness' in infants that required a sin offering) and you have the beginning of the doctrine of original sin as later taught by Augustine. Perhaps it can be summarized thusly: Origen developed the doctrine of inherited uncleanness in order to account for the practice of infant baptism.[12]

Tertullian (c.160-c.220), whose teachings also contributed to the growth of the doctrine of an inborn taint in all infants, arrived at his conclusions because of the influence of Stoic philosophy, in particular the belief in traducianism,[13] by which all the qualities of the parent are reproduced in the child. Since the race was conceived and born after Adam and Eve had sinned, it follows, Tertullian believed, that the qualities they passed on to their children were the fallen, corrupted qualities they had after the curse had been pronounced on them by God.

Thus, none of the three church leaders – Irenaeus, Origen, and Tertullian – whose teachings eventually resulted in the doctrine of original sin got their doctrines from Scripture. For one, it was the recapitulation theory; for another it was infant baptism; and for another it was Stoic philosophy that led to the doctrine's formulation.

By the time of Athanasius (c.297-373), the development of this doctrine took another turn. Now, instead of its being some kind of corruption of human nature that is passed on, what is inherited is a loss of supernatural graces with which the man was endowed at first, but which were lost in the Fall. Athanasius apparently arrived at his teaching by combining one idea learned from Tatian and one learned from Irenaeus. Tatian taught that Adam lost any communion with the Holy Spirit (though he said nothing about a similar loss for any of Adam's descendants). Irenaeus made a distinction between the "image of God" (which he affirmed belonged to man's nature, and was not lost when Adam sinned), and "the likeness of God" (which he equated with certain supernatural endowments that were lost in the Fall).[14] From Athanasius' combination of these two men's ideas comes the doctrine

---

[12] It is rather uniformly admitted by scholars that Origen did not get his later doctrine either from Paul (Romans 5), or from Irenaeus, or even Tertullian.

[13] Traducianism is the belief that the soul of an infant is procreated or transmitted to the child by the parents in the act of procreation.

[14] The expressions Irenaeus used come from Genesis 1:26, where God says, "Let Us make man in Our *image*, according to Our *likeness*." It has been a matter of debate through the ages whether there is any difference intended between "image" and "likeness." The synonyms do have different meanings, but this verse is most likely an example of Hebrew parallelism. However, as Irenaeus used the two terms, "image of God" was understood to be a bodily form or shape that God has, and of which man's body is a copy; whereas "likeness of God" was some sort of spiritual possession or endowment. Some Catholic theology has modified Irenaeus' definition of *imago dei*, while keeping his definition of *similitudo dei*. Instead of speaking of God's body, what is spoken of as being the "image of God" is man's natural endowments of reason and free will which remained intact after the Fall. As will be seen later in this study, the Protestant Reformers rejected this distinction between "image" and "likeness," and argued instead that the "image of

that is still taught by Catholics and many Protestants, as being the essential heart of what the "Bible" says happened to the race when Adam sinned.

In the Western church, no other teacher said anything of significance on the subject, until the time of Augustine. However, in the east, teachings that are quite incompatible with "original sin" were being put forth, until at least as late as the 5th century.

> *Gregory of Naziansum* [330-390, in Constantinople] maintained that both the *nous* [mind] and the *psuche* [soul] have been considerably impaired by sin, and regarded the perversion of consciousness seen in idolatry, which previous teachers had ascribed to the influence of demons, as an inevitable effect of the first sin. But he was far from asserting the total depravity of mankind and the entire loss of free will. *Athanasius* [c.297-373, in Alexandria] maintained man's ability to choose good and evil, and even allowed exceptions from original sin, alleging that several persons prior to Christ were free from it. *Cyril of Jerusalem* [c.315-386] assumes that the life of man begins in a state of innocence, and that sin enters of the free will. *Chrysostom* [c.347-407, in Constantinople] insisted upon the liberty of man and his self-determination.[15]

Theological positions have often come about as the result of controversy. It was the attempt to refute the teachings of Pelagius that led Augustine and others to formulate the doctrine of original sin that would influence church thinking for hundreds of years. Pelagius (c.354-c.420) came from Britain to Rome in his early twenties and soon became a highly regarded and influential leader in church circles. Before 410, Pelagius went to Africa along with his friend and helper Coelestius. Pelagius soon moved on to Palestine, while his friend stayed behind in Africa, teaching the doctrines Pelagius taught. From Pelagius' extant writings we learn these elements of his system:

- Physical death is not a punishment for Adam's sin, but is something that is part of human nature.
- Adam's sin influences the race only as a bad example.
- Since all babies are born without sin (i.e., they are in the same state Adam was before the Fall[16]), infant baptism is useless, and infants who die without being baptized go directly to heaven.
- Freedom of the will was not lost (either for Adam or his descendants) when Adam

---

God" which was lost was Adam's "original righteousness," so that it is a depraved nature that is inherited, rather than an absence of supernatural endowments that is inherited.

[15] John McClintock and James Strong, "Sin, Original," in *Cyclopedia of Biblical, Theological and Ecclesiastical Literature* (New York: Harper and Row, 1891), Vol.9, p.766.

[16] Pelagius evidently taught "creationism," the view that at the moment of conception or birth, God creates a new soul for each person born. (Compare footnote #13 above, where the other prevalent view, "traducianism" was explained.) Holding to creationism, Pelagius could affirm that each soul is created just as Adam was before he fell – pure and innocent, with no bent or inclination either toward sin or holiness.

sinned, and therefore a man's will is equally ready to do either good or evil.[17]

- God's grace is something external to the man (just as are the precepts of the Old and New Testaments), and is intended merely to aid the will to do what it could do by itself.
- Grace is given according to a man's merits.

In AD 411, the local bishop had summoned Coelestius to a local council, and ordered him to retract his statements about original sin and infant baptism. Coelestius refused and was excommunicated and exiled. Shortly thereafter, at a meeting in Jerusalem, Pelagius was charged with heresy, but in the debate on the topic, Pelagius defeated his accuser. By now, Jerome, who lived in Bethlehem, entered the controversy against Pelagius, trying to show that it just was not possible that fallen man could have or acquire a "justice"[18] which is as perfect and equal as that which God Himself has. Several attempts were yet made to get Pelagius to recant or be excommunicated. In December of AD 415, Pelagius was forced to disavow some of the points Coelestius had taught, especially the one about grace being given according to man's merits, but he was not excommunicated. The African bishops kept up a constant attack, with letters to Innocent I in Rome, in which they insisted that the Pelagian doctrines of freedom of the will and infant baptism were erroneous. Shortly before his death, Innocent I excommunicated both Pelagius and Coelestius. Innocent's successor at first reinstated Pelagius, but again the African bishops prevailed; and in AD 418 Pelagius was again excommunicated, and this time expelled from Palestine. Julian of Eclanum became the new leader of Pelagianism, and one of the points he constantly made was that the doctrine of original sin, as taught by the African bishops, was a revival of Manichaeism.[19]

During this running debate, Augustine, in North Africa, changed his doctrine. Before the Pelagian controversy, Augustine taught freedom of the will, though he did hold to the solidarity of the race with Adam. In his later anti-Pelagian writings, he emphasized that freedom of the will was lost when Adam sinned, that all men inherit moral corruption

---

[17] Pelagius taught that each soul chooses for itself its own destiny when it voluntarily chooses good or evil, right or wrong. He explained that the fact that all men do in fact become sinners is due to the example and influence of those who surround the young from their earliest years. The other side of this doctrine, of course, is that it is possible (at least in theory) that a man could live his whole life without sinning, in which case he would have no need for a Savior.

[18] "Original Justice" (or "original righteousness") is a technical term among Catholics for the perfectly righteous condition of man in Eden before the Fall, a condition that included happiness and immortal life. In truth, Jerome overstated what Pelagius supposedly taught on this point, for Pelagius constantly affirmed that men were inferior to God. Nevertheless, the way Jerome worded it, everyone could "see" that what Pelagius taught was patently false.

[19] Manichaeism is a "dualistic oriental religion combining pagan and Christian elements. It sees a continuing struggle between the kingdom of light and kingdom of darkness, to be resolved after 1468 years when fire destroys the earth and the kingdom of evil. The Manichees saw women and matter as inherently evil. Augustine was at one time a Manichee before becoming a Christian." Donald T. Kauffman, *The Dictionary of Religious Terms* (Westwood, NJ: Fleming H. Revell Company, 1967), p.301.

from Adam,[20] that this corruption or depravity is complete so that fallen man cannot even will what is good, that man can do no good whatever and therefore continually needs God's grace in order to be saved, and that grace is something internal that is done to change the fallen man.[21]

Semi-Pelagianism, a theological movement in the 4th and 5th centuries, held a position between that of Pelagius and Augustine. Whereas Augustine held that God's grace (which is absolutely necessary for salvation) preceded regeneration, and was given to those whom God had elected to be saved, the Semi-Pelagians held that God's grace followed regeneration. Each of these positions was the logical conclusions to which their adherent's views of freedom of the will led. If, with Augustine, it is believed that a corruption is inherited from Adam so that fallen man is unable even to will what is good (i.e., there is no freedom of the will), then God must act first. If, with the Semi-Pelagians, there is still a freedom of will that men may exercise, there does not need to be a prevenient act of grace to save the man.[22] After Augustine's death, Faustus of Riez declared that Adam's sin resulted in man's physical death, but not his spiritual death, and that predestination is merely God's foreknowledge of what man himself has freely decided. These views, contrary to what Augustine had taught, were suppressed by decree from Pope Hormisdas, who instructed church leaders to adhere to the views expressed in the writings

---

[20] "In Augustine's thought, original sin is not merely a psychological state, but a metaphysical one; that is, man's fall was a fall in the order of being. Once having fallen, therefore, man cannot by his own efforts regain his former status in being. This is expressed in Augustine's notion that before the fall, angels and men possessed the ability not to sin (*posse non peccare*) as well as the ability to sin (*posse peccare*), but after the fall they possessed only the latter. Adam's sin, then, has corrupted the entire human race and it is a mass of sin (*massa peccati*) and justly subject to damnation. By this Augustine means not only that man inherits a tendency to sin but that he inherits guilt. How this comes about is not so clearly stated by Augustine, since he accepted the idea that every soul is freshly created by God (i.e., he held to creationism rather than traduciansm)." Van A. Harvey, *A Handbook of Theological Terms* (New York: The Macmillan Company, 1964), p.222.

[21] Augustine has been called "the Doctor of Grace," because his teachings on this topic have become the doctrinal position of the Catholic Church. Here we see how the doctrine of original sin, as taught by Augustine, has become the fountainhead of the idea that in salvation, fallen (depraved) man is wholly passive, and salvation is all 'grace' (something done for and to man by God). Moses E. Lard ("Original Sin," in *Lard's Quarterly*, January 1866 [Kansas City, MO: Old Paths Book Club, 1950 reprint], Vol.3, p.136-154) has suggested that the devil deliberately introduced the doctrine of original sin into theological debates because, after the Fall, it has proven to be the devil's best tool to thwart God's plan, since it has led to a continuing practice of infant baptism which really does not put a man into the church, but instead gives lost man a false sense of security. Also, the idea that salvation is something done to man has led many to reject the idea that the faith that saves is an obedient faith, and this too may well result in many well-meaning people failing to actually exercise that faith which is the condition of being justified by God.

[22] How easy it is to have some things right, and some things wrong, as we would understand and proclaim the Christian faith. One Semi-Pelagian's (John Cassian) doctrines were these: "The beginning of faith or the impulse to do good sometimes comes from man's will, unaided by grace; for, in spite of original sin, the will is still capable of performing good and salutary acts. Supernatural grace is necessary for salvation, but no special help from God is needed to persevere to the end; a fixed number of the elect is contrary to the universal salvific will of God; infants who died without baptism were punished because God foresaw the sins they would have committed if they had lived longer." S.J. McKenna, "Semi-Pelagianism," *The New Catholic Encyclopedia* (Washington, DC: Catholic University of America, 1967), Vol.13, p.75.

of Augustine. Thus it was that Augustine's theology became normative in the Western church, though his views never did gain a secure footing in the Eastern church.

In the Middle Ages, the Scholastics modified some of Augustine's teachings. Aquinas (13th century) built his system on Aristotelian philosophy, and where this conflicted with Augustine, he abandoned the latter's doctrine. Aquinas denied that there was a natural goodness forfeited at the Fall, that free will was impaired, or that concupiscence[23] is the real nature of sin. Both Aquinas and Duns Scotus taught that Adam's sin resulted in a loss of "original righteousness"[24] or "superadded graces," but that it did not affect man's nature. The views of the Scholastics became, at the Council of Trent (1543-63), the official doctrine of the Church of Rome.

> The decrees of that Council affirm that the fall caused loss of original righteousness, infection of body and soul, thralldom to the devil, and liability to the wrath of God; that such original sin is transmitted by generation, not by imitation; that all which has the proper nature of sin, and all guilt of original sin, is removed in baptism; that concupiscence remains after baptism, but this, though called "sin" by St. Paul, is not sin truly, but only metonymically.[25]

Of course, the Council of Trent was in many ways a reaction against the Protestant Reformation, and indeed an effort to stop it. Protestants were teaching a different doctrine on original sin than Rome's official line; most Protestants taught the Augustinian ideas that the Scholastics had rejected. Luther and Calvin both asserted that the depravity of Adam's descendants was total.[26] For Calvin, concupiscence was the nature of sin (and it is often expressed popularly that "man sins because he is a sinner," that is, out of his perverted *state* proceed his evil *acts*), while for Luther and Melanchthon, unbelief (lack of fear of God) was the essential nature of sin, while concupiscence was seen as a consequence of unbelief. The Formula of Concord also emphasized that human cooperation in salvation (sometimes called synergism) is wholly excluded because of the corruption and depravity inherited from Adam.

---

[23] "Concupiscence" is a word that means "desire," or "longing in the soul." Patristic writers often presented this "desire" as being pitted against the will, hindering any free decisions. It was Augustine's views on concupiscence that were made official Catholic Doctrine at the Council of Trent, in its *Decree on Original Sin*. Paul will say something about "desire [for forbidden things?] being sin," Romans 7:7,8, but this desire is not inborn (as the theory of original sin has it); rather, it is something stimulated from without as the devil presents his temptations.

[24] See footnote #14 above.

[25] F.R. Tennant, "Original Sin," *Hastings Encyclopedia of Religion and Ethics*, Vol.9, p.562.

[26] Not only were the Reformers in opposition to Catholic dogma, but they were in opposition to the "humanists" such as Erasmus, who emphasized man's freedom of will.

Some did break from the Augustinian doctrine. Zwingli denied that total depravity is inherited from Adam, but he did admit a possible inclination to evil, which God punished only if it resulted in a man's willingly acting out the sinful thing. To Zwingli, it is the act, not the desire, that is the nature of sin. The Anabaptists also broke from the Augustinian position. Some avoided the term "original sin" because it is not found in the Bible, while others appealed to an urge for good that every man feels as proof that the doctrine of total depravity inherited from Adam is wrong. Still other Anabaptists rejected the doctrine because of their strong beliefs in the freedom of the will, and others taught that the rebirth of the spirit in conversion counteracted whatever penalty was imputed to the race when Adam sinned. Not a few of these Anabaptists went back to the Scriptures to ascertain what the Bible said on the subject!

> Hubmaier's booklet *Concerning Free Will* (1527) refers expressly to a passage by the prophet Ezekiel (18:4,20) that "the soul that sins shall die" (i.e., the soul may either sin, or not die) and he quotes Ezekiel's dictum that "the son shall not bear the iniquities of the father nor shall the father bear the iniquities of the son." This reference to Ezekiel is particularly significant for Anabaptist thought because it removes the fatalistic character of "inherited" sin which became so oppressive in Protestant orthodoxy and so hopeless as to life's possibilities.[27]

Sebastian Frank, in 1531, succinctly stated the Anabaptist position:

> Concerning original sin nearly all Anabaptists teach as follows: just as the righteousness (*Gerechtigkeit*) of Christ is to no avail to anyone unless he makes it a part of his own being through faith, so also Adam's sin (i.e., original sin) does not impair anybody except the one who makes it a part of his own being through faith, and likewise brings forth fruit of his sin. For as foreign righteousness does not save anybody, so will foreign sin not condemn anybody either.[28]

The earlier Arminians[29] taught something happened to Adam's physical body when he sinned, and this body, now susceptible to the ravages of disease and death, is what his descendants inherit. The later Arminians, however, particularly the followers of Wesley, taught that something corrupting happened to Adam's inner man, and this "bent to sinning"

---

[27] N. van der Zipp, "Original Sin," *The Mennonite Encyclopedia* (Scottdale, PA: Mennonite Publishing House, 1959), Vol.4, p.80. The same article shows that those few Anabaptists who did embrace a doctrine of original sin learned it, not from Paul's writings, but from 2 Esdras (which, for some reason, was a favorite book among the Anabaptists).

[28] van der Zipp, *op. cit.*, p.80-81. The remainder of this interesting article goes on to show that in subsequent years some Mennonites (spiritual descendants of the Anabaptists) have adopted Calvinistic views on original sin, but the majority have rejected the idea of an inborn sinful nature.

[29] Jacob Arminius (1560-1609) was a mild-mannered Dutch Reformed preacher who reacted against the dogmatic Calvinism of his time. His teachings came to be known as "Arminianism," and one of the distinguishing characteristics is the stress on man's part in salvation.

is passed on to the race.   So, among these later Arminians, we hear the expression "saved and sanctified" – which is a popular way to express the idea that conversion ("saved") takes care of the forgiveness we need for our own personal sins and that a later experience ("sanctified") takes care of the moral infection we inherited by birth from Adam.

The Westminster Confession of Faith, produced at the Westminster Assembly (1643-47), is the basis of the doctrine of most Presbyterian and Congregational[30] churches, and has deeply influenced Protestantism.   The Westminster Confession explicitly declares,

> By this sin [referring to the sin of Adam and Eve] they fell from their original righteousness and communion with God, and so became dead in sin, and wholly defiled in all the faculties and parts of the soul and body.   They being the root of mankind, the guilt of this sin was imputed, and the same death in sin and corrupted nature conveyed to all their posterity, descending from them by ordinary generation ... Man, by his fall into a state of sin, has wholly lost all ability to any spiritual good accompanying salvation, so that a natural man, being altogether averse from that good and dead in sin, is not able by his own strength to convert himself, or prepare himself thereunto.[31]

This Confession was one of the last of the great creeds and confessions that the church produced down through the centuries.   But when its presentation of original sin is compared with Scripture, it can be seen why many of the leaders of the Restoration Movement rejected all creeds, and expressed their beliefs in words like these: If the creed says more than the Bible, it says too much; if it says less than the Bible, it says too little; if it says the same as the Bible, why have the creed in the first place?

Liberal Protestant theologians in the 18th-20th centuries, and Neo-orthodox and Neo-liberal theologians in the 20th century, have largely abandoned any idea of original sin, and many have even abandoned what the Bible says about the nature of personal sin.   Most of these theologians have started with the currently popular philosophy of their day, and tried to make the Bible match it, in hopes that by this process the Bible would be made more acceptable to modern man.   In one sense, the use of current philosophy as a starting point from which to build one's world view is nothing new.   Augustine derived his views from Greek philosophy, and attempted to make Christian doctrine match.   Aquinas, too, tried to assimilate Christianity to Aristotelian philosophy.   However, when the more recent theologians and philosophers went to work, the prevailing philosophy was not Platonism, Neo-Platonism, or Aristotelianism, but Rationalism, Hegelianism, or Existentialism. Starting with these philosophical presuppositions, and trying to assimilate them with Chris-

---

[30] Congregationalism includes the Separatists and Pilgrims, and these groups deeply influenced church history and doctrine in England, the Netherlands, and New England.

[31] Philip Schaff, ed., *The Creeds of Christendom*, 3 vols. (Grand Rapids: Baker Book House, 1966). Vol.3, p.615,623.

tianity, has proven to produce even less satisfactory results.[32]

This historical sketch of the doctrine of original sin has revealed several important conclusions:

- The doctrine as formulated by Augustine and taught by Calvin is more the result of philosophy than of deductions from Scripture.
- Many churchmen through the years have rejected the idea of inherited depravity from Adam by Adam's posterity.
- What in one generation is intended only as a defense of orthodoxy becomes crystallized as dogma in the next.

Were it not for Augustine and the dominance of the Roman church (and the Roman church admits her doctrine was developed more by the church than found in Scripture), one wonders if Western Christianity would have been agitated by the doctrine of an inborn sinful nature.

III. INTERPRETATIONS OF SOME OF THE BIBLICAL PROOF TEXTS FOR ORIGINAL SIN

In Psalm 51:3-6, as David confesses his sin to God, it will hardly do to make him say, "God, I couldn't help myself, because I was born that way," yet this is exactly what

---

[32] Leibniz, Kant, Schleiermacher, Hegel, Julius Muller, and Ritschl, all were philosophers who set forth their own views of what "sin" is and what "original sin" means (see these views summarized in Tennant, *op. cit.*, p.563-564). For some it was selfishness, for others it was a defect in nature, for others it was social injustice. Liberal Protestants rejected the doctrine of original sin as being incompatible with scientific knowledge (man's origins were brutish, and a moral state like Adam's took ages to evolve) as well as with moral insight (a man can be held to be guilty only for his own deliberate acts). The evolutionary theory of Herbert Spencer and Charles Darwin ruled out any responsibility to God for sin, for there was no sin *per se*. In America, Ralph W. Emerson's transcendentalism in effect denied any moral evil in human experience, while Walter Rauschenbusch's Social Gospel supplanted the idea of personal sin with social evil. Next came the environmental and behavioristic psychology of Thorndike and Watson, where man is a product of his heredity and environment; since he has no control over these, he is not morally responsible for his actions. For Freud and his followers, sin is simply an illusion. Liberal churchmen adapted these ideas, and now talked about how man by his own efforts was approaching closer and closer to being perfect (ideas which were envisioned by William James and John Dewey). Two world wars, the Great Depression, violent crime and political corruption caused a loss of faith in the inevitability of human progress. C.S. Lewis' *Screwtape Letters* (New York: Macmillan Co., 1961) helped churchmen once again to see that a real devil and actual personal sins are indeed a problem. In more recent times, Neo-orthodoxy (Barth, Brunner, and Tillich) has denied there was any historic Adam to whom any inherited sinfulness could be connected. Neo-orthodox ideas about sin and original sin are summarized nicely in Bernard Ramm, *A Handbook of Contemporary Theology* (Grand Rapids: Wm. B. Eerdmans Publishing Co., 1966), p.117-119. Neo-liberalism, beginning with Bultmann, has tried to demythologize the Bible. Sin becomes a myth, with Adam in the Genesis 3 account being a sort of religious everyman, for the account there is not believed to be history, but only a pictorial presentation of what happens to every man on earth. For Bonhoeffer, original sin simply expressed the idea of social injustice. In the radical theology of the 1960's (Robinson, Altizer, Hamilton), with its deification of humanity, there is no personal sin, nor any moral responsibility to God. These Neo-liberal ideas are nicely summarized by Martin E. Marty and Dean C. Peerman, eds., *A Handbook of Christian Theologians* (Nashville: Abingdon, 1965), and Stanley N. Gundry and Alan F. Johnson, eds., *Tensions in Contemporary Theology* (Chicago: Moody Press, 1976).

David would be saying if verse 5 teaches inborn depravity inherited from one's parents. How much better to understand verse 5 to be an acknowledgment that no matter what influences to evil one finds in other people, still (as verses 4 and 6 indicate) God still expects each individual to conform to His will.[33]   Still, it must be admitted, when a reader consults the commentaries on Psalm 51:5, he will find the comments to be slanted so as to agree with the denominational position of the individual author on original sin.[34]

Psalm 14:2,3 should not be used to prove an inherited sinful nature, as it sometimes is.   It plainly reads "they have all turned aside ... become corrupt."   If a man is born in sin, how is it possible to go aside?   The fact that they went aside is evidence they were not born that way.   Indeed, if the definition of sin given in Special Study #3, that it is an act, a violation of God's law, is correct, then it is impossible for sin to be inherited.

Ephesians 2:1-3 give a picture of what life was like before the readers of that letter became Christians.   They were "dead in ... trespasses and sins," that is, they were "dead *because of* their own trespasses and sins," not because of something inherited from their parents.   And when it says they were "by nature" children deserving God's wrath, "by nature" means because of long practice,[35] rather than that they used to sin just because it came naturally as a result of inborn fleshly depravity.

Those verses where "flesh" is opposed to "spirit" can be understood in the light of the fact the devil has the ability to stir up the desires of the flesh, and thus induce the man to do something opposite of what his "spirit" might otherwise prompt him to do.   Some men's understandings do become darkened, but Romans 1 has indicated this is because of their own personal sins, not Adam's.

---

[33] The traditional view is that David was the last child born to Jesse.   Perhaps the mother of David was different from the mother of the older sons, and the union of she and Jesse was not in good taste.   "Nothing is known concerning his mother; the references in Psalms 86:10 and 116:16 to David himself as 'the son of thy handmaid' are too uncertain of identification to postulate for her the virtue of 'godliness.'   Dean Stanley suggests David's mother may have been the wife or concubine of Nahash, and then married Jesse.   This, he thinks, will agree with the difference of age between David and his sisters.   [David's sisters were some years older than he, for David had some nephews, sons of his older sister Zariliah, who were about the same age as David.]   The later rabbis represent him as born in adultery (Psalm 51:5)."   George L. Robinson, "David," in *International Standard Bible Encyclopedia* (Grand Rapids: Wm. B. Eerdmans Publishing Co, 1949), Vol.2, p.790.

[34] For example, Adam Clarke gives a paragraph on "conceive" to show that it speaks of the time the baby is in the warmth of the womb, and so must refer to depravity or corruption being present to the embryo while still in the womb.   He writes, "As my parts were developed in the womb, the sinful principle diffused itself through the whole, so that body and mind grew up in a state of corruption and moral imperfection."   *The Holy Bible ... With Commentary and Critical Notes* (Cincinnati: The Methodist Book Concern, nd), Vol.3, p.384.   On the other hand, several writers note that "conceive" is the word usually used of animals in heat, and so suppose that the conception of David was the result of a lustful union.   See Lange's *Commentary on Psalms* (Grand Rapids: Zondervan Publishing House, nd), and Gesenius, *Hebrew and Chaldee Lexicon* (Grand Rapids: Wm. B. Eerdmans Publishing Co., 1963) on *yacham*, p.346.

[35] See comments on "by nature" at Romans 2:14.

CONCLUSION

It is likely true that it is because there are a few verses that might (at first glance) teach the doctrine of hereditary depravity that the debate has raged for so long in the church. But it is also true that the majority of the early proponents and defenders of the doctrine of original sin taught it, not because it was clearly set forth in Scripture, but because their presuppositions or philosophical systems demanded some such doctrine if they were going to be logically consistent. It also seems evident from our historical study that certain parts of the doctrine resulted from the heat of controversy rather than from a clear word of Scripture. Once this history is understood, and it is seen that it was clearly not until post-apostolic times that churchmen "found" original sin to be taught in the Bible, it helps remove any hesitation one might have about presenting Romans 5:12ff (as was done earlier in this commentary) as teaching that what is hereditary (i.e., imputed to the race by God) is physical death, and nothing more. To be sure, the Augustinian-Calvinistic hereditary depravity theory is widely taught and widely accepted, but that does not necessarily make it right.

Worded popularly, the consequence of Adam's sin to the race is this: the moment a baby is born it begins to die physically. Disease and sickness are the means by which physical death is finally victorious.

SELECTED BIBLIOGRAPHY

Babcock, Wm. S., "Augustine's Interpretation of Romans (AD 394--396)," *Augustinian Studies*, 10 (1979), p.55-74.

Barth, Karl, *Christ and Adam: Man and Humanity in Romans 5*. New York: Harper and Row, 1956.

Bultmann, Rudolf, "Adam and Christ According to Romans 5," in *Current Issues in New Testament Interpretation*, edited by W. Klassen and G.F. Snyder. London: SCM, 1962, p.143-165.

Burns, J.P., "The Interpretation of Romans in the Pelagian Controversy," *Augustinian Studies*, 10 (1979), p.43ff.

Danker, F.W., "Romans 5:12: Sin Under Law," *New Testament Studies*, 14 (1967-68), p.424-439.

Denny, James, "Fall," *Hastings Encyclopedia of Religion and Ethics*, edited by James Hastings. New York: Charles Scribner's Sons, 1921. Vol.5, p.701-705.

Duke, David N., "Schleiermacher: Theology Without a Fall," *Perspectives in Religious Studies*, 9 (1982), p.21-37.

Garcia, Albert L., "Original Sin and the Unborn," *Concordia Theological Quarterly*, 47:2 (April 1983), p.147-152.

Johnson, S.L., "G.C. Berkouwer and the Doctrine of Original Sin," *Bibliotheca Sacra,* 132 (1975), p.316-326.

Kirn, O., "Sin," *The New Schaff-Herzog Encyclopedia of Religious Knowledge*, edited by Samuel Macauley Jackson. Grand Rapids: Baker Book House, 1957. Vol.10, p.432-439.

Lard, Moses E., "Original Sin," *Lard's Quarterly*, 3 (January 1866). Kansas City: Old Paths Book Club, 1950 (reprint), p.136-154.

Marcus, Joel, "The Evil Inclination in the Epistle of James," *Catholic Biblical Quarterly*, 44:4 (October 1982), p.606-621.

Murray, John, *The Imputation of Adam's Sin*. Phillipsburg, NJ: Presbyterian and Reformed Publishing Co., 1979. (This material originally appeared in *The Westminster Theological Journal,* XVIII/2, XIX/1, XX/1.)

Oehler, Gustave F., *Theology of the Old Testament*. Grand Rapids: Zondervan Publishing House, reprint nd. (Originally published in 1873-74). p.229-245.

Quek, Swee-Hwa, "Adam and Christ According to Paul," *Pauline Studies*, edited by Donald A. Hagner and Murray J. Harris. Grand Rapids: Wm. B. Eerdmans Publishing Co., 1980. Chapter 5, p.67-79.

Scroggs, R.J., *The Last Adam: A Study in Pauline Anthropology*. Oxford: Basil Blackwell, 1966.

Tennant, F.R., "Original Sin," *Hastings Encyclopedia of Religion and Ethics*, edited by James Hastings. New York: Charles Scribner's Sons, 1921. Vol.9, p.558-565.

Turner, David L., "Ephesians 2:3c and *peccatum originale*," *Grace Theological Journal*, 1:1 (Fall 1980), p.195-218.

Van der Zipp, N., "Original Sin," *Mennonite Encyclopedia*. Scottdale, PA: Mennonite Publishing House, 1959. Vol.4, p.79-83.

Weaver, David, "From Paul to Augustine: Romans 5:12 in Early Christian Exegesis," *St. Vladimir's Theological Quarterly*, 27:3 (1983), p.187-206.

C. God's Plan of Salvation (Justification by Faith) Involves Blessed Effects on Slaves of Sin. 6:1-23.

Summary: "The sin" entered the world when Adam sinned, and eventually gained dominion over all men. That God's way of saving men delivers men from this reign of sin in their lives is demonstrated by a reminder of the significance of baptism (6:1-14), and by an illustration drawn from the world of slavery (6:15-23).

6:1 – *What shall we say then? Are we to continue in sin that grace might increase?*

What shall we say then? Since this is almost the same question with which chapter 4 began, some outline Romans as though chapter 6 were Paul's answer to another supposed objection a Jew might raise to his doctrine of justification by faith (3:21-28).[1] Others note the close connection with the thought about how grace super-abounds where sin increases (expressed in 5:20), and suppose Paul is anticipating an inference that someone might erroneously deduce from this teaching. Paul clearly teaches that it is not a proper inference to draw from 5:20,21 that justified men are at liberty to plunge on in sin.

Are we to continue in sin.[2] Before a man is converted, he is under the dominion of sin.[3] To continue "in sin" would be to continue to commit sin as he had committed sins before his conversion.

---

[1] In chapter 3, Paul has clearly indicated that salvation is conditioned on faithfulness. Maybe then, since it does not demand sinless perfection, it encourages a man to go ahead and sin. Paul's detractors might ask, "If there are no 'laws' that must be kept, what controls a man's behavior?" Paul will show that the Christian is free from the bondage of sin, free to control his own behavior (with the help of the indwelling Holy Spirit).

[2] A subjunctive mood verb (such as is used here) could be translated as hortatory ("Let us continue in sin!") or as deliberative ("Are we to continue?"). The translators must decide which it is. Here the deliberative idea is best; it leads the reader to turn this question over in his mind, to meditate on it, and to ponder its ramifications and consequences.

[3] Ever since 5:12, with the exception of 5:13, Paul has been using the expression "*the* sin" (there is an article in the Greek before the word *hamartia*), and seems to mean by it the idea of sin's power or dominion. It would seem beneficial at this point to explain the concept of "bondage to sin" from which (as chapter 6 shows) justified men are freed. When a man commits his first sin, he dies spiritually (chapter 7 will show), and at that point he becomes what the Bible calls a "slave to sin." His spirit is no longer able consistently to control the body in which he lives. We also tend to believe that the devil no longer has to seek permission before he tempts the man who has become such a slave to sin (though he may ask as he did in the case of Job and Peter). When the devil tempts a man who has died spiritually, the man responds to the desires the devil has stirred up in his body, and the man sins, because his spirit is no longer able to control consistently. More will be said on this topic of slavery to sin at Romans 6:6.

That this concept of "bondage to sin" may be better understood, several contrasting thoughts should be pondered. 1 Corinthians 10:13 seems to suggest that there is "the way of escape" provided for the Christian, right at the moment he is tempted, that is not provided in the case of the unconverted man who still is in bondage to slavery. Romans 8:1-3 will show that, for the Christian, God puts some limits on the devil. Jesus evidently implied the same thing in the Model Prayer when He taught His disciples to pray, "Do not permit us to be tempted, but deliver us from the evil one." Also, the fact that repentance can lead to a change of behavior, will show that even for the slave of sin, the bondage is not absolute.

That grace might increase? This purpose clause may express the motive behind the suggestion to continue on in sin, namely, in order that God may have opportunity to demonstrate His super-abounding grace. An objector could draw this inference from Paul's teaching: if when sin abounds, God has opportunity to show how His grace super-abounds, then does it not follow we should sin more, thus giving God an opportunity to be more gracious?

6:2 – *May it never be!   How shall we who died to sin still live in it?*

May it never be![4]   Paul's rebuttal of any such false inference that someone might draw from his teaching is in strong and indignant language. Reasons why such a conclusion is unthinkable are given in the following verses. Men who have been justified by faith are positively *not* to continue living in sin!

How shall we who died to sin still live in it?[5] "We" would include both Paul and his readers, all of those who have been justified by faith. The pronoun translated "we" (*hoitines*) carries the idea of "being such as" those who died to sin. To continue to live in sin is completely inconsistent for people "such as" we are. "We who died to sin" is a strong expression denoting the fact that "*the* sin" no longer has the power it once did. "The moment a man is dead he ceases to respond to stimuli. Coax him, command him, threaten him – no response, no reaction. The sphere in which he once moved is his sphere no longer."[6] Verses 3 and 7 will help us understand the time in the past when Paul and his readers "died to sin." This dying to sin, this liberation from the power of sin, takes place when a man is baptized, those verses will show. To Paul, any notion that a liberated slave would deliberately want to voluntarily and habitually submit to his old master is disgusting and revolting.[7]

6:3 – *Or do you not know that all of us who have been baptized into Christ Jesus have been baptized into His death?*

Or do you not know.   This verse gives in expanded form one reason for not continuing in sin. The thread of thought begun in verse 2 continues. 'We Christians indeed have died to sin, or are you really ignorant of what our very baptism involved?' "Do you not know" is Paul's characteristic way of appealing to a well-known truth,[8] and simple reflec-

---

[4] See this expression explained at Romans 3:4.

[5] The KJV, "we that are dead to sin," might leave the reader with an improper idea of the meaning of this question, for it might imply a "state of being" rather than simply (as the Greek does) a definite act in the past time.

[6] Lenski, *Romans*, p.389-90.

[7] "For a Christian, continuing to <u>live</u> in sin is impermissible and impossible. Of course, Paul knows that even a believer commits random acts of sin until the day of his release from this earthly existence." Hendriksen, *Romans*, p.195.

[8] It certainly is to be inferred that the instruction given to penitent believers before their baptism included an explanation of the significance of the act of baptism. One thing Paul expected all the Roman Christians

tion on that truth should have kept any of his readers from drawing the false inference raised in verse 1.

That all of us who have been baptized into Christ Jesus. The Christians Paul addresses in this passage were all distinctly and perfectly conscious that they had been baptized.[9] There certainly was no infant baptism in the Roman church.[10] This passage also speaks to those 21st century Bible teachers who would treat baptism as though it were really nothing more than an outward sign of an inward grace. Remember, such teaching presupposes that in salvation man is wholly passive, and is saved (justified) the moment God gives the man faith. Even if that were true (and it hardly is, if it is a fact that "faith comes by hearing the Word of God"), this passage would still affirm that the dominion of sin, the slavery to sin, is not broken until baptism![11] Precisely because this verse, in no uncertain terms, connects "baptism" with "died to sin" (i.e., it was when the penitent believer is baptized that this death to sin takes place), those teachers who would downplay the importance of baptism in water must find some way to explain away its clear meaning. (1) One popular attempt is to draw it to our attention that Paul nowhere mentions "water" in chapter 6. Therefore, it will be alleged, it is not at one's baptism in water that he dies to sin, but rather at the time of one's being "baptized in the Spirit" as 1 Corinthians 12:13 talks about.[12] (2) Another popular attempt is the allegation that "into" (in "baptized *into*

---

to know is that it is at baptism that the old slavery to sin is broken. Since Paul has never been to Rome, the only way they could be expected to know this is if candidates for baptism were universally so taught in the early church.

[9] There is no intimation in "all of us who have been baptized" that there were some Christians at Rome who had not been baptized. Such an interpretation might be given to the English translations at this place, but it is an improper interpretation, for the Greek does not at all suggest any such meaning.

[10] T.E. Watson, *Baptism Not for Infants*, p.50, maintains that it is impossible to understand Romans 6:2-4, "except on the supposition that *all* those to whom Paul was writing had been baptized as professed believers." Quoted by Wilson, *Romans*, p.99.

[11] "From this and other references to baptism in Paul's writings, it is certain that Paul did not regard baptism as an 'optional extra' in the Christian life, and that he would not have contemplated the phenomenon of an 'unbaptized believer.' ([Paul's] references to baptism in 1 Corinthians 1:14-17 do not mean that he regarded the sacrament itself as unimportant, but rather that the identity of the baptizer was unimportant. [Paul] takes it for granted that all the members of the Corinthian church were baptized, 1 Corinthians 1:13, 6:11, 10:1ff.)

"In apostolic times it is plain that baptism followed immediately upon confession of faith in Christ. The repeated accounts of baptism in Acts give ample proof of this ... Faith in Christ and baptism were, indeed, not so much two distinct experiences as parts of one whole; faith in Christ was an essential element in baptism, for without it the application of water, even accompanied by the appropriate words, would not have been baptism." Bruce, *Romans*, p.136. Bruce's comments are correct, but the use of the word "sacrament" may be suspect; we would prefer to call baptism an 'ordinance of Christ.' The use of the expression "application of water" is also perhaps overly vague, since immersion is the form universally taught in the New Testament. See James Gilchrist Lawson, *Did Jesus Command Immersion? An Exhaustive Study of the Word "Baptize"* (Cincinnati: Standard Publishing Co., 1947).

[12] 1 Corinthians 12:13 does read, "for by one Spirit were we all baptized into one body," but it is doubtful that the "Spirit" is the element into which people were immersed. Rather, most commentators understand this to be a dative of agent, and so explain the verse to teach that "by the agency of the Holy Spirit, we were all led to the place where we wanted to be baptized (in water) into the body (the church)." Such an

Christ") really means "in connection with." That is, because they were already in connection with Christ by faith, they were later baptized (in water).[13] Neither of these attempts to circumvent the plain meaning of what Paul wrote can be tolerated. On the first, how is someone who has never been immersed to know (as Paul's Roman readers knew!) if he has ever been "baptized in the Spirit"? The way these teachers explain "baptized in the Spirit," it is something mysterious, rather than something a convert is consciously aware of. Not only do they explain away the real import of baptism, but they have robbed Paul's argument of any force. Only if the word "baptized" has reference to an immersion in water (such as Jesus commanded as He gave the Great Commission, and which has always been the initiatory act by which one enters into Christ and His church), does Paul's argument in chapter 6 have any cogency.[14] On the second, how are we to harmonize this alleged meaning of verse 3 with the clear affirmation of verse 7? The alleged meaning (i.e., that a person is 'in union with Christ' before he is baptized) of verse 3 would have a man saved (justified) before he is dead to sin, yet verse 7 clearly affirms a different time sequence for "died (to sin)" and "justified" – either the two are contemporaneous, or a man is 'dead' before he is "justified."[15]

---

explanation is in harmony with those verses that teach how the Holy Spirit works through the Word to bring men to the conviction of their sins and of their need for justification. It is also in harmony with the accounts of conversion in Acts where we are plainly told that it was "in water" that penitent believers were baptized.

[13] The word translated "into" is *eis* in the Greek, and it regularly signifies motion toward. In Koine Greek, the preposition *en* is the one that usually is translated "in." Even while agreeing that the meaning of this preposition *eis* is changing as we move from Classical to Koine to Modern Greek (indeed, *en* has disappeared from Modern Greek, and *eis* is regularly used in its stead), so that *eis* no longer signifies motion toward, but simply rest in a place (i.e., it is an example of what is called static *eis*), it still would not be proper to interpret *eis* in Romans 6:3,4 as though it were static. Let us for the moment attempt to translate here as though *eis* were static, with the resultant meaning that a man is already in union with Christ before he is baptized, and notice the difficulties that immediately result. Romans 6:2,3 taken together tell us that it is at baptism that one dies to sin. Baptism and death to sin are vitally connected. No baptism, no death. No death, still in slavery to sin. Now if "into (*eis*) Christ" means because a man is already in Christ he should be baptized, then it would follow that a man in Christ can still be a slave to sin, for the slavery is still not broken till baptism. This is clearly an unacceptable position to hold or teach! How much better to present it just as Paul does, that baptism is essential to being freed from the old slavery to sin. In other words, in Romans 6, *eis* (as it regularly does) signifies motion towards. Again, we might appeal to Galatians 3:26,27, where *eis* appears. While some might wish to argue it is another example of static *eis*, this clearly will not do, for the Galatians passage goes on to say that in baptism one "puts on Christ," not before. *Eis* in Galatians must denote motion toward. And if even but one passage teaches "motion toward" as being connected with baptism, then baptism is one of the essential conditions a man must meet if he would be saved. One final piece of evidence can be obtained by examining the English translations (RSV, Phillips, NEB, TEV, NASB, NIV, etc.) that have been made since it was known there is such a thing as static *eis*, and it will be seen that there is almost universal agreement that *eis* in Romans 6:3 denotes motion toward. These modern translations render *eis* as "baptized into Christ" and "baptized into (or into union with) His death."

[14] Vine, *Romans*, p.87, has written this explanatory paragraph about "baptized." "The word *baptizō* was necessarily transliterated into English, as there was no equivalent in our language. 'To immerse' would be simply 'to plunge into.' To baptize is to put into water and take out again. It involves immersion, submersion, and emergence, – death, burial and resurrection." Vine's comment is in the main correct, save for his statement about "no equivalent in our language." It is to be noted that *baptizō* was not transliterated at Matthew 26:23, but was translated "dipped."

[15] It is just possible that "died" (an aorist participle) in verse 7 precedes the being "justified" (verse 6).

Since the attempts to explain away the vital importance of baptism are specious, let it once more be affirmed that "baptized" here has reference to the same baptism Jesus commanded as He gave the Great Commission, namely, an immersion in water.[16]   And let it once more be affirmed that such a "baptism" puts the candidate "*into* Christ Jesus."[17]

Have been baptized into His death?   In chapter 3:24,25, Paul has demonstrated how the death of Christ was a "redemption" and a "propitiation" that made it possible for God to justify the man who has faith in Jesus.   Chapter 5 has emphasized how the "one act of Christ" has resulted not only in "justification of life to all men" but made it possible that "grace might reign through righteousness to eternal life."   Now Paul says that when a man is baptized into Christ, he also is baptized into the benefits that were wrought by Christ's death.   Jesus died to make it possible for God to justify believers, and at baptism a man enters into the salvation that God has provided.   At baptism, the man has fulfilled the initial condition on which God imputes righteousness.[18]   It is when a penitent believer in Jesus is baptized that Christ's death becomes efficacious for that believer; the time of his baptism is when he is justified, has his sins forgiven, and is reconciled to God, all of which were made possible because of the death of Christ.

6:4 – *Therefore we have been buried with Him through baptism into death, in order that as Christ was raised from the dead through the glory of the Father, so we too might walk in newness of life.*

Therefore we have been buried with Him through baptism into death.   "Therefore" seems to introduce a consequence of having been united with Christ in His death.   Scripture everywhere emphasizes the fact that Christ not only died, but He also was buried.   Thus, if a man is united by baptism into His death, he is also united in burial.   The expres-

---

It is regularly true that the time of the action in a participle is related to the time of the action of the main verb on which the participle depends.   For instance, a *present* participle indicates action contemporaneous with the action of the main verb, whereas an *aorist* participle means that the action indicated by the participle preceded the time of the action indicated by the main verb.   Since "died" (in verse 7) is an aorist participle, and "justified" (verse 6) is the main verb in the verse, it may be that Paul is affirming that the "dying" (at baptism) preceded the time of being "justified."

[16] It is true that "water" is not specifically mentioned in this context, nor is it mentioned in some of the conversion accounts in Acts when we are informed that the penitent believers were "baptized."   Just as it can hardly be disputed that what Jesus commanded was baptism in water, so it can hardly be doubted that what the converts submitted to (as recorded in Acts) was baptism in water.   It has been rightly said that every time the word "baptism" appears in the New Testament, if the reference is to something other than immersion *in water* (e.g., "baptism of suffering" or "baptism of the Holy Spirit"), the context specifically tells us.

[17] Some New Testament scholars have affirmed that there is something deliberate in the way the names for the Son of God are used in the New Testament.   "Jesus Christ" is thought to emphasize the fact that the "man" Jesus was none other than the oft-promised and long-awaited Messiah, while "Christ Jesus" puts emphasis on the exalted and glorified One (Christ) who had previously come into the world for our salvation (Jesus).

[18] Review the notes at Romans 3:22-28 on God's imputing or reckoning righteousness on the condition of "faith," and review the notes in chapter 4 where it was demonstrated that it is an "obedient faith" that meets the definition of the *faith* that saves.

sion "we have been buried" is likely to have reference to the momentary burial beneath the waters of baptism, as the person is baptized into Christ.[19]   The words "into death" likely are best connected with "baptism" rather than "buried;" at least that is what a comparison with what was said in verse 3 would suggest, for there it spoke of "baptized into His death." However, because the Greek at Romans 6:4 reads *the* death" instead of "*His* death" as verse

---

[19] Though the inference is disputed by a few (for example, Murray, *Romans*, p.215, footnote), the list of Bible scholars who find reference to the apostolic practice of immersion in water as the mode of baptism is almost endless.   We quote some of these, not as though immersion must be true simply because of the sheer number of men who so teach, but in order that some of these men's spiritual children may ponder whether they have done what their own denominational teachers have admitted the Bible teaches.

Chrysostom on John 3 (*Hom.* xxv) wrote, "When we sink our heads in the water as if in a tomb, the old man is buried, and, going down, is wholly hid once for all."

Philip Schaff (Lange's *Commentary on Romans*, p.302) writes, "All commentators of note [except Stuart and Hodge] expressly admit or take it for granted that in this verse the ancient prevailing mode of baptism by immersion and emersion is implied, as giving additional force to the idea of the going down of the old and the rising of the new man."

Albert Barnes [Presbyterian] wrote, "It is altogether probable that the apostle in this place had allusion to the custom of baptizing by immersion."   *Romans*, p.148.

John Wesley [Methodist] said, "We were buried with him – alluding to the manner of baptizing by immersion."   *Explanatory Notes upon the New Testament*, (published by G. Lane and C.B. Tippett, for the Methodist Episcopal Church at the Conference Office, 220 Mulberry St., Joseph Longking, Printer, 1846, New York).   p.220.

Adam Clarke [Methodist] wrote, "It is probable that the apostle here alludes to the mode of administering baptism by immersion, the whole body being put under the water, which seemed to say: the man is drowned, is dead; and when he came up out of the water, he seemed to have a resurrection of life; the man is risen again; he is alive."   *Commentary on Romans*, p.78.

Conybeare and Howson [Church of England] say, "This passage cannot be understood unless it be borne in mind that the primitive baptism was by immersion."   *Life and Epistles of St. Paul*, p.511.   Or again, "We know from the Gospels (Matthew 28:19) that the new converts were baptized 'in the name of the Father, and of the Son, and of the Holy Ghost' ... It is needless to add that baptism was ... administered by immersion, the convert being plunged beneath the surface of the water to represent his death to the life of sin, and then raised from the momentary burial to represent the resurrection to the life of righteousness." *Op. cit.*, p.345.

Martin Luther ("Sermon on Baptism," Vol.2, p.75 of his works edited in 1551) said, "The term 'baptism' is a Greek word; it may be rendered into Latin by *mersio*: when we immerse anything in water, that it may be entirely covered with water.   And though the custom be quite abolished among the generality (for neither do they entirely dip the children, but only sprinkle them with a little water), nevertheless they ought to be wholly immersed, and immediately drawn out again, for the etymology of the word seems to require it.   The Germans call baptism 'tauf' from depth, which they call 'tief' in their language; as if it were proper those should be deeply immersed, who are baptized.   And truly, if you consider what baptism signifies, you shall see the same thing required, for it signifies that the old man and our native character that is full of sin, entirely of flesh and blood as it is, may be overwhelmed by divine grace.   The manner of baptism, therefore, ought to answer to the signification of baptism, so that it may show forth a sign that is certain and full."   (Quoted by Grubbs, *Romans*, p.87,88.)

At Romans 6:4, the *Confraternity Edition of the Challoner-Rheims New Testament* [Roman Catholic] notes, "St. Paul alludes to the manner in which baptism was ordinarily conferred in the primitive church, by immersion.   The descent into the water is suggestive of the descent of the body into the grave, and the ascent is suggestive of the resurrection to a new life.   St. Paul obviously sees more than a symbol in the rite of baptism.   As a result of it we are incorporated into Christ's mystical body and live a new life."

Similar statements and teachings might easily be multiplied, but there is no need.   When, therefore, a man says the mode of baptism is unimportant, he is saying that it is not really important to do things the way Jesus commanded and the way the apostles practiced as they carried out His commands.   Rather than deliberately setting about to avoid what the Bible says, it would be much better to simply submit and obey.

3 did, there is some question whose death (Christ's, or the baptismal candidate's) verse 4 is referring to. The article ("the") before death might be an article of previous reference, namely, to Christ's death just specified in the close of verse 3. On the other hand, the omission of "His" might be intended to remind us that the main topic of the whole paragraph is the death to sin (verse 2) that breaks the old slavery to sin, and this expression "baptized into death" would then be telling us where and when that death to sin took place. The penitent believer has "died to sin" when he is buried in baptism.[20]

This is but one part of Paul's argument that the Christian may *not* continue in sin; namely, that in baptism a man becomes dead to sin and buried! "Baptism, according to Paul, while ... it is no magical rite effecting *ex opere operato* that which it signifies, is no empty sign but a decisive event by which a man's life is powerfully and unequivocally claimed by God."[21] Those who say that "baptism is but an outward sign of an inward grace," and mean by it that the man already is in Christ (forgiven, justified, reconciled) before he is baptized, and that baptism is just a picture of what has already happened previously in his heart, are not presenting it the way Paul does here in Romans. If, on the other hand, one wishes to say baptism is an outward sign of an inward grace, and mean by it that baptism pictures what is happening (death, burial, and resurrection) right at the time the baptism is being administered, then he would be speaking as Paul himself words it.

In order that as Christ was raised from the dead.[22] Here is a second consequence or result of being baptized into Christ. Not only is there a "burial," but just as He was raised from the dead, so the one being baptized is raised up out of the waters of baptism to walk in newness of life. Just as a burial demonstrates the reality of a death having occurred, so a burial would help demonstrate the reality of a resurrection. The expression "we have been buried" declares in the strongest manner our union with Christ in death and our entire separation from the former life in which sin reigned. That we have also been raised after

---

[20] Not a few writers object to this second interpretation of "baptism into death" on the grounds that a man is not buried until after he is dead. Thus it would be most unusual, it is alleged, if Paul were actually saying that the death to sin takes place only as the burial itself takes place. The idea is then advanced that the death to sin actually takes place at repentance. However true it may be in the physical world that death regularly precedes the burial by some time, it may not be true in the case of death to sin. Paul's presentation in verses 2-4 appears to say that the death and the burial are both tied together in the same act of baptism.

[21] Cranfield, *Romans*, p.304. Wording what Cranfield says in popular phraseology, Paul is *not* teaching what has come to be called "baptismal regeneration." That is, Paul is not saying that the mere act of dipping a man in itself produces or causes or results in his regeneration. ("Regeneration" in the expression "baptismal regeneration" is usually defined to mean the whole completed process of salvation.) Instead of defining regeneration as the whole process of salvation, this commentator tends to make "regeneration" synonymous with "conception," and understands 1 John 5:1 to say that the man who believes has been *conceived* (ASV). The one who has been conceived can become a "son of God," but he is not one yet. (John 1:12-13 say that the one who believes has been conceived.) And in Titus 3:5, Paul (instead of teaching that baptism produces regeneration) appears to teach that regeneration (i.e., coming to believe that Jesus is the Christ) precedes the washing (baptism), for he speaks of the "washing of (i.e., that results from) regeneration."

[22] The fact of Jesus' bodily resurrection from the dead has been expressed at Romans 4:24.

being buried is even more significant in showing that the old dominion of "the sin" (see notes at 5:20) is a thing of the past.

Through the glory of the Father. In this verse, "glory" seems to be synonymous with God's power or God's strength.[23] In some New Testament passages, the resurrection of Jesus is something Jesus Himself could accomplish, as He says in John 10:18; but in the majority of passages, as here, the resurrection is attributed to the operation of the Father.[24] The two explanations of how Jesus was raised are not inconsistent, but are easily understood in the light of His oneness with the Father in the Godhead.

So we too might walk in newness of life. "So" means "in like manner." Perhaps what is implied here is what is clearly stated in Ephesians 1:19,20 and Colossians 2:12, where it is stated that the same power that was used to raise Jesus from the dead is exerted to raise a man to walk in newness of life.[25] "Newness (*kainos*) of life" indicates a life new in quality, a life different from the "old life" which was characterized by continuance in sin or domination by the power of sin (verse 1). God's way of saving man includes the marvelous blessing of emancipation from the old slavery to sin! This change from slavery to freedom takes place at baptism. "If any man is in Christ, *he is* a new creature," 2 Corinthians 5:17, and both Romans 6 and Galatians 3:27 tell us that a man gets into Christ at the time of his baptism. "The beginning of the new life of believers, with the power as well as the obligation to lead such a life, is ever regarded as dating from their baptism."[26] Because of what was accomplished by Christ's death, burial, and resurrection, if a man is baptized into Christ, that baptism act accomplishes his death to sin, his burial as being dead to sin, and his resurrection to a new way of life. How monstrous, then, to entertain for even one moment, the idea that for some reason or another one might "continue in sin."

6:5 – *For if we have become united with* **Him** *in the likeness of His death, certainly we shall be also* **in** the likeness *of His resurrection,*

For if we have become united with *Him* **in the likeness of His death.**[27] "For" tells us that verse 5 is an explanation of what was just said in verse 4, a restatement of the same

---

[23] In Romans 3:23, "glory" was explained as being synonymous with "God's approval." It is possible that "glory" here in 6:4 also means "God's approval;" that is, God showed His approval of Jesus by raising Him from the dead.

[24] See Acts 2:24,32; 3:26; 10:40; 13:30; 2 Corinthians 4:14; Ephesians 1:20; Colossians 2:12; 1 Peter 1:21.

[25] On "walk," meaning "to conduct one's self" or "to live," see notes at Romans 4:12, though the word used here differs from the Greek word used at that place.

[26] Barmby, *Romans*, p.157.

[27] The NASB supplies "Him" in italics because there is no corresponding word in the Greek. In fact, "with" comes from the preposition *sun* in the compound *sumphutos*. However, since it is *His* death and *His* resurrection being talked about in the context, the sense is not materially affected by the insertion or omission of "Him."

idea in other terms. The word translated "united" (*sumphutos*) does not occur elsewhere in the New Testament. The KJV rendering, "If we have been *planted together*" is evidently not quite the right idea.[28] The word evidently comes from the process of grafting a shoot onto a tree, and so "united" or "grown together" is closer to the concept Paul is expressing. In baptism, the person who was immersed (baptized into His death, verse 3) becomes "grafted into" Christ.[29] "Likeness" tells us that the two deaths, Christ's and ours, are not absolutely identical. His was a physical death and resurrection; ours is a death to sin and a resurrection to spiritual life. Both deaths, nonetheless, are real, historical events.[30]

Certainly we shall be also *in the likeness* of His resurrection. "Certainly" translates *alla*, a word usually rendered by the adversative "but," though here it is more likely continuative and climactic, and the "certainly" of the NASB catches the idea nicely. "We shall be" is simply the way a consequence is expressed (*if* such a thing *is* the case, such other thing *will* follow).[31] To think the future "shall be" means that this "resurrection" was still off in the future for Paul's readers would be to misread what Paul is writing.[32] Again, verse 5 is a rephrasing by Paul of what he has just said in verse 4. As in verse 4, this "resurrection" in verse 5 is something the Christians had already experienced as they had come up out of the waters of baptism, rising to walk in newness of life.[33] As it meant when

---

[28] The Greek word *sumphutos* does not signify "planted." Were it from *sumphuteuō*, it might have this idea. But it is from *sumphuō*, which means "to grow together" or "to be brought forth together" and not "planted together." Arndt-Gingrich, *Lexicon*, p.788, suggests the word is one used by men in primitive times of their relationship to their divinity.

[29] Sanday and Headlam, *Romans*, p.157.

[30] For the past two centuries, critics have been anxious to find the "sources" behind Paul's teaching, whether it be on the Lord's Supper, or baptism into Christ, or the resurrection of Jesus. Starting from the preconceived notion that there is no supernatural, and ignoring or summarily dismissing Paul's own statements about the origin of his teaching (Galatians 1:11,12), these critics attempt to find natural sources that Paul must have reworked and then woven into the fabric of his theological system. Several favorite hunting grounds for these critics are the pagan mystery religions, Gnosticism, and Jewish apocalyptic writings. When something even remotely close is found, it is proclaimed that the source of Paul's material has been found. Barclay's note (p.85, *Romans*) about a pagan god (in the Greek mystery religions) who suffered, died, and rose again, is but a reflection of this critical search for naturalistic sources. J. Gresham Machen, *The Origin of Paul's Religion* (Grand Rapids: Wm. B. Eerdmans Publishing Co., 1925), long ago demonstrated that there is no evidence of a dying-rising savior god in mystery religions until 200 years *after* Paul. Lenski, *Romans*, p.397-98 also has a good paragraph on this same topic.

[31] Understanding the future to express simple *consequence*, the verse says, "If we have been united in the likeness of His death [and we were when we were plunged beneath the surface of the baptismal water], the consequence is that we are also united in the likeness of His resurrection [assuming, of course, that there was an emergence from the baptismal water]. Some have rejected the idea of consequence, and have supposed that the future tense here expresses an *obligation* – if we have been united in His death, we have an obligation to realize our position in our daily lives by refusing to continue longer in sin.

[32] There is a resurrection of the body still in the future, at the second advent, but this is not the verse to prove it. 1 Corinthians 15:22-28, or 1 Thessalonians 4:16, or even Romans 5:18 are some of the verses one should appeal to for the resurrection of the body.

[33] The concept expressed by "newness of life" in verse 4 is here expressed in the words "likeness of His resurrection."

used earlier, "in the likeness"[34] shows that Christ's and our "resurrections" are not absolutely identical. His was a physical resurrection, a reanimation of the body that had been buried; but as verse 8 explains, ours is not so much physical as it is spiritual, a new kind of life because the old dominion of sin has been broken.[35] And as before, there is also a sense in which both are alike. After His resurrection, Jesus' life was different from before; He was no longer subject to the pressures of temptations by the devil, because God put limits on the devil. Likewise, the Christian is no longer a slave to "the sin," and he does not need to succumb to the temptations offered by the devil, for God also puts limits on the devil (Romans 8:3).

One more comment is needful on this whole verse: do not fail to observe that this verse is a conditional sentence. It reads "*If*" we have been united.[36] If a man has not been immersed into Christ (united in the likeness of His death), he has no promise of being united with Christ in the likeness of His resurrection either!

6:6 – *knowing this, that our old self was crucified with* **Him,** *that our body of sin might be done away with, that we should no longer be slaves to sin;*

Knowing this. This participle is likely causal – i.e., "because we know this." *Ginōskō* is knowledge that comes by experience. What happened to us when we were baptized is something we are fully conscious of. We realize what has died as we were baptized, and we have experienced the truth that it is in newness of life that we have risen.

That our old self was crucified with *Him.* The term "old self" or, better, "old man", also occurs at Ephesians 4:22 and Colossians 3:9, and denotes man's condition when unregenerate, when under the dominion and condemnation of sin.[37] "Our 'old man' is the opposite of 'the new man' (Ephesians 4:22-24) and of 'a new creature' (2 Corinthians 5:17; Galatians 6:5)."[38] The "old man" is the whole man as he was before conversion but after committing his first sin, and coming under the power of sin. Thus "old man" is not the same thing as "outer man" only, or "inner man" only, about which Paul writes in 2 Corinthians 4:16. The word "crucified" is a reflection of the way Jesus died, into which men are

---

[34] Some would also supply the verb from the preceding clause, so that it reads "we shall also be *united with Him in the likeness* of His resurrection." The underlying doctrine is the same, whichever way we read it.

[35] Such a figurative use of the word "resurrection" is not without warrant in the New Testament. Something similar is done at John 5:24,25 and Revelation 20:5.

[36] Marshall J. Leggett, writing in the *Christian Standard*, 116/8 (February 21, 1981), p.10,11, has given an excellent, contemporary presentation of the "necessity of baptism for salvation." In it he pleads for a "Biblical, undenominational view" and presentation of the *meaning* of baptism.

[37] Those theology students who write from an original sin/total depravity standpoint often are inclined to identify the "old man" with what they call "sinful propensities" or the "old sinful nature." One is almost suspicious that "old *self*" in the NASB reflects such a theological viewpoint.

[38] Lenski, *Romans*, p.400.

baptized.[39]   "Crucified with Him" in this verse is just another way of saying what was expressed in the words "baptized into His death" in verse 3.   Whether or not there is any intimation by Paul (in his choice of this word) that the "old man" dies slowly and painfully as a man becomes a Christian is debated.[40]

That our body of sin might be done away with.   The person being baptized is not only perfectly conscious, Paul has said (verses 3-5), that as he was being baptized a death, burial, and rising again was taking place, but he also was aware that in his baptism the body of sin was made powerless.   "That" (*hina*) is likely a purpose clause.   One purpose, the recipient knew, of his baptism, was that the "body of sin might be put out of action."[41]

As the reader might guess, understanding this expression "body of sin" (along with the previous expression "old man") is crucial to an understanding of this passage.[42]   The easiest way to understand what Paul speaks about is this: (1) Remember that "*the* sin" all through this passage is pictured as being a power that wants to exercise dominion in the world.   (2) Remember that a man's body is one area where the devil has the ability to attack.   The devil has the ability to stir up bodily desires (verse 12 speaks of the "lusts" of the body), and if these desires are indulged, they result in acts of sin.   (3) Remember that until a man is baptized he is a slave to "the sin" (as the next phrase tells us).   (4) Finally, observe that Paul substitutes "mortal body" (verse 12) for "body of sin," and then goes on to describe how the members of the body can be ruled by and used by sin.[43]   Thus the "body of sin" is man's physical body to which the devil has access, the desires of which he can excite, and which he uses, as he ever works to extend his dominion of darkness over the whole world.[44]   As he writes "done away,"[45] what Paul is affirming is that the devil's

---

[39] The aorist tense in the verb "crucified" points back to the time of baptism.   Compare the use of the similar expressions ("buried with Him in baptism" and "nailed ... to the cross") in Colossians 2:12,14.

[40] Not a few of the writers who hold the doctrine of an inherited sinful nature are also men who have been sprinkled instead of immersed.   One wonders if their comments about how "painfully" the old man dies do not reflect the truth that without immersion there has not been experienced any real emancipation from the old bondage to sin.   Without immersion into Christ, they are not able to "know" what Paul says here in Romans 6:6 a man can "know by experience (*ginōskō*)."   "If Paul's language seems exaggerated, it is because we who were baptized as unconscious infants can hardly realize what baptism was to the adult believer in the apostolic age."   Gifford, *Romans*, p.128.

[41] Herein is suggested part of the content of the teaching regularly given to candidates for baptism in the early church.   No less content should be included in 21st century instructions on 'How to Become a Christian.'

[42] Lange, *Romans*, p.203-4, presents at least ten different interpretations.

[43] Paul does not reflect the old Greek philosophy that the body of man is evil in itself (the Greeks thought all matter was evil), or that the body is inherently sinful.   He does show that the body may be used either in the service of sin (6:13) or in the service of God (12:1,2).

[44] The reader is referred back to Special Study #3 on "The Doctrine of Sin" included at the close of chapter 5, where the method the devil uses was explained in some detail.

[45] The word is *katargeō*, and it means "to render inactive," or "powerless," or "ineffective."   Arndt-Gingrich, *Lexicon*, p.418.   The same word is translated "nullify" at Romans 3:3 and 4:14.

ability to use the "body" to get a man to sin is greatly limited when the man is baptized into Christ. No longer must the man be subservient to the body that has been made a slave of sin; he can regain control over the house he lives in, after that slavery to sin is broken at baptism.

That we should no longer be slaves to sin. Here we have stated the result that comes when the body of sin is done away with.[46] The old slavery to sin has been broken. That is, the result of being baptized into Christ (or as it is phrased earlier in this verse, of being "crucified with Him") is that the body no longer has to respond to "the sin" like a slave who was obligated to serve a master with no choice as to the kind or duration of the service. Sin does bind a man – and more and more, as he continues to sin. But in baptism into Christ, that bondage is ended. The slave has been set free! There is no further obligation or need to "continue in sin" (verse 1). Of course, just as slaves in the United States sometimes voluntarily chose to stay on and serve their old masters after Lincoln freed the slaves, so it is possible for an emancipated slave of sin to go back and serve his old master instead of the One who freed him. This, however, is a course of action that Paul will attempt to dissuade his readers from pursuing (verses 12-14).

6:7 – *for he who has died is freed from sin.*

For he who has died is freed from sin. This verse is evidently intended to provide a reason why it can be said they were no longer slaves to sin. In the world of slavery, when the slave died, his old master could get no more slaving out of him. Death freed him from the dominion of the master. The same is true when it comes to slavery to sin. "The sin's" old dominion over a person ends when that person has died, and remember that verses 2-4 have shown that this "death" takes place in baptism into Christ.[47] "Freed from sin" does not mean sinless perfection. Scripture in a number of places (one might point to this very context, verse 12-22) teaches that men in this life do not reach such a degree of holiness that they completely stop committing sins. There is a vast difference, however, between (a) committing an occasional sin, and (b) being a slave to sin. It is freedom from being a slave to sin that Paul is talking about in this verse.

---

[46] The construction is an articular infinitive in the genitive case, and this can express either purpose or result. Dana and Mantey, *Grammar*, p.213.

[47] Adverting for a moment to the topic introduced in footnote #40 above, it might be useful toward a complete understanding of how Paul's writings are explained, to observe that those students of Augustine and Calvin who believe there is an old sinful nature that lingers on after one becomes a believer and subsequently is sprinkled or poured, are often also likely to teach that there is an experience which follows what they call "conversion," that is needed before a man can get control of his old sinful nature. This experience involves heartfelt repentance, and is regularly called "sanctification." Could it be that such believers do get some relief from their habit pattern of sin, because repentance is a change of action; but could it also be that these religious people have substituted an experience resulting from repentance for the real "freedom" from slavery to sin that takes place when a man is baptized into death? In the light of these questions, it is very instructive to read Frew's footnote in *Barnes Notes on Romans*, p.147, to the effect that Paul *must* mean "dead only in a measure and not dead *altogether*," since, in his observation, it is men's experience to still have a *sinful nature* to struggle with after coming to faith. May we be so bold as to say that "faith minus immersion" or "faith plus sprinkling/pouring" is not the same kind of "faith" Paul teaches as being the condition of justification?

Before leaving this verse, it should be observed that the word translated "freed" is the same word elsewhere in Romans translated "justified." Since God is the one who imputes righteousness, it may be said that God is the Great Emancipator. When He justifies a man, God not only reckons righteousness to him (see 4:6-22), but He also puts certain limits on the devil. In the light of all that God does when He "justifies" a man, the translators were probably not far from the truth when they picked "freed" as the word to express what this verse says. And it should be included in our thinking that whereas Romans earlier makes "faith" the condition on which justification is reckoned, this verse words the condition as "he who has died (been baptized)." The two ideas must in some respect be complementary, and that is not surprising, for Galatians 3:26,27 also shows that the "faith" which is a condition for justification involves baptism.[48]

6:8 – *Now if we have died with Christ, we believe that we shall also live with Him,*

Now if we have died with Christ. This "if-clause" summarizes what has been presented about being "united with Him in the likeness of His death" in the preceding verses. The "if" does not express any doubt; rather, it is merely used to introduce (again) the main thought of this whole paragraph: a Christian, because of the blessing of being freed from slavery to sin, does not even consider continuing in sin (verse 1)!

We believe that we shall also live with Him. Again, as in verse 5, the future tense expresses consequence more than simple futurity. It is not talking about the remote future, after the second advent of Christ, but it is talking about living in "newness of life" (verse 4), beginning at the moment of baptism, and lasting all the rest of the days of this life. It is the very opposite of the living in the sin we did when still slaves of sin (verse 2). More of what is involved in living with Him is detailed in the verses following. After being raised with Christ, if Christians are to continue this being united with the likeness of Christ, they will have to live as He lives. And how is that? Jesus lives His whole life to please God (verse 10). This then is how the Christian believes he too is expected to live!

6:9 – *knowing that Christ, having been raised from the dead, is never to die again; death no longer is master over Him.*

Knowing that Christ. This phrase would be better translated "Since we know ...."[49] Our

---

[48] Note that Galatians 3:27 begins with "for," and thus verse 27 is giving a further explanation of what was just said in verse 26 about being "justified by faith." In light of what Paul writes in Romans 6 and Galatians 3, it can hardly be acceptable to affirm that the Bible teaches that a man is saved before he is baptized. Earlier at 6:4 (especially footnote #20), the whole question of when a man's "ethical death" occurs was introduced, but perhaps the issue should be addressed once more. Even were it to be admitted that a man dies to sin when he repents (and repentance is a change of mind and a change of action, a determination to be done with sin), still that would not meet God's revealed conditions for salvation, or deliverance from slavery to sin. Paul's closely reasoned presentation of "died to sin ... baptized into death ... he who has died ... is justified from sin" indicates that the deliverance from slavery to sin occurs as one is immersed, not before. And the "justification" also occurs at baptism, not before.

[49] Thayer, *Lexicon*, p. 174, shows that *oida* (know) followed by *hoti* (that) is used to introduce something that is "well known or acknowledged."

belief about Christ includes the known fact that He is alive forevermore. It is because of His never-ending life that Christians have assurance that their being united with Him means "continual living with Him." If He were liable to come again under the dominion of death, then it would follow that the Christian too (because of that union with Him) is liable to come under the dominion of sin again.[50]

Having been raised from the dead, is never to die again. "Dead" is plural, just as it was in verse 4, and suggests that when Christ was raised, there were many dead bodies left behind.[51] He need not ever die again, for the atoning death He has already suffered is sufficient for all! But more than that, He is now (since His resurrection) in a position where "death" cannot get control over Him.

Death no longer is master over Him. This implies that death once had dominion over Christ.[52] God cannot die, but Jesus incarnate could die because He was in a body like ours, a body inherited from Adam and therefore subject to the same physical death that has been passed on to the whole race (5:12-18a). Remember that verse 7 has specifically told us that death brings an end to the dominion of a master over his slave. Once the slave has died, the old master can exert no more mastery or dominion. Likewise in the case of our Lord: once He has died and has risen in His glorified body, that is the end of death's dominion, yea, the end of even the possibility of any further dominion.[53]

The point being developed is that Christians are very definitely *not* to continue in sin (verse 1). Just like death and resurrection brought a change in Christ's existence (He is no longer subject to dominion by death, or to temptation to sin), so when the old man died and the new man rose (as baptism into Christ took place), that brought a change in existence to one who up to that time had been in bondage to sin. Sin's dominion is broken, and there is help available to master the temptations the devil still puts forth.[54] If Christians were

---

[50] Verse 16 will show that there is a danger that continual sinning *will indeed* bring the Christian back under the dominion and bondage of sin. But continual sin that results in a return to slavery is something far different from the (one) first sin committed after reaching the age of accountability which resulted in slavery to sin.

[51] "Dead" is a plural adjective, and we must supply a noun to complete the sense; hence "dead bodies."

[52] "Master" represents *kurieuō* in the Greek, a word that signifies to have the power of a lord (*kurios*) over another. Some of the older English versions read, "death no more *hath dominion* over Him." It must not be forgotten that death lorded it over Christ with His consent. Of His own will He laid down His life (John 10:18). This fact of Christ's consent does not in any way change the fact that Jesus would never have been liable to die had He not become incarnate.

[53] "Him" is emphatic in the Greek, showing that there is a contrast between Jesus and some others. Over them death lorded it, but not over *Him*! "Others who had been raised from the dead [think of those raised by Jesus during His earthly ministry] returned to that common life of men in which death still had dominion over them, but with Christ it was not so." Gifford, *Romans*, p.128.

[54] Chapter 8 will detail how the Holy Spirit is available to help. 1 Corinthians 10:13 tells about the limitation God puts on the devil so his temptations are not so overpowering that there is no way to resist, and it also tells about the way of escape (from the temptation) that God provides every time the devil comes to tempt one of His children.

obliged to fear that Christ were still subject to the power of death, and to temptations from the devil, this help available to live the Christian life would not be very comforting or reassuring, for even with it, he would still have to fear that it might be all for nought.[55]

6:10 – *For the death that He died, He died to sin, once for all; but the life that He lives, He lives to God.*

For the death that He died, He died to sin, once for all. Verse 10 (as the first word "for" indicates) is further explanation of what all is implied in the fact that Jesus died and rose again.   As He died, He died "unto sin;" that is, His previous relation to "the sin" came utterly to an end.[56]   Just as sin tried to extend its dominion over every man, so it tried to get dominion over Jesus, too.   That is what the temptation in the wilderness (Matthew 4) was all about.   And if we take at face value Jesus' statement to the disciples as He entered the Garden of Gethsemane ("pray that ye enter not into temptation," Luke 22:40, ASV), we can also affirm that during the time in the garden, Jesus was being tempted again.   "The sin" was trying to gain mastery over Jesus.   Before His death, during His earthly days, Jesus was subject to temptation.   The devil was able to plant thoughts in His mind, and stir up the desires of His body, just as he does when he tempts any man.   But when Jesus died, this verse tells us, He was no longer subject to temptations.   Jesus' death and resurrection made a difference in His relationship to sin.   It was different after His death than it was before.   The same thing can be said for the one "united with Him in the likeness of His death."   There is a changed relationship.   No longer must the man who is baptized into Christ continue in sin.   The old dominion has been abruptly ended.   "Once for all"[57] says there was a finality, a completeness, to the changed relationship in the case of Jesus' death.   Likewise, one would anticipate a similar, decided break with sin in the life of the Christian.   Indeed, the Christian may not continue in sin as before.

But the life that He lives, He lives to God.[58]   Having risen from the dead, Christ now lives, and each moment He is pleased to do simply that which is in absolute harmony and union with God the Father.   It is, of course, not implied that before He died, when on earth, He lived in some other way than in harmony with God.   The contrast as this very context has shown is between the state of His humiliation when He could be stimulated by the devil's temptations, and the state of the changed relationship since His resurrection, when

---

[55] More will be said about the security of the believer in notes on chapter 8.

[56] Because the Greek reads "*the* sin" – i.e., the same expression that has been used since 5:12 to indicate the power or dominion of sin in the world – we tend to reject the interpretation of this verse which suggests that "Jesus died *for* sin," that is, to atone for it.   That is a true doctrine, but this is not the verse that teaches it.   For the doctrine that Jesus' death was an atonement for sins, see Romans 3:21-25 and 5:6-9; 2 Corinthians 5:21; Hebrews 7:27, 9:12,24-28, 10:10; and 1 Peter 3:18.

[57] *Ephapax*, "once for all," once and completely, is distinguished from *pote*, "once upon a time," and is a strengthened form of *hapax*, which also means "once for all."   Vine, *Romans*, p.91.

[58] It should be remembered that in the words "He lives!" we have the testimony of one who had seen Jesus after His resurrection.   On the Damascus Road, and more than once after that, the Risen Lord (He who was alive, was dead, and is alive evermore) appeared to Paul.   Paul could speak from experience when he testified that "He lives!"

only what God wills is all He must pay attention to. No other suggestion, no other enticement, no other stimuli, even interests Him. Christ's whole purpose in living is to promote the glory of God. How all of this relates to the topic at hand, about whether or not a Christian may continue in sin, the next verse will explain.

6:11 – *Even so consider yourselves to be dead to sin, but alive to God in Christ Jesus.*

Even so. Now we have the application of verse 10 to the reader. As Christ now lives only to bring glory to God, so should the powers of the Christian be exerted to promote the glory of God. Having died, been buried, and risen from the watery grave, the Christian is bound to live a different life. He cannot continue in sin on the pretext of making grace to abound.

Consider yourselves to be dead to sin, but alive to God in Christ Jesus. "Consider" is an imperative, a command – a command that continually must be carried out by the Christian. That in being baptized into Christ a man becomes dead to sin (i.e., sin's old mastery or dominion over the man has been abruptly ended) is a matter that has just been established by revelation. What happened in Jesus' case also happens in the convert's case. But perhaps it could be said that what was *absolute* in Jesus' case (i.e., death has no more dominion, the liability to temptation is ended, after His resurrection) is only *potential* in the Christian's case (i.e., the Christian must cooperate with God in this matter of control of the mind and body when the devil tempts). That is why the Christian is commanded to think, plan, and take into account ("consider") not only that he has died to sin, but that he is henceforth to live to God.[59] When a man keeps reminding himself that he is "dead to sin," he is really saying, "I will not respond to sin's allurements; I will not succumb to any stimulus to do evil." When, on the other hand, he keeps reminding himself "I am alive to God," he is really saying, "I will be open to spiritual stimuli, for I have an obligation to promote God's purposes and glory, and I will be quick to bring glory to God by my response."

6:12 – *Therefore do not let sin reign in your mortal body that you should obey its lusts,*

Therefore. Two lines of behavior will result if a man "thinks" in the manner that he has been commanded to think (verse 11). First, he will stop letting sin reign in his body, and stop using his body to commit sins. Secondly, he will yield only to God, and will use his body to do right things. A man's baptism is but the beginning of his new life. Whether or not sanctification follows depends both on "thinking" (verse 11) and "action" (verses 12,13). Paul's readers are here exhorted to cooperate with God so that what was potential in their initial salvation might become actual as their lives in Christ continue.

Do not let sin reign in your mortal body. The Greek prohibits the continuance of an ac-

---

[59] The fact that the Christian must continually reckon himself dead to sin and alive to God shows that the *possibility* of sinning is ever present. If he is to avoid the sinning, he must think positively and intentionally about how to respond to God's will. Just as "alive unto God" meant that Jesus now seeks to promote the purposes and glory of God, so when the Christian is commanded to consider himself "alive unto God," it means that he is bound to live and promote God's purposes and glory.

tion already going on.[60]   "Stop letting sin reign!" would be a good way to catch this implication.   A Christian still has temptations to sin; otherwise, this exhortation would be pointless.   But he is no longer a slave to "king sin" (verse 6), and thus he does have a responsibility to resist and refuse to do as tempted.   Because his spirit is alive in Christ, he can control the house he lives in (his "mortal body").   That the body is called "mortal" reminds us of 5:12 where mortality was decreed for the whole race because of Adam's sin, and now we learn that the Christian still is subject to that physical mortality even though he has risen to walk in newness of life.   A day is coming in the future when these mortal bodies will be given life (Romans 8:11), but until that future redemption of the body occurs (8:23) only the Christian's spirit can be said to be "living."[61]   The Christian is exhorted to control what happens in his body, indicating there is a difference between the inner man (2 Corinthians 4:6) and the mortal body in which the inner man lives.

For a number of verses now, it has been noted that Paul writes "*the* sin," and this has been explained as being a reference to the power or dominion of sin.   Perhaps another way to word it is to suggest that we substitute "devil" for all these places "the sin" has appeared, for it is the devil who has been trying to usurp dominion over God's creation ever since the beginning.   The devil is the one who stirs up the lusts of men's bodies (as the next phrase will specify), plants thoughts in their minds, and induces them to sin.   The Christian is encouraged to stop letting the devil have his way, and this is possible since the old man has been buried with Christ and risen to walk in newness of life.

That you should obey its lusts.   This is a purpose clause,[62] and seems to state the purpose "*the* sin" has in mind when it reigns over a man's body.   Sin's (read, the devil's) purpose is to stir up bodily desires[63] and through them to control the man's whole behavior.   "Its" refers to the body's desires, not sin's.[64]

> Sin is personified as a tyrant whose sphere of influence is the human body. This tyrant reigns in or rules over the body, but only as the desires of the body have control of it and lead it into sin.   Objects of temptation act upon the de-

---

[60] This is a present imperative with *mē*.   A present imperative differs from an aorist subjunctive in prohibitions in this way: the present imperative prohibits the continuance of an action already going on; the aorist subjunctive forbids one to even begin to do a thing not yet begun.   Dana and Mantey, *Grammar*, p.301-302.

[61] A review of what was said about "spirit" in footnote #42 on chapter 1, and footnote #3 on chapter 6, may help make clear what is here written about the inner man (or "spirit" of man).   The "old man" of verse 6 would be the man whose spirit is "dead" because of sin; the "new man" would be the one whose "spirit" is again alive because of righteousness (8:10).

[62] The construction is *eis* followed by an articular infinitive in the accusative case, and this construction expresses purpose.   J. Gresham Machen, *New Testament Greek for Beginners* (New York: Macmillan Co., 1923), p.138.

[63] See notes at Romans 1:24 on "lusts" meaning "desires."

[64] In the Greek, "its" is neuter.   "Sin" is feminine; "body" is neuter.   Thus it is decided that it is the body's desires.

sires and excite them. These desires now seek to be gratified. The will yields, and the result is sin. Such is the process. But [Christians] are not to allow these desires to become so excited as to impel us to obey them.[65]

It does not seem to be a doctrine of Scripture that the body, or the spirit, of itself, is able to offer temptations to sin. Instead, those temptations have to be excited from without, as the devil comes to tempt men.[66]

6:13 – *and do not go on presenting the members of your body to sin* as *instruments of unrighteousness; but present yourselves to God as those alive from the dead, and your members* as *instruments of righteousness to God.*

And do not go on presenting the members of your body to sin. This verse continues the prohibition begun in verse 12 – a prohibition against continuing an action already being done. Before their conversion, slaves of sin regularly presented the members of their physical bodies to sin. But they are not to continue in sin. The "members" of the body would be such things as the hands, feet, tongue, ears, and eyes. When the devil exercises his reign over men, he wants first this member, now that, now all of them. The devil is trying to regain the dominion he lost when we died to sin. Paul is attempting to dissuade Christians from continuing to put their bodily members at the disposal of the devil.

***As* instruments of unrighteousness.** This is what the devil wants men to use their bodily members to do. "Unrighteousness" is everything that contradicts God's standard of right, especially in our relations to other men.[67] The devil wants his slaves to use their hands, tongue, ears, eyes, and all their bodily members, as tools or instruments[68] by which unrighteous acts are done.

But present yourselves to God as those alive from the dead. The verb tense now changes to aorist imperative. It evidently is intended to convey the idea that this presentation is to be a definite, once-for-all, commitment. The inner man, who has died and risen with Christ (verses 4,8,11), is the one who is here given the responsibility of controlling the whole man's behavior, of decisively putting his whole being at the disposal of God.

And your members *as* instruments of righteousness to God. This phrase is just the opposite of what was said in the first half of the verse. Here is what God wants men to do

---

[65] Lard, *Romans*, p.207.

[66] What Paul writes here, about how sin works, is in harmony with what James writes in chapter 1 of his epistle, comments on which are included in Special Study #3 on "The Doctrine of Sin" found between chapters 5 and 6 of this work.

[67] The Greek word *adikia* was explained in comments at Romans 1:18.

[68] *Hoplon* is a word that means "any tool or implement." Thayer, *Lexicon*, p.449. In a context where warfare is the subject, the word is often translated "weapon," but otherwise, "weapon" is not a proper translation.

as they present the members of their physical bodies to Him. The apparent contrast (in the second half of this verse), with what sin wants a man's members to do (first half of the verse), leads to the suggestion that the "righteousness" here that God wants means "right conduct."[69]   Both God and Satan are looking for men who will choose them as masters, and who will then use the members of their bodies in service to their chosen master. Each man who is alive from the dead is faced with the tremendous alternative of making himself a tool in the hand of God, or a tool in the hand of Satan. Which alternative is the correct one is not left to doubt. Christians are *not* to continue in sin. They are to present their members to God to be used exclusively in His service.

6:14 – *For sin shall not be master over you, for you are not under law, but under grace.*

For sin shall not be master over you. With "for" Paul introduces a reason why the readers should and could do as commanded in verses 12 and 13. In the first half of the verse God promises that sin shall not be permitted to lord it over His children. If the readers but cooperate with God in this matter of controlling the desires the devil stirs up, if they but present themselves to God to be used in His service, then God promises that an occasional act of sin will not result in the devil regaining his old mastery over them.[70]   The point of this verse is this – sin will tempt and harass and ensnare; it will be a powerful, dangerous, and too-often victorious enemy. And yet sin could have no authority over us if we would make it our purpose to *not* use our bodily members as instruments of unrighteousness, but instead to use them as instruments of righteousness.

For you are not under law, but under grace. The last half of this verse gives a reason for the promise that "sin shall not be master over you." "Law," while it shows what acts and desires are sin, gives no help to overcome the desires or to avoid the acts. "Grace" does provide such help. Because "law" is anarthrous,[71] it is not easy to decide whether the reference is limited to the Law of Moses, or whether this verse is stating a much broader principle. It may be saying only that the Law of Moses gave no such help to the man who was trying to overcome temptation and sin that "grace" now gives. Or, in light of what is

---

[69] The difficulty a student of Romans has trying to determine the meaning of *dikaiosunē* has been alluded to in previous notes, e.g., 1:17, 3:5, 3:21-26. In addition to an imputed righteousness (God's way of saving man), and righteousness as an attribute of God, it may be that here in chapter 6 we have a third meaning for "righteousness," namely, right living.

[70] The comments have attempted to reflect two noteworthy changes in the Greek words used in this verse. For the first time in many verses, "sin" has no article. So it is not so much talking about the power or dominion of "*the* sin" as it is individual acts of sin, or anything that has the quality of sin. There is also a change of verbs of which we should be aware. In verse 12, the word translated "reign" is *basileuetō*. The word translated "master" here in verse 14 is *kuriesei*. In verse 12, we are exhorted not to let sin *reign*. We are to own no allegiance to it as a *king* whose rule we must obey. Here in verse 14, the word speaks of not letting "sin" *lord* it over us. In ancient times, each king had many lords under him, who carried out his will. The change in nouns and verbs thus imply this thought – this or that sin would like to lord it over us, draw us into this or that vice or passion or habit. And if the "lord" can lord it over us, it will not be long until the "king" will be reigning again!

[71] The problem presented to the commentator by the presence or the absence of the article before "law" was explained in notes at Romans 2:12.

taught in chapter 7 (i.e., that the presence of any rules or law gives the devil greater opportunity to work his evil ways in us), this verse may be saying that because a Christian has fewer rules and laws to live by than did, say, a man under Moses' Law, he has a better chance of living in the way that rising to walk in newness of life would suppose he would. One reason he has the better chance is because the absence of a multitude of rules already tends to limit the devil's opportunities to attack and lord it over the Christian.[72] Another reason is that he has God's help ("grace") to overcome temptation and sin.[73]

6:15 – *What then?* *Shall we sin because we are not under law but under grace?* *May it never be!*

What then? That is, what conclusion is to be drawn from what has just been said? If it is true that God promises sin shall not lord it over you, does it not seem to follow that a man under grace is free to sin and never have to pay any penalty?

Shall we sin because we are not under law but under grace? This question reminds us of verse 1 and also verse 14, and the answer is based on the teaching given in verses 2-14. Since the man who has died to sin is under grace, does this mean that a man is free to commit a sin here and there?[74] Does not the fact that in Christ a man is not under law but under grace mean that there is no danger of sin ever becoming our master again?[75]

May it never be![76] To believe a man is free to sin now and then because he is under grace is not far from what Jude 4 condemns when he writes about "persons who turn the grace of our God into licentiousness." The following verses, which set forth what is sometimes called "the slave market analogy," will give the reason for the strong negative here. It would be a misuse of the freedom a man has in Christ to suppose he can submit now and then to "lord sin" and yet remain in no danger of coming again under the bondage of slavery

---

[72] There are rules or laws (i.e., certain God-given standards) by which the Christian is expected to live. The Christian is not free from all laws; as 1 Corinthians 9:19-21 plainly show, the Christian is "under law to Christ." There are also certain lists of sins, repeated several times in Paul's epistles, that the Christian is warned to avoid. So anarthrous *nomos* here does not say the Christian has "no law at all" to guide his behavior.

[73] The same idea of God's help is worked out in detail in chapter 8 of this letter, and in Ephesians 3:14-20.

[74] Note that the verb is an aorist subjunctive in verse 15, whereas it was a present subjunctive in verse 1. Verse 1 asked about continual sin; verse 15 asks about random acts of sin now and then. In both verses the subjunctive is likely an example of what is known as a "deliberative subjunctive;" the question is asked to get the reader to think carefully on the subject, without necessarily expecting a vocal answer to be given.

[75] Each of the expressions ("under law," "under grace") in verse 15 that is a restatement of what was said in verse 14 is to be explained the same way in both verses. If "law" (anarthrous *nomos*) meant "Law of Moses" in verse 14, it also means that in verse 15. And if this is a reference to the Law of Moses, it may be the first time in Romans that Paul has categorically set aside the Law of Moses (see 3:21 and 4:13).

[76] See this expression explained at 3:24.

to "king sin."[77]

6:16 – *Do you not know that when you present yourselves to someone* as *slaves for obedience, you are slaves of the one whom you obey, either of sin resulting in death, or of obedience resulting in righteousness?*

Do you not know. Here begins the reason for the strong negative answer to the question asked in verse 15. "Do you not know" is Paul's way of saying "I remind you."[78] Paul is saying, "I assume you are acquainted with the laws and customs of slavery, and with the servitude that results even when a slave changes masters." In the early verses of chapter 6, the point was that a master can get slaving out of a slave only until the slave dies; once the slave has died, the master could go on giving orders to the corpse but the corpse will pay no attention nor give any response. In this and the following verses, the illustration changes. Now the thing contemplated is that the slave has become someone else's property. When this happens, the former master has no further authority over the slave, nor can he get any more service out of his former slave. The slave must give all his time and energies to his new owner.[79] A 21st century employee who, after working 8 hours for his employer, has his evenings and weekends to himself, or even takes another part-time job (so he has two "bosses"), may have a hard time appreciating the line of argument here. It must be remembered that slaves had no time they could call their own; every moment belonged to the master.

That when you present yourselves to someone *as* **slaves for obedience.** "Present" is the same word used in verse 13, and denotes a voluntary, willing presentation. "For obedience" is what the one presenting himself has in mind; he will obey whatever the master commands. Christians are dead to sin by virtue of their baptism into Christ, and thus have changed masters. Yet their new master allows them a certain freedom, so that they are free to present themselves to God to be His slaves, or to present themselves to sin

---

[77] A word needs to be said about the *freedom* men in Christ have, in the light of the expressions "present yourselves to God" and "not under law, but under grace." Batey, *Romans*, p.84, introduces this topic with these words. "The ideal of pure freedom totally uncommitted to any values or demands soon leaves one the victim of arbitrary choices made without consideration of life's ultimate meaning. The uncommitted life turns into a chaos of meaningless decisions which lead to frustration and despair. The desire for pure freedom results in slavery to arbitrary choice. How can one know what he should do with his life if he remains uncommitted to any meaning, if he has no goal toward which to press or purpose for which to live?" The freedom we have in Christ is a freedom to choose any one of several beneficial uses for our lives – and this choice, once made, does indeed give purpose to life. But the man is *not* controlled by the requirements of law, nor is he a slave to a religious legal system, nor does he have to be a conformist to certain external, man-made rules of piety, like the Jew did.

[78] See notes on this expression at Romans 6:2.

[79] Bruce, *Romans*, p.140, summarizes the paragraph with these words. "This is what happened to you. You have passed from the service of sin into the service of God; your business now is to do what God desires, not what sin dictates. There is a big difference between the kind of thing you will do as servants of God and the kind of thing you used to do as servants of sin. And not only is there a difference in character between the two kinds of service; there is a great difference between the ends of these forms of service. Sin pays wages to its servants – the wages being death. God gives us not wages, but something better and much more generous ... eternal life ...."

and become its slaves.

You are slaves of the one whom you obey.   Jesus Himself used to teach that "no one can serve two masters!"   If a man continually chooses to serve sin, the time will come when he is again enslaved.[80]   Only if he chooses to present himself to God, his new master, will he continue to be God's bond-servant.

Either of sin resulting in death, or of obedience resulting in righteousness?   The two incompatible masters are here called "sin" and "obedience."   "Sin" is anarthrous (as in verse 14), and seems to denote individual instances of sin, done in obedience to the evil one.   If a man continues to commit certain acts of sin, making no effort to stop letting sin reign in his mortal body, the result eventually is that he will sink back into the very slavery from which he was freed at his baptism.   "Obedience," the other possible master, by analogy, would speak of individual instances of obedience, done in response to God.   Of what the obedience consists is delineated in the following verses.   The final outcome of serving each master is here called "death" and "righteousness," with each term evidently being an exact antithesis of the other.   "Righteousness" (*dikaiosunē*) is used throughout Romans to denote something attainable in this present life; thus "death" too seems to be something that can happen again in this life, namely, "spiritual death," "dead in trespasses and sins."[81]   Paul does not say that committing one act of sin after a man becomes a Christian will cause him to change masters.   He does say that continual sinning will have such a result.   The "newness of life" (verse 4) can be lost by the man who presents himself to sin as its servant; obeying sin will result in "death."[82]   "Righteousness" can either be initial justification, or continual justification.[83]   The two words, "either" and "or," show that a man has but two ways open before him.   Jesus once spoke of a wide and of a narrow way as being the two ways open to men (Matthew 7:13,14).   One or the other of these two ways every man must choose; there is no middle ground.

---

[80] "Sin has a tendency to enslave the sinner.   The first time he lies, he may be horrified; the second time, only somewhat shaken; the third time, lying seems far more natural and easy.   At last the sin of telling untruths has him in its grasp. For other sins the story is similar.   At last this person is living in sin, has become enslaved by it."   Hendriksen, *Romans*, p.204.

[81] Some writers do indeed try to make both "death" and "righteousness" refer to the next life – hell and heaven.   While it is true that "death" sometimes refers to what is called the "second death" (Meyer, Gifford, and others so interpret), to so explain it in this case destroys the parallelism (or antithesis) that is so evident in this verse.   Since the context following (6:17-23) shows "righteousness" in this paragraph is something attainable in this life, it does not seem to be the right thing to do to make "death" something attainable only after this life.   (It may be that when we come to verse 23, we have arrived at a verse that deals with the servant's final destiny, but it is possible that even verse 23 speaks of this life rather than the next.)

[82] Of course, the reference is not to "physical death," since that is a consequence, not of individual sins, but of Adam's sin, as we learned in chapter 5.

[83] That "justification" is not just a one-time thing, see notes at Romans 3:24,28 and 4:19.   For initial justification, which takes place when one is baptized into Christ, see notes at Romans 6:7.   In reply to those writers who suppose *dikaiosunē* here cannot mean "justification" because that is "by faith" (Romans 1:17, 3:22) whereas this verse speaks of "obedience," let it once more be noted that there is no difference in Scripture between "righteousness by faith" and "righteousness by obedience," for the "faith" that saves is an obedient faith.

6:17 – *But thanks be to God that though you were slaves of sin, you became obedient from the heart to that form of teaching to which you were committed,*

But thanks be to God.   In verses 17 and 18, Paul gives thanks to God that the condition of being slaves to sin was a thing of the past for his readers.   The general truth stated in verse 16 is now given personal application to the readers.   Paul is full of delight that they have a new Master, and he will encourage them to present themselves to Him and to Him only (verse 19).

That though you were slaves of sin.   The marginal note shows that there is no word for "though" in the Greek, but it is very doubtful that Paul ever intended this verse to say, as the marginal note implies, "I am thankful that you were slaves of sin."   Most of the English translations add a word ("whereas" or "though") to the translation, so the reader sees the contrast between what they are now (servants of God) and what they were before (slaves of sin).   Indeed, many will point out that this verse (which is the last clause of a comparison) begins with "but," and thus infers that some such word as "though" must be supplied, so that the reader can easily discern (from the contrast in the two parts of the verse) that Paul's gratitude is for the fact that the slaving to sin was a thing of the past.   The expression "slaves of sin" has been explained in verse 6.

You became obedient from the heart to that form of teaching.   This phrase tells how the old slavery to sin was broken; the next verse will show how they have come to have a new Master.   "You became obedient" repeats this idea for the fourth time in two verses; the aorist tense verb points back to an act in the past, namely, to the time of their baptism.[84] As Paul looks back to the time of their baptism, he thinks of them as both having understood what was involved in it (verses 2,3), and also as having been heartily sincere.[85]

When one obeys, he must have some teaching, some command, to obey.   What the Romans had obeyed Paul here designates as "that form of teaching."

- Some think this phrase is just another name for the "gospel."[86]   The word translated "form" is *tupon*, and means "form, or shape, or type, or pattern, or model, or mold (cast) into which molten metal is poured so as to take its shape."[87]   Since it is not easy to explain in what sense the gospel can be thought of as having a cast or shape, not a few

---

[84] It will be remembered that verse 7 (which succinctly summarizes in the word "died" all that verses 2-4 say about being baptized into death) has clearly shown that it is in baptism that the old slavery to sin is ended, and the slave is freed.

[85] "From the heart" is the opposite of "eyeservice," Ephesians 6:6.   Their baptism was not a mere form; their hearts were in the act.   Their obedience was sincere.

[86] Paul could not say "you became obedient to the Word of God," for the Jews had been doing that, and were still slaves of sin.   Therefore, he had to specify more closely what teaching they had obeyed.

[87] See Arndt-Gingrich, *Lexicon*, p.837,838, and Vine, *Romans*, p.94.

writers reject the idea that the expression is another way of saying "gospel."[88]

- Others think Paul has specific reference to baptism since the idea that baptism is a model or picture or type of "teaching" is easy to demonstrate. If by "teaching" one means the "gospel," it need only be recalled that a significant part of the gospel is the death, burial and resurrection of Jesus (1 Corinthians 15:1-4), and baptism (with its immersion and emersion) neatly pictures this truth (as 6:2-4 has clearly demonstrated). Or, if it is said that the "teaching" in Paul's mind is the teaching given in verses 2-7, of which the readers were perfectly aware (verse 3), namely, that in baptism there is a death of the old man, a burial, and a resurrection to walk in newness of life, it can easily be seen how baptism in water pictures this doctrine.

To which you were committed. The pronoun "which" agrees with "form"; it was into this form that they were "delivered."[89] This expression succinctly pictures what happens as the candidate allows himself to be lowered by another into the waters of baptism.[90] Putting verses 16 and 17 together, we are told that the "form of teaching" is to be "obeyed" if one is to experience "righteousness." If our explanation of these verses has been correct, again we are driven to the conclusion that baptism is an essential part of the condition (faith) that God requires in a man before He imputes righteousness. We say "again we are

---

[88] In a moment, we shall read that the recipients of this letter have been "poured into this *tupon*." Vine makes a good effort to explain how the gospel can have a "mould" to it when he suggests that the truths of the gospel are the mould, and the believers are likened to molten material, whose character is shaped by the gospel. *Romans*, p.94.

   In certain liberal theological circles, this expression "*form* of doctrine" (KJV) has been used to prove that there were distinctive types or systems of doctrine taught by the writers of the New Testament. For example, George B. Stevens, *The Theology of the New Testament* (New York: Charles Scribner's Sons, 1953), finds one system in the Synoptics, another in John's Gospel, another in the primitive apostolic preaching, another in Paul, etc. There is little to be said in favor of the idea that the gospel had different (perhaps even contradictory) forms. The Jerusalem Conference (Acts 15, Galatians 2) shows there was no difference between Peter and Paul, or between those apostles and what Jesus taught. "The view that the Christian teaching itself had different forms (*types*), such as Pauline, Petrine, Johannine, is rightly rejected. The Romans had not adopted a peculiar type of the gospel or of gospel ethics, say the Pauline; some of them had been converted before Paul was converted (Romans 16:7)." Lenski, *Romans*, p.427-28. If there were different systems of doctrine, there is no way Paul could have known that the believers at Rome all knew and had "obeyed heartily" the *same* "form of doctrine."

[89] The idea of 'obedience in baptism' as a condition of righteousness is one that a number of commentators wish to avoid at all costs, for it would result in having to reject their whole system of teaching on 'how to be saved.' Having adopted the notion that "faith" is something given to the candidate by God, and having accepted as a corollary the idea that in salvation man is wholly passive, this verse just cannot be teaching that baptism (or any other act of obedience) is a condition of salvation. So they must find a satisfactory explanation for it while at the same time avoiding any reference to baptism. "Committed" (delivered) is a word that gives this group of interpreters a difficult time. Most will note that "deliver" (*paradidōmi*) is the verb form of the noun for "tradition" (*paradōsis*), and then they write about how this "body of [Christian] tradition" was delivered to the believers in Rome. However, understand that verse 17 does not say that the "form of doctrine" was delivered to them; it says they were delivered into the form of doctrine. As we work through this passage, let it be remembered that Christian liberty does not consist in freedom to amend the "doctrine," but in obeying from the heart the "form of doctrine."

[90] The verse itself does not say who delivered the readers into the form of doctrine. Arndt-Gingrich, *Lexicon*, p.620, suggest it was God who did the delivering, but when one reads through verse 17 and its context, it certainly appears that this is only importing an extraneous idea into the passage.

driven" because we understand verses 16 and 17 to be simply repeating (in different words, and to make a different point) the truth already expressed in verses 2-7.

6:18 – *and having been freed from sin, you became slaves of righteousness.*

And having been freed from sin.   "Freed" here is a different word from that used in 6:7, but the idea is evidently the same.[91]   Again, it is Paul's doctrine that such "freedom" comes as a man is baptized.[92]   "Imagery aside, to be freed from sin is to be pardoned.   In order to be pardoned, two things are necessary: (1) obedience to the model of teaching, and (2) 'hearty' obedience."[93]

> "Emancipated from sin" ... that is liberty indeed.   The sin power usurped authority over us (5:12), stole us from God and thus made us slaves.   We never rightly belonged to the sin.   We were not created for the sin power, to sin.   Freed from that power at last, we can fulfill the purpose of our being.[94]

You became slaves of righteousness.   "You became slaves" translates one word in the Greek, an aorist passive verb.   The aorist tense shows that the 'freeing' from sin and the "became slaves" took place at the same time, namely, as they obeyed in baptism.   The passive voice suggests that the change of masters was not something they did for themselves, but was done to them.   Since it is God who justifies, it is likely true that "God" is the suppressed subject, the One who wrought the change of masters.   "Righteousness" reads "*the* righteousness" in the Greek, and one wonders if righteousness is pictured as being a power exerting itself in the world, just like "*the* sin" (5:12) was.   Once again, the idea that a man can have but one of two possible masters is presented: either he is a slave of sin, or he is a slave of righteousness.   There is no middle ground; he is never completely independent.

6:19 – *I am speaking in human terms because of the weakness of your flesh.   For just as you presented your members as slaves to impurity and to lawlessness, resulting in further lawlessness, so now present your members as slaves to righteousness, resulting in sanctification.*

---

[91] Because the word translated "freed" in verse 7 is actually "justified," there is some hesitation about using "freed" to express its meaning in that verse.   Here the word is *eleutheroō*, the regular word used when the topic is the "freeing" of bondslaves.

[92] The verb tenses for "freed" in this verse and "became obedient" and "committed" in the previous verse indicate these two take place at the same time.   The KJV reads "being *then* made free," and we suppose the translators added the "then" to make it clear to the readers that the freeing of the slave of sin takes place in baptism.

[93] Lard, *Romans*, p.214.   Lard justifies his note about "pardoned" by noting that what is said in figurative language drawn from the metaphor of bondservice here in verse 18, is not greatly different from what was written in verse 16 about "obedience resulting in righteousness (justification)."   Thus, it can be seen that "freed" and "justified" are two ways of presenting the same idea.

[94] Lenski, *Romans*, p.428.

I am speaking in human terms because of the weakness of your flesh.   The expression "*slaves* of righteousness" is not literally true, Paul now says.   A bondslave has no freedom to choose his new master, as the Christian has (see verses 12 and 13, and what follows in verses 19 and 20).   "I am speaking in human terms"[95] thus means "I'm borrowing an illustration from everyday Roman life that is not true, in all its details, to the spiritual life."[96] It is doubtful that Paul really meant to equate the service of Christ to the thralldom of slavery.   "Weakness of your flesh" probably speaks of dullness of spiritual perception. The Roman readers, because of a limitation true of all men, namely, that they live in a body of "flesh,"[97] would have had difficulty understanding arguments and illustrations that were more strictly spiritual in character.

For just as you presented your members *as* slaves to impurity and to lawlessness. Paul is evidently here giving a reason why he just warned that his use of the term "slave" is not literally true.   Before they became Christians, their relationship to Satan was not slavery in the absolute sense.   Even before their emancipation, when it could be said they

---

[95] The ASV reads, "I speak after the manner of men," and some read into that the idea that Paul was using language that was human in nature in contrast to some other language he might speak.   Paul did when occasion demanded speak in foreign languages (1 Corinthians 14:18), and even uses the expression "tongues (languages) of angels" (1 Corinthians 13:1), but it is doubtful that this passage in Romans has such an emphasis on the word "human" (as though he said "*human* terms"), as to allow it to be used to prove that he sometimes spoke in languages other than human.   Instead, he seems to be telling his readers to beware because his illustration is not true-to-life in all its details.   Speakers and writers must always be on their guard lest the problem of verbalisms cause them to be misunderstood by their audience. So Paul pauses here, as he did at Romans 3:5, to warn us not to press all the details from this human example.

[96] Barmby, *Romans*, p.161, suggests that the detail that may not be quite true of the Christian life is to be found in the word "slaves."   "Paul may mean, 'In saying you were made *slaves* to righteousness, I am using human language not properly applicable to your spiritual relations.   Christians are called on to render a free, willing allegiance to righteousness: being, in fact, sons, not slaves.'"   Batey, *Romans*, p.86, points his readers to the word "freed," since a slave who had been freed was a man no longer under any master at all.   "Paul seems to recognize that his analogy from slavery creates a problem; the alternative to slavery would seem to be emancipation from the power of sin and the law.   And the Christian would thus seem to be free to live without any standard of values.   However, Paul points out that such is not the case.   The Christian is free only to be a slave of God and to serve God with his members."

[97] Beginning at Romans 1:3, we have questioned the rather widespread doctrine that "flesh" is inherently evil.   In harmony with this widespread doctrine, not a few explain "weakness of the flesh" here in verse 19 as denoting moral weakness.   "Some take 'weakness of the flesh' to denote *moral* weakness, which renders the attainment of holiness [see "sanctification," verse 22] difficult for man (cf. Mark 14:38), and then take 'I speak after the manner of men' as meaning, 'I require of you no more than is possible for your frail humanity; for I call on you only to render to righteousness the same allegiance you once rendered to sin.'   This interpretation gives a totally different meaning to the clause.   It has the support of Origen, Chrysostom, Theodoret, Calvin, Estius, Wetstein, and others; but it does not appear so natural or probable as the other [i.e., dullness of spiritual perception], which is accepted by most modern commentators." Barmby, *Romans*, p.162.   Even were we to admit that "flesh" here denotes a moral weakness, it should be clearly evident that the "flesh" is presented as darkening the readers' *understanding*, not as perverting the *will*.   Once this fact is observed, it soon becomes evident that Romans 6:19 does not give any support at all to the usual way the doctrine of an inborn sinful bent is presented.   Nor is the expression with which verse 19 opens to be understood as if it meant the Romans were on a lower level (either moral or intellectual) than other churches.

were slaves to sin, there still was a certain freedom to act. They still were the ones who "presented their members" to their old master for use in his service. In 6:13, Paul worded it, "presenting the members of your body *to sin*." Now the old master is called "impurity and lawlessness." It is doubtful that two different masters are intended; it would seem more satisfactory to explain the two terms as simply presenting the effect serving the old master had on the slave himself.[98] "Impurity" reminds us that sin defiles a man;[99] "lawlessness" reminds us that sin violates the laws of God, that it is rebellion and anarchy.[100]

Resulting in *further* **lawlessness.** This clause evidently states the result that comes from presenting one's members to sin.[101] "Sin leads to nothing positive; lawless conduct only results in a habit or state of lawlessness."[102]

So now present your members *as* **slaves to righteousness.** "Now" means now that you have been freed from the old slavery to sin. This member of the comparison repeats what was written in verse 13, with this one difference: whereas "righteousness" in verse 13 spoke of right living, "*the* righteousness" in here in verse 19 pictures "righteousness" as the new master, the new power, in the Christian's life.[103] A slave the Christian may be, but there is nothing degrading or demeaning about service to the Master.[104] A slave the Christian may be, but he is not free to use his freedom as an excuse to commit sin. Such would not be use, but abuse, of the new-found freedom!

---

[98] Some writers, because of an attempt to avoid having Paul say that "obedience" was a condition for "justification" ("righteousness," verse 16), have been wont to explain "righteousness" all the way through this paragraph (verses 15-23) as though it denoted man's relationship to man, i.e., righteous acts. Having explained "righteousness" as being how a Christian's conduct affects his fellow man, they then will explain "impurity and lawlessness" in terms of how these sins affect one's neighbors. While it is true that my sins are not only against God, but also against my fellow man, this may not be the verse to prove it.

[99] *Akatharsia*, "impurity," was explained at Romans 1:24.

[100] *Anomia*, "lawlessness," was explained at Romans 4:7. "*Anomia*, 'lawlessness,' signifies, not merely the abstract idea, but disregard for, or actual breach of, the Law of God. In 1 John 3:4, lawlessness is stated as a definition of sin." Vine, *Romans*, p.95. "Imagine giving one's own bodily members as slaves to such a tyrant! Too often we hide this horribleness from ourselves and shudder at it only when it reveals itself stark and naked in some fearful crime. Learn from Paul what this tyrant looks like so that you will not extend even one finger to him." Lenski, *Romans*, p.431.

[101] Actually, the Greek can be either purpose or result; only the context will decide. Since verse 21 speaks of "benefit deriving from [sinning]," it seems right to emphasize result in this instance.

[102] Barmby, *Romans*, p.162.

[103] As in verse 13, the aorist imperative ("present") means do so definitely, once for all. Now that there has been a change of masters, God's slave must present his members only to God.

[104] The Queen of Sheba thought it a great honor and privilege to be a servant of Solomon. Angels regard it as their glory to be servants of God and implicitly obey His will. David never thought of himself more honored than when he esteemed himself a Servant of the living God. The Christian likewise is to be of the same mind. It is an honor to be a servant of God.

Resulting in sanctification. Just as a habit pattern of service to impurity and lawlessness resulted in further lawlessness, so "sanctification" is here given as the result of a life of service to righteousness. Sanctification would seem to be a process,[105] a continual growth toward a more holy, God-like character, a growing dedication to God and His service. Paul urges his readers to use their bodily members as "righteousness" would direct, in order that they may attain sanctification.[106]

6:20 – *For when you were slaves of sin, you were free in regard to righteousness.*

For when you were slaves of sin. Verse 20 is probably best understood as introducing a reason for presenting one's members to righteousness. Verses 20-22 all go together, with verse 20 preparing the way, and then verses 21 and 22 actually expressing the reason or the motive for complying with the exhortation. "When you were slaves of sin" speaks of the time before a man is converted, as verses 17 and 18 have explained.

You were free in regard to righteousness. It reads "*the* righteousness" again, and once more personifies "righteousness" as though it were a master or a king who is trying to extend the area of his reign. In the everyday world of the 1st century, two masters could not at the same time demand slaving out of the same slave. Likewise, "sin" and "righteousness" were two masters trying to exert their power in the world; man could be expected to be obligated to but one at a time.[107] Before their conversion, "*the* sin" and not "*the* righteousness" was their master.[108]

---

[105] Greek nouns that end in -*mos* describe, not a completed state, but a *process*. Barclay, *Romans*, p.93.

[106] The student of Romans will find considerable variation in the commentaries when he searches to see what explanation is given for "sanctification." For details of the doctrinal points he is likely to find reflected in comments at this place, see Special Study #5 on "Sanctification" at the close of chapter 6. One matter not discussed in Special Study #5 is the question of whether "sanctification" (*hagiasmos*) and "holiness" (*hagiosunē*) are interchangeable terms. The only three places *hagiosunē* appears in the New Testament, it is translated "holiness" (Romans 1:4; 2 Corinthians 7:1; and 1 Thessalonians 3:13). Most understand that while *hagiasmos* speaks of a process, *hagiosunē* speaks of the result of the process, the completed state. Some would explain Romans 6:19 as though it were synonymous with *hagiosunē*, i.e., a completed process. Appeal is even made to such passages as 1 Thessalonians 4:3,4; 2 Thessalonians 2:13; and 1 Timothy 2:15, as being other instances where *hagiasmos* is alleged to speak of the *result* of the process, rather than the process itself. This commentator, however, is not convinced by these arguments. Of course, if "sanctification" is a process in verse 19b, then "lawlessness" in verse 19a, because of the parallel nature of this verse, would also be a process.

[107] In verse 19, Paul has already indicated that his analogy dare not be pushed in all its details. So it may be observed that there is no actual freedom from God's standards of right, even while the man is a slave to sin. The sinner merely disregards what God says, but he will still have to answer in the Judgment (as chapters 1-3 have shown).

[108] The observant student will find in the commentaries that writers who defend and espouse the doctrine of original sin/total depravity believe they have found in this verse another proof text for their doctrine. "Free in regard to righteousness" is understood to mean that men "were not at all under the influence of righteousness. They were entirely devoted to sin – a strong expression of total depravity. It settles the question, and proves they had no native goodness." Barnes, *Romans*, p.156. See Special Study #4 on "Original Sin" at the close of notes on chapter 5.

6:21 – *Therefore what benefit were you then deriving from the things of which you are now ashamed? For the outcome of those things is death.*

Therefore what benefit were you then deriving. "Therefore" continues the thought introduced by the previous verse. 'Granted that you were slaves of sin (and "free" from the master called "righteousness"), what did it benefit you?' There is a contrast between "then" in this phrase, and "now" in verse 22. "Then" speaks of the time before their conversion, the time when they were slaves of sin. "Benefit" translates the word that means fruit, as the margin shows. Paul usually uses the word "fruit" only in a good sense,[109] and in this fact may lie the impact of the question. The implied answer is that there was nothing, no good fruit, no real profit, no solid advantage, to a life of service to sin.

From the things of which you are now ashamed? The proper way to punctuate this verse, so that Paul's question is followed by an answer, has been debated from earliest times.[110] Following the lead of the NASB, this middle phrase is part of the question with which verse 21 begins, and the idea suggested by the question and its implied answer might be summarized thusly:

> The fact that when the disciples in Rome looked back over their past lives, they felt ashamed of the sin in which they had formerly delighted, which shows the deep change that had taken place in their minds, and implies how sincere and thorough their repentance had been. Moreover, if they had derived no benefit from their past sins, but, on the contrary, felt ashamed of them, they could certainly have no reason for returning to them; and this is what the Apostle is seeking to guard them against. The issue he is making with them is, that they are not to sin, because they are under grace.[111]

"'The things of which ye are now ashamed,' ... are 'the works of darkness' of Ephesians 5:11; and in both places they are declared to have no fruit."[112]

---

[109] See Galatians 5:22; Ephesians 5:9,11; Titus 3:14, for Paul's other uses of the word "fruit."

[110] In the Latin Vulgate, the KJV, ASV, and NASB, the question mark is placed after "ashamed," and this results in no specific answer being given to the question. The implied answer is "none," and the clause that begins with "for" immediately following is a reason why there was no fruit. The other way to punctuate the sentence is to put a question mark after "deriving," making all the middle phrase of the verse ["things of which you are now ashamed"] the answer to the question. This second suggestion for punctuation has against it the fact that it causes the translators to depart from a formal equivalent to a dynamic equivalent translation of the middle phrase of this verse. This second way of explaining the verse gives a different answer to the question asked in the first part of the verse. Instead of "none," there was "fruit," but only such fruit as that of which they were now ashamed.

[111] Lard, *Romans*, p.217.

[112] Barmby, *Romans*, p.163.

For the outcome of those things is death. Here is further answer to the question "Shall we sin?" asked in verse 15. They ought never to forget either the unprofitableness of their former unregenerate way of life, or the "death" in which it resulted. "Outcome" translates *telos*, a word that means "end, goal, final result." The result of sin is "death," a word that may point to a spiritual death that takes place in this life, or it may be a reference to everlasting punishment, called "the second death,"[113] or it may include both ideas.

6:22 – But now having been freed from sin and enslaved to God, you derive your benefit, resulting in sanctification, and the outcome, eternal life.

But now having been freed from sin and enslaved to God. "Now" is contrasted to "then" in the previous verse. Now that you have become Christians, now that you have changed masters,[114] is the idea. Paul is finishing up the reason why the Christian should present his members as slaves to righteousness (verse 19). Now that they have been freed from the bondage of sin, now that they have a new master, the situation is reversed. They can have some fruit (benefit) now, whereas before, when they were slaves of sin, they produced nothing of real value (verse 21). Paul used metaphorical language before to name the Christian's master (he used "obedience" in verse 16, and "righteousness" in verse 18). He now lays aside the metaphor and directly names the Master as being God himself.

You derive your benefit, resulting in sanctification. "You are no longer without fruit. Your fruit is [produced by] the new Christian life which leads on to sanctification and finally to eternal life."[115] Having risen to walk in newness of life (6:4), when they present their members as slaves to God, they do bear fruit,[116] and this in turn will result in "sanctification." Most efforts to specify in what the fruit consists have tended to allude to parallel passages where the same word is used – e.g., Galatians 5:22, the "fruit of the Spirit," or Romans 7:4, "fruit for God." If 7:4-6 is allowed to explain the "benefit" or "fruit" Paul has in mind, then it probably should be affirmed that "fruit" and "present your (bodily) members as slaves to righteousness" are interchangeable expressions. "Fruit for God" in that paragraph (7:4) is the opposite of the "fruit for death" (7:5); therefore, there seems to be some truth in the suggested explanation that "fruit" is metaphorical language meaning 'to present one's members as instruments of righteousness.' The man who consciously and regularly uses his members in service to God will soon see how this in turn leads to further sanctification.[117]

---

[113] The word "death" has already been used with a similar connotation at Romans 1:32. "Death" in this verse is a different concept than "*the* death" about which 5:12 spoke. "Death" is anarthrous in verse 21, whereas it had an article in 5:12.

[114] Again, as in verse 19, it is understood that service to God is not literally slavery. Paul is again using a human analogy that is imperfect, but nevertheless useful, to get his idea across.

[115] Sanday, *Romans*, p.77.

[116] The verb "derive benefit" is present tense; they are bearing fruit right now and continually.

[117] For "sanctification," *hagiasmos*, see notes at verse 19, including footnotes #105 and #106. A comparison of the verses that refer to "justification" and those that refer to "sanctification" in this chapter

And the outcome, eternal life. "Outcome," as in verse 21, translates *telos*, and has the same meaning. Continual fruit-bearing brings growth ("sanctification"), and this growth culminates in "eternal life." The strong suggestion in the verse is that "eternal life" is possessed conditionally, but this should not be surprising, for the security of the believer is always presented, in Scripture, as being conditional.[118] Also, in the Scriptures, "eternal life" is sometimes looked on as a present possession (as at John 3:36), and sometimes as a future reward (compare Romans 5:21). "Eternal" (*aiōnios*) describes a period of undefined duration, and often also implies the idea of "abundant," so that "eternal life" describes as much the *quality* of life as it does *duration*.[119] Lest the topic this whole paragraph deals with be forgotten, it seems proper to recall that Paul is answering a question about voluntarily, deliberately indulging in occasional acts of sin (verse 15). His answer has been a resounding *no*, for such behavior could result in coming under bondage to sin again, and this would in turn lead to the loss of eternal life.

6:23 – *For the wages of sin is death, but the free gift of God is eternal life in Christ Jesus our Lord.*

For the wages of sin is death. Beginning with "for," this verse expresses the reason why the outcome of one service is death, while the outcome of the other service is eternal life. Verse 19 has already indicated that the illustration drawn from the world of slavery is not true in all its details; perhaps it may be said that verse 23 gives still another one of these details. In the Roman world, bondslaves were unpaid; in the spiritual world, the slaves of sin do get paid! Sin always pays. The sinner may not want it, but the wages will be paid. "Sin" is still portrayed as being a master. The expression, "wages of sin," means wages paid by sin.[120] In this context, where it contrasts with "eternal life," "death" includes not

---

will show that the two concepts are different, and that justification precedes sanctification.

[118] One example here will suffice. See 2 Peter 1:5-7, where the Christians are exhorted to supply certain qualities or virtues. Then consult 2 Peter 1:8-11, where it is said if these qualities are present in the Christian's life, and increasing, it will guarantee his calling and election; he will never stumble; and it will result into an abundant entrance into the eternal kingdom for him. More will be said on the topic of "eternal security" in notes on chapter 8. In the meantime, let it be observed that the very passage now being studied in Romans places side by side the idea of "conditional" security and the expression "eternal life." This is one passage among many that must be dealt with by those who affirm that the security of the believer is *not* conditional, or else it could not be called "eternal."

[119] In Revelation 20:4-6, a passage that seems to describe the intermediate state of the righteous (showing all is well with them) just before final judgment falls, we find the terms "lived" and "lived not" (ASV) used to describe the contrasting condition of the righteous and the wicked. Remembering that John 5:24,25 also describe the present condition of the believer in Jesus as 'living,' and adding to this the profound statement Jesus made to Martha (John 11:25) about how a man who believes in Him "shall *live* (continue to live on, in the intermediate state) even if he dies," we can begin to comprehend some of the magnitude of truth contained in the expression "eternal life."

[120] "The word here translated 'wages' (*opsōnia*) properly denotes what is purchased to be eaten with bread, such as fish, flesh, vegetables, etc.; and thence, it means the pay of the Roman soldier, because formerly it was the custom to pay the soldier in these things. It means, hence, that which a man earns or deserves; that which is his proper pay, or what he merits. As applied to sin, it means that death is what sin deserves, that which will be its proper reward." Barnes, *Romans*, p.158. There is likely also the idea of the wage being deserved, and that it is a stipulated reward. This being true, it is highly improper to

only spiritual death, but it ultimately involves the "second death, the lake of fire" (Revelation 20:14).[121]   Since this is true, it becomes astounding that any freedman should ever contemplate returning to the service of the old sinful master!   It ought to cause any Christian to drop all thought of ever playing with sin.

But the free gift of God is eternal life in Christ Jesus our Lord.   Each form of servitude reaches a goal when finished, and in this respect the two are alike.   But there is a vast difference between the two goals.   One is "wages (earned);" the other is a "free gift."   One is "death;" the other is "eternal life."   In spite of a life of service to God, in spite of such a presentation of bodily members to God as resulted in sanctification, the Christian still has not earned eternal life; that life is a "free gift," a grace gift,[122] given by God to those who are "in Christ Jesus."[123]   That Christ Jesus is here identified as "our Lord"[124] is one more deterrent to a life of playing with sin.   For a man to go on sinning is tantamount to giving service to the wrong "master" (lord).   Christ Jesus is his new master, and He does *not* want His servants to be spending their time sinning.

Here ends the paragraph about how God's way of saving men results in some blessings to slaves of sin.   Their slavery is broken; they have a new master; their life is now productive; there are blessings in store in the future.

In the 1st century Roman world, there were three classes of people – the *liberi* (free men), the *liberati* (freed men), and the *servi* (slaves).   A freed man was no longer under the control of his former master; instead, out of gratitude, he would cling for the rest of his life to the one who redeemed him with silver or gold from his bondage.   In a somewhat similar way, when God justifies a man, He has bought him for a price (the precious blood of Jesus), and he is no longer in bondage to his former master.   In gratitude, with joyful and hearty willingness, they cling to their New Master, and live only to serve Him.   Freed men know what it was like to be a servant of sin, and they want no more of that way of life!   Thus it is that Paul answers the questions asked in verses 1 and 15.

---

affirm that there is no such thing as eternal punishment for the wicked, since "it is hard to believe that a loving God could ever send a man to hell."   The Bible plainly indicates that God never intended for sinners to be consigned to hell, a place created for the devil and his angels (Matthew 25:41).   But if men refuse His offer of pardon made available because of Calvary, if they refuse His overtures of love, if they persist in their sin, then God has no choice but to give them their stipulated and deserved "wages."   In reality, the men sentenced themselves to hell.

[121] The comments offered on the word "death" in verses 16 and 21 are also true for its use here.

[122] "Free gift" translates *charisma*, a word whose significance was explained at Romans 5:16.

[123] "In Christ" is an expression that was used at 6:11, and expresses that "union with Christ" in which a believer participates by virtue of his being baptized (with its threefold significance of death, burial, and resurrection to newness of life).

[124] This is not the first time in Romans that Jesus has been called "Lord."   See 1:4,7 and 5:1,11,21 for other uses of "Lord."   See notes at 3:24 for the distinction between "Jesus Christ" and "Christ Jesus."

SPECIAL STUDY #5

SANCTIFICATION

The word "sanctification" (*hagiasmos*) does not appear in the Old Testament, and is used but ten times in the New Testament.[1]   However, the root word from which it comes and its cognates appear more than a thousand times in Scripture; this makes it one of the most important concepts in Biblical and historical theology.

The importance of the subject could not be stated in clearer terms than one finds in Hebrews 12:14, "Pursue after ... the sanctification (*hagiasmos*) without which no one will see the Lord."

As long as the use of the word in the Bible is the topic of study, there is little disagreement among the lexicons. But when one passes from Bible times into church history, there is great difference of doctrine discernible. The goal of this Special Study is to help the student of the Bible to understand what the Bible says, and also to recognize what certain theologians are saying when they explain what "sanctification" or "holiness" means.

I. ETYMOLOGY AND DEFINITION OF TERMS

The Hebrew word meaning "sanctify" is *qadosh*, and seems to mean "to cut" or "to separate."[2]   "Separation," too, is the main idea found in the Greek words *hagios* (holy), *hagiazō* (to make holy, to sanctify, to consecrate), *hagiasmos* (sanctification), and *hagiosunē* (holiness).[3]   "Generally, sanctification (*hagiasmos*), as an act or a process, begun by God and ever going on 'in Christ,' is distinguished from holiness or sanctity (*hagiotēs*) and moral purity (*hagiosunē*), which are a state and quality respectively."[4]

---

[1] *Hagiasmos* is used at 1 Thessalonians 4:3,4,7; 2 Thessalonians 2:13; Romans 6:19,22; 1 Corinthians 1:30; 1 Timothy 2:15; Hebrews 12:14; and 1 Peter 1:2. A cognate, *hagiotēs*, occurs at 2 Corinthians 1:12 and Hebrews 12:10. Another cognate, *hagiosunē*, occurs three times, at 1 Thessalonians 3:13; Romans 1:4; and 2 Corinthians 7:1. Other cognates are the verb form *hagiazō*, and the noun *hagios*, often translated "holy" or "saint."

[2] G.A. Turner, "Sanctification," in *Zondervan Pictorial Encyclopedia of the Bible*, edited by Merrill C. Tenney (Grand Rapids: Zondervan Publishing House, 1975), Vol.5, p.265.

[3] The translations given are those found in the NASB. The KJV is not consistent in which English word is used. The KJV sometimes reads "sanctification" and sometimes "holiness" where the word is *hagiasmos*; it consistently uses "holiness" to translate *hagiosunē*.

[4] R.H. Coats, "Sanctification," in *Hastings Encyclopedia of Religion and Ethics*, edited by James Hastings (New York: Charles Scribner's Sons, 1903), Vol.11, p.181.

It soon becomes evident that whatever "holiness" or "sanctification" a thing or person has, it is derived from its relationship to God.   Each of the members of the Godhead are intrinsically "holy;"[5] God's children are "holy" only in that they are consecrated or separated to Him, separated to sacred service.   A sanctified person is one who is separated from a sinful world and put into a special relationship with God.   He is not *out* of the world; but while *in* it, he is consecrated or dedicated to God for divine service.

Thus far, there is fairly general agreement among Bible students.   It is only in regard to the questions of the manner by which sanctification is accomplished, the time it occurs (whether before or after justification), and the degree to which sanctification may be carried in this life, that there is dispute among the various theologians and churches.

II. THE DOCTRINE IN HISTORY

None of the questions in dispute were much of a topic of discussion until the time of Augustine.   His dispute with Pelagius, his doctrine of original sin, and his doctrine of the church all influenced his teaching about sanctification.   In opposition to Pelagius, Augustine taught that the whole process of sanctification was accomplished by the grace of God, and even man's cooperating effort was itself a divine gift.   His doctrine of an inherent taint in man's nature led him to explain sanctification as being a supernatural impartation of divine life to the believer.   Augustine's doctrine of the church led to the statement that God's grace which produced sanctification was available only in the church, and only through the sacraments.   Augustine allowed for the possibility of entire sanctification in this life, but also taught that it was never realized because God judicially so decreed it.[6]   Augustine's theology influenced the Roman Church for 1000 years.

Aquinas refined Augustine's doctrine, and this in turn became official Catholic doctrine at the Council of Trent.   Briefly summarized, this is the Catholic dogma: Because of a sinful human nature, supernatural grace is imparted by God to save lost man,

---

Besides this group of words related to *hagios*, there are some synonyms (*hieros, hosios, semnos,* and *hagnos*) sometimes translated "holy."   The idea in *hieros* is that something is associated with the gods, or belongs to them.   *Hosios* means that something is "godly," in harmony with the laws and nature of God.   *Semnos* implies the idea of deserving reverence or awe because the object of awe is magnificent or impressive.   *Hagnos* denotes freedom from sensual sins.   R.C. Trench, *Synonyms of the New Testament* (Grand Rapids: Wm. B. Eerdmans Publishing Co., 1953), p.327-334.

[5] That the Father is Holy, see Jesus' prayer, "Holy Father," in John 17:11, and see Revelation 4:8, 6:10, and 15:4.   That the Son is Holy, see Luke 1:35; Mark 1:24; Acts 4:27,30; and Hebrews 7:26.   And of course, the name by which we regularly call the third member of the Godhead is *Holy* Spirit.

[6] Augustine of Hippo, "On the Spirit and the Letter," chapter 63, in *Nicene and Post-Nicene Fathers*, edited by Philip Schaff (Grand Rapids: Wm. B. Eerdmans Publishing Co., 1956), Vol.5 (Anti-Pelagian Writings), p.112.   Some brief notes about Augustine's theology were also given in Special Study #4 on "Original Sin," p.207ff.

and raise the soul to a new level of being, in order that it may achieve its heavenly destiny and beatitude of knowing, possessing, and enjoying God. An inexhaustible treasury of grace, provided originally by Christ and increased as a result of the saints' works of supererogation, available only through the church and the sacraments, is what produces sanctification. The manner of sanctification has both a divine and a human side.

> From the divine side, the presence of this sanctifying or sufficient grace within the soul remits original sin, imparts a permanent habit of inherent righteousness, and carries within itself the promise and potency of all perfection. Out of it, as from a divine seed, emerges a tree of spiritual life, which branches out into the three theological and four cardinal virtues and yields ultimately the seven ripe fruits of the Holy Spirit. Only by mortal sin can its operations be neutralized or destroyed, the guilt which is contracted subsequently to baptism being removed by the eucharist in the case of venial sins and by the penitential system of the Church in the case of those that are more serious. From the human side, good works or supernatural acts of faith working through love have merit before God and secure increase of grace on that account: yet no such meritorious works are possible without the continuous assistance of actual, co-operating, or efficacious grace, which supplements the sanctifying grace originally bestowed, and mysteriously inclines the will, by its own effort, to give a free assent to righteousness. The resulting process and goal of holiness are spoken of, not as sanctification (which was already bestowed in God's initial act), but as justification, or the actual making just or righteous through infused grace leading to final perseverance, of him who was once a sinner but can now stand before the bar of God, deserving eternal life.[7]

It can be seen from this summary that in the Roman system, there likely is no entire sanctification in this life, sometimes not until considerable time has been spent in Purgatory after this life. It can also be seen that when a Catholic theologian reads these verses about "sanctification," and the ones previous about "justification," he usually thinks something considerably different from what a Protestant means when he talks about "justification" and "sanctification." Catholic theology has sanctification before justification, whereas Protestant theology has justification preceding sanctification. No wonder there is so much religious confusion in the world.

Following the Reformation there were two prominent views about sanctification in the Protestant world – often called the Wesleyan and Reformed views.

The Wesleyan View – "Saved and Sanctified"

John Wesley's doctrine was being formulated between 1739 and 1760. After that, in his sermons, he used such terms as "Christian Perfection," "Perfect Love," and "Holiness"

---

[7] Coats, "Sanctification," *op. cit.*, p.182.

to refer to an instantaneous act subsequent to conversion, wrought by the Holy Spirit, by which man's old sinful nature that lingered after his conversion was finally subdued, and entire sanctification (sinless perfection) resulted.

> Justification (salvation) was supposed to be the work of grace by which sinners are made righteous and freed from their sinful habits when they come to Christ. But in the merely justified soul there remains a corrupt principle, an evil tree, or a "root of bitterness," which continually prompts to sin. If the believer obeys this impulse and willfully sins, he ceases to be justified; therefore the desirability of its removal, that the likelihood of backsliding may be greatly lessened. *The eradication of this sinful root is sanctification.* It is therefore the cleansing of the nature from all inbred sin by the blood of Christ (applied through faith when a full consecration is made), and the refining fire of the Holy Spirit, who burns out all dross when all is laid upon the altar of sacrifice.[8]

Followers of this Wesleyan-Holiness tradition are accustomed to express it by the simple slogan, "Saved and Sanctified." "Saved" refers to initial justification, and "sanctified" refers to this second work of grace, this subsequent experience at which the old sinful root is eradicated. Even the hymnology from this movement reflects this second work of grace idea: "Take away our bent to sinning" ... "Let us find that second rest" ... "Make and keep me pure within" ... "Love divine, all loves excelling."[9]

The Reformed View

Calvin, like Luther, rejected the Catholic doctrine of sanctification. Instead, for Calvin, sanctification was a process aided by the indwelling Holy Spirit – a process of growth in grace and mastering fleshly lusts that is never entire or complete in this life.

> Sanctification is the work of God's free grace, whereby we are renewed in the whole man after the image of God, and are enabled more and more to die unto sin, and live unto righteousness. Sanctification is the same work which is commenced in regeneration and it is wrought by the Holy Spirit. It is a work of God in which the believer co-operates by use of the means of grace placed at his disposal. It occurs over the believer's whole life, and is never complete in this life but only at death. It consists of mortifying the old sinful nature and deeds by crucifixion and the quickening of the new nature unto good works affecting the whole man.[10]

---

[8] H.A. Ironside, *Holiness: The False and True* (Neptune, NJ: Loizeaux Brothers, nd), p.42.

[9] A good, brief summary of the Wesleyan doctrine of sanctification is found in Daniel Steele, "Sanctification – Wesleyan Doctrine," in *The International Standard Bible Encyclopedia*, edited by James Orr (Grand Rapids: Wm. B. Eerdmans Publishing Co., 1952), Vol.4, p.2685,2686.

[10] Harold J. Ockenga, *The Church of God* (Westwood, NJ: Fleming H. Revell, 1956), p.221.

The Reformed view may be differentiated from the Wesleyan in that there is no second work of grace, no single act of the Holy Spirit by which a man is made entirely holy. In Reformed theology, sanctification is a process that continues on through the whole life. There is also a similarity between the Reformed and Wesleyan views, in that both posit that there is an old sinful nature that lingers on after conversion that must be subdued, and this subduing (in one form or another) is sanctification.[11]

Rationalistic Views

For the sake of being current, it is necessary to briefly review how the doctrine of sanctification has been treated since rationalism and existentialism have become prevailing philosophies in the world.

Rationalism stressed man's efforts for his own moral perfection, rather than what "God" might do for man. Sanctification became a way of describing a man's inner disposition which resulted in behavior that would please God.

Kant rejected the idea of supernatural or revealed religion, so he had little use for the church's doctrine that "God" had something to do with a man's sanctification. Kant, and men like him, was trying to hold on to the values that Christianity taught without holding on to the sources from which Christianity springs. Thus, they talk about "moral law" and "holiness" and even "God." For Kant, the necessity for sanctification rested solely on the nature of the thinking, experiencing, acting self, and on the categoric claims of moral law. "Holiness" and "moral character" were almost equated, and since man must act in an ethical way, else he cannot be happy, sanctification was progressive, something a man could will to do, something to be striven for as long as a man lives.[12]

Schleiermacher's doctrine of sanctification was similar to the Catholic Church's, in that he conceived of sanctification as preceding justification, but different in that one need have no relationship to the church in order to be sanctified. To him, faith is a subjective thing (a religious attitude toward God), even mystical (a feeling of satisfaction and of communion with God, a feeling even people outside the church could experience), and was the seed or germ from which sanctification and justification grew. Perhaps there was a vague similarity to the Biblical doctrine of sanctification in his presentation, for he spoke of the progressive domination of the God-consciousness within us over the morally defective world-consciousness, and he also spoke of how the Holy Spirit rouses our free

---

[11] See Special Study #4 at the close of chapter 5 for more presentation and refutation of the idea that the Bible teaches all men receive an inborn sinful nature inherited from Adam.

[12] Immanuel Kant, *Critique of Practical Reason*, Vol.42, *Great Books of the Western World*, edited by Robert M. Hutchins (Chicago: Encyclopedia Brittanica, Inc., 1952), p.344-346.

loving surrender to the attractive and formative personality of the Redeemer.[13]   While Kant's sanctification implied a personal immortality in order to be completed, Schleiermacher's sanctification was something that could be completed in this life.

Ritschl's teaching was like the Reformers, as far as sanctification following justification was concerned. Ritschl also spoke about how the Holy Spirit helped the members of God's kingdom to have behavior characterized by goodness, righteousness, and love. However, to Ritschl, the "Holy Spirit" is not one of the members of the Godhead, not a person at all, but is an attitude produced by the "complete knowledge of God which is common to believers in Christ." He defined sin as a relative failure to do the good, right, and loving thing; in fact, there is no absolute standard of right that all are expected to conform to, and the breaking of which is "sin." Sanctification, the opposite of "sin," therefore is something that can be complete in the present life, since all one must do is fulfill his duties to his neighbors.[14]

Existential Views

Neo-orthodox and Neo-liberal theologians tend to understand that the Bible presents its message in terms of "symbolism." Expressions such as Christ's deity and incarnation are treated not as historical truths, but as symbols. In fact, in Tillich's theology, "Christ" is an ideal that men associate with the man Jesus. This ideal is called "New Being," and is simply another way of saying that wherever love is manifested in the world, "Christ" is there. For Tillich, sanctification is this "New Being" progressively overcoming evils in the church and in society.[15]

Reinhold Niebuhr also gives a symbolical interpretation to Biblical truths. He postulates that the image of God in man is man's "original righteousness," or simply the conscience. He explains that the law written in man's heart is *agape* or love. The best example of love in history is in Jesus, thus He is the Christ. For a man to be saved, he needs no relationship to the Jesus of history, but only to the symbol of the Christ.[16] Love, or the "hidden" Christ, is the original righteousness God gave to all men. As man grasps this truth he is converted, and sanctification is this "Christ" in us, growing more and more as man by his own effort comes to love more and more. There is no Holy Spirit within to lead, guide, transform, or help. "Christ lives in me" means that at last I have caught the

---

[13] Friederich Schleiermacher, *The Christian Faith*, edited by H.R. Mackintosh and J.S. Stewart, (Philadelphia: Fortress Press, 1976), p.100.

[14] Benjamin A. Ritschl, *The Christian Doctrine of Justification and Reconciliation*, edited by H.R. Mackintosh and A.B. Macauley (Clifton, NJ: Reference Book Publishers, 1966), p.605,606,652.

[15] "[Sanctification is] ... the process in which the power of the New Being transforms personality and community, inside and outside the Church." Paul Tillich, *Existence and the Christ* (Chicago: University of Chicago Press, 1957), p.179,180.

[16] Reinhold Niebuhr, *The Nature and Destiny of Man* (New York: Charles Scribner's Sons, 1943), Vol.2, p.109,110.

agape spirit.

This commentator has rejected both rationalistic and existential world views, and therefore also rejects the misguided efforts of some theologians to make the Bible fit such a world view.[17]

Still there remains the question – which of the other three views (Catholic, Wesleyan, or Reformed), if any, is an expression of what the Scriptures themselves say about sanctification?

III. SURVEY OF REPRESENTATIVE VERSES

People, things, and even the Lord are objects of sanctification. Inanimate objects, such as the Tabernacle's laver, altar, and vessels, were sanctified (Exodus 40:9,10, 19: 23); they were set apart to sacred service. But are we to suppose any change took place in the *nature* of these vessels, or that there was any evil element rooted out of them? Believers are called upon to sanctify the Lord in their hearts (1 Peter 3:15). How are we to understand an exhortation like this if sanctification implies an inward cleansing, or making holy what was before unclean and evil? The Christians addressed in 1 Corinthians 6:11 are already sanctified (set apart to God), yet they were also still "carnal" (1 Corinthians 3:1,3 ASV). Unbelievers are sometimes sanctified. In 1 Corinthians 7:14, the life-partner of a Christian, though unsaved, is said to be sanctified. Does that mean that such a one is free from sins?

The manner or means of sanctification is attributed both to God and to men. At times God is declared to be the One who sanctifies. Paul wrote, "May the God of peace Himself sanctify you entirely ..." (1 Thessalonians 5:23). The Holy Spirit has a "sanctifying work" He does as men become Christians (1 Peter 1:2; Romans 15:16; 2 Thessalonians 2:13). The Son was sanctified by the Father (John 10:36). Did the Son have an evil nature to be changed? Hardly, for the Bible indicates that Jesus was sinless perfect.[18] Jesus also sanctified Himself (John 17:9). Likewise, at 2 Corinthians 7:1, believers are exhorted to sanctify themselves in these words, "... let us cleanse ourselves

---

[17] Warren C. Young has given a thoughtful evaluation of several of these modern views. He points out that both liberalism and existentialism reduce "salvation" and "sanctification" to something akin to self-edification. If "Christ" is merely symbolic, then a man has nothing but his own feelings, his own strength, his own resources to draw on. And if Jesus is merely a man, who so far is the best example of love, what is there to keep a greater than "Christ" from appearing in history someday? The Christian gospel is robbed of any objective or historical significance by both methods of interpretation. "The Nature of Sanctification," in *Christian Faith and Modern Theology*, edited by Carl F. H. Henry (New York: Channel Press, 1964), p.371-86.

[18] In spite of the Scripture's clear teaching on the matter of Christ's sinlessness, there are holiness teachers who have alleged that the reason Jesus had to be born of a virgin was so he could avoid the inherited sinful nature (which, they believe) all men receive by virtue of descent from Adam. See the Special Studies on "Sin" and "Original Sin," included at the close of chapter 5, where this whole topic has been covered in detail.

from all defilement of flesh and spirit, perfecting holiness in the fear of God." And again in Romans 6:19-22, we read that when a Christian consciously presents his bodily members to God in order to do what is righteous, this results in his sanctification. Thus, the man himself had something to do with his own sanctification. In the Old Testament we read that men could sanctify themselves to do iniquity (Isaiah 66:17). How absurd the thought of any inward cleansing here, just because the word "sanctify" is used.

Given the teaching of these verses, it begins to appear that the word "sanctify" does not carry the implication of "inward cleansing" as the Wesleyans teach.

What about the "time" when sanctification is said to take place? In some verses, it is taught that there is a "sanctification" (setting apart to sacred service) at the time of conversion (e.g., 1 Corinthians 6:11; 1 Peter 1:2).[19] In other verses, persons already addressed as sanctified are afterward exhorted to be holy (compare 1 Peter 1:1,2 with 1:15,16; and compare Romans 1:7 ["saints"] with 6:19-22; and compare 2 Corinthians 1:1 with 7:1). The Hebrews are exhorted to continually pursue (present tense, continuous action) holiness (Hebrews 12:14), and perhaps 1 Thessalonians 5:23 suggests that sanctification is something that is not completed this side of heaven.

Thus, it begins to appear that neither the Catholic or Wesleyan doctrines present sanctification as the Scriptures themselves do. But does that mean that the Reformed view is wholly correct, and the one to be embraced and taught?

IV. IS SANCTIFICATION AN INSTANTANEOUS ACT, OR A LIFE-LONG PROCESS?

Standard Wesleyan arguments that sanctification is a one-time act that follows conversion include the following:

(1) If sanctification is something God wills (1 Thessalonians 4:3), and something God Himself does to a man (1 Thessalonians 5:23), why should not this sanctification be instantaneous and entire?

(2) There may be a gradual growth in grace and knowledge of the truth, but entire sanctification is instantaneous. For example, Romans 6:6 ("our old self was crucified") and Galatians 2:20 ("I have been crucified with Christ; and it is no longer I who live") present the picture of a sudden death.[20]

---

[19] The 1 Peter passage would appear to teach that the "sanctifying work of the Holy Spirit" is what leads a man to obedience to Christ. (One might suppose Peter is reflecting the fact that God's Spirit does convict a man of his sins, John 16:8-10, and does lead a man to the place where he wants to be baptized into the body, 1 Corinthians 12:13.) Does this mean that the Roman Catholic doctrine that sanctification precedes justification is correct? Not completely. For there are numerous verses that show there is a sanctification that follows conversion, too, and one rarely sees this side of the topic presented in Catholic theologies.

[20] The context of both these passages about "crucified" refer to the time of justification, not to a later time when a man is "sanctified." In the slogan "saved and sanctified," these verses from Romans and

(3) The aorist tense verbs (indicating a single act) found in 1 Thessalonians 5:23 ("sanctify") and in Romans 6:19 and 12:1 ("present") point to a definite, decisive moment in time.[21]

(4) The use of the word "perfect" or "mature" in certain passages (e.g., 2 Corinthians 7:1 and 1 Corinthians 2:6) is alleged to teach that the act of sanctification is past, and the person has been "perfect" ever since.[22]

Reformed theologians, in reply to these standard Wesleyan arguments, point to the fact that even in Thessalonians one finds that side by side with Paul's prayer for sanctification are admonitions to growth and progress (1 Thessalonians 3:12 and 5:14). Some verses may indeed look at sanctification as a one-time act, but those are verses which look back at the time of conversion, where a man is "sanctified" (set apart to the Lord) as he begins his Christian life. When a man becomes a Christian, when he comes out of the world, and with true faith and repentance dedicates himself to God in baptism, these very acts are sanctifying in their effect. The apostles, consequently, do not hesitate to characterize such persons as "saints." A second point used to show that sanctification is a process is the very use of the Greek word *hagiasmos*, since words with a *-mos* ending indicate a process. 1 Corinthians 1:30, in which Christ is called our "sanctification" (*hagiasmos*), likely means that Christ has become the cause or ground that makes sanctification possible. Reformed thinking, which says "Christ justifies no one whom He does not also sanctify,"[23] seems to interpret this verse incorrectly. It could mean that sanctification is automatically done by Christ to the Christian only if the Bible elsewhere teaches that man is wholly passive in the whole matter of salvation.

V. SANCTIFICATION DOES NOT MEAN "SINLESS PERFECT"

Sanctified people, like the Corinthians were (1 Corinthians 1:2), could still be contentious (1:11-13), carnal (3:1-6), puffed up (4:18,19), condone immorality in their midst (5:1), defraud one another (6:1-8), have domestic troubles (7:1-5), worship idols

---

Galatians should be explicated as having reference to "saved" rather than to "sanctified" as the Wesleyans are wont to do.

[21] While we agree that the aorist tense refers to a decisive moment, we still have not admitted the Wesleyan interpretation of these passages, for the verses do not speak of something God does to the man in a moment, but rather of a decision the man himself is exhorted to make once and for all.

[22] Paul himself repudiates the idea that he has reached perfection (Philippians 3:12), while at the same time claiming for himself and his readers a degree of perfection (Philippians 3:15). It would, in the light of these verses, be very precarious to claim that the connotation in the use of the word "perfect" is that an instantaneous moment of being sanctified has occurred in the past. It would hardly do to try to make "perfect" in 1 Corinthians 13:10 mean "sanctified" as Wesleyans would have the word mean in their slogan "saved and *sanctified*."

[23] John Calvin, *The Institutes of the Christian Religion*, 2 volumes, edited by John T. McNeill (Philadelphia: Westminster Press, 1960). III.XVI.1. Vol.1, p.798.

(8:1-13), partake of the Lord's Supper in an improper manner (11:20-34), and wrangle over spiritual gifts (12:1-31). This hardly can be harmonized with the Wesleyan doctrine that one who is sanctified is beyond sinning.[24] Romans, too, which is addressed to "saints," is filled with admonitions to stop sinning (as for example, 6:12).[25]

> There is no *terminus ad quem* for us in this world; no stage at which we may sit down and say it is enough. There are always heights beyond heights, and blessings beyond blessings – blessings whose affluent fullness would be too great for our present capacity, and which, therefore, await our approach to them, and our spiritual preparation to receive them ... There is no recorded example among men of perfect holiness. The best and brightest of Old Testament worthies were not spotless; and those who lived and walked with the Savior of men, and who drank deepest of his Spirit, never succeeded in reproducing his sinless and glorious character. Whatever their attainments in grace and goodness, they had still, even from their loftiest height of excellency, to look up with humble spirits and adoring praise to Him who, alike in the glory of his majesty and the shame of his humiliation, was pre-eminently *the* Holy One. John says, "If we say that we have no sin, we deceive ourselves, and the truth is not in us" (1 John 1:8). Paul remarks, "Not as though I had already attained, either were already perfect; but I follow after, if that I may apprehend that for which also I am apprehended of Christ Jesus" (Philippians 3:12). Surely if this was true of him, there is no one who may claim to have gone further, and to have attained more. The fact that God Himself is the standard model of perfect holiness should teach us to be at once humble in our pretensions and most aspiring in our aims. We may never in this world be holy as He is holy, but it is something ... to strive for; and even in the world to come, we may sit down with Abraham, Isaac, and Jacob in the kingdom of heaven, and enter into eternal fellowship and fraternity with the spirits of just men made perfect, even there we shall take up the strain of the four living beings – representative of the whole creation – and looking up to Him who is still infinitely above us, say: "Holy, holy, holy, Lord God Almighty" (Revelation 4:8).[26]

---

[24] Some in the Wesleyan tradition have recognized they have a problem with "perfectionism," and have tried to get themselves out of difficulty by using a different definition for "sin." The old expression "freedom from sin" has been replaced by expressions like "freedom from known sin," "entire consecration," or "Christian assurance." "Whether one can live sinlessly or not depends upon one's definition of sin. If sin is a voluntary transgression of the law, we may be faultless. If sin involves ignorant transgression or involuntary lack of conformity, then we cannot live without sin." Ockenga, *The Church in God*, p.226.

[25] Compare notes on Romans 1:7, "called *as* saints." The Wesleyan would rather translate it, "called *to be* saints," as though the holiness or sanctification were still a future event that would transpire in the lives of the readers. But it will hardly do to attempt to defend the proposition that the only people who are called "saints" in the New Testament are those who have not only been saved, but also, at a later time, been sanctified.

[26] J.S. Lamar, *First Principles and Perfection* (Cincinnati: Standard Publishing Co., 1891), p.251-253.

SUMMARY

The word "sanctify" carries the idea of consecration, devotion, or set apart to sacred service. As such, sanctification can be thought of as either an act or a process. If one looks back at the time of his baptism and consequent initial justification, "sanctification" (set apart to sacred service) can be viewed as an act in the past (as it is in 1 Corinthians 6:11). If one looks at the growth in grace and knowledge and the determination to pursue a right course of living (as Romans 6, or Hebrews 12:14 exhorts), then "sanctification" may be viewed as a process, and a life-long process at that.

There is both a negative and a positive side to the process. Negatively, there is to be a separation from sin; positively, there is to be a presentation of one's members to God to be used in His service.

> The sanctified are set apart or separated to a sacred service or purpose. It does not mean that they were sinless, or free from temptation to sin, but consecrated to the service of God. All who have entered into Christ, and have obligated themselves to serve him, are said to be sanctified in Christ Jesus regardless of their degree of consecration or perfection of character. There are degrees of sanctification just as there are degrees of Christian knowledge and fidelity to Christ. The growth in sanctification and holiness is to be attained by a constant and persistent study of God's will and a daily effort to bring oneself into obedience to the same.[27]

> Our chief concern while we remain here below is to "*follow after holiness, without which no man shall see God.*" And although we may not hope to reach here the ultimate state of that relative holiness which is possible to redeemed humanity, we may, by the help of the Holy Spirit, gradually approach unto it. And the pursuit itself, if faithfully and earnestly made, will cause us to be acceptable to God through Jesus Christ our Lord.[28]

---

[27] David Lipscomb, *A Commentary on the New Testament Epistles: First Corinthians*, edited by J.W. Shepherd (Nashville, TN: Gospel Advocate Co., 1960), p.21.

[28] Lamar, *First Principles and Perfection*, p.254.

SELECTED BIBLIOGRAPHY

Barber, Burton W., "Scriptural Studies in Sanctification," *Voice of Evangelism*, 9 (January 1954), p.4ff. (A nine-lesson series is found in the January through June issues.)

Bartlett, J.V., "Sanctification," in *Hastings Dictionary of the Bible*, edited by James Hastings. New York: Charles Scribner's Sons, 1903. Vol.4, p.391-395.

Berkouwer, G.C., *Faith and Sanctification*, Grand Rapids: Wm. B. Eerdmans Publishing Co, 1952.

Ironside, H.A., *Holiness: The False and the True*. Neptune, NJ: Loizeaux Brothers, nd.

Orton, H. Wiley, *Christian Theology*, Vol.2. Kansas City: Beacon Hill Press, 1960.

Rall, Harris F., "Sanctification," in *International Standard Bible Encyclopedia*, edited by James Orr. Grand Rapids: Wm. B. Eerdmans Publishing Co, 1952. Vol. 4, p.2681-2686.

Turner, G.A., "Sanctification," in *Zondervan Pictorial Encyclopedia of the Bible*, edited by Merrill C. Tenney. Grand Rapids: Zondervan Publishing House, 1975. Vol.5, p.264-267.

Weisiger, Cary N., *The Reformed Doctrine of Sanctification*. A 24-page booklet included in the Series "Fundamentals of the Faith," included at page 24 in *Christianity Today*, 11:23 (September 1, 1967).

Young, Warren C., "The Nature of Sanctification," in *Christian Faith and Modern Theology*, edited by Carl F.H. Henry. New York: Channel Press, 1964. Pages 371-386.

D. God's Plan of Salvation (Justification by Faith) Involves Blessed Effects on Those Who Struggled to Meet the Law's Demands. 7:1-25

Summary: In 6:14,15, Paul has made the statement that a Christian is "not under law but under grace." This was a very hard thing for Jews to accept. In verses 1-6 of chapter 7, Paul shows how it is true that the Law of Moses is no longer binding, and how this is in reality a blessing. Verses 7-12 explain that in actuality the presence of the Law gave the devil more opportunity to tempt and lead a man to ruin. Verses 13-25 will be a firm reminder that the Law gave a man no help to live by its requirements, but instead resulted in a constant inner conflict in the hearts of spiritually sensitive men.

7:1 – Or do you not know, brethren (for I am speaking to those who know the law), that the law has jurisdiction over a person as long as he lives?

Or do you not know, brethren. The way this verse begins shows there is a connection with the idea expressed in the closing verses of chapter 6.[1] In fact, since 5:20, an underlying theme has been the idea that the Law of Moses was never intended by God to be a permanent arrangement in the way men were to be led to redemption. As in 6:3, this wording of the question is Paul's way of reminding them of something they already knew well. Paul has just written that the Christian, freed from the service of sin and now being the servant of God, has fruit to sanctification, and as a final result, eternal life. This whole proposition could not be true if the Christian were still under the Law of Moses. Yet, to suggest to a people who had fought and died for the Law that it was no longer valid, was an emotionally loaded statement. Paul tries to ease the jolt by calling them "brethren" (a form of address not used since 1:13), to show them he understands how potentially explosive this topic is, and that he is affectionately concerned for them.[2]

(For I am speaking to those who know the law). The NASB translators left the word "law" in small letters. It is another example of anarthrous *nomos*,[3] and could be translated either "law" or "Law." Their decision is based on what they perceive to be the train of thought in this and the following verses. Simply stated, the supposed train of thought is this: verse 1 is a thesis, verses 2 and 3 are an illustration of this thesis, and verses 4-6 are

---

[1] At 6:14, we had the expressions "sin shall not be master over you," and "not under law, but under grace." The first of these two expressions was worked out in detail in 6:15-23. Indeed, the old slavery to sin has been broken, and individual sins, too, need not be surrendered to. Now, in 7:1-6, the second of the two expressions is worked out.

[2] This affectionate form of address occurs seven times in Romans, and a study of each will show that each time it occurs, it marks a topic of special concern on Paul's part, one that is even difficult (emotionally) for him to write about, knowing how delicate he must be in his presentation, lest the truth he shares be hotly rejected before it is even given a hearing.

[3] The technical term "anarthrous *nomos*" was explained, along with what the translator's decision must be each time he encounters this construction, in notes at Romans 2:12.

an application of the thesis to the readers.[4]   Paul's readers were not ignorant of the general proposition true of all law, that a man is subject to the laws of the land only so long as he lives.   They will understand the idea he is about to convey in the thesis and its illustration.

That the law has jurisdiction over a person as long as he lives?   This is the general thesis or proposition Paul is presenting at this point in his letter.   It is a universal principle, understood by Jew and Gentile alike, that legal obligations are binding only for so long as human beings are alive.[5]

7:2 – For the married woman is bound by law to her husband while he is living; but if her husband dies, she is released from the law concerning the husband.

For.   Verses 2 and 3 are an illustration of the general principle Paul has set forth in verse 1.[6]

The married woman is bound by law to her husband while he is living.   "Married woman" translates *hupandros*, a classical word meaning "one that is under a husband."[7] The whole Roman world had such a law about the relation of the wife to the husband; it was no more specifically Jewish than it was specifically Roman.   "Bound" translates the verb *deō*, a word also used elsewhere by Paul of the marriage relation (1 Corinthians 7:27). "While he is living" is a participial phrase, "to the living husband," and repeats the idea from verse 1 about how a law has jurisdiction over a man only "as long as he lives."

---

[4] If this be a true outline of Paul's thought, several conclusions follow: (1) "law" in verse 1 speaks of any law, of which the Law of Moses is but one example, and the NASB translators have pointed us in the right direction with their lower case "law."   (2) It would not be proper to use this verse to help prove that the majority of the Roman church members were of Jewish background.   Only if it reads, "I speak to people who know the Law," might it be evidence for a Jewish religious background for the readers.   See the Introductory Studies for greater detail on this question of the nationality and religious composition of the Roman church.   (3) Verse 1 should not be interpreted in such a way that reflection is cast on other churches, as though they were less acquainted with "law" than were the saints at Rome.   Paul is simply taking an example from the way the laws of men are applied, and anyone who knows anything at all about law knows that death brings release from the laws of the land.

[5] The word translated "person" in verse 1 is generic, meaning one of the human family, a man or a woman, a human being.   As far as the Greek is concerned, the last word could be rendered either "as long as *he* lives" or "as long as *it* lives."   If we translate "it," then the idea is that a law has dominion over a man only so long as the law is in force.   When the law is rescinded, people no longer are required to obey it. Origen, Ambrose, Grotius, Erasmus, and others, thinking the Law of Moses is specifically in Paul's mind, prefer to translate the verb by "it," and then explain that the verse is another evidence of the temporary nature of the Mosaic code.   The idea behind the NASB's "*he* lives" is that death releases a man from the laws of the land by which he was bound in life.   For example, here is a man being tried in court; in the middle of the trial, he dies.   The case is no longer prosecuted.   Death ends the jurisdiction of the law over the man.

[6] "This verse has cost most commentators a vast amount of trouble, and all (as it seems to this writer) without much reason.   Their whole difficulty has arisen (1) because they try to construe the verse as a sort of allegory (rather than a simple illustration), and (2) from attempting to trace a minute correspondence between all its parts, and certain facts [such as 'bearing fruit'] in the life of the Christian."   Lard, *Romans*, p.220

[7] Barmby, *Romans*, p.182.

But if her husband dies, she is released from the law concerning the husband.[8] The "law of the husband" is the law of marriage which binds her to her husband. "Released" translates *katērgētai*, a word that means "to make ineffective,"[9] and the perfect tense indi-

---

[8] Once again, it must be recalled that this reference to marriage is intended to be but an illustration of the thesis stated in verse 1. Those writers who attempt to make this an allegory (an allegory is a parallel in which all of the details are made to express some spiritual truth) have found it almost necessary to come up with some "wonderful" explanations. The problem allegorizers face is this: First impressions would lead the reader to think of the law as the husband, and the believer as the one who is freed from old relations so as to form a new union with Christ, because the former husband is dead. This interpretation runs up against a real difficulty in verse 4, for Paul goes on to speak, not of the death of the husband (as verse 2 and 3 would lead one to expect), but of the believer's having died to the law. Numerous suggestions have been proposed in an attempt to excuse Paul for using such a poor allegorical example.

(1) Some are of the opinion that Paul forgot his line of thought while dictating this letter: it really was the *Law* that he was going to write about as dying, and not the *man*. Ephesians 2:15 and Colossians 2:14 are regularly quoted to support this idea. (*Reply*: While it is true the Law of Moses was temporary, this is probably not the passage to be used to prove it. Instead of losing his line of thought, it will be noted that a death taking place in the man who becomes a believer, just as he writes in verse 4, has been the theme since early in chapter 6.)

(2) Some say Paul deliberately refrained from writing about the death of the Law, as a strict application of his allegory would require, lest he offend Jewish readers. (*Reply*: People of Jewish background who became Christians were regularly taught about the temporary nature of the Law. They would have known all about this matter before they ever read this letter from Paul.)

(3) Some write at length how the *wife*, as far as the marriage bond is concerned, really dies at the same time her husband dies. Meyer, for example, so interprets, and appeals to Ephesians 5:28 to support this interpretation. (*Reply*: To suppose such an idea is all the time implied beneath the surface of what Paul actually writes, and to add all this verbiage to comments on verses 2-3 just to get them to match verse 4, is unnecessary.)

(4) Not a few writers express the opinion that Paul is deliberately mistreating his illustration to gain the point he is trying to make. After all, he has already warned us in 6:19 that there were details in his slavery illustration that were not actually true to life. (*Reply*: Is it Paul – with the alleged discrepancy between his illustration and the application he is making [i.e., so that it is the husband who dies in the former, and we ourselves, as represented by the wife, in the latter] – who has made the mistake, or is it Alford and others who have tried to make an allegory out of a simple illustration?)

(5) Augustine arrived at a completely different and novel interpretation. The former husband represented not the law, but the "sinful passions" (verse 5) that were part of the old man. The wife represents not Christians but the souls of men. And the new husband ("so that you might be joined to ... Him who was raised from the dead," verse 4) is Christ. (*Expositio Quarumdam Propositionum ex Epistola ad Romanos*, Prop.33, in Migne's *Patrologia Latina*, Vol.35). (*Reply*: This whole approach appears to be, not an attempt to explain what Paul wrote, but an attempt to excuse Paul for what Augustine thought he wrote. There is some doubt Paul equates the "former husband" with "sinful passions" [verse 5], yet this equation must be made if Augustine's allegorical interpretation is to be maintained. Even if this equation is made, it still has not relieved what seems to be the real difficulty, that all of a sudden it is the "wife," not the former husband, who is spoken of as having died [verse 4]. Gifford, Sanday and Headlam, and Barth, though modifying Augustine's explanation in one or more details, have not really improved on it.)

(6) Beza slightly modified Augustine's spiritual application, by affirming that there are two marriages in view. "In the first, the old man is the wife; predominating sinful desires [are] the husband; transgressions of every kind [are] the offspring. In the second, the new man is the wife; Christ [is] the husband; and the fruits of the Spirit (Galatians 5:22) are the children." (*Reply*: In Paul's writing, the wife remains the same, but in Beza's application ["old man" vs. "new man"] she does not.)

Actually, none of these attempts at explaining the apparent discrepancy between the allegory and its application is necessary. Treat verses 2 and 3 as an illustration (i.e., one point alone is being illustrated), and this elaborate attempt to excuse Paul for a discrepancy within some allegorical presentation is no longer needed. The one point being illustrated is this: death brings release from the law.

[9] See comments on this verb at 3:3,31; 4:14; and 6:6.

cates a release from the claim of the husband's law over her that began the moment he died, and is still true. Whenever the husband dies, in the eyes of the law, the woman is free from the obligations she had to him as her husband while he was alive.[10]

7:3 – *So then if, while her husband is living, she is joined to another man, she shall be called an adulteress; but if her husband dies, she is free from the law, so that she is not an adulteress, though she is joined to another man.*

So then if, while her husband is living. This verse seems intended to be a confirmation of what was said in verse 2. That the woman is bound to her husband so long as he lives is true, and this can be seen from the fact that were she to be married to a second man while the first was still living, she would be an adulteress. The remainder of the verse will show that the opposite is also true; namely, that death ends a law's jurisdiction.

She is joined to another man, she shall be called an adulteress. "Called" translates *chrēmatizō*, a word that regularly means "divinely called."[11] Literally it reads, "she becomes [belongs] to a different husband," an expression used of the marriage relationship.[12] Because the woman in this example is still, by the law of marriage, bound to her former husband, the new relationship is adulterous.[13]

But if her husband dies, she is free from the law. In this phrase is the whole point of the illustration. Death brings release from the jurisdiction of the law, just as the thesis in verse 1 stated.

So that she is not an adulteress, though she is joined to another man. Because there has been a death, the law of the husband is no longer valid. The same law which renders the wife inseparable from the husband as long as there is life also sets her free from this union as soon as a death occurs. Since the old law is no longer applicable, there is no legal reason why she could not be joined to another man. In fact, the law pertaining to the situation before there was a death is now set aside. It has no relevance to the present situation.

---

[10] That the whole world had such a "law of the husband" reflects what was expressed in chapter 1 about how God's rules had been handed down from generation to generation. The basis of this law, as Jesus one day reminded the Jewish religious leaders (Matthew 19:4-6), is the original institution of marriage in the Garden of Eden (Genesis 2:24). It was at a much later time that the same idea was given legal enactment in the seventh commandment for the Jewish people (Exodus 20:14).

[11] See the author's *New Testament History: Acts*, p.420.

[12] Arndt-Gingrich, *Lexicon*, p.156, under *ginomai*, II.3. Also see footnote #18, below.

[13] Paul and Jesus are not contradicting one another when it comes to what it takes to end a marriage. Paul says physical death ends it. (In 1 Corinthians 7, Paul also seems to say that willful desertion by an unbeliever ends a marriage.) Jesus indicated that divorce resulting from a case of continued unfaithfulness also ends the marriage (Matthew 5:32 and 19:9). Paul is not dealing with the problem of marriage and divorce here in Romans 7, nor is Romans 7 to be used to prove that *only* physical death (and nothing else) ends a marriage. All Paul is doing in Romans 7 is using the example of marriage to show how death ends the jurisdiction that the law of the land has over a person.

7:4 – *Therefore, my brethren, you also were made to die to the Law through the body of Christ, that you might be joined to another, to Him who was raised from the dead, that we might bear fruit for God.*

Therefore, my brethren. This verse contains the beginning of the application of the thesis given in verse 1 and illustrated in verses 2 and 3. The gist of Paul's presentation is this: just as death ends the jurisdiction of men's laws, so it is in the case of the Law of God (Law of Moses). The death of Christ, into which we are baptized (6:3), frees baptized believers from any claims the Law of Moses might exert over them. This is another of the blessed effects of God's way of saving man.[14]

You also were made to die to the Law through the body of Christ. "You also" may mean "you as well as the wife in the illustration." "Made to die" is the same as "baptized into death" (6:4) and "united with Him in the likeness of His death" (6:5). The "Law" that had jurisdiction before there was a death, and now no longer is in force, clearly is the Law of Moses, as the context (verse 7) will show. Because there has been a death (Christ's death on Calvary), the Law of Moses has no further relevance as a particular code of God's will for the man who is united to Christ's death. "The body of Christ" is that which was nailed to the cross (compare "crucified with Him" in 6:6) as a sacrifice for sins (see 3:24,25 and 5:6). It was in order that He might die for the ungodly that Jesus became incarnate in a human body (Hebrews 2:14). Because of the redemption wrought by Jesus, when a man is baptized into the death of Christ, that man has died (the "old man" has died). And that death brings a release from any further subservience to the Law of Moses.[15]

That you might be joined to another, to Him who was raised from the dead. "That" indicates purpose,[16] apparently one purpose God had in mind when He chose to save man by the method He does (an atoning death on Calvary and justification by faith). God's purpose all along was to bring an end to the need for and jurisdiction of the Law of Moses; it was but temporary; God all along intended to end it when Christ came.[17] In its place, God intended (purposed) that believers in the Church Age should belong[18] to "another."

---

[14] Other blessed effects of God's way of saving man (justification by faith) have been presented at Romans 5:1, 5:12, and 6:1. Paul's use of "brethren" at important places in his letters has been explained in footnote #2 above.

[15] Many Jews, including the Judaizers, whom we believe Paul is anticipating as he writes this letter to the Romans, thought that the Law of Moses was of perpetual validity. Thus, in their opinion, even though a man was converted to Christ, he was still obligated to keep the Law of Moses. Paul is denying all this by arguing that death brings a release from law, and anyone who is immersed into Christ, be he Jew or Gentile, is free from any obligation to the demands of the Law of Moses.

[16] The Greek here is *eis* and the articular infinitive. See footnote #62 on chapter 6.

[17] See the discussion about the temporary nature of the Law of Moses at Romans 3:21,31.

[18] The Greek reads, literally, "that we should become (*ginomai*) to another." The same expression was used of the wife's relation to her husband in the LXX at Leviticus 22:12,13; Ruth 1:12; and Ezekiel 23:4. Translators and commentators must be careful here in the word chosen to translate *ginomai*. In verse 3, it was rendered "*joined* to another man." The NASB also uses "joined" in verse 4, but perhaps a better

As the woman is freed from the law of the husband by his death, and when married again comes under the authority of another, so we, when we are made free from the Law of Moses by the death of Christ, are brought under a new law of fidelity and obedience to Him with whom we are thus joined.[19]

A believer's relation to Jesus is of a "different kind"[20] than was the relationship of an Old Testament believer to the Law of Moses. Most translations, by one method or another, show that the "another" to whom the believer belongs is none other than Jesus, the One who was raised from the dead.[21] In what ways a believer's relation to Jesus is different from how it was to be under the Law of Moses will be explained in some detail in this and the next chapters.

That we might bear fruit for God. The "fruit" in Paul's mind is likely the same "benefit" (fruit) that he just spoke about in 6:22, namely, acts of obedience to Christ that result in sanctification.[22] The implication is that a man under the Law was left almost barren as far as sanctification (fruit) was concerned. But for the man under grace, it is at last possible to produce this blessed fruit.

7:5 – *For while we were in the flesh, the sinful passions, which were* **aroused** *by the Law, were at work in the members of our body to bear fruit for death.*

For while we were in the flesh. Paul is explaining how it is possible to "bear fruit *for God*," and the idea is that the new relation to Christ should be as fruitful as the old relation was (it bore fruit unto death, this verse will say), but the fruit is of a wholly different kind. Paul again is ready to take up the idea that men under the Law had little help with their sin problem; but now they do have help, since they have the aid of the indwelling Holy Spirit. "In the flesh" is another way of saying the "body of sin" (6:6).[23] It speaks of the time before

---

way would be simply to read "belong to" in both verses. In verse 4, the KJV reads "married to another," but this can be misleading (just as "joined to" can be), since the New Testament consistently presents the Christian as simply *engaged* to Christ, with the marriage feast (and the marriage) not taking place until the second advent. See 2 Corinthians 11:2 and Ephesians 5:25-29.

[19] Lipscomb and Shepherd, *Romans*, p.129.

[20] The Greek has two synonyms often translated "another." One is *allos*, which means "another of the same kind." The other is *heteros*, which means "another, but of a different kind." Berry, *Lexicon*, p.6. The word used here for "another" is *heteros*.

[21] See notes at Romans 3:24,25 and at 6:4,5,9 concerning the resurrection of Jesus from the dead.

[22] Some, who try to explain every detail of this passage as though it were an allegory, write about the "fruit" (children) that result from a marriage, and then go on to talk about how the Christian while united with Christ will be a soul winner.

[23] The different meanings of *sarx* ("flesh") were introduced in comments on Romans 1:3. There is a sense in which the Roman Christians were "in the flesh" even after their conversion, for they were still living on earth in flesh and blood bodies; therefore, it becomes evident that "in the flesh" in this place seems to mean something like "controlled by the flesh," controlled or motivated by it after the devil had stirred up some evil desires in the flesh.

conversion when the readers were "slaves to sin" (6:6); the body of the man was in control of the man, rather than his spirit being in control. The phrases following will also show these people were under the jurisdiction of the Mosaic Law while they were "in the flesh."[24]

The sinful passions. The Greek reads "the passions of sins," perhaps reflecting a Hebraism meaning "sinful passions" as the NASB translates. "Sinful passions" then would be desires which, if indulged, would lead to sins (plural). The passage also shows these desires are stirred up or aroused from without; they are not inherent in the flesh. "Sinful passions" and "flesh" are not equated in this passage,[25] but the flesh may be an occasion for sin, for there are many temptations that come our way because we have flesh and blood bodies.

Which were *aroused* by the Law. The word in italics is best omitted, for the inclusion of the word leads to the impression that the Law itself causes a man to have sinful desires,[26] and this is wholly contrary to what Paul himself writes in the following verses! It is possible that verse 7 explains what "which were by the Law" means. If verse 7 guides us, then this phrase means that by the Law men learn that certain desires are sinful. It is also possible that verses 9-11 explain what "which were by the Law" means. If verses 9-11 guide us, then this phrase means that the presence of the Law gave the devil (sin) an opportunity to tempt that he did not have when Law was not present. Either of these explanations is to be preferred to the one suggested by the insertion of the word "aroused."

Were at work in the members of our body to bear fruit for death. The sinful passions were what worked[27] in the members of our body,[28] and the result was "fruit" (i.e., sinful ac-

---

[24] This should not be taken to imply that in order to be what Paul calls "in the flesh" a man would also have to be living under the Law of Moses. It is presumed that anyone who has committed his first sin, wherein also his "spirit" died, would be living as the "flesh" directed, i.e., would be "in the flesh." The only reason for introducing the Law at this place is to point out how very little was the help it gave to the man who was "in the flesh" to control his actions, especially after the devil had stirred up some sinful passions.

[25] What Paul here writes tends to corroborate what was written earlier in the Special Studies on Sin and Original Sin. Paul does not regard the flesh as inherently sinful. "Indeed, this very passage proves the contrary. It implies that it is possible to be 'in the body' without being 'in the flesh.' The body, as such, is plastic to influences of either kind: it may be worked upon by Sin through the senses, or it may be worked upon by the Spirit. In either case the motive-force comes from without. The body itself is neutral. See especially the excellent discussion in Gifford, p.48-52." Sanday and Headlam, *Romans*, p.174.

[26] It is a very popular explanation of this passage to say that people do not get ideas about doing wrong things until they see a warning against it. You would not even think about touching the bench, except for the fact the painters put up a "Fresh Paint" sign. Now, all of a sudden, you must find out for yourself if the paint is still wet. In spite of what Paul himself writes in the following verses, it is rather disappointing to see how many modern English versions (including NASB, NEB, TEV, NIV, New KJV) render this verse in such a way that it seems to say that the "desires that lead to sin" are *caused* by the Law.

[27] "Were at work" treats *enērgeito* as though it were a middle voice verb, and the word often is middle voice when it occurs in the New Testament. But it is also possible that the form is a passive voice. If so, the verse would read "the sinful passions ... were wrought in our members," showing even more clearly that the evil desire is derived from an outside source, and is not inherent in the flesh.

[28] For the meaning "members of our body," see notes at 6:13,19, where the same expression occurred.

tions, impurity, lawlessness, as Paul wrote in 6:19) that in turn led to "death," the same "death" he has already warned about in 6:21.[29]   Instead of the Law giving the man help to control the desires and the members of his body, the presence of the Law instead gave the devil more opportunity to stir up those sinful temptations, more of an opportunity to exercise his dominion over the man.   How vain, then, to look to the Law for life or help.

7:6 – *But now we have been released from the Law, having died to that by which we were bound, so that we serve in newness of the Spirit and not in oldness of the letter.*

But now we have been released from the Law.   "Released" is the same word used in verse 2.   "Now" means "now that we have obeyed the gospel, now that we are united with Christ" (as chapter 6 has plainly demonstrated).   Because there has been a death, the Law of Moses has no authority over us.   Because of the absence of Law, there is also an absence of so many opportunities for the devil to tempt the Christian!   To the man who is justified by faith, it is a great blessing (chapter 7 says) to be free from the Law of Moses.

Having died to that by which we were bound.   It is not the Law that died, as the translation in the KJV, "that being dead wherein we were held," might cause a reader to think.[30]   It is the man who has been baptized into death who has died, an idea that has been repeated several times already in chapters 6 and 7.   "That by which we were bound" seems to be distinguished from the Law, and if so, it likely refers to the dominion of "the sin" that 6:7 indicates is ended when a man dies in baptism.   The aorist tense participle "having died" indicates that the "death" preceded the "release from the Law."

So that we serve in newness of the Spirit.   "So that" is a result that is tended to be produced,[31] the contemplated result.   Perhaps we should insert "God" after serve, for in chapter 6 just ended, Paul has written about being servants of God.   The fact that baptized believers are still slaving (serving) as slaves has been explained in 6:16-22, but it is a voluntary slavery of emancipated slaves in expectation of sanctification and eternal life.

---

[29] "Not only did these sinful desires work in our members when we were under the flesh; but to an extent they work in them still, for otherwise we [who are united with Christ] should be without sin.   The difference between our former state and the present is that these desires then [led to the flesh ruling us]; now we rule them [and our bodies].   It is true that we do not now suffer the flesh to control us, but still we are in it; and so long as this is the case, we shall be more or less influenced by it."   Lipscomb and Shepherd, *Romans*, p.130.   "The great, general fact of our Christian life must be that, with masterly will and the aid of the Holy Spirit, we control the flesh.   The exceptions are to be accidental and unwilled."   Lard, *Romans*, p.226.

[30] There is a Greek textual variation here, with the Textus Receptus, as published by the Elzevirs, reading *apothanontos*, as though it were the Law that died.   This reading is not supported by a single manuscript.   All the old Greek manuscripts read *apothanontes*, meaning that it is the people who have died (as they were baptized into Christ).

[31] *Hōste* followed by an infinitive expresses result, not the result actually produced [which is expressed by *hōste* followed by an indicative], but the result that tends to be produced.   Dana and Mantey, *Grammar*, p.286.   "*Hōste* with the indicative lays stress on the effect; *hōste* with the infinitive lays stress on the cause."   Sanday and Headlam, *Romans*, p.176.

Where Paul wrote "newness of life" before, now he writes "newness of spirit."[32]   Believers serve God as their "spirit" directs, now that it is alive again,[33] and able to control and direct the behavior of the whole man.   No longer need the man be controlled by the "sinful passions" like he was when he was still "in the flesh" (verse 5) with his spirit "dead because of trespasses and sins."[34]   Chapter 8 will eventually add the thought that the indwelling Holy Spirit aids the believer's spirit in this effort to direct and control the behavior.

And not in oldness of the letter.   "Letter" here refers to the Law of Moses, with its rules of conduct, both positive and negative.   The Law pointed in the right direction, but the old man could not make his behavior match the righteous requirements of the Law.[35]   Before explaining these last two phrases in more detail (i.e., verse 5 is the subject of 7:14-25; verse 6 is the subject of chapter 8), Paul will stop to make sure what he wrote in verse 5 is not misunderstood.

7:7 – What shall we say then?   Is the Law sin?   May it never be!   On the contrary, I would not have come to know sin except through the Law; for I would not have known about coveting if the Law had not said, "YOU SHALL NOT COVET."

What shall we say then?   As in 6:1, this question means "What inference are we to draw from the statement just made?"   As noted earlier, this is Paul's usual wording, with "May it never be!" following, when he is meeting and rejecting an anticipated possible objection to his teaching.

Is the Law sin?   This question is intended to remind us of some statement just made.   But which one?   Paul has just said in verse 5 that the Law is in some way connected with sinful passions.   Did he mean that the Law[36] was the thing that stimulated or aroused these passions?   If that is indeed what the Law did, then one could say the Law was bad, evil, "sin."[37]   Others point to a different statement which they suppose this question is intended

---

[32] As before, at 2:29, the translator must make a difficult decision whether or not to capitalize the word "spirit," thus making it a reference to the Holy Spirit.   As in the previous instance, the KJV and ASV read "spirit," while the NASB reads "Spirit."   Not a few would agree with the NASB translators, and then comment about how the indwelling Holy Spirit is the animating principle of the new life in Christ, as opposed to the old system that had merely external precepts and requirements to direct the life.

[33] Romans 8:10 will explain that the "spirit" is alive because of righteousness.

[34] Though Ephesians 2:1 reads, "And you were dead in your trespasses and sins," the margin explains it means "by reason of" the sins; i.e., the sins are what brought on the "death."

[35] The whole matter of how a man in his "old state" related to the Law's requirements will be set forth in detail in 7:13-25.

[36] The reference is to the Law of Moses (*nomos* has the article).   Still we admit that a case could be made for "the law" here as meaning all of God's revelation from the time of creation until now.   However, limiting it to the Law of Moses seems to us to be much more in keeping with the purpose of the epistle, and the argument of the context.

[37] Every once in a while, Bible writers used the word "sin" as though it were an adjective meaning "bad" or "exceedingly evil."   Used in this way, it becomes the strongest word for evil that one could employ.

to remind. Paul has written that when a man becomes a Christian he is released from the Law just like he was released from sin. Does this imply that the two, Law and sin, are somehow equally oppressive, and therefore release from both is desirable? In the light of verse 8 and following, it would appear that the first of these two options is the correct one. It is not the Law that arouses sinful passions, it is "the sin" (the devil trying to expand his dominion in the world) that arouses the sinful desires.

May it never be! Was it the Law that aroused the sinful passions? "Not at all!" is Paul's indignant response.[38] A person may have to be aware of God's law before sin has an opportunity to work (verses 8,11), but this is far from saying that the Law itself causes, or arouses, or stimulates a person's sinful desires. Someone or something else generates, or excites, such sinful desires. The Law plainly tells a person such desires are sinful, but the Law does not arouse the desires. Instead of the Law's being sin, Paul will say (as he closes this clarification of verse 5) the Law is holy and righteous and good (verse 12).

On the contrary.[39] One might suppose from the strong denial in the previous phrase that there is no connection at all between the Law and sinful desires. The adversative with which this explanation begins shows that such is not the case. There is a relationship between the two that we need to understand, so Paul goes on to explain that relationship. He has two major thoughts. On the one hand, without having the Law, he would not have known which acts and desires God calls sin (verse 7). On the other hand, the presence of the Law gave sin (Satan) an opportunity to deceive and thus kill (verses 8-11).

I would not have come to know sin except through the Law. The point of this verse is that if there had not been a revelation from God, how would any man know what is right and wrong? This may mean "I would have had no personal experience with sin, either to know what sin is, or to have seen the working power of sin in my life." In the following sentences, he will make both these points – first, that "law" helps him to understand what acts and desires are sin, and then also how the presence of "law" gives "sin" an opportunity to do its tempting and death-bringing work.[40] This commentator would differ with the NASB translators who capitalized "Law." In this phrase "law" is anarthrous,[41] and in this

---

[38] See this expression explained at Romans 3:4.

[39] The Greek word is *alla*, which is variously translated when it occurs at 3:31, 5:14, 7:7, and 8:32. The KJV uses "nay" at 7:7, "yea" at 3:31, and "nevertheless" at 5:14, to translate the same word. The NASB uses "on the contrary," "nevertheless," and "but" as translations. The word is an adversative, but it can have a continuative force, also.

[40] In verses 7-24, the question is much debated whether Paul, who writes throughout the passage in the first person singular, is describing simply his own personal experience, or whether what was true in his case is the experience of every human soul. "What is plain from the start is the fact that Paul's personal experience is offered only because it is typical of what happens to every man. Otherwise, there would be no sense in Paul's obtruding his own experience. Our individual experiences may differ in minor details, but they do not differ in the essentials here sketched." Lenski, *Romans*, p.461,462. It is not the Law of Moses alone that reveals what acts are sin, or that gives the devil opportunity to tempt, but some revelation (be it oral tradition or the New Covenant Scriptures) every man has. These revelations can serve just as the Law did when it comes to a knowledge of sin and giving sin an opportunity to tempt.

[41] This technical language concerning anarthrous *nomos* is explained in notes at 2:12.

phrase it would seem that "law" has a wider reference than simply the Law of Moses,[42] though even that Law would be an example of the kind of "law" Paul has in mind. A revelation from God to man has always been necessary if man would ever come to realize what sin really is. Yet as helpful as it is to know what God says on a subject, it is also to be remembered that once a man knows God's truth, that very realization is the time when the devil has an opportunity to tempt that he never had before. So "law" is not the cause of sin, but a man's awareness of what God says is right and wrong does provide an occasion for being tempted, and thus sinning.

For I would not have known about coveting if the Law had not said, "YOU SHALL NOT COVET." Paul uses the tenth commandment to illustrate the general idea just stated in the previous clause. He would have known from everyday experience that "desires"[43] in the body cry out to be satisfied. But without the word from God about "desires," he would not have known[44] that some desires are wrong. Men must always depend on a word from God if they are to have an infallible standard of right and wrong. One way it can be seen that there is a relationship between the Law and sin, is that in the Law one can learn what God calls sin, including even certain desires as well as actions.

7:8 – But sin, taking opportunity through the commandment, produced in me coveting of every kind; for apart from the Law sin is dead.

But sin. Here begins Paul's presentation of a second relationship between law and sin. God's law is not the thing that arouses sinful desires; His law is not the cause of sin; rather, its presence gives sin an opportunity to work. Here, as in many of the verses since 5:12, "the sin" is personified as a power trying to gain a mastery over the whole human race.

> There is, of course, no real, personal entity, called sin that acts upon the human family and causes violations of the law. Who then is it that performs the office here ascribed to sin? It is not our nature, for our nature is what is acted upon. Who is it then? It is *Satan.*[45]

---

[42] The train of thought in this verse seems to be this: this middle phrase of verse 7 is a general statement true of all times and places, while the final phrase is a specific illustration of the general statement.

[43] The word translated "covet" or "desire" (*epithumia*) is a difficult word for which to find an English equivalent, since there is no exactly corresponding English word. "Covet" and "lust" are too narrow, and "desire" lacks the idea of evil which the original often implies.

[44] Paul has used two different words for "know" in verse 7. In the previous phrase, he said "I would not have come to know (*ginōskō*) sin." In this phrase, he writes, "I would not have known (*oida*) about coveting." The difference between the two is this – *ginōskō* implies knowledge that is derived from personal experience, while *oida* denotes knowledge that is the result of mental perception. Thayer, *Lexicon*, p.118. Thus, what Paul has written is, 'I would have had no personal experience or acquaintance with the working power of sin, if I had no law given to me by God. And I would have had no head knowledge about desire being wrong, were it not for God's Law.'

[45] Lard, *Romans*, p.230.

Taking opportunity through the commandment. The word translated "opportunity" (*aphormē*) is a military word meaning a "base of operations" from which an attack was launched.[46] The awareness of what God had commanded gave sin a place from which to attack the soul. "Commandment" (*entolē*)[47] points back to the tenth commandment just quoted in verse 7.

Produced in me coveting of every kind. "Sin" is the subject of this verb; sin (the devil) stirred up sinful desires[48] in the flesh. He stirs up desires to do the very thing that the commandment prohibits. Sin thus has been presented as doing two things once a man becomes aware of God's law: the devil takes advantage of the opportunity afforded to him by men's knowledge of the law; and he stirs up all kinds of evil desires in men.

For apart from the Law sin *is* dead. Here is further evidence that it is not proper to interpret verse 5 as though the Law is the thing that arouses sinful desires in a man. Sin is the culprit, not "law." "Law" is anarthrous here; it is not just the Law of Moses that furnishes sin a base of operations; any law God has given will provide sin with the same opportunity.[49] "Dead" is a surprising and forceful way to word the idea that sin is powerless to try to do its killing work.[50] "Sin," too, is anarthrous here, and refers to this or that individual action or desire, rather than to "king sin."

7:9 – *And I was once alive apart from the Law; but when the commandment came, sin became alive, and I died;*

And I was once alive apart from the Law. There is little doubt Paul is referring to some past experience in his own life. He vividly can recall how he became aware of the very thing he is writing about here, namely, the relation of law to sin in his life. There was a time when he was not aware of any of God's laws. The most plausible explanation is that Paul is referring to the time of his childhood, those early years of his life[51] when he was without any awareness of what God requires of a man.[52] Modern writers use the expression

---

[46] Thayer, *Lexicon*, p.90.

[47] The word "command" (*entolē*) is often used in the Bible for divinely-given commands. *Nomos* is used for the Mosaic code as a whole, while *entolē* is used for the individual commands that made up the Law.

[48] "Coveting" is the same word used in verse 7, which see for an explanation of its meaning.

[49] Implied in this language is the additional idea that until a person becomes aware of God's law, it is not possible for him to be tempted. What is here implied is specifically stated in the next verse.

[50] Instead of explaining the unexpected word "dead" as though it meant "powerless" or "can't work," some commentators have reverted to the idea written in verse 7, namely, that sin is not "perceived" as sin without law to help the man's understanding of God's will.

[51] The verb "I was alive" is an imperfect tense in the Greek, and thus refers to a continuous experience in the past.

[52] Jewish customs defined age 12 as the time when a Jewish boy reached the age of accountability,

"the age of accountability" to express this same period of time in a young person's life when he neither knows God's requirements, nor is he held accountable by God for his actions.[53]

But when the commandment came.   The commandment "You shall not covet" (verse 7) is the one referred to, as far as Paul's own life was concerned.   In other men's lives, it might be some other command God has given that they become aware of, but the result is still the same.   "The commandment came" evidently means 'it came into my consciousness, and I became aware of God's command on this topic.'   It is the opposite of what "apart from the law" meant in the previous clause.   He is no longer "apart from the Law"; now he is perfectly aware of what God commands.

Sin became alive.   The NEB reads "Sin sprang to life."[54]   Before Paul became aware of the Law's requirements, sin was dormant.   But when the awareness of what God had commanded came, sin had the opportunity it had been waiting for, and so sprang into action.

And I died.   We suppose that this means the "spirit" part of him died, and thus was no longer able to control his desires and behavior.[55]   Of course, Paul did not "die spiritually" simply because he was tempted.   Implied is the admission that Paul sinned by doing the unlawful thing (coveting) that the temptation suggested, and because he sinned he "died."[56] Note how Paul has again answered the question posed in verse 7.   The Law was not the cause of sin, but the Law did give "the sin" an opportunity to spring into action.   Not only did Paul die spiritually, but his sin would also have resulted in an alienation from God, and

---

and was thence forward required to observe the requirements of the Law, having become a "son of the covenant."

[53] Not only do attempted explanations differ greatly, but numerous doctrines have been built on this expression, "I was once alive apart from the Law." (1) One idea is that Paul's soul was pre-existent, and that he was alive in Paradise before he was conceived by his parents. (2) Another idea is that Paul was for a little while completely free of any awareness of sin or any feelings of guilt at the time he was caught up to Paradise, about 14 years before he wrote 2 Corinthians (12:1-4) and Romans. (3) Another suggestion is that Paul is speaking of the whole human race, personified and encapsulated in their first parents before the Fall. (4) Another proposed explanation is that Paul is looking back at the time he was a self-satisfied Pharisee, completely unaware of any alienation from God. Proponents of this solution even appeal to Philippians 3:6, "as to the righteousness which is in the Law, found blameless."

[54] "There is no need for a discussion regarding the verb [*anazaō*], whether it means 'got alive' or 'got alive again.' It may mean either, and here evidently means the former." Lenski, *Romans*, p.466.

[55] A review of footnote #42 in chapter 1 may prove helpful at this point. Paul writes that it was "I" (emphatic) who died. In the rest of chapter 7, "I" is distinguished from his "flesh" (verse 18), i.e., from his "body" (verse 23). In chapter 8:10 it is the "spirit" that is alive because of righteousness. We suppose there is a close identification between Paul's "I" and his "spirit."

[56] If it is Paul, the self-righteous Pharisee, who was "alive apart from the Law," then a different explanation must be given to this verse. It would be saying that there came a time when his study of the Law showed him he was not righteous, but a sinner. This commentator has not been satisfied with the explanation of "died" that this interpretation requires. "Died," it seems evident, means more than 'No longer was I a self-satisfied, self-secured person, who thought I was getting along quite well morally and spiritually.'

a realization of personal guilt because of his disobedience.

7:10 – *and this commandment, which was to result in life, proved to result in death for me;*

And this commandment, which was to result in life. The tenth commandment, and indeed all of God's commandments, were intended by their Giver to be for man's spiritual benefit. God Himself had worded it, "This do and you shall live."[57] The "life" is probably not greatly different than the "life" Paul has said (in 6:4,10, and 6:22) results from God's way of saving men.

Proved to result in death for me. To realize "life" under the Old Covenant, one had to keep its commandments perfectly. Such perfect obedience is something Paul found a man cannot do. God intended only good for man when He gave them laws to live by, but the devil subverted what God wanted. He took advantage of the opportunity provided because of Paul's new knowledge of God's commandment, and stirred up all manner of sinful desires in his body. Because Paul succumbed to the devil's temptation, and failed to keep God's law, the result was spiritual death. Again Paul has answered the question posed in verse 7. It was not the Law's fault that Paul sinned. Lay the blame where it actually belongs, at the devil's feet.

7:11 – *for sin, taking opportunity through the commandment, deceived me, and through it killed me.*

For sin. The point of this verse is to explain that the "death" of verse 10 is not the fault of the Law. It was not the Law that killed him, but "the sin."[58] Paul restates the idea found in verse 8, and then gives further explanation about how sin took advantage of the presence of law to deceive and kill.

Taking opportunity through the commandment. Just as in verse 8, the presence of a commandment which the man clearly understood was just the springboard the devil had been waiting for. Now the devil has a place from which to attack the man, and he wastes little time going on the attack.

Deceived me. This is the same word that Paul uses in 2 Corinthians 11:3 when speaking of what Satan did to Eve in the Garden of Eden. "The sin" deceived Paul; the devil deceived Eve.[59] What Paul has written about his own first sin is interestingly parallel to

---

[57] See Leviticus 18:5;   Ezekiel 18:9,21; 20:11,13,21.

[58] "The sin" is placed first in the Greek for emphasis, whereas in verse 8, it was "opportunity" that was emphasized. It was *sin*, not the commandment; it was *SIN* that deceived and slew him. In passing, here might be another evidence that verse 5 does not mean that the Law *arouses* sinful desires.

[59] "Sin's deceit consists in presenting the object of desire as *a good*, though when obtained it at once proves to be *an evil*." Gifford, *Romans*, p.139. The thing Satan tempts men to desire is not really good for them, but the "desire" inspired by the tempter causes it to seem so. "The sinner, by breaking the law, does not really obtain what he expects; the fancied pleasure or gain seems worse than worthless by reason of the loss and suffering it brings upon him. In this sense the breaker of the law is always beguiled or

what happened to Eve, as recorded in Genesis 3. For a while, our first parents were "alive apart from law." Then the time came when God gave a commandment about the tree of the knowledge of good and evil, "You shall not eat of it, for in the day you eat of it you shall surely die." Satan now had a commandment present, and this was an opportunity he took advantage of. He came to the woman and deceived her when he said, "You shall not surely die!" Eve's desires for what was forbidden were aroused by the devil's temptation, she partook of the forbidden fruit, and she died.[60] This was just what happened to Paul: the commandment was the occasion, and with it present as a base of operation, the sin did the deceiving. Having been deceived, Paul sinned and died.

And through it killed me. "Killed me" means the same as "I died" in verse 9. James 1:14-15 teaches the same doctrine about how sin works that Paul has just presented. "The deceitfulness of sin led Paul to expect one thing, while he experienced another. He expected life, and found death. He expected happiness, and found misery; he looked for holiness, and found increased corruption."[61]

7:12 – *So then, the Law is holy, and the commandment is holy and righteous and good.*

So then. Verse 12 is a conclusion drawn from the whole of the last five verses, and finally answers the question verse 7 had posed about whether the Law is sin. Verses 7b-11 have shown that though there is a relationship between the Law and sin, the Law itself is not the cause of sin, nor is the Law evil. Verse 12 is a logical inference from what was said in verses 7b-11, and is an affirmation about the positive character of the Law, now that the devil has been shown to be the real cause of sin.

---

deceived." Lipscomb and Shepherd, *Romans*, p.134.

"Paul has one revealing word which he uses of sin. 'Sin,' he says, '*seduced* me.' There is always deception in sin. Vaughan says that sin's deception and delusion works in three directions. (i) We are deluded regarding the *satisfaction* to be found in sin. No man ever took a forbidden thing without thinking that it would make him happy, and no man ever found that it did. (ii) We are deluded regarding the *excuse* that can be made for it. Every man thinks that he can put up a defense for doing the wrong thing; but no man's defense ever sounded anything else but futile when it was made in the presence of God. (iii) We are deluded regarding the *probability of escaping the consequences of it.* No man sins without the hope, and even the certainty, that he can, as we say, get away with it. But it is true that, soon or late, our sin will find us out." Barclay, *Romans*, p.99.

[60] So it was in the case of Paul. Once, as a lad, he was alive apart from God's law. But there came a day in Paul's life when the force of God's commandment, "You shall not desire that which is forbidden!" came home to his mind. This realization of God's law furnished the devil with just the opportunity he had been seeking. The devil deceived Paul, and brought about an act of sin, and this resulted in Paul's spiritual death. No longer was Paul in a state of happy innocence. He was aware of his wretchedness and guilt and shame.

The careful student will remember the same passage ("you shall surely die") was alluded to when 5:12 was being explained. Not only did Adam's sin result in a decree of physical death to the race (5:12), so Adam and Eve's first sin also resulted in their own spiritual death (implied in the parallel between 7:11 and Genesis 3).

[61] Hodge, quoted by Wilson, *Romans*, p.119.

The Law is holy. "The Law" referred to is the Law of Moses. Originally given by God, the Law partakes of the character of God, who is holy. It is not possible to get something impure and unholy from something that is holy. The Law is not to be blamed. The Law is not the cause of sin.[62] "The moment we see how sin operates where the Law is present, it becomes perfectly clear that the law is not sin. The whole trouble is with sin!"[63]

And the commandment is holy and righteous and good. The commandment, in particular, is the tenth of the Decalogue (as the quotation of it in verse 7 has shown). Yet the assertion is also true of any and every part of the Law. Each one of the three words used to describe the commandment has a particular and appropriate meaning in this context. "Holy" again means that the commandment is pure within itself, without any taint that might be the cause of sin. After all, God who is "holy" does not tempt any man; we would expect that the commandment also, since it is like its Giver, would not tempt any man. "Righteous" tells us it requires of a man only what is right; it never requires him to do what is wrong. The commandment (whichever one you may think of) is not the cause of sin. "Good" says that the commandment is positively beneficial,[64] intended by its Giver to work for the welfare of those to whom it relates.[65] Given this characteristic, there is no way that the commandment (or the Law) is to be blamed for causing a man to sin.

This concludes the middle paragraph of chapter 7, in which Paul has shown that there is a relationship between the Law and a man's sin – the Law helps a man to know what acts and desires are sin; but when a man has a knowledge of God's law, this gives Satan an op-

---

[62] Once more, let it be emphasized that strong language like this about the real character of the Law should warn us not to add the word "aroused" back in verse 5, as the NASB and other translations have been wont to do.

[63] Lenski, *Romans*, p.469.

[64] "Good" is *agathos*, the same word used at Romans 5:7, which we have suggested may mean "bene-factor." Thayer, *Lexicon*, p.2, gives "useful, salutary, profitable" as the meaning of the word in 7:12.

[65] What Paul has written about the Law of Moses, and its commandment(s) in particular, certainly is a terrific polemic against the modernistic concept of the Old Testament. When the liberal theologian tries to criticize the Law of Moses, remember that Paul said, "the commandment is holy, righteous, and good." The liberal has been wont to say that the Old Testament is a production of the human mind, unaided by the Holy Spirit. And then it is not unusual to hear the liberal theologian find fault with the Old Testament. One example of such fault finding is in certain Disciples of Christ literature, where a certain command from God is called "one of the wicked laws of the Old Testament." "Wicked"?!? How can language like that be harmonized with what Paul here writes about the Law being holy? To be sure, liberal theologians will point to New Testament verses which, they assert, justify their criticism of certain parts of the Law. Hebrews 8:6,7 is one passage, where it reads "if the first covenant [Moses] had been faultless," which means that it certainly was faulty in some sense. (*Reply:* The context in Hebrews explains in what sense it was "faulty." It was faulty *only* in the sense that it did not provide a perfect sacrifice for sin. It could therefore not be a final revelation, and God had to introduce the second, the "new covenant," into the world. The Law was good for the purpose for which it was given, namely, to prepare the world for the coming of the Christ.) Others appeal to Jesus' abrogation of the Mosaic permission of divorce for any cause (Matthew 19) to show that the lower level of morality it tolerated is actually a "fault." (*Reply:* God makes His revelations to a man where he is. What God did when He granted the *permission* to give a bill of divorcement was to set the standards considerably higher than the people who received the Law were living by. To have asked more of them, at the time, would have led to a rejection of the whole statute. Again, the Law was appropriately God-designed for the purpose and age for which it was given.)

portunity to tempt that he did not have before. But the Law is not the cause of sin in a man's behavior. The final paragraph of chapter 7 will explain the relationship of the Law to the sinner. It tells a man what is right and wrong, but gives the man no help to prevent him from doing the wrong, nor does it give him any help to aid him in doing the right.

7:13 – *Therefore did that which is good become* a cause of *death for me? May it never be! Rather it was sin, in order that it might be shown to be sin by effecting my death through that which is good, that through the commandment sin might become utterly sinful.*

Therefore did that which is good become *a cause of* death for me? "That which is good" is a reference to the Old Testament Law, which has just been called "holy, righteous, and good" (verse 12). "Death" has the same meaning it did in verses 9 and 10. While demonstrating that the Law was not at fault, not the cause of his sinning, in verse 10 he has written that the "commandment proved to result in death for me." Lest someone misunderstand that expression and blame the Law for causing his death, Paul now asks whether such an understanding is correct.[66]

May it never be! Such a suggestion as presented in the question preceding is unthinkable.[67] The commandment God had given was not at fault. If Paul had kept the commandment, he would not have died.

Rather it was sin. We must supply a verb to complete the sentence. Most writers repeat the verb from the question above, so that the completed sentence is 'It was "the sin" that became *a cause of* death for me.' By omitting the predicate, Paul places emphasis on the subject. "The sin, the sin alone" was the real cause of death for me.

In order that it might be shown to be sin. This is likely a result clause. When sin became a cause of death, it lost the attractiveness it had when it was doing its deceiving work. The passive voice verb implies God as the agent who wanted this result to happen. After all, if there were no penalties connected with sinning, who would ever be sorry he sinned? Who would ever want to get out of the bondage of sin? But when sin resulted in death, then the hideous character of sin,[68] its real character, began to become evident.

By effecting my death through that which is good. How "the sin" (the devil) took advantage of the presence of the Law to tempt and seduce to sin, which resulted in death, has been explained in verses 8 and 9.

---

[66] A technical note is needed to help see the relation of verse 13-14 to the rest of the chapter. Some note that in verse 12, Paul wrote the first side (*ho men*) of an intended contrast between the law and sin; however, the second half (*ho de*) of the contrast is suppressed. Instead, it seems Paul digresses at the word "good" to meet a possible objection which might be urged against the goodness of the commandment. (How can it be "good" when you have just said it "proved to result in death"?) Others note verse 13 begins with "therefore," and suppose it is a second rejected inference (see verse 7 for the first) that might be drawn from what Paul said in verse 5.

[67] The indignant "May it never be!" has been used before. See notes at Romans 3:4.

[68] "Sin" is used as an adjective, just as it was in verse 7, "Is the Law sin?"

That through the commandment sin might become utterly sinful. Paul is showing what a heinous thing sin is. When sin uses the good thing (like the Law) to trap a man and kill him, that reveals how utterly horrible and warped sin is.[69] What sin is doing is taking the Law that God had intended for good, and wrecking all of God's plans and purposes. That is what is so horrible about it.[70] So the Law was not the cause of death, but the Law did help men see the enormity of sin. Only when the sinner is made to realize his need for deliverance, is the necessary preparation for such deliverance accomplished.[71]

7:14 – *For we know that the Law is spiritual; but I am of flesh, sold into bondage to sin.*

For we know that the Law is spiritual. In verses 14-23, Paul now confirms (*gar*, "for") his vindication of the Law and his exposure of sin as the real culprit by a profound analysis of the operation of sin in man. His presentation in verses 7-13 has been based on the distinction, "not the commandment, but sin ...." Now his argument is based on the distinction, "not I, but sin that dwells in me." The verb could be translated either "we know" or "I know."[72] Earlier in Romans (2:2 and 3:19) Paul has made a similar appeal to the religious consciousness of his readers. "The Law" refers to the Law of Moses, but what precisely "spiritual" means is open to question. Perhaps it speaks of the Holy Spirit's inspiration of the Law when it was originally given. Perhaps it is another way to denote the idea given in verse 12 that the Law was pure and holy. Perhaps, if we allow the context following to decide, it means that the Law was of such a nature that it appealed to the spirit of a man.[73] In any case, verse 14 is an affirmation that the Law of Moses was not the cause of his death.

---

[69] Matthew 22:15-17 and Luke 20:19-22 illustrate what we have here in Romans. To what depths the religious leaders have sunk, when they ask Jesus this question about tribute to Caesar. What was wrong with their question? What was devilish about their question? Simply this (Luke 20:21): they were relying on the fact that Jesus was a good man, that He would not be hypocritical in His answer; yet they intended to use His answer to ensnare and trap Him. Likewise, the Law was good. Along comes sin and uses that which was holy as a means of trapping a man and getting him to sin. There is nothing much worse than to act in such an unprincipled way just to ruin another.

[70] Where the NASB has "utterly sinful," the RSV has "sinful beyond measure." The word Paul used was *huperbolē*, which Arndt-Gingrich *Lexicon*, p.848, translates "excess, extraordinary quality or character, in the extreme." Men are so much in the world, and there are so many sins that we like to flirt with, that it often is not possible for us to see the utter sinfulness of sin. Trying to help his students see the real danger of sin, George Mark Elliott used to say, "We treat sin as a cream puff rather than as a rattlesnake!" John Trapp has written, "Sin is so evil that it cannot have a worse epithet given it. Paul can call it no worse than by its own name, 'sinful sin.'" Quoted in Wilson, *Romans*, p.120.

[71] Compare Galatians 3:19-22.

[72] The original manuscripts were written in all capital letters, with no break between words. Thus, it is not absolutely certain whether Paul wrote *oidamen*, "we know," or *oida men*, "I know."

[73] "Spiritual" is used some 25 times in the New Testament. Sometimes it is the opposite of "natural," as in 1 Corinthians 15:44. Sometimes it is the opposite of "carnal" or secular, as in 1 Corinthians 9:11 (KJV). Sometimes it is the opposite of "material" things, as at 1 Corinthians 10:3,4. Sometimes it pertains to "spirits," as at Ephesians 6:12. Sometimes it speaks of consistent Christian lives, such as a man whose "spirit" is alive could prompt, as in 1 Corinthians 3:1. This last one seems to be the one the context of Romans 7 requires for the use of the word "spiritual" here in 7:14.

The remainder of chapter 7 has been the subject of a continuing controversy among commentators. The question at issue is whether it is Paul the Jew or Paul the Christian whose religious consciousness is here presented. If it is his experience *before* conversion, then he is giving his own experience as an illustration of what is common to all men who have been deceived and killed by sin. If it is his experience *after* conversion, then what he writes would be true of all Christians. The verses vividly portray an inner struggle going on, with the spirit not being able to control because of the power of sin. Do slaves of sin have such struggles? Do Christians continue to have such struggles? The answer given to this debated question will necessarily affect the comments given in a number of places in these verses. The arguments for and against each proposed answer are given in Special Study #6, "What State of the Soul has the Apostle Portrayed in Romans 7:14-24?" included below after the comments on chapter 7. The conclusion there reached is that Paul is describing the struggles with sin that a man under the Law had.[74]

But I am of flesh.[75] Perhaps it can be said that this is the Pauline way of wording what Jesus said to Nicodemus, "that which is born of the flesh is flesh" (John 3:6). Paul is speaking of the fact that he lived in a flesh and blood body. When his spirit died as a result of his first sin, the flesh became so predominant over the rest that he could speak as though

---

[74] Two thoughts not included in the Special Study need to be included here. (1) The NIV does not even translate the "for" (*gar*) with which verse 14 begins. They cannot, and at the same time consistently hold that 7:14-18 speaks of Paul the Christian, and the Christian's struggles with sin, i.e., that the Christian (even after being baptized into death) still has an old sinful nature. We affirm that the reason the NIV translators left the "for" out is because it would result in a contradiction in their theology. They hardly dare show that verse 14 continues the idea given in verse 13, for verse 13 speaks about "sin bringing death," something that obviously can*not* be true if it is Paul the Christian speaking. (Remember, Calvinistic writers also teach "eternal security" for the Christian.) The student of the NIV translation is aware that this is not the only place that translation pushes Calvinistic theology at its readers simply by the choice of words made as they translated. (2) If verses 14-25 refer to the Christian, then this paragraph would also imply that the Law of Moses is still something binding on the Christian. Indeed! With all the Pauline statements to the contrary, and even the Jerusalem Conference (Acts 15) showing that the Law of Moses was but temporary, intended for the dispensation between Moses and the Cross, are we not driven to the conclusion that Paul is vividly describing his pre-Christian state?

[75] The correct reading is *sarkinos*, and not *sarkikos*. The Greek adjectives ending in *-inos* describe the material out of which anything is made. (The ending *-ikos* denotes "quality.") The NASB's "I am *of flesh*" catches the idea that he is speaking of the material of which he is made. The KJV "carnal" was satisfactory at one time, since it is from a Latin word meaning "flesh," but the word "carnal" now has moral overtones which Paul may not have intended at all.

Three views have been advanced concerning Paul's use of *sarkinos* here. Each is based on a previously understood relation between *sarkinos* and *sarkikos*. (1) Paul purposely chose a very strong word, thus excluding any reference to the regenerate, spiritual man. According to this view, *sarkinos* is a stronger word than *sarkikos*. In the commentator's opinion, this first view is the correct one, as a study of the use of both words in 1 Corinthians 3:1 and 3:3 seems to verify. (2) Some hold the view that both words are of equal strength. This view is often adopted by those writers who are interested in making 7:14-25 have reference to the Christian's struggles with sin. (3) Delitzsch finds *sarkinos* a weaker word than *sarkikos*. Were he right, this would be easiest to harmonize with the view that 7:14-25 is the Christian's struggles with sin. Otherwise, one almost has to tamper with the text, making it read "I *was* carnal" but, of course, now that I am in Christ I am not as carnal as I was.

he were wholly made of flesh.[76]   The body was an occasion for sin, but the flesh was not sinful in itself.   Flesh is not inherently sinful.[77]

Sold into bondage to sin.   It is Paul's "I" (his spirit) that was in bondage.   The word "sold into bondage" is significant.   "It denotes, not our having been originally slaves (*vernae* [Lat.]), but our having been sold into slavery (*capti* [Lat.]).   Slavery to sin is not the rightful condition of our nature."[78]   Men had not been slaves from the beginning, even from birth, but had been sold into slavery.   We are not left to figure out for ourselves what "sold into bondage to sin" means.   In verses 15-25, Paul himself explains at length just what he means.   In verses 15-17, he explains that his inner self is impotent to prevent him from doing wrong.   In verses 18-21, he shows that his inner self is impotent to make him do the right.   Finally, in verses 22-25, he shows that while the Law could not deliver him from this inner conflict, Christ can and does.

7:15 – *For that which I am doing, I do not understand; for I am not practicing what I would like to do, but I am doing the very thing I hate.*

For that which I am doing, I do not understand.   Here begins Paul's proof that the "I" is indeed "sold into bondage to sin."   The idea is, 'Am I not a slave when, as I feel is the case with me, I am not my own master?'   "Observe, the state that goes on to be described is that of an unwilling bondslave, not of one who likes his bondage, and has no desire to be free."[79]   "That which I am doing" is *katergazomai*,[80] one of three different Greek verbs in verses 15-21 that are translated "do" or "practice" in the English versions.[81]   In the con-

---

[76] In our comments we have consciously tried to maintain a distinction between Paul's "I" (his spirit), and the fleshly house the spirit lives in.   We have done so, lest we contradict what is clearly stated in verse 23, where the "I" and the "body" are distinguished as two separate entities.   Perhaps it is needless to note that many who teach that man has an innate sinful nature inherited from Adam are wont to find some justification for their theory in that Paul seems to equate his "I" and the "flesh" in this one verse.   It is rather standard to find explanations that suggest that before conversion a man's whole being, his *egō* and his *sarx* are sinful, while after conversion, the *egō* ("I") is no longer under the control of sinful flesh.   Lenski, for example, argues that before conversion the *egō* was "flesh" (carnal, being taken ethically to mean "not submissive to the will of God"), whereas, after conversion the *egō* was no longer "flesh" – so the only thing the Christian has to do is overcome the taint of sin left in the body in which he lives, which overcoming is done by a masterful exertion of the will and the help of the grace of God.   *Romans*, p.474ff.

[77] The comments offered here are still denying the Augustinian-Calvinistic doctrine of original sin, just as the Special Studies at the close of chapter 5 led us to conclude, following a long scrutiny of the relevant Scripture verses and the history of their interpretations.

[78] Barmby, *Romans*, p.189.

[79] Barmby, *Romans*, p.189.

[80] The possible reason for the change from aorist tense verbs in verses 7-13, to all present tense verbs in verses 14-23, is addressed in Special Study #6 at the close of comments on this chapter.

[81] The three verbs are *katergazomai, prassō*, and *poieō*.   *Katergazomai* speaks of single acts, deliberate acts, thoroughly carried out.   *Prassō* speaks of habitual or repeated practice, something done consciously or with a special purpose or aim.   *Poieō* speaks of general performance or accomplishment of a single act; it could be mechanical or unconscious.   Trench, *Synonyms*, p.361ff, or Berry, *Lexicon*, p.127.

text, each is used to speak of sinful acts. "Understand" is the NASB's rendering of *ginōs-kō*,[82] and it likely would be better rendered "approve."[83] It hardly seems likely that Paul is saying 'I don't know what I am doing.' To so interpret this phrase, and then to have him in the very same verse proceed to make the most careful discrimination in his thoughts and actions, is unreasonable. If he does not approve of the acts, why does he do them? This is the very point! This is evidence that he is a bondslave ("sold into bondage to sin").

For I am not practicing what I *would* like *to do*. With "for" Paul introduces a reason why he does not approve of his own practice. The "not" in the Greek goes with the verb "like," so that it actually reads, "I am practicing what I would *not* like to do." His inner self was impotent to make him avoid the wrong. "Practicing" denotes the constant activity, the habitual, or repeated practice. In his heart, Paul wished[84] to avoid the wrong, and if he were free from the bondage to sin, he would avoid it. This is the picture of the struggle that goes on between the "I" (spirit) and the fleshly body to rule the life of the man who is attempting under the Law of Moses to serve God.

But I am doing the very thing I hate. "Do" this time translates *poieō*, which looks at the whole series of acts as almost unconscious and mechanical.[85] Verse 16 will show that the reason Paul's heart or spirit has an aversion to these acts is because the Law condemns them. Paul did not sin from love of sin. On the contrary, he hated sin.[86] Yet he was so

---

[82] See notes on this word at Romans 2:2.

[83] Such a meaning for *ginōskō* would be paralleled in Matthew 7:23 where Jesus warns that to some He will have to say, "Depart from me, I never knew (approved) of you." That the word means "approve" is what lies behind the KJV's "I do not allow." However, since not all agree that "approve" is the proper idea here, it is well to present several variations on the theme that *ginōskō* should be translated "know." (1) As a slave obeys his master without heeding the result of the act he performs, so Paul says, 'I do not discern the true nature and moral bearing of that which I perform at sins's bidding. The moral sense is not wholly lost nor inactive, but it is confused and overpowered, and so rendered ineffective.' (2) Calvin preferred the idea "I don't recognize" the enormity of what I am doing. Not a few would agree, basing their conclusion on the fact that approval may accompany recognition, but it is never directly expressed by the word used here. (3) "For he that is mastered by pleasure, or intoxicated with the passion of anger, has not a clear discernment of the sin. But, after the subsidence of the passion, he receives the perception (*aisthēsin*) of the evil." (Theodoret). Gifford, *Romans*, p.140-141.

[84] The verb translated "like" in the NASB is *thelō*. The translation of this word and its synonym *boulomai* is disputed, especially since both are sometimes translated "I will." Does the word *thelō* regularly have any reference to the *will* in the strict sense, or does it merely mean "I wish" or "I desire." Since "like" in this clause is contrasted with "hate" in the next clause, it may be that we are not speaking of the *will* in verse 15. "The exact distinction between *thelō* and *boulomai* has been much disputed, and is difficult to mark. On the whole, it seems that, especially in New Testament usage, *boulomai* lays greater stress on the idea of purpose, deliberation, and *thelō* on the more emotional aspect of the will. In Romans 7:15 it is evidently something short of the final act of volition, and practically equal to 'wish' or 'desire'." Sanday and Headlam, *Romans*, p.182. With this agree both Thayer and Grimm, but not Cremer or Berry.

[85] See footnote #81 for the distinction between *poieō* and the other verbs used in this verse.

[86] When some writers appeal to this verse as evidence that Paul is speaking of a Christian's struggles against sin, it soon becomes evident that the argument is not convincing. It has been alleged that no unregenerate man (let alone one under the Law of Moses) had desires to do that which is good, and hates that which is evil. But note these quotations from the heathen writers (copied from Barnes, *Romans*,

powerfully inclined to it by the temptations that attacked through his body of flesh that he committed sin, even when he didn't wish to.   And the Law was powerless to help.   If Paul had not been "sold into bondage to sin," he would have acted differently than he did.[87]

7:16 – *But if I do the very thing I do not wish* **to do,** *I agree with the Law,* **confessing** *that it is good.*

But if I do the very thing I do not wish *to do.*   Verse 16 carries on the argument begun in the previous verse, from which then verse 17 is further inferred.   There were certain things the Law of Moses prohibited.   Yet Paul, being "sold into bondage to sin", found himself doing them.

I agree with the Law, *confessing* **that it is good.**   "Good" is *kalos*, morally and spiritually excellent, attractive.   This is a re-affirmation of what was said about the Law in verse 12.[88] If Paul recognizes that he ought not to be doing the sinful thing, because such behavior is falling below God's standards as revealed in the Law of Moses, that recognition is an admission that the Law (the standard of right) is good.

7:17 – *So now, no longer am I the one doing it, but sin which indwells me.*

So now.   "Now" is logical.[89]   Here comes the true reason why Paul sinned; no other logical answer is possible from what has been said in the previous verses.

No longer am I the one doing it.   "Doing" is *katergazomai*, as in verse 15.[90]   "I" is again Paul's inner man, his better self, his resolving self, his spirit.   Paul is saying, 'It is not my

---

p.171).   Xenophon (*Cyrop.* vi.1); Araspes, the Persian, says, in order to excuse his treasonable designs, "Certainly I must have two souls; for plainly it is not one and the same which is both evil and good, and at the same time wishes to do a thing and not to do it.   Plainly then, there are two souls; and when the good one prevails, then it does good; and when the evil one predominates, then it does evil."   Epictetus (*Enchixid.* ii.26) says, "He that sins does not do what he would; but what he would not, that he does."   Ovid (*Meta.* vii.9) writes, "Desire prompts the one thing, but the mind persuades to another.   I see the good, and approve it, and yet pursue the wrong."   Clearly, what we have in Paul's writing is similar to what many *unconverted* men think and feel about their sin.

[87] In passing, we cannot resist the opportunity to point out how this verse contains a rather solid refutation of the doctrine of total depravity.   Paul, before his conversion, wished or desired or would have liked to do the right and avoid the wrong.   He was not totally bad.

[88] "Good" (*kalos*) here is not the same word rendered "good" (*agathos*) in verse 12.   "Here it is not the beneficent aim of the law which was ordained unto life, but its moral beauty and excellence that is asserted." Gifford, *Romans*, p.141.

[89] The comment by Gifford is typical of what one finds in the commentaries.   "It is now almost universally admitted that the expressions 'now' and 'no more' ['no longer,' NASB] are not *temporal*, as distinguishing the speaker's present condition from his former state before grace, but *logical*: 'this being the case ('now'), there is no room left to say it is I'."   Gifford, *Romans*, p.141.

[90] See footnote #81, above.

inner man who leads me to do what the Law prohibits. I do not want to break the Law –
yet something leads me to break it. That something is sin – and this shows that I am a
slave of sin.'[91] Paul is not saying that he is not personally responsible for his sins. Rather,
he is saying that it was not his spirit that prompted him to sin.[92]

But sin which indwells me. It is the sin which dwells in his flesh (as verse 18 shows)
that causes him to break the Law. "Or rather, it is the sin which excites the flesh in order
to cause him to do the sin. For, if left to himself, unmoved by the flesh, he would do only
what he wishes to do – which is what the Law requires, and therefore not sin."[93] "So it
was not his inner self that did the evil, but sin that dwelt in his members. And unless he
was delivered from the sin that controlled him, it would [continue to] defile his spirit and
drag him down to ruin."[94] Note that in these last two clauses, Paul distinguishes between
his inner self which he calls "I" and the outer self (the flesh) which he here calls "me."[95]

*7:18 – For I know that nothing good dwells in me, that is, in my flesh; for the wishing is
present in me, but the doing of the good is not.*

For. "For" shows that this verse is designed to confirm the statement that it was sin which
dwelt in him that caused him to do what he did. Having shown that his inner self was a
slave to the sin at work in the flesh by indicating how his inner man was incapable to
prevent him from doing the wrong, Paul now makes the same point about slavery to sin by
appealing to the fact that his inner man could not make him do the right, either (verses
18-21). The parallelism of the two arguments is marked by the repetition of the same
conclusion in the same words (compare verses 17 and 20).

I know that nothing good dwells in me, that is, in my flesh. The last few words of this
clause show that we have correctly interpreted "me" in the preceding verse. Such a consciousness as this language displays was exactly what the Law was designed to produce;

---

[91] Once more, in the light of chapter 6, which shows that the old slavery to sin is broken when a man
becomes a Christian, it seems hard to reconcile what Paul here says with the oft-defended idea that 7:14-
25 speaks of Paul the Christian and his struggles with sin after conversion. It makes much more sense if
it is a non-Christian speaking his feelings.

[92] It is only by dragging this verse out of its context that anyone today can use it as an excuse for sinning
on the pretext that he cannot help himself – there is just some inner compulsion that drives him to it.
Indeed, the man may be a slave of sin, but he is still responsible and answerable for his own sin, for the
whole line of argument is that even after sinning, there is a bitter realization that such acts are culpable,
and the sinner needs deliverance or he will perish.

[93] Lard, *Romans*, p.239.

[94] Lipscomb and Shepherd, *Romans*, p.137.

[95] The indwelling sin of this chapter corresponds to the indwelling Spirit in the next chapter. This is
further proof that the power which exerts so baneful an influence is not merely an attribute of the man
himself (i.e., we deny the idea of inherent evil propensities), but has an objective reality. Sanday and
Headlam, *Romans*, p.182.

the Law helped men to be conscious of their sin, and of their need for a deliverer. As in verse 17, so here again, Paul distinguishes between his inner man (the "I") and the outer man ("me," "my flesh"). "Good" here is *agathos*, which means (as in 7:12) beneficial, helpful – helpful, that is, to control his sin problem. Paul, of course, is still speaking of the man under the Law, and is saying that the Law gave no help with the sin problem, nor was there anything in his physical body that gave any help to resist the seductive temptations and desires aroused by the devil.[96]   But as will be presented in chapter 8, when the old slavery to sin is broken, and a man has the help of the indwelling Holy Spirit, it can be a different story when it comes to controlling the impulses of the flesh.[97]

For the wishing is present in me. Here comes Paul's proof of the foregoing statement about "nothing good (helpful) dwells ... in my flesh." "Wishing" is *thelō*,[98] and Paul is about to say, 'I cannot turn my wish into action. I have the power to wish to do right. My desire and my purpose are not interfered with, but I cannot turn my wish into action.'

But the doing of the good *is* not. On "doing" see *katergazomai* in verse 15, and on "good" see notes on *kalos* at verse 16. "It was easy for Paul to will the morally and spiritually excellent thing, but it was not easy to bring it to completed action."[99]   His difficulty lay, not in the wishing, but in the executing. Paul is not saying that he never did anything that was right. He is saying he could not habitually do it (present tense, continuous action). In the days of the Law, only Christ had such absolute, perfect control over His body. Paul did not have that.

---

[96] Attention again is called to Special Study #6 at the close of this chapter, wherein this phrase about "nothing good dwells in me" is shown to be one of the decisive expressions by which one can determine if it is Paul the Jew or Paul the Christian whose struggles are vividly portrayed in this paragraph. Could a Christian, who has received the gift of the indwelling Holy Spirit at his baptism, and in whose body the Holy Spirit continues to live and work, could the Christian say, "*Nothing* good dwells in me"? Hardly! This paragraph must therefore be understood as portraying the struggles a Jew under the Law had with his sin problem.

Just as objectionable is the use made of this expression "nothing good dwells in me" by the Calvinists to prove their doctrine of total depravity. Barnes, for example, wrote, "There could not be possibly a stronger expression of belief in the doctrine of total depravity. It is Paul's own representation of himself. It proves that his heart was wholly evil." *Romans*, p.172. But we reply to Barnes with a question. Are "flesh" (in which no good thing dwells) and the "heart" (which Paul has represented as wishing to do the right) the same thing? If they are not, if there is a distinction between Paul's "I" and his "flesh," then it will take more than this verse to prove total depravity. (For greater detail on this topic, the reader is again referred to Special Studies #3 and #4 at the close of chapter 5.)

[97] As is documented in Special Study #6 following this chapter, the Christian is not free from temptations that come through the flesh. Indeed, the devil still works the same way, save that certain limits have been imposed on him, and certain helps are available to the Christian so he need no longer succumb to the devil's desires.

[98] The word evidently would have the same meaning here that it did in verse 15. "It is essential that the Apostle's language concerning the will [wish] towards good should be weighed with moderation and candor. He does not use a word expressing the deliberate and final choice which is immediately followed by action (*proaireisthai*, 2 Corinthians 9:7); nor a word expressing a conscious preference and purpose (*boulomai*), but *thelō*, which simply means 'I am willing [wishing, desiring]'." Gifford, *Romans*, p.142.

[99] Lenski, *Romans*, p.482.

7:19 – *For the good that I wish, I do not do; but I practice the very evil that I do not wish.*

For the good that I wish, I do not do. Verse 19 is confirmatory of the idea that Paul had the ability to "wish" – but not the ability (while under the Law) to carry the wish into completed action continually. He could not habitually do (*poieō*, present tense, continuous action) the good he was wishing to do.[100] "Good" is again *agathos*, for which, see 7:12,18. The fleshly body he lived in was in control, and hindered his doing the good things in the Law that his mind approved.

But I practice the very evil that I do not wish. The evil things his mind condemned, these things the flesh led him to do. Example: Resolved, I am not going to sin with the tongue. Yet then he went out and did it. "Practice" is *prassō*, for which see notes at verse 15. "Evil" is emphatic in this clause, just as "good" was in the previous clause. Clearly, Paul had the power to *wish*. It was the ability to *practice* what he wished, what was in harmony with God's revealed will, that he lacked. And he lacked it because of his being sold into bondage to sin. Paul is showing the absolute necessity of being under grace, and not under Law. The man apart from grace is wretched and miserable because the Law gives no help with his sin problem.

7:20 – *But if I am doing the very thing I do not wish, I am no longer the one doing it, but sin which dwells in me.*

But if I am doing the very thing I do not wish. For some reason Paul found himself (before conversion) doing other than his inner man wished to do. He now tells why.

I am no longer the one doing it, but sin which dwells in me. Compare notes at verse 17, where the same expression was used. Paul once more has arrived at the conclusion that he has been sold into bondage to sin. This is the only explanation for his inner man's failure to control his behavior. Satan is the cause of the sin and death, not the Law. Satan tempts the man, and by means of sinful desires for a moment gains control of the man's body (the flesh); the body then causes the man to disobey the very Law he wishes to keep. This is the way it was as long as Paul was under the Law, as long as he was a slave to sin.

7:21 – *I find then the principle that evil is present in me, the one who wishes to do good.*

I find then the principle that evil is present in me. In verse 21, Paul summarizes the whole wretched experience he has been sketching.[101] The word translated "principle" is *nomos*, the word usually translated "law" up to this point in Romans. There have been two leading interpretations of this passage. (1) Many suppose Paul has reference to the Law of Moses. If so, a slightly different punctuation is needed. The verse could read, "I find then that the Law was designed for me, for it helps me to will to do good, but still evil

---

[100] The KJV translates both verse 15 and verse 19 as though they said the same thing. They do not. Verse 15 spoke of doing what he wished not to do. Verse 19 deals with not doing what he wishes to do.

[101] The word "then" (*ara*) shows this is a summary of the previous verses, likely 14-20.

is present and controls." Another suggestion for completing the broken sentence, while making reference to the Law of Moses would be that perhaps Paul intended to write, "I find therefore the Law, when I desire to do good, *unable to help me*"; but he changes the form of the sentence as he writes so that instead of saying "I find the Law unable to help me," he says, "I find that evil is at my side." (2) Others affirm that the word "law" here is used as it was in 3:27, meaning a rule that governs actions, a principle of procedure. Translating it this way, there is no reference to the Law of Moses. In fact, the contrast between "principle" here and "Law *of God*" in verse 22 seems to show that some other sense is intended for *nomos* here in verse 21. In addition, *nomos* here seems to mean the same as "law in the members of my body" in verse 23, so "principle" seems the best preference for translating *nomos* in verse 21.[102]   Sold into bondage to sin as he is, Paul, who wishes to do the right, finds this principle or rule to be true, that evil is right there beside him, at hand[103] and ready to do its sinful thing.

The one who wishes to do good. He has already told us in verses 15 and 19 that he has the ability to wish; he just does not have the ability to control his behavior so it matches what he wishes. Why? Because he lives in a fleshly body, and is a slave to sin, being enticed to do evil by the devilish influences that excite the desires of his body. Paul has now demonstrated by a second argument that indeed he was a slave to sin before his conversion, and this is proven by the fact that his inner self was not able to make him do the right. What follows is a portrayal of the constant conflict a man under the Law experienced, a conflict which the Law gave no help to stop, a conflict from which the Law could not deliver him.

7:22 – *For I joyfully concur with the law of God in the inner man,*

For I joyfully concur with the law of God. Verses 22 and 23 explain the two thoughts contained in verse 21. I have "wishes to do good," "for (verse 22) I joyfully concur with the law of God." "Evil is present in me," for (verse 23) "there is a different law in the members of my body." "Joyfully concur" is an expression of approval, consent, an emotion of pleasure when the Law is contemplated.[104]   "Law of God" is another name for the Law of Moses.[105]   Paul's wish to do good was prompted by his delight in what the Law

---

[102] The Greek does read *ho nomos*, but the presence of the article does not absolutely require us to understand that the Law of Moses is what Paul has in mind, for the article also occurs in verse 23, where it is rather certain he is *not* speaking of the Law of Moses. There are times when the article has the force of a demonstrative pronoun, and one might render verse 21 as "*this* principle."

[103] "In me" represents the verb *parakeimai*, a word which occurs only here in the New Testament. It means to "lie alongside," to "be at hand," to "be near," or to "be ready." Arndt-Gingrich, *Lexicon*, p.623.

[104] The idea in "joyfully concur" (with its emotional overtones) has a slightly different connotation than "I agree with the Law" in verse 16. "The 'delight in the law' differs from the 'consent' (verse 16), as belonging to the sphere of feeling rather than of intellect; it thus expresses a stronger moral sympathy with what is good." Gifford, *Romans*, p.143.

[105] The Law of Moses is designated as "Thy law" (i.e., God's law) numerous times in the Psalms. The phrase "the Law of the Lord" is used in Exodus 13:9, Psalm 1:1, and many others. The exact expression Paul uses, "Law of God," is used to designate the Law of Moses at Nehemiah 8:8,18 and Hosea 4:6.

required. People under the Law did delight in its requirements; this language is in in harmony with how a man living under the Law might feel.[106] Psalm 119:97, "O how I love Thy law. It is my meditation all the day." Psalm 1:2, "his delight is in the Law of the Lord." Psalm 19:7-11 is full of expressions of delight in the Law, including "the precepts of the Lord are right, rejoicing the heart." Job 23:12 reads, "I have treasured the words of His mouth more than my necessary food."

In the inner man. Up to this point, Paul has used the word "I" to denote his spirit, his inner man, what we have called the resolving self, the better self. Now he uses the expression "inner man," which we have already used (by anticipation) in the comments earlier. Other terms that are closely related to the inner man are heart, mind, and spirit.[107] The "inner man" is distinguished from the "outer man" (the body and its members) in 2 Corinthians 4:16.

> It is now admitted by all candid and competent interpreters that this expression is *not in itself* equivalent to "*the new man*" (Ephesians 4:24, Colossians 3:10), or "*new creature*" (2 Corinthians 5:17, Galatians 6: 15): it indicates the "*mind*" (*nous*, verse 23 and verse 25), the "*spirit of man*" (1 Corinthians 2:11) as contrasted with "*the outward man*," the body or flesh (2 Corinthians 4:16). This "*hidden man of the heart*" (1 Peter 3:4), without which man would not be man, is the spiritual, willing, reasoning being, in which the regenerating power of the Holy Ghost begins to form "*the new man*," Ephesians 3:16. The context only can decide whether "*the inward man*" is regarded in his natural or in his regenerate state.[108]

---

[106] Again, let it be noted that those commentaries that think 7:14-25 speak about Paul the Christian, and the Christian's struggles with sin, are required by their thesis to explain this verse as though the Law of Moses is still a ruling principle in the lives of Christians. Is this where many denominationalists get the idea the Law is still binding, in spite of what the New Testament clearly says elsewhere on the temporary nature and present abrogation of the Old Testament? Is this debatable interpretation the cause of the lack of distinction between the Law and the gospel that we see in so many commentators – a lack that results in great confusion when one tries to explain those verses that say Law was intended only for the time between Moses and Christ, and has been abrogated by the New Covenant? How much better, in this commentator's opinion, to have Romans 7 be a reference to Paul the Jew, and the Jew's inner conflict, a conflict because of slavery to sin, a conflict from which deliverance is possible in Christ; and at the same time be able to harmonize all the verses that teach the temporary nature of the Law of Moses, because Romans 7 no longer contradicts such a doctrine. (Some commentaries, like Hendriksen, *Romans*, p.235, have attempted to avoid having Romans 7 teach the abiding validity of the Law of Moses by suggesting that the "law of God" in verse 22 means the law of God in general, even though this expression elsewhere is used of the Law of Moses in particular. Is this not an exigency he is forced into by his misunderstanding of 7:14-25 as speaking of Paul the Christian, rather than as we have proposed, Paul the unconverted Jew?)

[107] The expression "inner man" is not equivalent to the "new man" of Ephesians 4:24, or to the "new creature" of 2 Corinthians 5:17, for both those terms refer to a man after conversion. This is one of the places where the question of what state of the soul (is Paul speaking of the man under the Law, or the man under the gospel?) Paul is viewing, has bearing on the explanation. Those who believe he is portraying Paul the Christian as having struggles with sin, *will* make the "inner man" and the "new man" equivalent.

[108] Gifford, *Romans*, p.143.

7:23 – but I see a different law in the members of my body, waging war against the law of my mind, and making me a prisoner of the law of sin which is in my members.

But I see a different law in the members of my body.   The inner man can act as an onlooker, watching his bodily members as though they were at a distance from him.   As Paul watches, he sees that "different law,"[109] different, that is, from the Law of God, at work in the members of his body.   The principle he saw at work in his body was the constant tendency to sin, whenever his desires were excited by sinful objects.   Later in the verse this "different law" will be identified as "the law of sin."   "My members" signifies my fleshly members, such as hands and eyes and tongue, and stands in contrast to the "inner man," the mind.   Take notice again that "law" and "members" are not equated; again, we are guarded from the idea that flesh is inherently sinful.

Waging war against the law of my mind.   "The law of my mind" is another way of saying what verse 22 says, "I joyfully concur ... in the inner man," or what verse 19 says, 'I wish to do good.'   This constant inclination to do the right has been prompted by the requirements he learned from the Law of Moses.   The different law that wages war against the desire to do right is none other than the power that sin exerts over the slave of sin, working through the desires that are excited in the fleshly body, overpowering the inclination to do right and to avoid the wrong.

And making me a prisoner of the law of sin which is in my members.   The same idea is expressed in "making me a prisoner" as was expressed by the statement that he was "sold into bondage to sin" (verse 14).   Now, in verse 23, what he meant when he wrote that previous statement has been more fully clarified.   To make one a prisoner, a victory must be gained over him by sin.   The man living under the Law of Moses had two things to contend with.   One was the Law's requirements, with which he heartily agreed and in which he delighted, and which his inner man wished to do.   The other was the action of sin on the body (here designated as "the law of sin which is in my members"), stirring up its lusts, and overpowering the inner man's wishes.   And since the Law gave no help here, he became a slave to sin.[110]

7:24 – Wretched man that I am!   Who will set me free from the body of this death?

Wretched man that I am!   Literally, "Miserable man I!"   This wail of anguish wrung from the heart, this cry for help, is the result of constantly losing the conflict with the "law of sin" (verse 23).   The slavery of the inner man, his better self, his spirit, to the law of sin in his flesh brought a feeling of distress and grief.

Who will set me free from the body of this death?   The freedom Paul longs for is not to be completely rid of his body, such as occurs when a man dies physically and his spirit en-

---

[109] The Greek word is *heteros* (a different kind), and not *allos* (another of the same kind).   Galatians 1:6,7 serves to explain the difference between *heteros* and *allos*.   As there, *heteros euangellion* (a "different gospel") is not a true gospel; so here, this *heteros nomos* is not true law.

[110] This statement about the failure of the Law to give any help anticipates what Paul will write in 8:3.

ters the disembodied intermediate state.   Rather, Paul is anxious for freedom from the old slavery while still living in his flesh and blood body here on earth.   Paul wants someone to help him overcome the fleshly desires when they are excited and cry out to be satisfied in this or that act of sinning.[111]   The phrase "body of this death" has prompted a good deal of discussion in the commentaries.   Some would translate it "out of this body of death" (see NASB margin), as though Paul were speaking of his mortal body.   Though this is a possible translation, the context seems to be against it.   The NASB text is the reading to be preferred.   The "body" would then be identical with "my members" in verse 23 (in which the law of sin works), and identical with "my flesh" in verse 18 (with which he serves the law of sin).   "This death" (according to the NASB text) would be identical with the death he has already written about in 6:21 and 7:5.   Death seems to mean the whole condition of helplessness, guilt, and misery just described, which is, in effect, spiritual death.[112]

7:25 – *Thanks be to God through Jesus Christ our Lord!   So then, on the one hand I myself with my mind am serving the law of God, but on the other, with my flesh the law of sin.*

Thanks be to God through Jesus Christ our Lord!   This is the reply to the foregoing question, "Who will set me free?"   There is obviously an omission of part of the statement, but the question being answered leaves little doubt as to what the omission is.   We might fill in the missing words in this manner, "Thanks be to God,[113] *He will set us free* through Jesus Christ our Lord!"[114]   When and how this deliverance is effected will be explained in

---

[111] The word translated "set free" has not been used before in Romans.   It is a very strong word, *ruomai*, and while it means to "save, rescue, deliver, or preserve," it also suggests that some considerable power or force will be needed to accomplish the deliverance.

[112] Paul is contrasting a man's position under the Law and his position under grace.   Under the Law, the only hope a man had was to fulfill perfectly the conditions of the legal system.   Resting on Law, we can only say, "Wretched man that I am!"   But under grace, a man does not have to be perfect in order to have hope.   If we rest on grace, we may say (verse 25), "Thanks be to God!"   Throughout this whole paragraph the Deliverer has been kept out of view, that man's absolute need for such a Deliverer as indispensable to life and happiness may be understood.   Unless he has a Deliverer, the slavery to sin, and the constant victory of the devil, will continue to produce misery in the mind and spirit of the man.   (If those writers were correct who view this whole passage as the Christian's struggles with sin, it would seem to follow that Paul here teaches that a man's "sinful nature" is never mastered during this lifetime; there is no deliverance from the propensities planted in us (as they teach) by original sin.   If what Jesus did on Calvary does not make it possible to be delivered from the old sinful nature, there is certainly no such thing as deliverance this side of death.   This whole paragraph, arguing *ad hominem*, would also seem to be a powerful argument against any doctrine of complete sanctification [see Special Study #5 at the close of chapter 6]).

[113] Instead of "Thanks be to God," the Vulgate, Wycliffe, Rheims, Douay, and some Greek manuscripts read, "the grace of God."   This requires a slight change in the Greek, but it does give good sense.   After asking, "Who will set me free?" Paul answers, "The grace of God through Jesus Christ our Lord shall set me free!"

[114] See notes at Romans 1:4 for the significance of the title "Jesus Christ our Lord."   It is "the full soteriological name of the Mediator; his person (Jesus), his office (Christ), his relation to us Christians (our Lord)."   Lenski, *Romans*, p.490.

chapter 8.[115]

So then. Some would start chapter 8 with this phrase. We prefer to think of it as the concluding summary of 7:14-24, as do the ASV and NASB translators. Here, speaking of how it was when a man lived under the Law of Moses, Paul sums up in two terse phrases the state of things prior to the entrance of Christ into the picture.[116]

On the one hand I myself with my mind am serving the law of God. "I myself" is the inner man, the spirit, the resolving self, the one who was constantly wishing to do the right.[117] The expression "the law of God" is without a definite article in the Greek, and though the reference again is to the Law of Moses (as in verse 22 and footnote #105), in this place the absence of the article has the effect of stressing the nature of this law, that it was given by God. Here is a man living under the Law of Moses,[118] telling us that his inner man wished to do what the Law required, but he found that he could not consistently do it because of the overpowering effect his body had over his spirit (which had "died" when he committed his first sin). The reason his "body" acted contrary to the will of God is summarized in the next phrase.

But on the other, with my flesh the law of sin. "Law of sin" has been explained in verse 23. Paul is saying that though he desired to do right, he was sold into bondage to sin. The devil would stir up sinful desires in his body, and while he was under the Law, he never had perfect control over his body – instead, his body controlled him. The flesh was stronger than the wishes of the inner man; so he did the sins to which he was tempted through the flesh, rather than doing what the inner man wished to do. That is the way it was under the Law of Moses. But for the man who is "in Christ," this condemnation to

---

[115] This is another verse where one's view of that state of the soul Paul has been portraying will have an influence on the comments offered. Those who believe it is the Christian's struggles with sin will write about the second coming of Jesus as the time when this deliverance takes place, for that is when the body will be redeemed, and when all opportunity for the devil to tempt the redeemed will forever be past. (It is admitted that there are references to the second coming in chapter 8, but we also understand those references are incidental rather than the chief point being explicated. The chief point is that the indwelling Holy Spirit can help the believer *in this life* to master the temptations the devil offers.)

[116] "It is unnecessary to treat this sentence as misplaced [as certain liberal and Neo-liberal theologians have been wont to do]. Moffatt makes it stand as a parenthesis after verse 23, which, he says, 'seems its original and logical position before the climax of verse 24' – a transposition which C.H. Dodd says is 'surely right.' G. Zuntz thinks that it 'may be an addition by Paul himself or a summing up by some early reader; in any case its present position is unsuitable and suggests that a marginal gloss has been inserted into the text' (*The Text of the Epistles*, p.16). [J.B. Phillip's translation simply omits the latter half of the verse. F.F. Bruce goes on to affirm that the sentence is *not* misplaced.] It appears in its present position in our earliest authorities; and it is a precarious procedure to rearrange the words of Paul in the interests of [what we may think is] a smoother logical sequence." Bruce, *Romans*, p.156.

[117] For notes on "I," see Romans 7:9 ("*I* died") and 7:14 (especially footnote #76); for notes on "the mind" and the "Law of God," see comments on these expressions at verses 22,23.

[118] This statement about "serving the law of God" is one of the decisive expressions in this paragraph to help us understand that it is Paul the Jew (not Paul the Christian) who is opening up to his readers the inner struggle between spirit and flesh. It was the Jew, not the Christian, who is obligated to follow Moses.

slavery to sin is a thing of the past (8:1-4).[119]

---

[119] What Paul writes here, about how the slave of sin could not control the fleshly body he lived in, will be completely reversed in his presentation in chapter 8. The Christian's spirit is alive, and with the help of the indwelling Holy Spirit, *can* control the fleshly house he lives in. No longer is the Christian at the mercy of "king sin."

SPECIAL STUDY #6

WHAT STATE OF THE SOUL
HAS THE APOSTLE PORTRAYED
IN ROMANS 7:14-24?

What happens if a Bible teacher regularly gives a verse a wrong explanation?   For example, Luke 18:1-8 was originally told (verse 1 tells us) to illustrate the need for persistence in prayer.   Verse 8 closes with these words, "When the Son of Man comes, will He find faith on the earth?"   If this verse is regularly used to prove that there will be a falling away from the Christian faith before the return of Jesus, it is very possible to miss what it is really saying about faith to continue in prayer.   In other words, if we use a verse out of its context to prove what may be a true doctrine, we never learn what the verse really says to us, and we are impoverished.

Bible teachers do need to speak as the oracles of God (1 Peter 4:11).   It is necessary to speak it as rightly as we can as we teach or preach.   Instead of 'right sermon – wrong verse,' the intent must always be to strive for 'right sermon – right verse.'

Romans 7 has been a disputed passage for hundreds of years.   It is doubtful that this study can settle the dispute.   What is intended within this Special Study is to collect in a convenient order the arguments pro and con for some of the more popular interpretations, so that the student may more easily evaluate the arguments, and thus arrive at his own studied conclusion on this controverted subject.

I. DOES IT PORTRAY THE STRUGGLES WITH SIN THAT EVERY CHRISTIAN EXPERIENCES?

According to this interpretation, Paul speaks of his own experiences because they are representative of the struggles with sin and with the sinful fleshly nature that every Christian experiences.   The citadel (often identified as being the "will") has been freed (by redemption), but there are still battles in the outer works (because the sinful fleshly nature still remains after conversion); and, according to the usual interpretation, deliverance from this continual struggle will not be complete until the Christian is no longer living in his fleshly, mortal body.

A. Bible Students Who Have Held and Taught this View

The truth or error of any theological position is not ultimately decided by the number of scholars who can be amassed on either side of a question; rather, the truth of a position is determined simply by what God Himself said on the subject.   However, it can be instructive to study history, to see how a theological viewpoint came to grow and be passed along to succeeding generations.

Methodius (c.260-c.311 AD), a Greek church leader who opposed Origen, in his *Discourse on the Resurrection*, shows his belief that the Christian struggles with his evil nature until the time of his physical death.[1] Augustine, as a result of his battle with Pelagius, eventually came to interpret Romans 7 as the Christian's struggles with his evil nature.[2] In AD 394, prior to the Pelagian controversy, Augustine's stated view was that Romans 7:14ff pictures the struggle with sin in an unregenerate person (see his *Expositio Quarundam Prop. Ep. Rom*, Prop. 45). This same view was repeated in *Ad Simplicianus*, about AD 397, and in *Confessions*, vii.21, c.AD 400. The Pelagian controversy began about AD 412. It was not until c. AD 420 that Augustine's view, that Romans 7:14ff pictures the Christian's struggles with sin, was presented in *Contra duas Epistolas Pelagianorum ad Boniface*, i.12. This changed view was then repeated in *Retractiones*, i.23, written c. AD 427, and in *Contra Julianum*, vi. 13, written about the same time.[3] The Latin church leaders (Hilary, Gregory, Ambrose, Anselm, Aquinas) generally followed Augustine's lead. After the Reformation, Luther, Melanchthon, Calvin (and those Reformed scholars who follow in Calvin's train), and Beza all opted for the interpretation that Romans 7 reflects the Christian's struggles with sin. Likewise taught the Scotch theologians, Brown, Haldane, and Chalmers. Eighteenth and nineteenth century writers who defended this interpretation include Delitzsch, Alford, Barnes, Lard,[4] Philippi,[5] and Fraser.[6] Twentieth century writers include Barth, Barrett, Batey, Bavinck, Berkhof, Berkouwer, Bruce, Cranfield, Hamilton, Lenski, Nygren, Vine, and Wilson.

B. Arguments Alleged to Demonstrate the Truth of this Interpretation

1. *There Is a Change of Verb Tenses Which Must be Explained.*

In verses 7-13 the aorist tense is used, and in 8:1ff the aorist tense is used. But in

---

[1] Methodius, "On the Resurrection," in *The Ante-Nicene Fathers*, edited by Alexander Roberts and James Donaldson (Grand Rapids: Wm. B. Eerdmans Publishing Co., 1951), Vol.6, p.371ff.

[2] See page 235ff, above, where the history of Augustine v. Pelagius was briefly rehearsed.

[3] Meyer and Lange attribute this change in Augustine's views to the exigencies of the Pelagian controversy. And with them, this commentator agrees. Calvin and Hodge, on the other hand, attribute the change "to a deeper insight into his own heart, and a more thorough investigation of the Scriptures."

[4] Moses E. Lard is one of the few early Restoration Movement writers who taught this view, but because his commentary on Romans was long a standard work in the Movement, the idea has been widely taught since.

[5] F.A. Philippi, *Commentary on the Epistle to the Romans* (Edinburgh: T&T Clark, 1878), is a good reference for a detailed presentation of the interpretation that Romans 7 is the Christian's struggles with sin.

[6] James Fraser, *A Treatise on Sanctification* (London: Bliss, Sands & Co., 1898), p.254ff.

verses 14-24 the present tense is used. Since verses 7-13 (where the verb is past tense) spoke of the time under the Law, verses 14-24 must speak of the time since being freed from the Law (i.e., the present time even as Paul the Christian is writing). In this way the change of verb tense easily can be explained, it is argued.[7]

2. *Every Expression in this Whole Paragraph is a Statement to which even the Holiest of Men Can Agree.*

Not only the personal experience of every Christian attests to the continuing struggle with sin, but the Bible elsewhere specifically affirms that such a contest between the Christian and temptations to sin is a continuing fact of life. Romans 6:12-23 has implied this when the Christian is exhorted to stop presenting his members to sin as tools of unrighteousness. Galatians 5:17, that well-known passage about the flesh versus the Spirit, is written to warn Christians that continued living as the flesh prompts will end in eternal punishment. Unless there is a continuing struggle with sin, this warning is pointless. Christians are exhorted to mortify the deeds of the flesh (Colossians 3:5).[8]

3. *There are Statements in the Paragraph that No Unconverted Man Could Say.*

The expressions often appealed to are "we know that the Law is spiritual" (verse 14); "I joyfully concur with the law of God in the inner man" (verse 22); and "with my mind I am serving the law of God" (verse 25). In addition, the person portrayed is one who wishes to do that which is good (verses 15,18,19,21), and this is alleged to be totally unlike the unconverted man.[9] Furthermore, verse 25 must be a Christian thanking God for his deliverance; and if verse 25 is a Christian speaking, then the whole paragraph must be a Christian speaking. The argument thus says that, since there are statements a non-Christian could not make, this passage must picture the Christian's struggles with sin.

C. Arguments Offered to Show the Impropriety of this Interpretation

1. *The Unusual Explanation that Must be Given to "the Law"*

---

[7] In reply, proponents of other views ask, Is the change of tense a sufficient reason to justify so marked a change of subject as this interpretation implies? Is it not possible that in 7:14-23, Paul is answering some standard Jewish objections to Christian doctrine, and to make his point emphatic, Paul puts the verbs in the present tense, to make the reminder of every Jew's experience even that much more vivid and real?

[8] The careful reader must observe that the question under discussion is *not* "Does the Christian still have to practice a control over his flesh after the devil tempts?" but whether or not Romans 7 is one of the passages to be used when teaching on this topic of the Christian's struggles with sin. Remember, if one takes the position that Romans 7 is the Christian's struggles with sin, then one must also teach that such struggles are "in vain" (cf. Bruce, *Romans*, p.152) because the adversary (sin) is so overpowering. Does this last conclusion ring true with the presentation in the rest of New Testament, e.g., 1 Corinthians 10:13?

[9] The reader will observe that the presupposition behind this argument is that total depravity, inherited from Adam, renders an unconverted man totally unable to say such things as this.

To interpret verses 14-24 as being the Christian's struggles with sin requires an unusual interpretation to be given to the words "the Law" and "the Law of God" (verses 12,14,16,22,25). This unusual interpretation must be given to keep this passage from contradicting those clear New Testament references which show that the Law of Moses is not binding on the Christian. To be forced by the theory being defended to say that the verses in question do not have particular reference to the Law of Moses, but refer to "God's laws in general," is a serious, and likely fatal, problem for this proposed interpretation.

2. *The Context, both Preceding and Following, is Against this Interpretation.*

It is true that in chapters 5 and 6, some blessed results of God's way of saving man (justification by faith) have been brought into view, including the fact that in baptism into Christ a man is "freed from sin." But on the other hand, it must be admitted that 7:7-13 refer to the pre-Christian position of a man. And 8:1 contrasts "now" (how it is *now* with the Christian) with what was said in 7:14-25. The context on both sides of the paragraph in question would lead the reader to think that 7:14-25 also spoke of the experiences of a man under the Law, before he became a Christian.

3. *The Arguments Given to Substantiate the Other View*

All the arguments in favor of the interpretation that it is the unconverted man whose struggles with sin are pictured in Romans 7:14-24 are, in fact, arguments against the idea that this paragraph speaks of the Christian's struggles with sin.[10]

II. TWO MINORITY VIEWS

Not all writers hold either to the unregenerate man or to the Christian man view. There are some "intermediate" views. Since relatively few writers have proposed and/or defended these views, we might call them "minority" views.

A. An Enlightened Jew, in the Process of Being Converted

Hodge and Gifford both opt for this method of explaining the verses, and illustrate it by suggesting Paul is revealing his inner struggles and torment while on the way to Damascus. To this commentator, it seems this is but a variation on the theme that it is Paul the Jew whose experiences are being portrayed. However, since such an interpretation is hard to harmonize with Augustinian and Calvinistic views of inherited sin and total depravity, have Hodge and Gifford tried to get around that problem by suggesting that we are looking at a man who has already experienced what would be called (by them) a first work of grace? If so, this would allow them to hold the doctrines of inherited sin as taught in the creeds (such as the *Westminster Confession of Faith*) and at the same time

---

[10] See Part III, section B, below, where these arguments are listed.

give a plausible commentary on the paragraph in question.

B. An Immature Christian

Hendriksen presents this option, only to reject it in favor of the usual Reformed view his comments represent. According to this proposed method of explaining the passage, three stages of religious development are pictured by Paul: (1) A person still unconverted and in slavery to sin (7:5,9); (2) The babe in Christ who is struggling; he hates his sin, but is not very far advanced on the road to sanctification (7:14-25); and (3) The mature believer for whom there is no more condemnation (8:1-4). Hendriksen then rejects this view by observing that it is the mature believer who hates his sin the most, and who is most distressed by it when he does sin.

III. DOES IT PORTRAY THE STRUGGLES WITH SIN THAT AN UNREGENERATE MAN EXPERIENCES?

According to this method of explaining the verses, for the time being (until 8:1), the redemptive work of Christ is left out of the picture because Paul wanted to show what the Law of Moses could and could not accomplish with reference to a man's sin problem. The Law could not redeem. It could not even remove the feeling of guilt. In fact, a man aware of the requirements of the Law and comparing them with his own behavior was "wretched" and looking for deliverance "from the body of this death."

A. Bible Students Who Have Held and Taught This View

The Greek church leaders, generally, such as Origen, Tertullian, Chrysostom, and Theodoret, held this view. So did Augustine before his controversy with Pelagius,[11] and Jerome (who seems to have changed his views, much as did Augustine). Erasmus, Faustus Socinus, Arminius, and others so explained it in the time of the Reformation. Post-Reformation theologians espousing this view include Muller, Neander, Tholuck, Hengstengberg, DeWette, Ewald, Whitby, Stuart, Lechler, Meyer, Bengel, Godet, Sanday and Headlam, Denney, Ellicott, Doddridge, Macknight, Conybeare and Howson, and the Restoration Movement writers, Grubbs, B.W. Johnson, Lipscomb, and McGarvey. Twentieth century scholars who have held that 7:14-24 is a picture of the unregenerate man

---

[11] "Augustine was for a time involved in the common error, but having more thoroughly examined the passage, not only retracted what he had falsely thought, but in his first book to Boniface proves, by many forceful arguments, that what is said cannot be applied to any but the regenerate." John Calvin, *Romans*, p.264. Calvin's language not only gives what he thought caused Augustine to change, but also expresses his own attitude toward any other interpretation. "What weighed with Augustine was that in verses 17,20,22, more propension to good is implied than his doctrinal theory allowed to the natural man ... If, however, St. Paul's intention, obvious from his own writing, does not fit in with Augustinian or Calvinistic theology, so much the worse for the latter." Barmby, *Romans*, p. 185.

and his inner struggles with sin include W.G. Kummel, Ridderbos, Bultmann, and C.H. Dodd.[12]

B. Arguments Alleged to Demonstrate the Truth of this Interpretation

1. *Appeal is Made to Certain Expressions Not Suitable for a Christian to Say.*

"I am of flesh" (verse 14). Does not this mean the same as "in the flesh" as stated in verse 5? If so, it speaks of a man under the dominion of sin at a time in history when the Law was present, but was of no help.[13]

"Sold into bondage to sin" (verse 14). Is this not synonymous with being what was called a slave to sin in 6:6? Is not a slave the opposite of being under grace (6:14)?[14]

"The wishing is present in me, but the doing of good is not" (verse 18). Are we to suppose that the man in whom the powers of grace are operative (as is true of the regenerate) is destitute of good works which are the fruit of the Spirit?

"Wretched man that I am!" (verse 24). Surely this complaint is far from being the state of mind of one who has entered into the joy and liberty of the gospel (7:6, 5:1-5).

"Nothing good dwells in me" (verse 18). This can hardly be harmonized with what Paul himself writes about the indwelling Holy Spirit in chapter 8, especially verses 9-11.

2. *The Relation to the Law of Moses Assumed in Verses 14-24 Would Hardly be Different from that in Verses 7-13.*

The "for" (*gar*) which connects verse 14 with the preceding verses denotes a continuance of thought. Verses 14-25 continue the same line of thought that was in verse 13

---

[12] In certain conservative circles, the reader's attention would be drawn to the fact that in the 19th and 20th centuries, many of the scholars who have espoused this interpretation of Romans 7 have been theologically liberal, and of course, their comments would be influenced by their presupposition that man has greater natural abilities than the Bible (seen through Calvinistic eyes) is thought to allow. This commentator would reply to both, that neither dogmatic theology nor the currently popular philosophy should be permitted to color a man's comments on Scripture if he expects to understand what God Himself has said on the subject.

[13] It might be noted here that Calvin circumvented this argument by regarding the transition to the regenerate man's struggles as taking place at verse 15. If Calvin's view is adopted, then the difficulties of applying the expressions of verse 14 – "I am of flesh" and "sold into bondage to sin" – to a regenerate person disappear. In reply to Calvin's proposed point of transition, why is it that the verb tenses change at verse 14 and not at verse 15, if the transition really is at verse 15 as he urges?

[14] This does not deny what was said in 6:16 about how a Christian can relapse into the old slavery, but it is hard to see how "sold into bondage to sin" is the same thing that 6:16 spoke of, namely, a *voluntary presentation* of one's self to sin, a presentation made after the old slavery had been broken.

and before.   Further, we find in 7:5 and 7:6 the obvious theses of the two major sections that follow (in the remainder of chapter 7 and chapter 8, respectively).   7:5 distinctly expresses the state of being under Law (which the rest of chapter 7 discusses) and 7:6 speaks of the state of being delivered from the Law (which chapter 8 will develop).

3.   *Parallels to the Expressions Paul Uses are Found in Pagan Literature.*

Far from being expressions that only a born-again Christian could make, statements similar to verses 14-24 have been found in such non-Christian writers as Ovid, Euripides, Xenophon, Seneca, Epictetus, and others.[15]

> The verses in question (verses 17,20,22) do not, in fact, express more than the apostle elsewhere allows man to be capable of, and what observation of fact allows him to be capable of, though not having yet attained to Christian faith; viz., approval of, longing for, and even striving for, what is good.   It is not more than sincere and earnest men, even in the Gentile world, have been already credited with in chapter 2 of this epistle (verses 7,10, 14,16,26,29).[16]

4.   *The Change of Verb Tense Can Be Explained.*

Paul's deliberate change from past tense verbs to present tense verbs in verses 14-24 may be the strongest argument against the idea that he is portraying a time long past in his life.   However, this change can be given a plausible explanation.   The use of the present tense is deliberate, in order to dramatically bring home to the consciousness of his readers what they had all personally, and sadly, experienced.   Each of his readers knew all too well what Paul was talking about.

5.   *Total Depravity is a Dogma Not Likely Supported by Scripture.*

"However 'far from original righteousness' man outside the gospel may be, still that utter depravity attributed to him by some theologians is neither consonant with observed fact nor declared in Holy Writ.   The image of God in which men were created is represented as defaced, not obliterated."[17]   Interpreting 7:14ff as a portrayal of the Christian's struggles with sin forces the interpreter to speak of the evil propensities in the flesh

---

[15] "Paul's contemporaries well knew this feeling, as indeed, we know it ourselves. Seneca talked of 'our helplessness in necessary things.' He talked about how men hate their sins and love them at the same time. Ovid, the Roman poet, had penned this famous tag, 'I see the better things, and I approve them, but I follow the worse.' No one knew this problem better than the Jews. The Jews had solved it by saying that in every man there were two natures, two tendencies, two impulses. They called them the *Yetser hatob* [mind of good] and *Yetser hara* [mind of evil]." Barclay, *Romans*, p.101. See also the quotes cited in footnote #86 associated with the comments at 7:15.

[16] Barmby, *Romans*, p.185.

[17] Barmby, *Romans*, p.185,186.

with which the Christian has to contend.   Such an interpretation leaves much to be desired, as far as accurately reflecting what the apostle Paul wrote.

6.   *Between 8:1 and 7:14-25, There is a Sharp Contrast.*

8:1 begins with "now" and draws a sharp contrast with the deplorable condition that existed before, about which 7:14-25 spoke.   If 7:14-25 is the Christian state, how do we explain the contrast introduced in 8:1?   But if 7:14-25 is the unconverted state, the contrast introduced in 8:1 makes beautiful sense.

7.   *7:14-25 Must Surely Harmonize with Statements Already Made in Chapter 6.*

The view that 7:14-25 pictures a slavery, a bondage, that still remains after a man becomes a Christian seems to conflict with statements already made in chapter 6.   Sin is a dethroned master, the slave to sin has been freed, he has risen to walk in the same newness of life that Jesus did following His resurrection.   How can such statements in chapter 6 be harmonized with the idea of some that the "I" (inner man) of 7:14-25 represents the new man, redeemed by Christ, but still a slave to evil propensities, a slavery he will not escape until he leaves this life to enter Heaven?

CONCLUSION

Given the arguments pro and con, and seeing how some of them fit into historical and dogmatic contexts as much or more than simply being exegetical comments, this commentator has concluded that 7:14-25 speaks of the struggles with sin that the person under the Law of Moses had, indeed the struggles that any unregenerate man may have as he tries to abide by the Light he has.   Those struggles are vividly displayed here, and as we look into the Word Paul has written, we can see ourselves reflected in this mirror. Having reached an accountable age, we too have seen the devil deceive us and make us slaves who do hurtful and ruinous things to ourselves and to others.   We too can identify with the wretchedness that cries out for a Deliverer!

As has also been stated in the comments, although Romans 7 is not the chapter to use to prove it, there is no absolute exemption from temptation for the Christian, nor does the practice of self-control as the Christian is tempted always come easily.   The devil keeps trying to regain his old mastery over the citizens of the Kingdom of Heaven.   But there are limitations put on the devil, by God, for the Christian's benefit, and the old forced slavery to the devil is a thing of the past.   What is needed now is for the Christian to watch his mind and desires for those temptations, and when they occur, to resist in the power of the Holy Spirit (Romans 12:1,2).   This holy resistance, coupled with a conscious presentation of one's whole self to God for His service, will put an end to the immediate temptation, and an end to the struggle until the devil is again permitted to tempt God's child.   But talking about the need for the practice of self-control when the devil tempts is very far different from the doctrine that says the tendency to evil is inherent in the fleshly body we live in, and therefore always present to harass and cause us grief. To present the doctrine that the Christian can be victorious over temptation to sin, rather than always having to be helpless in its power, is as different as night and day.

SELECTED BIBLIOGRAPHY

Cranfield, C.E.B., *A Critical and Exegetical Commentary on the Epistle to the Romans*. Edinburgh: T&T Clark, 1975.

Dodd, C.H., *The Epistle of Paul to the Romans*. London: Hodder and Stoughton, 1932.

Espy, John M., "Paul's 'Robust Conscience' Re-Examined," *New Testament Studies*, 31 (1985), p.161-188.

Jewett, R., *Paul's Anthropological Terms: A Study of their Use in Conflict Settings*. Leiden: E.J. Brill, 1971.

Lloyd-Jones, D. Martyn, *Romans: An Exposition of Chapters 7:1-8:4*. Grand Rapids: Zondervan Publishing House, 1973.

Martin, B.L., "Some Reflections on the Identity of *ego* in Rom. 7:14-25," *Scottish Journal of Theology*, 34:1 (1981), p.39-47.

Mile, D.J.W., "Romans 7:7-12. Paul's Pre-Conversion Experience," *Reformed Theological Review*, 43:1 (1984), p.9-17.

Mitton, C.L., "Romans 7 Reconsidered," *Expository Times* 65 (1953,1954), p.78-81, 99-103, 132-35.

Wenham, David, "The Christian Life: A Life of Tension?" in *Pauline Studies*, edited by Donald A. Hagner and Murray J. Harris. Grand Rapids: Wm. B. Eerdmans Publishing Co., 1980. p.80-94.

E. God's Plan of Salvation (Justification by Faith) Involves Blessed Effects On Those In Whom the Holy Spirit Now Dwells.   8:1-30

Summary: The indwelling Spirit, whom the justified man receives as a gift at the time of his justification, helps the Christian to control the desires the devil excites, because God has condemned sin in the flesh, verses 1-11.   The indwelling Spirit witnesses to the believer's having been adopted into the family of God, verses 12-17.   Believers have a hope of glory which, coupled with the aid of the indwelling Spirit and God's over-ruling providence, is sufficient to sustain them through all sufferings, verses 18-30.

8:1 – *There is therefore now no condemnation for those who are in Christ Jesus.*

There is therefore now no condemnation.   Chapter 8 has been called a triumphant hymn of hope, for it speaks of "the happy condition of a man in Christ."   "It is a continuation of the subject discussed in the previous chapter, and is intended mainly to show that the gospel does for men what the Law was incapable of doing."[1]   "Therefore" shows that 8:1-4 is an inference drawn from what has just been written in chapter 7.[2]   "Now" is temporal, and contrasts how things are now that the gospel has come, now that deliverance in Christ is a fact.   "No condemnation"[3] is explained in the next verse to mean "set free from the law of sin and death."   The sentence of condemnation to sin and death has been repealed or cancelled for all those who are in Christ Jesus.[4]

For those who are in Christ Jesus.[5]   In 6:3-11, Paul has explained how a man comes to be "in Christ Jesus."   "Those are meant who have been immersed into Christ."[6]   This is a reminder that God's way of saving man (i.e., He provided Jesus as a propitiatory sacrifice,

---

[1] Barnes, *Romans*, p.175.

[2] Commentaries are not wholly in agreement when they attempt to specify what in chapter 7 this inference is derived from.   (1) Some, such as Hodge, Haldane, Hendriksen, affirm that 8:1 is connected with the whole discussion about justification and freedom from the old slavery to the power of sin, 6:1-7:25.   (2) Others, such as Bengel and Stuart, think 8:1 is connected with 7:6, where it speaks of serving in newness of the Spirit [note the capital "S"] and not oldness of letter.   (3) Still others, such as Augustine, Alford, and Gifford, connect 8:1 to 7:25's thanksgiving for the deliverance in Christ Jesus.

[3] "Condemnation" translates *katakrima*, a word that has been explained at 5:16,18.

[4] The careful reader will observe that the absence of condemnation is something that is related to *this* life.   It does not therefore seem proper to use this verse to prove what will or will not be the "sentence" God pronounces at the final judgment.   The Bible indeed may teach that those in Christ will be confessed before the Father, rather than denied and condemned to everlasting torment (e.g., Matthew 10:32), but this is not one of the verses properly used to show that truth.

[5] The KJV has one more phrase in verse 1, "who walk not after the flesh, but after the Spirit."   These words are evidently an interpolation from verse 4.   They are not found in Sinaiticus, Vaticanus, Ephraemi, etc., as a part of verse 1.

[6] Lard, *Romans*, p.246.

and He justifies those who believe in Jesus, 3:21-26) is the reason the sentence to condemnation can be rescinded.[7]

8:2 – *For the law of the Spirit of life in Christ Jesus has set you free from the law of sin and of death.*

For.   Verse 2 explains what verse 1 means when it says "no condemnation."

The law of the Spirit of life in Christ Jesus.   "Law" here seems to be used with the same meaning it had in 3:27 and 7:21, a 'rule that governs actions, a principle of procedure.'   The "Spirit of life" is evidently one of some forty different Biblical names for the Holy Spirit.[8] Thus the "law of the Spirit of life" is what Paul will go on to describe in the following verses – that is, living the new life as the Holy Spirit directs our human spirit.[9]   This is but the second time Paul has made reference to the Holy Spirit[10] in this letter: not only does the Holy Spirit flood the hearts of believers with the love of God (5:5), but once His help is introduced into the life of the believer, there is no further talk of the believer's being defeated or being mastered by sin against his will.[11]   The phrase "in Christ Jesus" can be

---

[7] In comments on 6:20 and 6:22, it was noted that Catholic and Protestant scholars have different concepts of "sanctification" and "justification."   That debate is reflected in many commentaries as we begin chapter 8.   Does 8:1ff speak of justification or sanctification, it is often asked.   If chapter 8 deals with the help to live the Christian life that the Holy Spirit gives the man who is in Christ Jesus, then the topic is "sanctification."

[8] The different names, "Spirit of truth," "Spirit of holiness," "Spirit of God," "Spirit of Christ," "Holy Spirit," "Comforter," all seem to emphasize some special characteristic or function of the Spirit.   Just what is intended by the designation "Spirit of *life*"?   Is it because He helps convict a man of his sins and encourages the sinner to come to Christ for forgiveness and newness of life (all of which is called 'the begetting work' of the Spirit)?   Is it because He will have something to do with raising the believer's dead body at the resurrection (8:11)?   Is it because the Spirit helps the one who has been freed from his old slavery to sin to *live* the life of service to Christ?   Is it because the Spirit has inspired the gospel, which is God's power to salvation?

[9] One very complex problem translators and commentators face when working through chapter 8 is how to translate *pneuma*, which appears 19 times.   Should it be translated "spirit" [making it a reference to a man's spirit], or should it be translated "Spirit" [making it a reference to the Holy Spirit]?   The KJV, ASV, RSV, NASB, and TEV consistently capitalize it each time it appears (though some read "spirit" one time, at verse 10).   The ERV, Phillips, NEB, Lard, and Campbell (*Living Oracles*) at times chose to use the lower case "s" – particularly at verses 4,5,6,9a, and 13.   There are two basic approaches to this difficult question: (1) Examine the context and the probabilities each time the word *pneuma* appears, and make a separate decision in each case;   and (2) Consult the old Greek manuscripts, and see whether the abbreviation *PNA* occurs, or whether the word is spelled out completely, *PNEUMA*.   The abbreviation occurs (supposedly) when it is a reference to the Divine name, while the full spelling occurs when it is a reference to the human spirit.   Caution must be observed, for we do not know if the abbreviations were in the autograph copies, or whether the abbreviation merely shows the copyist's belief (which would have little more authority than any other reader's opinion).   This whole matter can be pursued in Philip W. Comfort's "Light from the New Testament Papyri Concerning the Translation of *Pneuma*," *Bible Translator*, 35:1 (1984), p.130-133.

[10] *Pneuma* was used at 1:4,9; 2:29; and 7:6, but none of those were interpreted in this commentary as a reference to the Holy Spirit.

[11] Certain scholars in the Christian Churches and Churches of Christ have been wont to explain that the Holy Spirit works *only* "through the Word" as He leads a man to become a Christian, and then as He

connected with "life" or with "set you free." If we think of the "life in Christ Jesus," there is stress on the union with Christ about which the previous verse reminded us. If we think of free in Christ, His atoning (and perhaps also His mediatorial) work is the thing in view.

Has set you free from the law of sin and of death. "Set free" is an aorist tense, and thus points back to a definite time in the past, namely, the deliverance from the domination by sin and death which took place at baptism (Romans 6:3-7, especially verse 7). Paul also wrote about this freedom in 6:18 and 6:22. In 8:1, too, he has spoken of being "in Christ;" that happens when a man is baptized into Christ; that is when he is "set free."[12] The "law of sin and of death,"[13] as the context would require, is the same law of which 7:14-24 spoke, the law of sin in my members, the "different law" of 7:23. The "death" likewise is the death spoken of in 7:11,13,24, spiritual death.[14] The whole last half of the verse, therefore, means that the Christian is freed from slavery to sin; the Christian is freed from the bondage to sin into which he had been sold. Verse 3 will say that God's way of saving men – justification by faith – does something the Law of Moses could never do. This freedom from the law of sin and death is the realization of what was yearned for in 7:24.

The rest of the paragraph is a development of the thought introduced here in verse 2. It is shown, first, how God, in Christ, has done for us what was necessary that we might be freed. It is shown, secondly, how we ourselves must "walk according ... to the Spirit" if we would continue this freedom.

8:3 – *For what the Law could not do, weak as it was through the flesh, God* did: *sending His own Son in the likeness of sinful flesh and* as an offering *for sin, He condemned sin in the flesh,*

---

helps the man to live the Christian life. While the former is in harmony with Scripture, the latter may not be. One reason it may not be is because it requires a special understanding of this passage to justify the theory that the Spirit works only through the Word on the Christian. First, the "*law* of the Spirit of life" must be explained to be a 'complex name for the gospel.' (Proponents of this idea often are, to a degree, legalists, saying that just as the Jews had a Law to obey, so the Christian has a new law to obey. One set of laws [Moses'] is replaced with another [gospel].) Then the whole expression is further explained to mean that the Spirit dwells in and works through His "law" (gospel); this is why (this explanation affirms) it is called the law "of the Spirit of life."

The foregoing should cause us to search the Word to see what it says about the leading of the Spirit in the life of the Christian. Does the Spirit lead *only* through the Word, or does He lead both through the Word and sometimes apart from, but in harmony with, it? (Answers will be found later in Romans 8.)

[12] The KJV reads "made *me* free," where the NASB reads "set *you* free." Since the Sinaiticus and Vaticanus manuscripts both read "you," that likely was the original reading in the autograph.

[13] The Greek reads '*the* sin' and '*the* death,' and we are reminded of the power of sin that tries to gain dominion (about which Paul has said much since 5:12) and about the "death" which results from sin (which also has been a topic since 5:12).

[14] In the light of what Paul writes in 8:11-15, perhaps "set free from ... death" also includes a deliverance from the penalty of physical death to the race, which is realized in the resurrection of the body. However, caution must be observed again, lest it be implied that *only* those "in Christ" are raised from the dead, for that would contradict what has already been written in 5:18 about "justification of life to *all* men." It might better be maintained that "set free from ... death" means exemption from any liability of experiencing the "second death" (Revelation 21:8), as well as being freed from spiritual death.

For what the Law could not do.   Since both verses 2 and 3 begin with "for," it would appear that each verse is intended to give part of the explanation of how it is possible that there is "now no condemnation for those who are in Christ Jesus."   The Law of Moses never could and never did make it possible for men to be "free from the law of sin and death."[15]   Instead of condemning sin in the flesh, instead of delivering men from the dominion of sin, chapter 7 has shown that the presence of the Law gave sin more opportunity to effect its deadly work and thereby increase its domination.

Weak as it was through the flesh.   This in a sense is a summary of what has been set forth in detail in 7:14-24.   The inner man was sold into slavery, and thereafter was controlled by his fleshly body whose desires were excited by various devilish temptations. The inner man wanted to avoid the wrong, and do the right, but he was not able to control the house in which he lived.   The Law of Moses was weak, too, and so gave a man's spirit no help in controlling his flesh.

God *did*.   God did what the Law could not do.[16]   He has given the man in Christ some help to control the fleshly house he lives in.   He sets men free from "the law of sin and of death," and replaces that with "the law of the Spirit of life."   How it is justly possible for Him to do this is explained in the following clauses.   The Law was weak, but God was not!

Sending His own Son in the likeness of sinful flesh.   God the Father is the One who sent "His own Son" to become incarnate and to be a sin offering.   The initiative in the whole process of redemption must be traced to the love and grace of the Father.   "His own Son" indicates the uniqueness of Jesus' relationship to the Father,[17] and the fact that the Father sent Him also is a clear declaration of Jesus' pre-existence.   The human body that Jesus entered when He became incarnate is here described (in the NASB margin) as "the likeness of the flesh of sin."[18]   His physical body was just like the body other men have, made of

---

[15] Besides what Paul here says the Law could not do, the New Testament elsewhere points out some other ways the Law was weak or imperfect.   It provided no perfect sacrifice for sin (Hebrews 9:22, 10:4). It could not fully reveal the sinfulness of sin (as it can now be seen through Calvary).   It did not provide a perfect exemplar for men to imitate (there were men, the tenor of whose lives were right, but there was no perfect exemplar in the Old Testament).

[16] The translators supplied the verb "did" from the context, since it is the opposite of "could not do."

[17] At Romans 1:3,4, the meaning of "Son," when used of Jesus, has been set forth.   The language Paul uses here in 8:3 nearly corresponds to the Johannine "only begotten" [*monogenēs*], cf. John 1:14,18; 3:16,18; 1 John 4:9.   Jesus was the only One of His kind there is.

[18] Each of the words in this expression (which occurs nowhere else in Scripture) has been the subject of debate.   (1) The word "likeness" [*homoiōma*] must not be understood as indicating any unreality in Christ's body.   That would be docetism, the idea that Christ was a phantom, without a real material body like other men have.   Against such a docetic Christology, John writes "every spirit that confesses that Jesus Christ has come *in the flesh* is from God" (1 John 4:2).   By using the word "likeness" here and at Philippians 2:7, Paul is not teaching Gnostic docetism.   On the contrary, elsewhere, Paul plainly affirms that Jesus was "born of the seed of David according to the flesh" (Romans 1:3, 9:5), and that He was "manifested in the flesh" (1 Timothy 3:16, ASV).   By using "likeness," Paul is saying the body Jesus lived in was just like the body all other human beings inhabit.   Paul uses "likeness" not to express semblance;

flesh, and capable of being tempted to sin through desires stirred up by the devil, yea, even capable of becoming the dominating power in His life, as it would have if Jesus had committed even one sin.

And *as an offering* for sin.   Here is the purpose for which the Son was sent by the Father to become incarnate.   The Son came to deal with sin.   The words in italics may be right, for the Greek word used here is the one regularly used in the LXX for "sin offering."[19] This expression "offering for sin" reminds us of Romans 3:25, where Christ is said to be a propitiation, a covering, an atonement for sins.

He condemned sin in the flesh.   Many and various suggestions have been advanced as to *how* God condemned sin in the flesh.[20]   The preceding context, which speaks of being "set free from the law of sin and death," would tend to cause us to believe that "condemned sin in the flesh" means that, for the man in Christ, sin has been deposed from its rule in the flesh.   When a man becomes a Christian, the old slavery to sin is broken.   Sin is unable, freely and at will, to exercise its old sway in the flesh any longer.   It must not be overlooked that "God" is the subject of this clause.   Our concept of the work of Christ is truncated unless we take into account the action of God the Father in those events which lie at the center of man's redemption and emancipation from "the law of sin and of death."

---

reality.   (2) The expression "sinful flesh" cannot mean that flesh is inherently sinful, for the sinlessness of Jesus is jealously guarded everywhere in the New Testament.   To interpret "flesh of sin" (NASB margin) to mean that Jesus inherited a sinful nature from His mother would be Ebionitism.   (It is instructive to observe how those writers who hold and defend the doctrine of original sin with its inherited sinful nature attempt to defend Jesus' sinlessness at the same time.   Some have even argued that the virgin birth was necessary to keep Jesus from inheriting any evil propensities, basing their doctrine on the idea that it is the father who passes these on, rather than the mother.)   (3) "Flesh of sin" reminds us that sin acts through the desires excited in the fleshly body, just as chapter 7 has demonstrated.   Jesus provided mankind with a perfect example of how to control those desires.   In Christ, His flesh did not lead to sin, not because it was better than, or different from, other men's flesh, but because it was kept in perfect subjection.   He controlled it so it could not lead Him to sin

[19] Sanday, *Romans*, p.88.   The Greek word is used for "sin offering" some 50 times in Leviticus alone. See also 2 Chronicles 29:24; Psalm 40:6; and Hebrews 10:6,8.   If we omit the words in italics, so that it reads simply "for sin," we are given a slightly different thought in this verse.   It is a sobering and thrilling thing to contemplate that God sent His Son, so that I could have help practicing self-control.   He sent Him to help me with my sin problem.   He sent Him "for sin."   If self-control was so important to God the Father, how important should it be to me?!?

[20] There is a partial truth in several of these comments men have offered, for each is related somehow to the context – either to "flesh," or "for sin," or "an offering for sin."   (1) Christ's days in the flesh revealed the sinfulness of sin in such a way that it was condemned as never before.   (2) Christ, by His own sinless life, condemned sin by way of contrast.   ("And ... for sin" in Romans 8:3 indicates that the action of condemning sin is more than by good example; it must be construed in redemptive terms.)   (3) Christ was victorious over the attempts of sin to dominate His life, and thus condemned sin in the flesh.   By sending Jesus in a body just like other men have, God proved that men do not have to sin just because they live in fleshly bodies.   (4) Christ destroyed the dominion of sin and death over the flesh.   (Cp. Romans 6:6-11 and 8:1.)   The death of Christ and His resurrection and glorification are involved in the devil's being dislodged from his usurped place of dominion on earth.   (Cp. John 12:31 and Colossians 2:15.)   (5) Because Christ took our human nature, and died under judgment due to our sin, it can be said that sin was condemned in the (Christ's) flesh.

8:4 – *in order that the requirement of the Law might be fulfilled in us, who do not walk according to the flesh, but according to the Spirit.*

In order that the requirement of the Law might be fulfilled in us. Here we are told the purpose God had in mind when He condemned sin in the flesh. He wanted to make it possible for men to live the kind of holy life which the Law all along had revealed as being pleasing to God.[21]

Paul has already written much on the temporary nature of the Law of Moses, how it was nailed to the cross, and how it is no longer a binding code of statutes for those in Christ; therefore, unless we suppose Paul is now contradicting what he wrote earlier in this very letter, this verse must not be explained in such a way as to imply that Christians must obey the Law of Moses. Furthermore, he did not write 'fulfilled *by* us' but "fulfilled *in* us." It is the human spirit, alive because of righteousness (verse 10), aided by the indwelling Holy Spirit, that produces the holy living the Law aimed for, but which it could not achieve because it was "weak ... through the flesh" (verse 3).

Who do not walk according to the flesh. "Walk" is used metaphorically in both Testaments to indicate behavior, a course of life.[22] To behave "according to the flesh" would be to live as the devil prompts a man to do by exciting the desires of his body.[23] Such a course of behavior is open to a man after he becomes a Christian, but it is a foolish course to pursue; remember that 6:16 has warned that continuing to walk according to the flesh will result in slavery to sin again and also in death. There will be no holy life for the man who walks according to the flesh.

But according to the Spirit. Shall we capitalize the word "spirit"[24] or not? If we read "spirit," it refers to man's spirit (aided and prompted by the indwelling Holy Spirit, as verses 12-14 will show), and a good case can be made for this way of understanding the verse.

---

[21] The word translated "requirement" is *dikaiōma*, a word that has been used before in Romans, and with several different meanings. See 1:32, 5:16, and 5:18. It is doubtful that the connotation "the sentence a judge passes" is the idea here at 8:4, as it was at 1:32 and 5:16. The KJV here reads "the *righteousness* of the Law" and in so doing, the translators have given the word *dikaiōma* the same meaning here in 8:4 that it had at 5:18, i.e., right conduct. We are following the KJV's lead when we talk about holy living in our comments.

[22] Psalm 1:1,2; 2 Corinthians 10:2, 12:18; Galatians 2:14; Ephesians 2:2.

[23] This is but one of many verses in the New Testament which plainly indicate Christians still will have temptations to face and master, even after their old slavery to sin has been broken. The note of encouragement found in this chapter is that the *hopeless* wishing, the *wretchedness* resulting from the constant defeat of his better self because of the operation of "the sin" in the flesh that was man's lot before conversion, is all a thing of the past. Temptations to be faced? Yes. But hopelessness and defeat? Not any longer for the man in Christ.

[24] See footnote #9, above. Sometimes it makes a great difference whether you capitalize or not. Other times, you come out about the same place. This is one of the verses where you come out about the same place. Even if we read "Spirit," it is implied that the human spirit is no longer dead or dormant or still enslaved, but is alive again and able to respond to the guidance of the divine Spirit.

"Flesh" and "spirit" are here the "outer" and "inner man" of the Christian, and stand opposed to each other as the two great principles of action, which decide life to be good or bad, acceptable or not with God. To walk according to the flesh is to be carried away by its tendency to sin; to walk according to the spirit is to be obedient to its constant wish to do right.[25]

On the other hand, most modern English versions capitalize the word, perhaps because the context goes on to speak much of the Holy Spirit's work in the life of the Christian. The Christian thus has a choice to make between the two powers that would direct his life – whether sin through the flesh, or the Spirit through the inward man. It is by the indwelling and direction of the Holy Spirit that the goal intended by the "requirement of the Law" is fulfilled (or approached) by (in) the believer.[26] Christian holiness is not so much a matter of painstakingly trying to conform to a long list of external laws such as were contained in the Law of Moses, but of cooperating with and taking advantage of the help offered by the Holy Spirit.

8:5 – *For those who are according to the flesh set their minds on the things of the flesh, but those who are according to the Spirit, the things of the Spirit.*

For. "For" introduces a detailed explanation (verses 5-8) of what has just been said about walking according to the flesh and walking according to the Spirit.

Those who are according to the flesh set their minds on the things of the flesh. "According to the flesh" is the same thing as "walk according to the flesh" in verse 4. But who are intended by the word "those" – are they non-Christians or Christians? As has been earlier concluded, this commentator believes chapter 8 speaks of sanctification, and therefore deals with what it is possible for the Christian to do.[27] The Christian can still walk after the flesh (though not without penalty, of course), or he can walk after the Spirit. The choice is up to him. The Christian's behavior will reflect what he fixes his attention on, what he sets his heart on.[28] "The things of the flesh" here do not include *all* the hungers

---

[25] Lard, *Romans*, p.252. We would phrase the last sentence a bit differently, since the language "its tendency to sin" could be misunderstood to mean inherent evil propensities that still remain after conversion, a doctrine that has been rejected in notes on chapter 7. The general substance of Lard's comment, however, shows how what has been said in chapter 7 can be used to help decide on "spirit" rather than "Spirit" at this place. Campbell and Goodspeed are two translators who have made it small "s" here, a reference to the human spirit.

[26] This is not saying that a state of sinless perfection will be reached in this life. As we read on in Romans, we shall learn more about this goal, and also how the Spirit leads and aids the believer toward this goal.

[27] If these verses deal with the topic of sanctification – and that is what fulfilling the Law's requirement spoken of in verse 4 appears to mean – rather than justification, then comments similar to Wiersbe's would be incorrect. Wiersbe writes, "Paul is not describing two kinds of Christians, one carnal and one spiritual. He is contrasting the saved and the unsaved." *Be Right*, p.89.

[28] The verb *phroneō*, translated "set the mind on," means "to think, to feel, to direct one's mind to a thing, to seek or strive for, to side with." Thayer, *Lexicon*, p.658. Compare its use in Matthew 16:25; Romans 14:6 ("observes," "regardeth [ASV]"); and Colossians 3:2.

and appetites of the fleshly body, for many of these are lawful and it is therefore right to gratify them.[29]   In this context, the phrase then must signify only those desires and appetites which have been excited by the devil, and which, if gratified, would lead to sin. This passage, we believe, shows that even in the Christian, there remains the problem of practicing self-control over the fleshly body – the body which the devil still has the ability to influence by stirring up its desires.   Though no longer a slave to the body, the Christian is in danger of succumbing to these temptations; if he does succumb, he has not fulfilled the conditions involved in the human side of redemption.   The key to his behavior, then, is what the Christian *wills* to do.   If he sets his mind on what the Holy Spirit wants him to do, he can control his body; but if he sets his mind on what the devil wants him to do, he will find sin beginning to conquer and to lord it over him again.

But those that are according to the Spirit, the things of the Spirit.   The last half of this clause lacks a verb.   We would supply "set their minds on" from the previous clause, so that the last part of verse 5 reads, 'those that are according to the spirit[30] set their minds on the things of the Spirit.'   God's indwelling Spirit is able to plant thoughts in the mind, just as is the devil.   The Christian must be careful whose promptings he pays attention to, for his holiness or lack of it depends on where his affections are placed.   By exciting the desires of his body, the devil would lead the Christian away from God.   By prompting and helping him to control the desires of the body, the Holy Spirit would lead the Christian closer to God.   This last part of verse 5, paraphrased in the light of the comments above, says, 'the man who would live as his inner man (his regenerated spirit) wishes him to, will carefully pay attention to the promptings and leadings of the indwelling Holy Spirit.'

8:6 – For the mind set on the flesh is death, but the mind set on the Spirit is life and peace,

For the mind set on the flesh is death.   The connection of verse 6 to the preceding is disputed, especially by those who take both *pneumas* in verse 5 as a reference to the Holy Spirit.[31]   If the comments on verse 5 were correct, then this verse gives a reason why the

---

[29] It is clear that Paul is using "flesh" as was explained in 7:5.   Paul does not have in mind the man who has worked for hours, and who is in need of food and rest – that when he sits down to eat, or lies down to rest, that he is 'minding the things of the flesh' and cannot be pleasing to God while he eats and rests.   "Paul enumerates the works of the flesh: 'Fornication, uncleanness, lasciviousness, idolatry, sorcery, enmities, strife, jealousies, wraths, factions, divisions, parties, envyings, drunkenness, revellings, and such like' (Galatians 5:19-21).   As indicated by 'and such like,' there are many similar evil dispositions, vices, and vanity which destroy the spiritual life."   Lipscomb and Shepherd, *Romans*, p.145.

[30] Again, the commentaries and versions are divided on whether or not to capitalize "spirit" the first time it appears in this clause.   This commentator inclines to the view that it is a reference to the human spirit that has been regenerated, and therefore the "s" should be lower case.   This best continues the parallelism and contrast with the first part of verse 5:   in each part of the comparison, the first member ("according to the flesh" and "according to the spirit") is something that is part of the man himself (i.e., his "outer man" and his "inner man"), while the second member of the comparison in each case speaks of an influence from outside of the man.

[31] Some make verse 6 to be an explanation of "He condemned sin in the flesh" in verse 3.   Others connect verse 6 to verse 4b, and thus it explains how the "requirement of the Law" comes to be fulfilled.

Christian listens to and follows the leading of his Holy Spirit-energized spirit. The reason is that the Christian has his ultimate destiny in view. "Mind" here is *phronēma*, with the suffix *-ma* putting emphasis on the result of the action of minding.[32] We might therefore render it, "the result of walking according to the flesh is death."[33] "Death" is probably the same "death" spoken of in 7:24. It would include both spiritual death in this life, and eternal death in the world to come. Why the "mind set on the flesh" results in "death" is explained in verses 7 and 8.

But the mind set on the Spirit is life and peace. Just as "mind set on the flesh" takes up the first half of verse 5 ("according to the flesh"), so this part of verse 6 takes up the second half of verse 5 ("according to the spirit").[34] Again, the result of minding the spirit is the thing emphasized. "Life" in this clause is the opposite of death in the previous one, and the explanation given in verses 9-11 shows that not only does it involve the spirit continuing to live, but there also is a resurrection body involved. "Peace" was explained at 5:1 as a holy calm breathed over the soul by the Holy Spirit pouring forth God's love on the heart. Peace includes "(1) the state of reconciliation with God, and (2) the sense of that reconciliation which diffuses a feeling of harmony and tranquility over the whole man."[35] "The more we mind the things of the spirit, the fuller, richer, and stronger will be our spiritual life, the sweeter and deeper our peace, and the more will uncertainty and fears be expelled."[36] How the "mind set on the spirit" results in "life and peace" is detailed in verses 9-11.

8:7 – *because the mind set on the flesh is hostile toward God; for it does not subject itself to the law of God, for it is not even able* **to do so;**

Because the mind set on the flesh is hostile toward God. Verses 7 and 8 are proof of 6a, that the result of minding the flesh is death. "The mind set on the flesh," as in verse 5, is the same as "walk[ing] according to the flesh," a behavior discussed in verse 4. "Mind" again is *phronēma*, and emphasizes a result of setting the mind on the flesh. 'Hostility to-

---

[32] The "mind" that does the minding is *phren*; the action of minding or thinking is *phronēsis*. As explained earlier in these comments, words ending in *-ma* place emphasis on the result of what the rest of the word speaks about.

[33] Whereas it takes but one sin to result in spiritual death when a man comes to the age of accountability, after a man's spirit has been regenerated, it takes *continual* sinning to bring about spiritual death again. See notes at Romans 8:13.

[34] Again, the problem of translating *pneuma* as "Spirit" or "spirit" must be addressed. Whichever way the word is rendered the first time it appears in verse 5, is how it likely should be understood here in verse 6. What Paul writes shortly, in verses 9-10, tends to support the conclusion that it should be "spirit" in this place.

[35] Sanday and Headlam, *Romans*, p.196. The emphasis in "peace" is not so much on the act of reconciliation, but the enjoyment of the condition that results after a man is reconciled.

[36] Lenski, *Romans*, p.506.

ward God' is what results from continual walking according to the flesh. In order for the believer[37] to continue to walk according to the flesh, he must develop a certain animosity, dislike, or hostile attitude toward God.[38] Otherwise, how could the believer refuse to acknowledge His claims?

For it does not subject itself to the law of God. This clause gives a reason why it is said that hostility to God is the result for the believer who sets his mind on the flesh. "It" is the mind that is set on the things of the flesh. The present tense verb "subject" says this failure to submit to God's law is a continuous thing. The verb is in the middle voice, and suggests that a voluntary submission would benefit the person submitting. The "mind" that constantly refuses voluntary submission to God must not want the benefit – indeed, there is hostility present after all! The "law of God" (the second edition of the NASB uses a lower case "l" here, and reads "law of God") is the same expression used at 7:22 and 7:25, and the phrase evidently continues the same idea about holy living that 8:4 denoted.

For it is not even able *to do so.* The full sense of this last clause is "the mind set on the flesh is not able to subject itself to God's law." The reason this is true is "no one can serve two masters." A man cannot serve the flesh and at the same time submit to God's law.[39]

8:8 – *and those who are in the flesh cannot please God.*

And those who are in the flesh cannot please God. Verse 8, beginning with "and," con-

---

[37] "A popular exposition of this passage deserves incidental remark. Many think the passage is speaking of justification, rather than sanctification. Those who do, speak of the 'mind of the flesh' being the innate corruption of human nature, resulting from the Fall, and removable only by a direct and powerful operation of the Holy Spirit. Previous to this operation of the Holy Spirit, man is held to be totally depraved, and as incapable of any act of acceptable obedience. Without the work of the Holy Spirit, he is lost; with it, he is regenerate and fitted for the Master's use." Lard, *Romans*, p.255.

[38] Christians who are continuing to sin may have no notion that they are exhibiting a hostile attitude toward God; in fact, many will profess to love Him. But God's testimony is that there must be a certain enmity or hostility toward Him if a man is to live according to the flesh. "This [attitude towards God] is the all-important matter. To that point Scripture in all its teaching leads. The Bible is not a book of moral philosophy. Everything hinges upon God's view of things and upon the condition of persons in His sight." Vine, *Romans*, p.115.

[39] Calvinistic interpreters have been accustomed to explain the "reason" why there is no submission in different terms than these comments. "Is not able" has been used to prove the doctrine of "total inability," and this total inability (thought to be inherent in human nature) is the reason a man cannot submit to God's law. For the sake of discussion, let us for the moment suppose the Calvinistic interpreters are right, and the verse is indeed talking about a man's state before conversion. Does it then prove the doctrine of total inability? If it did, it would be contradictory to 7:18b, where it has been clearly demonstrated that a man's "I" is *not* totally disabled. The "I" can see and delight in and wish to do the right! The "I" may be a slave to sin before conversion, but the doctrine of total inability (that it cannot even want to do right, let alone produce it) is surely not supported in Romans.

Once more, remember that our comments have followed the supposition that these verses speak *not* about the man's state before he becomes a Christian, but rather of the sanctification of the *Christian*. If this is correct, this passage neither teaches total inability, nor the need of a first work of grace before the man (minding the things of the flesh) can even want to do right.

tinues the thought of the first part of verse 7, and gives a second reason why those who are living "according to the flesh" will find that the result of such behavior is "death" (verse 6). First, appeal was made to the man's own hostility toward God. Now, appeal is made to God's attitude toward the man's behavior – He is not pleased! "In the flesh" is another way of saying what verse 4 did, where Paul wrote "walk according to the flesh." It means to live in accordance with the sinful desires that are stirred up (by the devil) in the fleshly body.[40] When a believer habitually decides to pursue the course of behavior the devil prompts, he is all the time sinning against God. That is the reason he cannot please God. God is never pleased when men sin, and even less pleased when ex-slaves of sin choose to serve their old master instead of their Redeemer.

8:9 – *However, you are not in the flesh but in the Spirit, if indeed the Spirit of God dwells in you. But if anyone does not have the Spirit of Christ, he does not belong to Him.*

However. Verses 7 and 8 explained verse 6a. Verses 9-11 will detail the thought of 6b.

You are not in the flesh. Paul is writing to Roman Christians who were living in flesh and blood bodies, so it will hardly do to take "not in the flesh" literally. When he says they were "not in the flesh," he is saying that the Roman Christians are not habitually allowing their bodies (after being excited by the devil) to control them; they were not habitually sinning under pressure of the influences of their fleshly bodies.

But in the Spirit. As we did in verse 6b, it is best to translate it "spirit" (small "s").[41] Paul is saying the Christians at Rome were controlling their bodies, doing what the inward man (their "spirit") prompted them to do, rather than what the "flesh" prompted them to do. As "in the flesh" was another way of saying "walk according to the flesh," so "in the spirit" is another way of saying "walk according to the spirit."

If indeed the Spirit of God dwells in you. The preposition "if indeed" expresses slight doubt.[42] In all charity, Paul assumes that all his Roman readers are walking according to the spirit, but he does not want to be their judge. They are to judge themselves, and Paul

---

[40] In light of 1 Thessalonians 4:1 and Galatians 2:20, where people living in flesh and blood bodies did "please God," it seems evident that "flesh" is used in the same sense it has been for several verses now, namely, how it is a place where the devil ("the sin") does his work, and which results in behavior displeasing to God, if submitted to.

[41] There are some difficulties to be faced if *pneuma* (the first time it occurs in verse 9) is taken as a reference to the Holy Spirit. (1) It would almost amount to tautology to say that a man is governed by the Holy Spirit provided the Holy Spirit dwells in him – yet this is what the verse would say, if *pneuma* in the first part of the verse means "Spirit" rather than "spirit." (2) To make the first *pneuma* mean "Spirit" could lead to the doctrine that the Holy Spirit *forces* the Christian to live the holy life, which is, of course, not true. The idea that justification results in an infused righteousness, which programs a man automatically to live a holy life, has already been shown to be an incorrect interpretation of the doctrine of justification.

[42] *Eiper*, the word used here, may be thus distinguished from *eige*. *Eiper* may be translated "provided that" and expresses slight doubt, while *eige* expresses rather an assurance in the sense of "if indeed." See Thayer, *Lexicon*, p.172, under *ei*, III.13.

gives them the criterion by which they may easily determine the matter. Are they walking as the indwelling Holy Spirit prompts? From whom are they getting their directions? Both in this clause and in the next, we have two different names for the Holy Spirit ("Spirit of God" and "Spirit of Christ"). He is called the "Spirit of God" because He proceeds from God. The New Testament often speaks of the bodies of Christians as being a dwelling place of the Spirit.[43] "Dwells" here probably means more than just living there; in this context dwelling involves the Spirit's influence, guidance, direction, or prompting. The heart (the spirit, the inner man) hears the Spirit's promptings, and when it moves in accordance to that prompting, then the behavior that results is such as will please God. One way in which the Holy Spirit "helps the Christian is by strengthening his spirit, Ephesians 3:16. The Christian's being successfully under control of his inward man is conditional – the condition being that the Holy Spirit shall dwell in him and help him."[44]

But if anyone does not have the Spirit of Christ, he does not belong to Him. 'You do have the Holy Spirit dwelling in you, if you have been converted,' is the idea. The only people who do not have the Holy Spirit indwelling, to help and aid them to live pleasing to God, are those who have never become Christians. Here is another of the many passages in the Bible that imply the pluralistic unity of the Godhead, for the Holy Spirit is both the Spirit of God and the Spirit of Christ.[45] The nearest antecedent to "Him" is Christ, and the doctrine would be that all who belong to Christ are also recipients of the gift of the Holy Spirit whom Christ Himself sends to dwell in them.[46] Shortly, in verse 12, Paul will draw the conclusion toward which he is building – there is no real reason why the Christian should live according to the flesh, not when you consider that his spirit is alive and that he has the Holy Spirit to help.

---

[43] Acts 2:38 and Ephesians 1:13 suggest that this indwelling begins when a believer is immersed into Christ. 1 Corinthians 6:19; 2 Corinthians 6:16; and Ephesians 2:22 speak of a man's body as being a "temple" in which a Deity dwells. Galatians 4:6 tells how the "Spirit" was sent into the "hearts" of believers.

[44] Lard, *Romans*, p.257.

[45] "Spirit of Christ," as indicated earlier, is but another name for the Holy Spirit. And if "Spirit of God" (earlier in verse 9) meant that the Holy Spirit proceeds from God, then "Spirit of Christ" means that the Holy Spirit also proceeds from Christ. Compare 1 Peter 1:11 and John 15:26. These passages served as the basis of the *Filioque* clause in the Western versions of the Nicean Creed.

[46] Once more, the question of whether the passage deals with justification or sanctification must be addressed. This last clause of verse 9 has been used by those who suppose Paul is contrasting the unregenerate and the regenerate life in order to substantiate their supposition. They would explain that "walk[ing] according to the flesh" is here identified as being something done by the man who does not have the Spirit of Christ, the man who does not belong to Christ. This commentator wonders whether such an explanation results from dealing with the text Paul wrote, or whether it results from an attempt to make Paul match dogmatic theology. Most Calvinistic writers hold the doctrine of the unconditional eternal security of the believer. This passage has been affirming that men who live according to the flesh will die. But if the believer can never be lost, then, of course, this passage cannot be talking of believers. It would have to be interpreted of the unregenerate, or the doctrine of unconditional eternal security would be shown to be unscriptural, and would have to be abandoned. More will be said about the doctrine of eternal security in Special Study #7 at the close of comments on chapter 8.

8:10 – *And if Christ is in you, though the body is dead because of sin, yet the spirit is alive because of righteousness.*

And if Christ is in you. Verse 10 is the middle member of this three-verse explanation of verse 6b, about how the "mind set on the spirit results in life and peace." Earlier in chapter 8, Paul used "in the flesh" as an abbreviation for "walking according to the flesh." Now he substitutes another abbreviation, "Christ," for the phrase "Spirit of Christ" used in the previous verse.[47] The thing being talked about is the indwelling of the Holy Spirit, through whose help the flesh can be controlled by the Christian.

Though the body is dead because of sin. Different interpretations have been offered for this phrase. (1) One suggestion is that the "body is dead in respect to sin," that is, that sin has no more power to excite evil desires in the fleshly body.[48] (2) Another suggestion is that it means the physical body is a drawback to the development of the spiritual life.[49] (3) The generally accepted interpretation is that even though the Holy Spirit indwells it, the physical body is still subject to the physical death that came to the whole race as the result of Adam's sin (Romans 5:12-21).[50] The body is "dead" in the sense that it is still mortal, subject to death.[51]

Yet the spirit is alive because of righteousness. "Spirit" here is not the Holy Spirit,[52]

---

[47] Perhaps also in Ephesians 3:16,17, "Christ" is substituted for the "Spirit of Christ," where Paul writes, "that He would grant you ... to be strengthened with power by His Spirit in the inner man, that Christ may dwell in your hearts through faith." It will be observed that Paul uses the designations "Spirit of God," "Spirit of Christ," "Spirit" (verse 4), and "Christ," for the Holy Spirit, in this passage, and the expressions are interchangeable.

[48] This interpretation has in its favor the fact that the words "dead" and "sin" are given meanings they have had in the immediately preceding context. Against it is the fact that it would be very strange to make *dia hamartian* mean anything but "because of sin." Nor would such an interpretation match in a favorable manner with the words "mortal body" in verse 11.

[49] Against this interpretation is the fact that it strains the word "dead." Nor is it easy to find the Bible teaching that the mere possession of a human body is, *ipso facto*, a hindrance to holy living.

[50] In technical language, the interpretation of this phrase rests on the answer to the question, What is the apodosis that goes with the 'if-clause'? (1) It seems best to take the middle clause of verse 10 as a subordinate clause, and make the last part of verse 10 the apodosis of this conditional sentence, just as the RSV, NEB, and NASB do. (2) If the middle clause is part of the conclusion to the if-clause, then one of the first two interpretations offered in the verse is likely correct. (3) If the middle clause is a subordinate clause, then the third of the suggested interpretations is likely the right one. Notice that the RSV, NEB, and NASB all make the middle clause subordinate by the use of "though" or "although" to introduce it.

[51] The reason we take it to be "mortality" (physical death, rather than spiritual death resulting from trespasses and sins) is because of the context in verse 11, which not only speaks of "mortal bodies" but also introduces that idea that resurrection (by the Spirit's operation) will remove even the physical limitation that Christians now experience.

[52] Chrysostom, Calvin, Hendriksen, and others suppose the reference *is* to the Holy Spirit, but even those versions that have been wont to capitalize "Spirit" in this chapter treat "spirit" here as a reference to the inner man. See ASV, NASB, RSV.

but the human spirit.[53]   ("If Christ is in you" in the previous phrase is the reference to the Holy Spirit in this verse.)   "Righteousness" is God's way of saving men, a concept explained in the earlier chapters of Romans.   Involved is Calvary, and the imputation or reckoning of "righteousness" to the one who is an obedient believer in Jesus.   "Because of righteousness" gives the reason why the "spirit" can lead to 'life.'[54]   Apart from God's way of saving men, there would be no 'life.'[55]   When Paul says the "spirit is life," he is saying that living as your better self directs will lead to life sanctification here, and glorification ultimately.   Understood in this way, this verse thus implies that it is at the time God initially imputes righteousness to the believer that a man's "spirit" becomes alive from the dead, and is thereafter able to control the body it lives in, by the help of the indwelling Spirit.   Paraphrasing the verse, Paul's meaning is this – 'But if the Holy Spirit dwells in you and is allowed to help you, even though the body is still subject to physical death because of the penalty to the race that resulted from Adam's sin, the inner man can lead the justified believer to live a holy life.   This ultimately leads to glorification (verse 11-13).'

8:11 – *But if the Spirit of Him who raised Jesus from the dead dwells in you, He who raised Christ Jesus from the dead will also give life to your mortal bodies through His Spirit who indwells you.*

But if the Spirit of Him who raised Jesus from the dead dwells in you.   Rather than "but," it would be better to translate *de* as 'moreover,' since verse 11 continues the thought begun in verse 9.   Not only will there be spiritual life (sanctification) resulting from the work of the Holy Spirit as He aids a justified man's spirit, but there is also a resurrection body to look forward to.   "The Spirit of Him who raised Jesus from the dead" has been called "the longest title of the Holy Spirit in the New Testament."[56]   The condition "if Christ is in you" (verse 10) is now repeated, but with a slight change of emphasis in order to highlight another consequence to believers of having the Spirit of God indwelling them.   "Him who raised Jesus from the dead" is God the Father,[57] and since there is a unity and harmony among the members of the Godhead, the Holy Spirit, too (this title implies), is in-

---

[53] The word "spirit" stands in a contrast to "body" in the first part of this verse, and therefore we would expect a reference to the inner man, the "spirit."

[54] Literally, the verse reads "the spirit is *life*."   Since we have opted for sanctification as the topic of chapter 8, "life" has reference to holy living after one becomes a Christian.   (Those who find justification to be the topic of chapter 8 explain "life" to mean "eternal life," and it is not unusual to find those interpreters writing about how this principle of life is inalienable, or never again can be lost.)

[55] It is true that apart from God's way of saving man, the spirit (which dies when a man commits his first sin, 7:9) would never be alive again.   And it is true that when a man is immersed, he rises to walk in newness of life (chapter 6).   So when we comment on "the spirit is alive" or "the spirit is life," we are combining both ideas – that the spirit has been regenerated, and that (because it is alive again) it can now direct and lead to holy living.

[56] Vine, *Romans*, p.117.

[57] For the subject of the resurrection of Jesus, and for the fact that each member of the Godhead was involved in that resurrection, see comments at Romans 1:4; 4:24,25; 6:4,9; and 7:4.

volved in the work of raising bodies from the dead.[58]   He was active in the resurrection of Jesus (1 Timothy 3:16; Hebrews 9:14); He will be active in the resurrection of believers, too.

He who raised Christ Jesus from the dead will also give life to your mortal bodies. "Mortal bodies"[59] is one expression which helps lead to the conclusion that "give life to" is a reference to the future resurrection of the bodies from the grave.   "Raised Christ Jesus from the dead" also prepares our minds for a discussion of the future resurrection.   Shortly, verse 23 will also speak about that same resurrection body.[60]   Furthermore, the New Testament does seem to distinguish between the resurrection of the righteous and the resurrection of the wicked, as though one precedes the other.   In the Bible, one reads of "resurrection *of* the dead," and "resurrection *from* the dead."   The suggestion that "resurrection *from* (*ek*) the dead" is that of the righteous being raised first, leaving the wicked behind, may be correct.   The "resurrection *of* the dead" is the resurrection that leaves none behind.[61]   It will be a resurrection like that of Jesus, a resurrection "from the dead," when the mortal bodies of those in whom the Holy Spirit has lived are quickened by God.

Through His Spirit who indwells you.   The marginal note "because of" shows the variant reading found in the manuscripts at this place.[62]   If we read "because of," the verse says

---

[58] As in other places, so here, "dead" is a plural adjective, and we must supply the noun "bodies."   This is the same grammatical approach Paul employs in 1 Corinthians 15.   Also implied is that when Jesus was raised "from among (*ek*) dead (bodies)," that there were others that were left behind.

[59] "He does not say 'dead bodies,' but 'mortal bodies;' because in the resurrection our bodies shall not only cease to be 'dead' (verse 10), i.e., subject to a necessity of death, but also shall cease to be 'mortal,' i.e., capable of dying, such as was Adam's body before his sin.   After the resurrection, our bodies shall be altogether immortal."   Gifford, *Romans*, p. 151.

[60] Those writers who affirm "justification" is the topic of chapter 8, and who believe that a second work of grace helps a man to overcome his sinful propensities after he has become a Christian, will find that doctrine taught in this verse.   "Life to your mortal bodies" is explained to mean that "the body, the corrupt, carnal body, so long under the dominion of sin, is made alive and recovered to the service of God." Barnes, *Romans*, p.184.   Barnes never tries to explain how this idea is to be harmonized with the comments written on 7:24,25, which would say that the dominion of sin is never mastered in this life. Instead of treating the passage as related to justification, if we explain the passage from the standpoint of sanctification, all the difficulty is gone.   "For the word *zoōpoieō* ['give life to'] see note at 4:17.   It does not denote reinvigoration.   The reference is not to the impartation of some special energy of life and power to our bodies in the present state, but to the effect upon them of the shout of the Lord at the time of the Rapture (1 Thessalonians 4:17; Philippians 3:20,21; 1 Corinthians 15:52,53).   What is mortal will then be 'swallowed up of life'."   Vine, *Romans*, p.117.

[61] A brief word about the eschatology of this commentator is probably in order here.   He holds to what might be styled a modified amillennial view.   The traditional amillennial view usually has but one general resurrection, followed by one general judgment, followed by eternity in heaven or hell.   This commentator would propose that the Bible does teach two resurrections, with the resurrection of the righteous preceding the resurrection of the wicked, though without 1000 years between the two, as modern premillennialists would teach.   See the booklet, *Let's Study Prophecy* (Moberly, MO: published by the author, 1982).

[62] The difference is slight between the genitive *dia pneumatos* ("through His Spirit") and the accusative *dia pneuma* ("because of His Spirit").   The readings are about equally supported, with Sinaiticus, Alexandrinus, and Ephraemi, having the genitive, and Vaticanus and Beza having the accusative.

that God will raise our bodies in the future resurrection because our body has been a place where the Holy Spirit lived.[63]   If we read "through," the passage teaches that the Holy Spirit will have an active part in the actual raising of the mortal bodies in that future resurrection.   Just as the Holy Spirit was active in the resurrection of Jesus, so the Spirit is to be active in the resurrection of the saints.   A study of Scripture as a whole will show that the Father, Son, and Holy Spirit are all active – in creation, in the new birth, and in the future resurrection of the body.   The persons of the Godhead were co-active in the acts of redemption, and will be co-active also in the consummation.

8:12 – *So then, brethren, we are under obligation, not to the flesh, to live according to the flesh –*

So then, brethren.   Verses 12 to 17 are an inference drawn from the preceding verses.[64] "Before carrying out the thought suggested by these last two verses (which will be done in verses 18ff), the apostle now draws a conclusion (verse 12ff) from what has been said so far, so as to press the more the obligation of a spiritual life in Christians."[65]   Paul will unfold the operation of the indwelling Spirit as He aids the inner man to control the body, and he will tell about the testimony given by the indwelling Spirit regarding the believers' adoptions as sons of God.

We are under obligation.   This word has been explained at 1:14.   This is a matter of solemn obligation, and the following verses will give reasons why Christians have this obligation.   There is a difference between a "duty" and an "obligation."   A duty is imposed by an outside authority; an obligation is a debt imposed from within.

Not to the flesh, to live according to the flesh – .   The dash indicates there is a broken sentence in the original.   Half of the verse has been suppressed, but the context easily suggests what we should mentally supply: "We are under obligation, not to the flesh ...

---

[63] "It cannot be thought that God would leave in the grave the body in which His own Spirit has dwelt." Sanday, *Romans*, p.91.   If this reading is correct, then the raising of the bodies of the believer to be with God in heaven is conditioned on whether the Holy Spirit has been living in them.   Compare Acts 2:38 and Ephesians 1:13, 14.   The indwelling of the Holy Spirit is a down payment, "a pledge" that God will give the resurrection body (2 Corinthians 5:5).   God does not save the whole man at baptism.   The inward man is freed, and is made alive, but the redemption of the body must wait its future resurrection on the Resurrection Morning.   Of course, it should also be remembered that the Spirit can be grieved (Ephesians 4:30; 1 Thessalonians 5:19). If a man quits Christ after being baptized, if he continues to offer his members to sin as instruments of unrighteousness, it may very well be that the Holy Spirit will cease to live in his body; if this happens, there is no promise that that man will be included in the resurrection of the righteous, even though the Spirit did once live in his body.

[64] Perhaps the inference is based on the whole paragraph (8:1-11).   If so, Paul is saying, 'Since God has condemned sin in the flesh, and since a continued behavior pattern based on the mind of the flesh is hostile to God, and since we have the help of the indwelling Spirit to overcome sin in our lives, we are debtors to live as the Spirit leads.'   Perhaps the inference is based only on verse 11, and the idea would be, 'Since a resurrection body is pledged to those whose bodies are temples of the Spirit, we are debtors to live as the Spirit leads.'

[65] Barmby, *Romans*, p.208.

but we are under obligation to the spirit, to live according to the Spirit of God." Christians do not owe the devil a thing! There is no valid obligation for serving the devil. Actually, by suppressing the positive half of the Christian's obligation, the reader is caused to pause and think, and this makes the positive obligation (that we *are* under obligation to live according to the Spirit) all the more emphatic. What it means to live "according to the flesh" has been explained at 8:4; likewise, what it means to live "according to the Spirit" was also explained in 8:4.

> We are of the spirit, led by the Spirit; we are sons, children, heirs, co-heirs with Christ, to be glorified with him. Can we, then, live as though we were none of these, as though we were still entirely led by the flesh, and going forward to nothing but death?[66]

How contradictory for Christians, having been delivered from the law of sin and death, and being indwelt by the Holy Spirit, to yield obedience and service to that from which they have been emancipated.

8:13 – *for if you are living according to the flesh, you must die; but if by the Spirit you are putting to death the deeds of the body, you will live.*

For if you are living according to the flesh, you must die. Again, Paul repeats what he said in 6:16, about how serving sin results in death. He repeats the penalty for voluntarily serving sin, in order to enforce the idea that the believer has no obligation to live according to the flesh whatsoever. "Living" is a present tense verb, and pictures a continual living, a habitual living. Such a habit pattern of living "according to the flesh," that is, living as the devil prompts a man to do through the desires of the flesh, will end in death. "Die" is placed in contrast to "live" at the end of the verse, and so indicates that the death in Paul's mind is not merely that of the body. It is spiritual death that ultimately ends up in eternal separation from God. Either the Christian kills sin (the temptations to sin), or sin will kill him. Concerning the word translated "must," Paul did not write *dei* (the Greek word meaning "it is necessary") but he wrote *mellete* (the Greek word meaning "you are about to"). The word implies imminence, for no one knows but that he will die spiritually, perhaps when he commits the very next sin, if it is one of a long series in a habit pattern of sin.[67] A Christian who supposes he can live according to the flesh has death hanging over him like the sword of Damocles.[68]

---

[66] Lenski, *Romans*, p.515.

[67] "Christians lose spiritual life in proportion as they indulge the appetites and desires of the flesh that are contrary to the teachings of our Lord. If, for example, a Christian indulges in anger, or malice, or any of these passions that our Lord condemns, he is not only violating the word of the Lord, but he is destroying the spiritual man, and weakening it every day, and giving the flesh greater power over the spirit; and so the flesh will dominate and control the whole man, while the spiritual man languishes and dies." Lipscomb and Shepherd, *Romans*, p.149.

[68] "We should not fail to note the clashing terms in this verse – 'If you *live*, you are about to *die*.' Paul intends to reverse these terms in the next sentence, and thus emphasize the clash. Men ever think they are really living when they give way to the flesh, whereas in reality they are heading straight for eternal

But if by the Spirit. Does the word *pneuma* here denote the Holy Spirit or man's spirit? The translators have capitalized the word, and this seems to be the better way of explaining this verse. If we make it a reference to the human spirit, then we have a difficult time explaining the word "you" in the next clauses – for previously the "I" and the "inner man" have been used interchangeably. Furthermore, the next verse seems to require a reference to the Holy Spirit in this verse. Thus "by the Spirit" means by the aid of the Holy Spirit who dwells in you. The verse is saying that by the aid of the indwelling Spirit the Christian can practice self-control.

You are putting to death the deeds of the body. Similar expressions of man's responsibility for self-control are found in 1 Corinthians 9:27 and Colossians 3:5-10.[69] The word translated "putting to death" was used in Romans 7:4 of something God did on the believer's behalf; but here, the believer's own activity is emphasized. Christians who are freed from condemnation to slavery to sin must nevertheless make it their business all their days to master the fleshly body's desires when these have been excited by the devil. "The believer's once-for-all death to the Law and to sin does not free him from the necessity of mortifying sin in his members; it makes it *necessary* and *possible* for him to do so."[70] It is not necessary to explain the "deeds of the body"[71] after all that has been said by Paul about how "the sin" stirs up the desires of a man's body in an effort to get him to use his body to commit acts of sin. The devil tempts, and the human spirit says "No!" to the sinful thing the devil wants the believer to do. This refusal is the "putting to death the deeds of the body," and this refusal is aided by (prompted by?) the indwelling Spirit.

You will live. Whereas "you must die" meant that death would come, or it was about to happen, "you will live" means that the life the believer already has will continue. The Christian has life abiding in him, ever since he rose to walk in newness of life (6:4,8,11). If the Christian continually puts to death the deeds of the body, he will continue to live.

8:14 – *For all who are being led by the Spirit of God, these are sons of God.*

For. "For" introduces a reason for something just said, or a further explanation of something just said. Is "led by the Spirit" another way of saying "by the Spirit" in the previous verse? Does "sons of God" take up and expand the "you will live" of the previous verse?

---

death. Paul states this fact as being most certain. He states it as a motive, as one that must impel every Christian away from yielding to the flesh. The motive is most powerful. Who wants presently to end in death? We have become Christians for the very purpose of escaping this death. How, then, shall we live so as after all to run into this death?" Lenski, *Romans*, p.517.

[69] The Colossians passage speaks of conversion (verse 9), "laid aside the old self with its evil practices," and of a continual growth in Christlikeness (verse 10), which is the result of "consider[ing] the members of [the] earthly body as dead to [various sins]" (verse 5).

[70] Murray, *Romans*, p.294.

[71] There is a manuscript variation here, some reading "flesh." But the better supported reading is "body." The latter is supported by Sinaiticus, Vaticanus, Ephraemi, Alexandrinus, and other major uncials.

All who are being led by the Spirit of God. "Spirit of God" is one of the names for the Holy Spirit.[72] "Led by the Spirit" is one of a number of almost synonymous expressions in this chapter. In verse 4, Paul has spoken of believers who "walk according to the Spirit." In verse 5, he has said they "set their minds on ... the things of the Spirit." In verse 9, he has said the "Spirit dwells in" them. In verse 13, he introduced the concept about "putting to death the deeds of the body by the Spirit." Now we have this phrase about being "led" by the Spirit. "Are being led" is present tense, led all along, led continually.[73] The verb is passive; the Spirit does the leading, though without impinging on the freedom of the will, as verse 13 shows. This passage then has demonstrated how the human spirit (alive because of righteousness, verse 10), prompted and led by the indwelling Spirit, conquers the lusts and desires that are stirred up by the devil, thus helping the believer to live the Christian life.[74]

These are sons of God. To be led by the Spirit implies a special relationship to God – that of sonship. Further, the expression seems to be related to "you will live" in verse 13. Because the original puts emphasis on "these," as though it meant "these, and these alone," it seems to be saying that the man who continually puts to death the deeds of the body is the only man who continues that special relationship. A man becomes a "son of God" (in

---

[72] See Romans 8:9.

[73] The passage is expounding one of the blessings available to Christians. This leading is something available to those who are "sons of God." But just how does the Spirit lead? In earlier notes, we have suggested that the Spirit has the ability to plant thoughts in the mind (see verse 5), and that 'prompted by' might be a good way of explaining how the Spirit aids the human spirit to put to death the deeds of the flesh (verse 13). Is it possible that "the way of escape" that God makes available when a man is tempted (1 Corinthians 10:13) is none other than the Holy Spirit's "leading"? The Christian regularly is aware that "the way of escape" (to avoid the sin the devil has suggested) almost instantly pops into his consciousness right after the tempting thought does; and before he sins, he must deliberately choose either to sin, or choose to take the way of escape. Lard, *Romans*, p.264, has explained that this leading is both internal (in the man's heart), and external (somehow related to the Scriptures), as he wrote, "This leading is both internal and external. To whatever extent the Holy Spirit by his indwelling strengthens the human spirit to enable it to control the flesh, to that extent the leading is internal; to whatever extent the motives of the 'law of the Spirit' [Romans 8:2: note Lard's explanation of this phrase differs from that offered in explanation in this commentary], when brought to bear on the heart in the New Testament, enlighten and strengthen, and so enable the human spirit to keep the body in subjection, to that extent the leading is external." This commentator would modify Lard's explanation just slightly. It could be said that not only does the Holy Spirit have something to do with "the way of escape" coming into focus in a man's consciousness, but also He may help the man to recall some of God's explicit prohibitions on the particular temptation the devil is offering, so that the believer has a Scripture to quote to the devil, and thus can come off victorious from the temptation, just as Jesus did, Who also quoted Scripture to the devil as a part of His resistance to the temptations (Matthew 4:1-11).

[74] Care should be exercised that "led by the Spirit" is explained in the same terms as was "*by the Spirit* putting to death the deeds of the body." It seems rather evident that in this context, the language "led by the Spirit" should not be used to substantiate a doctrine that the Holy Spirit leads individual Christians like He led the apostles when they spoke by inspiration. The word for "lead" in the case of the believer is *agō* (cp. Romans 2:4 and Galatians 5:18), while the word used of God's special mouthpieces' being "led" is *pherō* (see 2 Peter 1:21). Nor is it likely the leading of the Spirit as He helps a believer practice self-control is to be made synonymous with His leading as, for example, when He directed the steps of the apostles away from Asia and Bithynia and toward Philippi on the Second Missionary Journey (Acts 16:6-10).

the special sense this context requires[75]) by being adopted into the family of God at the time he was justified; he continues that relationship by putting to death the deeds of the body through the leading of the Holy Spirit. What a motivation for living, not according to the flesh, but according to the Spirit. None but the latter can expect to continue to be a son of God.

8:15 – *For you have not received a spirit of slavery leading to fear again, but you have received a spirit of adoption as sons by which we cry out, "Abba! Father!"*

For. In verse 15, Paul makes an appeal to the consciousness of Christians, to confirm the statement he has just made that they were "sons of God" (verse 14). Then, before pursuing the discussion to the next step, that sonship implies heirship (verse 17), Paul will pause in verse 16 to show how the indwelling Spirit confirms the Christian's awareness that he is a child of God.

You have not received a spirit of slavery leading to fear again. The aorist tense verb "received" (both in this clause and the next) looks back to the time when they became Christians. *Pneuma* has already been used with two different meanings in Romans 8 – sometimes it speaks of the Holy Spirit, and sometimes it has referred to the inner man, the human spirit. In light of this fact, some try to explain verse 15 as though it were a reference to the Holy Spirit;[76] others try to make it a reference to the human spirit. Neither gives a very satisfactory interpretation. Therefore, it is quite common in the commentaries on verse 15, to find that *pneuma* is given a third meaning in chapter 8, namely, 'a frame of mind, feeling, attitude, temper of mind.' A "spirit of slavery" would then be an attitude or spirit such as is found in men who are slaves. In this context, the "spirit" of defeat and wretchedness that chapter 7 delineated, when the man was still a slave to sin,[77] would be an illustration of the feeling the word denotes. It is the attitude of mind a man has before he has been liberated by the gospel, a disposition accompanied by fear. "Again" tells us the feeling was present before (and this was true even for the man under the Law). Before a man is converted, when his inner man would prefer to live differently, his slavery to sin

---

[75] There is a sense in which it can be said that all men are by creation the "sons of God," as in Acts 17:28,29. But this whole context has been talking about the new creation. "This idea of 'sonship' is also worked out in the Epistle to the Galatians (3:26-4:7). It is the Christian transformation of the old theocratic idea. The Israelite had stood in this special relation to God; now it is open to *spiritual* Israel, of whatever race they may be." Sanday, *Romans*, p.91. Verse 14 has shown that not every man is a "son of God" but only as many as have the indwelling Holy Spirit to lead them.

[76] So interpreted, this verse gives two more names by which the Holy Spirit is designated in the Bible, namely "Spirit of adoption" and "Spirit of slavery." The weakness of this interpretation is that it is difficult to see what the meaning of "Spirit of slavery" might be. Even were we to suppose that "Spirit of slavery" is somehow related to the Spirit's work (say His inspiration of the Old Testament writers) in the Old Testament age, when the presence of the Law gave sin an opportunity to spring to action (7:8), and the action often resulted in bondage for those under the Law, it is still difficult to see how the Spirit Himself could be thought of as being responsible for the bondage (slavery), and thus be styled "Spirit of slavery."

[77] The slavery (or bondage) that everywhere in this epistle is contrasted to the freedom enjoyed by the sons of God, is the bondage of sin (6:6,16,17,20; 7:25).

produces a dread of punishment and a feeling of fear of death and of the future.[78] This is no longer the case with those who have the spirit of adoption.

But you have received a spirit of adoption as sons. Though "spirit" is capitalized in the KJV, unless "spirit of bondage" is a reference to the Holy Spirit, it is doubtful that "spirit of adoption" is either, for the parallelism in the two expressions would lead us to understand that "spirit" in both probably refers to the same thing.[79] If "spirit of slavery" is a frame of mind characteristic of those who are slaves of sin, then "spirit of adoption" is a frame of mind characteristic of[80] those who have become God's adopted sons. "Adoption" speaks of the method by which men become "sons of God."[81] The figure of adoption is probably

---

[78] This "fear" is reflected in the pagan idea of retributive justice, as in Acts 28:4, and is specifically stated in Hebrews 2:15, where it talks about "fear of death" while a man is subject to bondage.

[79] The careful reader will have noticed that we have rejected all those comments which attempt to personify "spirit of bondage" (as though he were some kind of evil spirit) and "spirit of adoption." Augustine, for example, believed "spirit of bondage" was another name for the devil, because the devil leaves his followers in a state of bondage and slavery. However, the verb "received" is difficult to explain – when could it be said that the devil had been "received"? Augustine did have in his favor the fact that his proposed explanation did make "spirit" in both clauses refer to the same kind of "spirit." And Augustine could also point to Galatians 4:5,6, where the Holy Spirit and the idea of adoption as sons are closely related. Gifford, *Romans*, p.153, has a brief presentation of other attempts to personify the two expressions in Romans 8:15.

Other proposals have been set forward in an attempt to explain this difficult verse. (1) One proposal would disallow the argument that "spirit" must have the same sort of meaning in both phrases. The result is that "spirit of bondage" is thought to be a human disposition, but "Spirit of adoption" is thought to be a name for the Holy Spirit. (Most writers whose theology would lead them to believe man is wholly passive in salvation would urge that "sonship" is something the Holy Spirit produces, and therefore "Spirit of adoption" must be a reference to the Holy Spirit.) If there were some compelling *Biblical* reason for giving "spirit" a different meaning in the two phrases, there would be no hesitation on this commentator's part to do so; but he hardly would allow an *a priori* theological position to determine how Bible verses should be explained. (2) Another proposed explanation of the passage suggests the key phrase, "you have not received a spirit of slavery [bondage]," does not imply the actual existence of a "Spirit of slavery." Murray, for example, urges that the phrase "'Spirit of bondage' is negative and there is no reason why we should not interpret the thought to be, 'You did not receive the Holy Spirit as a Spirit of bondage but as the Spirit of adoption'." *Romans*, p.297. Cranfield, *Romans*, p.396, opts for Murray's interpretation, and appeals to 1 Corinthians 2:12 and 2 Timothy 1:7 as similar sentence forms. However, against this proposal is the position of the word "not" in the Greek: it negates the *verb* in Romans 8:15 and 2 Timothy 1:7, whereas it negates the *noun* in 1 Corinthians 2:12. If it negated the *noun* here in Romans, then Murray and Cranfield might be right in their proposed explanation.

[80] The Greek genitive case may be interpreted two ways in this place – it could be a subjective genitive (where the noun in the genitive case *produces* the action) or an objective genitive (where the noun in the genitive case *receives* the action). In our comments we have opted for the subjective genitive, but not a few commentators opt for the objective genitive, and so construe the expressions as though the "spirit" makes men slaves, or adopted sons, as the case may be. "'The Spirit of adoption' or sonship (*huiothesia*) is, in other words, the Spirit who makes believers sons of God and enables them to call God their Father." Bruce, *Romans*, p.165.

[81] "*Huiothesia* is, literally, 'son-placing' (from *huios*, 'a son,' and *tithēmi*, 'to place'), i.e., a place and state of a son, given to one to whom it does not belong by natural descent (see 9:4)." Vine, *Romans*, p.119. There is the possibility that Paul coined this word, found for the first time in ancient literature here in Romans and Galatians 4:5. After New Testament times, the writers tend to make "adoption" synonymous with baptism – that is the place or time when one becomes "adopted" into God's family. See Gifford, *Romans*, p. 152.

not taken from Jewish customs so much as from Roman customs, since the Law of Moses contained no provision for such a practice.[82]   Adoption was essentially a Roman practice, and was closely connected with the Roman ideas of family.   This is the idea Paul wants us to have come to mind when he speaks of the believer's adoption into the family of God.

> The term "adoption" may smack somewhat of artificiality in our ears, but in the first century AD an adopted son was a son deliberately chosen by his adoptive father to perpetuate his name and inherit his estate; he was no whit inferior in status to a son born in the ordinary course of nature, and might well enjoy the father's affection more fully and reproduce the father's character more worthily.[83]

So the "spirit of adoption" is the frame of mind, the attitude, the disposition felt by a man who has been adopted into the family of God.

By which we cry out, "Abba! Father!"   Whereas "fear" was the product of the frame of mind when still in bondage to sin, "loving trust" is the product of the frame of mind after a conversion has taken place.   This loving trust (as of a son toward his father), this intimate relationship, is reflected even in the words the son uses when he addresses the Father.   "By which" refers back to the "spirit of adoption,"[84] and it means that the cry "Abba! Father!" is something that results from the consciousness of having become one of God's adopted children.   "Father" is the language of a son, not a slave; indeed, among the Jews, slaves were forbidden to use the term "father" in addressing the head of the family.[85]   "Cry out" portrays a boy in distress, crying out for "daddy" to come help!   So, in prayer,[86] both public and private, the children of God, in loving trust, call on their Father to come provide protec-

---

[82] Hendriksen, *Romans*, p.259, argues that the Jews did indeed have adoption practices. He appeals to the case of Moses being "adopted" by Pharaoh's daughter (Exodus 2:10), to the case of Esther being brought up by Mordecai (Esther 2:7), and to certain expressions in the Old Testament where God promises faithful men that "He would be a Father to them, and they would be His sons and daughters," as evidence that the Jews did understand and practice "adoption," albeit, not in the formal or technical or legal sense the word came to have in the Greek and Roman worlds.

[83] Bruce, *Romans*, p.166.

[84] Instead of referring back, some translators and commentators make this phrase an introduction to verse 16, so that it reads, "When we cry, 'Abba! Father!' the Spirit Himself bears witness with our spirit that we are children of God."   This breaks the balance found in two parts of verse 15, leaving nothing to parallel "leading to fear again" in the second part.   Further, it tends to imply that the Spirit's testimony is dependent on man's initiative, and such an implication is probably fatal to this method of interpreting the passage.

[85] Vine, *Romans*, p.120.

[86] Not all writers would explain "cry out" as though it meant urgent prayer.   Cranfield, *Romans*, p.399 enumerates other proposed interpretations – such as "Spirit-inspired prayers (cf. 1 Corinthians 14:15)" or the "invocation" at public worship, or the publicly spoken prayer as contrasted with the whispered prayer prescribed by Jewish customs.

tion and help.   "Abba" is an Aramaic word, and denotes familiarity, much as the English word "daddy" does.   "Father" is a Greek word, and it seems to convey a little more formal relationship between child and father.   The idea of calling God "Father" when addressing Him in prayer was something not found among worshiping Jews or Gentiles until after Jesus introduced this method of calling on God.   In the Model Prayer, Jesus taught His disciples to pray, "Our *Father*...," but it was after Gethsemane, where Jesus used both words, "Abba! Father!" that the use of both in crying to God entered the practice of the early church.[87]   Before Jesus came, men had many concepts and ideas of God, but they did not call Him "Father."   Now that Jesus has come, and made it possible for men to be adopted into the family of God, how natural to call Him "Father!"   Lest we forget the point Paul is discussing (verse 12-17), we might ask these questions: Are we God's sons?   Do we address Him as Father?   We certainly, then, are not debtors to the flesh.

8:16 – *The Spirit Himself bears witness with our spirit that we are children of God,*

The Spirit Himself.   The very similar passage in Galatians 4:6 seems to be conclusive in favor of this being a reference to the Holy Spirit.   "Himself" is a better translation than the "itself" of the KJV, since the Holy Spirit is a person.[88]

Bears witness with our spirit.   The translation of the Greek here is disputed.   It may be "bears witness *with*" or it may be "bears witness *to*."   Both are possible translations of the Greek.   If we take the former, verse 16 says there are two witnesses (the Holy Spirit and our spirit), both of whom are bearing witness to the fact of our sonship.[89]   If we take the latter, verse 16 says that one witness, the Holy Spirit, keeps giving assurance to our inner man that we are God's child.[90]

---

[87] That Jesus actually used *both* words, even in Gethsemane, is questioned.   Mark, alone of the Gospel writers, tells us that Jesus cried "Abba!" when He was in Gethsemane (Mark 14:36).   (Did Mark learn this from Peter, who was but a stone's-throw away from Jesus, and could hear His outcries, Hebrews 5:7?)   Mark writes, "*Abba ho patēr*."   Whether Jesus cried "Abba! Father!" or whether *ho patēr* is simply Mark's translation of "Abba" for the sake of his readers, and then both the Aramaic and the Greek translation was picked up and used by the church in prayer, is not known for sure.   Did Jesus speak Aramaic regularly, so that even the Model Prayer would have begun with "Abba"?   Did He use two different words for "Father" as He prayed to His Father in Heaven?   (*Ho patēr* is in the nominative case, rather than the vocative [the usual case denoting direct address], but Blass, deBrunner, and Funk, *Greek Grammar of the New Testament and Other Early Christian Literature* (Chicago: University of Chicago Press, 1961), p.81, affirm that the nominative with the definite article was used instead of the vocative.)

[88] See the author's *New Testament History: Acts*, p.89,90, where the Spirit's attributes of personality are outlined.   The KJV rendering follows the Greek construction exactly, where the pronoun *auto* ["itself"] is neuter because it agrees grammatically with *pneuma* which is also a neuter word in the Greek.

[89] The KJV, ASV, NASB, NKJV, NEB, and JB are translations that have rendered it "with our spirit," and among recent writers, Hendriksen, *Romans*, p.260,261, defends it, by affirming, among other things, that the verb "bear witness with" is regularly used elsewhere in Romans of *two* witnesses testifying to the same thing.

[90] The Vulgate would translate it "to our spirit," and among recent writers, Cranfield, *Romans*, p.403, defends it, by reminding us that the knowledge that we are God's children is something that we cannot impart to ourselves, so our own "spirit" would hardly be presented as testifying to such a fact.   In reply, does not Cranfield miss the thrust of this whole context when he rules out a man's "spirit" as being a

Not only is the translation disputed, but the answer to the question 'How does the Spirit so witness?' is also disputed.[91]   The context may help us to decide this question.   In the context (see verse 14), the leading of the Spirit has been the topic; that is, the Spirit's prompting of the inner man to control the body he lives in.   Should we not, then, say that the Holy Spirit's help to live the Christian life is the way He bears witness with our spirits that we are children of God?[92]   Our "spirit," now that it is alive because of righteousness (verse 10), is also able to testify to the fact that a new birth has taken place (see the word "children" in the next phrase).   Our "spirit" knows whether it is alive or not.

That we are children of God.   This is what the Holy Spirit and our spirit both say – "We are children of God."   In verse 14, Paul wrote "sons," and the word reflects the fact that an adoption has taken place.   Now he uses the word "children," and the word reflects the fact that a "birth" has taken place.[93]   Probably no further contrast is intended (e.g., "children" implies immaturity, while "sons" implies responsible adulthood[94]); indeed, it seems plain

---

possible witness, especially in the light of the vast change from slavery (which was personally experienced by the spirit) to freedom in Christ?   The inner man (the spirit) knows whether it is slave or free.   It can testify to that fact.

[91] Once again, the relationship between verse 16 and verse 15 must be taken into account.   If verse 16 begins with "by which we cry 'Abba! Father'" [see footnote #84], then the Spirit would bear His witness when the Christian prays.   On the other hand, punctuated as the NASB does it, verse 16 is understood to be a confirmation of the fact that an "adoption" (verse 15) has indeed taken place, and God has become the "Father" (in a spiritual sense) to the believer.   Under this interpretation, the Spirit's witness could be either internally (as He helps the inner man to control the fleshly body), or externally (through the Scriptures).

[92] Probably we are *not* to think of a *miraculous testimony* by the Spirit to our spirits, no matter how we read the verse.   Nor would we limit the Spirit's testimony to the witness He bears through the Scriptures (the Written Word), though this has been a popular view among certain Christian Church and Church of Christ authors.   The reason we tend not to limit it to the Word is that the context has said nothing about the Written Word.   It will also be remembered that Romans 5:5 has spoken about a witness of the Holy Spirit in men's hearts.   Lard, long ago, questioned the popular Christian Church view in these words: "The passage is sometimes interpreted differently.   It is maintained that the Holy Spirit lays down the conditions of the new birth, and declares that upon compliance with them, we are children.   This, it is alleged, is the Spirit's testimony.   And, on the other hand, it is held that we know within ourselves whether we have or have not complied with these conditions.   This, it is said, is the testimony of our spirits.   Most of what is here said is certainly true, but to put such an explanation on Romans 8:16 is to misapply the passage." *Romans*, p.266.   Lard is correct, because Romans 8:16 is not dealing with *becoming* a Christian, but with the help the Holy Spirit gives to a man who is *already* a Christian.

[93] "*Teknon* [child] and *huios* [son] both point to parentage.   *Teknon*, however, emphasizes the idea of descent, giving prominence to the physical and outward aspects; while *huios* emphasizes the idea of relationship, and considers especially the inward, ethical, and legal aspects."   Berry, *Lexicon*, p.137. *Teknon* is related to the verb *tiktō*, "to beget," and so the word calls to mind the new birth (see John 3:1-8 and Titus 3:5).

[94] In Galatians 3:23-4:7, Paul does make a distinction between a period of infancy and a period of adulthood, but the words there translated "children" and "sons" are *nepioi* ("infants," not *tekna*, as in Romans 8:16) and *huioi*.

that "children" and "sons" are used interchangeably, save for the implied notion of how they came into this relationship with God. Christians are both "sons" and "children." Because of adoption and because of the new birth, the Christian is certainly *not* a debtor to live according to the flesh (see verse 12).

8:17 – *and if children, heirs also, heirs of God and fellow heirs with Christ, if indeed we suffer with* **Him** *in order that we may also be glorified with* **Him.**

And if children, heirs also. The thread of thought begun at verse 13 is now resumed. "You will live!" he wrote, and this living includes being a child of God, and that involves all the privileges that a child or a son enjoys. "One characteristic of the son is that he is his father's heir. So it is with the Christian. He, too, has an inheritance coming."[95]

Heirs of God. An "heir" is one who succeeds to an estate. God has, as it were, an estate, and Christians will inherit it. "Heirs of God" can involve nothing less than that the sons of God are heirs of the inheritance which God Himself has laid up for them. But it is difficult to exclude the richer and deeper thought that God Himself is the inheritance of His children (Psalm 73:25,26; Lamentations 3:24). All that the Father has belongs to the sons.

And fellow heirs with Christ. Conformable to Roman practice, where adopted sons were treated the same as natural sons, the Christian receives the same inheritance that Jesus does. Whatever inheritance awaits Jesus as the Son of God also awaits the adopted sons.[96] There is a majesty, a glorified body, a new heavens and a new earth, access to the Holy City, the New Jerusalem, to the tree of life and the water of life. How foolish it would be to so live now as to jeopardize the receiving of this inheritance. Yet that is exactly what Christians who walk according to the flesh are in danger of doing!

If indeed we suffer with *Him*. As in verse 9, "if indeed" implies slight doubt. Most believers will be called on to suffer with Christ. The doubt involves when the suffering may come, and of what sort it may be.[97] Still, such suffering is here given as a condition upon which the attainment of the inheritance by the children of God is contingent. "To suffer with Him" is probably another way of expressing the idea that these people suffer because they belong to Christ and remain in Christ – such remaining in Christ being the op-

---

[95] Sanday, *Romans*, p.92.

[96] "There are marked differences between the conditions attaching to this inheritance and those relating to an earthly inheritance. A natural inheritance is most frequently possessed upon the death of the father. The inheritance to be enjoyed by believers is to be bestowed by and shared with One who never dies. Again, under Jewish law, the eldest son received the largest share [a double portion], and daughters were excluded, unless there were no sons. Under Roman law sons, daughters and adopted children shared an inheritance equally. All believers will share Christ's inheritance. Moreover, the inheritance has been won for them by His death ...." Vine, *Romans*, p. 121.

[97] Different kinds of suffering, besides physical torture, would include mental anguish, ridicule, false accusations, hatred, and misrepresentation, among others.

posite of walking according to the flesh whereby relationship can be forfeited. If they would walk according to the flesh, then the world would not so act as to cause suffering for the Christians. By word and example, Jesus rebuked sin, and because of this, He was hated and persecuted.[98] When the Christian reproduces the life Jesus lived, the Christian is hated and persecuted for the same reason.[99]

In order that we may also be glorified with *Him*. In His high priestly prayer, Jesus prayed that the Father would glorify Him with the glory He ever had with the Father before the earth was created (John 17:5). When this prayer was answered in the affirmative, Jesus was glorified. He also prayed that those men who come to believe on Him through the words of the apostles might also be with Him in glory (John 17:24). This portion of Jesus' prayer yet awaits its complete affirmative answer at the consummation of the age. But it will be fulfilled, as the following verses in Romans 8 show. It is "in order that" (a purpose clause) we may be glorified that we share in suffering with Him. It is either God's purpose that suffering is the way to glory,[100] or it is the purpose the Christian has in mind when he suffers with Christ – namely, he would share in the coming glorification. Sharing in Christ's glory is an incentive to share in Christ's sufferings.[101] "Glorified with Him" brings us again to the subject of the future glory at the return of Christ that was introduced at verse 11.

8:18 – *For I consider that the sufferings of this present time are not worthy to be compared with the glory that is to be revealed to us.*

For. We now enter upon that part of chapter 8 where Paul shows that believers have a

---

[98] The sufferings of Jesus are presented from two different viewpoints in Scripture. (a) He was hated because He rebuked sin. See the plural "sufferings" in passages like Philippians 3:10 and Hebrews 2:10. John 15:18 and 15:20 speak of hatred and persecution. Hebrews 12:3 urges the readers to "consider Him who has endured such hostility of sinners against Himself." (b) Scripture also presents His sufferings as being a vicarious atonement for sins. See the word "suffer" in such passages as Luke 24:26,46; Acts 17:3; and Acts 26:23. Christians never can suffer as an atonement for their own sins or anyone else's; His alone was the sacrifice that resulted in forgiveness of sins. Nevertheless, even when this difference (some of His suffering was vicarious whereas the Christian's can never be) is taken into account, still it is true that there is this similarity between His suffering and that of the Christian. For Jesus, the road to glory involved suffering. Likewise, the road to glory for the man who is united with Christ involves suffering.

[99] There are sufferings that come upon the Christian just because he belongs to Christ. See John 15:18,19; 2 Corinthians 1:5, 4:10; Philippians 3:10; 1 Peter 4:13.

[100] Hodge notes that this is a good verse to point out the error of those theologies which suggest some of men's sufferings serve to satisfy the demands of God's justice. This verse would show that suffering, instead, prepares men to participate in glory. Suffering is a refining process through which men must pass. See Hebrews 12:4-11 and 1 Peter 4:1,2.

[101] In passing, it might be profitable to consider what Romans 8 has emphasized by way of answer to the question, "How can a man know he is saved?" (1) "Children" has reminded us of the necessity of the new birth. (2) There is the putting to death the deeds of the body, which results in continued "living." (3) There is the leading of the indwelling Holy Spirit. (4) There is a man's own consciousness, the "spirit of adoption." (5) There is the man's own "spirit," which is aware of what happened at the time of conversion. (6) There is joint-suffering with Christ. These are not all the answers that might be assembled, but these are sufficient to show that there is more to the knowledge of salvation than just a hunch or a feeling.

hope of glory which, coupled with the aid of the indwelling Spirit and God's overruling providence, is sufficient to sustain them through all sufferings. Paul just spoke of sufferings in verse 17. "For" introduces the first reason why the present sufferings should not discourage the believer.[102] Lenski connects verse 18ff with both the suffering and glory of verse 17.

> "For" = in order that you may understand the better what has just been said about our suffering together with Christ and our also being glorified together with him. All of this will become clearer when we view ourselves in the midst of the entire suffering creature world which longs for our glorification at the last day. Do not occupy your mind exclusively with the little suffering which you individually endure but see this vast creature world groaning, and we with it.[103]

The same writer also reminds his readers that this paragraph in Romans reflects Paul's worldview, and thus is a help to us who would have our own worldview match that of the Scriptures.

> [Paul] presents a worldview that is at once so lofty and so profound as to leave behind all non-scriptural conceptions. The whole creature world is made to depend on what God does with his children. Going back to the fall of Adam which plunged the creature world into vanity and corruption, the Christian hope is made nothing less than the fulfillment of the expectation of even this creature world [an expectation of being done with the vanity and corruption to which it was subjected]. In the midst of a groaning world we pray, but one far greater, the Spirit himself, makes our prayers what they should be. Far above this vast whole, so sadly deranged, is the hand that makes all things work together for good to us according to his eternal purpose, and that purpose will be realized for sure.[104]

I consider. The same word was used at 3:28 ("maintain"), and expresses a doctrine that Paul is asserting. It is more than just an opinion or supposition. It is a considered judgment expressed for the purpose of leading his readers to the same conclusion.

That the sufferings of this present time. The word "sufferings" (*pathēma*) speaks of

---

[102] Three reasons are given for the believer to be encouraged to patiently endure the sufferings of this present age. (1) His sufferings are just a part of the suffering experienced by all of creation, and these sufferings really point forward to glory (verses 18-25). (2) The Holy Spirit helps support us through our infirmities (verses 26,27). (3) God overrules the very trials that seem to hinder us, and makes all things to work together for our ultimate good (verses 28-30).

[103] Lenski, *Romans*, p.529.

[104] *Op. cit.*, p.528,529.

evil, afflictions, misfortunes, calamity, persecutions, sicknesses.[105]   Some attempt has been made to restrict these "sufferings" to the suffering with Christ that the previous verse introduced, but it seems better to think that "the sufferings of the present time" are not limited to just the ones suffered for the cause of Christ, but rather refer to sufferings in general.[106]   When a man is suffering with Christ, he knows the reason for the suffering; but when he is experiencing other suffering, he needs comfort and assurance, perhaps even more.   The "present time" is *chairos*, a season, a period marked by special features, and seems in this passage to extend to and end with Christ's second coming.

Are not worthy to be compared.   "Not worthy" means 'not of corresponding weight.' Weights were used on a balance scales.   Place all the sufferings a man experiences on one pan of the scale, and place the coming glory on the other pan, and there is no comparison. The sufferings, however many they may be, are of no weight in comparison with the glory to come; the sufferings do not even balance on the scale with the glory.   The pan with the glory in it plunges down so quickly it would seem there was nothing at all in the other pan.

> When sufferings and glory are held against (*pros*) each other, the sufferings amount to nothing, no matter how many and how severe they are.   When we are in the midst of sufferings we often give them too much consideration, fail to look at the coming glory, and lose our balance and proportion.   Here we have Paul's corrective.[107]

With the glory that is to be revealed to us.   The "glory" contemplated in this passage is that of the final resurrection, and of the age to come (heaven).   As noted in verse 17, Jesus has already begun to share in this glory, and the day is coming[108] when those who are in Christ will share it, too.[109]   This glory is of much more weight than any possible suffering,

---

[105] Thayer, *Lexicon*, p.478, and Barnes, *Romans*, p.188.

[106] The reasons men suffer include the following: (1) The whole creation was subjected to vanity and futility when Adam sinned (verse 20).   (2) Some suffering is due to our own sins and faults which necessitate chastisement (Hebrews 12:4-11).   (3) Some suffering is the result of the sins of others (murder, war, robbery, torture).   (4) Some suffering is for the glory of God (John 9:3).   (5) Some suffering is the temporal punishment for sin that by God's design automatically accompanies or results from the sin (Romans 1:27).   (6) If a man lives for Christ, there is going to be suffering (Romans 8:17).

[107] Lenski, *Romans*, p.530.

[108] "Is to be" represents the verb *mellō*, which does not express just simple futurity, but rather presents the idea that the "glory" is ever approaching, and is therefore ever nearer at hand.   (See comments on this same verb at Romans 8:13.)   The actual time of the revealing is the second advent of Christ (Colossians 3:3-4; 1 Peter 1:4-5), but the way Paul words the phrase here in 8:18, the time is not definitely stated when God's plans shall be consummated, neither is it stated in such a way that it is necessarily relegated to the distant future.   What is emphasized is that the glory *is* approaching.

[109] The Greek reads "revealed to usward."   The idea is that of Christ appearing in His glory, and bathing the redeemed in that glory.   Compare 1 John 3:2.   Believers are not mere spectators beholding this glory; they are participants in it, glorified by it.   (These notes have tended to understand *eis hēmas* as meaning "revealed *to* us" rather than "revealed *in* us."   "*In* us" would carry the idea that this glory would come to the believer, enter him, fill him, and then be seen by others [angels and other redeemed men] to be in him.)

and by this thought the Christian may be sustained.

> Their sufferings may seem great; but they should remember that they are nothing in comparison with future glory. They are nothing *in degree*, 2 Corinthians 4:17. They are nothing *in duration*. These sufferings are but for a moment; the glory shall be eternal. The sufferings will soon pass away; but the glory will never become dim or diminished – it will increase and expand forever and ever.[110]

The redeemed, as they are living in the midst of the glories of heaven,[111] will never look back on this life and be sorry that they suffered as they did, in order that they might gain the glories.

8:19 – *For the anxious longing of the creation waits eagerly for the revealing of the sons of God.*

For. Considerable difference of opinion exists as to the precise element of verse 18 with which verse 19 is to be connected. Some suppose verse 19's statement about the sympathetic longings of creation all around us is proof of the certainty that the glory is coming. Others suppose it is proof that the glory is still future. Still others suppose that it is the greatness of the glory that is being illustrated in verse 19. "The coming glory must be very great. Indeed, so surpassingly great is it that even creation is looking forward to it with intense eagerness."[112]

The anxious longing of the creation. The verb means "to look for something with outstretched head."[113] It denotes eager anticipation, leaning forward and stretching the neck to get a first glimpse of something coming into sight. The word "creation" was used in 1:20 of God's act of creating. Here, as it did in 1:25, "creation" refers to what was created. When it speaks of the product created, and when there is nothing in the context to limit it, the word encompasses all of creation, rational and non-rational, animate and inanimate. Since the context determines the meaning of the word, how comprehensively does the context here permit us to take the word? What things do verses 20-23 require us

---

[110] Barnes, *Romans*, p.188.

[111] Some have supposed that the "glory" here contemplated is to be received in the *intermediate state*. Hendriksen, in his book, *The Bible on the Life Hereafter* (Grand Rapids: Baker Book House, 1959), p.53-57, shows there is such glory to be received and enjoyed in the intermediate state, but not even he thinks that is the glory referred to in Romans 8:18. The "glory" is received in the *eternal state*. Verses 19 and 23 make it plain that Paul is referring to what will transpire at the time of the "revelation of the sons of God," when the redeemed receive their "redemption (glorious, resurrection) bodies."

[112] *Lard, Romans, p.268.*

[113] Thayer, *Lexicon*, p.62.

to exclude? Unfallen angels are excluded, because though they are created beings, they were not "subjected to futility" (verse 20), nor to "the slavery to corruption" (verse 21). Satan and the demons are not included because, though they are created beings, they cannot be regarded as longing for the "revealing of the sons of God" (verse 19), and they will not share in the "freedom of the glory of the children of God" (verse 21). Redeemed men are not included, because they are distinguished from the creation that is waiting with anxious longing in verses 19,21, and 22.[114] Lost men, the unredeemed, cannot be included, for these are not to be "set free from its slavery to corruption into the freedom of the glory of the children of God" (verse 21).[115] We thus have been led to the conclusion that *all of rational creation is excluded* by the terms of verses 20-23. What is left of God's creation is the whole world of nature, both animate and inanimate, what we would call *all nature*. Verse 20 will show that "creation" includes as much of the creation (other than man) as fell under the original curse on account of Adam's sin (Genesis 3:17,18).

Waits eagerly for the revealing of the sons of God. "Waits eagerly" could be rendered "waits patiently."[116] Creation is personified[117] as waiting it out, patiently and assiduously, until the expected thing actually arrives. The "revealing of the sons of God" is closely related to "the glory that is to be revealed to us" (verse 18). The redeemed from among all the nations of the earth are included in the designation "sons of God." Previous verses in Romans have identified Christians as being "sons" and "children" of God. When Jesus Christ Himself is revealed in all His glory (2 Thessalonians 1:7; 1 Peter 4:13), then the sons of God will have their "revealing" too. And when this moment in history comes, there will also be a renovation of the universe, resulting in a new heaven and a new earth.[118] This

---

[114] Barnes tries to make "creation" be a reference to redeemed men. He is right in saying that the same word is used of the "creation" to whom the gospel was to be preached (Mark 16:15; Colossians 1:23), and he is right when he says it is applied to the "new creation" (2 Corinthians 5:17; Galatians 6:15). But because the context requires it, "creation" and redeemed men are evidently two different groups here in Romans 8:19.

[115] Were the unbelieving included in "creation" that is waiting with anxious longing, then this passage would assert universal salvation. Since such a doctrine, so contrary to other clear passages, would be the result, the interpretation that leads to it must be rejected as a possible valid interpretation of this passage.

[116] The word is *apekdechomai*. Arndt-Gingrich, *Lexicon*, p.82, give the former meaning. Thayer, *Lexicon*, p.56, gives the latter meaning.

[117] It is undoubtedly personification here, when irrational creation (all nature) is spoken of as having "anxious longing" and 'eager waiting.' Such personification, where the inanimate is invested with life and feeling, is quite common in Scripture (Deuteronomy 4:34; Psalm 19:2, 68:17, 106:11; Isaiah 2:1, 14:8, 24:5-7; Habakkuk 2:11; Job 12:7-9). "Paul personifies the world, just as the prophets did when they make the floods and trees to clap their hands, Psalm 98:8 and Isaiah 55:12. It is one of the frequent figures of speech thus to make nature sympathize with man. When the Assyrians were overthrown, Jehovah said, 'I caused Lebanon to mourn for him, and all the trees of the field fainted for him,' Ezekiel 31:15. In the passage before us, human feelings are ascribed to inanimate things." Lipscomb and Shepherd, *Romans*, p.152.

[118] Revelation 21:1; 2 Peter 3:10-13; Isaiah 66:22.

will mean no less than a removal of the curse to which creation was subjected when Adam sinned.   No wonder "all nature" looks forward to the revealing of the sons of God.   There is something wonderful in store for nature, too, when that day comes.   Is it not implied that part of the "glory" which is to be revealed (verse 19) involves this renovated universe in which the redeemed shall dwell?

8:20 – *For the creation was subjected to futility, not of its own will, but because of Him who subjected it, in hope*

For the creation was subjected to futility.   This verse gives three reasons why the creation has a longing, an earnest expectation, and is waiting for the revelation of the sons of God: (1) it was subjected to futility, (2) it was subjected not of its own will, and (3) it was subjected in hope that it would be set free.   "Creation" is the same "creation" spoken of in verse 19, with the same limitations.   God is the One who did the subjecting,[119] as the phrases following will show.   The time when He did the subjecting of creation to futility was evidently the time of man's Fall (see Genesis 3:17-19 for the sentence that followed the Fall).[120]   All things were created "good" (Genesis 1:1 and 1:31), but when man sinned, creation was subjected[121] to futility and to slavery to corruption.   "Futility" translates *mataios*, which means "failing to reach or accomplish its intended purpose."[122]   The creation evidently was originally intended by God to serve man, to help the man fulfill the purpose for which God put him here in the midst of the creation.   But since it has been subjected to futility, the creation nowhere accomplishes the perfect service God originally intended.   Instead of perfect service, what one sees is "slavery to corruption" (verse 21) and groaning and travailing (verse 22, ASV), even a longing on creation's part for that renewal that will allow it to once again accomplish the purpose for which it was created.

> [When Adam sinned] the creature world was compelled by God to fail in its divinely intended purpose of glorifying God by serving man in a perfect way. [Since the Fall] man eats the fruits of the earth and dies; that was not what these fruits were made for.   Man uses the animals, and his life ends by perishing; that was not God's intent.   This "futility" has even entered the creatures themselves, so that they even help to hurt and to destroy man.[123]

---

[119] The verb "subjected" is taken as though it were passive, rather than middle voice.   Hodge (*in loc.*), taking it as a middle voice, accordingly ends up with this meaning for the verse: the creation submitted to the yoke of bondage in hope of ultimate deliverance.

[120] Romans 5:12 has already shown that "physical death" entered the world when Adam sinned.

[121] The aorist tense verb points to one act in the past.

[122] A study of synonyms helps us understand the meaning of "futility."   *Kenos*, "empty, vain," emphasizes the lack of contents, empty.   *Mataios*, "aimless, purposeless," emphasizes the lack of result. Berry, *Lexicon*, p.55.   *Mataios* is the opposite of *teleios*, "goal."

[123] Lenski, *Romans*, p.534.   An excellent source for further study on the topic of "futility" is James Orr, *The Christian View of God and the World* (Grand Rapids: Wm. B. Eerdmans Publishing Co., 1948), p.195.

Thus we have the first reason for the "anxious longing" and eager waiting that characterize creation. "If creation were perfect (*teleios*), and were fulfilling the noblest possible purpose, there would be no cause for looking forward hopefully to the future."[124]

Not of its own will. That is, it was not through its own fault, or because of its own will, that the creation was subjected to futility. This does not imply that "creation" possesses a "will," or that creation could have willed its own subjection to futility. This is simply a statement to emphasize the fact that it was wholly on account of the will of another (i.e., because God willed it) that the subjection took place.

But because of Him who subjected it. The creation was subjected to futility because God so arranged it and so ordered it in pursuance of His divine purpose and counsel.[125] This was not just an arbitrary act on God's part, an act devoid of any ultimate reason. When man sinned, God could have removed man from the creation, but that would have thwarted His purposes for creating this world. Nor could God allow the sinner to continue to live in a perfect creature world, nor could He allow the creature world to serve the fallen man as though nothing had happened. As part of His plan to lead man to repentance, God so worked it that the whole creation now reminds man of his sin and his guilt. The second reason the creation waits for the revelation of the sons of God, and its own future freedom from corruption, is that it was subjected to this corruption not of its own will.

In hope. These last two words of verse 20 are best connected with the main verb ("was subjected") and also with verse 21, so the thought is that God subjected creation to futility in hope that it would one day be set free from that futility. God's hope of setting creation free from its bondage to corruption was the condition God had in mind when He subjected creation to futility. Without this anticipation of future deliverance, God's act of subjecting might be viewed as a senseless act.[126] Further, the present state of futility, slavery to corruption, groaning and travail is not the final state of the creation. God's providence and government will see that His hopes for the future are realized.

8:21 – *that the creation itself also will be set free from its slavery to corruption into the freedom of the glory of the children of God.*

That the creation itself also will be set free from its slavery to corruption. If we read "that,"[127] then verse 21 gives the content of the hope God had in His heart – namely, that

---

[124] Sanday, *Romans*, p.93.

[125] That "God" is the "Him" who "subjected" the creation to futility is evident from the context. Men could not do it; the devil would not do such a thing "in hope ...." This passage also has some bearing on our ideas of the origin of evil in the world. The ancient Greek ideas (1) that matter is essentially evil while spirit is good, and (2) that a demiurge (i.e., some creature other than the supreme God) created the evil world, are precluded. What Paul says is in harmony with what the Scriptures teach elsewhere (e.g, Romans 5:12), that the beginning of evil in the world is connected with Adam's Fall.

[126] Verses 24 and 25 will present Paul's own explanation of how he is using the word "hope."

[127] Because of a manuscript variation, the KJV reads "because" rather than "that." Indeed, if we adopt

the creation would be delivered from its futility. "Corruption" would explain why creation fails to reach its intended purpose, for instead of serving men, creation not only at times proves futile because it is itself subject to decay and death, but creation also, at times, actively brings harm to men – think of floods, draught, hurricanes and tornados, earthquakes and tidal waves.[128] Note how in this verse (as well as in verse 23) "creation" is distinguished from the "children of God," a fact used in verse 19 to help define the word "creation" in this context. The creation then, with its futility and corruption, everywhere tells man that something is desperately wrong with our world, and helps produce a longing in the heart for something better. "Also" says that the creation, *as well as* the children of God, is going to be set free from slavery to corruption.[129] Just as creation shared in the curse because of Adam's sin, so creation will share in the deliverance from the curse, a deliverance that coincides with the second advent and the final resurrection. "Set free" implies that creation will continue to exist after the second advent, but in a new form – no longer subject to decay and death.

Into the freedom of the glory of the children of God. "Freedom" is the very opposite of "slavery." The old slavery to corruption and death will be removed. Who is intended by the expression "children of God" has been made clear in verses 14,16, and 19 above. The "glory" that these children of God are going to experience has been introduced already in verses 17 and 18. When Christ returns, the slavery to corruption which has hindered all nature from accomplishing the purpose for which God made her will be removed, and in its place will be the "freedom of ... glory."[130] God has anticipated (and promised) all along that the very creation which He subjected to futility and corruption will be set free

---

the reading *dioti* (following Sinaiticus, Beza, etc.) we would have to translate "because," and verse 21 would be giving a reason why there was hope in God's heart – namely, because creation was going to be set free from its bondage to corruption. *Hoti*, "that," is the reading found in Alexandrinus, Vaticanus, Ephraemi, etc., among the uncial manuscripts.

[128] "Corruption" (*phthora*) is used with several different meanings in the New Testament. Sometimes, as here, it means decay and death in the physical sphere (cp. 1 Corinthians 15:42,50 and 2 Peter 2:12). Other times, it means moral decay or degeneracy (2 Peter 1:4). In Galatians 6:8, the word *phthora* ("destruction," NASB) may have the connotation of loss of salvation, eternal misery. 2 Peter 2:12 is a verse in the New Testament where the word "corruption" seems to have an active meaning, rather than passive. The phrase "will in their destroying they will be destroyed" has regularly been interpreted to mean that the false teachers about whom Peter warns will be destroyed because of the destruction they themselves have caused. If we give a similar active meaning to the word here in Romans, the verse would say that creation often harms and destroys men, rather than serving them.

[129] "Slavery to corruption" literally reads "slavery of corruption," with the words "of corruption" being in the genitive case. Now this construction may be either a subjective or an objective genitive [see these genitive constructions explained in footnote #80 at Romans 8:15]. If subjective, then the corruption produces the slavery; if objective, then the slavery results in or consists of corruption. The NASB translators (correctly, it would seem) have opted for the latter meaning when they translated "slavery *to* corruption."

[130] To translate as does the KJV, which makes this construction a hendiadys – "a glorious freedom" – tends to obscure the beautiful contrast in the verse between "slavery to corruption" and "freedom of glory."

from this temporary condition, and that emancipation will occur at the same time the children of God are glorified (verse 18).[131]   Thus we have the third reason why creation is looking forward to the revelation of the sons of God; it is looking forward to its own renovation and to its unhindered opportunity to serve redeemed man.

8:22 – *For we know that the whole creation groans and suffers the pains of childbirth together until now.*

For we know.   Two elucidations of what has just been said in verse 20 are introduced by "for."   The first (verses 22,23) tells us more about the extent of the subjection to futility.   The second (verses 24,25) tells us more about the meaning of the word "hope."   We know?   How do Christians know about the groanings of the creature world?   By observation.[132]   Everywhere a man looks he can see that things are wrong.   All of nature shows it.

That the whole creation.   The "whole creation" denotes so much of all creation as has been cursed because of sin.   Whether the expression is broader than what was included in "creation" in verse 19 depends on how one reads verses 22 and 23 taken together.   If it reads "even redeemed men groan," then the "*whole* creation" that "groans" could include men (yes, even redeemed men) as well as nature.

Groans and suffers the pains of child birth together.   Both verbs are compound verbs with the preposition *sun* ("together") added.   Thus it says "groans together and suffers pains together."   Creation in all its parts unites in this groaning and travailing.   Here again we have personification.   Paul attributes "groans" and consciousness of "pains" to all of creation, nature as well as men.   Groaning, "to express grief by inarticulate or semi-articulate sounds,"[133] for something better is one evidence that creation has been subjected to futility.   Just like it is hard to understand "crooked" unless one knows what "straight" is, so unless the creation once enjoyed a better condition from which it has been deprived,

---

[131] It should be noted that Paul here teaches the renovation, not the annihilation, of the universe. Creation is pictured as continuing on, but in a new, free, glorious state.   "What Paul says in this section settles the question raised by other passages (e.g., Psalm 102:27; 2 Peter 3:10; Revelation 20:11; Isaiah 34:4; Job 14:12) as to whether the creature world will be annihilated or renovated.   The 'liberty of glory' cannot have a double meaning: blessed, eternal glory for the children of God, and annihilation for the creation ... It has been well said that not the *kosmos* [world] itself will pass away, but only the *schema tou kosmou touto* [form of this present world] (1 Corinthians 7:31).   The fire mentioned by Peter must be the fire of purification (2 Peter 3:10).   The 'new heaven and new earth' mentioned in Revelation 21:1 are not *neos*, 'newly created and never existing before,' but *kainos*, 'fresh, new in contrast with the old, different from what heaven and earth ... formerly were.' ... Many questions regarding details confront us in this connection.   Will the animals, plants, insects be raised to life?   What about the noxious creatures, the bacilli, for instance?   We have no answers.   [But do not let our lack of answers dim our hope!]   He who made Paradise for Adam will make heaven and earth new, far beyond Paradise, in the consummation. For 'the tabernacle of God is with men, and he will dwell with them' (Revelation 21:3) in a way that is beyond what Paradise [the Garden of Eden] ever knew."   Lenski, *Romans*, p.538,39.

[132] The Greek word "know" is *oida*.   See footnote #8 at Romans 2:2.

[133] See Thayer, *Lexicon*, p.347, where he explains the different synonyms of *klaiō*, "to weep audibly, to lament."

there would be no such groans as here are attributed to the creation. The whole creation, too, is suffering birth pains, and out of these a new condition of creation is to be born – elsewhere (2 Peter 3:13) called the "new heavens and new earth." One might view the pains simply as another evidence that creation has been subjected to futility, but when the pains are called "pains of child birth," Paul is reminding us of the "freedom of the glory" to come, to which the creation (under God's control) is about to give birth.

Until now. Ever since creation was subjected to vanity, up to the time when Paul wrote, creation has been unintermittent in its groaning and travail. In fact, the pains and groaning will not cease until the last trumpet sounds and Jesus returns in glory. Then God's anticipation of a new order will be realized.

8:23 – *And not only this, but also we ourselves, having the first fruits of the Spirit, even we ourselves groan within ourselves, waiting eagerly for* **our** *adoption as sons, the redemption of our body.*

And not only this. That is, not only does creation groan and suffer pain, but we Christians do, too. "We Christians, too, though we possess the first fruits of the Spirit, nevertheless inwardly groan, sighing for the time when our adoption as the sons of God will be complete, and even our mortal bodies will have been transfigured."[134] Let it be recalled that the principal thought of this whole paragraph is not the deliverance of creation, but the future glory of the children of God (verse 18), and that verses 22 and 23 are detailing the extent of the "futility" to which creation was temporarily subjected.

But also we ourselves. "We ourselves" evidently means "we Christians," and is not limited, as some have supposed, to "we apostles." Since the whole context has been dealing with Christians in general, it is proper to suggest that Paul's "we" here includes all the redeemed.

Having the first fruits of the Spirit. First, what is the correct translation of this phrase? The ASV ("*who* have the first-fruits...") and NASB treat it as though it were an attributive participle, further defining the subject, but this is not quite right.[135] Since the Greek construction is a circumstantial participle,[136] it would be better to give it a circumstantial

---

[134] Sanday, *Romans*, p.95.

[135] Attributive participles usually have an article before the participle, and the whole construction is translated (as the ASV does) as a relative clause. There is no article before "have" in the Greek. (Dana and Mantey, *Grammar*, p.224ff, designate "attributive participles" as "adjectival participles.")

[136] Dana and Mantey, *Grammar*, p.226ff, call this construction "The Adverbial Participle." Henry L. Crosby and John N. Schaeffer, *An Introduction to Greek* (New York: Allyn and Bacon, 1949), p.65, explain about circumstantial participles: "A participle, when used without an article and in agreement with a noun or pronoun expressed or implied, is called the *circumstantial participle*. It may denote *time* ["when"], *manner* ["by"], *means* ["by"], *cause* ["because"], *condition* ["if"], *concession* ["although"], or any *attendant circumstances* ["since"] of an action." (This writer has supplied in brackets the usual English word used to help translate the circumstantial participles.)

translation – so we suggest "*though* having the first fruits of the Spirit" as a good way to capture what the Greek says. The groaning of the children of God is thus introduced as something surprising. Even though we Christians have the indwelling Holy Spirit, yet we join in this groaning for the dawning of the day of glory.[137] "First fruits," used figuratively, signifies the assurance of more to come.[138] The indwelling Holy Spirit[139] is evidence that there is more to come for the Christian, and the verse will go on to identify the resurrected, glorified body as being one thing Paul has in mind when he writes of more to come (first fruits).[140]

---

[137] If we read this verse as do the KJV, ASV, and NASB, the idea of the phrase would be that the indwelling Holy Spirit is the one who arouses within the Christian the sense of longing for something better, which then expresses itself in groanings. But not only is this *not* an attributive participle, the words "even we" (with which the next phrase begins) are also against such an interpretation.

[138] "In acknowledgment of the fact that all the products of the land came from God, and in thankfulness for His goodness, Israelites brought as an offering to Him a portion of the fruits that ripened first, these being looked upon as an earnest of the coming harvest." Tenney, *Zondervan Pictorial Bible Dictionary*, p.284. Such offerings were brought at different times of the year. The first sheaf of barley harvested was brought and offered at Passover time, with the anticipation that the remainder of the crop would be harvested after the celebration of Passover; at Pentecost it was the coming wheat harvest that was similarly celebrated, etc. "The first fruits were that portion of the productions of the earth which were offered to God (Exodus 23:19, 34:26; Leviticus 23:10-12). From the nature of the case, they contained the evidence and assurance of the whole harvest as being secured. The idea, therefore, of an earnest or pledge is included in the phrase, as well as that of priority. This is the general, if not the constant, use of the word in the New Testament. Thus Christ is called 'the first fruits of them that sleep' (1 Corinthians 15:20), not merely because he rose first, but also because his resurrection was a pledge of the resurrection of those who 'are Christ's at His coming.' In the following passages – Romans 11:16, 16:5, 1 Corinthians 15:15, James 1:18 – both ideas [pledge and priority] may be, and possibly ought to be, retained." Lipscomb and Shepherd, *Romans*, p.154.

[139] Those who think "we ourselves" is limited to the apostles give a different explanation for what measure of the Holy Spirit is here called "first fruits." They also give a different explanation of the 'more' that is to come. (1) For example, the modern Pentecostal and Charismatic movements have opted for this explanation: the "more to come" is a second outpouring of the Holy Spirit, toward the close of the church age, sometimes called the "latter rain" in distinction from the "early rain" which the apostles received. In order to justify this interpretation, the genitive construction "of the Spirit" must be taken as a partitive genitive – that is, the Spirit Himself was partially given in the early days of the church; there is more Spirit to come in the latter days. While this is a possible translation of Greek, it hardly contributes to the argument Paul is making in this context. How would a preliminary giving of the Spirit to the apostles, to be followed by a complete outpouring later, help his argument that the whole creation is subjected to futility and therefore is groaning? (2) The suggestion that there will be a fuller outpouring of the Spirit in heaven (fuller than what was done for Paul and the other apostles) would better fit Paul's argument that there is a future glory coming. Still, this is taking the genitive as partitive, and it gives "we ourselves" a meaning not supported by the context. (3) Support for the Wesleyan second work of grace is sometimes found in this verse, as though it meant that when they are converted, believers possess a part of the Holy Spirit, and then at the time of the experience that follows conversion, they receive Him fully. It is difficult to see how this idea of more Holy Spirit to come in this life would contribute anything to the argument Paul is making, and is therefore to be rejected as a viable interpretation for this verse.

[140] This method of explaining the phrase treats "of the Spirit" as a genitive of apposition, that is, that the Holy Spirit is Himself the gift of first-fruits. Those who interpret as footnote #137 explains would object to this explanation on the following grounds: first fruits of the barley harvest meant more barley to come; first-fruits of the wheat harvest meant more wheat to be harvested later. Would not we expect "first-fruits of the Spirit" to mean more "Spirit" to come later? Answer – yes, unless the one using the word explains what he means, and this, it is affirmed, is exactly what Paul does in the latter part of verse 23.

Even we ourselves groan within ourselves. As it did in verse 22, "groan" here is the expression of the longing which feels that it is delayed in its course toward its object, or of the burden of the effort that must be expended constantly in order to contend with the obstacles in the way. At first sight, it is surprising that Christians too ("even we ourselves") are groaning – after all, they have been redeemed, freed from the old slavery to sin, and have the indwelling Spirit (a pledge of more to come) to help them live the Christian life. Why then should they be groaning? Well, they still live in a body that is dying physically. In this they share in common with all creation the futility that leads to the utterance of these groans. "Within ourselves" may mean that the groans of the Christian are not spoken out loud, but are felt and thought in the mind.[141]

Waiting eagerly for *our* adoption as sons. The word "adoption" is applied to two different events in the life of the redeemed. (1) In 8:15 it was applied to their entrance into the family of God at their conversion. (2) In this context it is applied to their entrance into the glorified family of God at the time of the resurrection from the dead and the putting on of glorified bodies. This use of "adoption," both for something that happens in this life and for something that relates to the next, is not unusual. "Salvation" and "redemption" are two other words that are used with the same double signification.[142] "Sons of God" (8:14) we have become, but there is a part of the wonderful blessing included in our adoption that is yet future, and is eagerly awaited.[143]

The redemption of our body. By this appositional statement, Paul explains how those who are already the adopted sons of God (8:15) can still be waiting for "adoption." Here is where we learn he is using the word "adoption" with a different meaning than before. Or perhaps it should be said that "adoption" includes more than the present privilege of sonship; it also includes the resurrection of the body. Christ died for the body as well as the soul, this passage reminds us. The salvation taught in the Bible is the salvation of the total personality, body and soul and spirit. Greek philosophy taught that salvation consisted of getting rid of the body, which was considered to be a sort of prison house for the soul. Christianity teaches that salvation involves the removal of the decaying and dying limitations of the fleshly body that have resulted from sin, by the transformation of the body into a glorified spiritual body similar to the glorified body of Christ. It is at the time of Christ's return that the resurrection takes place, and the sons of God will be clothed with an immortal and incorruptible body.[144] "Christians are waiting for the redemption of

---

[141] Lenski, *Romans*, p.540, is probably correct when he warns that no distinction between how creation groans and how Christians groan, as though one were audible, and the other inaudible, is intended by the use of the words "within ourselves" for the Christians.

[142] For the use of "salvation" and "redemption" with reference to what a man in Christ has in this life, see Romans 1:16, 3:24, 11:11; and Ephesians 1:7. For their usage with a future orientation as something that happens at the second advent of Christ, see Romans 13:11; Philippians 2:12; Luke 21:28; and Ephesians 1:14, 4:30.

[143] The verb "waiting eagerly" here in verse 23 is the same verb used (and commented on) in 8:19.

[144] Romans 8:11; 1 Corinthians 15:50-55; 2 Corinthians 5:2,3; Philippians 3:20,21. Those "sons of God" living on earth at the time of Christ's second coming will be transformed into their glorified bodies

their bodies from mortality and suffering. Their redemption in Christ will not be completed until their bodies are raised from the dead and glorified and are become like Jesus in His glorified and immortal body."[145]

8:24 – *For in hope we have been saved, but hope that is seen is not hope; for why does one also hope for what he sees?*

For in hope we have been saved. As indicated earlier, verses 24 and 25 explain how the word "hope" was used in verse 20. They also show that God's hope for all nature, that it will one day be set free from the present slavery to corruption, is a hope equally shared by Christians.[146]

Though enjoying the relationship indicated in the expression "adoption as sons,"[147] Christians are still waiting and hoping for the fulfillment of all that is involved in the expression "adoption." "Hope" in this clause seems to be used in its subjective sense. As explained in notes at 5:2, this "hope" is a complex emotion, made up of an earnest desire for and an expectation of obtaining something in the future. Here in verse 24, the thing anticipated is the redemption of the body.

---

without having to experience death; all whose bodies have died and been buried, will find themselves (their souls) accompanying Jesus as He returns (1 Thessalonians 4:14) and being clothed upon with glorified bodies that have been raised from the grave in this glorified condition.

[145] Lipscomb and Shepherd, *Romans*, p.155.

[146] Whose hope (God's, or the Christian's) is it that is spoken of in verse 24? Verse 24 might be explained exactly as verse 20 was, of God's hope (anticipation) of the future deliverance of creation from futility and bondage. Or if we allow verse 25 (which reads "if *we* hope") to influence our conclusion about verse 24, then verse 24 deals with a hope entertained in the heart of each redeemed person, a hope of what each person one day will possess.

Another difficult decision faces the translator and interpreter of this passage. How should this simple dative case (with no preposition in the Greek to guide us) be translated? It has been done three ways: (1) "by hope" (KJV), (2) "in hope" (NASB), and (3) "to hope" (so Moffatt, essentially). If we take the first option, then it seems to say that God saved us by hope – that is, not all that is involved in a man's salvation is made immediately available to him when God counts him as justified. God hopes or anticipates that more will be done for His child at the time Jesus returns. ("By hope" can hardly mean that hope is the instrument or condition by which a man is saved. The Theology of Hope as propounded by Jurgen Moltmann and others can find no corroboration here. See James DeForest Murch, "Today in Christendom," *Christian Standard*, 103/7 [February 17, 1968], p.105.) If we take the second option (as indeed the comments on the verse reflect), the verse seems to say that a condition, not of attainment, but of hope, is the normal condition the child of God experiences in this life. The salvation the believer now is in possession of is incomplete, and he still waits for his adoption (to wit, the resurrection of the body). If we take the third option, then "hope" is used (not as a subjective feeling, as it was in the first two options) in its objective sense, meaning "the thing hoped for." When a man is justified, salvation was not delivered to him complete in one package. On the contrary, instead of being lifted at once to glory, the hope of glory is something yet to be realized. ("Salvation" is viewed as something past, something present, and something future, in various Bible verses. See comments at Romans 1:16 and 5:9.)

[147] The verb tense in "we have been saved" indicates that the reference is back to the time of conversion. See 8:14-16 on "adoption" as "sons" and what "children of God" means.

But hope that is seen is not hope. Beginning with the word "but," the rest of verse 24 is Paul's definition of the word "hope" which he has been using. "Hope" can have both a subjective sense (a desire for, an expectation or anticipation of), and an objective meaning (the thing hoped for). Can we say that the first use of "hope" in this phrase takes it as objective, and the second as subjective? If so, the idea would be when the hoped-for thing is seen (i.e., possessed, being enjoyed) there is no longer any need for anticipation. What a man already possesses, he cannot be said to hope for. Christians are still living a life characterized by hope, hope for the glory, liberty, and resurrection of the body. The day is coming when for the faithful this expectation will become a realization.

For why does one also hope for what he sees? This clause is intended as confirmation of the preceding remark. If something hoped for is already possessed and being enjoyed, "hope" has ceased and fruition has set in.

8:25 – *But if we hope for what we do not see, with perseverance we wait eagerly for it.*

But if we hope for what we do not see. This verse seems to continue the confirmation begun in the preceding clause. Hoping for what we do not yet see – this is precisely what believers are now doing. Though freed from slavery to sin, they still live in a dying body. A glorified body is still something in the future, and therefore it is a proper object of hope.

With perseverance we wait eagerly for it. "Wait eagerly" is the same word used in verses 19 and 23. The "it" for which believers are waiting and hoping is the deliverance of all creation from the slavery to corruption, which for them also specifically includes the redemption of the body. Paul's use of the word "perseverance"[148] suggests that there will be adverse circumstances facing the believer until he possesses his resurrection body. "Perseverance" or "fortitude" is a fitting finale to the whole previous paragraph (verses 18-25). God will bring about the consummation of redemption (setting creation free and ushering in the new heavens and new earth) in His own good time, according to His plan. Patience (perseverance) on our part shows that we are in harmony with God's way of doing things. Impatience (lack of conquering the adverse circumstances) would show dissatisfaction with God's design. God has revealed that there is a liberty, a glory, and a resurrection body in the offing for each of His children. For the time being, the child of God may face adverse circumstances, but even these sufferings (being part of the creaturely suffering all around) are evidence of the coming glory, so he faces them with fortitude.

8:26 – *And in the same way the Spirit also helps our weakness; for we do not know how to pray as we should, but the Spirit Himself intercedes for* **us** *with groanings too deep for words;*

And in the same way. Here begins the second reason for courage and comfort in the face of adversity and suffering for the child of God.[149] Verses 26 and 27 will show how the

---

[148] See notes on *hupomonē* at footnote #17, at Romans 2:4.

[149] See the summary paragraph for chapter 8, on page 329, the introductory note at 8:18 on page 355,

Holy Spirit helps sustain[150] the believer through the sufferings which are the precondition of being glorified together with Christ.   Without His aid, the believer would find it difficult to persevere; more likely he would succumb.

The Spirit also helps our weakness.   "Spirit," as the following context evidently requires, is the Holy Spirit, so the word is capitalized in our versions.   "Weakness" is singular[151] in the better manuscripts, and speaks of the same condition the context has been dealing with, namely, the "futility" and "slavery to corruption" (verses 20,21).   The word translated "helps" is a compound form that means "to take hold of anything with another," "to give assistance by sharing a burden," or "to come to the aid of."[152]   Along with the believer, the indwelling Holy Spirit takes hold of the "weakness" in order to help the believer through it.   How the Holy Spirit does this assisting is explained in the rest of the verse.

For we do not know how to pray as we should.   In our creaturely state, with its pervasive futility, harm, and decay in and all around us, it is very difficult to analyze any given situation in order to pray intelligently about it.   There is a neuter article in the Greek that is often left untranslated; translated, the idea is '*the what* we shall pray as necessary, we know not.'   The Greek does not say we do not know how to pray; it says we do not know *for what* to pray; that is, the thing that is most needful in the given situation is hard to know. When a man is hurting because of his own dying body, or because in his case "nature" was not helpful but rather harmful, for what should he ask?   Our petitions,[153] though they may appear to be in accord with what the pressing needs of the moment dictate, may not be in harmony with God's ultimate wisdom, love, and grace.[154]   What we are asking from our limited perspective may not be in accord with what God wants to do in a person's life. Such a limitation results in hesitation to pray for the situation at all.   In this moment of hesitation and destitution on our part, the Holy Spirit comes to help.

---

and footnote #102 on page 355 where the thread of Paul's argument is outlined in bold strokes.

[150] "The same way" connects verses 26,27 to something in the previous context.   Some make this connection: the creation groans, Christians groan, and in the same way, the Holy Spirit groans.   Others think the connection is to the word "hope."   As "hope" (verse 24) sustains the believer and helps him to persevere, so also the Holy Spirit helps sustain the believer and helps him to persevere.

[151] It is the Byzantine text that has the plural, which then found its way into the KJV.

[152] See *sunantilambanomai* in Thayer, *Lexicon*, p.601, or Arndt-Gingrich, *Lexicon*, p.792.   It may help us to appreciate the meaning when we consider that "help" is the same word used in Luke 10:40, where Martha asks that Mary be bidden to help her, i.e., to take hold of the task with me.

[153] The word translated "pray" is *proseuchomai*, a word regularly used of requests addressed to God, while a synonym, *deomai*, may be used of requests addressed to man as well.   *Proseuchomai* carried with it the notion of worship, and is a more general word for "pray" than *deomai*, which tends to emphasize the particular benefit being requested.   Berry, *Synonyms*, p.20.

[154] "We want many things; and it may be that we actually pray for things which, were they granted, would prove our greatest misfortune, while we do not want, and never ask for, many things which would be our greatest blessings."   Lard, *Romans*, p.277.

But the Spirit Himself intercedes for *us*.   Because of our "weakness," we do not know for what to pray; but the Holy Spirit knows, and He offers the requests we would be offering if we but knew for what to ask.[155]   "Intercedes" is a present tense verb, indicating continuous, habitual action, whenever it is needed.   Jesus promised His apostles that, if He left, He would send them "another Helper" (John 14:16,17).   Here in Romans 8, we see that a promise of One to come alongside to help (*paraklētos*) is also true for all the children of God; the promise of a Comforter is not limited to just the apostles.[156] "Intercedes" (*huperentungchanō*) is a word that occurs nowhere else in the New Testament, though its root form (*entungchanō*) is used several times.   The root form means to 'turn to, approach, appeal, petition' someone on behalf of another.[157]   While the Christian knows not for what relief to plead for, the indwelling Holy Spirit offers up just the right plea to the Father.   How this plea is offered, and why it is just the right one, Paul goes on to explain in the following words.

With groanings too deep for words.   This tells how the Spirit offers just the right request to the Father.   "Groanings" is the same word used at 8:22,23; perhaps the word "yearning" or "sighing" would better catch the idea here, such being the feelings or wishes prompted by the Spirit in the heart of the believer.[158]   Extenuating situations come to all the children of God, and we know not what is the proper thing to pray for.   When because of "weakness" the Christian is without words, then the Holy Spirit has opportunity, and He prompts the Christian to 'yearn.'   "The Holy Spirit of God dwelling in us, knowing our wants [and needs] better than we, Himself pleads in our prayers, raising us to higher and holier desires

---

[155] "The Spirit Himself" is best taken as a reference to the Holy Spirit.   Some de-capitalize this, and make it speak of the human spirit.   Campbell (*Millennial Harbinger*, Vol.1 [February, 1830], p.111-116) did this, but it raises too many difficulties to make it a reference to the human spirit.   How can it be said that the human spirit makes intercession for us, as though the spirit's activities were wholly separate from the other activities of the man, which, after all, are directed by that same spirit?

[156] One of the regular rules for interpreting Scripture, taught to English speaking people as long ago as when Wycliffe made the first translation into English, is that one must pay attention to who is speaking, *to whom*, for what purpose, and for what age (Patriarchal, Mosaic, or Christian).   A careful interpreter, then, would apply to all Christians what Jesus spoke to the apostles, only if the Scripture elsewhere makes the same promise to all.   Apparently, Romans 8:26 does expand to all Christians the promise of "another Helper" which in John 14:16,17 was a promise to the apostles.

[157] Arndt-Gingrich, *Lexicon*, p.269.   A "lawyer" (an advocate, an intercessor) can do two things for his client: he can plead the case for his client, and he can prompt the client what to say.   Children of God have two divine intercessors.   Jesus is Himself their intercessor in the courts of heaven (Romans 8:34; Hebrews 7:25; 1 John 2:1), speaking on their behalf to the Father.   The Holy Spirit, here on earth, prompting the Christian's yearnings and sighings (Romans 8:26), is, as it were like a lawyer, prompting his client what to say.   When Jesus promised the Comforter, He used the words "another (another just like Me, another of the same kind) Comforter."   The intercessory activity of the Holy Spirit has often little been taken into account.   The glory of Christ's intercession in heaven should not be allowed to place the Spirit's intercessory work in eclipse.

[158] That the "groanings" (yearnings) are to be found in the heart of the believer is evident from the next phrase which tells how the Father searches the "hearts" and sees these sighs and groanings.   We are not to get the idea that the Spirit 'groans' without using the hearts of the believer in whom He dwells.   Yet be sure that the yearnings, sighs, groans are the product ultimately of "the Spirit Himself."

than we can express in words, which can only find utterance in sighings and aspirations."[159] Neither the Christian nor the Spirit actually says any words; all there is to this request is a "sigh" heaved from the heart.[160]

8:27 – and He who searches the hearts knows what the mind of the Spirit is, because He intercedes for the saints according to the will of God.

And He who searches the hearts.　"He who searches the hearts" is God.[161]　The hearts are the hearts of believers, the very hearts in which the groanings prompted by the Spirit have registered.　God, the omniscient, is able to read the thoughts and motives of the Christian.　Just because they are unutterable is no hindrance to His knowing what is being felt and thought.

Knows what the mind of the Spirit is.　"Mind" here is *phronēma*, and emphasizes the result of the Spirit's thinking.　The indwelling Spirit had the believer's best interests in mind when He prompted the believer to "yearn" in his heart.　God not only knows what the believer is thinking, He also knows (and approves[162]) what the Holy Spirit was thinking (before He did His prompting).　As God searches the hearts of men, he finds unuttered and unutterable groanings in the hearts of His children.　Though they are just sighs heaved toward heaven, there is a meaning in them that is perfectly discerned by God.

Because He intercedes for the saints according to *the will of* God.　In verse 26, Paul wrote "the Spirit Himself intercedes for *us*;" now he words it, "He intercedes for saints."[163] The intercessory work of the Spirit is something done for the people of God, and for them only.　The yearnings that the Spirit prompts, as He goes about His "intercessory work," are

---

[159]　Alford, *Romans*, p.397.

[160]　"Too deep for words" translates *alalētois*, "unutterable." Paul does not write *alalois* (lacking the facility of speech, dumb, silent); he uses a word which means "cannot be expressed by any words or language so as to convey the meaning." See Thayer, *Lexicon*, p.25. This fact has evidently escaped the modern charismatic movement, which appeals to this verse as proof that there is a prayer language use of 'tongues' (often designated as the language of angels), as well as an evangelistic use of 'tongues.' The indwelling Spirit does indeed intercede for the Christian, but it is not in any "words" at all, whether we think of tongues of men or tongues of angels!

[161]　This is a title repeatedly used of God the Father. Matthew 6:4; 1 Chronicles 28:9; Psalm 7:9, 139:1,23; Proverbs 17:3; Jeremiah 11:20, 17:10; Acts 1:24; 1 Corinthians 4:5; 1 Thessalonians 2:4; Hebrews 4:13; Revelation 2:23.

[162]　"Know" in this place may just have the meaning of "approves," since the next phrase begins with "because" (*hoti*). It is possible that *hoti* should be translated "that," in which case the next clause gives the content of the Spirit's mind (thinking). But if we translate *hoti* as "because," then the next clause gives the reason God "knows" (approves) what the Spirit is thinking (and prompting) – namely, because what He is requesting is in perfect harmony with the will of God.

[163]　The absence of any article in the Greek brings out the essential quality of those for whom the Spirit intercedes – it is for "*saints*" (*hagiōn*) that He so pleads. The word "intercedes" has been explained in comments on verse 26. On the meaning of the word "saint," see notes at Romans 1:7.

in strict accordance with God's will for our lives.[164]   This is the reason why the Spirit offers up just the right plea to the Father.   He is in harmony with the Father in all things.   In this way, Paul has explained how the Holy Spirit helps the believer through his temporary stay in this imperfect, "futile" world.

8:28 – *And we know that God causes all things to work together for good to those who love God, to those who are called according to* **His** *purpose.*

And we know.   Here begins the third ground of encouragement for the support of the Christian in the midst of sufferings that he is called upon to endure in this life.[165]   Verses 28-30 will teach about God's overruling providence that is operative for the benefit of His children.[166]   He can take the very things that seem to hinder His children, and make them work out together for the eternal good of His children.   Despite their temporary "weakness" (verse 26) and the "futility" and "slavery to corruption" (verses 20,21) in all of nature around them, Christians need not be dismayed or depressed.   According to God's eternal purpose, He has already determined they will be glorified.   He can then be counted on to do what is needed to help them reach that eternal goal.[167]   Christians "know"[168] this by revelation.   "The great fact, 'that for those loving God, He works all things together for good,' is a fact known only to Christians from the Word.   If it were not for this Word, they, too, would think that only too many things worked for their evil instead of their good."[169]

That God causes all things to work together for good.   "All things" should be limited to the things Paul himself enumerates in the context.   It certainly includes no less than the adversity and suffering that causes creation, Christians, and even the Holy Spirit to "groan," about which the preceding context has said much.   But how much more of the context may we include?   May we include the items listed in verses 29 and 30?   May we include the listing found in verses 38 and 39?   Certainly, none of these is outside of His providential oversight, and any and all of them could be turned by Him[170] into what is beneficial ("good")

---

[164] As the italics in the NASB show, the phrase "according to *the will of* God" is literally "according to God" in the Greek, and the phrase stands at the beginning of the clause, so that there is emphasis on it. What the Spirit does is *according to God*, i.e., is in harmony with what the Father is doing in His world.

[165] See notes at 8:18 and 8:26 for the first two grounds of encouragement.

[166] Special Study #2, page 66-75, has introduced the doctrine of God's providence and government.

[167] Special Study #7 at the close of chapter 8 takes up the matter of the security of the believer, about which much is said in 8:28-30.

[168] The word for "know" is *oida*, which means to learn by instruction.   See footnote #8, at Romans 2:2.

[169] Lenski, *Romans*, p.550.

[170] There is considerable variation in the readings found at this verse in the manuscripts.   (1) Some read as do the KJV and ASV, "all things work together for good."   "All things" is taken to be a neuter plural nominative, and a neuter plural subject may have a singular verb [Machen, *Grammar*, p.70].   If this reading (found in Sinaiticus, Ephraemi, Beza, and the Byzantine text) were followed, then it would certainly modify what has been said earlier about "weakness," "futility" and "slavery to corruption."   The curse is not so dev-

for His children, beneficial in the sense that it promotes their eternal salvation.   The Old and New Testaments contain examples of how God made seeming evil contribute to good, even in this life.   The account of Joseph being sold into slavery by his brothers is one. They intended it for evil, but Joseph can see in it how God was contributing to the good (Genesis 50:20).   The persecution of the church by Saul of Tarsus led to the scattering of the Jerusalem church to distant parts of the Roman world (Acts 8:4).   It looked like a calamity, and many people did indeed hurt and suffer from the havoc he caused, but the persecution served only to plant the church in a hundred new places to flourish more than ever.   Knowledge of how God makes things (even adverse things) contribute to the ultimate good of the saints will help sustain them through the trials and sufferings.[171]

To those who love God.   Paul uses a present tense verb, those who continually love God. In the Greek, this clause is the first one in the verse and Paul puts it forward for emphasis, so there will be no mistake about who are the ones for whom God works all things together. "Loving God" reminds us of 6:13 where the ex-slaves of sin are exhorted to present themselves to God.   It recalls 6:22 where love-slaves of God grow in sanctification which results in eternal life.   It recalls all that chapter 8 has said about walking according to the Spirit, and about being "sons" and "children" of God.   It is for such as these, and these alone, who continually express their love for God both in attitude and action, that such a guarantee that God will overrule even the adverse circumstances for their good holds true.[172]

To those who are called according to *His* purpose.   This phrase is a further description of the ones for whom God causes all things to contribute to their ultimate good.   Men are

---

astating as to produce spiritually and eternally adverse effects on mankind.   "All things" still "work together for good" at least for the Christian.   Hendriksen, *Romans*, p.279-80, defends this translation.   (2) Some read "He [meaning the Holy Spirit] works for good to those who love God."   The Holy Spirit, who was the subject of the preceding verses, is made the subject of this one too, and besides prompting the Christian to yearn, He also actively is involved in events so that their result is ultimately beneficial to the Christian. So the NEB translates the third person singular verb in this verse (though, rather arbitrarily, it seems, "God" is inserted as the subject of the next verse, though it is still the third person singular verb there, nor is there any noun for "God" in the Greek).   (3) The reading "God causes all things to work together for good," found in P[46], Vaticanus, and Alexandrinus, has been rather widely accepted as the true reading since the discovery of the Chester Beatty Papyri.   See RSV, NASB, TEV, NIV, etc.   "All things," which can either be nominative or accusative plural, is taken as accusative, the object of the verb "works together."   This latter is the reading accepted by the commentator, and the comments on the verse reflect the view that this is the true reading.

[171] A Christian does not need to be very old to be able to look back on life and see things that at first looked like disasters, but which in time worked out for the good; things that at first looked like disappointments worked out to greater blessings.   And as the Christian looks back, he can see a guiding and directing Hand in it and through it all.   How very comforting it is to have experienced God's providence in the past, and to be able to count on it in the future.

[172] The above comment needs to be modified in one respect.   While it probably can be said that not all adverse circumstances are worked together for good by God for the unregenerate, yet it is true that some adversities have helped lead some unregenerate to repentance.   So Lard's comment is right when he states, "No others [save those who constantly love God] have the guarantee that the adverse events of life shall work them good.   Such events may tend to bring the unrenewed to Christ, as no doubt in many instances they do; but only as they do this, do they work them good."   *Romans*, p.280.

"called" (invited to salvation) through the gospel,[173] and in this context it is implied that the invitation has been accepted and obeyed.[174]   Furthermore, this "calling" was extended or offered to men in harmony with God's "purpose."[175]   "According to *His* purpose"[176] has reference, without doubt, to the "plan" God made back in eternity before creation.[177]   This clause "according to *His* purpose" is very important!   It furnishes the clue to the meaning, as we shall see, of the next two verses.

8:29 – *For whom He foreknew, He also predestined* to become *conformed to the image of His Son, that He might be the first-born among many brethren;*

For whom He foreknew.   This verse and the next give the reason why Paul can say that

---

[173] See notes at Romans 1:1-7 and 8:30, and the Special Study #1 at the close of chapter 1, for detailed comments on the word "call."

[174] "'Them that are called' cannot be understood as limiting 'those that love God,' as though among those that love God, only some are 'the called'." Barmby, *Romans*, p.213.   Perhaps it is true, in some sense, that God's invitation (call) to men to become Christians preceded their "love for God," since the Scriptures elsewhere tell us that "we love Him because He first loved us" (1 John 4:19).

[175] While the NASB has correctly put "His" in italics since there is no word in the Greek corresponding to it, nevertheless, the only other passage in Romans where Paul uses the word "purpose" (9:11), it is distinctly called "*God's* purpose."   Therefore, likely, the same idea is in Paul's mind here at 8:28.

[176] *Prothesis*, "purpose," means "to place something before one's mind," that is, to plan, purpose, resolve.   Arndt and Gingrich, *Lexicon*, p.713.   This commentator does not think it right or helpful to call this "plan" (purpose) a "covenant," as some covenant theologians are wont to do.   He can find no specific verse in Scripture where the plan made back in eternity is called a covenant, as though such a covenant, supposedly made between God and Christ, is the key that unlocks the rest of Bible history and theology. It contributes to a wider understanding of God's word to attempt to call Bible things by Bible names, and it contributes little to our understanding to call this "plan" (purpose) by some other name such as "covenant." Let us save "covenant" for what the Bible itself calls a covenant.

[177] Other verses that speak of God's "plan," besides Romans 9:11, are Ephesians 1:11, 3:11, and 2 Timothy 1:9.   When it was, back in eternity, or how long before He began to create this world and fit it up for a dwelling place for the man He was about to form, that God formulated this plan, cannot be decided with certainty.

What all did this "plan" embrace?   In bold strokes, it may be summarized in this manner: back in eternity God wanted a family who would love Him, not because they had to, but because they wanted to. God set before His mind's eye the whole human race with their entire destiny.   He would create a man with the power of choice, and put him in a world suitable for his habitation.   If the man should exercise his freedom of will and choose to sin, there would have to be appropriate penalties – death to the race, a curse pronounced on creation, a series of covenants made with men, culminating in the new covenant (remember Romans 5, where sin entered, death entered, and the Law entered).   Also part of the predetermined plan included this divine necessity – if the man should decide to rebel, God would even send Jesus to be their redeemer (He was foreordained before the foundation of the world to be a lamb slain for men's sins, 1 Peter 1:20; Revelation 13:8), that the man might have another opportunity to repent of his rebellion and become one who voluntarily loves God instead, just as God wished.   It was determined at that time that if man should rebel, then only those "in Christ" would be saved (Ephesians 1:4-11).   All things pertaining to man's redemption were included in the plan, including the predetermination that men should be "called" by the gospel.   Romans 8:29 will give more of the items included in the plan – that there should be a family of sons, all conformed to the image of the Firstborn Son.   This is the goal toward which God, step by step, is moving all things.

God works all things together for good in harmony with His eternal plan (purpose), and as that reason is unfolded we learn in greater detail some of the elements included in God's "purpose."[178] Paul is revealing some of the eternal counsels of God, as those ideas and plans pertained to the people of God.

"Whom" is plural, not singular. Paul is thinking of a group here – composed of individuals, to be sure – but nevertheless a group of individuals who constitute a corporate whole.[179] This group would be none other than the ones earlier designated as "those who love God" (verse 28). Now we are told that this group was foreknown. "Foreknew" is a compound verb in the Greek, made up of the preposition *pro* ("before") and the simple verb *ginōskō* ("to know"). The addition of the preposition does not change the meaning of *ginōskō*; it just dates it – dates it "before" certain other actions God planned or did (as verse 30 will show). Most agree that the 'knowing' took place at the same time God made His plan (verse 28), and in fact the knowing formed one element of the plan. When God planned the human race, long before their actual existence, it was then that He "foreknew." "Foreknew" likely has the meaning "to approve beforehand."[180] That is, when God made

---

[178] Perhaps as many as five different elements are specified in this and the next verses: foreknowledge, predestination, calling, justification, and glorification.

[179] Paul's use of the plural is identical with his procedure in Ephesians 1:4, where he wrote "just as He chose us (plural) in Him (i.e., in Christ) before the foundation of the world." God's foreknowledge and predestination were concerned with "those (plural) who are in Christ" and what would happen to them. Individual predestination – whether or not certain individuals were or were not "in Christ," and that irrespective of their own response to the gospel – is something not contemplated in the verses we are studying.

[180] The word *proginōsko* ("foreknew") has been explained in four different ways by the commentators, depending at times on the theological system being defended, and depending at times on the particular connotation that *ginōskō* is capable of expressing.

(1) "To know beforehand," is one suggestion. It is true that the word does have this sense in the New Testament, as at Acts 26:5 and 2 Peter 3:17. God's knowledge is such that He knows the end from the beginning; He knows what will happen before it does happen. (a) Lange explains how certain theologians have adapted this meaning, and then built their systems on it, thusly: "The 'knowing beforehand' was understood by the Greek and Arminian expositors in an anti-predestinarian sense as the foresight of faith; and by the Lutheran writers of the foresight in perseverance in bestowed faith." *Romans*, p.278. God saw beforehand those who would believe, and these are the ones foreordained to salvation, is how Arminians explain "foreknew and predestined." (b) Calvinistic writers, in direct opposition to this presentation which allows mankind to exercise the freedom of will, use "foreknew" to defend the doctrine of divine election. They would ask, Whence comes this faith that God foresees? Their answer: the faith which He foresees is the faith which He Himself creates. Appeal is made to the following passages to substantiate the presentation: John 3:3-8, 6:44,46,65; Ephesians 2:8; Philippians 1:29; and 2 Peter 1:2. For these Calvinistic writers, foreknowledge carries with it automatic foreordination to salvation. To this commentator, the effort to include faith as part of the theological meaning of *proginōsko* is unwarranted, and merely leads us into theological complications. Furthermore, it tends to confound two ideas which Scripture keeps distinct, namely, foreknowledge and election, e.g., 1 Peter 1:2, "elect according to the foreknowledge of God."

(2) "To select or choose beforehand," is another suggestion. It is said that God's foreknowledge is a loving, favorable knowledge. The idea that *ginōskō* sometimes implies that the knower has a personal relationship to the one known, probably can be defended. See Psalm 1:6; Hosea 13:5; Amos 5:2. Indeed, in God's plan for the future, some such personal relationship would ensue, but it is questionable whether the word *proginōsko* should be used to substantiate this doctrine. Why not use "child of God" or "son of God," to express it?

His plans for man, He determined He would "approve" those who were in Christ.

He also predestined.   The word translated "predestined" also is a compound verb, meaning "to decide (or plan, or determine, or ordain, or mark out, or destine) something beforehand."[181]   For the moment, Paul omits the intermediate steps between God's foreknowledge and the destination to which He has determined they will be carried, and instead tells us what that destination is – namely, that the believers are to be conformed to the image of His son.   God decided on this destination for believers, evidently, at the same time He made His original plans (verse 28) to create.   'Foreknowledge' and 'predestination' are two different things, this verse would suggest.   Foreknowledge focused attention upon God's approval for those in Christ, but it did not inform us what destiny was in store for those whom God approved.   It is precisely that information that is now given.

To become **conformed to the image of His Son.**   If we allow the context (verse 23 as well as the phrase following) to influence our comments, then "image of His Son" seems to be a reference to the final resurrection, and implies that in that final resurrection the bodies of the redeemed will be of the same form as the glorified body of the Son of God.[182] God's plan, made back in eternity previously, was that the redeemed should be like His Son in form and appearance.   This likeness to the Son is the thing this passage says was predestined.[183]

---

(3)   "To determine beforehand," is a popular explanation found in comments at this place. Calvinistic writers are apt to include an explanation about how God from all eternity, out of the mere good pleasure of His will, selected certain individual persons out of mankind He was about to create to be heirs of glory. "Commenting on 'foreknew,' Calvin writes, 'It is an *adoption* to the estate of children, whereby he has separated us forever from the rejected'." (Quoted in Lenski, *Romans*, p.557.) The objections to the interpretation that "foreknew" is equivalent to "predestined" is that this very context uses the two words as distinct, and to say that certain *individuals* are the object of this foreknowledge ignores the fact that "whom" is plural, denoting *a group* constituting a corporate whole.

(4)   "To approve beforehand" is thus the likely meaning for *proginōskō* in this passage. "Know" does mean "approve" in a number of passages, including Matthew 7:23; 1 Corinthians 8:3; Galatians 4:9; 2 Timothy 2:19; and 1 John 3:1. And, of course, the book of Romans has already shown that God approves of those who are faithful. It has developed the thesis that justification is by faith. Or as Ephesians 1:4 tells us, God decided (when He made His plans ahead of time) that He would approve those who would be in Christ.

[181] See *prooridzō* in Thayer, *Lexicon*, p.541, or Arndt-Gingrich, *Lexicon*, p.716. The English words predestine and foreordain are practically synonymous.

[182] Two different explanations for "image of His Son" are found in the commentaries. Some suggest that two things, one present (in the heart) and one future (the body), are involved in this process of transformation; so it is not unusual to read that "image" includes being like the Son both in character and in destiny. Others opt for one thing, the future transformation of the body at the second coming of Christ, as being in Paul's mind when he writes about "image of His Son."

[183] The determination beforehand, the predestination, has nothing to do with God predetermining certain acts of obedience or disobedience for each individual man who might live on the face of the earth. "Foreordained" does not make men act in any given way. In this passage, we are specifically told that the thing foreordained is that those whom God "approves" would be conformed to the image of His Son. It is

The same idea, that the redeemed will have bodies just like Christ's glorified body, is taught in Philippians 3:20,21. It should not be overlooked that "conformed" includes the Greek word *morphē*, which suggests that this change into the likeness of Christ is inward and thorough, not simply an outward and superficial resemblance.[184] It should cause the reader to pause for contemplation and marvel when he reads that the destiny God has planned for the redeemed is no less than to be conformed to the image of His Son!

That He might be the first-born among many brethren. Paul here tells us about the ultimate purpose God had in mind. God did all this planning because He wanted a family.[185]

> The [eternal] kingdom is here conceived of as being a family. In this family Christ has the rights of primogeniture, but all Christians are his brothers. And the object of Christ's mission and of the great scheme of salvation (in all its states – foreknowledge, calling, justification, etc.) is *to make men sufficiently like Him to be His brethren*, and so to fill up the number of the Christian family.[186]

"First-born" is one of the words over which theological battles have raged. What is at issue is the question of whether or not Jesus is a created being. Some have tried to make "first-born" mean that Jesus was the first person to be created by God.[187] However, comparing the six passages in the New Testament where the word is used of Christ results

---

bringing in extraneous material to attempt to make this verse say that individual men's *actions* are predestined. See more on this topic in comments on verse 30.

The doctrine of "unconditional eternal security" for the redeemed is also found by some in these verses, a topic about which more will be said in Special Study #7 at the close of comments on chapter 8. The argument for such an unconditional perseverance of the saints is allegedly found in the idea that since God has predestined the believer to be conformed to the image of the Son, nothing can intervene to stop what God has foreordained – therefore, the unconditional security of the believer must be implied in this language.

[184] A knowledge of Greek synonyms is helpful here. Both *morphē* and *schēma* denote "outward appearance, outward form," but they express something more than that. "In *morphē* it is also implied that the outward form expresses the inner essence, an idea which is absent from *schēma*. *Morphē* expresses the form as that which is intrinsic and essential, *schēma* signifies the figure, shape, as that which is more outward and accidental." Berry, *Synonyms*, p.134.

[185] Compare Ephesians 1:4-11, where we are told of God's desire for a family to love Him, not because they have to (as would be true if they had no freedom of choice), but because they want to. When it is said that God's ultimate purpose was to have a family, we are placing emphasis on the words "many brethren." If we place emphasis on the word "first-born," then we would say that the great object God had in mind was that His Son receive the priority, dignity, and supreme honor due Him.

[186] Sanday, *Romans*, p.97.

[187] This topic has been introduced before in our comments on Romans. See footnote #9 in chapter 1, for example. That Jesus is not a created being, but is co-eternal with the Father, seems beyond dispute, once a passage like John 17:5 is taken into account – where Jesus speaks about the glory that He *ever* had with the Father before the creation of the world (NASB).

in the observation that, in most of them, the topic the context deals with is the future resurrection of the dead; perhaps it can also be said that in none of the six passages is Jesus' pre-existent relationship to the Father even discussed.[188]   Certainly, in this passage, it is out of place to use the word "first-born" as though it meant that Jesus was the first being the Father created.   The future resurrection (much more than the beginning of God's creative work) is certainly the main topic here in Romans 8, but whether it is Christ's priority in time (i.e., He was the first to come out of the grave in a glorified, spiritual body), or whether it is Christ's supremacy and sovereignty in that future world where all will have resurrected and glorified bodies like His, cannot be determined with any degree of certainty.   Still, the expression "among many brethren" would seem to point to priority in time in this passage.

In any case, it is thought-provoking to find the redeemed called "brethren" of Christ, just after His priority and/or supremacy has been pointed out.   It certainly adds to the highness and distinctiveness of the predestined state to which God is leading the redeemed.   At the same time, the designation "many brethren"[189] emphasizes the community and union of the redeemed with Christ.   There is a marvelous dignity to be bestowed upon the people of God.   For this reason, Jesus is not ashamed to call them "brethren" (Hebrews 2:11,12).

8:30 – *and whom He predestined, these He also called; and whom He called, these He also justified; and whom He justified, these He also glorified.*

And whom He predestined.   Having paused to explain the destiny that God has in mind for those He approves, Paul now shows the steps that intervene between the time God made these plans and their ultimate fulfillment.   In order that the "foreknown" ones who were destined to be glorified might reach that goal, God planned to call men, then justify them, and then glorify them.   It appears that verse 30 is still telling us what God's thinking was as He made His plans back in eternity, for the word "predestined" in this verse picks up the same theme just spoken about in verse 29.   In other words, "according to His purpose" (verse 28) is the phrase that verses 29 and 30 expand as they tell us some of the elements

---

[188] In Colossians 1:18, Revelation 1:5, 1 Corinthians 15:20, and this passage in Romans 8 (in a context where "glorification" and "redemption of the body" is the topic), the context in which "first-born" appears clearly has reference to the future day of the resurrection.   In one of the other two passages, Colossians 1:15, some have argued that the topic is Christ's pre-existent state, since verse 16 goes on to talk about how "in Him all things were created."   However, it can just as plausibly be demonstrated that verses 16-18a should be taken together as giving reasons why He should be *preeminent* – namely, His activity in creation, and providence, and in the re-creation (the church).   The other passage where "first-born" is used of Christ is Hebrews 1:6, a verse whose punctuation is disputed, so one cannot tell for sure whether it refers to His incarnation, or to His second advent.   If we read it, "And again, when He [God] brings the first-born into the world ..." all the word "again" does is introduce another quotation on the same subject (His incarnation) from the Old Testament.   If we read it, "And when He again brings the first-born into the world," the word "again" would be a reference to the second advent, since it would mean that God was bringing Jesus into the world one more time.   (In Old Testament times, Jesus was active in the world [see 1 Corinthians 10:4 where Jesus is credited with being the One who provided the water to the wandering Israelites in the wilderness, and John 12:40,41 where John says it was Jesus that Isaiah saw in the vision recorded in Isaiah 6].   Those, plus His incarnation, were His previous entrances into the world.)

[189] Although, in comparison to the number who have populated the earth through all the ages, only a few are saved (Matthew 7:14), still "*many* brethren" conveys the idea that the Son will be surrounded by a great multitude of redeemed people (Revelation 7:4,9,11-15).

that make up God's "plan."[190]   Perhaps the following diagram will help to grasp what Paul is saying:

GOD MADE A PLAN BACK IN ETERNITY – verse 28

He said, "I'll approve ... and I'll destine ... some ... to glory" – verse 29

"*Approve*" comes from "foreknew."
"*Destine*" comes from "predestined."
"*Some*" are specifically "those who love God," i.e., those who are in Christ.
"*Glory*" is another way of saying "conformed to the image of His Son."

In order that the foreknown ones, who were destined to be glorified, might reach that goal, God also planned to 'call' men, then 'justify' them, and then 'glorify' them – verse 30

These He also called.   Paul now lists some of the steps that lie between the beginning of the plan (foreknowledge and predestination) and the grand conclusion to the plan (glorification).   His decision to approve and destine some to glory was made back in eternity; these "steps" in verse 30 are actions God planned to take (and indeed does take) in time, steps by which His eternal purpose would be brought to actual fruition.   One of the things God does is offer men an invitation[191] to surrender their lives to His will.   This invitation is presented to men as they hear the gospel preached – it is presented through the

---

[190] A failure to see that "according to *His* purpose" (verse 28) is the clue to the interpretation of this whole passage has led theologians into one of the most difficult of all the topics that occupy their studies, namely, the knotty problem of predestination vs. free will.   (This topic has also been briefly touched upon in the author's *New Testament History: Acts*, in the Special Study on pages 130-134.)   More will be said on freedom of the will in Special Study #8 at the close of this chapter, but suffice it to say here that there can be no question that Paul fully recognizes the freedom of the human will, and this is true both of the redeemed and the unredeemed.   Nor is there any question but that Paul also recognizes the sovereignty of God.   God has so arranged things that there are two roads, and only two, that a man is free to choose to travel.   He must choose one or the other, but the choice is his.   God does not force the man to choose the one he does, although, in His mercy, God may bring pressures to bear, trying to lead the man to repentance (Romans 2:4).   It should be emphasized once more that Romans 8 does not say anything about certain individuals being predestined to salvation, and because of this predestination God was therefore obligated to call and justify them.   This passage must not be interpreted in such a way as to cause it to impinge on the doctrine of free will.

[191] On the word "call" see notes at verse 28, and Special Study #1 at the close of chapter 1.   The aorist tense is used (for "call" and for the other verbs in this verse) because when God plans something, it is as good as done!   Past tense verbs are often used in passages which deal with the future, for this very reason.

It seems appropriate, at this point, to comment briefly on some misleading ideas that are sometimes given in comments on calling.   Hodge, and Calvinistic writers generally, tell us that "called" here in Romans 8:30 means 'effectually called.'   "Calvin uses [verse 28] to posit a difference in the call extended to men;

Word (Romans 1:16). The fact that some respond positively to the invitation and are saved, while others reject the invitation and are lost, has proven to be a philosophical difficulty for some. Some express this felt difficulty by asking, "Why even call those whom God could foresee would reject the invitation?" Answer: If God offered the invitation only to a certain, select few, then He could be charged with arbitrary partiality. That there is no such partiality with God, has already been demonstrated (Romans 3:21-26). Others express this felt difficulty by asking, "If God could foresee that some would reject the invitation and be lost, wouldn't it have been better not to have created man in the first place? Since He created man with the freedom to choose, isn't God ultimately responsible for certain men being lost?" Answer: Not only does the questioner have no way of knowing whether or not (looking at things from God's point of view) it would have been better not to create, the questioner also has ignored the fact that Matthew 23:37 and similar passages show that God, rather than arbitrarily excluding some, has gone to great lengths to woo and win men's affections; and despite all that God could do, the men themselves excluded themselves.

And whom He called, these He also justified. Much has already been said in Romans about God's way of saving men, namely, "justification by faith" (see especially Romans 3:24-30). The only ones justified are men of faith, so it is implied that the invitation God offered has been responded to in a positive way.[192]

And whom He justified. It has been pointed out by numerous writers that the steps Paul lists are not quite exhaustive on the subject. Included in God's plan for mankind was the sending of Jesus as a sin offering. Also included, but not specifically mentioned in this context, is the step called "sanctification" (see 6:19,22).[193]

These He also glorified. Strictly speaking, the glorification of God's children is still future, but it is here spoken of as already past, because Paul is speaking of what God planned and determined, when, back in eternity, He was purposing His family.[194]

---

one call is 'according to God's purpose' and converts irresistibly and is extended only to the elect. Another call is 'not according to God's purpose' and never converts and is extended to the non-elect, the reprobate." Lenski, *Romans*, p.554. *Reply:* No verse of Scripture allows us to think that the call extended to some men is different from the call extended to others. In fact, the very opposite is true. The Parable of the Sower (Matthew 13) shows that the same "seed" goes to all – the difference is made because of the difference in "soil" the seed contacts. Even Matthew 22:14 indicates that the *same* "call" goes to all.

[192] "'Justified' (*edikaiōsa*) means the participation in God's 'righteousness' (*dikaiosunē*), the passing into a 'state of salvation' through faith in baptism." Barmby, *Romans*, p.213.

[193] There are some writers who find "sanctification" included even in this context. Some assert that the following word, "glorify," really has reference to sanctification. Others affirm that sanctification was included in the previous phrase, "conformed to the image of His Son."

[194] As suggested in footnote #191, the past tense verbs can be explained by suggesting that when God plans something, it is as good as done.

We are almost back to the place we started.   When man sins, he "falls short of the *glory* of God."   Now, at the end of His purpose, God *glorifies* those whom he foreknew, destined, called, and justified.   "Not only will God's children receive gloriously transformed bodies (Romans 8:11,23; 1 Corinthians 15:43-53; Philippians 3:21), but on and after the day of resurrection they will shine forth in all their glory in both body and soul, these having now become reunited."[195]   Because God has a plan (a purpose formed back in eternity) – to sum up all things, to bring all things together in Christ, things in heaven and things upon earth (Ephesians 1:10,11) – and because His plan of salvation involves blessed effects on those in whom the Holy Spirit dwells, He is able to work all things together for good to those who continually love Him.   Believers are on a journey that is part of the plan of God; when they begin to see the whole "panorama that stretches from the love of God before times eternal to the grand finale of the redemptive process," (Murray, *Romans*, p.322) then their hope of glory, coupled with the aid of the indwelling Spirit and God's overruling providence, will prove sufficient to sustain them through all sufferings.

F. God's Plan of Salvation (Justification by Faith) Involves Blessed Effects on Those Who are God's Elect, and Who Thus are Objects of His Love.   8:31-39

Summary: With the proof of God's love before him, the Christian has nothing to fear. No matter what comes, God, the Judge, is on his side, and the ascended Christ intercedes for him.   Christ's love, also, is so strong that nothing is powerful enough to intercept it, or to bar the Christian's triumph and glorification.

8:31 – *What then shall we say to these things?   If God is for us, who is against us?*

What then shall we say to these things?   As it did in 3:5 and 4:1, the question "What shall we say?" means 'What inference can we draw?'   But to what in the previous context does "these things" refer, from which we are to draw this inference?   Perhaps the following expression, telling us "God is for us," focuses our attention on all that was said since 5:1. Since 5:1, Paul has been enumerating one after another many of the blessings that accompany God's way of saving a man – all of which are evidence that God indeed is "for us."   "These things" then would remind us of all those blessed effects, about which we have been reading now for several chapters.[196]

---

[195] Hendriksen, *Romans*, p.285.

[196] This all-inclusive suggestion for "these things" seems more satisfactory than the less-inclusive references suggested in other commentaries on Romans.   One points particularly to "called, justified, and glorified" of verse 30 as being what Paul has in mind as he writes "these things."   Or again, another suggests that 8:31-39 is a commentary on verse 28, about how God causes all things to work together for good.   Still others include 8:18-30, or all that has been said from 8:1, as being the teaching from which we are to pause and draw an inference.

If God *is* for us, who *is* against us?   "God is for us" is the inference or conclusion Paul would have us draw after we have paused and thought about what he has previously written. The "if" is not the "if" of uncertainty, but the "if" of presupposition.   We could read it, "Since God is for us!"   Without any gainsaying, God is on the side of the redeemed.   He is their friend.   What He planned back in eternity and carries out in time had men's ultimate good in mind.   Whether it is pronouncing and removing a curse, or sending His Son to be a propitiation, or breaking the power of slavery to sin, or giving the indwelling Spirit to help live the Christian life, or overruling even the circumstances that seem to militate against us, all these plainly show that God, in His Person and in His providence, is for us![197] "Who is against us?" does not mean that there are no adversaries at all, for verses 35,36, and 38,39 refer to the most violent kinds of opposition.   But the sense of the question is, What adverse power can there possibly be that is stronger than God?   Christians do have enemies (Satan, evil men, evil spirits, adverse circumstances), but none are mightier than God who is for us.   None can thwart God's purpose of blessing and saving the believer, as long as the believer remains loyal to Christ.[198]   In the following verses, Paul will proceed to illustrate the truth of the inference (God is for us) and the resulting conclusion (who is against us?).

8:32 – *He who did not spare His own Son, but delivered Him up for us all, how will He not also with Him freely give us all things?*

He who did not spare His own Son.   Here Paul reminds his readers of the most conclusive proof he could give that God is for us.   It is in the form of an argument from the greater to the lesser.   If God has done for our good the greatest that is conceivable, will not all other lesser blessings follow?   Paul's choice of words to show what God has done for us would stand out to any Jew who knew his Old Testament, especially the story of Abraham's sacrifice of Isaac, for Paul used the very language of Genesis 22:16.   What God acknowledged as the highest proof of Abraham's love for Him, God Himself furnished to men – He actually "did not spare" His own Son.[199]

---

[197] In light of this inference that "God is for us," and in light of verses which plainly state that God does not wish for any to perish, it is probably right to affirm that God never purposed the damnation of any man. That He wants all to be saved, however, does not mean that all will be ultimately saved.   Some men indeed will be lost, but it will be in spite of all God has done to keep them from misusing their freedom of choice. More will be said on this matter in a Special Study #8, "The Doctrine of Predestination" included at the close of notes on chapter 9, but it would seem that this inference ("God is for us") should keep anyone from ever saying that God unconditionally predestined certain men to be lost.

[198] That there is a security for the believer, and that this security is conditional, is the topic of Special Study #7 at the close of this chapter.

[199] At Romans 8:3, the expression "His own Son" has already occurred.   It means that there is no other who stands in the same relation to the Father, as does Jesus.   This is the force of the Greek word *idios*, translated "own."   It intimates that the Son was and is of one nature with the Father.   Paul has also shown that God has many "sons" by adoption (Romans 8:14-16), but Scripture allows no confusion to exist between the "Sonship" of Jesus and the "sonship" of the adopted.   Jesus is unique in His sonship. (Lenski is reflecting on, and rightfully objecting to, the unfounded assertions made by certain Liberal and Neo-orthodox theologians, when he comments, "What do some interpreters mean by saying that Paul never called Jesus God's Son?   He began this epistle by calling Jesus this (1:2), [repeated it at 8:3], and here he even emphasizes it by writing 'His *own* Son'." *Romans*, p.565.)

Sparing refers to suffering inflicted. Parents spare their children when they do not inflict the full measure of chastisement due. Judges spare criminals when they do not pronounce a sentence commensurate with the crime committed. By way of contrast, this is not what God the Father did. He did not withhold or lighten one whit of the full toll of judgment executed upon his own well-beloved and only-begotten son.[200]

God could not spare His Son, and still carry out His plan of redemption.

But delivered Him up for us all. The truth summarized here has been fully set forth at Romans 4:25. Instead of sparing His Son, God delivered Him up to suffering and death, thus showing He is for us, since the reason He delivered Jesus was to benefit "us all." The incarnation, the suffering, the death, and the resurrection of Jesus is intelligible only when it is viewed as being something done vicariously – it was "for us all" that Jesus was delivered.[201] In this context, "us all" may well be limited to those who are in Christ, the ones who were foreknown, predestined, called, justified, and who will be glorified (as verses 28-30 so aptly say); but this limitation should not be pressed so as to make Paul teach the doctrine of limited atonement.[202] While it is true that Christ's death is potentially effective to every person who ever lives (Romans 5:6-8; 1 Timothy 2:6, "[He] gave Himself as a ransom *for all*"), Romans 8:32 is likely taken out of context if it is used to prove the doctrine of universal atonement.

How will He not also with Him freely give us all things? The greatest gift – that He delivered up His Son to die for us – ensures that the lesser "things" will also be given. There is a definite article before the word "all things" in the Greek. Does the presence of this article mean we are to limit "all things" to those that have to do with salvation and glorification (verse 30), or shall we understand that the article is an article of previous reference, and thus we are pointed back to the "all things" in verse 28? If we take the second option, then we are told that even those things that at first seem to oppose us will in

---

[200] Murray, *Romans*, p.323.

[201] On the preposition, *huper*, translated "for," see notes at Romans 5:6. It means "in behalf of."

[202] Those commentators whose theological background would cause them to think in terms of limited atonement, indeed tend to emphasize the idea in their comments at this place. Murray, *Romans*, p.325, for example, makes reference both to the preceding and following context to show that "us all" is limited just to the elect. But unless one is aware of the doctrine of limited atonement (Christ died only for the elect) in the background, it might not even be clear why there is this emphasis on limiting "us all" to the elect. To say Christ died 'for His people' is Scriptural, Ephesians 5:25. To say Christ died "for all" is also Scriptural, as has been shown in the notes above. And while it is Scriptural to say that Christ died "for every one" (Hebrews 2:9), it is also Scriptural to say that Christ died "for many" (Matthew 20:28 and 26:28). It surely would be pressing the truth if one were to attempt to use the expression "for many" to prove limited atonement. "No stress can be laid here or at Matthew 26:28, on the term *many* as distinguished from *all*; nor need it be said that *pollon* ['many'] is used for *panton* ['all']. The language is in substance that of Isaiah 53:12, where the contrast is merely between Christ as one and mankind as many, without any reference to a limit of the number." H. L. Mansel, "Matthew," in *The Bible Commentary*, edited by F.C. Cook, p.109.

fact be given to us, that is, made to be a blessing.   Earlier in the verse, Jesus the Son was said to be delivered *"for* us."   Now the language changes a bit.   "With Him" represents Christ as being given *"to* us," just as surely as "all things" are given "to us."[203]   "Freely give" is a translation of the verb *charizomai*, and suggests that the gift is bestowed as a matter of grace.   To "give freely" is agreeable to God's nature, and not only that, it reminds us that God cares for His children, just like Jesus taught He does (Matthew 6:25-30).   Paul wrote this reminder in the form of a question that expects a positive answer.[204]   The following verses will go on to show that, for the believer, both God and Jesus will be active so that this positive answer about "all things" is actually realized.

8:33 – *Who will bring a charge against God's elect?   God is the one who justifies;*

Who will bring a charge against God's elect?[205]   The expression "bring a charge against"

---

[203] Both Thayer (*Lexicon*, p.598) and Arndt and Gingrich (*Lexicon*, p.789) take "with Him" as being associated with the *object* ("all things") of the verb "give."   Now it is just possible that "with Him" is intended to associate the exalted Jesus with God (the *subject* of the verb) in the act of giving all things to the believers.   It is the lexicographer's opinion that is reflected in each of their choices of examples of the different possible uses of the preposition *sun* ("with"), and both also give examples of passages where this dative preposition denotes association together with the *subject* of an active verb in the doing of the action.   One could even appeal to the closing phrases of verse 34 for a specific statement of what Jesus is doing as He joins together with God in seeing that "all things" are given to the believer.

[204] In Greek, questions that expect a positive answer are written with the particle *ou*; questions that expect a negative answer have the particle *mē*.   In this case, Paul wrote *ouchi*, a strengthened form, suggesting this is a truth that no one would deny.   Thayer, *Lexicon*, p.469.

[205] The punctuation and arrangement of verses 33 and 34 are somewhat difficult and have long been the topic of comment.   Several possibilities have been put forth and defended, including:

(1) Cranfield, *Romans*, p.437, alludes to the fact that there is some ancient support for reading the whole (verses 33 and 34, as indeed all of verses 31 to 37) as a series of questions.   Thus verses 33 and 34 would read, "Who shall bring a charge against God's elect?   Shall God who justifies?   Who is the one who condemns?   Shall Christ Jesus who died?   Who rather was raised?   Who is at the right hand of God?   Who also intercedes for us?"

(2) The ASV margin suggests it should be so punctuated as to produce 4 questions; Barnes, *Romans*, p.201, also defends this arrangement, as he writes, "This may be read with more force as a question, 'Who shall lay anything to the charge of God's elect?   Shall God who justifieth?' ... The passage implies that there would be a high degree of absurdity in supposing that the same Being would both justify and condemn at the same time ... 'Who is he that condemneth?' ... 'Shall Christ, who has died, etc., condemn them?'   The argument here is, that as Christ died to save them, ... He will certainly not condemn them."

Lenski, *Romans*, p.567-68, urges that to take it as four questions is not suitable.   Though admitting that such punctuation of the English is possible, since there was no punctuation in the most ancient Greek manuscripts, he still objects on the basis that the second of the four questions yields a sense that is incongruous.   "Before what judge would God bring an accusation?" he asks.   "And would God as a judge also be the accuser?"

(3) The KJV, NIV, and TEV punctuate these verses so that we have two questions followed by two answers, thusly; "Who shall lay anything to the charge of God's elect?   It is God that justifieth.   Who is he that condemneth?   It is Christ that died ... who makes intercession for us."   Various points have been presented as proof that this is the proper way to translate.   Hendriksen, *Romans*, p.289, appeals to Isaiah

is a metaphor taken from the courts of justice. The mental image suggested is that of a court room, where the judge is sitting at the bench, and the accuser is standing before the judge, presenting his case against the accused who is here identified as "God's elect."[206] There is little reason to restrict this 'accusation' to the time of the final judgment. God hears such accusations all the time, for the devil, the accuser of the brethren, accuses them

---

50:8,9 as likely being in the background, and if so, it settles the problem of punctuation, for it has two questions and two answers. Lenski, *Romans*, p.570, argues that the two questions introduced by "Who" are decisive, and also calls attention to the parallel answers, "God who justifies" and "Jesus who died." A third evidence is found in the participle "who justifies." As far as the original Greek (which had no accent marks) is concerned, it could be either a present tense participle, or a future tense participle (since both would be spelled exactly alike, save for accent mark). Both Lenski and Sanday and Headlam (*Romans*, p.221) urge that the participle must be taken as a future tense, since that better fits the verb forms found in the context. If they are right, the verses should be read as two questions followed by two answers.

Perhaps one of the strongest objections to this third way of punctuating is that it tends to complicate the task of identifying the one who is thought of as doing the 'condemning.' It cannot be God, because He has already been alluded to as the Judge who justifies. It can hardly be the devil, for if his accusations got nowhere, it is certain he couldn't go on to condemn. Lenski tries to solve the problem by introducing the suggestion that "all God's judgments, both his acquittals and condemnations, are by God Himself subjected to the whole universe of angels and of men for judgment as to whether they are righteous in every way." (*Romans*, p.569.)

(4) The ASV, RSV, and NASB punctuate it so that the second and third phrases form a question which is seen as being the answer to the first. "Who will bring a charge against God's elect? God is the one who justifies; who is the one who condemns? Christ Jesus is He who died ... who also intercedes for us. Who shall separate us from the love of Christ (verse 35)?" Among the evidences marshaled to defend this method of punctuation is the fact that two early Greek church fathers (Origen and Chrysostom) so understood the passage. Murray, *Romans*, p.327, objects to any treatment of the passage that finds verse 34b the answer to the question, "Who is the one who condemns. Murray states, "If the clause, 'Who is he that condemns?' finds its answer in the latter part of the same verse, then Jesus Christ would, by implication, be represented as the justifier. This is not Pauline usage ... God, not Jesus, is the justifier ...." A third argument favoring this system of punctuation is that verse 34b thus provides an appropriate introduction to the question asked in verse 35a.

Lenski has objected to this fourth method of punctuation. He thinks that putting the second and third phrases together to form one question, requires reading "the one who condemns" as if it were a present tense participle, which is out of place with the other verb forms in the context. It also requires making the words "God who justifies" a "strange pendant nominative."

Though this commentary is based on the NASB, the third suggested punctuation is the one that will be reflected in the comments offered on these verses. Where different punctuation would produce a different interpretation of the verse, that interpretation will be included in the appropriate footnotes.

[206] Vine, *Romans*, p.132, suggests, "In the case of the prisoner at the bar, there are, so far as this passage goes, (1) the accuser, (2) the accused, (3) the judge, (4) the executioner." We have no great difficulty agreeing with (1), (2), and (3) for they are clearly indicated in the questions. (4) must be found in the words "who is he that condemneth?" or in "Who shall separate us from the love of Christ?" and there certainly is some doubt whether or not the executioner is the person indicated in either of these expressions.

before God day and night.[207]   "Elect" is a new word in this passage,[208] used evidently as a brief and convenient way to designate those who before have been identified as "sons of God," "children of God," "those who love God," "those who are called according to His purpose," who are "foreknown" and "predestined," those who are "justified" by faith.   It is sobering to contemplate that even after all God has done for those who are now His adopted children, that the devil can still make accusations against them.[209]   The Bible just hints at all the mighty struggle going on in the unseen world for the souls of men; but it makes it very plain that in the case of those whom God is justifying, the devil's accusations are unsuccessful.

God is the one who justifies.[210]   In the expression "the one who justifies" lies the entire doctrine of justification as presented at Romans 3:21-28, etc.[211]   It has been shown in chap-

---

[207] Revelation 12:10. For other verses detailing the devil's activities as accuser, see Job 1 and 2; Zechariah 3:1; and the Greek word translated "devil" (*diabolos*, *i.e.*, to throw down, to accuse). The thoughtful reader will have observed in the comments on this verse that God has been identified as the "judge" before whom this accusation is made, and that parallel Scriptures have been used to suggest that the devil is the accuser. Many commentators have supposed that the identity of the accuser is implied in the following phrase, and that it is God (not the devil) who is to be thought of as being the accuser. This proposed exposition leaves the identity of the judge unexplained (or, on the assumption that the "trial" is the final judgment, goes on to make Jesus the judge). Neither of these last two options is as satisfactory as the conclusion offered in the notes.

[208] The word *eklegō* is also translated "chosen," as in the expression "chosen people." God's choice or election took place back in eternity before the creation of the world (Ephesians 1:4,5). See also comments on "His purpose" at Romans 8:28, especially footnote #177.

   "'Chosen' is from *eklegō*; and it means to select or pick out from; that is, to select some and reject the rest. But it means to select or pick out for a reason, and not arbitrarily. [Sometimes the reason is service to be done for God; sometimes it is for salvation. See notes on chapter 9.] In all cases of the saved, it means to select or accept because of obedience. They who obey are chosen; they who disobey are rejected. This exhausts the subject. The old theory that obedience is consequent on election, and not election on obedience, is without foundation in the Bible. Even in the original purpose of God, in His 'plan' (verse 28), He chose only whom He foresaw would obey Christ." Lard, *Romans*, p.287. Lard's comment is satisfactory, if the last phrase means no more than that God predetermined that those who were in Christ would be saved, while leaving men free to choose whether or not they will be "in Christ."

[209] Cranfield (*Romans*, p.438), having opted for the punctuation of the ASV/NASB, views this first question of verse 33 as though it were a rhetorical question that needs no written or stated answer. It would be equivalent to an emphatic denial that any one will even dare to make any accusation (to God the judge) against the elect, he suggests. However, such an implication seems to be incongruous with what the New Testament says elsewhere about the devil's activities. He certainly dares to make such accusations. Because of this fact, it can be observed that most writers, who are commenting on the ASV/NASB text, opt for the suggestion that an answer to the first question is implied in the second (thus making God the accuser). This raises the serious difficulty already alluded to in footnote #207 above. Instead of leaving the accuser or the judge unidentified, the comments in the text propose that an identification of both accuser and judge is possible and plausible.

[210] Remember, the KJV, NIV, and TEV make "It is God who justifies!" the answer to the question about "Who will bring a charge against God's elect?"   The answer is, God is constantly acquitting the very people being accused, and that justification clears them of every charge which anyone might bring against them.

[211] This is the last occurrence in Romans of the verb "justify" which has been one of the main key-words in the first eight chapters.

ter 4 that justification is something that is done over and over by God for the faithful.[212] Christians still are liable to sin, and when they do, it gives the devil even more opportunity to accuse them before God.   However, instead of the accusation being acknowledged and condemnation being pronounced, in the case of the faithful, God again pronounces "justified!"   He can do this because of the work of Jesus.   "A charge against God's chosen would amount to nothing; for if made, He is sure to acquit.   Should the charge be false, it will not be entertained; should it be true, his chosen will repent, and He will justify.   There is therefore no chance for the 'traducer' (devil) to secure the condemnation of the brethren."[213]

8:34 – *Who is the one who condemns?   Christ Jesus is He who died, yes, rather who was raised, who is at the right hand of God, who also intercedes for us.*

Who is the one who condemns?   There is no appeal from God's court.   If He has justified, then there is no superior court or judge who could reverse His sentence of acquittal.   When God is constantly saying "Not guilty!" there is no one who can successfully set aside His verdict and pronounce in its place a sentence of condemnation on the accused.[214]   The devil's accusations are evidently an attempt to persuade God to no longer protect or be "for" the elect (verse 31), like God protected Job in the Old Testament (Job 1:10,11) – but his accusations fail, and instead of condemning, God continues to be "for us."   Lest it be recalled again (see Romans 4:5) that a judge who acquits the guilty is a crooked judge, the following phrases will explain how God can be righteous in character while at the same time He forgives and justifies the sinner.

---

[212] See the notes at 4:19 and 4:24.

[213] Lard, *Romans*, p.287.   Lest it be thought surprising that the devil's name is introduced in the comments at this place as being the accuser, let it be remembered that his activities against God and His Anointed, as well as against the redeemed, are matters already alluded to several times in Romans, even though the devil himself has not been specifically named.   See comments at Romans 1-3 about how all have sinned (which implies the devil's activities) and how God's marvelous plan to redeem men was implemented; at 5:12 where we were told that "sin" entered the world when Adam sinned; at chapter 6 which spoke not only about being dead to sin but also about freedom from sin; and especially at chapter 7 which used the same language about "deception" that was used of the devil's tricking of Eve in the Garden. In few, if any, of those places was there any hesitancy about the explanation offered, namely, that in the unspoken background of what Paul was writing was the assumption that God was thwarting the devil's rebellious plans and actions.   So the introduction of the devil's accusatory work here should not be thought incongruous or implausible.   In fact, in his final warning in this letter, Paul for the first time specifically names Satan as he tells us that the devil's activities have been on his mind, but that "the God of peace will soon crush Satan under your feet" (Romans 16:20).

[214] The word "condemns" is a stronger word than "accuse."   It is the sentence rendered by a judge, a condemnation to punishment pronounced against the accused who has been found guilty.   The identity of the one doing the "condemning" is related to the larger problem of how these verses are punctuated.   We are probably limited to two choices, either it is the devil (the one who brings charges against God's elect) who is trying to condemn, or it is the Judge who is thought of as either condemning or justifying.   While either of these is to be preferred to the interpretation that requires the introduction of another party in addition to the accuser and the Judge, it must also be admitted that it is hard to see how it can be said that the accuser both brings charges against and also condemns the elect.

Christ Jesus is He who died.   It is very likely that the perceived connection of 34b to the context has affected the punctuation and translation,[215] and has itself been affected by comments given to previous expressions.[216]

- Perhaps it contains an implied answer to the previous question, namely, "Though there are some people whom Jesus condemns, it is not those whom God continually justifies."[217]
- Perhaps these four phrases in verse 34b go with what precedes, and give reasons why God the judge will not be pronouncing condemnation on believers.[218]

---

[215] The options from which a translator must choose have been set forth above in footnote #205.   Here the translator must decide: Is it a statement ("Christ Jesus is He who died") or is it a question ("Shall Christ Jesus who died?")?   Is it intended to answer the question "Who is the one who condemns?" or is it intended to prepare us for what verse 35 will ask?   Or is it transitional, so that it relates both to what precedes and what follows?   The comments herein given, which treat 34b as transitional, depart slightly from what the punctuation found in the NASB text might suggest.

[216] The comment made earlier at verse 33, about not restricting the time when the accusation is made against the Christian to the final judgment, also exerts an influence on how this verse is understood.   If the whole text were talking about the final judgment, then (in harmony with what the Scripture elsewhere often states) Jesus would be the One pictured as being the judge, and He would be the One who "condemns" to eternal punishment (verse 34).

[217] Just as the punctuation of the ASV/NASB would make the second question contain an implied answer to the first, so that same punctuation would tend to make the phrase "Christ Jesus ... who died ... intercedes" an implied answer to the second question about who condemns.   That implied answer could be expanded in this manner: 'Though it is true that there are some whom Jesus condemns, it is not those whom God justifies.'

Perhaps a further word about the Exalted Lord's activities during the church age is in order at this place.   As verse 34 will go on to specify, Jesus is involved in intercessory work on behalf of the redeemed.   Would such intercessory work rule out any possibility of a "condemnation" also being pronounced by Him?   Do the Scriptures elsewhere even suggest that Jesus "examines" believer's everyday activities and thoughts, let alone pass a sentence of "condemnation"?   Indeed, they just may.   It has often been observed that Paul's letters fall into four groups, and that each group has a similarity of topics covered.   1 Corinthians was written about the same time as Romans, and falls into Group Two of Paul's letters, along with 2 Corinthians and Galatians.   1 Corinthians 4:4,5 tell us that the Lord (evidently a reference to Jesus, as verse 5 ["until the Lord comes"] shows) examines Paul (and others?) habitually, continually ("examines" is a present tense verb).   While there is a final judgment, too, to be faced, as verse 5 implies, that is not when the "examination" takes place that verse 4 is talking about.   Verse 4's examination takes place before the time of the final judgment.   Thus, Scripture not only has God watching and passing judgment daily on men's actions; so evidently does Jesus.   Thus, if 1 Corinthians has Jesus making daily examinations, then it just might be possible to make a case for identifying <u>Jesus</u> as the One in Romans 8:34 who is thought of as possibly condemning the person against whom accusation had been made.   If a believer were to involve himself in habitual sin of some sort, we can be sure Jesus would condemn.   But if God's elect child is faithful, then not even Jesus would condemn when He makes His preliminary, daily, habitual inspections of men's actions, thoughts, and motives.

While it may be true that Jesus daily "examines" and in some cases "condemns," to propose that verse 34b actually *implies* that Jesus is the One who might condemn after the devil accuses, requires that we treat 34b differently than we treated 33b.   The idea that verse 33b contains an implied answer to the question "who accuses?" was rejected.   Shall we now, just a few words later, adopt the idea that 34b contains an implied answer to the question of "who condemns"?

[218] Those who opt for the punctuation found in the KJV/NIV/TEV tend to explain verse 34b as being the answer to the question "Who is the one who condemns?"   A suppressed idea must be implied to make the connection.   'No one (certainly not God!) will condemn, not where the four great evidences from Christ's

- Perhaps the four phrases are intended to introduce verse 35, and give reasons why the elect can be confident that Jesus continues to love them.[219]

Whichever is the correct idea, Murray's note about the first reason is worthy of contemplation:

> Here there is no express reference to the purpose for which Christ died nor to the persons on whose behalf He died. The apostle had sufficiently dwelt on these aspects (cf. 3:21-26; 4:25; 5:8-11; 6:4-10; 8:3,4). The terseness of this point draws attention to the stupendous significance of the death of Christ in the series of redemptive facts instanced in this verse. That Christ Jesus should have died is in itself so arresting a fact that the simple statement summons to reflection on its implication.[220]

Yes, rather who was raised.[221] The addition of "yes, rather" seems to suggest that reasons two, three, and four, are climactic.[222] Not only did He die, but His resurrection and His continuing position and work in heaven are also needed to accomplish the end for which God sent Jesus to die.[223] "Raised" is passive voice, and thus may suggest that the agent who raised Jesus is none other than God Himself (see 4:25, 6:4, 8:11), with the resurrection then being the evidence that God accepted His sacrifice for sin. Perhaps it is correct to say that God and Jesus (who is alive evermore) are both active, both thus personally guaranteeing that the beneficiaries of the new covenant actually receive the benefits of the death of the sacrificial victim (Hebrews 9:16,17).

---

redemptive work are introduced.' Because of what Jesus has done and continues to do, God has no moral need to condemn; instead He can be true to Himself while at the same time continuing to justify the believer.

[219] It is usually those who prefer the ASV/NASB punctuation who tend to take verse 34b as preparatory and introductory to what will be presented in verse 35. Instead of thinking of 34b as being an answer to the question asked in 34a, it introduces four pivotal elements of Christ's redemptive work in order to remove all uncertainty about the fact that Christ loves us.

[220] Murray, *Romans*, p.328.

[221] The marginal note adds the words "from the dead," and it is possible these words were in the original, since they are found in Codices Sinaiticus, Alexandrinus, Ephraemi, 33, and others.

[222] In a few instances, the Greek translated "yes, rather" introduces a correction or retraction of a previous statement (Thayer, *Lexicon*, p.388). In most cases where it is used, it introduces something that is greater, something to be more preferred, "what moreover is of greater moment" (Thayer's rendering at this passage).

[223] The resurrection, as indeed His reigning and His intercession, are inseparable and indispensable in the accomplishment of redemption. See 4:25, 5:10, and 6:5.

Who is at the right hand of God. Though Jesus' sacrifice for sins was complete at Calvary, there were and are activities on behalf of the redeemed that He still performs in heaven. Hebrews speaks of Him offering (once and for all) His blood on the antitypical mercy seat in heaven.[224] Having done that, He took His seat beside the Father. His being seated at the right hand of God not only focuses on the present glory of the One who was once crucified, it also serves as a reminder of what is more succinctly expressed in the word "Lord," namely, that Jesus is involved in providentially controlling what happens in the world.[225] No wonder that Paul could write (verse 31) that "God is for us!"

Who also intercedes for us. Here is the fourth reason why no one can condemn[226] the ones who are justified – Jesus constantly intercedes for them. A few verses earlier (verse 27), Paul wrote that the Holy Spirit intercedes for the redeemed. To the intercessory work of the Spirit now is added that of Jesus Himself. Only here and at Hebrews 7:25 is the word "intercession" used to explain about Christ's high priestly work on behalf of the saints.[227] "Intercedes" sometimes carries the connotation found in the word "beg," namely, that of someone on bended knee, and with outstretched hands, humbly supplicating for a favor. It is highly doubtful that such a mental image is to be conjured up when one thinks of Jesus' making intercession to the Father. Instead we should remember John 17:24, where Jesus prayed, "Father, *I desire* that they also, whom Thou hast given Me, be with Me where I am." Numerous verses suggest that Jesus now has His glorified body, but that it still bears the marks of His suffering for sin. This obvious reminder would be all that is needed to assure that the Father will continue to grant what Jesus requests.

8:35 – *Who shall separate us from the love of Christ? Shall tribulation, or distress, or persecution, or famine, or nakedness, or peril, or sword?*

Who shall separate us from the love of Christ? This is the fourth in a series of questions, all introduced by the affirmation (verse 31) that God is for us.[228] Each question highlighted and emphasized a facet of the wonderful truth that is implicit in the fact that

---

[224] Compare Hebrews 1:3, 2:9, 7:26-8:2, 9:11-14.

[225] See notes on "Lord" at Romans 1:4. Many suppose that this third expression reflects Psalm 110:1, where Jesus' present exaltation and rule over all things was long ago predicted.

[226] This comment reflects the punctuation of this passage as found in the KJV/NIV/TEV, which treat verse 34b as though it answered the question asked in 34a.

[227] Christ's high priestly intercession is also hinted at or implied in John 14:16, 1 John 2:1, and even at Romans 5:9,10 (where we learned that we are saved by His "living"). Examples of Jesus' intercessory work are His prayer for Peter when the devil asked permission to "sift" the apostle to see if his faith could be shaken (Luke 22:31,32), and His high priestly prayer recorded in John 17. Hebrews 4:14-16, 9:24, and 1 John 2:1 should also be studied to ascertain more about Christ's intercessory work.

[228] Each of the questions ("who is against us?" [verse 31], "who will bring a charge against God's elect?" [verse 33], and "who is the one that condemns?" [verse 34]) beginning with *tis* (who?), matches in form this fourth question (which also begins with *tis*), thus showing that they are intended to be coordinate.

God is for us.[229]   Here the facet held up for special contemplation is the truth that Christ continues to love us.[230]   Not only do hard times (resulting from "vanity" in the natural world, 8:18-22) come to the Christian, but evil men (at the instigation of the devil) also cause grief and hurt.[231]   It seems to be almost universal, that when these "evils" come, somehow the Christian has a vague feeling that Christ has forsaken him, or that God no longer loves him.   Nothing could be further from the truth.   And to demonstrate it beyond a doubt, Paul continues by stating several hurts that evil men cause God's people, and then asserts that none of them is proof that Christ or God has ceased to love.

Shall tribulation, or distress, or persecution, or famine, or nakedness, or peril, or sword?   These things would appear, to the ones suffering them, to belie the idea that Christ still loves them.   "When these things come upon one for Christ's sake, they certainly do not look like the tender caresses of love.   They look as though no Christ existed, or as though He had abandoned [his servants]."[232]   Paul himself had already experienced all of these trials (save the last one), yet he could triumphantly affirm his own awareness that Divine love toward him continued to flow uninterrupted.   To one who knew what it was to be persecuted by wicked men, there is a sort of natural order in the things specified in this verse.   "Tribulation" is a feeling of pressure, while "distress" is the inner distress and anxiety that comes from being penned up in a very narrow place, while not knowing quite where to turn.[233]   "Persecution" is the pursuit or hounding by enemies, sometimes includ-

---

[229] Given the way the ASV/NASB is punctuated [see note #207 above] in verses 33 and 34, verse 35 rests on what was said in 34b.   The connection would be this: Christ is still acting on behalf of the redeemed (34b) because He loves them (35), and nothing is ever to be thought of as being able to stop Christ from continuing to so love and so act on behalf of the redeemed.

Other interpreters suggest a different thread of thought in this passage.   If verse 34 introduces the question in verse 35, then it may be supposed to say that Jesus, who will uninterruptedly continue to love the ones being justified, will never be one to condemn them, even when they are accused by the devil.

By now, the careful student has almost been bewildered trying to follow all the possibilities and their ramifications that this passage presents.   In trying to grasp the central thrust of Paul's writing, many careful students likely decide that these verses form one of the "difficult passages" Peter alluded to (2 Peter 3:15,16), which men are apt to wrest and distort.   Yet, prayerfully, we press on, if perhaps some little bit of the profound message herein contained may become clear.

[230] While it is admitted that "love of Christ" could be either a subjective genitive or an objective genitive (which would speak of our love for Christ), the context makes it rather clear that it is to be taken as a subjective genitive.   Verse 37 speaks of "Him who loved us," and verse 39 uses the phrase "the love of God which is in Christ Jesus."   What is more, the passage has been speaking of what God and Christ have done and are doing for us, so we would naturally expect this to also refer to Christ's love for us.   (It perhaps should be noted, too, that there is a manuscript variation here, with Vaticanus and Sinaiticus reading "of God" rather than "of Christ," though most textual scholars suppose this is an assimilation from verse 39, and that "of Christ" is what Paul originally wrote.)

[231] Verse 35 begins with "who," so we expect him to have people (more than things) in mind.   God is for us.   Verse 33-34 have shown that the devil fails when he tries to accuse and get a condemnation of God's people.   Verse 35, therefore, likely tells what evil men do as they try to hinder the Christian.

[232] Lenski, *Romans*, p.573,574.   Remember, Romans 5:3-5 has already clearly implied God does not shelter the redeemed from the difficulties of this life, when such difficulties are needed for spiritual growth.

[233] Both "tribulation" and "distress" were explained in notes at 2:9.

ing bodily harm. "Hunger"[234] follows when you are fleeing in an effort to escape your pursuers. "Nakedness" is the lack of proper clothing when one's property is confiscated, or when he has to flee, leaving his possessions behind. "Peril" speaks of the dangers one is in when finally caught by the persecutors. "Sword" denotes the death that finally happens to the pursued.

8:36 – *Just as it is written, "FOR THY SAKE WE ARE BEING PUT TO DEATH ALL DAY LONG; WE WERE CONSIDERED AS SHEEP TO BE SLAUGHTERED."*

Just as it is written. Psalm 44:22 is quoted to show that such trials[235] have ever been the lot of God's servants, and they never did separate the saints of old from God or His love for them. To be sure, they suffered at the hands of evil men, but those Old Testament heroes (even the ones who suffered martyrdom) still continued to be the object of God's love. Of this, the record is quite plain.

"FOR THY SAKE WE ARE BEING PUT TO DEATH ALL DAY LONG. Pause to let the meaning of "For Thy sake" register! There is emphasis on it.[236] "For Thy sake" in Psalm 44 pictures Israel, not as being punished for sins they committed, but because they were being faithful to God. Likewise, verse 35 has pictured those whom Christ loves as being severely persecuted and even killed, and instead of the suffering being evidence He had stopped loving, it was just the opposite. They were suffering precisely because they were *still* objects of His love! "All day long" expresses well the thought of the Greek; it is not simply "every day," but "the whole day." Persecution and violence unto death, at the hands of devilish men, is always present.

WE WERE CONSIDERED AS SHEEP TO BE SLAUGHTERED." In Psalm 23, the Psalmist pictured God's people as being led to a green pasture and beside still waters. Now the picture has changed. The sheep are no longer in the pasture, but have been rounded up to be sold to be butchered. The figure of being rounded up and herded like sheep is all too familiar to those Christians who face persecution and death "for His name's sake."

8:37 – *But in all these things we overwhelmingly conquer through Him who loved us.*

But. Here comes the answer to the question asked in verse 35.[237] None of those things

---

[234] Thayer, *Lexicon*, p.378, notes that *limos*, translated "famine" in the NASB, is often used for "hunger" in the LXX.

[235] Taking the Psalm as being applicable to the whole list seems better than trying to limit it just to "sword."

[236] The writer of 2 Maccabees 7 applied Psalm 44:22 to the martyrdom of the mother and her seven sons, save he substitutes "for His (i.e., God's) laws" where the Psalmist had "for Thy sake." In a similar manner, "for Thy sake" can be applied to the Christian, whom Jesus pictured as suffering "for My sake and the gospel's" (Mark 8:35), as it might be also to the apostle John, who was exiled to Patmos "because of the word of God and the testimony of Jesus" (Revelation 1:9).

[237] The NASB reads "but," which is a literal translation of *alla*. The negative answer ("Nay!") that begins verse 37 in the ASV is actually only implied in the Greek, and what actually is true as the Christian meets

can separate us from Christ's love!   Several writers comment on the remarkable difference of tone between the Psalmist and Paul.   In Psalm 44, the Psalmist cannot understand the chastening, and is complaining that the trials are too bitter and extreme.   Paul, instead of complaining, exhibits a sense of rejoicing.   There is no real discrepancy.   The trials and persecutions are the same in both cases, but the difference in tone is due to the death and resurrection and high priestly work of the exalted Lord.   Through His help, the opposition of the adversaries can be turned into a means of triumph.

In all these things we overwhelmingly conquer.   "All these things" are the things just listed in verse 35.   "We are more than conquerors," as the ASV renders it, is an excellent translation, first introduced in the Geneva Bible, 1557.   We gain a victory that is more than a victory, is the idea.   We are in the process of conquering, or we keep on achieving brilliant victories.   "Not only are our adversaries deprived of power to snap the tie of the love of Christ, but their opposition is turned to our account, enhancing the power of our victory through Christ."[238]   Appearances to the contrary (the one suffering persecution is often the object of pity; we may cheer if the prisoner merely escapes; martyrdom is often seen to be a defeat), the designs of the adversaries of the Christian are completely and wholly overthrown, and the Christian comes off with all the laurels of conquest.

Through Him who loved us. Instead of drawing back from suffering for Jesus' sake, or thinking that we are no longer loved just because we are suffering, we are actually enabled by Christ to continually achieve brilliant victories.   The ones whom God justifies are the ones whom Jesus holds on to and helps.   In every encounter with adversity, even when the hostility ends in the martyrdom of the believer, the victory is unqualified.   Unbelievable? Yes, were it not that Jesus loved[239] us in the past, and continues to love and help the objects of His love.

8:38 – *For I am convinced that neither death, nor life, nor angels, nor principalities, nor things present, nor things to come, nor powers,*

For I am convinced.   Now Paul adds his own personal declaration of assurance that Christians, relying on Him who loves us, can be more than conquerors.   Paul shares his

---

those trials is affirmed instead. 'No, we are not separated from Christ's love, *but* we are more than conquerors ...' is perhaps the suppressed thought that "but" implies.

[238] Vine, *Romans*, p.134.

[239] The aorist tense participle indicates that the reference is to one particular act in the past, whereby the reality of love was proven. Undoubtedly, the event in the past is none other than Calvary. Yet it is difficult to decide if it is God's love or Jesus' love that is here intended. For several verses Paul has been demonstrating that *God* is for us. Verse 39, too, will speak of God's love for men. Perhaps it is God who is actively aiding the Christian to gain glorious victories even as seemingly impossible hardships are faced. On the other hand, if verse 35 reads "love of Christ," then it can also be equally true that it is *Jesus* whose love was demonstrated. Scriptures elsewhere could be appealed to as being parallel. Romans 5:6-8 has already told us of God's love. Galatians 2:20 tells us that Christ's love was demonstrated at Calvary. In either case, one should not read this aorist participle as though it suggested that the love (be it God's or Christ's) is all in the past; for the context has presented this love as still abiding.

conviction to encourage his Christian readers to join him in making the same declaration. "We, too, are confident!" he would have them affirm. Having followed carefully the presentation in the first eight chapters of Romans, Christians should be able to affirm with perfect confidence that *no condition of existence* (whether death or life); *no beings* (whether they be angels or principalities); *nothing in time* (whether in the present or in the future); *nothing in the way of powers or forces*; *nothing in space* (whether in the heights or depths); *nothing in all creation*; can separate him and his fellow Christians from God's saving love by placing a barrier between them and that love, so that it cannot reach them.

That neither death, nor life. For the most part, the expressions that follow occur in pairs, but it is not always the case, nor does any specific pattern or order seem to be followed. First, Paul names two conditions of man's existence. Nothing in either of these can separate the Christian from God's love by placing a barrier between them and it, so that His love cannot reach them. At first sight, it might seem surprising to find "death" listed here, for the New Testament shows that for the redeemed death puts them into the very presence of God.[240] But without the resurrection of Jesus and its implications to help men to have a clear understanding on the topic, it is perhaps true that an Old Testament saints' views of death were imperfect. It just may be that those men before Christ looked on death as being particularly hostile, because it was viewed as something that would separate them from God's fellowship (see, for example, Psalm 6:5, 30:9, 88:5,10-12, 115:17; Isaiah 38:18). If so, this erroneous view[241] is what Paul here refutes. There is nothing about death for the Christian that precludes God's love from reaching him. "Life" (remember, verse 35 has already specified some of its trials and distresses, its persecutions and martyrdoms) no more can put a barrier between God's love and the Christian than death can.

Nor angels, nor principalities. No beings, not even angelic or demonic, can put a barrier between Christians and God's love so that it cannot reach them. It is likely these two terms denote different ranks or orders of angels, just as they do elsewhere in the New Testament,[242] but whether they are good angels or evil angels, or both, is not easy to deter-

---

[240] Philippians 1:23; 2 Corinthians 5:8; Revelation 6:9.

[241] Extreme caution here is necessary. The doctrine of plenary-verbal inspiration is clearly taught in the New Testament (2 Timothy 3:16; 2 Peter 1:20,21; 1 Corinthians 2:6-13). Therefore, our comments on certain Old Testament passages, and in particular about the writer's own understanding of what he was speaking or writing by the help of the Spirit's inspiration, must not be stated in such a way as to leave the impression that the statements recorded in the Old Testament Scriptures are simply the product of man's knowledge and effort. Inspiration does not imply omniscience on the part of the speaker, or rule out an imperfect understanding of what he was prompted to speak (1 Peter 1:10,11).

[242] Sometimes it is classes of good angels, sometimes it is classes of evil (fallen) angels, that are so denoted. See Philippians 2:10; 1 Corinthians 15:24; Ephesians 6:12; 1 Peter 3:22; 2 Peter 2:4,11; Colossians 1:16. "Principalities" are angels of greater power and might than "angels," as Ephesians 6:12 and 2 Peter 2:11 show. ("Principalities," of course, as far as the Greek word itself is concerned, could denote "civil authorities," or "magistrates," but in the context here in Romans, "angels" seems to suggest a like explanation for "principalities.")

mine.[243]   The reason why no angels can separate the Christian from God's love is because Christ has once and for all won the decisive battle against such spirits (Colossians 2:15; Ephesians 1:21,22), and therefore these spirits are now subject to Him (1 Peter 3:22).

Nor things present, nor things to come.   Nothing in time, whether in the present or in the future, can prevent God's love from reaching the believer.   The present time may be grievous at times, as it was for Paul.   In those difficult moments, let it never be thought that God no longer loves His suffering children.   In one sense, the future, too, had its gloomy prospects, for the Lord's second coming is to be preceded by an apostasy, the appearance of the man of lawlessness, and perhaps a time of intense persecution directed against the saints.[244]   Yet none of these future things can separate believers from God's love for them.

Nor powers.[245]   "Powers" likely does not refer to angelic powers, nor to miracles,[246] but

---

[243] Barclay, *Romans*, p.123,24, has a long section on Rabbinic beliefs about angels, and suggests that Paul is countering the Rabbinic beliefs at this point.   He writes, "At this particular time the Jews had a highly developed belief in angels.   Everything in the world had its angel.   There was an angel of the winds, of the clouds, of the snow and hail and hoarfrost, of the thunder and the lightning, of cold and heat, and of the seasons ... According to the Rabbis there were three ranks of angels.   The first rank included thrones, cherubim, and seraphim.   The second rank included powers, lordships, and mights.   The third rank included angels and archangels and principalities.   Now the Rabbis ... believed that these angels were grudgingly hostile to man.   They believed that the angels had been angry when God created man.   It was as if they did not want to share God with anyone and they had grudged man his creation and his share with God.   The Rabbis had a legend that when God appeared on Sinai to give Moses the law, He was attended by His hosts of angels, and the angels grudged Moses the law, and assaulted Moses on his way up the mountain and tried to stop him, and would have stopped him had not God intervened.   So Paul ... says, 'Not even the grudging, jealous angels, can separate us from the love of God, much as they would like to do so'."

If Barclay's presentation of Jewish beliefs is accurate, then it is evident from the New Testament that some of those beliefs were confused and some erroneous.   The New Testament does present fallen angels as hostile to God and His plans (see, for example, Revelation 12:9), but the good angels (i.e., those who are thought of as submissively and obediently fulfilling their divinely-appointed roles in the ordering of the universe and the affairs of men) certainly are not presented as being hostile to redeemed men.

Comment must also be made on the view, stated in some commentaries, that when the Scriptures use "angels" (without any qualifying adjective), it means only good angels.   This view is not well-founded.   Cf. Acts 23:8; 1 Corinthians 4:9, 6:3; Hebrews 2:16.

[244] 2 Thessalonians 2:1-12; Revelation 20:7-10.

[245] It seems best to regard "powers" as a single item (the other terms have been given in pairs), and it also seems best (on the basis of where the word is found in the older manuscripts) to place it after "things to come" as the ASV/NASB do, rather than to place it after "principalities" as the KJV does.   The reading "angels, principalities, powers" likely has been influenced by the idea that all three terms refer to classes of angels (as indeed they do in 1 Peter 3:22; 1 Corinthians 15:24; and Ephesians 1:21).

[246] "Powers" in the New Testament, at times, is used in a context where the topic is miracles.   See Matthew 11:21; Acts 2:22; 1 Corinthians 12:10,28,29; 2 Corinthians 12:12.   Some have even alluded to 2 Thessalonians 2:9, which speaks of "false wonders," to explain how "powers" could be hostile to believers.

to human rulers, earthly potentates.[247]   None of these, even when instigating persecution on the church, have so interposed as to make it unable for God's love to continue to reach the redeemed.

8:39 – *nor height, nor depth, nor any other created thing, shall be able to separate us from the love of God, which is in Christ Jesus our Lord.*

Nor height, nor depth.   Nothing in space can keep God's love from reaching us.   Some commentators who take these terms as designating "space" appeal to Isaiah 7:11 as a parallel passage.   Others appeal to Psalm 139:7,8 as showing that the two terms were commonly used to express the limits of space.[248]

Nor any other created thing.   This concluding expression seems intended to make the list completely comprehensive, leaving no loopholes.[249]   Nothing – not any being or thing – in all of creation can block God's love from reaching the child of God.

Shall be able to separate us from the love of God.   This is the grand conclusion to which the argument of chapter 8 has been building.   Based as it is in God's love, the plan of God for redeeming faithful men will issue in glory – not because the men, of their own determination and effort, will endure, but because to God's continual justification of those faithful men is added the indwelling Spirit's aid to live the Christian life, plus God's overruling providence, plus the love of Jesus which prompts Him to continue His intercessory work until it is time for His second advent.

---

[247] "Powers" evidently is used here, like its synonym "authority" (*exousia*) at Romans 13:1,2, to designate earthly, civil leaders.   "Powers" (*dunamis*) would signify power in general, whereas *exousia* would denote the ability to use such power.   Yet it must be admitted that both Thayer and Arndt and Gingrich do not even give "earthly rulers" as a possible meaning for "powers" in this passage; both opt instead for the word here being a reference to angels of extraordinary power.

[248] Both Barclay, *Romans*, p.124, and Geoffrey W. Bromiley, *Theological Dictionary of the New Testament* Vol. 8 (Grand Rapids: Wm. B. Eerdmans, 1964), p.611ff, note that "height" and "depth" were commonly used technical terms in the world of astrology.   Barclay writes, "The ancient world was haunted by the tyranny of the stars.   They believed that a man was born under a certain star and thereby his destiny was settled.   There are some who still believe that; but the ancient world was really haunted by this supposed domination of a man's life by the influence of the stars.   Height (*hupsōma*) was the time when a star was at its zenith, and when its influence was greatest; depth (*bathos*) was the time when a star was at its lowest, waiting to rise and put its influence on some man.   Paul says to the haunted men of his age, 'The stars cannot hurt you.   In their rising and setting they are powerless to separate you from God's love'."

Since the "powers" that astrologers suppose inhabit the stars and planets are actually demonic, if Paul did have astrological beliefs in mind as he wrote "height and depths," the meaning of this expression would not differ greatly from what he meant as he wrote "angels and principalities" earlier in this list.

"Height and depth," at a later time than Paul, became technical terms in Gnosticism, but it is doubtful if an appeal to what Gnostics believed will help us to assign a definite meaning to the terms here in Romans.

[249] On the basis of this last expression, some have proposed the idea that the Bible implies there are universes other than the one "earth" is located in, and that these universes are likewise populated with intelligent life.   Sanday and Headlam (*op. cit.*, p.244), on the other hand, after noting Origen's comment about another creation besides the visible one ("in its nature visible though not as yet seen"), wonder if this is not an anticipation of what the microscope and telescope have helped men to discover.

Now we have a better idea about what Romans 5:5 meant, when Paul wrote that "the love of God has been poured out within our hearts through the Holy Spirit who was given to us." It may be observed that, whereas in verse 35 Paul wrote "the love of Christ," now he writes "the love of God, which is in Christ Jesus our Lord." The substitution of one phrase for the other leads us to see that Christ's love for man cannot be truly comprehended until it is recognized as being the love of God Himself; and neither can the love of God be understood until it was fully manifested in Jesus Christ. This is the "love" which allows no external obstacle or hostile circumstance[250] to get between the Lover and the object being loved.

Which is in Christ Jesus our Lord. God's love, from which the redeemed cannot be separated, is here specifically identified as the love which is resident in Jesus and which operates through Jesus (Romans 5:8). "It is only in Christ Jesus that it exists, only in Him that it has been manifest, and only in Him that it is operative, and only in Christ Jesus as our Lord can we know the embrace and bond of this love of God."[251]

Since Romans 5:1, Paul has been carefully enumerating and underscoring the blessed effects that result from God's way of saving men. While more yet remains to be said, there is no doubt that God is for us (8:31), that peace with God is available (5:1 and 8:6), that the vanity and death to which creation was subjected when Adam sinned will be removed (5:12-19 and 8:18-21), that the hope of the glory of God will give way to fruition (5:2 and 8:20,21) in a special sense to those who have risen to walk in newness of life (6:4 and 8:4), this walking itself being aided and helped by the indwelling Spirit (8:12-17). "God's love so sure, will still endure," until the redeemed, having conquered over all obstacles, stand on the sea of glass, and sing the song of Moses and the Lamb (Revelation 15:2-4). And even then, those in the intermediate state still have all the new heavens and new earth to look forward to (Revelation 21:1-7).

---

[250] Observe, it is *external* powers and influences, not our own failure in faithfulness, that are in view. Cannot the believer fall away? Cannot he cease to be faithful? The answer is well-given by Godet: "In the moral life freedom has always its part, as it had from the first moment of believing. What Paul means is that nothing shall pluck us out of Christ's arms *against our will*, and as long as we refuse not ourselves to abide in them." *Romans*, p.333 (emphasis mine, GLR). "In both lists [verse 35, and verses 38,39], no item such as our own unbelief, obduracy, or apostasy appears. Paul is not teaching irresistibility to or amissibility of grace or an absolute predestination. As Judas separated himself from God's love in Christ, so will others. But Paul is not dealing with this possibility, since he depicts the love that makes us conquerors. He is speaking to those who need this comfort for their valiant conquering and not to possible apostates." Lenski, *Romans*, p.576.

[251] Murray, *Romans*, p.335.

SPECIAL STUDY #7

ONCE SAVED, AM I ALWAYS SAVED?[1]

The theological doctrine embraced under the titles "Eternal Security," "The Security of the Believer," or "The Perseverance of the Saints" is popularly referred to as "once in grace, always in grace," or "once saved, always saved." In a brief statement, what is being affirmed is that once a person has become a Christian, there is no possibility of that person subsequently falling away and being eternally lost. When it is affirmed that a saved person cannot fall from grace, "grace" is equivalent to the care and preservation God's Spirit exercises on behalf of the child of God, so that he cannot fall outside the realm where "grace" would be operative in his life to produce salvation.

In commentaries on Romans 8, written from a Reformed viewpoint, one finds explanations given to these verses that either assume or espouse the *unconditional* security of the believer. Thus, it seems appropriate to study this doctrine – its history, its major component ideas, the usual arguments pro and con, and concluding with a brief presentation of the *conditional* security of the believer.

I. THE HISTORY OF THE DOCTRINE OF ETERNAL SECURITY

It is helpful to a right understanding of this question to know a few historical facts that lie in the background. The origin and history of a doctrine are important to the proper understanding of it. Many eminent names are connected with this debate, but the four most prominent during the Church Age are Augustine, Pelagius, Calvin, and Arminius. It is also helpful to be acquainted with what happened at the Synod of Dort, AD 1618-19.

A. Pre-Reformation Views

Patristic thought (roughly AD 100-500) was largely in agreement that the security of the believer is conditional.[2] However, during this period, one influential voice for the other view, namely, that the security of the believer is unconditional, was Augustine (AD 354-430).[3] This man's influence on church dogma extended for more than a thousand years

---

[1] This study, here presented in edited and abbreviated form, was originally prepared for and delivered at the North American Christian Convention, held in Atlanta, Georgia, in July, 1984.

[2] W. Boyd Hunt, "The Perseverance of the Saints," *Christianity Today*, 6:17 (May 25, 1962), p.18. The same material was later included in *Basic Christian Doctrines*, edited by Carl F.H. Henry (New York: Holt, Rinehart and Winston, 1962), p.234-240.

[3] The reader may find it beneficial to review the historical information about Augustine and Pelagius that was included in the earlier study on "Original Sin."

after his death. Starting with the idea that God's predestination is the *cause* of salvation, Augustine saw that when God elected a person to eternal life, that inevitably involved final perseverance; unconditional security was a necessary corollary. Since Augustine taught that salvation is always God's gift, he entitled his work on perseverance "On the Gift of Perseverance."[4] In order to arrive at his notion of predestination, it is very likely that Augustine violated the very rules of interpretation of Scripture that he required of others.[5] If so, since his major premise is erroneous, his view of unconditional perseverance is likely flawed. Augustine's chief opponent was Pelagius, and the debate between them brewed for several years. Pelagius' key argument was his assertion of the freedom of the human will to do good or evil. While we tend to agree with the idea of freedom of the will, it is evident that Pelagius attempted to defend his belief with faulty arguments.[6] Augustine succeeded in pointing out that some of Pelagius' arguments were patently un-Biblical, and this in turn led to Augustine's views carrying the day.

Medieval Catholic theology was heir, not of Augustinian predestinarianism and unconditional security, but of a semi-Pelagian optimism regarding man's freedom and ability. Semi-Pelagianism arose because of a reaction against some of the stricter teachings of Augustine, in particular his rigid predestination, his idea of the priority and irresistibility of grace, and his doctrine of absolute and infallible perseverance.[7] Catholic theologians continued to wrestle with this issue, with first one and then the other idea being reasserted, until the Council of Trent (1563), when the doctrine that man freely cooperates with justifying grace was asserted. "God does not forsake those who have been once justified by grace 'unless He be first forsaken by them.' This leads to a doctrine of apostasy, 'By every mortal sin grace is lost,' and of restoration, '...those who, by sin, have fallen from the received grace of justification ... may be again justified ....'"[8]

---

[4] Augustine's doctrine is quoted by Reinhold Seeberg, *Textbook of the History of Doctrines* (Grand Rapids: Baker Book House, 1958), Vol.1, p.351,352, as follows: "Therefore, whoever have in the most provident ordering of God been foreknown, predestinated, called, justified ... are now the sons of God and can by no means perish. The unpredestinated, or [un]foreknown, on the other hand, under all circumstances, fall into ruin, as parts of the *massa perditionis*. Even if they appear to be real Christians, called, justified, regenerated through baptism, renewed – they will never be saved, because they are not elected. No blame attaches to God; they are alone to blame, as they simply remain given over to their fate."

[5] Guy F. Duty, *If Ye Continue* (Minneapolis, MN: Bethany Fellowship, 1966), p.15.

[6] In an attempt to vindicate freedom of the will, Pelagius and his followers maintained that Adam's Fall involved only himself, that none of his descendants was affected. This is hardly compatible with Romans 5. In their arguments that man's "freedom of will" was not lost, they confined grace to forgiveness, and were perhaps overly optimistic in their views about how much spiritual good a man unaided by divine grace is capable of doing, even after years of evil habits and behavior. When all Pelagius' arguments are summarized, it is perhaps correct to say that he attributed to man too much ability to save himself – that all a man has to do is exercise his free will, and the result would be that he would be upright.

[7] Geoffrey W. Bromiley, "Semi-Pelagianism," in *Baker's Dictionary of Theology*, edited by Everett F. Harrison (Grand Rapids: Baker Book House, 1960), p.479,480.

[8] Hunt, "Perseverance," p.18.

B. Reformation and Post-Reformation Views

In their laudable effort to correct the corrupt religious doctrines and practices of their day, the Reformers appealed to the teachings of Augustine as a model of what the church should be. (How much better it would have been if they had gone back four more centuries to the New Testament for their model!). Thus, many of Augustine's views began to show up again in the church doctrine taught by the Reformers. On this particular matter of the perseverance of the saints, Luther and his followers taught a conditional perseverance, including the possibility of apostasy.[9] Melanchthon taught that the human will cooperates with the divine will in salvation, a doctrine that is often designated as 'synergism.' In this he was perpetuating a belief similar to the semi-Pelagian view of the Council of Trent. Thus, Lutheranism tends to teach a conditional security for the believer.

The Protestant churches that trace their doctrinal ancestry to Calvin, on the other hand, regularly teach an unconditional security or perseverance of the elect. Calvin got his inspiration on predestination from Augustine, and from this starting point worked out his other doctrines. "Calvin, like Augustine, defined predestination as God's eternal decree by which God's absolute sovereign will decided the eternal destiny of every individual."[10] The idea that each individual's destiny is absolutely decided by God logically leads to the doctrine of unconditional perseverance. Once He has elected and saved a person, there is no way short of another act of God which could undo what God had decreed; therefore, the man's salvation is sure, and certain also is his assurance of salvation.[11] Calvin's writings on predestination and unconditional election greatly intensified the debate among theologians which had been raging for a thousand years.

One important theologian who opposed Calvin's views was Jacob Arminius, a Dutch preacher who at first defended Calvin, until further study led him to adopt the doctrine of conditional security of the believer.   His followers, called Arminians or Remonstrants,

---

[9] See Martin Luther, "The Greater Catechism," edited and translated by Henry Wace and C.A. Buchheim, in *Luther's Primary Works Together with His Shorter and Larger Catechism* (London: Hodder and Stoughton, 1896), p.141f. The Lutheran confessions also plainly allow for the possibility of apostasy, e.g., Article XII of *The Augsburg Confession*; Article IV, Negative III of *The Formula of Concord*; and Article IV, III of *The Saxon Articles*.

[10] Duty, *If Ye Continue*, p.17. See also Calvin's *Institutes*, Book 3, Chapter XXI.

[11] It has been shown that at times Calvin was not consistent in his presentation of this doctrine, but the predominant view that comes through loud and clear is "the inflexible constancy of election." See *Institutes*, Book 3, Chapter XXIV.10, and Book 3, Chapter II.16,40. "Calvin ... made inconsistent and self-contradictory statements ... It seems strange that Calvin, the law student, did not see the 'multitude of inconsistencies and self-contradictory tendencies' in the Augustinian theology he adopted. 'Calvin, honest as he meant to be, found ... the fatal facility of reading into Scripture what he wished to find there' ... '[Calvin] had a manner in which he explains away every passage which runs counter to his dogmatic pre-possessions'." Duty, *If Ye Continue*, p.18,19. The quotations about Calvin's methods, Duty observes, come from a historian friendly to Calvin, namely, F.W. Farrar, *History of Interpretation* (Grand Rapids: Baker Book House, 1961), p.351,343.

carried matters considerably further than Arminius had done in his writings. In 1610, they set forth their non-Calvinist views in a document called "Remonstrance," and the Dutch Protestant ministers who signed the document came to be known as "Remonstrants." Its five articles are summarized by Roger Nicole:

I.   God elects or reproves on the basis of foreseen faith or unbelief.
II.   Christ died for all men and for every man, although only believers are saved.
III.   Man is so depraved that divine grace is necessary unto faith or any good deed.
IV.   This grace may be resisted.
V.   Whether all who are truly regenerate will certainly persevere in the faith is a point which needs further investigation.[12]

After considerable discussion, these views were condemned at the Synod of Dort (1618-19).[13] Dort's answer to Arminianism was formulated in five canons that have popularly been expressed by the acrostic "TULIP" – namely, Total depravity, Unconditional election, Limited atonement, Irresistible grace, and the Perseverance of the saints. These five points have become the classic definition of Calvinism since.

Dort did not actually settle the 1300-year-old debate, for both conditional and unconditional security continued to be taught and championed.[14] The Westminster Confession (1647) carried on the classic Calvinistic views of unconditional security. "This perseverance of the saints depends, not upon their own free will, but upon the immutability of the decree of election ...."[15] John Wesley, on the other hand, vexed by the careless living of some Calvinists (after all, if one's salvation is unconditionally guaranteed, it does not really matter how one lives, does it?), stressed the necessity of careful living in harmony with the exhortations in the Word of God, and he allowed for the possibility of apostasy if one failed consistently to demonstrate Christian character and life. Later Methodist writers have tended to be synergistic, but with some tending toward Calvin by

---

[12] Roger Nicole, "Arminianism," in *Baker's Dictionary of Theology*, edited by Everett F. Harrison (Grand Rapids: Baker Book House, 1960), p.64,65.

[13] The Synod of Dort was meant to be a general council of all Calvinistic churches to sit in judgment on Arminianism. The Arminians were summoned before the council and given a hearing, but the council was biased from the start and the foregone conclusion was predictable. The Arminian doctrine of conditional perseverance (predestination) was examined and condemned. Arminius, who had died before the council was held, was branded as a heretic. Two hundred Arminian preachers were deprived of their pulpits, and those who refused to be silent were banished from their country. Calvinists were determined to crush the Arminian "heresy." Arminian leaders were persecuted, imprisoned, beheaded, or burned at the stake.

[14] Nicole, "Arminianism," notes that in the Netherlands after Dort, Arminianism continued to have its proponents, such as Hugo Grotius. However, the rationalism of the 18th century adversely affected the Remonstrants' views of inspiration and the Trinity. Summarizing its influence outside of Holland, Nicole wrote, "Arminianism exercised considerable influence in France, Switzerland, Germany, and England, and hence throughout the world. In a number of cases this point of view gained the upper hand in spite of Calvinistic confessions of faith."

[15] "Westminster Confession," Cap.XVII.II, in Philip Schaff, ed., *Creeds of Christendom* (Grand Rapids: Baker Book House, 1966), Vol.3, p.637.

emphasizing the need for grace, while others tend more toward Pelagius by emphasizing the freedom of the will.[16]

C. Modern Developments

The debate between Calvinists and Arminians entered the American theological scene along with the colonists who came from Europe. On the Calvinistic side were the Reformed, Presbyterian, Free, Puritan, Congregational, and most Baptist groups. On the Arminian side (in the matter of conditional security) were the Lutheran, Anabaptist (Mennonite), General and Free Will Baptist, Methodist, Holiness, and Restoration Movement churches.

Since many of the early Restoration Movement preachers came out of Calvinistic backgrounds, their own inner struggles as they tried to reconcile the five points of Calvinism with what they could read in their own Bibles are exciting to read about and ponder. A typical example is "Raccoon" John Smith, whose parents were rigid Calvinistic Baptists, so this is the heritage in which Smith grew up. The incisive questions he began asking about the points of dogma he heard and the way he found answers to his questions makes for delightful reading.[17] The reasons why he came to reject the five points of Calvinism have pretty much become standard in the Christian Churches.[18]

Recent decades have witnessed a revival of interest in Puritan theology. Book clubs and publishing houses have issued reprints of the classic Puritan works. In these, Calvinistic doctrine is making a comeback, after it had declined somewhat in the middle decades of the 20th century.

D. What History Has Shown

It can be said that the doctrine of unconditional security is a step-child of Augustine's predestination theology, rather than being exegetically derived straight from the Word of God. Augustine's dogmas have prospered and declined as the debate about them has raged among theologians through the centuries. The doctrine received a "booster shot" from Calvin (after he revived it from Augustine), from which it has gone into its Protestant orbit. Down through history, as one reads the positions defended and the arguments put forth to substantiate each side of the debate, one thing impresses us – in the heat of controversy, defenders and proponents often claimed things not Biblically defensible while trying to jus-

---

[16] Hunt, "Perseverance," p.19.

[17] See John W. Wade, *Pioneers of the Restoration Movement* (Cincinnati: Standard Publishing Co., 1966), p.49-60; John A. Williams, *Life of Elder John Smith* (Cincinnati: Standard Publishing Co., 1904). Louis Cochran's *Raccoon John Smith* (New York: Duell, Sloan & Pearce, 1963), while presented as an historical-fiction novel, is a convenient place to read many of William's paragraphs.

[18] Debates between the "Reformers" and Calvinistic teachers have included the *Bogard-Warlick Debate* (Shreveport, LA: Lambert Huffman Press, 1915), proposition #4; the *Franklin-Fisher Debate* (Louisville, KY: G.W. Robertson & Co., 1858. Reprinted Joplin, MO: College Press, 196?), proposition #4; and the *Kelley-Garner Debate* (Reynoldsville, TX: Published by M. Kelley, 1953), proposition #3.

tify the position they had staked out in the debate. Those "extreme positions" then became the "orthodox" or "non-orthodox" views going into the next round of debate, and these in turn were what later generations fought to defend or destroy.

In summary, the doctrine may be stated on this fashion: the doctrine of the unconditional security (the impossibility of apostasy) of the elect grows out of, and is the logical outcome of, the doctrine of predestination. It is that God decreed before the world began that a certain elect number should be saved and a number just as fixed and certain could not be saved. Neither class is to be increased nor diminished, having been determined by God, irrevocably and unalterably, before the foundation of the world. Of course, if a man's salvation has been settled from all eternity, then he is bound to persevere; the man is made that way. God has made him a certain way, either a vessel to be saved, or a vessel to be damned. Once God has so made the man, he could not be or do otherwise than how God has made him.

This doctrine of unconditional security requires as one corollary the denial of any free moral agency to man. Man can have no choice or volition in the matter of salvation. He is a mere machine in the hands of God. His salvation on the one hand, or his damnation on the other, is simply a matter of naked omnipotence! The man could not do anything one way or the other that would affect his salvation. If he is predestined to be saved, he could not be lost, no matter what he does. And if he is predestined to be damned, a reprobate, then he could not do anything to be saved, and could not be saved no matter what he did. There is a second corollary required, namely, the direct converting power of the Holy Spirit. Man is wholly passive in salvation. In the matter of salvation or in the matter of damnation, God saves or God damns. No man can do anything to be saved, because the theory requires the direct operation of the Holy Spirit to regenerate man. After conversion, no man can do anything that would result in his being damned, for no man can successfully undo what God has done. Therefore, the dogma of eternal security (as inherited from Augustine and Calvin) teaches that a saved man cannot fall from grace.

II. THE DOCTRINE OF UNCONDITIONAL ETERNAL SECURITY IN DETAIL

A. The Doctrine – As Stated by Its Defenders

Theologically considered, the doctrine signifies "that they whom God has regenerated and effectually called to a state of grace can neither totally nor finally fall away from that state, but shall certainly persevere therein to the end and be eternally saved."[19] This perseverance is possible because the indwelling Spirit keeps those whom God has redeemed. Passages cited to support the doctrine are John 3:36, 5:24, 10:27-30, and Philippians 1:6.

---

[19] Louis Berkhof, *Systematic Theology* (Grand Rapids: Wm. B. Eerdmans Publishing Co., 1941), p.545.

The *Westminster Confession of Faith* words the doctrine in this manner: "They whom God hath accepted in His Beloved, effectually called and sanctified by His Spirit, can neither totally nor finally fall away from the state of grace; but shall certainly persevere therein to the end, and be eternally saved."[20] According to the Calvinistic theory of regeneration, the soul is chosen by God from eternity, its conversion and regeneration are wholly the work of the Holy Spirit, and the work, having been begun by God for His own good pleasure, will not and cannot be abandoned by Him. Or, to quote again the words of the *Westminster Confession of Faith*:

> This perseverance of the saints depends not upon their own free will, but upon the immutability of the decree of election, flowing from the free and unchangeable love of God the Father: upon the efficacy of the merit and intercession of Jesus Christ; the abiding of the Spirit, and the seed of God within them; and the nature of the covenant of grace – from all which ariseth also the certainty and infallibility thereof.[21]

Some Calvinistic presentations of the doctrine of unconditional security have almost permitted carnal living. J. Oliver Buswell quotes what he designates as pseudo-Calvinistic speakers who have told young people, "Dear young people, there are two ways to go to heaven: the spiritual way and the carnal way. It is so much better to take the spiritual way."[22] The November 19, 1948 *Sword of the Lord* carried a sermon in which one finds this paragraph:

> We take the position that a Christian's sins do not damn his soul! The way a Christian lives, what he says, his character, his conduct, or his attitude toward other people, have nothing whatever to do with the salvation of his soul ... All the prayers a man may pray, all the Bible he may read, all the churches he may belong to, all the services he may attend, all the sermons he may practice, all the debts he may pay, all the ordinances he may observe, all the laws he may keep, all the benevolent acts he may perform, will not make his soul one whit safer; all the sins he may commit, from idolatry to murder, will not make his soul in any more danger.[23]

Harry A. Ironside delivered an address in the Moody Memorial Church a few decades ago

---

[20] Chap. XVII.I, Schaff, *Creeds of Christendom*, Vol.3, p.636.

[21] Chap. XVII.II, Schaff, *op. cit.*, p.636,637.

[22] J. Oliver Buswell, *A Systematic Theology of the Christian Religion* (Grand Rapids: Zondervan Publishing House, 1962), Vol.2, p.146.

[23] Quoted by O.L. Mankamyer, in his tract *Once in Grace, Always in Grace, in the Light of God's Word* (Yellville, AR: published by the author, 1953), p.3. John H. Gerstner, "Perseverance," in *Baker Dictionary of Theology*, edited by Everett F. Harrison (Grand Rapids: Baker Book House, 1960), p.403,404, would insist that such an antinomian presentation is a perversion of the doctrine of eternal security. "... perseverance not only does not, but cannot, lead to antinomianism because, by definition, it means persevering in holiness and not in unholiness," he writes.

in which, as he presented his understanding of the doctrine of eternal security, he offered this "meaning" or definition of the doctrine:

> When we speak of the eternal security of the believer, what do we mean? We mean that once a poor sinner has been regenerated by the Word and the Spirit of God, once he has received a new life and a new nature, has been made partaker of the divine nature, once he has been justified from every charge before the throne of God, it is absolutely impossible that that man should ever again be a lost soul. Having said that, let me say what we do *not* mean when we speak of eternal security of the believer. We do not mean that it necessarily follows that if one professes to be saved, if he comes out to the front in a meeting, shakes the preacher's hand, and says he accepts the Lord Jesus Christ as his Savior, that that person is eternally safe. It does not mean that if one joins a church or makes a profession of faith, is baptized, becomes a communicant, takes an interest in Christian work, that that person is forever secure. It does not mean that because one manifests certain gifts and exercises these gifts in Christian testimony, that that person is necessarily eternally secure.
>
> Our Lord Jesus Christ said to the people of His day, as recorded in Matthew 7:21-23, "Not everyone that saith unto Me, Lord, Lord, shall enter into the kingdom of heaven; but he that doeth the will of My Father which is in heaven. Many will say to Me in that day, Lord, Lord, have we not prophesied in Thy name? And in Thy name have cast out devils? And in Thy name done many wonderful works? And then will I profess unto them, I never knew you: depart from Me, ye that work iniquity." Such people then may have been very active in what is called Christian work – they have preached, they have cast out demons ... they have professed with their lips, they have accomplished many wonderful works, but they are found in that day among the lost, and when they plead their great activity and their earnestness in Christian testimony, the Lord says to them, "I never knew you." Notice, He does not say to them, "I used to know you, but you have forfeited My favor and I do not know you any longer." He says, "I *never* knew you."[24]

B. Summary of the Major Component Ideas Involved in the Doctrine of the Unconditional Security of the Saints

1) The salvation of the sinner is all God's doing. Man is wholly passive, simply a recipient of the salvation God provides. Ephesians 2:6-8 ("[God] raised us up with Him, and seated us with Him in the heavenly places ... by grace you have been saved"), 1 Corinthians 3:6-9 ("God was causing the growth. ... You are God's field, God's building"), and other similar passages, are appealed to as Biblical evidence that salvation is something God does to the sinner.

---

[24] H. A. Ironside, *The Eternal Security of the Believer* (New York: Loizeaux Brothers, Publishers, 1934), p.6,7.

2) The choice of who will receive salvation was made by God back in eternity before creation, and is irrevocable. God decided who – individually – would be saved, and who would be lost. Any freedom of choice on man's part is wholly rejected. These ideas are affirmed to be gleaned from passages such as Revelation 13:8 ("every one whose name has not been written from the foundation of the world in the book of life") and Romans 11:29 ("the gifts and the calling of God are irrevocable").

3) Faith and justification by faith are a one-time act. When saving faith is given to a man by God, that man's salvation is once-for-all taken care of. The only 'belief' that counts for salvation is the initial act of believing. To demonstrate this one-time aspect, appeal is made to the aorist tense verb[25] "drinks" in John 4:14 ("whoever *drinks* of the water that I shall give him shall never thirst"), and to the aorist tense verb forms in Ephesians 1:13,14 ("heard," "believed," "sealed", ASV).

4) The exhortations to Christian living found in the New Testament are not based on the possibility of losing one's salvation, but are based on appreciation for what God has done and plans to do in the Christian's life. For example, the appeal to Christian living found in Romans 12:1 (which begins with "therefore...") shows the appeal is based on all that has gone before in Romans 1-11. Likewise, Titus 2:11,12 ("the grace of God has appeared, bringing salvation to all men, instructing us to deny ungodliness and worldly desires and to live sensibly ..."); Colossians 3:1-3 ("if then you have been raised with Christ, keep seeking the things above"); and 2 Corinthians 5:14,15 ("the love of Christ controls us ... that they who live should no longer live for themselves, but for Him").

5) Sins committed by Christians may sever fellowship with the Father, but not relationship. A man's son can never cease being a son; a child of God can never cease being God's child. Habitual sins may rob a man of his opportunity to serve or minister (as for example, 1 Corinthians 9:24-27, which is interpreted to mean that the runner is "disqualified" from further participation). Habitual sins may rob a man of his reward, but they do not endanger his salvation (as for example, 1 Corinthians 3:12-15, where the man's work is burned up, but the man's soul is still saved). The sense of fellowship with the Father that is broken by sin may be restored by confession (as taught in 1 John 1:7-9, "if we confess our sins, He is faithful ... to forgive and cleanse us"). The "crowns" promised to believers may be lost, but not salvation, is how it is taught by those who espouse unconditional eternal security.

6) Persistent sin after profession of faith reveals the lack of genuine conversion. 1 John 3:6-10 is appealed to for proof: "no one who sins has seen Him or knows Him ... the one who practices sin is of the devil ... no one who is born of God practices sin," where all the verbs are present tense, implying continuous action. If a man quits Christ and the church after years of service, he was never saved in the first place. 1 John 2:19 ("they went out from us, but they were not *really* of us, for if they had been of us, they would have

---

[25] The aorist tense denotes a completed act in the past time.

remained with us") and Matthew 7:23 ("I never knew you"), are the standard verses used to show they were never saved in the first place.

7) Sins committed by Christians will result in "discipline" from the Father, but not in eternal punishment. Hebrews 12:5-13 ("whom the Lord loves He disciplines"). Of what this disciplining consists is found in those passages that threaten "death" as a consequence of sinning – but observe carefully, these passages are interpreted to mean that it is a premature *physical* death, so that a man's further service is hindered, and not the "second death" that is threatened.

III. HOW THE DOCTRINE OF UNCONDITIONAL ETERNAL SECURITY IS DEFENDED

A dozen or more standard arguments, marshaled to convince the doubters, can be found repeated over and over in popular presentations of the Calvinistic doctrine of eternal security. Among them are the following:

A. Eternal Security is the Plain Teaching of the Bible

A number of verses can be alluded to, with the affirmation that they indeed do teach unconditional security. John 10:27-29 includes these words spoken by Jesus Himself, "I give eternal life to them; and they shall never perish." Romans 8:29-30 is seen to flatly affirm that every believer is unconditionally foreknown, predestined, called, justified, and glorified. Philippians 1:6 is appealed to in order to show that what God begins, God finishes. After Romans 8:35-37 has demonstrated the continuing love of Christ and God for the believer, it is reasoned that for a believer to be lost, he would somehow have to be separated from the love of God, and become instead an object of God's wrath, the very thing being denied as possible in this passage. 1 Peter 1:5 ("protected by the power of God"), 2 Timothy 4:18 ("the Lord ... will bring me safely to His heavenly kingdom"), and 1 Corinthians 1:7-9 ("our Lord Jesus Christ ... shall also confirm you to the end, blameless ... God is faithful"), are likewise said to substantiate the doctrine of the unconditional security for the elect. Appeal is also made to Jesus' promise found in John 6:37-40 ("the one who comes to Me I will certainly not cast out"). Even the 23rd Psalm is pressed into service to support this doctrine, where we read, "And I will dwell in the house of the Lord *forever*." "The true Christian is no temporary visitor, but a permanent dweller in the house of the Lord. How those rob this Psalm of its deeper and richer meaning who teach that the grace of God is but a temporary thing."[26]

B. Eternal Life is a Present Possession

John 3:16 says the believer already has "eternal life." Likewise read John 3:36 and

---

[26] Loraine Boettner, *The Reformed Doctrine of Predestination* (Philadelphia: Presbyterian and Reformed Publishing Co., 1968), p.199.

5:24.   Once this fact has been duly noted, then it is argued, 'If the one who now possesses eternal life could in any way lose it, then it wasn't *eternal*, was it?'

C. "No Condemnation" is the Promise Held Out to Believers

Romans 8:1 reads, "There is therefore now no condemnation for those who are in Christ Jesus."   John 3:18 (KJV) reads, "He that believeth in Him is not condemned."   John 10:28 promises "they shall never perish."   John 5:24 (KJV) reads, "he that believeth ... shall not come into condemnation."   Once these verses have been pointed out, it is customarily observed, 'If one who is saved could later be lost, then it would be possible for him to be condemned, to perish.   Such a possibility is plainly ruled out by the verses just quoted.'

D. Knowledge of Salvation Excludes the Idea That It Could Be Lost

The Bible does affirm that it is possible for a man to know he is saved.   1 John 5:13 ("that you may know that you have eternal life"), 1 John 3:2 ("we are children of God"), and 2 Corinthians 5:1 ("we know ... we have a building from God") are typical of the passages which indicate the Christian's inner awareness of his relationship with God. Teachers of unconditional eternal security allege that if it were possible for a believer (at some time in the future) to lose his salvation, then such present knowledge or awareness would be impossible.[27]

E. A "Son of God" Will Always Be a Son

When a person is once born into a family, can he ever be unborn, it is asked?   The prodigal son was still a "son" when he returned (Luke 15:22-24); he never lost his sonship. A born son will always be a son.   He may sin and need "chastening," but he can do nothing to destroy the fact that he is a son.[28]

F. Our Citizenship is in Heaven

Born-again believers have been registered (enrolled) on the heavenly citizenship list

---

[27] "A consistent Arminian, with his doctrines of free will and falling from grace, can never in this life be certain of his eternal salvation.   He may, indeed, have the assurance of his *present* salvation, but he can have only a *hope* of his final salvation.   He may regard his final salvation as highly probable, but he cannot know it as a certainty.   He has seen many of his fellow Christians backslide and perish after making a good start.   Why may not he do the same thing?   If Arminianism were true, Christians would still be in a very dangerous position, with their eternal destiny suspended on the probability that their weak, creaturely wills would continue to choose right."   Boettner, *op. cit.*, p.193.

[28] Arminians would respond, "Didn't you ever hear of a child dying?"   Indeed, he was born into the family, but though it may not be possible to be un-born, it is possible to die.   There is a physical death and there is a spiritual death.   John 6:53 says, "Unless you eat the flesh of the Son of Man and drink His blood, you have no life in yourselves."   What is the state of a man who has "no life"?   He is dead!   It apparently is a doctrine of the New Testament that continued, habitual sin will kill even a 'son' of God.

per Philippians 3:20 ("our citizenship is in heaven") and Hebrews 12:23 ("the first-born who are enrolled in heaven"), whereas the names of the lost have not been written in the book of life, Revelation 17:8 ("whose name has not been written in the book of life from the foundation of the world"). Believing that the names of the saved were inscribed in the book of life before creation, and also that the names of the lost never have been nor will be written in the book of life, the defender of unconditional security asks, "If it is possible that a person once saved could be lost, then did God make a mistake when (back in eternity) He registered the person's name on the heavenly citizenship list?" Such a doctrinal presentation that would require God to have made a mistake just cannot be right, he thinks. Jesus told His disciples to rejoice in the fact that their names were written in heaven (Luke 10:20). How could a person rejoice if there was the possibility that his name was only temporarily written in the Lamb's book of life? God cannot be thought to have made the mistake of writing a name in the book of life that He later would have to blot out.

G. God's Foreknowledge and Election are Seen to Issue in Eternal Security

Romans 8:29,30 tell us that whom God foreknew, He predestined to be conformed to the image of His Son. 1 Peter 1:2 shows that election was done "according to the foreknowledge of God the Father," while Ephesians 1:4 is said to demonstrate that this election took place "before the foundation of the world." Once these verses have been called to mind, proponents of unconditional perseverance of the saints hasten to drive home their point. They reason thusly, 'Those who teach a person may be saved and then lose his salvation must also teach that God's election can be a temporary thing; indeed, they must teach that God's foreknowledge must have been faulty, for if He knew the person would eventually end up lost, why save him in the first place?'

H. The Gift of the Holy Spirit is Evidence of Eternal Security

Believers are indwelt by the Holy Spirit (Romans 8:9), and are sealed by the Spirit (Ephesians 1:13,14). Furthermore, it is pointed out that Jesus even promised that the Spirit would "be with you forever" (John 14:16). For one to be saved and then lost would mean that the Spirit no longer dwells within, the seal is broken, and Jesus' promise has failed.

I. Christ's Advocacy and Intercession Insure the Believer's Security

The ascended Christ does make intercession on behalf of His people, Romans 8:34 and Hebrews 7:25. John 11:42 affirms that the Father always hears Jesus' prayers. Hence, the Arminian, holding that Christians may fall away, must deny either the passages which declare that Christ makes intercession for His people, or he must deny the passage which declares that Jesus' prayers are always heard.

J. God's Love is a Reason to Believe in Eternal Security

Romans 5:8-10 tell us that God loved us when we were sinners. Verses 9-11 tell us that "much more" will He love us now that we have been justified, and save us from wrath.

Does God's love blow hot and cold?   Are we to think that while we were sinners we could *not* provoke Him so that He ceased to love, but that after we have been saved we *can* so act as to provoke God to change His mind and stop loving, and therefore wholly withdraw His grace?   Others ask, Wouldn't God be "cruel" if he allowed a person once saved to live long enough to be lost again?   This, too, is an appeal to the love of God as an evidence of security.

K. The Fact that Salvation is "By Grace" is Another Evidence for Eternal Security

When it is affirmed that salvation is "by grace," what is meant is that salvation is something that is entirely God's work.   The believer does not cooperate with God in any way in the accomplishing of personal salvation.   The believer is a new creation, 2 Corinthians 5:17 ("if any man is in Christ, he is a new creature"), something God has made. When Paul wrote, "By grace you have been saved through faith, and that not of yourselves, it is the gift of God, not as a result of works ..." (Ephesians 2:8,9), he is affirming that God is the one who did the saving without any help from man.   2 Timothy 1:9 ("who has saved us ... not according to our works") likewise is said to rule out any cooperation by man in the matter of salvation.   Once this major premise is established, then the minor premise that follows goes like this: if nothing a man does contributes to his salvation to begin with, then it follows that nothing a man does could detract from his salvation later.   It all depends on God, and He has saved – therefore the salvation is guaranteed!   Perseverance in salvation is not dependent on a man's good works, but on God's grace.   Romans 6:14 says, "You are not under law, but under grace."   "Since they are not under law, they cannot be condemned for having violated law. ... Sin cannot possibly be their downfall, for they are under a system of grace and are not treated according to their deserts."[29]

L. The Nature of Regeneration is Seen to Guarantee the Security of the Believer

In Calvinistic thought, regeneration is defined as being a supernatural act of God, by which man's fallen inner nature is re-created.   The argument for unconditional eternal security follows thus: if it took a supernatural act by God to save a man, it would take another supernatural act by God Himself to remove that salvation and change the inner nature back again.   That God would ever reverse the inner change and cause the new life He had implanted to be lost is something unthinkable and completely incongruous with the verses that speak of God's love, the indwelling of the Spirit, and the intercession of Jesus.

M. The Believer's Position "In Christ" Insures His Security

Among the New Testament verses that show the believer is "in Christ" are Romans 8:1 and 12:5; 1 John 5:20; and Colossians 1:28.   Because a believer is "in Christ," the believer's eternal future is linked with that of Christ.   If He can ever be lost, then so can the believer.   If He cannot be lost, then neither can the believer.

---

[29] Boettner, *Reformed Doctrine of Predestination*, p.184.

It can be seen by now that if one grants the major premise that back in eternity before creation God elected and predestined certain individuals to salvation, one could also marshal a number of verses to demonstrate that this selection unconditionally guarantees the security or perseverance of the elect.

At the same time, it can also be seen that there are some parts of the whole idea that are hard to accept, not only because the opposite of election to salvation (namely, election of certain individuals to damnation) must either be defended or explained away, but also because they require an unexpected 'twist' to be given to those verses that, on the surface at least, seem to be not harmonizable with the doctrine of unconditional eternal security.

Certainly, the Bible says too much about the security of a Christian to dismiss the topic altogether as a figment of the imagination. What is needed is a presentation of the doctrine that allows the Scriptures themselves (rather than some previously held doctrinal position) to determine the content of our belief. This is what the rest of this Special Study shall attempt to do.

IV. THERE IS A *SECURITY* FOR BELIEVERS TAUGHT IN THE BIBLE

"Security" is used in the broad sense that it means 'freedom from danger, care, or fear; feeling or condition of being safe; certainty; something that secures or makes safe; confidence; safety, protection, defense.'

A. "Security" is Present in the Idea of the Providence of God

"Providence" has reference to that care, preservation, and government that God exercises over all things that He has created, so that they accomplish the purposes for which they were made.[30] Among the items that are usually classified as "special providence," the ones which contribute to the security of the believer especially, are answered prayer and deliverance from temptation, including the way of escape.

B. The Bible Affirms that the Believer is "Kept, Guarded, Protected"

Jude 24 speaks of how God is "able to keep you from stumbling, and to make you stand in the presence of His glory blameless." In a similar vein, Romans 16:25 offers praise "to Him who is able to establish you (i.e., has power to make your standing sure)." 1 Peter 1:5 reminds us that those who will in the future obtain the imperishable inheritance are in the meantime "protected by the power of God." As he begins his letter, Jude expresses his confidence of being "kept for Jesus Christ." Paul prays that God will sanctify and preserve the Thessalonian Christians, and then he expresses confidence that

---

[30] See Special Study #2, at the close of chapter 1, where the doctrine of God's "providence" has been presented in detail.

"He also will bring it to pass" (1 Thessalonians 5:23,24). In his last letter, Paul again proclaims his certainty of the Lord's continuing help, when he writes, "The Lord will deliver me from every evil deed, and will bring me safely to His heavenly kingdom" (2 Timothy 4:18).

C. Jesus Indeed is Active in Intercessory Work

Just before Jesus returned to heaven to be with the Father, He prayed that God would (in the future) put limits on the devil with reference to the evil one's ability to tempt the apostles (John 17:15). Romans 8:34 suggests that Christ is not idle now that He has resumed His place in heaven, but that He continues to make intercession for the saints. So likewise affirm Hebrews 7:24,25, and 9:24. John uses the word "advocate" to designate this activity of Christ, when he speaks of Him as our "Advocate with the Father" (1 John 2:1). Perhaps much of Jesus' intercessory work is similar to what He did for Peter while He was still on earth. "Simon, Simon, behold, Satan has demanded *permission* to sift you like wheat; but I have prayed for you, that your faith may not fail; and you, when once you have turned again, strengthen your brothers" (Luke 22:31,32).

D. Limits Have Been Placed on the Devil After the Old Slavery to Sin is Broken

Romans 6:7 and 6:14 show that the old slavery to sin, which lasted ever since the person committed his first sin, is broken when he becomes united with Christ. Likewise, Romans 8:1 indicates that the condemnation to slavery to sin is a thing of the past for the one who is in Christ Jesus. These verses better help us to understand the Model Prayer, too, where Jesus taught His disciples to pray, "Do not permit us to be tempted, but deliver us from the evil one" (Matthew 6:13, GLR's translation). It requests God to put limits on the devil's efforts to tempt the disciple. Because of this help from God, the one who has been born again does not go on sinning habitually. The Son of God appeared for this purpose, that He might destroy the works of the devil (1 John 3:6-9).

E. Sins Really Have Been Atoned For

The believer can have a sense of well-being, a sense of security, because for him it is not like it was when only the blood of bulls and goats could be offered (Hebrews 10:1-10). Indeed, through Calvary, God "has perfected for all time those who are sanctified" (Hebrews 10:14).[31] However, let it be noted that there is a vast difference between God's *provision* in the atonement, and man's *appropriation* of what God has provided.[32]

---

[31] "Perfect" is a word that has been used in Hebrews (e.g., 7:19, 10:1) to mean 'qualify a man to come into the presence of God because his sins have been covered.'

[32] This last sentence, with its word "appropriation," anticipates what shall be developed in the next major point of this study, namely, that the security of the believer is *conditional*.

F. A Goal is Promised to Believers.

There is security in the knowledge that God is moving all of history toward a goal, the second advent of Christ, and the eternal kingdom to follow. A number of things will happen to believers at that great day. Jesus will "present to Himself the church in all her glory, having no spot or wrinkle ... blameless" (Ephesians 5:27). Jesus Himself promises not to lose or cast out any one who comes to Him, but rather that He will raise up the believer from the dead on the last day (John 6:37-40). On another occasion, He promised to give eternal life to the sheep who hear his voice; such sheep will "never perish, and no one shall snatch them out of My hand," He said (John 10:25-30). Paul picked up this theme from Jesus' teaching, when he promised the Corinthians that "Jesus Christ ... shall also confirm you to the end, blameless in the day of our Lord Jesus Christ" (1 Corinthians 1:7,8).

There *is* a security promised to the believer – and it is far more pronounced in the New Testament than the frequency of sermons on the topic in Christian churches might lead one to think.

V.   IT IS A *CONDITIONAL* SECURITY THAT THE BIBLE TEACHES

In fact, it is not the matter of security itself that is the item of dispute; rather, it is the nature of its bestowal that is the point of controversy. Does the Bible present this security as being unconditionally granted from all eternity only to certain elect individuals,[33] or does the Bible make the security contingent on a person's continuing to believe (i.e., on a person's faithfulness)? The remainder of this Special Study shall be occupied with the presentation of the position that it is a *conditional* security that is offered by God to people.

A. How Election, Predestination, and Grace are Related to the Security of the Believer

Ephesians 1:4,5 present the doctrine of election in its clearest light. "He chose us (i.e., elected us) in Him (Christ) before the foundation of the world ... In love He predestined us to adoption as sons ...," Paul writes. In other words, back in eternity, God wanted a family of children who would love Him, not because they had to, but because they wanted to. The people He created would love Him, not because it was all they *could* do by virtue of the way He created them; instead, they would be *free to choose* whether or not they would love Him. In His plan, God determined that all who were "in Christ" would be part of that family. But whether or not a person is "in Christ" is a result of that person's own choice. Ephesians 1:13ff tells about that choice as it delineates how a man comes to be "in Christ" – it is by hearing the gospel, believing in Jesus, and being sealed with the Holy Spirit. God's "election" in no way overrules a person's freedom of choice in the matter. His election does not automatically involve membership in the family.

---

[33] Such "unconditional security" has been presented above in Parts II and III of this Special Study.

Perhaps at this place a review of Romans 8:28-30 would be in order. Back in eternity, God made a plan ("according to *His* purpose"). His plan was this: 'I'll approve (foreknew) and I'll destine (predestined[34]) some to glory (to be conformed to the image of His son).' The "some" are those "who love God," the same group designated as "those who are in Christ" in Ephesians 1:3-6. In order that the foreknown ones, who were destined to be glorified, might reach that goal, God planned to "call" (offer an invitation to) them, "justify" them, and then "glorify" them. So explained, "foreknowledge and predestination" do not automatically and unconditionally involve membership "in Christ," but they do very much suggest a security, a moving toward a goal, for the person who continues to "love God."

In Special Study #1 on "Grace" at the close of comments on chapter 1, it was shown that, when the Bible says we are saved by grace, "grace" is sometimes God's favorable and unmerited attitude, and sometimes it denotes His action toward men. But it would seem to be improper to appeal to God's grace as evidence of unconditional eternal security, for Hebrews 12:15 warns that it is possible for believers to fail (or come short) of the grace of God, and the specific way to come short of the grace of God (the preceding verse tells us) is to fail to "pursue ... sanctification (holiness)." In other words, the grace of God is conditional. A believer's security is conditioned on faithfulness.

Thus, the way that "election," "predestination," and "grace" are presented in key Scriptures leads us to see that the believer's security is conditional, for each of those key passages also clearly sets forth a condition God expects the people He has elected, destined, or graced to continue to meet.

B. Salvation Requires Both God's Provision and Man's Response

God's provision and man's corresponding response are regularly found side-by-side in Scripture after Scripture. 2 Peter 1:3-11 first tell of God's generous provision of all things necessary for life and godliness, and then, "for this very cause" (namely, God's provision), the believer is on his part exhorted to supply all diligence to develop certain qualities, with the promise that if the qualities are present and increasing, then he will never fall, and an entrance into the eternal kingdom is guaranteed. 1 Peter 1:5 says that believers are kept "through faith" for the inheritance that is undefiled and won't fade away. Colossians 1:23 promises the readers that they will be presented to Christ "*if* you continue in the faith ... and not moved away from the hope of the gospel." John 10:25-30 first of all notes that Jesus' sheep continue to hear His voice ("hear" is a present tense verb), and on this condition Jesus says "I give eternal life to them." Revelation 3:8,10 put man's response

---

[34] More will be said on the topic of "predestination" in succeeding chapters of Romans. Special attention will have to be given to Romans 9:21. In passing, it should be observed that since that verse speaks of predestination to "honorable *use*" or "common *use*," it is hardly likely that that verse, or its context, speaks of individual and unconditional predestination to salvation or damnation. If the doctrine of unconditional predestination (and by parity of reasoning, unconditional security) is not to be found in either Romans 8 or 9, it is exceedingly doubtful that it is to be found at all in the New Testament, for all admit that those two passages are pivotal.

and God's provision side by side when Jesus promises, "because you have ... kept My word, and have not denied My name ... I also will keep you from the hour of testing ...." 1 John 5:18 tells of God's provision: "We know that no one who is born of God sins; but He who was born of God (i.e., Jesus) keeps him and the evil one does not touch him." But close by, in verse 21, is this admonition, "Little children, guard yourselves from idols." 1 Thessalonians 5:23,24 (which promises that God will sanctify the readers, and faithfully preserve them until the second coming, which He also will bring to pass) also contains 3:1-10. In those early verses of chapter 3 (just before 3:11-13, where Paul prays a prayer similar to 5:23,24, that the Lord would "establish your hearts unblameable in holiness before our God and Father at the coming of our Lord Jesus with all His saints"), he emphasizes the corresponding responsibility resting on the Thessalonian Christians, to "stand firm in the Lord" and in their faith.

Only if man's corresponding response in salvation is important can the verses that show man is held accountable mean anything. Jesus said, "The Son of Man is going to come in the glory of His Father with His angels; and will then recompense every man according to his deeds" (Matthew 16:27). Paul said that God "will render to every man according to his deeds" – salvation or damnation (Romans 2:6-10). Peter said that the Father "impartially judges according to each man's work" (1 Peter 1:17). John saw the sea and death and Hades give up the dead that were in them, "and they were judged, every one *of them* according to their deeds" (Revelation 20:13). If the doctrine of *unconditional* election or reprobation were true, if man were wholly passive in the matter of salvation or damnation, because those matters were the result of absolute foreordination and predestination, how can any of these verses about judgment "according to deeds/works" be true? But, on the supposition that salvation depends not only on God's provision but also on man's response, there is no problem with these verses about judgment according to works. Instead, they harmonize beautifully with the idea that after God has made gracious provision, He expects man to fulfill certain conditions if the man would benefit from the gracious provision He offers. Furthermore, all these verses require us to understand that man still is a free moral agent. He is free to choose or reject – otherwise how could he be held accountable?

C. The Faith that Saves is Not a One-Time Thing[35]

In John 3:15-18,36, five times a present tense verb form is used in the Greek where "believes" occurs in the NASB. Instead of speaking of a single act of believing, the present tense conveys the idea of continuing action. Verse 18 says "he who believes (continues to believe) in Him is not judged (condemned)." But what happens if the person ceases to be a believer? It is only to the one who continues to believe that the promise of not coming into judgment (condemnation) is made. The faith that saves in John 3 is not a

---

[35] See summary point #3 on page 405, where it was shown that the doctrine of unconditional security also requires us to understand that the faith that saves is a one-time act. In fact, each of these paragraphs under Part V of this study, showing that the Christian's "security" is *conditional*, refutes one of those "summary points" (pages 404-406) either in part or in whole.

one-time thing. The promise is conditional! Verse 36 reads, "He who believes in the Son has eternal life; but he who does not obey the Son shall not see life, but the wrath of God abides on him." If proponents of unconditional eternal security are right – if when they claim the first part of the verse means that the 'believer can never become an unbeliever, can never be lost' – then it seems only proper, by parity of reasoning, to conclude that when John says the unbeliever "shall not see life," that it must mean it is impossible ever for the unbeliever to become a believer and be saved. If the first part of the verse is unconditional, so is the second. If the second is conditional, so is the first. John 5:24 and 7:37,38 likewise speak of "belief" as a continual thing, rather than a one-time act. The salvation, the security, the assurance is promised on the condition of continual believing.[36]

D. The New Testament Everywhere Requires Faithfulness as a Condition of Continuing Salvation

In this connection a study of the five warning passages[37] included in the book of Hebrews is most enlightening. One half of the whole book is warning, lest the readers cease being faithful to Jesus, return to the old Jewish religion, and find that because of their lack of faithfulness their salvation has been forfeited. Chapter 4 draws a lesson from Israel's history: saved from Egypt, yes, but they fell in the wilderness, and failed to enter the promised land. They fell because of unbelief! Do not let someone say the Israelites who fell in the wilderness never really believed in the first place. Turn to Psalm 106. It is a chapter on Israel's deliverance from Egypt. In verse 12, David tells us that Israel believed. Then in verse 24, he says that they believed not. Between those two verses it describes how they made the molten calf, rebelled against Moses, lusted and envied, forgot God their Savior, and "believed not." So they first believed, then they believed not. The same ones who once believed afterward believed not. The believers turned into unbelievers, and did not enter Canaan. The same expressions are found in Hebrews 4 – verse 3 speaks of believed, and verse 11 speaks of disbelief (disobedience), and how if a believer becomes a disbeliever he forfeits opportunity to enter God's heavenly rest. Faithfulness is the condition of entering that rest! Hebrews 6:4-9 threatens burning (Hell) to those who were once Christians (enlightened, were made partakers of the Holy Spirit), but who afterward "have fallen away." Hebrews 10:35-39 (and chapter 11, too, with its

---

[36] Proponents of unconditional eternal security are apt to point to John 4:13,14, where a "one-time drinking" (it is an aorist tense) is affirmed to be what Jesus meant when He said to the woman at the well, "Whoever drinks (aorist tense) of the water that I shall give him shall never thirst." At first glance, it might be a defensible position to suppose that Jesus taught that one act (of drinking) results in security (never thirsting again). But when, on another occasion (John 7:37,38), Jesus required continual drinking ("come to me and drink [present tense, continual action]") and continual believing ("He who believes [present tense] in Me ..."), interpreters should be slow to affirm that the faith on which salvation or assurance is based is a one-time act. Before too much of a case is made for the aorist tense meaning only one act of drinking, a careful study should be made of 1 Corinthians 10:4 where an aorist and an imperfect tense (continuing action in the past) of the verb "drink" are used interchangeably. Furthermore, it is possible the aorist tense represents action that requires an extended period of time to complete, as "building" in John 2:20, or "dwelt" in John 1:14, or "explained" in John 1:18 [where the verb refers to Christ's entire manifestation of God throughout His earthly life and ministry], or "walk" in Romans 6:4.

[37] The 5 passages are Hebrews 2:1-4, 3:7-4:13, 5:11-6:20, 10:26-39, and 12:18-29.

roll call of the ones who were faithful) exhorts the Christians to beware lest they throw away their confidence. They presently had it, and with it the promise of great reward, but they could lose it. They have need for endurance in the faith (endurance in doing the will of God), for those who shrink back (return to Judaism) find that God has no pleasure in them, and their end is perdition (destruction). The writer of Hebrews closes chapter 10 by stating that it takes "faith" (faithfulness) if the soul is to be preserved. The same idea is echoed and illustrated in chapter 11, where he says (verse 6) "Without faith (i.e., faithfulness) it is impossible to please Him."

Romans 4,5 show that Christians are saved the same way Abraham was, and his "faith" was not a one-time thing. What is depicted is continuing faithfulness over a whole lifetime, as appeal is made to Genesis 15 (Romans 4:3), to Genesis 17 (Romans 4:18,19), and to Genesis 22 (Romans 4:22). These events, over a number of years, show that Abraham's faith was not a one-time thing; instead, over and over again, he believed. He was faithful! And on this condition of faithfulness God continued to justify him.

The same "if-condition" (the same expectation of faithfulness) is found in Jesus' own teaching. Matthew 10:32-33 (KJV), "Whosoever (an "if" clause) therefore shall confess me (continuous action) before men, him will I confess (one-time act) also before my Father in Heaven."[38] In the Parable of the Sower, it can be seen that perseverance is needed. Jesus, in Luke 8:13, speaks of those who "believe for a while, and [then] in time of temptation fall away." If one is saved by faith, that is, when he believes, what happens to him when he loses his faith, that is, quits believing? Jesus said they "believe for a while." Now it will not do to affirm 'they never did believe in the first place,' because Jesus said they did! If a man is saved by faith, these were saved for a while. If a man is saved by faith, he is saved while he believes. If that faith is lost, salvation is lost also, is it not? If a man's faith can be lost, and he is still saved, then what becomes of the doctrine of justification by faith? If his faith is lost, it would be a justification without faith! One must either surrender the doctrine of the impossibility of apostasy, or the doctrine of justification by faith. Posit the idea that faithfulness is the condition of continuing salvation, then the teaching of Jesus in Luke 8 and the doctrine of justification by faith in Romans are beautifully harmonious. On another occasion, Jesus made continuing in His word the condition of continuing discipleship. "Jesus therefore was saying to those Jews who had believed Him, 'If you abide in My word, then you are truly disciples of Mine, and you shall know the truth, and the truth shall make you free.'" (John 8:31,32). In a similar vein, man's being forgiven by God is conditioned on man's forgiving the one who sins against him. In the Model Prayer, Jesus taught His disciples to pray, "Forgive us ... just as we have forgiven those who have sinned against us" (LNT). And in Matthew 18:21-35, the parable of the unmerciful slave, Jesus emphatically shows that forgiveness is conditional. "So shall My heavenly Father also do to you, if each of you does not forgive his brother from your heart." Over and over again, the New Testament clearly portrays that "faithfulness" is the condition of a man's continuing salvation.

---

[38] Compare 2 Timothy 2:12, "If we endure, we shall also reign with Him. If we deny Him, He also will deny us."

G. New Testament Passages Also Show Believers were "Cut off" for Lack of Faithfulness.

One important passage to consider is John 15:1-6, where Jesus is recorded as giving the metaphor of the vine and the branches. Several key points made by Jesus include: (1) The same relation exists between Christ and the Christian as exists between the vine and the branch. (2) In the words "every branch in Me" (verse 2), Jesus plainly stated that the branch was once part of the vine. In fact, without a vine from which it can grow, there will be no branch. Some proponents of unconditional eternal security have tried to say that the branches that 'burn' never were in the vine. Such a notion hardly matches either Jesus' illustration or the observable facts in the world of nature. In the spring, owners of a nearby orchard trim off branches that do not produce, pile them up, and eventually burn them. If one drives by the orchard at the right time, he can see those piles of branches that have been cut. Now it is hard to imagine that any of them just grew by themselves, and never were part of a parent stock! No, they were once all part of the vine. In verse 5, Jesus identifies the vine as being Himself, and His followers (in the context, He is speaking to the apostles) as the branches. Further, in that same verse, He again affirms that the branches are "in Him," that is, the branch that is in the vine represents the man who is in Christ. (3) The branch that does not bear fruit is cut off. In real life, does this not teach that a person truly united to Christ may afterward be cut off, if there is a failure in fruit bearing? (4) Note what Jesus says about the branch that fails to produce. It is "cut off," "thrown away," "dries up," is "cast into the fire" and "burns." Separated from Christ, a man withers, and eventually is eternally lost ("burns" is present tense, continuous action). Did Jesus give this metaphor to teach that it is impossible for a child of God to fall away and be lost? If so, He went at it in reverse. It is very probable that there is not a man on earth who can harmonize the vine and the branches with the doctrine of the impossibility of apostasy. (5) God does cut off branches that fail to produce. If a man fails to produce over a long period of time, God cuts him off. Like a newly cut branch, he may look green for a while, but he will wither. Furthermore, one seldom, if ever, sees one of these cut off branches grafted back into the vine; the excision tends to be permanent. (6) Several times in these verses, Jesus uses the words "abide in Me" or "abide in the vine." It is something the believer may choose to do, or not do. "Abiding in Christ" is expressive of a life-long commitment, a continuing, habitual pattern of life (note the verb is present tense, inferring continuing action). Perhaps it could be said that the cardinal axiom of the Christian life is "abide in Christ!" It is a matter of faithfulness over a period of time, not a one-time thing.

Romans 11:21,22 likewise speak of branches broken off, cut off, because of unbelief. God even threatens to "cut off" Paul's Christian readers unless they "continue" in His kindness. 1 Corinthians 3:17 records the warning that God will "destroy" those Christians who by their continued divisiveness destroy the (temple of God) church. 1 Corinthians 9:24-10:12 also hold out the warning that those once saved may lose that salvation. Those who defend the doctrine of the impossibility of losing salvation interpret 9:27 as though Paul were speaking of being disqualified from further service as a minister of the gospel.

In fact, the NASB reads "disqualified" where some of the older translations read "castaway" (KJV) or "rejected" (ASV).[39] However, the context on both sides of 9:24-27 shows that Paul is talking about participation in salvation. In 9:23 he explains that he behaves in such a non-selfish way as to be helpful and supportive of others, so that he may save them (verse 22) and thus be a fellow-partaker with them in the benefits of the gospel. In 1 Corinthians 10, what happened to Israel in the wilderness is held up by way of example to warn the Christians lest they commit the same kinds of sins that barred some Israelites from the Promised Land. They had escaped Egypt, and had shared in the Christ-provided blessings in the wilderness, and still they perished.

Galatians 5:20, written to "brethren" in Christ (verse 13), plainly affirms that if they habitually indulge in deeds of the flesh (drunkenness, immorality, idolatry, sorcery) they shall "not inherit the kingdom of God." If they cannot inherit the kingdom of God, how are they going to be saved? Here is another verse which shows it is possible for a man once a Christian to become lost because of lack of faithfulness.[40]

2 Peter 2:18-22 also show that lack of faithfulness results in believers' being cut off, by making these points: (1) They had escaped the defilements of the world by the knowledge of the Lord and Savior Jesus Christ. (2) They had again become entangled in those defilements and are overcome. (3) Their last state was worse than the first. (4) It would have been better for them not to have known the way of righteousness, than having known it to turn away from the holy commandment delivered to them. (5) Their "turning away" is compared to the proverb of a dog returning to its vomit, and a hog to wallowing in the mire. Now it cannot be claimed that these people "never had it," for Peter says they "escaped" and were "entangled *again*." It will not do to say that the problem is that the hog never became a sheep and so never was saved, for the verse says 'washed.' They had known the way of righteousness and turned away from it, is how Peter puts it. The last state is worse than the first – either because their abandonment to sin is more complete after

---

[39] The word so translated is *adokimos*, translated "reprobate" in the KJV/ASV at Romans 1:28 ("depraved," NASB); 2 Corinthians 13:5,6,7 (NASB, "fail the test," "unapproved"); 2 Timothy 3:8 ("rejected," NASB); Titus 1:16 ("worthless," NASB). To attempt to make the word mean 'unqualified for further competition, but still eligible for the prize' is hardly a satisfactory explanation.

[40] Galatians 5:4, "You have fallen from grace," is a well-known text in Galatians that is often appealed to by non-Calvinistic interpreters, as proof that "once in grace, always in grace" is an unbiblical doctrine. Though not specifically stated, it would seem that the Galatian Christians (to whom Paul wrote) have *not* already lost their salvation, for in 5:1 Paul pleads with them to "keep standing firm." (It is assumed that once a Christian dies spiritually, and thus has reverted to a lost condition, there is no way to reclaim that person for Christ. See notes at Romans 6:16,21.) Indeed, they were in danger of losing their salvation if they did not heed his warnings to abandon the course they had embarked on after listening to the Judaizers. If this presentation of the condition of the Galatian Christians is correct, then "you have fallen from grace" does *not* mean they are already lost, and again on their way to eternal punishment as they had been before their conversion; nor would it be proper to use *this* passage to contradict the "once in grace, always in grace" doctrine. Instead, "you have been severed from Christ" would say only that the Galatians who did as the Judaizers taught were foolishly seeking to be saved in a way totally different from what Christ taught (compare Galatians 1:6-8). Likewise, "you have fallen from grace" would mean that the Galatians were foolishly trying to continue in the Christian life without the help (grace) that the Holy Spirit provides, rather than that they were already excluded from any further possibility of benefiting from the grace of God that results in salvation.

quitting Christ than it was before they became Christians; or, as seems more likely, because (degrees of punishment in hell) their punishment will be greater since they had greater opportunity (compare Luke 12: 47,48).

Passages could be multiplied where it is clearly supposed that it is possible for people once saved to be "cut off" and again lost, if faithfulness (the condition of justification) should ever be found by God to be lacking.

F. It Takes Continual Sinning to "Kill" the Christian's Spirit

As has been explained in comments on several verses[41] of Romans, a man's first sin causes his spirit to die. When the new birth takes place, it is the spirit part of the man that is reborn (John 3:6; Romans 8:10). Both Romans 6:23 (addressed to Christians!) and 8:13 show it is possible for the spirit to die again; should this occur, the man has reverted to the lost condition that was the case between the time the first sin was committed and the time of the new birth. The one difference is that whereas it took one sin to kill the spirit the first time, for the Christian it is continual, habitual sinning that causes the spirit to "die" again.[42]   James 1:15, Galatians 6:7-9, and Romans 8:12-14 declare that spiritual death is the inevitable consequence of habitual sinning as a deliberate pattern of behavior.[43]

G. The Logical Conclusions to which Calvin's Doctrine of Eternal Security Lead are Unacceptable

These conclusions are unacceptable because they require an 'exegete' to give peculiar 'twists' to many passages seeming to assert salvation is conditional and can be lost.

---

[41] See footnote #42 at Romans 1:9 and comments at Romans 7:9 and 8:10.

[42] What death is threatened to Christians who sin? Premature physical death (without salvation being lost), or spiritual death (with the corollary of punishment in Hell)? Proponents of unconditional eternal security tend to teach that the death threatened is premature physical death. Now Romans 8:13 reads, "If you are living according to the flesh, you must die; but if ... you are putting to death the deeds of the body, you shall live." Paul had just called them "brethren," so he was addressing members of the church, children of God, saved people. It is hard to believe that the death there threatened is physical death, because Romans 5 has shown that men die physically anyway, no matter how they live. "Die" (in the context) refers to spiritual death, the opposite of "live." Eternal punishment is implied, and this threat is addressed to people who were spiritually alive. This would show that a child of God can die, spiritually die, die in sin, and be lost.

[43] The Bible does not teach that a man is in and out of grace (saved, lost, saved, lost, etc.) several times every day. The Bible does teach that God chastens His children for their sin, and if the sin continues, His children become lost, disinherited, outside of grace. Some proponents of unconditional eternal security have appealed to Romans 8:1 ("there is therefore now no condemnation for those who are in Christ Jesus") as proof that no child of God ever is in danger of dying spiritually and thus being condemned as lost. It should be observed that the statement is qualified (verse 4) by the expression "who do not walk according to the flesh, but according to the Spirit." True, the ASV omits this clause from verse 1 (where the KJV has it), but it is in verse 4, and is repeated in verse 13. So the argument that 8:1 is proof of *unconditional* security does not hold. It should be further recognized that, in its own context, Romans 8:1 has nothing to do with the final judgment. It is speaking of 'no condemnation to a life of slavery to sin' – something the Law of Moses could not provide for a man, but the death of Christ did. Limits are put on the devil as the man continues to meet the qualification of "walking according to the Spirit."

1) "Apostates" must be explained (by advocates of unconditional eternal security) as being people who never were Christians, but who have come to repudiate the fundamental doctrines of the Christian faith.   H.A. Ironside's handling of 2 Thessalonians 2:3, "Let no one deceive you for *it will not come*, unless the apostasy comes first, and that man of lawlessness is revealed ...," is an example.   He illustrates the meaning of the word "apostasy," as he uses it, by giving the statistic that 75% of the ministers in the Church Federation in Chicago signed a questionnaire saying they do not believe some of the great fundamental truths of the Bible.   "There you have apostasy," he interjected.   Ironside then speaks of a certain preacher who made a blatant attack on the doctrine of the blood atonement, and calls him an apostate.[44]   Could one say that these ministers were all Christians once, but that now some are no longer saved?   "My dear friends, I am afraid the whole trouble is that most of them have never been born again at all.   They do not know anything of regenerating grace, and therefore are quite ready to apostatize from the doctrines held sacred by the great evangelical denominations."[45]   This commentator has difficulty thinking that "apostate" means someone who never believed in Christian doctrines in the first place.   That is certainly giving an unexpected "twist" to the definition of the word.

While attempting to explain Hebrews 6:4-6, Ironside made this comment:

> If you will keep in mind the difference between an apostate and a backslider, it will save you a lot of trouble over many scriptures.   The apostate knows all about Christianity, but never has been a real Christian.   The backslider is a person who has known Christ, who did love Him, but became cold in his soul, lost out in his spiritual life.   There is not a Christian who has not often been guilty of backsliding.   That is why we need the Lord as our Advocate to restore our souls.   When backslidden, it is not our union with Him that is destroyed, but it is our communion ... The apostate is always a man opposed to Christ.[46]

Some thought should be given to the possibility that a teaching is wrong if it requires its defenders to come up with a peculiar definition like this in order to maintain that teaching.

2) "Free moral agency" must be denied by the advocates of unconditional eternal security.   If one is going to advocate unconditional security, he must of necessity deny any free moral agency to man, for it would be very inconsistent to admit that a man is a free moral agent, and then deny he can ever exercise his freedom so as to fall away and be again lost.   Let Ironside again be a representative of this matter, and hear him as he denies that man is a free moral agent:

> Is man an absolutely free moral agent?   He was when God created him, but is he now?   Is the sinner a free moral agent?   What does the Scripture say?

---

[44] Ironside, *The Eternal Security of the Believer*, p. 28,29.

[45] *Ibid.*

[46] Ironside, *op. cit.*, p.38.

"You are led by the devil captive at his will." What! A man who is led by
the devil captive at his will, a free agent! ... Man is a slave to sin and Satan;
he is not free.[47]

The fact of the matter is that man is not an "absolutely free moral agent." In
his unsaved state he is a slave of sin, "led by the devil captive at his will."
When regenerated he is the servant of Christ, delighting in holiness and
indwelt by the Spirit of the living God.[48]

Contrary to what Ironside has affirmed about the absence of freedom of the will or freedom
of choice, there are numerous verses which teach the very opposite.[49] Isaiah 53:6 reads,
"All we like sheep have gone astray." 2 Peter 1:10 tells the Christian to give all diligence
(by developing the qualities of moral excellence, knowledge, self-control, etc.) to make his
calling and election sure. Without this diligence, without these qualities growing and
abounding, the Christian is in danger of perishing. Romans 6:12 tells Christians to stop
letting sin reign in their mortal bodies – which certainly implies freedom of the will.
Romans 6:16 likewise involves freedom, when the Christian is pictured as presenting
himself to someone as a slave. When a Christian sins, God chastens (disciplines) him, as
Hebrews 12:4-12 teaches, with the intent that the man will stop his sinning and become
more holy (verse 10), but God's purpose in discipline is not always realized, for a man can
respond to chastening in one of two different ways (verses 5 and 9).[50] Now the very fact
that he can respond in different ways implies he still has freedom of choice. The parable
of the steward in Luke 12:41 presents the steward as having two possible courses of
conduct open to him in his Master's absence. That certainly involves freedom of choice.

Surely, a doctrine that requires one to give up the clear teaching of the Word of God
that man is a free moral agent is suspect in the highest degree. Ought not the doctrine of
unconditional eternal security be surrendered instead?

3) The "book of life" must be distinguished from the "Lamb's book of life" by the
advocates of unconditional eternal security. In the case of the "book of life" (Revelation

---

[47] Ironside, *op. cit.*, p.25.

[48] *Op. cit.*, p.22. Ironside goes on to show that the slave of Christ is not free to choose what he will do,
but rather is under the control of God (he quotes Philippians 1:6 to prove it), or under the control of the
indwelling Holy Spirit. He further asserts that Christ's sheep are not free to "destroy themselves" (as John
10:28, with its middle voice verb might be translated).

[49] Even Ironside (*op. cit.*, p.25) admits that when a man hears the gospel he is *free* to choose; he has
the power of decision. Now if a man is a free moral agent as he becomes a Christian, what happened to
him that he lost his freedom of choice after becoming a Christian. What happened that reduced man to a
mere robot, moving only at the impulse of God or the Holy Spirit? It seems that Ironside is not consistent
in his presentation. Either a man is free, or he is not.

[50] Calvin erred in interpreting the covenant with David, Psalm 89:31-34. He read it as though it proved
that chastening of necessity *always* restores erring believers. This is not true anymore than God's
covenant with Israel ensured that chastening would always save all the Israelites.

3:5), it is possible to have one's name entered therein and later erased.   In the case of the "Lamb's book of life" (Revelation 13:8), names of some were deliberately not entered therein before the creation of the world, just as the names of others were entered before the creation.   Ironside is again representative of how proponents of unconditional eternal security are forced by their doctrine to make an unwarranted distinction between the two books.

> Is there any difference between the book of life and the Lamb's book of life? Yes, the book of life is the book of the living.   It is the record too of profession.   From this book names may be blotted out.   The Lamb's book of life is the record of the eternal purpose of God.   Names inscribed there are written from the foundation of the world.   In other words, one book speaks of responsibility, the other of pure grace.   No Christian will ever have his name blotted out of the Lamb's book of life, for all such have eternal life – which is unforfeitable and everlasting.[51]

The only reason that famous preacher had for making this distinction is because of his preconceived notion that once a man is saved, he can never be lost.   He had to explain away Revelation 3:5, lest it contradict his cherished doctrine.[52]   But his effort fails to carry conviction, when it is observed, (a) that it is the "book of life" (not the *Lamb's* book of life, as was true in Revelation 13:8) wherein names were not written from the foundation of the world (Revelation 17:8); (b) that it is the "book of life" that is produced, and out of which men are judged in the final judgment (Revelation 20:12); and finally, (c) that a man's eternal destiny depends on whether or not his name is in the "book of life" (Revelation 20:15).   If Ironside's explanation of the "book of life" were true, namely, that it is a record that a man is living for a while on earth, then Revelation 20:15 would teach the absurd notion that the reason a man is cast into the lake of fire is because he never lived on earth.

H. Eternal Life is Not Only a Present Possession, but Also a Future Promise

Indeed, some New Testament verses teach that eternal life is something the believer enjoys during the present life.[53]   Were it also true that no verses held out eternal life as a

---

[51] Ironside, *op. cit.*, p.48.

[52] In the KJV, Revelation 22:19 also speaks about "taking away his part from the book of life," but there is a manuscript variation here, and so the NASB reads "tree of life."   Still, Revelation 3:5 does speak of one's name being erased from the book of life!

[53] See notes at Romans 5:21 and 6:22.   [Some have denied the presentation made at those verses. Because so many verses hold out "eternal life" as something future even for the Christian, a different explanation is given to those few verses that seem to say eternal life is a present possession.   The explanation is based on a well-known use of past tense verbs when a prophecy is being uttered.   In the Old Testament, Isaiah said, "the people that walked in darkness have seen a great light" (Isaiah 9:2).   The prophet used a past tense verb to predict an event 700+ years in the future (compare Matthew 4:16). Again, in Isaiah 9:6, "unto us a child is born, unto us a son is given," he used the present tense to predict an event seven centuries later.   In the same way, it is suggested, the verses that speak of eternal life in the past or present tense are actually only promises yet to be fulfilled, predictions of what will be for the faithful when this life is ended.]

future promise, then the argument for unconditional eternal security based on the expression "eternal life" might have some validity. (If it could be lost, it was not eternal, was it?) However, our study of Romans 6:22 has already produced one place where eternal life is a future promise. To this could be added Mark 10:30 (which records Jesus' promise to those who followed Him that they would receive blessings 100-fold in this present age, and "in the age to come, eternal life"), 1 Timothy 6:12 (where Paul exhorts Timothy to "take hold of the eternal life"), Titus 1:2 (which speaks of the "hope of eternal life"), and Galatians 6:8 (where the Christian who sows to the Spirit will reap "eternal life"). Both ideas – present possession and future promise – are taught in Scripture. Eternal life, while in a measure attained and enjoyed here by the believer, is conditional, and is also to be gained hereafter. It is something to be attained and enjoyed by the faithful.

The conclusion to which all this has been leading is this – **The Bible does teach "security," but it is security for the "believer." It is a conditional security.**

VI. SOME PRACTICAL CONSIDERATIONS RESULTING FROM THIS STUDY

A. Bible Students Must be Careful in their Preparation to Teach and Preach.

There are evidently some verses to which the teachers of unconditional eternal security give an erroneous explanation. An example would be 'disqualified from further competition' at 1 Corinthians 9:27. There are also some verses that they do correctly. An example would be 1 Corinthians 3:11-15, where it is possible for a saved man to lose some of his reward, and still be saved. If the above presentation of conditional security is true, then Christians may have eternal life abiding in them now, and still could lose it because of unfaithfulness. Their names are in the book of life, but they also can be erased.

B. Christians Must Take Heed to the Words of the Songs they Sing.

Some expressions found in certain songs reflect the doctrine of unconditional eternal security. In "How Firm a Foundation" occur the words "the soul that on Jesus hath leaned for repose; I'll never, no never, no never forsake." The chorus, "Now I Belong to Jesus," sung often at baptismal services, has the phrase "not for the years of time alone, but for eternity." One wonders whether this expresses the doctrine of once saved, always saved; or whether it expresses the newly-baptized person's determination to belong to Jesus now and forever?

C. Prayers Asking for Forgiveness Should Be Included in Our Requests to God.

Several preachers, advocating the doctrine of the unconditional security of the saints, no longer include petitions for forgiveness in their prayers, because they perceive that all of a man's sins, past, present, or future, were taken care of at one time, at Calvary. It somehow would be inconsistent, they suppose, to pray for forgiveness if all were forgiven once for all time when Christ died. There is something wrong with such a presentation, since the New Testament is filled with examples of followers of Christ asking for forgiveness, e.g., Mark 11:25,26; Luke 11:4; Acts 8:9-24; James 5:16; and 1 John 1:9 and 2:1. Perhaps what is amiss is that while the atonement for all sin (Romans 3:25,26; Hebrews 9:14,15, and 10:14) was made once for all time at Calvary, its application to individual situations depends on that individual's initial response to the gospel and, subsequent to that, his asking for forgiveness after repentance.

D. What About the Problem of the "Nominal" Church Member?

Since a Christian's continuing salvation is conditioned on his faithfulness, it becomes all the more imperative that Christians encourage one another to love and good works (Hebrews 10:24), and that in cases of habitual sin, that the proper steps of discipline (Matthew 18:15-18) be lovingly undertaken. The "nominal" church member just cannot be allowed to continue unimpeded on his "nominal" way.

E. The Steps of Salvation include "Christian Living."

The five-finger presentation made popular by Walter Scott (though now modified slightly) – faith, repentance, confession, baptism, and *Christian living* – is a right presentation of Biblical truths. However, care must be exercised, lest the idea be left in the hearer's mind that acts of Christian living are somehow meritorious, or that if we turn in a "poor paper" today that we somehow have failed the whole course.

F. Believers in Unconditional Security can be Taught and Convinced Otherwise.

When one reads through carefully-reasoned presentations of the doctrine of "once saved, always saved," the arguments can be pretty convincing. One book, for example, quotes all the pertinent verses, and puts the words teaching eternal security in italics, so the reader is impressed with all the promises.[54] Then when one turns to books written against the doctrine, he finds they use some of the same key verses, only interpreting them differently.[55] How is one to know what is actually the truth in this matter? Perhaps each Bible student will have to do something similar to what Robert Shank has done – namely, study the Scriptures themselves, and let them speak. He will find fewer verses hard to harmonize with the doctrine of conditional security than the defenders of unconditional security have found they must wrestle with.

---

[54] Harold Barker, *Secure Forever* (New York: Loizeaux Brothers, 1974).

[55] One could only wish that Barker, as he quoted and italicized his verses, would have put in bold print all the expressions in the same verses that present the conditional element that is attached to the promise of security.

CONCLUSION

The question is not, "Do I believe in the security of believers?" I do! The question is, "Is that security conditional or unconditional?" The answer: it is conditional. Robert Shank has worded it succinctly:

> Please excuse me from the company of any who maintain that the believer is insecure. It is abundantly evident from the Scriptures that the believer is secure. But *only* the believer. Many who have debated "the security of the believer" have missed the issue. The question is not, Is the believer secure? but rather, What is a *believer*?[56]

Eternal life is free, but not without cost; it is by grace, but not without conditions. It is promised to those who "by perseverance in doing good seek for glory and honor and immortality" (Romans 2:7). Unbelievers are told the conditions of salvation; believers are told the conditions of continuance in salvation; these conditions are declared by God to be the appointed means of enjoying eternal life.

Robert Milligan's analogy seems to convey the sense of Scripture. He explained the safety and security of the Christian on this fashion:

> The argument of the apostle, in this case, is just such a one as you would severally employ if you were endeavoring to persuade your friends and relatives of other lands to become citizens of this Republic. In such a case, you would, of course, say much about the fertility of our soil, the salubrity of our climate, the vast resources of our country, the enterprise, intelligence, and moral character of our citizens. But you would dwell particularly, and with special emphasis, on *the liberal provisions of our Constitution*, on the *chartered rights and privileges* of every faithful American citizen. You would assure your friends that if they would renounce their allegiance to all other governments, and become citizens of these United States, that in that event, all the powers and resources of this vast and mighty Republic would then be pledged for their security and protection.
>
> Now, suppose that your arguments should prevail, and that many of your friends should really leave their foreign homes, and become American citizens; would anyone in his senses even imagine that there was anything compulsory in the case? That this change of citizenship was owing to any decrees of necessity or fatality passed by the framers of our Constitution? Would any one suppose that these persons were deprived of their free agency, and made the mere tools and chattels of our Government? That their being once citizens of our Republic implies, of necessity, that they shall always remain so? That henceforth they have no power whatever to expatriate them-

---

[56] Robert Shank, *Life in the Son: A Study of the Doctrine of Perseverance* (Springfield, MO: Westcott Publishers, 1961), p.55.

selves; and that even if they should do so, our Government would still be under obligations to extend over them the shield of our Republic? That they could rightfully claim the honors and protection of our flag in a foreign land, even after they had renounced their allegiance to our Government, and become the sworn and naturalized citizens of another nation? No one would so reason. No one would so imagine. The most that could be claimed for these persons, in any case, would be the protection of our Government so long as they remained in the relation of its faithful citizens and subjects.

And just so it is in the kingdom of heaven. There is nothing in its constitution, or its laws, or its administration that in the slightest degree interferes with the personal liberty and voluntary agency of any man, whether he be a citizen or an alien. But, so long as he is loyal to its King, and faithful to its laws, all the powers and resources of the universe are pledged for his safety and security.[57]

SELECTED BIBLIOGRAPHY

Adam, D.S., "Perseverance," in *Encyclopedia of Religion and Ethics*, edited by James Hastings. New York: Charles Scribner's Sons, 1917. Volume 9, p.769-771.

Barker, Harold, *Secure Forever*. New York: Loizeaux Brothers, 1974.

Beckwith, C.A., "Perseverance," in *The New Schaff-Herzog Encyclopedia of Religious Knowledge*, edited by Samuel M. Jackson. Grand Rapids: Baker Book House, 1956. Volume 8, p.470.

Berkouwer, C.G., *Faith and Perseverance*, translated by Robert Knudsen. Grand Rapids: Wm. B. Eerdmans Publishing Co., 1958.

Boettner, Loraine, *The Reformed Doctrine of Predestination*. Philadelphia: Presbyterian and Reformed Publishing Co., 1968.

---

[57] Robert Milligan, "The Safety and Security of the Christian," in *The Living Pulpit of the Christian Church*, edited by W.T. Moore (Cincinnati: R.W. Carroll, 1865), p.374,375.

Boswell, Ira M., "The Safety of the Elect," in *Flaming Hearts and Other Sermons*. Cincinnati: Standard Publishing Co., 1939, p.175-191.

Duty, Guy, *If Ye Continue: A Study of the Conditional Aspects of Salvation*. Minneapolis: Bethany Fellowship, 1966.

Gibbons, James E., "Once in Grace, Always in Grace?" in *The Sword and Staff*. Vol.2/3 (March 1958), p.3,6.

Gromacki, Robert, *Is Salvation Forever?* Chicago: Moody Press, 1973.

Hunt, W. Boyd, "The Perseverance of the Saints," in *Christianity Today*. Vol.6/17 (May 25, 1962), p.61,62.

Ironside, H.A., *The Eternal Security of the Believer*. New York: Loizeaux Brothers, 1934.

Mankamyer, O.L., *Once in Grace, Always in Grace, In the Light of God's Word!* Yellville, AR: Published by the author, 1953.

Marshall, I. Howard, *Kept By the Power of God: A Study of Perseverance and Falling Away*. London: Epworth Press, 1969.

Milligan, Robert, "The Safety and Security of the Christian," in *The Living Pulpit of the Christian Church*. Cincinnati: Standard Publishing Co., 1868.

Owen, John, *Works of John Owen*. London: Richard Barnes, 1826. Vol. VI, p.xxxi-533; and Vol. VII, p.2-324
    In this material is a complete discussion of the subject, with both Calvinistic and Arminian positions set forth, with the Calvinistic idea defended.

Rice, John R., *Can a Saved Person Ever Be Lost?* Wheaton, IL: Sword of the Lord Publishers, 1941.

Shank, Robert, *Life in the Son: A Study of the Doctrine of Perseverance*. Springfield, MO: Westcott Publishers, 1961.

West, J.W., *Once in Grace, Always in Grace: or The Eternal Security of the Saints, Refuted*. No publication information in the tract except date, 1941.

IV. GOD'S ETERNAL PURPOSE TO PROVIDE THE UNIVERSALLY NEEDED SALVATION TO ALL MEN EXPLAINS HIS DEALINGS WITH ISRAEL IN THE PAST, PRESENT, AND FUTURE. 9:1-11:36

A. Paul's Concern Because of the Jews' Tragic Rejection of Christ. 9:1-5

Summary: Paul expresses his heartfelt sorrow that many Jews are rejecting the gospel, for he loves his countrymen and remembers their exalted privileges, not the least of which was to be the channel through which Messiah came into the world.

9:1 – I am telling the truth in Christ, I am not lying, my conscience bearing me witness in the Holy Spirit,

I am telling the truth in Christ, I am not lying. There is a rather abrupt change of subject. Paul closes his presentation of the blessings inherent in God's way of saving man with his Triumphant Hymn of Hope (chapter 8), and without a word of transition (there is not so much as a particle in the Greek), comes to this note of keenest and deepest sorrow.[1] Paul does not directly state the subject he is now going to discuss; only gradually does the topic become evident. He is about to discuss an extremely delicate theme, a theme that already has caused many Jews to become Paul's violent opponents. In a sentence, this theme could be summarized thus: Paul is brokenhearted that so many of his Israelite kinsmen have rejected the gospel, for since Calvary, an Israelite's relationship with God depends on whether or not he has accepted Jesus as Savior and thus has become one of those who are justified by faith. The double affirmation[2] by Paul that he is telling the truth

---

[1] Two extremes to be avoided when dealing with chapters 9-11 are these: (1) The chapters are an unnecessary appendix to the argument that would not be missed if one simply read 12:1 immediately after completing chapter 8. (2) The section is the main part of the book of Romans, and all else is subordinate to the topic here covered.

In every age, opponents of the gospel have posited what seem (to them) to be logical and cogent reasons that the gospel can be safely ignored. It well might be that in chapters 9-11 Paul is dealing with one of these "reasons" that many in the 1st century would appeal to. "The Problem of the Jews" was one that had to be explained for both Jewish and Gentile hearers of the gospel. The Jews had been God's chosen people; they had a unique and special place in God's purposes. Yet when God's Son came into the world they had rejected Him and crucified Him. If Christianity really is of God, how does one explain why the majority of Jews have not recognized and accepted it as such? "If the Jew, who has had every opportunity to know, does not see a need to accept the message about God's Son, why should we Gentiles?" the Gentile unbeliever might ask. On the other hand, the unbelieving Jew would think, "Since we Jews already are God's chosen people, isn't that sufficient to ensure us a continuing place in God's purposes and favor?" Such objections had to be met if men were to be convinced of the truth and of their need for the righteousness of God that is revealed in the gospel. This is exactly what Paul does as he demonstrates how God has been working out his eternal purpose (Romans 8:28-30) in history. What has happened to believing and unbelieving Jews (as well as to believing and unbelieving Gentiles) is in complete harmony with God's anciently-formed and -revealed plan to justify men by faith.

[2] Though Paul at times does take an oath to guarantee the truth of some statement he makes, it is not

evidently reflects the fact that his opponents have accused him not only of abandoning the law and the religious traditions of the Jewish people but that he is no longer even concerned for his own people (for how else, his opponents might ask, could all the time he spends going to Gentiles be explained?). Responding to such false charges, "the truth in Christ" means, 'Far from being hostile, or unconcerned, my relationship with Christ makes such an attitude impossible.' Jesus did not have such an attitude; how can one of His followers?

My conscience bearing me witness in the Holy Spirit. "Conscience" is used here, as it was in Romans 2:15, of that innate faculty which sits in judgment upon one's actions, and assigns to them moral qualities of praise or blame. Paul calls upon both the witness of his conscience and the activities of the Holy Spirit as evidence he is telling the truth.[3] The topic about which he is telling the truth is introduced in the next verse.

9:2 – *that I have great sorrow and unceasing grief in my heart.*

That I have great sorrow and unceasing grief in my heart. Far from what his detractors have charged, namely, that Paul no longer cares about his own race, Paul here affirms their lostness from Christ was for him a painful subject, every time he thought about them. Even in verse 3, where the reason for this sorrow and grief is finally hinted at, Paul does not actually say that their rejection of Christ is what burdens his heart, for the tragedy of their opposition to the gospel, and the thought of their peril both now and in eternity to come, cause his emotions to churn so much that he can write about it only in broken sentences. It is only as we read on in chapters 10 and 11 that the real reason for his sorrow, namely, the Jews' rejection of Christ and of God's way of saving man, becomes clear.

9:3 – *For I could wish that I myself were accursed,* **separated** *from Christ for the sake of my* **brethren,** *my kinsmen according to the flesh,*

For I could wish that I myself were accursed, *separated* **from Christ for the sake of my brethren.** We likely are to understand that Paul is expressing his *present* feelings as he writes, rather than what his feelings were before his conversion.[4] "Accursed" (literally,

---

certain that the language of verses 1-3 is such as would actually be used in an oath. ("In Christ" might be an oath, but it is hardly likely that the corresponding "in the Holy Spirit" in the latter part of verse one is.) Still, his language here in verses 1-3 reminds us of the solemn affirmations he makes when he is suspected or directly accused of lying. Compare Galatians 1:20; 2 Corinthians 1:23, 11:31; and 1 Timothy 2:7.

[3] Perhaps it is Paul the Christian, who is aware of the promptings of the indwelling Holy Spirit, who here speaks. 'My conscience is in harmony with the leading of the Holy Spirit; I am walking not according to the flesh, but according to the Spirit, so that in this matter I am incapable of falsehood or self-deception,' would be the idea. Or perhaps it is Paul the apostle, who is aware of the Spirit's "inspirational" activities, who here speaks. 'As I write this letter, the Holy Spirit, who moves me to write just what God wants, would not permit me to write a lie. Therefore, I know that in this case my conscience isn't deceiving me,' would be the idea.

[4] The imperfect tense verb (best translated, "I was wishing") could have reference to his own feelings about Christ, before his conversion, when he was busy persecuting Christians. 'I was wishing myself to be separated from Christ as far as possible. I wanted nothing to do with Him!' While it is true that Paul tried to get men to blaspheme Christ, and he himself did many things contrary to Christ, it is also true that

anathema[5]) involves damnation in Hell, and by using this expression, Paul shows the intensity of his love for his kinsmen. He says, in effect, if his being sent to eternal punishment would result in their salvation, then he was willing to be lost.[6] Paul goes farther than Moses once did. Moses' love for his people was so great that he did not want to be saved without them (Exodus 32:30-32). Paul's love is such that he wanted them saved even if he were lost. Here is a great truth – the man who would save the sinner must love the sinner!

My kinsmen according to the flesh. Since "brethren" (in the previous clause) can be brothers in Christ, or brothers in Adam, or brothers in Abraham, Paul must specify how he has used the term. He tells us he is talking about physical descendants ("according to the flesh") of Jacob (Israel). Both he and they were members of the Jewish nation. Paul's grief arises not only from the fact of physical kinship, but from the remembrance of all the privileges God had granted to the Jews since the time of Jacob.

9:4 – *who are Israelites, to whom belongs the adoption as sons and the glory and the covenants and the giving of the Law and the* **temple** *service and the promises,*

Who are Israelites. Just as in chapter 3, where Jewish objections to Paul's doctrine about sin and justification by faith also were being answered, so here, Paul begins by alluding to the distinct privileges shared by the Jews.[7] "Israelites" emphasizes the fact that they were

---

in order to assign such an interpretation to this passage requires one to ignore the infinitive that precedes "myself" in the Greek. Therefore, the Greek construction and the context both seem to require a reference to the present, to Paul's feelings toward the Jewish people now, after years of preaching the gospel as the apostle to the Gentiles.

[5] "The Greek word *anathema* frequently translates, in the Septuagint, the Hebrew *cherem*, which signified a thing devoted to God, whether for His service, as in the case of the sacrifice (Leviticus 27:28), or for its own destruction, e.g., an idol (Deuteronomy 7:26) or Jericho (Joshua 6:17). [These latter uses caused the] term to thus acquire the more general meaning of the disfavor of God as in Isaiah 34:5 or Malachi 4:6. This is its meaning here, as also in Acts 23:14; 1 Corinthians 12:3, 16:22; or Galatians 1:8,9." Vine, *Romans*, p.137,138. Sanday and Headlam, *Romans*, p.228, explain how the variation of spelling (long "e" or short "e" in "anathema") found in Greek literature and in the New Testament has resulted from the influence of differing dialects.

[6] This Greek construction is sometimes called an unattainable wish. In light of Special Study #7 on "Eternal Security," the impossibility of Paul's being lost is not the reason the wish is unattainable. The real reason such a wish is unattainable is that it is the death of Christ, and not the salvation or damnation of Paul, that has essential bearing on other men's eternal destiny.

[7] Vine (*Romans*, p.136,137) has observed that the parallelism extends even further. The three questions that the objector asked (chapter 3:1ff) as he attempted to refute Paul's teaching that Jew and Gentile alike were sinners and needed the salvation offered in the gospel, were each answered in turn. The first objection, that Paul's doctrine was contrary to the distinct privileges God had granted to the Jew, was answered in 3:2 (they did have privileges abundant!). Similarly, Romans 9:4,5 presents a continuation of the list of privileges. The second objection, that the validity of God's promises was called in question by Paul's doctrine, was answered in 3:4 ("Let God be found true!"). Similarly, 9:6-13 will affirm that the rejection of unbelieving Israel does not mean that God's promises have failed. The third objection, that Paul's doctrine implied that God was acting unrighteously, was answered in 3:6-8 (God will judge the world, and do it impartially). Similarly, in 9:14 the question is asked, "Is there unrighteousness with God?" [ASV], and this is answered in verses 14-29.

descended from Israel (Jacob).   One could be a descendant of Abraham (like the Ishmaelites were), and not be an Israelite; one could be a descendant of Isaac (like the Edomites were), and not be an Israelite.   "Israelites" were the ones who were a select nation, a kingdom of priests.   "Israelites" is a name that betokens a very special place before God (Genesis 32:28).[8]

To whom belongs the adoption as sons.   The Jews in Old Testament times were God's adopted sons.   See Exodus 4:22, where God first announced this privilege for Israel, when He said, "Israel is My son, My firstborn."   What is involved is that Israel now, following the Egyptian bondage, is to have a peculiar relationship to God, in contrast to other nations.[9]   "Adoption," as applied to Israel in the Old Testament, is a different idea than when the word is applied to Christians, as it just was in Romans 8:15,23.   It is the difference between a "national" sonship and a "spiritual" sonship.   The people of Israel are collectively called the "son" of God, whereas for Christians, it is an individual thing.

> Sonship with an Israelite was purely national, not individual, and, therefore, no guarantee of salvation.   Its mark was in the flesh, not in the spirit; and though a peculiar distinction within itself, and implying much, it is entitled to no honor under Christ.   To his hereditary sonship, an Israelite had still to add sonship to Christ, as really as the humblest Gentile; otherwise he was lost.[10]

And the glory.   The Shekinah, the visible symbol of God's presence with them, is the thing signified.   The Shekinah led Israel through the wilderness (Exodus 13:21,22, 16:10); rested on Mt. Sinai (Exodus 24:16,17); covered and filled the tabernacle after Moses built it according to the pattern (Exodus 40:34-38); and rested over the mercy seat in the holy of holies (Leviticus 16:2).   Later, when Solomon built the temple, the glory[11] of the Lord filled that building (1 Kings 8:10,11).   What a privilege the Israelites had, as God revealed Himself to them as He did to no other peoples.   God met them and spoke to them from the "glory" in the holy of holies (Numbers 7:89).

And the covenants.[12]   Since "covenants" is distinguished from "the Law" (see the next

---

[8] Mention perhaps could also be made of Hosea 12:3 and Galatians 6:16, where the expression "Israel of God" implies a contrast between the true and the false Israel.   Paul himself will take up this matter in subsequent verses.

[9] Compare Hosea 11:1, "Out of Egypt I called My son."

[10] Lipscomb and Shepherd, *Romans*, p.166.

[11] For the various uses of the word "glory," see comments at Romans 1:23.

[12] There is a manuscript variation here, and some weighty manuscripts (among them P[46], B, D, G) read it singular, "the covenant."   (a) One-covenant theologians are happy with the singular, and usually comment about the "one covenant of grace" as being the covenant Israel participated in.   In reply to this attempted identification of the "covenant," one wonders how this supposed "covenant of grace" could be thought of as a special privilege for Israel, since it is something that is true for all men since Adam sinned (at least, according to usual Covenant Theology presentations).   (b) Having rejected Covenant Theology's definition of the singular "covenant," if we accept this singular reading, the reference would be to the Mosaic

phrase), we no doubt should think of (1) the covenants God made with Abraham (Genesis 15:18, 17:4, 22:16), which are called "covenants of promise" in Ephesians 2:12; (2) the covenant of circumcision (Acts 7:8); and (3) the Davidic covenant (2 Samuel 23:5; Psalm 89:28), which promised the Messiah would be a descendant of David. God was entering into a covenant relationship[13] with these peoples in a way He did not do with other peoples.

And the giving of the Law. Not only was the possession of the Law of Moses itself a real privilege (Romans 3:1,2), but when Paul adds the verb "giving," he likely alludes to the manner in which God gave it. Never before was Jehovah manifested with such marvelous miracles that inspired a sense of both terror and majesty. "Have any people heard the voice of God speaking from the midst of the fire, as you have heard it, and survived?" (Deuteronomy 4:33).

And the *temple* service. The Greek has but one word, *latreia*, a word specially used of the worship that was conducted first in the tabernacle and later in the temple. The translators have added the word "temple" to help the English readers understand what the original readers would have known by long practice.[14] This reminds us of the prescriptions for the worship (*latreia*) of God that are recorded in the book of Leviticus, on which the temple ceremonies at Jerusalem were still based when Paul was dictating these words. All the other nations were left to worship according to the way the Patriarchs had been instructed by God,[15] to which, in many cases, had been added many superstitious inventions.

And the promises. Likely the promises in view are those which foretold the coming of Messiah – promises given not only to Abraham, Isaac, and Jacob, but also repeated often by the writers of Psalms and the Old Testament prophets.[16] The more one contemplates

---

covenant made with Israel at Sinai (Exodus 24:8), but we then would be hard put to explain the difference between this expression and the one immediately following ("the giving of the Law"). Thus, internal considerations, as well as the manuscript evidence supporting the plural, lead us to accept the plural reading "covenants."

[13] Two different Greek words are translated "covenant." *Suntheke* implies that the parties who make the covenant are equals. *Diatheke*, the word used here, implies that the parties to the covenant or agreement are unequals. In a *diatheke*, God sets all the conditions, and the individuals involved are free to accept or reject the conditions, but not to alter or change them. Because the word carries the idea that one party to the covenant is greater than the others, the word "promise" is often used almost interchangeably with "covenant," as in Galatians 3:16,18.

[14] Compare what is said at Hebrews 9:1-6.

[15] At Romans 1:32 it has been pointed out that the Patriarchs had numerous revelations from God which are only implied in the Scripture record. That Melchizedek was a priest of the Most High God implies a revelation about priesthood. That Abel, by faith, offered a more excellent sacrifice than Cain implies God had given specific instructions about sacrifice. Worship did not begin as merely a human invention, though by Paul's time, many of the practices in non-Jewish worship ceremonies were of human origin, rather than divine.

[16] The Bible student can produce for himself a list of these promises by referring to the Gospel of Matthew, wherein are some 40 different Old Testament Messianic prophecies quoted, as Matthew tries to

this impressive list of privileges the Jews enjoyed, the more it serves to emphasize the tragedy of their rejection of the One to whom these promises and privileges pointed. No wonder Paul is so brokenhearted.

9:5 – *whose are the fathers, and from whom is the Christ according to the flesh, who is over all, God blessed forever. Amen.*

Whose are the fathers. One thinks of the three great patriarchs, Abraham, Isaac, and Jacob, after whom God was pleased to call Himself (Exodus 3:6,13; Luke 20:37), and also of the twelve sons of Jacob, and of the tribes that descended from each (1 Corinthians 10:1; Hebrews 1:1, 8:9). The whole panorama of Hebrew history comes flooding to mind at the mention of the "fathers."

And from whom is the Christ. Of all the privileges granted to Israel, this was the crowning one – that they should be the channel through whom the Hope of the world, the long-expected Messiah, came into the world.[17]

According to the flesh. That is, only His human nature ("flesh") was derived from Israel through the fathers. As in Romans 1:3, this phrase "according to the flesh" implies there was another, higher nature, in respect to which Messiah was not "from" the Jewish nation. Although Jesus was of Jewish descent physically, He was also much more than a Jew.

Who is over all, God blessed forever. Amen. Jesus was much more than human, the writer tells us; He is also God! Just as Romans 1:3 spoke of both Jesus' human and divine natures, so 9:5 speaks of both.[18] Paul here expresses Jesus' essential divine nature. The

---

show to his Jewish readers that Jesus is the promised Messiah since He fulfilled all these prophecies. In the *Thompson Chain Reference Bible* is a special section entitled, "Prophecies Concerning Jesus and their Fulfillment." The chart mentions both prophecies of a kingly Messiah, and of a suffering Messiah. Frank Charles Thompson, compiler, *The New Chain-Reference Bible*, Third edition (Indianapolis: B.B. Kirkbride Bible Co., 1934), p.246-249. Hendriksen, *Romans*, p.313,314, also gives a parallel listing of prophecies and fulfillments.

[17] "From whom" (*ex hōn*), which differs from "whose" (*hōn*) in the two instances preceding, is most exact in showing that Jesus did not belong to the Jews as though He were their special property. Jesus was a descendant of Abraham, through Jacob, and David, and others of the chosen people. He was only derived from them, of course, as Paul goes on to say, on His human side.

[18] The careful reader will have observed that several modern translations (ASV margin, RSV, NEB, NIV margin) render the closing words of verse 5 as though they had reference to the Father, rather than to Jesus. There is no manuscript variation here to cast any doubt on the wording of this passage. But the manuscripts originally had no punctuation marks, and the difference between the words being a description of who Jesus is and a doxology to God the Father depends entirely on the punctuation of the passage by the translators. Before a translator can punctuate it, he has had to interpret it. The suggestion that a whole new sentence (i.e., a doxology to the Father) be made up of the words "God over all be blessed forever" is the one that draws the most criticism. In some cases, the RSV for example, the punctuation and translation chosen reflect a definite bias against the deity of Christ. O.T. Allis, *Revision or New Translation?* (Philadelphia: Presbyterian and Reformed Publishing Co., 1940), p.116, affirms that the RSV text, "God who is over all be blessed forever," is "a definite triumph for the Unitarians who have long contended that these words must be regarded as a benediction to God and not as ascribing Deity to Christ." It is pertinent to note that the belief in the deity of Christ does not depend on passages like Romans 9:5,

present participle (translated "who is") expresses not only what Jesus is since His resurrection and ascension – exalted "over all" – but actually is a statement of what always was, is, and will be the essential and characteristic nature of the One who came into the world to be its Savior.[19]   Paul quickly has said three things about the Christ who became incarnate – He is over all, He is God, and He is blessed forever.   What a stupendous privilege to be a part of such a One's activities in the world!

---

which might be ambiguous. See for example the first chapter of Hebrews, where not only are seven characteristics of deity ascribed to Him (verses 2,3), but where the Father expressly calls Jesus "God" (verses 8,9). It is perhaps significant that it was Erasmus, the great humanist, who first suggested that these words in Romans 9:5 are addressed to the Father. Until then, "it was universally referred to Christ in the ancient church, by all the Reformers, and by almost all of the modern interpreters who believe in the divinity of Christ." Hodge, *Systematic Theology*, 3 vols. (Grand Rapids: Wm. B. Eerdmans Publishing Co., 1952), Vol.1, p.511.

Modern theologians and translators defend their work with the following objections against making Romans 9:5 a reference to the deity of Jesus: (1) Paul never, they allege, calls Jesus "God" in any of his writings.   (2) To say Jesus is not only God, but is "over all," is at variance with the rest of the New Testament wherein Jesus is dependent on the Father.   (3) Doxologies in the Pauline letters are addressed to the Father, not to Jesus.   [As to (1), Paul does call Jesus "God" in Titus 2:13 and 2 Thessalonians 1:12, and this is in complete harmony with what the rest of the New Testament writers affirm.   As to (2), Jesus' dependence on the Father is limited to His function as Savior, not to His essential being.   Where essential being is the subject, Scripture everywhere makes Jesus equal with the Father, even to the point where both can equally be said to be "over all."   As to (3), this objection misses the point, for if the phrase is so translated as to be a designation of who Messiah is, it would not any longer be thought of as a doxology.   Yet even if we admit it is a doxology, it could still be shown to be in harmony with Paul's usage elsewhere, for we do have a doxology addressed to Christ in a Pauline epistle – 2 Timothy 4:18.   However, the word order here is against this being a doxology at all, whether addressed to the Father or the Son.   In doxologies, the word "blessed" regularly precedes the predicate; but here, if this were a doxology, the word "blessed" would uncharacteristically follow the predicate "God."   Were we to admit that Paul varies his usual word order, and does here address a doxology to God, we are hard pressed to be able to indicate a reason why he inserted such a doxology at this place.   He would hardly say, "I'm full of sorrow because the majority of my people reject Jesus," and then immediately say, "Praise the Lord!"].

It should not be thought incongruous or inharmonious with what Paul elsewhere writes about Jesus that he here in Romans 9:5 calls Him "God."   He does apply to Jesus all the attributes of deity.   He is creator (Colossians 1:16).   In Him dwells all the fulness of the Godhead bodily (Colossians 2:9).   Jesus always exists in the form of God (Philippians 2:6).   Jesus is the image of the invisible God (Colossians 1:15).   And it is likely that what is called "the judgment seat of God" in Romans 14:10 is styled the "judgment seat of Christ" in 2 Corinthians 5:10.   "Moreover, when Paul gives Christ the title 'Lord,' he does so because God the Father Himself has given Him that title as 'the name that is above every name' (Philippians 2:9-11).   The title 'Lord' is given to Jesus by Paul as the equivalent of the Hebrew *Yahweh* (Isaiah 45:23 and Romans 14:11).   The way Paul applies Isaiah 45:23 to Jesus in Philippians 2:10-11 indicates that to him, the confession 'Jesus Christ is Lord' means 'Jesus Christ is Jehovah'." Bruce, *Romans*, p.187. Furthermore, Jesus is called God elsewhere in the New Testament, as at Hebrews 1:8; John 1:1,18, 20:28; and 2 Peter 1:1.

"When we review the history of the interpretation, it cannot but be regarded as a remarkable fact that every objection urged against the ancient interpretation [that Jesus is here called 'God'] rests ultimately on dogmatic presuppositions, and that every alternative that has been proposed is more or less objectionable both in the form of expression and in the connection of thought." Gifford, *Romans*, p.179. Paul has been listing the privileges God had extended to the Israelites.   The highest of all was that Messiah, who is one of the members of the Godhead, and who is no less a being than One who is "over all," entered into human form through Jewish lineage.

[19] Similar present tense Greek verbs, indicating durative action, are found at John 1:18 (where it speaks of Jesus as being ["who is"] in the bosom of the Father) and Philippians 2:6 (where we are told that Jesus "exists in the form of God").

B. God's Dealings with Israel *In the Past* Are Just as God Revealed They Would Be – It Has Always been the "Remnant."   9:6-29

Summary: God has not been unfaithful to His Word when He used the 'Israel within Israel' to accomplish His purposes, 9:6-13. Paul then gives three reasons why men cannot accuse God of being unjust in thus dealing with 'Israel within Israel,' 9:14-29.)

9:6 – *But* it is *not as though the word of God has failed.   For they are not all Israel who are* descended *from Israel;*

But *it is* **not as though the word of God has failed.**   Paul's readers must not draw a wrong inference from his grief concerning Israel's rejection of their Messiah.   While he has been expressing his grief over the actions of his Jewish kinsmen, such sorrow and grief should never be interpreted to imply that Paul thought God's promises to the fathers ("the word of God," i.e., the declared purpose of God) had failed to come true.[20]

For they are not all Israel who are *descended* **from Israel.**   Here Paul assigns the reason why he can say the word of God has not failed.   Likely the idea governing this paragraph is what in verse 5 was called the crowning privilege granted to the Jews – that of being the channel through whom God accomplished His purpose of bringing His Son into the world. If this is true,[21] then the underlying connection of verse 6 to the context is this: when God made the promise to Israel (Jacob) that in his seed all the nations of the earth would be blessed (Genesis 28:14), God never did include all the physical descendants of Jacob.[22] There was an 'Israel within Israel' whom He intended to be the ancestral line through which Messiah (according to the flesh) sprang.   The "seed" was limited to the 'Israel within Israel.'[23]

---

[20] "'The word of God' should be understood in a more specific sense and not in the sense of Scripture as a whole or of the word of the truth of the gospel.   It is the word of promise in the covenants alluded to in verse 4." Murray, *Romans*, Vol.2, p.9.

[21] Some confirmation of this view is found in 9:7-13, where the limitation of the word "descendants" is clearly explained by a reminder of Old Testament history.   In several instances, the line through whom the coming "Seed" (Christ) was to come is clearly limited to but one out of several possible lines of descent. The line through whom Messiah was eventually to come is the thread that ties these verses together.

[22] One of the points being made in the whole book of Romans is that God has always purposed to include Gentiles in His plans and purposes.   The phrase "which are descended from Israel" reminds us that not all who were born to Jacob were included in the "true Israel," the people of God.   Israel does not consist simply of the natural descendants of Jacob.   We are reminded of Romans 2:28,29, where we learned we must be careful in our definition of the terms "Jew" and "circumcision" if we would use them with the same meaning God assigned to these terms.

[23] It is not forgotten nor ignored that in Galatians 3:16 Paul points out that "seed" ultimately and supremely refers to Christ.   But it is also true that the promise made to the patriarchs included their nearer physical descendants, with the line ultimately finding its fulfillment in the coming of Christ into the world. It is with this matter of nearer physical descent the context here in Romans emphasizes.

9:7 – *neither are they all children because they are Abraham's descendants, but: "THROUGH ISAAC YOUR DESCENDANTS WILL BE NAMED."*

Neither are they all children because they are Abraham's descendants. Just as not all Jacob's physical descendants were in the line through which Messiah was to come, so neither are all the physical descendants of Abraham in the line. It is expressly stated from the first that the line through which Messiah was to come was confined to one particular branch of Abraham's posterity. It was through Isaac, and not Ishmael, or any of the sons of Keturah, that the ancestry of Christ could be traced.

But, "THROUGH ISAAC YOUR DESCENDANTS WILL BE NAMED." This is a quotation of Genesis 21:12, where God instructed Abraham not to oppose Sarah's demand that Hagar and Ishmael be sent away, because his "seed"[24] was not to be reckoned through Ishmael, but through Isaac. God's limiting the line through which the seed would come implied a selection, a choice (see verse 11) made by Him; therefore, the doctrine of divine election[25] to service was illustrated in the very commencement of the history of the nation.

9:8 – *That is, it is not the children of the flesh who are children of God, but the children of the promise are regarded as descendants.*

That is, it is not the children of the flesh who are children of God. What has just been said is now further explained. In the case of Abraham, the "children of the flesh" would be such physical offspring as Ishmael and Keturah's children. Mere physical descent did not qualify any of them to be called "children of God," i.e., the children God had chosen to use as the line through whom Messiah was to come.[26]

But the children of the promise are regarded as descendants. The next verse will specify what promise Paul particularly has reference to. It was one made to Abraham just one year before Isaac was born. Isaac was the line through whom the "seed" was to come. It was God himself who made the choice of Isaac.[27]

---

[24] The NASB carries a marginal note that the word they have rendered "descendants" is literally "seed," and it is a matter of interpretation whether the singular is understood of one, or collectively of a group.

[25] The verb translated "named" is *kaleō*, the word sometimes translated "call, summon, call aloud, name, etc." See Special Study #1 at the close of chapter 1 on "'Call' and 'Grace'."

[26] It might be instructive to compare "children of God" here in verse 8 with the "adoption" spoken of in verse 4. God adopted the nation Israel to do a special job He wanted done in the world.

[27] The word translated "regarded" here in verse 8 is the same word translated "reckoned" at Romans 4:3-5. Perhaps it is time to make several pertinent comments. (1) Readers who have also read Paul's "seed" argument in Galatians 3:16-29 and 4:22-31 will perhaps wonder why hardly any reference has been made to those verses in the course of explaining Romans 9. The reason is this: the topics being discussed by Paul are not quite parallel. In Romans, Paul is talking simply about God's selection of some (not all) of Israel's (or Abraham's) descendants to perform an historic function – namely, to be the line through whom Christ comes. In Galatians 3:16, on the other hand, we are shown that the word seed (because it is singular in the promise "in your *seed* all the nations of the earth shall be blessed) has reference ultimately to Christ. In Galatians 3:29, because the word "seed" can be a collective noun, the topic is who is included in the group that today could be named "Abraham's seed." The allegory of Ishmael

9:9 – *For this is a word of promise:* *"AT THIS TIME I WILL COME, AND SARAH SHALL HAVE A SON."*

For this is a word of promise. In the next phrase, Paul quotes Genesis 18:10, and thereby reminds his readers that God Himself had plainly and specifically declared which one of Abraham's physical offspring was the one He had chosen to be the lineage through whom Christ came.[28] "Promise" is the first word in the Greek, and it is placed forward for emphasis. "Pay special attention to the *promise* that was made just before Isaac was born, and you will see the truth of the point I am making," is what Paul is saying.

"AT THIS TIME I WILL COME, AND SARAH SHALL HAVE A SON." God is speaking to Abraham, and says, "I will surely return to you in the spring (or at this time next year[29]), and Sarah your wife shall have a son." By this promise made by God to Abraham, God Himself specified the "seed" line. The promise which He had made earlier (Genesis 15:4-6, 17:16-27) is now made specific. The son born next year to Sarah is the one!

9:10 – *And not only this, but there was Rebekah also, when she had conceived* **twins** *by one man, our father Isaac;*

And not only this.[30] Paul is going to appeal to another instance where God made special choice of the one through whom the lineage of Christ was to continue. What happened in the case of Isaac (his being chosen rather than Ishmael) also happened in the case of Jacob (he was the child of promise rather than Esau). Verse 10 is supposed to be a stronger argument ("and not only so" [ASV]) to prove his point than was verse 9.

---

and Isaac, Hagar and Sarah, which follows shows that spiritual descendants are what God intended, not just physical. (2) Readers of many popular commentaries on Romans will have observed, especially in those by Calvinistic authors, that many allusions to predestination *to salvation* are regularly included among the comments on these verses. Already one will have read statements like, "The Divine choice was made according to God's own will." "The immediate point in the argument is the sovereignty of God in His selection of one and rejection of another." "The choice made by God depended not upon the works of the flesh but on His own promise." "'In Isaac shall your seed be reckoned' speaks of a decree that was issued by the sovereignty of God which excluded Ishmael, Esau, etc., from the covenant and from salvation." Following our comments on chapter 11 is Special Study #8 on the topic of predestination, which the reader will want to consult. For the moment, let it be observed that all Romans 9 has spoken of is predestination *to service*. "Seed" – the line through whom the "Seed" (Christ) came – is the thought running all through these verses. This is election *to service*, election to be the channel through whom the Seed came into the world. It will be several verses, yet, before the topic of "salvation" is taken up.

[28] There is an article before "word" in the Greek, but none before "promise." The KJV evidently did it right when it translated, "This is *the* word of promise."

[29] "At this time" (or, "at this season," ASV) equals "at the corresponding time next year." "At this time next year" is how we would say it.

[30] The sentence begun in verse 10 is not formally completed. (Note the dash at the close of verse 10 in the ASV; note that verse 11 in the KJV is in parentheses.) What Paul does first is to give a brief reminder of the Old Testament record about the birth of the twins. Having done that, he quotes the "promise" made to Rebekah (verse 12), which was really his main point of emphasis. God revealed His choice of Jacob to be the "seed" in the words He spoke to Rebekah.

But there was Rebekah also. In the likelihood that some would find a flaw in the previous illustration, Paul also reminds his readers of the birth of Jacob and Esau. In the case of Ishmael, the person who wanted to quibble could point out the fact that Ishmael was not a fully legitimate child as was Isaac (after all, Hagar was a bondwoman!); and, therefore, he could say, it was because Ishmael and Isaac had different mothers that God chose to use one and not the other. By reminding that Jacob and Esau had the same mother, Rebekah, Paul can drive home the principle suggested earlier that God's choice has been involved in the "seed" line all along. There was no such thing as different mothers, or even a different time of birth, in their case.

When she had conceived *twins* **by one man, our father Isaac.** Jacob and Esau were twin children, conceived by the same father. The expression "by one man" guards against an objector finding some human cause in the choice God made that Jacob would be the line through whom Messiah came, and not Esau.[31] Paul has already ruled out any difference in mothers as being the possible cause of the preference, for, in Rebekah's case, the children were of the same mother. The only possible difference then, if some physical reason could be found to justify the preference, would have had to be on the father's side, but that too is ruled out by the fact that Isaac was the common father.

9:11 – *for though* **the twins** *were not yet born, and had not done anything good or bad, in order that God's purpose according to* **His** *choice might stand, not because of works, but because of Him who calls,*

For though *the twins* **were not yet born.**[32] The selection of Isaac was not specifically stated until after Ishmael's birth. The selection of Jacob was made before either he or his brother was born.

And had not done anything good or bad. Again, one who wished to quibble about the choice of Isaac over Ishmael might argue that Ishmael had done something bad, and so forfeited the opportunity to be in the lineage of the Messiah. Well, no such argument can be made when it comes to God's choice of Jacob over Esau. That choice was made before either had been alive to do anything either good or bad. The reason for the choice, therefore, must lie in the mind of God, rather than being conditioned on something man is or does.

---

[31] Lenski finds a reason in these verses to reject the usual "predestination to salvation" comments found in most Calvinistic authors. "Paul does not allegorize or produce types: as Isaac was born physically in a wonderful way, so we are born spiritually in a wonderful way. This breaks down when we come to Jacob. Isaac and Jacob cannot be separated, the one to typify one thing, the other another thing; for Paul combines them as illustrating the same thing, namely promise: 'And not only she (Sarah) but also Rebecca.' Nor can these promises be made absolute decrees that are illustrative of God's absolute sovereignty which predestines to salvation whom he will (Isaac, Jacob) and reprobates whom he will (Ishmael, Esau); and thus also reprobates the mass of Jews and likewise the mass of Gentiles. Paul's two illustrations have nothing to do with eternal election or predestination to salvation or reprobation." *Romans*, p. 597.

[32] The fact that verses 10-12 are a broken sentence in the original, which the KJV tried to indicate by putting verse 11 in parentheses, has been alluded to earlier. Some have objected to putting all of verse 11 in parentheses, because it tends to destroy the connection with the following verse.

In order that God's purpose according to *His* choice might stand. The real, underlying reason for God's actions is here stated. In a word, the reason is simply that God chose to carry out His purpose this way. "Purpose" was explained at 8:28 as being the 'plan' formed by God in eternity before He ever set about to create. Included in that plan was God's intention to save mankind if sin's entrance into the world made such salvation necessary. Now Paul tells us that God's 'purpose of the ages' also included His choice[33] of some for service – so the rest could be blessed. Before He ever began to create, God decided (He elected, He chose) who would be in the line of physical descent that would culminate at Bethlehem with Mary giving birth to Jesus.[34] "Might stand" is the opposite of "failed" in verse 6. The verb here is a present tense, indicating that the principles acted upon all through the ages are still in force as Paul writes.

Not because of works, but because of Him who calls. Evidently these words are intended to make it perfectly clear that God's choice of whom He will use in His service is absolutely dependent only on the way God wants to do it – and not on anything in man. Jacob could not point to anything he had done (he was not born yet) that would entitle him to the privilege of being in the Messianic line. In fact, when we remember his later life, his faults and sins, it is almost surprising that God used him. But the point is, He did, simply because He decided to do it that way. The reason for the choice lies wholly within the mind and will of God.[35]

---

[33] "Choice" is translated by "election" in some versions. This results in long notes in many of the commentaries about God's "election" of some to salvation or damnation. (This topic has been covered extensively in Special Study #1 on "Call" and "Grace" at the close of notes on chapter 1.) Most of these comments tend to treat "the purpose of God" and "according to election" as two separate items – whereas the entire expression "the purpose of God according to election" is a unit. Cranfield, *Romans*, p.478, explains it to mean "God's purpose which is characterized by election."

[34] It is instructive to consider the particulars that made up Paul's philosophy of history – particulars that still are valid! (1) His use of the word "mystery" gives us one clue to his philosophy of history. That is, as the ages passed, God revealed little-by-little exactly what He was doing in history. Ephesians 1: 4-11 is one passage where we learn of the foreknowledge and plan which God had before the creation of the world, a plan that has now been revealed through the gospel as preached by the apostles. Paul even enumerates some of the major features of God's purpose for the ages in that Ephesians paragraph. (2) From Romans 5:12ff, we come to understand that there are a succession of ages in God's plan for the history of the world. Beginning with Adam we have what is customarily called the Patriarchal age; after Moses' time we have the Mosaic age; and with the coming of Jesus the Christian age is introduced. In each of these ages, God has revealed Himself more than in former times. (3) In Romans 8:28-30, 9:11, and Ephesians 1:11, we are told that God has had a plan or purpose which He has been working out just as He chose to do it. God could have redeemed mankind by a simple act, even by a nod, if he had wished. Instead, He chose to work in harmony with the human limitations and conditions which He Himself created, and in some cases He even has used men in order to accomplish His purposes when the men did not particularly want to be used. He chose first this man, then that; this people, then that, in order to make Himself known to others, and through them, in time, that the whole world might come to have a saving knowledge of their Creator. (4) Why did God choose to do it this way? He had two things in mind – the completion of the Messianic Kingdom, and the exhibition of His divine mercy. This latter purpose – the exhibition of Divine mercy – suggests the solution to another class of questions. Why does God allow sin? Why does He shut up men under sin? It is that ultimately He may exhibit the depths of His divine mercy. (5) Paul's philosophy of history also includes the idea that all of history is moving toward a goal, the second advent of Christ and the new heavens and new earth. God is moving it there. See 8:19ff.

[35] A word of caution needs to be extended. In theological debates, much attention is given to the

9:12 – *it was said to her, "THE OLDER WILL SERVE THE YOUNGER."*

It was said to her.   Paul is about to quote Genesis 25:23, where God's selection of Jacob for service is made known to Rebekah.

"THE OLDER WILL SERVE THE YOUNGER."   According to the custom of the day, by leaving the womb first (Genesis 25:24-26), Esau should have been the greater, and should have been regarded as the first-born and the father's chief heir.   But God chose Jacob, the second-born, and He did so simply because He was pursuing the plan He had chosen.   God's choice of Jacob also meant that the "fathers from whom is the Christ according to the flesh" (verse 5) would be the Israelites, rather than the Edomites (the descendants of Esau).[36]   That the Israelites (the race that descended from Jacob) were to be the privileged people, and not the Edomites, was implied in God's explanation to Rebekah recorded in Genesis 25:23, where the whole verse reads, "Two nations are in your womb; and two peoples shall be separated from your body; and one people shall be stronger than the other; and the older shall serve the younger."[37]   That the Israelites (and not the Edomites) were the privileged people is also documented by a quotation from Malachi, which is alluded to in the next verse.

9:13 – *Just as it is written, "JACOB I LOVED, BUT ESAU I HATED."*

Just as it is written.   Paul continues his argument about how God has been faithful to His promise, and that He has acted in absolute harmony with what He Himself had revealed He would do, by a quotation from Malachi 1:2,3.   Malachi prophesied 1400 years after Jacob and Esau were born, so he was in a position to look back over the centuries to see if

---

relation between God's sovereign choice and God's foreknowledge.   (The ideas of "call" and "foreknowledge" are related in Romans 8:28-30; the ideas of "choice" and "foreknowledge" are related in 1 Peter 1:1,2.)   We suppose that it is in error to affirm that God's choice was limited by His foreknowledge of what man would do or not do.   Such an explanation ignores what Romans 9:11 says about the choice *not* being based on what man does or does not do.   The *choice* for service finds its reason in God alone, Paul says here in Romans 9.   Likewise, God's choice of who would be saved (per Ephesians 1:4, He decided that those who would be *in Christ* would be the saved ones) is a choice that lies wholly within God's mind and will.   But whether or not a man is "in Christ" is left up to individual men to choose, as they exercise their freedom of choice either to accept or reject God's overtures of love, and His call (invitation) to become members of the family of God.

[36] Many paragraphs are written at this place on the question of whether or not the nations that sprang from Jacob and Esau were automatically involved in God's choice of the founder of the nation.   Some authors are attempting to defend the doctrine of the election of *individuals* to salvation; others are trying to defend the idea that God elects *nations* to be His covenant people, but that His election does not extend to which individuals in those nations are involved.   If this passage is talking about election to *service*, rather than election to salvation or covenant relationship, much of what has been written in the commentaries on the topic is beside the point.   "What is here in question is not eschatological salvation or damnation, but the historical functions of those [nations] concerned and their relations to the development of the salvation-history."   Cranfield, *Romans*, p.479.

[37] Again, a number of commentaries recall the fact that, in subsequent history, the Edomites were in bondage to Israel or Judah, even citing a number of Scriptures where this is made plain.   In this writer's opinion, it is beside the point to recall this fact.   All the writer of Romans is interested in showing is that there was a selection process used by God, and that "seed" never did include all the physical descendants.

God's word had proven true.   Before the birth of twins, God had said He would use Jacob (and his race) to do the world the great service of bringing Messiah into the world.   Now, by quoting Malachi, Paul is appealing to history as recorded in Scripture to demonstrate that God has done exactly as He said He would do.   It was Jacob, not Esau, that He used.

"JACOB I LOVED, BUT ESAU I HATED."   The context of this passage in Malachi indicates that it is the nations of Israel and Edom, rather than their individual founders, Jacob and Esau, that are in view.   The aorist tense verbs (loved, hated) are probably intended to summarize God's different use of the two nations down until Malachi's time. How are we to understand the words "loved" and "hated"?   "Loved" is God's attitude that led Him to choose Jacob for His special tool.   "Hated" is the attitude that led Him to decide not to use Esau.[38]   Once more, it is necessary to keep these things in mind with reference to the selection of Jacob.   Was Israel elected to eternal *salvation*, and the Edomites rejected?   No!   Israel was elected by God to an *historical function*, in the interest of His worldwide redemptive scheme, that they might be a blessing to all peoples.   This election to service had no reference to eternal destiny.   Whether or not Jacob is saved, that depended on Jacob.   Whether or not Esau was damned, that depended on Esau.   But whether Messiah comes through Jacob or through Esau, that depended on God.

Paul's argument, so far, is one with which few Jews would find fault.   The Arabs were the descendants of Ishmael who was a flesh and blood descendant of Abraham, but the Jews would never dream of saying that the Arabs are included in the "seed."   The Edomites were the descendants of Esau, and Esau was a true son of Isaac, and the twin brother of Jacob; but no Jew would ever have included the Edomites in the "seed."   They could hardly disagree with Paul's emphasis that God has been making choices all through history, selecting this one and bypassing that one, without being unfaithful to the promise about "seed" that He made to the patriarchs.

9:14 – *What shall we say then?   There is no injustice with God, is there?   May it never be!*

What shall we say then?   That is, what conclusion shall we draw from what has just been said?   The question supposes one of Paul's Jewish readers might ask, "Is it right of God to pursue a policy of selection like He has done?"[39]   Having shown that God was not unfaith-

---

[38] The human emotion of "hate" is un-Christ-like and sinful when there are elements of malice, vindictiveness, or bitterness involved in it.   (a) Such attitudes are completely foreign to God's "hate," so many have preferred to explain it to mean "loved less."   Murray, *Romans*, Vol.2, p.21, cites Genesis 29:32,33; Deuteronomy 21:15; Matthew 6:24, 10:37,38; Luke 14:26; and John 12:25 as examples where this meaning of "to love less, to regard and treat with less favour" is likely the correct explanation of "hate." (b) Others take the word literally, after observing that there is such a thing as a holy hate.   "There is a hate in us that is the expression of holy jealousy for God's honour and of love to him (cf. Psalms 26:5, 31:6, 139:21,22; Jude 23; Revelation 2:6).   This hate is the reflection in us of God's jealousy for His own honour." Murray, *op. cit.*, p.22.   (c) Earlier in Romans, it was learned that God's "wrath" has effects that can be seen in men's lives (Romans 1:18ff).   In similar fashion, perhaps it can be affirmed that there is in God a holy hate which also has its effects in our world, whereby some are rejected as God chooses which individuals and nations he will destine to do a special service for Him.

[39] Several times before (Romans 3:5, 6:1, 7:7) the same question has been asked.   Cranfield, *Romans*, p.482, suggests that Paul uses this question when he recognizes that a possible false conclusion could be

ful to his word (9:6-13), Paul now gives three reasons why men dare not accuse God of being unjust when He chooses some to do a special service, and not others. (1) Scripture reveals the principle of God's free will, verses 15-18. (2) Mere man is not competent to criticize the Creator (like a man would be doing if he accused God of being unjust), verses 19-21. (3) Instead of thinking about injustice, men should be contemplating the motive behind God's actions – His *mercy*, verses 22-29.

There is no injustice with God, is there?   When God "loves" one and "hates" another, is there any injustice or wrong actions on His part? Since His selection is dependent on nothing else than His own will to do it that way, when He chooses one and rejects another, is there any possibility that He is being unfair?

May it never be!   When God chose Jacob to be in the Messianic line, simply because His planning for the ages included making such a selection, was God doing something wrong? No! The thought is not to be entertained.[40] Paul will now appeal to passages in the Scripture to show that God has always made such choices, and no one ever accused Him of being unjust in the choices Paul is about to enumerate.[41]

9:15 – *For He says to Moses, "I WILL HAVE MERCY ON WHOM I HAVE MERCY, AND I WILL HAVE COMPASSION ON WHOM I HAVE COMPASSION."*

For He says to Moses.[42]   The verse about to be quoted comes from Exodus 33:19. After Israel's sin of the golden calf, Moses wanted to know if Israel still had a place in God's plans. The quotation is part of God's answer to Moses' prayer about this matter. Whether or not God extended "mercy" to Israel depended not on Israel's behavior, but on God's sovereignty to choose whom He would to carry out His plans.

"I WILL HAVE MERCY ON WHOM I HAVE MERCY, AND I WILL HAVE COMPASSION ON WHOM I HAVE COMPASSION."   God's statement to Moses is quoted with the intent of demonstrating that when God chooses some course of action (like His selection of Isaac and Jacob to be in the "seed" line, spoken about in the preceding verses), He cannot be accused of doing something wrong. In fact, a long time ago, God

---

drawn from what he has just said. The question is followed by a statement of the possible false conclusion, its rejection, and then the correct idea is presented.

[40] For the expression, "May it never be!" see notes at Romans 3:4.

[41] We are probably to understand that Paul is already beginning to lay the foundation on which he can build his affirmation that God has regularly limited His dealings to a "remnant" (Romans 11:5).

[42] "According to Origen, followed by many fathers and some few modern commentators, the section of verses 15-19 contains not Paul's own words, but a continuation of the objection put into the mouth of his opponent, finally to be refuted by the indignant disclaimer of verse 20. Such a construction is quite contrary to the structure of the sentence and of the argument. In every case in which 'God forbid!' occurs, it is followed by an answer to the objection, direct or indirect. Moreover, if this had been the construction, the interrogative sentence would not have been introduced by the particle *mē*, expecting a negative answer, but would have been in a form which would suggest an affirmative answer." Sanday and Headlam, *Romans*, p.253.

claimed the right to do just as He chose to do; yea, to be free to do just as He wills to do.[43] Of course, it is understood that God's attributes of holiness and righteousness are not violated by any of the things He chooses or wills to do. God does not act in a manner inconsistent with His very being, so men certainly cannot find any injustice in God, even when He does those things that are determined simply by His absolute sovereignty.

9:16 – *So then it* does *not* depend *on the man who wills or the man who runs, but on God who has mercy.*

So then. Verse 16 sums up the argument made in verses 14 and 15. From the one instance where God spoke to Moses about His right to act as He willed to act, Paul infers what is the general principle behind all God's acts of selection or choosing.

It *does* **not** *depend* **on the man who wills or the man who runs.** "It" has reference to God's reasons for choosing as He does.[44] His choice is not based on men's actions, either actual or foreseen. Commentators have had difficulty explaining the unusual words "wills" and "runs" in this verse.[45] Lipscomb suggests that Jacob and Esau are still in the background (since they were last spoken of a verse or two earlier).

He illustrates what he means by the case of Jacob and Esau. Isaac willed that

---

[43] When reading this quotation from the Old Testament, put emphasis on the personal pronouns ("I"), and God's claim to be free to do as He chooses will be conveyed to the mind of the hearers.

This passage is often misunderstood by Calvinist theologians, and is made a proof-text for absolute and unconditional election and predestination to salvation. It is done, (1) by putting particular emphasis or stress on the relative clauses ("on whom") as the passage is read; and (2) by ignoring the Romans 9 context, which is election to *service* rather than to *salvation*. Calvinism reads "I will have mercy on whom I will have mercy" to mean, "I will not demand works or that any other condition be met by man (Romans 9:11). I will just save the few 'on whom' I wish to have mercy." To this commentator, Calvinism has made this passage say the very opposite of what it actually does. Calvinism has God extend mercy and pity to only a few of the wretched and lost. For the great mass of the lost, God has no pity ("compassion") but only condemnation and damnation. Mercilessly, pitilessly He lets them perish in their wretchedness, and even decrees that they shall perish. Instead of a sovereignty that operates within the bounds of mercy and pity, Calvinism attributes a peculiar sovereignty to God, a sovereignty which instead of being generous is greatly constricted and limited since He has mercy on only the few "on whom" He wishes to have mercy. On the contrary, God's words to Moses, while emphasizing His freedom to do as He wills, have the opposite implication. Instead of restricting and limiting His mercy, God is promising to have mercy and compassion in such a wide generosity as to be almost utterly amazing. To interpret as Calvinism does – that God's mercy is extended only to the few, and the rest are condemned even when they are not personally responsible for their sinful condition – would be, in this commentator's opinion, the very embodiment of unrighteousness and injustice that Paul insists cannot be laid to God, because God does not act that way.

[44] Calvinist writers affirm that the "it" is salvation, rather than a selection to service. However, there is a legitimate doubt whether salvation has yet come into the scope of this presentation in Romans 9. It is not easy to determine where the topic changes from service to salvation in chapters 9-11, but it is hardly possible that the change occurs before 9:29. This whole question is taken up and examined in Special Study #8 on "Predestination" at the close of chapter 11.

[45] Calvinist writers, who insist this passage deals with how men are saved, will explain the two words as excluding any human volition or action as conditions for salvation. Salvation, they affirm, is simply a matter of God's predestination; it is all God's doing; it results from His election; synergism (man's cooperation with God in the matter of salvation) is completely ruled out.

Esau should inherit the blessing, and Esau ran with haste to obtain the venison for his father that he might have the blessing; but neither Isaac's will, nor Esau's running could defeat the purpose of God to bless Jacob.[46]

But on God who has mercy.   That is, God's choice of some for service is wholly a matter of God's own volition.   That choice does not depend on what the man does or does not do.

9:17 – *For the Scripture says to Pharaoh, "FOR THIS VERY PURPOSE I RAISED YOU UP, TO DEMONSTRATE MY POWER IN YOU, AND THAT MY NAME MIGHT BE PROCLAIMED THROUGHOUT THE WHOLE EARTH."*

For the Scripture says to Pharaoh.   Another illustration from God's actions in history will show that God cannot be accused of injustice even when He chooses to use someone like Pharaoh.   The passage about to be quoted is from Exodus 9:16.[47]   In that place, it is actually Moses who is speaking to Pharaoh, but Moses is acting as God's mouthpiece.   So, when Paul says "Scripture" speaks, it is tantamount to identifying "Scripture" as being the place where God speaks to men today.

"FOR THIS VERY PURPOSE I RAISED YOU UP, TO DEMONSTRATE MY POWER IN YOU.   God directed Moses to address these words to Pharaoh after the sixth plague (boils).   In the Hebrew, the verb translated "raised up" suggests that God prevented Pharaoh from being slain by the boils in order that He might more completely exhibit His power as He dealt with Pharaoh in the future.[48]   God chose to use Pharaoh (as He has chosen to use other men throughout the course of history) "in order to demonstrate His mighty power."[49]   If Pharaoh had died in the plague, men would have had some idea of God's power; but God kept Pharaoh alive and on the throne with the express design of providing a more notable demonstration of His power.   God displayed His power in the miracles He wrought in delivering Israel from Egypt, so that Israel might see the mighty hand of God at work, and also (as the next phrase tells us) so that the whole earth would come to know about Jehovah.   God had chosen Pharaoh for service; the ruler of Egypt was

---

[46] Lipscomb and Shepherd, *Romans*, p.174.

[47] It is not quoted from the LXX, but is Paul's own free translation of the Hebrew.

[48] The Hebrew at Exodus 9:16 has the hiphil stem of the verb 'amad, which could have two meanings. It could mean "let you recover" (from the plague of boils, instead of letting him die in the plague), and it could mean "raised you up" (continued to permit him to be ruler of Egypt at this time).   The LXX used *dieterethes* ("you were carefully kept"), the first of these two possible meanings; Paul uses *exēgeira* ("you were raised up"), the second of the two possible meanings.   Either way we translate the hiphil, it was the hand of Providence that kept Pharaoh alive or on the throne longer than he would have lived or reigned otherwise.   It does not mean God deliberately aroused Pharaoh to act as he did because Pharaoh had been predestined to so act, so that God could then demonstrate His power against him.   It does speak of something God chose to do after Pharaoh already was on the scene of history.

[49] Cranfield, *Romans*, p.487, observes that Paul uses *dunamis* for "power" where the LXX had *ischuros*. He supposes that the change was deliberate, so that the word "power" here in 9:17 is exactly the same as the word "power" (unto salvation) in 1:16.   Cranfield thinks that it is God's saving power that is the thing He wished to demonstrate so uniquely in Pharaoh.

involved in God's merciful plan of the ages.[50]

AND THAT MY NAME MIGHT BE PROCLAIMED THROUGHOUT THE WHOLE EARTH." That God elects for service can be seen in the case of Pharaoh. He was a man whom God used as His sword (Psalm 17:13), and as the rod of His anger (Isaiah 10:5). God wanted all the earth to know about His power and name, and Pharaoh was the channel God chose through whom these things could be made known. Not even in Pharaoh's case can God be accused of injustice. It was mercy that God was extending when He acted as He did in Pharaoh's case.

> The judgment of God on the Egyptians consisted in the plagues, whereby the nation was well-nigh destroyed; and the fame of these plagues, and the safe passage of the Israelites through the Red Sea, and the destruction of the Egyptians therein, struck terror in the nations around, as is indicated by the many references to them. It is seen in the words sung after the passage of the Red Sea: "The nations have heard, and they tremble with fear; the Philistines were seized with terror. The leaders of Edom are terrified; Moab's mighty men are trembling; the people of Canaan lose their courage" (Exodus 15:14,15). Also consider the words of Rahab to the spies sent by Joshua: "I know that the Lord has given you this land. Everyone in the country is terrified of you. We have heard how the Lord dried up the Red Sea in front of you when you were leaving Egypt. We have also heard how you killed Sihon and Og, the two Amorite kings east of Jordan. We were afraid as soon as we heard about it; we have all lost our courage because of you. The Lord your God is God in heaven above and here on earth" (Joshua 2:9-11). See also the words of the Gibeonites: "We have come from a very distant land, sir, because we have heard of the Lord your God. We have heard about everything that He did in Egypt, and what He did to the two Amorite kings east of Jordan: King Sihon of Heshbon and King Og of Bashan" (Joshua 9:9,10). [See also 1 Samuel 4:8 for the effect produced on other nations by the news of the Exodus and attendant events.] Thus it was that the catastrophe which distinguished the going out of Egypt, provoked by Pharaoh's blind resistance, paved the way for the conquest of Canaan.[51]

From the passages of Scripture just alluded to, it is evident that God's purpose in "raising up" Pharaoh was accomplished. Men all over the Mediterranean world were talking about Jehovah in reverent (and even fearful) tones.

---

[50] "The light in which Calvinism sets the case deserves a note. It represents God as rearing up Pharaoh from his cradle to be the monster he was, and then as punishing him for being and doing precisely what he was impelled to be and do. No wonder the world is shocked with the blasphemy. The circumstance that so many have been deluded into the persuasion that the Bible teaches it, is exactly what has led so many to eschew the Bible. But the Bible knows it not." Lard, *Romans*, p.308.

[51] Lipscomb and Shepherd, *Romans*, p.175. Note that the wording found in the TEV has been substituted for the ASV originally quoted by the authors of this note.

9:18 – *So then He has mercy on whom He desires, and He hardens whom He desires.*

So then.   Just as verse 16 summed up the argument about God's freedom of choice based on the case of Moses, so verse 18 sums up the argument from the illustration of Pharaoh. Once more, God's freedom to choose whom He wishes, and use the chosen ones as tools to accomplish His purpose in the world, has been clearly demonstrated.

He has mercy on whom He desires.   There is stress on the words "whom He desires." "Mercy" is a repeat of the idea stated in verse 15.   When the men, whom God had chosen, freely and voluntarily cooperated in the task God chose them to do, they were recipients of further mercy from Him.

And He hardens whom He desires.   When men, like Pharaoh, obstinately rebel and refuse to be used in the historical way God has chosen to use them, God goes ahead and uses them anyway.   But instead of enjoying His mercy, they find they are the objects of His judicial hardening.[52]   Note that this judicial hardening is not something done by God

---

[52] In most places where the word is used in the New Testament, "hardening" speaks of something done to a rebellious sinner, that makes him more nearly a soul condemned for hell.   Indeed, not a few writers, at this place, word their comments as though this passage, too, talked of judicial hardening that leads to damnation.   We would postulate that it is not until later in Romans – at Romans 11:7 – that we come to hardening of the heart that involves salvation or damnation.   We still affirm that Romans 9 is speaking about election to service, not election or hardening with reference to salvation.

"This whole passage has been used in support of Calvinistic views of the original absolute reprobation of individuals irrespectively of their deserts.   [Calvin himself, in his commentary on Paul's Epistle to the Romans at 9:18, draws this conclusion.]   It is important, therefore, to consider carefully both the original meaning of the verse, quoted from Exodus, and the apostle's application of it.

"First, with reference to Pharaoh himself, what is meant by 'I raised thee up (*exēgeira*)'?   Not 'created thee;' nor (as the Vulgate, Augustine, Calvin, and some others) 'stirred thee up' to resist my will, that I might exhibit my power in confounding thee.   Whether or not Paul's *exēgeira* would bear this sense, it is quite inadmissible in the Septuagint (from which, in this expression, he varies), and also in the Hebrew, of which the proper rendering is 'I made thee to stand.'   Both in the Hebrew and the Septuagint, the idea is that Pharaoh had been kept alive instead of being at once cut off, that God's power might be displayed in him. Thus the expression cannot mean, either that God had brought Pharaoh originally into existence for the sole purpose of destroying him, or that he had from the first irresistibly incited him to obduracy in order to condemn and destroy him.   How is God's purpose in raising Pharaoh up defined?   'That I might show in thee My power, and that My Name might be declared throughout all the earth;' i.e., as is evident from the history, by the deliverance of Israel in spite of Pharaoh's opposition through the judgments sent on him and his people to that end.   There is plainly nothing in the original history to imply Pharaoh's individual reprobation with regard to his own eternal salvation, but only his discomfiture in his opposition to the Divine purpose of mercy to Israel.

"Secondly, with a view to such execution of his purposes, God Himself is said to have hardened Pharaoh's heart; and it is to this that the apostle draws special attention in conclusion, as denoting that which it is his design to show.   It is thus certainly declared that this hardening was from God.   But even so, it is nowhere said God had made Pharaoh's heart hard from the first, so that he had been all along incapable of acting otherwise than he did.   The inference, rather, is that, after willful resistance to appeals, final obduracy was sent on him as a judgment.   And it is further to be observed that in some verses in Exodus (7:15,19,21; 9:34) Pharaoh is said to have hardened his own heart, with the addition, in Exodus 9:34 of 'he sinned yet more;' while in others (7:14,22; 9:7,35) it is only said generally that his heart was hardened.   The two forms of expression seem to denote two aspects of final obduracy in man – according to one as being self-induced, according to the other as judicial. (Cp. 1 Kings 22; Isaiah 6:9; Matthew 13:15).

"Thirdly, another important thing to be kept in view for a proper understanding of the drift of the passage is that, though Pharaoh was himself an individual, his case is adduced in no connection with the

before man is born. In this context, it is something that is God's response to man's rebellion to God's choice of that man for service.[53] God could have stricken Pharaoh dead at the very beginning, when he first refused to let Israel go. Instead, God hardened Pharaoh's heart, kept him alive and on the throne, and then proceeded to show all the world that He was greater than any Pharaoh – yea, was One whom all the world should fear (worship).

9:19 – *You will say to me then, "Why does He still find fault? For who resists His will?"*

You will say to me then. Having finished his presentation that God cannot be accused of injustice when He exercises His freedom to choose (verses 15-18), Paul now takes up the matter that mere men are not competent to criticize their Creator. Paul's last statement (verse 18) included the affirmation that God hardens whom He desires, as well as extending mercy to whom He desires. Since nearly all men have difficulty reconciling in their own minds the doctrines of Divine omnipotence and human free will and responsibility, if any of Paul's opponents should pause on the word "hardens," as though there really were something unfair or unjust in God's choosing of some men for certain historical functions, Paul now shows that such thoughts are completely out of place.[54]

"Why does He still find fault? Even though men like Pharaoh are used by God to accomplish His purposes in the world, such men are still held responsible by God for their own obstinate actions. "Is this fair?" is the gist of the question Paul's imaginary objector is asking. 'They didn't ask to be used; they didn't even have a voice in the matter of whether or not they were chosen by God for the particular historical function. Why should God find fault with them (i.e., hold them as guilty of rebellion) if they refuse to be a tool in His hands?'

For who resists His will?" The implied answer to the imaginary objector's question is "no one!" "Resists" is a word commonly used to denote the resistance offered by soldiers or armed men (cp. Ephesians 6:13; Luke 21:15; Acts 13:8). No mere man, not even one

---

question of individual predestination [to salvation or damnation], but in illustration of the principle on which [men or] nations, or races of men, are elected to or rejected from the enjoyment of Divine favor [for it is a favor or privilege to be selected by God to do an historical task for Him in the world]. This is the real subject of the whole chapter; and hence, to build on this part of it a doctrine of individual election or reprobation is to bring into it what is not there." Barmby, *Romans*, p. 266,267.

[53] It is obvious that for the individual concerned, God's choice for honorable use, or menial use, is a matter of tremendous consequence. To miss the inestimable privilege of being a part of what God is doing in history, or to miss what can be experienced and enjoyed when one is a voluntary and grateful "vessel," is far from being a trivial loss.

[54] The NASB has a paragraph break at verse 19. In our comments, verse 19 has been treated as a continuation of the topic begun in verse 14. While it is not easy to produce an outline of chapters 9-11, perhaps Paul himself has given us some indication of his own progression of thought within these chapters. Why not take Paul's use of *oun* ("therefore") at 9:14, 9:30, 10:14, 11:1, and 11:11, as being his indicators of movement to a new thought. This is what has been attempted in the outline presented in the text for this long section.

so powerful as Pharaoh (in that we have just been reminded of his effort to resist God's will) could offer any effectual resistance to an omnipotent God! Since mere man cannot but do what the absolute sovereign of the universe wills, how then can God be just and at the same time find fault with the man whom He has just overpowered? Is not God at fault for willing to use some for service, rather than man being at fault for failing to carry out some function, some task, some service he never asked for in the first place? After all, God is so powerful that no one can resist His will. Once more, let it be remembered that the context has been talking about service – God's using certain men so that many others might come to know Him. It is His will to so use men that is being talked about, and whether or not men submit to being tools in God's hands.[55]

9:20 – *On the contrary, who are you, O man, who answers back to God? The thing molded will not say to the molder, "Why did you make me like this," will it?*

On the contrary. *Menounge* is a strong corrective. Paul will indicate that the attitude of heart that prompts such a question that would find fault with what God wills is wrong. Men are not to question God, or act as if He had done something wrong. Every man still stands in the relationship of creature to Creator, and instead of accusing the Creator of injustice, the creature should be submissive to the will of the Creator. Any refusal to so submit is blameworthy.

Who are you, O man, who answers back to God? There is something wrong with the whole question in verse 19. When anyone begins to question the justice of God, or to find fault with God's dealings with His world, there is something wrong with the questioner.[56] It borders on presumptuousness and arrogance to suppose one can sit in judgment of God.[57]

---

[55] In verse 18, Paul used the word "desire" (*thelēma*); now he uses the word "will" (*boulēma*). (See Romans 7, footnote #84, for the possible connotations of these two synonyms.)

Further explanation is needed at this place. Instead of its being "service" that is desired or willed by God, Calvinist writers, for several verses now in Romans 9, speak of "salvation or reprobation" as being the thing desired or willed. ["If God Himself hardens the heart, why does He yet find fault with man? What justice is there in continuing to lay blame on a creature who goes on sinning because God so wills and he cannot resist?" is one typical example of Calvinistic comments on verse 19.] Yet even Calvinist commentaries recognize a certain incongruity in comments that have God "willing" that a man "goes on sinning." So, since Paul has used two different words here (*thelēma* and *boulēma*), Calvinist writers are wont to distinguish between God's secret (decretive) and revealed (perceptive) wills. They then write, "Man can, of course, do nothing about the former [*boulēma*]. But he certainly and rightly is held responsible for what he does about the latter [*thelēma*]. This two-fold fact is clearly set forth in two easy-to-remember passages: Deut. 29:29 and Luke 22:22." Hendriksen, *Romans*, p.327. Or again, "Man is able to resist the will, the *thelēma*, of God, but whatever takes place, God's determinate counsel, *boulēma*, is never prevented from fulfillment." Vine, *Romans*, p.146. In this way, they suppose, they have explained away the apparent incongruity. How much more satisfactory to stay away from any such incongruity by recognizing that it is *service* and not *salvation* that is the immediate topic in Romans 9.

[56] After observing that Barrett and the NEB treat *anthrōpos* ("man") as if it were contemptuous, Cranfield urges that this vocative case (*ō anthrōpe*), the first word in the sentence, is used in conscious contrast to *tō theō* ("God"), the last word in the sentence, so that the translation "man" or "O man" is required. *Romans*, p.490.

[57] Some have supposed that the objection of verse 19 is repelled rather than refuted. There is a severe rebuke to the one who would presume to ask such a question, but there is also a logical refutation of the

The thing molded will not say to the molder, "Why did you make me like this," will it? That God's dealings should be questioned at all is a breach of the reverence due to God. Mere man is not competent to criticize the Creator. It is possible that this part of verse 20 is a free rendering from Isaiah (29:16; or 45:9; or 64:8). If so, Paul makes use of both Isaiah (this verse) and Jeremiah (next verse) to reply to the one who presumptuously thinks he can criticize God for using as tools whatever man He wants to. "What makes the Prophet's language so exactly appropriate to the Apostle's argument is that they are both dealing with the same subject, namely, God's formation of Israel as a nation, and His consequent unquestionable right to deal with it as seems good to Him."[58]

9:21 – *Or does not the potter have a right over the clay, to make from the same lump one vessel for honorable use, and another for common use?*

Or does not the potter have a right over the clay. "Or" suggests an alternative to what was said in verse 20. 'If you do not accept what was said in verse 20 about the sovereignty of the Creator over His creatures, then you must deny that the potter has complete control over his clay – an absurd idea.' It is helpful to an understanding of Paul's illustration to recall Jeremiah 18:3-10. In order that he might appreciate God's way of dealing with nations, God directs Jeremiah to go to the potter's house, and watch the potter at work at his wheel. As he works with a lump of clay, with the intention of making a vessel of it, "the vessel ... was spoiled in the hand of the potter." "So he remade it into another vessel, as it pleased the potter to make" (Jeremiah 18:4). Here is one point of comparison with Romans: the right of the maker to decide the use of the vessel he makes – be he a human potter, or the Creator of all. In Jeremiah 18:6, we read God's own application of the object lesson to Jeremiah: "Can I not, O house of Israel, deal with you as this potter does? ... Behold, like the clay in the potter's hand, so are you in My hand, O house of Israel." In verses 7-10, God goes on to explain how He could cause nations to rise or fall, and how His plans sometimes were altered because of a nation's repentance or rebellion. The context following in Jeremiah 18 warns Israel that she would be rejected as a tool for God's service if she was not faithful. God even threatens a "day of calamity" if they proved unfaithful, and one can hardly avoid being reminded of the calamity that happened to Pharaoh when God wanted to use him for a tool (Romans 9:17).

To make from the same lump one vessel for honorable use, and another for common use? Commentaries take up much space as attempts to identify the "same lump" are set forth and defended. A hidden agenda behind much of the rhetoric is either a pro- or an anti-Calvinistic position to be defended.[59] What Jeremiah and Paul insist is that the Divine

---

objection. That refutation is found in the real relationship of every creature to its Creator.

[58] Gifford, *Romans*, p.173. It should be remembered that God formed Israel to be a nation of priests, who would help others get to God (Exodus 19:6).

[59] Calvinist writers usually identify the "same lump" as being a reference to "sinful humanity." "Calvinism finds its peculiar sovereignty of God in this verse. Supralapsarian Calvinism [holding that God determined to save some and permit others to be damned before He decided to permit the Fall] finds the sovereignty which created some men to fall and to be damned, and some to be saved despite their fall, both according to an absolute decree. Infralapsarian Calvinism [holding that in the Divine mind the fall of

craftsman could put his lump of humanity to any providential use for which He sees there is a need, without first asking the man's permission. The key problem for Calvinistic and anti-Calvinistic interpreters is how to understand the words "to honor" and "to dishonor."[60] For some reason, many immediately think of salvation or damnation. However, we have here in verse 21 the very same ideas we had in verse 11 – in which Jacob's selection and Esau's rejection (as far as a use, a historical function, was concerned) depended on "God's purpose according to His choice" rather than any inherent qualities of their own. In fact, the very same idea being expressed here in verse 21 was expressed of Pharaoh in verse 17 – in which God raised up Pharaoh in order that His name might be proclaimed throughout the whole world. "A vessel is honored or dishonored by the use to which it is put."[61] A "vessel to honor" designates the finished product that the potter intends will be used for some special purpose or on special occasion. A "vessel to dishonor" describes the finished product that the potter intends will be used for menial purposes.[62]

9:22 – *What if God, although willing to demonstrate His wrath and to make His power known, endured with much patience vessels of wrath prepared for destruction?*

What if God. Literally, it reads "But if God," and while verses 22-24 form the "if clause," there is no conclusion clause to complete this conditional sentence. Our English versions supply the word "what" at the beginning of the "if clause," meaning "What (are you going to say) if God wills ...?"[63] The "but" indicates there is a contrast intended. Evidently the contrast is between what Paul's opponent has charged (God has been unjust, verse 14) and what has actually been the case (God has been very merciful in His actions).

---

man preceded the decrees of election and reprobation] finds the sovereignty which from the same fallen lump of humanity decreed and shaped some to salvation and decreed and shaped some to damnation. Calvinism assumes that the whole story as to why some are saved and others are lost is figuratively described in this verse." Lenski, *Romans*, p.620.

Anti-predestinarians seem to struggle with this verse, too. Concerning Paul's use of Jeremiah 18, Barclay quotes with approval, "One great New Testament commentator has said that this is one of the very few passages we wish Paul had not written." *Romans*, p.140. He goes on to defend Paul as writing this poorly worded argument out of anguish of heart over the Jew's situation. Another speaks of the potter doing what he will with the clay "according to the fitness of the material" (Lipscomb and Shepherd, *Romans*, p.179). But how can one harmonize "same lump" with the proviso about "fitness of the material"?

Both schools of interpreters miss the key point that it is not predestination to salvation that is the topic, but God's determination to use people and nations for a special service.

[60] The NASB margin shows that the Greek behind "honorable *use*" and "dishonorable *use*" is literally "to honor" and "to dishonor."

[61] Arndt-Gingrich, *Lexicon*, p.425, in comments on "honor" as used at Romans 9:21. In the case of the use God assigns to men and nations, God is the one who decides whether the function they will serve is "to honor" or "to dishonor."

[62] "It should be noted that *eis atimian* implies menial use, not reprobation or destruction. The potter does not make ordinary, everyday pots, merely in order to destroy them." Cranfield, *Romans*, p.492.

[63] Other attempts at completing the suppressed member of this sentence are: "What right do you have to find fault with God?" "What can you say against the Divine conduct, if He should be willing to do as He wishes?" For similar examples of sentences beginning with *ei de*, and left incomplete, see Acts 23:9, and Winer's *Grammar*, #64.

As we come to verse 22, we seem still to be developing the idea that was begun in verse 14, namely, that there is no unrighteousness with God. Instead of charging Him with injustice, men should be contemplating the motive behind His actions – His *mercy*! Instead of being arbitrary or unfair, He has been patient even with obstinate 'tools,' all because He wanted to make His power known more widely.[64]

Although willing to demonstrate His wrath. As in Romans 1:18, "wrath" apparently does not so much speak of the wrath the wicked will experience in hell (cp. Romans 2:8), as it does His "wrath" experienced in this life. What God did to Pharaoh after that monarch determined not to submit to God's will is an example of such temporal "wrath." "Willing" is a present participle in the Greek,[65] indicating His "willing" and His "enduring" took place at the same time. This long if-clause tells us there were three purposes God had in mind as He endured with patience those vessels of wrath.[66] He wanted to demonstrate His wrath, reveal His power, and reveal the riches of His glory on vessels of mercy.

---

[64] It is from verse 22 through verse 29 that it is hardest to sustain the presentation these notes have attempted to present, namely, that it is "choice for service" rather than "election to salvation." Indeed, because a new sentence begins at verse 22, some think that Paul himself changes topics from service to salvation here, rather than at verse 30, as these comments will suggest.

[65] "The present participle, therefore, is used if the action denoted by the participle is represented as taking place at the same time as the action denoted by the leading verb." Machen, *New Testament Greek for Beginners*, p.105. In other words, the "willing" and the "enduring" (the leading verb in the "if-clause") took place at the same time. If this circumstantial participle were taken as temporal (rather than causal, or concessive, compare next footnote), it would simply be translated "*while* willing ... [God] endured ...."

[66] The explanation offered for the phrase rejects the fact that it begins with "although" in the NASB. Neither the KJV nor ASV has any helping word at all before the participle "willing." "There has been much discussion as to whether this [circumstantial participle with which this phrase begins in the Greek] should be translated [as a causal participle], 'because God wishes,' or [as a concessive participle], 'although God wishes.' In the former case the words mean, 'God, because He wishes to show the terrible character of His wrath, restrains His hands, until, as in the case of Pharaoh, He exhibits His power by a terrible overthrow.' In the latter case, 'God, although His righteous anger might naturally lead to His making His power known, has through His kindness delayed and borne with those who had become objects that deserved His wrath.' That the second is the correct interpretation is shown by the words 'with much longsuffering' which are quite inconsistent with the former interpretation, and by a similar passage, Romans 2:4, where it is distinctly stated 'that the goodness of God leads to repentance'." Sanday and Headlam, *Romans*, p.261.

Gifford, on the other hand, opts for the translation "because." In essence, his comments include these thoughts: (1) Verses 22,23 are Paul's interpretation and generalized application of the passage about Pharaoh quoted in verse 17, and this interpretation helps us understand that previous quotation. (2) The comment "endured with much patience" shows that "I have raised you up" meant "I sustained you and kept you alive," just as we have explained it. (3) The words "for this very purpose I raised you up that I might show in you My power" make it certain that, when Paul writes "God, willing to demonstrate His power," he means "because He willed" and not "although He willed." (4) It was because God desired to demonstrate His wrath, that is, to warn men about it, that He gave a long series of warnings and judgments, before He brought on the final catastrophes (as in Pharaoh's case). *Romans*, p.174. Cranfield, too, defends the causal participle by making these points: (1) It is not unnatural to couple a final clause [verse 23] with a causal participle, but it is unnatural to couple such a final clause with a concessive participle. (2) The concessive participle would leave us with the idea that part of God's will is yet unfulfilled, but this seems inconsistent with what Paul has said about the revelation of God's wrath in Romans 1:18, and the implication of 1:16b-17 that God's power is being made known as the gospel is proclaimed. (3) Taking it as a causal participle yields a better parallelism between verse 17 and verse 22. *Romans*, p.494.

And to make His power known.   He wanted to reveal to men His "ability to do things."[67] One is reminded, for example, of the plagues, where God made a distinction between the Israelites and the Egyptians as He brought the various plagues on one but exempted the other.   This was an impressive lesson about what God is able to do.

Endured with much patience vessels of wrath prepared for destruction?   "Patience" is God's longsuffering when being provoked by people.[68]   "Vessels of wrath" can be a subjective genitive,[69] meaning vessels that are instruments by which God executes His wrath (manifests it to the world);[70] or it can be an objective genitive, meaning vessels that are the recipients of His wrath.[71]   In Pharaoh's case, both ideas are true.   Pharaoh experienced God's wrath, and he also was a means by which God demonstrated His wrath and power to all men.[72]   But how shall we understand "prepared for destruction"?   It is a middle or passive participle in the perfect tense.   Since the construction is deliberately different from the passive voice verb which follows in verse 23, where God is named as the agent, the suggestion that "prepared" should be taken as a middle voice is likely correct, and thus it is implied that these "vessels" prepared themselves for destruction.   As in the case of Pharaoh, whenever someone refuses to be a tool in God's hand, God gets another tool!   He also discards the one that refuses to be used.   Lenski's comment catches the idea expressed by this perfect tense verb:

> The perfect participle [with present continuing results implied] means that for
> a long time they have already been ripe for "destruction."   God should have

---

[67] The same word, *dunatos*, is translated "able" at Romans 4:21.   *Dunatos* is a different word than was used at 1:16 or 1:20, yet all three words are rendered "power" in the NASB.   *Dunatos*, as it is used at Romans 9:22, means "what his power could do."   Thayer, *Lexicon*, p.160.   [Arndt-Gingrich, *Lexicon*, p.208, in contradiction to this, suggest that *dunatos* in verse 22 is equal to *dunamis* in verse 17.]

[68] See comments about *makrothumia* at Romans 2:4, footnote #17.

[69] The Greek construction called objective or subjective genitive was explained at Romans 8:15, footnote #80.

[70] In Isaiah 13:5, 54:16; and Jeremiah 50:25, "vessels of wrath" has the subjective meaning, i.e., instruments of His wrath by which He works destruction on others.   Gifford (*Romans*, p.174) urges that the word "vessel" taken from the figure of the potter (Romans 9:21) implies some kind of use which the vessel is to serve; thus, "vessels of wrath" and "vessels of mercy" are such as fitly serve God's purpose of showing His wrath and His mercy.

[71] The NIV's "objects of wrath" and "objects of mercy" (verse 23) treat the genitives as being objective.

[72] Shall we explain "wrath" as being eternal punishment?   No, not if our notes earlier in this verse are correct, that "wrath" is something that can be seen and experienced in this life, as well as the world to come.   Who are the recipients of this "wrath" in this life?   Is Pharaoh still in view, as is suggested in the comments?   Or are the Jews in view, too?   Remember, Paul is about to discuss the fact that the Jews have forfeited the high privilege of being God-used channels of blessing, or service, to the world.   Like He "endured with patience" a Pharaoh who was rebelling against the purpose to which God wished to assign to him, so the Jews, for several centuries, had been endured with patience by a God who was wishing to use them as channels of blessing, but whose wishes were being by and large ignored.   Gifford writes, "'vessels of wrath' without the definite article.   Though his language is still full of allusions to the previous passage (v.17-21), Paul has now passed from the particular example of the hardening of Pharaoh to the general principle which connects it with his immediate subject, the rejection of Israel."   *Romans*, p.174.

destroyed them a long time ago, but delayed and delayed. God exercised his longsuffering because of his immense mercy. We think at once of Pharaoh. At the first meeting with Moses he hardened himself, but God delayed. Pharaoh hardened himself after each of the first five plagues, and still God bore with him. Even after God's judicial hardening had set in, the delay continued. We are told of its purpose in verse 17; now we see it again. Egypt and all the world got to see, not only God's wrath and power, but especially also "the riches of his glory on vessels of mercy," Israel.[73]

The word "destruction" (*apoleia*), used only here in this letter, means "not the destruction of being, not annihilation," but "the destruction of well-being, its ruin so far as the purpose of its existence is concerned."[74] An example of such destruction would be Pharaoh, who found himself and his armies destroyed because of his refusal to heed the Creator's will.

9:23 – *And* **He did so** *in order that He might make known the riches of His glory upon vessels of mercy, which He prepared beforehand for glory,*

And *He did so.* This verse continues the (broken) sentence begun in verse 22, and further explains God's action so as to silence any objection the imagined opponent might raise to Paul's doctrine. God has not been unjust (verse 14) in any of His choices for service.

In order that He might make known the riches of His glory upon vessels of mercy. "In order that" tells us that this was the primary or final purpose of God's enduring patience with the vessels of wrath. Not only has God shown great patience in bearing with those vessels of wrath who disqualified themselves for service (verse 22), but He did so in order to be able to make known the riches of His glory upon vessels of mercy. "Upon" tells us that God first shows mercy to the vessels He will use, and then in turn they become vessels of mercy who make His mercy known to others. "Vessels of mercy" can, like "vessels of wrath," be either an objective or subjective genitive. It can speak of vessels who experience mercy, or it can speak of vessels through whom God's mercy is manifested to the world.[75] Between Moses and Christ, it was a remnant,[76] the 'Israel within Israel,' that

---

[73] Lenski, *Romans*, p.623.

[74] Vine, *Romans*, p.148. While agreeing with Vine's comment that the word *apoleia* does not involve annihilation, it should be remembered that elsewhere the word "destruction" is used (not only of destruction in this life, but) of punishment in hell, and even then it does not mean annihilation. 2 Peter 3:6 is a good place to see this: the Noahic world was "destroyed," Peter writes. Now if "world" means people, they were not annihilated, for 1 Peter 3:19,20 show them still in existence in the intermediate world; and if "world" means "globe, earth," it was not annihilated; it is still here, though its outward form has changed.

[75] The noun *eleos* and the verb *eleeō* have appeared in the text since 9:15. Thayer defines this word "mercy" as "kindness or good will towards the miserable and afflicted, joined with a desire to relieve them." *Lexicon*, p.203. There is a synonym, *oiktirmos*, and a comparison of the two helps to grasp the meaning of *eleos*. "Both words denote sympathy, fellow-feeling with misery, mercy, compassion. *Eleos*, however, manifests itself chiefly in acts rather than words, while *oiktirmos* is used rather of the inward feeling of compassion which abides in the heart. A criminal might ask for *eleos*, mercy, from his judge; but hopeless suffering may be the object of *oiktirmos*, compassion." Berry, *New Testament Synonyms*, p.128.

[76] The argument about the "remnant" and the 'Israel within Israel' will be introduced in verses 25-29,

God used[77] as His vessels of mercy; since Christ, as verse 24 will specify, God's vessels of mercy are those whom He has called from both Jewish and Gentile backgrounds. The phrase "riches of His glory" is one of Paul's favorite expressions.[78] The term "riches" (*ploutos*) speaks of bountifulness, a term particularly suitable when God is thought of as a giver. "Glory"[79] seems to refer to God's gracious character, and would be a way of summing up in a single word such attributes as His love, grace, and mercy. God chose some "vessels of mercy" because He wanted to reveal more of His character to men than they could learn about through a study of the creation (Romans 1:19,20).

Which He prepared beforehand for glory. There is no question, as before, as to the agent who does the preparing: it is God. God is nowhere said to be the cause of "fitting men for destruction," but He certainly has been the active agent in preparing men to glorify Him. Assuming that the illustration of the potter is still in view (verse 21), then the "glory" for which these vessels are prepared corresponds to "honorable use," and would also be the opposite of "destruction" in verse 22. Thus, the idea conveyed by "glory" in this phrase would not quite be the same as in the previous expression "riches of His glory." "Glory" here would be something similar to praise (glory) being given to God. When a man voluntarily submits to the historical function which God had in mind when He created mankind, then the result is praise offered to God,[80] both by the man himself and by those he influences toward the knowledge of God. Another intriguing topic is brought to mind by the word "prepared."[81] What all is involved in God's preparation of these "vessels" for

---

and then, after a long explanation, be summarized in 11:5.

[77] "Salvation is of the Jews," Jesus told the woman at the well (John 4:22). They were the ones He chose to be the channels through whom He could reveal Himself to the whole world. And if some were rebellious, then like Pharaoh, they too would become "vessels of wrath prepared for destruction," and God would find some other people to be his "vessels of mercy."

[78] See Ephesians 1:18, 3:16; Philippians 4:19; Colossians 1:27.

[79] The reader is reminded that the numerous connotations expressed by "glory" have been a topic of comment already at Romans 1:23 and 3:23. "His glory" (verse 23) is likely contrasted with "His wrath" in verse 22.

[80] Perhaps one of the most difficult things in the way of ready acceptance of the idea that "glory" here corresponds with "praise offered to God" is the fact that in 2:7,10, 5:2, and 8:18, "glory" spoke of heaven, rather than something in this life. But before we can say that "glory" equals "heaven" here in 9:23, we must first show where in the passage the topic has changed from "service" to "salvation." Just as "destruction" (verse 22) spoke of missing the real purpose of one's existence in this life (and not of punishment in hell), so we believe "glory" here speaks of something in this life, namely, giving glory to God and thus fulfilling one's real purpose for existing (rather than having reference to the glory of heaven). [Note: if we were to explain "glory" at Romans 3:23 as being "praise offered to God," then we might also ponder whether there is some relationship between the "glory" for which God prepares His vessels, and the "glory" from which man falls short because of his sinning.]

[81] Strict Calvinists appeal to this verse, among others, to show that salvation is monergistic, that is, that God does it all – He causes the new birth, He elects certain ones to salvation, He gives them saving faith, He preserves them unconditionally unto the end. After all, does it not say that "God prepared them beforehand for glory"? Where, they ask, does this passage leave any room for synergism, for man's cooperation with God in the matter of salvation? Indeed, if the topic of this paragraph is salvation, rather

glory? And what does "beforehand" mean? As the potter first plans the vessel of honor, and then forms and produces it, the same is likely true regarding God's use of men. Is Paul saying God first made His plan about what historical use each vessel should serve and then, here in time, carried out His plan? He worked "upon [the] vessels of mercy," and when they function according to His plan, then He gets the glory.[82]

9:24 – even *us, whom He also called, not from among Jews only, but also from among Gentiles.*

***Even* us, whom He also called.** As he begins to make the application toward which this presentation of God's dealings with Israel in the past has been leading, Paul now specifically identifies the "vessels of mercy" spoken of in the previous verse, save now it refers to all those whom God has chosen to use as vessels of honor in this age since Calvary.[83] "Also called" seems to be something *in addition to* "prepared beforehand:" in the case of "vessels" chosen for honorable use in the Christian age, God *also* calls them through the gospel[84] – something in addition to what He did when He chose and prepared Abraham or Isaac or Israel to be His honorable vessels in Old Testament times.[85] The rest of the verse

---

than service, they have a rather convincing argument.

[82] Predestinarians may be partially correct when they date the "beforehand" back in eternity. The "before" in "prepared *before*hand" likely points us back to eternity before God created. Verse 11 has spoken of "God's purpose according to choice" and Romans 8:28-30 has spoken of God's "purpose," and both of these have been explained to refer to God's planning before He actually created. However, it would be difficult to limit the "before" to eternity before creation. Unless we understand the perfect tense "fitted for destruction" (verse 22) to mean something done back in eternity – which is surely doubtful – there is no need to limit the aorist tense "prepared beforehand" to eternity either. Both the aorist and perfect tenses could reach only back in history, into the lives of the vessels concerned.

[83] "Us ... Jews ... Gentiles" certainly involves individuals, as well as nations or groups. Calvinist writers have relied on this language to show that God's predestination is the predestination of individuals; non-Calvinistic writers have insisted that His predestination (like that of Jacob) is only of nations. It surely appears the Calvinist commentators are correct in their identification of "individuals" as being the objects of God's predestination (though they are in error when trying to identify that to which the individuals are predestined). Likewise, it appears that non-Calvinistic writers are in error when (in their effort to disprove Calvinism) they try to defend the thesis that it is *only* nations, *not* individuals, that are the objects of God's predestination. How much better to reflect what Paul here suggests, that both men *and* nations are the objects of God's predestination to service. Paul's "us" would include both himself and his readers among the chosen vessels in the present age. (Cranfield, *Romans*, p.497-98, explains the various attempts scholars have made to relate what is said in verses 23-26, and to show this relationship by punctuation, or the addition of words such as "even" in the NASB. His conclusion, with which this commentator agrees, is that "us," with which verse 24 begins, stands in apposition to "vessels of mercy" in the previous verse.)

[84] On God's calling of men, see Romans 8:28-30. In Special Study #1, both God's call to salvation and His call to specialized service have been explained. The comments given above reflect the idea that "called" here in 9:24 is a call to salvation. However, it would not be difficult to defend the idea that it is a call to service that Paul has in mind, and that God Himself predicted the day was coming when Gentiles as well as Jews would get such a call.

[85] Those who think the topic of this whole paragraph has been salvation are wont to debate which comes first, the preparation of verse 23, or the call of verse 24. Gifford, *Romans*, p.175, urges that the preparation precedes the call. Murray, *Romans*, Vol.2, p.37, argues that the call precedes the preparation, since most Calvinist theology would see the call as the beginning of the preparatory process.

will show that both Jews and Gentiles, whom He calls through the gospel, are God's present-day "vessels of mercy," channels through whom "the riches of His glory" are made known to the world, in order that the world might in turn offer glory to God.

Not from among Jews only, but also from among Gentiles.   That some from among the Jews would be called is assumed as a given, since the covenant made with Abraham has not failed (9:6).   However, that God was going to use people from among the Gentiles, too, as His special instruments, is the point of the following verses, where the writer weaves together a wonderful selection of Old Testament passages to prove the statement here asserted.   God's dealings with Israel have been just as God predicted they would be.   God even explained to Israel, long ago through the prophets, that the time was coming when Gentiles, too, would be more actively included in His plans for the world.[86]

9:25 – *As He says also in Hosea, "I WILL CALL THOSE WHO WERE NOT MY PEOPLE, 'MY PEOPLE,' AND HER WHO WAS NOT BELOVED, 'BELOVED.'"*

As He says also in Hosea.   In the expression "from among Jews" (verse 24), Paul has inferred that only *some* from among the Jews would be included.   Plus, he has plainly stated that *some* from among the Gentiles would also be included.   Since both these ideas were so foreign to most Jews' thinking, they needed special treatment before they would be accepted as true.   Thus, Paul proceeds to show from Scripture that both these facts were predicted.   By referring to two passages found in the book of Hosea, he will establish that Gentiles are included.   Then, by appealing to Isaiah, he will show that only a remnant of the Jews was predicted to be involved.

"I WILL CALL THOSE WHO WERE NOT MY PEOPLE, 'MY PEOPLE,' AND HER WHO WAS NOT BELOVED, 'BELOVED.'"   This is a quotation of Hosea 2:23, and Paul uses it to justify his assertion that Gentiles, too, would become tools in God's hands, His "vessels of mercy."   In the 8th century BC, Hosea was a prophet to Israel, the northern kingdom, before they were taken into captivity.[87]   It is helpful to recall the background of Hosea's prophecy in order to feel the force of Paul's statement taken from Hosea. Hosea's own tragic domestic life is a parable of the relation between God and Israel.   God told the prophet to marry a wife.   So he married Gomer, the daughter of Diblaim, and she in due course gave birth to a son.   He acknowledged the child as his and named him Jezreel, in obedience to God's command.   There is the possibility (implied by the names given to them, and what is said in Hosea 2:1-5) that Hosea was not the father of the second or third child she gave birth to.   The second he named Lo-ruhumah ("one for whom no natural affection is felt"), and the third he named Lo-ammi ("no kin of mine," or "not my

---

[86] In a sense the topic here in chapter 9 differs from the one in 4:12-17, where it was the matter of being justified by faith that was emphasized.   But while the topics differ, yet the fact that "Gentiles" are vitally concerned is common to both passages.   A review of the comments at 4:16-18 will show that the promise to Abraham about "all the descendants" would certainly involve the Gentiles.   Likewise, God's plans for some to be vessels of mercy also includes the Gentiles, the very thing 9:24-29 develops.

[87] Grubbs and Plummer are both mistaken when they date Hosea's ministry.   His ministry was to the ten tribes *before* they went into captivity.

people"). In Hosea 1:10-2:23, we then learn that the names of the last two children were eventually changed, and that the names of all three enshrine prophecy. Jezreel, meaning "God shall sow (scatter) seed," was a prediction of the scattering of the ten tribes because of their sin – but God was also sowing seed in order to get a harvest in the future. The names of the other two were object lessons to Israel, predicting that during the captivity, the house of Israel would be a people on whom God had no compassion; in fact, He would not even claim them as "My people." Hosea 2:23 takes up the idea of a harvest in the future as a result of the captivity, and the New Testament shows that the name change from Lo-ammi to Ammi ("My people") embraces the acceptance of Gentiles (who once were not the people of God) into the circle of God's people.[88] In a similar fashion, the other child's name change suggests that those who once had received no mercy now are the recipients of mercy.[89]

9:26 – *"AND IT SHALL BE THAT IN THE PLACE WHERE IT WAS SAID TO THEM, 'YOU ARE NOT MY PEOPLE,' THERE THEY SHALL BE CALLED SONS OF THE LIVING GOD."*

"AND IT SHALL BE THAT IN THE PLACE WHERE IT WAS SAID TO THEM, 'YOU ARE NOT MY PEOPLE.' As noted above, this is a quotation of Hosea 1:10. "In the place" spoke of the country into which the ten tribes would be taken as captives.

THERE THEY SHALL BE CALLED SONS OF THE LIVING GOD." In God's sight, they were "not My people" when they went into captivity; but a day was coming when repentance would change that. Some from Israel (together with some from Judah, Hosea 1:11) would again be God's people. When the name is changed from "Lo-ammi" to "Ammi," that would involve some from among the Jews, too, as well as from among the Gentiles. Jehovah is called the "living" God, in opposition to all the idols that were not "living" (i.e., alive and/or life giving).[90] When a man becomes a "son" of the living God, he is a member of God's family, one of the class of men whom God acknowledges as "My people." Paul's argument has once again returned to what was said in verse 6, that the covenant promise did not include or guarantee that every descendant of Israel was automatically included among the "vessels of mercy." "They are not all Israel that are descended from Israel."

9:27 – *And Isaiah cries out concerning Israel, "THOUGH THE NUMBER OF THE SONS OF ISRAEL BE AS THE SAND OF THE SEA, IT IS THE REMNANT THAT WILL BE SAVED;*

---

[88] Both Paul, here at Romans 9, and Peter, in 1 Peter 2:10, explain this passage in Hosea as involving the inclusion of the Gentiles among the people of God, after Messiah has come.

[89] Perhaps the fact that Hosea took Gomer back into his love – after her time of infidelity – is also a prediction that God will not allow the broken relationship between Himself and the Jews to stand forever. Even clearer is the verse about to be quoted from Hosea 1:10, that a day was coming when "Israel" again would be "God's people," that is, some from among the Jews, also, would be included in God's people.

[90] Compare 1 Thessalonians 1:9; Jeremiah 10:10.

And Isaiah cries out concerning Israel. The prophecies now about to be quoted are more concerned with the exclusion of all Israelites except a remnant, than they are to show that Gentiles are also included. The second passage quoted from Hosea (verse 26) does not specify how many Israelites would again be included in the group God calls "My people." One might conclude that all Jews would be involved, until he recalls the passages from Isaiah where it is clear that it is only a few – a remnant. Paul characterizes Isaiah, not as just speaking, but "crying" this message. While the word "cry" often is used to designate the message as a prophetic utterance,[91] such an impassioned utterance was intended to arouse greater attention, lest the message be missed.

"THOUGH THE NUMBER OF THE SONS OF ISRAEL BE AS THE SAND OF THE SEA.[92] The verses now brought to the reader's attention come from Isaiah 10:22,23, though Paul has modified the passage to "number of sons" (rather than "people") to match what was just quoted from Hosea about "children" ("sons"). When the Israelites went into captivity, there was a great number of them.[93] From time to time, during the reign of Ahaz, king of Judah, God sent Isaiah to the king with a message of reassurance. Pekah, king of Israel, and Rezin, king of Syria, had formed an alliance against the Assyrian empire, and were determined to bring Judah into their coalition, even though it meant deposing Ahaz. So they have come up to Jerusalem to make war against Judah. Isaiah 7 begins a series of messages given to the king and the people about the future. On one visit, Isaiah took his son, who bore the symbolic name Shear-jashub ("a remnant shall return") with him. God not only promised deliverance from Rezin and Pekah, but it was during that visit that God spoke to Ahaz and told of the Son who would be born of a virgin, who would be Immanuel ("God with us"). A short while later, after another son had been born to the prophet and named Maher-shalal-hash-baz ("Haste to the spoil, speed to the prey"), God indicated that Assyria would hasten to strike down both Rezin and Pekah, and also would take Judah captive. Then comes chapter 9 with its prediction of the birth and reign of the Prince of Peace, followed by a warning to Judah about the coming Assyrian invasion which God Himself would turn back. Judah did not need to fear Assyria, but Israel did. Where Israel was once a proud and stately forest, there would be only a few trees left when Assyria got done with them, so few that even a child could count them (Isaiah 10:19). Then Isaiah begins to speak of this "remnant" who would return in penitence to God.

IT IS THE REMNANT THAT WILL BE SAVED. There is emphasis on the word "remnant." The word "remnant" means "that which is left," that which may remain after a battle or a great calamity.[94] Only a remnant, a small minority, will survive the impending

---

[91] Compare John 1:15; 7:28,37; and 12:44.

[92] The original NASB read "children." The margin read "sons," which is what the Greek *huiōn* literally means. In fact, later editions of the NASB have changed the reading to "sons of Israel."

[93] "As the sand of the sea" is an expression that denotes a large and innumerable multitude. It reminds us of the promise recorded in Genesis 22:17, about the number of Abraham's children.

[94] Barnes, *op. cit.*, p.221. Compare 2 Kings 19:31; Judges 5:13; Isaiah 14:22. The "remnant" idea in the Old Testament (when one puts together all the passages where the language appears) involves the union of the north and south after the return from the captivities. Some from all the tribes (from the ten

judgment (when God will use the Assyrians as His agents). But if only a remnant survives, at least a remnant will survive,[95] and continue to be God's tools, His "vessels of mercy."

9:28 – *FOR THE LORD WILL EXECUTE HIS WORD UPON THE EARTH, THOROUGHLY AND QUICKLY."*

FOR THE LORD WILL EXECUTE HIS WORD UPON THE EARTH. This is still part of the quotation from Isaiah 10:22-23. In a passage where God's ability and freedom to fashion and use men as His instruments has been emphasized (Romans 9:14-18) there is something very appropriate about this claim made for God and His use of Assyria as an instrument of judgment by which Israel is cut down, leaving only a remnant. "The word" that the Lord executes is none other than His threatened judgment.

THOROUGHLY AND QUICKLY." The RSV reads "with rigor and dispatch." God's threatened judgment will be severe and decisive. That is why only a remnant will be left.

9:29 – *And just as Isaiah foretold, "EXCEPT THE LORD OF SABAOTH HAD LEFT TO US A POSTERITY, WE WOULD HAVE BECOME AS SODOM, AND WOULD HAVE RESEMBLED GOMORRAH."*

And just as Isaiah foretold. The NASB translators have supposed that verse 29 continues the Scriptural evidence for the truth affirmed in verse 24, namely, that only some would be called from among the Jews to be God's chosen vessels. It has happened "just as Isaiah foretold,"[96] and then Isaiah 1:9 is reproduced, so all can read the predictions themselves, so as to grasp its message.

"EXCEPT THE LORD OF SABAOTH HAD LEFT TO US A POSTERITY. "Sabaoth" transliterates the Hebrew word meaning "hosts, armies."[97] "Posterity" ("seed")

---

that were called "Israel" and the two called "Judah") would return and welcome the long-awaited Messiah, a promise that was fulfilled when Jesus became incarnate. Here in Romans 9-11, Paul will show that the "remnant" idea continues even after Messiah has come.

[95] The words "save" and "salvation" are used with at least five different meanings in the Scripture. (1) Deliverance from danger (Matthew 8:25, 14:30, 23:37,39). (2) Deliverance from disease (Matthew 9:21, 22; Luke 8:36; Mark 5:23; John 11:12). (3) Keep or preserve something in good condition (Luke 17:33). (4) Deliverance from the power of sin (Matthew 1:21). (5) Deliverance from the final condemnation of God (Matthew 10:22, 18:11; Luke 13:23). Since the "saved" that Isaiah was promising was something other than forgiveness of sins, we have used the word "survive" to express the idea of their preservation through the calamity God was sending on the unfaithful nation.

[96] The older translations read, "As Isaiah hath said before." It is not unusual to find comments explaining the "before" to mean Isaiah's other pertinent statement is found in the book of Isaiah, at a place *before* the passage just quoted from chapter 10:22,23.

[97] Sometimes the "hosts" may refer to the host of stars in the heavens (Deuteronomy 4:19; 2 Kings 23:5). Sometimes, the "armies" are the armies of heaven, the hosts of angels who do God's bidding (1 Kings 22:19; Psalm 148:2; Luke 2:13). Sometimes, the armies are composed of human soldiers, whether it be the armies of Israel (1 Samuel 17:45) or foreign armies like Assyria whom God sent to chastise His people. He is called their Lord because He is their commander. When all the ideas are combined, one

is the word used in the LXX for the Hebrew word for "small remnant." Thus, both Isaiah 1:9 and 10:22,23 deal with the same topic, the remnant.[98] The point is this: but for the remnant left behind, the rejection of Israel would have been utter and complete. Implied is the idea that the preservation of the remnant was an act of mercy on God's part.

WE WOULD HAVE BECOME AS SODOM, AND WOULD HAVE RESEMBLED GOMORRAH." Sodom and Gomorrah were two of the cities of the plain that were wiped out completely when God sent destruction on them, after He warned Lot to flee (Genesis 19:24,25). Isaiah's language means, "If God had not spared a few in Israel, it would have as completely disappeared as did the cities of Sodom and Gomorrah." But God did spare a "remnant," and through these few He continued to carry out His purposes in the world. Once more, Paul has demonstrated from Scripture that not *all* Jews are included in the covenant promise, only a remnant.

In 9:6-29, a number of passages from the Old Testament have been produced to substantiate Paul's thesis that God's dealings with Israel *in the past* have been just as He predicted they would be. He had made a covenant with Abraham and his descendants that involved their being used as the channel through whom Messiah (with all the blessings that would entail) would come into the world. But that covenant never did include all the descendants – just the 'Israel within Israel.' In accordance with what He revealed numerous times about His intentions, and in perfect harmony with His covenant promise, God rightly could and did choose to make use of *some* of the descendants as "vessels of mercy." He has so acted all through time since Abraham, and still continues to so act.

C. God's Dealings with Israel *In the Present* Are in Harmony with the Doctrine of Justification by Faith. 9:30-11:10

> *Summary:* The real reason why any Israelite is excluded from the "remnant" during this age since Messiah has come is the Israelite's rejection of God's way of saving man – justification by faith.

9:30 – *What shall we say then? That Gentiles, who did not pursue righteousness, attained righteousness, even the righteousness which is by faith;*

What shall we say then? That is, what summary[99] could one give of the message present-

---

is reminded that God is the great king who alone commands – a thought wholly appropriate to this context where God's freedom to choose instruments for His use is the topic being expounded.

[98] Cranfield, *Romans*, p.503, points out that the Hebrew term found in Isaiah 1:9 is not the regular term Isaiah uses for the "remnant," and offers this explanation: "he possibly refrained from using *se'ar* here because he did not regard the survivors of 701 BC as the purified remnant of Israel." The difference in terms, however, does not destroy the validity of using this passage as Paul does, as one of several that teach the "remnant" idea.

[99] Though the words, "What shall we say then?" are the same as those in 9:14, their meaning here is

ed by Paul thus far in Romans? The answer to the question asked in the first part of verse 30 "consists of two parts: 1) a statement of facts (30,31) drawn from the whole preceding discussion, and expressed as a striking paradox; and, 2) a declaration of the cause (32,33), by which the paradox in the case of the Jews is explained."[100]

That Gentiles, who did not pursue righteousness, attained righteousness. All during the Old Testament centuries when God was working specially through His chosen vessels, the Israel within Israel, the Gentiles, as a whole,[101] were not actively interested in God's way of saving man. The first chapter of Romans has already shown how Gentiles had exchanged the worship of God for the worship of idols, and how they had ignored the "ordinance of God." Now, surprisingly, in view of their lack of pursuit of righteousness, and in view of their lack of privileges such as the Jews had, they have responded to the gospel in great numbers, and have been reckoned "righteous" by Him.[102]

Even the righteousness which is by faith. Righteousness, God's reckoning a man as "just," the earlier chapters of Romans have abundantly demonstrated, is attained when a man accepts the offer of justification by faith contained in the gospel (Romans 1:16,17). Even though the Gentiles did not have a schoolmaster to bring them to Christ (Galatians 3:24), many of them obeyed the gospel when the opportunity to do so was offered to them.

---

not quite the same, since the construction that follows them is not the same. In that place, a possible erroneous inference is stated and refuted; in this case, he simply states the only logical conclusion the doctrine taught in chapters 1-9 allows. Sanday and Headlam, *Romans*, p.279, show that there are two possible ways to construe the rest of chapter 9. (1) One way is to take verses 30 and 31 (following the question "What shall we say then?") as the answer to the question. They opt for this explanation, though with hesitancy: "This interpretation is probably right. The difficulty, however, is that nowhere else in the epistle, where Paul uses the expression, 'What shall we say then?' does he give it an immediate answer. He follows it by a second question, as for example 9:14." (2) The other way is to take verses 30 and 31 following the question as a second question, "Shall we say that, while Gentiles who did not seek righteousness have obtained it, Israel has not obtained it?" Verses 32 and 33 would then be explained as the positive answer to that question. "Yes, but why? etc." Sanday and Headlam urge that this second way of construing these verses has against it the awkwardness of the appended phrase "even the righteousness which is by faith."

[100] Gifford, *Romans*, p.177. Verses 23 and 24 have spoken about "vessels of mercy" and how "(some) would come from among the Jews" and "(some) from among the Gentiles." To become a chosen vessel that God can use in His service in this Church Age, one must be justified by faith, whether he be Jew or Gentile. Paul's whole previous presentation in this letter ("we maintain that a man is justified by faith apart from works of the Law," 3:28; or "the righteous man shall live by faith," 1:17) has prepared us for the conclusion he himself will present in the following verses.

[101] Along the way, there were a few Gentiles whom God reckoned as righteous. We think of Melchizedek, of Rahab (after she learned about God from what He did to the Egyptians), of Job, and some others. But the majority failed to learn about the Heavenly Father, in spite of His wishes and efforts to reveal Himself through His chosen vessels.

[102] "Gentiles" does not have an article in the Greek; it is not "the Gentiles" (i.e., all of them), but simply "Gentiles" (i.e., some Gentiles, namely, those who have believed the gospel). As indicated in the Introductory Studies, this epistle to the Romans was written in the winter of AD 58, and already multitudes of Gentiles had embraced the Christian religion, Paul here says. It has been less than 20 years since the first Gentile, Cornelius (Acts 10,11), heard the gospel, believed, and was reckoned as justified by faith.

9:31 – *but Israel, pursuing a law of righteousness, did not arrive at* that *law.*

But Israel. With all their privileges (9:3-5), and with the gospel having been taken first to the Jew, one would have expected Jewish people to have responded in greater numbers than Gentile people did.   But Israel's behavior is so different from what God's dealings with men in the past would lead us to expect.   How are we to explain it?

Pursuing a law of righteousness. In contrast to how the Gentiles lived, not pursuing righteousness, Israel had pursued "a law."   That there was something faulty about the object Israel was pursuing is implied in the expressions Paul uses.   Instead of saying that Israel pursued "righteousness (by faith)," Paul writes that Israel pursued a "law of righteousness."[103]   Since Paul is talking about Israel, it seems reasonable to suppose that "law" has some reference to the Law of Moses.   But what is meant by the expression "law of righteousness"?   If we allow 10:3 to guide us, "law of righteousness" must be understood as expressing the same thing that "going about to establish their own righteousness" does; something different from actually "subjecting themselves to the righteousness of God."   If we allow 9:32 to guide us, "works" that were somehow related to the Law, are included in the expression "law of righteousness."   Ostensibly, then, "pursuing a law of righteousness" means they supposed that their zeal for "law" was the way to demonstrate right standing with God.[104]

Did not arrive at *that* law.[105] Much less than arriving at righteousness, they did not even

---

[103] Some commentators affirm the different qualifying phrases used with "righteousness" in these two verses should be disregarded.   Once this is done, it is then asserted that the "righteousness" Israel was aiming at was not something different from the approval of God to which the Gentiles attained.   But Paul does not write that Israel was pursuing righteousness; he says they were pursuing a *law* (somehow related to righteousness).

Another difficult matter is encountered as one tries to determine if "law of righteousness" is simply another way of saying "righteousness of law" (see footnote #104, below).   Meyer's first comment on "law of righteousness" is "Quite erroneous is the view of Chrysostom, Theodoret, Calvin, Beza, Piscator, Bengel, Heumann [and Lard] that it is a *hypallage* for *dikaiosunē nomou* ["righteousness of law"]." (*Romans*, p.391).

[104] Most readers of Romans would expect "righteousness" to have the same meaning in both verse 30 and 31, unless the passage specifically warns that the words are used with different connotations.   The comments thus far offered have attempted to give "righteousness" the same meaning each time it occurs in this context – namely, "right standing before God," "justified," "reckoned as righteous by God."   In earlier verses in Romans, it has been demonstrated that the Jew "boasted" that the mere possession of the Law was evidence that he already had a right standing with God.   It was not a case that he needed to be reckoned as righteous; as far as he was concerned, he already had that, and the privileges God had extended to him proved his favored status in God's eyes.   May we then suppose that "law of righteousness" reflects the complacent Jewish belief that the "law was given because (as they thought) they already were righteous in God's judgment"?

[105] The Byzantine text, as reflected in the KJV, adds the phrase "of righteousness" after this second occurrence of "law," so that it reads, "(Israel) hath not attained to the law of righteousness."   Those expositors who were explaining the King James text usually identified the first occurrence of "law of righteousness" as being a reference to righteousness with God under the Mosaic law, while they made the second "law of righteousness" to be synonymous with "righteousness in the Christian dispensation." However, the additional phrase should probably be rejected on the basis of the manuscript evidence.

arrive at "law."[106] "Did not arrive" expresses the idea of continually failing to reach what was continually being pursued.[107] The next verse will explain that the real problem with Israel was a wrong idea of the conditions on which God reckons righteousness.[108] The point of "did not arrive at law" is that Israel failed to attain to the thing toward which the Law was pointing them, namely, faith in Christ. God had intended the Law, when He gave it, to aid Israel in its quest for righteousness before God; but their failure to understand it, and make proper use of it, left them outside the group of people whom God now (since the advent of the Messiah) reckons as righteous.[109]

9:32 – *Why? Because* **they did** *not* **pursue it** *by faith, but as though* **it were** *by works.* *They stumbled over the stumbling stone,*

Why? Why[110] did Israel fail to arrive at the law? The reason is simple. Verses 32 and 33 will tell us the real problem with Israel was that they had a wrong idea of the conditions on which God reckons righteousness.

The thoughtful reader will have recognized that a series of decisions must be made before one can comment on this passage. (a) Shall we understand "righteousness" to mean "God's way of saving man" or as "man's right way of living"? (b) Shall we understand the genitive in "law of righteousness" to be an objective, subjective, or an attributive genitive? (c) Is the expression "law of righteousness" different from or synonymous with the expression "righteousness of law" (Galatians 3:21; Philippians 3:9)? (d) "Law" is anarthrous *nomos*. Shall we translate it "Law" or "law" or "principle" (as at 3:27b)? Each of these options has been tried by some commentator, with the resulting comments carrying varying degrees of conviction.

Also involved is another far-reaching consequence of how we explain this passage – namely, what was Paul's real point of contention with 1st century Judaism? Was the Mosaic religion (as originally given and intended by God) now wholly abrogated by the New Covenant? Or was Paul simply contending with a perversion of what Moses actually required of men? Or are both true?

[106] Observe that Paul did not write, as might have been expected from the previous phrase, "did not arrive at the law of righteousness"; instead, he wrote "did not arrive at law." (The NASB has interpreted the verse by adding the word "that" before "law" in this final phrase. This differs little from the Byzantine text that reads "law of righteousness." The only problem is that, as the text now stands, Paul did not write "that" – he simply wrote "law.")

[107] Of course, it can be said that in the centuries before the advent of Christ, some few among Israel were indeed justified by faith (there were some whom the Bible calls "righteous," e.g., Luke 1:6). Since the gospel has been preached, some few Jews have obeyed the gospel and been justified by faith (see 11:1-10), but the mass of the Jewish people failed to arrive at that place.

[108] "Error is often a greater obstacle to the salvation of men than carelessness or vice. Christ said that publicans and harlots would enter the kingdom of God before the Pharisees. In like manner the thoughtless and sensual Gentiles were more susceptible of impression from the gospel, and were more frequently converted to Christ, than the Jews, who were wedded to erroneous views of the plan of salvation.

Let no man think error in doctrine a slight practical evil. No road to perdition has ever been more thronged than that of false doctrine. Error is a shield over the conscience, and a bandage over the eyes." Hodge, *Romans*, p.331,332.

[109] On the assumption, then, that verses 30 and 31 reiterate what has been written earlier in this epistle about "Law" (e.g., Romans 2:17-29; 3:20-4:15; 5:20; 6:15; 7:1-6), Israel's pursuit of righteousness failed because of a wrong use of the law.

[110] "*Dia ti* asks for a reason; *hina ti* [had Paul written it] would ask for the purpose." Lenski, *Romans*, p.636.

Because *they did* not *pursue it* by faith, but as though *it were* by works. Paul explains the reason why Israel did not arrive.[111]   "As though by works" introduces a subjective idea here – what Israel thought regarding the way the "law" was to be observed.[112]   "By faith" would suggest listening carefully to what God was saying, and faithfully performing what He prescribed.[113]   "By works," since it is contrasted to "by faith," indicates that the "works" they were doing were something other than what God had revealed He wished or required of men under the Mosaic law.

Is it possible to identify these "works" with greater precision? Should we perhaps think of religious activities done mechanically, without the worshiper's heart in them? Such an attitude would readily present itself when, as the Jews did, a man thought he already (by virtue of his descent and the privileges granted to him) was in right standing with God. More likely, we should think of the "works of the Law" such as 3:20,28 and 4:2 have already indicated do not meet the condition on which God reckons men as righteous. Such religious traditions, invented by men rather than being specifically commanded by God, resulted in a pride which led the Jew to suppose he was superior to men who did not have such works of the Law. Such works included the meticulous tithing of even the minutest garden vegetables, fasting twice a week, the traditions of the elders about washing of hands before eating, what constituted work on the Sabbath, the straining of gnats out of beverages lest unclean food be ingested, etc.[114]

---

[111] Note the italics.   The Greek is very succinct and clear in meaning; the italics and punctuation chosen by the translator are intended to help the English reader to get the idea conveyed by the Greek. (a) In such instances it is customary to repeat the subject, verb, and object from the previous sentence.   The real problem is what is the "it" that was pursued – "righteousness" from verse 30, or "law" from verse 31? One would normally expect the nearer antecedent to be the word supplied – in this case "law."   In addition, for those wishing to pursue the matter of punctuation, helpful notes occur in Sanday and Headlam, *Romans*, p.280, and Cranfield, *Romans*, p.508.   (b) Another textual variation occurs here, also.   Readers who compare the KJV and NASB will see that verse 32 in the KJV reads "but as it were by the works of the law."   The genuineness of the concluding "of the law" here is doubtful, since the manuscript evidence is against these words being part of what Paul originally wrote.

[112] Wording it as he does, Paul plainly separates himself from any such belief that "works" accomplished what the Jews thought they did.   It will also be evident to all who are trying to think their way through this difficult passage that the explanation given to "by works" depends greatly on decisions already made, not only in Romans 3 and 4, but also in 9:30-32.   At least four different explanations of "works" can be found in the commentaries, each put forth as an attempt to explain why Paul found fault with the Jews' behavior. The thing wrong with the "works" was (a) there was a perverted quality in their endeavor, or (b) they were trying to earn righteousness [i.e., meritorious works], or (c) the works resulted from a rule of life that would produce righteousness, or (d) they were simply legalistic works with no corresponding attitude of heart.

[113] Earlier, this commentary has proposed that "faith," or "faithfulness," is "doing what God says."   If the "works" of Israel had been "of faith," they would have been meeting the conditions on which a man is granted a right standing with God.   The fact that Paul here specifically says Israel's pursuit was "of works" and not "of faith" indicates that Israel had a wrong idea of the conditions of justification.   Israel could have known that mere possession of the Law was not of itself evidence of right status with God.   Israel could have known about every man's individual need for justification by faith from a careful reading of the Old Testament; they could have discerned the same truths Paul has pointed out in earlier chapters of Romans.

[114] Some have appealed to Philippians 3:3-11 for an illustration of such "works" – where Paul says his former self-confidence in the flesh resulted partly from privileged status (circumcised, Israelite, Benjaminite) and partly from personal accomplishment (zealous, blameless).   Paul surely uses himself, in that passage, as an illustration of what the majority of his Jewish contemporaries felt and believed.

They stumbled over THE STUMBLING STONE. Evidence of Israel's lack of faith was a matter the prophets had predicted, and the pertinent passages are introduced by use of the expression "stumbling stone."[115]   Christ is held up as the One in whom men were to believe, and He would prove to be a stone of stumbling to those who withheld belief.[116]

9:33 – *just as it is written, "BEHOLD, I LAY IN ZION A STONE OF STUMBLING AND A ROCK OF OFFENSE, AND HE WHO BELIEVES IN HIM WILL NOT BE DISAPPOINTED."*

Just as it is written. There are two passages taken from Isaiah and fused together in this quotation.[117]   Some of the language comes from a threat found in Isaiah 8:14, and some of the language is taken from a promise made in Isaiah 28:16.   Wrapping his presentation in Biblical language (so that "they stumbled over the stumbling stone" is substituted for "not of faith but of works"), Paul now affirms that what Isaiah had predicted is exactly what has happened to Israel.

"BEHOLD, I LAY IN ZION A STONE OF STUMBLING AND A ROCK OF OFFENSE. Not only does the New Testament verify that this language is Messianic,[118]

---

[115] There is no need to weaken the meaning of the term "stumbled," as though it meant "to be annoyed with" or "to show irritation at," as Sanday and Headlam, *Romans*, p.280, have done.   *Skandalon* is something one stumbles over, trips over.   It was originally the name for that part of a trap to which the bait was attached, which when the tempted animal tried to eat, became the trigger by which the animal was snared.

[116] C.K. Barrett has written concerning Romans 9-11, "Perhaps the most common view is that, after a predestinarian account of the fall of Israel in 9:1-29, 9:30-10:21 provides a complementary account of the same lapse in which the fault is laid squarely at Israel's door, and in turn leads to a synthesis in chapter 11 in which Paul states his hope for Israel's future."   "Romans 9:30-10:21:   Fall and Responsibility of Israel," *Essays on Paul* (Philadelphia: Westminster Press, 1982), p.132.

   What Barrett does not say is that the common view of chapter 9, predestination *to salvation*, has left God's actions in a bad light, so predestinarians are delighted to be able to lay the blame for being lost on man himself (9:30-33).   In this manner, they suppose, they have relieved God of the terrible stigma that He deliberately predestined some to be lost.   Hence, God is not at fault, man is (as 9:30-10:21 plainly shows).   However, if chapter 9 dealt with predestination *to service*, there is no stigma attached to God's choice of some to honorable use and some to menial use; and 9:30-33 shows how it is that the majority of Israel is outside of the "Israel" that God is presently using for "honorable service."   Not that they were unconditionally predestined to be, but that their unbelief (a personal, deliberate choice) is the real cause.

[117] Paul's technique of scriptural argumentation is to tie together passages where the same word(s) or theme(s) is found.   In the present case, the words "stumbled," "rock," and "believes" are the terms that show the passages quoted from Isaiah are relevant to the summary just given in 9:30-32a.   (The same principle was followed in the citation of passages in 9:6-29 – a theme or word was the common thread tying all of the verses together.)   Some have found fault with the way Paul cites passages – first one from the Hebrew, then one from the Septuagint, then a paraphrase strictly following neither the Hebrew nor the LXX – urging that what he does borders on deliberate manipulation of what the Old Testament text actually says.   A more satisfactory explanation is that Paul's exposition of these Old Testament passages is not only the result of the Holy Spirit's revelatory and inspiratory actions, but also is in perfect harmony with what Jesus Himself did when (after His crucifixion and resurrection) He opened and explained all the Scriptures that pertained to Himself (Luke 24:44-48).   The student who would see the particular problems involved in the different versions and quotations from Isaiah here in 9:33 should consult Cranfield, *Romans*, p.511,512.

[118] Three "stone" passages from the Old Testament are regularly alluded to in New Testament writings,

but it was so understood in Judaism.[119]   Isaiah 28:16 reads, "Therefore thus says the Lord God, Behold, I am laying in Zion a stone, a tested stone, a costly cornerstone for the foundation, firmly placed.   He who believes *in it* will not be disturbed."   Isaiah 28 is a promise about a rock sanctuary in the time of storm.   In the midst of this verse, Paul has substituted the ominous warning language from Isaiah 8:14 about "a stone of stumbling and a rock of offense."[120]   Zion was one of the hills upon which Jerusalem was built.   It was at Jerusalem one would find the Rock that would either save or crush.   How a person responded to God's word in Isaiah's time, or (considering the Messianic implications of Isaiah's prophecy) how a person responds to the Messiah in Paul's time, will determine whether He is a sanctuary, a refuge in the midst of storm, or whether He is the rock of stumbling, the dangerous obstacle against which one comes to grief.

AND HE WHO BELIEVES IN HIM WILL NOT BE DISAPPOINTED.   This phrase from Isaiah is the one which provides Paul with a tie-in to his statement about "by faith" (verse 32).   Like the LXX before him, Paul writes "in *Him*" where the Hebrew had "He who believes."   The personal pronoun is a reference, ultimately, to the Messiah.   Whether or not a man is of faith depends on what he does with Jesus.[121]   "The meaning [of 'will not

---

all of them as having Messianic intents.   The same two Isaiah passages (with the same variation in text) are combined in 1 Peter 2:6-8, and applied to Jesus.   Psalm 118:22 is a second "stone" passage explained by Peter (Acts 4:11; 1 Peter 2:6-8) as being a prediction of Christ.   Daniel 2:34 is the third "stone" passage shown to be Messianic in Luke 20:17ff.

[119] Because of the use of the "stone" passages by Jesus (cf. Matthew 21:42) and Christians to demonstrate that a rejection of Jesus as Messiah by Jewish people is a faulty approach to God, some attempts have been made to deny the Messianic import of the "stone" passages.   Some appeal to the Dead Sea Scrolls, where the Qumran community or Council is seen to be the fulfillment of Isaiah's prediction.   See 1QS 6.26ff and 1QS 8.7, or G. Vermes, *The Dead Sea Scrolls in English* (Baltimore: Penguin Books, 1962), p.38.   More recently, Paul Meyer, "Romans 10:4 and the End of the Law," in *The Divine Helmsman: Studies on God's Control of Human Events*, edited by J.L. Crenshaw and Samuel Sandmel (New York: KTAV, 1980), p.64, has urged that the stumbling stone is the Torah which misleads (his interpretation of Romans 7), and that "believes in Him" refers to faith in God, so that Paul's argument in Romans is Theocentric rather than Christocentric.   To find Christ in 9:33, Meyer argues, "one must ... simply read Paul as anticipating here his mention of Christ in 10:4."   All this is a departure from what one finds in the LXX and the paraphrase of the passage in the Targum (see Cranfield, *Romans*, p.511).   F.F. Bruce (*Romans*, p.199) explains that the stone appears initially to be a reference to the righteous remnant, and then came to be embodied personally in the promised Prince of the House of David.

[120] These two passages from Isaiah have the same historical background as did the two previous quotations (verses 27-29).   The Assyrian invasion of Israel and Judah, and the efforts of those two lands to defend themselves, is the immediate context wherein these two prophecies are found.   Isaiah 28 is part of a message to the pro-Assyrian party in Judah that their foreign policy attempts to bribe Assyria will fail – that only God, not Assyria, was Judah's real Protector.   In verse 16, God declares that the true basis of Judah's safety was the person and work of the Messianic Redeemer.   The prophecy recorded in Isaiah 8 is an exhortation not to fear the alliance between Israel and Syria.   The Assyrians will sweep over Israel like the waters of a great flood, but there will be one place of refuge – God Himself will prove a "sanctuary" to all who put their trust in Him.   Those who would spurn His word would perish.   The Isaiah 8 passage is a reference to the Father; Paul applies it to Jesus, in perfect harmony with the deity of Jesus.

[121] "What vv.32b and 33 have done is to add an explicitly Christological dimension to the definition of the disobedience of Israel and of the obedience of some Gentiles which has already been given in vv.30-32a.   That disobedience and that obedience are essentially a matter of relationship to Christ." Cranfield, *Romans*, p.512.

be disappointed'] is that those who trust in God need never fear that their trust in Him will prove ill-founded. God vindicates His people's faith, so that they need not feel embarrassed on His account."[122] By fusing these two passages, Paul shows that Scripture foretold both the faithfulness of some among Israel and the stumbling of others. The real cause of Israel's rejection is their unbelief – Israel has rejected Christ, and so stumbled over the stone of stumbling. The word "believes" gives Paul the theme which will occupy the next several verses.

A chapter break now occurs in our Bibles, but there is no break in Paul's thought; the explanation of Israel's "not by faith" continues in chapter 10. A preview of the rest of the paragraph about God's dealings with Israel in the present would include these major ideas:

- Ever since the call of Abraham, God has been selecting certain of His descendants to do a special job for Him in the world. God is still following the same procedure, now using Israel (though not all of Israel, but the Israel within Israel) as a vessel of mercy. According to God's plan for the ages, the members who comprise this select Israel are those who have responded to God's call, whether of Jewish or Gentile background.

- That many of physical Israel, who might have been God's special vessels by which He extends mercy to the world if they were saved themselves, have been rejected by God so that they are no longer the chosen instruments He is using. This is due to their own fault. The concluding verses of chapter 9 and the whole of chapter 10 are devoted to showing Israel's personal responsibility in this matter. They had failed to listen to what God was saying to them, and rejected the Messiah.

Overcome with the sadness of the subject, Paul pauses in the opening verses of chapter 10 to express his grief again over the majority of Israel's failure to continue to be the "Israel of God" (10:1,2a). He returns to the idea introduced in 9:30,31 pointing out that Israel adhered to their own method of "righteousness" instead of accepting God's method (10:2b-3). Israel went about trying their own method in spite of these facts: (1) The Law on which they based their own method had been done away in Christ (10:4). (2) Their own method was exclusive whereas God's way is clearly universal and intended for all alike (10:11-13). (3) Believing was something Israel had had plenty of opportunities to do. The gospel had been preached over the entire Roman world and Israel had the capacity to understand what was preached, so their failure to be men "of faith" was not due to lack of opportunity. In fact, they had been warned by their own Old Testament prophets about the possible failure to believe.

The opening verses of chapter 11 will conclude this paragraph about God's dealings with Israel in the present by showing two things: some Israelites are believers and are part of the remnant of Israel God uses today; and a judicial hardening has been visited upon those descendants of Israel who have refused to accept Jesus, the Messiah.

---

[122] Bruce, *Romans*, p.200.

10:1 – *Brethren, my heart's desire and my prayer to God for them is for* **their** *salvation.*

Brethren. The theme does not change. The subject being discussed in chapter 10 is the same as at the close of chapter 9 – how it is that men become a part of the real "Israel" of God. "Brethren" speaks of Christian brethren, the church members at Rome to whom Paul is writing this letter. One should be sure to note that the "Israel" that has been rejected by God is in antithesis to "brethren."[1]

My heart's desire and my prayer to God for them. As he did in the beginning of chapter 9, Paul affirms his intense concern for his own race in order to allay any doubts that might be created by his affirmation about their failure. There is a slight difference of emphasis, however, in chapter 10. In 9:4,5, Paul writes about the privileges and prerogatives that had been granted from God's hand to Israel; now, in 10:2, he emphasizes something subjective, Israel's "zeal for God." Both these emphases make Israel's failure all the more heart-breaking. There is no exact English equivalent of the word translated "desire," a word which has the connotation of delight or pleasure.[2] Paul seems to be saying that there was not much that would give him greater pleasure than to see more of his own race being saved.[3] "Prayer" is the word often rendered "supplication," a petition for some particular benefit.[4] The "them"[5] that Paul speaks of are his kinsmen in the flesh, the Jews who have not obeyed the gospel.

Is for *their* **salvation.** The "salvation" he desires for them is the "justification" (right-eousness) about which this epistle has had much to say, including most recently at 9:30. Paul is not praying for a miracle to save the Jews, nor was he praying for a special dispensation on their behalf (so that they might be saved in some other way than the "justification

---

[1] "The position of the word 'brethren' in the Greek increases the emphasis of a word always used by the apostle when he wishes to be specially emphatic. The thought of the Christian brotherhood intensifies the contrast with the Israelites who are rejected." Sanday and Headlam, *Romans*, p.282.

[2] The word is *eudokia*, and the commentaries and lexicons do not agree in their attempts at conveying its meaning. Some urge that "good will" or "good pleasure" is a better choice than "desire." (See Sanday and Headlam, *Romans*, p.282, who opt for the first, and admit that others [such as Lightfoot, at Philippians 1:15; Thayer, *Lexicon*, p.258; and, we can add Arndt-Gingrich, *Lexicon*, p.319,320, to the list] take the opposite view. *Eudokia* is "what would give the greatest pleasure and satisfaction," Lenski, *Romans*, p.611. "Wish" or "desire" are not exactly adequate translations, but we do not have a better English word.

[3] The Greek has an untranslatable particle (*men*) at the beginning of verse 1, which shows that there is a contrast coming. Already in the writer's mind is the fact that there was something that was not in harmony with what would give him such great pleasure. Verse 3 will specify what that opposite fact is.

[4] Berry, *New Testament Synonyms*, p.20, shows that while *proseuchē* is a general word restricted to prayers to God, the word used here, *deēsis*, is a word that means a prayer *for a particular benefit*, and can be addressed either to God or to man.

[5] Instead of "for them," the KJV reads "for Israel." The better supported reading in the manuscripts is as the NASB reads. Perhaps "Israel" was added in the margin by some early scribe as an explanatory note, and this marginal gloss then made its way into the Byzantine text. The reading "for them" shows the relationship with chapter 9:31-33 much better than does the reading "Israel."

by faith" that has always been the way of right relationship with God). He certainly was praying that God would send messengers to them, and that when preachers of the gospel came, they would listen and respond positively to the invitation.[6] Implicit in Paul's language here in chapter 10 is the fact that it is entirely possible to be a physical descendant of Abraham, Isaac, and Jacob, yet still be in need of salvation. During the centuries when Israel lived under the Mosaic Law, men were part of Mosaic covenant simply by virtue of their physical birth. However, the fact they were 'children of Abraham' did not guarantee they would also be saved. As they grew to responsible age, they had to be taught to know the Lord, and a failure to be faithful to what they were taught would result in an unfavorable verdict from God.

10:2 – *For I bear them witness that they have a zeal for God, but not in accordance with knowledge.*

For I bear them witness. 'I can testify on their behalf' is the idea. This verse gives the reason for Paul's desire and prayer for Israel. Having been an Israelite himself, and having been "extremely zealous for the ancestral traditions" (Galatians 1:14) and "zealous for God" (Acts 22:3), he knew only too well the extent of Jewish zeal and how misdirected that zeal could be, and the tragic consequences of such misdirected zeal.

That they have a zeal for God. "Paul selects the very word which the Jew himself would have chosen to express just that zeal on which more than anything else he would have prided himself."[7] Zeal for God "refers to the Jewish hatred of idolatry, their fanatic rever-

---

[6] What about offering prayers for the lost today? "In 1723 Robert Millar ... wrote *A History of the Propagation of Christianity and the Overthrow of Paganism*, in which he advocated intercession as the primary means of converting the heathen. The idea soon caught on. Twenty years later prayer groups were to be found all over the British Isles. Their chief petition was for the conversion of the heathen world." J. Herbert Kane, *A Concise History of the Christian World Mission* (Grand Rapids: Baker Book House, 1982), p.83. Kane goes on to show that Jonathan Edwards tried to make the idea popular in America, and by the 1780's a tract he had written had sparked some churches to have intercession for the non-Christian world the first Monday of each month. In the last half of the 20th century, some advocates of strictly Biblical mission methods have begun to question whether such prayer for the lost is even Scriptural, urging that it is difficult to find any relevant examples of such prayers being commanded or offered. It is probable that Romans 10:1 and 1 Timothy 2:1-4 are the only possible candidates for inclusion as prayers for the lost. The content of the prayers desired in Timothy are that government leaders so govern that Christians may carry out their tasks of giving God His due, and reaching lost men. It does not seem that the prayer there is "for the lost" only, since God was being asked to influence government leaders so as not to hinder the attempts to evangelize the lost. Here in Romans, Paul is hardly asking God to somehow act on the hearts of the lost Jews so that they may be saved apart from hearing and obeying the gospel. Such an explanation would be in direct opposition to what is about to be set forth in chapter 10.

It seems pertinent, in passing, to observe that 10:1 also has some bearing on the Calvinist interpretation of chapter 9 (that God elected some to salvation or damnation, and did the electing back in eternity, and that the number cannot be increased or decreased). If the Calvinist doctrine is true, then this prayer "for their salvation" makes no sense. If certain men are predestined to be lost, why is Paul praying for their salvation? But if it is 'whosoever will may come,' then Christians are right when they pray "for salvation" for the lost.

[7] Sanday and Headlam, *Romans*, p.283. Compare the use of the same word at Acts 21:20.

ence for the Temple, their outward obedience to the Law and the rabbinical traditions, and to crown all of these, their hatred of Christ and Christianity."[8]

But not in accordance with knowledge. The Jews intended to serve God by means of reverence for the temple, avoidance of idolatry, etc. They were not deliberately resisting God's will. They just did not understand what His will was, especially with reference to the subject of justification (as the next verse will explain). The word translated "knowledge" is the word often used for "the true knowledge of God."[9] "Had they read the law of Moses and the prophets correctly, they would at once have recognized in Jesus their long-expected Messiah and would have hailed Him with great joy. Their lack of knowledge, being due to their own stubborn refusal to either see or hear, was inexcusable."[10]

---

[8] Lenski, *Romans*, p.642. "It would be difficult to find a more happy description of the state of the Jews at this period. They had a 'zeal for God.' Josephus wrote, 'The Jew knows the Law better than his own name ... The sacred rules were punctually observed ... The great feasts were frequented by countless thousands ... Over and above the requirements of the Law, ascetic religious exercises advocated by the teachers of the Law came into vogue ... Even the Hellenised and Alexandrian Jews under Caligula died on the cross and by fire, and the Palestinian prisoners in the last war died by the claws of African lions in the amphitheatre, rather than sin against the Law. What Greek would do the like? ... The Jews also exhibited an ardent zeal for the conversion of the Gentiles to the Law of Moses. The proselytes filled Asia Minor and Syria, and – to the indignation of Tacitus – Italy and Rome.' The tenacity of the Jews and their uncompromising monotheism was seen in some conspicuous examples. In the early part of his procuratorship, Pilate, seeking to break through their known repugnance to everything that savored of image-worship, had introduced into Jerusalem ensigns surmounted with silver busts of the emperor. Upon this the people went down in a body to Caesarea, waited for five days and nights in the marketplace, bared their necks to the soldiers that Pilate sent among them, and did not desist until the order for the removal of the ensigns had been given. Later Pilate caused to be hung up in the palace at Jerusalem certain gilded shields bearing a dedicatory inscription to Tiberius. Then, again, the Jews did not rest until, by their complaints addressed directly to the emperor, they had succeeded in getting them taken down. The consternation that was caused by Caligula's order for the erection of his own statue in the Temple is well known. None of the Roman governors dared to carry it into execution. Caligula himself was slain before it could be accomplished. Justice must be done to the heroic spirit of the Jews. But it was zeal directed into the most mistaken channels. Their religion was legal and formal to the last degree. Under an outward show of punctilious obedience, it concealed all the inward corruption described by the Apostle in Romans 2:17-29, the full extent of which was seen in the horrors of the great insurrection and the siege of Jerusalem." Sanday, *Romans*, p.111.

[9] *Epignōsis* is the word used here. "The Jews were destitute, not of *gnōsis*, but of the higher disciplined knowledge, destitute of the true moral discernment by which they might learn the right way. *Epignōsis* (see Lightfoot on Colossians 1:9, to whose note there is nothing to add) means a higher and more perfect knowledge, and hence it is used especially and almost technically for knowledge of God, as being the highest and most perfect form [of knowledge]." Sanday and Headlam, *Romans*, p.283.

[10] Lipscomb and Shepherd, *Romans*, p.186. Here we have one Biblical answer to the idea, held by many in the 20th century, that if a man is sincere and zealous for what he believes, he must, of course, be acceptable to God. Well, the Jews were zealous, but their zeal was misdirected, and they were not accepted. Zeal, not regulated by a right knowledge, leads to the substitution of error (note how the Jews sought a "law of righteousness") and can inspire a persecuting spirit (remember Paul's example before his conversion). Romans 10 will go on to show that what is believed is an important criterion, too, in addition to zeal.

10:3 – *For not knowing about God's righteousness, and seeking to establish their own, they did not subject themselves to the righteousness of God.*

For not knowing about God's righteousness. "For" shows that verse 3 is related to what has just been said, and is either a reason or an explanation of the statement about "not in accordance with knowledge." "God's righteousness" is God's plan of saving men, which elsewhere in Romans has been designated as 'justification by faith.'[11] Paul, at this point in his presentation, simply states the fact of the misunderstanding, the lack of knowledge on the part of the Jews. Whether this ignorance is culpable is a point not made until later (verse 14ff).

And seeking to establish their own. "Establish" does not so much mean "to procure it for the first time" as it does "to cause a person or thing to keep his or its place; to uphold or sustain the force or authority of anything."[12] In this expression, Paul reflects the sad fact that 1st century Judaism had departed from what God revealed through Moses, and had tried instead to devise their own way of being righteous in His sight, rather than submitting to the conditions that God had already revealed. Not only had Judaism changed and modified their religion through the years since the captivities, but they also supposed that they continued to enjoy right standing with God through the system, constantly changing as it was, that they themselves had devised.[13]

They did not subject themselves to the righteousness of God. Confident they already had 'righteousness with God,' they went about endeavoring to sustain the position they supposed they had, rather than yielding their hearts in obedient faith to God's way of saving man.[14]

---

[11] See Romans 1:17 and 3:21, and the comments there made. Some commentators suppose that God's "righteousness" here stands for God's attributes of character, instead of His plans and counsels and acts whereby He reckons righteousness to those who believe. But the context rather requires that we emphasize how men come to have a right standing with God.

[12] Thayer, *Lexicon*, p.308.

[13] In the Introductory Studies of this book, pages xxix-xxxi (Pre-Christian Interpretation of Scripture), and pages lxii-lxix (Paul and Judaism) explain the changes made in Judaism. When the various commentaries are compared, it soon becomes evident that at least three explanations of this phrase in Romans 10:3 are proposed. (a) "Their *own* righteousness" sometimes is thought to mean "of their own devising, rather than God's." (b) Sometimes it is explained to mean "self-righteousness," that is, a right standing with God "wrought by their own works," and in opposition to God's way of saving men, wherein no meritorious works are required. (c) Recently, the possessive pronoun has been given an exclusive connotation (as though this righteousness were only for Jews, exclusive of all others) by E.P. Sanders in *Paul, The Law, and the Jewish People* (Philadelphia: Fortress Press, 1985), p.38. In this, one would properly object that the real reason Sanders has been forced to give "own" such a meaning (imported from the following context, e.g., verse 12) is because he has opted for a wrong explanation of the "works" (he limits such works to certain "identity markers") that Israel was faulted for pursuing (9:31,32).

[14] "Did not subject themselves" treats the Greek verb as though it were middle voice. Lenski, *Romans*, p.644, notes that many second aorist passive verbs, like *hupetagēsan*, were used in the place of aorist middles. A similar middle voice sense for a passive form of *hupotassō* can be seen at Romans 8:7, 13:1; Hebrews 12:9; James 4:7; and 1 Peter 2:13.

10:4 – *For Christ is the end of the law for righteousness to everyone who believes.*

For.   Three verses in a row begin with "for," and the exegete must determine the relationship of these verses to the preceding thought.   Do we have three reasons given why it can be said of Israel that their zeal was "not in accordance with knowledge" (verse 2)? Or does verse 4 give a reason for what was just said in verse 3 about Israel not subjecting themselves to God's way of saving men?   While both these explanations give a true sense, it is the latter we shall pursue.[15]   Taking verse 4 as an expansion of what verse 3 said, the thread of thought connecting both is this: "Christ" is an integral part of God's way of saving man, and a person who rejects Him cannot possibly have right standing in God's sight!

Christ is the end of the law.   Here we have come to one of the places in the New Testament where a person's theology is likely to color his comments.[16]   This is true since two of the key terms have several possible meanings. (a) Since "Law" is anarthrous. is the reference to the Law of Moses[17] or to law in general?   And what is the connection of verse 4 with 9:31 where "law" was last used?   (b) Shall we render *telos* as "end"[18] or "goal"[19] (as the NASB margin has it)?   The word *telos* is first in the Greek sentence, showing that there is a special emphasis on this word.   How careful an exegete must be at

---

[15] It is not easy to see how verse 5 (where for the third time in a row "for" begins a verse) can be explained as being a third reason for what was said in verse 2.   It is much easier to suppose that verse 5 gives a reason (or further explanation) for something just said in verse 4.

[16] Romans 10:4 is one of the passages where battles between one-covenant and dispensational theologians have been fought.   One-covenant theologians would prefer "goal."   Dispensational theologians, by contrast, would tend to prefer "end," so that they can demonstrate once more that the Law of Moses was temporary, and ended when Messiah came.   Cranfield, *Romans*, p.518,519, insists Paul does not mean the Law of Moses was terminated or abolished in Christ.   "We are convinced that there is no statement in any of Paul's epistles which, rightly understood, implies that Christ has abolished the Law," he writes, and even has a special essay on Paul's theology which includes a study on "The Old Testament Law," p.845-861, wherein this thesis is defended.

[17] For an explanation of the technical language "anarthrous *nomos*," see notes at Romans 2:12.

[18] Gifford, *Romans*, p.183, Meyer, *Romans*, p.405, and others urge that the following context in Romans, where there is an emphatic contrast between righteousness "of law" and righteousness "of faith," shows that the only possible way to translate *telos* (so that it agrees with the context) is "end, termination, conclusion."

Three possible meanings for *telos* are suggested in the lexicons and commentaries: (1) goal, (2) end, and (3) meaning or fulfillment.   The third is probably to be rejected.   Jesus does *fulfill* the Old Testament prophecies of the Coming One, but that is not the point emphasized by *telos* ("end, goal").   "It is quite true that Christ is the *teleiōsis* of the Law, that in Him what was typical has its fulfilment; but *telos* never means *teleiōsis* (as it is taken here by Origen, Erasmus, etc.)"   Sanday and Headlam, *Romans*, p.285.   Similarly, while it is true that Jesus was sinless perfect, it would not be a relevant comment on this passage to suggest its meaning is that "Jesus in his life fulfilled (*telos*) perfectly the righteousness required by the Law."

[19] The word *telos* was translated "outcome" (goal) at 6:21,22.   Vine suggests that Romans 6:21,22 "expands precisely and succinctly how the Jews were mistaken."   *Romans*, p.154.

this place, lest his preconceived notions determine his comments.[20]

If what has been written since 9:32 is correct, then we suppose that "goal" would be the proper idea here. The aim, or goal, of the Law was to show men their sin, their need for a Savior, and their need of the righteousness by faith which is made possible by Him.[21] By this short statement about "Christ being the goal of the Law," Paul summarized the evidence that Israel's knowledge was faulty (verse 2) and that their works (9:32) actually failed to arrive at God's righteousness. What Israel failed to see was that the Law[22] was intended to lead a man to Christ, and in relationship to Him one would find that he was now in right standing with God, having been justified by faith.[23] "Christ" (Messiah) here stands for all He is and does as He becomes incarnate so He can be a perfect sacrifice for sin, and then serves as high priest and intercessor for His people after His resurrection and return to Heaven.[24]

---

[20] This commentator is not sure his own comments are wholly free of bias in this regard. He does teach, in harmony with Galatians 3 and Hebrews 7-10, that the Law of Moses was never intended to be anything but temporary. Four hundred years after the covenant made with Abraham, the Law was added to the Abrahamic Covenant until the Seed (Christ) should come; then it was abrogated and a new priesthood and the new covenant came into force. Such a view of the Law is a New Testament doctrine everywhere taught; even Colossians 2:14 shows that the Mosaic Code ended when Christ was nailed to the cross. Romans 3:21-25, 6:14, and 7:6 have made the same point already in this letter. So the doctrine that the Law was temporary does not depend on how 10:4 is interpreted.

[21] See Romans 2:19-21, 5:20, 7:7,22-23, and 8:3 for Paul's own statements about the purpose of the Law.

[22] "Law" (anarthrous *nomos*) certainly includes the Law of Moses (something just for the Jews), especially in light of the word "everyone" in the last part of this verse. Even if we suppose that "law" in 10:4 has the same meaning it did in 9:31, we still have the Mosaic code in the background.

If those writers were correct who insist that anarthrous *nomos* here is not a reference to the Law of Moses, but is a reference to law in general, whether that possessed by Gentile or that possessed by the Jew, there would be a slightly different turn given to the explanatory comments. The passage would then mean that the "end" or "goal" God had in mind when He gave various "laws" to any of mankind was that they eventually be driven to see their need for the verdict of righteousness based on faith and made possible by Messiah.

[23] "Since Christ is the end to which the law brings everyone that believeth for righteousness, if one is not brought by the law to accept Christ, it shows that he has mistaken the end and purpose of the law. The same idea is expressed in Galatians 3:24,25, 'So that the law is become our tutor to bring us to Christ, that we might be justified by faith. But now that faith is come, we are no longer under a tutor.' Those who claim to follow the law, yet reject Christ, are ignorant of the end and teaching of the Law." Lipscomb and Shepherd, *Romans*, p.187. (It will be observed that Lipscomb has used the word "end" as though it means "goal" or "purpose," which indeed is one of the connotations of the English word "end.") Sanday and Headlam, *Romans*, p.285, object to all of this as they comment, "... but *telos* is only used once in this sense (i.e., "goal") in St. Paul's Epistles (1 Timothy 1:5), *Christos* would become the predicate, *telos* would then require the article, and *nomos* would have to be interpreted of the Jewish Law." Their first argument about *telos* as meaning goal has already been shown to be in error – see Romans 6:21,22. Of the others, only the one about an article being needed causes the student to hesitate. However, even that can be satisfactorily explained by remembering that a noun without the article often emphasizes the quality of the noun.

[24] Compare what has been said earlier about "Christ" in Romans, especially at 1:4,7, 3:24,25, and 5:11.

For righteousness to everyone who believes. That is, righteousness (as provided in Christ's sacrifice for sin) is the goal to which the Law pointed. The word order in the Greek, "For goal of law [is] Christ unto righteousness to everyone who believes," makes this clear.[25] Right standing with God is vitally related to Messiah and His work. Such right standing is not limited to one race; it is for "everyone who believes."[26]

10:5 – *For Moses writes that the man who practices the righteousness which is based on law shall live by that righteousness.*

For Moses writes. Once more the line of Paul's thought must be given special consideration, as this is the third verse in a row that begins with "for." Verse 5 is probably to be understood as the first of several Scriptural proofs for what has just been said in verse 4 about righteousness being available to *"everyone* who *believes."*[27] Paul himself has indicated that "everyone who believes" is the topic of this whole paragraph by the fact that he both introduces and summarizes the paragraph (9:33 and 10:11) by referring to the words from Isaiah 28:16 about how the one "who believes in Him will not be disappointed."[28]

That the man who practices the righteousness which is based on law shall live by that

---

[25] The word order seems to be against the interpretation of Murray, *Romans*, Vol.2, p.50, and others, where it is proposed that "unto righteousness" should be taken very closely with "law," so that the whole meaning that results would be "Christ is the end (termination) of the Law as the way of attaining righteousness before God." The fact that "unto righteousness" is more closely associated with "Christ" (than with "law") leads to the explanation given in the comments above.

   Ernst Kasemann's effort in his *Commentary on Romans* (Grand Rapids: Wm. B. Eerdmans Publishing Co., 1980), p.283) to show that "righteousness" does not go with "goal," but with "all that precedes," comes across as a piece of special pleading.

[26] Perhaps there is a sense in which "goal" and "end" are both correct meanings for *telos*. Once the goal has been reached, there is no further need for the means of reaching the goal. In addition, if "Law" remained in force as a condition of salvation, then salvation could not be extended "to everyone;" it would be available only for those who were "under Law."

[27] Other interpreters have suggested different ways of outlining this material. (1) Some begin a new point in the outline of Romans with verse 5. 10:1-4 is taken as a sort of parenthetical statement, with verse 5 taking up where 9:33 left off, with its topics of "stumbling" and "believers not being put to shame." As proposed earlier, it seems proper to let Paul's use of "therefore" at 9:14,30, 10:14, 11:1,11 point us to his own major shifts in thought and topic. (2) Some think verse 5 is a second reason (the first was found in verse 3, with verse 4 being further elaboration of that first reason) for what was said in verse 2 about Israel's zeal for God not being "in accordance with knowledge." Their lack of knowledge can be demonstrated by a simple appeal to some passages from their Old Testament Scriptures (e.g., 10:6-8).

[28] The comments offered in the text will reflect the opinion that verses 5-13 are an appeal to Old Testament Scriptures to substantiate what has been said in verse 4 about the universality of the righteousness Christ has wrought (i.e., it is to *everyone* who believes). At the same time, since God has set forth this condition of belief for *everyone* ('whosoever'), it will also show that one who does not believe has stumbled over the Messiah, and has disqualified himself for inclusion among the righteous.

righteousness.[29]   Paul will cite two Old Testament passages where the same doctrine he is presenting (that "righteousness" is conditioned on faithfulness) has already been set forth.   First, he cites a passage from the opening verses of Leviticus 18, and attributes it to Moses.[30]   Repeating the message God had given him, Moses did not limit it to Israel.   He said "the man who [and that can be anyone!] practices the righteousness ... shall live."[31]   Paul has not forgotten what he has already written in 2:6-26 and 3:28-30; in fact, what he here writes agrees perfectly with what he wrote earlier.[32]   What God has always required as a condition for "living" (having right standing with Him) is faithfulness to the revelation

---

[29] There are some manuscript variations here that raise questions for the interpreter.   The Nestle text has *hoti* ("that") after "writes."   Someone has said that *hoti* is Greek for quotation marks, and when it is so intended it is left untranslated.   Thus, the NASB takes the *hoti* as being the start of the quotation, so that we read, "For Moses writes *that* ..."; or leaving the word untranslated, it says, "For Moses writes, 'The man who does righteousness ....'"   The United Bible Society text, however, has a different reading.   It has the *hoti* after the word "law," and this would be translated "For Moses writes concerning the righteousness which is based on law, *that* the man who does it ...."   On the basis of the textual evidence cited, this commentator would opt for the UBS reading being what Paul originally wrote.   Furthermore, the Nestle text is rather difficult to translate smoothly.

Not only is there a question of the location of "that," but at least one manuscript reads "righteousness of *faith*" rather than "of law."   Several other variations also occur in the quotation from Leviticus, including one that reads "them" (*auta*) after the participle "does" (*poiēsas*).

Another thing to observe is that the LXX of Leviticus 18:5, from which Paul quotes a portion, reads in the former part of the verse, "You shall therefore keep *all* my statues and *all* my judgments."   If we were to accept the reading of this verse found in the Nestle/NASB text, which makes even the first part of verse 5 to be something Moses writes, then for the expression "keeping of *all* the statutes and judgments" found in Leviticus, Paul substitutes "the righteousness which is of law," as though to him they were synonymous statements.   Such a result would be objectionable, in our opinion, because it would cause Paul to be contradicting here what he has written at Romans 2:13 about faithfulness (rather than sinless perfection) being the condition of salvation.

[30] In an age when the Mosaic authorship of the Pentateuch is often questioned or denied, it is well to note what Paul and Jesus say on the subject.   As they both quote various passages from the first five books, they both attribute them to Moses.   A denial of the Mosaic authorship, then, is tantamount to questioning the truthfulness of both Jesus and Paul.

[31] Observe that these comments on Leviticus 18:5 are in harmony with what has been written at Romans 2:13, where the same Old Testament passage was paraphrased.   Moses is not pictured as holding out a promise that he knew (when he spoke it) was unattainable, that he knew no one could fulfill.   Rather, Moses is saying that if a man is faithful to the revelation he has been given, God will count him as justified.

At 10:5, not a few commentaries offer explanations that have Moses offering an impossible condition – that the way to righteousness under the Law is sinless perfection.   Such comments would tend to be worded in this fashion: "'Practices' is an aorist tense verb, and pictures a man's whole past life being under review.   The 'doing' has been lifelong, and never for a moment fell under the Divine standard.   The way one escapes condemnation under a legal system is to comply with that system.   He must continually refrain from breaking the law if he would be counted as 'not guilty'."   As will be demonstrated shortly, comments of this nature immediately put the commentator in a difficult spot, as he would try to harmonize what he has just written with what Scripture indicates elsewhere.

[32] Commentators who find verse 5 to state something in contrast with verses 6-8 usually have to explain how it is that Paul seemingly misinterprets or misapplies the passage from Leviticus 18.   Paul is accused of reversing the natural meaning of the words Moses wrote.   On first sight, one who reads the words of Leviticus would likely understand them to mean that 'God's law given to Israel consisted of statues and judgments which *might be kept*, and by keeping which, they could enter into life.'   Furthermore, the refer-

He has given – perseverance in doing what He says is right. Leviticus 18 is one Old Testament passage that teaches this. Neither Judaism's departure from the Mosaic revelation nor their rejection of the Messiah is compatible with the *practice* of righteousness!

10:6 – *But the righteousness based on faith speaks thus, "DO NOT SAY IN YOUR HEART, 'WHO WILL ASCEND INTO HEAVEN?' (that is, to bring Christ down),*

But the righteousness based on faith speaks thus. "But" shows the translator's opinion that there is a contrast between what is set forth in verse 6ff and what was said in verse 5.[33] However, in harmony with what has been written above, we would translate it "and," thus making verses 6-10 a second proof from the Old Testament that righteousness is based on faithfulness to God's revelation concerning His Messiah.[34] Paul's method of introducing

---

ences to Leviticus 18 by Ezekiel (20:11,13,21) and Nehemiah (9:13,29) clearly show that in their view there was nothing about the condition that was impracticable, nor was the promise unattainable. Did then Paul misrepresent or misunderstand the passage, or deliberately reverse its meaning? That is exactly what some Neo-orthodox and Neo-liberal interpreters affirm has happened. Now such a conclusion surely impinges on the inspiration, either of Moses or of Paul. This commentator, on the basis of Divine inspiration for both Moses and Paul (which would lead both to speak only pure, holy truth), rejects any idea that Paul is inventing a new interpretation for the passage, an interpretation which actually misapplies or reverses the real meaning of the passage. Any supposed disharmony between Moses and Paul on the topic of how anyone is "justified" in God's sight might be the result of our failure to understand what either one or both of those men wrote, but it cannot be attributed to the idea that Paul deliberately reversed what Moses wrote.

Nor is this accusation that Paul misrepresented what the Old Testament taught a matter of interest only in the 1st century. Just as Paul has been accused of misrepresenting Leviticus, Christian missionaries attempting to evangelize Jewish people in the 20th century are still accused by Jewish leaders of misrepresenting what the Jewish Bible says (*Christianity Today*, 28:17 [Nov. 23, 1984], p.40,41). It is of great importance, then, that when Christians would share the real meaning of the Old Testament, they do it only as the Master and His inspired apostles did it.

[33] George E. Howard, "Christ the End of the Law: the Meaning of Romans 10:4-8," *Journal of Biblical Literature*, 88 (1969), p.335,336, has urged that it is not the Greek of this passage, but a preconceived notion of the relationship between verse 5 and verses 6-8, that leads translators and commentators to affirm that verse 6 introduces a contrast to verse 5. "*De*, however, does not always imply 'but:' sometimes it implies 'and.' There are many examples where the very construction which appears here, i.e., *gar ... de*, demands the rendition 'for ... and' [see, for example, Romans 7:8f, 10:10, 11:15f]. Since there is no *a priori* rendition for this set of particles, the context must determine their proper meaning. One particular point of view toward Paul's theology will make vss. 5 and 6-8 antithetical; another will make them conjunctive." Howard then goes on to attempt to demonstrate how the passage neatly fits the conjunctive idea, much more so (in his opinion) than the antithetical.

Kasemann, *Romans*, p.284, notes that those theologians who prefer "goal" as a translation for *telos* in verse 4 will contest the view that there is a contrast between verse 5 and verses 6-8; on the other hand, those who opted for "end" are more likely to emphasize the contrast between the verses.

[34] It is sometimes objected that the interpretation offered in the notes, that verses 6ff *continue* the idea already begun in verses 4 and 5, which also involves an interpretation of Leviticus 18:5 as being a condition that could be fulfilled, is not in harmony with Paul's own use of the same Leviticus passage in Galatians 3:10-12. Surely, it is argued, Galatians treats "He who practices them shall live" as something impossible; therefore, ought we not read the same meaning into Paul's words here in Romans 10? (As noted in footnote #32, not a few writers on Romans present the possibility of Romans 10:5 "reversing" the real meaning of Leviticus 18:5. However, no commentator on Galatians [with the possible exception of F.F. Bruce, *The Epistle to the Galatians*, in The New International Greek New Testament Commentary series

this second proof text is unusual, but is probably an abbreviated way of saying, "Scripture

---

(Grand Rapids: Wm. B. Eerdmans Publishing Co., 1982), p.157-168] that this writer has studied even deals with the matter of the relationship of Galatians to Leviticus when they treat Galatians 3:12 as being something impossible.) If indeed, Galatians uses Leviticus 18:5 to prove that practicing the Law was something impossible, then we would be compelled to retreat, and admit that Romans 10:5 is in contrast to what is affirmed in 10:6ff.

One attempt to harmonize Galatians 3:12 and Romans 10:5 has been set forth rather succinctly by George E. Howard in "Christ the End of the Law: the Meaning of Romans 10:4-8," *Journal of Biblical Literature*, 88 (1969). He has proposed that the usual Protestant interpretation of this passage, namely, that the contrast in Galatians is between the *doing of man* and the *faith of man*, or between salvation by works on the one hand, and salvation by faith on the other, is based on a wrong understanding of the word "faith." He wrote (p.335), "Since the time of the Reformation, NT faith has been understood almost exclusively as man's faith in Christ. It has been recently argued, however, that the phrase *pistis christou*, which appears seven times in Paul (Rom.3:22, 26; Gal 2:16 (twice); 3:22; Eph. 3:12; and Phil. 3:9), refers to Christ's faith as opposed to man's faith in Him. The faith ... [which is the condition of justification] refers to the divine faithfulness to the promise given to Abraham that in him all the nations of the earth will be blessed ... The accepted premise of Paul's theology as it stands today is: *the faith of man vs. the works of man.* The reformulation of the premise in line with the new understanding will be: *the faith of Christ vs. the works of man.* ... Consequently, [Galatians 3:10-12] is not one which discusses the psychological differences between law and faith, but rather it explains God's plan to include the gentiles in the kingdom of God and thus to fulfill his promise to Abraham." Karl Barth, *Church Dogmatics* II:2 (Edinburgh: T&T Clark, 1957), p.245, and Cranfield, *Romans,* p.521,522, attempt the same interpretation for Romans 10:5. While it is possible, in some cases, that "faith of Christ" might refer to the faith Christ Himself exhibited, it would be difficult to show that when the word "faith" appears by itself (without the additional phrase "of Christ") it too means Christ's faithfulness, rather than man's faith in Christ. Furthermore, it is expecting too much to think that the average reader would automatically think of Christ's faithfulness when he reads "faith" in either Romans 10 or Galatians 3. It seems to us that this whole attempt to make it Christ's faithfulness is really unnecessary, since, in our opinion, it results from a faulty understanding of Paul's quotations of Leviticus, as though he understood Leviticus to offer an impossible condition for righteousness.

Let us take a closer look at Galatians 3 to see what Paul is saying, and what 3:12 especially means in its larger context. First, it seems proper to list a few of the given conclusions we work from. (1) Leviticus 18:5 is quoted in both Romans and Galatians with the same meaning. It will not do to say that in Romans it is given a "possible condition" emphasis, while in Galatians it is "impossible." One verse of Scripture (18:5) should not be expected to have two possible and at the same time contradictory meanings. If this were possible, the Bible would end up being nonsense. (2) Galatians and Romans were written within 6 months of each other (both from the third missionary journey, just before the offering was delivered to Jerusalem), so it will not do to say that Paul changed his theology between the writing of the two letters. Even were we to grant that Paul's doctrine was of human origin and subject to change and development (which we do not!), this close proximity would lead us to believe Paul used the Old Testament verse with the same meaning in both books. Even were we to grant that Galatians was written early (say, AD 45) and Romans later (say, AD 58), the matter of inspiration would preclude the verses being contradictory. (3) The Law of Moses was only temporarily added to the covenant given to Abraham (Galatians 3:15ff), and has been abrogated at Calvary. The New Covenant (Jeremiah 31:31ff; cf. Hebrews 8:8ff) that Christ died to ratify and inaugurate (Hebrews 9:15ff) is different from the Mosaic Covenant, or Law (Hebrews 8: 8,9). Since the Law has been canceled, no man has to obey it, either to become a Christian, or to stay a Christian. (4) "Faithfulness" has always been the condition on which God counts men as righteous. And that is faithfulness to the revelation from God that the man has, or has opportunity to know. (5) The topics in Romans and Galatians are slightly different. Romans 10 deals with requirements *Jewish* people must meet in order to right standing with God. Galatians 3 deals with what a *Gentile* who is already justified by faith is required to do to *continue* in right standing with God. (6) The usual Protestant explanation of these passages, with its dichotomy between "faith" and "works," has yielded a wrong idea of the Bible's teaching on what "faith" is. We have suggested using "faithfulness" as often as practicable to avoid this false notion.

says with reference to righteousness conditioned on faithfulness."[35]   Paul's usual method of documenting something from Scripture is to find a common term in the passages he quotes.[36]   "Faithfulness" (faith) to the revelation one has been granted is the current topic.

---

(7) It would appear that Leviticus 18:5, as spoken by Moses, held out an attainable condition. To Israel, he said, "Be faithful to the Mosaic Law, and you will live (eternal life)." The references to Leviticus 18 by Ezekiel (20:11,13,21) and Nehemiah (9:13,29) also clearly show that in their view there was nothing about the condition that was impracticable, nor was the promise unattainable. It is very doubtful Paul reverses this meaning, or misinterprets it.

Now, with these working conclusions in mind, let's examine Galatians 3:10-12. The context (Galatians 3:3) deals with what is demanded of Gentile converts to remain in right status with God. The Judaizers were demanding circumcision, food, days, etc. as found in the Mosaic Law. Paul says these rules are no longer binding! Verses 1-14 are part of the argument that, like Abraham, the Galatian Christians were justified by faith, not by law. Verse 8 says that the promise to Abraham (that in his Seed [Christ] all the nations [Jew and Gentile] would be blessed [have their sins forgiven]) never was limited by Law-keeping. Verse 9 shows that anyone who is faithful can be blessed with Abraham (the Gentile). Verse 10 shows that the Law pronounces a "curse" (not a blessing) on those who do not abide by all the things written in the Book of the Law. (Does this reflect the fact that the Judaizers no longer demanded compliance with *all* the ordinances and statutes in Moses, e.g., bloody sacrifices as sin offerings were no longer required since Christ had offered a once-for-all sacrifice for sin? Or does it reflect the same argument that Galatians 5:3 does, that the demands of the Judaizers will prove to be progressive? If Paul's readers accept the first requirement the Judaizers were demanding [i.e., circumcision, food, days, etc.], where would it lead? Why, soon the Judaizers would be demanding conformity to the whole Law, and freedom in Christ would be gone!) Verse 11 quotes Habakkuk 2:4 as predicting justification on the basis of faithfulness (and faithfulness is something that is not limited to Law-keepers). Verse 12 would then assert that faithfulness has never been defined by, or limited to, Law-keeping. Faithfulness is something anyone can do, whether he has the Law of Moses or not. Leviticus 18:5 is quoted to show that "Law" is limited to one group – the one which has such commands and statutes. "Faithfulness" and "Law-keeping" are not co-terminous ideas. Verse 13 shows that Christ has redeemed men from the curse of the Law (the curse for breaking it, pronounced in verse 10). That there was a "curse" for breaking "law" is something equally true for both Jew (with his Law) and Gentile (with his ordinances and rules given by God (Romans 1:32). Verse 14 says that now (since Christ redeemed us from the curse) the blessing of the Spirit promised to Abraham (verse 8) is available to all, to Jews and to Gentiles, too.

In this way, the Leviticus 18 passage is shown to be interpreted the same way by Paul both in Galatians and in Romans (and indeed is in harmony with Jesus' quote of it, Luke 10:28). Paul and Moses both treat the promise ("He who practices them shall live") as holding out a possible condition of righteousness, as long as the Law was valid. But with the coming of Christ, that way to life is now closed. Where the gospel has been heard, Law is no longer valid as a revelation to which one must be faithful; but "faithfulness" (to the revelation one has) is still a valid condition.

---

[35] In this way we would account for the unexpected way this second passage from Moses is introduced. (In the eyes of the historical-critical commentator, to personify the "righteousness based on faith" as though she were speaking, rather than attributing the quotation to Moses who actually wrote it, is a violation of the literal sense of Scripture. Some, like Kasemann, *Romans*, p.285-287, go on to build a whole rationale for the way the modern "exegete" handles Scripture, ignoring, where it seems right to them to do so, what the Scripture itself says, in deference to whatever their reconstruction of Scripture and history seems to require.) It is not necessary to suppose that Paul is simply using the words of Scripture by way of accommodation (as Sanday and Headlam, *Romans*, p.288,289, affirm). Nor is it necessary to suppose that Paul has interpreted the passage by rabbinical methods, whereby something other than the original meaning has been squeezed out (as Meyer, Bruce, and Batey suggest). Nor is it necessary to see in the passage in Deuteronomy a prophecy of the gospel (as George Mark Elliott taught). T.H. Horne, *Introduction to the Critical Study and Knowledge of the Scriptures*, 8th edition (Grand Rapids: Baker Book House, 1970), Vol.2, Part 1, p.344, answers this latter view.

---

[36] For example, see how he just used "live," which he found in Habakkuk 2:4 and Leviticus 18:5, as the common word that ties these two passages together.

He has already used Abraham as an example of justification by faith, but the Jew might argue that that was *before* the Law was given. So Paul must appeal to a passage in the Law or the book of the Law where "faithfulness" to that revelation is likewise expected. In addition to the verse just quoted (verse 5), where else in Moses can he find a text that would exclude such changes in the Mosaic religion as Judaism had presumed to make? The passage Paul quotes to show that God expected faithfulness to what He had revealed is Deuteronomy 30:12-14.

"DO NOT SAY IN YOUR HEART. Paul introduces the following quotations from Deuteronomy 30 by using the language of Deuteronomy 9:4. By using this introduction, he narrows the reference to Jewish (not other people's) behavior. To "say in your heart" is a Hebraism meaning to think to himself, to think secretly.

'WHO WILL ASCEND INTO HEAVEN?' These words from Deuteronomy 30:12, as originally spoken by Moses, were prefaced by this encouragement, "For this commandment which I command you today is not too difficult for you, nor is it out of reach." All they needed to do was be faithful to Moses' revelation. Instead of climbing up to heaven to try to discover God's will, they already had the revelation God expected them to observe (and it kept pointing them to Christ, Romans 10:4).

(That is, to bring Christ down). Three times, in verses 6-8, Paul uses this expression "that is" to interrupt his quotation of Deuteronomy 30, in order to introduce his Christological interpretation[37] of that Old Testament passage. Remember, Christ is the goal of the Law! The Jew who supposes he can be righteous before God while at the same time rejecting the Messiah who has become incarnate is hardly being faithful to the revelation he has in that Law.

10:7 – *or 'WHO WILL DESCEND INTO THE ABYSS?' (that is, to bring Christ up from the dead)."*

Or 'WHO WILL DESCEND INTO THE ABYSS?' Instead of quoting verbatim the text of Deuteronomy 30:13 (which talks of a futile voyage across the sea) Paul substitutes the language of Psalm 107:26, where the word "abyss" (depths) is found. "Abyss" is some-

---

[37] We must pause for a moment on the word "interpretation." Not a few commentaries speak of Paul's employing an old Jewish method of Bible exposition called *pesher* (= "interpretation"). By this, it is supposed, one can excuse Paul's forcing onto the Deuteronomy verses a meaning they never had – Paul was simply doing something any Jew would do as he explained Scripture, trying to make it relevant to his own day. After noting that one finds "that is, ..." (i.e., *pesher*) in the Qumran literature, Cranfield goes on to ask, "But what are we to make of Paul's treatment of Deut. 30:11ff as biblical interpretation? Is it merely arbitrary, like much of the exegesis of Qumran – a matter of forcing upon an OT passage a meaning essentially foreign to it? So it has certainly seemed to many. Even as sympathetic a commentator as Gaugler can speak of it as 'a specially crass example' of the typological method of interpretation." *Romans*, p.524. Nor is C.H. Dodd, *Epistle of Paul to the Romans* (New York: Harper and Brothers, 1932) to be followed when he suggests Paul is unfolding the greater "inwardness" of Deuteronomy 30:11ff.

Paul is simply reminding his readers that to properly understand the Old Testament, one must see it as pointing men to the coming Christ. To fail to see its connection to Christ is like trying to read the Old Testament blindfolded: the only way to remove the "veil" is to see Jesus in the Old Testament (2 Corinthians 3:14-18).

times used interchangeably for "sea" (as Genesis 1:2), but there are also times (as in Psalm 71:20) when "abyss" refers to a portion of the intermediate world and thus is related to "Sheol."[38]   It is this fact that allows Paul to interpret "abyss" Christologically.

(That is, to bring Christ up from the dead)." As in verse 6, "that is" introduces Paul's Christological application of the Deuteronomy passage.   To refuse to accept Jesus as the Messiah, as the unbelieving Jews were doing (an action that demonstrated a lack of faithfulness to the revelation given to them), was tantamount to acting as if Christ had never risen from the dead.[39]   It is the word order ("bring Christ down" followed by "bring Christ up") that leads us to believe that Paul here speaks of the two grand stages in the great work of redemption – the incarnation and the resurrection.[40]   Both were required in order that the "righteousness which is by faith" might effectively be brought "near" to us.

10:8 – *But what does it say?   "THE WORD IS NEAR YOU, IN YOUR MOUTH AND IN YOUR HEART" – that is, the word of faith which we are preaching,*

But what does it say?   By this question, which is not part of the Deuteronomy 30 passage, Paul asks the reader to give some thought to the passage.   What does it say in the very next verse following the ones just quoted?   Does it not talk about faithfulness to the revelation you have been given?

"THE WORD IS NEAR YOU, IN YOUR MOUTH AND IN YOUR HEART."   The "Word" that Moses was speaking about, namely, the Law of Moses, which was a revelation of the will of God, was easily accessible, so that a man could know what God expected and faithfully observe it.   The Jewish people were not free to change or alter it, but were commanded to speak it to others ("in your mouth") and memorize it ("in your heart").

That is, the word of faith which we are preaching.   Once more (cf. verses 6,7), Paul introduces his Christological application of the text from Deuteronomy.   The "faith which we are preaching" is nothing other than the gospel,[41] a more recent revelation of God's will than the Law.   "Word of faith" equals the message which emphasizes faithfulness as the

---

[38] "Abyss" is elsewhere used in the New Testament to denote the abode of the demons (Luke 8:31; Revelation 9:1), and seems to be pictured as the "depths" of Hades (which is the intermediate place of the wicked).   The abyss and Tartarus (2 Peter 2:4, Greek) seem to be two words for the same place.

[39] In the close juxtaposition of "abyss" and "rise from the dead," we likely have reference made to Christ's descent to Hades (between His death and resurrection) which is probably alluded to in Acts 2:27 and 1 Peter 3:19.

[40] Hebrews 13:20 is the only other place in the New Testament where "bring up" is used of the resurrection of Jesus.   Some have suggested that Paul has adopted the language of Psalm 71:20 to express the idea of Christ's departure from the abyss.   Remember, his style is to take single words or topics found in several passages, and show how they tie together to express the message of Scripture.

[41] The Greek reads "*the* faith," but the article is the article of previous reference.   Paul is talking about the same "faith" that he has been talking about in this whole context.   In fact, it would be profitable to compare the expression found in 3:27, "a law of faith."   (There are times in the New Testament when the expression "the faith" refers to the body of Christian doctrine, but that is not, it seems, the case here.)

condition on which God counts men as righteous (cf. 10:17).[42]   It can even be shown that the "word ... we are preaching" is "near you," since Christian preachers have been preaching it far and near to everyone.   The word "preaching" suggests the theme which is worked out more fully in verses 14-18.   But in the meantime, he will pause to detail some of the content of the preaching.

10:9 – *that if you confess with your mouth Jesus* as *Lord, and believe in your heart that God raised Him from the dead, you shall be saved;*

That if you confess with your mouth Jesus *as* **Lord.**   We prefer to translate *hoti*, with which this verse begins in the Greek, by the word "that," rather than "because."   This makes verse 9 specify the contents of the preaching.[43]   Two things 1st century gospel preachers emphasized were "belief" and "confession."[44]   "Confess" means to say the same thing, to speak that which agrees with something which others speak or maintain.[45]   Here it may mean to say the same thing about Jesus that God says, namely, "Jesus is Lord!"[46] Since the following context deals with how a man is initially justified by God, it seems likely that this "confession" is one made at the time of conversion,[47] a confession that con-

---

[42] The justification for Paul's identification of "the word" in Deuteronomy 30:14 with the gospel message, is the fact that the Word of the Law had Christ as its goal (Romans 10:4).   Again, there is a thematic connection between Deuteronomy and Paul's use of it, and Paul should not be accused again of importing something into Moses' words that Moses never intended.

[43] In technical language, this is a case of indirect discourse after the word "preach," and what follows "that" is an indirect quotation of the "word about faith" that the apostles have been preaching.   (To translate *hoti* as "because" would make verse 9 to be a reason for something just said.   What might that something be?)

[44] The order ("confess" and then "believe") found in verse 9 is such because of the passage just taken from Deuteronomy 30, which used this same order ("mouth" and then "heart").   In Romans 10:10, Paul will state the order as it actually is for the New Testament age.

[45] Thayer, *Lexicon*, p.446.

[46] In the Greek, both "Lord" and "Jesus" are in the accusative case, after "confess."   It is not unusual to have a double accusative after the verb "confess"; see John 9:22.   Compare also 2 Corinthians 4:5 and Philippians 2:11.

[47] Christians "confess" in multiple ways and at multiple times.   (a) There is a "confession" that the Christian makes, not only at the time of his baptism, but all the rest of his life.   (See 1 Corinthians 12:3 [where the confession was something Christians were doing]; Matthew 10:32 [where "[he] who shall confess Me" is a present tense verb, indicating continuing action]; and Philippians 2:11 [which seems to speak of Christian worship].)   (b) Lipscomb and Shepherd, *Romans*, p.190-91, urge that Romans 10:9 is not a reference to a formal confession of faith before baptism, but is rather a lifelong confession, and a continual believing, unto righteousness.   While it is true (as has been shown in notes on chapter 4) that God's reckoning of a man as righteous is not a one-time thing, but something that happens over and over again during the man's life on earth, it is also doubtful that 10:9 addresses this subject.   (c) The context and the aorist tense verb (a one-time act) meaning "confess" tend to support the idea that this is the confession made in order to become a candidate for baptism.   If this is the meaning, then this verse contains the earliest formal confession of faith (since Acts 8:37 does not enjoy integrity).   It appears to have been a practice in the apostolic age to have the candidate make a confession before he was immersed.   For example, 1 Timothy 6:12 suggests Timothy had made a public confession before his immersion into Christ.   And even though the manuscript evidence is against the integrity of Acts 8:37,

veys the content of what one has come to believe about Jesus.[48]

Much has been written in recent years about both the actual wording of the early Christian confessions, and the actual meaning intended in the words.[49]   Through the years, the formula has grown from "I believe Jesus is Lord" to "I believe Jesus is the Christ, the Son of the living God."   Both formulas are intended to convey the same belief about the historical Jesus – including His incarnation, death, bodily resurrection, and exaltation to supreme lordship and universal dominion.   To believe both in the resurrection (Romans 4:24) and that Jesus is now Lord[50] is no mere intellectual exercise.   It involves the shattering realization that God has miraculously entered into history and inaugurated the reign of Messiah over all the creation.   After such a realization, no man can ever be the same as he was before!   Surely no Jew could be giving heed to what Moses said about the Prophet (Deuteronomy 18:15) and at the same time continue to reject Jesus as the Messiah.

And believe in your heart that God raised Him from the dead. The construction translated "believe ..." has been used before in Romans 6:8, and in both these places it speaks of

---

there is evidence as early as Irenaeus' day, and as early as Cyprian, that these men were familiar with the variant reading of Acts 8:37. (I.e., as early as AD 200 or 250, some 100 years before our oldest uncials, here were church fathers who knew the reading now found in the Byzantine text.)

What is the value of such a public confession?   Confession is one way to tell if a man believes. Before we baptize him, we want evidence of the candidate's faith.   A confession is evidence of faith.   It is one way to know what the candidate is thinking and what his convictions are.   The confession by mouth is not in the same category as faith – in one sense.   A man might not be able to speak (he is "dumb" either from birth or disease or act of man), and that would not hinder his being baptized.   He could signal his confession another way.   However, if a man does not have faith (convictions as to who Jesus is, and that God has raised Him from the dead and exalted Him to His right hand – convictions that are accompanied by appropriate repentance), that would hinder his being eligible to be baptized.

[48] Though the content of the confession and the belief are stated in different terms in this verse, Paul does not mean to imply that the mouth confesses something other than what the heart believes.   Instead, the two "content" statements complement each other, and help define what is included in the "faith" that is the condition on which God reckons righteousness.

[49] Cranfield, *Romans*, p.528,529, has a delightful summary of the salient points.   The ascription of the title "Lord" to Jesus is not a Hellenistic addition to the early apostolic tradition, but was used in the Aramaic-speaking church before there were any Hellenistic Christians.   The use of "Lord" more than 6000 times in the LXX for the Tetragrammaton (Jehovah) is also a key point.   Paul applies Old Testament Jehovah passages to Jesus.   Philippians 2:10,11, where "Lord Jesus" is described as a "name above every name," attributes Deity to Jesus.   Prayers are offered to Jesus, and Jesus is associated with God the Father as being a source of all blessing.   He concludes with this paragraph, "We take it that, for Paul, the confession that Jesus is Lord meant the acknowledgment that Jesus shares the name and the nature, the holiness, the authority, power, majesty and eternity of the one and only true God."

[50] The content of "Lord," when applied to Jesus, has been indicated earlier at Romans 1:4; 4:24,25; 5:10,11; and 6:4,5,9,10.   A.T. Robertson, *Word Pictures in the New Testament* (Nashville, TN: Broadman Press, 1931), Vol. 4, p.389, writes, "No Jew would do this [make a confession that 'Jesus is Lord'] who had not really trusted Christ, for *kurios* is used in the LXX of God.   No Gentile would do it who had not ceased worshiping the emperor as *kurios*.   The word *kurios* was and is the touchstone of faith."

conviction; the content of what is believed is indicated by the "that" phrase.[51]   The "heart" here, as often, stands for the mind.   One thing that a prospect must believe in order to be eligible to become a Christian is that the resurrection of Jesus was an action performed by God.[52]   After all, the validity of Christianity stands or falls with the resurrection.   Because the resurrection proves His claims, the gospel (no longer is it the Law) is the present revelation from God which men are expected to believe and confess.

You shall be saved.   There is reason to believe that this verse refers to initial salvation (justification) rather than continuing or final salvation.[53]   The context has been dealing with the *practice* of righteousness (faithfulness to the revelation granted) being the condition on which God reckons a man "righteous."   This *practice* has a starting point. Both "believe" and "confess" in this verse are aorist tense verbs, likely signifying a single act.   This would be harmonious with the idea of being reckoned righteous initially, but not so easily made to fit the condition of continuing or final salvation.   "Confess with your mouth" and "believe in your heart" are not separated in this presentation, as though one without the other had any consequence as far as "salvation" is concerned.   Faithfulness, the condition which God looks for as He justifies men, would require *both* belief in the resurrection and confession of the deity of Jesus.

10:10 – *for with the heart man believes, resulting in righteousness, and with the mouth he confesses, resulting in salvation.*

For with the heart man believes.   It is difficult to find a satisfactory explanation of the point of verse 10, or its connection to the argument that precedes, in any of the commentaries.   It begins with "for," and thus is a reason for, or a further explanation of, something just said.   If we treat it as a reason for something just said, then verse 10 gives a reason why the apostles preach (verse 8) what they do (verse 9).   They preach what they do because this is part of the condition men must meet if they would be reckoned "righteous" by Him.   If we treat it as an explanation for something just said, Paul is explaining the actual order ('faith' first, then 'confession') in the Christian age.   Now that

---

[51] Leon Morris, *The Gospel According to John*, New International Commentary on the New Testament (Grand Rapids: Wm. B. Eerdmans Publishing Co., 1971), p.335-337, has a note showing that *pisteuō* followed by the dative case indicates simple, mental assent, credence (like Matthew 21:25, where "believes him" means "believe the man who was speaking"), whereas *pisteuō* followed by *eis* and the accusative indicates an obedient faith (like John 3:16, "believes in Him").   The construction here, *pisteuō* followed by a *hoti* clause, is slightly different from the former construction.   In this case, instead of believing the man, the emphasis is on believing *what* the man said (with the *hoti* clause specifying what it was that was said).

[52] See notes at Romans 4:24 on God raising Jesus from the dead, and what all is involved in this statement (including God's acceptance of Christ's sacrifice for sins).   Jesus, the historical Jesus, crucified under Pontius Pilate, was dead, buried, rose, and appeared.   There is more implied in the language "raised ... from the dead" than the mere reinhabitation (by the soul and spirit) and revivification of a dead body. He was designated as both Lord and Christ in a way that is unmistakable, and not only that, He is the "firstfruits of those who are asleep" (1 Corinthians 15:20).

[53] For "saved," see "salvation" in 1:16 and "saved" in 5:9,10.   "Saved" denotes the fact that the man has sinned, and needs the salvation offered in the gospel, which involves 'justification by faith.'

Messiah has come, belief in the heart of who Jesus is, and public confession of that belief, are inherent in the 'faithfulness' prerequisite to being reckoned as "righteous" by God.[54]

Resulting in righteousness. Literally, it reads "unto (*eis*) righteousness." "Unto" is telic, and denotes the end (or motion toward) for which a thing is done.[55] This commentator believes that "righteousness" and "salvation" (since verse 4 in this context) are merely two different terms for the same thing.[56] While it remains true that initial justification (and Israel's lack of it) is the main emphasis in these verses, it is also true that 'belief-confession' are necessary conditions to 'righteousness-salvation' at any stage along the way from initial justification to final glorification.[57]

---

[54] The verb tenses in verse 10 are present tense (whereas the verbs "believe" and "confess" in verse 9 were aorist tense). The present tense verbs evidently speak of something God expects continually, yea, has always expected, from a man, if that man would meet the conditions of salvation. This explanation appears to be more satisfactory than the one that suggests it is belief and confession all through life that is in Paul's mind (see footnote #47). It has even been proposed that the following verses are quotations from the Old Testament to show that belief and confession were something taught in the Old Testament. Verse 11 will quote an Old Testament passage concerning belief; verse 13 will quote one that speaks of confession, it is suggested.

[55] The same telic use of *eis* has already been observed at Romans 5:18 and 10:4. Care must be exercised here, for it is not implied that any appreciable time intervenes between compliance with the condition of obedient faith ('belief-confession') and the result (justification).

[56] In verse 9, Paul used the word "saved," and both "confess and believe" were linked to it. Now he uses both "righteousness" and "salvation" in verse 10, and while one is linked to "believes" and the other to "confesses," it is difficult to make any intelligible distinction between the terms "righteousness" and "salvation" to which they are linked.

Not all commentators agree that "righteousness" and "salvation" are interchangeable terms in this verse. In fact, a number have asserted that "righteousness" speaks of initial justification (becoming a Christian in this life), while "salvation" speaks of final salvation (glorification). It appears to this commentator that the ones who are forced to make such a distinction are the ones who have attempted to defend the thesis that justification is on the basis of faith alone (as distinct from obedient faith or faithfulness). If one is justified the moment he believes (mental assent), of course you could not also include a confession made *after* he believes as being part of the essential condition of justification. Note how this comes through clearly in Barmby's comment, "By faith alone we are justified; but by confession in actual life, which is the fruit of faith, our salvation is secured." *Romans*, p.294. Not only has Barmby contradicted himself (he wrote on verse 9 about a "living operative faith"), and not only has he missed the distinction between "belief in the heart" (meaning mental conviction) and "faithfulness" (the condition of justification), but he also is out of harmony with the usual Calvinist explanation (i.e., since the *Pulpit Commentary* is Anglican, one might expect it to follow Thirty Nine Articles of Faith which tend to be Calvinistic) of the security of the believer, for by his comment he makes the security of the believer conditional.

If Romans 10:9,10 were the only passage that speaks to the subject of 'faith' (the condition requisite for being declared righteous by God), we might interpret it as Barmby, Lenski, Alford, and others do. But since other passages deal with the subject, and since those passages show that the faith that saves is an obedient faith (i.e., something other than just belief in the heart), we find it difficult to agree with the interpretation given to the passage by the faith-only writers.

[57] Again, recall that in chapter 4 it has been shown that justification by faith is something that happens over and over through the Christian's life. The 'belief in the heart-confession with the mouth' condition is something God continually looks for as He would reckon men as "righteous." Compare Hebrews 4:14 and 10:23 for other examples of continual confession of one's beliefs in Jesus as a necessary condition of right status before God.

And with the mouth he confesses, resulting in salvation. "Salvation" (i.e., the forgiveness of sins) and "righteousness" (i.e., justification by faith) are here indicated to be interchangeable terms, and Paul, as is his custom, has linked them together in this passage because of their thematic agreement.[58] If a man would be saved (justified), what he must believe and what he must confess have been made plain in verse 9.

10:11 – *For the Scripture says, "WHOEVER BELIEVES IN HIM WILL NOT BE DISAPPOINTED."*

For the Scripture says. For the second time in just a few verses (see 9:33), Paul is going to quote Isaiah 28:16, perhaps with a slight shift in emphasis. Having demonstrated from the Old Testament itself that the Jewish people, if they were to have right standing with God, were *not* free to change or alter the Law God gave (their only option was to faithfully observe it, until it led them to Christ, its goal, 10:4), Paul will now demonstrate that such right standing is available to *anyone* who would meet the God-given conditions. Worded another way, Paul first took the word "believes" from the Isaiah passage and expounded its meaning. Now he will take "he who" from the Isaiah passage and emphasize its meaning. There is a universal element in "he who" that includes the *Jew* as well as the *Gentile!*

"WHOEVER BELIEVES IN HIM WILL NOT BE DISAPPOINTED." We are still in the paragraph where Paul is presenting the thesis that God's dealings with Israel in the present are in harmony with justification by faith.[59] Even though the invitation is extended to all, not all have responded to the invitation via belief in order to be counted as righteous. Paul supplies "whoever" at the beginning of the quotation, substituting it for "He who."[60] Israel's problem is not because God has arbitrarily excluded them. Israel's problem is that

---

[58] "But why does the apostle connect belief and justification together, and confession and salvation together? He cannot intend to imply that belief without confession will secure justification, nor that confession without belief will secure salvation. Neither is justification one thing to be secured by belief, and salvation a different thing to be secured by confession. No man can be justified and be unsaved, or be saved and be unjustified. I therefore can not think that the apostle meant anything special [by the different terms]. It is, I doubt not, a mere peculiarity of style, not of doctrine – a probable imitation of Hebrew parallelism." Lard, *Romans*, p.333.

[59] In harmony with what was given above in footnote #51, note that Paul's language changes from "believes in the heart" to "believes in Him." This shows that both "believe in the heart" and "confess with the mouth" are together encompassed in the more inclusive expression "believes in Him." Again, it is demonstrated that the faith that saves is an obedient faith.

[60] Instead of the article and a participle with which the phrase opens (see 9:33), Paul adds the adjective *pas* ("all", "every") to the construction, so that the Greek reads "everyone who believes." Our translators use "whoever" to convey the same idea. "It may be that, quoting from memory, he had forgotten that this word *pas* was not in the original; or he may have purposely added it in order to express more clearly what the original – in which there is no limitation on *ho pisteuōn* – really implied. The latter supposition is probable, inasmuch as (according to the best supported readings) he had previously (Romans 9:33) quoted the text without this addition. Further, he will follow out the idea of *pas* (everyone) by giving a reason for it (verse 12); and then, in verse 13, he adds a text from Joel in which *pas* does occur, so as to intimate that the 'calling on the name of the Lord,' spoken of by Joel, implies the 'believing' spoken of by Isaiah, and hence the two texts must be equally universal in their application." Barmby, *Romans*, p.294. In any case, we may affirm that *pas* is here in this verse because the Holy Spirit wanted it here.

by their own unbelief they have stumbled over the Stone of stumbling,[61] and so excluded themselves.

10:12 – *For there is no distinction between Jew and Greek; for the same* **Lord** *is Lord of all, abounding in riches for all who call upon Him;*

For there is no distinction between Jew and Greek. Verse 12 appears to be an explanation of the word "whoever" in the previous clause.[62] "No distinction" says that when it comes to the condition that men must meet to be reckoned as righteous, there is just one, and it applies to all men equally.[63] Just as 3:22 has said there is "no distinction," so here again Paul reverts to the same idea. "Jew and Greek" is a religious designation for the whole world (see notes at 1:16), and does not differ from "Jews ... Gentiles" found in 3:29.[64]

For the same *Lord* **is Lord of all.** "For" introduces a reason why there is no distinction; this is why there is a universality to it. Here, it is not easy to tell whether "Lord" is a reference to the Father or to the Son. In 3:29, a similar expression meant that God is God of the Gentiles as well as God of the Jews. Perhaps the topic is God's reckoning men righteous, and this phrase says God does it just one way for all men, since He is Lord of all men. Or, perhaps the topic is faith in Jesus, and this phrase says that faith in Jesus is the condition of justification for all men, since He is Lord of all (compare verse 9).[65]

Abounding in riches for all who call upon Him. "Riches" here equals " abounding in spiritual wealth."[66] In Ephesians 3:8 we read of Christ's riches. No matter who (it may be Jew or Gentile) calls on Him for salvation, He lavishes His riches on that person. The

---

[61] The context helps us decide that Paul meant "Jesus" when he wrote this verse about "believing in Him," and for this reason the NASB capitalizes "Him."

[62] Four verses in a row, 10-13, begin with "for," and each gives a reason for, or an explanation of, something said in its predecessor.

[63] "Here, in verse 12, the apostle comments on the text from Isaiah, so as to show the universality of its application. It is (he would say) in itself applicable to Jew and Gentile alike; and it must needs be so, since the one God is the same to all that call upon Him, even as the Prophet Joel also testified (see the next verse). The thought thus expressed was one deeply fixed in Paul's mind. He elsewhere speaks of the very unity of God as implying the necessity that He is the same alike to Jews and Gentiles (see notes at Romans 3:29)." Barmby, *Romans*, p.294.

[64] Notes have been given at 2:17 on the meanings of "Jew" and "Israel," and how the terms came to be used interchangeably by New Testament times. In this context, it would be difficult to make a meaningful distinction between "Israel" in 9:31 and "Jew" in 10:12.

[65] Jesus is elsewhere in the New Testament designated as the Lord of all. See Acts 10:36; Romans 14:9; Ephesians 4:5; and Philippians 2:9-11.

[66] "In 11:33 and Philippians 4:19, Paul speaks of God's riches absolutely. Elsewhere we read of the riches of God's kindness, longsuffering, glory, etc., (e.g., 2:4; 9:23; Ephesians 2:7), and of God's being rich in mercy (Ephesians 2:4)." Cranfield, *Romans*, p.531.

emphasis has shifted slightly from the universal provision for justification to the lavish generosity of the Provider, but there is still a universal quality to the generosity.[67] It is "for all who call upon Him." "Call upon Him" will be explained in detail in the following verses. Here it has to do with becoming a Christian, a faithful follower of Jesus, the One who is Lord of all.[68]

10:13 – *for* **"WHOEVER WILL CALL UPON THE NAME OF THE LORD WILL BE SAVED."**

For **"WHOEVER WILL CALL UPON THE NAME OF THE LORD WILL BE SAVED."** Paul undergirds his argument that there is no distinction, that the way to right standing with God is open for all, by quoting the well-known passage found in Joel 2:32.[69] The same passage was quoted by Peter on the day of Pentecost, as he held out the offer of salvation in Christ for all who call upon the name of the Lord. Peter also quotes the preceding verses in Joel which show that this offer is good during the "last days," i.e., between Pentecost and the great and glorious day of the Lord. Paul's emphasis on "whoever" does not differ in meaning from the words "all flesh" found in Joel 2:28. "Whoever" and "all flesh" show that *Israelites* as well as *Gentiles* are included; there is no distinction. The risen Lord has been given universal dominion, and He has riches (enough and to spare) for any who appeal to Him for salvation.[70]

How carefully Paul has shown to the Jew that the way to right status with God is faithfulness to the revelation one has been granted. All these Old Testament quotations are intended to show the Jew that Jesus is the goal of the Law for righteousness to everyone who believes. In essence, this passage in chapter 10 is an appeal to Israel to abandon the way of their own devising (10:3) and embrace the Messiah to whom their Law and Prophets pointed. After all, if it is a way open to every man, it is surely open to them.

---

[67] Observe how often the word "all" is repeated in verses 11-13.

[68] It is instructive to run the references where "calling on the name of the Lord" occurs in Scripture. Sometimes "call upon the Lord" has reference to prayer (Acts 7:59). Sometimes it has reference to worship (1 Corinthians 1:2; 2 Timothy 2:22). Sometimes it speaks of becoming a Christian (as here and in Acts 2:21). In at least one place, it seems to be a designation for "Christians" (Acts 9:14,21). In Acts 22:16, it is difficult to tell if the phrase is a reference to prayer or to initial salvation. (If the latter, then the passage, as the immediately preceding words show, includes "baptism" in the expression "calling on the name of the Lord.") "In Scripture, 'calling upon God' is always a habit, not a single act. Cp. Genesis 4:26; Zechariah 13:9; Acts 2:21, 9:14; 1 Corinthians 1:2; 2 Timothy 2:22; 1 Peter 1:17." Vine, *Romans*, p. 157. "From the habit of beginning addresses to a deity by mentioning his name, it became a technical expression for the suppliant to a god, and a designation of his worshipers. Hence the Israelites were 'those who call upon the Lord' or 'the name of the Lord.' They were in fact specially distinguished as the worshipers of Jehovah. It becomes therefore very significant when we find just this expression used of the Christians as the worshipers of Christ (the Lord)." Sanday and Headlam, *Romans*, p.291.

[69] Here is another instance in the New Testament where an Old Testament 'Jehovah-passage' is applied to Jesus. In the passage in Joel, "the Lord" is God the Father. In the New Testament, the passage is applied to Christ as the Lord on whom men call for salvation. This interchangeable use of Old Testament verses for God or Jesus is a clear testimony to the Deity of Jesus.

[70] "Shall be saved" has been explained at 10:9.

10:14 – *How then shall they call upon Him in whom they have not believed? And how shall they believe in Him whom they have not heard? And how shall they hear without a preacher?*

How then shall they call upon Him in whom they have not believed? How can Israel become believers in the Messiah, so they will call upon Him for salvation? They will have to obey the gospel that, since Pentecost and the conversion of Cornelius, the heaven-sent messengers have been preaching. With a series of four questions, Paul turns from the "whoever" aspect of faith to the means by which any man may become a believer.[71] Each of the four questions assumes that the opportunity to hear and obey is something open for everyone, Gentile and Jew alike.[72] Justification by faith is the basis of God's dealings with Israelites and Gentiles in this present age. He is treating them all alike.

And how shall they believe in Him whom they have not heard? These four questions imply that there is a distinct order to the conditions antecedent to calling on the name of the Lord.[73] Preaching, hearing, believing, and calling are the steps specified in this series

---

[71] One difficulty in these verses is to know where to make a paragraph break. The NASB starts a new one with verse 16. Some start a new one with verse 11, making verses 11-21 a proof of the extension of the gospel to the Gentiles. Many commentaries start a new paragraph with verse 14. The problem of outline has been discussed in footnote #97 on chapter 9, and footnote #27 on chapter 10. The *oun* ("therefore") construction here is not quite the same as at 9:14 or 9:16 or 9:30, so we do not make a major paragraph break here. At the same time, it likely is true that the decision on the question of outline depends on the opinion the commentator has formed about the line of argument in the whole passage. Those commentators who have explained chapter 9 as being predestination by God to salvation or damnation are wont to emphasize in this paragraph in chapter 10 that Paul is giving further proof that the fault of Israel's exclusion from salvation lies in themselves – thus excusing God's predestination as being the real cause of some men's damnation. More will be said on this in Special Study #8 at the close of chapter 11, where the thesis that Romans 9 talks about predestination to *service* rather than salvation will be expounded (in the light of chapters 10 and 11).

[72] Another difficulty an expositor faces, as he comments on verses 14-21, is to attempt to explain the object for which Paul quotes the string of passages from the Old Testament. James W. Aageson, "Scripture and Structure in the Development of the Argument in Romans 9-11," *Catholic Biblical Quarterly*, 48 (1986), p.265-289, has made a recent attempt to show the connection and object of these Old Testament quotations. Sanday and Headlam summarized the prevailing opinions in their time (*Romans*, p.294,295). (1) Calvin saw the object as being to justify the preaching of the gospel to the Gentiles. "God must have intended His gospel to be preached to the Gentiles, for a duly commissioned ministry [and Paul is thinking of himself] has been sent out to preach it." (2) The Roman Catholic view is that the words are introduced in order to justify an apostolic or authorized ministry. However, it is difficult to harmonize the fact that God commissioned the early gospel preachers with the Catholic idea that the hierarchy has the authority to commission preachers today. It is true that the verses speak of messengers who have been "sent" (*apostellō*). But the context indicates that it is not the church but the Lord who has sent the missionaries. (3) Chrysostom saw the object as being to prove that Israel could not plead, in defense, a lack of opportunity or warning, for the gospel had been fully and universally preached (verses 14-18), and Israel had been warned beforehand by Isaiah that they would reject God's message (verses 19-21). Grubbs, *Romans*, p.135, calls the passage an "Erotetic Sorites (a question chain) exhibiting the [fact that the] antecedent condition of calling upon the Lord for salvation [has been fulfilled]." The Jews, it has been shown, have neglected God's method of obtaining righteousness; and they did it out of ignorance (verse 3). That ignorance was culpable, for they had every opportunity of knowing. All the conditions necessary for "call[ing] upon the name of the Lord" have been fulfilled.

[73] To add to a topic which was considered during the study of chapter 6, it is all the more evident that admittance to a right standing with God (after a person has personally sinned and come short of the glory of God) is something intended for believing, consenting *adults*. Romans 10, which speaks of hearing and

of questions.[74]   Each question in this four-question chain is an argument, the conclusion of which is tacitly assumed, and the assumed conclusion then becomes the ground for the next question.   To believe, it is necessary to have something to believe, and this implies the necessity of hearing Christ speak through his gospel messengers.[75]

And how shall they hear without a preacher?   If people are going to hear the voice of Christ, someone is going to have to preach in His behalf.   "Preacher" is a translation of the word meaning "herald."   A herald acted as a public announcer, delivering some message from a king.   He simply heralded the message he was sent to deliver, adding nothing, subtracting nothing, altering nothing.   If the herald had made any change, it no longer would have been the voice of the king or the message from the king.[76]   This is another of the conditions that has been fulfilled by the time Paul writes to the Romans.   Israel and Gentiles both have heard gospel sermons.

10:15 – *And how shall they preach unless they are sent?   Just as it is written, "HOW BEAUTIFUL ARE THE FEET OF THOSE WHO BRING GLAD TIDINGS OF GOOD THINGS!"*

And how shall they preach unless they are sent?   As has been indicated earlier, the One who commissioned the preachers to go preach is no less than Deity Himself.   Whether it is the Father, or the Lord Jesus Christ, or the Holy Spirit who has actually sent the preachers, likely depends on which "heralds" one has in mind at the moment.[77]   Lest this

---

believing and confessing with the mouth, certainly excludes infants from any need to be initiated into church membership.   It would seem, instead, that until each person commits his own first act of sin, he has a right relationship with his Creator.   It is only after he sins that he needs justification by faith in order to have again a right standing with God.

[74] That several steps (in the process of attaining a right standing with God) are here specified causes us to pause and reflect what other steps have been specified.   Worded another way, since a man is justified by 'faith,' it must be that the 'faith' involved is inherently capable of having all these antecedent steps as component parts or constituent elements.   What has been set forth in Romans as being included in these steps of salvation, or in the 'faith' that saves?   It has been popular in the Restoration Movement to express the steps with a "five-finger exercise" mnemonic device.   They are: (1) hear, (2) believe, (3) repent, (4) make the good confession, (5) be immersed.   As to (1), it is taught in 10:14,17.   As to (2), belief in the heart was specified in 10:9,10.   Step (3), it will be recalled, in Romans 2:4 was made one of the preconditions to salvation.   As to (4), confession with the mouth was included in 10:9,10.   That (5) is involved was made abundantly clear in 6:1-11.   Thus, the five-finger exercise is a convenient way of summarizing and remembering what several passages in Romans have taught.

[75] The verb *akouō* ("hear") followed by the genitive case ("whom") means to "hear Him" rather than to "hear about Him."   There is a sense in which Christ Himself is speaking as His messengers preach.

[76] There is still truth in this for the 21st century.   Men who are heralds for Christ allow Christ to speak through them to others only when His word is transmitted exactly as He gave it to the heralds.

[77] For example, it was the Holy Spirit who said to the church at Antioch, "Set apart for Me Barnabas and Saul for the work to which I have called them" (Acts 13:2).   Yet it was Jesus Himself who gave Paul his call on the Damascus Road (Acts 26:16-18).   On the other hand, the evangelist Timothy was "ordained" by the elders of the congregation in which he grew up (1 Timothy 4:14).

One thing these notes (about who commissions the preachers) have tried to avoid is the idea of apo-

point be missed, note that if the One who sent the preachers is Christ, and if the preacher has heralded the exact "word of Christ" given him to dispense, then the person who rejects what the preacher says is really rejecting Christ Himself (cp. Luke 10:16).

Just as it is written. A portion of Isaiah 52:7 is about to be quoted, and the purpose of the quotation is to show that conditions one and two ("preachers" have been "sent") have been fulfilled. Isaiah 52 is recognized as having reference to the Messianic Age, even in rabbinic literature. This is an important link in Paul's presentation; he is saying that this Messianic prediction has already been fulfilled in the preaching done by 1st century apostles and prophets. They were the duly authorized messengers and their message was authentic.

"HOW BEAUTIFUL ARE THE FEET OF THOSE WHO BRING GLAD TIDINGS OF GOOD THINGS!"[78] In their original context, these words were spoken about the runners who were carrying the news home to Jerusalem from Babylon that the days of exile were past and restoration was at hand. In the New Testament, this whole section of Isaiah (i.e., chapters 40-66, from which this passage is taken) is interpreted of the Messianic Age. The "Suffering Servant Poems" are uniformly applied to Jesus by the apostles. The deliverance from Babylon under Cyrus, like the deliverance from Egypt in the days of Moses, is treated as foreshadowing the greater and perfect deliverance wrought by the Servant, Jesus. "How beautiful are the feet" means simply "how welcome is their coming!"[79]

10:16 – *However, they did not all heed the glad tidings; for Isaiah says, "LORD, WHO HAS BELIEVED OUR REPORT?"*

However, they did not all heed the glad tidings. Israel did not "obey" the glad tidings.[80] This is the reason many in Paul's time are not in right standing with God![81]   There were

---

stolic succession, as though a line of ordination services, that can be traced back to Jesus, is the only true authorization a man has to preach or 'administer the sacraments,' as some churches teach it. Another thing avoided is the idea that a secret, Divine call to preach is necessary in this age. See Special Study #1 about "call to the ministry" at the close of chapter 1.

[78] The KJV adds some words, "preach the gospel of peace," not included in the more recent versions. The words are omitted from the older manuscripts of Romans, and should not be included in the text. The whole of the passage found in Isaiah is not quoted by Paul – just the words that are pertinent to his argument – and the words he uses are taken from neither the Hebrew nor the LXX, but are freely rendered.

[79] Other explanations for "beautiful" have been proposed. Lard, *Romans*, p.338, urges the word should be translated "timely," as though the messengers had come at just the appropriate time. "Feet" are mentioned, Lard thinks, because the primitive preachers traveled mostly on foot. Cranfield, *Romans*, p.535, suggests that the joyfulness of the tidings the messengers bore was indicated by their "eager and buoyant walk."

[80] The verb translated "[give] heed" is *hupakouō*, a word regularly translated "obey." Thayer, *Lexicon*, p.638. It is the same word (only in noun form) encountered at Romans 1:5, where we read about the "*obedience* of faith."

[81] These comments follow what seems to this commentator to be the better of two possible explanations of verse 16. The other is that verse 16a is Paul's statement of a possible objection to his argument, and verse 16b is the answer to this objection. The objection would be, "But not everyone has heard; therefore,

four links in the chain covering the gap between God's offer of salvation and man's appropriation of it – one sent, preaching, hearing, and believing in Him. It is at the fourth link that many of the Jews broke the chain. They did not obey; they did not submit (see 10:3).[82] "Glad tidings" is *euangelion*, the word often translated "gospel." In Paul's application of Isaiah's prediction, Isaiah's "glad tidings" of the end of the exile becomes a prediction of the gospel news of redemption in Christ.

For Isaiah says. The text about to be quoted is Isaiah 53:1, the same passage John alludes to (John 12:38) to account for the people's failure to believe in Jesus as the Messiah during His ministry in Jerusalem. Israel's failure to obey Jesus (verse 16a) had been foretold by the prophet Isaiah.

"LORD, WHO HAS BELIEVED OUR REPORT?" Isaiah, in the midst of the best known of the Suffering Servant Poems, "complains that his declarations respecting the Messiah had been rejected by his countrymen. The form of expression, 'Who hath believed?' is a mode of saying emphatically that few or none had done it. The great mass of his countrymen had rejected it."[83] Notice how "believed" in this passage corresponds to "obeyed" ("heed") in the previous clause. Again, it demonstrates that saving faith is an obedient faith. God's part in salvation was done; the real problem was Israel's refusal to obey (2 Thessalonians 1:8) the gospel message.[84]

10:17 – *So faith* **comes** *from hearing, and hearing by the word of Christ.*

So faith *comes* **from hearing.** Verse 17 is probably best understood as being an explanatory statement, or a brief summary, lest we miss the thought Paul has been trying to convey by the quotations from the Old Testament.[85] It will be useful to observe that "hearing" in this verse and "report" in the previous verse are the same words in the Greek.

---

it appears, your argument that the messengers have been divinely commissioned is false!" The answer would be, "Yes, the messengers were divinely commissioned. The real problem is as Isaiah predicted – a deliberate rejection of the message." Cranfield, *Romans*, p.536, notes that to indicate the introduction of a possible objection by the use of the Greek word *alla* ("however") would be very uncharacteristic of Paul.

[82] "Not all" is perhaps a deliberate understatement. A few did obey (11:1-5), but the great majority of Israel had refused the gospel.

[83] Barnes, *Romans*, p.237.

[84] The Greek translated "report" means, literally, "our hearing." Thus it comes to mean the message preached, for that was what the people heard as the prophet spoke.

[85] Commentators have offered various proposals in an effort to trace the line of Paul's argument through these verses. Verse 17 begins with *ara*, a Greek word usually used to indicate a conclusion from something just said. Some (e.g., Barrett, *Romans*, p.205) are not happy with Paul's arrangement, and suppose verse 17 should follow immediately after verses 14-15a. Some (e.g., Bultmann) are confident there is a problem with the text here, and that Paul did not write as we now have it. Still others will take the text as we have it (since there is no evidence in the manuscripts of a textual variation with regards to verse 17), and try to explain its appropriateness right where Paul put it. With this latter approach, this commentator heartily agrees.

If there is going to be faith, there must be something "heard," a message to believe. Such a message has been delivered, the next phrase will affirm. So, if the majority of the Jews were unbelievers, the fault is their failure to believe, not that there has been a lack of message or messengers to deliver it.[86]

And hearing by the word of Christ.[87] The message men are to hear and believe is the gospel, first delivered by Christ, then propagated by His heralds. We have had the word "herald" before (verse 14, "preacher"), delivering the message another commissions one to deliver. Here we are told that it is Christ's own message that is shared by the preachers.[88] The "word of Christ" is another way of saying what was said in verse 8, "the word of faith which we are preaching." The gospel has been preached; the prerequisites to being the kind of believer that God counts as just have been clearly set forth. If any Israelites are outside the pale of right standing with God, the fault is theirs; they withheld belief; they refused to submit; they would not obey. After all, the gospel went to the Jews first!

10:18 – *But I say, surely they have never heard, have they? Indeed they have; "THEIR VOICE HAS GONE OUT INTO ALL THE EARTH, AND THEIR WORDS TO THE ENDS OF THE WORLD."*

But I say. Both verses 18 and 19 begin with this phrase. In each case, it introduces a possible argument that might be advanced to excuse Israel's unbelief. Remember, step three ("hearing") has been passed over in the previous verses (wherein it is being demonstrated that the prerequisites needed in order to be able to call upon the Lord have been fulfilled). Paul has affirmed that Israel's failure was at step four; now, in case someone would object that the failure was really at step three, Paul deals with that.[89]

"Surely they have never heard, have they?" The question expects an affirmative answer, "Yes, that's it! They have never heard."[90] Had the Jews not heard the gospel, this would have been the real reason for their unbelief.

---

[86] What is here affirmed, about the way "faith" comes to a man, surely is not compatible with the Calvinist doctrine that saving faith is a "gift" that somehow is supernaturally implanted in a man's heart if he is one of the elect. (Ephesians 2:8, a verse sometimes used to prove that faith is indeed such a gift, does not support the doctrine it is alleged to prove. "Faith" is a feminine noun; the "it" in the phrase "it is the gift of God" is neuter; so it is not "faith" that is the gift Paul has in mind. The marginal note is correct in the NASB; it explains that "saved" is the thing that is the gift of God. Nor should 1 Corinthians 12:9 be appealed to in order to prove that the faith which is the condition of being justified is a gift from God, for 12:9 speaks of one of the *charismata* [supernatural gifts] given to people after they are saved.)

[87] Some manuscripts read "word of God," but the better reading is "word of Christ."

[88] Some writers think "word of Christ" means "word about Christ" (cp. NASB margin), rather than the word Christ authorized to be preached. Either way, the reference is ultimately to what we call the "gospel."

[89] There is something basically wrong with any supposition that the fault is to be found in step three. Since faith comes by hearing, a failure at step three would imply that the responsibility for Israel's unbelief rested either on those who were sent to herald the message, or on the One who sent them, for failing to see that they got to Israel.

[90] The word "heard" is *akouō* as in verse 14; not *hupakouō* ("obey," "heed") as in verse 16.

Indeed they have: In the Greek, Paul uses the same emphatic corrective translated "on the contrary" at 9:20.   The Jew cannot plead that the gospel has never been preached in his hearing.   It had been preached to the Jew, and to much of the Gentile world, by the time Paul wrote this letter to the Romans.   Paul will state this fact in some words taken from Psalm 19.

"THEIR VOICE HAS GONE OUT INTO ALL THE EARTH, AND THEIR WORDS TO THE ENDS OF THE WORLD."   Without any note that he is quoting Psalm 19:4, Paul uses words originally written about the heavenly bodies to convey the idea that the gospel had been "heard" throughout the Greco-Roman world.[91]   Jesus had indicated that before the destruction of Jerusalem occurred (i.e., AD 70), the gospel would have been preached to the whole inhabited world (Matthew 24:14).   Likewise, Colossians 1:5-23, written about AD 63, affirm that the whole world has heard.[92]   Now, it is true that Paul is planning a missionary trip to Spain (Romans 15:24,28), which indicates that the Gospel has not been widely proclaimed in that nation.   So, we should not press the words of the Psalm with literal exactness.   Still, it can be affirmed that when the gospel has been quite widely preached to Gentiles, a man would be hard pressed to substantiate the proposition that there were places in the Diaspora where the gospel had not also been heard by the Jewish people who lived there.   Paul's contention stands: The Jews have heard.

10:19 – *But I say, surely Israel did not know, did they?   At the first Moses says, "I WILL MAKE YOU JEALOUS BY THAT WHICH IS NOT A NATION, BY A NATION WITHOUT UNDERSTANDING WILL I ANGER YOU."*

But I say.   As in verse 18, this expression introduces a second possible way to escape the notion that the Jews are responsible for their own unbelief.   Paul is still showing that step three ('hearing,' see verses 14 and 17) in the prerequisites to an obedient faith is not where the fault lies.

Surely Israel did not know, did they?   This question, too, like the one in verse 18, expects an affirmative answer.   "Yes, that's it!   Israel heard, but they didn't understand the message!"[93]   Without using the strong corrective ("on the contrary") this time, Paul will

---

[91] Psalm 19 deals with God's revelation in "the heavens" (verses 1-6) and in His word (verses 7-11). Paul borrows poetic language from the Psalm to describe how the "sound" of the preachers of the gospel has "gone out into all the world," just like the rays of the sun or the beauty of the constellations are seen all over the inhabited world.   ("'Their sound' follows the LXX as against the Hebrew 'their line'; possibly the LXX translators read *qolam* ('their voice') in the Hebrew copy before them instead of *qawwam* ('their line')." Bruce, *Romans*, p.209.)

Commentators are divided regarding Paul's use of Psalm 19.   (1) Some think Psalm 19 is an Old Testament prediction (or, if not a prediction, at least a type or symbol) of the gospel's worldwide spread. (2) Others suppose Paul simply uses the language by way of accommodation (since there is no formal introduction of this Old Testament passage).   I.e., he uses the words of Psalm 19 to express the idea he is asserting, that the gospel had been preached widely enough that the Jews have had opportunity to hear.

[92] In Romans 10:18, Paul uses the word *oikoumenē* for "world."   It denotes the "inhabited earth," or more particularly, the Roman Empire, which ruled the whole Mediterranean world in the 1st century.

[93] Paul has not forgotten what he wrote about Israel "not knowing" in 10:3.   The word translated "know"

use Old Testament Scriptures to answer this possible objection, too. 'No,' says Paul, 'it was not that the message was too difficult to understand. They understood well enough. Their real problem was that they just refused to obey.' Their failure was at step four, not at step three. "Israel" is introduced into the text in a rather emphatic way, and for the first time since 9:31. He did use the word "Jew" at verse 12, so the change may be meaningful.[94] "The real reason for the introduction of the word 'Israel' is that it gives an answer to the question, and shows the untenable character of the excuse. Has Israel, Israel with its long line of prophets and its religious privileges and its Divine teaching, acted in ignorance? When once 'Israel' has been used, there can be no doubt of the answer!"[95]

At the first Moses says. By quoting three Old Testament prophecies, Paul shows that there was no reason why Israel should have failed to understand the message. The first passage is taken from the Song of Moses (Deuteronomy 32:21), and follows the LXX.[96] In order of time, and in the order the books are located in the canon, Moses stands "first."[97]

"I WILL MAKE YOU JEALOUS BY THAT WHICH IS NOT A NATION, BY A NATION WITHOUT UNDERSTANDING WILL I ANGER YOU." The general

---

here is the verb *ginōskō*, and both Thayer and Arndt-Gingrich give "understand" as a possible meaning for the word. Thayer (*Lexicon*, p.117) lists the word under "to learn to know, come to know, get a knowledge of," and adds in this instance the object that is known must be determined from the context. From the context, what was it that Israel did not "know"? (1) Was it the universality of the gospel (that it was for Gentiles, too) that they did not know? The quotations following, from Moses and Isaiah, are taken to mean that they certainly should have known it, for it was predicted in the Old Testament. (2) Was it the "word of Christ" (the message that is to be believed) that Israel did not know? The quotations from the Old Testament are then interpreted to mean that there is no reason they should have failed to know.

Neither of these attempts at supplying the understood object from the context is quite as satisfactory as the results produced by translating *ginōskō* as "understand." "The Greek mind requires statement of the objects of verbs even less than does the English. Yet the Greek omission of the object also means that there is stress on the verbs, and not on the objects. Was there not *hearing*? Was there not *understanding*?" Lenski, *Romans*, p.672.

[94] Some have tried to maintain that the Bible (in New Testament times, even) makes a clear distinction between "Jews" and "Israel." The 20th century Identity Movement, for example, maintains the thesis that Anglo-Saxons are the "Israel" of the Bible (and the people of God), whereas "Jews" always designates those enemies of God who "lie when they claim they are Jews" (Revelation 3:9). That something is amiss in all of this is seen when the Identity Movement also affirms that the gospel is only for Israel, and not for Gentiles or Jews. Such a theory is hardly compatible with Romans 10.

[95] Sanday and Headlam, *Romans*, p.299.

[96] C.F. Keil, *Biblical Commentary on the Old Testament*, Vol.3 on the Pentateuch (Grand Rapids: Wm. B. Eerdmans Publishing Co., 1949), p.465, has analyzed this Song of Moses, and has answered the critics who deny its Mosaic authorship and date, and place it in the time of the kings by some unknown writer.

In his Song, Moses is reminding the Israelites that God was provoked when they worshiped idols ("no-gods," Hebrew, *lo'-'el*), and so rebuked them by calling the "no-people" (Hebrew, *lo'-'am*) to receive the blessing He had earlier granted to Jacob. We are reminded of Luke 20:15,16, where God takes away the vineyard from the wicked vine dressers, and gives it to others who bring forth fruits worthy of repentance.

[97] Cranfield, *Romans*, p.538, notes that Richard Bently has proposed a different punctuation for these verses, so that it reads "Did not Israel know first?" That is, was Israel not the first of all the nations to get the gospel? While this is true, it is doubtful that it is the point of the passage, for it is difficult to connect such a question to the passages quoted from Moses and Isaiah.

idea of the passage is that if "foolish" Gentiles could understand the message, then surely "wise" Israel could.[98]   No, the problem was not with step three, i.e., with understanding. Israel's problem was at step four (see verse 14, and 16):   it was willful unbelief, a stubborn refusal to obey.   The reason for the "jealousy"[99] was that someone else (the no-nation) was getting God's blessing.   The Jews were "angered" by the fact that the no-people (the Gentiles[100]) were accepted without having to be like the Jews.[101]

10:20 – *And Isaiah is very bold and says, "I WAS FOUND BY THOSE WHO SOUGHT ME NOT, I BECAME MANIFEST TO THOSE WHO DID NOT ASK FOR ME."*

And Isaiah is very bold and says.   Isaiah is introduced as a second witness to the fact that Israel has understood what they heard (verse 19).   But how shall we understand "very bold"?   Does it tell us what Isaiah was feeling as he delivered this prophecy (that he knew he was risking his life to do it)?   Or does it tell us the content of his message is even more astonishing than that of Moses (just quoted)?   Verses 20 and 21 are from Isaiah 65:1,2. Paul applies verse 1 (quoted here in 10:20) to the Gentiles, who, after long centuries of living without a written revelation and not particularly pursuing righteousness (9:30), have nevertheless turned to God.   God is represented as saying about the Gentiles, "I was found by them who sought Me not."   Then He applies verse 2 (quoted in 10:21) to Israel.   God is represented as saying about Israel, "You are a disobedient and obstinate people."

"I WAS FOUND BY THOSE WHO SOUGHT ME NOT, I BECAME MANIFEST TO THOSE WHO DID NOT ASK FOR ME."   After the manner of the Old Testament prophetic utterances, Isaiah speaks of future things as though they had already taken place. This passage from Isaiah 65:1 repeats the idea just drawn from the Song of Moses about the Gentiles.   Isaiah's words are a prophecy of Gentiles coming to Messianic salvation.[102]

---

[98] To the Jew, the Gentiles were a "no-people" and were "without understanding" because they did not have the Law of Moses to guide them.   The Jews, on the other hand, in their own estimation, were the 'people' of God, and they were a 'people of understanding.'

[99] The sense in which "jealousy" is used here is debated.   Some think it is used in a good sense, as in 11:11, where it is a "provocation to emulation."   Others think that here in 10:19, because of the "anger" in the second member of the Hebrew parallelism, it is an angry jealousy.

[100] The word *ethnos*, often translated "nation," is also the same word often translated "Gentile."

[101] If "without understanding" means "cut off from the knowledge of God" because they had not received the same special revelation the Jews had, namely, the Mosaic Law, then in verse 19 we have about come full circle to where we were verse 3.   In spite of all the changes the Rabbis had introduced to their religion, Jews supposed their zealousness proved they still had "knowledge."   It galled them to think that people who were "without understanding" (i.e., without the Law, and without similar zealousness) should be the recipients of God's blessings.

[102] Whether or not there may have been a reference in Isaiah to apostate Jews, Paul by inspiration applies the words to the Gentiles of his day.   "The idolatrous Gentiles, being wholly occupied with the worship of their idols, never once thought of inquiring after or worshiping the true God.   Nevertheless, to them, while in this state, God, by preaching the gospel, made Himself known and offered Himself as the object of their worship, and they gladly responded.   They broke their idols, burned their books, surrendered to the authority of Christ, and began to walk in newness of life."   Lipscomb and Shepherd, *Romans*, p.197.

10:21 – *But as for Israel He says, "ALL THE DAY LONG I HAVE STRETCHED OUT MY HANDS TO A DISOBEDIENT AND OBSTINATE PEOPLE."*

But as for Israel He says. The "but" and "as for Israel" with which this verse begins, tells us there is a contrast between verses 20 and 21, and for this reason we have explained verse 20 as having reference to the Gentiles. The exact opposite of the response of the Gentiles (who accepted Christ) has been the response of the Jews. As noted above, verse 21 is taken from Isaiah 65:2.

"ALL THE DAY LONG I HAVE STRETCHED OUT MY HANDS TO A DISOBEDIENT AND OBSTINATE PEOPLE." "All day long" could cover all the days of Israel's existence. To 'stretch out the hands' is a gesture of supplication or invitation.[103] God is pleading with Israel to come to Him for redemption. But for the majority of Israel, His pleading is in vain. "Disobedient" (a word used earlier at 2:8) is likely the opposite of submission (10:3) and heeding (10:16). "Obstinate" is the opposite of "confess" (10:9,10). Again, it has been shown that the real problem with Israel was not a lack of understanding. The real problem with the Israel of Paul's day, just as it was in Isaiah's day, was a stubborn refusal to obey what they understood. In the present, God is dealing with men on the basis of justification by faith. Any man, be he Jew or Gentile, who refuses to be a man of faith, just cannot have right standing with God.[104]

We are not yet finished with the section begun at 9:30, entitled "God's Dealings with Israel *in the Present* are in Harmony with the Doctrine of Justification by Faith." While it is true that many Israelites have rejected the gospel's offer of justification, this fact does not mean Paul's message is wrong, or his missionary zeal misguided. There is still a remnant (11:1-5) of faithful Israelites with whom God is working.

---

[103] Conybeare and Howson think it is the gesture of a mother opening her arms to call back her child to her embrace. *Life and Epistles of St. Paul* (London: Longmans, Green, and Co., 1873), p.525. Once more the topic of predestination must be called to mind. If certain men are absolutely and unconditionally predestined to be lost, why does God stand, all day long, with outstretched hand, imploring them to come to Him? (It will not do, as some have tried in order to avoid the force of this passage against their doctrine of the predestination of the elect, to say that the people Isaiah [or Paul] is addressing are already saved people whom God is trying to recall from backsliding, lest they lose part of their reward. Such a notion of the people's standing with God will not fit the context, either of Isaiah or Romans 10.)

[104] A note about the evidential value of what has just been studied. The student will want to pay close attention to the twelve citations from the Old Testament that Paul has used in 9:30-10:21. The passages cited are Isaiah 28:16, Isaiah 8:14; Leviticus 18:5; Deuteronomy 30:12ff; Isaiah 28:16 (again, at 10:11); Joel 2:32; Isaiah 52:7; Isaiah 53:1; Psalm 19:4; Deuteronomy 32:31; Isaiah 65:1; and Isaiah 65:2. No major portion of the Hebrew Bible is absent. Paul cites from the Law, the Prophets, and the Holy Writings. And pay careful attention to the six passages cited from Isaiah. Three come from the first part (chapters 1-39), and three come from the second part (chapters 40-66). Liberal theologians have been accustomed to assign part two to some author other than Isaiah himself; such language as "Deutero-Isaiah" and even "Trito-Isaiah" have been coined to express this theory. But see how Paul introduces these passages. "The Scripture says." "It is written." "Isaiah says (verse 16)," where few liberal theologians would assign Isaiah 53 to Isaiah's authorship. "Isaiah is very bold" introduces a chapter from the so-called "Trito-Isaiah." What we have here in Romans is definitive evidence against the speculative theories offered by the historical-critical scholars.

11:1 – *I say then, God has not rejected His people, has He?   May it never be!   For I too am an Israelite, a descendant of Abraham, of the tribe of Benjamin.*

I say then.   The first paragraph of this chapter (11:1-10) continues Paul's exposition of the thesis that "God's Dealings with Israel *in the Present* are in Harmony with the Doctrine of Justification by Faith."[1]   Having shown (in chapter 10) that the majority of Israel does not have right standing with God because of their stubborn disobedience, he now shows that those Israelites who are part of the present-day "remnant" are still God's chosen vessels.   On the other hand, those who are disobedient will find that a divine judicial punishment has descended upon them.

God has not rejected His people, has He?   Chapter 11 has proven to be an exceedingly difficult chapter to explain satisfactorily, and so has been a great theological battleground. Comments made on verses in the first part of the chapter tend to determine how verses in the latter part of the chapter are explained, so the exegete and reader must both be very cautious.   God's "people" in the context evidently has reference to the Jewish people.[2] But what is involved in the verb "rejected"?[3]   The answer given to this question in the commentaries is determined to a large extent by the writer's notion about the underlying topic of the context.   Some perceive that "justification" is the underlying theme, so the question is interpreted to mean, "Can it be said God has no further interest in saving Jewish people?"   Some remember that the whole section began with a discussion of God's choice of some for service, so the question is interpreted to mean, "Does God no longer use Jewish people as His chosen vessels to make His mercy known to others?"   Others, reading in the following verses that some Jews are still included in the remnant, interpret the question to mean, "Has God cast off *all* Jewish people?"   Still others, remembering 9:6 where a possible false inference (if Paul's doctrine is right, the word of God must have failed!) is

---

[1] On several previous occasions, during the discussion of chapters 9-11, it has been necessary to pay special attention to the outline of the material, so that following the line of Paul's argument can be more easily discerned.   While calling attention to Paul's own use of *oun* ("therefore") as marking his movement from one major thought to another, thereby helping us discern the outline, it is also admitted that when we come to chapter 11 the content of the paragraphs has had an influence on how the major points of the outline have been worded.   Both 11:1 and 11:11 begin with the same construction ("I say then," followed by a question expecting a negative answer), and thus are conclusions logically related to what was said in chapter 10.   Someone has outlined the first two paragraphs of chapter 11 on this fashion: The unbelief of the majority of Israel is neither (1) total, nor (2) permanent.

[2] There is a connection between 11:1 and what is written before (chapters 9 and 10).   The last verse in chapter 10 spoke of "Israel" being "a disobedient and obstinate people."   9:32 has spoken about Israel stumbling over the Stumbling stone.   9:31 has stated that Israel failed to attain right standing with God. These all sound so final!   Yet there were also faint echoes of hope amidst all these verses.   9:24 has spoken of vessels of mercy being called both from among Jews and Gentiles.   9:27-29 have introduced the "remnant" idea.   10:1 tells of Paul's prayers for Israel.   10:11,12 have held out the absolute lack of distinction between Jew and Greek – whoever believes in Him will not be disappointed.   In light of these verses of hope, it ought not to be implied that *all* Israel is involved in the disobedience and stumbling.

[3] The verb translated "rejected" is *apōtheō*, a word which means "to push aside, reject, repudiate." Arndt-Gingrich, *Lexicon*, p.102,103.   It is the word used in Acts 7:27,39 of the Hebrews' treatment of Moses, both in Egypt and at Mt. Sinai.   It is the word used to describe the negative (disdainful[?]) response to the gospel by certain Jews in Antioch (Acts 13:46).

corrected, think that 11:1 is intended to answer another possible false inference, only with reference to a different Old Testament Scripture.[4]

May it never be!   With an emphatic denial,[5] Paul repudiates the suggestion that God has rejected His people.   At the same time, alongside this denial must be placed the fact that there is a sense in which it can be said that the "unbelieving Jews" have been rejected. 11:15 speaks of "their rejection."   11:20 says they were "broken off."   Perhaps now we have a partial answer to the question about the meaning of "rejected His people" in the previous phrase.   "His people" is interpreted by the context to mean "*all* His people." Israel has not been rejected *in toto, en masse.*   The proof Paul offers for this emphatic denial is himself and other faithful members of the "remnant."

For I too am an Israelite, a descendant of Abraham, of the tribe of Benjamin.   By these claims of pure Jewishness, Paul offers himself as proof that not all Israelites have been rejected.[6]   No one can deny that Paul is an Israelite – a lineal descendant of Abraham,[7] of the tribe of Benjamin.[8]   He is an Israelite, all right.   Not only that, he is the apostle to the Gentiles[9], a "vessel of mercy" chosen from among the Israelites whom God is using to make His name known among the Gentiles.

---

[4] Whereas 9:6 seemed to have reference to the promised "seed-line" included in the covenants God made with the Patriarchs, not a few writers believe 11:1 has a reference to God's promise found in Psalm 94:14 (or 1 Samuel 12:22), where it is stated categorically that "God will not abandon [reject] His people."

[5] See notes at Romans 3:4 for the explanation of this expression.

[6] The majority of commentators understand the phrases at the close of verse 1 to be a proof given for Paul's emphatic denial that God has rejected His people.   However, there is another way the verse has been explained, in which these three phrases are part of the emphatic denial.   Paul is conceived as saying, 'God forbid that I, an Israelite, etc., should ever teach that Israelites are rejected by God!'   Paul is thus reminding his readers that he, too, is an Israelite; and therefore, to him, as much as to them, the supposition seems almost blasphemous.   It seems to this commentator that the majority have it in this place.   If God had rejected His people *in toto,* then Paul, too, would be rejected, for he surely was a Jew.   But Paul, the Christian, was enjoying and sharing the Messianic blessings.   So it can be said that the rejection of Israel is only partial – just the unbelieving Israelites are rejected.

[7] While "seed (sons, descendants) of Abraham" sometimes has a spiritual significance in the New Testament (as at Galatians 3:7,29 and Luke 19:9), more often it refers to physical descent from Abraham (as at 2 Corinthians 11:22).   In this place "seed of Abraham" would distinguish Paul as being of pure descent, and not a proselyte or descended from a proselyte.

[8] When a man was stating his Jewish pedigree, "of the tribe of Benjamin" meant "of the purest blood, because the tribes of Judah and Benjamin alone kept the theocratic continuity of the race after the Exile [Ezra 4:1, 10:9]." Sanday, *Romans*, p.116.   Reconstructing what may have gone through the minds of the parents of the apostle Paul, Bruce writes, "It is not surprising that parents who traced their descent from the tribe of Benjamin and cherished high ambitions for their new-born son should give him the name borne by the most illustrious member of that tribe in the history of Israel – 'Saul the son of Kish, a man of the tribe of Benjamin' (Acts 13:21)." *Romans*, p.213.

[9] Acts 26:17; Romans 1:13, 15:16; Ephesians 3:8; 1 Timothy 1:11, 2:7.   Paul's appeal to his God-given mission, rather than to his personal experience of salvation, would seem to be better evidence that God has not rejected His people.

11:2 – *God has not rejected His people whom He foreknew.   Or do you not know what the Scripture says in* **the passage about** *Elijah, how he pleads with God against Israel?*

God has not rejected His people whom He foreknew.   "Foreknew" in some sense is a guarantee that God has not rejected His people; but just what is the meaning of the word, and how does it apply to Israel?   According to comments at 8:29, where the word "foreknew" was used before by Paul, God foreknew (approved ahead of time) those who would be "in Christ."   In harmony with this plan God made, those who are "in Christ" – whether they be Gentile or Israelite – have not been rejected.   God has not changed his plans or purposes.   Whether it be Paul, or Peter, or Barnabas, or some of the readers of this letter in Rome who also happen to be descended from Abraham – if they have accepted Jesus as the Messiah and are justified by faith, they are still God's "chosen people."[10]   Nor should it be forgotten that God's choice was for service,[11] not just for salvation, so some from among "His people" will still be used to carry out His missionary purposes in the world.[12]

---

[10] This verse, which speaks of "His people whom He foreknew" as not being rejected, has been thought to teach several different things, depending on who is commenting upon it.   (1) Calvinist interpreters, who tend to make "foreknew" and "predestined" to be synonymous terms, here find proof that back in eternity God determined that certain peoples were to be the objects of His special delight, and verse 2 tells us that God's eternal predestination does not change.   This whole theological view has been touched upon in comments on chapter 9, and will be given more attention in Special Study #8 at the close of comments on chapter 11.   (2) Some think the reference is to Israel as a nation.   'The Jews as a nation always were and always will be God's chosen people,' the theory goes.   While it is true that God did choose Israel to do a special service for Him in the interest of His world-wide redemptive program, it is not true that the whole number of descendants of Israel was so chosen.   Nor does this theory do justice to the understanding that God's "foreknowledge" (His approval ahead of time) had to do with those who were "in Christ" rather than the whole number of physical descendants taken indiscriminately.   (3) Some writers of premillennial or dispensational persuasion have found in these words a New Testament promise that the Jews as a nation will return to Palestine (at a time shortly before the second coming of Christ).   They read verse 2 as though it said "God has not (permanently) rejected His people."   In this commentator's opinion, such an interpretation can be put on this passage only by ignoring the context which speaks of the Christianization of the Jews, not their nationalization.   (4) A fourth suggestion (the one followed in the comments on these verses) is that there is reference to the remnant with whom God is working, a theme which is developed in the context following.   This interpretation treats "whom He foreknew" as a limitation put on the words "His people."   There were some people (even from among Israel) whom God approved beforehand; and these, Paul says, have not been rejected.   Whether or not a person belongs to the remnant depends on whether or not he has accepted Christ.

[11] Chapter 9 has developed the theme that God's choice of some to be vessels of mercy was free and sovereign, and always involved some from among Israel as well as some from among the Gentiles.   Some commentators have objected to the interpretation given in the notes, that "whom He foreknew" modifies "His people," and serves to restrict the expression "His people" to just a remnant.   The objection is based on the idea that "His people" in verse 1 has a reference to the nation as a whole, and to restrict "His people" to the remnant in verse 2 would be unusual.   In reply, it should not be thought unusual that "His people" should be used in two different senses in this context, when we have already been reminded there is an 'Israel within Israel' (Romans 9:6), and verses 4 and 5 refer directly to the remnant.

[12] Let it be remembered that before Paul is finished with this letter, he is going to make known his plans to go to Spain, and his desire that the Roman Christians help support this planned missionary venture (15:24).   Is this one of the ways that the converts from Judaism in Rome could carry out their "honorable use" as vessels of mercy?   We think so.

Or do you not know what the Scripture says. As at 6:3, "do you not know" is Paul's characteristic way of appealing to a well-known truth, simple reflection on which would have kept the readers from drawing any such false inference as the one raised in 11:1. The readers are given one of two possible choices: you must admit that God works with a remnant, or else you must be ignorant of what the Scripture says.[13] The passage about to be quoted comes from 1 Kings 19:10-14, and it is not until Romans 11:5-7 that the real thrust of the quotation becomes evident.

In *the passage about* Elijah. The Greek reads simply "in Elijah." Before it was divided into chapters and verses to make it easy to refer to a certain passage, the Bible was divided into paragraphs or sections, to which titles were given,[14] the titles being derived from the subject matter in the paragraph. "In Elijah" was one of these titles. Compare Mark 12:26 where another famous Old Testament passage is referred to by its title, "In the Bush."

How he pleads with God against Israel? Elijah charged the Israelites with crime against God and pleaded with Him for their rejection.[15] In the next verse (where phrases from 1 Kings 19:10-14 are quoted), Paul quotes the words used by Elijah when he accused Israel.

11:3 – *"Lord, THEY HAVE KILLED THY PROPHETS, THEY HAVE TORN DOWN THINE ALTARS, AND I ALONE AM LEFT, AND THEY ARE SEEKING MY LIFE."*

"Lord, THEY HAVE KILLED THY PROPHETS, THEY HAVE TORN DOWN THINE ALTARS, AND I ALONE AM LEFT, AND THEY ARE SEEKING MY LIFE." The time is just after the contest with the prophets of Baal on Mt. Carmel. Ahab has told Jezebel that all the prophets of Baal have been killed, and she sent a message to Elijah threatening to kill him within 24 hours. So Elijah fled from Jezebel. First, he ran south to Beersheba, then into the wilderness. In time he arrives at Mt. Horeb, still discouraged and disillusioned, and makes this plea against Israel. His accusation is that all of Israel is apostate;[16] he alone is faithful. God, in His answer, will point out that Elijah

---

[13] On "what the Scripture says," see notes at Romans 9:17.

[14] Many examples of these paragraph titles for Biblical passages taken from the Talmud and from Hebrew commentators are given by Sanday and Headlam, *Romans*, p.310,311.

[15] "The verb *entunchanein* ["pleadeth"] means (1) 'to meet with,' (2) 'to meet for the purposes of conversation,' 'to have an interview with,' Acts 25:24; hence (3) 'to converse with, plead with,' ... either on behalf of some one ... Romans 8:27,34; Hebrews 7:25, or against some one ... and so (4) definitely 'to accuse' as [it is used] here ...." Sanday and Headlam, *Romans*, p.311.

[16] Jezebel had killed some of God's prophets (1 Kings 18:4). There were altars of burnt offering in the Tabernacle, and later in the Temple at Jerusalem, but that is not the thing referred to by Elijah. "The Jews were not forbidden to make altars elsewhere. Hence, they are mentioned as existing in other places, 1 Samuel 7:17; 16:2,3; 1 Kings 18:30,32. These were the altars of which Elijah complained as having been thrown down by the Jews." Barnes, *Romans*, p.245. "Altars, by the law of Moses, were required to be made of earth or unhewn stones, Exodus 20:24,25. Hence the expression 'to dig them down' means completely to demolish or destroy them." *Op. cit.*, p.244. Things were bad in Israel. "Ahab the son of Omri did evil in the sight of the Lord more than all who were before him" (1 Kings 16:30). He erected an altar for Baal. He made the Asherah. "Thus Ahab did more to provoke the Lord God of Israel than all the kings of Israel who were before him" (1 Kings 16:33).

has drawn a false conclusion from what he has been observing. There were some pious men still left in the nation, a remnant with whom He could work.

11:4 – *But what is the divine response to him?* *"I HAVE KEPT for Myself SEVEN THOUSAND MEN WHO HAVE NOT BOWED THE KNEE TO BAAL."*

But what is the divine response to him? At Mt. Horeb, Elijah has been living in a cave. God commanded him to go out of the cave, but the prophet apparently disregards the command. Nevertheless, "The Lord was passing by."[17] Then follow some tremendous and awe-producing manifestations: the whirlwind, the earthquake, and the fire. Then when there was "a sound of gentle blowing," Elijah went to the mouth of the cave, and God spoke to him.[18] It was in this "divine response"[19] where God spoke about the 7000 who have not bowed the knee to Baal.

"I HAVE KEPT for Myself SEVEN THOUSAND MEN WHO HAVE NOT BOWED THE KNEE TO BAAL." These words are taken from 1 Kings 19:18, though there is nothing in the Hebrew or LXX that corresponds to "for Myself." By inserting "for Myself," Paul shows that the theme in 1 Kings is the same as his theme in Romans 11, namely, that there were people whom God had decided to use in His service. In Elijah's time, Israel was in a life and death struggle with Baal worship.[20] Yet even in the apostate

---

[17] One is reminded of another prophet of God, Moses, who, having dealt with a case of idolatry, was also on Mt. Horeb, and who was granted a similar manifestation of God (Exodus 34:1-9). In both cases the message was the same – God will by no means clear the guilty, but He will continue to work through the righteous remnant so that His plans and purposes are accomplished.

[18] "God now gave Elijah a threefold commission: (1) to anoint Hazael king over Syria (cf. 2 Kings 8:7-15); (2) to anoint a new king for Israel, Jehu the son of Nimshi (cf. 2 Kings 9:1-10); (3) to appoint his own successor, Elisha the son of Shaphat. These three individuals, though differing in vocation and character, would yet be united in the humbling and desecrating of the house of Ahab." John T. Gates, "1 Kings," in *The Wycliffe Bible Commentary*, edited by Charles F. Pfeiffer and Everett F. Harrison (Chicago: Moody Press, 1963), p.334.

[19] "Divine response" is a felicitous translation of *chrēmatismos*, a stem regularly used in the New Testament for a "divine message" or an "answer from God." See Matthew 2:12,22; Luke 2:26; Acts 10:22, 11:26; Hebrews 8:5. See the notes on "called" in this commentator's *New Testament History: Acts*, p.420.

[20] "Bow the knee" is an expression denoting worship (cf. Ephesians 3:14; Philippians 2:10). "The word *Baal* in Hebrew means 'Lord,' or 'Master.' This was the name of an idol of the Phoenicians and Canaanites, and was worshiped by the Assyrians and Babylonians under the name of *Bel* (cf. the Book of *Bel* in the Apocrypha). This god was represented under the image of a bull or a calf; the one denoting the Sun [god], the other the Moon [god]." Barnes, *Romans*, p.245,246. See also the article on "Baal" by Steven Barabbas in *The Zondervan Pictorial Bible Dictionary*, edited by Merrill C. Tenney (Grand Rapids: Zondervan Publishing House, 1963), p.87,88, for more detailed information about Baal and Baal worship.

The KJV reads "to *the image of* Baal." The reason for the italics is that the word "Baal" is masculine, but the article ("the") in the original is feminine. The KJV translators supplied a feminine noun to correspond to the feminine article. How the feminine came to be used is uncertain. "Some have thought that the deity was androgynous; others have conjectured that the feminine is used contemptuously. Baal was originally the sun-god. The sun, it may be remembered, is feminine in German and some other languages. [Perhaps the feminine came from some similar ancient usage.]" Sanday, *Romans*, p.116. Hendriksen gives a different suggestion to explain the feminine-masculine grammar. "When Scripture was read aloud, the name of god was not pronounced. Instead, the reader would say 'shame;' Greek,

Northern Kingdom which was full of Baal worship, a remnant, a few of the Israelite people, 7000 men,[21] had not been involved in the worship of that idol.[22]   These made up the remnant who would continue to be tools in God's hands.[23]

11:5 – *In the same way then, there has also come to be at the present time a remnant according to* **God's** *gracious choice.*

In the same way then.   Verses 5 and 6 are Paul's exposition of the verses just quoted about Elijah, so that their relevance to the question at hand ("God has not rejected His people, has He?") can be clearly seen.   As there was a remnant in Elijah's day, an Israel within Israel, so there is a remnant in my time, Paul is asserting.   And if this is so, then the suspicion that God has "rejected His people" is not true!

There has also come to be at the present time a remnant.   The "present time" is the period since Christ came.   The "remnant"[24] would consist of Christians of Jewish descent.[25]   Just as the remnant He reserved for Himself in Elijah's time was proof that God was keeping His word about not rejecting Israel, so the same is true in Paul's time.   The

---

aischunē; Hebrew, *boseh*; both feminine."   *Romans*, p.361.   Cranfield, *Romans*, p.547, gives references where the substitute words are actually found in the text of 1 Kings 18:19,25 and Jeremiah 3:24; 2 Samuel 2:8 compared with 1 Chronicles 8:33.

[21] The Greek is *andras*, "male, husband," not the general word *anthrōpos*, "man, mankind."   Hendriksen urges that "7000 men" is "probably to be understood in the sense of 'in addition to the women and children,' for it would be hard to imagine a situation in which only the men had remained faithful to God. ... To be sure, these seven thousand constituted only a remnant of Israel's population, but it was a *significant* remnant."   *Romans*, p.362.   Cranfield offers the suggestion that "7000" is a symbolic number "in the light of the special significance attaching to the number seven and to multiples of seven in the Bible and in Judaism, as a symbol of completeness, perfection."   *Romans*, p.547.

[22] When Hazael, Jehu, and Elisha had finished their work of chastisement, God says "I will leave 7000 ..." (1 Kings 19:18).   The future tense verb suggests that God will providentially cause the remnant to survive the slaughter wrought by the three leaders Elijah was commissioned to appoint.

[23] "Though the number [7000] corrects Elijah's mistaken estimate of the situation, and is far in excess of what his complaint would imply, yet it should be noted that the seven thousand were only a remnant. This fact underscores the widespread apostasy in Israel at that time and points to the parallel between Elijah's time and the apostle's.   This is a consideration basic to the use Paul makes of the Old Testament passage."   Murray, *Romans*, Vol.2, p.69.

[24] See notes at Romans 9:27 on the word "remnant."

[25] There were about 3000 Jews converted on the day of Pentecost (Acts 2:41).   Soon, the number grew to be about 5000 men (Acts 4:4).   Still later, we read, "You see, brother, how many thousands there are among the Jews of those who have believed" (Acts 21:20).   In this last reference, the Greek word is not "thousands" but "myriads" (tens of thousands).   In most communities where new congregations were planted, the first converts were Israelites.   These thousands of Jews made up the "remnant" as Paul writes this letter.   It is sobering to recognize that even with these myriads of converts, still the great mass of Jewish people was disobedient and obstinate.

spiritual condition of Elijah's day and Paul's day were the same. The nation as a whole, then as now, rejected God's message. But now as then also there is a faithful remnant left; there are still people of Jewish descent who have embraced Jesus as the Messiah, and these make up the "remnant" in the present time.[26] A negative answer to the question asked in verse 1 is justified on the basis of the differentiation between national Israel (the majority) and spiritual Israel (the remnant).

According to *God's* gracious choice. The older translations read "according to the election of grace." That there was a remnant at all, either in Elijah's time or Paul's, is the result of God's choice or election.[27] "It was an election of grace, a choice proceeding from, or arising out of grace."[28] Earlier in our study of Romans, we learned that "grace" is both an attitude and an action on the part of God.[29] Likewise, in 9:11, Paul has written about "God's purpose according to His choice," and what he writes here in chapter 11 certainly recalls what was alluded to earlier. Back in eternity, as God was planning how He would act, because He wished to be gracious to His creation, He chose to make salvation available to any who were faithful to His revealed will. The number of the faithful may be but a remnant, but God will continue to act in their behalf just as He graciously elected (chose) to do it.

11:6 – *But if it is by grace, it is no longer on the basis of works, otherwise grace is no longer grace.*

But if it is by grace, it is no longer on the basis of works. The explanation of how a remnant has come to be is here continued. Verses 5 and 6 are Paul's own exposition of how God acts, whether in Elijah's time, or in the age since Messiah has come. His actions result from His grace. "No longer on the basis of works" reminds us of what Paul already wrote in 9:11, "not because of works,[30] but because of Him who calls." How is it that there is a remnant whom God deigns to bless and use as His chosen instrument to do a spe-

---

[26] The idea of the "remnant" is an important theme in Scripture, and the serious Bible student will want to make a special study of it. Some helpful ideas can be gleaned from Sanday and Headlam, *Romans*, p.316ff. A purview of current handling of the topic can be found in Ronald E. Clements, "A Remnant Chosen by Grace" in *Pauline Studies*, edited by Donald A. Hagner and Murray J. Harris (Grand Rapids: Wm. B. Eerdmans Publishing Co., 1980), p.106-121.

[27] Reformed theologians put their familiar explanation on verses 4,5. "As in the time of Elijah, it was because *God had received them unto Himself* that *any* were saved from idolatry (verse 4), so now it was by the same gracious sovereignty that any were saved from the prevalent unbelief ... The apostle thus shows that neither *all* the ancient people of God were cast away, nor that *any* whom He *foreknew* were rejected ... It is of God that *all* are not corrupt and lost. It is owing only to the election of grace, to His merciful choosing, that *any* are saved." Barnes, *Romans*, p.246.

[28] Lard, *Romans*, p.349.

[29] See Special Study #1 on "grace" at the close of comments on chapter 1.

[30] Whatever comments were offered in the commentaries at 9:11 are likely repeated here, e.g., if the "works" there were thought to be meritorious, likely the comments offered here will also talk about meritorious works.

cial service in the world? That remnant does not result from anything in man! That remnant is the result of something in God Himself! "No longer on the basis of works" likely reflects a Jewish conceit that Paul rejects. Perhaps it reflects Jewish pride in their descent from Abraham, or their boast in the Law (Romans 2:23). Perhaps it reflects what was alluded to in 10:3, their efforts to establish their own righteousness. Whatever these "works" were, it is obvious that they were something other than simple faithfulness to what God had commanded through Moses.

Otherwise grace is no longer grace.[31] If something man devises (works) is included as part of the basis by which one becomes part of the remnant, then the remnant no longer is based on "grace." "Grace" is *God's* attitude and action, not something man invents or produces.

11:7 – *What then? That which Israel is seeking for, it has not obtained, but those who were chosen obtained it, and the rest were hardened;*

What then? This question, stated here in an abbreviated form, so often asked in this letter, prepares us for a summary or a conclusion drawn from what has just been written (verses 1-6).

That which Israel is seeking for, it has not obtained. Israel (as a nation, as a whole) is still seeking (present tense verb), and what it did not obtain in the past, it still has not obtained. This repeats what was already said about Israel in 9:31,32 and 10:3. "Righteousness" was the thing being sought, those previous verses have indicated.

But those who were chosen obtained it. "Israel" was used in 9:31,32 in such a way that it could be misunderstood. Now, we see that Paul did not intend for his language to be taken as being "all inclusive."[32] The remnant, the "chosen[33] people," the Israel who have

---

[31] After this phrase, which ends the verse in the NASB, the KJV has another long part to this verse, which reads, "But if it be of works, then it is no more grace; otherwise work is no more work." The addition is not sustained by the manuscript evidence (it is not found in P^{46}, Sinaiticus, A, D, G, etc.), and should be omitted. Bruce opines that it was a marginal gloss that accidentally became incorporated into the text of later copies. *Romans*, p.214.

[32] Actually, a little reflection on what has been written in chapter 9 would keep anyone from taking "Israel" in 9:31,32 in an all-inclusive sense. No one would take "Gentiles" in verse 30 as all-inclusive. Paul is talking only about those who are "righteous *by faith*." But Jewish readers (and we too!) are helped in our understanding of God's ways and purposes as a result of Paul's explication of the "remnant" idea.

[33] "Chosen" in verse 7 should be given the same meaning that "choice" was given in verse 5. "Election" (chosen) does not mean that some obtained righteousness because of an irresistible election back in eternity. The use of this verse that Reformed theologians make of it, to prove their doctrine that God's election back in eternity determines whether or not a man is saved or hardened, is not justified. What God "chose" was that those who were "in Christ" would be justified, and would be vessels for honorable use; but He did not unconditionally predestine who would, and who would not, be "in Christ." That is determined by a man's response to God's invitation; it is conditioned on man's "faithfulness" to the revelation God has granted to him.

become Christians, are no longer seeking. They have right standing with God, and are being used by Him to help win the world to Christ.

And the rest were hardened. The "rest" would be all of the nation Israel who are not part of the "remnant," not part of the "chosen" ones. Remember, God's "elect" are those who choose to be in Christ. So the opposite of that would be those who choose not to accept the offer of salvation in Christ. These are the ones who are hardened. Why were they hardened? 9:31,32 has shown that they were not listening to God. 10:3 has said they would not subject themselves to the righteousness of God. 10:16 says they did not obey the glad tidings. 10:21 has indicated that there was disobedience and obstinacy involved, and this in spite of God's outstretched hands. God (as verse 8 makes clear) is the one who hardened[34] them, and this hardening is judicial. They have not failed because they were hardened, but they have been hardened because they have failed.[35]

---

[34] The verb translated "hardens" at 9:18 was *sklērunō*. The word used here is *pōroō*, a word that (in its noun form, *pōrōsis*) is also used in 11:25. The noun also occurs at Mark 3:5 and Ephesians 4:18. Romans 9:18 had to do with a hardening that resulted from refusal to "serve." Here in 11:7, it has to do with hardening that results from rejecting "salvation." *Pōrōsis* is a word used of many things; it can be the "callus" that forms on the hands when they are exposed to pressure or work; it can be a stone that is harder than marble; it can be the new growth that unites the ends of a broken bone, a growth that is harder than the bone itself. From these literal meanings, the word came to have a figurative meaning – "unfeeling, not sensitive." Applied to the spiritual realm, it speaks of the dulling of our true nature, the loss of spiritual sensitivity so that an appeal from God is very difficult to hear. (The KJV reads "blinded" at this place, from a confusion of two similar Greek verbs. In 1611, "blinded" did not have the connotation of "moral insensitiveness" that the Greek word does; yet in modern English, this is exactly the connotation the word has come to have, so "blinded" is not a bad translation of *pōroō* in this place.)

[35] In Romans 1:21 we were told that the Gentiles had suffered a judicial penalty for their refusal to heed the revelation they had. Now a similar thing has been done to the majority of Israel who refuses to heed the greater light offered in the gospel. No doubt, Israel first blinded their own spiritual eyes and were willfully ignorant of much they should have known (as chapter 10 has spoken of the gospel being preached to all – in understandable terms). But beyond all reasonable doubt, there is a reference to a judicial act by God, by which they were further hardened. No man can reject the gospel without being hardened – God has made it work that way! There are temporal punishments for sin, as well as eternal ones.

God never by effectual causation makes a man to sin; nor by His own first omnipotent act does He harden a man's heart. Pharaoh hardened his heart first by his own act; then God hardened Pharaoh's heart. Five times we are told Pharaoh hardened his own heart (Exodus 7:13,14,22; 8:15,32; 9:7) before we read that God hardened his heart (Exodus 9:12). Even after that, as if a remnant of liberty still remained to him, it is said for the last time that he hardened himself (Exodus 9:34,35). Then, at length, as if by way of terrible retribution, God hardened him five times more (Exodus 10:1,20,27; 11:10; 14:8). The same heat that cooks the meat will dry the sand, burn the shavings, melt the wax, and harden the clay. It depends on the make-up of the object being heated. In a similar way, the gospel works different ways on different people. One of God's great moral laws is that if a man steels his heart against the truth, his heart will be hardened. If a man refuses food for a long enough time, he gets to the place he cannot eat. If a man does not use his arm for a long period of time, he gets to the place he cannot use it. So the gospel and man have been so constituted that the same gospel will either melt or harden the man, depending on the man's response – and the response of the man is a matter of the man's own free choice – save that God in His sovereignty has so made man that he has only one of two choices – either to accept or reject the gospel.

11:8 – *just as it is written, "GOD GAVE THEM A SPIRIT OF STUPOR, EYES TO SEE NOT AND EARS TO HEAR NOT, DOWN TO THIS VERY DAY."*

Just as it is written. In verses 8-10, Paul will show that such hardening, instead of being proof that God's promises to His people have failed, is exactly what Scripture long ago indicated to be God's way of dealing with disobedience and obstinacy.   In what follows in verse 8, we have a composite of verses from Isaiah 6:10 and 29:10 and Deuteronomy 29:4. To quote a composite like this is equal to saying that the Scriptures speak on the topic of "judicial hardening" in a number of places.[36]

"GOD GAVE THEM A SPIRIT OF STUPOR.   "Stupor" is another word that denotes a dull insensibility to things spiritual.[37]   This portion of verse 8 comes from Isaiah 29:10 (though similar language is found in Isaiah 6:9,10), and is part of a rebuke the prophet administered to his guilty, unrepentant countrymen.   Isaiah 29:9, the verse immediately preceding, shows that, like the drunkard could have avoided his besotted condition by abstaining from liquor, so the Israelites could have avoided their condition of sin and unbelief.   Because they did not, God was going to send further punishment on them, in the form of a "spirit of stupor."

EYES TO SEE NOT AND EARS TO HEAR NOT.   This part of verse 8 comes from Deuteronomy 29:4.   Moses is about to turn over to Joshua the leadership of the people of Israel.   Before him stands a new generation (for the one that came out of Egypt has died in the wilderness), with whom God is going to enter into covenant relationship (Deuteronomy 29:10-13).   By way of reminding this new generation what happens to people who do not keep the covenant they promise they will, Moses recalls what happened to the earlier generation.   After seeing what God did in Egypt, and the Red Sea, and in the wilderness, you would have expected that generation to give themselves in wholehearted love and devotion to the Lord.   But they did not, and so God caused their eyes to see not, and their ears to hear not.   Again, the topic is dull insensibility to everything spiritual.

DOWN TO THIS VERY DAY."   This phrase too is part of the quotation from Deuteronomy 29:4, and is common Old Testament language to denote the permanence of a result or situation or event.   Stephen made a similar accusation to his accusers when he said, "You men who are stiff-necked and uncircumcised in heart and ears are always resis-

---

[36] It will be remembered that similar composites, or combinations of, and free quotations of Old Testament texts were produced at Romans 3:10-19 and at 9:32,33.   The thing that allows Paul to tie the passages together is the fact that a similar word or theme runs through all of them.

[37] The word translated "stupor" is *katanuxis*, "which literally means 'pricking' or 'stinging,' and hence comes to be used of the numbness which results from certain kinds of sting."   Bruce, *Romans*, p.215. Others suggest the word pictures the stunned bewilderment a person experiences after a sharp blow on the head.   Such a stunning effect also can result from such emotion as leaves one speechless.   It is used of a drunken "stupor," where the person is awake, but has little awareness of what is going on around him. Thayer, *Lexicon*, p.334, writes that men with a spirit of stupor are "so insensible that they are not affected at all by the offer made them of salvation through the Messiah."

ting the Holy Spirit; you are doing just as your fathers did" (Acts 7:51). Behind Stephen's words, as well as behind Paul's quotation here in Romans, is the underlying assumption that the Israelite people have throughout their history demonstrated an obstinacy that has resulted in judicial punishment from the hand of God.[38]

11:9 – *And David says, "LET THEIR TABLE BECOME A SNARE and a trap, AND A STUMBLING BLOCK AND A RETRIBUTION TO THEM.*

And David says. Verses 9 and 10 are taken from (for the most part) the LXX of Psalm 69:22,23. Psalm 69 is a Messianic Psalm; it is often so quoted in the New Testament.[39] So there should be no question about the relevance of the Psalm to the situation in Paul's day. In Psalm 69:20-28, David is praying to God,[40] asking Him to pour out His wrath against those who have made themselves enemies of the Divine will, especially as they have heaped reproach on the Messiah.

"LET THEIR TABLE BECOME A SNARE and a trap.[41] The general idea in the prayer is David's wish that God will cause punitive things to happen to His enemies. Just how a "table" would be a "snare" has been variously explained. One idea is that it is figurative language for presumptuous security. The enemies are pictured as feasting, thinking all is secure, only to have their enemies overtake them amidst the eating. Another reminds us that the "tables" of nomads in David's time were "skin or cloth, spread out on the ground ... upon which the feast was laid, which could entangle the feet of the feasters,

---

[38] Hodge, *Romans*, p.358, tries to help us see the seriousness of such judicial punishments. "The design of such citations is to show that what was fulfilled partially in former times, was more perfectly accomplished at a subsequent period. The Jews had often before been hardened, but at no former period were the people so blinded, hardened, and reprobate, as when they rejected the Son of God, and put Him to an open shame. It had often been predicted that such should be their state when the Messiah came. The punitive character of the evils here threatened cannot escape the reader's notice. This blindness and hardness were not mere calamities, nor were they simply the natural effects of the sins of the people. They were punitive inflictions. They were so announced. God says, I will give you eyes that see not. It is a dreadful thing to fall into the hands of the living God. The strokes of His justice blind, bewilder, and harden the soul."

[39] Psalm 69:4 is used at John 15:25. 69:9 is used at John 2:17 and at Romans 15:3. 69:21 is used at Matthew 27:34 and John 19:29. 69:25 is used at Acts 1:20. Sanday, *Romans*, p.118, for some reason, argues against the Davidic authorship of Psalm 69. He writes, "It appears highly improbable that this Psalm was really written by David. Nor can the Davidic authorship be argued strongly from this passage, as 'David' merely seems to stand for the Book of Psalms, with which his name was traditionally connected." This commentator sees no reason to deny the Davidic authorship of the Psalm, when Paul here says David said it. Compare notes at Romans 4:6.

[40] There are imprecatory Psalms in the Old Testament, where God's punishment is called down on God's enemies. The Psalmists were Holy Spirit-inspired, and there was no hate in their hearts when they asked for such doom on the enemies who continually opposed God's ways. They were asking that the wicked men be removed so that God's program could flourish as it ought. Compare Acts 4:29,30, which may be an imprecatory prayer.

[41] "'Trap' does not appear in either the Hebrew or the Septuagint, and appears to be added by Paul. Translate rather, 'Let them be for a chase,' i.e., instead of feasting, let them be hunted and persecuted'." Sanday, *Romans*, p.118.

if they sprang up suddenly at the approach of danger."[42]

AND A STUMBLING-BLOCK AND A RETRIBUTION TO THEM. "Stumbling-block" represents the same word translated "offense" in 9:33.[43] "Retribution" (a deserved punishment, one in return for an evil done) is one of the reasons it is said that the "hardness" in this context is "judicial." Rather than choosing an interpretation that says the hardness is a result of divine sovereignty and even preceded men's own sins, "retribution" says that the sins came first, then the divinely appointed punishment came into force.

11:10 – *"LET THEIR EYES BE DARKENED TO SEE NOT, AND BEND THEIR BACKS FOREVER."*

LET THEIR EYES BE DARKENED TO SEE NOT. Here David prays for the same thing to happen to his enemies that Deuteronomy 29:4 (see verse 8) says God has caused to happen to disobedient and obstinate people in Moses' time. It is a spiritual blinding from the hand of God, intended as a penalty for refusing to see the truth when the opportunity was offered.

AND BEND THEIR BACKS FOREVER." The Hebrew reads "Let their loins totter and shake," as one does when he has a heavy burden placed on his back. What the LXX translators had in mind when they translated "bend their backs" is not certain, whether it is bent under the heavy burden, or whether it pictures a man stooping to grope on the ground because his eyes are blind. Either way, it is a sore punishment for sin that the Psalmist prays that God will inflict on the enemies. The ASV had the word "always" where the NASB has "forever."[44] What the original says is that the bending of the back is not to be intermittent, but continuous and sustained. "Always" fits this idea better, since "forever" has the connotation that the condition can never change, even into eternity, and that seems to be out of harmony with what follows in verse 11-24.

That portion of chapters 9-11 which sets forth God's dealings with Israel *in the present* as being in harmony with the doctrine of justification by faith has now been completed. That God acts in harmony with the doctrine of justification by faith does not signal a change in His attitudes toward Israel. Instead, it is just exactly what one would expect who knows about the "remnant" and "hardening of the disobedient" and God's "election (choosing) of some according to grace."

---

[42] Cranfield, *Romans*, p.551. Some have tried to identify the "table" as though it were the Paschal table, or as if it figuratively stood for "the sum of all God's favors," but this seems to gain us little by way of understanding.

[43] *Skandalon* is "that over which one falls," "a cause of destruction." It is the "moveable stick or tricker ('trigger') of a trap, ... a snare; any impediment placed in the way and causing one to stumble or fall." Thayer, *Lexicon*, p.577.

[44] The Greek is *dia pantos*, "through all (time)," while the usual phrase translated "forever" is *eis tous aiōnas*, "unto the ages."

D. God's Dealings with Israel *in the Future* Will be in Harmony With the Doctrine of Justification by Faith.   11:11-32

Summary: The rejection of the majority of Israel is only temporary.   Their fall has a special purpose, namely, the introduction of the Gentiles, which in its turn will have the effect of awakening unbelieving Israel to a realization of what they are missing.   If Jewish people will submit to God's way of saving men, they can and will be restored to Divine favor.

11:11 – *I say then, they did not stumble so as to fall, did they?   May it never be!   But by their transgression salvation* **has come** *to the Gentiles, to make them jealous.*

I say then.   The question which follows repeats the same general idea as the question in 11:1, and thus the remainder of chapter 11 is intended to help the readers understand what was affirmed about Israel in 10:20,21.   Gentiles are indeed included in God's "gracious choice," and Israel is "disobedient and obstinate."   But let's see how God, in His providence, uses all of this to His ultimate glory.   Though 11:11-32 is related to what was affirmed in the closing verses of chapter 10, there is, however, a difference in emphasis as far as Israel is concerned.   Whereas 11:1-10 dealt with things *in the present* (as Paul wrote), 11:11-32 deal with *the future*; and whereas the hardening was partial (it was inflicted only on unbelieving Israel), it is also only temporary (it will be removed if they become believers).

They did not stumble so as to fall, did they?   "They," who are the subject of this question, are those who have been hardened (verse 7).   "Stumble" reminds us of 9:32, where they "stumbled" over the stumbling stone.   It speaks about the majority of Israel who have disobeyed the gospel.   The form of the question in the Greek is the one that expects a negative answer.   It should probably be read so that the emphasis rests on the word "fall."[45]   "Fall"[46] is not a lasting, permanent position for Israel, is it?   You are not saying that there is no further hope or possibility of reversing God's decision of "rejection" for unbelieving Israel, are you?   Once again, we must be so very careful in our comments, for the idea expressed in this question dominates the following verses.   If we have misunderstood the thrust of the question, our comments on verses following will be flawed.

---

[45] "So as to fall" is a translation of a *hina* clause in the Greek.   A *hina* clause can express either purpose or result.   Commentators who have opted for *purpose* have spoken of God's purpose in this (as though the fall of unbelieving Israel was predestined).   Commentators who have opted for *result* have spoken of this as being the "contemplated result" God had in mind.   Was the state indicated by the word "fall" the contemplated final result God had in mind?   No. The rejection of Israel was not final.   They could repent and come back.   Israel had stumbled, but "stumbling" did not leave them without remedy for their exclusion from the Messianic redemption.

[46] The direction of Paul's argument depends on the contrast between "stumble" (*ptaiō*) and "fall" (*piptō*). The majority of Jews have stumbled, but what shall be the outcome of the stumble?   A man may stumble (trip over something) and recover himself; or he may stumble and fall completely.   Is there no one to help him up?   Is there no getting up from the fall?   Is it permanent and irremediable?

May it never be!   With an emphatic denial, Paul repudiates the suggestion that the "fall" of the majority of Israel is a permanent condition.   He will go on to make two statements as he explains his "May it never be!"   (1) Their stumbling is temporary, and God overrules it so as to benefit the Gentiles.   (2) Even those out of the majority who become believers will be grafted back in.

But by their transgression salvation *has come* to the Gentiles.   "Transgression" is the way the NASB translators have chosen to render *paraptōma*[47] at this place; the ASV reads, "by their fall," which left the reader with no doubt which of the words ("stumble" or "fall") in the previous phrase this one is related to.[48]   The majority of Israel was transgressing, yet God overruled it so that His purposes to redeem as much of mankind as possible have been accomplished.   "Salvation" has come to the Gentiles.   How this was done is indicated over and over again in Acts as we see the rejection of the gospel message by the Jews result in the preachers going to the Gentiles with the message.[49]

To make them jealous.   We have had an "angry jealousy" at 10:19, but here "jealousy" seems to have its good connotation, "emulation."   When the Jews see what blessings ("the riches of His glory upon vessels of mercy," 9:23) the recipients of the gospel are enjoying, they will become envious and want what they are missing.   This will in turn lead them to desire the salvation which they have been rejecting, and to a restoration to divine favor where they are again a part of the chosen people.

11:12 – *Now if their transgression be riches for the world and their failure be riches for the Gentiles, how much more will their fulfillment be!*

Now.   The last statement in verse 11 might give the wrong impression, that the only importance of the salvation of the Gentiles was to lead to the salvation of the Jews.   This verse restores the balance – Gentiles who have become believers and God's chosen vessels are not just afterthoughts, second class citizens in the kingdom.   Unbelieving Gentiles are just as much the objects of God's redemptive interest as are lost Jews.

---

[47] We have had *paraptōma* before, at Romans 4:25 and 5:15-18,20.   It is a deviation from truth, a sin, a transgression.   (Some commentators have treated *paraptōma* as though it were used here for the condition Paul designates as "stumbling," and suggest we should render it "by their trip" or "by their false step."   No one reading the Greek, especially in light of the difference between *ptaiō* and *piptō*, would expect Paul to be using *paraptōma* as though it meant the same as *ptaiō*.   "Transgression" or "fall" is a much better rendering here.)

[48] Thayer, *Lexicon*, p.485, indicates the word *paraptōma* has its derivation from *parapiptō*, not from *ptaiō*.   Thus, it is related to "fall" rather than to "stumble."   The result of Israel's "stumble" is "sin," this word says.

[49] See Acts 8:1-40; 13:45-48; 18:5,6; 28:24-28.   Remember, too, that it was "to the Jew first and also to the Greek" (Romans 1:16).   Lipscomb and Shepherd, *Romans*, p.202,203, suggest that "stumble" refers to the time before Christ (as much as it does to Paul's own time), and that when Israel stumbled and fell into idolatry, God then scattered them over the whole world.   This exile from the homeland came to be called the Diaspora (a word that in the Greek means to "scatter seed").   It is true that scattered Israelites became the "seed beds" that God used to help the spread of Christianity when Christ came; however, it is not certain that this idea was in Paul's mind as he wrote about the "fall" of his contemporary Israelites.

If their transgression be riches for the world. "Transgression" is the same unbelief (and "fall") indicated in verse 11 where this same word was used. "Riches for the world" seems to be synonymous with "salvation has come to the Gentiles" in the latter part of verse 11.[50]

And their failure be riches for the Gentiles. "Failure" is another of the synonyms in the Bible for 'sin.'[51] The word really means to be defeated, to be diminished as a result of a battle. Having written earlier about how Israel came to be reduced to a remnant, this word continues that imagery nicely. As compared with all the people who make up Israel as a nation, the number of people who have become Christians is a "small number." Sin ("failure") has diminished the "Israel of God" to a small number. Yet notwithstanding its size, it was this remnant that had brought "riches" (the gospel) to the Gentiles.[52]

How much more will their fulfillment be! The words "failure" and "fulfillment" are in contrast to each other; "fulfillment" must be the opposite of "failure" (defeat, diminishing). If "failure" was the sin of rejecting Jesus as the Messiah (as verses 11 and 12a have indicated), then "fulfillment" would be the obedience of faith in the Messiah.[53] The idea expressed in the verse is this: if those Jewish people who are presently disobedient to the gospel would recognize Jesus as their Messiah and obey the gospel, what glorious results might be expected from that! If the "fall" of Israel had been the occasion of so much blessing to the Gentiles, what would result from Israel's revival and restoration?[54] "This

---

[50] "The word riches means wealth, abundance of property, more than is necessary to supply our wants. Hence, it means also anything that may promote our comfort or happiness. The gospel is called riches as it is the means of our highest enjoyment and eternal welfare. It is the means of conferring numberless spiritual blessings on the Gentile world." Barnes, *Romans*, p.251.

[51] Berry, *New Testament Synonyms*, p.117,118.

[52] Commentators use different methods to explain what distinction (if any) is intended in the two phrases, "riches for the world" and "riches for the Gentiles," that occur in verse 12. We tend to reject Barth's (*Church Dogmatics*, Vol.2, p.279) explanation that the "transgression" in the previous phrase was the action of the Jews in nailing Jesus to the cross, which in turn activated the reconciliation of the world (his explanation of "riches of the world"). Barth gets his explanation from verse 15, where "rejection" and "reconciliation of the world" are written by Paul, as though these were his own explanation of the words "transgression" and "riches for the world" just written in verse 12.

[53] "Fulfillment" ("fulness") is used again, except with reference to the Gentiles, in verse 25. In that place it has to do with the conversion of large numbers of Gentiles. One would expect the word to have the same meaning (i.e., conversion) here in verse 12.

[54] That such a revival had not occurred at the time Romans was written is obvious. But when, in the future after Paul wrote, did he contemplate such a return to Jesus as Messiah? Is it something that happens all through the church age, as one by one Jews turn to Christ, or is it something that happens toward history's close? The answer to this difficult question will be looked for in the verses following, to see if Paul gave any intimation to guide us.

Several interpretations have been assigned to "fulfillment." (1) It talks about the conversion of the whole majority of national Israel who are now unbelievers. There has even been a division of opinion whether it includes all Jews through all the centuries, with those who have died being given a second opportunity to obey the gospel, while those living will as a body obey the gospel; or whether it refers to some future generation toward the close of the Church Age, all of whom will be converted by the gospel. (2) It designates a "full number" which have been elected to salvation. (3) It is a New Testament prediction of the national restoration of Israel to the Promised Land, just before the millennial reign of Christ begins. (4) The interpretation adopted in the notes is that it speaks of the obedience of many who were before their

hope, that the restoration of Israel would be the source of great joy and blessing to the world, was already contained in that prophetic song of Moses which Paul has quoted at 10:19, and which he again quotes in 15:10, 'Rejoice, O Gentiles, with his people'."[55]

11:13 – *But I am speaking to you who are Gentiles. Inasmuch then as I am an apostle of Gentiles, I magnify my ministry,*

But I am speaking to you who are Gentiles. What has been written in verses 11 and 12 is a point to be given careful consideration by the Gentile Christians.[56] Verses 13 and 14 may be intended to impart to his readers some of his own evangelistic zeal. If they, too, would be about the evangelization of the Gentiles, with the same energy and commitment that motivated him, perhaps the sooner the Jews will be moved to "jealousy," and the sooner will dawn the day of the final consummation to which all Christians look forward.

Inasmuch then as I am an apostle of Gentiles. "Inasmuch then" likely introduces something like, "contrary to what you may think."[57] It would be natural to think that in going to Gentiles as he did, he had no further interest in the unbelieving Jews. The New Testament has numerous references to Paul's commission to be the "apostle of Gentiles," i.e., to the Gentiles.[58] Not that other apostles (with the possible exception of James, the Lord's brother) did not preach to Gentiles, or that Paul did not preach occasionally among the Jews; but his commission was especially to carry the gospel to the Gentiles.[59]

I magnify my ministry. 'I work hard at my ministry' is the idea.[60] He works hard to carry out his commission to evangelize the Gentiles, because their conversion will provoke the

---

conversion included in the majority. Again, it is debated whether this conversion occurs during the whole Church Age, or whether it has to do especially with the generation(s) living just before the second coming, who are pictured as obeying in large numbers.

[55] Gifford, *Romans*, p.194.

[56] Whether this phrase can be used as evidence to demonstrate the ethnic backgrounds of the church at Rome has been disputed. There certainly was a Gentile element in the congregation; perhaps the majority of the congregation was from Gentile backgrounds. (See this question discussed in the Introductory Studies to this letter.)

[57] There is an untranslated particle (*men*) in the Greek, a particle that usually introduces a contrast (the contrasting member is introduced by *de*). However, there is no contrasting statement actually written here, so it seems best to suppose that it is implied. Furthermore, there is no agreement as to what two statements are being contrasted. Gifford, *Romans*, p.194, suggests that Paul is implying that his work with the Gentiles was but one part of the ministry to which he was called.

[58] See footnote #9, at Romans 11:1.

[59] See Acts 26:15-20 and Galatians 2:9.

[60] George Mark Elliott used to say that this verse would be a good text for a message to preachers. We need to work hard to accomplish what God has set before us. "The minister does not magnify *himself*; he magnifies his *office*." Barnes, *Romans*, p.253.

Jews to emulation, and in faith to accept the Messiah, and this would bring untold blessings both to Jew and to Gentile.

11:14 – *if somehow I might move to jealousy my fellow countrymen and save some of them.*

If somehow I might move to jealousy my fellow countrymen.[61]   Here is why Paul works hard at his ministry. "Jealousy" means "emulation," as at 11:11. The next phrase helps us to understand the sense of "jealousy" in both verses.

And save some of them. Paul hopes that his evangelization of the Gentiles (i.e., his magnifying his ministry) will also serve to win some of the Jews to Christ.[62]   "Those who are instruments of [other men's] salvation are said to save. 1 Corinthians 7:16, 9:22; 1 Timothy 4:16. Only by speaking thus can we realize the grandeur of the work of those who turn sinners from the error of their way."[63]   "Paul's sense of the difficulty of persuading his fellow countrymen is apparent in the modest phrase 'some of them.' (Cp. 1 Corinthians 9:22)."[64]

11:15 – *For if their rejection be the reconciliation of the world, what will* their *acceptance be but life from the dead?*

For. Verse 15 appears to be connected to verse 14. If so,[65] it is giving a reason why he wants to save some of his fellow countrymen, as well as Gentiles.

---

[61] The Greek reads "my flesh," where the NASB has "my fellow countrymen." Paul has reference in "flesh" to his Jewish kindred, as the context shows, so "fellow countrymen" is not a bad rendering. "For this use of *sarx* compare the use of *basar* in Hebrew in the sense of 'kindred' and the corresponding use of *sarx* in the LXX (e.g. Genesis 37:27; Leviticus 18:6; 25:49; Judges 9:2; 2 Samuel 5:1)." Cranfield, *Romans*, p.561.

[62] For "save" meaning "to convert," see notes at Romans 5:10.

[63] Lipscomb and Shepherd, *Romans*, p.205.

[64] Gifford, *Romans*, p. 195. It should be observed that Paul's hope of saving "some" during his lifetime does not impinge on the idea that a conversion of a large number of Israelites (who before their conversion were included among the number whom God rejected) is a thing that will happen years in the future after his own ministry is finished. (This future conversion is implied in "their acceptance" [verse 15], "grafted in" [verse 24], and "all Israel will be saved" [verse 26].)

   Liberal theologians can find no support in this passage for their attempted reconstruction of Pauline theology, wherein that Paul's doctrine and life were adversely affected by a theory (that we now know was mistaken) that the *parousia* (and before that, the conversion of "all Israel") was going to occur before his lifetime ended, and thus he must drive himself to get the gospel preached to all the Gentiles in a decade or so. How much more plausible to suppose Paul entertained the same 'I do not know when the second coming will be' doctrine elsewhere presented in the New Testament, for, after all, in some passages he includes himself among the living when Jesus returns (e.g., 1 Corinthians 15:51) and in some passages he thinks of himself as among those who have died before Jesus returns (e.g., 1 Corinthians 6:14).

[65] Some would take verses 13 and 14 as a sort of parenthetical note, and would connect verse 15 with verse 12. This results in verse 15 being a restatement, in stronger terms, of what was said in verse 12.

If their rejection be the reconciliation of the world. In 11:1-10, Paul has indicated that God had rejected those Jewish people who had refused to obey the gospel.[66] Such unbelievers are not His "chosen people." In Romans 5:10,11, Paul has shown how the hostility between sinners and God is the thing that is removed when "reconciliation" takes place. "Reconciliation" is what is offered to the world as the gospel is preached to all.[67] The Bible elsewhere indicates that such a thing as universal salvation is not going to happen – many will reject the offer of salvation given in the gospel.[68] Therefore, "reconciliation of the world" should not be interpreted to mean that all men will be reconciled. It does suggest that in God's mind, the scope of the offer of reconciliation is the whole world.

What will *their* acceptance be. "Acceptance" is the opposite of "rejection" in the first part of this conditional sentence.[69] In an epistle where justification by faith has been the theme, God's acceptance of some who are now among the rejected implies they have become believers. This is one of the expressions in Romans 11:11-24 that seems to point to a time after Paul's life and ministry are completed. In that future time is when "their acceptance" will occur.[70]

But life from the dead? Two very different interpretations have been assigned to this phrase. Some take it in a figurative sense, as signifying a spiritual revival.[71] If a few Jewish evangelists (like Paul) had accomplished so much among the Gentiles in so short a time,

---

[66] The words translated "rejected" in 11:1,2 and 11:15 differ. In the former, it was the verb *apōtheō*; now, it is the noun *apobolē*. However, Thayer gives "cast off, reject, repudiate" as possible meanings for both. Those who are designated as being "rejected" are the same ones who earlier were said to have stumbled, fallen, and been defeated ("transgression," verse 11).

[67] The gospel could not be preached to the Gentiles until it had first been offered to the Jews (so God had planned it back in eternity). The Jews had now heard, and because of their rejection of the message, they had been "rejected" by God, as far as being "chosen people" or "chosen vessels" is concerned. So their rejection might be said to have opened the door to the preaching to the Gentiles, and thus has resulted in the reconciling to God of the many from the world of the Gentiles. If the evangelistic endeavors among the Gentiles by the few Jewish preachers who are part of the remnant have proven to be such a blessing to the world, what would be the result if there were a whole host of Jewish (as well as Gentile) preachers?

[68] "The gate is wide, and the way is broad that leads to destruction, and *many* are those who enter by it." Matthew 7:13.

[69] "The noun *proslēmpsis* is not used elsewhere in the New Testament, but the meaning is shown by the parallel use of the [cognate] verb (cf. Romans 14:3, 15:7)." Sanday and Headlam, *Romans*, p.325.

[70] The pronoun "their," which occurs twice in verse 15, seems to include a greater number of Paul's "fellow countrymen" than is involved in the "some" he hopes to provoke to emulation and salvation. Out of the great mass who have been rejected, he will try to win a few to Christ, anticipating that the same process will be carried on in the generations to follow (should the Lord tarry). The day will come when many will turn to Jesus as their Messiah.

[71] So it was understood by Augustine, Melanchthon, Calvin, Barnes, Bengel, Clarke, Macknight, Lard, Plummer, Gifford, Hodge, Lipscomb and Shepherd, George Mark Elliott, Murray, Vine, and others. Lenski argues that "life from the dead" means the same thing here in chapter 11 that it did in chapter 6 – a rising from spiritual deadness to walk in newness of life. He urges that Ezekiel 37:1-10 uses the same image of "life from the dead" to denote a great moral change among the people.

think what a revival would result from the preaching of hundreds or thousands of such "chosen vessels"! Others take it in its literal sense, as signifying the resurrection from the dead.[72] Two reasons are often given to justify this second interpretation: (1) "Life from the dead" must be something more stupendous than was signified in "salvation" (verse 11), "riches for the world" and "riches for the Gentiles" (verse 12), and "reconciliation of the world" (verse 15).[73] The resurrection of the dead, and the new heavens and earth that follows, would be such a stupendous blessing. (2) The idea of "revival" among Gentiles is inconsistent with verse 25ff, which seem to date the "fulness of the Gentiles" as taking place *before* the conversion of the mass of Israel.

This commentator tends to agree with the literal interpretation, and understands that the Bible presents this timetable for the future: the conversion of large numbers of Jewish people shortly before the second coming is the last thing on God's schedule of history before the resurrection from the dead,[74] and the ushering in of the eternal kingdom of God. Perhaps it could be said that Paul uses "life from the dead" because more is intended than

---

[72] Among the commentators who so interpret have been Origen, Chrysostom, and most commentators before the Reformation, plus Meyer, Alford, Sanday, Cranfield, Bruce, and others. Elliott, noting that Paul did not use the word "resurrection" but "life," urged that the apostle would hardly have used the phrase "life from the dead," thus predicatively, if he had meant by it a fixed and predetermined event like the final resurrection.

[73] It is difficult to see 'spiritual revival' as a climax befitting the first half of verse 15. "Reconciliation of the world" follows the conversion of the Gentiles (or is included in it). "Life from the dead" follows the conversion of the Jews. There must be more to "life from the dead" than simply "conversion," for a moral and spiritual renewal is a necessary prerequisite to readmission to God's favor.

[74] At Romans 8:11 it was explained how there may be a difference in the expressions "resurrection *of* the dead" and "resurrection *from* the dead." If it is true that "resurrection *from* the dead" is something that speaks of the resurrection of the righteous, then "life *from* the dead" just might have reference to that same resurrection of the just. The resurrection takes place at the second coming, 1 Corinthians 15:21 (where it is resurrection *of* the dead), 15:23-28 (where the consummation follows the second coming and the defeat of the last enemy [death] by resurrection); and 1 Thessalonians 4:16.

If this interpretation of "life from the dead" is adopted, the reader must be careful to guard against a presentation, popularly given in the 20th century, that the conversion of the Jews is something simultaneous with the second coming of Jesus. (It is sometimes affirmed that the conversion will take place as the Jews see Jesus coming on the clouds of heaven. "They will look on Him whom they have pierced" is the verse used to document this theory. However, the apostle John says that Old Testament prediction was fulfilled at Calvary, John 19:37). If the Jews were converted at their first physical glimpse of the returning Christ, their conversion would not be a justification "by faith;" it would not be what Paul in Romans anticipates, for he says that the faith that saves comes by hearing (10:17), not by seeing. What Romans anticipates is that the Jews will hear and obey the gospel, and then be justified in God's sight.

A second caution is in order. If "life from the dead" is the resurrection of the righteous, such an interpretation does not automatically imply that one thousand years elapse before the resurrection of the wicked, as some millennial systems teach. (Review footnote #61 in chapter 8.) Furthermore, Vine's (*Romans*, p.165, 166) identification of "life from the dead" as being millennial blessings granted to the Jews is also seriously suspect. Modern premillennialists are hard pressed to find many of the major details of their system taught in the New Testament; typical, therefore, is Vine's comment at this place: "In this verse the four dispensational events intimated in verse 12 are recalled, but in a different way: (a) the fall of Israel is now spoken of with reference to their 'casting away;' (b) 'the riches' of the world is now called 'the reconciling;' (c) 'the fulness' of Israel is here spoken of as 'the receiving of them' into God's favor, i.e., in Millennial blessing." (Vine does not have a (d), but one must assume from a comparison of the verses that "life from the dead" and "millennial blessing" is the fourth of his "dispensational events.")

simply the resurrection of the righteous.   Think of the new life in the world to come, the final development and glorious consummation of the kingdom of Christ, the "new heavens and new earth, in which righteousness (righteous people[?]) dwells" (2 Peter 3:13).

11:16 – *And if the first piece* of dough *be holy, the lump is also; and if the root be holy, the branches are too.*

And if the first piece *of dough* be holy, the lump is also. In language reminiscent of two Old Testament metaphors ("first fruits" and "olive tree"), Paul now gives the reason for his confidence in the future conversion[75] of many Jewish people.[76]   The word translated "first piece" here is the same word translated "first fruits" at other times in the New Testament (e.g., Romans 8:23).   The fact that "lump" appears in the next phrase makes it likely there is an allusion to Numbers 15:17-21, and that in this place it should be translated as the NASB does, since it refers to the first portion of dough removed from the whole kneaded lump of dough.[77]   "Holy," as it often does, denotes "consecrated, or set apart to sacred service."[78]   Perhaps here it even has the technical connotation 'consecrated to God as a holy nation.'   Whenever one reads the word "first fruits" or "first piece," the immediate idea implied is that there is 'more to come.'

Once the proper translation is determined, the next thing is to decide upon a meaning. Several have been suggested, but the one that seems most likely is the one that takes "first piece" and "root" (in verse 16) and "fathers" (verse 28) as all being designations for the patriarchs (Abraham, Isaac, and Jacob); and which also takes "lump" and "branches" (verse 16) and "enemies" (verse 28) as all being designations for the majority of Israel who are presently unbelievers, but whose conversion is anticipated in this paragraph.[79]

---

[75] Such a future for Israel has been implied in several expressions in verses 11-15.   See verse 11, where his answer to the question about a permanent fall was "May it never be!"   See verse 12, where "their fulfillment" is anticipated.   See verse 15, where "their acceptance" is looked forward to.

[76] Verses 16-24 also serve as a second part of his explanation for the "May it never be!" in verse 11. The first part was that 'the rejection of the Jews had benefitted the Gentiles.'   The second part is that 'many Jews will return, one day.'

[77] "The allusion here is to the custom, described in Numbers 15:17-21, of dedicating a portion of the dough to God.   The portion thus taken was to be a 'heave-offering,' i.e., it was to be 'waved' or 'heaved' [Nehemiah 10:37] before the Lord; and then the whole lump was given to the priests."   Sanday, *Romans*, p.120.   It is often asserted (though it is difficult to document) that the first fruit, thus offered (waved) before the Lord, imparted its consecration to the whole mass from which it was taken to represent.   Thus, it was "holy" and could be given to the priests without defiling them.

[78] Compare the comments on "saints" at Romans 1:7.   "Holy" is but another translation of the adjective *hagios*, there translated "saints."

[79] Two other interpretations have been suggested besides the one given in the notes.   (1) Some think it has reference to Christ, as the word "first fruits" does in 1 Corinthians 15:23.   Christ, the seed of Abraham according to the flesh, is the pledge that there is more to come, and the more to come involves the future conversion of many of Abraham's fleshly seed.   (It should be observed that while the Greek word is the same, *aparchē*, the "allusion [in 1 Corinthians] is rather to the sheaf of the first fruits of the barley harvest which was 'waved' before the Lord on the Sunday following Passover, thus consecrating the whole harvest [Leviticus 23:10ff]."   Bruce, *Romans*, p.217.)   (2) Others think it has reference to Jewish converts, as the

In any case, it is in the 'more to come' connotation of "first piece" (first fruits) that Paul finds confirmation of his assertion that many Jews one day will have "acceptance" with God.

And if the root be holy, the branches are too. This is a second metaphor used in this verse to prove that there will be a future conversion of many of the Jews.[80] Already Paul is beginning his allusion to the "olive tree," with its "root" and "branches." "Root" has reference to Abraham (or the patriarchs[81]), and "branches" has reference to the Jews who will become Christians one day. The unbelieving majority of the Jews (the "branches") are still considered "holy" in God's sight, Paul here tells us. They are "holy" in the sense that Israel (since the time when God made His plan for mankind) constitutes a holy nation, out of which some (the Israel within Israel) have been chosen by God as His special vessels. He remembers His promise about "seed;" thus, the branches, because of their relationship to the patriarchs, will have an opportunity in the future to obey the gospel and thus become acceptable to Him.

11:17 – *But if some of the branches were broken off, and you, being a wild olive, were grafted in among them and became partaker with them of the rich root of the olive tree,*

But if some of the branches were broken off. "Some of the branches" is a deliberate understatement,[82] for it is the majority of Jewish people who have been broken off. But broken off from what? Before the verse ends, Paul will tell us that he has the "olive tree" in mind. No doubt Paul wants his readers to recall the Old Testament figure of an olive tree as representative of Israel,[83] the true people of God.   God is likely the One who is

---

word "first fruits" does in Revelation 14:4 (compared with Revelation 7:3-8). The first converts (the first piece of dough) into the church (as the Book of Acts shows) came out of Jewish background; the "lump" (the more to come) has reference to the future conversion of the Jews that this context has been talking about. See this interpretation presented and defended in Cranfield, *Romans*, p.564; Barrett, *Romans*, p.216; and Lipscomb and Shepherd, *Romans*, p.206. In this commentator's opinion, this view has against it the fact that it confuses the "lump" with the "remnant," which has not been the emphasis for several verses now. Since verse 11, the topic has been the majority who were not part of the remnant. (The explanation offered in the text can be seen in more detail in Sanday and Headlam, Murray, and Vine, *in loc.*)

[80] The serious student will find numerous interpretations of "first piece" and "root" in the commentaries. (1) Both figures represent the Patriarchs, especially Abraham. (2) Both figures represent Christ. (3) Christ is the first fruit, and Abraham is the root. (4) Both figures represent the 1st century Jewish Christians. (5) Jewish Christians are the first fruit; the patriarchs are the root. There appears to be no valid reason for making any distinction between "first piece" and "root" as many commentaries are wont to do. It would be just like Paul to validate his argument by appealing to several Old Testament figures in which there is a common topic or theme.

[81] Abraham was the progenitor of Israel, yet Romans 9:6-13 has reminded us that the seed-line was specially designated, too.

[82] A similar use of deliberate understatement was made at Romans 3:3.

[83] See Jeremiah 11:16; Hosea 14:6. Certainly, unbelieving Israel was not broken off from the church, for Jews who rejected the gospel were never in the church which Christ said He would build.

thought of as breaking the branches off – because He found them to be disobedient to the gospel, and therefore unsuitable for His purposes.

And you, being a wild olive, were grafted in among them. "Among them," that is, among the branches that were not broken off. The branches that were not broken off stand for the same believing Jews who before were designated as the "remnant." "And you" is emphatic in the Greek, and it singles out each individual Gentile Christian, first of all with reference to how he came to be part of the olive tree, and later with reference to a warning lest any Gentile Christian adopt an unchristian attitude of superiority toward the other branches, whether they be in the church or out of it.[84]

In most arboricultural practice, a slip (a "shoot," or a scion) from a cultured tree is grafted onto a wild root. Thus it is that Paul has been charged, by some critics, with making a great blunder when he has a wild slip grafted onto a cultured root. As has often been the case, it appears the critics are the ones who have blundered, for the practice (as far as olive trees are concerned) was known both in ancient and in modern times,[85] just as Paul describes it.

> At any rate, Paul's parable is clear. Here are two olive trees – a cultivated olive and a wild-olive. The latter produced poor fruit which contained little oil; the former normally produced good fruit. The olive is Israel, the people of God; the wild-olive is the Gentile world. But the olive began to grow weak and unproductive; old branches were therefore cut away and a graft was made from the wild-olive. "The cutting away of the old branches was required to admit air and light to the graft, as well as to prevent the vitality of the tree from being too widely diffused over a large number of branches" (Ramsay). The graft from the wild-olive is the sum total of Gentile believers, now incorporated into the people of God; the old branches which were cut away are those Jews who refused to accept the Gospel.[86]

---

[84] Paul uses second person singular verbs from verse 17 through 24.

[85] Among the ancients, Columella, *De re rustica* 5.9.16; and Palladius, *De insitione* 53f, are examples which show that the grafting of a wild olive slip into a cultivated tree, which had become unproductive, would reinvigorate the tree so that it again would bear fruit. And as for modern times, "Sir William Ramsay does, indeed, quote Theobald Fischer as saying that it was customary in Palestine sixty years ago 'to reinvigorate an olive-tree which is ceasing to bear fruit, by grafting it with a shoot of a wild-olive, so that the sap of the tree ennobles this wild shoot and the tree now again begins to bear fruit'." *Pauline and Other Studies in Early Christian History* (Grand Rapids: Baker Book House, 1970), p.223,224.

The reader should be aware that not all writers agree that Paul here describes a common 1st century practice. Sanday and Headlam, from verse 24's "contrary to nature," argue that Paul is here describing a "wholly unnatural process – for grafts must necessarily, in our experience, be from cultivated stock inserted into wild stock, the reverse process being one which would be valueless and is never performed." *Romans*, p.328.

Cranfield, *Romans*, p.566, finds the whole exercise of defending or criticizing Paul to be unnecessary since verses 23 and 24, in his opinion, describe a process, "a parallel to which ... is hardly likely to be discovered," that of grafting a broken-off branch back into the live tree. More will be said on this in comments at verses 23-24.

[86] Bruce, *Romans*, p.218.

Unsaved Gentiles do make up the wild olive tree, but we are not to think that all the Gentiles have been grafted into the cultured olive; only those "branches" (verse 24) of the wild olive that have become believers are pictured as having been cut off from the wild olive and grafted into the cultivated tree.

And became partaker with them of the rich root of the olive tree.   The root of the tree is still good; some of the branches (Jewish Christians) are still good, but some of the branches are unfruitful.   These unfruitful branches have been removed, and new branches (Gentile Christians) have been grafted in.   The new branches receive their life from the root.   Pictured here is "the rich flow of sap in which the wild olive partakes, but which does not belong to the wild olive itself, but is all drawn from the root."[87]   "In such unusual grafting ... both the graft and the stock on which it was grafted were affected; the old stock is reinvigorated by the new graft, and the new graft in turn, fed by the sap of the olive stock, is able to bear such fruit as the wild-olive could never produce."[88]   Of the attempts to identify what the "root of fatness" stands for in the application of the symbol to the church, that of Vine is most satisfactory.   "The Gentile believer had become a spiritual descendant of Abraham, partaking of the spiritual life and blessing which belonged to him and his descendants by Divine covenant."[89]

11:18 – *do not be arrogant toward the branches; but if you are arrogant,* **remember that** *it is not you who supports the root, but the root* **supports** *you.*

Do not be arrogant toward the branches.   What is being prohibited is a feeling of superiority,[90] whether towards their fellow Jewish Christians, or towards the unbelieving Jews.[91]   "Stop being arrogant"[92] is the first of the applications Paul makes of the metaphor

---

[87] Sanday, *Romans*, p.121.

[88] Bruce, *Romans*, p.218.   Bruce's comments reflect his decision about the genitive phrase found in this passage that is rendered "rich root" in the NASB, but "root of fatness" in the margin.   "Fatness" may be an attributive genitive, thus a root whose essential quality is fatness; or it might be an objective genitive, where the "fatness" receives the action from the root.   Bruce, with his note about sap and producing fruit, has evidently opted for the latter.

[89] Vine, *Romans*, p.167.   Others have opted for "divine election," or "the blessings promised to the patriarchs," or "the grace they enjoy" as being signified by the 'fatness of the root.'

[90] The word *katakauchaomai*, a compound word including not only to "boast" but also "down," pictures putting someone else down, to triumph over, to exult over.   Arndt-Gingrich, *Lexicon*, p.412.

[91] It is not easy to decide whether the "branches" are those among whom the Gentiles have been grafted (i.e., the good ones, the Jewish Christians), or whether the "branches" are the ones who have been broken off.   Both views have been defended.   The former view supposes that there was some friction between the Jewish and Gentile elements in the congregation at Rome (perhaps such friction is again reflected in Romans 14:1-15:13), and Paul is anticipating the need to warn against such prejudice if the unity of the congregation was to be preserved.   The latter view supposes that verse 19 identifies the "branches" as being the non-Christian Jews, and that this passage warns Christians about entertaining the same anti-Jewish prejudices that were common in the Roman world.   How many of our contemporary unbelieving Jewish neighbors have an antipathy toward Christianity because in the long centuries since Paul wrote, it has been the "church" that has encouraged and participated in the persecutions non-Christian Jews have experienced.   Those who profess to follow Christ have not always listened carefully to one of

of the olive tree.   After developing this theme, he will make a second application in verses 23,24.

But if you are arrogant.   Some of Paul's readers were entertaining uncharitable feelings toward the branches, maybe without admitting it to themselves.   This conditional sentence would cause them to search their own hearts, to ascertain their real feelings.   And if the feelings were wrong, what Paul writes next would help them come to a right perspective.

***Remember that* it is not you who supports the root, but the root *supports* you.**   Jesus worded it on this fashion, "Salvation is from the Jews" (John 4:22).   The privileges that converted Gentiles enjoy are derived, not original.[93]   In fact, the believing remnant of Israel did not make themselves what they were; they were part of the cultivated olive tree that God had been working on since He called Abraham, and gave him the covenant, "In your seed all the nations of the earth shall be blessed."   Instead of haughty feelings of superiority, Christians should entertain feelings of appreciation toward the "branches," and especially toward the "root."[94]

11:19 – *You will say then, "Branches were broken off so that I might be grafted in."*

You will say then.   The Gentile Christian is anticipated as trying to justify some of his feelings of superiority.   Maybe he cannot boast over the branches still in the tree, but is not he better than the *unbelieving* branches that have been broken off?

His apostles, who warned against such behavior.

[92] The present imperative with *mē* prohibits the continuance of an action already going on.   (See this explained in footnote #60 at Romans 6:12.)

[93] "We do not do justice to this place if we narrow it to the reception of the Gentiles among the spiritual seed of Abraham; it seems rather to mean that the whole scheme of redemption had its foundation in the Jewish economy.   Not only was Abraham the spiritual father of all the faithful; not only was the Redeemer a Jew and all the apostles and first teachers of the gospel of Christ Jews, but all books of the Scriptures, both of the Old and New Testaments, were written by Jews."   Lipscomb and Shepherd, *Romans*, p.209.   (The thrust of the quotation is right, but the last statement needs correction.   Luke, the author of the third Gospel and Acts, may well have been a Greek.)

[94] A word needs to be said about the rather common conception that 'the church has taken the place of the Jews as God's chosen people.'   Both Ephesians and 1 Peter 2 make it plain that the church does indeed have the special privilege of being God's 'chosen people,' while unbelieving Israel has been rejected.   But 'the church has taken the place of Israel' must be modified by what Paul writes both here in Romans 11:18, and in Ephesians 2:15.   The 'church' that takes the place of the Jews is made up of believers, from both Jewish and Gentile backgrounds.   There is a sense in which the church is the continuation of God's activities during the ages before Bethlehem.   The new covenant is the Abrahamic covenant renewed.   The "tree" with the unbelieving branches removed, and wild branches ingrafted, retains its identity, and is never regarded as a different tree from the one which sprang from the root.   Care should be exercised here: the statement about continuation should not be taken as though it reflected one-covenant theology.   The Mosaic covenant, as Romans (and the rest of the New Testament) has taught all along, was a temporary thing, added to the Abrahamic covenant until the Seed should come (Galatians 3:15-22).

"Branches were broken off so that I might be grafted in." The feeling expressed is, "I must be better than the broken-off branches, since they were broken off to let me in!" "God must think I am of more value than they, or He would not have extended His special providence to me." Ah, if the Gentile Christian is not careful, he will develop the same pride the ancient Jew was condemned for; it is a pride that looks at one's position ("I've been grafted in!") and begins to think he must be somebody special for God to do such a thing as that. No! The following verse will show that it is not personal worth or special privilege granted to a favored few – but that "faithfulness" is the condition to being grafted in, and remaining in, the cultivated olive tree.

11:20 – *Quite right, they were broken off for their unbelief, but you stand by your faith. Do not be conceited, but fear;*

Quite right. Paul grants the part of the argument about some being "broken off" and some being "grafted in." But he goes on to remind his readers that "faith" and "unbelief" were involved, too, and that leaves no room for inordinate pride or arrogance.[95] Thus, it appears, the attempted justification by the Gentile Christians for their attitude was based on a half-truth. Paul goes on to emphasize the other part of the truth they were ignoring.

They were broken off for their unbelief, and you stand by your faith.[96] God's dealings with Gentiles, as well as with Israel in the past and in the future, are in harmony with the doctrine of justification by faith. His "gracious choice" (11:5) still requires faithfulness on the part of those who would be His 'chosen people.' Men "stand"[97] by faith. This is a truth that no man dare ever ignore or forget!

Do not be conceited, but fear. 'Stop minding the high things!' 'Habitually have reverence (for God)!'[98] In light of what shortly will be written, perhaps the idea is that men should fear God, because His kindness is not to be presumed on, and His severity is not to be trifled with (verse 22).[99]

---

[95] Cranfield reminds us that "in order that I might be grafted in" was not the whole purpose of the breaking off of the branches. God's purpose includes also that which verse 11 indicated, "to make them jealous." Gentiles ought not to forget this truth. *Romans*, p.568.

[96] One wonders why the NASB (1960 edition, but removed in later editions) added the word "only" at this place. "By faith" is emphatic in the Greek, but the emphasis can be indicated to English readers, just as well as it was to Greek readers, by using the same word order as found in the original, as the NEB did it, "By faith you hold your place."

[97] "Stand" is from *histēmi*, a word that means "to cause to stand." God is the implied agent who "caused them to stand." Compare notes at Romans 5:2.

[98] Both imperatives are present tense; thus, the prohibition forbids the continuance of an action already going on, while the positive command requires habitual action. We have had the word "fear" in the sense of "reverence" at Romans 3:18, where we learned that its absence is one reason why men sin. "God" likely is the object of the fear, as the following verses go on to speak about God's actions toward men.

[99] It should be noted that Paul does not represent "fear" as an emotion which is incompatible with the exercise of faith. On more than one occasion, he puts forward the fear of failure (the fear of displeasing

11:21 – *for if God did not spare the natural branches, neither will He spare you.*

For if God did not spare the natural branches. Verse 21 gives a reason for the injunctions (in verse 20) to stop being conceited, and to be reverent habitually. "Natural branches" has reference to the disbelieving Jews, who by physical descent might be thought to have some kind of claim on being eligible to be part of the tree.[100] "Did not spare" is another way of wording what happened to the unbelieving branches; they were "broken off" (verse 17).

Neither will He spare you.[101] 'If there is a failure in your faithfulness,' is the implied condition. "You" reminds the Gentiles that they are alien branches; they do not even have a physical claim to being part of the tree, as the Jew had (cp. Ephesians 2:11-13). The Gentile Christian's security was conditional; like the Jew, he too is liable to be broken off for the same cause (unbelief). What has presently happened to the Jews, partly because their presumption led them to ignore the need for faithfulness, should engender a healthy fear in the Gentiles who were beginning to have the same superior, complacent attitude. After all, God will no more tolerate unbelief in the Gentiles than He did in the Jews.[102]

11:22 – *Behold then the kindness and severity of God; to those who fell, severity, but to you, God's kindness, if you continue in His kindness; otherwise you also will be cut off.*

Behold then the kindness and severity of God. Paul here urges his readers, instead of nourishing feelings of superiority, to contemplate these characteristics God has displayed in His dealings with men. After all, such contemplation can result in a man's own improvement and benefit. Verse 22 also serves to sum up what has been written since verse 11. "In the grafting in of Gentiles and the breaking off of unbelieving Jews are to be recognized the kindness and the severity of God."[103] Paul used the word "kindness" at Romans 2:4. "Severity"[104] is a word that occurs only here in the New Testament, but ex-

---

the Creator) as a proper stimulant to Christian endeavor. 1 Corinthians 2:3; Philippians 2:12; Ephesians 6:5; Hebrews 4:1; 1 Peter 1:17.

[100] That some Jewish people prided themselves about being superior to others simply because of their descent from Abraham seems to be reflected in John the Baptist's admonition at Matthew 3:9, "Do not suppose that you can say to yourselves, 'We have Abraham for our father!'"

[101] The KJV reads, "*Take heed* lest he also spare not thee." There is a manuscript variation here, with the Textus Receptus carrying the word "lest" that the older text does not. The addition of this word considerably weakens the force of Paul's warning.

[102] Special Study #7, "Once Saved, Am I Always Saved?" following the comments on chapter 8, has addressed the matter of the security of the believer.

[103] Cranfield, *Romans*, p.569.

[104] The Greek is *apotomia*, from *apo* (off, away from) and *temnō* (to cut). Thus, the word means "to cut off," but there is also implied a sharpness, rigor, roughness, in the action. Thayer, *Lexicon*, p.69. The English word "severity" now has a connotation of harshness, or even cruelty, that it did not formerly have. A vine dresser, or tree trimmer, while cutting off decayed or dead branches, exercises a firmness to do what is best for the vine or tree.

presses the same thought found in the words "broken off" (verse 17) or "cut off" (later in this verse). "As providence had been appealed to (verse 17), the apostle states the true providential aspect of God's dealings. It had a double side – one of goodness toward the Gentile, and one of deserved severity towards the Jew."[105]

To those who fell, severity. "Those who fell" are the Jewish unbelievers.[106] The severity which God exhibited is a consequence of their unbelief, not an antecedent.[107] For the time being, God has turned toward the Jew the severe side of His providence.

But to you, God's kindness. For the time being, while His severe side is turned toward the unbelieving Jews, the gracious side of His providence is turned toward the believing Gentiles.

If you continue in His kindness. We might have expected Paul to write, "If you continue in faith."[108] That he can substitute "kindness" here for "faithfulness" shows the real nature of the faith that saves – it is a *continual living* in the sphere where God extends His kindness.

Otherwise you also will be cut off. It is by faith that membership in the true people of God is acquired and maintained; it is by unbelief that it is forfeited. That principle, says Paul, is applied without partiality, to Gentiles as well as to Jews. Branches that were grafted in when they became believers will be "cut off" if they quit being men of faith. Again, we have it clearly set forth that a man's standing before God is conditional.

11:23 – *And they also, if they do not continue in their unbelief, will be grafted in; for God is able to graft them in again.*

And they also. As suggested at verse 18, it is likely that verses 23 and 24 are Paul's second application of his metaphor of the olive tree. The reason he appealed to this symbol in the first place was to substantiate his presentation that a future conversion of many Jewish people is to be anticipated. Now he tells us the conditions which they must meet if they would again stand in right relationship with God. Not only should Gentile Christians bear in mind that they continue to stand by faith; they should also be aware that if the unbelieving Jews quit their unbelief, they will be grafted back into the olive tree.

---

[105] Sanday, *Romans*, p.121.

[106] The Greek word "fell" here in verse 22 is the same word translated "fall" in verse 11. It is the opposite of "stand" in verse 20.

[107] To look at it as an antecedent is Calvinism.

[108] Consider the fact that he has just written in verse 20, "you stand by your faith." Compare Colossians 1:23, "If indeed you continue in *the faith* ..."; or Hebrews 3:6, "if we hold fast our confidence;" or Hebrews 3:14, "if we hold fast the beginning of our assurance ...."

If they do not continue in their unbelief.   Ever since the days of Paul, whenever one of Abraham's descendants has heard the gospel, believed in his heart that God raised Him from the dead, and confessed with his mouth that Jesus is Lord, he has been grafted into the olive tree.   The same holds true for the great majority of unbelieving Jews who one day will become "acceptable" to God.

Will be grafted in.   It does not say all living Jews will be grafted in, but it does say "if they do not continue in their unbelief," they will be grafted in.   Again, let it be noted Paul is dealing with the Christianization of the Jews, not their nationalization.   The "fall" of the Jews as a race (verse 11) is not a permanent and irrevocable thing.   As many individual Jews as will repent, will find they are included among the people of God (the olive tree).

For God is able to graft them in again.   Paul here explains how it is possible for God to graft them in.   He is "able" to do it.[109]   But why does Paul stress God's ability (power) to graft them in?   What is there about grafting them in that requires the power of God to do it?   We probably should take our clues from the word "again" in this clause, and from the following verses, which begin with "for," and so seem to be intended to explain this affirmation that God is able to graft them in.   "Again" reminds us that men do not ordinarily graft a branch from the same tree back on to the parent stock.   The reason the old branches had been cut off from the olive tree was that they had quit producing.   Simply cutting such a branch off, and then grafting it in again, would not cause it to begin to produce again.   It would take the power of God to graft an old branch "again" into the parent stock with the result that it would begin to produce fruit again.   The underlying idea of verse 24 seems to be this: When one considers that God could graft Gentiles in, who up until shortly before their conversion had not even been pursuing righteousness, He surely is able to so work it out that the Jews can become believers, too.[110]   Surely, He faces difficulties.   When one considers the Jews as a nation, having rejected Jesus as their Messiah and being so inveterately set against the gospel as they are, with the result that they have been "hardened" even further, it seems impossible they could ever become believers.   But do not forget that the gospel is the power of God unto salvation to everyone who believes.   Verse 25 then says that such an ingrafting of Jewish people who become believers is exactly in harmony with what God has promised in His Word He will do.[111]

---

[109] In Romans 4:21, Abraham had a similar assurance about God's "ability" to do things.

[110] In the word "able" (*dunatos* speaks of strength, might, power) there is no support for the view sometimes taught that saving "faith" is a gift given by God to the elect.   That would be completely foreign to Romans 10:17, as has been emphasized earlier in these comments.   While He does not implant faith apart from the Word, it still is true that He providentially arranges for preachers and prospects to get together; He so has arranged things that the Jews will be provoked to emulation; He shuts "up all in disobedience that He might show mercy to all" (verse 32).   These are some of the things in mind when it is written that God can so work it that the Jews can become believers.   He is not to be pictured as doing anything for the Jews (to lead them to faith) that He has not done for the Gentiles.

[111] Why does Paul appeal to God's ability to graft them in?   The likely answer is that He can do it and at the same time be consistent with Himself.   If the Jews should change their current attitude of rejection of Christ, then God can graft them in, for He would be acting in harmony with the principles of His administration, which include justification by faith, keeping His promises to the patriarchs, and acting in a way that is consistent with His own moral attributes.

11:24 – *For if you were cut off from what is by nature a wild olive tree, and were grafted contrary to nature into a cultivated olive tree, how much more shall these who are the natural branches be grafted into their own olive tree?*

For if you were cut off from what is by nature a wild olive tree. This verse seems intended to expand on the "ability" God has to graft branches into the olive tree. It will take God less "power" to reingraft the broken off natural branches than it did to graft in the wild olive branches.[112] The wild olive tree stands for the Gentiles, individual branches from among whom have become believers and have been grafted into the only cultivated olive tree God has.[113]

And were grafted contrary to nature into a cultivated olive tree. The phrase "contrary to nature" has been the one that has caused the commentators difficulty.[114] It has only been in recent years that a few grafts have been successfully made between different families; grafts are usually unsuccessful unless plants of the same or closely related kinds are used.[115] Even when grafts are made within the same family, the fruit produced on the grafted branch is that of the scion type, not that of the stock to which the scion is newly attached. That wild Gentiles could be grafted into God's olive tree, and produce spiritual fruit (just like the remnant branches were producing) is most unusual.

How much more shall these who are the natural *branches* **be grafted into their own olive tree?** If the Gentiles were accepted by God when they accepted Christ, certainly the Jews will be accepted when they obey Christ. Paul does not picture a cultivated branch from one tree being grafted onto another cultivated tree; he writes that the branches are grafted into the same tree from which they had been cut off. The scion and the stock are certainly compatible, once the scion has become a believer.

---

[112] The KJV treats "by nature" as though it explains the word "wild" – "If thou wert cut out of the olive tree which is wild by nature." "But there is no point in saying that a wild olive tree is by nature a wild olive tree; for it can hardly be a wild olive tree otherwise than by nature. Paul's point is rather that the wild olive tree is that to which the branch that has been cut out belongs by nature." Cranfield, *Romans*, p.571. The phrase *kata phusin* here ought not be given a different meaning than was given in 11:21.

[113] That God has but one olive tree is in harmony with what has been said in the early verses of chapter 11, how there has always been a "remnant" to carry on the "chosen people." Footnote #94 (at Romans 11:18) should be reviewed, lest "one olive tree" be used to prove a false theory about the continuing validity of the Mosaic covenant, as one-covenant theologians are sometimes wont to do.

[114] There is no need to see this phrase as Paul's apology for using his illustration about grafting a wild shoot into a cultivated stock, as though he knew it was an "unnatural" illustration. In light of what both modern and ancient writers have said about the actual practice of grafting a wild olive scion into a cultivated plant, we probably must look for a different explanation of "against nature."

Cranfield, *Romans*, p.571, having insisted we should understand "by nature" and "against nature" in light of the contrast made in this very context, then explains, "... the Gentile Christian has been cut out of the wild olive tree, which is the tree to which by nature he belongs ..., his native tree, and grafted into the cultivated tree to which by nature he does not belong ("against nature") ...."

[115] See the article on "Grafting," in *Funk & Wagnalls Standard Reference Encyclopedia*, edited by Joseph L. Morse (New York: Standard Reference Works Publishing Co., 1959), Vol.12, p.4180,4181.

11:25 – *For I do not want you, brethren, to be uninformed of this mystery, lest you be wise in your own estimation, that a partial hardening has happened to Israel until the fulness of the Gentiles has come in;*

For. As expressed in comments on verse 23, it appears that verse 25 (as was true also for verse 24, since both begin with "for") is intended to explain, or give a reason for, the phrase "God is able to graft them in."[116]

I do not want you, brethren, to be uninformed of this mystery. As in 1:13, this opening formula is Paul's way of emphasizing what he is about to say. "Brethren" is usually included as part of the formula; but it should be noted here that whereas "you" was singular in verses 17-24 (where he was speaking specially to the Gentile portion of his readers), now the "you" is plural. "You, brethren" suggests he is speaking to the entire congregation, not just its Gentile portion. A "mystery," as the word regularly denotes in the New Testament Scriptures, is something not clearly revealed in the Old Testament Scriptures, but now (by the New Testament apostles and prophets) is.[117] The truth that is called a "mystery" is something that would not even be known except by divine revelation.[118] Paul will first summarize the contents of the "mystery" he is about to reveal and then (verses 26 and 27) share some of Old Testament passages where this truth was dimly foreshadowed.

Lest you be wise in your own estimation. He has earlier warned the Gentiles to "stop being arrogant" (verse 18), and it was there noted that arrogance is often based on ignorance of some truth, and at times even on a half-truth. Without proper information to help them

---

[116] It is not unusual, in the commentaries, to find the writers beginning a new, major point of their outline for Romans at this verse. But it is hardly likely that a main point would begin with "for."

[117] The word "mystery" occurs some 30 times in the New Testament, with 20-plus of those times being in Paul's writings. The meaning of the word is best illustrated in Ephesians 1:9-12 and 3:4-7. In classical Greek, the word did convey the idea of secrecy, or incomprehensibility. But as J.B. Lightfoot writes in *St. Paul's Epistles to the Colossians and to Philemon* (Grand Rapids: Zondervan Publishing House, nd), p.168, "Thus the idea of *secresy* [sic] or *reserve* disappears when *musterion* is adopted into the Christian vocabulary by St. Paul: and the word signifies simply 'a truth which was once hidden but now is revealed,' 'a truth which without special revelation would have been unknown'."

"Mysteries" was also a word used for certain secret religious ceremonies to which only the initiated were admitted in the mystery religions of the Greek world. Liberal theologians, who have ignored or denied Paul's own statements as to the origin of his religion, have been wont to point to the ceremonies and language in Paul that are similar to the mystery religions, and claim they have found proof that he simply adapted certain of these into his new religious teachings, and therefore there is nothing supernatural about Pauline Christianity. A half-century ago, J. Gresham Machen, *The Origin of Paul's Religion* (Grand Rapids: Wm. B. Eerdmans Publishing Co., 1925), answered these naturalistic allegations.

[118] A number of topics are called "mysteries" in the New Testament. Among these are: (1) the eternal purpose of God concerning the redemption of man, 1 Corinthians 2:7; (2) the incarnation of Jesus, 1 Timothy 3:16; (3) the admission of the Gentiles, Ephesians 3:3; Colossians 1:26,27; Romans 16:25; (4) the mystical union of Christ and His church, Ephesians 5:32; (5) the transformation of the "living" at the time of the resurrection, 1 Corinthians 15:51; (6) the opposition of antichrist to the gospel, 2 Thessalonians 2:7; (7) here in Romans 11:25, God's purposes that are behind His dealings with Israel. In this Christian age, something that was a mystery is no longer a mystery after it has been explained by an inspired apostle or prophet.

form their beliefs and attitudes, the readers of this epistle, whether Jew or Gentile, might come to have a self-laudatory attitude about their own response to the gospel. Paul therefore makes known the contents of the "mystery" lest they get conceited about their supposed superior wisdom.

That a partial hardening has happened to Israel. "Israel" speaks of Israel as a nation, rather than of "spiritual Israel."[119] It was the majority of the race who disbelieved who were hardened (verse 7), not the remnant. Romans 11:7-10 has explained what is involved in this judicial hardening.[120] "Partial" may mean either that the hardening was not complete (the individual Jews who have suffered this judicial punishment are not so hardened that there was no further chance of recovery), or that the hardening extended only to a part of Israel (those Jews who have heard the gospel but have not become converts to the Christian religion are the ones who have been hardened).[121]

Until the fulness of the Gentiles has come in. "Fulness" is the same word translated "fulfillment" in verse 12, where it was used of the Jews. In that earlier verse, the word apparently was used in the sense of "conversion," and not just of conversion, but conversion "in great numbers."[122] What is it that the Gentiles in large numbers[123] are pictured as enter-

---

[119] "Spiritual Israel" is a convenient way to designate what was called the Israel within Israel at Romans 9:6, or what has been designated as the "remnant" in chapters 9:27ff and 11:5.

[120] The word translated "hardening" here in verse 25 is the same word used in 11:7. There is a possibility that this "hardening" is part of the contents of the "mystery" that Paul is here explaining. "While Israel's unbelief was something plain for all to see, and not needing to be revealed, the fact that a divine hardening was involved was something which could properly come under the heading of *musterion*. It could not be known by unaided human reason." Cranfield, *Romans*, p.575.

[121] If we take the second of the two options, namely, that only a part of Israel has been hardened, that is something we have already been told in Romans 11:7-10. Thus, the real thrust of the "mystery" has yet to be stated; it will follow in the words "until the fulness of the Gentiles has come in."

[122] It will be recalled that "fulfillment" (fulness) was the opposite of "failure" (diminishing, defeat). The failure was the rejection of the gospel, which greatly reduced the numbers of God's chosen people. Thus, the opposite would be conversion, which would greatly increase the numbers.

[123] While not rejecting the idea that "fulness" (among its several implications) includes a numerical connotation, we have carefully worded the comments so as to avoid any semblance of the idea that the number of the redeemed (whether from among Gentiles or Jews) is fixed and determined by the election of God, and is so absolute that it cannot be added to nor subtracted from. While there is a truth that God wants His banquet hall full (Luke 14:23), and while Acts 3:19,20 and 2 Peter 3:11,12 suggest that the second coming of Jesus awaits the addition of large numbers to the people of God, we doubt that the number is absolutely fixed in God's mind. Certainly, "fulness" cannot be so construed. Contextual considerations would tend to direct us away from such an interpretation. In verse 12, "fulness" did not refer to *all* the Jews who will ever be converted through the ages, but seemed to point to large numbers at just one time in history. Likewise, Romans 11:12 has indicated how much greater the "riches" will be for the Gentiles when the fulness of Israel comes in. The option certainly must be considered that this speaks of the conversion of still more Gentiles (though the total number converted would not be as great as during the ages when Israel was partially hardened, and God was working especially with the Gentiles).

ing? "Come in" is a word that Jesus often used of entering the Kingdom,[124] while the immediate context here in Romans has been dealing with being grafted into the 'cultured olive tree.' Thus, "come in" has reference to Gentiles entering into right standing with God and being used as His chosen vessels.[125] "Until" most likely is intended to put a time limit on how long the hardening to Israel will continue.[126] When the fulness of the Gentiles has come in, then the hardening of Israel will also be ended. Now if a man is hardened because he rejects the gospel, it certainly must be inferred that the reason God no longer hardens many in Israel is because they no longer are committing the sin of rejecting Jesus as their Messiah. As we see it, verse 25 is holding out the same promise (already expressed in verses 12 and 15) that the rejection of Jesus by a majority of Israel is but a temporary thing, and one day that will all change, as that future generation acknowledges their allegiance to the Lord Jesus Christ.[127]

---

[124] See Matthew 5:20; 7:13-21; 18:3; 19:17; Mark 9:43-47; John 3:5.

[125] In the opinion of most commentators, this passage deals with (what is) unfulfilled prophecy. Therefore, the reader who is making a thorough study of Romans will find several options offered as explanations of this phrase. (1) Some say the words picture a time when the ingathering of the Gentiles will be *running high*. (2) Some say the phrase pictures a time when the ingathering of the Gentiles will be *ended*. "Come in" is an aorist subjunctive, and would tend to look on the action as completed. (If "life from the dead" in verse 15 speaks of the final resurrection, then we may think of the conversion of Gentiles as having ended before the fulness of Israel comes in.) (3) Some say the phrase pictures a time when the ingathering of the Gentiles will be *nearly ended*. (If "life from the dead" in verse 15 means "spiritual life," then we must understand that some Gentiles will be converted even after the "fulness of the Gentiles has come in.")

In addition to these three options, another question that proves difficult to answer with any degree of certainty, and yet has a considerable bearing on how the student constructs his system of eschatology, is whether the time indicated in "until the fulness of the Gentiles has come in" is the same as that to which our Lord's words (Luke 21:24) point, "Jerusalem will be trampled under foot by the Gentiles until the times of the Gentiles be fulfilled."

One important thing to keep in mind as comments are made on these verses is this: nowhere in the passage does Paul specifically mention the second coming of Christ. (Granted, it may be implied in "life from the dead" in verse 15; and "fulness of the Gentiles *has come in*," verse 25, surely gets one near the end of the church age; but it is still true that no specific mention of the second coming is here made.) What then are we to think of those interpretations that speak of a future generation, or generations, just before the *parousia* (second coming)? At best they are but *possible* explanations.

[126] "Until" (*achri hou*) certainly must be understood as a temporal clause. A.T. Robertson labels it a temporal clause meaning "until which time." "Its basic meaning is 'up to'." *Grammar of the Greek New Testament in the Light of Historical Research* (Nashville: Broadman Press, 1934), p.639. Thayer, *Lexicon*, p.91, says that *achri* is a "particle indicating the *terminus ad quem*."

[127] If we knew exactly what verse 25 means, we could go a long way toward making an outline of events that can be expected to occur before the second coming of Christ. We can, on the basis of the interpretation given, make a tentative outline, saying that before Christ comes, several things can be expected to happen. The "fulness of the Gentiles coming in" is one of the things to look for. Following that, we expect the conversion of a great number of Jewish people to Christianity. Then follows the return of Christ, the resurrection, and the consummation.

Thinking students usually ask further questions at this point, such as, "Doesn't the Bible picture the return of Jesus as being possible at any moment? If we have to await a conversion of Jewish people toward the end of history, how can the return be imminent?" Consider two thoughts as this question is pondered. One, 2 Thessalonians 2 indicates there is an apostasy and a revealing of the man of lawlessness that must occur before the second coming. That certainly does not look like an imminent coming was anticipated by Paul. Second, lest anyone become complacent, thinking "I've not seen a multitude of

11:26 – *and thus all Israel will be saved; just as it is written, "THE DELIVERER WILL COME FROM ZION, HE WILL REMOVE UNGODLINESS FROM JACOB."*

And thus all Israel will be saved. "And thus" refers back to what was just said in verse 25. It means "in the manner just explained," namely, when the fulness of the Gentiles has come in, the hardening in part that has happened to Israel will be ended. God's intent that they be roused to jealousy (verse 11) will yet be accomplished. This phrase, too, reveals part of the contents of this "mystery" that Paul is sharing with his readers. "Israel," if verse 25 has any influence at all on how the word is understood in this context, must be national Israel.[128] "All" will have to be given a less than absolute connotation.[129] He hardly means

Jewish people converted, therefore I have plenty of time yet before Christ returns," it is very difficult to know how many are being converted at any time, and where, in our world. Maybe the conversion of many Jewish young people in California in the past two decades is part of the "fulfillment" of the Jews.

Thinking students often ask another question, "Are we living in a post-Christian world?" They have noted the decline in the number of conversions from among Gentile peoples, and are wondering if "the fulness of the Gentiles" has already come in, so that we are very near the time of the end. In reply to this question, it could be noted that the center from which the gospel radiates has moved several times in the course of history – from Jerusalem to Antioch to Europe to America. It moved each time God needed some new vessels to make His mercy known. The old centers declined as far as Christian influence was concerned. Perhaps what we are witnessing is God's rejection of America, and His calling of a new people from among the races of Gentiles to be His vessels. If so, we have no indicator of the nearness or remoteness of the second coming.

A third request thinking students make is for further explanation of this commentator's idea of "fulness" and how "Gentiles" and "Jews" fit into God's plan of history. What this commentator pictures in his own mind is this: Now, while the fulness of the Gentiles is coming in, what he sees is that the majority of converts are of Gentile background, though a few Jews are included. He expects the situation to be reversed when the "until" time limit is reached and the time has come for the fulness of the Jews to come in. The majority of converts will then be Jewish, with just a few Gentiles also being won. He does not anticipate that this "revival" will be long in duration, for he rather holds the view that "life from the dead" (verse 15) is reference to the resurrection, followed by the new heavens and new earth. But he also admits that we are dealing with prophecy, and since we are human, there is always the possibility of error in our understanding of the pertinent passages.

[128] Lenski, *Romans*, p.726, reminds us the word "Israel" was used with two different meanings in one short sentence in 9:6; why could it not be used with its national meaning once here in verse 25, and then with its spiritual meaning in verse 26? (Lenski's interpretation of Romans 11 is severely influenced by the fact that his eschatology is such that no time or activities are thought of as occurring on earth after the "fulness of the Gentiles" comes in. However, he has erroneously interpreted Matthew 24:14 as teaching that the final judgment follows the fulness of the Gentiles, whereas Matthew 24:14 is a prediction of the destruction of Jerusalem that happened in AD 70, some 40 years after Jesus made the prediction. See this commentator's work, *Let's Study Prophecy* [Moberly, MO: Published by the author, 1982], p.52,53.) In reply to Lenski, with the single exception of 9:6, every time "Israel" has been used in chapters 9-11, the reference has been to national Israel. That meaning is what one would expect as he reads verse 26, too.

[129] It becomes evident to the interpreter, as he works his way through this difficult passage, that some word in verse 26a must be given a secondary meaning. If we take "Israel" to mean spiritual Israel, as some opine we should, then we have given it a different meaning than the word had just a few phrases earlier in verse 25. If we take "Israel" to mean national Israel, then "all" is the word that must be explained in a less-than-absolute sense. There are a number of places in the Bible where "all" is not absolute: E.g., 1 Kings 12:1; 2 Chronicles 12:1; and Daniel 9:11. The passage in Mark 1:5 – where it is stated, "All Jerusalem came out" to where John the Baptist was baptizing – is one where it means simply "a large number." On the whole it seems better to choose "all" rather than "Israel" as the word whose meaning must be taken in a secondary sense.

that all Israelites in the past will be saved; it must mean the Jews living on earth at the time.[130] Furthermore, it is doubtful that Paul means every Jew then living will become a convert. "'All' often signifies, in Scripture, the greater part, very many, a large number. This is its import here. The meaning is that the great body of Israel shall be saved."[131] "Saved" has its usual import of the forgiveness of sins, becoming Christians, or being justified by faith.

---

[130] Lenski, *Romans*, p.695-728, has objected to this whole presentation as has been given in our comments. He insists that it is the remnant, and that only, during all the centuries since Paul, that is the topic of this "mystery." It is the remnant that is involved in the "their fulfillment" (verse 12, i.e. fulness of the Jews); it is the remnant whose acceptance results in spiritual life (verse 15); it is the remnant that makes up the part of Israel that is not hardened (verse 25) and is the real topic about which the "mystery" is concerned; and it is the remnant that makes up the "all Israel" who are saved (verse 26). Perhaps this following paragraph summarizes what Lenski thinks is the chief weakness of the interpretation followed in the notes above: "That exegesis is one-sided which centers only on the petrified part, makes that the subject of the mystery, and makes the mystery itself what shall be done with this part ... And these millennialists and these conversionists who claim to deal with the petrified part deal only with the last generation or a few generations of this petrified mass, for only a few extremists claim that all the petrified Jews who have died will be raised up and also be converted." *Op. cit.*, p.722.

Were it not for the apparent intimations of a coming conversion of many Jews in the future that we have had all along since verse 11 (e.g., see verses 12, 15, and 25), it would be very tempting to agree with Lenski, and interpret "all Israel" as meaning simply the sum of all those Jews who, through the centuries, have become Christians. These are members of the real Israel of God, and by the time God consummates history, "all Israel" will have been saved.

Hendriksen, *Romans*, p.379, lists other arguments often marshalled against the interpretation presented in the notes. (1) Does not "all Israel" sound very strange as a description of the (comparatively) tiny fraction of Jews who will still be living on earth just before Christ's return? (2) The reader of Romans has not been prepared for the idea of a mass conversion of Israelites. For the past three chapters, the emphasis has been on the "remnant" – not on the great masses. Is Paul now saying (in effect), "Forget what I told you previously"? (It seems to this commentator that Hendriksen forgets what Paul has written in verse 12, where there *is* a clear distinction made between the remnant, which has been the theme for many verses, and the majority, who are the ones involved in the "fulfillment.") While each of Hendriksen's objections has been answered in the literature, they are presented here lest any reader become dogmatic in his statements about what Romans 11:11-32 predicts.

[131] Lard, *Romans*, p.370. Modern premillennial writers have tried to show that "thus all Israel will be saved" actually is a New Testament prediction of the return of the Jews to the Promised Land. This surely is another case of special pleading, for if the return of the Jews to the land is not taught in this passage, it is not taught in the New Testament (see the additional comments on this same topic in footnotes #10 and #54, earlier in chapter 11). Further, their argument is seriously impaired by the fact that the Old Testament predictions of a return can be looking forward simply to the return from the Babylonian exile. Nothing in the context has prepared us for a discussion of the restoration of Israel to the land. Instead, we have been reading of Israelites becoming "believers" (verse 23). Amillennial and premillennial writers even agree on this matter. Amillennialist Floyd E. Hamilton, *The Basis of the Millennial Faith* (Grand Rapids: Baker Book House, 1972), p.52,53, wrote, "Notice that it is the *salvation* of the Jewish race, not its restoration to national prosperity under the Messianic king, that is here promised." Similarly, historic premillennialist Henry Alford, *The Greek Testament* (London: Rivingtons, 1871), Vol.2, p.436, wrote, "I have not mixed with the consideration of this prophecy the question of the restoration of the Jews to Palestine, as being clearly irrelevant to it; the matter here treated being, *their reception into the Church of God*."

If these comments have been correct,[132] the import of this passage is: When the fulness of the Gentiles has come in, then the turn of Israel will come around again; then the prophecies that dimly foreshadowed their conversion will be fulfilled.[133]

Just as it is written. The rest of verse 26 and verse 27, which quote passages from the Old Testament, are some of the places in the Old Testament where this "mystery" was dimly foretold. Verse 26 cites Isaiah 59:20; verse 27 is a citation of Isaiah 27:9.[134]

"THE DELIVERER WILL COME FROM ZION. In the Hebrew, the word "deliverer" is *Go'el*, the Kinsman, the Redeemer, the Vindicator, the Avenger.[135] Job 19:25 shows that the *Go'el* is the Redeemer Jesus Christ.

- The Hebrew of Isaiah 59:20 reads "to Zion." The LXX reads "for Zion's sake." Paul writes "out of Zion." How shall we explain this change?

- What does the word "Zion" mean? Zion was the name of one of the hills on which the city of Jerusalem was built (2 Samuel 5:6-9). In time, Zion came to be a name for the whole of Jerusalem (2 Kings 19:21). When Jerusalem became the capital city of the Jewish people, the name Zion frequently was used figuratively for the Jewish people. Yet it also is a name applied to heavenly Jerusalem (Hebrews 12:22; Revelation 14:1).[136] Of all these options in translation and meaning, which shall we choose? Does Isaiah picture Messiah as coming from heaven, or to Jerusalem, or from the Jewish people, or for the benefit of the Jewish people?

---

[132] One of the matters that has helped convince this commentator that the "conversionist" interpretation should be given serious attention is what was said in verse 11 about the majority of Jews who are unbelievers being provoked to jealousy, and so coming to Christ themselves. Perhaps this "jealousy" has not happened yet. Perhaps what is needed is for the fulness of the Gentiles to come in, and then when such large numbers of Gentiles are turning to Christ and participating in His Messianic blessings, the Jewish majority will see this and finally come to feel that jealousy that Paul seems to anticipate.

[133] Henry Alford, *The Greek Testament*, Vol.2, p.435, gives a helpful summary of the history of the interpretation of this passage. Among others quoted, he notes that Augustine taught a future conversion of the Jews, while Jerome denied it. At the time of the Reformation, the passage was a great battlefield. The Millenarians generally took the ground that the passage spoke of the future conversion of the Jews. Their opponents (including Luther and Calvin) took the opposite ground, contending that all that was predicted was that the door of mercy should still be kept open to the Jews and that many of them should return. To what Alford wrote could be added a note about the 19th and 20th centuries. 19th century postmillennialism, as represented by Hodge, *Romans*, p.584, understood the passage to predict a future conversion of the Jews. 20th century dispensationalism also holds the viewpoint that Israel as a nation has a future in God's plans, including a restoration to the Holy Land, their restoration as a nation to God's favor with Messiah ruling over them for 1000 years. See John F. Walvoord, *The Return of the Lord* (Findlay, OH: Dunham Publishing Co., 1955), p.93.

[134] As he has a number of times before, Paul combines several passages from the Old Testament, using a key word or theme that is found in each passage alluded to, as the thread that ties them together. Paul follows the LXX with a few variations, rather than the Hebrew.

[135] The Greek has an article and a participle, and would be translated, "the One who delivers."

[136] Steven Barabas, "Zion," in *Zondervan Pictorial Bible Dictionary*, edited by Merrill C. Tenney (Grand Rapids: Zondervan Publishing House, 1963), p.914.

- Which coming, His incarnation or His second coming, is Isaiah predicting?

It is clear that Paul is here not directly quoting, but is gathering up various Old Testament passages in one statement. "It may be that the whole citation is intended to express the sense of prophecy rather than the wording of any one single passage, and that the apostle has, in the words 'out of Zion,' summed up the prophecies which declare that the Redeemer *should spring out of Israel.*"[137]

HE WILL REMOVE UNGODLINESS FROM JACOB." The reference to removing ungodliness from Jacob is the way the LXX reads, and it differs considerably from the Hebrew of Isaiah 59:20. We picture these verses from Isaiah as being another case of "mountain-peak prophecy."[138] In one panoramic sweep, Isaiah takes in the whole Messianic Age, from incarnation to consummation. The part of the verse that talks about the Deliverer coming out of Zion has already been fulfilled in the first coming of Christ.[139] The part of the verse that tells about turning ungodliness[140] from Jacob has yet to be fulfilled in the future conversion of the Jews. It is in this phrase where the "mystery" about "thus all Israel will be saved" is found. "Saved" refers to Jacob's forgiveness and salvation.

11:27 – *"AND THIS IS MY COVENANT WITH THEM, WHEN I TAKE AWAY THEIR SINS."*

AND THIS IS MY COVENANT WITH THEM. For the first few words of verse 27, Paul continues the quotation from Isaiah 59:21. The rest of the verse is either from Isaiah 27:9, or as Bruce suggests,[141] from the classic new covenant prophecy found in Jeremiah

---

[137] Alford, *The Greek Testament*, Vol.2, p.436.

[138] See Gareth L. Reese, *New Testament History: Acts* (Moberly, MO: Scripture Exposition Books, 2002), p.62. W. Kay, "Commentary on Isaiah," in *The Bible Commentary*, edited by F.C. Cook (London: John Murray, 1898), p.19, has an excellent discussion of what he calls "the law of perspective shortening."

[139] A large number of commentators deny that the "Deliver will come from Zion" phrase is a reference to the first advent. It is not at all unusual to see comments to the effect that the reference is to the second coming of Christ, and that the conversion of the Jews will take place at the same time as when Christ comes. While it is admitted that "from Zion" might mean "from heaven," it is difficult to believe that seeing Jesus return on the clouds of heaven is the thing that causes the Jews to believe, for that would seem to contradict the thesis of Romans that the faith that is the condition of justification comes by hearing the gospel. This is true for everyone, the Jew first as well as the Greek. (In this connection, a review of Romans 11:15, especially footnote #74 might prove to be profitable.) Nor should Acts 3:19-21 and 2 Corinthians 3:16 be admitted as evidence of the conversion of the Jews as resulting from the second coming, for it requires a misinterpretation of those passages to make them teach that the return of the Lord is the thing that will convert the Jews.

It is much more in harmony with the rest of Isaiah to see 59:20 as a reference to Christ's first coming. Messiah did come (Isaiah 2:2,3). The Messianic kingdom was established on Pentecost (Acts 2). God laid the foundation in Zion. That foundation consisted in the death, burial, resurrection, and appearances of Jesus. The law did go forth from Jerusalem.

[140] See Romans 1:18 for the meaning of "ungodliness."

[141] Bruce, *Romans*, p.222.

31:31-34.[142]   The covenant that God made first with Abraham, and which has been renewed several times, involves in its fulfillment the removal of Israel's sins.

WHEN I TAKE AWAY THEIR SINS."   The future conversion of the Jews, Paul says, is part of what is involved in the covenant God made with Israel.   Objection is voiced to having the last line of verse 27 state the contents of the covenant, on the basis that it begins with "when."   But it should be remembered that this is a citation of an Old Testament passage, and this accounts for the inclusion of the word "when."   In fact, the taking away of sins is the heart of the covenant God made with Abraham, and renewed with Jacob (Israel).   God "takes away" sins when He justifies by faith.

11:28 – *From the standpoint of the gospel they are enemies for your sake, but from the standpoint of God's choice they are beloved for the sake of the fathers;*

From the standpoint of the gospel.   What follows, to verse 32, are some statements that emphasize several of the implications involved in what is predicted for Israel in the preceding section.   "According to [from the standpoint of] the gospel" must mean as far as the evangelization of the world has thus far proceeded.[143]   Jews, at least the majority of them, were still disobedient, transgressing, rejected, and thus at enmity with God.

They are enemies for your sake.   At the time Paul was writing, the majority of the Jewish people were rejecting and opposing the gospel, and thus God looked at them as being His enemies.   Their sin had led to an estrangement between them and God, and they were in need of reconciliation.[144]   "For your sake" reminds us of what was written in verse 11, "by their transgression salvation has come to the Gentiles."   What has happened to Israel is in harmony with the character of God and the way He providentially planned to move history toward its ultimate goal.

---

[142] The meaning of the word "covenant" was explained at Romans 9:4.   The new covenant, ratified by Jesus' blood shed on Calvary, seems to be synonymous with the Abrahamic covenant; i.e., the new covenant is the Abrahamic covenant renewed.   Galatians 3 shows that the Abrahamic covenant ("in your seed all the nations of the earth shall be blessed") has never been set aside.   It is still the one under which God is operating, and under which Christians have a relationship to God, for the "Seed" is Christ, "all nations" include Jew and Gentile, and "blessed" means the forgiveness of sins.   Compare Acts 3:24,25. For more information about this new covenant, and its fulfillment of the pristine promise made to Abraham, see notes at Hebrews 8:8-12 and 9:1-10:18.   The Greek word translated "new" in the phrase "new covenant" is regularly *kainos*, a word that means "renewed."   The new covenant under which Christians live is the Abrahamic covenant renewed.   (The only time *neos* is used of the new covenant, Hebrews 12:24, it is deliberately used to remind the readers that the new covenant was just recently inaugurated.)

In order to clearly understand the distinction between the Mosaic covenant which was temporary, and the new covenant which is abiding, the reader may find it profitable to review footnotes #20 and #34 in chapter 10, and footnote #94 in chapter 11.

[143] It will hardly do to say that "gospel" is used here for the message preached, thus making part of the message preached the statement, "Jews are enemies of God!"   It might be defensible to say that part of the gospel message dealt with the place of the Jews in God's system of things.

[144] Compare Romans 5:10,11.

But from the standpoint of _God's_ choice. If the parallel phrase in the first part of this verse ("from the standpoint of the gospel") meant "as things stand right now," then this matching phrase has the same connotation. How does God's "choice" stand right at the moment? The "choice" being referred to, of course, is the choice of Israel to be God's special vessels, referred to in Romans 9:11. The "remnant" of 11:5,7 shows the choice has not been abandoned as Paul writes during the 1st century. The majority to be converted will lend further credit to the truth that God did choose "Jacob" (Israel).

They are beloved for the sake of the fathers. "Beloved" by God is the idea. God still has an affectionate interest in the Jewish people, even those whom He has had to harden. God is not willing that any should perish. "This does not mean that he approved of their conduct or character, or that he had for them the same kind of affection which he would have had if they had been obedient."[145] For the sake of the fathers," the patriarchs Abraham, Isaac, and Jacob (see 9:7-13), presents the same doctrine as found in Romans 11:16. First having chosen them, God made certain promises to the patriarchs. He will honor those promises, and even help the unbelieving Jewish people to come to faith by the way He graciously arranges history and the spread of the gospel. God still wants to pour out blessings on the people of His choice (Deuteronomy 7:6-8, 9:5, 10:15), and He will, once they have come to accept Jesus as the Messiah.[146]

11:29 – _for the gifts and the calling of God are irrevocable._

For. Verse 29 gives a reason why we can believe God will not quit loving the people whom He chose. The choices God made back in eternity are not something to be withdrawn or revoked, nor even to be regretted by God.

The gifts and the calling of God are irrevocable. "Gifts" is _charismata_,[147] and likely has reference to those supernatural blessings enumerated in Romans 9:4,5. The "calling of God" would be the call God gave to the patriarchs (e.g., God's call of Abraham out of Ur of the Chaldees) to be His special servants.[148] In many passages, the Bible presents God

---

[145] Barnes, _Romans_, p.261.

[146] "These words have been interpreted in terms of the 'merits of the fathers' (Hebrew, _zekhuth ha'aboth_) – the Jewish doctrine that the righteousness of the Patriarchs constitutes a store of merit which is credited to their descendants. But this is not Paul's meaning here ...." Bruce, _Romans_, p.223. See Sanday and Headlam, _Romans_, p.330ff, for a short article on "The Merits of the Fathers."

[147] Because _charismata_ is regularly used in the New Testament for the special gifts of the Holy Spirit (i.e., spiritual gifts) which were given to the church after Pentecost, some writers see verse 29 (not as proof of His continuing interest in the Jewish people, as we have interpreted in the notes, but) as proof that the enmity between Jew and God has worked out to the Gentiles' advantage. On the other hand, the word has been used twice before in Romans, at 1:11 and 5:15, and in but one of these is the reference possibly to spiritual gifts. So there is nothing hindering us from explaining _charismata_ in 11:29 as we did at 5:15.

[148] Those writers who interpret "gifts" as being the spiritual gifts given since Pentecost are inclined to refer to 9:24 for an explanation of "calling" – and explain it as having reference to the calling of some Gentiles and Jews to be His present-day servants. This verse would then have to be a reason why the gospel is going to continue to be preached universally as it now is, even if it results in many Jews becoming enemies because of their refusal to obey it. God does not revoke what He has started.

as being faithful, unchanging, constant, when it comes to His eternal purpose (8:28, 9:11) and to the declaration of His purpose (9:6). In harmony with His purpose to choose Israel, God has no regret; He is not going to change and choose another people at this late date.[149]

11:30 – *For just as you once were disobedient to God, but now have been shown mercy because of their disobedience,*

For. Verses 30 and 31 (which together make up one conditional sentence) are intended to be a further explanation of what was said in verses 28 and 29.[150] At the same time these verses introduce several more of the implications regarding God's plans for Jew and Gentile that Paul has been emphasizing since verse 28. Once these implications are known, it can be seen that God has not repented of the gifts and calling of the fathers. God's purposes to show mercy remain constant; in some cases, it has been completed; in other cases, it has not. As one reads these verses, he recognizes the carefully constructed balance between the statements made about both Gentiles and Jews. "Once ... disobedient" (verse 30) matches "now ... disobedient" (verse 31). "Now ... shown mercy" (verse 30) matches "they also may now be shown mercy" (verse 31). The first member in each case speaks of Gentiles; the second member speaks of Jews. There is a balance in a third set of statements: "because of their disobedience" (verse 30) matches "because of the mercy shown to you" (verse 31); in this third set the first member speaks of the Jews, and the second of the Gentiles.

Just as you once were disobedient to God. The Gentile converts were once like the disobedient Gentiles described at length in chapter 1, and who were characterized as not pursuing righteousness in 9:30. "Once" speaks of the time before their conversion, the time before the gospel age, when they were disobedient to the revelation from God which they had.[151]

Other writers, observing that nothing specifically has been said about the "call" of the patriarchs, have supposed that the construction "gifts and calling" is another example of hendiadys (cp. Romans 1:5, "grace and apostleship") and means one thing, "the benefits of being called."

[149] Some have supposed that the statements about God "repenting" (e.g., Genesis 6:6; 1 Samuel 15:11,35; Psalm 90:13; Jeremiah 18:8; Jonah 3:10) are somehow contradictory to the ones that emphasize His faithfulness and constancy. While God's purpose remains constant, it does not force Him to be inflexible in the means He uses to arrive at His purpose. The methods by which history is led to reach the goals He has set may change, but not the goals. In addition, the fact is that many of God's promises to men are conditional on man's response; therefore, change in man is followed by a corresponding change in God's treatment of him. While this change in God's actions (looked at from a human standpoint) might look as though God changed His purpose, God has declared that His covenant with the patriarchs should have a long time to run, terminating only with time (Genesis 17:7; Psalm 105:8-11). The New Testament helps us to see how the Abrahamic covenant is still the one under which God is working with mankind, in His effort to redeem them.

[150] The "if-clause" in the condition is introduced by "just as" (*hōsper*) in verse 30; the conclusion clause is introduced by "so also" (*houtōs kai*) in verse 31.

[151] See notes at Romans 1:32 and 2:12, where it is demonstrated that the Gentiles did have a revelation from God, albeit not a written revelation like the Jews had after Moses' time. In notes at Romans 2:8, the significance of the fact that "believe and obey" (disbelieve and disobey) are interchangeable terms in the

But now have been shown mercy because of their disobedience. "Now" means since the gospel age has begun. The fact that Jewish people rejected the gospel led the evangelists to go to the Gentiles with the message of reconciliation (compare what was said in Romans 11:12). When the Gentiles responded positively to the gospel invitation, God was merciful and forgave their sins. He justified them by faith.

11:31 – *so these also now have been disobedient, in order that because of the mercy shown to you they also may now be shown mercy.*

So these also now have been disobedient. The Jews were disobedient to God in their rejection of His Son, and the gospel message the Son came to reveal. This first phrase in verse 31 reminds us of Romans 10:14-17,21. "Now" seems to have a temporal significance here, just as it did in verse 30.

In order that because of the mercy shown to you they also may now be shown mercy. Romans 11:11 has indicated that the sight of the admission of the Gentiles was intended to act as a stimulus upon the Jews, and lead them to an obedient faith. "As the rejection of the gospel by the Jews proved a blessing to the Gentiles, so in turn, its reception by the Gentiles is to prove a blessing to the Jews."[152] The door of mercy is wide open for the Jews to return.[153] Jews have not been cut off irrevocably. God will not damn a man just because he is a Jew. If that Jew will repent, God will receive him.[154] Just like the Gentiles received mercy after a time of disobedience (verse 30), so the Jews too will receive mercy after a time of disobedience (verse 31).

11:32 – *For God has shut up all in disobedience that He might show mercy to all.*

For God has shut up all in disobedience. Since it begins with "for," verse 32 is giving a further explanation of verses 30,31, and at the same time summarizes the presentation of

---

New Testament has been pointed out. It is instructive to note that the Greek word (*apeitheē*) is translated both "disobey" and "disbelieve." Properly and usually, *apeitheia* conveys a different idea from *apistia*. As noted earlier, *apeitheia* is a stubborn refusal to be persuaded (cp. notes at Romans 10:21), while *apistia* denotes merely a lack of faith or belief. In light of "disobedience" being used to describe their actions, what the Gentiles were doing was deliberate rebellion against what God had revealed His wishes were.

[152] Lipscomb and Shepherd, *Romans*, p.215.

[153] There is a manuscript variation on the second "now" in verse 31. Sinaiticus and Vaticanus include it; P[46], Alexandrinus, and the Byzantine family omit it. With it included, some have used this verse to prove that the salvation of all Israel is not something at the end of the age, but something going on all through the church age. With it omitted, a stronger case is made for the salvation of all Israel being yet future, near the end of the age. The "showing of mercy" to the Jews, the context seems to imply, is something that has not yet happened, as it one day will happen. Those who accept the "now" as being the correct reading usually take it as logical (rather than temporal) in this case, in order to make it match the fact that the showing mercy is yet future.

[154] The Jews have retained their national identity through the centuries, for some reason, while other races and nationalities have lost theirs. Are we to infer from the present passage that one reason the Jews have not lost their identity is that God has a future job planned for the descendants of Abraham?

chapters 9-11, by emphasizing the principle that lies behind all of God's providential action.[155]   "Shut up" is a word used of enclosing fish in a net (Luke 5:6) and of imprisoning people in a building (1 Maccabees 5:5).[156]   God is not the efficient causation of men's disobedience, but in His providential ordering of His world, He can so decree that the man who sins will become a slave to sin, and He can "give them over" (as we learned in 1:24,26,28).[157]

> He is not thus represented as plunging men into inevitable infidelity, having given them no choice.   As in the case of the *hardening* spoken of in previous verses, his dealings are *judicial*; the state into which the Jews are now by Him shut up has not been undeserved.   And, further, His ultimate purpose is here declared to be one of mercy.[158]

In the word "all," Paul includes both Jew and Gentile.   Paul is looking across the whole span of human history, and is summing up what God's plans and purposes were.   We might tend to think that God has not been fair when He has dealt with first one people, then another – working with the Jews for a while, while seemingly ignoring the Gentiles, and then being gracious to the Gentiles while seemingly ignoring the Jews.   But that is not the case.   There was divine purpose behind it all.

That He might show mercy to all.   God's ultimate purpose[159] for mankind is now revealed; all along it has been His purpose to show mercy to Gentile and Jew alike.   This is the way of escape from the prison-house of disobedience, namely, God's mercy.   Any man, whether Jew or Gentile, can throw himself on the mercy of God, and he will find his

---

[155] Note how themes of human disobedience (9:1-5,31; 10:3,16,21; 11:3,7,11,20,30,31) and God's mercy (9:15-18,23; 10:21; 11:5,22,30,31) have recurred throughout these last three chapters. God's providential and sovereign action (9:5,7-13,15-16,17,20-24,25,28,29,33; 10:9,12,15,19,21; 11:1-5,8, 11-12,16-24 [especially 21],25,29) likewise have been called to mind, over and over in these chapters.

[156] The only other place *sungkleiō* ("shut up") occurs in the New Testament is at Galatians 3:22,23 ("the Scripture has *shut up* all men under sin," "being *shut up* to the faith which was later to be revealed"). Cranfield, *Romans*, p.586, observes that like the Hebrew *sagar* (for which the LXX uses *sungkleiō*), in the Piel and Hiphil stems, can also mean "deliver up," so the Greek word too can have this meaning (as at Psalm 78 [LXX: 77]:50,62; Amos 1:6).

[157] Various methods of softening the expression, of what this verse says God did, have been proposed. Chrysostom and the Greek Fathers in the early church tended to explain "shut [them] up" as meaning 'declared' them to be unbelievers, or 'convicted' them of being disobedient.   Others have tried to explain it as though God simply 'allowed' them to become so imprisoned in disobedience.

[158] Barmby, *Romans*, p.324.

[159] In the Greek, it is a *hina* clause, expressing purpose.

sins forgiven and his iniquities pardoned.[160]

> The way in which the apostle regards such present judicial dealing as conducive to final mercy appears to be such as this. It is the doctrine of the whole Epistle that salvation is to be attained by man's renouncing his own imagined righteousness, and submitting himself to the righteousness of God. It conduces to this end that his "disobedience" should have its course and consequences; so that, conscience being at length awakened, he may long for deliverance from his hopeless state, and appreciate the offered salvation (see chapter 7). So the Gentile world was long shut up in its self-induced, but also judicial, "disobedience" (see 1:18ff); that, "the wrath of God" being at length revealed to it from heaven, the "righteousness of God" might also be revealed to it and laid hold of. In like manner God deals now with the Jews, who still persist in going about to establish their own righteousness instead of submitting themselves to the righteousness of God. He shuts them up for the present in their disobedience, to the end that at length, after their long judgment, and stirred up by the fulness of the Gentiles coming in, they may feel their need, and accept salvation.[161]

All God's dealings with mankind are in accordance with His purpose to show mercy to all. Whether in the past, present, or future, whoever would respond to God's revelation and be a man of faithfulness will find himself reckoned as righteous by God. Whoever refuses to submit to God's way of righteousness will find himself judicially punished. But even then, God has not given up completely on that man. He will continue to attempt to lead the man to repentance. However harsh, then, His dealings may seem, when we contemplate His real purpose of showing mercy, we can only burst forth into thankfulness to God, just as the apostle does in the following verses.

---

[160] Believers in the final, universal salvation of all men have used this verse (as indeed they use Romans 5:18) as one of their proof texts. They insist that the "all" on whom God showers His mercy is as universal as the "all" whom He has shut up in disobedience. If all have sinned, then all are saved, is their conclusion. However, to reach their conclusion, they have to tear the verse away from its context. Chapter 11 has been dealing with belief and unbelief, and grafting in and breaking off, depending on whether there is belief or unbelief. The whole section has been illustrating how God uses "chosen vessels" to extend His offer of mercy to the whole human race; what need is there for this if all are going to be saved anyhow? In the present age, by the preaching of the gospel, the offer of justification by faith is made to all alike, without any distinction of nationality. What a waste of time and effort, if all are to be finally saved, whether or not they are in right standing with God.

With universalism becoming a pervasive philosophy in the World Council of Churches, it is not surprising (though it is heartbreaking) to find a call for a moratorium on missions (e.g., Bangkok '73); or to find a de-emphasis on personal evangelistic work (since, in modern thinking, men have all been redeemed at Calvary; they just do not know it yet, so this is the real message the church has to proclaim) that would lead men to forsake their idolatrous ways, and confess Jesus as Lord, and their only Savior. Perhaps the most tragic thing about this "universalism" is that men claim it is what is taught in the Bible. (It is a low view of Scripture, similar to Barth's, that permits a man to say universalism is what the Bible teaches.) The student who wishes to pursue this topic, will find helpful information in Arthur Johnson, *The Battle for World Evangelism* (Wheaton, IL: Tyndale House Publishers, Inc., 1978).

[161] Barmby, *Romans*, p.324,325.

E. A Hymn of Praise to God.   11:33-36

> *Summary:* When we contemplate God's purposes and providential control of His creation, spread out before us in vast panorama as they have been in chapters 1 to 11, we are awed by His marvelous wisdom and knowledge by which it was all planned; we properly recognize His relationship to His creation; and we break out into praise to Him.

11:33 – *Oh, the depth of the riches both of the wisdom and knowledge of God!   How unsearchable are His judgments and unfathomable His ways!*

Oh. If (as the NASB does) we spell it "Oh" it is an exclamation of admiration. If (as the ASV did) we spell it "O," it is like an adjective describing immensity.[162] Verses 33-36 form a doxology,[163] and the key to understanding these four verses is to recognize they are the conclusion to the argument which Paul has been pursuing since Romans 1:16.

The depth of the riches both of the wisdom and knowledge of God! "Depth" is used metaphorically to mean inexhaustible, profound, immense. "Riches" carries the idea of wealth, abundance.[164] The translator must make a decision whether to translate *kai*, the first time it appears in this phase, by "both" or "and."[165] Because it is difficult to find a distinct and definite meaning for "riches,"[166] like can be assigned to "wisdom" and "knowledge," most translators prefer "both." "Wisdom" would be the choice of the best methods to accomplish the best ends,[167] and at the same time knowing how these methods would relate to each other in such details as cause and effect. "Knowledge" would be the ability to perceive exactly what was needed in every case ('immeasurable wealth of know-

---

[162] The one letter Greek interjection (ō) occurred before in Romans 2:1 (ASV), 2:3, and 9:20, where it was prefixed to words in the vocative case, and so was translated "O." (Cp. "O Theophilus," at Acts 1:1 [ASV] and "O Jews," at Acts 18:14.)   The lexicons usually treat the interjection here at Romans 11:33 as an exclamation of admiration.

[163] There are many grand doxologies in the Bible.   See Jude 24,25 and Romans 16:25-27.   Doxologies deserve special emphasis and study, for they are soaring leaps made by God's inspired men.

[164] Compare the use of the word "riches" at Romans 2:4, 9:23, 10:12.

[165] The KJV, ASV, and NASB all render it "both," so that "riches" modifies "wisdom and knowledge," and the whole phrase tells us that the riches of God's wisdom and knowledge are inexhaustible ("depth," *bathos*, means "without bottom").   If we translate as the NASB margin suggests, then the word "depth" modifies all three nouns, and we would read, "O the depth of the riches, and of the wisdom, and of the knowledge of God."

[166] Those who take all three genitives as separate and independent substantives, usually explain "riches" by an appeal to 9:23 or 10:12.   It is not unusual to see "riches" explained as a 'wealth of divine grace.'

[167] As verse 32 has explained, the end or design God had in view was to bestow mercy on all, and the method was to work first with this people, and then with that remnant, using them as vessels of mercy. There was a profound wisdom behind it all, Paul says.

ledge' is another way to say omniscience).[168]

How unsearchable are His judgments and unfathomable His ways!   This phrase is also an exclamation.[169]   "Unsearchable" means that which cannot be investigated or fully understood.[170]   "Unfathomable" means that which cannot be comprehended or investigated thoroughly.[171]   Here is one of the passages in the Word where we are told that some of God's plans and doings are not discernible simply by unaided human research. Even those judgments and ways which He has revealed may be beyond human comprehension.[172]   "Judgments" refers to the result[173] of "decisions" He made, such as the one that made the entrance of the Law necessary when man sinned (5:20), and that by which Israel was excluded and the Gentiles admitted.   "Ways" denotes the mode or manner of executing His decisions, such as His arrangement by which He justifies those who have faith in Jesus (3:26), frees the slaves of sin (6:17,18) and makes available the indwelling Spirit to aid the Christian to live faithfully (chapter 8).

11:34 – *For WHO HAS KNOWN THE MIND OF THE LORD, OR WHO BECAME HIS COUNSELOR?*

For.   In verses 34 and 35, Paul appeals to some Old Testament passages to demonstrate the truth of the exclamations just made about the wisdom and knowledge, the judgments and ways of the Lord.[174]   The passage quoted in verse 34 is Isaiah 40:13,[175] and varies

---

[168] George Mark Elliott used to say, "The more knowledge we have, the more God's ways amaze us. It staggers the imagination to realize what God must have to know."

[169] The relative adverb *hōs* ("how") is used here, as at Romans 10:15, to introduce an exclamation. Arndt-Gingrich, *Lexicon*, p.907.

[170] The Greek word, which occurs only here in the Scriptures, is from the verb *ereunaō* (meaning to search, to examine) compounded by the preposition *ek* (meaning "out"), preceded by an alpha-privative, which negates what the rest of the word says.

[171] The adjective *anexichniastos* is made up of the verb *exichniazō* (meaning to trace out, to investigate, to research thoroughly), plus an alpha-privative.

[172] Mortal men ought not be offended by such language, but rather should rejoice that all around may be seen evidences of God's wisdom and invisible hand at work.

[173] The word is *krima*, and at chapter 5, footnote #111, it was noted that nouns ending in *-ma* emphasize the result of the action signified by the noun.

[174] The commentaries are not agreed on how much of verse 33 that verses 34 and 35 are intended to explain or give a reason for.   Gifford, *Romans*, p.202, says that the three ideas of verse 33 (knowledge and wisdom, judgments, and ways) are here justified in inverted order.   Vine, *Romans*, p.174, indicates that verse 34 is related to only the last exclamation in verse 33, so that the first question has reference to the judgments of God, and the second question has reference to His ways.

[175] Paul quotes this same Isaiah 40:13 passage at 1 Corinthians 2:16.   In 1 Corinthians, Paul applies this passage to Christ.   Here in Romans, he applies it to God.   Isaiah himself was making reference to Jehovah.   (It has already been called to the reader's attention that it is common to find Old Testament "Jehovah" passages applied to Jesus in the New Testament.   See Romans 1, footnote #21, and Romans

only slightly from the LXX.

WHO HAS KNOWN THE MIND OF THE LORD. Wisdom, knowledge, and judgments are the product of the mind. Long ago, Isaiah indicated that no man can know what God is thinking, unless God reveals His mind. In 1 Corinthians 2:16, where Paul claims for himself and the other apostles to "have the mind of Christ," it becomes clear that God has deigned to reveal (to the apostles and prophets) some on the subject of His own designs and purposes. But until this is done, and His inspired messengers have spoken what they have had revealed to them, there is no knowing the mind of the Lord.

OR WHO BECAME HIS COUNSELOR? With whom did God consult when it came time for Him to make His decisions? "Earthly monarchs have counselors of state, whom they may consult in times of perplexity or danger. But God has no such council. He sits alone; nor does He call in any or all of his creatures to advise him, for none of those created beings is qualified to contribute anything to enlighten or to direct him."[176] Did God ask advice from any created being so that He would know how to act? Hardly!

11:35 – Or WHO HAS FIRST GIVEN TO HIM THAT IT MIGHT BE PAID BACK TO HIM AGAIN?

OR WHO HAS FIRST GIVEN TO HIM. This verse is an echo of Job 41:11.[177] Perhaps Paul intends this quotation to be illustrative of the "immeasurable wealth of wisdom and knowledge" alluded to in verse 33. The means by which God works are not supplied to Him from without, but proceed from the boundless stores of His omniscience and omnipotence.

THAT IT MIGHT BE PAID BACK TO HIM AGAIN? Nothing in God is derived from without, so as to be claimed back again by its owner.[178] The questions Paul has asked in the past few verses expect an answer of "No one!" On those occasions (back in eternity

---

10, footnote #69.)

[176] Barnes, *Romans*, p.266.

[177] This passage is found at Isaiah 40:14 in some manuscripts of the LXX, but the poorly attested reading is pretty well agreed to be a gloss into Isaiah from this passage in Romans. The words are found in the Hebrew of Job 41:11, though the Hebrew is quite different from the LXX at that place. The fact that one other time, when Paul deviates considerably from the LXX, he is quoting Job 5:13 (at 1 Corinthians 3:19), has caused some critics to wonder if there was another Greek translation of the Old Testament, besides the LXX, to which Paul had access. In this commentator's opinion, it is more likely that while Paul usually quoted from the LXX, he was familiar also with the Hebrew text, and exercised judgment in his citations (inspired judgment, no doubt). (Cp. at Romans 3:10, footnote #27, and at Romans 9:33, footnote #117.)

[178] Those commentaries which have emphasized the unscriptural character of the idea of human merit and works, regularly remind the reader (again) at this place that such human merit is ruled out. Typical would be Cranfield, *Romans*, p.591, who writes, "The purpose of the quotation is to underline the impossibility of a man's putting God in his debt."

before creation, and even after creation) when God has made plans and choices and decisions, no one has given God any advice.[179]   No one, therefore, either from experience or research, is able to explain God's wisdom, knowledge, judgments and ways.   What was affirmed in verse 33 stands true; Scripture itself confirms it.

11:36 – *For from Him and through Him and to Him are all things.   To Him* **be** *the glory forever.   Amen.*

For from Him and through Him and to Him are all things.   Verse 35 has affirmed the truth that nothing in God is derived from without.   Now, by a reminder of creation's relationship to its Creator, this statement is justified.   In other words, verse 36a is a reason for what was just said in verse 35.[180]   Created things cannot contribute any "how-to-do-it" ideas to their Creator – not when they themselves all proceed from Him,[181] are made or wrought by Him,[182] and exist to carry out His ends.[183]   Subordinate, they are, and dependent on Him, rather than He on them.[184]

To Him *be* **the glory forever.   Amen.**   This doxology is a fitting conclusion, not only for chapters 9-11, but also for the whole doctrinal portion of the epistle, which has now been finished.   God is worthy of receiving praise from men, now and forever.

---

[179] This language, "no one has given Him any advice," is intended (as the context clearly shows) to mean "no created being."   It does not rule out the idea that the Godhead as a whole (Father, Son, and Holy Spirit) planned the universe and all its inhabitants, and carried out the plan.   God (not necessarily the Father only) is the source and Creator and goal of all things.

[180] The verse begins with "because," *hoti* in the Greek.

[181] "From Him" (*ex autou*) is a genitive of source.   "God is the personal source, the first cause of all things.   See also 1 Corinthians 8:6.   This lends no support to the pantheistic doctrine that everything is an expression or phase of the Deity.   On the contrary, all things owe their existence to Him."   Vine, *Romans*, p.174.

[182] "Through Him" (*di' autou*) expresses (intermediate) agency.   First, God had the idea or the plan to create (all things are "from Him"); then God did the actual work of creating; He was the agent of creation.

Because some verses (e.g., John 1:3,10) attribute the work of creating to Jesus as the intermediate agent, some of the older commentators have supposed there is a reference to the Godhead in Romans 11:36a.   "It is a mistake to see in this, as some of the older commentators have done, an allusion to the Trinity.   This can hardly be.   The subject of the whole verse is God the Father." Sanday, *Romans*, p.125.   The third in the series of prepositions, "to Him," is only with difficulty explained as being a reference to the Holy Spirit.

[183] "To Him" (*eis auton*) might mean that God is the goal toward whose praise and glory all things were made.   While that certainly is a Biblical doctrine, having been offered as a possible interpretation of the verse about "fall short of the *glory* of God" (Romans 3:23; see also Colossians 1:15, where the same thing is said about Christ), in light of recent verses about God's providential use of His creation, it might be preferable to think about creation carrying out His ends.

[184] Those writers who constantly are looking for Paul's sources are apt to suggest that Paul borrowed verse 36a from pagan sources.   See Cranfield, *Romans*, p.591, who, while suggesting a pantheistic or Stoic source, nevertheless credits Paul with pouring new meaning into the formula.

The "Amen" may first have been Paul's own heartfelt agreement with what he had just written by inspiration.[185]   In time, when the letters were read out loud in the public worship services, these "Amens" (found with some regularity in Paul's letters) were places the whole audience was accustomed to voice their agreement with what has just been read.

---

[185] "God is in control" is an underlying theme in all eleven chapters of the doctrinal portion of Romans. While not every question that a man could ask about God's purpose and providence has neatly and completely been answered, enough has been written, as the Spirit led, to enable Paul and us to see that God has all along been quietly and surely working out His determination to extend His mercy to all who will submit to His way of righteousness.   "Let God continue to carry out His will, and praise Him for how He does it!" is the idea in this doxology.

SPECIAL STUDY #8

THE DOCTRINE OF PREDESTINATION

INTRODUCTION

The terms "predestination," "foreordination," "determinate counsel," "foreknowledge," "purpose," and "election" are all expressions found in our English Bibles. What do they signify? How are they related to each other, if they are not synonymous? Whatever the Bible teaches on these matters is as true as what it teaches on any other subject or term. Any student of the Bible will want to know what the Scriptures say on the subject; he may disregard what men have said on the subject, and even reject what human creeds say, but he cannot disregard what the Scriptures themselves say.[1]

Predestination is a Biblical term, as we shall see. Those who wish to call Bible things by Bible names will surely wish to use the term as God Himself has used it. But how has He used it? And involving whom? These are matters this Special Study will address. Through much of theological history, the doctrine of predestination has been a constant cause of comment and controversy. Positions have been advanced, and then defended or objected to, often using technical terms with which many modern readers are unfamiliar. It is therefore also intended that the information here given will help give a perspective on the topic that will aid the reader to understand comments he finds offered for many passages, not only in Romans,[2] but in other Bible books.

---

[1] A brief introduction to this topic has been offered in the Special Study, "Predestination and Foreknowledge," found in the author's *New Testament History: Acts* (Moberly, MO: Scripture Exposition Books, 2002), p.130-134.

[2] Any commentator who is perfectly honest will admit that comments made on numerous passages in Romans reflect decisions and conclusions about the doctrine of predestination. To list just a few:

(1) The outline of chapters 9-11 may well reflect a peculiar view of predestination. For example, in harmony with Lutheran theology, the following outline is rather standard: Chapter 9 shows the predestinating hand of God in the present hardness of the non-believing Jews, and sharply rejects any human claim to membership among the elect that they may assert (9:14-18). After God's predestination has been emphasized in the early part of chapter 9, 9:30-33 and chapter 10 make it clear that the unbelief is man's fault, not the result of God's predestination. Chapter 11 makes it clear that the present obduracy does not involve the final predestination of unbelieving Israel to damnation.

(2) The discussion of an age of accountability at Romans 7:9 raises the question of the salvation of unbaptized children. Has God predestined them to salvation or damnation?

(3) Consider what was written about "foreknowledge" and "predestination" at Romans 8:28,29. Is foreknowledge synonymous with omniscience? Does God's foreknowledge precede His predestination?

(4) Does the phrase "the Law came in besides" at Romans 5:20 have anything to do with predestination?

(5) See what was said on "purpose" and "predestined" at Romans 8:28,29. Are "purpose (plan)" and predestination but two different words for the same thought or action of God?

(6) Several times the topic of "faith" versus "works" has been discussed, as has the matter of how saving faith is produced or arrived at in the heart of man. The explanations given often reflect a previously-made decision about the doctrine of predestination.

The explanation given at Romans 8:28-30, about how God made a plan back in eternity, how that plan involved approving those who were "in Christ," how those "in Christ" were to be destined for glory, and about how that plan also included intermediate steps (call, justify, glorify) to help men get to the goal, differs from most Protestant and Catholic presentations of predestination. Thus, it seems needful, in an effort to think God's thoughts after Him, to pause to make a rather detailed study of this whole matter.[3]

I. DEFINITION OF TERMS

A. Hebrew Terminology

The English words "predestine" and "foreordain" are compound words, and the Hebrew language does not admit such terms, so we do not find either word in our English Old Testaments. What we do find are words that may have some relationship to the ideas embraced in each. Theologians have pointed to such words in the Hebrew Old Testament as '*etsah* (to plan, to counsel, as at Jeremiah 49:20, 50:45; Micah 4:12); *ya'ats* (to purpose, as at Isaiah 14:24,26,27; 19:12; 23:9); *ya'ad* (to appoint, to ordain, to plan, as at Psalm 139:16; Isaiah 22:11); and *bahar* (to choose, as at Numbers 16:5,7; Deuteronomy 4:37, 10:15; Isaiah 41:8; Ezekiel 20:5).[4]

---

(7) The explanation offered for Romans 5:12 ("death spread to all men, because all sinned") is likely bound up with the commentator's view of predestination.

(8) The conclusion one reaches on the whole matter of eternal security – and the search for certainty of salvation – is likely influenced by beliefs about predestination.

(9) The presentation in Romans 9:6-29, whether it is election of some for *service* or of some for *salvation*, is inseparably related to the doctrine of predestination.

(10) If the Bible teaches predestination, is it of individuals, or of groups?

(11) Does Romans 8:30 ("whom he predestined") teach a predestination of some to salvation? And if so, does it logically follow that some are also predestined for damnation? (This is often referred to as either "single predestination" or "double predestination.")

(12) Is there any truth to the statement sometimes heard, that God predestines the plan, but not the man?

(13) Comments have been offered on the synonyms for "will" (*boulē* and *thelēma*). Does God have two kinds of "will," so that some things which He wills inexorably happen, while other things willed do not?

(14) In Romans 11, opinions have been expressed about the terms "fulness of the Gentiles" and "fulness" (fulfillment) for the Jews. Does predestination involve a fixed number, determined by God, which cannot be added to nor subtracted from?

(15) Sin has been spoken of as a 'power' in the world, and in the lives of men. Was this predestined by God, or simply permitted?

(16) Freedom of the will has been emphasized in the comments offered on Romans. How is this doctrine to be harmonized with God's predestination?

[3] It can safely be said that several complete systems of theology start with the doctrine of God's predestination. While it is not the present commentator's practice to base his system of doctrine wholly on this one concept, it is certainly true that what one thinks about predestination does influence comments on scores of verses.

[4] B.B. Warfield, "Predestination," in *Hasting's Dictionary of the Bible*, edited by James Hastings (New York: Charles Scribner's Sons, 1911), Vol.4, p.47,48, lists these and several other Hebrew words of

B. Greek Terminology

The English words "predestine" and "foreordain" are used to translate the Greek word *proorizō* at Acts 4:28; Romans 8:29,30; 1 Corinthians 2:7; and Ephesians 1:5,11. It is certainly useful to see how the word is used in each of these places.

> For truly in this city there were gathered together against Thy holy Servant Jesus, whom Thou didst anoint, both Herod and Pontius Pilate, along with the Gentiles and the peoples of Israel, to do whatever Thy hand and Thy purpose predestined to occur. (Acts 4:27,28)

> And we know that God causes all things to work together for good to those who love God, to those who are called according to His purpose. For whom He foreknew, He also predestined to become conformed to the image of His Son, that He might be the first-born among many brethren; and whom He predestined, these He also called; and whom he called, these He also justified; and whom He justified, these He also glorified. (Romans 8:28-30)

> But we speak God's wisdom in a mystery, the hidden wisdom, which God predestined before the ages to our glory. (1 Corinthians 2:7)

> Blessed be the God and Father of our Lord Jesus Christ, who has blessed us with every spiritual blessing in the heavenly *places* in Christ, just as He chose us in Him before the foundation of the world, that we should be holy and blameless before Him. In love He predestined us to adoption as sons through Jesus Christ to Himself, according to the kind intention of His will ... In all wisdom and insight He made known to us the mystery of His will, according to His kind intention which He purposed in Him with a view to an administration suitable to the fulness of the times, that is, the summing up of all things in Christ, things in the heavens and things upon the earth. In Him also we have obtained an inheritance, having been predestined according to His purpose who works all things after the counsel of His will, to the end that we who were the first to hope in Christ should be to the praise of His glory. (Ephesians 1:3-12)

Theologians also often include such Greek words as *protassō* ("having determined their appointed times," Acts 17:26); *protithēmi* ("which He purposed in Him," Ephesians 1:9); *prothesis* ("purpose," as in Romans 8:28, 9:11; Ephesians 1:11, 3:11; 2 Timothy 1:9); *prohetoimazō* ("prepared beforehand," Romans 9:23); *problepō* ("provided," Hebrews 11:40); *proeidon* ("looked ahead" or "foreseeing," Acts 2:31; Galatians 3:8); *proginōskō* and *prognōsis* ("foreknew" or "foreknowledge," as Romans 8:29, 11:2; 1 Peter 1:2,20; Acts 2:23), and others.[5]

---

similar meaning (such as *chasab* [purpose, plan, devise], *gezerah* [decree], *zamam* [purpose], and *chaphets* [to be pleased, to desire, to will]) that he thinks express "predestination" in the Old Testament.

[5] Warfield, *op. cit.*, p.48, also lists "appoint" (Acts 22:14, 26:16), "chosen beforehand" (Acts 10:41), and terms designating the "will, wish, or good pleasure" of God (Acts 2:23 [*boulē*]; Romans 9:18,22 [*thelō*]),

C. More on the English Terminology

The word "predestine" has come into Biblical translations through the Latin Vulgate, which used *predestinare* (to destine [to set apart, or devote to a particular use, condition, or end] beforehand) to translate the Greek word *proorizō*. (The Latin Vulgate used *predestinare* for the Greek *proorizō* at every place except Acts 4:28, where the Latin has *decerno*.) In Latin, *predestinare* denotes an act of the will, rather than the actions by which that which is willed is carried into effect.

Certainly, not all scholars are happy with the choice of *predestinare* for *proorizō*, some thinking *praefinire* (to set a goal beforehand, to predetermine the end in view) would have been a better Latin word.[6] Because of some unfortunate connotations, theologians have introduced some synonyms, each of which has carried a special meaning to the theologian. When talking of *things* that God has predestined, theologians prefer "foreordained" or "decreed" (like God decreed that the sun should shine). They have tried to save "predestine" for God's supposed determinations respecting the destinies of *men* in the future world. In fact, the Westminster Confession used "predestine" only for the saved; it used "foreordination" when speaking of the destiny of the wicked.[7] In Reformed theology, predestination of some to salvation has been made synonymous with "election."

Translators making English versions have struggled to find a suitable term. Wycliffe did not bring "predestinate" over from the Latin at all, but used "before ordain."[8] Tyndale used "predestinate" only at Ephesians 1:11; otherwise, he used "ordain before," "appoint before," and "determined before." The Geneva Bible used "predestinate" at both Ephesians 1:11 and 1:5. The Rhemish version, closely following the Vulgate, used "predestinate" except at Acts 4:28, where it read "decreed." The KJV, influenced by the Rhemish, used "predestinate" except at Acts 4:28 ("determined before") and 1 Corinthians 2:7 ("ordained"), where it followed Tyndale. The ERV/ASV do not use "predestinate" at all; instead, "foreordained" is preferred at every place.[9] The NASB uses "predestine" at

---

and the terms for "election" or "choice" as being similar.

[6] As Hermann Cremer points out, the question "is not *who* are the objects of this predestination, but *what* they are predestinated to." *Biblico-Theological Lexicon of New Testament Greek* (Edinburgh: T&T Clark, 1880), p.462.

[7] A.S. Martin, "Predestination," in *Hasting's Encyclopedia of Religion and Ethics*, edited by James Hastings (New York: Charles Scribner's Sons, 1919), Vol.10, p.225.

[8] That Wycliffe did not use "predestinate" in his translation is thought by some to be surprising, since he was a predestinarian of the most deterministic type. E.F. Karl Muller, "Predestination," in *The New Schaff-Herzog Encyclopedia of Religious Knowledge*, edited by Samuel Macauley Jackson (Grand Rapids: Baker Book House, 1957), Vol.9, p.196.

[9] While some have supposed that the English translators were influenced by the Westminster Confession's usage of predestinate for eternal life, and foreordain for eternal death, the real reason is likely the change that is taking place in connotations of words. As a result of Calvinistic influence, "predestinate" has come to be thought of as a precise synonym for "election." Since not all of the verses where *proorizō* occurs speak of this single concept, the more general word "foreordination" was preferred. When the student consults the newer translations, he finds it almost impossible to recognize that the same word is

all the places *proorizō* occurs in the Greek. *The Expositor's Greek Testament* favors "foreordain" as the best translation.[10]

D. Definition of Terms by Various Theologians

Augustine (AD 354-430) was the first theologian to develop a detailed doctrine of predestination. He even coined the term "predestination" on the basis of the Vulgate translation at Romans 1:4.[11]   Perhaps Augustine tried to make his new word "predestination" cover too much.

> Historically, Augustine of Hippo formulated triple predestination, that is: general predestination or providence, which magnifies God's wisdom in governing all things; special predestination or election in which His free grace is seen in the choice of His people; and preterition or reprobation by which He passes by or leaves other sinners to the due desert of their guilt for the manifestation of His power and justice.[12]

In Roman Catholic theology, "Predestination is the plan eternally conceived by God whereby He conducts rational creatures to their supernatural end, that is, to eternal life."[13] Augustine worded it a bit differently, so that he defined predestination as "the foreknowledge and preparation of those gifts of God whereby they who are liberated are most certainly liberated."[14]

---

being translated, because of the variety of methods used to represent the word in any given context.

[10] S.D.F. Salmond, "The Epistle to the Ephesians," in *The Expositor's Greek Testament*, edited by W. Robertson Nicoll (Grand Rapids: Wm. B. Eerdmans Publishing Co., 1967), Vol.3, p.251.

[11] Wilfred Joest, "Predestination," in *The Encyclopedia of the Lutheran Church*, edited by Julius Bodensieck (Minneapolis: Augsburg Publishing House, 1965), Vol.3, p.1952. "Both Hebrew Wisdom and Christian theology worked out a large conception of God's relation to the world and to man as part of the world, which it was found difficult to embody in a single word. Accordingly, in both developments there occur a number of terms each of which conveys some special *nuance* of the general idea, for that is how the religious consciousness works. The philosophic consciousness, on the other hand, desiderates a term for the idea in its largest breadth; that is its nature. In Hebrew probably the nearest equivalent is *'etsah.* In Greek in the NT there is none; hence, Patristic thought coined 'predestination' precisely as in the case of another doctrine, that of the Person of Christ, is coined *homoousios.*" A.S. Martin, "Predestination," *Hasting's Encyclopedia of Religion and Ethics*, Vol.10, p.226.

[12] William C. Robinson, "Predestination," in *Basic Christian Doctrines*, edited by Carl F.H. Henry (New York: Holt, Rinehart, and Winston, 1962), p.49,50.

[13] A.G. Palladino, "Predestination (in Catholic Theology)," in *New Catholic Encyclopedia* (Washington, DC: Catholic University of America, 1967), Vol.11, p.714. He goes on to explain, "Of necessity this plan is very complex. It must be concerned, first of all, with the supernatural order: its end, which is eternal life; its means, the complexus that we term supernatural grace (sanctifying and actual, efficacious and sufficient grace, the infused virtues, and the gifts of the Holy Spirit). Predestination also closely involves the divine foreknowledge of future free acts, the exercise of the free will of man, and divine predilection."

[14] *Ibid.*

According to Augustine, the object of predestination is salvation, the freeing from servitude of sin, and all the benefits through which salvation is attained, i.e., efficacious graces, including the gift of final perseverance ... the subject of predestination is all men who are in fact saved.[15]

The medieval revival of learning, from around 1050, produced schools and universities in which theology was held to be the "Queen of the Sciences." The Scholastics were attempting to harmonize Christianity (as it had come down to them) with the newly rediscovered heritage of classical philosophy. Over a period of about 300 years, predestination was ascribed either to God's intellect, or to His sovereign will.

By the late 1200's ... several Scholastic systems, differing in detail [were] available. Predestination generally was handled in the context of God seen as Supreme intellect, who predestined on the basis of His foreseeing the choice the individual would make ... But this "solution" was soon attacked ... God was seen as Sovereign Will, and the problem of predestination shifted. How can man's choice be free, if foreseen? How can God be called fully sovereign, if He is bound to follow a future which is already determined?[16]

Aquinas' definition is similar: "Predestination is a plan existing in the divine mind for the ordering of some persons to eternal salvation."[17] Aquinas further distinguished three different operations by God that were part of predestination – dilection, election, and formal predestination.

Dilection is the absolute decree of the divine will whereby God wills eternal life, that is, a determined measure of eternal happiness for a select group of men. Election is the same act of the will, insofar as through it God chooses a certain group of men to be saved rather than others whom He could have chosen. Formal predestination is the plan existing in the divine intellect according to which God accomplishes the salvation of those whom He has chosen.[18]

John Calvin, basing his doctrine on the absolute sovereignty of God, developed a theory of predestination that has been dubbed "double predestination" because it has God not only decreeing the salvation of certain ones, but also the damnation of others.

---

[15] *Ibid.*

[16] Dirk Jellema, "Predestination," in *The New International Dictionary of the Christian Church*, edited by J.D. Douglas (Grand Rapids: Zondervan Publishing House, 1974), p.798.

[17] Palladino, *ibid.*

[18] *Op. cit.*, p.717. Be sure to observe the use of both "intellect" and "will" as being involved in God's predestination.

His position may be summarized as follows: (1) From all eternity, God chooses a certain portion of mankind to be saved; the others He positively and antecedently wills to condemn.   (2) God not only wills the damnation of the latter, but also directly wills moral evil or sin itself in the same way that He wills moral goodness.   (3) Predestination, therefore, is nothing more than the eternal decree of God by which he has decided upon the fate of each man. Some are preelected to eternal life, and others positively are preordained to eternal damnation.[19]

Calvin made the doctrine of predestination one of the cornerstones of his whole system of theology.   From it developed his views on limited atonement (Christ died only for the elect), irresistible grace, and unconditional eternal security.

Jacob Arminius and his followers assigned "predestination" to the overall plan of God.   In contrast to Calvin, Arminians taught a universal atonement, that grace can be resisted, and that a man can fall from grace.

It does not predict the fate of any individual.   God decided that man would be saved through faith in Christ.   In any specific case, a man determines his own destiny by whether he allies himself with Christ or rejects Him.   Such a view preserves both God's final control over creation and man's free will in regard to his eternal future, the Arminians contend.[20]

Early Lutheran theologians generally distinguished between a narrow and a wider predestination.   Predestination in the narrow sense is God's decree to save all persevering believers in Christ.   Predestination in its wider sense has to do with God's will that "desires all men to be saved" (1 Timothy 2:4).[21]   W.S. Reid has given a different definition to the wider and narrower aspects of predestination.

In its wider reference it refers to the fact that the Triune God foreordains whatsoever comes to pass (Eph. 1:11,22; cf. Psm. 2).   From all eternity God has sovereignly determined whatsoever shall happen in history.   The narrower aspect or use of the term is that God from all eternity has chosen a body of people for Himself, that they should be brought into eternal fellowship with Him, while at the same time He has ordained that the rest of humanity should be allowed to go their own way, which is the way of sin, to ultimate eternal punishment.   These are known as the doctrines of election and reprobation.[22]

---

[19] *Op. cit.*, p.716.

[20] Young Oon Kim, *Unification Theology and Christian Thought* (New York: Golden Gate Publishing Co., 1975), p.155.   Chapter 5 deals with "Predestination."

[21] John McClintock and James Strong, *Cyclopedia of Biblical, Theological and Ecclesiastical Literature* (New York: Harper and Brothers, Publishers, 1891), Vol.8, p.496,497.

[22] W.S. Reid, "Predestination," in *The Evangelical Dictionary of Theology*, edited by Walter A. Elwell (Grand Rapids: Baker Book House, 1984), p.870.

Karl Barth attempted to formulate a definition of predestination that rejects both Calvinism and Arminianism.[23] It has been called "the Christological way" of election. Jesus Christ is at the same time the electing God, the elect man, and the rejected man.

> According to the Basle theologian, predestination primarily means that God freely and graciously decided before the creation to unite Himself with man in the person of Christ and through Him with all the people He represents. God elected Himself to fellowship with man and elected (predestined) man to fellowship with Him. From all eternity He is the Electing God. God does not simply predestine mankind. *More importantly He predestines Himself.* God resolved once and for all to determine Himself in Christ for sinful man and sinful man for Himself. In the overflow of His love and freedom of His grace, He determined to be gracious toward man even though man would rebel against Him.[24]

In this brief study of the terminology, it has become clear rather quickly that ideas are imported from near-by phrases and verses, from verses thought to be on the same topic, and even from the currently prevailing philosophy, and included in the overall doctrine called "predestination." It is also clear that theological controversy has played a part in present-day attitudes and positions, so that what some call "predestination" may be a long way separated from the Biblical use of the term. This calls for more detailed study.

II. IS PREDESTINATION IMPLIED IN THE OLD TESTAMENT?

The answer to this question rather depends on how many of the allegedly related terms one includes in a definition of predestination. If predestination is one facet of the *plan* (Grk., *prothesis* or *boulē* [?]) for history that God made back in eternity, and then carries out in time (Romans 8:28; Ephesians 1:11; Acts 4:28), it certainly can be said that the idea of predestination underlies much of what is read in the Old Testament Scriptures. If one considers that predestination results from the *will* (Grk., *thelēma*) of God (Ephesians 1:5,11), then verses that speak about His will would be related to the doctrine. If we include God's *operation* of all of creation, rather than limiting predestination to "salvation history," an even larger number of Old Testament verses would present ideas similar to predestination.

What men can know about God's purposes and plans is limited to what God has revealed about Himself, in creation, in the Word, and in Christ. Two things God reveals about Himself in the Old Testament are the facts that He is omnipotent and personal.[25] He

---

[23] Bernard Ramm, *Handbook of Contemporary Theology* (Grand Rapids: Wm. B. Eerdmans Publishing Co., 1966), p.40.

[24] Kim, *op. cit.*, p.158. (Emphasis mine, GLR)

[25] "Throughout the Old Testament literature ... the fundamental conception of God remains the same, and the two most persistently emphasized elements in it are just those of might and personality." Warfield,

is the One who created all things, and He is the One who sits as Ruler of all that He has made (Psalm 29:10).   The doctrine of divine providence is "spread over the pages of the Old Testament ... Heaven and earth and all that is in them are the instruments through which He works His ends."[26]   There is a vivid sense of dependence on God in every area of life.   Historical events, occurrences in nature, all are indicated to be part of the plan God has for His world.[27]

God revealed His counsel to men, insofar as it was necessary for them to know it, to the patriarchs, and through the prophets of the Old Testament.   In the very opening verses of Genesis, the reader gets the impression that the reason for the creation is that God has a purpose He is carrying out, though the purpose is not stated in those early chapters. Adam has a freedom of choice, either to obey or disobey, but he must make the decision. When Adam sins, the whole record rather centers on God's attempts to recover fallen man to Himself.   From the proto-evangelium in Genesis 3:15, to the preserving of the race from destruction in the Flood, to the call of Abraham, to the giving and repeating of the covenant to Abraham, Isaac, and Jacob, there is the promise of the coming Messiah who will help man with his sin problem.   Even His choice of Israel as His peculiar people had the purpose of making His name known to all the world (Isaiah 45:4-7).

III. JEWISH IDEAS ON PREDESTINATION

In the centuries after the close of the Old Testament canon, as the different Jewish sects were aborning and developing their peculiar tenets, there are some rather specific statements about predestination and free will in Philo, the Apocryphal books, and in Josephus.[28]

- The Essenes, whose beliefs were a mixture of Jewish, Greek, and Eastern ideas, were absolute predestinationists, affirming that "fate" (Grk., *eimarmenē*, "destiny, regulated by fate, inevitable necessity") is the mistress of all, and that nothing occurs to men which is not in accordance with her destination.

- The Pharisees were material predestinationists, teaching that the material world is predestined by divine decree, but allowing that while some of men's actions are predestined, some also are the result of their own power as to whether they are done or not.

"Predestination," *Hasting's Dictionary of the Bible*, p.48.

[26] Warfield, *op. cit.*, p.48,49.

[27] Warfield, *op. cit.*, p.49,50, has a section entitled "Cosmical Predestination in the Old Testament," wherein he details many of the things specifically identified as fulfilling God's plan.

[28] Warfield, *op. cit.*, p.53, as he presents the Calvinistic position of unconditional predestination, laments this appearance of emphasis on man's freedom of will in the post-canonical Jewish writings.   He attributes it to pagan Greek influence on Jewish thinking.

- The Sadducees were hostile to all forms of predestination, and they traced all events to chance. For the Sadducees, human affairs and actions are entirely under the power of men themselves, so that men are the causes of what is good, and receive what is evil from their own folly.[29]

Each of these sects would certainly insist that their beliefs were informed by what the Scriptures themselves teach on the subject. Perhaps each sect arrived at its beliefs by overemphasizing one facet of the whole doctrine. If one notices all the Old Testament passages where the control of all His creation is claimed by the Creator, it would be possible to think all is predetermined, and that no freedom exists to man. On the other extreme, once a man has sinned against God, and for the moment (seemingly) suffered no ill effects, he may soon come to think God can be safely ignored. If a man refuses to acknowledge any dependence on God, it will not be long until he thinks that man himself is the measure of all things, and that man himself controls his world.

IV. NEW TESTAMENT VERSES RELATED TO THE IDEA OF PRE-DESTINATION

A. In the Gospels

The assumption behind Jesus' many statements on this topic is that God is providentially guiding nature in all of its operations, whether it be God causing it to rain on the just and the unjust (Matthew 5:45), or clothing the flowers of the field (Matthew 6:30), or feeding the little birds (Matthew 6:26), or answering the prayers of men (Matthew 6:6, 9:37,38). Jesus' announcement that the Kingdom of God/heaven is at hand (Matthew 4:17; Mark 1:14,15) implies that something that has long been predicted is about to be fulfilled. This, in turn, requires a view of history that is teleological. The expression that is found dozens of times, "that it might be fulfilled which was spoken by the prophet," likewise implies that the One who made the prediction is actively involved in seeking that it comes true. Jesus' presentation of the final judgment, at which some men are told "Come, inherit the kingdom prepared for you from the foundation of the world" (Matthew 25:34), implies that God has had a destiny planned for the righteous since before He created. Many times, it is stated that Jesus came to do the will of the Father (John 4:34, 5:30, 6:38-40). Jesus came to offer an invitation to sinning men to return to God (Matthew 9:13; Mark 2:17). His death as a sacrifice for sins is something that had long been revealed as part of God's plan ("the Son of man is to go, just as it is written of Him, but woe to that man by whom the Son of man is betrayed!" Mark 14:21). Jesus' oft repeated dictum that "many are called but few are chosen" (Matthew 22:14) implies freedom to reject the invitation, and thus exclude one's self from the "chosen ones" who will share in that kingdom.[30] Whosoever will may come (John 3:16, 6:37, 7:37), and it is of inestimable

---

[29] It is to Josephus, *Antiquities*, XIII.v.9; XVIII.i.3, and *Wars*, II.vii.14, that we are indebted for these characterizations of Jewish beliefs in his own time.

[30] The idea that men are free to accept or reject the invitation ("call") is sometimes disputed by an appeal

value to have one's name written in heaven, since those whose names are entered in the book of life are the ones who will share in the goal God has been working out for the redeemed (Luke 10:20). Jesus warns the Jews who were rejecting Him that God would take the kingdom away from them and give it to a people (Grk., *ethnē*, "nation, Gentiles") who would produce fruit (Matthew 21:43). God has a special task for these "elect" to do, and so He orders even the duration of historical events like the siege and fall of Jerusalem (AD 70) for their benefit (Matthew 24:22). There is a danger that they may be misled by false Christs and false prophets (Matthew 24:24), and get involved in the revolt against Rome that will end in the destruction of the city of Jerusalem. There have to be stumbling-blocks, if there's going to be a moral universe wherein men are going to have any freedom of choice (Luke 17:1). And at the close of the church age, Jesus says the angels will be sent forth to the "four winds" to gather the "elect" (Matthew 24:31). In harmony with this worldwide gathering of the elect, Jesus often emphasized that His mission was to seek and to save the lost from the whole world (John 3:16, 6:51, 12:47, 17:21). As the risen Lord, He sends His messengers with an offer of salvation to all the nations (Matthew 28:19,20). He also often talked about the final judgment, at which men would have to give an account of their "stewardship" (John 12:47,48; Matthew 24:45-51, 25:31-34; Luke 16:1-13). In the meantime, His mediatorial work in heaven is directed toward the salvation of men (John 17:24-26). On the supposition that what he wrote was inspired, and therefore reflects God's own thoughts, John's statement of his reason for writing his Gospel reflects God's purpose of salvation of the believer (John 20:30,31).

B. In Acts and the non-Pauline Epistles

The apostles and New Testament prophets continue the same themes Jesus had taught, including those related to predestination. *Peter*, both in his sermons recorded in Acts and in his two epistles, has much to say on the subject. The crucifixion of Jesus was something that happened in harmony with the predetermined plan of God (Acts 2:23, 4:28), and was "foreknown before the foundation of the world" (1 Peter 1:20). Peter can look at the fulfillment of prophecy concerning Jesus as something that had to occur (Acts 1:16, 2:24). Jesus' present stay in heaven is something that must continue until the restoration of all things about which the prophets spoke (Acts 3:21). God's redemptive interest includes Gentiles (Cornelius, Acts 10,11) as well as Jews, and He "calls" (i.e., offers an invitation to) men of both classes (Acts 2:39). 1 Peter 1:1,2 show how men become part of the "chosen people" in this Christian age – it is in harmony with God's foreknowledge (I'll "approve" those who are "in Christ," cp. Romans 8:29), and results from the sanctifying work of the Holy Spirit that produces obedience to Jesus, which in turn is accompanied by a cleansing from sin (as the obedient are sprinkled with His blood). Those who disobey the gospel are appointed to certain damnation (1 Peter 2:8).

---

to those verses where God is said to "draw" (John 6:44, 12:32, cp. 6:65) people to Himself, with the related claim that they cannot come unless they are drawn. However, instead of such language meaning that some "calls" are effectual while others are not (as Calvinist interpreters explain), suppose that the call is made through the gospel, and that the Holy Spirit does His convicting, converting work through the preached word. If so, then all Jesus is saying is that God determines when men (in this land, or that) will have their opportunity to hear the gospel, and so have their opportunity to choose to be "in Christ" or not. God may "draw" men to Himself, but it is still man who is described as "coming" (John 3:21; 6:35,44; 14:6).

Barnabas will encourage men "with resolute heart to remain true to the Lord" (Acts 11:23).   Men still have a freedom to obey or disobey, even after becoming Christians.

Stephen, as he reverently rehearses Israel's history, endorses a teleological concept of history (Acts 7), in which God is accomplishing His goal, whether in the calling of Abraham, or the sojourn in Egypt, or in the promise to raise up a Prophet like Moses, or in punishing the disobedient as in the incident of the golden calf, or in commanding the people to build a place of worship "according to the pattern."

Luke, the writer of Acts, adds his summary statement about the Lord adding to their number daily those who were being saved (Acts 2:47), and an explanatory note about the Lord opening Lydia's heart (Acts 16:14).   He also has the contrasting statements that record the results of Paul's and Barnabas' evangelistic ministry in Antioch of Pisidia.   While the Jews were filled with jealousy, repudiated the word of God, and judged themselves unworthy of eternal life, the Gentiles, on the other hand, rejoiced, "glorified the word of the Lord; and as many as had been appointed to eternal life believed" (Acts 13:45-48).[31]

James, the Lord's brother, tells how every good and perfect gift comes from the Father of lights (James 1:17), and how in the exercise of His will both James and his readers had become Christians through the word of truth, and that as Christians they had a purpose as the first-fruits among His creatures (James 1:18).   He writes about how God chose men who were rich in faith[32] to be heirs of the kingdom "which He promised to those who love Him" (James 2:5).   James also encourages a healthy sense of dependence on the Lord (James 4:11, 5:7-11).

The apostle *John*, especially in Revelation, writes about the omnipotence of God, calling Him "Almighty" (Grk., *pantokrator*, 1:8, 4:8, 11:17), and presents history as being guided by God's hand (e.g., in Revelation 4, God on His throne is true, whatever may be the appearances to the contrary in the world).   John also has a theme we have heard before, namely, the Lamb's Book of Life, save that John has an addition about the names being inscribed there "from the foundation of the world" (Revelation 13:8, 17:8),[33] plus some in-

---

[31] In the author's commentary on Acts, he suggests that the "appointed" (which can be either middle or passive, as far as the Greek original is concerned) should be translated as a middle voice.   The verse then reads, "As many as were *determined* to have eternal life believed."   What the Jews did who rejected the message is contrasted with what the Gentiles did who accepted it, in balanced statements exactly corresponding to each other.   Freedom of choice is upheld; there is no predetermination or coercion exercised by God in either response to the gospel.   See *New Testament History: Acts*, p.490,491.

[32] The words added in italics in the NASB rendering, "He chose the poor of this world *to be* rich in faith," reflects a predestinarian bias in the translators.

[33] It is possible that in 13:8 (but not in 17:8) that the thing that was done from the foundation of the world is the crucifixion of Jesus (a "lamb slain from the foundation of the world" is the translation offered in the margin of the NASB).   Calvinist writers are quick to seize on the idea of "written in the book before creation" as evidence of God's predetermination of the destiny only of certain individuals (the 'elect').   But why do those same writers deny what is said in Revelation 3:5 about the conditional aspect of keeping one's name in the book?   (It is the overcomer who is promised his name will not be erased.)   Is not the reason this, that their theology demands such an interpretation be attached to what the Word says at these places,

formation about the future destiny of those whose names are in that blessed book (20:12-15, 21:27).   John tells how Jesus is the propitiation for the sins of the whole world (1 John 2:2), and says that God sent Jesus to be the Savior of the world (1 John 4:14).   This is all in harmony with God's plans when He made the world.

C. In the Writings of Paul

This commentator has regularly attributed the authorship of the epistle to the Hebrews to Paul.   It has some significant statements related to predestination.   Hebrews 2:9,10 tells how Jesus has tasted death for every man, and that this was necessary if God was going to bring many sons to glory (the destiny He had in mind for those "in Christ").   Already in Mosaic times, God had revealed that the blood of bulls and goats could never take away sin, but that a body was being prepared for Jesus, in which He could offer the perfect sacrifice for sins, once and for all (Hebrews 10:5-10).   It takes faith and patience to inherit the promises (6:12), and God can be counted on to be unchanging with reference to what He has promised to those who are faithful (6:17,18).   A "Sabbath rest" awaits the people of God (4:9), and "those who have been called" can "receive the promise of the eternal inheritance" (9:15).   This calling Christians have received is a "heavenly calling" (3:1), i.e., either from heaven, or to heaven.   By responding to this invitation, the readers have come to the "church of the first-born (new birth?) ones," who "are enrolled in heaven" (in the Book of Life?) (12:23).   If they do not remain faithful to Jesus, now that they have come to Him, they will be again lost (Hebrews 6:4-6, 10:26-31).

In the undoubted sermons and writings of Paul, occur some of the clearest references to God's will, plan, choice, and predestination of men and things.   For example, in Paul's sermon preached in Athens (Acts 17:22-31), we are told that God is creator of the world and all things in it, and that He is Lord of heaven and earth.   He gives life and breath and all things to all men.   His creation is intended to point men to the Creator, giving them some idea of what He is like (17:28,29).   He has made from one (i.e., Adam) every nation of mankind to live on the face of the earth.   God then determines when nations rise and fall, and how far their boundaries spread (17:26),[34] and He does so to assist men to find Him

---

rather than letting their theology be informed by the Word?   (Otherwise, they would have to abandon their doctrines of unconditional predestination and unconditional security for the elect, would they not?)

[34] Now, all of a sudden, a number of verses in the Old Testament are seen in a new light.   Daniel 2 and Daniel 7,8, where God foretold the next several hundred years of history – Babylon, Medo-Persia, Greece, and Rome, make sense.   So does the prediction that "Seventy weeks have been decreed for your people and your holy city" (Daniel 9:24).   "Greece" can be called by name 200 years before there was a nation of Greece (Daniel 8:21-27); Alexander the Great's exploits can be foretold (Daniel 11:3,4), as well as those of Antiochus Epiphanes, including how the Romans would come and stop his advance into Egypt (Daniel 11:21-30), because God has a plan for history that is going to be carried out.   He even has chosen the "tools" He will use to accomplish His purposes.   "Cyrus" can be called by name, 200 years before he was born, and designated as the one who would permit Israel to return from captivity and rebuild the temple (Isaiah 44:28 and 45:1), because God is moving history toward a goal.

and serve Him. The ages before the Gospel Age were "times of ignorance" which God looked beyond (17:30), implying His plan for the future was in the process of being carried out. He also told that audience that God has fixed a day in which He will judge the world through Jesus (17:31), and that in the meantime He is declaring to men (through gospel preachers?) that all everywhere should repent (17:30), which surely sounds like freedom of the will is still recognized and honored by Him.

What we read in this sermon is underscored in Paul's later letters. The creation was intended to point men to the Creator (Romans 1:20,21). A deliberate refusal to acknowledge Him to whom Creation points, results in wrath (Romans 1:18). Without submission to God, men will find themselves living in an evil age, from which they need deliverance; this deliverance has been provided according to God's will in Jesus Christ (Galatians 1:4). God loves us, and did not withhold his Son, so that sinners might be reconciled and be saved by His living (Romans 5:6-11). God desires all men to be saved and to come to knowledge of the truth, for there is one God, and one mediator also between God and men, the man Christ Jesus, who gave Himself a ransom for all, the testimony about which was to be born at the proper time (1 Timothy 2:4-6). God chose some pretty unlikely candidates (from a human standpoint) to bear that testimony, but He did it deliberately, lest men's faith rest in something other than God (1 Corinthians 1:27-31). If the vessels He chooses for service rebel, they will find themselves hardened (Romans 9:17, 20-23). The men who hear the message are free to accept it, or reject it, but those who reject it will find themselves hardened (Romans 11:7-10). God is moving history toward a goal, a judgment (in which Jesus will be the judge), a consummation that occurs after God has abolished all His enemies (1 Corinthians 15:20-28; 2 Corinthians 5:10).

Of course, the three key passages on predestination in Paul's writings are in Romans 8:28-30, Ephesians 1:1-11, and Romans 9-11. The outline offered at Romans 8:28-30 should be referred to, as a reminder of what that passage said about predestination. It was the end in view ("to become conformed to the image of His Son") that was predestined. This goal was to be shared in by all who were "in Christ."[35]

When we turn to Romans 9-11, we find that the idea of "predestination" underlies numerous verses: "through Isaac your descendants will be named" (9:7), "God's purpose according to election" (9:11, ASV), "the older will serve the younger" (9:12), "I will have mercy on whom I will have mercy" (9:15, KJV), "for this very purpose I raised you [Pharaoh] up" (9:17), "He has mercy on whom He desires, and He hardens whom He desires" (9:18), "does not the potter have a right over the clay?" (9:21), "which He prepared beforehand for glory" (9:23), "a remnant according to *God's* gracious choice" (11:5), "those who were chosen obtained it" (11:7), "He will remove ungodliness from Jacob" (11:26), "from the standpoint of God's choice they are beloved" (11:28), and "God has shut up all in disobedience that He might show mercy to all" (11:32).

---

[35] The "whom He predestined" (Romans 8:30) should not be taken as proof that only some particular individuals have been divinely predestined to be saved, as has been done by Catholic and Calvinist theologians. Nor is it likely that the phrase "whom he foreknew" (verse 29) teaches that God's choice of some to be saved was based on His foreknowledge of what they would do.

It will be remembered that in chapter 9 the comments spoke about God's election to service, while in chapter 11, the comments had to do with salvation. It is not unusual to hear several objections to such a presentation.

(1) It could well be asked concerning chapter 9, in a book that has been expounding "justification by faith," why have we all of a sudden begun to talk about service? *Answer:* Because the passage itself seems to demand it. Verse 5 ("whose are the fathers, and from whom is the Christ") has introduced the subject we have called "service" – the idea that God had a job He wanted done in the world, and He chose someone to do it. Verse 7 ("in Isaac shall thy seed be called" [ASV]) speaks of Isaac being in the line through whom the promised Seed (Christ) should come. This, too, speaks of "service." Verse 17 ("that My name might be proclaimed throughout the whole earth") is a use, a function, a "service," in which Pharaoh was involved. Verse 21 ("honorable use ... common use") expresses the idea of "service," a use God had for those vessels.

(2) Haven't you found some verses in chapter 9 that are hard to make harmonize with your idea that the topic is predestination to service? *Answer:* Admittedly, two passages must be explained in an unexpected way: (a) Hosea's prophecy (9:25-26, "not my people" become "my people") is explained as dealing with salvation (more than service) in the other place where it is alluded to in the New Testament, 1 Peter 2:9,10. (b) The expression "hardens" (Romans 9:18) is usually understood to speak of salvation or damnation, depending on man's response to God's commands. To take it as referring to service, as we do in our comments, some think is peculiar.

(3) Where in chapters 9-11 does the discussion change from "service" (which you claim is found in the early verses of chapter 9) and turn to "salvation" (which you claim chapters 10-11 deal with)? The question infers that chapter 9 also deals with salvation, since no change of topic is easily discernible. *Answer:* In the comments, the break has been made at 9:30, since Paul himself indicates a change of topic at this point.

In the face of the objections that are mustered against the idea of predestination to *service* in Romans 9, it seems only equitable to list some of the problem verses the other interpretation (that chapter 9 is predestination to *salvation*) must struggle with.

1. Why speak of salvation in the early verses of chapter 9, when there is no mention by Paul that that is his topic, as he talks of Isaac, Jacob, or Pharaoh?

2. Why treat "honor" and "dishonor" (verse 21, ASV) as though they were describing an eternal destiny, rather than the use to which vessels are put in this life?

3. Why explain "I raised you up" (verse 17) differently from the way the Old Testament passage teaches? The Old Testament means "spared, kept alive" – not "brought onto the scene of history" as predestination-to-salvation interpreters explain it.

4. The usual, Biblical meaning of "patience" (verse 22), namely, that God's patience is intended to lead men to repentance, must be ignored by those whose comments are support predestination-to-salvation. "God is *kind* even to the lost," these commentators are required to say, before He sends the lost to their predestined eternal doom! Are

they trying to dispel some of the seeming harshness toward the lost that their interpretation of the passage attributes to God? But of what value, and indeed what comfort is it, that God's mercy extended to the lost is ultimately wasted, since they were predestined from all eternity to be damned?

5. Is hardening (and mercy) an arbitrary act on God's part, with no regard to the will of men? The Calvinist answer would be "Yes!" Four lines of thought[36] show the fallacy of this thinking, that hardening is an arbitrary act on God's part, apart from conditionality.   (a) The doctrine of unconditional predestination violates the fundamental thesis of Romans (cf. 1:16,17). (b) It would be contrary, or in opposition to the connotation of "patience" (Romans 9:22). (c) It would falsify Paul's argument for the rejection of the Jews (9:30-33).   (d) It would render meaningless the universality of the gospel (10:11-13).

Because there are fewer problems that are difficult to answer, the comments offered on chapter 9 – that it deals with predestination (of men and nations) to *service* – seem to be the most plausible.[37]

We now turn to the famous passage in Ephesians 1. Especially in verses 5 and 11 do we have statements about God's predestination. The former informs us that those who are in Christ are predestined to adoption as sons, because God was pleased to do it this way. The latter tells us that God operates all things according to the counsel of His will and, in particular as one part of His plan (Grk., *prothesis*, purpose), has predestined Jewish people (who are in Christ) to be His inheritance. Just as the outline offered at Romans 8:28-30 helps to visualize what is there set forth, perhaps the following outline will help us to grasp some of the many ideas in the exalted language of this passage.

Spiritual Blessings in Heavenly Places

1. Planning for a Family of Adopted Sons.   Ephesians 1:4-6a

    God selected those who would be "in Christ" to be His family members, and He did it before creation. He expects His chosen ones to be holy and blameless,[38] as they stand before Him. In love, He predestined the chosen ones to adoption as sons through Christ,[39] because it pleased Him to do it this way.   He desired and

---

[36] These four lines of thought are suggested by Grubbs, *Romans*, p.123.

[37] A similar presentation is found in Jack F. Cottrell's chapter on "Predestination," in his *What the Bible Says about God the Ruler* (Joplin, MO: College Press, 1984), p.331ff. Cottrell notes that "This is a revised version of an earlier essay entitled 'Conditional Election'" which appeared in *Grace Unlimited*, edited by Clark Pinnock (Minneapolis: Bethany House Publishers, 1975).

[38] God's choice was not because He foresaw holiness that would earn the choice, but in order that men might become holy and without blemish. Holy = separated, different. Without blemish = something fit to offer to God.

[39] God determined beforehand that the family members would be "adopted." He determined beforehand that Jesus would be the mediator of this adoption. "Adoption" was a Roman practice, whereby a

anticipated that those chosen ones would offer praise to their Benefactor.[40]

2. Execution of the Plan in History.   1:6b-8a

God bestowed grace "on us" in His beloved Son, whose blood was shed that there might be redemption, and the forgiveness of sins.   Such redemption and forgiveness is in harmony with the riches of His grace which He has lavished on us.[41]

3. Publication of the Plan.   1:8b-10

God then made arrangements, as seemed best to Him, to reveal to mankind the mystery of His will, a revelation He all along had planned to make, after Jesus had offered Himself to redeem lost men.   God was continually administering[42] the ages[43] as a good steward would manage his charge, intending in the end to sum up in Christ all things in heaven and earth.[44]

4. Application of the Plan of Salvation to Mankind.   1:11-14.

Verses 11,12 (which begin with "we") speak about Jewish participation in the fam-

---

child was legally transferred from one father's power to another's, and often a nobody became a somebody simply because of the status of the adoptive parent.   The adopted child then had the same rights and obligations and privileges as a child naturally born to the adoptive parents.   Thus, "adopted" says Christians have come to have the same status in God's sight as Jesus has – not deity, but elevated to be "somebodies," who one day will receive a body just like the one Jesus now has (Philippians 3:21), and who will inherit the same as Jesus inherits.

[40] When what God has done is considered by man, it should cause man to praise and honor God.

[41] The degree of God's forgiveness was controlled by, dominated by, the riches (Grk., *ploutos*, wealth, abundance, plenitude) of God's grace.   The phrase "In all wisdom and insight" can go either with what precedes or with what follows.   If taken with what precedes, it says that His grace was guided within the limitations of His wisdom and prudence.   If taken with what follows, it says that the revelation of His plan was guided by His wisdom and prudence.

[42] God has been planning and thinking and administering and arranging history, so that it comes out where He wants it to.   "Administration" is *oiknomia*, a "stewardship."   Like a *steward* managing the family affairs so they run smoothly and uninterruptedly, is how God is pictured as managing the ages.

[43] "The fulness of times" means a succession of ages (e.g., Patriarchal, Mosaic, Christian) has come to a close in the plan of God, when we come to the Christian age.   It is the Christian conviction that history has a plan, a purpose, that it is the working out of the will of God.

[44] What is reflected here is our fragmented society, with its suspicions and racial prejudices, its animosity between the haves and the have-nots, and its strife between family members.   This is all to be ended and solved in Jesus.   God is going to gather together objects now apart and unrelated into a final, perfect unity.   All things in heaven and earth are included.   Creation will be restored to its former state, before sin entered and all things were subjected to futility.

ily, while verses 13,14 (beginning with "you also") refer to Gentile participation in the same family. In accordance with God's plan, the Jewish people (who were God's special heritage[45]), heard the gospel first, and some responded positively, hoping in Christ, and this brought praise to God. Then the gospel message was taken to the Gentiles, and some of them also responded positively, believing the message, and as a result were sealed with the gift of the Holy Spirit who had been promised. This gift is a pledge of further inheritance yet to come, the resurrection body ("the redemption of the purchased possession" [KJV]).[46] This too would result in praise to God.

"Thus ... we have brought before us the whole ideal history of salvation in Christ from eternity to eternity – from the eternal purpose as it lay in the loving heart of the Father, to the eternal consummation, when all things in heaven and earth shall be summed up in Christ."[47] It is implied that God expected (not predestined) the man He was going to create to sin, and need redemption, and adoption as sons. It is also evident (by way of contrast) what would be the situation of those who were not "in Christ" (because of their own failure to hope in Him, or believe in Him). They would end up not being holy or blameless. They would not be forgiven. They would not be redeemed. They would not be part of the family of God. They would be excluded from the summing up of all things in Christ. They would fail to praise Him. They would not be sealed by the Holy Spirit, nor would they have any down payment on an inheritance yet to be received from God.

V. A BRIEF REVIEW OF THE DOCTRINE OF PREDESTINATION IN CHURCH HISTORY

Now that a detailed review of many of the pertinent verses of Scripture has been completed, we are in a position to sit in judgment of history, as we review how men have interacted with the Scriptures.

---

[45] As the marginal note shows, it is not easy to decide what *kleroō* asserts about the Jews. It might mean that they were assigned a lot (a heritage, a task to do) in the process of the revelation of His will. It might mean that they were assigned the position of being God's private possession, a heritage He gets. It does not (as some might think, after reading "we have obtained an inheritance" in the NASB text) have reference to something the Jews get from God, as though they were predestined to a heavenly home from the very beginning.

[46] As was true in Romans 8:28-30, so here in Ephesians 1:13,14, Paul sees several stages in God's administration of the Gentile's affairs. There is hearing the gospel (the good news that salvation is available). There is believing the gospel (not faith only, but an obedient faith). There is a sealing by the Holy Spirit (the seal is a mark of ownership, a pledge of protection). There is eventual "glorification," indicated by the words "inheritance" (Grk., *klēronomia*, that which one receives as a bequest) and "redemption of the purchased possession" (KJV).

[47] Warfield, "Predestination," *Hasting's Dictionary of the Bible*, p.60.

A. The First 400 Years

In both the Eastern and Western Churches, the extant writings show a harmony with the doctrines of conditional predestination and freedom of the will. "Justin Martyr, Irenaeus, Clement of Alexandria, Origen, and Chrysostom – all in clear and decisive statements – give their adherence to the theory of conditional predestination, rejecting the opposite as false, dangerous, and utterly subversive of the divine glory."[48] "In the Western Church all the early theologians and teachers were equally unanimous," and then direct reference is made to Tertullian, Hillary of Portiers, and Ambrose.[49] Instead of certain individuals being predestined by God's decree to salvation, the destiny of man is conditioned on the use or abuse of his free will. While many of the writings were intended as a refutation of the Gnostics (whose theory required a denial of free will and an assertion of determinism), so that the arguments might be extreme positions espoused in the heat of debate, it appears to this commentator that those early writers were (for the most part) presenting the divine thoughts on this topic just as they were revealed in Scripture.

B. Augustine and the Catholic Church

As has been indicated elsewhere, Augustine's doctrine was at first the same as held by other churchmen in the first 400 years.[50] It was his running debate with Pelagius that led Augustine to present a completely different view. Pelagius taught that man had the freedom to accept or reject God. Augustine attempted to counter this by advancing three arguments: that man's will was enslaved by sin, that grace was needed before the man could choose for God, and that this grace was given only to those whom God had predestined.[51] He eventually came to teach that God predested evil, that the non-elect were likewise predestined by God's decree to be damned (sometimes called "double predestination"), and that God also grants the gift of perseverance to His elect.

Augustine's views came to be accepted in the Western Church, though from time to time various theologians offered amendments or objections to individual details. Jerome held to the doctrine of free will. The Semi-Pelagians taught that God's grace and the human will cooperate in the salvation of men. While Augustine taught that God's grace preceded regeneration, the Semi-Pelagians held that grace followed regeneration. The Semi-Pelagians also argued that it was impossible to harmonize Augustine's view of the predestination only of some with the clear Biblical statements that God wills the salvation

---

[48] McClintock and Strong, "Predestination," p.498. Not all the quotations are documented, so the student may wish to consult Muller, "Predestination," p.192,193, for the sources.

[49] McClintock and Strong, *op. cit.*, p.498,499.

[50] See a brief presentation of the debate that led to the change in Augustine's doctrinal position, in Special Study #4 about "Original Sin," at the close of chapter 5.

[51] Muller, "Predestination," p.193,194.

of all men. Others assailed the idea of predestination to evil, and still others the doctrine of reprobation of the impenitent wicked.

In the 9th century, Gottschalk revived Augustine's double predestination, only to have it rejected by the Synod of Quiercy, AD 849. Though following Augustine's theology, they could not accept the view that God willed the non-elect to be damned. Next came Aquinas[52] and the Scholastics,[53] whose views have been detailed earlier in this study, as we attempted to define terms. Thomas Bradwardine, a rigid Augustinian, stressed God's predestination as basic to understanding our universe. Wycliffe and John Huss stressed God's election as the key theological concept; they saw the church as made up of the elect who are already saved, in distinction to the usual Catholic view that the church is the source of the desperately needed aids (merit or grace) to salvation.

The debate among Protestants after the Reformation had little effect on official Catholic doctrine on predestination. The formulation at the Council of Trent,[54] the views of Molina,[55] Banez,[56] and others are tolerated, though not necessarily sanctioned.[57] In more recent times, there has been "an unmistakable tendency toward the Semi-Pelagian Jesuit position" in Catholic theology.[58]

---

[52] "Predestination is, to Aquinas, a part of Providence, and it presupposes election in the order of reason. Though Divine goodness in general be without election, Aquinas thinks that communication of a particular good cannot be without election. Predestination has, for him, its foundation in the goodness of God, which is its reason." James Lindsay, "Predestination," in *International Standard Bible Encyclopedia*, edited by James Orr (Grand Rapids: Wm. B. Eerdmans Publishing Co., 1949), Vol.4, p.2435.

[53] In Scholastic theology, "the prevailing doctrine, while carefully avoiding both Semi-Pelagian terms and the extreme deductions of Augustinianism (irresistible grace and perseverance), exalted the operation of grace alone and constantly repeated the formulas of Augustine on foreknowledge and predestination to good, but mere foreknowledge of evil." Muller, "Predestination," p.195.

[54] "The Council of Trent formulated the doctrine of salvation ... [along this line]: undeserved prevenience of grace which man by his own free will may accept or reject and continued operation of grace in accordance with man's response." Joest, "Predestination," p.1953. This is very similar to the Semi-Pelagian position.

[55] Toward the end of the 16th century, there was a debate in the Catholic church about predestination, between the Thomistic Dominicans and the Semi-Pelagian Jesuits. Louis Molina was a Spanish Jesuit who tried to reconcile human freedom with divine predestination by stating God foreknows but does not cause men's actions. The Dominicans rejected this because they felt it denied God's grace, and also because Molina's views differed much from Aquinas' views.

[56] Domingo Banez was a Spanish theologian who staunchly defended Aquinas' views in that late 16th century debate. The views of both Molina and Banez are set forth in Palladino, "Predestination," p.717,718. The Jesuits tended to give man's will a role in the process of salvation; the Dominicans opposed such a doctrine.

[57] In the 17th century, Jansenism was a revival of rigid Augustinian doctrines of predestination and irresistible grace. Cornelius Jansen was a strong opponent of the Jesuits, and his writings (and those of his supporters) led to a minor schism in the Catholic church, resulting in the "Old Catholic Church" in the Netherlands.

[58] Muller, "Predestination," p.196. See also Palladino, *op. cit.*, p.718-19. "The post-Tridentine Roman Catholic theologians formulated their doctrine of Predestination with particular emphasis on the freedom of

C. Protestant Views

The two men who played key roles in the early part of the Reformation, Luther and Calvin, were both influenced by Augustine's theology, as well as the thinking of influential Scholastics. Luther first accepted the solution that was common among the Scholastics, that God's foreknowledge of man's conduct in some way explains predestination. He gradually changed, until he was teaching the same doctrine Augustine had. Luther came to teach "The Bondage of the Will" and double predestination, and in his commentary on Romans 9 uses Paul's references to the election of Isaac, Jacob, and the rejection of Ishmael and Esau, (plus the election of David and the rejection of Saul) as Scriptural proof of the doctrine of irrevocable election of some to salvation.[59] He also taught that the Fall of Adam was divinely decreed.[60] "In the Lutheran churches the fierce 'synergistic' controversy of the later 1500's resulted from Melanchthon's attempt to save some role for the human will."[61] The Lutheran church today holds a slightly different doctrine. The *Formula of Concord* teaches single predestination, and rejects any type of cooperation of the human will in the process of salvation.[62] Other Lutheran theologians affirm that God's predestination to salvation was from the beginning contingent upon faith; that is, God decrees salvation for all men on the condition that they believe in Christ.[63] American Lutheranism has been disturbed by a controversy over predestination.[64] Karl F.W. Walther, a German immigrant to the United States, who founded the Lutheran Church –

---

the human will." F.L. Cross, ed., *Oxford Dictionary of the Christian Church* (London: Oxford University Press, 1958), p.1009.

[59] A.G. Palladino, "Predestination (In Non-Catholic Theology)," in *The New Catholic Encyclopedia* (Washington, D.C.: Catholic University of America, 1967), Vol.11, p.719.

[60] Muller, "Predestination," p.196.

[61] Jellema, "Predestination," p.798. The Augsburg Confession, in the formation of which Melanchthon played a key role, deliberately avoids the question of predestination.

[62] Lutheran theology agrees with Calvin in that salvation is *sola gratia*, by grace alone, since they see man as totally depraved, and God as magnificent in His grace. Lutherans put little emphasis on God's sovereignty, as did Calvin. Lutheran theology differs from Calvin in that it teaches the *gratia universalis* principle, that is, that grace is as universal as is sin, and the death of Jesus was a universal atonement. See *Formula of Concord*, XI.

[63] Joest, "Predestination," p.1954. The presently-accepted Lutheran doctrine states that God's foreknowledge deals with both the good and evil, but that predestination deals only with salvation. Those whom God foresees will believe, He eternally elects. If certain men are not elected, the fault is their own. Thus, a majority of Lutherans hold views different from those of Luther himself.

[64] "It was the doctrine of election in the last century that split Lutherans in the United States right down the middle and it more than any other doctrine is responsible for the manifold divisions in Lutheranism in America that last to this day." David P. Scaer, "The Doctrine of Election: A Lutheran Note," in *Perspectives on Evangelical Theology*, edited by Kenneth S. Kantzer and Stanley N. Gundry (Grand Rapids: Baker Book House, 1979), p.106.

Missouri Synod in 1847, was critical of other Lutherans for teaching synergism in opposition to Article XI of the *Formula of Concord*. He taught that election was to faith, rather than on the condition of faith. He further asserted that God would bring the elect to faith, even if they willfully resisted His efforts.

It was over the doctrine of predestination that Erasmus split away from Luther. Erasmus had published "The Freedom of the Will," and it was in reply to this that Luther wrote his "The Bondage of the Will" in which he systematically set forth his recently-developed doctrine of predestination. Erasmus defended the view that there must be some room for man's will in deciding the issue of salvation. About the same time, Zwingli (while espousing double predestination) advanced some extreme views, declaring that all evil, as well as all good, is due to the causality of God.[65]

Calvin's contribution to the debate was made when this second-generation reformer was but 25 years old. He was influenced in many of his ideas by Luther's and Zwingli's writings. Calvin's doctrines, as well as Arminius' opposite views, have been summarized above, as we were defining terms. The Dutch Reformed Church became a stronghold for Calvinistic theology, though it has seen and continues to see vigorous debate on predestination. Arminius and his followers raised serious objections to Calvin's doctrine of predestination. Out of their protest grew the Remonstrants, a group of Dutch preachers and churches. In 1610 they drew up the Remonstrance, an Arminian doctrinal statement setting forth non-Calvinistic views on such matters as predestination and the extent of the atonement.[66] For them, predestination was concerned solely with the overall plan of God; it did not predict the fate of any individual. God decided that men would be saved if they were believers in Christ. In any individual case, the man determines his own destiny by whether he obeys or rejects Christ. Thus, the Remonstrants sought to preserve both God's final control over creation, and man's freedom of the will.[67] The Synod of Dort was convened in 1618 for the purpose of silencing the Remonstrants. The strict Calvinistic members of the synod won the day. Jan van Olbenbarneveldt, a statesman favoring Arminius, was beheaded; Hugo Grotius, the famous jurist, was condemned to life in prison.

---

[65] Muller, *op. cit.*, p.196.

[66] The Remonstrants presented five Articles expressing their views. This is the origin of the famous "Five Points" in the controversy between Calvinism and Arminianism. Martin, "Predestination," *Hasting's Encyclopedia of Religion and Ethics*, p.233. Since most are familiar with the acrostic TULIP used to express the five points of Calvinism, George E. Failing has proposed an acrostic for the five points of Arminianism: ABCDE – **A**tonement for all; **B**elievers alone are elected; **C**onvicting grace; **D**eliverance from sin; **E**ndurance of believers. His proposal is quoted in Wilber T. Dayton, "A Wesleyan Note on Election," in *Perspectives on Evangelical Theology*, edited by Kenneth S. Kantzer and Stanley N. Gundry (Grand Rapids: Wm. B. Eerdmans Publishing Co., 1979), p.100.

[67] Kim, "Predestination," p.155. Though the doctrines held by the Remonstrants are indeed very similar to those to which this commentator has come as a result of his study, he was not aware of their staunch defense of conditional predestination until after he had formed his own views.

Many Remonstrants were banished from Holland until about 1630, when the government gave them liberty to return to their land.

Among the strict Calvinists at the Synod, there were two distinct views regarding the order of events in the divine plan. These views have come to be designated as Infralapsarians and Supralapsarians. *Lapsus* is Latin for the Fall of Adam, and the prefixes express the time when God elected some to be saved, whether *after* the Fall, or *before* the Fall.

> The order of events [for the Infralapsarian] then is: God proposed (1) to create; (2) to permit the fall; (3) to elect some out of this fallen mass to be saved, and to leave the others as they were; (4) to provide a redeemer for the elect; and (5) to send the Holy Spirit to apply this redemption to the elect. According to this plan, election follows the fall.

> According to the Supralapsarian view the order of events is: God proposed (1) to elect some creatable men (that is, men who were to be created) to life and to condemn others to destruction; (2) to create; (3) to permit the fall; (4) to send Christ to redeem the elect; and (5) to send the Holy Spirit to apply this redemption to the elect. According to this plan election precedes the fall.[68]

D. Post-Reformation Views

"The Puritans of England and those who early settled in America, as well as the Huguenots in France, were thoroughgoing Calvinists. In more recent times the doctrine has been set forth by Whitefield, Hodge ... Shedd, Strong, Kuyper and Warfield [Boettner and Berkouwer]."[69] Calvinist notions were spread over New England by the Puritans, and through most of the middle and western United States by the Reformed Dutch and other Presbyterian bodies. While the Westminster Confession has come to be the official doc-

---

[68] Loraine Boettner, "Predestination," in *Baker's Dictionary of Theology*, edited by Everett F. Harrison (Grand Rapids: Baker Book House, 1960), p.417.

[69] Boettner, *op. cit.*, p.416. See also Loraine Boettner, *The Reformed Doctrine of Predestination* (Philadelphia: Presbyterian and Reformed Publishing Co., 1968). This volume was first published in 1932.

"C.G. Berkouwer attempts a contemporary defense of the older doctrine in *Divine Election* (Grand Rapids: Wm. B. Eerdmans Publishing Co, 1960). He is sensitive to all the harsh things said about the doctrine, to some of the unlovely expositions of it by those who are within the historic Reformed camp, and to Barth's and Brunner's criticisms. Berkouwer attempts to give the traditional view a restatement that is thoroughly Christocentric, and that shows by rather lengthy expositions that the traditional view contains no determinism, no shadows, no dealings with a hidden and therefore threatening God, no lessening of the need for the gospel preaching, and no cause for uncertainty concerning one's salvation." Ramm, "Predestination," p.41,42.

A decade after Ramm wrote, Berkouwer published another book, *A Half Century of Theology* (Grand Rapids: Wm. B. Eerdmans Publishing Co., 1977), which makes it very evident that Berkouwer is no longer sympathetic to the Canons of the Synod of Dort.

trinal position of the Church of England, and also of much of Presbyterianism, there has always been a strong movement within Anglicanism against Calvin's doctrines (as evidenced by the group that drew up the Lambeth Articles).[70]   Jonathan Edwards also had a profound influence on American theology, as his Calvinist doctrines and eloquent preaching led to the Great Awakening in New England.[71]

While in the Netherlands, among the Dutch Reformed Churches and the Reformed Churches of the Netherlands, there has been a decided change in attitude away from Calvin's doctrine of predestination, the opposite has been true among their denominational relatives in the United States, the Christian Reformed Church, who have been most critical of the Dutch developments.[72]

Arminian theology was widely disseminated by John Wesley;[73] thus, Methodism and related movements tend to be Arminian.   An interesting aside is that George Whitefield, the great Methodist evangelist and a contemporary of the Wesleys, was a strict Calvinist. Among the Baptist churches, one finds a varying degree of adherence to the five points of Calvinism.[74]   By the mid 1800's Congregationalists in America had lost their enthusiasm

---

[70] See McClintock and Strong, "Predestination," p.500,501.

[71] His theology is set forth in *The Freedom of the Will* (reprint edited by Paul Ramsey [New Haven: Yale University Press, 1957]).   Edward's contribution was the reconciliation of the divine decrees and free will, and the exposition of the divine motive for predestination as resting in the divine glory.   Martin, "Predestination," *Hasting's Encyclopedia of Religion and Ethics*, p.233.

[72] Fred H. Klooster, "Predestination: A Calvinistic Note," in *Perspectives on Evangelical Theology*, p.81-89.   Klooster attributes the change in Netherlands' theology to Barth's influence, and that may be true of some recent critics of Calvin, though not of all, for some of the Dutch involved in the controversy antedate Barth.   Klooster also notes two notable exceptions to the Christian Reformed Church's defense of Calvin.   One is Harry Boer, and the other is James Daane, whose views were published in *The Freedom of God: A Study of Election and Pulpit* (Grand Rapids: Wm. B. Eerdmans Publishing Co., 1973).

[73] "The only system on election, if one could call it such, that Wesley built has two affirmations.   The first meaning of election, to him, is a 'divine appointment of some particular men to do some particular work in the world.'   The second is 'a divine appointment of some men to eternal happiness.'   But Wesley hastens to say, 'But I believe this election to be conditional, as well as the reprobation opposite thereto.   I believe the eternal decree concerning both is expressed in these words: 'He that believeth shall be saved; he that believeth not shall be damned' (Mark 16:16)."   (The quotations come from "Predestination Calmly Considered," *Works of John Wesley* [Grand Rapids: Zondervan Publishing House, 1958-59], Vol.10, p.210.).   Dayton, "A Wesleyan Note on Election," p.95,96.

[74] Frederick E. Mayer, *The Religious Bodies of America*, 4th edition (St. Louis: Concordia Publishing House, 1960), p.258ff, speaks of two groups of Baptists, the General (Arminian) Baptists, who believe in universal atonement, and freedom of the will; and the Particular Baptists, who have always favored Calvin's theology of a limited, or particular, atonement.   Among the former he lists The Free-Will Baptists and Regular Baptists.   Among the latter he groups the American Baptist Convention, The Southern Baptist Convention, Primitive ("Hard Shell") Baptists, and The General Association of Regular Baptists.

for Calvin's views, and by 1900 were denouncing them.[75]

    In the 20th century, Karl Barth's attempted rejection of both Calvinism and Arminianism in favor of his own "Christological way of election" has raised again the theological issue of predestination.   Barth's ideas on God's election are discussed under three topics: (a) the election of Jesus Christ;   (b) the election of the Community (Israel and the Church); and (c) the election of the individual man (the number of the elect is indeterminate).[76] Barth's conclusions are less than Biblical, since they lead to a belief in universal salvation.[77] The tragedy is that his influence is such that his theology has become the doctrinal position of the World Council of Churches, and this theology is inimical to any attempts to evangelize men in the traditional sense of the word.[78]   Other Neo-orthodox theologians, such as Paul Tillich[79] and Emil Brunner,[80] have also rejected Calvin's idea of double predestination.

---

[75] Kim, "Predestination," p.159ff, cites Washington Gladden, *How Much is Left of the Old Doctrines?* (Boston: Houghton and Mifflin, 1899) as one vocal example of such repudiation of Calvinist predestination.

[76] Barth's doctrine of predestination can be found in his *Church Dogmatics*, II/2 (Edinburgh: T&T Clark, 1957), p.3-506.

[77] "Since Barth states that all men are elect in Christ, the basic difference between believers and unbelievers is only that the unbeliever does not yet know that he is elected.   Moreover, since Jesus took upon Himself the rejection of all men, no man therefore is rejected by God ... It is difficult to see how Barth can escape from the charge of universalism, the doctrine that holds that all men are *de facto* eventually saved." Palladino, *op. cit.*, p.722.

[78] See Arthur Johnston, *The Battle for World Evangelism* (Wheaton, IL: Tyndale House Publishers, 1978), p.100ff, "Divergency in Evangelism Appears in the WCC."   Also consult footnote #106 in chapter 11.

[79] Paul Tillich, *A History of Christian Thought* (New York: Simon & Schuster, 1972), p.262-275.   Tillich doubts that the doctrine of predestination is the beginning point of Calvinism, since the idea was not developed in the first edition of Calvin's *Institutes*.   For Tillich, the central doctrine of Calvinism is the majesty of God.   Predestination, then, is nothing more than God's providence applied to mankind.   He is moving them to a goal, just as He is history.   But the idea of predestination to damnation Tillich found hard to harmonize with the idea of God's love.

[80] Heinrich Emil Brunner, *Dogmatics* (Philadelphia: Westminster Press, 1950), 3 Vols.   Volume 1 covers the doctrine of God, and page 303 and following is where he presents his understanding of predestination (election).   He rejects the double predestination of Calvinism as nothing more than iron-clad determinism, and insists that man can neither believe in nor love God like that.   It is much easier to object to someone else's theory than it is to formulate a new one and then explain it.   This is certainly true of Brunner's attempt to find a new way to understand and express the doctrine of election.   Part of what he writes is, "... in the Christian revelation of eternity ... my eyes are opened to perceive the truth that God, *my Lord*, regards *me*, from all eternity, with the gaze of everlasting love, and therefore that my individual personal existence and life now receive an eternal meaning" (page 305).   What makes many of these Neo-orthodox writers hard to understand is that they give old words completely new meanings.   "Eternity" does not mean "before creation" as theologians usually to define it when dealing with "predestination," but is a dimension of the present reality.   Therefore, God's election was not a pre-temporal decree, as Calvin thought of it, but is something that happens every day in the present reality.

SUMMARY AND CONCLUSIONS

The conclusion published in this commentator's previous study of this topic bears repeating:

> God, in eternity, determined that those "in Christ" should be saved. God also determined that those not "in Christ" should be damned. God brings various influences to bear on a man's life, but He never forces the man to go against his own free will. The sovereign God determined that there would be two, and only two, ways a man could walk, either a life of belief, or one of disbelief. Man is free to choose whether he will be "in Christ" or not.
>
> Irrational creation is predestined as God willed it, with no freedom to choose its own way. Rational creatures do have a choice. God has predestined the plan to be followed, but He does not predestine individuals (in the Calvinist sense of the word).[81]

As a result of this much longer and more detailed study of this perplexing problem, there is not much in that previous statement that needs changing.[82]

- Perhaps, like the Patristic writers, we have tried to find one term that will express a whole range of Biblical ideas, only to end up with asking that term to do too much.

- Perhaps we should separate the ideas of providence and predestination, in which case we would omit from the quote above the sentence about "irrational creation being predestined."

- Perhaps we need to continue the search for the exact Biblical terms to use as we express Biblical ideas. Have the theologians really gained anything by making "election" and "predestination" synonymous terms? Nor is anything added to our understanding when we find "foreknowledge" and "predestination" treated as synonymous terms. Do we not add to the confusion when we use "plan (purpose)" and "predestination" as interchangeable terms, especially if Romans 8:28,29 show that "predestination" is but one facet of the "plan"?

- Perhaps as we read passages like Genesis 8:21,22 and Acts 17:26, we should rethink our views about when God "planned" certain events in history. Maybe instead of predetermining how all His world would work, God (in His marvelous wisdom and prudence) did some of the ordering as history passed, as for example after the Flood (when He said, "seed time and harvest, as long as the world shall stand") would be when He has set in motion what we now recognize as the uniformity of nature. The verb in

---

[81] Gareth L. Reese, *New Testament History: Acts*, p.134.

[82] It is our intention to try to repeat Biblical thoughts just as God has revealed them. Our rejection of Calvin's doctrines, therefore, is not based on current philosophy (remember, Erasmus was influenced by his humanistic friends), but on what (to our mind, at least) the Scriptures themselves say. Acts 17:11 is still a helpful suggestion as it encourages us to compare what we hear men preach and teach to the Word of God, and accept only what matches, rejecting all that does not.

Acts 17:26 about His "determining" when nations rise and fall, is not *proorizō* (*pre-* destined), but simply *orizō*. Could this refer to a moment in time, rather than a determination made back in eternity before creation?

"We only remark, in passing, that no fact is more striking or significant in the whole history of Scripture exegesis than the steady gravitation of all sound expositors to the exegetical views of the early Remonstrants."[83]   God has been working out His plan for history.   He has determined to have a family of adopted sons, made up of those "in Christ," whom He can forgive and justify because of the redemption that was wrought at Calvary. God also determined the conditions which when complied with He would reckon a man as "in Christ."[84]   God did not predestine sinful acts (that Jesus later was sent to die for), for such an idea cannot be harmonized with the punishment for evil that God sends because He holds men responsible for their own evil acts.   God's family will be huge (Revelation 7:9), but the number of those who are saved is smaller than the number of those who are lost (Matthew 7:13,14, 22:14).

SELECTED BIBLIOGRAPHY

Berkouwer, G.C., *A Half Century of Theology*.   Grand Rapids: Wm. B. Eerdmans Publishing Co., 1977.

-----, *Divine Election*.   Grand Rapids: Wm. B. Eerdmans Publishing Co., 1960.

Boettner, Loraine, *The Reformed Doctrine of Predestination*.   Philadelphia: Presbyterian and Reformed Publishing Co., 1968.

Buis, Harry, *Historic Protestantism and Predestination*.   Philadelphia: Presbyterian and Reformed Publishing Co., 1958.

Cottrell, Jack, *What the Bible Says About God the Ruler*.   Joplin, MO: College Press, 1984. p.331ff.

Hodge, Charles, *Systematic Theology*. Grand Rapids: Eerdmans Publishing Co., 1960.   Vol.1, p.535ff.

---

[83] McClintock and Strong, "Predestination," p.498.

[84] It is at this point that the very thoughtful students have difficulty accepting the views herein presented. No matter how it is worded, making membership in God's family "conditional on man's response" seems to detract from God's sovereignty and lordship over all things, for it surely does seem to make more depend on man's ability to choose, than on what God does; in fact, a wrong choice by man can almost be seen as frustrating God's will.   Perhaps, if it is remembered that even in Adam's case (and that before he ever sinned), being what God intended him to be was made conditional, then it will not be so hard to see that God's majesty and sovereignty is not diminished when He grants to men the freedom to act.   Instead, it should enhance our appreciation of, and dependence on, a God who can overrule even willful men's attempts to frustrate His will and plan.

Joest, Wilfried, "Predestination," in *The Encyclopedia of the Lutheran Church*. Minneapolis: Augsburg Publishing House, 1965. Vol.3, p.1951-57.

Kim, Young Oon, *Unification Theology and Christian Thought*. New York: Golden Gate Publishing Co., 1975. p.149-163.

Klooster, Fred H., *Calvin's Doctrine of Predestination*. Grand Rapids: Baker Book House, 1977.

-----, "Predestination: A Calvinistic View," in *Perspectives on Evangelical Theology*, edited by Kenneth S. Kantzer and Stanley N. Gundry. Grand Rapids: Baker Book House, 1979. p.81-94.

Martin, A.S., "Predestination," in *Hastings Encyclopedia of Religion and Ethics*, edited by James Hastings. New York: Charles Scribner's Sons, 1911. Vol. 10, p.225-35.

McClintock, John, and Strong, James, *Cyclopedia of Biblical, Theological, and Ecclesiastical Literature*. New York: Harper Brothers Publishers, 1891. Vol.8, p.496-502.

Muller, E.F. Karl, "Predestination," in *New Schaff-Herzog Encyclopedia of Religious Knowledge*, edited by Samuel M. Jackson. Grand Rapids: Baker Book House, 1957. Vol.9, p.191-98.

Palladino, A.G., "Predestination (In Catholic Theology)," in *New Catholic Encyclopedia*. Washington, D.C.: Catholic University of America, 1967. Vol.11, p.714-19.

-----, "Predestination (In Non-Catholic Theology)," *Op. cit.*, p.719-22.

Reid, W.S., "Predestination," in *Evangelical Dictionary of Theology*, edited by Walter A. Elwell. Grand Rapids: Baker Book House, 1984. p.870-72.

Robinson, William C., "Predestination," in *Basic Christian Doctrine*, edited by Carl F.H. Henry. New York: Holt, Rinehart and Winston, 1962. p.49-55.

Scaer, David P., "The Doctrine of Election: A Lutheran Note," in *Perspectives on Evangelical Theology*, edited by Kenneth S. Kantzer and Stanley N. Gundry. Grand Rapids: Baker Book House, 1979. p.105-115.

Warfield, B.B., "Predestination," *Hastings Dictionary of the Bible*, edited by James Hastings. New York: Charles Scribner's Sons, 1911. Vol.4, p.47-65.

V. EXHORTATIONS AND PRACTICAL INSTRUCTIONS BASED ON THE FORE-GOING DOCTRINAL EXPOSITIONS. 12:1 - 15:13

A. Concerning the Christian's Relation to God. 12:1,2

12:1 – *I urge you therefore, brethren, by the mercies of God, to present your bodies a living and holy sacrifice, acceptable to God,* **which is** *your spiritual service of worship.*

I urge you therefore, brethren.   God is looking for men of faith, the first eleven chapters have told us. "Therefore," with which chapter 12 begins, gathers up all that has been written thus far,[1] and at the same time shows there is a vital connection between the doctrine that went before and the practical exhortations that now follow.[2] After a man becomes a Christian, if he would continue to be a man of faith, he has new responsibilities and new privileges.   Some of the specifics involved in "faithfulness" for the Christian are set forth in this practical section of Romans.[3]   The word translated "urge" (*parakaleō*) can be rendered "beseech" (as when one begs for a favor), "comfort" (in the sense of "cheer up"), or "exhort" (as when one encourages another to do what is right).[4]   Of these, the third one is evidently the idea in this place.   Paul is expressing an earnest, affectionate appeal to his brethren,[5] so "exhort" or "urge" are good choices.

By the mercies of God.   The word "mercies" denotes the sum of the provisions which God has made in the gospel for our salvation.   Each of these provisions is an expression of His mercy.   Hence, the whole are called "mercies."[6]   It is on these mercies that Paul

---

[1] "Therefore" looks back to what has been written earlier in the letter.   Some would refer it to chapters 9-11 (because that is where we read about "the mercies of God").   Others would include all that has been written since 1:16, since these chapters have been concerned with God's way of saving man (the action of a merciful God).

[2] Without the doctrinal, there is no practical.   A man who disbelieves what divine revelation teaches will be difficult to exhort concerning how he should live.   "Doctrine is never taught in the Bible simply that it may be known; it is taught in order that it may be translated into practice."   Bruce, *Romans*, p. 225.

[3] Paul's letters, for the most part, break down neatly into two major points, doctrinal and practical.   "An equally marked division between the theoretical and the practical portion is found in Ephesians (chapter 4), and one similar, although not so strongly marked, is found in Galatians (5:1 or 5:2), Colossians (3:1), 1 Thessalonians (4:1), and 2 Thessalonians (3:6).   A comparison with the epistles of Peter and John will show how special a characteristic of Paul is this method of construction."   Sanday and Headlam, *Romans*, p.351.   Chrysostom long ago noted that Paul has already paused, here in Romans, to offer some exhortation.   See 6:12-14, and also 8:12-17.   (Hebrews, which this commentator attributes to Paul, also has its exhortations [warnings] interspersed through the whole letter.)

[4] Arndt and Gingrich, *Lexicon*, p.622,623.

[5] "Brethren" likely has the same force as at 1:13 and 11:25.

[6] The New Testament reflects the influence of the Old when it comes to referring to God's compassion. The Hebrew word for "mercy" has no singular form; it regularly appears in the plural *rachamim*; the LXX

bases his appeal.[7] The "mercies of God" are the reason why they should listen to his appeal to present their bodies as living sacrifices.

To present your bodies a living and holy sacrifice, acceptable to God. This is how a person who appreciates what God has done should live. Romans 6:13 spoke of presenting ourselves and our bodily members to God. 6:19 talked about presenting the bodily members as slaves to "king righteousness." Now, the same verb[8] is used again, and instead of "members" it is the whole body[9] that is to be presented as a sacrifice. This presentation[10] is something one does *after* he becomes a Christian, and indicates the Christian is free to determine to which master he will present his body. Paul's appeal is for a free and voluntary offering to God! Their "bodies" are the sacrificial victims[11] the Christians offer. Likely the three adjectives – "living, holy, acceptable" – all explain the kind of sacrifice it is to be. In the Jewish worship, the animal had to meet certain standards before it would qualify to be a sacrifice suitable to offer to God. Likewise, the Christian's sacrifice has to meet certain standards. The first word, "living," perhaps is intended to suggest the contrast between the Christian's sacrifice (where the "victim" is not actually

---

translates it by the plural "mercies." Some have thought that Paul has direct reference to what he has just written in 11:30,31, about God's mercy now being extended to the Gentiles; they suppose the connection is this – since God's mercy is at present being poured out on the Gentiles, I base my appeal to you Gentile Christians at Rome on this fantastic truth! Others appeal to verse 32, where God has mercy "to all," and think of Paul as addressing both Jewish and Gentile Christians in this appeal. The fact that Paul changes words (he used *eleos* in chapter 11; here he has *oiktirmos*) leads us to think he has in mind all God has accomplished in an effort to redeem people.

[7] "Calvin's comment is apt. Paul here 'teaches us,' he says, 'that men will never worship God with a sincere heart, or be roused to fear and obey Him with sufficient zeal, until they properly understand how much they are indebted to His mercy.'" Cranfield, *Romans*, p.596.

[8] *Parhistēmi* can have the sense of "place (someone or something) at another's disposal," and at times it also is a technical term for the religious practice of "offering (a sacrifice)." Arndt and Gingrich, *Lexicon*, p.633. When the word has its technical sense, the offering presented was thought of as passing from the offerer's possession, and becoming wholly God's property.

[9] Commentators debate whether 'body' is used for the whole person (though this commentator is not convinced those passages regularly pointed to – Philippians 1:20, Ephesians 5:28 – as examples of such a use of *sōma* are legitimate), or whether Paul has a special reason for speaking of the 'body' (the instrument of the soul, 2 Corinthians 5:10) in particular. Perhaps there is a tacit reference to what has been written in chapters 5-7, about how the devil has the ability to stir up the desires of the body, and thus get the man who lives in it to sin with it. The very bodily members that used to be utilized to do the devil's bidding are now to be presented to the Lord (see 6:19).

[10] The verb "present" is an aorist tense verb, which usually speaks of a one-time act. If that is its meaning here, this passage urges the Christian to make a definite surrender to the will of God, once and for all. An aorist tense likewise occurs in 6:13,19; but in 6:16 it is a present tense verb, indicating continuous action. Perhaps this is why Cranfield, *Romans*, p.600, writes, "And this self-surrender has, of course, to be continually repeated." Perhaps each time a Christian is tempted to use his body for the old master, Sin, is when he is to make a decisive presentation of his body to God instead.

[11] Paul does not use the word *prosphora*, which refers to sacrifices in general; instead, he uses *thusia*, the word that implies a sacrifice that was slain.

killed), and the Jewish sacrifices (where the animal victim was killed).[12]   The idea would be that the Christian's sacrifice was to be constant; there was to be a dedication about his lifestyle, with all his living energies and powers directed consciously to God's service. "Holy" does not just mean set apart and devoted to God, as the word often does in the New Testament,[13] for "sacrifice" and "present" already have suggested that idea.   In this context, there is no doubt an ethical connotation to the word – the body offered to God must be one whose lusts and appetites are carefully restrained, one free of immorality.[14] Like the Jewish sacrifice had to be unblemished and without spot (Deuteronomy 15:21; Leviticus 22:2-10; Malachi 1:8), so the Christian's sacrifice must be pure and free from the stains of passion, its sensual desires and appetites mastered by self-control, or the sacrifice is blemished.   "Acceptable to God" designates the sacrifice as being one that is true and proper, one that God has specified as being acceptable, and which therefore will please Him.   Since Calvary, the Christian's presentation of his "body" to God is the kind of sacrifice that has His approval.[15]

Which is your spiritual service of worship.   The presentation of the body as a sacrifice is the thing that is designated as a "spiritual service of worship."[16]   "Service of worship" is the NASB's way of rendering *latreia*, a word whose proper significance is "worshiping,

---

[12] Attempts to explain the word "living" have not been altogether satisfactory.   Three different approaches have been offered: (1) As given in the notes, there is a contrast between the animal being killed and the Christian's sacrifice continuing to live.   (2) The Christian's everyday activities, his concrete living, are offered to God.   An example would be Barclay, *Romans*, p.168, who sums up his thought-provoking paragraph in this manner, "So, Paul says, take your body, take all the tasks that you have to do every day; take the ordinary work of the shop, the factory, the shipyard, the mine; and offer that as an act of worship to God."   (3) Some suggest there is a reference to the "newness of life" that Romans has said much about, especially in chapter 6.   However, it was not the *body* that rose to walk in newness of life, yet it is the *body* that is here said to be "living."   The next phrase about "spiritual service" would be the better place to talk about "newness of life," or the spirit being alive.

[13] For "holy," see notes at Romans 1:7 ("saints"), 7:12, and 11:16.

[14] Those who thought "body" meant "the whole man, the worshiper himself," are likely to talk about spiritual growth at this place, and it is not uncommon to find references to Hebrews 12:14 ("Pursue holiness [sanctification, NASB], without which no one will see the Lord") and to Romans 6:19 ("resulting in sanctification") in an effort to explain what is meant by "holy" at this place.

[15] Perhaps there is a reflection that the Mosaic sacrifices, such as Jewish worshipers offered, were no longer valid.   "The animal sacrifices of an earlier day have been rendered forever obsolete by Christ's self-offering, but there is always room for the worship rendered by obedient hearts.   The new order has its sacrifices, which do not consist in the lives of others, like the ancient animal sacrifices (cf. Hebrews 13:15ff; 1 Peter 2:5)."   Bruce, *Romans*, p.225.   Perhaps there is a reflection that Gentile sacrifices are not pleasing to God.   "The offerings of the heathen; the pilgrimages of the Mohametans; the self-inflicted penalties of the Roman Catholics, uncommanded by God, cannot be acceptable to Him.   Those services will be acceptable to God, and only those, which He appoints.   Cp. Colossians 2:20-23."   Barnes, *Romans*, p.270.

[16] It is the *act* of offering, and not the *thing* offered – the sacrifice – that constitutes the "service."

i.e., the *action* of worshiping."[17]   The word *logikos* (translated "reasonable" in the KJV, "spiritual" in the NASB) is a word whose meaning is determined by its use in its context.[18] Perhaps what Paul intended is that such "service" rendered to God is 'demanded by reason.' After all that God has done for lost man (see Romans 3-11), such a presentation of his body to God is the only reasonable, or logical, response a man can make.   Perhaps Paul meant that such "service" is what is expected of a man whose "spirit" is alive (see Romans 8:10) and able to control the house (body) in which he lives.[19]

12:2 – *And do not be conformed to this world, but be transformed by the renewing of your mind, that you may prove what the will of God is, that which is good and acceptable and perfect.*

And do not be conformed to this world.   The Greek construction prohibits the continuance of an action already going on, so "Stop being conformed to this world" would be a good rendering.   This prohibition deals with one area that will need attention if they are going to render "spiritual service" by presenting their bodies to God.   It is not possible to be conformed[20] to this world and to present one's body to God at the same time.   A man's

---

[17] Cranfield, *Romans*, p.601. We have had the word "service" before at Romans 9:4, and the corresponding verb was used at 1:9. Barclay, *Romans*, p.168,169, tells us this word has an interesting history. "Originally, it meant *to work for hire or pay.* It was the word which was used of the laboring man who gave his strength to a master or an employer in return for the pay the employer would give him. It denotes not slavery, but the voluntary undertaking of a work. It then came to mean quite generally *to serve*; but it also came to mean *that to which a man gives his whole life.* For instance, a man could be said ... *to give his life to the service of beauty.* In that sense, it comes very nearly to mean *to dedicate one's life to.* Then, finally, the word came to be the word which was characteristically and distinctively used of *the service of the gods.*"

The one who said "Worship is a verb!" was rightly trying to express the truth that the word has the connotation of action in it; think of the whole range of sacrifices and offerings the Old Testament saint brought to the temple where he offered them to express the devotion of his heart.

The sign seen above some church building doors, "Enter to Worship. Depart to Serve." could be misleading. It is true that vital Christianity is more than just two hours on a Sunday morning; "Depart to serve" reminds us that it is something lived every day. But it is not true, as the slogan might suggest, that "worship" and "service" are two separate and wholly unrelated things.

[18] The word occurs in 1 Peter 2:2, and is translated "of the Word," in the phrase "long for the pure milk of the word." If that meaning were assigned to the word here in Romans 12:1, the verse would be saying that such presentation of our bodies as a living sacrifice is a service demanded 'everywhere in the Word.'

[19] Not only did Christians offer this everyday "service" (worship) to God, there were also special meetings or assemblies where Christians gathered together to sing hymns to Jesus, to hear the apostles' doctrine, and to commune in the Lord's Supper. It would not be a proper conclusion from Romans 12:1 to say that after making a presentation of one's body to the Lord (as Paul here urges), that there is neither time nor need for regular times of "worship" such as Acts 20:7 and Hebrews 10:25 implies the church observed.

[20] "Conformed" translates *suschēmatizō*, the stem of which is *schēma*. There is a well-known difference between the Greek synonyms for "form," *idea*, *schema*, and *morphē*. "*Idea* denotes merely *outward appearance.* Both *morphē* and *schēma* express something more than that. They too denote outward form, but as including one's habits, activities and modes of action in general. In *morphē* it is also implied that the outward form expresses the inner essence, an idea which is absent from *schēma*. *Morphē* expresses the form as that which is intrinsic and essential, *schēma* signifies the figure, shape, as that which is more outward and accidental. Both *schēma* and *idea* therefore deal with externals, *schēma* being more

behavior can be influenced away from God if he simply copies the present, fleeting, popular-at-the-moment fads and fashions.[21]   A Christian will have to keep eternity's values in view if he will live each day consistently for Jesus.[22]

But be transformed by the renewing of your mind.   This is a present tense imperative verb – constant inward transformation is the thing commanded.[23]   'Continue to allow yourselves to be transformed' might catch the flavor of the original.[24]   In the army, part of basic training is to rid the new recruit of his civilian ideas, and fill him instead with new, army-oriented ideas, and thus change the 'boot's' behavior.   Paul is telling these Christian 'recruits' at Rome that if a man (who used to be a sinner) would serve God, he must undergo a change, not just of outward form, but of inward personality, at the very essence of his

---

comprehensive than *idea*, while *morphē* deals with externals as expressing that which is internal."   Berry, *Synonyms*, p.134.   Cranfield, *Romans*, p.605-607, argues against placing much emphasis on the difference in synonyms at this place.

[21] "This world" is a translation of *aiōnos* ("age"), not *kosmos* ("world").   The expressions "industrial age," or "atomic age" or "space age" catch the idea – something that is the chief emphasis for a short period of time.   The period is marked or identified by this characteristic idea.   As time passes, the emphasis changes.   What the prohibition warns against, then, is "worldliness," or what might be called living a "this worldly life."   "He is warning the membership then and now against yielding to the various manifestations of worldliness by which they are being constantly surrounded: such as the use of dirty or offensive language, the singing of scurrilous songs, the reading of filthy books, the wearing of tempting attire, engaging in questionable pastimes, association (on intimate terms) with worldly companions, etc. There is hardly any end to the list."   Hendriksen, *Romans*, p.404.

[22] In the Scriptures, time (*chronos*) is looked on as divided into a succession of "ages" (*aiōnes*).   We usually call them Patriarchal, Mosaic, and Christian.   The idea of "eternity" to come (after the second coming of Jesus) is often expressed by the Greek phrase "unto the ages of the ages"; it pictures a succession of ages stretching into the endless future.   In Old Testament times, the Messianic age was often designated by the expression "the age to come."   It is obvious that in this prohibition about being conformed to this age, "age" means something different from what "age" meant in the expression "the age to come" or the "Messianic age."   "This age" in Scripture often has a negative connotation.   Galatians 1:4 calls it "this present evil age," and 2 Corinthians 4:4 speaks of life dominated by "the god of this age" (i.e., the devil).   "This age" can thus designate the state of the world as it exists until the second coming of Christ, much of it alienated from God.   Christians may well be living in this age, but their behavior does not have to conform to this world's behavior; Christians can remember they are citizens of a heavenly kingdom, and can act like children of the King.   In the words of Peter, "I urge you as aliens and strangers to abstain from fleshly lusts, which wage war against the soul.   Keep your behavior excellent (winsome) among the Gentiles ..." (1 Peter 2:11,12).

[23] The word here is *metamorpheuō*, and the stem *morphē* can be seen in it.   From this word we get the English word metamorphosis.   It is the verb translated "transfigured" at Matthew 17:2.   From the explanation given above in footnote #20, it can be seen that the thing commanded is not just outward conformity in behavior, but a thorough inward change which manifests itself in outward actions and appearance.   "The only other place the word appears in the New Testament is 2 Corinthians 3:18, where it is used of believers being 'changed' into the likeness of Christ 'from one degree of glory to another' by the operation of 'the Lord who is the Spirit' – a passage which is a helpful commentary on this present one." Bruce, *Romans*, p.227.

[24] A reminder that both verbs in verse 2 are present tense verbs, indicating continuing action, will help us to think of this behavior change as a progressive thing.   The perfect Christian character is not formed all at once at the time of conversion, even though the old slavery to sin has been broken.

being. "Transformed" is a passive voice verb; the Christian is being acted upon.[25] The "renewing of the mind" is the thing that will produce the inner-motivated behavior that pleases God. The noun "mind" is used in the New Testament about like we use it in popular speech – sometimes for the mental faculties, reason, understanding,[26] and some-times for moral and spiritual vision or perceptiveness.[27] The Christian's whole conduct will be different from the conduct of the men of the world, because the Christian's whole thinking is different.[28] No longer are the standards of the present age a satisfactory guide; instead the renewed mind is interested in what the "will of God" is. The "will of God" is the thing on which the Christian fixes his thoughts, and the result is a transformed life.[29]

That you may prove what the will of God is. "That"[30] indicates purpose; the purpose the renewed mind is intent on is to "prove what the will of God is."   "Prove" (*dokimazō*) denotes a "double process ... (1) that of deciding what the will of God is, and   (2) that of

---

[25] Some commentaries allude to the work of the Holy Spirit as the cause of this "transformation." He is the One (these commentators suggest) whose influences transform the man and his behavior. Chapter 8 has already alluded to the help the indwelling Spirit gives to the Christian to help him live the Christian life. But chapter 6 has also indicated that the Christian himself has some submitting and some mortifying to do, now that his spirit is alive because of righteousness. One ought not therefore suppose that a man is wholly passive in this business of transformation of behavior. Furthermore, it might be better to wait until the word "renewing" to make reference to the Spirit's activities in this whole process of transformation.

[26] "The mind (i.e., the mental faculties, reason, understanding) is in itself neutral. When informed by an evil principle, it becomes an instrument of evil. When informed by the Spirit, it is an instrument of good. It performs the process of discrimination between good and evil, and so supplies the *data* to the conscience." Sanday, *Romans*, p.127.

[27] "The renewal of the mind means the adjustment of our moral and spiritual vision to the mind of God." Vine, *Romans*, p.175. Some writers of Calvinistic bent use this passage as proof that men's minds are depraved as a result of Adam's Fall, and will not work right until they are renewed. Instead of men's minds being affected by Adam's sin, the other passages in Romans that have touched the topic of how sin affects the mind have focused on the man's own sins as being the cause of the mind's not working right.

[28] "Renewing" is *anakainōsis*, whose root is *kainos*, with the preposition *ana* intensifying the idea in the root. (See footnote #131 at Romans 8 for the meaning of *kainos* and of its synonym *neos*.) Paul evidently coined this word; at least it is first found in Paul's writings.

[29] It is rather surprising to see how readily the commentaries attribute this changed thinking to the work of the Holy Spirit, especially in light of the fact that Paul does not (in this context) name the Spirit as being the agent who does the renewing. We have had Romans 7:6 ("we serve in newness of the Spirit"), where some find a reference to the Holy Spirit's work. Titus 3:5 is appealed to as being a parallel passage, and it does indeed speak of the "renewing" work of the Spirit, an activity of the Spirit in the man's life after his baptism ("the washing of regeneration"). 2 Corinthians 4:16 and Colossians 3:10, which tell about the "inner man" (or "new self") being "renewed," are also alluded to as parallel references. To be honest, this commentator is still studying how the Spirit helps the believer. That He gives the inner man help to control the body seems rather clearly to be a fact. How He does it is not so clearly explained. Does He plant thoughts in the mind? Does He somehow 'renew' the mind? Does He aid our inner man to overcome and master what the devil has tried to do in our bodies as he has offered his enticements and temptations? This is a topic that deserves more study.

[30] At Romans 6, footnote #62, we have had an explanation of *eis* followed by an infinitive as expressing purpose.

choosing and acting upon it."[31]   The present tense indicates that there is a continual effort to determine and to demonstrate the will of God in the behavior.   Here, "the 'will of God' is not the divine attribute of will, but the thing willed by God – the right course of action."[32] The three adjectives in the next clause further limit and define this will of God, this course of action that the Christian is interested in pursuing, now that he has presented his body to God as a sacrifice.

That which is good and acceptable and perfect. "Good" may have its sense of morally good, or it may have its sense of that which is beneficial to man.[33]   "Good" is not just what men may decide is good, but rather is that which God has revealed He calls "good." "Acceptable" means that which is pleasing to God, or that of which He will approve. "Perfect" may be used here in the sense of "complete."   It is not just part of God's will that the renewed mind is interested in producing in the life of the believer; it is His complete will.   As the body is presented to God as a sacrifice, there is to be no inconsistency in the practice of the "will of God."

Having stated the broad principle which is to govern the conduct of the Christian, Paul now goes on to make application of the principle to certain specific areas of life.

B. Concerning the Christian's Relation to the Church.   12:3-16

12:3 – *For through the grace given to me I say to every man among you not to think more highly of himself than he ought to think; but to think so as to have sound judgment, as God has allotted to each a measure of faith.*

For through the grace given to me.   "For" indicates a connection of what follows to what has just been said.   "For" equals 'Let me explain further what I mean about demonstrating the will of God.'   What does it mean, for example, to the other members of the local congregation, when I present my body to God, especially when I consider that I have received some special gifts (verse 6)?   As it likely did in Romans 1:5, so here "grace" seems to refer to Paul's apostolic office.   It is in virtue of his being an apostle that he gives these following admonitions; as God's commissioned messenger, he is merely explaining what God wills in this area of one's behavior.

I say to every man among you not to think more highly of himself than he ought to

---

[31] Sanday, *Romans*, p.127.   *Dokimazō* was previously used at Romans 1:28 and 2:18.

[32] Sanday, *Romans*, p.127.

[33] We have had the word "good" before at Romans 2:7,10 and 7:13.   (It is not easy to decide if "good" is used as a noun in this place, as Thayer, *Lexicon*, p.3, believes; or whether the article before "good" picks up the article before "will," so that the construction is what is called an attributive adjective, meaning "the will – namely, the good, acceptable, and perfect one."   See Machen, *New Testament Greek*, p.36, for an explanation of attributive adjectives.)

think. Each individual member of the congregation is pointedly commanded[34] by the apostle to be careful how he regards himself, lest constantly, habitually,[35] he allow himself to have either too high an opinion[36] of his own importance, or too low an estimate of his value to the congregation.[37]   When a particular job is offered, the Christian should not try to shirk responsibility by thinking himself too good for the job.

But to think so as to have sound judgment.[38]   Here is the true standard by which a man is to think of himself – his place and value in the congregation should be estimated in the light of "sound judgment," sober judgment.   Sober and sane thinking neither exaggerates nor depreciates such gifts as God Himself has bestowed on the believer.   God had dealt to each man a measure of faith (the next phrase will tell us), and sober thinking would lead a man neither to overestimate his own gifts, nor underestimate those of others.[39]   Just what constitutes sound judgment is further delineated in the following phrases.

As God has allotted to each a measure of faith.   Paul is saying that when a man recognizes thoughtfully the "measure of faith" he and the other Christians have received from God, then he will be able to propose for himself the proper behavior in relationship to other members of the congregation.   That each Christian has been given a "measure of faith" is an unexpected expression.[40]   The word "faith"[41] (for the moment not taking the context into account) could mean 'faithfulness,' or 'personal faith,' or 'the faith' (i.e., a body of doctrine), or it could have reference to one of the supernatural gifts called "faith" (as at

---

[34] "I say" was Jesus' characteristic way of presenting a teaching, and the people who listened to Him thought of Him as "One who spoke with authority" (Matthew 5:34,39 and 7:28,29).

[35] The Greek *huperphronein* ("to think too highly, to be haughty") is a present infinitive, and so pictures having the thoughts habitually turned in a certain direction.

[36] "*Huperphronein* means to have high thoughts, to be high-minded, proud, which of course leads to looking on others, especially the humble in station and life, as inferiors and beneath notice.   Such pride is wholly inconsistent with the example and spirit of Christ, and needs to be completely subdued." Lard, *Romans*, p. 382.

[37] "Sound judgment" would certainly exclude underevaluating and undervaluing one's place and purpose within the congregation.

[38] There is a play on words in the Greek.   Four words in this text – "think highly," "think" (twice), and "sound (sober) judgment" – all are from *phroneō* (or some related form of it).   David Brown's effort at reproducing the paranomasia in English is "not to be high minded above what he ought to be minded, but so to be minded as to be sober-minded."   Wilson, *Romans*, p.200.

[39] When it is remembered that Romans was written from Corinth, and that at Corinth there was considerable unsober thinking about gifts (see chapters 12-14), one wonders if Paul is trying to head off (before it starts) similar misbehavior at Rome that he had experienced at Corinth.

[40] In verse 6, Paul uses the expression "according to the proportion of ... faith," and in Ephesians 4:7, he uses "to each ... grace was given according to the measure of Christ's gift."

[41] See comments on "faith" at Romans 1:5,8,12; 3:3; and 10:8.

1 Corinthians 12:9 and 13:2).[42]   "Measure" (*metron*) can mean either the means of (i.e., the instrument for) measuring something, or the standard by which something is measured, or the amount or quantity of something after it is measured.[43]   Given all these options, several explanations could be offered for the expression "measure of faith."[44]   Perhaps this Greek phrase is a genitive of source, so that "measure of faith" means that one gets his "measure" (amount, quantity) as a result of becoming a Christian (a believer, a man who is justified by faith).   Such an explanation enables us to take "faith" in the sense it often has in Romans, and it also aids us as we try to allow the following verses to explain what is here said (since we notice that verses 4-6 begin with "for").   "Measure" would then be explained by "gifts that differ according to grace" (verse 6), which expresses the idea that the gifts are distinguished from each other, in that one gift results from this measure (amount) of grace, while another's gift results from a different measure of grace.[45]   This "measure of faith" was "allotted"[46] to each of Paul's readers at some time in the past.   The thought that "God" had done the allotting, should keep anyone from thinking too highly of himself, or too poorly of the other church member, for such thoughts would border dangerously on complaint and criticism of God for what He had allotted by grace.

---

[42] There was a time when this fourth meaning of "faith" was the one this commentator thought Romans 12:3 spoke about, especially in light of Paul's reference to "gifts" in verse 6.   However, this results in "faith" being used in a different way here in Romans than it is used in 1 Corinthians 12 and 13.   That is, in Romans "faith" must be turned into a general term covering all the special gifts, whereas in 1 Corinthians it is a specific term for but one gift.   In those passages where "faith" is a "special miracle-working faith," it seems to be distinguished from other similar spiritual gifts (see 1 Corinthians 12:8-10; 13:2).   Further, if "faith" here in verse 3 is a supernatural gift, it is difficult to harmonize this Romans passage with 1 Corinthians, because Romans indicates "faith" is something "each man" receives, whereas 1 Corinthians indicates not everyone has the gift of faith.   The apparent problems inherent in trying to use this fourth meaning for "faith" have caused this commentator to seek a better solution for this difficult passage.

[43] Thayer, *Lexicon*, p.408.

[44] One of the many interpretations that deserves special attention is the one that says "faith" in this verse is the "faith" which results in a man's being reckoned righteous by God.   Since the verse says the "measure of faith" is "allotted by God," it is not uncommon to find some commentaries teaching that the faith that saves is a gift from God.   The reader should observe that this interpretation just assumes "measure of faith" is a partitive genitive (see Dana and Mantey, *Manual Grammar*, p.79), so that it is "faith" rather than "measure" that is allotted.   In light of what Paul wrote at 10:17, how can anyone affirm that faith is a gift, rather than being the person's free, individual response to the message he has heard preached?   It seems that what was written at 10:17 should warn us against any interpretation of this verse that makes "faith" (if it be understood as the faith that saves) as being given by God.   Even the verb "allotted" is difficult to explain on this supposition.   Are we to think of saving faith as being apportioned to believers, with some getting more, and others getting less?   This is difficult to accept.

[45] In the author's commentary on Acts, this phenomenon called "measure" is called "the different activities of the Holy Spirit."   *New Testament History: Acts*, p.101.

[46] *Merizō* means "*divide* into its component parts; to *distribute* something to people; to deal out, assign, *apportion* something to someone."   Arndt and Gingrich, *Lexicon*, p.505.

   As the following verses are studied in detail, it will be observed that some describe the gifts apportioned by the laying on of an apostle's hands (the temporary, supernatural gifts), while others describe the gifts that were evidently assigned at the time of one's immersion for the forgiveness of sins (spiritual gifts, which are still available to believers after the apostles and their laying on of hands have become a thing of the past).

12:4 – *For just as we have many members in one body and all the members do not have the same function,*

For just as we have many members in one body. Here begins several verses where an explanation of "sound judgment"(verse 3) and "allotted ... a measure of faith" is given. Using the relationship of the different parts of the human body to illustrate how members of a congregation are to relate to each other is one of Paul's favorite analogies.[47]

And all the members do not have the same function. As a man studies his physical body, he can see both unity and diversity, and both are essential. Each part of the human body has its own distinctive work to do,[48] yet in a healthy body all the parts function harmoniously and interdependently for the good of the whole body. The members of the human body do not argue with each other, or envy each other, or dispute about their relative importance, or withhold from each other what they can contribute to their neighbor's welfare. Why, then, in the church, should any think more highly (or lowly) of himself than he ought to think? Is it not easy to see that such individual estimation of importance is not "sound judgment"?

12:5 – *so we, who are many, are one body in Christ, and individually members one of another.*

So we, who are many, are one body in Christ. Individual believers, those who are "in Christ," viewed collectively, make up "one body," the church. The unity of the individual believers is supplied by their relation to Christ, the head of the body (Ephesians 1:22,23; see also John 15:1-7). "Viewed individually, Christians stand to each other in the same sort of relation as the different limbs and organs of the natural body, as hand and foot, or hand and eye."[49]

And individually members one of another. That is, "we, as individuals, are fellow-members with one another in the body." Each member must recognize it is but one of many members, and must contribute to the welfare of the other bodily members, and a desire to do such is "thinking soberly" (verse 3). In the human body, one member has one task assigned to it, while another member has a different assignment; and when all do their appointed tasks, the body lives and grows. In the same way, Paul is picturing each individual member of the congregation functioning with the special gift he or she has received, benefitting the fellow members who are also part of the body, with the result that the congregation lives and grows. Our relationship, in Christ, to the other members of the body, involves mutual responsibility to and for each other. In the following verses, we have some specific examples of such mutual responsibility in action.

---

[47] See 1 Corinthians 12:12-27; Ephesians 4:25, 5:30.

[48] The word translated "function" is *praxis*, and means a "task, an activity, an office, a function." Arndt and Gingrich, *Lexicon*, p.704. It is the same word translated "deeds" at Romans 8:13.

[49] Sanday, *Romans*, p.128.

12:6 – *And since we have gifts that differ according to the grace given to us,* **let each exercise them accordingly***: if prophecy, according to the proportion of his faith;*

And since we have gifts that differ according to the grace given to us. It is this phrase, in our opinion, that helps define the word "measure" in "measure of faith" (verse 3). It is this phrase that also shows how it comes to be that the individual members in the body of Christ have different "functions," just as the members of the human body have different functions (verse 4). God has given differing gifts to Christians, usually one gift to each believer.[50] "Gifts" is *charismata,*[51] the same word used for "spiritual gifts" in 1 Corinthians 12-14. The gifts differ in value and importance, and evidently also differ in how they were imparted. 1 Corinthians 12:31 and 14:5 indicate some gifts were more valued, or greater than others, because more people in the congregation were benefitted when those particular gifts were exercised. The temporary supernatural gifts were received by the laying on of an apostle's hands (cp. Acts 8:17, 19:6; Hebrews 2:4),[52] while the spiritual gifts that are available through the whole church age evidently are imparted as a person becomes a Christian (1 Corinthians 12:13[53]). It is God's unmerited favor in action

---

[50] 1 Corinthians 12:8-10 seems to indicate one gift per person. However, at times the man who had the gift of speaking a foreign language could also translate it into the local dialect (1 Corinthians 14:5, 13); that is, he had two gifts, "tongues" and "interpretation of tongues." There were also times when someone else had to do the translating (1 Corinthians 14:27). This limitation of one gift per person would be the rule for non-apostles; apostles had several of the gifts – they could speak by inspiration, speak a foreign language, work gifts of healings, etc. It is doubtful any of the listings of "gifts" in the New Testament, whether here in Romans, in 1 Corinthians 12, in Ephesians 4, or in 1 Peter 4, is exhaustive. Upwards of 27 different gifts are named in those chapters, and it is not even certain that this covers the total number of such gifts.

[51] *Charismata* has occurred several times in this Roman epistle, at 1:11; 5:15,16; 6:23; and 11:29. Perhaps one of these (Romans 1:11) has the same meaning it does here in 12:6.

[52] Hebrews 2:4 notes several divine credentials an apostle could display in order to demonstrate the truth of his message – among them, the "distributions of the Holy Spirit" (so the Greek reads), which would seem to be similar to what elsewhere is designated as spiritual gifts given by the laying on of an apostle's hands. This commentator teaches that the office of apostle was a temporary office in the early church, as indicated by the qualifications that one had to meet to be an apostle of Jesus (Acts 1:21,22), and by the expression in Ephesians 2:20. Therefore, those spiritual gifts that were imparted by the laying on of an apostle's hands would last only as long as there were apostles, and people on whom they laid hands, still living on earth. Among the spiritual gifts, some specifically are identified (1 Corinthians 13:8) as being of the temporary kind – prophecy, tongues, and knowledge. This commentator is also of the opinion that 1 Corinthians 13:8 abbreviates the list of gifts given in 1 Corinthians 12:8-10 and 12:28. Therefore, he would conceive all those in both lists as being temporary, the kind received by the laying on of an apostle's hands.

If it should be wondered how Christians at Rome could have spiritual gifts when no apostle is there or has been there yet, see what was said on this matter at footnote #50, on chapter 1 of Romans.

[53] The first half of 1 Corinthians 12:13, "By one Spirit we were all baptized into one body," evidently says that the Holy Spirit leads a man to the place that he wants to be baptized into the body (as Romans 6 pictures). It is the latter half of the verse, "and we were all made to drink of one Spirit" that suggests that every Christian receives a "gift" at the time of his conversion. It is not easy to discern, however, whether the measure of the Spirit that 1 Corinthians 12:13b refers to is the indwelling of the Holy Spirit, or whether it might refer to such spiritual gifts as did not require the laying on of an apostle's hands to receive. In Romans 12:3, "allotted" is an aorist tense, looking to a specific time in the past when this apportionment was made; the conversion of each Christian would fit this figure. In 1 Peter 4:10, which speaks about spiritual gifts being received, likewise uses an aorist tense verb, and could point back to the time of conversion.

("grace")[54] that determines which gift and who receives it.   It is in harmony with His royal freedom to dispense the grace-gifts in different measures on different persons.

Let each exercise them accordingly.   We have the gifts; what is to be done with them? The answer to this question has been implied by the illustration of the body in verses 4 and 5.   Out of the received gift comes the function the individual Christian is to perform in the body.[55]   The rest of verse 6, and the two following verses, will give examples of some of the different "gifts" Christians received, and were expected to use for the benefit of the other members in the body.

If prophecy.   The gift of prophecy was the highest gift available to ordinary church members.[56]   This gift is listed next in order under apostles in Ephesians 4:11; it is listed second in 1 Corinthians 12:28, and is assigned a place superior to tongues in 1 Corinthians 14:1,5,39.[57]   Prophecy was inspired preaching[58] in the language of the people; the content

---

[54] See comments at Romans 1:7 for the meaning of the word "grace."

[55] Perhaps, in light of this passage, it is not in harmony with Scripture to preach that every individual church member is to measure up to the same standard if he would be thought of as "spiritual."   Before we say that every Christian is expected to "teach" (verse 7), or that every Christian is to "show mercy" (verse 8), etc., we may need some careful definition, lest we hold up a standard God never did.

Since the early 1970's, sparked by Ray Stedman's *Body Life* (Glendale, CA: Regal Books, 1972), dozens of books have been published whose emphasis has been on helping church members discover which "gift" each has received, and then encouraging each to use it, as a means for revitalizing a dying church, or turning what otherwise is a personally disappointing ministry into an exciting one in that community and church.   C. Peter Wagner's *Your Spiritual Gifts Can Help Your Church Grow* (Glendale, CA: Regal Books, 1979) is perhaps a good summary of all that has been said in these books.   In this commentator's opinion, a fatal flaw in most of these presentations (including Bill Gothard's "Basic Youth Conflicts [Series Two]") is that no distinction is made between the temporary and permanent gifts, nor is there a careful definition of many of the gifts, so that they match what one reads in the Bible.   (For example, as they cover the gift of "prophecy," which in the Bible is inspired speaking, it is made to mean nothing more than uninspired preaching today.   This hardly leaves the reader with a clear, Biblical concept either of prophecy, or spiritual gifts today.)   If Bible teachers would speak God's thoughts after Him, then surely they should use Bible words in a Bible way.   If this is done, then helping people to recognize the gift each has been allotted, and encouraging each to use it, is a profitable exercise for all the members of the congregation.

[56] A question that is most difficult to answer satisfactorily is whether men and women both held the office of prophet in the New Testament church.   Philip's daughters (Acts 21:9) were prophetesses, and Joel predicted that in the church age "sons and daughters" would prophesy (Joel 2:29; cp. Acts 2:17).   Is there a difference between the *office* of prophet and the *function* of prophet in the New Testament, like there apparently was in the Old Testament?   (This distinction might explain why Daniel, who had the function of prophet, is placed among the "Holy Writings" in the Hebrew Canon rather than with the "Prophets," i.e., with those who held the office of prophet.)   If there is a difference, which position did women hold in the New Testament?   Did they hold the office along with the male prophets, or did they at times function as a prophet without holding the office?

[57] "Prophet" and "prophecy" are treated at length in the author's commentary on Acts, at 11:27,28.   The New Testament prophet (who was second in rank after the apostles) differs slightly in rank or authority from the position the Old Testament prophets occupied, which was one of priority (Numbers 12:6-8; Deuteronomy 18:15-18; Hebrews 1:1).

of the message could refer to the past, the present, or the future.[59]   From 1 Corinthians 14, we learn that a prophecy could result in the church's being instructed and exhorted (verse 31), edified, exhorted, consoled (verse 3), and unbelievers being convicted and converted (verses 24,25).   The message the prophet was burdened to deliver evidently came as a special revelation to the prophet's mind, giving the message a certain sense of immediacy and importance, which even allowed the prophet with the latest revelation to take precedence over one who was speaking (1 Corinthians 14:30).[60]

According to the proportion of his faith.   For a number of verses now, until verse 14 in fact, Paul uses only participles, and no verbs.   Most translators supply the verbs needed to make a complete sentence, as for example the ASV, which reads "whether prophecy, *let us prophesy* according to the proportion of our faith."   In this way, all these verses are made exhortations to do well what God has given us the gift to do.[61]

If it is wondered why the office of apostle is not mentioned in this list in Romans, several answers may be suggested.   There is no apostle at Rome (see Romans 15:15-29).   Furthermore, Paul has already alluded to his own apostolic "grace" (Romans 1:5 and 12:3).   "It would scarcely be in accord with the pattern indicated in the New Testament for one apostle to give directions to another respecting the conduct of his office.   The priority of the apostleship makes it thoroughly appropriate, on the other hand, for Paul to enjoin a prophet to exercise his gift 'according to the proportion of faith'."   Murray, *Romans*, p.121.

[58] We would, in a very similar vein, attribute the inspiration of Luke's writings, and Mark's, and Jude's, to the gift of prophecy.   Apostles could speak and write by inspiration by virtue of having received the measure of the Holy Spirit called 'the baptism of the Holy Spirit.'   Those apostles could also lay hands on others, and some would receive the gift of prophecy, enabling them to speak by inspiration the message they have received by revelation (cp. 1 Corinthians 2:12,13).

[59] "Prophecy" has come to have the connotation in modern English of 'prediction of the future,' but if we try to read this definition back into the Biblical passages, we will be left with the wrong idea.   Prophets did sometimes predict the future (cf. Agabus who predicted a coming famine, Acts 11:27,28).   They could also announce something that God wanted done now (cp. the prophets who were instructed to see that Paul and Barnabas were sent off on the missionary journey, Acts 13:1-3).   Prophets could encourage and strengthen congregations with their preaching (cp. Judas and Silas at Antioch after the Jerusalem Conference, Acts 15:32).   They could sometimes even tell what was done in the past (cp. Jude telling about Enoch's prophecy, Jude 14,15).

[60] In the early congregations, the temporary spiritual gifts took the place, and answered the purpose of, the present written New Testament.   "By them the churches were built up and kept in order.   In a word, every thing was done by them – the gospel was preached, the disciples instructed, the churches ruled.   They were then indispensable; but now they are not, the New Testament supplying their place."   Lard, *Romans*, p.384.

[61] The other way of taking these participles is to make them all dependent on "having gifts" in verse 6, treating each participle as an example of one kind of gift, but without any stated exhortation about using the gifts.   That the method of interpretation found in the ASV is to be preferred is shown by the fact that few commentators have the hardihood to carry the other method as far as verse 8, let alone to verse 13 where the participles end.

"Proportion" is a translation of *analogia* in the Greek, a word used nowhere else in the New Testament.[62]   It means "in right relationship to," "in agreement with."[63]   We tend to take "the faith" as meaning "that which is believed, a body of doctrine,"[64] so that the exhortation here to the prophets is to make sure the message they deliver is in agreement with already admitted Christian doctrine.[65]   If it be questioned why such an exhortation is even needed when the preaching is inspired by the Holy Spirit, the answer may lie in this:

---

[62] It is a word from the world of mathematics, and "means the ratio or proportion which results from comparison of one number or magnitude with another.   In a large sense, therefore, as applied to other subjects, it denotes the measure of anything."   Barnes, *Romans*, p.176.

The Peshitto Syriac translators thought this phrase is related to what was said in verse 3, for the Syriac uses the same word to translate both "measure" in verse 3 and "proportion" here in verse 6 (Cranfield, *Romans*, p.620).   This leads to an explanation along these lines: If prophecy is the measure or proportion we have been given now that we have become Christians, then God expects us to preach. This interpretation has against it the fact that, in verses 7-8, each of the phrases following the designation of the gift received seems to designate *how* the gifts are to be used.   It would be out of place then, here in verse 6, to interpret this as meaning *what* gift the prophets are to use.

If we must explain this phrase by a corresponding phrase in the context, a better choice might be that "proportion of faith" is somehow related to "according to grace given to us" in verse 6.   Better still is the interpretation offered by the NASB translators, that "proportion of faith" is related to an understood "let us exercise them accordingly."

[63] Arndt and Gingrich, *Lexicon*, p.56.

[64] Arndt and Gingrich, *Lexicon*, p.669.   The Greek reads "the faith," i.e., there is an article present. Sometimes the article does serve as a possessive pronoun (the NASB so treats it here, when they render "*his* faith").   Machen, *Grammar*, p.148.   But it is doubtful that it should be so translated here, for it rather requires that "faith" be understood as being subjective faith, and this in turn leads one into difficulty when it comes to offering an interpretation.   It makes Paul say that how much "prophecy" one gets to deliver depends on how much faith he has.   It is hard to believe that what this verse teaches is that one prophet might be more inspired than another simply because he is a more faithful Christian than the other.   Neither in Caiaphas' case (John 11:51) nor in that of Balaam's ass (Numbers 22:21-35; cp. 2 Peter 2:16) did inspiration depend on how much "faith" the mouthpiece exhibited.

(Admittedly, [a] the "prophecy" in the two examples just cited may not be the same kind of inspiration a prophet experienced as he prophesied.   Considerable debate has raged as to the meaning of "prophesied" in the case of Caiaphas, though John makes it plain that the priest did not "speak on his own initiative."   In the case of the ass, the specific term 'prophesy' is not used, though we are told "the Lord opened the mouth of the donkey," and she "spoke with a voice of a man."   The animal was simply used as a tool, without any of the freedom to compare spiritual things with spiritual words that 1 Corinthians 2 emphasizes occurred when apostles or prophets spoke.   Also, [b] the objective sense assigned to "the faith" in the notes is not an ancient one, having perhaps originated with Thomas Aquinas [so Barmby, *Romans*, p.345 affirms].   So, it is with some hesitation that the comments offered have been adopted.)

[65] This interpretation amounts to explaining 'analogy of faith' as though it were similar to what has come to be designated as 'the analogy of Scripture,' i.e., the principle that Scripture is to be interpreted in accord with Scripture.

We are hesitant to accept, as the reason why Paul added "according to the proportion of faith," the interpretation that suggests some men's inspiration came from the devil, and therefore even a true prophet had to be careful of what he spoke, lest the devil intrude a false message along with the true.   Indeed, there were messages received from evil spirits (1 Corinthians 12:3; 1 John 4:1) as well as from the Holy Spirit, so a man did have to be careful from which source his "message" came.   But is that the point of "according to the proportion of faith"?   It seems that this interpretation is based on a confusion of the terms "revelation" and "inspiration," and the terms are not synonymous.   See this further explained in the author's Special Study, "The Doctrine of Inspiration," in *New Testament History: Acts*, p.127-29.

the Spirit did not overpower the human messenger.[66] The human messenger had a considerable personal responsibility when it came to acting as God's mouthpiece.[67] When the prophet spoke, his words were not just words which his own wisdom might choose, but were words which the Holy Spirit helped him choose, as he searched his vocabulary to find just the right word to express the truth he had learned by revelation.[68]

12:7 – *if service, in his serving; or he who teaches, in his teaching;*

If service, in his serving. The ASV reads, "Or ministry, *let us give ourselves* to our ministry." "Service" appears between "prophecy" and "teaching" in this listing, and this causes us to question whether "service" is likewise a special leadership function, or whether the word has simply a general sense, 'practical (voluntary) service.'[69] Assuming it is a special leadership function, and because the word is *diakonia*, some have supposed that the office of deacon is referred to.[70] Still others have proposed that it indeed refers to a special leadership function, but should not be limited just to the office of deacon. The evangelist's work is sometimes called a "ministry" (Colossians 4:17; 2 Timothy 4:5). An apostle's work

---

[66] 1 Corinthians 14:32 (ASV) indicates that the "spirits of the prophets" (i.e., the message they have just received) "are subject to the prophets" (i.e., the prophets are still in control of whether or not they speak – they are not being used by the Holy Spirit simply as a public-address system).

[67] What, for example, would keep him from withholding part of what had been revealed to him? This exhortation may be intended to say, 'Do not withhold any of the doctrine ("the faith") you have been commissioned to deliver.' Compare Acts 20:20, where Paul asserts that he has been faithful in this regard, not shrinking from declaring anything that was profitable to his listeners.

[68] 1 Corinthians 2:13 indicates the *words* as well as the ideas were the subject of Holy Spirit activity. After the special messenger had received a revelation, he would "compare spiritual things with spiritual words," and as long as he chose the right word, the Holy Spirit allowed/encouraged him to speak it. This is what is meant by "not in words taught by human wisdom, but in those taught by Spirit." When the speaker was about to choose a wrong word, somehow (the Bible nowhere explains this 'somehow') the Spirit hindered him, until he came up with the right word. In this way, each inspired speaker's/writer's own personality and vocabulary can be discerned in his message, but the message itself is exactly what God wants said.

[69] Those who take it in what might be called a 'general sense,' write about service that might be offered personally to the poor, the sick, the stranger, the widow. Perhaps it is true some have a 'gift' for this kind of ministry, but it also would appear that it is verse 8b that covers such acts of generosity and mercy. If, however, one were to think of "service" as what is involved in administering such gifts on behalf of the congregation, then it might not be completely out of place to talk about service to the poor, widow, etc. In harmony with this, observe that Paul uses the word "service" of his own trip to Jerusalem with an offering (Romans 15:31). Nor should "varieties of ministries" be overlooked (1 Corinthians 12:5).

(The careful reader will quickly observe that each commentator makes an educated guess as to the nature of the "gift" in as many as three or more of these seven "gifts" listed in verses 6-8. Most of these guesses are based on the analogy of Scripture along with the lexical meanings of the particular words. Certainly, this must be done for "service," "exhorts," and "leads.")

[70] Arndt and Gingrich, *Lexicon*, p.183. It is instructive to note that the 'deacons' in Acts 6 were endowed with spiritual gifts (Acts 6:6,8). It is also noteworthy that in 1 Peter 4:11, Peter uses two gifts to illustrate his exhortation (in verse 10) about using whatever spiritual gift one has received, those two being "speaking" and "serving." (Are these the same as Paul's "prophecy" and "service"?)

is sometimes called a "ministry" (Acts 20:24; Romans 11:13; 2 Corinthians 4:1).[71]   In other words, whatever opportunity of service you have been allotted, give yourself wholly to it,[72] for the church (the body) needs it.

Or he who teaches, in his teaching.   "Compare 1 Corinthians 12:28, Ephesians 4:11, 1 Timothy 5:17.   It would seem from these passages (especially 1 Corinthians 12, 'thirdly teachers') that teaching was considered a special office in the early church"[73] – and certainly in the Corinthians passage it was a supernaturally endowed office.   "There were specially gifted teachers in the church.   They were a lower order than the apostles, prophets, or evangelists; and here they are admonished by Paul to diligently work according to their gift."[74]   It is not easy to precisely differentiate between what "prophets" and "teachers" did.[75]   Perhaps the teacher's particular function was to carry out the second part of the Great Commission, "teaching them to observe all that I commanded you" (Matthew 28:20).

12:8 – *or he who exhorts, in his exhortation; he who gives, with liberality; he who leads, with diligence; he who shows mercy, with cheerfulness.*

Or he who exhorts, in his exhortation.   As with the word "service," so here the question must be considered, does "he who exhorts" refer to a special leadership function in the church,[76] and was it a temporary or a permanent kind of spiritual gift?   Barnabas was one

---

[71] The way the Bible calls special leadership functions a "ministry" or "service" should be pondered. These functions are not just "professions" (an occupation, a job to be done to earn a living); they are, instead, ways one can be of service to people who need the service.

[72] Whatever meaning we assign to "in his serving" will determine how we explain "in his teaching" or "in his exhortation" in the following phrases, because the Greek phrases are all alike.

[73] Sanday, *Romans*, p.129.

[74] Lipscomb and Shepherd, *Romans*, p.223.   We are reminded of Acts 13:1, where the men who were prophets and *teachers* in the church at Antioch are named.

[75] Among the suggestions offered are these: (1) The source of the prophet's message was an immediate inspiration, while the source of the teacher's message was the Old Testament Scriptures.   (2) The prophets simply *proclaimed* the message; the teachers *explained* it.

[76] Those writers who are under a "clergy" system, and who feel the need to defend it as being Scriptural, are accustomed to explain "he who exhorts" as being a reference to a special position, but they also limit the role because they cannot have a non-clergyman 'administering the sacraments.'   A typical example would be Barnes, *Romans*, p.277.   "Perhaps the differences between the prophets, the ministers, the teachers, and the exhorters was this, that the *first* spake by inspiration; the *second* engaged in all the functions of the ministry properly so called, including the administration of the sacraments; the *teachers* were employed in communicating the instruction simply, teaching the doctrines of religion, but without assuming the office of ministers; and the *fourth* exhorted, or entreated, Christians to lead a holy life, without making it a particular subject to teach, or without pretending to administer the ordinances of religion."

If we could discard this denominational baggage, we would be left with the idea that some people in the early church had a particular ability to admonish, or to encourage, Christians to practice their known duties.   In an earlier generation in Missouri, it was not unusual for an itinerant evangelist to preach a message, only to be followed by an "exhorter" (often one of the local elders) who could make personal applications to individuals in the congregation, because their lives were known to him, where they were not

who excelled at "exhortation," or encouragement (Acts 4:36); we certainly may think of his work with Paul (Acts 9:27) or with Mark (Acts 15:37-41, after Mark had quit his task as "helper" in the midst of the first missionary journey) as examples of such 'rescue' work. Barnabas took people who found themselves in situations that very well might lead to quitting the ministry and quitting Christianity, and supported and encouraged them until they were strong enough to stand on their own again. Twice, Paul tells the young evangelist Timothy that his work includes both "exhortation" and "teaching" (1 Timothy 4:13, 6:2). The prophet also could function as an 'exhorter' (1 Corinthians 14:3). It would seem from such examples, and from the relationship of "he who exhorts" with the following context, that "he who exhorts" is not necessarily limited to any one special office, nor that it was simply a temporary gift. However, in truth, there is very little information in Scripture to guide us at this point.

He who gives, with liberality. "He who gives" probably speaks of the person who gives out of his own substance, rather than the one who distributes another person's gifts.[77] If the word does refer to the giver, rather than one entrusted with dispensing others' gifts on behalf of the congregation, then it would appear very probable that in this and the following phrases, Paul has passed from those gifts that related to special *leadership* functions in the church, and is now dealing with those gifts distributed generally amongst all members of the congregation, not just the leaders. While the Scriptures seem to suggest that each individual Christian has a responsibility to be a good steward of what God has entrusted to him, we have already suggested that not every Christian gets each one of these spiritual gifts. Therefore, we think that this special grace of giving is something not every member of the congregation is expected to exhibit. It does seem that God not only entrusts to some people greater material possessions, but also gives them a knack of knowing where and how to distribute them for the good of the cause of Christ. "With liberality" suggests the spirit or manner in which the giving is to be done. The basic thought is "singleness, simplicity, sincerity, mental honesty,"[78] with no thought of self-exaltation, ostentation, credit, praise, or reward. "Giving requires the simplicity, which without ulterior motives or secondary purposes is wholly directed toward the other person's need and has no other

---

always known so intimately by the itinerant evangelist.

[77] Sanday and Headlam, *Romans*, p.357, suggest that the difference between *metadidous* (the word used here) and *diadidous* is that the former speaks of giving out of one's own substance, whereas the latter speaks of distributing another person's substance. In contrast, Cranfield, *Romans*, p.624, gives examples he thinks tend to show that *metadidous* can mean distributing what is not one's own as well.

[78] Thayer, *Lexicon*, p.57. The Greek word is *haplotēs*. Arndt and Gingrich, *Lexicon*, p.85, give the definitions of "generosity, liberality" for Romans 12:8. Because the word seems to have the connotation of "liberality" when Paul uses it in 2 Corinthians 8:2 and 9:11,13, many suppose the same meaning should be assigned here. The attitude of generous giving is the thing that will help the body. "Neither liberality nor simplicity of purpose appears to be the most appropriate injunction with reference to the distribution of funds from the treasury of the church. Whereas when one's own possessions are in view, either of these virtues is particularly relevant." Murray, *Romans*, p.126.

consideration than that of relieving the need."[79]

He who leads, with diligence. It is doubtful that "he who leads" is limited to the function of elder, though that certainly would be included.[80] A number of areas in the life of a congregation (e.g., committees, meetings, youth work, choir, benevolence) call for someone to lead. Perhaps "leadership" is not even the right idea. Another possible translation would be "protector, guardian, to care for, give attention to."[81] If this translation were adopted, we should then think of those who are "on behalf of the church, a friend and protector for those members of the community who were not in a position to defend themselves (e.g., the widows, orphans, slaves, strangers)."[82] Whether it is leadership or protection, some people are gifted with these abilities. These people are expected to enter into their tasks with zeal and energy.

He who shows mercy, with cheerfulness. "If you are helping others who are in distress" is how the NEB reads. Most commentaries suggest that the distress is sickness, or the infirmities of old age, or disability of some kind. We wonder if "mercy" is not a general word that covers such supernatural abilities as "gifts of healings, helps" that Paul writes about in 1 Corinthians 12:28. It has also been suggested that when James instructs sick people to call for the elders, who will anoint the sick with oil, and offer a prayer of faith which will restore the sick (James 5:14,15), that those elders may well have had "gifts of healing." Whenever such spiritually gifted men were called on, and the calls could be so numerous as to become burdensome, the "mercy" was still to be extended in a cheerful manner. "He is to greet each opportunity for a merciful deed as a great find that makes him jubilant."[83] Such "cheerfulness" is not merely a matter of temperament, but is an atti-

---

[79] Cranfield, *Romans*, p.625. Another question would seem pertinent at this place: is the giving contemplated an instance of private charity, rather than giving through the treasury of the congregation? It would seem to be so. The idea that is popular in many quarters, that all monies a Christian gives should go through the local church (so the elders can have supervision of it, lest the members spend on causes which the elders do not approve) may be difficult to sustain either from command or example in the Scriptures. Members should welcome the elders' spiritual and doctrinal concerns, and elders who have properly instructed their flock in the faith should trust Christians to have the wisdom to give to worthy causes. Both members and elders should be granted the freedom in Christ to give on the spur of the moment, as perceived need and answer to prayer might prompt.

[80] In some passages where this same word (*prohistēmi*) appears, it has particular reference to the leadership in the congregation. In one verse, it does deal with the function of elders (1 Timothy 5:17). In one place it might be elders, but it cannot be certain it is limited solely to elders (1 Thessalonians 5:12). In another passage, it is used of the one who is "ruling" his own house, whether he be elder or deacon (1 Timothy 3:4,5,12). If we were to limit Romans 12:8 to the office of elder, it would not be proper to infer from it that but one elder is in charge of the congregation. We would not limit the function of prophecy to one person (cp. Acts 13:1) in each congregation; we would not limit teaching, or serving, or giving to one person. Why then (when the New Testament elsewhere indicates a plurality of elders in every congregation) would anyone suppose Romans envisions a one-man, ruling-elder type of polity?

[81] Thayer, *Lexicon*, p.539.

[82] Cranfield, *Romans*, p.626,627.

[83] Lenski, *Romans*, p.765. The Greek is *hilarotēs*; one can see "hilarity" in it.

tude that can be cultivated.[84]

12:9 – *Let love be without hypocrisy.   Abhor what is evil; cling to what is good.*

Let love be without hypocrisy.   After a plural participle introduced the list of gifts ("since we have," verse 6), the instructions in verses 6-8 were addressed, one after another, specifically to the person specially gifted with one of seven different gifts.   Beginning with "Abhor what is evil," the plural participles resume, showing us that the instructions in verses 9-13 are addressed to all, whatever the gift may be that each one has.[85]   These are qualities of character that all Christians are to exhibit, and the behavior inculcated still is concerned with the relationship of members of the congregation toward each other.

The initial phrase is this sentence ("let love be without hypocrisy") is in the singular, and is directed to each individual, just as the instructions of verses 6-8 were directed to the specific individuals.[86]   Love is *agapē*, and no better commentary on what *agapē* is, and how it acts, can be found than is given in 1 Corinthians 13.[87]   The better way of "love" in 1 Corinthians 13 was an instruction about how the Corinthians were to exercise their gifts – in such a way as to be spiritually helpful to the other fellow.[88]   We suppose Paul had a similar intent in his exhortation here, lest the Roman congregation be rocked by strife, like

---

[84] Barnes writes, "If anywhere a mild, amiable, cheerful, and patient disposition is needed, it is near a sickbed, and when administering to the wants of those who are in affliction.   And whenever we may be called to such a service, we should remember that this is indispensable.   If moroseness, or impatience, or fretfulness is discovered in us, it will pain those whom we seek to benefit, embitter their feelings, and render our services of comparatively little value.   The needy and infirm, the feeble and the aged, have enough to bear without the impatience and harshness of professed friends."   *Romans*, p.279.

[85] That we write about "instructions" (plural) indicates a decision has been made about the perceived line of thought in what Paul here writes.   That decision is that we should *not* take "Let love be without hypocrisy" as if it were the main thought, and that all the rest of the phrases (through verse 13) are examples or explanations of how genuine love works.   We are still working our way through a series of participial thoughts (through verse 13), and it is doubtful that nine of them are treated as subordinate to one of them. It may, however, be possible that the two that occur in verse 9 are related to "Let love be without hypocrisy."

[86] There is no verb or participle in the Greek, so one must be supplied.   One other place ("not lagging behind in diligence") in this passage a verb or participle must be supplied, but the nouns in that phrase are all plural.   Here in verse 9a, where the noun and adjective are singular, we would expect a verb or participle in the singular to be supplied also.   Thus, we take it to mean that the exhortation about "love" is addressed pointedly to each specifically-gifted individual.

[87] *Agapē* has been used of God's love for man in Romans 5:5,8 and 8:35,39.   Now it is used of a Christian's love for fellow man.   It is an attitude that can be developed and nurtured if a man will work on it.

[88] 1 Corinthians 12-14 deal with the nature and utility of spiritual gifts; so chapter 13 (right in the midst of these three chapters) surely has as its initial thrust a correction of the way the gifts were being exercised, lest the Corinthians continue to display selfishness in their use of the gifts.   Some gifts were intended to benefit the unbelievers more than the believers (1 Corinthians 14:22), so those commentators who write that "love here has as its object all men, as contrasted with love for the brethren (verse 10)," are not completely wide of the mark.   Nevertheless, we would still abide by the paragraph title offered for this section, that it has reference to the Christian's relation to the *church*.

the Corinthian church had been. "Without hypocrisy" ("without dissimulation," KJV) means without show, without pretense, without sham. The word "hypocrite" was originally used of an actor on a stage, who wore a mask that covered his real identity, and who acted out a part other than that of his true character. Thus, 'love that is without hypocrisy' would be "the real thing, genuine, and not counterfeit."[89] Its possessor would evidence his real interest in people by his actions.

Abhor what is evil. "Abhor" is a compound verb in the Greek, and no word expresses stronger aversion.[90] The proper Christian attitude toward evil is to shrink from it, shudder at it, have a strong feeling of horror about it. It is something that is to be constant and habitual, as are all the remaining instructions in this paragraph.[91]

The NASB makes this a new sentence, though it is a participial phrase in the Greek. It is difficult to know with any certainty how to treat this phrase and the next, whether as a separate sentence, or as subordinate to "Let love be without hypocrisy."[92]

▪ If we take them as subordinate, we would translate, "Let love be without hypocrisy, abhorring that which is evil, clinging to that which is good." If there is such a connection, and if "love" has to do with how church members were to exercise their gifts,[93] then the exhortation to "abhor what is evil" is a warning to the person doing the

---

[89] Cranfield, *Romans*, p.630. He also quotes Calvin, who wrote, "It is difficult to express how ingenious almost all men are in counterfeiting a love which they do not really possess."

[90] The verb here is *apostugeō*, and there is the possibility that the preposition *apo* not only intensifies the meaning, but expresses the idea of separation. Get away from the evil! Cf. Thayer, *Lexicon*, p.68.

[91] The participles are all present tense, indicating continuing, habitual, customary, repeated action.

[92] In favor of taking them as *subordinate* are these factors: (1) Both "abhor" and "cling" are participles in the Greek, and it is not easy to see how participles can be translated as imperatives. [Dana and Mantey, *Grammar*, p.229, do give Romans 12:9 as one of the few examples where a participle is used as an imperative in the New Testament.] (2) Beginning in verse 10, the participles are found conspicuously at the end of each phrase, whereas in verse 9 the participle begins the phrase. It could be argued that the change is deliberate, to show us *not* to treat 9b and 9c as separate ideas, but as subordinate to 9a.

In favor of taking them as *separate* instructions are these factors: (1) In the Greek, no verb appears at all in the expression about love. Our translators understand that some form of the linking verb is implied, and so have supplied, "Let (it) be." Is the understood subject in "*You* let (it) be..." singular or plural? Unless we take it as plural, the plural participles which follow are hard to treat as subordinate. (2) Each of the seven gifts was expressed by a singular participle. Now, at verses 9b-13, we have a series of plural participles. It is the first time since verse 6 ("we have") that the participle has been plural. Does not this significant change indicate separate instructions, rather than subordination?

[93] The student will not find many commentaries who make the connection between "love" and spiritual gifts (so that "love" governs how the gifts are to be exercised, as it does in 1 Corinthians 13) as our notes have done. Most writers treat "Let love be without hypocrisy" as a more general admonition dealing with how to behave toward others in whom "evil" (or "good") is perceived. Those who see "abhor what is evil" as a further explanation of "unfeigned love" tell us this phrase implies that "love which makes no discrimination between good and evil is merely sentimental and worthless" (Vine, *Romans*, p.180), or that "Christian love detests the evil in the person loved and only attaches itself to the good in him" (Sanday and Headlam, *Romans*, p.360).

loving, not to permit any "evil"[94] in his own heart to limit his use of the gift he has.

- If, as seems more likely, we begin a new sentence here (because the plural participles are resumed in this place), this exhortation is yet another way the Christian demonstrates God's good and acceptable and perfect will (verse 2) to other members of the body (verse 5). So interpreted, the "evil" that is detested would not be limited simply to a wrong use of spiritual gifts, as the other interpretation might suggest, but would speak of abhorring perceived "evil" in the fellow members of the body.

Cling to what is good. Get involved in the good the brother is doing.[95] Embrace it, encourage it, participate in it together with him.[96]

12:10 – *Be devoted to one another in brotherly love; give preference to one another in honor;*

Be devoted to one another in brotherly love. "Brotherly love"[97] denotes the mutual affection of those who are members of the same family. Here we are dealing with love for fellow Christians. Members of the body of Christ are no longer strangers to each other, or isolated units. They are brothers and sisters because they have the same Father. The body of Christ is not made up of a collection of acquaintances, or people who are simply friends; it is the family of God. And between members of the family there is a strong family affection, warm, tender love, the family spirit.[98] Paul may be simply reflecting the words of Jesus who instructed His disciples to love one another. He said, "By this all men

---

[94] This is the first time in Romans we have had this particular word (*ponēros*) for "evil," though we have had a cognate word (*ponēria*) which was translated "wickedness" at Romans 1:29, where it was shown that *ponēria* is a word which implies not only doing evil yourself, but delighting in getting others to do evil, too. Thus, *ponēros* could, in this context, refer to the destruction and danger that would result to other bodily members' spiritual welfare when only a selfish use of gifts was permitted or encouraged.

[95] If the final phrases in verse 9 are subordinate to "unfeigned love," then this passage would have to speak of "good" in the heart of the person doing the loving, for the nominative participle would agree with the subject of "Let love be ..." rather than the object of the love.

[96] "Cling" is from the Greek *kollaō*, which means "to join closely together, to associate with, to cling to" (Arndt and Gingrich, *Lexicon*, p.442), or "to glue, to glue together, fasten together, cement" (Thayer, *Lexicon*, p.353). It is used of dust 'clinging' to a person (Luke 10:11). It is used of 'hiring out' to someone (Luke 15:15). The same word is found at Matthew 19:5, where a man is said to be "glued" to his wife. "Glue yourselves together with the good" is the word picture. Be attached to it; be devoted to it.

[97] "Brotherly love" translates *philadelphia*. Compare Hebrews 13:1 and 1 Peter 1:22-23 for the doctrine of brotherly love.

[98] The word translated "devoted to" is *philostorgoi*, a word which "signifies the love as parents love their children. It hence denotes the tenderest kind of love." Lard, *Romans*, p.389. The word teaches us much about the brotherhood of the Christian family. It speaks of being helpful even to the family members who sin. (The boy does something wrong. His father may be hurt; but he does not hate the son, or freeze him out of the family circle. The father does not approve the wrong, but he tries to bind up the hurt.) When a man in the church does wrong and sins, we other family members are hurt. But he is our brother; and if we have the family spirit, we shall try to bind up the hurt. "No doubt, the idea is that Christians should love each other with the same sincerity and tenderness as if they were the nearest relatives." Hodge, *Romans*, p.396.

will know that you are my disciples, if you have love for one another" (John 13:35).[99]

Give preference to one another in honor. "The Christian is to take the initiative, and to show honor or respect to others without waiting for them to show it to him."[100] The word "give preference" means "to go before and show the way, to lead, to set an example."[101] The instruction to Christians is, not to see which could obtain the most honor, but which could confer the most honor on others.[102] Somewhere in his *Book of Martyrs*, Foxe says, "It is a greater honor to make a king than to become a king." Perhaps the attitude here taught is similar to Philippians 2:3, "let each of you regard one another as more important than himself." In this matter of who gets honored or praised, it is more important that *you* are appreciated and honored than that *I* am.

12:11 – *not lagging behind in diligence, fervent in spirit, serving the Lord;*

Not lagging behind in diligence. It is striking that as one reads these exhortations about relationships within the body, that this one about "not lagging behind" is one of the few negative expressions. It is almost as if Paul were causing it to stand out by deliberately wording it differently from all the other positive exhortations. The three expressions in this verse are very close together in meaning, and define the manner in which Christians are to exercise their spiritual service to God and man.[103] "Lagging behind" pictures the person who tries to get by with as little work and inconvenience as possible. Jesus used the word in one of His illustrations when He characterized a slave as "lazy" (Matthew 25:26). "Diligence" could also be translated "zeal."[104] In areas of service to his brothers, the Christian must avoid procrastination. Instead he is constantly to show earnestness, hastening to accomplish the necessary tasks.

---

[99] Nor is this love to be confined to members of the particular congregation to which we happen to belong. It must embrace the universal brotherhood of the redeemed.

[100] Sanday, *Romans*, p.130.

[101] Thayer, *Lexicon*, p.539.

[102] Barnes indicates that Christians have "to be studious to show to each other all the respect which was due in the various relations of life; children to show proper respect to parents, parents to children, servants to their masters, etc. How different this is from the spirit of the world; the spirit which seeks, not to confer honor, but to obtain it; which aims, not to diffuse respect, but to attract all others to give honor to us." *Romans*, p.281. Barclay observes that a failure in this attitude of conferring honor is one of the major causes of trouble in our congregations. "More than half the trouble that arises in churches concerns rights and privileges and places and prestige. Someone has not been given his or her place; someone has been neglected or unthanked; someone has been given a more prominent place on a platform than someone else – and there is trouble." *Romans*, p.178.

[103] The KJV "not slothful in business" could be misunderstood, since the word "business" now has the connotation of commerce with its buying and selling. If one remembers the context, then "business" is seen to have reference to the active relationships between members of the body.

[104] *Spoudē* is translated not only "haste, speed" but also "eagerness, earnestness, diligence, zeal (in matters of religion)." Arndt and Gingrich, *Lexicon*, p.771.

Fervent in spirit. "Fervent" is the word meaning "to boil with heat, to be hot." Thus, "the temperament of the Christian is compared to water bubbling and boiling over the flame,"[105] manifesting warmth and enthusiasm for the work of the Lord. Now that the man's spirit is alive (Romans 8:10), he must allow it to move him to action, like steam in an engine. The poet has caught the idea in the joyous words of the song "To the Work." First he says, "With the balm of His counsel our strength to renew, Let us do with a might what our hands find to do." Then he goes on to exult in opportunities for "toiling on." That is fervent in spirit!

Serving the Lord.[106] Jesus is the Lord (Master), and each Christian is His "slave." In the whole range of his activities, the Christian is simply submitting to the will of his Master.[107] If, with reference to his fellow members in the body of Christ, the Christian has as his basic philosophy of behavior the idea that "I am going to serve Jesus," his actions cannot be anything but such as will be spiritually beneficial.

12:12 – *rejoicing in hope, persevering in tribulation, devoted to prayer,*

Rejoicing in hope. "Let your hope be a source of joy to you!" Paul has given instructions about hope in 5:2-5 and 8:20-25. The thing for which the Christian hopes is to be allowed to produce a feeling of joy. The future resurrection and eternal life with God, Christ, and the redeemed brings joy beyond measure. Contemplation of these hoped-for blessings will bring a joy immeasurably greater and more lasting than the joy which being conformed to the present age may produce. Just as Peter's delightful paragraph about hope (1 Peter 1:3-9) is addressed to believers who are pilgrims on earth, and who are facing affliction and persecution from their unchristian neighbors, perhaps also in this verse and the next Paul is explaining to the Christian what to do when he or other Christians are afflicted or persecuted.

Persevering in tribulation. The word "persevering" has been explained at Romans 5:3 as meaning more than just passively enduring troubles when they come. It is an instruc-

---

[105] Sanday, *Romans*, p.130. Observe that Sanday uses "temperament" to translate *pneuma* here. Some have supposed that it is a reference to the Holy Spirit, and should be translated "Be aglow with the Spirit," or "allow yourself to be set on fire by the Holy Spirit." Since the very same expression ("fervent in spirit") is used of Apollos before he became a Christian (Acts 18:25), and therefore before he would have been influenced by the Holy Spirit, there is no real reason to make Romans 12 a reference to the Holy Spirit, either, even though Romans 12 instructs Christians who have the indwelling Spirit.

[106] Some manuscripts read "serving the opportunity" (*kairō*, "time," instead of *kuriō*, "Lord"). If this reading were correct, the exhortation would be for the Christian to eagerly seize each opportunity to serve as it presents itself. Barclay suggested some scribe confused the contraction he found in his text. But this explanation for how this variant reading occurred ignores the rather well-accepted dictum that such abbreviations were limited to a special group of 15 "theological" words, of which "Lord" (*kurios*) was one, but "time" (*kairos*) was not.

[107] Earlier in Romans (6:13-18), the idea of "slaving" was used to explain how a man lives. The connotation in the English word "slave" is to work exceedingly hard (and often for a harsh and impossible master). The Greek idea of "slave" was one whose entire work is directed by his master's will.

tion to take hold of the troubles and turn them into spiritual victories.[108] This tribulation results from the world's resistance to Christ and His gospel. Scripture regularly exhorts Christ's followers to expect such troubles and distresses.[109]

> The summons to be "patient in tribulation" is significantly sandwiched between the call to rejoice in hope and to continue instant in prayer. The Christian does not shrink under present trials because he is buoyed up by the hope of future glory and the divine strength which is imparted to him through prayer.[110]

Devoted to prayer. "Devoted" translates *proskartereō*, a word which means to "persist in, to adhere to, to busy oneself with, be busily engaged in, be devoted to."[111] The Christian lives in an atmosphere of prayer. "The meaning of this direction is that in order to discharge aright the duties of the Christian life, and especially to maintain a joyful hope, and to be sustained in the midst of afflictions, it is necessary to cherish a spirit of prayer, and to live near to God."[112] "Communion with God is essential as a controlling influence in our joy and in our patience under trial;"[113] otherwise, the Christian will find his spirit distressed and his mind succumbing to the anguish and pressure.

12:13 – *contributing to the needs of the saints, practicing hospitality.*

Contributing to the needs of the saints. Help to relieve the needs of the saints is the idea. "Saints" is used here, as elsewhere in the New Testament, of Christians still living alongside us, rather than of those "saints" who lived and died generations ago. "Contributing" comes from the word *koinōneō*, the cognate of which is translated "fellowship, communion, or joint participation in (something)."[114] It is an attitude toward the living

---

[108] "If life hands you a lemon, make lemonade," is the way one writer illustrates the idea in the word "persevere."

[109] See for example John 16:33 and Acts 14:22. See further the comments on "tribulation" at Romans 5:3.

[110] Wilson, *Romans*, p.204.

[111] Arndt and Gingrich, *Lexicon*, p.722. The word is often used to express the frequency of prayers to God (Acts 1:14, 2:42, 6:4; Colossians 4:2).

[112] Barnes, *Romans*, p.282. "We are to persevere in prayer. Is it not the case that there are times in life when we let day add itself to day, and week to week, when we never speak to God? When a man ceases to pray he despoils himself of the strength of Almighty God. No man should be surprised if life collapses if he insists on living life alone." Barclay, *Romans*, p.180.

[113] Vine, *Romans*, p.181.

[114] Thayer, *Lexicon*, p.351-52. *Koinōneō* is used with the same sense of sharing together to relieve needs in Romans 15:26; 2 Corinthians 9:13; Philippians 4:15; Hebrews 13:16; and very probably Acts 2:42. It includes the giving of money, and the doing of whatever one can to help supply the things the saints need. As Paul writes this letter to the Romans, he is on the eve of leaving for Jerusalem with an offering for the saints there (Romans 15:26). Paul is not here asking the Romans to have a part in this offering,

saints (my brothers and sisters in Christ) that treats their necessities[115] as one's own when it comes to relieving them. The church at Jerusalem has furnished a wonderful example of such "fellowship" (Acts 2:44,45; 4:34,35). The offering for the needy saints at Jerusalem provided by the churches in Macedonia, Achaia, and Galatia (Romans 15:26; 1 Corinthians 16:1-3; 2 Corinthians 8,9) likewise demonstrates the proper concern for the needs of the saints.[116] When we recall that we are listing some of the ways a renewed mind transforms a Christian's behavior, the matter of being involved in relieving a fellow Christian's needs is not surprising, for in a world which is bent on getting, the Christian is bent on giving.[117]

Practicing hospitality. Aggressively seeking to be hospitable is the idea in the word *diōkō*, which is here translated "practicing."[118] "Hospitality" comes from the Greek *philoxenia*, "love for strangers." From this literal meaning, it was but one step to the idea of being a host and entertaining them. Not only would brethren (in town on business or fleeing from their own homes as refugees) need a place to stay, but they would need a place to worship; and in the absence of specially built meeting places, the homes of the local brethren would become the places of worship. "Without complaint," added to the exhortation to be hospitable in 1 Peter 4:9, indicates that it takes extra effort to show this love to strangers, and sometimes it is repaid with abuse and disappointment. Nevertheless, as many have remarked, the Christian does not wait for the stranger to present himself at

---

but is giving instructions about the regular necessity any Christian has for such fellowshipping whenever he sees the need. "Whenever the children of God fall into want, take a part of their wants upon yourselves. Make their wants your wants, to the full extent of your ability to relieve them." Lard, *Romans*, p.391.

[115] A number of Graeco-Latin manuscripts and fathers read *mneia* ("memories") of the saints, rather than *chreia* ("needs"). The source of the different reading is unknown, but it did encourage the idea of having festivals in honor of the dead saints and martyrs, that one still finds observed in some churches (e.g., Roman, Eastern). The idea of presenting an offering of money as though it would benefit the souls of those saints already departed from this life is far from being Scriptural doctrine. Even the idea that it teaches 'prayers' for the departed saints (i.e., remembering them in prayer, rather than by monetary contributions), misses the idea in the word *koinōneō*. "Needs (necessities)" refers to such things as basic food, shelter, and clothing, help for the sick, and such like.

[116] Let it be observed that the Christian's special concern is for the needs of the *saints*. "While we have opportunity, let us do good to all men, but especially to those who are of the household of faith" (Galatians 6:10) helps the Christian keep his priorities right when it comes to helping the needy. American Christians, who in relation to Christians in other lands, are exceedingly affluent, have been granted a marvelous opportunity and responsibility and privilege in this area of alleviating the needs of the saints, while not ignoring their unconverted neighbors' needs either.

[117] Lard has a thought-provoking devotional note at this place. "It is much to be feared that this precept will never again be revived; for I am assuming that where it is not wholly forgotten, it has at least fallen into desuetude. I have never seen it practised except on a scale so parsimonious as to render it a virtual nullity. The scanty manner in which the rich disciples of the present day share the wants of the poor is a sham. From their thousands, they dole out dimes; and from storehouses full, mete out handfuls. This is no compliance with the precept; and it were better for a Christian that he were without a coat to his name than to have two, and not to give to his brother who has none. Such precepts as the present one will, in the day of eternity, prove a fatal reef on which many a saintly bark has stranded." *Romans*, p.391.

[118] The word *diōkō* was used at Romans 9:31 of Israel's pursuit of "a law of righteousness." The word can even have the connotation of "persecute" from the idea of the relentless pursuit the persecutor exhibits toward the object of his vengeance. In fact, the same word is translated "persecute" in the very next verse.

the door; rather, the Christian goes out and eagerly looks for those to whom he can show hospitality.[119]

12:14 – *Bless those who persecute you; bless and curse not.*

Bless those who persecute you; bless and curse not. Paul evidently makes an allusion to one of Jesus' own teachings (Matthew 5:44; Luke 6:28).[120] There is some evidence (including that of P[46] and Vaticanus) for the omission of "you" after "persecute": in that case, Christians are exhorted to call down blessings on persecutors, whether they themselves are the victims of the persecution or not. If we put verses 13 and 14 together, the refugees to whom the Christians are to extend hospitality may be the ones thought of as being persecuted. Not only are the Christians to practice hospitality, they are to pray for the ones who have been persecuting these brethren of theirs, whose flight now gives special necessity for such hospitality. It is not sufficient to avoid any desire for retaliation against those persecutors; Christians must take pains to see to the welfare of the persecutors.[121] Without a renewed mind, the inclination would be to call a curse on the persecutors.[122] Such behavior is emphatically rejected by the repetition of the command to bless,[123] as well as by the negative "curse not."[124]

12:15 – *Rejoice with those who rejoice, and weep with those who weep.*

Rejoice with those who rejoice. "With" is *meta*, and means 'rejoice in company with rejoicing ones.' Our suggested outline for this passage indicates that the rejoicing ones (or

---

[119] Not only is the elder to be a hospitable person (1 Timothy 3:2; Titus 1:8), but every believer is to be.

[120] How did Paul know about Jesus' sayings such as this? On the assumption that the traditional dates are correct, Luke's Gospel will not be written for another two or so years after Romans, so he did not repeat this saying from Luke. (In fact, tradition has it the other way: Luke writes what Paul has been preaching). Matthew's Gospel had been written about 8 years before Paul wrote Romans, but it is not necessary to suppose that Paul had seen a copy of Matthew's Gospel, and then here repeats what he had read therein. Jesus' own teachings circulated in oral form before they were written down, but not even oral tradition is the source of Paul's information about the life of Christ. If we trust Paul's own statement of the source of his gospel, he received it by direct revelation from Christ (1 Corinthians 11:23; Galatians 1:11,12). In passing, that Jesus' teaching is repeated by the New Testament writers is evidence that His teachings were intended for the Church Age, as well as for the generation who heard Him with their own ears.

[121] Cranfield, *Romans*, p.640, reminds us that one way to show that the desire (for good toward the persecutor) is no mere pretense, is by actually praying for God's blessing upon them.

[122] The prohibition, written with the Greek negative *mē* and the present imperative, prohibits an action already going on. The Christians are to stop cursing the persecutors. (In verse 14, the form of the admonition changes from the use of participles to the use of imperative mood verbs. In verse 15, Paul will use infinitives, and in verse 16 revert again to the use of participles, as earlier in this paragraph.)

[123] Though P[46] omits the second "bless," it should probably be granted that Paul originally included it.

[124] "In cases of cruel persecution, where the disciples would feel themselves outraged, they would naturally become very much exasperated. The consequent temptation to imprecate evil on their enemies would be very great. But the apostle allows nothing of the kind. On the contrary, Christians are to bless their persecutors; that is, they must invoke blessings upon them." Lard, *Romans*, p.392.

the weeping ones in the next phrase) are our fellow Christians, the fellow members of the body of Christ.[125]   Just why the fellow Christians are rejoicing or weeping is not indicated. Is it because of some special occasion (e.g., a wedding) or some earthly honor[126] that they are rejoicing?   Is it because of bereavement that they are weeping?   Can the rejoicing and weeping be the Christian's heartfelt response over the spiritual salvation or waywardness of friends and family members?   Like the rejoicing of the angels in heaven over a sinner who repents, perhaps Christians are also encouraged to rejoice[127] with other Christians in their time of joy over the repentance of loved ones.   Absence of selfish interests and overcoming disinterestedness in others (the two are closely related) is a noble character trait each Christian can develop.

And weep with those who weep.   Again, it is 'weep in company with weeping ones.' Empathy, to feel with, is the attitude the Christian is trying to develop.   A heartfelt interest in the brother's state is the way the Christian's behavior exhibits the will of God (verse 2).[128]

12:16 – *Be of the same mind toward one another; do not be haughty in mind, but associate with the lowly.   Do not be wise in your own estimation.*

Be of the same mind toward one another.   This verse has been variously interpreted. Does it continue the thought of verse 15?[129]   Does it introduce a new thought?   If it introduces a new thought, is it part of the paragraph that deals with relationships within the body (verse 3-15), or is it the beginning of a new paragraph about relationships with those outside the body?   For reasons which will soon become apparent, we think it is part of the paragraph that began in verse 3.   Paul will repeat this same formula in 15:5 as he gives instructions to the strong and weak brothers in the congregation at Rome.   The NEB renders it, "Care as much about each other as about yourselves,"[130] i.e., have the same attitude

---

[125] That the admonition concerns relations between Christians would not rule out proper sympathy toward Jews or Gentiles, even though they are not (yet?) our brothers in Christ.   In a moment (see verses 16,17), we shall have to address the matter of where the subject changes from relationships between Christian and Christian, to relationships between Christian and non-Christian.

[126] "It is indeed difficult to congratulate another on his success, especially if his success involves disappointment to us [we would like to have been recognized publicly, too!].   It is only when self is dead that we can take as much joy in the success of others as in our own."   Barclay, *Romans*, p.182.

[127] A technical note is needed here.   "Rejoice" and "weep" are both infinitives in the Greek, and an infinitive cannot be the main verb in a sentence.   Perhaps their meaning is rightly understood if we supply some verb from the context.   For example, we could use "I urge" from 12:1, and now verse 15 reads, "I urge you ... to rejoice," etc.

[128] "The feeling of sympathy is perhaps more under the control of the will than might be supposed." Sanday, *Romans*, p.131.

[129] Verse 15 has called for fellow-feelings.   A great hindrance to such fellow-feelings would be to have too high an estimation of oneself.   Hence, in verse 16, Paul goes on to condemn such pride.

[130] The 2nd edition of the NEB is here quoted.   A literal translation of the Greek would be "Minding the same thing toward each other," that is, "what you regard or seek for yourself, seek also for your brethren." Barnes, *Romans*, p.286.   The 1st edition of the NEB had "Have equal regard for one another."   Perhaps

about your brothers as you have for yourselves. Philippians 2:3,4 would be a good commentary: "Do not merely look out for your own personal interests, but also for the interests of others." The command speaks of attitudes that govern behavior. It does not require unanimity in matters of opinion (as chapters 14 and 15 will show) to carry out this command, but there will have to be mutual unselfishness, mutual helpfulness, if there is to be the harmony in the body (verses 4,5) that will cause the world to take notice.

Do not be haughty in mind. Literally the Greek reads, "not minding the high things." It can prohibit haughtiness,[131] or ambition. A person who is constantly pushing himself into higher positions simply out of conceit or for the prestige it affords is very destructive of the harmony that ought to prevail in the body.

But associate with the lowly. The margin reads, "accommodate yourself to lowly things" because the adjective "lowly" can be either masculine or neuter. It is easy to see that "associate with the lowly (humble)" nicely contrasts with "Do not be haughty."[132] It is also easy to see that when "high things" is recognized to be a neuter form, "lowly" could be so understood too, thus accounting for the marginal reading. "Allow yourselves to be carried along by the humble tasks (janitor, usher, preparing the loaf, laundering the linen or the baptismal robes, preparing food for a sick family)."[133] As the poet has put it, "The trivial round, the common task, will furnish all we need to ask: room to deny ourselves, a road to bring us daily nearer God."[134]

Do not be wise in your own estimation. This is not quite the same expression used at Romans 11:25, yet both phrases are translated the same way in the NASB.[135] (The phrase is an echo of Proverbs 3:7.) The English rendering also does not allow us to see the play on words occurring in verse 16 — "mind," "mind," and "wise" are from the same root. 'Stop

---

this choice of translation depends on how the following phrases are interpreted. If they are taken as explaining "Be of the same mind toward one another," then the idea is that Christians are to have the same mutual good feeling towards each member of the body, whatever their position or status.

[131] It is the same Greek words that at Romans 11:20 were rendered, "Do not be conceited."

[132] In favor of this interpretation is the fact that *tapeinos* ("lowly") is not elsewhere in the New Testament applied to things, but is regularly applied to persons.

[133] George Mark Elliott, classroom lectures on Romans, *in loc.*

[134] Quoted in Sanday, *Romans*, p.132, who also observes that to read the phrase "accommodate your-selves to lowly things," requires us to give a secondary meaning to *sunapagomenoi*, which he thinks is not quite so expressive or natural as when we translate "associate with men of lowly estate." It might also be observed that, when the KJV was translated, "condescend" was a good word, though now it has come to have a different connotation (namely, "to patronize" or "to put on an appearance of association with people beneath you, when everyone can see you are self-conscious about doing it"). In its good sense, "condescend" meant a friendly and unselfconscious association with ordinary and unimportant people.

[135] The prepositions are different: 11:25 is *en heautois*, whereas 12:16 is *par' heautois*. Thayer treats both alike (*Lexicon*, p.477), as having reference, metaphorically, to something done in the mind. "*Para* with the dative indicates something is or is done either in the immediate vicinity of someone, or (metaphorically) in his mind."

minding your own wisdom' or 'stop relying on your own wisdom,' we could translate.[136]

This injunction forms the climax of the paragraph about the Christian's relationship with fellow members of the body. If a man 'minds his own wisdom,' the instruction (verse 2) about behaving as a 'renewed mind' would prompt him to behave cannot be followed; nor can the injunction (verse 3) to "not to think more highly of himself than he ought to think."

C. Concerning the Christian's Relation to Those Outside the Church. 12:17-21

12:17 – *Never pay back evil for evil to anyone.   Respect what is right in the sight of all men.*

Never pay back evil for evil to anyone.   "From the mutual duties of brethren in Christ, Paul passes to the wider relations of the Christian towards all men, and especially towards his enemies."[137]   This instruction against retaliation is not limited to one's enemies, or to those outside the church.   There are times when Christians do unlovely things to each other, but if the brothers are practicing brotherliness, there should be no evil from that quarter that one would be tempted to repay.   Yet even if it is an unbeliever who has done evil, there still is to be no retaliation,[138] for this matter of getting even is simply not Christian.   What Paul writes reflects what Jesus Himself taught in the Sermon on the Mount.[139]   When a man has received injuries, his feelings are aroused, and his judgments are clouded.   In this condition, he is just not qualified to determine either the kind or degree of punishment due for the injuries.   Retaliation, therefore, is not permitted.

Respect what is right in the sight of all men.   Christians are not only to do what they know to be right in the sight of God (verse 2), but they are also to give forethought[140] to how men will view their conduct so that they may avoid justifiable suspicion and criti-

---

[136] Again, the present imperative with the Greek negative particle *mē* prohibits the continuance of an action already going on.   One commentator has noted that the word "wise" occurs in the Corinthian correspondence, in the rather sarcastic "*You* are wise" (1 Corinthians 4:10; 2 Corinthians 11:19).   It is a lack of sober thinking (Romans 12:3) that lets a man be "wise in his own estimation."

[137] Gifford, *Romans*, p.209.   Cranfield, *Romans*, p.629, makes the paragraph break at verse 14, mostly on the basis of the change from participles to the use (in that one verse) of an imperative verb.   The NASB treats verses 9 to 21 as one paragraph, making this prohibition of retaliation another result of the principle of unhypocritical love.   It is on the basis of Paul's use of "all men" in verses 17 and 18 that we have chosen to make the paragraph break at this place.

[138] "To no man" is emphatic in the Greek.   "Not one man" is to be the recipient of retaliation.

[139] Matthew 5:38-48; Luke 6:29-35.   Peter (1 Peter 3:9), as well as Paul (see also 1 Thessalonians 5:15), regularly repeated these precepts Jesus taught.

[140] *Pronoeō* suggests foresight, careful thought ahead of time, take into consideration.   It is the thought which precedes and controls actions, and is another manifestation of the renewed mind (verse 2).

cism.[141]   Paul has likely adapted Proverbs 3:4 as he writes this instruction, and Peter echoes the same idea as he urges his readers to keep their behavior excellent (winsome) among the Gentiles (1 Peter 2:12).[142]   The last word, "all men," also is emphasized in the Greek.   Whether it is a Christian or a non-Christian who will view or be affected by the behavior, before the action is done, it is to be made the subject of forethought as to how it will be interpreted.   If the interpretation may be adverse, the behavior is to be avoided.[143]

12:18 – *If possible, so far as it depends on you, be at peace with all men.*

If possible, so far as it depends on you, be at peace with all men.   Two qualifications are given that limit the attempts toward peace.   (1) "If possible" implies that being at peace cannot always be done.   There may come times when the claims of Christian principle will have to be defended vigorously.[144]   (2) "So far as it depends on you" implies that over what others will do, the Christian may have no control; if another breaks the peace, there is nothing the Christian can do about it.   "You" is emphatic.   The Christian is responsible (in the matter of peacekeeping) for himself.   So far as he is concerned, he is continually to do his best to keep the peace.[145]   Feelings of bitterness that may be aroused in the hearts of others, or desire for retaliation, or any cause that might lead to discord and strife, is not to be the fault of any Christian's behavior.

12:19 – *Never take your own revenge, beloved, but leave room for the wrath* **of God,** *for it is written, "VENGEANCE IS MINE, I WILL REPAY," says the Lord.*

---

[141] Other explanations proposed for this phrase include "Take thought how you may do good to all men" and "Let your actions be such as all men agree are good."   Against the former is that it treats an accusative case as though it were dative, in order to get "to all men."   Against the latter is the fact that the Christian's standard of behavior is not what the majority thinks is right (a sort of moral consensus), but is rather what God has declared to be right.

[142] "Here is a great precept of loyal jealousy for the Heavenly Master's honor.   His servant is to be nobly indifferent to the world's thought and word where he is sure that God and the world antagonize.   But he is to be sensitively attentive to the world's observation where the world, acquainted with the word of the Lord and conscious of its truth and right, is watching, maliciously, or it may be wistfully, to see if it governs the practice of His professed followers.   In view of this, the Christian will never be content even with the satisfaction of his own conscience.   He will set himself not only to do right, but to be seen to do it ... He will not only mean well toward others; he will take care that his manner and bearing, his dealings and transactions, shall unmistakably breathe the Christian air."   Lipscomb and Shepherd, *Romans*, p. 230,231.

[143] The topic of freedom of the will has been debated in these notes earlier.   This instruction, about taking forethought before we act, is another verse that makes little sense unless the Christian is both free to act and is also responsible for his actions.

[144] This verse does not teach peace at any price, for such would contradict the plain teaching of the Word elsewhere.   In Hebrews 7:2, we learn that Melchizedek was first king of righteousness, and then king of peace.   Righteousness has a priority over peace.   Paul is certainly not teaching that a man is to compromise right in order to be at peace.   James 3:17 tells us that wisdom (from above) is first pure, then peaceable.   If being loyal to Christ disturbs the peace, then the peace will have to be disturbed.   A man dare not be disloyal to Christ for the sake of peace with men.

[145] The Greek present participle "*being* at peace" indicates continuous action.

Never take your own revenge, beloved. Here again the present participle indicates a habit pattern. "To avenge" (*ekdikeō*) is to take satisfaction for an injury received by inflicting an injury in return on the offender.[146] There may be a connection to the thought of verse 18. If someone else breaks the peace by sinning against you, it is not the Christian's prerogative to avenge that injury. It is only God's prerogative to avenge wrongs, as the next phrase will show. "It was perhaps because he recognized that in 'avenge not yourselves' he was enjoining something very hard even for Christians ... that Paul inserted the affectionate 'beloved' at this point."[147] God loved them; He would see that they were taken care of, and that their enemies received their due recompense.

But leave room for the wrath *of God*. The NASB translators have taken this phrase to mean "Let God take care of those who have injured you." "Make room for the law of Divine retribution to operate, whether now or on the day of wrath (2:5)."[148] "Stand aside yourself as a mere spectator, and let the wrath of God have free course to accomplish itself as He shall think well."[149] "Of God" is in italics, but the quotation from the Old Testament immediately following makes it relatively certain that it is "God's" wrath that is here in Paul's mind.[150] In the following verses, Paul will give three reasons for keeping ourselves from all thought of vengeance: (1) Vengeance is God's prerogative. (2) To treat a man with kindness rather than vengeance is the way to heap coals of fire on his head. (3) To stoop to vengeance is to be ourselves conquered by evil.

---

[146] "In a savage society, vengeance is immediately taken, if possible, or it is pursued for years, and the offended man is never satisfied until he has imbrued his hands in the blood of the offender." Barnes, *Romans*, p.288. Christianity teaches us to avoid a spirit and purpose of revenge for injuries.

[147] Cranfield, *Romans*, p.646. Often when the Bible writers use the word "beloved" (dearly loved) by itself in the vocative case, the idea is that the readers are Divinely-loved ones.

[148] Bruce, *Romans*, p.230.

[149] Sanday, *Romans*, p.133. There is an article in the Greek (it reads "*the* wrath") and this tends to show, as does the context, that our translators have interpreted correctly. See Romans 1:18, 2:8, and 5:9 for "the wrath" of God, which was explained to be 'God's holy displeasure toward sin.' God is essentially gracious and desires that all be saved. But God must bestow His grace in harmony with His total perfection. In the case of an impenitent sinner, God cannot bestow mercy on that man because of His holy displeasure against sin – a displeasure that has effects that are felt by sinners both in this life and the life to come. The Christian must be careful of his attitude as he makes room for the wrath of God to operate; it would not be far from a feeling of "vengeance" if the Christian were to anxiously *desire* God to quickly and surely take vengeance on the offender. What the language implies is that if punishment *is* due, the Christian must leave it to the righteous God to inflict it; it is not something the Christian is to do for himself.

[150] All the Greek says is "Give place unto wrath." Not only has it been interpreted to mean "God's wrath," but it has been interpreted at least three other ways. (1) The wrath is that of the injured person. Instead of indulging his wrath, he is to abstain from vengeance, and let his wrath cool down. (This is probably more than the Greek says.) (2) Allow the enemy to exhaust his wrath on us without resisting. (The Greek could mean this, but it does not fit the context. Not all peace-breaking results from an enemy's *wrath*; nor does this interpretation fit the following quotation from the Old Testament.) (3) 13:4 will speak of the wrath that a civil official inflicts on criminals. Instead of taking justice into our own hands, we are to permit the proper authorities to exact the penalty for the crime. (This view at least is supported by the remote context. But in this commentator's opinion, it confuses the topic of chapter 12:17-21 [personal relations and prerogatives] with the topic of chapter 13 [the prerogatives and functions of the civil magistrate].)

For it is written.   The words about to be quoted are taken from the first part of Deuteronomy 32:35.[151]

"VENGEANCE IS MINE, I WILL REPAY, SAYS THE LORD." "Vengeance" comes from the same root word translated "revenge" earlier in this verse.   It is the infliction of deserved punishment on an offender for something evil he has done.   The right to punish those who are persecuting or injuring God's people belongs absolutely with God, and in no sense or degree is "vengeance" the personal prerogative of the people being injured.[152] The Christian is not to attempt to take matters into his own hands.   Although it is the Christian who is being injured, it is God alone who must redress the wrong, and He will surely do it.   The Christian must be patient, and wait for Him to avenge.

12:20 – *"BUT IF YOUR ENEMY IS HUNGRY, FEED HIM, AND IF HE IS THIRSTY, GIVE HIM A DRINK; FOR IN SO DOING YOU WILL HEAP BURNING COALS UPON HIS HEAD."*

"BUT IF YOUR ENEMY IS HUNGRY, FEED HIM, AND IF HE IS THIRSTY, GIVE HIM A DRINK.   The verse is taken from Proverbs 25:21,22,[153] and this instruction prevents the Christian from hoping or praying that God's vengeance will quickly strike the offender.[154]   It would be difficult to harbor a resentment that results in praying for a quick punishment to befall the enemy, and at the same time to be looking for ways to meet the enemy's needs.   The absence of the disposition to offer practical help is a kind of indirect retaliation.   "Food" and "drink" surely stand for kindness of any sort.   Being kind to one's enemy when he is hungry or thirsty is God-like.   God does it daily, and He is our example.

FOR IN SO DOING YOU WILL HEAP BURNING COALS UPON HIS HEAD." What is meant by "burning coals"?

---

[151] The form of this quotation, which differs both from the Septuagint and from the Hebrew, is precisely similar in wording to Hebrews 10:30, where this same verse from Deuteronomy is adduced as a warning to Christians lest they abandon their allegiance to Christ.   This resemblance in language has been used as evidence for the Pauline authorship of Hebrews, since he is known to have written Romans.

[152] Care must be exercised at this point, for it is in the matter of *personal* grievances and hurts where vengeance is left to God.   The limitation taught in verse 19 in no way contradicts the following teachings found elsewhere in Scripture: (1) Romans 13:4 – the civil ruler is an avenger of wrath.   This speaks of the proper process of law by the proper authority.   In such cases there is no need to wait for God's punishment to fall.   (2) 2 Corinthians 7:11 – the congregation took a firm hand in the matter of discipline of the flagrantly sinning member.   The church does not wait for God to act in such cases where church discipline is needed.   When a group, under the authority of God, punishes, that in no way contradicts what Paul is here speaking about.   Here in Romans, Paul is speaking about personal desire to get even.

[153] This is the third time in just a few verses that Paul has alluded to Proverbs.   See notes at verses 16 and 17 for the previous two references.

[154] "The 'but' sets what follows in contrast to the self-avenging mentioned in the preceding exhortation." Vine, *Romans*, p.184.

- *Does it mean greater punishment[155] for the enemy?*   In verse 19b, God has threatened wrath on the enemy.   The Christian's kindness, having been rejected, will aggravate his guilt and lead to greater punishment from God on the enemy.   One might also appeal to the portion of Proverbs 25:22 not quoted by Paul, where "coals of fire" is contrasted with a reward from the Lord to the one who is a benefactor.   Still others appeal to passages in the Psalms where "coals of fire" seem to refer to punishment from God.[157]   One strong objection to the notion that "coals of fire" means "greater punishment" is that it is rather easy to read the verse in such a way as to have Paul advocating an odd motive for benefaction.   Do good to your enemy so his punishment will be greater?   Is that not the very "vengeful disposition" this passage prohibits?

- *Does it mean the enemy is led to change his mind and action[156] toward the Christian?*   Verse 21 stresses the idea is that evil is overcome.   One of the best ways to get rid of an enemy is to convert him to Christ, thus making him a friend.   The commentaries usually turn "heap burning coals upon his head" into "convert" in one of two ways.   Some think of the 'burning heat of feeling ashamed' which leads to repentance.[158]   Others treat "burning coals upon the head" as a 1st century proverb for a change of mind that results from a deed of love.[159]   An objection advanced against this explanation is that kindness does not always result in a change in the enemy's attitude or actions.

Perhaps "coals of fire" mean either punishment or repentance, depending on the enemy's response to the kindness received from the Christian.

12:21 – *Do not be overcome by evil, but overcome evil with good.*

Do not be overcome by evil.   Do not let the evil done to you tempt you to abandon Christian principles (verse 17a), so that you would rather get even than be helpful to the one who injured you.[160]

But overcome evil with good.   "The good" would be the kindness offered to the enemy

---

[155] This was the interpretation of Chrysostom, and many of the Greek church fathers.

[157] Psalm 11:5; 18:12-14; 140:10.

[156] Origen, Pelagius, Augustine, and others so interpreted.

[158] If a Christian is beneficent toward his enemy, that man would have to be very hardhearted not to be impacted and changed by such action.   The kind actions have awakened in the adversary the pangs of shame and remorse and repentance.

[159] Some believe the expression originated from an "Egyptian ritual in which a man gave public evidence of his penitence by carrying a pan of burning charcoal on his head."   Bruce, *Romans*, p.230.   See also William Klassen, "Coals of Fire: Sign of Repentance or Revenge?" *New Testament Studies* 9 (1962-63), p.337-50.

[160] It is not easy to decide if the "evil" is the injury done by the offender, or whether it is the "evil" of retaliation to which the injured person may be tempted.   If we choose the latter, then one way the devil's temptation is resisted is by doing good to the enemy.

(verse 20). Even if the enemy is not converted to Christianity, the Christian has won a victory in his own soul.[161]

Verse 21 summarizes the whole paragraph (verses 17-21) dealing with the Christian's relationship with "all men," especially those outside the church. It takes a renewing of the mind (verse 2) to put into practice the exhortations included in this paragraph.

D. Concerning the Christian's Relation to Civil Authority. 13:1-7

13:1 – *Let every person be in subjection to the governing authorities. For there is no authority except from God, and those which exist are established by God.*

Let every person be in subjection to the governing authorities. "Every soul"[1] is emphatic in the Greek; no Christian is to think of himself as exempt from what is here commanded. "Let (him) be in subjection" denotes voluntary submission to the governing authorities.[2] Wycliffe used "higher powers" at this place, a rendering which leaves somewhat open the question of the identity of the "authorities."[3] The NASB translators

---

[161] In revenge, he is the loser who is the victor. The one who masters the temptation to retaliate vindictively has overcome (won a victory). And perhaps the enemy will be introduced to Jesus, who can help him overcome the evil he has been practicing.

[1] The marginal reading shows that the Greek actually reads "every soul." "'Every soul' is a Hebraism for 'every person,' though at the same time, here, as in chapter 2:9, there is a slight stress upon the fact that a man is a conscious and intelligent being, capable of moral relations; and it is especially with reference to these relations that the phrase is used." Sanday, *Romans*, p.136.

[2] *Hupotassō* in the passive means "subject oneself, be subjected or subordinated, obey." Arndt and Gingrich, *Lexicon*, p.855. Of course, the word does not inculcate blind obedience, for we must assume in the background what Jesus taught about rendering "to Caesar the things that are Caesar's; and to God the things that are God's" (Matthew 22:21). There is the idea of 'order' in the root of the word, and what the Christian is to do is to recognize and accept the 'order' or 'arrangement' that God has made for society, and to attempt to fulfill one's duties to that arrangement in a responsible way.

[3] For some time, a running debate has been held as to the identity of the "authorities" – whether they be human or angelic (with the angelic [demonic] powers being behind the scenes, influencing and acting through the civil authorities).

- Oscar Cullmann, *The State in the New Testament* (New York: Charles Scribner's Sons, 1956), p.95ff, offered the opinion that the "powers" are both human and angelic. Perhaps his most convincing argument is that the word elsewhere in Scripture usually refers to angelic or demonic beings.

- See Murray, *Romans*, p.252-256, and Hendriksen, *Romans*, p.430-31, for refutations of this idea. Perhaps their most telling refutation is that it is hard to find any verses that make Christians subject to powers in the spirit world. Though there are passages where demonic powers influence some government officials (Daniel 10:13; Ephesians 6:12; 1 Peter 5:8 [where the suggestion is that the devil instigated the Neronian persecution in which Christians were thrown to the lions]), it surely would be out of place to interpret Romans 13 so that Paul is commanding Christians to obey demonic powers. It would furthermore be hard to believe that the "powers" which are represented as God's ministers to promote good and restrain evil (as is done in Romans 13) would have reference to demons, who (after being subdued by Christ, Colossians 2:15) have been recommissioned by Him into government service; in the New Testament, demons are everywhere represented as inimical to all God is doing in His world.

- If not demonic, then, could the spirit powers be angelic? While good angels may be sent by God to

were right, in this commentator's judgment, to limit the reference to human civil authorities.[4]   The whole matter of a man's obligations and responsibilities to civil government officials is another specific area where the man with the renewed mind will demonstrate the good and acceptable and perfect will of God (12:2).[5]

For there is no authority except from God.   Beginning with "for," this clause and the next state two reasons why the Christian voluntarily submits himself to the governing officials.   This phrase says that the idea that society should be governed originated with God.   Christians honor God by honoring the arrangement He has instituted for the government of mankind.[6]

And those which exist are established by God.   "The governing authorities" presently in power are there because God has permitted it, or arranged it.[7]   The Christian who decides

---

influence governments (especially in answer to the prayers of the saints), does the Bible represent good angels as *regularly* being present behind the scenes and influencing government? Do 1 John 5:19 ("the whole world lies in the power of the evil one") and Revelation 13:1-10 (where the old dragon gives the beast out of the sea his power and throne and authority) have any bearing on what regularly is the spirit-world activity that would persuade and manipulate government officials?

[4] Some have tried to defend the position that "governing authorities" refer to church authorities, but this interpretation involves difficulties inexplicable to this commentator's mind. In the context it talks about taxes being given to the "higher powers." Do men pay taxes to church authorities?

[5] Critics have long pondered why Paul (Romans 13:1-7; 1 Timothy 2:1-3; Titus 3:1) and Peter (1 Peter 2:13-17) found it necessary to especially emphasize the Christian's duties in reference to government officials. We reject the view that Romans 13:1-7 is a parenthetical note, perhaps not even original, since it allegedly interrupts the flow of thought from 12:21 to 13:7. There is no manuscript evidence that these verses are not part of the original. But which of the other plausible reasons that have been advanced may be nearest correct, we have no way to determine. (1) One suggestion is Jews were notorious for their turbulence and restlessness under foreign domination. In those early years, when Christianity was regarded as merely another Jewish sect, it was very important that Christians show no such rebellious temper or insubordination toward the 'powers that be' as they were rightfully exercising their authority. (2) Another suggestion is that since Jesus taught on this subject (Matthew 22:16-22; John 19:10,11; Matthew 17:24-27), it should not be thought surprising that Paul and Peter would teach the disciples what the Master expected. In Luke 20:22-25, the Jews asked Jesus whether it was God *or* Caesar. Jesus replies that His followers have an obligation to both God *and* Caesar. Christians are citizens of a heavenly kingdom, and as such have an obligation to it; they are to be familiar with its ordinances and laws and render obedience to its King. Christians are also citizens of an earthly kingdom. As such they have an obligation to know the laws that regulate conduct, to be obedient to these, to give proper honor and respect to government officials, and to pay their taxes. (3) A third suggestion is that, in light of the fact that God's people had difficulty with this topic of submission to (foreign?) governments (see all the questions asked of Jesus about it), Christians needed this special help (further revelation) in order to be able to draw the line between the obedience to civil authority that obedience to the Lord demands, and the disobedience which the same loyalty to Christ would require (cp. Acts 4:19,20; 5:29).

[6] It has not been implied that a particular kind of government (be it democracy, republican, parliamentary, monarchy, or totalitarian) has God's approval more than another. It simply says that the idea that men should be governed is from God, rather than being of human origin or invention. Society must have some regulatory laws (and people to enforce them) in order to protect the rights of its members ("life, liberty, and the pursuit of happiness"); better still, to enable them to "lead a tranquil and quiet life in all godliness and dignity" (1 Timothy 2:2); and to discipline or punish those who violate these laws (Romans 13:4).

[7] The teaching that God sets up rulers, keeps them in office (cp. Romans 9:17), and removes them from

he will be insubordinate and lawbreaking is actually setting himself in rebellion to God.

13:2 – *Therefore he who resists authority has opposed the ordinance of God; and they who have opposed will receive condemnation upon themselves.*

Therefore he who resists authority has opposed the ordinance of God. The Greek words in verses 1 and 2 translated "subjection," "established," "resists,"[8] and "ordinance," all have the same root; it has to do with the "order" that God has established. Instead of "ordinance" we might use 'disposition' or 'arrangement.'[9]   Since civil government of society is God's idea, and since those men who hold office derive their position from Him, the man who is demonstrating God's will (verse 2) submits to His arrangement in this area of life, too.   The Christian is a law-abiding citizen, submitting to the governing authorities, or he has, in effect, set himself in opposition to God.

And they who have opposed will receive condemnation upon themselves. *Krima*, here translated "condemnation," was rendered "judgment" (sentence of a judge, verdict) at Romans 5:16.   Whether the "condemnation" here is human or divine is not specified, and both interpretations have been defended in the commentaries.   The preceding context has emphasized the "ordinance of God;" He might well be the One to whom Christians have to

---

office, has not been an easy one for men to accept.   Yet Paul expressly states that "the powers that be (the ones presently all around us) are appointed by God" (KJV).   God does not set Himself apart from history; He is working in and through it.   In the early years in Canaan, "He (God) gave them judges" to rule and defend the people (Acts 13:20).   When Israel demanded a king, God permitted it (1 Samuel 8:1-22, 12:13-18), and "gave them Saul the son of Kish ... for forty years" (Acts 13:21).   "After He had removed him, He raised up David to be their king" (Acts 13:22).   Years later, Daniel told Nebuchadnezzar that God "removes kings, and sets up kings" (Daniel 2:21, ASV).   He told this same king at a later time that he would live in the fields like an ox "until you recognize that the Most High is ruler over the realm of mankind, and bestows it on whomever He wishes" (Daniel 4:25).   Even Revelation 17:12 reflects the same divine control, when it is said "authority" to rule as kings was received (from God); also, in the context, these "ten kings" are evil.   It should not be inferred that God *approves* all forms of government (He certainly does not approve of the "ten kings"); still, these people are holding office because God *permits* it.   They have not defeated Him in order to get into office.

[8] *Antitassō* means "to range in battle against," or, in the middle voice, "to oppose one's self, to resist." Thayer, *Lexicon*, p.51.   Paul's statement sounds rather absolute.   Are there no instances at all where the Christian may oppose the government officials currently in power?   (An earlier footnote was addressed to the matter of what happens when God and government contradict.)   When it comes to making personal application of what Paul here teaches, one of the most difficult questions is faced in time of political revolution.   Can a Christian actively participate in the overthrow of the current government?   Commentators are divided on this topic.   Lipscomb and Shepherd would be an example of those who teach it is wrong to help overthrow a government.   "To seek to resist or overthrow civil government ... would be to resist the ordinance of God ... Then it is wrong for Christians to resist or seek to overthrow or destroy the power ordained of God, and they who resist will fall under the condemnation of the power and of God Himself." *Romans*, p.234.   Hendriksen, on the other hand, does not believe the passage establishes an absolute rule against participation in a revolution.   "It is clear, then, that in writing as he does here in Romans 13:2, the apostle is thinking of the ruler who is performing his duty of preserving order, approving good behavior, and punishing evil.   In *that* case he who opposes the authority is, indeed, resisting the divine ordinance ... The apostle is not establishing a universally valid principle that opposing the authority and disobeying a command issued by a civil magistrate is always wrong ... That the apostle was referring to normal, and not to outrageous or mistaken, governmental functioning, is clear from verse 3." *Romans*, p.434.

[9] Thayer, *Lexicon*, p.142.

answer when they have been guilty of civil disobedience. The KJV translators, with their rendering "damnation," certainly thought that it threatened punishment in hell to the Christian whose life is characterized by habitual rebellion to governing authorities. The following context emphasizes the sentence pronounced by the civil authorities against the lawbreakers. Christians who oppose the laws and law-enforcement officers will find themselves sentenced to punishment just as surely as will non-Christians.[10]

13:3 – *For rulers are not a cause of fear for good behavior, but for evil. Do you want to have no fear of authority? Do what is good, and you will have praise from the same;*

For rulers are not a cause of fear for good behavior, but for evil. "For" introduces a reason for something just said. Perhaps it is a third reason why Christians voluntarily submit to governing authorities (verse 1). Perhaps it is intended to introduce an explanation of "receive condemnation" (verse 2). "Fear" points to threatened punishment for civil disobedience.[11] "Rulers" is to be taken as a general reference; most rulers do not treat law-abiding citizens in such an abusive and repressive way as to cause fear; most carry out their office as God intended government officials to, treating only evildoers in such a way as to cause them to fear. Of course, there have been (and tragically, still are) exceptions to what is here said about how government officials act.

Do you want to have no fear of authority? "You" is singular; each individual's reasonable desires are appealed to. Verse 4 indicates that "fear" is the fear an evildoer experiences after doing the evil. There is the fear the fugitive from justice experiences as he constantly worries that the law will catch up with him. After the evildoer is apprehended, there is the fear of the penalty to which the magistrate sentences the evildoer. The way to avoid such fear is to break no laws.[12]

Do what is good, and you will have praise from the same. The "good" means the same as verse 1, "be in submission to the governing authorities." From time to time, the governing authority who is fulfilling his office as God intended will deliberately praise or honor the law-abiding citizen. Paul is not making this truth known for the first time; it was something well understood in the ancient world.[13]

---

[10] Sanday and Headlam make an effort to combine both human and divine in their comments. "The logical result of Paul's teaching as to the origin of human power is that resistance to it is resistance to the ordering of God; and hence, those who resist will receive *krima* – a judgment or condemnation which is human, for it comes through human instruments, but divine as having its origin and source in God." *Romans*, p.367.

[11] "This fear can be of two kinds, the fear that inhibits wrongdoing and the fear that results when wrong has been committed. It would appear that the latter is particularly in view. In the next clause the question, 'wouldest thou have no fear of the power?' enjoins the absence of the fear that is the result of wrong doing." Murray, *Romans*, p.150.

[12] It would certainly appear to be true that Paul holds out the fear of punishment as a deterrent to crime. It is one motive, though others (e.g., see verse 5) are also held out.

[13] Cranfield, *Romans*, p.665, in a footnote, calls attention to a fascinating collection of material illustrative of this fact, made by W.C. van Unnik.

13:4 – *for it is a minister of God to you for good.   But if you do what is evil, be afraid; for it does not bear the sword for nothing; for it is a minister of God, an avenger who brings wrath upon the one who practices evil.*

For it is a minister of God to you for good.   The ASV reads "*he* is a minister."   The reference is to the government official.[14]   In the original, "minister of God" is placed first in the sentence for emphasis.   He is no less than *God's* minister, *God's* servant, when he functions in his official capacity.[15]   "For good" seems to repeat the idea in "good" found in verse 3; that is, the governing official's task is to encourage and promote good behavior among the citizens.[16]

But if you do what is evil, be afraid.   The Christian is not exempt from the punishment prescribed by the law, should he transgress the law.

For it does not bear the sword for nothing.   The Roman magistrate wore a sword,[17] and it was intended for more than mere decoration.   It was worn to be used when necessary. That in the New Testament, "sword" involves the idea of the death penalty is clear.[18]   Not only does it imply the right of capital punishment, it may also reflect the government's pow-

---

[14] It is true, all through this passage, that Paul uses "authority" more often than he uses the word "rulers" to refer to the governing men.   Perhaps Lenski is right when he suggests Paul deliberately preferred to write about the authority exercised by the men, rather than to the men themselves.   "Paul does not say that '*the rulers*' are God's ministers, for they may abuse the authority, may wreck the state.   He calls *the authority* 'God's minister,' for he refers to its exercise which accords with God's own arrangement (*diatagē*, institution, verse 2)."   Lenski, *Romans*, p.791.

[15] The governing official may not even know Jehovah, but the task he performs is ultimately one God wants carried out in His world.   In that sense, he is God's servant.   The idea reflects what was said in verses 1 and 2.

[16] Another interpretation of "for good" is that the service the governing official renders is for the welfare of the citizens under him.   For example, the policeman giving a ticket is the agent of God, ordained of God to keep us from killing ourselves and others, by driving dangerously – even if few recognize this at the time. Barnes, *Romans*, p.293, explains it thusly: "For your benefit.   That is, to protect you in your rights, to vindicate your name, person, or property; and to guard your liberty, and secure to you the results of your industry."   Lipscomb and Shepherd, *Romans*, p.234, even suggest that all the persecutions that came upon Christians from the side of the government (like those from Nero, Trajan, and others), were needed by the Christians to promote their true and eternal welfare (cp. Hebrews 12:5-11).   Cranfield, *Romans*, p.666, urges that "you" specially singles out the Christian, and that "good" is used in the sense found in 8:28, where "God causes all things to work together for good."   He then goes on to write about how the government official helps the Christian toward the "good" which God has in store for him, namely, salvation.

[17] Paul is writing to Romans, who were used to seeing governing officials in their official dress.   He uses *machaira*, the Roman short sword, which was used for executing citizens on whom the death penalty was pronounced.   "It would not be necessary to suppose that the wielding of the sword contemplates the infliction of the death penalty exclusively.   It can be wielded to instill the terror of that punishment which it can inflict.   It can be wielded to execute punishment that falls short of death.   But to exclude the right of the death penalty when the nature of the crime calls for such is totally contrary to that which the sword signifies and executes."   Murray, *Romans*, p.152.

[18] See Luke 21:24; Acts 12:2, 16:29; Hebrews 11:34; Revelation 13:10.

er to quell political rebellion, and to put down lawlessness with force, if need be.[19]

For it is a minister of God.   The governing authority is as much a minister of God when he is wielding the sword in punishment of the criminal as he is when he is actively encouraging good behavior.   It is part of God's plan for the government of society that evildoers be punished, and when the official carries out the punishment, he is serving God, just as much as when he promotes the good.[20]

An avenger who brings wrath upon the one who practices evil.   "Avenger" (*ekdikos*) is the same root translated "revenge" and "vengeance" in 12:19.   It denotes one who deals out justice, one who exacts a penalty from someone.[21]   Thus, the state is charged with a function which has been explicitly forbidden to the individual Christian acting personally and merely on his own behalf.   "Wrath" here likely expresses the familiar idea of God's wrath against evil doing.[22]   God's wrath is something that can be experienced by evildoers in this life, as well as the life to come.

---

[19] Capital punishment in every dispensation is approved by God (yea, ordered by God, Genesis 9:6). When a criminal is executed for his crime, the death penalty does not violate the commandment that says, "You shall not commit murder."   There is a difference, as far as the act contemplated, between capital punishment and premeditated murder.   The sanction that the Bible everywhere gives to the forcible restraint of evil, some have found difficult to harmonize with what is often perceived to be Christ's way of love and nonresistance of evil.   There is a time and place for nonresistance (e.g., personal hurts suffered at the hand of a Christian brother), but there is also a time and place for wielding the sword.   "In order effectively to discharge this duty, the State is armed with the sword.   In these degenerate days when the poison of humanism has directed sympathy to the criminal instead of his victim, it ought to be particularly noted that the Apostle describes the restraints imposed by the law in terms of retributive vengeance. 'Nothing shows the moral bankruptcy of a people or of a generation more than disregard for the sanctity of human life.   And it is this same atrophy of moral fibre that appears in the plea for the abolition of the death penalty.   It is the sanctity of life that validates the death penalty for the crime of murder.'   (John Murray, *Principles of Conduct*, p.122).   The state is also armed with the sword in order to defend its frontiers and the lives of its citizens against the aggressor.   Dr. Gordon Clark aptly remarks, 'Christ said, "Render unto Caesar the things that are Caesar's."   Of course, the immediate reference was to taxes, but Christ knew that Caesar had an army.   He did not refuse to pay taxes to Rome on the ground that some of the tribute would be used to support the army.' ... Pacifism receives no encouragement from the New Testament.   It is true that harlots are commanded to 'go and sin no more,' but soldiers are not asked to resign from the army! [Luke 3:14]."   Wilson, *Romans*, p.212.

[20] "The repetition of the phrase, 'minister of God,' emphasizes the double purpose of the state.   It exists positively for the well-being of the community, negatively to check evil by the infliction of punishment; and both these functions are derived from God."   Sanday and Headlam, *Romans*, p.368.

[21] The idea that what the governing official does (as he praises the good and avenges the evil) is right, is an idea that is assumed all through this passage.   Now the thought occurs, how is this truth to be explained by those writers who teach total depravity?   How is it possible that these unconverted men in government positions get anything right?   Some have tried to argue that civil government is *per se* evil, and serves good only in the sense that as a lesser evil it restrains and counteracts greater evils.   (*Reply*: Is it possible that civil government is evil, when, as this context has affirmed, it is ordained of God, serves the good, and is called "a minister of God"?)   While it is true that God has at times permitted evil men to remain in office (even overruling their evil for His glory), it is hardly true of all governing officials that they are "bad fellows" (as Luther described them when he said it is God's way to hold the world which is full of bad fellows in check by means of bad fellows as rulers).

[22] Compare what was written at Romans 12:19.

13:5 – *Wherefore it is necessary to be in subjection, not only because of wrath, but also for conscience' sake.*

Wherefore.   Verse 5 states a summary conclusion drawn from what has been said in the first four verses.   It gives the Christian view of civil authority.

It is necessary to be in subjection.   Two reasons (one external, and one internal) why it is "necessary"[23] for the Christian to be submissive to civil authority[24] will be given by Paul.

Not only because of wrath.   Verse 4 has just defined what wrath is in Paul's mind.   Fear of punishment by the bearer of the sword, if he does not obey the law, is an external reason why Christians of necessity must be law-abiding citizens.

But also for conscience' sake.   Now we have the second reason, the internal one, why the Christian is a law-abiding citizen.   "Conscience" is used with at least two different meanings in the New Testament.

- In Romans 2:15 and 9:1 it spoke of that innate faculty that prompts a man to do what his mind thinks is right, and criticizes when the man does what his mind thinks is wrong. That might be the idea here – when a Christian breaks civil laws his conscience bothers him, and a man who goes against his conscience is sinning (Romans 14:23).

- 1 Peter 2:19 is an example of a second use for the word "conscience," namely, with the connotation of "knowledge, awareness, consciousness."[25]   If this is the idea here, then what the Christian is aware of is the presentation that government is appointed by God, and that governing authorities are God's ministers, and that as such they have certain rights (to honor and punish).   This is a new way of looking at governing authorities; it is part of the "renewed mind" that helps direct the Christian's behavior (12:2).

The Christian, who is committed to honoring God with his body, and submitting to His will, will of necessity be in submission voluntarily to civil authority.

13:6 – *For because of this you also pay taxes, for* **rulers** *are servants of God, devoting themselves to this very thing.*

For because of this you also pay taxes.   After several verses where "you" has been singular (pointedly making personal application of the instruction), Paul now returns to the plural.   This is something all Christians do.   "Taxes" in this verse is "tribute," the yearly

---

[23] Several Greek words are translated "it is necessary."   *Dei* is a word that indicates a necessity that grows out of the nature of things.   *Opheilō* denotes a personal obligation, something that is proper, that ought to be done (Berry, *Synonyms*, p.136).   The word used here, *anangkē*, denotes a necessity imposed either by the external condition of things, or by the law of duty, or regard to one's advantage. Thayer, *Lexicon*, p.36.

[24] See Romans 13:1 under "be in subjection to the governing authorities."

[25] Arndt and Gingrich, *Lexicon*, p.794.

tax that Rome levied on persons and property in the lands they had subjected, in order to operate the government. The question about paying taxes, even if they are taxes paid by a subject people to a foreign potentate (a question that vexed the Jews, Luke 20:22), has been answered by Paul the same way Jesus answered it. The reason why Christians pay taxes ("because of this") may be found in all that has been written[26] since 13:1, or it may be found in "for conscience' sake" in verse 5. As they pay taxes,[27] each Christian acknowledges the divinely-approved and -appointed character of the civil power which entitles it to obedience. Christians pay their just share of the costs of government.[28] Taxes are a cause of almost universal complaint. But without taxes there would be no government, and anarchy would reign in the land.

For *rulers*[29] are servants of God. A different word is used here for "servant" than was used in verse 4. The word here is *leitourgos*, a word that once had the connotation of special service or ministry on behalf of the people but rendered to the gods. In the Jewish world it came to be used of the priest who was thought of as doing a service for God as he represented the people.[30] By using this word of the civil authorities, Paul implies that they are doing a service for God (whether they realize it or not) on behalf of the people. This is why the Christian supports them with his taxes. "Civil governments are ordained of God; and if so, taxes are too, for governments cannot be carried on without them. Consequently, we dare not refuse to pay taxes, for, in so doing, we disobey God."[31]

Devoting themselves to this very thing. The "thing" may be God's service (*leitourgos*,

---

[26] "For this cause" ("because of this") would include: (1) because government officials are God's ministers; (2) because the Christian is law-abiding; (3) because of fear of punishment; (4) because of conscience' sake. For all these reasons, the Christian pays his taxes.

[27] The Greek verb can either be indicative (a statement of fact) or imperative (a command). It is best to treat it as indicative (Christians do, as a matter of fact, pay taxes, whether living in the Roman empire or under whatever government jurisdiction) since "for" would be hard to explain if we tried to make this a command. Those who take it as imperative often suggest that for a number of reasons some of the Roman Christians were disinclined to pay their taxes, and Paul here orders them to do so.

[28] Because of their "knowledge" of God's will about government, and because a Christian is honest and law-abiding, it should not require anything to be said about the corresponding obligation Christians have not to cheat on their income tax. Many countries collect the taxes in a far different way than in America. In America, the amount of tax paid is computed by each individual, taking into account his income and the relevant tax laws. The only thing (in many cases) that prompts the individual to report all his income is his desire to please his Maker. Even if Godless men cheat on their taxes, the Christian does not.

[29] The Greek reads simply "They are God's ministers." It is not easy to decide if it is the ones who are collecting the tax, or the ones whose programs are paid for by the taxes being collected, that are called "God's ministers." Not too many tax payers regard the tax collector as a God-send; but, quite literally, he is that. His work provides the money which maintains order, health, safety, and provides necessary services such as roads, drainage, defense, etc. Who would care to live in a country which was not cared for?

[30] Thayer, *Lexicon*, p. 375,376. The use of *leitourgos* rather than *diakonos* (as at verse 4), if anything, enhances the dignity of the ministry of these civil officials.

[31] Lard, *Romans*, p.401.

"servants," verse 6); or it may be the punishing of evildoers and preserving order among the citizens (verses 3,4); or it may be the collecting of taxes (verse 6). If we take the latter, the idea is that Christians will not evade their taxes, since it is as God's servants that the government officials busy themselves with the receipt and disbursement of the taxes.[32]

13:7 – *Render to all what is due them: tax to whom tax* **is** *due; custom to whom custom; fear to whom fear; honor to whom honor.*

Render to all what is due them. Verse 7 is an exhortation to Christians to perform all the duties taught in verses 5 and 6. There is certainly a good possibility that verse 7 is Paul's expansion of what was implied when Jesus said, "Render to Caesar the things that are Caesar's and to God the things that are God's."[33] Anyone who in any way exercises civil authority is included in this first statement. Whatever is due (and the following phrases will give some specific examples), the Christian will gladly give.[34]

Tax to whom tax *is due.* The word "tax" again is the Greek word for "tribute" (*phoros*, see verse 6), and this exhortation would tell Paul's readers (remember the letter would eventually be circulated in occupied areas outside of Rome) to continue to pay tribute to the conquering nation who now governs them.[35]

Custom to whom custom. The word here is *telos*, and refers to taxes levied on goods and merchandise, whether imported or exported. "There were customs duties, import and export taxes, taxes … paid for the use of main roads, for crossing bridges, for entry into markets and harbors, for the right to possess an animal, or to drive a cart or a wagon."[36]

Fear to whom fear. Verse 3 has just said governing authorities are not a cause of fear to law-abiding Christians. Now the same word "fear" is used of something Christians are to confer on those who deserve it. It would thus seem the word "fear" is not used with the same connotation in both verses. Thus, some write about a wholesome fear toward those

---

[32] Many commentators have quoted Calvin's words at this place. Just as civil officials can learn from verse 3 and 4 what their God-given responsibilities are, so there is something to be learned from verse 6. When governing authorities claim taxes and dues, they certainly ought "to behave in a way worthy of God's officials, and (in Calvin's words) 'to remember that all that they receive from the people is public property, and not a means of satisfying private lust and luxury'." Cranfield, *Romans*, p.669.

[33] Observe that both statements include the word "render," *apodidōmi*, that is, pay back what is due.

[34] "Due" is from *opheilō*, an obligation. See footnote #23 above.

[35] In the Roman empire, subject nations paid three different kinds of "tribute" to the Roman government each year. "There was a *ground tax,* by which a man had to pay, either in cash or in kind, one-tenth of all the grain, and one-fifth of the wine and fruit produced by his ground. There was an *income tax*, which was one percent of a man's income. There was a *poll tax*, which had to be paid by everyone between the ages of 14 and 65." Barclay, *Romans*, p.190.

[36] Barclay, *op. cit.*, p.190. Matthew, before he became an apostle of Jesus, was a collector of such taxes (Matthews 9:9). A present-day application would speak of sales taxes and the value-added tax. Christians do not smuggle goods into a land in order to avoid import duties; nor do they look for ways to avoid the hidden taxes (sales, excise, amusement, and the like).

who administer the law, a fear that leads the Christian to do right and avoid evil. Others tell us that fear here means respect or reverence – "a reverential awe for the one who has power in his hands."[37]   Still others remind us that Scripture everywhere enjoins "fear" as something due to God and Christ (cp. Luke 1:50; 1 Peter 3:15; Revelation 19:5), and treat the verse as though it were synonymous with 1 Peter 2:17, "Fear God, honor the king."

Honor to whom honor. It is generally granted that "fear" in this verse denotes a greater degree of respect, and "honor" a lesser degree of respect, and that the official who is due "fear" is a higher official than the one to whom is due "honor." "Honor" means to value, to esteem. It is an attitude that is due toward governing officials generally; if the current holder of the office is a dishonorable man, it is still possible for the Christian to honor the office or position.[38]

With this exhortation, the section about the Christian's relation to civil authority ends and a new paragraph begins. The new paragraph is related, however, for Paul shows that the words about "fear" and "honor (respect)" have behind them the broader principle of love – seeking to act in the best interests of the other man.

E. Concerning the Christian's Relation (Love) to all Men.   13:8-14

13:8 – *Owe nothing to anyone except to love one another; for he who loves his neighbor has fulfilled* **the** *law.*

Owe nothing to anyone except to love one another. Christians are to render to all what is their due, whether tax, custom, fear, or honor. Yet even when all these are taken care of, there is still one more debt,[39] and it is one that can never be completely taken care of,

---

[37] Sanday and Headlam, *Romans*, p.368. This is the generally accepted interpretation.

[38] "What Paul probably means is something on this order: 'Simply paying your taxes is not enough. Telling the officials, "Here's your money, and now get out!" will never do. You should *respect* these men for the sake of their office, and *honor* them in view of their faithful devotion to their task. Remember, they are *God's ministers*! And by means of what is done with this money not only the people in general, including you yourselves, are benefited, but so is the cause of the Gospel'." Hendriksen, *Romans*, p.437,438.

[39] "Owe" (*opheilō*), in the Greek, can either be indicative or imperative. It is a present tense verb, indicating habitual or continuous or repeated action. If it is indicative, it is a statement that Christians do indeed owe nothing to any man. If it is imperative, it says, "Do not continue to owe anything to any man." Most translators opt for the imperative.

In a time when many of us tend to purchase all our goods and possessions on the installment plan, some (including Hudson Taylor, missionary to Japan, and Charles H. Spurgeon, London preacher) have supposed this passage prohibits purchases on the installment plan. "Owe no man anything" means "Pay cash, or don't buy it!" it is alleged. The argument against installment debt is then reinforced by an appeal to those passages (e.g., Exodus 22:25; Jeremiah 15:10) which prohibit God's people from charging or paying interest. However, this whole treatment of the phrase in verse 8 seems quite extraneous to what Paul has actually written. We would affirm the context has been nowhere close to saying anything about going into debt to purchase something. And we would affirm that what the Bible elsewhere prohibits is not the charging of interest, but the charging of exorbitant interest; in fact, in one of Jesus' illustrations, His

namely, the debt of love.[40] "One another" reminds us that Christians are surrounded by people other than government authorities to whom they have responsibilities. How is the Christian to behave toward all these people? Love them! That is the Christian's perpetual obligation. That is how the man with a "renewed mind," a new way of looking at things and people, takes care of his interpersonal relationships. He loves them with *agapē* love. The way to know whether one is loving as he should be is to compare his behavior with God's commands (such as the ones referenced in verse 9) on the subject.[41]

For he who loves his neighbor has fulfilled *the* law.   The reasons why it is so important to act out of love are two: (1) love fulfills the law of God (verses 8b-10); and (2) selfish indulgence (i.e., the absence of love) is completely out of harmony with the time in which we are living (verses 11-14).   As the marginal reading indicates, "his neighbor" is a rather free translation of the Greek ("the other") at this place.   The translator must make several key decisions at this place:

- Shall he translate "The one who loves has fulfilled the other law," or shall he translate "The one who loves the other has fulfilled the law"?

- If we choose the former, how shall we explain "the other (*heteros*, different) law"[42]? If we choose the latter, how shall we harmonize this apparent appeal to the Mosaic Law[43] with what the New Testament says elsewhere about the Law being abrogated at the cross?

---

servants are chided for not putting the money He entrusted to them into the bank so it could earn interest (Luke 19:23). While it might be needful to express a warning to Christians about installment debts (for one can so obligate himself and his future income that he has no free funds with which to do special things for God when opportunities to do so present themselves from time to time), this is not Paul's subject in verse 8. (As a more egregious example of misreading a text and fundamentally missing its true import, some twist the Model Prayer's statement, "Forgive us our debts" (Matthew 6:12), into a proof text that Christians can ignore making payments on the financial debts they have incurred. The New Testament is clear that Christians are to be transparently honest. It is the opposite of faithfulness to evade paying one's financial debts, or even to refuse to pay on them regularly as promised.)

[40] See notes at Romans 12:9 on "love." See also C.S. Lewis, *The Four Loves* (New York: Harcourt, Brace, and World, 1960).

[41] In a previous decade, much was said about "situation ethics" as taught by Joseph Fletcher (*Situation Ethics*, Philadelphia: Westminster Press, 1966) and James A.T. Robinson (*Honest to God*, Philadelphia: Westminster Press, 1963). Both suggested that "love" is the motive that regulates Christian behavior, but a fatal flaw in their presentation is that they never gave the word "love" its Biblical definition, nor did they permit God's Word to determine in advance that some situations were sin and were to be avoided. In Romans 13:10, as he summarizes some of the commandments (no adultery, no stealing, no coveting), Paul says "love" includes these prohibitions. When a man injures his neighbor in any of these ways, he simply is not loving. Love to fellow man requires a Christian to do to his fellow man just what the law of God requires him to do.

[42] Several suggestions have been advanced: (1) The Mosaic Law is different from the civil law that has been the topic in 13:1-7. (2) The "other law" is the "second law" of Matthew 22:39 and Mark 12:31. "And a second is like it: 'You shall love your neighbor as yourself.'" (3) The "other law" is Paul's way of saying what James writes, when he calls it "the royal law" (James 2:8).

[43] "Law" is anarthrous, and could specify 'any law,' though one would naturally suppose it is a reference to the Mosaic Law in the light of the quotations in the next verse, which are taken from Moses.

Perhaps the reason we get ourselves into trouble in this verse is that we try to make it a reference to the Law of Moses, even though nothing has been said about the Mosaic Law since Romans 10:5. Why not let the context help our understanding? The farther context (verses 1-7) has implied there are laws about behavior that magistrates must adjudicate. The nearer context (verse 8a) deals with our 'debts' to others. Why not make "law" (anarthrous *nomos*) refer to whatever law there is which regulates conduct between 'me' and 'the other.' Then, in verse 9, Paul will illustrate this truth by taking examples from the Law of Moses. "Fulfilled" is a perfect tense in the Greek.[44] So certain is he who loves another to fulfill the law to which he is subject, that the verb tense regards him as having already done it. The thing is treated as done, because it is sure to be done.

13:9 – *For this, "YOU SHALL NOT COMMIT ADULTERY, YOU SHALL NOT MURDER, YOU SHALL NOT STEAL, YOU SHALL NOT COVET," and if there is any other commandment, it is summed up in this saying, "YOU SHALL LOVE YOUR NEIGHBOR AS YOURSELF."*

For this. "For" introduces a confirmation of what was just said about law being fulfilled. The word translated "this" is the neuter definite article ("the") and it has given rise to diverse methods of explaining it. Several modern versions paraphrase at this point, similar to Phillips who has, "For the commandments ...," even though the article is singular and the usual Greek words translated "commandment" are feminine.[45] Lard suggests some word like *gegramenon* ("the thing which has been written") should be supplied.[46] We suppose what Paul means is, 'Let me give you an example of the kind of laws I am talking about by appealing to some well-known ones in the Decalog.'

"YOU SHALL NOT COMMIT ADULTERY.[47] Adultery is illicit sexual intercourse with someone else's wife or husband.[48] No one will commit adultery against one whom he

---

[44] The significance of the perfect tense was explained at Romans 2:25 ("become") and 3:21 ("manifested").

[45] *Entolē* (used later here in verse 9), *epitagē*, *parangelia*, are all feminine. There are some neuter words (seldom used in the Scripture), such as *parangelma, diatagma,* and *entalma.*

[46] Lard, *Romans*, p.404.

[47] The reader who has memorized the Ten Commandments from Exodus 20 will notice that Paul lists them in a different order. Paul has not followed the order of the Hebrew text (which in both Exodus 20 and Deuteronomy 5 has "murder, adultery, steal") but the LXX of Deuteronomy 5. (The manuscripts of the LXX differ. In Exodus, Sinaiticus reads "adultery, steal, murder," while Codices A and F read in the Hebrew order. In Deuteronomy, Sinaiticus reads "adultery, murder, steal," while the others read as does the Hebrew order.) The KJV also includes the ninth commandment, "You shall not bear false witness"; but it is absent from the better authorities for the text, so it is not included in the NASB.

[48] The student of the Old Testament will notice that we have broadened the meaning of the word, as compared to its meaning in the Mosaic age. "In the Old Testament, [adultery was] sexual intercourse, usually of a man, married or unmarried, always with the wife of another." Emmet Russell, "Adultery," in *Zondervan Pictorial Bible Dictionary*, p.17. By this definition, for a married man to have relations with a concubine was not adultery. The New Testament seems to broaden the definition ("fornication," the wider term for sexual offenses, is used almost interchangeably with "adultery"), so that any sexual relationship outside the marriage relationship is adulterous (cf. Hebrews 13:4).

loves.   It is self-love, selfishness, that leads a person to so behave, not love.[49]

YOU SHALL NOT MURDER.   What is prohibited is premeditated murder, killing with malice aforethought.   The Mosaic legislation treated accidental killing, manslaughter, differently than was murder.   The deliberate murderer, even if he fled for asylum to the city of refuge, was to be removed from the city and put to death (Exodus 21:14; cf. 1 Kings 2:28-34).   The man who had accidentally committed manslaughter was given a trial. Unless two witnesses could be found to convict him of deliberate murder, he was acquitted and granted asylum in the city.   If he was found guilty of murder, he too was taken and executed.   In the New Testament age, the man who loves the other (the neighbor) will not deliberately murder, and will even take special care lest there be accidental deaths.[50]

YOU SHALL NOT STEAL.   The argument behind this command is the same as with the other prohibitions included in this verse.   The man who loves will not hurt others by unlawfully taking what does not belong to him.   Stealing is concerned with getting; love is concerned with giving.

YOU SHALL NOT COVET." Compare notes at Romans 7:7, where we learned that the word may be translated "desire," and that it is left up to the context to determine if the desire is good or bad.   Because "desire" is such a neutral word, it would seem our translators deliberately chose the word "covet," which has a bad connotation to it, thus matching the context.   It is desire for evil things, or desire for what belongs to someone else, that is prohibited. When we read the last two prohibitions together, we learn that the motive, as well as the act, can be sin.   It is not possible to "desire" (in the bad sense of the word), and "love" at the same time.

And if there is any other commandment.   That is, if there is any other commandment respecting relationships between 'me' and 'the other.'   It is this statement that shows that Paul has simply selected examples from the Mosaic Law to illustrate his point.

It is summed up in this saying.[51]   "Summed up" is "a rhetorical term used of the summing up of a speech or argument, and hence of including a large number of separate details under one head."[52]   While it is true that one can find the "saying" about to be quoted in Leviticus 19:18, we like the suggestion that just like Paul reminded his readers that his teaching about

---

[49] "When two people allow their physical passions to sweep them away, the reason is, not that they love each other too much, but that they love each other too little. In real love, there is at once respect and restraint which saves a man from sin."   Barclay, *Romans*, p.191.

[50] Careful driving of automobiles and other motor vehicles; building without using shoddy materials, lest lives later be endangered; watching out for the welfare of other participants in sporting events that could be dangerous, are examples of the way a loving person behaves, lest others be harmed and killed.

[51] The ASV adds "namely," and reads, "It is summed up in this word, namely."   In some manuscripts, there is a phrase in the Greek, *en to*, which probably does not enjoy integrity, since it is not included in P[46] or Vaticanus, that the ASV translators used "namely" to represent.

[52] Sanday and Headlam, *Romans*, p.374.

government and taxation (13:1-6) simply reflected Jesus' teaching (verse 7a), so Paul is repeating the Master's instruction about loving the brother (Matthew 22:34-40) as he gives men with 'renewed minds' directions about how to govern their interpersonal behavior.[53]

"YOU SHALL LOVE YOUR NEIGHBOR AS YOURSELF."   In the Old Testament, among Israel, "neighbor" was understood to mean fellow-Israelite.   Jesus broadened the scope of the word "neighbor" as he illustrated His meaning by telling the parable of the Good Samaritan.   To the man who has heard Jesus teach, anyone in need is his neighbor. For years, it has been disputed whether self-love ("as [you love] yourself") is legitimate.[54] Verses like Galatians 2:20 ("I have been crucified with Christ; and it is no longer I who live, but Christ lives in me; and the life which I now live in the flesh I live by faith in the Son of God ...") are alleged to teach that for the Christian there is no 'self' to love any more. Instead, it is Christ within who is loved, and the Christian treats his neighbor just like he would treat Christ.   On the other hand, proponents of the legitimacy of self-love tell us that 'self-love' is not to be equated with selfishness or egotism.   Self-love is simply the normal creaturely interest in bodily needs being taken care of.[55]   Jesus wants His followers to express the same interest in the needs of others as they do for their own needs, instead of being so absorbed with their own needs that they are oblivious to the needs others have.

13:10 – *Love does no wrong to a neighbor; love therefore is the fulfillment of* the *law.*

Love does no wrong to a neighbor.   Paul repeats, in negative form,[56] what was said in verse 8.   Love moves a man to do good to others; it likewise keeps him from doing them

---

[53] Perhaps it should again be emphasized that the modern disjunction between law and love is quite foreign to Paul's thought. Laws (rules, prohibitions) help us judge whether or not we are loving as we ought. Law prescribes the action, but love it is that constrains or impels the action involved. See John Murray, *Principles of Conduct* (Grand Rapids: Wm. B. Eerdmans Publishing Co., 1957), p.22,24.

[54] We do not read Jesus' saying as though He were commanding men to love themselves; He simply assumes that they do. The whole debate about whether such assumed behavior is legitimate or not, hinges on whether such self-love is corrupt and wicked, the result of a 'sinful nature' affecting each man's behavior, or whether it is part of every creature's own self-protection mechanism, and so is not necessarily wicked. We are inclined to believe that those writers who believe in a sinful nature, inherited from Adam, with which even the Christian is obliged to struggle, are the ones who have tried to persuade the rest of us that 'self-love' is always something sinful and to be avoided. (See this matter of a 'sinful nature inherited from Adam' discussed in comments on chapter 5, and in the Special Studies following chapter 5.)

[55] "It is unnatural and impossible for us not to love ourselves. 'No man ever hated his own flesh' (Ephesians 5:29), and in accord with this Paul says: 'He that loveth his wife loveth himself' (Ephesians 5:28) ... We are never asked to love God as we love ourselves or our neighbor as we love God.   To God our whole being in all relationships must be captive in love, devotion, and service.   To conceive of such captivity to our own selves or to any creature would be the essence of ungodliness.   Of this distinction our Lord's words are eloquent: 'Thou shalt love the Lord thy God with all thy heart, and with all thy soul, and with all thy mind, and with all thy strength ... Thou shalt love thy neighbor as thyself' (Mark 12:30,31)." Murray, *Romans*, p.163.

[56] Cranfield suggests that the negative form is due to the negative form of the commandments just quoted. *Romans*, p.678.

harm. Hendriksen believes that we have a deliberate understatement, and that "love does no wrong" really means "love greatly benefits the neighbor."[57]

Love therefore is the fulfillment of *the* law. This phrase forms the conclusion drawn from the argument in verses 8 and 9. The context has indicated that the "law" in view refers to whatever laws there might be to regulate relationships between people.[58] As it was in verse 8, "law" is anarthrous.[59] It is not just the second part of the Law of Moses that is fulfilled by loving; it is all law respecting personal relationships between men, even the "law" set forth by Jesus who said "You shall love your neighbor as yourself."[60] "Fulfillment" means to carry into effect, to realize, to execute, to perform."[61] The man who loves puts into practice what the law guiding interpersonal relationships teaches him to do.

13:11 – *And this* **do,** *knowing the time, that it is already the hour for you to awaken from sleep; for now salvation is nearer to us than when we believed.*

And this do. "This" refers to what the apostle has been teaching, and gives a second reason (cp. verse 8b) why the readers should behave toward others as love for the neighbor would lead them to.[62] Some verb must be supplied to complete the sense. Perhaps the most appropriate word is a word of exhortation, "*Let us do* this."

---

[57] "In the words, 'Love does no harm to the neighbor,' we have an example of a figure of speech called *litotes*. This means that a negative expression of this type implies a strong affirmative. So, 'He's no fool' may mean 'He is very shrewd.' Similarly, 'Love does no harm to the neighbor' means 'Love greatly benefits the neighbor.' '... does no harm' is an understatement for 'greatly benefits'." Hendriksen, *Romans*, p.440.

[58] If we remember the context as we explain "love is the fulfillment of the law," there will be little need to go into a long paragraph explaining that there is a greater law, about love to God, that has priority in our attention even over the one about love to the other. Nor will we need to explain that love for the brother implies that a man already has his relationship with God right, or else he could not "love" his brother like he is here commanded to do. There is no need to advert to this topic here in chapter 13, for a man's relationship to God has already been the topic in Romans 12:1,2.

[59] See notes at Romans 2:12 for the meaning of "anarthrous *nomos*."

[60] The same truth, about "love your neighbor as yourself" as "fulfillment of the law," is also found in Galatians 5:14. In that book, Paul has been teaching that the Law of Moses is no longer binding on Christians, but that it was a temporary thing, added to the promise (covenant) made to Abraham. Freedom from the Law of Moses, to which Christians are called, however, does not give the Christian a license to sin. He still must abide by Jesus' teaching about loving the neighbor; and the Christian who does that will not indulge his own flesh, but will serve the other (Galatians 5:13).

[61] Thayer, *Lexicon*, p.518.

[62] Some commentators begin a new paragraph here at 13:11 (as does the NASB), and suggest that verses 11-14 give a motive for all Paul's practical instructions since 12:1. Lard, for example, wrote, "The meaning is, Let us be obedient to ruling authorities; let us pay tax; let us love our neighbor; let us do all this because we know the season." *Romans*, p.407. Gifford takes a mediating position: "*And this.* Compare 1 Cor. 6:6,8 and Eph. 2:8. It recalls with fresh emphasis the preceding thought 'Owe no man anything but love,' which is itself the comprehensive summary of all the Christian duties in the preceding chapter and this one." *Romans*, p.214

Knowing the time.   The reason Christians "know" the time is because of Divine revelation.[63]   "Time" is a translation of *kairos*, a word that connotes a definite, suitable time, the time of some decisive event, opportunity, or crisis.[64]   The word refers to a certain *extent* of time which is in some way marked to distinguish it from other such stretches of time.   "'Time' here is not time in general but a time with distinct significance, a time charged with issues of practical moment ...."[65]   If "salvation" (later in the verse) has something to do with the second advent of Christ, then "time" (a distinct, significant time) reminds the readers that the Church Age is the last in the succession of ages in God's dispensation of things,[66] and that next on God's calendar is the consummation.

That it is already the hour for you to awaken from sleep.   This is one of the issues involved in knowing the significance of the time.   "Already" indicates there is to be no delay, no neglect in this matter of awakening from sleep so as to carry out the command to love one another.   If we propose to do anything in this area, it is time already to be about it.   "Hour" (*hōra*) is often used, not to designate sixty minutes, but a specific time; the moment has arrived, the alarm clock is ringing, the "hour" for action is here.   "The image of awakening out of sleep is often used in the Scriptures to designate the rousing up from a state of comparative inaction to one of strenuous effort.   (See 1 Corinthians 15:58; Ephesians 5:14; 1 Thessalonians 5:6.)"[67]   Indifference to sin (sleep) must be replaced with alertness.[68]

For now salvation is nearer to us than when we believed.   Since it begins with "for," this phrase gives a reason why it is imperative to awake from sleep.   "When we believed" has reference to when we first became Christians.   "The salvation is not the one from sin, which the Romans already had (Romans 6:3,4,17), but speaks of the completion of it in the glorification awaiting them when the Lord should come."[69]   In Romans, Paul has spoken before of this same "salvation" in these terms: "our adoption as sons, the redemption of our body" (8:23); "the revealing of the sons of God" (8:19); "glory, honor, immortality, eternal life" (2:7); "the outcome, eternal life" (6:22).[70]   Each Lord's day, even today, right

---

[63] The word "know" is *oida*, whose meaning has been explained in comments at Romans 7:7 (footnote #44).

[64] *Kairos* has been used before in Romans, at 3:26, 5:6, 8:18, 9:9, and 11:5.

[65] Murray, *Romans*, p.165.

[66] Ephesians 1:10.   The Church Age is designated "the last days" in Acts 2:17.   See also 2 Timothy 3:1, Hebrews 1:2, and 2 Peter 3:3.

[67] Lipscomb and Shepherd, *Romans*, p.240.   The word *hupnos* is used six times in the New Testament; five times it refers to natural sleep; once, here, it is used figuratively of spiritual lethargy.

[68] Some of the sins to be alert about will be listed in verse 13.   "Awaken" is an aorist tense verb, and has the significance "to awaken at once."

[69] Lipscomb and Shepherd, *Romans*, p.240.

[70] This future salvation, in 1 Peter 1:4,5, is ready to be revealed in the last time.   Peter includes in it "an

"now," we are one day nearer to the consummation than when we were first baptized.[71] We are to live in the light of this tremendous fact.   The amount of time left in which men will have opportunity to do loving things for their neighbors, as they help each other prepare for the judgment, grows shorter each calendar day.   Just how near the new day of final salvation is will be pictured in the next verse.

13:12 – *The night is almost gone, and the day is at hand.   Let us therefore lay aside the deeds of darkness and put on the armor of light.*

The night is almost gone, and the day is at hand.   In the last few hours of the night before the sun comes up over the horizon, there is a reddish tint in the east.   The darkness is giving way to the light of the new day.   In just a short time the sun will be up.   That is the mental picture Paul paints for us as he tells us about the significance of the "time" we live in (verse 11).   Christians are viewed as already being able to see the first streaks of light on the eastern horizon that signal the dawn of the eternal new day.[72]   Whatever prep-

---

inheritance, which is imperishable and undefiled and will not fade away, reserved in heaven."   Hebrews 9:28 tells us that Jesus will appear a second time, and then this salvation will be manifested.

[71] Because almost 19 centuries have passed since Paul wrote "now salvation is nearer ...," some have accused him of making a mistake here.   C.H. Dodd, *The Epistle of Paul to the Romans* (New York: Harper and Brothers, 1932), p.209, suggests that in Paul's earliest epistles (1 and 2 Thessalonians) he thought the second coming would occur within a few months, certainly within the lifetime of most present members of the church.   He thinks Paul's language here in Romans 13 is a tip-off that Paul's views have changed, and he no longer thinks of the second advent as being imminent.   (Some questions immediately come to mind: Did Dodd forget 2 Thessalonians 2, where certain things had to happen before the return of Christ?   If Paul was wrong about the time of the second coming, and wrote that error into his letters, how many more errors are there?   What does this alleged change in doctrine do to the idea of revelation and inspiration as the source of Paul's religion?   If in Paul's earlier letters he thought of himself as still living when Christ returns, how shall we explain 1 Corinthians 6:14, where he includes himself among the dead when Christ returns?   And since 1 Corinthians was written just a few months before Romans, has Paul now changed his mind again, so that in Romans 13 he again expects to live to see it?   Certainly, some early Christians did misunderstand the apostles' preaching about how soon the Christ's return would be, 2 Thessalonians 2:2; 2 Peter 3:3-13.   But how can it be affirmed the apostles were mistaken when they were the ones to attempt to correct the misunderstandings?)   Sanday and Headlam, *Romans*, p.378, try to ease the problem by saying that "the language is that befitting those who expect the actual coming of Christ almost immediately, but it will fit the circumstances of any Christian for whom death brings the day."   John Murray, *Romans*, p.168, suggests that the New Testament does teach that the day of the Lord is at hand, without implying that it is imminent.

All that must be remembered is that, from the perspective of the prophets (who foresaw the sufferings of Christ and the glories to follow), the next thing on God's calendar is Christ's return to judge the living and the dead.   Hendriksen, *Romans*, p.446, uses 2 Peter 3:8 to show that men's time calculations are faulty – instead of thinking of 19 centuries, we should think of but a day or two (looking at it as God counts time).   Jesus and His apostles are ever consistent in their instruction about the time of the second advent.   Not knowing the time, they sometimes present it as occurring soon, possibly within their lifetimes; at other times, they present it as something off in the distant future.   What they did say was worded in such a way that whether men lived in the 1st century or the 21st, they would take care to so live as to be ready to stand before the judgment seat of Christ, to answer for the deeds done in the body (2 Corinthians 5:10).

[72] The second coming of Christ is here, as elsewhere, presented under the figure of a day dawning. (Cp. 1 Corinthians 3:13; Ephesians 5:14; 1 Thessalonians 5:4; 2 Peter 1:19.)   The ages previous to that day are regarded as the time of night.

aration needs to be made for that day must be done quickly.[73]

Let us therefore lay aside the deeds of darkness. "Lay aside"[74] is in the middle voice in the Greek, "Let us lay (them) aside for our own benefit." And the verb is an aorist tense, indicating a decisive act. The word picture is to "lay them off" as we lay off clothes worn during the night.[75] "Darkness" may be another way to speak of the "night" of the present age.[76] Or "darkness" may be taken literally, and the "deeds" would be the sort of things (prompted by the prince of darkness) indulged in during the night by unsaved people, six of which deeds are specified in the next verse. Often, the reason such deeds are done in the dark is that people are ashamed to do them in the light, where they might be seen by others (cp. John 3:20,21).

And put on the armor of light. Again, the verb is aorist middle subjunctive, and denotes something done for one's own benefit, and done decisively.[77] "Armor of light" has been explained two ways. (1) If we follow the analogy of the previous clause, then "light" here would be a reference to the "day" of the coming eternal age. Instead of "the deeds" which characterized the life of darkness, Paul here writes "the armor,"[78] as though in his mind's eye he pictured each believer as a Christian soldier, arrayed for battle. The garments ("ar-

---

[73] Each of the main terms in this verse, "night, day, darkness, light," may have a metaphorical sense. "Night," metaphorically, would speak of the present age between the ascension and the return of the Messiah. "Day," if taken metaphorically, would stand for the coming age that will dawn with the second advent of Christ.

[74] "The verb *apotithēmi*, 'to put off,' or 'put away,' is used in the New Testament only once of material things, in Acts 7:58, with reference to clothes. In the seven other passages, as in the present one, it is used metaphorically." Vine, *Romans*, p.191,192.

[75] We admit the comment may be a bit anachronistic, for many people in the ancient world did not have special garments that were worn at night, different from what they wore in the day time. Compare the angel's instructions to Peter at Acts 12:8, which imply he would wear the same clothes while awake as he did while asleep. However, it should be noted that in this passage Paul is not speaking of the common man, but of the soldier, putting off his night clothes, and putting his armor on. Soldiers did not sleep in their armor.

[76] "Darkness" often has a metaphorical sense denoting "the ignorance respecting divine things and human duties." Thayer, *Lexicon*, p.580. "To hate one's brother is to walk in darkness (1 John 2:9,11), and with such a condition fellowship with God is incompatible (1 John 1:6). Again, the believer is to have 'no fellowship with darkness' (2 Corinthians 6:14; Ephesians 5:11)." Vine, *Romans*, p.192.

[77] Object lessons and mnemonic devices are very helpful when we would impress a truth upon our hearers. How shall we get men to remember their need for changed behavior? Perhaps the use of a "catchword" would help. We suppose "put on" and "put off," words used with frequency in passages dealing with morals, are examples of such catchwords. Since the words for "put off" and "put on" are the regular words for dressing, or changing clothes, every time a man did these common acts he would be preaching himself a sermon about giving up the habits of the old unregenerate life, and about allowing Christ's life to be reproduced daily in his own.

[78] The same word, *hopla* (armor, weapons), was translated "instruments" in 6:13.

mor") the Christian would want to be wearing when the great day dawns[79] should be put on now!   (2) If we take "light" figuratively, as denoting "truth and its knowledge, together with the spiritual purity congruous with it,"[80] then "armor" might have the same meaning it does in 1 Thessalonians 5:8 and Ephesians 6:10-18.   People walking in the light are to put on a different kind of clothing than they used to wear while they were in the unregenerate state.[81]   Just like "deeds of darkness" are enumerated in verse 13, so it is possible that "armor of light" is further explained in verse 14.

13:13 – *Let us behave properly as in the day, not in carousing and drunkenness, not in sexual promiscuity and sensuality, not in strife and jealousy.*

Let us behave properly as in the day.   "Behave" is a translation of a Greek word that literally means "to walk around."   Perhaps this is another of the catchwords used to help memorize the practical duties of the new life in Christ.   And if so, every time a man went walking, he preached himself a sermon.   "Properly" could also be rendered "honestly, decently, becomingly."[82]   The three couplets that follow are examples of behavior that is not proper, honest, or decent.   "As in the day" likely means that we are to live as we would if the Lord had already returned and we were living in His presence.[83]

Not in carousing and drunkenness.   Here begin three pairs[84] of examples of "the deeds of darkness" which the Christian who is behaving properly avoids.   Both words in this pair are in the plural, suggesting frequent repetition of the sinful behavior.   The nature of "carousing" is generally agreed on.[85]   Involved is a gathering of a number of persons in a

---

[79] If one were to wonder what need there would be for "armor" or weapons when the second advent occurs, it might be fruitful to study Revelation 19:14 and 20:7ff.

[80] Thayer, *Lexicon*, p.667.

[81] "The day is on us in which, as soldiers of Christ, we must battle for the life to come. This battle we wage, not in darkness, but in light. Let us then be appropriately clad for the conflict. In a word, let us lay aside the deeds of the old unregenerate life, and enter thoroughly on the duties of the new life in Christ." Lard, *Romans*, p.408.

[82] Arndt and Gingrich, *Lexicon*, p.327.   "Originally referring to elegance of bearing, outward gracefulness (*eu* + *schēma*), they [the noun *euschēmonōs* and its cognate verb] came to be used frequently in pagan Greek in a metaphorical sense with reference to conduct." Cranfield, *Romans*, p.687.

[83] What the interpreter must decide is whether "day" in verse 13 has the same meaning it did in verse 12, or whether "day" is used literally of "daylight" in distinction to "darkness" (which some also took literally). If this latter interpretation were adopted, then the verse encourages Christians to behave in the way respectable men do in the daytime.

[84] "The relation between the two nouns in each pair is very close: each pair may, in fact, be understood as suggesting one composite idea (e.g., drunken revelries) rather than two distinct ideas." Cranfield, *Romans*, p.687.

[85] "The *kōmos* was a sort of carousal in which a number of persons participated, and which commonly ended by the whole party parading the streets with music, songs, and dancing ... The *kōmoi* were very common among the idolatrous Gentiles, particularly among the devotees of Bacchus. The *kōmos*, especially in its grosser forms, was invariably attended with drunkenness." Lard, *Romans*, p.409.

boisterous party, where music and dancing and often drinking were accepted and expected behavior. This activity is classed as a work of the flesh in Galatians 5:21, and is forbidden both in that passage and in 1 Peter 4:3. "Drunkenness" or "intoxication" is the result of overindulgence in wine or other intoxicating drink.

Not in sexual promiscuity and sensuality. Both words in this pair are in the plural in the Greek, suggesting, as before, frequent repetition of the sinful behavior. Paul here warns Christians to avoid the unholy satisfaction of sexual lusts through illicit acts. "Sexual promiscuity" is an excellent choice to render the Greek *koitē*,[86] which in this context denotes illicit sexual intercourse. Phillips gives "playing with sex" as the meaning of the word in this place. "Sensuality" also is a good choice, for some of the older words, "licentiousness," "debauchery," "wantonness," though they expressed the meaning, are no longer in the common man's vocabulary.[87] "Unbridled lust" also would convey the idea. It denotes lascivious sexual behavior in public with no concern about whether or not public decency is shocked.[88]

Not in strife and jealousy. Both words in this final pair are singular. "Strife" was explained at Romans 1:29 as meaning "fighting, brawling;" it is not unusual to see a drunken revelry end in fighting and brawling. "Jealousy" is used here[89] in its bad sense, meaning secret envy, enmity, bitter rivalry. Such attitudes are often the result of infidelity. The

---

Donnegan's *Lexicon* (p.789) gives, "a jovial assembly of friends, who met at an entertainment or to celebrate a festival with music, dancing, and singing – a band of revelers, who after a feast, go through the streets and visit their friends, or mistresses, singing, dancing, and indulging in wanton and boisterous merriment. It then comes to mean the music, singing, or dancing at festive gatherings." Thayer has, "rioting, a revel, a carousal, in the Greek writers, a nocturnal and riotous procession of half-drunken and frolicsome fellows, who after supper, parade through the streets with torches and music in honor of Bacchus or some other deity, and sing and play before the houses of their male and female friends; hence used generally of feasts and drinking-parties that are protracted till late at night and indulge in revelry." *Lexicon*, p.367.

[86] The literal meaning of the word is "bed, "couch," and euphemistically it denotes sexual intercourse, or seminal emission. Arndt and Gingrich, *Lexicon*, p.440,441. The word was used at Romans 9:10, and was translated "conceive." "The word has in it the meaning of the desire for the forbidden bed ... The word brings to mind the man who sets no value on fidelity, and who takes his pleasure when and where he can." Barclay, *Romans*, p.149.

[87] "Licentious" means "disregarding commonly accepted rules or principles," "lawless, immoral, lewd." "Debauchery" means "excessive indulgence in sensual pleasures." "Wantonness" is a "reckless disregard for right, or justice, or morals," "no restraint in behavior."

[88] "*Aselgeia* is one of the ugliest words in the Greek language. It does not describe only immorality; it describes the man who has lost his shame. Most people seek to conceal their evil deeds and try to sin in secret; but the man in whose heart there is *aselgeia* is long past that. He does not care who sees him; he does not care how much of a public exhibition he makes of himself; he does not care what people think of him; reputation, and honor and decency, mean nothing to him." Barclay, *Romans*, p.194.

[89] *Zēlos* was used in its good sense at Romans 10:2, and was translated "zeal."

fact that certain sins beget further sinful attitudes should not be taken to mean that Christians will necessarily be free of "strife" or "jealousy" if they avoid the other sins mentioned in this verse.[90]

13:14 – *But put on the Lord Jesus Christ, and make no provision for the flesh in regard to its lusts.*

But put on the Lord Jesus Christ. According to Galatians 3:27 and Romans 6:3, we put on Christ at baptism. Here (and in Ephesians 4:24 and Colossians 3:12), "put on ... Christ" has a slightly different meaning, for it is something done after conversion. To "put on Christ" is to order our conduct in the exact opposite of what has just been described in verse 13. It is not a greatly different concept than "put on the armor of light" in verse 12. It is to be a decisive act, done for the believer's own benefit.[91] The meaning of this language is, 'Let your whole exterior life, as seen by the world, and your interior thoughts and motives, as seen by the Father, be but a reproduction of the temper and conduct of Christ.' Paul calls on his readers to make a once-for-all determination in their minds to be all that Christ requires them to be, and to do all that He requires them to do.[92]

And make no provision for the flesh in regard to *its* **lusts.** The Greek prohibits the continuance of an action already going on: 'Stop making provision for the flesh!' Rather than Romans 7 (see its discussion of "flesh"), this is the passage in Romans which teaches that the Christian still has struggles with "the sin" that seeks to regain control through the desires stirred up in the flesh. By desires of the flesh, Paul clearly means those unlawful desires or those desires for unlawful objects which are everywhere prohibited in the Bible, and which are aroused in our bodies by the devil, just as he aroused them in our bodies before our conversion (Romans 7:7). The reason the Christian can control his body and not just give in to the evil desires stirred up by the devil is that (in the case of the Christian) some limitations have been placed on the devil (Romans 8:3,4) and the old slavery to sin has been broken (Romans 6:7). The 'renewed mind' (12:2) can control the behavior, so that the world is forsaken, and the whole body is presented to God as a living sacrifice.[93]

---

[90] People are wont to classify sins, some as bad, and some not so bad. The problem is that we do not always see sin as God sees it. To many, it is perfectly amazing to see the sins that are classed alongside strife and jealousy (see the previous portion of verse 13). Is this our attitude toward strife and jealousy, that they are no more refined and genteel than sexual promiscuity and sensuality? Men who "behave properly as in the day" no more permit themselves sins of attitude than they permit themselves the other sins here condemned.

[91] The Greek verb is an aorist tense, middle voice.

[92] "The phrase to put on a person, which seems a harsh expression in our language, was one not unfrequently used by Greek writers [e.g., see Dionysius, Lucian, etc.], and means to imbibe his principles, to imitate his example, to copy his spirit, to become like him." Barnes, *Romans*, p.301.

[93] The word translated "provision" is *pronoia*, and literally means 'forethought.' (Compare what is said about the cognate verb *pronoeō* at Romans 12:17, footnote #140.) After the devil has offered his temptation (stirred up the desires of the body), the man must premeditate how he will carry out the suggested sin. Such premeditation is the thing Paul commands the readers to stop doing.

With this exhortation, the paragraph (which began at 13:8) dealing with "love one another" comes to a close.   "It is impossible not to feel how sublime Christian life would be, were it closely modeled after the precepts herein laid down."[94]

F. Concerning the Christian Relationship Between Strong and Weak Brothers. 14:1-15:13

14:1 – *Now accept the one who is weak in faith,* **but** *not for* **the purpose of** *passing judgment on his opinions.*

Now accept the one who is weak in faith.   The *de* that is translated "now" marks a transition to a new section of practical application of the doctrine taught in chapters 1-11. The renewed mind (12:2) will affect on the behavior of the weak brother toward the strong, and the strong brothers toward the weak.   The strong brothers are instructed to accept the one who is weak.[1]   What the strong brothers are instructed to do to the weak brother is to welcome and embrace him, to stretch out a hand of friendship, in order to make the weak brother feel at home in the congregation.[2]   This 'acceptance' deals with relationships between those who are already brothers in Christ (see 14:10).[3]

What is meant when we characterize a brother as being "weak in faith"?   In light of the following context (see verses 2,14,22,23), we suggest it means "weak in subjective faith, lacking the moral courage to stand for his convictions."[4]   'Acceptance' (a way of dem-

---

[94] Lard, *Romans*, p.410.

[1] The singular "the one who is weak" suggests any individual who is "weak" is to be accepted. Commentators are in general agreement that the weak brothers made up a minority in the congregation at Rome, while the strong brothers made up the majority.

[2] "Accept" in the Greek is *proslambanō*, a present tense verb, indicating continuous action.

[3] The suggestions of some, that this speaks of receiving new converts who are seeking admission into church membership for the first time, or that it speaks of receiving those who are seeking "transfer of membership," seem to miss the thrust of the context.

[4] It is not an easy thing to decide what is a "weak brother."   *Pistis* ("faith") can have a number of different meanings, as was explained in comments at Romans 12:3.   "Faith" has already been used with several of these different connotations in Romans.   (1) At times (e.g., Romans 1:17, 3:3), it has been synonymous with "faithfulness."   (2) At times (cp. footnote #41 at Romans 10:8), perhaps, it has signified a "body of doctrine."   This is what is meant by those commentaries that mention "objective faith" at this place.   (3) At times (e.g., 4:18-21, 10:17), it stands for personal faith or belief, and it is somewhat akin to our word "assurance."   It is this personal faith which is what is meant in those commentaries that explain "faith" to be "subjective faith" at this place.

Which of the three ideas is intended when Paul writes "weak in faith"?   Each could be defended.   In making our decision, all we have to guide us is the present context and the analogy of Scripture.   1 Corin-

onstrating "love [to] one another," Romans 13:8) of such a "weak brother" would involve so behaving toward him that he never need to act in a way that violates his conscience, nor ever be caused to feel ashamed about his convictions.[5]   While some of the particular topics

---

thians 8-10 is a passage that likewise deals with weak and strong brothers, though the matter in dispute (i.e., meats offered to idols) does not seem to be identical with any of the matters disputed in Rome.

If we were permitted to ignore the analogy of Scripture, then here in Romans it might be possible to affirm that the weak brother is weak in objective faith.   Being a relatively new Christian (?), or one who is not very well taught, the weak brother just does not have a very good understanding of Christian doctrine, and therefore does not realize the freedom and privileges he has in the gospel.   The strong brother, on the other hand, would be the well-taught Christian, who because of his larger knowledge of Christian doctrine knows that he has certain privileges.   However, it is not possible to use 'strong in objective faith' and 'weak in objective faith' as a working definition when we come to 1 Corinthians, for in 1 Corinthians the "weak brother" is the one who (in one matter, at least) is doctrinally *right*!   The "strong brother" at Corinth was doctrinally *wrong*!   (At Corinth, in the matter of going to the idols' temple, the "weak brother" was doctrinally right; he believed it was wrong to go to the idol's temple and participate in feasts offered to the idol.   The "strong brother" was the one insisting that it would not hurt him to go.   1 Corinthians 10:20-22 shows that the "weak brother" was doctrinally right on this topic.   Later in 1 Corinthians, it is also possible that it is a "weak" brother who wrongly believed that meats purchased in the market, after being offered to idols, should not be eaten at home.   1 Corinthians 10:27,28 show that Christians could eat whatever was served, unless someone with a conscience about the matter called the Christian's attention to the origin of the meat.   So, if it is possible for a "weak" brother to be either doctrinally right or doctrinally wrong, it becomes obvious that it is not a matter of how much instruction a brother has received that determines who is weak and who is strong.)   If we are going to be guided by the analogy of Scripture, we will have to reject as oversimplification the interpretation that would define "weak in faith" as meaning weak doctrinally.

We are left either with "faithfulness" or "subjective faith" as the area where the brother was "weak."   Perhaps it says he is having trouble with being steadfast, faithful, in what he believes he should do, because of the example of the strong brother.   Perhaps it says he is weak when it comes to assurance that a certain course of behavior is proper, especially when the strong brother's behavior is so opposite.   Either way, the weakness is not doctrinal, but is in the area of moral courage (i.e., he is too "weak" to stand for his convictions ["faith"]).   This is a definition of "weak in faith" that works both in Corinthians and Romans.   (The fact that the Greek reads "weak in *the* faith" has been used to show that subjective faith cannot be the meaning, but rather it must refer to "*the* faith," i.e., objective faith.   We reply that the article before "faith" does not prove that "faith" here means a body of doctrine.   Compare the same expression at Romans 4:19, where it was personal faith, personal conviction, even though the article is used there also.)

Whether or not the weak brother's doctrine is right (and remember, in Corinth it was right, while in Rome it was not), it is possible for him to be so weak in his personal convictions on one matter or another that these convictions are not lived out in real life, if doing so would bring ridicule from others.   When any opposition is faced, the weak brother behaves in a way that is contrary to how he believes he should act, and as a result his conscience is violated and his spiritual life is harmed.   (Conversely, there are many who could be designated as "strong in the faith" [subjective faith] who are doctrinally wrong.   Many men, doctrinally wrong, have the moral courage to stand for what they think is right.)

[5] Considerable attention has been focused on attempts to identify with more precision exactly who the weak brothers in Rome were.   The information we have to help us decide includes: (1) meat eating vs. vegetarianism, 14:2; (2) observance vs. non-observance of days, 14:6; (3) clean vs. unclean meats, 14:14; (4) abstinence vs. non-abstinence from wine, 14:21; (5) there was something Jewish vs. Gentile, 15:8-12.   We are not convinced that these five areas of dispute are to be looked for in one person, as if the one and same "weak brother" at the same time was of Jewish background, a vegetarian, observed special days, and abstained from wine and other "unclean" foods.   We see no reason why all five must be looked for in one "weak brother."   Instead, we see these five examples as typical of the various, individual matters concerning which any brother could be "weak"?

that were matters of debate at Rome may not be live issues in the 21st century, the instruction about the way strong and weak brothers are to treat each other is still valid.[6]

***But* not for *the purpose of* passing judgment on his opinions.** Welcome the weak brother into your fellowship, yes; but do not let the weak brother find that what happens regularly at these meetings is that his "faulty notions" are the topic of discussion and criticism.[7] Paul will specify several examples of such "opinions" in the following verses.

Those who have tried to put them together have proposed various identifications of the weak brothers in Rome. Some think they are Jewish Christians offended by meats offered to idols. (This is difficult to harmonize with vegetarianism. Vegetarians eat no meat at all; they do not avoid just what had been sacrificed to idols, while eating other flesh.) Others suggest they are Jewish Christians who are offended by any meats forbidden as unclean in the Law, and by others' failure to continue to observe Jewish holy days. (Vegetarianism and abstinence from wine have caused difficulty to this attempted identification.) Others have suggested they were Jewish ascetics (Essenes, perhaps) before their conversion to Christianity, who brought their old beliefs with them into the church. (It is difficult to explain "no meat" as being somehow related to "unclean meats.") Still others have supposed they were Jewish Christians (Judaizers) who were enamored with the idea that the Law of Moses was still binding on Christians. (While most Judaizers could hardly be characterized as being weak in their convictions, it is possible to point both to Peter and Barnabas, at Antioch, as being men who did not have the courage to stand for their convictions at one point in their Christian experience, Galatians 2:11-13.) The reader who wishes to pursue this matter at length will find help in Barmby, *Romans*, p.407-409; Lange, *Romans*, p.414-416; and Cranfield, *Romans*, p.690-698.

[6] Observing the similarity of topics in Galatians (special days, Galatians 4:10; "through love serve one another," 5:13; no "challenging one another," 5:26) and Colossians (special days, Colossians 2:16; "touch not, taste not, handle not," 2:21 [KJV]), and also observing a difference in Paul's attitudes (compassionate toward the weak brethren in Romans and Corinthians; firm and uncompromising opposition toward those troubling the churches of Galatia and Colossae), some have supposed that there is of necessity a marked difference in the identity of the group at Rome who are "weak" on these matters, and the groups at Galatia and Colossae. Perhaps the difference in Paul's handling of the different cases is related to the attitudes of the people involved. To those (like the Judaizers at Galatia, and the ascetics at Colossae) who with a pushy brashness would force others to their beliefs, Paul has little patience. But to those (like the "weak" at Rome) whose cautious convictions are barely able to govern behavior, he is tender and helpful. "A battered reed he will not break off" could be said of Paul, as well as of Jesus (Matthew 12:20). To word this matter in present-day language, may we not explain the difference in Paul's handling of the different situations in this way – Paul's handling of the matter depended on whether the other person was holding a certain belief simply as a personal opinion, or whether he not only held the view but also tried to make that matter of opinion a test of faith (or fellowship) incumbent on all.

As an example, consider the matter of circumcision. Now that Christ has come and being a member of God's covenant people is no longer limited to Jews, the mark of the old covenant is no longer meaningful. It thus falls in the realm of opinion, as 1 Corinthians 7:19 shows. How Paul exercised his liberty in Christ in this matter is illustrated in the cases of Titus (Galatians 2:3) and Timothy (Acts 16:3). If someone insists on circumcision as a test of fellowship, Paul will adamantly refuse, as in the case of Titus. If it is done out of deference to scruples of those whom there is no need to needlessly offend, he will do it, as in the case of Timothy. A much more detailed study of this whole matter of faith and opinion is included in Special Study #9 following comments on 15:13.

[7] Actually, though the above note appears to be the idea, this clause is one that is not easy to give a perfectly satisfactory rendering to. Indeed, no two critics appear to agree in regard to it. "Passing judgment" comes from *diakrisis*, whose root meaning is "to separate, distinguish, decide, take issue, interpret, judge, be at odds with." Arndt and Gingrich, *Lexicon*, p.184. "Opinions" comes from *dialogismos*, which signifies "thought, opinion, reasoning, design, doubt, dispute, argument." Arndt and Gingrich, *op. cit.*, p.185. Luke 24:38 shows that the word often has the idea of doubt, hesitation, as to what is thought or believed. This is why many translations use "scruples" at Romans 14:1, for the dictionary says a "scruple" is "a doubt or uncertainty regarding a question of moral right or duty."

To persecute a man for an opinion he holds is to wed him to it, for he will feel the attachment of a martyr to that in which there may be little value, but for which he has had to suffer.

14:2 – *One man has faith that he may eat all things, but he who is weak eats vegetables* **only.**

One man has faith that he may eat all things. Paul here begins to specify one point over which weak and strong brothers may be divided. The strong brother has confidence or assurance that he may eat meat as well as vegetables.[8]

But he who is weak eats vegetables *only.* "Herbs" (vegetables) excludes *all* meat, not merely that of Levitically unclean animals, or the flesh sacrificed to idols, or the meats abstained from on feast and fast days (though it is not uncommon in the commentaries to find such limitations offered as explanations of what Paul wrote here). The weak brother eats *no* meat; he is a vegetarian. Nor is there any pressing reason why the weak brother who is urging vegetarianism should be identified as of Jewish background. Greeks, too, could be ascetics.[9] The weak brother in Romans is doctrinally wrong, and Paul will delicately state that fact in Romans 14:13-17,[10] but it is not a matter that the strong brother

---

[8] The Living New Testament reads "meat offered to idols." That is interpretation, and very likely not even a plausible one. We grant that in a similar passage in 1 Corinthians 8-10, the "strong brother" was insisting on his right to eat meat offered to idols. But it is difficult to affirm that this was the problem in Rome, for in order to avoid "meat offered to idols" one does not necessarily have to be a vegetarian.

[9] Commentators have tried, without much success, to ascertain the origin of the weak brother's beliefs that God requires vegetarianism as far as diet is concerned. Barnes is typical of those commentators who think the weak brother was Jewish and he tells us is about all there is to be known on the matter of where Jews might get the idea that they should be vegetarians. "Josephus says that in his time there were certain [Jewish] priests of his acquaintance who 'supported themselves with figs and nuts' (*Life*, 3). These priests had been sent to Rome to be tried on some trifling charge before Caesar, and [for some reason they abstained from meat]. It is expressly declared of Daniel while in Babylon, that he lived on pulse [vegetables] and water, that he might not 'defile himself with the portion of the king's meat, nor with the wine which he drank,' Daniel 1:8-16)." *Romans*, p.303,4. Vegetarianism was also a customary religious practice for some ascetics in the 1st century. It was characteristic of the Orphic and Pythagorean sects among the Greeks, and of the Essenes among the Jews. Behind this asceticism was Greek philosophy. "At Colossae the error which Paul controverts was basically gnostic and posited, as F.F. Bruce observes, 'a clear-cut dualism between the spiritual and material realm' and regarded salvation as consisting in the liberation of the spiritual from the material. Thus 'asceticism was commonly regarded as an important element in this process of liberation'." Murray, *Romans*, p.173. It is not difficult to suppose that what people in Colossae believed, people in Rome (influenced by Greek culture and philosophy) could believe, too.

[10] Other Scriptures, such as 1 Timothy 4:4, indicate that the weak brother in Rome is doctrinally mistaken. God has said that meat-eating is permissible with Him, if it is eaten with thanksgiving. Yet it must be remembered that there is no *commandment* that a man *must* eat meat. In the Gospel Age, what a man eats by way of food is in the realm of Christian liberty. (Of course, believers should have adequate reasons for eating or not eating, and there are limitations on one's liberty. See 1 Corinthians 6:12-20 and Romans 14-15.)

should bring up for debate all the time.   For the moment, the right or wrong of the matter is not the important thing; for the moment, Paul is concerned with the feelings involved.

14:3 – *Let not him who eats regard with contempt him who does not eat, and let not him who does not eat judge him who eats, for God has accepted him.*

Let not him who eats regard with contempt him who does not eat.   These words are addressed to the strong brother, and he is instructed not to ridicule the weak brother, not to look on him with contempt, not to despise him as not being worth taking seriously.[11]   If the weak brother can be reasoned out of his position (especially if it is doctrinally wrong), it is well; but to attempt to laugh him out of it is unkind, and will tend only to confirm him in his views.

And let not him who does not eat judge him who eats.   This prohibition is addressed to the weaker brother.   He has a responsibility in the matter, just as much as the stronger brother does.   The prohibitions in both parts of this verse are present imperatives – and prohibit the continuance of an action already going on.   Both the strong and weak are at fault in this matter.   The strong are to stop treating the weak with contempt; the weak are to stop criticizing the strong.   Does not this prohibition remind us of Jesus' own prohibition of "judging" (Matthew 7:1-5)?   The weak brothers, who for religious reasons have adopted a vegetarian diet, were to receive the strong as "brothers," instead of treating them as just a "little less religious" because their diet included meat.   Whether a brother eats meat and/or vegetables is not a test of fellowship.   In the early church there was room for much variety, and yet there was to be harmonious unity.

For God has accepted him.   The nearest antecedent of "him" is "him who eats."   We suppose, therefore, that this phrase states the reason the weak brother must stop criticizing the strong brother.   God has welcomed[12] the meat eater; should not the vegetarian do the same?   Or will the vegetarian require more for acceptance than God Himself does?

---

[11] "We must avoid the attitude of *ridicule*.   No man remains unwounded when that which he thinks precious is laughed at.   It is no small sin to laugh at another's beliefs.   To us they may seem to be prejudices rather than belief; that does not matter; no man has a right to laugh at that which some other man holds sacred.   In any event, laughter will never woo the other man to the wider view; it will only make him withdraw still more determinedly into his rigidity."   Barclay, *Romans*, p.196,197.

[12] It is the same word translated "accept" in verse 1.   "God has accepted him" means that his continuing salvation is not based on any such condition as the critic (vegetarian) assumed.   Conditions for salvation there may be, but avoidance of meat is not one of them.   "Accepted" is an aorist tense, and perhaps looks back to the time of conversion.   God accepted him then (he was justified by faith).   His diet since then (just because it includes meat) has not caused him to be reckoned as unfaithful.

14:4 – *Who are you to judge the servant of another?   To his own master he stands or falls; and stand he will, for the Lord is able to make him stand.*

Who are you to judge the servant of another?   This also is addressed to the weak brother who has been judging (criticizing) the meat eater.   Observe the emphatic "you."   'You! Who do *you* think *you* are ...?' is the connotation.[13]   "Servant" here translates *oiketes*,[14] which means "domestic, household slave," and differs from *doulos* (bond-servant, slave) which we had at Romans 1:1.   'If I have a domestic, and I am pleased with how he cooks my food and washes my clothes, why should you take it upon yourself to criticize and condemn the way he cooks and does the laundry?'

To his own master he stands or falls.   This is a sharp rebuke.   It is the height of presumption when a weak brother sets himself up as if he was the real master in the Lord's house, and then proceeds to pass judgment on a fellow household servant.   When it comes to applying this illustration to the topic at hand, the idea is that the strong brother is answerable to the Lord[15] – it is to Him (and not the weak brother) that the strong must show whether he has used or misused his freedom.   The servant shall be approved ('stand') or condemned ('fall') by his own Master.   If his conduct pleases his Master, he shall be approved.   If not, he will be condemned.[16]   And the criterion He uses will be His own, not the rules some man (be he weak brother, as in this case, or strong) has devised.[17]

---

[13] See this construction explained in comments on "you" at Romans 2:3.

[14] The choice of *oiketes* is felicitous, for a "domestic" was one who belonged to the immediate family, and was in personal contact with the master.   That is exactly the position of the strong brother; he belongs to God's family, and is in personal contact with the Master.

[15] The Greek word translated "master" is *kurios*, the word often translated "Lord" as the NASB margin shows.   It is not clear whether Paul has in mind the Father or Jesus as the "Lord" to whom the servant answers.   On the basis of verses 3 and 10, some have opted for the Father; on the basis of verses 6 and 9, some have opted for Jesus.

[16] It is not possible to decide whether it is in this life or the next that the "Master" is judging the servant. If it is something done in this life (and Romans has shown that "justification by faith" is not a one-time thing), "stands" speaks of continuing in faithful obedience and thus having the Lord's approval.   If it is the final judgment that is in view, then the passage promises some servants that they will have God's approval ("stands," cp. Revelation 6:17), and it threatens others who once were servants with being condemned ("falls") at the judgment.   (It is not unusual to find that a commentator's beliefs regarding whether the security of the believer is conditional or not, affect his comments at this place.   Of course, if it is impossible for a man once saved to ever be lost, then the "servant" adjudged to have 'fallen' certainly means something other than eternal punishment.   "Falls" is the same word, and used with the same meaning, as at 11:11.) Whether or not a fellow-servant of the Lord has fallen into sin (and into condemnation) in the use of his liberty is something for God to decide, not the fellow-servant, and certainly not the weaker brother.

[17] Even if the weak brother were doctrinally right (which at Rome, he was not), he still would be out of place to criticize the strong brother.   This does not mean there is nothing a man can do who sees behavior in another that seems to him to be out of place.   It is, of course, not presumption, but a tremendous service to point out to each other what the Master has *commanded* in His Word, and to remind each other what His Word really requires.   This positive way of helping another servant to carry out his Master's will is something completely different from the criticism or contempt that is here prohibited.

And stand he will.   The strong brother's use of his liberty to eat meat as well as vegetables was regarded by the weak brother as a falling down in the strong brother's devotion to the Lord.   Paul here assures all concerned that the strong brother had not thereby subjected himself to the Lord's disapproval.

For the Lord is able to make him stand.   This statement gives the reason why Paul can promise the strong brother will "stand."[18] The strong brother is not standing by his own strength; he has the help of the Lord.[19]   Does anyone imagine that the Lord needs the assistance of the weak brother (if that 'assistance' amounts to 'criticism,' verse 3) to help the strong brother stand?

14:5 – *One man regards one day above another, another regards every day* **alike.**   *Let each man be fully convinced in his own mind.*

One man regards one day above another.   Here we come to a second matter[20] over which brothers may show an absence of love for each other, either ridiculing or censoriously criticizing the other's beliefs and behavior.   It is not certain whether it is the weak or strong brother who esteems one day more than another,[21] nor is it possible to decide what days the brother thought special.[22]

---

[18] "Stand" has been used three times in this verse, and likely has the same meaning in each place. It still is not possible to determine with any degree of certainty whether it is the final judgment or a judgment during this life. Even if it is standing in this life that the Lord helps the strong brother to do, the passage should not be used to prove that God unconditionally causes men (e.g., the 'elect') to stand. The context has been discussing the conditions of standing, and whether or not eating meat or vegetables is one of the conditions. (Some have supposed that "make him stand" refers to picking up a brother who has fallen, but while it is a possible translation of Greek, it requires the second and third uses of "stand" in this verse to be given a different meaning than in its first occurrence, and this is not likely to be right.)

[19] The KJV reads "God is able ...," but the better attested reading is "The Lord is able ...." May we assume that help of the Holy Spirit to live the Christian life (chapter 8) is included in this statement about the Lord's ability to make the man stand?   The Lord has the "power, ability" (*dunatei*) to exert influence on His servants, to help them stay in the sphere of His approval.

[20] The explanation assumes that the *gar* ("for") which occurs in some manuscripts (Sinaiticus in the first hand, Alexandrinus, and others) does not enjoy integrity (since it is omitted in P[46], Sinaiticus in the third hand, Vaticanus, and others).   If it were original, we would have to explain that the weak brothers all had two points of weakness, respecting both meats and days.

[21] Some suppose Paul follows the same order as in verse 2, where the strong brother is named first; so it would be the strong brother who esteems one day above another.   Others affirm that verse 1 sets the tone for the passage, and it is the weak brother's scruples that are prominent; therefore, it is the weak brother who esteems one day above another.

[22] Commentators have offered multiple suggestions for identifying the special day: (1) The Jewish Sabbath. So Lenski. The weak brother is pictured as worshiping on Sunday with the church, but also closing shop and ceasing to work on the Sabbath. (2) Jewish religious festivals, such as Passover, Pentecost, Tabernacles, Purim, Dedication, and Trumpets. So Hodge. (3) Jewish fast days, Mondays and Thursdays of each week, cp. Luke 18:12. So Ridderbos. (4) Ex-pagans, now Christians, were insisting on distinguishing between lucky and unlucky days. See Kasemann. (5) Ex-pagans, now Christians, were doubting the necessity of observing the Lord's Day each week. (6) Jewish Christians were insisting on keeping the Sabbath (and not the Lord's Day) on the supposition that the Mosaic Law was still valid.

Another regards every day *alike.*[23] This brother is, of course, not insisting that every day is a day when he can act as he pleases, but rather is one who treats every day as a special opportunity to serve the Lord. "Since this difference of conviction among believers is in the same category as the difference respecting the use of certain kinds of food, we must conclude that the observance of the days in question did not proceed from any continuing divine obligation."[24] Just as God had not *commanded*[25] that certain foods be eaten, so we suppose that God has not *commanded* that certain days be observed in the New Covenant Age, like He had *commanded* observance of the Sabbath in the Mosaic Age (Exodus 20:8; Deuteronomy 5:12,15). He could have, on the other hand, just as He did in the case of meats, indicated what was acceptable in His sight with regard to special days, leaving it to each individual Christian (as the next phrase indicates) to determine what was best for him as he would dedicate his life to the Lord.[26]

Whether or not Galatians 4:10,11 and Colossians 2:16,17 deal with the same problem is also debated. (a) It is not certain that Galatians and Colossians themselves discuss the same problem, let alone that their problem is somehow related to the problem in Rome. Paul is rejecting the Judaizer's claims in Galatians; the Colossian heresy is not exactly the same, being a mixture of eastern mysticism, Judaism, and asceticism. (b) Is it possible the problem at Colossae and Rome are identical? It is possible to find Judaism, and maybe asceticism, in Romans 14 and 15, but it is not easy to find oriental mysticism in the examples of points of contention Paul gives. (c) Is it possible the problem in Galatia and in Rome is the same? In order for the problem to be the same, it must be "Jewish" in nature, and somehow related to the belief that the commands in the Law of Moses must be observed if a man is to continue to have God's approval. Some suppose they could show this similarity. In Galatians, Paul is dealing with the situation where some – the Judaizers – had tried to bind on Christians the keeping of the Sabbath, circumcision, and table fellowship, as a matter of faith or test of fellowship. Paul abruptly and summarily dismisses the claims of the Judaizers as being inconsistent with the gospel of Christ, and warns the Galatian readers that if they give in to the Judaizers on these initial demands, they will soon find the Judaizers demanding they keep the whole Law (Galatians 5:3,4). Likewise, in Rome, those who advocated the keeping of certain days could be alleged to think them necessary to salvation (remember the presentation in chapter 4 dealing with the Law and circumcision), and were making them a wedge by which the door was opened to demanding that Christians keep the whole Law of Moses. (d) On the other hand, even if old Jewish beliefs are behind the debates in both places, the two cases may not be similar at all. It has already been pointed out in footnote #6 that the cautious scrupulosity of the weak brothers at Rome was a far different attitude than the demanding authoritarianism of the Judaizers.

[23] "There is no word in the Greek corresponding to 'alike,' although it is added here in the ASV, RSV, NEB, as well as the KJV, to complete the sense." Bruce, *Romans*, p.245. It should also be noted that the same Greek word is translated "judge" in verse 3 and "regards" in verse 5. "Here we have a good example of the way in which the apostle can change from one shade of meaning to another in the use of the same term. In verses 3 and 4, *krino* is used in the depreciatory sense of censorious judgment. In verse 5 it is used in the sense of 'esteem' to which no criticism belongs." Murray, *Romans*, p.177.

[24] Murray, *Romans*, p.178.

[25] Refer again to what was said in footnote #10, above, where there is a distinction between what God *commands* and what He says is acceptable.

[26] A most difficult question to answer is whether what is here written about observance of special days includes the Lord's Day as one of the special days. Christians surely will want to worship when and how God has shown is acceptable in His sight. Therefore, the conscientious believer approaches this passage with caution and prayer, so he may ascertain just what the Lord is saying. There is no doubt that several rather persuasive reasons can be given for observing the Lord's Day. Jesus rose on the first day of the week (Mark 16:9; Luke 24:1-12); the church began on the first day of the week (Acts 2:1-42); while the apostles were still living and guiding her, the Church observed the first day of the week (Acts 20:7; 1

Let each man be fully convinced in his own mind. Instead of the strong regarding the weak with contempt, and instead of the weak criticizing the strong, with the result that each has hurt the other, what is the proper course of action in such adiaphoristic matters? Let each brother, first of all, look to himself (verse 5), and then look to the Lord (verse 6). "Let each man be fully convinced" is a rule that applies to both strong and weak brothers. In fact, once the weak brother has developed full conviction on the matter, he may no longer be weak. His convictions will produce the courage to behave as he believes the Lord wants him to. He will then be demonstrating the acceptable will of God as his renewed mind transforms his behavior (12:2). If the strong and weak brothers will both follow the instructions of Paul here, it will lead to their "receiving" each other. Each brother's action should be determined not simply by another man's opinion, but by his own careful study of what God has revealed.[27]   When these instructions are carried out, we will find a harmony in the congregation, but not conformity or uniformity on all issues.[28]   "The

---

Corinthians 16:1-2); there was something special about the Lord's Day (Revelation 1:10); and early Christian literature shows the post-apostolic church observing the first day of the week as the day of worship (Justin Martyr, *Apology*, I.67; Pliny, *Epistles*, Book 10). In spite of this impressive array of evidence showing what the Christians customarily did, it is not possible to find a *command* about keeping the Lord's Day, like one can find a command about the Sabbath for those who lived under the Mosaic covenant.   Still, the church uniformly observed the Lord's Day, we affirm, because the apostles taught the new converts this was what was acceptable to their new Lord.

We are now ready to make some further observations. (1) It certainly is not in harmony with the New Covenant Scriptures to transfer the Sabbath Day taboos to the Lord's Day. The two days are not even the same day of the week.   Whether or not a Christian works at his regular occupation on the Lord's Day is not something prohibited by the Sabbath commandment in the Decalog. It would seem to be something that falls into the realm of opinion, something about which each individual must be "fully convinced" in his own mind, as he tailors his own behavior in the way he thinks he must to serve the Lord. (2) If some should wish to observe special days (think of days like Resurrection day or Christmas day), that too is something that falls within the purview of what Paul here writes, for he condemns neither the one who esteems one day above the other, nor the one who esteems every day alike. (3) The Pharisees had made a tyranny of the Sabbath, surrounding it with a jungle of rules and regulations and prohibitions. Did Paul fear a similar attitude might attach itself to the observance of the Lord's Day? There is more to Christianity than the observance of any particular day. And while Christians will want to express their devotion and allegiance to their Lord, and participate in His Memorial Supper with at least a weekly regularity, it is not the day that Christians should worship, but He who is the Lord of all days.

[27] Paul should not be interpreted to be saying, 'It makes no difference what a man believes, as long as he is sincere.' When God has *commanded*, it *does* make a difference what one believes. Paul is not in this section dealing with what God has commanded, but with the realm of the permissive. "Mind" here is *nous* (not *pneuma*), the same word used at 12:2. The use of *nous* shows that reflection, judgment, and the proper exercise of reason are all called for in the decision on the question of personal duty. Of course, in those matters where God has *commanded*, all that is needed is obedience. It is in the areas of the permissive that the strong brother and weak brother alike need to study the Word until they are fully assured in their own minds what God would have them do in the case in question.

"Fully convinced in his own mind" does not mean that each is fully assured that he himself is right and his brother is wrong. It means he is convicted from his study of the Word that his course of action is right for him – without casting any reflection on the other's course of action.

[28] The immediate context deals with the observance of special days. If one Christian (having carefully studied out what is best for him in his service to the Lord) wants to keep the days, it is not wrong, providing he does not violate his conscience (verse 23) in the matter. He has the right, and no one can interfere. If another esteems all days alike, and conscientiously chooses not to keep some day as special, he is not wrong. He has the right, and no one can interfere. The liberty that is part of the Christian system allows for this diversity among brethren.

plea is for acceptance of one another despite diversity of attitude regarding certain things. Compelled conformity or pressure exerted to the end of securing conformity defeats the aims to which all the exhortations and reproofs [in this section] are directed."[29]

14:6 – *He who observes the day, observes it for the Lord, and he who eats, does so for the Lord, for he gives thanks to God; and he who eats not, for the Lord he does not eat, and gives thanks to God.*

He who observes the day, observes it for the Lord. Here is the 'Look to the Lord!' part of determining what is the proper course of behavior in the adiaphoristic matters. The more each brother seeks to sanctify his opinion religiously, the more he brings it before the Lord, the more he will distinguish between the true and the false. "Observes" is a translation of the verb *phroneō*, a word which was translated 'set the mind' at Romans 8:5. "The day" recalls the previous discussion of verse 5a about esteeming certain days as special. What the phrase pictures is that the man has 'set his mind that he must esteem this day as special,' and he has reached that decision because it is part of his response to the Lord. His behavior is determined, not by irreligious feelings of what he would like to do, but by a desire to serve the Lord in this action.[30] This expression "for the Lord" is unfolded in verses 7-9.

And he who eats, does so for the Lord, for he gives thanks to God. "He who eats," we suppose, reflects what was first said in verses 2,3 about eating meat. This brother (we no longer make distinctions between strong and weak, once each is fully persuaded in his own mind [verse 5]) eats his meat, persuaded that his eating is in harmony with his Lord's will, and will tend to serve the interests of the Lord. His giving of thanks is evidence that the man is fully assured that it is right to use what God has given him for food. Christians commonly pause to give thanks to God for their food. While we know of no specific New Testament *command* that this must be done, pausing to offer thanks to the One who provides food and shelter and clothing is part of what is involved in a proper response to the Lord.[31]

---

[29] Murray, *Romans*, p.178.

[30] The KJV has another phrase about observing days that is not carried in the NASB. It reads, "He that regardeth not the day, to the Lord he doth not regard it." The phrase does not enjoy integrity, and probably was added by some scribe who thought a balance was needed concerning 'days' like follows concerning 'eating.' (The student will notice, as he studies the commentaries, that the writers are divided with reference to whether or not this additional statement is appropriate, or not in harmony with Paul's argument. Those who tend to see only Jewish holy days being observed by the weak brother affirm that the added phrase does not suit Paul's argument, for [they suppose] Paul would not be suggesting that such days be observed as set apart for God. We wonder if this type of comment has not missed the whole thrust of Paul's presentation about freedom in Christ. After all, Paul himself did Jewish things at times, such as taking vows [Acts 18:18] and participating in certain sacrifices connected with vows [Acts 21:22-26].)

[31] 1 Timothy 4:4,5 ("For everything created by God is good, and nothing is to be rejected, if it is received with gratitude, for it is sanctified by means of the word of God and prayer"), as well as these verses in Romans where both strong and weak brothers pause to offer thanks for their food, suggest that it was a custom rather universally practiced among the early Christians to have prayers at the table at meal time.

And he who eats not, for the Lord he does not eat, and gives thanks to God. This brother sits down to eat his vegetables, and he pauses to give thanks to God for his food. His giving of thanks is evidence that this brother is fully assured that it is proper (as part of his response to the Lord) for him to be a vegetarian.[32] Both the meat-eater and the vegetarian are pleasing to Christ.[33]

14:7 – *For not one of us lives for himself, and not one dies for himself;*

For not one of us lives for himself. "For the Lord" was repeated three times in verse 6. Verses 7-9 will give the reason why Paul has just said the Christian's[34] whole life is lived with the knowledge that he is responsible to the Lord, and that his behavior must please his Lord. If a man "lives for himself," his only object in his behavior would be his own gratification.[35] The Christian, with his renewed mind (12:2), has a different object than that. "No Christian considers himself as his own master, or at liberty to regulate his conduct according to his own will, or to his own ends. He is the servant of Christ, and, therefore, endeavors to live according to His will and for His glory."[36]

And not one of us dies for himself. Just as a believer has a transformed attitude about his everyday living, so the believer has a transformed attitude about death. When it comes to living, the believer intends to glorify Christ; when it comes to dying, he intends to keep glorifying Him.[37]

---

[32] The phrase about "gives thanks to God" should not be treated as though it were parallel to the Pharisee's prayer, "God, I thank Thee that I am *not* as other people, ... I fast twice each week (I abstain from meat!)." That is not what is meant by "gives thanks to God."

[33] Though in its original context it has a different meaning (being intended as a flat rejection of the heretic's doctrine that Mosaic commands were still obligatory, instead of being but a shadow of things to come, Colossians 2:17), the words of Colossians 2:16 might be quoted here by way of accommodation: "Therefore, let no one act as your judge in regard to food or drink or in respect to a festival or a new moon or a Sabbath day."

[34] In the words "Not one of us," the subject passes from particular cases of believers who regard days and foods, to the case of every believer and his everyday relationship with Christ as Lord.

[35] Cranfield, *Romans*, p.707, gives examples from both Greek and Latin where "lives for himself" denotes "living selfishly, caring only for one's own interest and comfort." While it is true that Christians must be concerned about their own behavior, lest it prove to be a stumbling-block to others, as verse 13 clearly shows, that is not the topic here in verses 7-9. It is not until verse 13ff that Paul takes up the matter of obstacles and stumbling-blocks. It is therefore a mistake, we believe, to use this passage as a funeral text, intended to show that the way we live and die has a strong influence upon others. That may be true, but this is not the text to prove it.

[36] Lipscomb and Shepherd, *Romans*, p.245.

[37] There are verses that suggest a Christian's service for Christ goes right on, even after his few years of physical existence in this life are ended by death. Philippians 1:20,21 is one of these passages. We propose that "to die is gain" does not mean that Paul gets great reward for his own personal enjoyment, but rather that physical death has opened up a whole new area of service for Christ – i.e., it is gain for Christ! 1 Peter 3:18 suggests that just as Christ's death opened up a whole new world of service ("He went and preached to the spirits in prison," etc.), so the Christian's death opens a whole new world of service for Him, too.

14:8 – *for if we live, we live for the Lord, or if we die, we die for the Lord; therefore whether we live or die, we are the Lord's.*

For if we live, we live for the Lord.   This verse explains what Paul had in mind in verse 7, when he said that none of us lives, or dies, unto himself.   While the Christian is living this life, he lives to do Christ's will, and to promote His glory.   The Christian makes it his great aim to subordinate all his own personal desires to what Christ desires.   That is how a renewed mind works.

Of if we die, we die for the Lord.   The grave is not an asylum where we get away from and are exempt from serving the Lord.   Barnes may be right when he suggests "the passage proves that the soul does not cease to be conscious at death.   We are still the Lord's, even when the body is in the grave; and [we are] His in all the future world, see verse 9."[38]

Therefore whether we live or die, we are the Lord's.   This statement summarizes ("therefore") what has been affirmed.   This is why we live and die "for the Lord" – because we belong to Him[39] both in life and in death.   Christ's authority over believers continues on, whether in this life or in the life to come.   The reason why He has such authority will be stated in the next verse.

14:9 – *For to this end Christ died and lived* again, *that He might be Lord both of the dead and of the living.*

For to this end Christ died and lived *again.*[40]   The reason why Christians are Christ's possession, and why He has authority over them, is found in His death and resurrection.[41]

---

[38] Barnes, *Romans*, p.308.   Not many passages in Scripture tell in detail what life in the future world will be like.   Therefore, believers diligently search for any passage that might give a hint.   We wonder if Romans 14 is such a passage.   It has been showing that believers have a marvelous freedom to determine what course their behavior will take in this life as they present their lives in service to Him.   May we also suppose that in the world to come, this similar freedom, and the resulting diversity of service, will be continued?   If "live for the Lord" involves this responsible freedom now, is it possible that "die for the Lord" implies that such responsible freedom continues in the next life?

[39] Both verbs "live" and "die" are in the present tense, indicating continuous action.   Thus, "die" suggests also what follows in the intermediate state.   "Lord" in verse 8 has been consistently explained as being a reference to Christ, because of what is immediately affirmed in verse 9.

[40] The KJV reads, "Christ both died, and rose, and revived."   If the reading were adopted, the "revived" could be explained as a reference to Christ's living in heaven and serving as Mediator, as was explained at Romans 5:10 ("we shall be saved by His life").   The best attested reading is like that in the NASB, and "Christ died and lived again" corresponds very nicely with the following clause, "that he might be Lord both of the *dead* and the *living*."

[41] "Lived," though an aorist tense, points to the resurrection (the NASB translators inserted "again" to show that this interpretation was their understanding of the word), rather than to the life of Christ here on earth previous to His death.   While the Greek does have a compound form of this verb (*anazaō*), which sometimes may mean "lived *again*," the word used here is the simple verb, *zaō*.   *Zaō* is often used of the new life into which Christ entered after His resurrection (Revelation 1:18, 2:8; Romans 5:10; 2 Corinthians 4:10,11).

It seems to us that the word order in verse 9 precludes "lived" as being a reference to His life before

"To this end" suggests a purpose in view, but we cannot tell if it was something God purposed in His mind, or if it was one purpose Christ had in mind when He came to earth to suffer, and die, and rise again.[42]

That He might be Lord both of the dead and the living. That Jesus Christ is called "Lord" is inexplicable if Jesus were a mere man.[43]

> Christ is here – in the most emphatic terms – held up as the supreme Object of the Christian's life, and of his death, too; and that by a man whose horror of creature worship was such, that when the poor Lycaonians would have worshiped him, he rushed forth to arrest the deed, directing them to "the living God" as the only legitimate object of worship (Acts 14:15). Nor does Paul *teach* this here [for the first time], but rather *appeals* to it as a known and recognized fact of which he had only to remind his readers. And since the apostle, when he wrote these words, had never been at Rome, he could only know that the Roman Christians would assent to this view of Christ, because it was the *common teaching of all the accredited preachers of Christianity*, and the common faith of all Christians.[44]

By His death and resurrection, Christ has established His claim of Lordship over all alike, both dead and living. Responsibility to Him, therefore, no one can escape. The "dead" would be the souls in the intermediate state at the time Paul wrote.[45] "The living" would be those to whom Paul wrote, and their contemporaries, and by parity of reasoning, us too. Whether or not men have voluntarily yielded allegiance to Him will be one of the topics in the final judgment (verses 10-12).

Calvary. (See also the comment in footnote #40.) Furthermore, in New Testament theology, the lordship of Christ is connected with His resurrection and glorification (cp. Acts 2:36; Romans 8:34; Philippians 2:9-11; Hebrews 2:5-9).

  Most commentators appeal to this aorist tense verb as being an example of an ingressive aorist; that is, the beginning of the act is emphasized. The aorist "lived" points, perhaps, to the first moment when the soul animated His body in the tomb. Instantly, at that point of inception, Christ became Lord of the dead and the living.

[42] It is commonly stated that Jesus gave His life when He died; it was something He did voluntarily (John 10:15-17). Paul in this verse attributes both His death and His resurrection to Jesus Himself. While the resurrection of Jesus is frequently represented as accomplished by the agency of the Father (e.g., 1 Corinthians 15:15), there are also instances where Jesus Himself claims to be the agent in His own resurrection (John 2:19; 10:17,18).

[43] The deity of Jesus has at least twice been the topic before in our study of Romans, at 1:4 and at 9:5.

[44] Wilson, *Romans*, p.222.

[45] As we have noted before in the quotation from Barnes (at verse 8), this passage refutes the old doctrine of soul sleeping, for Christ is Lord over something more than insensible matter (the bodies in the graves). Those who have died physically are not annihilated; they continue to exist in the spirit world, and are still under the dominion of Jesus. Jesus Himself taught the same doctrine when he showed that though long dead physically, Abraham, Isaac, and Jacob were still living (Matthew 22:32).

14:10 – *But you, why do you judge your brother?   Or you again, why do you regard your brother with contempt?   For we shall all stand before the judgment seat of God.*

But you, why do you judge your brother?   With these words, Paul returns to the thought of verse 3, that the weak brother is not to judge the strong nor the strong to ridicule the weak.   Having suggested in verse 4 that the weak brother is being presumptuous to set himself up as judge of another master's servant, he now repeats that idea.   This first question is addressed to the weak brother.   The "but you" is emphatic and connects verse 10 with the thought expressed in verse 9; it is intended to show him that how he is acting toward the strong brother is something contrary to the lordship of Christ.   If we read it with emphasis on both "you" and on "brother," the idea will be clear.   Since Christ is Lord of the dead and the living, it is a usurpation of His prerogative for the weak brother to presume to sit in judgment, and it is inconsistent with the relationship of believers to one another (note, Paul asks the weaker one why he is judging his "brother").   The latter part of verse 10 will show the weak brother that his critical behavior also should be abandoned, for if it is not, it will be a topic for which he will have to answer to God in the judgment.

Or you again, why do you regard your brother with contempt?   "You again" is also emphatic, and is addressed this time to the strong brother; it likewise is intended to show him that how he is acting toward the weak brother is also opposed to the idea of the lordship of Christ.   Jesus died and lives for "your brother;" how dare you claim to be responsible to Christ, and at the same time regard your brother (note the word "brother" again[46]) with contempt?   As before, the latter part of verse 10 will show the strong brother that his negative behavior should be abandoned, for if it is not, it will be a topic for which he will have to answer to God in the judgment.[47]

For we shall all stand before the judgment seat of God.[48]   This phrase begins with "for," and so is intended to give a reason Christians ought not judge or ridicule their brothers.   "We ... all" is universal; it is placed forward for emphasis.   It is a universal judgment; unbeliever and Christian alike will be there;[49] strong and weak brother alike will stand be-

---

[46] "Brother ... brother ...."   "The repetition of the word 'brother' not only indicates the equality of their standing, but is also a timely reminder that their relationship should be distinguished by that mutual love which delights to cover a multitude of faults."   Wilson, *Romans*, p.223.

[47] A special appeal to readers from the Restoration Movement seems in order.   The brethren who use musical instruments in worship, and those who do not, have often debated each other over what is the proper course of conduct for followers of Christ.   Let both sides, in this controversy, hear these words about judging and regarding with contempt our brothers, as each seeks to be fully persuaded in his own mind, and also orders his behavior as he does because he thinks he must to please the Lord.

[48] Some manuscripts read "judgment seat of Christ," as does the KJV, apparently in an attempt to harmonize this passage with 2 Corinthians 5:10.   But "God" here is the better attested reading.   Still, the KJV reading goes back to the first half of the 2nd century, because the reading "Christ" was known to Polycarp and Marcion.

[49] Romans 2:3-16 and 3:6 have already emphasized the universality of the final judgment.   This passage in Romans, showing Christians will be judged individually, contradicts those systems of eschatology which say the Christian is exempt from the final judgment.   A perusal of judgment passages

fore the judgment seat[50] of God. While verse 4 implied that the strong brother should so live as to please the Master of the house, it said nothing about the weak, presumptuous brother, being judged. Verse 10 makes it clear that both strong and weak brother must answer to God. 'If a man holds a different opinion than mine, why should I judge him or ridicule him? Each of us will have to answer for our own use of the liberty we have in Christ. If I have been a strong brother who has disdained the other, or if I have been a weak brother who has been censorious, one of the questions I will be asked at the final judgment is "Why?" I would not then be able to give an answer, as even now I am not able to give one.'

14:11 – *For it is written, "AS I LIVE, SAYS THE LORD, EVERY KNEE SHALL BOW TO ME, AND EVERY TONGUE SHALL GIVE PRAISE TO GOD."*

For it is written. Paul cites Isaiah 45:23 as Scriptural proof that all will stand before the judgment seat of God.[51]

---

produces the following partial listing: Matthew 16:27 ("The Son of Man is going to come in the glory of His Father with His angels; and will then recompense every man according to his deeds"); 25:31-46 (Sheep and Goat Judgment – the righteous are there, for how Christ's brethren were active in good works to their brethren is the thing judged); Hebrews 13:17 (Christian leaders give an account of the shepherding of their church members); 2 John 8 (a warning that some reward could be lost); 1 John 2:28 ("Little children, abide in Him, so that if He appears, we may have confidence and not shrink away from Him in shame at His coming"); 1 Corinthians 3:12-15 (Christians lose some reward, yet are saved, and it is a judgment scene); 1 Corinthians 4:5 (the judgment will bring to light the hidden counsels of the hearts); Revelation 22:12 ("to render to every man according to what he has done"); 2 Corinthians 5:10 (in words written to Christians Paul says, "For we must all appear before the judgment seat of Christ, that each one may be recompensed for his deeds in the body, according to what he has done, whether good or bad"); James 3:1 (Christian teachers receive greater judgment [condemnation]); 1 Timothy 5:12 (widows sentenced because they were not faithful to their obligations); 1 Timothy 3:6 (novice elders, condemned for pride); 1 John 4:17 ("we may have confidence in the day of judgment"); Colossians 3:25 (Christians get the consequences of the wrong done by them); Revelation 20:11-15 (at the Great White Throne Judgment, the righteous are there, for the sea [i.e., the sea of glass, where the redeemed are, Revelation 15:2] gave up the dead in it, and they are judged). These are just a few of the verses which plainly show Christians are judged, just as everyone else is.

[50] Paul uses a term (*bēma*, "judgment seat") with which his readers would have been familiar. The *bēma* was a raised platform, mounted by steps, located in the forum, on which the highest Roman official in the town would be seated on a portable seat, and hold court, adjudicating those cases that were brought before him, and dispensing justice. The Romans would know well the sight of a man standing before the judge's judgment seat, while his conduct was examined publicly. This is precisely what we expect to see when Jesus makes His second advent. Each individual (until all who have ever lived on earth has had his turn) will be summoned before God the judge, and his behavior will be examined publicly. Saints will receive rewards for their faithfulness; some will lose many of the rewards they might have had; others will be given retribution for their evil deeds. If it were not that Christ was there, standing beside the believers, pleading the blood He shed on their behalf on Calvary, that they might be justified by faith, all would be found guilty.

[51] Actually, the citation is taken freely from the LXX (with variations), and a portion of it is from Isaiah 49:18. (It is noteworthy that Paul applies this same Old Testament passage to Christ, at Philippians 2:10,11.)

"AS I LIVE, SAYS THE LORD. Where Isaiah 45:23 (in both the Hebrew and LXX) reads "By myself I have sworn," Paul substitutes a phrase of equivalent meaning from Isaiah 49:18. "Says the Lord" identifies the Speaker.[52] God is taking an oath, insisting that as sure as He is the living God, and there is none else besides Him, that is how sure it is there will be a judgment!

EVERY KNEE SHALL BOW TO ME. In neither Isaiah, nor here, nor at Philippians 2:10,11, is "every knee" restricted to the ungodly. That "all" will appear before God is seen in the words "every knee shall bow to Me." What God says about "every knee" surely applies to the Christian, and in that inclusiveness is the connection to Paul's warning to the strong and weak brothers that they too will be there. When men bow their knees to God, it is symbolic of their recognition of and submission to His right over them as supreme Judge.

AND EVERY TONGUE SHALL GIVE PRAISE TO GOD." The marginal reading is "shall confess[53] to God," and this is closer to the Hebrew which reads "shall swear to God." What is pictured in the Hebrew is each man answering Him under oath concerning his conduct. What is pictured in the NASB is that special kind of "praise to God" that follows a finished act of divine decision; it is an acknowledgment that what God has done as Judge is exactly right! It is from this passage theologians get the first part of their definition of the judgment – "It is a final vindication of God for the rewards and punishments already in part bestowed."[54] As everyone sees the verdict, he will recognize that perfect justice has been done; and he will "give praise to God," and this even if the verdict has been adverse.

14:12 – *So then each one of us shall give account of himself to God.*

So then. Paul has come to a summary conclusion. "So then" equals 'in accordance with the doctrine taught in that passage just quoted from Isaiah.'

---

[52] Here is an example of *kurios* without an article being a reference to Jehovah.

[53] The Greek word *exhomologeō* is capable of either meaning, "confess" or "praise." Arndt and Gingrich, *Lexicon*, p.276. When used with the meaning "confess," it often means to confess sins. Modern scholars have urged that when *exhomologeō* is used with the dative case following, it means "praise" offered to the person whose name is in the dative case.

[54] When an unjustified man dies, his soul goes to a temporary place of torment (designated as "Hades" in the New Testament) to await the final judgment. The torment experienced is severe, but not what it shall be for those who are cast into the lake of fire (Revelation 20:14). In contrast to this, when a righteous man dies, his soul goes to a temporary place of bliss (often designated as "Paradise," or as being "present with the Lord") to await the final judgment. The souls of the redeemed will accompany Jesus as He returns (1 Thessalonians 4:14), receive their resurrection bodies, stand in the judgment, and then be escorted to the place where there is no more hunger or thirst or dying, where they have access to the springs of the waters of life, and they have access to the tree of life that grows beside the river that flows from the throne of God (Revelation 2:7; 7:16,17; 22:1-3). A man either has eternal life abiding in him now, or he does not; it is not the judgment that decides this. The judgment is a vindication of God for what He did with the soul when the man died – whether it went to temporary punishment or temporary blessing. Following the judgment, the final punishment or the final blessing will be each soul's lot.

Each one of us shall give account of himself to God. There are four ideas in this summary. (1) Each ... of us. Note: *each* of us. It is an individual judgment. Not one will be exempted. (2) "Shall give account." Strong and weak brothers both will have to account for their attitudes and actions toward their brethren. (3) "Of himself." It is his own actions, not those of his brother, for which he must answer. (4) "To God." Not to the strong or weak brother, but to *God*, the omniscient, the holy, the righteous One. All of this tells us that responsibility naturally involves accountability. There is a beautiful life of liberty in Christ, but each Christian is accountable to God for how he uses his own freedom. This sobering thought will help each brother to judge his behavior now, so the account at the judgment seat of God is made with joy rather than shame.

14:13 – *Therefore let us not judge one another anymore, but rather determine this – not to put an obstacle or a stumbling block in a brother's way.*

Therefore let us not judge one another anymore. This phrase sums up the whole preceding paragraph. It is likely addressed to both strong and weak brothers, since both had been "judging" their brothers before they could criticize or ridicule. The present tense verb in this negative exhortation indicates this judging is something that is not to be done at any time. Since we are to give an account to God, and since we are on the same level (brothers), let us not suppose we have a right to sit in judgment on our fellow Christians in matters of opinion.

But rather determine this – .[55] This marks the transition to a new step in the argument. The following paragraph is addressed mainly to the strong brother, and teaches that there is no Christian liberty apart from Christian love.[56] That is, there are times when even the strong man is not at liberty to exercise his liberty.

Not to put an obstacle or a stumbling block in a brother's way. "Obstacle" here translates the same word (*skandalon*) that was translated "offense" (NASB) or "occasion of falling" (ASV) at 9:33. "Stumbling-block" was also explained at 9:33. Literally, the words picture putting an impediment in the path another person is taking, over which he stumbles, or falls down. Figuratively, the words are used of that which becomes the occasion of another person being hurt or trapped by sin.[57] In this context, it is the strong

---

[55] The same Greek verb (*krinō*) is translated "judge" in the previous phrase, and "determine" in this one. In verses 3-5 we had a similar example of Paul's using the same word in one passage with two different connotations. In Greek, as in English, the one word *krinō* can mean either "criticize" or "decide." For *krinō* used with the connotation of "decide" or "determine," see 1 Corinthians 2:21; 2 Corinthians 2:1; or Titus 3:12.

[56] This is not the first time in the hortatory part of this letter that Paul's specific instructions have been an unfolding of what it means to "love the brother." See 12:9, 13:8-10.

[57] The commentaries debate whether "obstacle" and "stumbling-block" refer to the same thing, or whether some occasions of tempting others to sin are more serious than others (since one word literally means a "block" against which the foot strikes, and the other is a "trap" in which it is caught). Alford distinguishes: an occasion of stumbling, an *act*; and offence, a *thought*. *Romans*, p.454. Lenski distinguishes between the two as though one injures, and the other involves being killed. "Our resolve must stand: never to hurt our brother spiritually nor – which is much worse – to kill him spiritually. The

brother's example which, when followed, leads the weak brother into sin, that is categorized as being an "obstacle" or a "stumbling-block."[58]   The man who puts a stumbling-block or obstacle in his brother's way is sinning, both against the weak brother and against Christ (1 Corinthians 8:12).

14:14 – *I know and am convinced in the Lord Jesus that nothing is unclean in itself; but to him who thinks anything to be unclean, to him it is unclean.*

I know and am convinced in the Lord Jesus.   Paul here uses a triple expression (know, convinced, in the Lord Jesus[59]) to convey the certitude of his own position in this matter. He identifies himself with the strong brother's position, and explains it is one he has held for some time.[60]   He grants, in principle, that the stronger brethren are right, but immediately shows that there are some instances in practice where, were the strong brother to exercise his right, it would be evidence of a lack of love.

That nothing is unclean in itself.   Here, we suppose, is a third example (meats vs. vegetarianism, and special days, being the first two) of the kind of things that strong and weak brethren might debate.[61]   This affirmation is another way of reasserting the principle of liberty in Christ.   The use of "unclean" in this verse, and "clean" in verse 20, leads us

---

trouble is that, when we offend a weak brother, we can never tell in advance whether he will be only injured or will be destroyed." *Romans*, p.833.   In contrast to this, many (e.g., Hodge, Gifford, Murray) would say the terms are synonymous when used figuratively.   Having earlier seen it is possible for a sinner who has been freed from sin to become entangled again in the old slavery (if he voluntarily presents himself to his old master enough times, Romans 6:16), we see no problem with assigning different meanings to the two words.

[58] Some suppose the words of verse 14 are addressed to the weak brother who is the one who has been "judging" (verse 3).   The supposition is that the weak brother, insisting that his view of things is the only Biblical one, may cause the strong brother to have doubts arise in his mind.   He then acts as before, but now his conscience bothers him, and thus the strong brother has been caused to stumble and sin. While this interpretation can be carried through verse 15, it is very difficult to explain the rest of the verses on the supposition they are addressed to the weak brother.

Verse 13 reminds us that Cain's indignant question, "Am I my brother's keeper?" is not one the strong brother should ask, as though his weaker brother's situation were of no concern to him.

[59] The KJV reads "by the Lord," and this sounds like Paul has been taught by Jesus on this topic.   While that may be true (see Mark 7:14-19, where Jesus taught on the subject of clean and unclean foods), "in the Lord" is a solemn form of asseveration.   From the very depths of his Christian consciousness, as a result of his union with Christ, his fellowship with Christ, Paul knows this to be true.   His beliefs are not based on human reason, or on his association with various men; his beliefs find their source in the Lord.

[60] "Know" is *oida*, absolute, positive knowledge, gained from an outside source (see comments at Romans 2:2).   "Am convinced" is *peithō* in the perfect tense.   It is a past completed action, with present continuing results.

[61] We can find no compelling reason to suppose that the meat vs. vegetarian debate was somehow related to the Mosaic legislation about clean and unclean meats.   Romans 15:7-13 does indicate there was something "Jewish" in at least some of the topics of debate, and we suppose this topic about clean and unclean meats is one.

to understand that what Paul writes here is a repudiation of the distinction between clean (those fit for food or sacrifice) and unclean (those not fit for food or sacrifice) animals taught in the Mosaic Law.[62] His statement reflects the fact that the Mosaic covenant was temporary, and that the old Mosaic distinctions have been abolished since Christ has come and inaugurated His new covenant. These animals are no longer unclean in themselves.[63] Paul flatly says, 'I do not hesitate to declare my own decided view, which is completely in harmony with submission to Jesus as Lord, that the scruples of weak brethren on the topic of unclean meats[64] are unfounded.' "Nothing is unclean" must be limited to the realm of the adiaphoristic.[65] The whole context since 14:1 has been talking about the "resources of the created world which are available for men's use,"[66] and it would be out of harmony with the demands of the context to give any wider meaning to things here described as clean or unclean.

But to him who thinks anything to be unclean, to him it is unclean. Having asserted again the principle of freedom in Christ, Paul proceeds to affirm that there are exceptions to the principle. For the weak brother, there is the limitation of his own conscience. For the strong brother, there is the limitation on his behavior that a loving consideration for his brother would make obligatory. Paul first points out that not all men have the inward confidence that he has just expressed. Probably there were many in the early church who, because of their background in Judaism, still had some haunting beliefs that the flesh of certain animals was not to be eaten.[67] With this hesitation in their minds, if they should go

---

[62] The LXX used the word *akathartos* ("common, unclean") as equivalent to the Hebrew *tame'*, but that Greek word also has a connotation that the thing "unclean" has been connected somehow with idolatry, which was not necessarily the case with the Hebrew, as one can ascertain by reading Leviticus 11. *Koinē*, not having a connotation of "association with idolatry," proved to be a satisfactory substitute for *akatharsia*. See Mark 7:2; Acts 10:14,28, 11:8; and Hebrews 10:29.

[63] Acts 15:29 (and similar passages) would put a limit on "nothing is unclean in itself" (verse 14) and "all things indeed are clean" (verse 20). There are some things that the Christian is to avoid because God has said so. Of course, when God created, it was all "good." It would not be proper to so interpret what Paul here writes as implying that God the Creator was responsible for making some things that are intrinsically evil. In fact, if certain things were intrinsically evil, the strong would be required to abstain from their use, just as they must abstain from the four things Acts 15:29 declares inharmonious with God's will.

[64] We speak particularly about "meat" because Paul himself does at verse 21.

[65] A thing is "adiaphora" if it is neither commanded nor prohibited in Scripture, and on that account is held to be an affair of the individual conscience. (*Webster's New International Dictionary*, 2nd Edition, p.32.)

[66] Cranfield, *Romans*, p.713.

[67] Some writers reject the Jewish provenance we have attributed to this paragraph. Those who do so believe there is something similar to 1 Corinthians 8-10 in this passage. Much of meat that was displayed for sale in the butcher shops had come from the nearby idols' temples (where a portion had been sacrificed to the idol, a portion had been eaten by the people who attended the banquet in honor of the idol, and what remained became the portion of the priests who served in the temple, who in turn sold it to the local butcher, who in turn offered it to the local citizenry for their meals at home). Some Christians, aware of the origin of much of the meat, were hesitant to eat it. 1 Corinthians specifically declares Christians are prohibited from attending the feasts in the idols' temples, but there is no prohibition on purchasing the meat from the

ahead and eat, the result will be that their consciences are bothered. A man should not violate his conscience. Before finishing this paragraph (see verses 22,23), Paul will return to this matter, and show that the man whose conscience bothers him is actually sinning if he eats. Before he does, though, he urges the strong brother to be considerate of others' scruples. Even though the weak brother's convictions have no basis in Scripture, to him[68] the meat is unclean, and his conviction is entitled to respect.

14:15 – *For if because of food your brother is hurt, you are no longer walking according to love. Do not destroy with your food him for whom Christ died.*

For if because of food your brother is hurt. With "for," Paul takes up the ideas he had introduced in verse 13b – obstacles and stumbling-blocks. The "brother" who is hurt is the weak brother. "Because of food" pictures the strong brother eating what he has a freedom to eat,[69] but with no respect for the effect of his actions on the weaker brother. Verse 14 has prepared us to understand the word "hurt." It is more than mere hurt feelings; it is moral affliction, i.e., the vexation of conscience.[70] Of course, the hurt does not come simply from watching the strong brother eat. What is implied is that the weak brother goes ahead and eats too, because of the influence of the strong brother's example.

You are no longer walking according to love. Once again, "you" is singular, and by this change from the previous plurals, Paul drives home to each individual reader the need to be considerate of his brother. Love (doing what is spiritually best for the other person), it has been pointed out (13:8-10), is the supreme rule by which Christians are to guide their behavior. It is not possible to cause grief while exercising your Christian liberty and to be acting out of love at the same time.

Do not destroy with your food him for whom Christ died. Not only does the inconsiderate behavior "destroy" the weak brother, but it also treats the death of Christ with contempt. The Greek prohibits the continuance of an action already going on,[71] so "Stop

---

local shops and eating it at home (with the one exception of consideration for a weaker brother's scruples, if the brother lets it be known he has problems with the source of the meat).

[68] Objectively, in the realm of liberty, there is nothing which cannot be brought into relation to God. But subjectively, there are things that, in the judgment of certain people, are unclean. "To him" (*ekeinos*, that one, emphatic) the actions are what his convictions make them. Conscience alone is not an infallible guide as to the right or wrong of a thing. But to act against one's conscience, even when the beliefs behind its promptings and accusations are misguided, is always wrong.

[69] The older translations read "meat" at this place, though the Greek is *brōma*, food of any kind. In old English, "meat" was a general word for food, whereas it now has the connotation of "flesh."

[70] As in verse 13 Paul used two words, "stumbling-block" and "obstacle (trap)," so here in verse 15 he uses two words, "hurt" and "destroy." Most writers think there is a correlation, and that "hurt" = "stumbling-block" while "destroy" = "obstacle."

[71] It is a present imperative with *mē*. See Romans 6, footnote #60.

destroying ... him!" would catch the idea. "Destroy" involves spiritual ruin, and ultimately includes perishing in hell.[72] It is something more serious than "hurt (grieve)" in the previous clause. No conduct of yours should tend to undo what Christ died to accomplish.[73] If Christ loved that man enough to die for him, is it too much to ask the strong brother to give up some article of food for him?

14:16 – *Therefore do not let what is for you a good thing be spoken of as evil;*

Therefore do not let what is for you a good thing be spoken of as evil. We suppose that this verse is addressed to the strong brother.[74] The "good thing" may well be the principle of Christian liberty which is the underlying topic of the whole paragraph.[75] The ones who are doing the "evil" speaking could be either the weak brothers[76] or non-church members.[77]

---

[72] The verb "destroy" is *apollumi*, the regular word used for "perishing" in hell. See notes at Romans 2:12. To the question of how the eating of food by the strong brother could be connected to, or contribute to, the perdition of the weak brother, several answers have been suggested. (1) The conscience is one of the God-given aids to keep a man from being lost. If a man is encouraged to violate his conscience, the time will come that it will quit working, and then the man is much more liable to be lost. (2) Lard (*Romans*, p.425) suggests that the destruction comes about in this fashion: the weak becomes so grieved at the actions of the strong, that he feels unable to live with him in the church, and so quits attending the services. Thus, his spiritual life declines until he at last perishes. Perhaps other answers could be given, but it should be observed that both of those given picture the "perishing" as a process, and this is as it should be, for the verb is a present tense verb in the Greek.

[73] Those who hold to the doctrine of unconditional eternal security (as taught by Calvin) struggle greatly with this passage. The passage plainly says it is possible for a redeemed man to be lost. That is why the strong brother must watch lest he contribute to the "destruction" of the weak brother.

[74] Not all writers have this exhortation addressed to the strong brother. They prefer to think of it as addressed to strong and weak alike. Gifford, for example, urges that in this passage the "plural is used when Paul wishes to express general principles (see verses 1,7-9,13,16, 15:1); the singular is used when he wishes to apply the principles to special cases (see verses 2-6,10,15,20-23)." *Romans*, p. 219. Gifford's note, in the main, appears correct, but it is not quite true, either at verse 1, nor here in verse 16, in this commentator's opinion. The verses on both sides of 16 are addressed to the stronger brother; therefore, we incline to the opinion that verse 16 is as well.

[75] Not all writers identify the "good thing" as being Christian liberty. Meyer and Lange suggest that "good thing" anticipates the expression "kingdom of God" in the next verse. Others think the "good thing" includes the whole Christian faith, i.e., the gospel.

[76] As strong Christians, we may have the liberty to do many things which our weak brothers think wrong. And when in their presence – and we know their feelings – were we to do such things, it would subject our liberty to unfriendly criticism. For the moment, the strong brother must refrain from exercising his liberty.

[77] Those who identify the one who does the evil speaking as being the weak brother can appeal to verse 3, and also to 1 Corinthians 10:30, for corroboration. Some question whether the weak brother would call the strong brother's 'liberty' a "good thing," at least in those particulars where he was confident the strong brother was abusing it. Lenski, who believes that outsiders are the ones speaking evil, writes, "When Christians are divided because of eating and drinking and other adiaphora such as clothing, cut of their hair, etc., outsiders certainly make sport of them and their Christianity, and these Christians themselves furnish the occasion and the reason for this." *Romans*, p.839.

14:17 – *for the kingdom of God is not eating and drinking, but righteousness and peace and joy in the Holy Spirit.*

For the kingdom of God is not eating and drinking. "For" shows us that the point of verse 17 is to give a reason for what was just said in 15b and 16. The idea is, 'You must remember the important thing about liberty is not using it selfishly to get what you want to eat or drink, but using it to produce righteousness, peace and joy.' This is the only place in Romans where Paul uses the expression "kingdom of God," and it is one of the few places in all his writings where Paul uses the expression for something presently existing.[78] "The Kingdom of God is the sphere of God's rule. In view, however, of the rebellion that has been raised against Him, the phrase most frequently signifies the sphere in which at any given time His rule is acknowledged."[79] The idea denoted by this phrase is little different from what earlier was called the "will" of God (12:2). Where men acknowledge His rule over their lives, selfishness is a thing of the past. Instead, the principles that govern the heart and action of His servants are unselfish ones.

But righteousness and peace and joy in the Holy Spirit. The context has been describing a man's relationship to men, not his relationship to God, so we shall interpret this passage in harmony with the context. "Righteousness," then, would not have the technical meaning it often has in Romans, namely, "God's way of saving man."[80] Instead, it would refer to 'right living, right dealings with our fellow men, a faithful discharge of all the duties which we owe to men and to God.' "Peace" would not have its technical meaning of a right relationship with God (often called reconciliation).[81] Instead, it would speak of harmonious relationships between brethren, even if they differ with us in matters of opinion. It speaks of a considerate course of behavior toward others that results from unity of heart and purpose. "Joy in the Holy Spirit" may mean personal satisfaction,[82] or

---

[78] The other places in Paul's writings where there is no doubt the "kingdom of God" is presently existing are 1 Corinthians 4:20 and 15:24. (The expression "kingdom" is also used by Paul with reference to the present manifestation of the rule of God, e.g., Colossians 1:13.) In other places where Paul uses "kingdom of God," the reference seems to be to God's rule subsequent to the return of Christ (e.g., Acts 14:22; 1 Corinthians 6:9,10; Galatians 5:21; Ephesians 5:5; 2 Thessalonians 1:5). In two places, it is not easy to decide if the reference is present or future (Colossians 4:11; 1 Thessalonians 2:12).

Some writers attempt to make Romans 14:17 a reference to the future kingdom, but this is hard to connect to verse 16. Verse 17 is a reason for how we live here and now, not information about the future kingdom of God.

[79] Vine, *Romans*, p.201,202. A brief introduction to the long and difficult topic of the "kingdom of God" can be found in the author's *New Testament History: Acts*, p.34-38.

[80] So the word is often used in the first four chapters of Romans. See especially 1:17 and 3:21,22.

[81] At Romans 5:1,2, we have had "peace" used in its technical sense.

[82] There would be a certain 'satisfaction' if the strong brother were to eat and drink what he wanted to. But it is not a lasting, permanent "joy." It may well be that because there is a "joy" the world can give, Paul needed to specify that he had in mind a different kind of joy, and so calls it "joy in the Holy Spirit."

it may mean doing things the Spirit suggests that will bring joy to others,[83] or it may mean joy in one another kindled by the Holy Spirit.[84]   When these great principles that govern life in the kingdom of God are known and understood, then it is easy to see how wicked is any behavior that would "destroy the brother for whom Christ died."[85]

14:18 – *For he who in this* **way** *serves Christ is acceptable to God and approved by men.*

For he who in this *way* serves Christ.   Verse 18 seems to be connected to the rest of the passage as an explanation of what has been said in verses 16 and 17.   Instead of resulting in men "speaking evil," living as verse 17 calls for will result in their approval.   When men submit to the rule of God in their lives, they have the approval of God.   "In this way" surely points back to the behavior toward others signified in "righteousness, peace, and joy."[86]   "Serves Christ" may reflect Jesus' own words, "to the extent that you did it to one of these brothers of Mine, *even* the least *of them*, you did it to Me" (Matthew 25:40).   The verb "serves" is present tense: 'keeps serving Christ.'[87]   "He who feels free to eat meat may be serving Christ as much as the one who abstains, but neither one nor the other can serve Him if righteousness, peace and joy in the Holy Spirit are lacking."[88]

Is acceptable to God.   "Justification" is something God imputes over and over again in

---

[83] The interpreter must make a decision whether the words "in the Holy Spirit" are intended to qualify all three words (righteousness, peace, and joy), or just the third word alone.   The indwelling Spirit does help the Christian to live a life pleasing to God (Romans 8).   It may well be that we should read this verse as though all three actions are prompted by the indwelling Spirit.

[84] When strong brothers "welcome" weak ones without arguing over scruples; when weak ones receive the strong brothers without criticism; when each acts in such a way as to promote the other's highest good, there is a joy in each other.   It results from both strong and weak permitting the Holy Spirit to lead and guide them in all their actions.

[85] Modern religious liberalism has made much of verse 17, as though how one acts toward his fellow man is *all* there is to the kingdom of God.   To so handle the verses (and speak of spreading the kingdom by establishing a better social, economic, governmental, and personal justice in the world, by reforms, by abolition of wars, etc.) is to miss the context of the book of Romans in which this verse is found.   God's way of saving man comes before righteousness, peace, and joy in the kingdom of God.   It takes a right relationship with God to produce a right relationship with man.

[86] Some have supposed "in this way" refers back to the phrase "in the Holy Spirit" (verse 17).   Alford rightly objects to making a subordinate member of the previous verse the emphatic one in this verse.   It is this verse that helps us decide that, in this context, "righteousness and peace and joy" are active principles of the Christian life.

[87] *Ho douleuōn* ("the one who serves") reminds us of Romans 6:19, about presenting ourselves and our members as "servants" (*douloi*, slaves) to God, after being freed from the dominion of sin.   Too, the word *douleuō*, unlike *diakoneō*, means having no will of our own, but being controlled and directed by the will of our master, Jesus Christ.

[88] Vine, *Romans*, p.202.

the Christian's life. When God sees the Christian being faithful in his motives[89] and actions (when He sees "righteousness and peace and joy," for example), He is well-pleased, and He continues to reckon that man as "righteous." And when this life is over, and the Christian must stand before the judgment seat of God (verse 10), he need never fear.

And approved by men. The man who uses his liberty within the guidelines of "righteousness and peace and joy" will win the goodwill of his brother, rather than putting an obstacle or stumbling-block in his way. Of course, not all men will approve.[90] But if a Christian man has the disposition described in verse 17, chances are that not only his weak brother, but also his unconverted neighbors, will approve of the way he uses his liberty.

14:19 – *So then let us pursue the things which make for peace and the building up of one another.*

So then. As before (7:25, 8:12), "so then" introduces a summary drawn from what has just been said.

Let us pursue[91] the things which make for peace. On the basis of what has been said about the kingdom of God and serving Christ, this exhortation embraces one aim that all Christians should have. "Peace" here likely denotes peace with one's fellow Christians. Paul is encouraging all the brethren to lay aside their contentious ways, whether it be the strong thoughtlessly putting obstacles and stumbling-blocks in a brother's way, or the weak being critical and judgmental.

And the building up of one another. Such building up of one another can proceed effectively only under conditions of peace. "Building up" is here a figurative designation for promoting growth in the Christian's life and character. "To 'edify another' is to build up a stable Christian character in him,"[92] to spiritually strengthen all that pertains to faith and inner life. And observe that it is a mutual thing; it is something we are to do for one

---

[89] "Man looks at the outward appearance, but the Lord looks at the heart" (1 Samuel 16:7).

[90] "Approved" is *dokimos*, "put to the test for the purpose of being approved, and having met specifications, having the stamp of approval placed upon one."

[91] There is a difference of opinion as to whether the verb here is indicative (a statement, "we are pursuing," as the NASB margin reads), or subjunctive (an exhortation, "Let us pursue"). Somewhere along the way there has been the same kind of scribal error we learned about at Romans 5:1. The difference between the indicative and the subjunctive is one letter in the spelling of the Greek word, and the manuscript evidence is nearly divided evenly. In light of this, the interpreter must resort to the context for help. Since verse 20 is imperative, one could naturally conclude that Paul was exhorting in verse 19, too.

[92] Bruce, *Romans*, p.252. "The word has unfortunately lost its freshness of meaning, but we have no other single equivalent for it in English. It is the upbuilding, or mutual help and assistance in the spiritual life, which Christians receive from their [dealings and communion] with each other." Sanday, *Romans*, p.147. Compare 2 Corinthians 10:8, 13:10; 1 Corinthians 14:4. According to the context in each case, the individual, as here, or the church, or the whole Christian body, is a building of God (of which Christ is the foundation, 1 Corinthians 3:11), on which the work of building is to proceed until the second coming.

another. Both the strong and weak brother need to grow. Perhaps the strong brother needs to grow in love; the weak brother needs to grow in knowledge of God's Word. In the first part of chapter 14, the encouragement was to "accept (welcome) one another." Now it is "build up one another." If we stopped with the first encouragement, it might give the impression that Christians are to leave each other alone, and let the weak remain weak, and let the strong remain oblivious to others' needs. But this second admonition explains further. We do not leave each other alone. We try to help each other in the faith, and build up each other's spiritual lives.

14:20 – *Do not tear down the work of God for the sake of food. All things indeed are clean, but they are evil for the man who eats and gives offense.*

Do not tear down the work of God for the sake of food. This command is addressed to the strong brother, as the return to the singular suggests. 'Stop tearing down the work of God!' is Paul's admonition, prohibiting the continuance of an action already going on. What the strong brother has been doing in his insensitive exercise of freedom is the opposite of "building up."[93] The "work of God" being pulled down in the context is the other brother's spiritual life.[94] Any time the strong brother's eating of "food"[95] will tend to wreck the Christian life and character of another, the strong brother is not to eat.

All things indeed are clean. The same thought as in verse 14 is repeated in order to enter further into the meaning of "not ... for the sake of food." Paul has not relinquished one iota his conviction that Jewish dietary laws are no longer valid.[96] There is freedom in Christ in this matter; yet just as verse 14 indicated, there are limitations to a man's freedom to act. Paul now he indicates what it means to ignore these limitations.

But they are evil for the man who eats and gives offense. As the marginal note indicates, "gives offense" is an interpretation of what the Greek says, which is simply "with offense."[97] It is sinful[98] for the strong brother to eat (what otherwise he has a freedom in

---

[93] The word *kataluō* means "pull down, tear down" – like wrecking a building – and continues the figure of 'erecting a building' (build up) in verse 19.

[94] Other explanations have been proposed for "the work of God." Barnes understands it to be a reference to the whole congregation (rather than the individual's spiritual life) that was being wrecked by the strong brother's behavior. He appeals to 1 Corinthians 3:9-15 as being a parallel passage. Another suggestion is that the "work of God" is the extension of Christianity to new areas. It usually is true that where there is internal strife in a congregation, they are not much involved in mission work. One even wonders if Paul is fearful that the strong vs. weak contention at Rome may endanger his hopes of being sent by the Roman church on his planned evangelistic trip to Spain.

[95] See comments above at verse 15 on *brōma*, "food."

[96] This time he uses the regular word for "*clean* animals" found in the LXX version, *katharos*.

[97] "With offense as an attendant circumstance" is the idea in *dia* and the accusative case. "Offense" here is the same word translated "stumbling-block" in verse 13. Some have supposed that it is the weak brother who is hurting himself as he eats, rather than the strong brother offending someone else. We would reply that verse 23 deals with the weak brother's eating while his conscience bothers him. Verse

Christ to eat) in such a way as to put a stumbling-block in another's way.   After stating what is *wrong*, Paul will follow with a statement of what is *right*.

14:21 – *It is good not to eat meat or to drink wine, or* **to do anything** *by which your brother stumbles.*

It is good not to eat meat.   The whole subject since verse 2 is summed up in this one verse, which is a maxim addressed to the strong brother.[99]   In contrast to the sin ("evil") involved in eating in such a way as to be a stumbling-block, this abstinence is designated as "good," that is, morally right, noble, a beautiful thing to do.   "Meat" here is *kreas*,[100] flesh-meat, a word that is more specific than "food" in verse 20.   The strong brother, whose freedom in Christ permits him to eat any kind of food, has more room to maneuver than does the weak brother.   On occasion,[101] he can eat a whole meal of vegetables, and his conscience will not bother him.   But the weak brother who thinks God expects him to be a vegetarian cannot (on any occasion) eat meat with a clear conscience.   Who, then, should concede?   The only one who can, the strong brother.

Or to drink wine.   This phrase shows that drinking wine was a problem for some in the early church, and Paul puts this problem in the realm of the adiaphoristic in this context in Romans.[102]   It is not known for certain why the drinking of wine was seen to be objection-

---

20, we believe, deals with the strong brother.   To so understand verse 20 makes the transition to verse 21 easier.   Furthermore, the whole context immediately preceding has been addressed to the stronger brother (whenever the singular verb is used).

[98] The word is *kakon*, "evil."   It does not mean merely "hurtful" or "bad" (in the sense that it is not good for him).   Paul is asserting that the strong brother is sinning when he uses his freedom inconsiderately.   Compare 1 Corinthians 8:12, "And thus, by sinning against the brethren and wounding their conscience when it is weak, you sin against Christ."

[99] There is a contrast between the previous verse and this one.   "A thing in itself indifferent may be wrong if it injures the conscience of others; but on the other hand, to give up what will injure others is a noble act."   Sanday and Headlam, *Romans*, p.393.

[100] Wuest (*Romans on the Greek New Testament* [Grand Rapids: Wm. B. Eerdmans Publishing Co., 1955], p.241) asserts that *kreas* is the flesh of an animal offered in sacrifice to an idol.   However, Arndt and Gingrich, *Lexicon*, p.450, simply give the meaning as "meat."   See notes at Romans 14:2 and 14:14 where the particular problem that "meat" presented for some was discussed.

[101] "It is possible that aorist infinitives were used in this verse ["eat" and "drink"] because Paul was thinking of specific occasions when eating or drinking might cause a brother to stumble, rather than of continuous abstention ... but we should not care to put it more strongly."   Cranfield, *Romans*, p.724.

[102] For one whose personal convictions are total abstinence from alcoholic drinks, it is not easy to write with objectivity on this phrase.   It seems to this commentator that many are simply looking to justify and indulge in a desired behavior; thus, he is concerned that anything he writes may serve to encourage others to go ahead and drink.   In the spirit of verse 19, he urges all Christians to weigh seriously all the negatives that can be said about drinking wine, and to adopt the lifestyle of total abstinence as *the* way to go.

able by the weak brothers.[103]   But when some brother makes his qualms and hesitations known, the others will respect his convictions and abstain lest they put a stumbling-block or obstacle in their brother's path.   If occasional meatless meals are the thing encouraged in the previous phrase, then, by parity of reasoning, this phrase would teach occasional abstinence.[104]

Or *to do anything* by which your brother stumbles.   This statement broadens the application of the principle to more than the three or four items Paul has specifically mentioned as being scruples of the weak.   It requires the strong brother to abstain (as the occasion may demand) from any similar thing, any course of conduct, in the realm of the adiaphora.   A brother in Christ "stumbles" when he behaves in a fashion for which his conscience bothers him.[105]   The next verse will show that such "stumbling" is actually sin,

---

[103] Several attempts have been made to explain why "wine" was objectionable to some of the brothers. (1) Wine available in the markets had been used as libations in the idols' temples, just like most meat had been.   Those who thought the meat to be "unclean" would also think the wine to be no longer fit for Christian consumption.   (2) Perhaps the objection came from certain ascetics for whom their whole diet was a matter of serious concern.   It is supposed that the same people who were vegetarians also had scruples about wine.   Some have argued that the weak brothers at Rome tended to be ascetics; that is, Jewish Christians who had been influenced by some of the principles of the Essenes – principles which included a prohibition of marriage, vegetarianism, and abstinence from wine altogether.   (3) Nazarites were not allowed to drink wine (Numbers 6:3), and the Rechabites (Jeremiah 35:1-13) drank no wine. With these Old Testament examples of "holy" men to guide them, perhaps some Christians concluded it was unlawful for Christians to drink wine.   (4) Perhaps in the background were practices involved on Jewish holy days and festivals.   According to commentators on Acts 2:13-15, it was customary to abstain from wine during the festal seasons, and since this chapter in Romans also speaks of observing special days (Romans 14:5,6), perhaps this is the abstinence the weaker brother had in mind.

Since there is no way to know for sure whether it was ex-Jews or ex-Gentiles who now had a conscience about wine, any interpretation or application of the passage that depends on a specific identification is surely suspect.   For example, if one were to attempt to justify his own proclivities to drink by relying on the supposition that this objection (in verse 21) to drinking wine was some Jewish taboo, and therefore something that Christians should no longer be concerned about, would be to ask the passage to bear more than it likely should.

[104] As indicated in footnote #101, it is by no means sure that the aorist verbs "eat" and "drink" are limited to occasional acts or particular occasions.   Let us see how this question leads to two entirely opposite applications of this passage to today's readers.   (1) Those who think it is "occasional" would also make a present-day application that "drinking wine" is not in itself wrong.   "Many Christians today think that drinking wine is a sin in itself.   Some think that the Bible forbids its use even in moderation; others mistakenly identify drinking wine with drunkenness and thus wrongly conclude that because the latter is a sin, so is the former.   But inasmuch as Paul uses wine as an example of the kind of thing that a Christian is *free to use, unless it offends others*, it is evident that its use is not itself a violation of God's law and therefore is not a sin.   Note carefully that Romans 14:21 *does not read*:   'it is right not to eat meat or *get drunk* or do anything that makes your brother stumble.'   The reason is evident; *getting drunk is a sin* whether it offends a brother or not, whereas *drinking wine is not wrong unless* it results in drunkenness or causes others to stumble."   Wilson, *Romans*, p.227,228.   (2) Those who see Paul commanding continuous abstention for the rest of a man's life will find in this passage a prohibition of all wine drinking. "The caution here shows us what should be done now in regard to the use of wine.   It may not be possible to prove that wine is absolutely unlawful, but still many friends of temperance regard it as such, and are grieved at its use.   They esteem the habit of using it as tending to intemperance, and as encouraging those who cannot afford expensive liquors ... In this state of the case, does not the command of the apostle here require the friends of temperance to abstain even from the use of wine?"   Barnes, *Romans*, p.316

[105] See notes at Romans 14:13 and 14:15 on "stumbling-block."   Paul does not say "might stumble," for no one can know what might occur sometime, someplace.   He says "stumbles," present tense,

and thus Paul has spelled out the gravity of the strong brother's example which encouraged the weaker one to go ahead in the (what for the weaker brother is) questionable behavior.

14:22 – *The faith which you have, have as your own conviction before God.* *Happy is he who does not condemn himself in what he approves.*

The faith which you have, have as your own conviction before God. This is one verse that suggests the strong brother abstains only when in the weak brother's presence. "Faith" in this place is a "firm and intelligent conviction before God that one is doing what is right, the antithesis of feeling self-condemned in what one permits oneself to do."[106] It is the same "faith" spoken of in 14:1,2 and 14:23. "Have as your own conviction before God" says that you need not give up the principle of freedom in Christ as a general guide for behavior in matters indifferent, nor do you need to think anything is wrong which was not actually so, but there are times when God should be the only witness[107] to your free behavior. There is no reason why the stronger brother should hesitate to abstain in those moments when it will help the weaker brother to keep from stumbling; after all, in his private life, where he will give no offense to his brother, he may live according to the freedom God has granted him.

Happy is he who does not condemn himself in what he approves. "Happy" is a translation of the word *makarios*, which is the same word translated "blessed" in the beatitudes. It means spiritually happy, blessed, spiritually prosperous.[108] If we think of this statement as being closely related to what precedes, the beatitude would be pronounced on the strong brother, and the idea would be something like this: 'Happy is the man who abstains when he runs the risk of causing his brother to stumble, for he will be saved from passing sentence upon himself for his sinful actions.' If we think of this statement as being closely related to what follows (and notice that verse 23 begins with "but"), the beatitude would be pronounced on all men, strong and weak alike, and the idea would be something like this: 'Happy is the man who can eat and drink what he pleases,[109] without any qualms of conscience to condemn him for doing so.'

---

stumbles regularly, whenever the stumbling-block is placed in his way. The implication is that the strong brother knows the fact that the weaker brother is behaving in a way his conscience condemns.

[106] Bruce, *Romans*, p.253. There is a manuscript variation at this place which causes some to treat the first three words as a question ('You [emphatic], do you have faith?'), followed by an instruction how to live it: 'Have it to yourself before God!'

[107] "Before God" is explained as though He, rather than the weak brother, is the witness of the stronger one's behavior. It is conceivable that "before God" is also a reminder that men need to be reverent, remembering they are always being watched by God, who passes judgment on their acts now, and will do so at His judgment seat.

[108] The happiness meant is not so much the future "Messianic blessedness," as Meyer (*Romans*, p.521) thinks, but is rather the present blessedness that results from a clear conscience and an undoubting mind.

[109] Again, *dokimazō*, as in verse 18 (and 12:2), means "to approve after having put to the test and finding that what has been tested meets specifications." Compare Wuest, *Romans*, p.241.

14:23 – *But he who doubts is condemned if he eats, because* his eating is *not from faith; and whatever is not from faith is sin.*

But he who doubts is condemned if he eats. The connection is this: "It is indeed a happy thing to have no self-condemnatory scruples of conscience, but, on the other hand, it is fatal to have scruples and ignore them."[110] The one who "doubts" is the one who is not "fully convinced in his own mind" (verse 5). One moment he thinks it is permissible; the next moment, it may not be. The result is that he is uncertain in his mind what his course of action should be. Whether it is the man's own conscience that is thought of as "condemning"[111] him for his actions, or whether it is God who does the condemning, is not easily decided. It is not possible to rule out the meaning "liable to divine penal judgment," since the next phrase classifies his doubting action as "sin."[112]

Because *his eating is* **not from faith.** This states the reason he is "condemned:" his eating was not in harmony with his moral convictions.[113] There can be all kinds of influences contributing to one's lack of courage to stand for his convictions: he may sometimes do something because everyone else is doing it; he may do it because he does not wish to stand in a minority of one; he may do it because he does not wish to appear different; he may do it because he does not wish to court ridicule and unpopularity.

And whatever is not from faith is sin.[114] This last phrase is a "sentence about which there has been much controversy down the centuries and about which interpreters still differ extensively."[115]

- How widely may this statement be taken? Does it apply only to Christians and refer simply to the adiaphoristic matters which have been the topic of this section of Romans? Or can it be interpreted, as Augustine did,[116] to mean that all acts of non-Christians are nothing but sin? If we reject "all acts," can it be used to show all acts for which a man's conscience bothers him (whether he is a Christian or non-Christian),

---

[110] Sanday, *Romans*, p.147.

[111] The word in this verse is *katakrinō*, "condemn," whereas in the previous verse it was simply *krinō*, "judge."

[112] Wuest (*Romans*, p.242) declares in favor of both options: "It is not only that his own conscience pronounces clearly against him after the act, but that such action incurs the condemnation of God." The only change we would make is to change "after the act" to read "even during the act," for men's consciences do bother them even while they are acting in a way that to their own mind is doubtful.

[113] Whatever meaning is assigned to "faith" in Romans 14:1, the same meaning will apply here. We understand it to mean "subjective faith, a personal assurance or conviction."

[114] Some manuscripts have a doxology (the one that we have at 16:25-27) following this last phrase. See this problem discussed in the Introductory Studies.

[115] Cranfield, *Romans*, p.728.

[116] Augustine, *Contra Julianum*, 4.32.

are sin? Hardly! Such an interpretation would be to ignore the context, which is dealing with a Christian's behavior.

- Does "faith" mean objective faith or subjective faith. The only way it could be taken as objective faith is to completely ignore the context.[117] Especially in light of verse 14b, which says the same thing as verse 23c, note once more that the context is dealing with personal convictions. Verse 23 opens with the words "doubts" and "condemned." We ought not ignore what Paul wrote immediately prior to this last phrase.

- Finally, there is the word "sin" to consider. By using this word "sin" to characterize the act of the man who goes against his conscience, Paul is telling us how God views the act. Verses 20 and 23 have emphasized that it is possible for both strong and weak brothers to "sin" in this area of Christian liberty. The strong brother may abuse his freedom, and in so doing he sins (verse 20). And when the weak brother does what he thinks he should not, that too is sin (verse 23). Freedom in Christ is a blessed thing (verse 22), but it is fraught with serious responsibility.

15:1 – *Now we who are strong ought to bear the weaknesses of those without strength and not* just *please ourselves.*

Now.[1] The translators have treated the Greek particle *de* as though it were continuative, and this appears to be correct. Chapter 15, at least as far as verse 13, does not take up a new topic, but continues Paul's instructions to strong and weak brothers concerning their behavior toward each other in the area of Christian liberty.

We who are strong. As in 14:13-19, Paul identifies himself as being one of the "strong" brothers; this fact seems to imply that in the four areas of dispute identified in chapter 14, the strong brother was doctrinally right. In this verse, for the first time in this whole discussion, Paul uses the term "strong" for the brother who in 14:2,22 was identified as having "faith."

Ought to bear the weaknesses of those without strength. The Christian ethic includes more than simple avoidance of the wrong; there is also a positive action to be taken. Not only must the strong brother avoid using his liberty so as to give offense (14:20), but also the strong brother has an obligation to help the weak brother to bear his weakness. The

---

[117] To this commentator's dismay, he finds that many of the non-instrument Church of Christ brethren attempt to treat "faith" in this verse as objective faith. By taking "faith" in an objective sense, they find their basis for saying that unless God has commanded it, it is an innovation, and is therefore sin. The implications of such a treatment of "faith" are difficult to sustain. Would our non-instrumental brethren agree with Augustine, who also took "faith" as objective? As has been noted, his interpretation led to the suggestion that the whole life of the unbeliever is sin, even his morality and virtue. And how shall our non-instrumental brethren harmonize their ideas about strict conformity to a "blueprint" in all things with Romans 14-15, which allows freedom in Christ, along with its consequent differences in behavior? (More will be said on this matter of faith and opinion in Special Study #9 following notes at Romans 15:13.)

[1] Some manuscripts end Romans with chapter 14, except for the addition of the benediction now found at 16:25-27. For the student interested in critical problems, extensive notes have been given in the Introductory Studies concerning the problem of the integrity of chapters 15 and 16. Chapter 15 continues without interruption the thought of chapter 14.

word "ought" is the first word in the Greek sentence, and thus the moral responsibility[2] of the strong brother toward the weak is emphasized. "Without strength" is used to describe those who earlier were denoted by the expression "weak in faith" (14:1). "Weaknesses" would be the "hurts" (14:15), the scruples, the embarrassments, the doubts, the possibility of an accusing conscience, with which the weak brother found himself burdened. Paul uses the same word of 'bearing' the weaknesses of others that is used of Christ's bearing His cross (John 19:17).[3] In the world, men who are weak are often oppressed and made to suffer even more by those who have power; in the kingdom of God, the strong expresses his strength by helping the weak, not by making him suffer.

And not *just* please ourselves. Refusal to help bear the burdens of others is mere selfishness. "It is the pleasing of ourselves regardless of how this pleasing affects others that is here condemned."[4] If nothing more is at stake than mere self-indulgence, the Christian is not free to use his liberty if at the same time a brother is hurt by his actions. The strong brother will have to take some forethought on the matter, if his self-restraint and self-denial are to have the effect of bearing the weaknesses of those without strength.[5]

15:2 – *Let each of us please his neighbor for his good, to his edification.*

Let each of us please his neighbor for his good. The strong brother is exhorted to make it his aim to please his neighbor in those matters that will contribute to his neighbor's absolute good.[6] "Please" him is the opposite of "grieve" ('hurting') him (14:15). It pleases him because it removes a source of temptation for him to do that thing, and makes his attempt to live a life pleasing to God easier. "For his good" puts a limit on what Paul

---

[2] The word is *opheilō*, from the same root as "ought" in Romans 1:14, 8:12, 13:7,8. As Paul enforces this duty he does not say '*You* have an obligation'; instead, he writes '*We* have an obligation.' Psychologically, "We must do this!" is a much better way to encourage others in their behavior, than "You must do this!"

[3] We have previously had the word *bastazō* at Romans 11:18 (where the NASB translated it "supports"). The verb means "to take up and carry a load for someone." It does not suggest the idea of good humor in tolerating the weaknesses of the other, or of adjusting oneself to something that is a nuisance. It does speak of something that requires strength and sacrifice to do, but it is gladly shouldered in order to *help* the one who needs help. Galatians 6:2,5 speak of the mutual helpfulness we can render to each other. We are to bear our own burdens, and bear one another's burdens. Amos 3:2 also deals with 'the peril of privilege.' Those chosen of God, blessed above all nations, also have a greater responsibility. Likewise, God has ordained that in the area of liberty, those blessed by "strength" shall pay special attention to the conscientious scruples of the weak.

[4] Hendriksen, *Romans*, p.470.

[5] Compare 1 Corinthians 10:31-33, "Whether, then, you eat or drink or whatever you do, do all to the glory of God. Give no offense either to Jews or to Greeks or to the church of God; just as I also please all men in all things, not seeking my own profit, but the *profit* of the many, that they may be saved." That sentence summarizes Paul's instructions to the Corinthians in a similar circumstance regarding the use and abuse of Christian liberty.

[6] See notes at 8:28 and 13:4 for an explanation of "good."

means by "pleasing his neighbor."[7]   Paul does not mean that the strong must always defer to the whims and wishes of others, but he is to defer when such deferential actions[8] will help the other obey God's will, and contribute to his salvation.

To his edification.   The Greek simply reads "unto edification"[9]; whether it is the building up of the congregation, or the building up of the individual Christian's character, we come out at nearly the same place.   If it is the building up of the congregation, then this passage would imply that selfishness (such as 15:1 condemned) is one of the major causes of congregational disharmony and decline.   Not only are people judgmental and derogatory in their actions toward each other, but if the weak brother is wounded often enough, he will be driven from the congregation, away from the influences of the Lord and the church.   If it is the building up of the brother, then this passage implies that the strong brother need not abstain at all times – only when the weaker brother will be helped.   If the weak brother is not edified, there is no reason for the strong brother to forego his liberty.   If the weak brother is only flattered that his scruples are recognized, or if the strong brother's actions will only be wrongly interpreted as condoning of wrong doing, in such instances it may necessitate that the strong brother exercise his liberty.[10]   "To please my neighbor, in the sense of this verse, is not weakly to comply with his desires, but to act with a view to his lasting benefit."[11]

15:3 – *For even Christ did not please Himself; but as it is written, "THE REPROACHES OF THOSE WHO REPROACHED THEE FELL UPON ME."*

For.   Both verses 3 and 4 begin with "for," and we suppose they give a reason for what has just been said in verse 2.   In case someone replies "Why should I?" Paul holds up the example of Christ (verse 3) and the words of Scripture (verse 4) to enforce his exhortation to the strong brother.

Even Christ did not please Himself.   We might have expected Paul to write that Christ

---

[7] In some passages (Galatians 1:10; Ephesians 6:6; 1 Thessalonians 2:4), Paul condemns actions that are intended simply to please men.   Yet here in Romans 15:2 and in 1 Corinthians 9:20-23, Paul made the pleasing of men a leading principle of Christian conduct.   So there is a wrong way to please men, and a right way to please them.   It is wrong if it hurts them, or contributes to their possible condemnation; it is right if it helps them on their way to heaven.

[8] "Actions," in this context, refer to the realm of Christian liberty, the act of the strong Christian foregoing a legitimate act because the weaker brother thinks it to be wrong, and might be tempted to sin by violating his conscience while he copies the conduct of the stronger brother.

[9] See notes at Romans 14:19 on "building up" for the meaning of the word translated "edification."

[10] A word of caution seems appropriate.   Paul has already warned about not just pleasing ourselves (15:1).   It is so much easier to please ourselves than it is to bear the weaknesses of the weak.   And it is rather easy to justify such selfish actions in our own minds.   All one needs to do is to think to himself that "my behavior in this area of liberty is justified" because "if I were to act in a self-denying way, it would give my neighbor the wrong impression."   It is such a short step to disobedience of the spirit of what Paul here writes to the strong brother about how he orders his behavior.

[11] Vine, *Romans*, p.205.

was bearing other people's burdens when He went to Calvary, or that He was acting for other people's good in accomplishing salvation.[12]   Instead, in words that recall what was just written in 15:1 ("not just please ourselves"), he points to the motive that filled Jesus' heart and led Him to do what was best for those whom He loved.   His way was to consider others first, to be concerned with their interests, and help them in any way possible.   Now if Jesus did not just please Himself while He was incarnate, then neither should any of His disciples.

But as it is written.   Psalm 69:10 is quoted to show that Christ was not merely self-seeking while He was incarnate.[13]

"THE REPROACHES OF THOSE WHO REPROACHED THEE FELL UPON ME."   Now we understand that "did not please Himself" does not mean that Jesus suffered against His will, rather than voluntarily.   Now we understand that Jesus acted in such a way as to shield another from hurt.   The insults that might have been directed at the Father were borne by Jesus instead.[14]   Jesus could have avoided all this simply by choosing the selfish path, but He did not.   So devoted was He in His efforts to help others with their burdens that not even the reproaches of God's enemies would deter Him.   "What an obligation have we to abstain from self-gratification, submitting to the restraint involved therein in order to advance the welfare of others!   How insignificant is any inconvenience or suffering caused to us in comparison with the sufferings which Christ endured."[15]

15:4 – *For whatever was written in earlier times was written for our instruction, that through perseverance and the encouragement of the Scriptures we might have hope.*

For whatever was written in earlier times was written for our instruction.   The connection of verse 4 with the context is a bit obscure.   But as we commented on verse 3,

---

[12] Compare 2 Corinthians 8:9; Philippians 2:5-8; and see also Paul's appeal to the example of Christ in 1 Corinthians 11:1 (just after his summary of how to use one's Christian liberty in 1 Corinthians 10:31-33). Matthew 20:28 reads, "the Son of Man did not come to be served, but to serve, and to give His life a ransom for many."

[13] Psalm 69 is one of the Passion Psalms (Psalm 22 is another).   It is typico-Messianic – not relating entirely to Messiah, but it is often cited in the New Testament as having Messianic import.   Next to Psalm 110 and Psalm 22, it is Psalm 69 that is most-quoted in the New Testament.   Paul has told us in Romans 11:9 that David is the author of this Psalm.

Some have thought it surprising that Paul did not cite Jesus' own words rather than quoting an Old Testament verse.   However, Paul has already told us that the gospel was foreshadowed in the Old Testament (Romans 1:2, 3:21), and he has also shown that the suffering of Jesus was part of God's eternal plan to redeem men.   Furthermore, at this time, Paul's readers would have copies of the Old Testament available for study, and might not have many copies of the Gospels (only Matthew has been written, and its destination was Palestine).   Therefore, for his readers, especially those of Jewish background, the Old Testament Scriptures would be an effective appeal.

[14] In the Psalm, David speaks the words with regard to himself, saying that he is bearing wicked men's reproaches that, if he were not there, would have been directed against God.   Paul transfers the words to Christ, and has Him addressing this statement to God, just as David did.

[15] Vine, *Romans*, p.206.

we suggested that Paul appeals both to the example of Christ and to Scripture to enforce his exhortation to the strong brother.   Though Psalm 69 is Messianic, there is a truth there that will help the Christian who is expected to imitate Christ.   There is an enduring value in "whatever was written in earlier times," i.e., the Old Testament,[16] even though the Mosaic covenant was but a temporary arrangement.   Christians can receive "instruction" from a study of the Old Testament writings.[17]   God, the author of those Old Testament Scriptures, "had this purpose, had it when he first caused the writing; he thought of us and of our needs long centuries ago and stored up for us in a permanent form all this Scripture instruction so that it would not be lost."[18]

---

[16] The Old Testament books that make up the Psalms, the Prophets, and the Holy Writings were all written "in earlier times," that is, before the time in which Paul and his readers lived.   Henry R. Halley, *Pocket Bible Handbook*, 17th edition, pages 348,349, has a brief but excellent summary of information on "The Old Testament Canon."   Among other things, he quotes Josephus to the effect that Jews considered the Old Testament Canon as fixed ever since the days of Artaxerxes (i.e., the time of Ezra, c.430 BC).   Here are Josephus' words: "We have but 22 books, containing the history of all time, books that are believed to be divine.   Of these, 5 belong to Moses, containing his laws and the traditions of the origin of mankind down to the time of his death.   From the death of Moses to the reign of Artaxerxes the prophets who succeeded Moses wrote the history of the events that occurred in their own time, in 13 books.   The remaining 4 books comprise hymns to God and precepts for the conduct of human life.   From the days of Artaxerxes to our own times every event has indeed been recorded; but these recent records have not been deemed worthy of equal credit with those which preceded them, on account of the failure of the exact succession of prophets.   There is practical proof of the spirit in which we treat our Scriptures; for, although so great an interval of time has now passed, not a soul has ventured to add or to remove or to alter a syllable; and it is the instinct of every Jew, from the day of his birth, to consider these Scriptures as the teaching of God, and to abide by them, and, if need be, cheerfully to lay down his life in their behalf." *Against Apion* I.8.

[17] In Romans 4:23,24, the same idea was set forth.   One should also compare 2 Timothy 3:16 (where the same word, *didaskalia*, is translated "teaching"), 1 Corinthians 9:10, and 1 Corinthians 10:6,11.   After such an extensive use of Old Testament passages as is found in Romans, it may seem surprising that Paul should find it necessary to make such a statement as we find in verse 4.   Perhaps he was aware of the false charges made against him by certain Jews (reflected in Acts 21:21, "forsake Moses"), and so shows that the Old Testament writings do have a value to the Christian, even though the Mosaic covenant has been abrogated in favor of the New Covenant and its writings.

With the exception of the statements that all service that is acceptable to God is "commanded" (which contradicts what we have just read in Romans 14), and the implication that everything in the New Covenant is "law" as much as it was under the Old, the following note catches the idea Paul is writing.   "The Old Testament is full of examples showing that through self-denial and patient suffering for the honor of God and the good of man, blessings and happiness come to the servants of God.   They are recorded to teach us how God deals with men – how He applies His own laws.   No man can have a clear knowledge of how God will apply His laws without studying the lessons He has given in the Old Testament.   The examples of Abraham, Isaac, Jacob, Moses, David, and Solomon are given to teach us how God deals with men under His laws.   All His dealings with men are instructive to us and helpful in learning our duty and how God will regard our actions under His laws.   God's dealings with the unfaithful are just as much for our good as His dealings with the righteous.   His condemnation of Cain is as instructive to us as His blessing upon Abel.   That is given as a warning against serving God in a way not commanded by Him; this, an encouragement to serve God as He directs.   Man needs both warning against the evil and encouragement to the good.   [The Old Testament is rich indeed in commands to persevere and be of good courage, and in examples of men who were made brave and patient by the power of God in them as they took Him at His word.]"   Lipscomb and Shepherd, *Romans*, p. 256,257.

[18] Lenski, *Romans*, p.860.

That through perseverance and the encouragement of the Scriptures. This phrase tells us what particular lessons (as far as the present subject is concerned) Paul wants his readers to learn from the Old Testament. "Perseverance" is *hupomonē*,[19] "putting up with things," a quality needed by those who would help carry the 'weaknesses' of the weak. The Scriptures are full of examples of men who denied self, and patiently suffered for the honor of God and the good of man.[20] Likewise, the Old Testament Scriptures offer abundant instruction about "encouraging"[21] others on their way to heaven. Weak brothers need such encouragement; they do not need "stumbling-blocks and obstacles" (14:13) from their fellow Christians.

We might have hope. As we persevere in bearing the burdens of the weak, and as we continue to give them encouragement, *both* of us, the one helping and the one being helped, can continue to have hope, can continue to live as Christians.[22] "Hope" here is the same hope Paul has spoken of in Romans 5:4,5.[23] If there is an absence of "perseverance" and an absence of "encouragement" of others, then there is a danger of one's hope of salvation being forfeited.

15:5 – *Now may the God who gives perseverance and encouragement grant you to be of the same mind with one another according to Christ Jesus;*

Now. At some place in chapter 15, Paul's instructions pass from particular emphasis on the strong brother's responsibilities to instructions intended for both strong and weak brothers. It seems best to find that break here at the beginning of this prayer-wish.[24]

May the God who gives perseverance and encouragement. The NASB margin gives (in this commentator's judgment) the better translation, "the God of perseverance ...."[25] It

---

[19] See notes at Romans 2:4 and 5:3 for *hupomonē*.

[20] It is doubtful if the phrase "of the Scriptures" means that the Scriptures effect the qualities of perseverance and encouragement in the readers. Rather, the readers must develop in their own lives the qualities that God has revealed are pleasing to Him.

[21] *Paraklēsis* is a word Paul has used before, at Romans 12:8. The *-sis* ending emphasizes activity; admonishing, comforting, encouraging.

[22] "To speak of Christians as holding fast their hope is, in fact, a very appropriate way of indicating their continuing to live as Christians." Cranfield, *Romans*, p.735.

[23] The Greek reads "*the* hope," and the article is likely the article of previous reference. "Hope" has been an important theme in Romans – see 4:18; 5:2,4,5; 8:17-30; 12:12; 13:11-14; and 15:12,13.

[24] Some have thought the break should be made at Romans 15:2, and others have tried to put it at 15:7.

[25] "Of the patience" and "of the encouragement" (Greek) are in the genitive case, and could refer to God as the author, or source, or giver of these qualities (genitive of origin or source). But are such qualities simply *infused* into each believer's character? We think not. "The example of God, here, who bears long with his children, and is not angry soon at their offences, is a strong argument why Christians should bear with each other. If God bears long and patiently with our infirmities, we ought to bear with each other." Barnes, *Romans*, p.321.

seems to speak of God as Himself being 'patient' and 'encouraging' in His dealings with men, and holds out His example that it might be emulated by His servants.

Grant you to be of the same mind with one another. "You" is plural, and thus is likely addressed to strong and weak alike. "Same mind" repeats the exhortation voiced in Romans 12:16. It is doubtful that Paul is demanding agreement on those questions in the realm of liberty about which weak and strong have had problems. Perhaps he is asking his readers to have the same mind which Christ had (verse 3), which is ready to please others for their good.[26] More likely, he is asking the strong and weak alike to live in harmony with each other, while allowing each to continue his personal exercise of liberty, only unto the Lord (14:6-8). "The fulfillment of this would banish all bitterness, harsh judgment, recrimination, and petty controversies."[27] "Grant" is one of the few optative tense Greek verbs found in the New Testament, and it is why we call this sentence a prayer-wish. God (who is the "God of perseverance and encouragement") would grant this prayer, if He were to be patient with the readers, and encourage them along the way, until they begin to practice as the Scriptures teach. The readers must not presume on God's patience, as though they had forever to bring their behavior into harmony with God's will.

According to Christ Jesus. This phrase may mean either 'according to the example of Christ' or 'according to the will of Christ.' Harmoniousness, oneness among believers is something for which Jesus prayed (John 17:20-23). Such unity does not require absolute unanimity of conviction on matters of opinion, but it does require a loving attitude by both the strong and the weak toward brothers who differ on such matters. It does require a hearty determination on the part of each brother to "live for the Lord" (14:8).

15:6 – *that with one accord you may with one voice glorify the God and Father of our Lord Jesus Christ.*

That with one accord. "That" (a *hina* clause) can express either purpose or result. It may be that the brothers are to make it their purpose to glorify God together; it may be that the result of such 'same mindedness' (verse 5) among the brothers will be glory to God. "One accord" (*homothumadon*) speaks more of harmony of feeling than unanimity of opinion. It is just the opposite of the sentiment or feeling that results from judging and regarding with contempt (14:3).

You may with one voice. Strong and weak brother are pictured as together lifting up their

---

"Of the patience" and "of the encouragement" (Greek) include an article of previous reference, referring to the "perseverance" and "encouragement" just mentioned in verse 4. It is in God, as one reads the Old Testament Scriptures, that these qualities are best seen.

[26] Such an interpretation would rather require us to understand this prayer-wish to be addressed more to the strong brothers than to all the brothers.

[27] Vine, *Romans*, p.207.

voices in praise to God.[28]   Without the "one accord," the "one voice" (if indeed it even occurs) would be hypocrisy.   Unity of affection for each other is a prerequisite to harmony in worship, while unanimity of opinion in adiaphoristic matters is not.

Glorify the God and Father of our Lord Jesus Christ.   "Since God is truly glorified only when such spiritual harmony prevails among His people, this provides Christians with the great incentive to shun those dissensions which would mar their worship and spoil their service."[29]   The One who is glorified is here characterized as being both the God and Father of Jesus.[30]   Unity in worship and life, oneness in the local congregation, has a drawing power in the community, and this brings glory to God.   Furthermore, such harmony is exactly what God has all along been working to achieve; Ephesians 1:10 speaks about summing up all things in Christ, replacing with oneness the fragmentation in society that sin has caused.   When it is evidenced in men's lives, God is glorified.

15:7 – *Wherefore, accept one another, just as Christ also accepted us to the glory of God.*

Wherefore.   Paul begins the concluding paragraph of this section addressed to strong and weak brothers with a conjunction that implies, 'In order that the divine purpose (verse 6) may be attained as far as you are concerned.'

Accept one another.   In 14:1 the same command was addressed to the strong brother; now it is addressed both to the strong and to the weak, and the instruction is that they are to welcome one another even while differing with each other on matters of opinion.

Just as Christ also accepted us.   'If you have difficulty accepting the other, consider how Christ received you.'[31]   Christ despised none of them; neither should they despise and reject

---

[28] The Greek reads "with one mouth."   What is pictured is such a loving relationship between brothers that it is almost as if they all uttered their praise though one mouth.   (It hardly is proper to use this verse to show that in 1st century worship services, it was customary for the congregation to recite some creed, doxology, prayer, or confession, in unison.   While there certainly was congregational singing and public prayer in such services, what this context refers to is the idea that where oneness of mind and accord is missing, someone is not glorifying God, but himself.)

[29] Wilson, *Romans*, p.232.   "Being thus united in sympathy and love for one another, the strong helping bear the infirmities of the weak, the weak rejoicing in the help of the strong, you may all, as one man, with one voice and one mouth, glorify God."   Lipscomb and Shepherd, *Romans*, p.258.

[30] Some have tried to explain the *kai* ("and") as if it were epexegetic ("glorify God, *even* the Father ..."), but this ignores Sharp's rule of grammar.   Granville Sharp formulated the rule that says if two nouns or participles in the same case are connected by *kai*, and the first has an article and the second does not, both nouns or participles refer to the same thing, and the second denotes a further description of the first. Dana and Mantey, *Grammar*, p.147.   In this place the Romans are being encouraged to glorify the One who is both God and Father of the Lord Jesus Christ.   Compare Ephesians 1:17; Matthew 27:46; John 20:17; Hebrews 1:9; 2 Corinthians 1:3, 11:31; 1 Peter 1:3, where Jehovah is also styled as being the "God" of Jesus.   Such a designation, which was common in the apostolic church, does not impinge on the deity of Jesus.   It is explained by adverting to Jesus' temporary (between His incarnation and the consummation) subordination to God (in function, not in essential deity).

[31] There is a manuscript variation at this place, some reading "us" (*hēmas*) and some reading "you" (*humas*).   "You" is probably the right reading.

any of their brothers. The impropriety of rejecting those whom Christ has already received is manifest.

> The compassionate welcome which Christ gives to all who become obedient to the Gospel individually ought to be perpetually reproduced in the welcome of good will and tenderness which they give one to another in all the relations of life. And if there are some concessions to make, some antipathy to surmount, some injury to forgive, one thing ought to lift us above all these annoyances – the thought that we are thereby laboring for the glory of God, who received us through the grace of our Lord Jesus Christ.[32]

To the glory of God. "This is to be taken with the immediately preceding statement 'as Christ received you.' The glory of God was the object in view in the reception of each by Christ, and the same object is to govern the attitude of believers one toward another."[33] If Christ's example is followed, the welcome between brothers will be unreserved, and God will be glorified by the mutual love and kindness of His people. The purpose God had in mind (verse 6) will be realized in their lives.

15:8 – *For I say that Christ has become a servant to the circumcision on behalf of the truth of God to confirm the promises* **given** *to the fathers,*

For I say. Paul now explains what he meant when he said "Christ has accepted you" (verse 7), and this in turn gives an additional reason why the readers should accept one another. "I say" probably has the stronger declarative sense, such as 'I affirm,' or 'I maintain.'

> My doctrine is that Christ came with a two-fold purpose; on the one hand, with a mission to the Jews, the chosen and circumcised race, to vindicate to them the truthfulness of God in respect to His promises, by Himself confirming and fulfilling these promises, and, on the other hand, with the object to exhibit the mercy of God in rescuing the Gentiles from their state of condemnation, and giving them cause to glorify God's name.[34]

We cannot help but think that there is a special reason for Paul's affirmation about Christ's mission to both Jews and Gentiles. His readers, the members of the church in Rome, were of both Jewish and Gentile backgrounds. Perhaps this even gives some hint about the reason for the strife in the congregation over matters of opinion. Though it is not possible to identify which topics of dispute would have found Jewish Christians the weak brothers, and which would have found the Gentile Christians the weak brothers, it is certainly plausible to assume the old ethnic distinctions contributed to the current problems. Paul says that since Christ ministered to both alike, so should everyone in the church.

---

[32] Lipscomb and Shepherd, *Romans*, p.258.

[33] Vine, *Romans*, p.207. Cranfield, *Romans*, p.739, argues in favor of connecting "to the glory of God" with "accept one another" rather than with the subordinate clause "as Christ has received you."

[34] Sanday, *Romans*, p.151,152.

That Christ has become a servant to the circumcision. Several explanations have been offered for this very difficult phrase. (1) Origen thought there was reference to Romans 2:28,29 – "a minister of the true circumcision of the heart." But this would be introducing an idea quite alien to the context. (2) A second suggestion is that there is reference to the fact that Christ Himself was a circumcised Jew and lived His whole life on earth as a Jew. (3) A third idea is that it has reference to the area of Christ's personal ministry – by and large, He was a minister to circumcised persons, to the Jews. He Himself said, "I was sent only to the lost sheep of the house of Israel" (Matthew 15:24).[35] (4) A fourth suggestion is that "circumcision" designates one of the two major racial groups that comprised the population of the world, and that He came to minister[36] to one (the Jews, verse 8), as well as to the other (the Gentiles, verses 9-12).

On behalf of the truth of God. Jesus came to minister to the Jewish people so that the truthfulness of God might be absolutely maintained.[37] The area in which God's truthfulness might have been questioned, had Jesus not come, is immediately explained in the next clause.

To confirm the promises *given* to the fathers. Concerning these "promises" that Jesus' incarnation and ministry to Jewish people fulfilled, see Romans 9:4. The promises made to the fathers were not that Christ should minister exclusively to the Jews, but that in the seed of Abraham all the nations of the earth should be blessed. Jesus maintained the truth of God by making good God's promises to the patriarchs. "Now these promises to the fathers being thus made good, secured salvation to so many of the Jews as obeyed Christ. Thus Christ accepted them; and He did it from the heart, or without reservation. So must we Gentiles accept the Jews."[38]

15:9 – *and for the Gentiles to glorify God for His mercy; as it is written, "THEREFORE I WILL GIVE PRAISE TO THEE AMONG THE GENTILES, AND I WILL SING TO THY NAME."*

And for the Gentiles to glorify God. The difference between the NASB and the ASV points to the difficulty translators face at this place.[39] The ASV reads "And that the Gen-

---

[35] True, Jesus' ministry did take Him outside the Jewish world (Matthew 4:12-17; John 4:4; Matthew 15:21-28 [Tyre, Sidon], and 29-38 [Decapolis]); but His personal ministry was mainly among the Jewish people. (This is not to say that what He came to do was intended to benefit only Jewish people.)

[36] The noun translated "servant" is *diakonos*, "minister." Perhaps Paul reflects Jesus' own characterization of the reason for His incarnation, "For even the Son of Man did not come to be served, but to serve (*diakonesai*)," Mark 10:45; or "I am among you as the one who serves (*diakonōn*)," Luke 22:27. Cranfield, *Romans*, p.741, offers the suggestion that behind the designation "servant" here in Romans (as well as in Mark) is the Old Testament concept of the "servant of Jehovah," a designation that everywhere it is alluded to in the New Testament is applied to none other than Jesus (e.g., 1 Peter 2:24).

[37] We are reminded of the argument of Romans 3:3,4 and 9:6-13.

[38] Lard, *Romans*, p.435.

[39] The Greek word *doxasai* can be either an aorist infinitive, or an aorist optative active, third person

tiles might glorify ...."   Taking the main verb from verse 8, the ASV means, "I say that ... the Gentiles are to glorify God ...."   That Messiah's work was intended to benefit the Gentiles as well as the Jews was something that Paul has affirmed all along.   Gentiles are certainly included in the words "all nations" that are found in the promise made to Abraham; however, since many Jews questioned this truth, Paul will now spend several verses citing Old Testament passages where the truth was clearly taught in the Old Testament.

For His mercy. We are reminded of 11:30-32, where God's providential treatment of Jews and Gentiles had as its ultimate reason the fact that God wished to show mercy to all. Now that Gentiles have become aware of God's will, and have "attained righteousness, even the righteousness which is by faith" (9:30), these obedient Gentiles are pictured as already (even as Paul writes) praising God for His mercy.

As it is written. Paul appeals now to several Old Testament passages to support his assertion that it has all along been God's plan to accept the Gentiles along with the Jews. In fact, these passages picture Jews and Gentiles together praising God, the very point being emphasized in verse 6.   The first passage appealed to is Psalm 18:49.

"THEREFORE I WILL GIVE PRAISE TO THEE AMONG THE GENTILES. David is the writer of this Psalm, and he pictures himself as praising God among the Gentiles.   It is not just David (while living among the Gentiles, who are still benighted and separated from Jehovah) who is offering up solitary praise; rather, the implication is that the Gentiles have learned to fear and worship Jehovah, and together with David they are lifting up praise to God.   In Paul's Messianic interpretation, Christ the antitype of David, foretelling the conquests of His kingdom, declares that in the midst of the Gentiles (i.e., surrounded by them, and therefore together with them) He will give thanks to God for their conversion.[40]

AND I WILL SING TO THY NAME."   "When David represents himself as among the Gentiles, as confessing to God, and singing with them, he foreshows that the time was coming when Jews and Gentiles would mutually accept each other; nay more, that they would be so completely one as to recognize the same God and sing the same songs; and mutual cordial acceptance is the point before the apostle's mind."[41]

---

singular verb. If it is an infinitive, then "the Gentiles" would be the subject of the infinitive and the whole construction would be a case of indirect discourse after "I say" at the beginning of verse 8. If it is optative, then we have a neuter plural subject ("the Gentiles") as the subject of the third person singular verb, which is acceptable Greek. (A plural verb is used with "Gentiles" at Romans 15:12, but a singular verb is used with "Gentiles" at Romans 9:30.) If we take it as optative, verse 9 is a wish, "O that the Gentiles might glorify God for His mercy ...." Our notes follow the idea that it is an infinitive, dependent on "I say." The NASB treats verse 9 as though it were dependent on the phrase "to confirm the promises to the fathers."

[40] As at 14:11, the word *exhomologeō* can be translated either "praise" or "confess."

[41] Lard, *Romans*, p.435. The Hebrew word "sing" (*zamar*) would involve the use of instrumental accompaniment.

15:10 – *And again he says, "REJOICE, O GENTILES, WITH HIS PEOPLE."*

And again he says.   Most writers think the quotation comes from Deuteronomy 32:43,[42] though some opt for Psalm 67:3,5.   We might prefer to translate "it says," which would mean "Scripture says," as "it is written" (verse 9) would lead us to expect.

"REJOICE, O GENTILES, WITH HIS PEOPLE."   Moses is commanding the Gentiles to join the Jewish people ("His people") in rejoicing over the deliverance God has wrought.   In the previous verse cited, David represents himself as singing unto God among the Gentiles.   Here the Gentiles are represented as joining with the Jews in praise to God.

15:11 – *And again, "PRAISE THE LORD ALL YOU GENTILES, AND LET ALL THE PEOPLES PRAISE HIM."*

And again.   Psalm 117:1 is the third passage Paul adduces to show that the common language of the Old Testament anticipated a time when Jew and Gentile would together lift their voice in praise to God.

"PRAISE THE LORD ALL YOU GENTILES.   This time it is the Psalmist who is commanding the Gentiles to praise the Lord because He has accepted them, and filled them with a spirit of joy.

AND LET ALL THE PEOPLES PRAISE HIM."   "All peoples"[43] would include both Jew and Gentile alike; none is excluded from this common praise to God.   "This passage is conclusive proof that not the Jews alone, but also all nations were to share in the redemption of the Messiah.   The application is obvious: Christ has received all; do you then receive one another?"[44]

15:12 – *And again Isaiah says, "THERE SHALL COME THE ROOT OF JESSE, AND HE WHO ARISES TO RULE OVER THE GENTILES, IN HIM SHALL THE GENTILES HOPE."*

And again Isaiah says.   The words are taken from Isaiah 11:1 and 11:10.   Isaiah has many passages dealing with the Gentiles, some of which Paul has already alluded to in Romans 9-11.

---

[42] If it is taken from the Song of Moses, it would be the third time in Romans that Deuteronomy 32 has been quoted.   See 10:19, 12:19.   Also, if taken from Deuteronomy 32, "Paul follows the meaning of the LXX version, which varies somewhat from the Hebrew.   In fact, the sense of the Hebrew is disputed." Sanday, *Romans*, p.152.

[43] As one reads the Psalms in the ASV or NASB, where the distinction between "people" (Jews) and "peoples" (Gentiles, or Gentiles and Jews) is clearer than in the KJV, he should consciously notice whether the word is singular or plural, as it will aid his understanding of what was being written.

[44] Lard, *Romans*, p.436.

"THERE SHALL COME THE ROOT OF JESSE. The "shoot" out of the stump of Jesse is none other than Jesus Christ. Jesse was the father of David, and this is one Old Testament passage that predicts Messiah should come from the lineage of David. The prophet Isaiah has pictured the destruction of the Jewish kingdom as about to take place at the hands of the Babylonians. The Jewish kingdom is likened to a tree, which when the Babylonians get done with it, will be cut down, leaving only a stump. But out of the stump, a little "shoot" would grow. That little shoot was the coming Messiah.

AND HE WHO ARISES TO RULE OVER THE GENTILES. That Christ was to rise up, or be exalted to the throne of God, and be invested with dominion over all nations – Gentiles as well as Jews – is what Isaiah was predicting. This is the point, of course, that Paul is after, the fact that the Gentiles are included in the Messianic plans, and in the Messianic rule. Isaiah's prophecy definitely foretells the reign of the Messiah over the Gentiles.

IN HIM SHALL THE GENTILES HOPE." The Gentile's only hope of salvation is based in the Christ. Christ was to be the Lord and Savior of the Gentiles as well as the Jews. Paul has now produced four quotations from the Old Testament: one from the Law (verse 10), one from the Prophets (verse 12), and two from the Holy Writings (verses 9,11).[45] Thus the truth that God planned to include the Gentile together with the Jew in Christ through the gospel is shown to be something that is taught in every part of the Hebrew Old Testament. It will therefore require a repudiation of the "instruction" (verse 4) found in the pages of the whole Old Testament, as well as a rebellion against the explicit wishes of Christ, if Jewish and Gentile converts are to refuse to glorify God with one voice (verse 6).

15:13 – *Now may the God of hope fill you with all joy and peace in believing, that you may abound in hope by the power of the Holy Spirit.*

Now may the God of hope. How shall we understand this verse? When it is recognized that this verse closes the practical portion of the epistle, perhaps this prayer-wish is intended to neatly summarize all that has been written in the epistle thus far. Or, when it is recognized that this verse closes the section concerning the relationship between strong and weak brothers, perhaps this prayer-wish is intended to summarize all that has been said on this topic. In verse 5, God is called "the God of perseverance and encouragement." Here He is called "the God of hope." Isaiah (verse 12) spoke of the "hope" that would result from Messiah's work. Having made provision for Messiah to come to the world to redeem men, God is well-called "the God of hope;" that is, He is the author, or source, or inspirer, of hope.

---

[45] "These passages are not chosen in a haphazard fashion but are carefully selected and built up as a whole: 1) David brings Jehovah to the Gentiles. 2) They are told to praise God with His people (verse 10). 3) All nations and peoples, Jews and Gentiles, are of their own accord to join together in praise (verse 11). 4) And the cause of all this praise is 'the shoot of Jesse,' the Jew's own yet also the Gentiles' ruler and hope (verse 12)." Lenski, *Romans*, p.870.

Fill you with all joy and peace in believing.   The blessing Paul invokes on his readers is that their believing[46] may give them a life full of joy and peace, in order that in the power of the Holy Spirit they may abound in hope.   Depending on how this verse is related to what has gone before, "joy and peace" might be the opposite of the hurts and strife that result when brothers criticize and ridicule each other's beliefs in the realm of opinion.[47]   If such actions and attitudes are ended, if instead of putting stumbling-blocks and obstacles in the path of the weak, the strong will help the weak carry their weaknesses, there will be joy and peace in the life of the congregation.   Or, if this prayer summarizes the whole letter up until now, then "joy and peace" would be the result of right standing with God because of His reckoning them as justified.   Likewise, what Paul has in mind when he writes "in believing" depends on how the verse is construed in relation to the rest of the letter.   (1) Perhaps he means "believing *in Jesus*."   Throughout, the epistle has shown that "believing" results in justification.   *In Jesus* points to the One in whom the Gentiles hope (verse 12) and the One who is a servant to the circumcision (verse 8).   If this is the idea Paul is conveying, then continual faithfulness to Jesus' teaching and example will produce joy and peace in the lives of the believers.   (2) Perhaps it means 'believing what Paul has just written in this section.'   If they continue to believe (and practice) what he has encouraged them to do, they would desist from judging and despising one another over opinions; instead, they would be led to accept and love one another in Christ.[48]   That, in turn, would cause a joy and peace that would be very satisfying.[49]

---

[46] "Believing" in the Greek is a present participle, indicating continuing action, rather than a one-time belief.

[47] See Romans 14:17 for "joy" and "peace."

[48] A summary of the instructions to the strong brothers and to the weak brothers would look like this:

INSTRUCTIONS TO THE STRONG	INSTRUCTIONS TO THE WEAK
1. Receive the weak brother. 14:1	1. Receive the strong brother. 15:7 *(Actually, 15:7 is addressed to both strong and weak.)*
2. No constant arguing on the weak brother's scruples. 14:1	2. No (holier-than-thou) criticism of the strong brother's freedom. 14:3
3. No ridicule of the weak brother's scruples. 14:3	3. Freed from being brother's keeper in areas of opinions. 14:4
4. Be fully assured in your own mind. 14:5	4. Be fully assured in your own mind. 14:5
5. Give no occasion of stumbling. 14:13ff	5. Do not violate your conscience. 14:14,22,23
6. Concentrate on the things that make for peace and edifying. 14:19	6. Be of the same mind one toward another: 15:5
7. May practice your liberty in private. 14:22	7. Together glorify God. 15:6
8. Bear the infirmities of the weak. 15:1	
9. Be of the same mind toward one another. 15:5	
10. Together glorify God. 15:6	

REMEMBER: Both must appear before the judgment seat of God and give an account of himself to God, 14:10.

[49] "The Greek word for 'fill' [*plēroō*] is a very strong and graphic word, originally applied to the feeding and fattening of animals in a stall, used also of the multitudes fed with the loaves and fishes (Matthew 14:20 ["satisfied"]).   It expresses complete satisfaction." Lipscomb and Shepherd, *Romans*, p.261.

That you may abound in hope.   This phrase states the purpose Paul has in mind when he prays that God will fill them with joy and peace.[50]   On the condition of believing, and being filled with joy and peace, rests the promise that their hope will continue to abound.[51] We suppose that the "hope" here in Paul's mind is the same as introduced at Romans 5:2, namely, hope of life to come.   The more that peace and joy abound in the life of the believer, the more does the soul have hope of the joys of the future and the more does the soul look forward to those joys.

By the power of the Holy Spirit.   The reference surely is to the activity of the indwelling Holy Spirit.[52]   The hope that believers entertain is not of human origin, but is a creation of the Spirit of God.   This is the age of the Holy Spirit in the economy of Redemption.   The Spirit acts to bring to reality what Jesus (the "root of Jesse"), who "rules" at the right hand of the Father, wills.

---

[50] See footnote #62 on Romans 6 for an explanation of import of *eis* followed by an articular infinitive.

[51] "Abound" is a present tense infinitive, indicating continuing action.

[52] Compare Romans 8:14, 14:17, and Ephesians 1:13,14. All three members of the Godhead have been named in verses 12 and 13.

SPECIAL STUDY #9

FAITH, OPINION, AND LOVE

The doctrinal and practical portions of Romans have been finished. Before going to the personal allusions and concluding exhortations, it seems appropriate to pause to look at a matter that has proven to be a problem, not only for the Restoration Movement, but for the religious world at large. Romans 14 and 15 have urged a generosity toward others whose opinions differ, and a self-denying helpfulness to those whose convictions are too "weak" to determine their course of behavior in all circumstances, but not so weak but that their consciences bother them in some actions. Surely, a pertinent question at this place is, "How does one determine what is a matter of faith, and what is a matter of opinion?"

Early in the 19th century, Campbell, Stone, and others looked out on a divided church and a disbelieving world. The faith which had once been delivered to the saints had become rejected. Human opinion had been exalted. They realized something must be done, and they proposed to unite God's people in matters of faith and to abolish matters of opinion as tests of fellowship, while suggesting that love be practiced in everything. One of the cardinal principles of the Restoration Movement came to be summarized in this old slogan, "In Faith, Unity; In Opinions, Liberty; and In All Things, Love."[1]

Alexander Campbell considered the distinction between "the faith" and "opinion" as so important that, if it were properly observed by the Christian community, both a unity in matters of faith and a liberty in matters of opinion could be achieved.[2] Campbell believed this was the only 'philosophy of unity' that would have a chance of uniting a divided Christendom. He saw the creeds and confessions popular in his day as examples of binding men's opinions on others, and he insisted that only "the faith" be made binding as a test of fellowship. His idea was correct, we believe, but the way he defined and explained what is "the faith" and what is "opinion" led him into conclusions that seem to be almost arbitrary,[3] and this has caused his religious descendants to almost cease voicing

---

[1] "The slogan is not original to our own [Restoration] Movement. It goes back to around 1615, to one Rupert Meldenius, who was defending Lutheranism in the early days of the Reformation, who is quoted as saying in Latin something like this: 'If we would but observe unity in essentials, liberty in non-essentials, charity in both (or all things), our affairs would certainly be in the best possible situation.' This was later popularized by Richard Baxter, who urged that all believers follow the dictum: 'In fundamentals, unity; in non-fundamentals (or doubtful things) liberty; in all things, charity'." Leroy Garrett, "How to Overcome our Biggest Hangup," *Restoration Review* 17:4 (April 1975), p.71. John Mahoney, writing in the *Clarence Courier*, January 14, 1981, attributed the slogan to St. Vincent of Lerins who wrote about AD 400.

[2] Alexander Campbell and Nathan L. Rice, *Campbell-Rice Debate* (Lexington, KY: A.T. Skillman & Son, 1844), p.835-838.

[3] In the Campbell-Rice debate, Rice attacked two areas – Campbell's principle that every man has a right to read and interpret the Bible for himself, and the principle of the right to freedom in opinions – as being the most vulnerable points of Campbell's philosophy of church union. Rice zeroed in on the matter of how different men understand what the Bible teaches about immersion, as he said, "Now, let me ask,

the slogan.

It is the thesis of this study that the reason we have never been able to agree on what is "faith" and what is "opinion" is that we have had a faulty definition of these terms. For example, it has been customary (following Campbell's lead) to define "faith" as being whatever is commanded or prohibited in the New Testament (a thus saith the Lord, a clear New Testament statement, or even an approved apostolic example suffices[4]); everything else (where God has not spoken) is in the realm of opinion. Now this way of determining what is a matter of faith has never been quite satisfactory. For example, when the Restoration Movement tried to explain why the holy kiss, and feet washing, and certain kinds of holiness were optional, and not matters of "faith," it soon became evident that we were not consistent in how we applied our own rules of determining what is "faith" and what is "opinion."[5] After all, those items are plainly taught in the Word. Furthermore, this definition of "faith" does not match what has just been studied in Romans 14,15. God has, for example, plainly spoken on the matter of clean and unclean meats. How then (if our way of determining what is a matter of "faith" were correct) could meats be in the realm of opinion? Yet that is where Paul plainly includes clean and unclean meats in his treatment of the strong and weak brothers.

The absence of a proper definition, or the absence of a "Biblical" way, to determine what is a matter of faith has led to untold grief and countless factions and parties in the Restoration Movement.

> It amazes me that people can have so much in common *in theory* and yet be so divided *in practice*. An instance of this is that great principle that comes down to us out of our history expressed in that slogan, *In matters of faith, unity; in matters of opinion, liberty; in all things, love.* I have not met the brother yet who does not accept this principle: that unity can be based only on matters of faith and that opinions must be held as private property and not be made tests of fellowship.

---

do those Christians who refuse to be immersed, reject the Bible as their only infallible guide? Or do they only refuse to be bound by Mr. Campbell's opinion of what it teaches? They do not understand the Savior to have commanded immersion ... [and so are excluded from Campbell's church]." Rice had pointed out a place where Campbell was vulnerable, that honest men could not agree on what the Bible taught on some items which Campbell had designated as "matters of faith." And Rice charged Campbell with insisting that in such instances of honest disagreement that his own "opinions" should prevail. *Campbell-Rice Debate*, p.791ff.

[4] "... the 'unity of faith' for which [Campbell] pleaded was not confined to the simple gospel facts of 'the faith' [i.e., death, burial, resurrection, and appearances of Jesus, 1 Corinthians 15] which he so carefully enumerated on many occasions, but was to embrace the 'whole testimony of God,' including all of the 'facts testified in the Scriptures.' And this, too, despite the fact that [many of] the practices of the church were determined only by apostolic sanction." Granville T. Walker, *Preaching in the Thought of Alexander Campbell* (St. Louis: Bethany Press, 1954), p.63.

[5] How could we explain why commands to be immersed were required of men today, whereas commands about the holy kiss could safely be ignored? Or why the Lord's Supper was required, while feet washing (for which there is a command and an example) are ignored?

When it comes to putting this into practice we are confronted with what I consider to be our biggest hang-up: what I believe to be a matter of faith is viewed by others as a matter of opinion, and what they accept as a matter of faith I relegate to a matter of opinion.[6]

In matters of faith, unity; in matters of opinion, liberty; in all things, love. This is accepted by all our divergent groups, and, I dare say, by the Christian world at large, and yet we remain tragically divided. We have the answer to division *in theory.* It is all wrapped up in that slogan. Our hang-up is that we can't move from theory to practice. And this is because we are all fouled up on the meaning of faith and opinion.[7]

Surely if the Bible teaches that there are some matters that are in the realm of "faith" and absolutely indispensable (cp. Jude 3; 1 Corinthians 16:13), and if it also teaches that there are areas of "liberty" or "opinion" about which each individual is responsible to the Lord (Romans 14:7-12), then it could also be expected that the Bible itself will give us help in how to determine which is which.

The hypothesis this Special Study will attempt to document is simply this: **Only those matters which are designated as "gospel" in the Scriptures should be made matters of faith (and thus also tests of fellowship).** In the slogan, "In Faith, Unity," we propose to substitute "gospel" for "faith."[8]

The verse of Scripture which has suggested this approach is Ephesians 4:3, "Being diligent to preserve the unity of the Spirit in the bond of peace." Jesus prayed for the unity of His followers (John 17); Paul suggests that when men first became Christians this "unity" was a reality; otherwise, there would be little point in exhorting Christians to be diligent to preserve it. He even designated "peace" (being at peace with your brothers) as the "bond" (bindings, the glue) that would tend to keep them together, and help preserve the unity that the Spirit had already achieved by their conversion. Therefore, whatever it took to make them Christians (and that is the gospel) is all that is a test of fellowship, and all there is to the "faith" (body of doctrine) concerning which there is to be a "unity."

---

[6] Garrett, *Restoration Review* 17/4 (April 1975), p.71.

[7] Garrett, *op. cit.*, p.72. He notes that the Restoration Movement is divided into 15 or 20 different parties. A list of the things (some of which are taken from Garrett's article) that have divided us include: Sunday schools or Bible classes; missionary and benevolent societies; serving the Lord's Supper – cups vs. one cup, and grape juice vs. wine; minister system; charismatic gifts; premillennialism; instrumental music; literature instead of or in addition to the Bible; Sunday school classes instead of one large assembly being taught by an elder; Bible colleges; order of worship (as stated in Acts 2:42); centralized agencies (such as Herald of Truth); reimmersion of immersed believers. In each case, proponents insist these are "matters of faith," but their opponents hold them to be "matters of opinion."

[8] The author is aware that such a limitation is likely to have implications and ramifications that he has not yet thought of or considered. He therefore encourages his readers to wrestle with this topic, as he has, and to interact with him, so that together we may "speak where the Bible speaks."

I.   PREACHING AND TEACHING – A VITAL DISTINCTION

If "gospel" is synonymous with "faith" in the slogan "In Faith, Unity ...," then it is incumbent on us to define carefully what is "gospel" and what is "teaching" (doctrine).

A. The Distinction Stated

In Acts 5:42, it is said of the apostles, "they kept right on teaching and preaching Jesus as the Christ." Note the distinction between "teaching" and "preaching." In his 1857 address to the Christian Missionary Society, Campbell insisted, "This is no mere speculative distinction. It was appreciated, fully understood and acted upon, or carried out, in the apostolic ministry."[9]

In view of the whole matter of unity and fellowship, we should at the outset make clear how the distinction between preaching and teaching is related to the larger problem of a divided church. It is our position that oneness in Christ and the fellowship of the saints is rooted in the preaching of the gospel. That is, when one hears and obeys the gospel, he enters into Christ and is thereby in the fellowship with all others in Christ. It is therefore the gospel, the good news, or "the message preached" (as 1 Corinthians 1:21 puts it) that brings one into Christ.

The *gospel* (*kērygma* or *euangelion,* Grk.) is a specific message; it is made up of facts, not theories or interpretations. When these facts are preached, believed and obeyed, the result is a new-born child of God. That child is a brother or sister to all others throughout the whole world who likewise have responded to the gospel. He or she is in the church and in the fellowship.

Teaching (*didachē*, Grk., "doctrine"), in the majority of places this word occurs in the New Testament,[10] is something distinctly different from preaching. It is instruction or education that the newly-born child is to receive once he has entered God's family. While preaching, *kērygma*, brings one into the school of Christ, teaching, *didachē*, is the curriculum he is taught during his lifetime in the school. While it is the gospel that brings us into fellowship, it is teaching or doctrine that strengthens and enriches the fellowship.

---

[9] Alexander Campbell, *Popular Lectures and Addresses* (St. Louis: John Burns, Publisher, 1861), p.537.

[10] In a half-dozen or so passages where "teaching" appears, the reference may well be to what was taught to the man to instruct him about how to become a Christian, rather than having reference to teaching given to the already converted man. 2 Timothy 4:3 may be such a case (though it is rather difficult to decide if "sound doctrine" in verse 3 is identical with, or different from, "preach the word" in verse 2). In Romans 6:17, "form of teaching" seems to be a reference to the gospel facts of the death, burial, and resurrection of Jesus as pictured in the "form" called baptism. Titus 1:9 is another passage where it is difficult to determine exactly what is intended in the expression "holding fast the faithful word which is in accordance with the teaching." Likewise, how shall we explain "the words of the faith and of the sound doctrine" (1 Timothy 4:6) on which Timothy was to be constantly nourished? Romans 16:17 is another place where "teaching" may be a reference to gospel facts, rather than to what was taught to those who had already obeyed the gospel.

If this hypothesis can be sustained, it follows that unity and fellowship are not based on a correct understanding or adherence to *all* that the New Covenant Scriptures teach (or are supposed to teach), but rather upon one's relationship to Christ as reflected in his or her acceptance of and obedience to the gospel.   Again, if this hypothesis can be sustained, it means that the gospel is not synonymous with the whole of the "New Testament" as is so commonly believed among Christian Churches and Churches of Christ.   The New Testament (more correctly, the "New Covenant Scriptures") is mostly teaching, or *didachē*; that is, it is mostly instruction on how a Christian is to live.   Only that part that sets forth the good news of Jesus as the Savior of the world, only those matters that are specifically called "gospel" or are a part of an evangelistic message, should be designated as "gospel." When we come to see this distinction, the New Testament will become a new book to us, and we will have a more Scriptural view of unity and fellowship.

B. The Distinction Defended

Contemporary New Testament scholars, such as Krister Stendahl of Harvard, affirm that, in this generation, the overriding issue in New Testament studies is hermeneutics (questions related to interpretation); the issue in the previous generation was the nature of the *kerygma* (the gospel), spurred by the publication in 1936 of C.H. Dodd's *The Apostolic Preaching and Its Developments*.   The basic distinction that Dodd drew between "preaching" and "teaching" is now accepted as a significant contribution to the understanding of the New Testament – although there is no agreement as to what precisely falls into one or the other categories and the extent of possible overlap.[11]

What Dodd did in 1936 is very similar to what Campbell did in 1865, in the very last thing Campbell ever wrote after 40 years as an editor.   Both men came up with a rather similar summary of what they considered to be "gospel."

---

[11] Not all writers agree with Dodd's listing of the content of the apostolic *kērygma*. Some prefer to use the word *kērygma* to denote the action of preaching, rather than the content. Still others maintain that it is not possible to separate *kērygma* and *didachē* into neatly separate and identifiable categories, since they certainly were intermingled in much early Christian preaching. D.R. Jackson, "Gospel (Message)," in *The Zondervan Pictorial Encyclopedia of the Bible*, edited by Merrill C. Tenney (Grand Rapids: Zondervan Publishing House, 1975), Vol.2, p.781, gives a good summary of recent writing on all sides of this problem, as well as a fine bibliography for further study. Much of the same material, but in more detailed form, is available in C. Brown, "Proclamation, Preach, Kerygma" in *New International Dictionary of New Testament Theology*, edited by Colin Brown (Grand Rapids: Zondervan Publishing House, 1978), Vol.3, p.44-68.

[12] *Millennial Harbinger*, 1865, p.516.

[13] C.H. Dodd, *The Apostolic Preaching and Its Developments* (London: Hodder and Stoughton, 1936), p.7-75.

CAMPBELL'S LIST[12]

We shall now propound or declare the seven facts that constitute the whole gospel. They are:

1. The birth of Christ: God being His Father and the Virgin Mary being His mother.

2. The life of Christ: as the oracle of God and the beau ideal of human perfection.

3. The death of Christ: as a satisfactory sacrifice for the sin of the world.

4. The burial of Christ: as a prisoner of the grave.

5. The resurrection of Christ: "O grave! I will be thy destruction."

6. The ascension of Christ: "He ascended up far above all heavens, that He might possess all things."

7. The coronation of Christ: as Lord of the universe. God His father constituted Him absolute sovereign of creation.

DODD'S LIST[13]

We may recover it (the primitive gospel) somewhat after this fashion:

1. The prophecies are fulfilled, and a new age is inaugurated by the coming of Christ.

2. The ministry, death, and resurrection of Jesus – all according to the Scriptures.

3. Jesus has been exalted to the right hand of God as Messianic head of the New Israel.

4. The Holy Spirit in the Church is the sign of Christ's present power and glory.

5. The Messianic Age will shortly reach its consummation in the return of Christ.

6. Therefore repent, be forgiven, and receive the Holy Spirit.

Both lists are virtually the same, and both insist that there is a distinction between *preaching* (the public proclamation of the above points to a non-Christian world) and *teaching* (which in the large majority of cases is ethical instruction given to those who have already heard and obeyed the gospel).[14]

---

[14] Further testimonies to the truth of this distinction between "preaching" and "teaching" could be elicited.

- Campbell, writing in the 1853 *Millennial Harbinger* (p.541) said, "Preaching the gospel and teaching the converts are as distinct and distinguishable employments as enlisting an army and training it, or as creating a school and teaching it. Unhappily for the church and for the world, this distinction, if at all conceded as legitimate, is obliterated or annulled in almost all Protestant Christendom." He goes on to bemoan the fact that evangelists who proclaim the gospel to the lost and pastors who minister the doctrine to the church are alike and without distinction called *preachers*. He makes it clear that the real problem is that they do not know what *the gospel* is.

- W. Carl Ketcherside, "Gospel and Doctrine," *Mission Messenger* 35/2 (February, 1975), p.18, shows that Alexander Campbell was likely influenced to make this distinction by Dr. George Campbell (whose translation of the four gospels was incorporated into the *Living Oracles*). In his book on the four gospels,

Instead of appealing to the writings of men in order to demonstrate this distinction, it would be much more profitable to appeal to the Scriptures themselves.

- The Great Commission instructs Christ's messengers to "preach the gospel" to every creature (Mark 16:15). In obedience to this command, Peter and the Eleven fully preached the gospel on the day of Pentecost (Acts 2:14ff). In contrast, Acts 2:42 shows that "doctrine" was the regular fare for those who had already responded to the gospel.
- In his own account of what happened at the Jerusalem Conference (Galatians 2:2), we are told Paul "submitted to them the gospel which I preach among the Gentiles." This language points to a specific message easily identifiable as the same message Peter was preaching to Jews. We are not to suppose that Paul laid out the entire New Testament, even including the book of Revelation.
- 1 Corinthians 1:21 refers to "the message preached," an expression denoting "content."
- Perhaps it would be correct to explain 1 Corinthians 3:10 by suggesting that it shows how Paul "laid a foundation" by preaching the gospel, while others build on the foundation by teaching the apostles' doctrine.
- 1 Corinthians 4:15 is another passage in 1 Corinthians where the distinction between "preacher" and "teacher" might help to explain its import. In it, Paul assures the Corinthians that they had but one father in the gospel (preaching), while they may have many tutors or guides (teachers).
- Peter shows how it was the gospel (1 Peter 1:25) that was the seed by which his readers had been "born again" (1:23).

---

in Preliminary Dissertation Number VI, George Campbell took 13 pages to investigate the three Greek words translated "to preach" and the one translated "to teach." After showing that "preaching" is addressed to a lost world, and "teaching" to a saved people, he states, "And if teaching and preaching be found sometimes coupled together, the reason appears to be, because their teaching, in the beginning of this new dispensation, must have been frequently introduced by announcing the Messiah, which alone was preaching."

- In 1950, Alan Richardson in his book *A Theological Word Book of the Bible*, p.172,173, gives Dodd credit for his own understanding of these two terms "preach" and "teach." "The fundamental idea of these words [for 'preaching'] is telling of news to people who have not heard it before – 'evangelization.' In the New Testament, 'preaching' has nothing to do with the delivery of sermons to the converted, which is what it usually means today, but always concerns the proclamation of the 'good tidings of God' to the non-Christian world. As such it is to be distinguished from teaching (Gk, *didachē*), which in the New Testament normally means ethical instruction, or occasionally apologetics or instruction in the faith. ... Evangelists and teachers seem to have been distinct ministries in the early church."

- W. Carl Ketcherside, in his book *The Twisted Scriptures* (St. Louis: Mission Messenger, nd), p.51, finds seven facts included in the gospel – and also distinguishes between "gospel" and "doctrine." His summary of seven facts are "the life, death, burial, resurrection, ascension, coronation, and glorification of Jesus of Nazareth."

One serious flaw in modern use of Dodd's work is the tendency to exclude anything supernatural or miraculous from the "kerygma" and relegate that to "teaching." This results in Scriptures being dissected into three layers of information – what Jesus actually said and did (of which we know little, the scholars affirm), the apostolic preaching (*kērygma*), and the additions by the early church (*didachē*). These three layers of information are not (it is supposed by the scholars) of equal value. For example, there is a good possibility the church added many things the apostles never taught, and the church's accretions to the New Testament may be safely ignored since they were merely human. The practical result of this is that, for many, this leads to rejecting as authoritative any of the New Testament except Level 1 (Jesus), or perhaps Level 2 (the apostolic preaching).

- The distinction is also clearly made in Matthew 4:23, "And Jesus was going about in all Galilee, teaching in their synagogues, and proclaiming the gospel of the kingdom ...." (Compare Matthew 9:35 and 11:1.)

- Acts 28:31 tells us Paul spent the two years of his first Roman imprisonment "preaching the kingdom of God, and teaching concerning the Lord Jesus Christ."

II. WHAT IS THE GOSPEL?

A major hurdle to overcoming our sectarian divisions is, therefore, to understand what the gospel is and what preaching the gospel means. Interestingly, the Bible teachers just quoted (Campbell, Dodd, Ketcherside, and others) did not completely agree on the "content" of the gospel. The reason, we suggest, is because they took only a few passages of Scripture to get their information.[15] Earlier in the comments on Romans, it has been proposed that the way to understand what the Bible says on any subject is to take *all* the verses in the Bible on that subject, and see what is taught by them all. We propose to find out the content of the "gospel" by (1) examining the passages[16] where the word "gospel" (*kērussō, euangelizomai,* Grk.) appears, and (2) by looking at the examples of Peter's and Paul's preaching as found in Acts. In this way, we suppose, we will come nearer to understanding what the whole New Testament tells us is "gospel."

Footnote #61 in chapter 1 outlines some of the items that are specifically called gospel.[17] That outline now should be reviewed. To what is there given, it would be well to add the following passages from Romans:

---

[15] It has been popular in the Restoration Movement to appeal to 1 Corinthians 15 to answer the question "What is the gospel?" It also has been popular to truncate that passage. Restoration preachers have said the gospel consists of the death, burial, and resurrection of Jesus, whereas Paul wrote that four facts were included – Christ's death, burial, resurrection, and His post-resurrection appearances (verses 3-8).

[16] We must look at specific "passages" rather than entire "books." It was not until the writings of the apologists and the apostolic fathers (e.g., Didache VIII.2; 2 Clement VIII.5; Justin Martyr, *Apology* I.66) that we first find the word "Gospel" used for a *whole* book (wherein is set forth the life and teaching of Jesus).

[17] Several explanatory notes to elucidate what is there given seem appropriate. Observe that in 1 Timothy 1:10,11, the words "teaching" and "gospel" appear side by side. Observe that verse 11 (which begins with "according to" [ASV]) refers back to verse 9, where we are told the Law is not made for righteous men. In its context, the passage from Galatians 2:2 shows that liberty in Christ is part of the gospel Paul preaches; after all, the point of the Jerusalem Conference was that the Law of Moses is no longer a binding statute. In view of certain tendencies in the Restoration Movement to treat the writings of the New Testament as though they constituted a "law" which simply has been substituted for the Law of Moses now that Christ has come, it cannot be emphasized enough that grace and law (thus defined) are not co-existent concepts. The gospel includes, as one of its major themes, the doctrine of freedom or liberty in Christ. Acts 13:39 and 15:10,11 demonstrate that this was an emphasis in early preaching.

Another point also needs to be stressed, given that some modern scholars have tried to say that "resurrection" was not part of the original *kērygma*. This assertion is flatly contradicted by Paul in 1 Corinthians. While but four items or themes included in the "gospel" are specified in 1 Corinthians 15:3-8, one of them is resurrection ["He was raised"], and it is also important to notice that such an enumeration was common to all the apostles (verse 11, "so we preach").

1:1-5 – "The gospel of God" includes its announcement in the Old Testament prophecies. It deals with God's Son, a descendant of David, but also God incarnate. It involves the resurrection of dead ones. It concerns a glorified Lord Jesus Christ who extends grace to men and calls some to be His apostles.

1:15-17 – The gospel reveals God's way of saving man, and is the vehicle through which God exerts His power to save believers.

2:16 – The gospel includes the affirmation that there will be a general judgment, at which time God will judge the secrets of men, with the result that some will be granted eternal life, and others will be ushered into wrath and indignation, tribulation and distress (Romans 2:6-10).

10:8 – The apostles preached a message demanding faithfulness ("the word of faith").

10:15 – Preaching the gospel results in belief and confession.

In addition to these, one would want to add Acts 14:15, where we are told that included in the gospel is instruction to quit idolatry and worship the Creator instead; Acts 17:3, where the emphasis that Jesus is the promised Messiah is underscored; 1 Corinthians 11:26, where observance of the Lord's Supper is a means of 'proclaiming'[18] the Lord's death until He comes; 2 Corinthians 4:4,5, where both "the glory of Christ, who is the image of God" and the Lordship of Christ are identified as being "gospel"; Acts 20:24, where the "grace of God" is emphasized; and Ephesians 1:13, where we read about "the message of truth, the gospel of your salvation."

At this point in our study, we would propose that in those New Testament passages where "faith" speaks of a body of doctrine,[19] "faith" is synonymous in content with what we

---

[18] In the last two passages, the Greek word translated "proclaim" (NASB) or "preach" and "shew" (KJV) is *katangellō* (a compound form of *angellō*), "to tell thoroughly."

[19] That there was indeed a body of truth that was regularly presented to all who would hear, can be seen from the following statement taken from Colin Brown. "The New Testament epistles contain a variety of phrases which suggest a corpus of teaching. Among those found in the later writings are: 'the faith once delivered to the saints' (Jude 3); 'your most holy faith' (Jude 20, implying a body of beliefs); 'the pattern of sound words' (2 Tim. 1:13); '... the deposit [*tēn parathēkēn*]' and 'the noble deposit' (1 Tim. 6:20; 2 Tim. 1:14); 'the faith' (1 Tim. 1:19; Tit. 1:13); ['the words of the faith'] (1 Tim. 4:6); 'the confession' (Heb. 3:1, 4:14, 10:23); 'the word of life' (Acts 5:20; Phil. 2:16) ... In one of the earliest of his epistles, Paul could write: 'hold fast to the traditions [*tas paradoseis*] which you have been taught' (2 Thes. 2:15) ... The term 'the gospel' also occurs in Rom. 2:16, 16:25; Gal 2:2; cf. 1 Cor. 15:1. Paul speaks of 'the preaching [*kērygma*]' and 'preaching of Jesus Christ' (Rom. 16:25), not in the sense of the activity of preaching but in that of its content. Similarly, 'the faith' (Gal. 1:23; Col. 2:7) denotes not simply the act of believing but also what is believed (cf. Eph. 4:5). In various letters Paul refers to 'the word of the cross' (1 Cor 1:18) or the word of God and of the Lord (1 Cor. 14:36; Gal. 6:6; 1 Thess. 1:6; 2 Thess 3:1; Phil 1:14; cf. 1 Pet. 1:25)." Brown, "Proclamation, Preach, Kerygma," *NIDNTT*, Vol.3, p.61.

To this list given by Brown we might add the following: Acts 6:7, where "a great many of the priests were becoming obedient to the faith;" Acts 13:8, where Elymas' opposition to apostolic preaching is explained by the words, "Elymas ... was opposing them, seeking to turn the proconsul away from the faith;" Acts 14:22, where recent converts are encouraged "to continue in the faith;" and 2 Peter 1:1, where Jewish and Gentile converts are said to have "received a faith of the same kind."

have identified as "gospel." If this is true, we have gone a long way toward understanding the real meaning of the slogan "In Faith, Unity." It must be clearly stated, lest there be misunderstanding: *it is objective faith in which there is to be unity*, not subjective faith. While there can be and must be agreement on the great themes of the gospel, it is too much to ask to expect each person's own beliefs (subjective faith) to be the same as every other person's beliefs, once some time has passed since conversion. Opportunities for being taught and for personal study differ too much. My "faithfulness" will likely not be the same as your "faithfulness," even though both of us are conscientiously trying to be submissive to the Lord. Yet this is where some of the Restoration Movement's inheritors have gone wrong – they have interpreted the slogan to mean there must be uniformity in subjective faith as well as in objective faith.

III. WHAT IS MEANT BY "UNITY"?

What is meant by "unity" is simply this – that there is no room for hesitation, no room for quibble, no room for doubt, on any of these themes that are called gospel. The items in the body of faith constitute the least common content of what must be accepted if a person is to be recognized as a part of the church of Jesus Christ. None of these is optional. This is the heart of New Testament Christianity. These are the fundamentals on which there must be uniform and whole-hearted agreement as a prerequisite to fellowship. Before I can offer to another the "right hand of fellowship" (Galatians 2:9), and before he can continue to recognize me as a brother in Christ, there must be unanimity and conformity on these gospel topics. A few examples may help us appreciate this point.

"Resurrection" has been identified as one of the gospel themes. It is not possible to treat the resurrection as optional. Romans 4:24 has made this truth plain, as does 1 Corinthians 15.

"Baptism" has been identified as one of the gospel themes. If we are going to have unity in the faith, this command of Jesus cannot be treated as optional.

The "incarnation" has been identified as one of the gospel themes. It cannot be relegated to a matter to be believed or not, as each person may choose. 2 John indicates an individual who denies that God became flesh in the person of Jesus does not have God.

"Repentance," with its accompanying change of lifestyle, is one of the gospel themes. This is not optional. In fact, one of the legitimate occasions for the practice of church discipline is when a brother lives in habitual and unrepented sin (1 Corinthians 5). Is it too much to say that behind Paul's appeal to the church at Corinth to discipline the erring brother is the fact that if they did not, they would no longer be displaying "unity in the faith"? (Cp. 2 Corinthians 2:9, where Paul tells the Corinthians that he was putting them to the test to see if they would be obedient in all things.)

The "second advent" is one of the themes of the gospel. 2 Peter 3 indicates that this theme is not optional.

The "final judgment" is one of the themes of the gospel.   Romans 2:2-16 has shown how this is not simply a matter that can be believed or not.   So does Romans 3:6.

"Forsake idolatry" is another theme of the gospel.   The four "essentials" (Acts 15:28,29) that the Jerusalem Conference prohibits for Christians are all found in the milieu of idolatry.   These are not optional.   If Christians are going to be "united" in the gospel, these "essentials" will have to be observed.

"Holy Spirit" was still another theme of the gospel.   It is not optional, or the question Paul asked of the disciples of John the Baptist ("Did you receive the Holy Spirit when you believed?" Acts 19:2) would make no sense.

We could continue going down the list of the themes or facts included under our outline points (facts, commands, promises, see footnote #61, on chapter 1 in this book) of the gospel, and show that there must be acquiescence to these by all believers.   God expects no less; neither should his children.   "In Faith, Unity!" shall be our motto.   On these matters, and these alone, we shall ask for agreement and whole-hearted endorsement, as we appeal to men for unity in Christ.

IV. WHAT IS AN "OPINION"?

Because we are vitally interested in the unity of all believers in Christ, and because we believe this old slogan may be a way to express our ideas to others in a succinct fashion so they will be interested in such unity also, we are still trying to understand the slogan "In Faith, Unity; in Opinions, Liberty; in All Things, Love."   Now that we have come to understand what likely is meant by the first statement, it is time to look at the second part of the slogan.   Here the real problem is agreement as to what is an "opinion."   Just as the users of the slogan have not always been clear in their understanding that the "faith" in which we are to be united in our convictions is *objective* faith (the facts, commands, and promises of the gospel), so we have also been less than precise when it comes to identifying what is an "opinion."

It has become pretty standard in Restoration Movement thinking to identify "opinion" with the areas on which the Scriptures are silent.[20]   In this, it would seem, the lead of the Campbells has been followed.   Thomas Campbell had stated it in these words:

---

[20] Early in the Movement's history, Thomas Campbell had enunciated the slogan "Where the Scriptures speak, we speak; where the Scriptures are silent, we are silent."   Somehow this slogan's two points became superimposed on the first two points of the other slogan, so that "In Faith, Unity" became synonymous with "where the Scriptures speak"; and "In Opinion, Liberty" became synonymous with "where the Scriptures are silent."   Other religious groups had used "essentials" and "non-essentials" to express the same ideas, but Campbell "made the express word of Scripture the test, and so preferred the words 'faith' and 'opinion' as more Biblical."   Charles A. Young, *Historical Documents Advocating Christian Union* (Chicago: The Christian Century Company, 1904), p.36.

We dare not, therefore, patronize the rejection of God's dear children, because they may not be able to see alike in matters of human inference – of private opinion; and such we esteem all things not expressly revealed and enjoined in the word of God.[21]

Alexander Campbell, in the Campbell-Rice Debate, also identified "opinion" with "probable inference" which is reached in "the absence of good, well-authenticated testimony." The exchange between Campbell and Rice went like this:

> [CAMPBELL] We have long since learned the lesson, that to draw a well-defined boundary between *faith* and *opinion*, and, while we earnestly contend for *the faith* to allow perfect freedom of *opinion*, and of the expression of opinion, is the true philosophy of church union, and the sovereign antidote against heresy.[22]

> [RICE] The gentleman appears to attach great importance to a distinction he makes between *faith* and *opinion*. I DESIRE TO KNOW WHERE FAITH ENDS, AND OPINION BEGINS. I wish information on this subject particularly; because unless I greatly err, Mr. Campbell's church are [sic] constantly acting in violation of their own principles in relation to it.[23]

> [CAMPBELL] With us, then, faith is *testimony believed*; knowledge is our own *experience*; and opinion is *probable inference*. Whenever we have clear, well-authenticated testimony, we have faith, and this faith is always in the ratio of the testimony we have, or in our apprehension of its truth and certainty. Our personal acquaintance with men and things constitutes our knowledge; of which different individuals according to their discrimination and capacity, have various proportions. But in the absence of our own personal acquaintance, observation and experience, and in the absence of good and well-authenticated testimony, we have mere *opinion*. So I define and use these terms ... Now, as diverse in religion as in nature, are these terms and their associations. In religion, we have one Lord, one faith, one baptism, one body, one Spirit, one hope, and one God and Father. But we have many opinions. The church, then, may have opinions by thousands while her faith is limited to the inspired testimony of the apostles and prophets; where that testimony begins and ends, faith begins and ends. In faith, then, all Christians may be one ... In faith we must be one, for there is but one Christian faith; while, in opinions we may differ.[24]

---

[21] Thomas Campbell, "Declaration and Address," in Young, *Historical Documents*, p.134,135.

[22] *Campbell-Rice Debate*, p.797.

[23] *Op. cit.*, p.801.

[24] *Op. cit.*, p.835,836. The article on "Opinion" in McClintock and Strong, *Cyclopedia of Biblical Literature* (New York: Harper and Brothers Publishers, 1891), Vol.7, p.387, shows that there was a

In this commentator's perception, Campbell made a mistake not only in his handling of the topic of faith, but also in his method of determining what is an opinion. As for faith, it seems he did not carefully distinguish between objective and subjective faith. Observe how in the first quote he speaks of "the faith" (i.e., objective faith), while in the second quote, he seems to confound "testimony believed" (i.e., subjective faith) and "one Christian faith" (i.e., objective faith). This confounding of terms got him into trouble with Rice in the debate as it progressed, and it also came to create problems for following generations of the Restoration Movement as they tried to apply the ideas in the slogan consistently. Not only was there a problem with "faith," but it also would seem that his method of determining opinion (matters where there is no testimony) was in error.[25]

A third generation Restoration preacher, J.S. Lamar, suggested the way out of the difficulty by offering a different way to identify "faith" and "opinion." But it appears that few have heard his suggestion.[26] Instead of reducing Bible teachings to the two categories of "faith" and "opinion," he suggested three categories – "The Essential, The Important, and The Indifferent."[27] By "essential" he meant those things we have classed as gospel – the redeeming work of Christ and the way of salvation. These are essential; we may make nothing a test of fellowship that Christ has not made a condition of salvation. By "important," Lamar meant those things we have designated to be "teaching" – the doctrines

---

running debate in the 19th century about the nature of "opinion." Some held it to be a synonym of personal belief, and in a measure too, of personal knowledge. Others held that an "opinion" was "any proposition, the contrary to which can be maintained with probability;" that is, an opinion "is opposed not to a matter of *fact*, but to a matter of *certainty*." A third definition of opinion was to use the word "to denote knowledge acquired by inference, as opposed to that acquired by perception." No wonder Rice asked for a definition of terms. It is also of interest that Campbell chose a definition of "opinion" that differentiated it from "knowledge."

[25] Before it be construed that this is unfair criticism of the Campbell's thinking, it should be remembered how far the Campbells have come as they endeavored to realize in the church and in life what they could read in their Scriptures. They were having to jettison centuries of tradition and ecclesiastical baggage, and we would not expect that the first time they spoke on any new subject they would have everything instantly correct.

[26] This commentator would affirm that many of the topics of debate in the non-instrumental Churches of Christ have actually failed to grapple with this matter of "essential" being synonymous with the terms of salvation. And the study of faith and opinion among the instrument-using Churches of Christ and Christian Churches has done little better. James G. Van Buren (quoting Robert Richardson, *Millennial Harbinger*, 1852) approvingly offers this definition: "We distinguish, then: (1) *Opinions* as inferences of human reason in respect to things not actually revealed or treated of in the Scriptures. (2) *Faith*, as the belief or sincere reception of the divine testimony in its full meaning ...." *Christian Standard* 86/3 (January 21, 1950), p.45. W. Robert Palmer wrote a thesis in college on the topic, and since has lectured widely, and published a book on the topic, *What the Bible Says About Faith and Opinion* (Joplin, MO: College Press, 1980). In the book, p.163ff, he continued to define "opinion" as synonymous with the "areas of silence" in the Bible, even after he had been sharply quizzed about the correctness of his definition ("How do you harmonize your definition of opinion with Romans 14,15, where things specifically taught by Jesus are included by Paul as in the realm of opinion?") by students who heard him lecture here in Moberly, MO.

[27] J.S. Lamar lived from 1829-1908. His sermon by this title is included as the very first sermon in a three-volume collection of sermons by outstanding preachers of that era. The collection is titled *New Testament Christianity*, edited by Z.T. Sweeney (Columbus, IN: New Testament Christianity Book Fund, 1926).

(precepts, commands, examples) in the New Testament that help a man live out in his life the principles of the gospel. They are important to his continuing well-being; they are important to him personally. But they are not to be made tests of fellowship, for having been baptized into Christ, he is already in the fellowship. The "indifferent" would be those things on which the Scriptures do not speak at all (what some have identified as "opinion"). In his conclusion, Lamar seems to suggest that there is a sense in which both the "important" and the "indifferent" fall under the area of "opinion" in the old slogan.

Just as we appealed to the Scriptures to help us with our concept of the "faith" that is essential, and on which we must have unity, perhaps too we can get some help from the Word of God on this matter of "opinion." Our research has turned up two Greek words that can have the meaning "opinion." One is *dialogismos*, on which comments were made in footnote #7 on chapter 14. The other is *gnōmē*, a word which occurs about a half-dozen times in the New Testament. It sometimes is rendered "opinion" (cf. 1 Corinthians 7:25,40; 2 Corinthians 8:10), "judgment" (1 Corinthians 1:10), "purpose" (Revelation 17:13), and "determine" (Acts 20:3). These words all are efforts to express the personal nature of the judgment or determination or "mind" (disposition) denoted by the word *gnōmē*. At the same time, in 1 Corinthians 7:40, the word *gnōmē* is used in a context where the "opinion" had behind it the revelation of God's will made personally to Paul by the Holy Spirit. Besides these two words translated "opinion," we have also seen the word "faith" (in its subjective sense of personal conviction) used in Romans 14:1 as somehow related to "opinion," or to how a man "thinks" (14:14).

With this background, we are ready to show that "opinion" in the slogan ("In Opinions, Liberty") embraces both subjective faith based on the "doctrine" (teaching) received since conversion, and the things on which the Scriptures do not specifically speak.

V. MOST "TEACHING" IS BUT A LOGICAL OUTGROWTH OF ONE OF THE TRUTHS OF THE GOSPEL

In the Great Commission there is "teaching" to be given to those disciples who are baptized in response to the gospel ("preaching"); "teaching them to observe all that I commanded you" (Matthew 28:20). This is the "teaching" with which this part of our Special Study is concerned. We are using the word "teaching" instead of "doctrine" in this part of our study because men, through the years, have tended to give the word "doctrine" their own private, personal definitions. Because of this, were we to immediately use the word "doctrine" without any clear definition of terms, our readers might "hear" something entirely different from what we are trying to present.

> In our discussions of unity the word *doctrine* is a loaded word. One brother emphasizes the importance of holding "doctrinal" truth, and says that we cannot ignore or undervalue "doctrinal" issues. Another replies that our dif-

ferences are, after all, "mere doctrinal differences," and it is clear that he does not include these among weightier matters. And no one is quite sure what doctrine really is.[28]

The newer translations sometimes use the word "teaching" where the Greek has the word *didachē*, whereas the older versions used "doctrine."[29] So our use of "teaching" rather than "doctrine" is nothing novel nor unheard of.

One of the best places to turn to see how "teaching" is the logical outgrowth of one of the truths or facts or themes of the gospel is 1 Corinthians. The phrase "the word (message) of the cross"[30] occurs in 1 Corinthians 1:18, and sets the standard by which all the topics Paul will teach are measured. All the questions asked by the Corinthians in their letter to Paul (7:1ff), and all the matters that were learned from Chloe's people (1:11ff), are answered in the light of the "word (message) of the cross" (the Christ-event – His death, burial, resurrection). If the Corinthians' beliefs and behavior were in harmony with the message of the cross, they were correct. If their actions were such as would negate what was done to redeem the world, then their actions were wrong and needed correction. Let us see this logical outgrowth of the truths of the gospel in the following points:

---

[28] Harry Moore, "Doctrine and Unity," *Mission Messenger* 22/11 (November 1970), p.168. As footnote #10 above has indicated, the New Testament usage of the word "teaching" is not always clear-cut and precise when it comes to the specific "ideas" or "doctrines" or "themes" being taught.

[29] The NASB, for example, uses "teaching" at Acts 2:42 and 2 John 10; but it still retains "doctrine" at Titus 2:1; 1 Timothy 4:1 and 6:3.

[30] In the first two chapters of 1 Corinthians, several verses help us understand what the "word of the cross" involves.

- 1:17 shows that the manner of presenting the message is involved, "not in cleverness of speech." The same idea appears in 2:1-5, where we learn that human wisdom – superiority of speech, persuasive words of wisdom, wisdom of men – were avoided deliberately.

- 1:18 shows that power is involved. God exerts the same power to save a man that He used to raise Jesus from the dead (Ephesians 1:19-20). 1 Corinthians 2:5 speaks of "power" again – and in that connection may have reference to God's credentialing the apostolic preaching by miracle (see 2:4).

- 1:23 shows that Christ "crucified" is emphasized. Not a warrior Messiah, flashing His signs from the sky, breaking the heathen yoke, but a Messiah hanged on a cross is what the apostles preach for good news! It is a spiritual kingdom, not a political one.

- 1:24 (and other verses) shows that wisdom is involved in the message of the cross. God's ways of doing things are marvelous. 1:30 explains that this "wisdom" includes righteousness (justification), sanctification (growth in the Christian life), and redemption (the ultimate glorification of the body). God's wise plan was not a new invention – it was part of His eternal plan (2:7). It was revealed ever so dimly in the Old Testament (a "mystery"), and now through the apostles was clearly explicated (2:7).

- 2:7 indicates "our glory" – at the resurrection and consummation – is included.

- 1:26 shows the message of the cross includes a "call" (invitation).

- 1:20 shows that the message of the cross was not flashy, sensational, new; instead, it was different from what the world expected.

- 2:9 indicates the message was not understood by wise men, nor can unaided men discover the truths of God apart from divine revelation. Rather, God has gotten His message from His mind to the minds of men by revelation, inspiration, and illumination (2:10-13).

TEACHING ON THIS MATTER	BASED ON THIS GOSPEL THEME
Party spirit	Exalting men to be religious leaders is compared to Christ (only) being crucified for them (1:13, 2:2, 4:5).
Moral problems	The gospel theme here is Christ's Lordship over the kingdom of God. They are a part of the body of Christ. "Christ our Passover has been sacrificed" (5:7); therefore, the old leaven of malice and wickedness already should be purged out. The body must be disciplined so the soul is saved, for Christ so taught (5:4,5).
Legal problems	The theme by which this problem is measured is repentance. What happened when they became Christians precludes any litigation, selfishness, etc. (6:11). Bodily members care for each other – even the judged ones.
Avoid prostitutes	Christ's death, resurrection, and exaltation are all appealed to. If they give their bodies to another, they void the reason for Christ's death. He bought their body (all of it) with a price (6:20). Individual parts of it cannot live their own life. The God who raised Christ will raise their mortal bodies (6:14).
Concerning marriage	Now the gospel theme is the ministry of Jesus and the apostolic commission. Paul's advice is based on what Jesus Himself taught (7:10) and on what the Holy Spirit inspired Paul to say (7:40).
Christian liberty	Both the death of Christ and the Lord's Table are the great themes behind Paul's teaching. Do not hurt the brother for whom Christ died (8:7-11). It is impossible to consistently visit the Lord's Table and the table of demons (10:20,21). Paul's own example of forbearance in matters of liberty was based on Christ's own example (11:1).
Women in worship	Christ's emptying Himself at the Incarnation seems to be the theme here. It is a voluntary submission, just as Christ voluntarily submitted to the Father (11:3).
Lord's Supper	The Memorial Supper is to be observed in accordance with what Christ did at the time He was being betrayed (11:23). Improper partaking of the elements (without self-examination) involves sin against the body and blood of the Lord (11:27).

TEACHING ON THIS MATTER	BASED ON THIS GOSPEL THEME
Spiritual gifts	Each church member is part of the same body. The "body of Christ" needs all its members. Exercise the gifts in a way that expresses love (chapter 13). Self-discipline and edification of others is the important thing. Follow Christ's example of love (14:1).
Resurrection	The gospel theme of Jesus' resurrection is made the touchstone. Greek philosophy which had no place for the resurrection of men's bodies is wrong, for their own resurrection is tied to Christ's (15:48,49). Resurrection is part of the original gospel message (15:1-11). It is the heart of apostolic preaching (15:11,12). It is part of the final victory won for us by Christ (15:20-28,50-58).

It is likely that similar examples of "teaching" that simply unfold great gospel themes could be found in the other New Testament epistles. For instance, the gospel theme of the second advent and final judgment form the basis on which an appeal to holy living is made by Peter (2 Peter 3:10,11). Note, this present commentator does not claim originality for the idea that "teaching" is a logical outgrowth of the gospel. Robert Richardson stated the same idea 150 years ago.

> But what we would insist upon is this: that it is with the gospel facts we have first and chiefly to do; that it is by these we are first met on the part of heaven; and that these not only comprise all that is necessary, so far as the Christian faith, and the salvation of the sinner is concerned, but involve necessarily and immediately the consideration of all preceding and succeeding revelations ... In short, there is not a principle of action, or an exhortation to duty; a hope or a privilege; an institution or a doctrine of Christianity, which is not deducible from these simple facts, as the oak is evolved from the acorn, or the leaf enfolded in the bud. We would not be understood to say, however, that human reason could have made these deductions, any more than human power could bring an oak out of an acorn.[31]

VI. CONFORMITY ON ALL POINTS OF "TEACHING" IS NOT DEMANDED OF CHRIST'S FOLLOWERS

This title is but another way of saying "In Opinions, Liberty." In matters of gospel, there must be harmonious agreement; "In Faith, Unity!" But it would seem to be true that it would be difficult to show from Scripture that brethren must demand (as a condition of continuing fellowship) conformity of all believers on all points of teaching. At the time when Paul wrote to the Corinthians, he calls them "the church of God," "saints," and "brethren," yet they certainly were not in agreement on all points of doctrine. In fact, in

---

[31] Robert Richardson, "The Gospel – No.V," *Millennial Harbinger*, October 1839, p.434.

some matters at Corinth (eating meats offered to idols in the idol's temple, and denial of the future resurrection of the body), some of these brethren were doctrinally wrong! To be sure, he wrote to help them better understand the implications of the gospel, so (in time) there would come to be more agreement than there currently existed, but this is hardly to be compared with demanding absolute conformity. Also, before conformity could be demanded, it is necessary to take into account that in any congregation, some are babes in Christ, and have not had opportunity to be exposed to all the "teaching." Even where two Christians are relatively the same age spiritually, conformity is not demanded by the New Testament. If conformity in all points of subjective faith were demanded, all the verses about "liberty" in Christ would be meaningless.[32]

A. Verses Wrongly Interpreted to Demand Conformity

Through the years certain verses have been adduced to prove that the New Testament contains a pattern, or blueprint, for the church and the Christian life that must be followed, right down to the smallest details, or one has not been 'loyal to Christ.' No deviation from the "pattern" was permitted, even though hardly any two proponents of the idea could agree on what was and what was not in the pattern. While we teach that there must be unity (no disagreement about, or rejection of any) when it comes to the facts, commands, and promises of the gospel, and while admitting that a certain similarity was expected of all congregations,[33] and even admitting that a certain standard of personal behavior was expected of all individual believers, we have come seriously to question the use of the following passages to prove that the "Bible" teaches that God expects absolute conformity on all points of personal faith.

Amos 3:3 – "Do two men walk together except they be agreed?" (KJV). This passage has been used to prove that two brothers have to agree on everything before they can walk together in fellowship. But as the NASB translation shows, what the passage really says is that two men, if they wish to meet at a certain place to walk together, must make an appointment.

---

[32] We have not forgotten Paul's instructions to brothers of differing viewpoints that each one is to be "fully convinced in his own mind" (Romans 14:5), nor have we forgotten that each man has a personal responsibility to see that his beliefs and actions are "according to Christ Jesus" (Romans 15:5). Nor would we ignore for a moment the truth that the man who loves God will make every effort to keep all the commands of God that are recorded in the New Testament writings (1 John 5:3).

[33] Unless there was a certain likeness, an ideal, a norm rather expected of every congregation, it could not be urged that the behavior of Corinthians was out of line with what was found in any other church (1 Corinthians 14:36), nor could Paul appeal to a standard expected of "all the churches of the saints" (14:33). Paul could also announce Timothy's coming visit to Corinth, during which the young preacher would remind the Corinthians of Paul's ways in Christ, "just as I teach everywhere in every church" (4:17). One could also appeal the widespread appointment of "elders in every church" as a part of normal congregational life. "Body-life" was also something expected in each congregation, as is evident from Paul's use of his body analogy in several letters addressed to different audiences. Likewise, when it comes to personal response to the gospel, Paul can assume that every member of the Roman church had been immersed (Romans 6), even though he has not been there. "Household instructions" (Ephesians 5:22-33; Colossians 3:18-25; 1 Peter 2:18-3:7) also assume a norm of Christian living expected of each church, whether it be Paul or Peter who is writing the letter.

Galatians 1:6-9 – "A different gospel; which is *really* not another; only there are some who ... distort the gospel of Christ ... If any man is preaching ... a gospel contrary to that which we have preached to you, let him be accursed." If our distinction between "gospel" and "teaching" has been correct, then it would not be proper to brand everyone who holds a different view on some *teaching* (e.g., the meats vs. vegetarianism of Romans 14:2), as preaching a different gospel. Yet this is the use made of the passage by the defenders of conformity. Since Galatians was a warning against the Judaizers, we could easily presume that the "different gospel" was none other than the idea that "works of the Law" (Galatians 2:16) were obligatory for Christians. Similarly, today, someone who elevates some man-made religious rule to a binding statute would be guilty of preaching "a different gospel, and of distorting the gospel of Christ." This understanding of Galatians hardly permits us to use it to brand every detail of difference someone else holds as "another gospel." It hardly demands conformance on every point of "doctrine" (teaching).

Romans 15:5,6 – "May ... God ... grant you to be of the same mind with one another according to Christ Jesus; that with one accord you may with one voice glorify ... God ...." Advocates of conformity insist that all church members must say the same things on all points of "doctrine," or there cannot be "one voice." But again, observe the context. It is a portion of the section that runs from 14:1 to 15:13, a section that deals with differences of opinion about meats, special days, etc. It is certainly not conformity that Paul demands of all the brethren. In fact, the opening verses of chapter 14 insist that brothers are not to argue and harangue to try to get conformity in these matters. As the comments offered on this passage in this commentary show, what is demanded by Paul is a behavior on the part of the brothers that will allow all to have a feeling of harmony that will permit them to worship together with no feelings of animosity or ill-will, even though they are not agreed on such things as meats vs. vegetarianism, clean vs. unclean meats, etc.

1 Corinthians 1:10 – "I exhort you ... that you all agree, and there be no divisions among you, but you be made complete in the same mind and in the same judgment." On first sight, this passage seems to demand conformity of all believers on all topics on which the Bible speaks, and so it has often been explained. But let us take a second look at the passage. Chapters 1-4 of 1 Corinthians deal with partisan strife and its consequences. Church members had gathered themselves into little cliques, which bragged about themselves and their leaders, and treated other parties with disdain. When Paul writes that they are to "all agree," "the phrase he uses is the regular phrase which is used of two hostile states of parties reaching agreement."[34] Whereas they are now acting out of hostile attitudes toward other parties, he asks them to make up their differences. When he urges them to be of the "same mind" he has reference to a unity of purpose – that these party cries ("I am of Paul, I am of Apollos, ... ") be stopped. When he asks for the "same judgment," he is speaking about the method – how to stop the cries – by exalting Christ only.

---

[34] William Barclay, *The Letters to the Corinthians* in the Daily Study Bible Series (Philadelphia: The Westminster Press, 1957), p.15.

Romans 16:17 – "Keep your eye on those who cause dissensions and hindrances contrary to the teaching which you learned, and turn away from them." This passage has often been used as a proof text for a congregation's withdrawing fellowship from a brother whose opinions differ from the majority's. However, so much must be read into the passage to get it to teach such an action. The better understanding of this verse is that it summarizes one of Paul's intentions for writing to the Romans. He was worried how some (Judaizers?) who may come to Rome will affect the brethren there. "The teaching which you learned" may be something they had been instructed in before Paul wrote to them, or it may include some of the gospel themes enunciated in Romans 1-11. It likely has something to do with the gospel by which they were led to know Christ as Savior, for the words "your obedience" (in verse 19) seem in some way an explanation of "the teaching which you learned" (in verse 17). "Keep your eye on those" means to look out for them. They have been visiting other churches; expect them to come to Rome too. "Dissensions" refers to alienations between men. The 'contrary teachings' would cause men to have divided loyalties, to be alienated from one another, because some were out of harmony with the gospel. "Hindrances," we've learned in Romans 14:13 ("obstacle"), means to be trapped into committing sin. "Turn away" means to "avoid their instructions." It does not talk of excommunication of some already in Rome. It warns the Roman readers not to give an audience to those false teachers who are about to come to Rome.

2 Thessalonians 3:6,14 – "Now we command you, brethren ... keep aloof from every brother who leads an unruly life and not according to the tradition which you received from us ... And if anyone does not obey our instruction ("word," Grk.) in this letter, take special note of that man and do not associate with him, so that he may be put to shame." These verses have been used as proof texts to justify public congregational acts of excommunication of brothers who are accused of not conforming to the locally accepted understanding of apostolic teaching. But neither "keep aloof from" nor "take special note of" are regular words for church discipline. Further, an "unruly life" (instead of being some deviation in doctrine) is explained in the context to designate those individual Christians who had quit working (because they thought the second advent was imminent) and who were living in idleness and sponging off the rest of the church. What the brethren are commanded to do is to avoid or shun these people; do not give them any help or encouragement to continue that "unruly" lifestyle. Able-bodied brethren were expected to earn their own food, not depend on the charity of other members. "Take special note" (in the middle voice, present tense) instructs the Christians to observe the unruly course of conduct over a period of time before they act. Then, when they do refuse hospitality, it is to be done with the intent of encouraging repentance ("put to shame"). While the offender is refused help, he is not to be treated as an enemy, but as a brother (verse 15).

1 John 1:7 – "But if we walk in the light as He Himself is in the light, we have fellowship with one another, and the blood of Jesus His Son cleanses us from all sin." Fellowship is conditioned upon walking in the light. Some have used "light" to prove there must be complete conformity of personal beliefs before two people can be in "fellowship." We think this misses the point John is writing. Instead, we would propose that "light" stands for the gospel message (and 2:2-6 might suggest this), and John encourages his readers to conform their lives to the major themes of the gospel. One of the themes is the love of God, and if believers reflect this truth, they will practice brotherly love (cp. 2:9-11, and 3:14-18). John writes what he does to promote fellowship, not to limit it.

2 John 10,11 – "If any one comes to you and does not bring this teaching, do not receive him into *your* house, and do not give him a greeting; for the one who gives him a greeting participates in his evil deeds." The "teaching" that is not to be supported or encouraged by the readers of this letter is the Gnostic doctrine that denied the incarnation of Jesus (see verse 7). Thus, it is one of what we have designated as "gospel themes" that is in John's mind. The eternal verity expressed in the first part of the slogan "In faith, unity" would be violated if the doctrine of the incarnation is abandoned. 2 John does teach its readers to avoid false teachers, but it carefully identifies what the false teaching is: it is a denial that Jesus Christ has come in the flesh. Such a denial is of the antichrist (verse 7, and 1 John 4:1-3).

Jude 3 – "Beloved, while I was making every effort to write you about our common salvation, I felt the necessity to write to you appealing that you contend earnestly for the faith which was once for all delivered to the saints." It hardly will do to suggest, as some have been wont to do, that Jude changed topics; he had intended to write about "salvation;" instead, he writes about "the faith." Instead, "faith" and "common salvation" are one and the same theme. Or, worded in the language of our slogan, "faith" equals "gospel" – contend for the facts, commands, and promises of the gospel. See that your life exemplifies those truths. The way to contend for the faith is to avoid the licentious life styles the false teachers (Gnostics?) advocated (verse 4ff). Holiness of life is required of those who would be properly ready for the second advent (verses 20,21).

B. What Kind of Unity Can We Have?

A little thought on each of these passages will show that the unity we are to have is related to the facts and commands and promises of the gospel. While there is to be agreement on these points by which all become part of the kingdom of God, once we are in Christ, ours will be a unity in diversity. The members of the body will differ from each other, and not have the same function (Romans 12:4,5). The members will have a diversity in understanding (1 Corinthians 3:1).[35] There will be room for personal choice in many practices as individuals attempt to live out in life the great themes of the gospel. (For example, per Acts 21:20, the Jerusalem church observed many of the old Jewish cus-

---

[35] We would suppose that there was a vast difference between Paul's understanding of the teaching of Christ and that of the jailer he baptized in Philippi. But the jailer and Paul were one in Christ because both had believed and obeyed the gospel. Now compare the jailer with other members of the Philippian church, such as Lydia whom Paul also baptized, or a bit later, to Luke (the brother who was famous for the way he heralded the gospel, 2 Corinthians 8:18), who became the preacher at Philippi for about 5 years. It is very doubtful if any of these attained the same level of understanding as any of the other brethren in the congregation. There will always be differences in personal beliefs, but this in no way has to impinge upon the beauty of being in Jesus together.

toms. Congregations composed of converts from Gentile backgrounds did not.) Because they are brothers in Christ by virtue of their obedience to the gospel, even the strong and weak brothers can so live as to produce righteousness and peace and joy in the Holy Spirit.

VII. CONSIDERATION OF POSSIBLE OBJECTIONS TO THIS PRESENTATION

We have suggested substituting "gospel" for "faith" in the slogan "In Faith, Unity," and have proposed that the great gospel themes are absolutely essential for all followers of Christ. We have proposed that into the area of "opinion" (in which room for "liberty" must be granted) would fall those personal beliefs gleaned from the teaching one receives after becoming a Christian, plus all those matters on which the Scriptures are silent. But this proposal is so different from how the concepts embodied in the slogan have usually been explained, that many have difficulty accepting the proposal. Objections regularly raised include the following:

A. It is Hard to Accept the Idea that "Teaching" is Relatively Unimportant.

"Unimportant" in what sense? Unimportant as tests of fellowship? Perhaps. There certainly are habitual sins for which a brother must be disciplined, in order to bring him to repentance (1 Corinthians 5, especially verses 3-5,11,12). If the attempts of the concerned Christians do not bring the sinning one to change, he must be formally excluded from the fellowship (1 Corinthians 5:13). But this passage hardly gives license to exclude a brother over every difference of belief or conviction he may hold. Unimportant to one's personal devotion to Jesus? Acts 2:42 surely shows that it is important in some sense to continue steadfastly in the apostles' "teaching." Paul's instructions to Timothy about his need constantly to be nourished on "sound doctrine" (1 Timothy 4:6) makes it vitally important. If I am to know whether or not I am carrying out in my life the implications of the gospel, what Jesus says and what the apostles write are not only important but crucial.

B. Why Make any Effort to Teach People in the Denominations if Differences in Opinion are Permissible?

Who among us does not have some areas where his understanding of what is involved in the gospel and in the "teaching" is faulty? Is it not a great boon to have someone else who has spent a lifetime of study share his insights in the Word with us? "Teaching them to observe all things" (ASV) is still part of the responsibility of Christ's followers. All of us need to grow until we "attain to the unity of the faith, and of the knowledge of the Son of God, to a mature man, to the measure of the stature of the fulness of Christ" (Ephesians 4:13, ASV). Verses 12 and 16 of this same chapter explain that this growth comes through the interaction of saints who have been equipped for service. Only in this way will we come to the place where we are no longer children, tossed here and there by every wave of doctrine.

Some discrimination will need to be made in this matter. Some of the current religious groups, more than others, get it right to a greater extent on gospel themes. Those groups, sects, and cults that have numerous areas where they are at odds with the facts of the gospel (e.g., a denial of the deity of Jesus, or of His atoning death, or of His resurrection, etc.) will need to be treated as unbelievers,[36] whose real need is to come to faith so that they may be justified by God. Those groups whose members have purified their souls in obedience to the truth (1 Peter 1:22), but who differ on some matter of teaching in the realm of opinion, will be treated as brothers who may need encouragement and help.

C. How Will This Affect our Handling of Doctrinal Disputes in our Congregations?

It all depends on the topic being disputed. If it is a gospel matter, such as the incarnation, or immersion, or liberty in Christ, or the resurrection, we shall have to be firm as we insist on agreement with the Word of God. If it is a "teaching" matter – say, someone wishes to observe special days – it will obligate me to treat him as a brother who understands one point of teaching differently from what I do. If I practice what Paul teaches in Romans 14-15, I will welcome him and not all the time pick on his beliefs so long as he does not try to push his opinions onto the whole congregation as though they were tests of salvation or fellowship. Neither may I push my opinions and understandings on the whole congregation. But I do have an obligation to help my brother for his good, to his edification (Romans 15:2), where he will let me.

D. What do the Verses That Warn About False Teachers and Heresy Mean, if the Falseness Does Not Lie in Doctrinal Areas?

The point of the question reflects the fact that a broad definition has been given to "false teacher" and "heretic," as though anyone who teaches error, even innocently, were guilty of this crime. In the Restoration Movement, people have always attempted to "Call Bible Things by Bible Names." The proper thing to do would be to examine the passages where these terms in question are used, find out what they mean, and then use the terms to express the same ideas.

The Greek word "false teacher" (*pseudodidaskalos*, Grk.) occurs but once in the New Testament, at 2 Peter 2:1. The word *pseudo* means "to lie;" it speaks of deliberate and intentional falsehood. The rest of 2 Peter 2 describes the "false teacher" as not only lying, but also as conscious of the fact he is lying (verses 3,13). He deliberately plans how he can deceive the unwary and how he can beguile unstable souls (verses 13,14). He is moti-

---

[36] "Unbeliever" is a word one must be careful how he uses, especially if he wishes to call Bible things by Bible names. In the light of what we have learned in Romans, a man is a "believer" when he is obedient to the faith and is reckoned as just by God. No man should be branded as an "unbeliever" who is in Christ Jesus, regardless of any mistaken opinions or different point of interpretation on some topic of teaching since he became a Christian. It is the unconverted to whom the designation "unbeliever" is given in the Scriptures. In 1 Corinthians 6:6, Paul makes a clear distinction between erring brothers and unbelievers. "But brother goes to law with brother, and that before unbelievers?" Likewise, in 2 Corinthians 6:15, Paul asks, "Or what has a believer in common with an unbeliever?"

vated by love for financial gain and prestige (verse 15). He uses the promise of sexual promiscuity as a lure to entrap young converts (verse 18). He denies the Master who bought him (verse 1). In popular usage, the designation "false teacher" simply means the teacher is teaching something that is false. In contrast, as used in Scripture, the word means something other than simply that the teacher is teaching something that is doctrinally wrong (false).

> May I suggest that it is not the *teaching* that makes one a *false teacher*, a term that appears but once in the New Testament scriptures. One may misinterpret some scripture (and who among us does not?) and teach the misinterpretation. The teaching may be dead wrong, false and even injurious, and yet the individual would not be a *pseudodidaskalos* ... The *pseudodidaskalos* ... is conniving, underhanded, insincere, insidious, factious, eager to form a party around himself, willing to disrupt the peace of a congregation to have his way.[37]

"Heresy" is another word that has both a popular meaning and a Biblical meaning. In popular meaning, a "heretic" is one who teaches a false doctrine, and "heresy" is popularly defined as "Religious opinion opposed to the authorized doctrinal standards of any particular church ... and tending to promote schism or separation ... An opinion held in opposition to the commonly received doctrine, and tending to promote division or dissension."[38] However, its Biblical meaning is quite different, since there apparently is no passage in the New Testament where "heresy" appears in connection either with "preaching" or "teaching." The word *hairesis* occurs ten times in the New Covenant Scriptures, and for only one of these does Thayer assign the popular meaning. Thayer then refers to Dr. George Campbell's *Preliminary Dissertations on the Gospels*, and the following is taken from dissertation number 9.

> Neither here [referring to 2 Peter 2:1] nor anywhere else in Scripture, I may safely add, nor in any of the writings of the first two centuries, do we ever find the word *hairesis* construed with *didaskō, kerussō*, or any word of like import; or an opinion, true or false, denominated *hairesis*. As far down indeed as the fifth century, and even lower, error alone, however gross, was not considered as sufficient to warrant the charge of heresy. Malignity or perverseness of disposition was held essential to this crime.[39]

If one were to consult a Greek dictionary, he would find comments very similar to what is given in *An American Commentary on the New Testament* on the word *hairesis* at 1 Corinthians 11:19:

---

[37] Leroy Garrett, "Who is a Heretic?" *Mission Messenger* 25/3 (March 1963), p.38.

[38] *Webster's International Dictionary*, Second Edition, p.1167,1168.

[39] Garrett, *Who Is A Heretic?*, p.35.

"Heresies" is a transliteration, but not a translation of the Greek word, which has come over into English with a different meaning from its ordinary Greek, or New Testament meaning. It means, originally, a taking; then, introducing the idea of selection, the taking of what one desires and leaving the rest, election, choice; then, a chosen way of living or thinking; then, a body of men choosing the same way of thinking or living; and finally, dissensions between different bodies of this kind. Its use in the New Testament is divided between the last two meanings, sects and their dissensions ... In Titus 3:10, the word translated "heretic" means in the same way, one who causes division, a sectarian ....[40]

Instead of being a peculiar teaching, a "heresy" (in its Biblical meaning) is a sect or party, deliberately chosen. For example, in Judaism one finds the different sects known as Pharisees, Sadducees, Essenes, etc. Such parties are not a proper expression of Christianity or the church, for *hairesis* is one of the works of the flesh (Galatians 5:20, "factions"). In fact, such parties or "heresies" are destructive of the church and the heavenly destiny of their members (2 Peter 2:1). Another word, *schisma*, is related. It means a "tear, division, dissension." In 1 Corinthians 11:18,19, *schisma* and *hairesis* appear to be almost synonymous. The difference is one of degree: "*schisma* is *actual division*, separation [cf Mark 2:21; 1 Corinthians 1:10]. *Hairesis* is rather the *separating tendency*, so it is really more fundamental than *schisma*."[41]

A heresy is a sect. A sect is a party formed for the purpose of separating some of God's children from the rest. Sects are formed by factionalists, those under the insidious influence of the party spirit. No one who is honestly mistaken about some matters of scriptural interpretation is a heretic. To be a heretic one must make a test of fellowship out of his opinion or interpretation and attempt to establish a party to promote or protect that view.[42]

This brief study of the two terms "false teacher" and "heresy" has resulted in this: it is not proper to use the terms to prove there must be conformity of personal beliefs (among all believers) derived from the teaching received after becoming a Christian, or be in danger of being branded as a false teacher or a heretic.

E. Does not the Bible Teach the Need for Church Discipline in Cases of Doctrinal Deviation?

If the Scriptures do instruct believers to discipline their brethren over matters of personal belief derived from teaching following conversion, then it might be urged that unity of personal belief is essential to remaining in fellowship. The passages sometimes

---

[40] E.P. Gould, "Commentary on 1 Corinthians," in *An American Commentary on the New Testament*, edited by Alvah E. Hovey (Philadelphia: American Baptist Publication Society, 1887), p.97,98.

[41] Berry, *Synonyms*, p.129.

[42] W. Carl Ketcherside, "What is Heresy?" *Mission Messenger* 25/3 (March 1963), p.41.

used to show the propriety of such discipline are Romans 16:17 and 2 Thessalonians 3:6,14, which have been explained above.

On what basis, then, may Christians withdraw from a brother and no longer extend to him the right hand of fellowship?   Harold Key has worded it well:

> So far as I know, a brother is to be withdrawn from only for two possible reasons.   [1] If he deliberately and distinctly repudiates the confession that he once made of his belief in the deity of Jesus Christ, obviously he renounces the very basis of fellowship (2 John 7-10).   To deny either the humanity or the divinity of Jesus is to destroy for one's self the very basis of spiritual life ... [2] The only other basis for withdrawing from a brother is if he denies the Lord by the way he lives.   If his manner of life is an obvious repudiation of the Lord's control over him, he shows in practice that the Son of God and Savior of man means nothing to him.   Therefore, if he walks disorderly by behaving scandalously, either as a deadbeat (2 Thess. 3:6), or a fornicator, or covetous, or an idolater, or a reviler, or a drunkard, or an extortioner (1 Cor. 5:11), obviously he refuses to let the Spirit of Christ control his life ... So then, fellowship is destroyed either by disbelief in the deity of Christ or by rejecting the control of the Lord in leading a life of holiness.[43]

Such are some of the more common objections to the presentation of faith and opinion made in this Special Study.   Most of the objections are based on popular misconceptions, rather than on actual verses of Scripture.   Since none contradicts the general tenor of the presentation, we wish to present it to the brethren for their consideration.

VIII. IN ALL THINGS, LOVE!

Just a word on this closing phrase of the slogan whose real meaning and intent we are trying to discern.   We have carefully tried to discriminate and clarify in our minds what the Bible calls "faith" and what it would include under the category "opinion."

This third summary statement calls for each Christian to act in a loving fashion, whether it be in his dealings with others in matters of "the faith," or whether it be in areas of "opinion."   Love, as was learned at Romans 12:9,10, is doing what is spiritually best for the other person.   Here, then, are some suggestions as to how love would act.

- If that other person is an unbeliever, love would make every effort to get the gospel to him.
- If that other person is a believer who may be mistaken in one or more of the gospel themes (such as the Corinthians were about the final resurrection of the body, chapter

---

[43] Harold Key, "Basis for Disfellowship," *Mission Messenger* 25/4 (April 1963), p.60,61.

15), love would seek to correct their mistaken beliefs.[44]   It is not a violation of Jesus' prohibition of judging to call men's attention to the facts, commands, and promises of the gospel, and expect them to 'see the Bible alike' on these matters.

- If the other person is a believer who has not yet learned some of the implications for his own life of the gospel facts, commands, or promises, love would (in a kindly and gracious manner) try to help the brother to appreciate those truths inherent in the glorious gospel.   Differences of interpretation there may be regarding some of the "apostles' teaching," and these differences may at times place a strain upon fellowship, but it is a tragic error to suppose that unanimity of personal beliefs is the basis of continuing participation together in the cause of Christ.

- If, in an area of Scriptural silence on some topic, should the other person hold an opinion that differs from mine, he should be allowed to hold it.   To His own Lord he stands or falls.   If his convictions are so weak, that in some matters his conscience would be offended if he were to act, love helps the weak brother bear his weaknesses.

- Differences in judgment as to methods may at times be so sharp and incompatible that it is better for brethren to separate geographically for a time in order to keep the unity of the Spirit in the bond of peace.   That is what Paul and Barnabas did over the question of taking John Mark on the second missionary tour (Acts 15:36-41).   But even after separating, they still treated each other as fellow workers in the same gospel cause (1 Corinthians 9:6), and they spoke highly of one another as servants of Christ (2 Timothy 4:11).

CONCLUSION: A PLEA FOR UNITY

Our desire is to realize in our generation the church as Jesus envisioned it and as the apostles taught it. This is a grand conception, and one worthy of all acceptance. In a fragmented society, one of the most needed emphases is the unity of all believers, the unity for which Jesus prayed. We think the time is just right to reiterate the Restoration Plea for unity. Let it be based on the New Testament Scriptures as a rule of faith and practice. Let all alike embrace the gospel facts, commands, and promises therein presented. "In Faith, Unity!" Nothing should be made a test of fellowship that is not included in the gospel. Let all who obey the gospel be tolerant of other converts who are just learning what for each is implied in the great gospel themes. "In Opinions, Liberty!" So long as the other man's opinion does not stand in the way of his obedience to God, it will not interfere with his salvation. And where it does not interfere with his salvation, he should be permitted to enjoy it. Yea, more than simply being tolerant, let each brother look for ways to be spiritually helpful to all his brothers. "In All Things, Love!"

---

[44] While the Ecumenical Movement and the Restoration Movement are alike in their abhorrence of schism among followers of Christ, and both have a goal of but one church on earth, the Ecumenical Movement's stated theological positions (e.g., a moratorium on missions; Christianity is simply cultural, and therefore no better or no worse than the other major world religions; a denial of the deity of Jesus; a doubt about a visible, personal, return of Christ on the clouds of heaven) would make it difficult for a gospel believer to endorse the Ecumenical Movement or get involved with it, save to help its leaders to an agreement with the gospel themes.

The union of all God's people in one harmonious body, as they were in the apostolic age, is a thing for which every one who loves the Lord should both work and pray. The necessity of this in order to the world's conversion [is obvious] ... (1) Our plea for Christian union implies that there are Christians to unite. It has ever been admitted that God has children among the denominations – those who have obeyed the Gospel and are serving Him in the spirit of humility. To deny that there are Christians apart from those who stand identified with us in our work of restoration would be to make our plea for Christian union both meaningless and senseless. While we believe that many identified with the denominations are Christians, they have taken on much that is neither Christianity nor any part of it; and this we labor to have them put away ... It will be seen, therefore, that while we claim to be Christians only, we do not claim to be the only Christians ... (2) Our plea for the union of God's people implies that the Church of God includes more than those engaged in this work of restoration ... God's church is composed of individual Christians, wherever they may be. Of His church they became members by obedience to the Gospel. They do not forfeit their membership in God's Church till they cease to be His children. As long as they are children of God, they are members of the body of Christ. Hence, if there are children of God outside of what the world calls Campbellism, the Church of God extends beyond the same boundary ... That God's people in ancient times belonged to but one Church is simply an admitted fact; and His people now should belong to that, and that only, to which they belonged then.[45]

We find many immersed brethren in the denominations who are sick of the party rivalry and suspicions. They long for one harmonious body, to speak with one voice to a lost and dying world. Can it be that the old slogan, "In Faith, Unity; In Opinions, Liberty; and In All Things, Love!" contains the missing, unifying idea that will help us all to "see the Bible alike" on those matters that are eternal verities, which in turn would enable us to present that united voice to call a world to Christ? We would like to think, after our study of Romans, that we have learned how to distinguish between faith and opinion, and with Paul are better able to "preach the gospel," for after all, it is still true that "faith comes by hearing the word of Christ." It is still when the gospel (not opinions) is preached that God's power to save is exerted in the hearers' hearts and lives.

General Douglas MacArthur once said, "There is no substitute for victory!" Jesus Christ said that there is no substitute for unity (John 17:21). The question is, am I in harmony with Jesus' thinking and priorities on this?

On August 29, 1955, the USS Forrestal, the greatest ship ever built (up to that time), majestically sailed down the James River, made her turn out into Hampton Roads, then out into the Chesapeake Bay, on her test-trial run. This mighty ship – as long as three and one-half city blocks, as high as a 25-story building, capable of providing steam and power

---

[45] F.G. Allen, "Our Strengths and Our Weaknesses," in *New Testament Christianity*, edited by Z.T. Sweeney (Columbus, IN: New Testament Christianity Book Fund, 1926), Vol.2, p.244-246.

equivalent of 200,000 horsepower, built to take care of 3,500 officers and men – as she sailed down Hampton Roads, was indeed a thing of beauty and majesty and strength.   On August 30, 1955, the ship limped back into harbor.   In her test-trial run, two of the four main thrust bearings burned out.   She was still the largest ship in the world; she was still the greatest warship ever built, but her power was gone!   Immediate repair was necessary.

On the day of Pentecost, AD 30, Jesus Christ gloriously launched His church, and she sailed forth from Jerusalem.   Over 2000 years had been used in preparing her for launching.   She was equipped to conquer the world.   The words of Jesus were written deep upon her bow: "Go into all the world and preach the gospel to all creation."   "Make disciples [of them by] baptizing them in the name of the Father, Son, and Holy Spirit, [and by] teaching them to observe all I have commanded you."   As the church of Jesus Christ made her way into the world, the eyes of heaven and hell were upon her.   So much depended on her success.   And for one fleeting moment it seemed the world would be conquered and Satan defeated.   We read that 3000 were baptized, 5000, then multitudes, both of men and women.   The church was the joy of heaven, the hope of earth, and the envy of hell.   As the 20th century dawned, the church was still a divine institution.   Jesus Christ was still the captain and the head.   But it did not take an inspired apostle to see that something was wrong.   The old ship was almost dead in the water.   While the population exploded, the church remained only about where she was the previous year as far as total numbers were concerned.   The diminishing of power and failure to make headway did not take place in a day.   Through the centuries, men slowly but surely 'burned out her bearings' as they wrangled and fought over human opinions.   It is this commentator's prayer that God will help us to make the immediate repair the ship of Zion needs.   Let us individually and collectively work for the needed unity in "the faith," allow men to hold their opinions in private, and be ruled in all things by love!   In the 1st century, God's program worked!   It will work today, whenever it is given the opportunity to work according to His design.

VI. CONCLUSION OF THE EPISTLE, WITH PERSONAL ALLUSIONS AND CHRISTIAN SALUTATIONS. 15:14-16:27

A. Apology for Admonitions. 15:14-21

Summary: Lest the readers be offended by Paul's bold admonitions, he explains that what he has done in this letter is in perfect harmony with his duty as an apostle to the Gentiles.   His aspiration as he fulfilled that commission was to take the gospel to unevangelized places, a task which before now has kept him from Rome.

15:14 – *And concerning you, my brethren, I myself also am convinced that you yourselves are full of goodness, filled with all knowledge, and able also to admonish one another.*

And concerning you, my brethren.   Paul begins his concluding remarks with a reference, as at 1:8, to the good report he has heard about the brethren[1] in Rome.   This is not flattery, as though he were "buttering them up" before asking for an offering; it is a courteous explanation of the tone in which he has written, with special reference to the exhortations since 12:1.   After all, he has never been to Rome, though he knows some of the brethren there personally (16:3-16); therefore, what he has written should not be taken as an implication he thought of them as being defective in knowledge, or love, or both.

I myself also am convinced.   Usually, the emphatic expression "I myself" would imply that Paul himself is so convinced, in contrast to some others who are not.   However, most commentators do not so interpret it here; instead, it is treated as an emphatic way of stating his own conviction.   "Convinced" is in the perfect tense, 'I have come to this conviction a while ago, and still have the conviction.'   "Not only do others tell me, but I am convinced myself that you possess all the qualifications which would fit you to teach others instead of receiving instructions yourselves."[2]   So what Paul has written, he himself tells us, is not to be interpreted as though he thought the Romans were themselves deficient in these areas; rather, if there was any deficiency, it was in their knowledge of Paul and his message and his mission.   So that they could make an intelligent decision whether or not to support him in his mission to Spain (verse 28), they needed this information.

That you yourselves are full of goodness.   "Goodness" (*agathōsunē*) sometimes denotes moral goodness quite generally, and sometimes denotes a disposition to do good, to show kindness toward others.[3]   "Full of" suggests that on the whole their lives are characterized by this quality.[4]   If we let the immediately preceding context guide us, then "full of good-

---

[1] On the term "brethren," compare comments at 7:1.   The NEB's "my friends" catches the intent.

[2] Sanday, *Romans*, p.153.

[3] Thayer, *Lexicon*, p.3.

[4] The same term was used in 1:29 to express the regular behavior of the unsaved.

ness" means 'full of kind and conciliatory feelings,' the Christian love which bears the weaknesses of the weaker brother. If we let the following context guide us, then the thought might be of generosity in heart and action which would be displayed as they help Paul on his way to Spain.

Filled with all knowledge. "Filled" is a perfect tense participle in the Greek; the filling took place in the past, and the results are continuing. It is because they are "filled with all knowledge" that they as a result are full of goodness. Their kindly disposition toward others has been produced by the knowledge. The original also reads "all *the* knowledge;" that is, knowledge of the gospel, about which he has been writing in the earlier portion of this epistle.[5] "No doubt the Apostle had really much to teach his readers – he does not say that he had not – but he courteously gives them credit for all they know."[6]

And able also to admonish one another. *Noutheteō* can be translated "admonish, warn, or instruct."[7] "What is denoted is the earnest attempt by words spoken (or written) to correct what is wrong in another, to encourage him to do what is right and to refrain from what is evil."[8] It means "to direct (another) with brotherly feeling."[9] Goodness resulting from knowledge is a prerequisite for effective instructing and admonishing. No doubt, in the back of Paul's mind is the idea that the influence of the Roman church would be great on those going to and from Rome. Paul writes to them, not so much because of their defects, but because of their strengths and because of their potential for good (stemming from their strengths and their strategic geographical location) for the kingdom of God.

15:15 – *But I have written very boldly to you on some points, so as to remind you again, because of the grace that was given me from God,*

But I have written very boldly to you.[10] "I have written" is an epistolary aorist, a literary

---

[5] That Paul can be confident they have a grasp of the great themes of the gospel implies that there was a standard content to the preaching, no matter who the preacher was. (Some writers have supposed that "knowledge" here has reference to one of the temporary spiritual gifts – cp. 1 Corinthians 12:8, 13:8 – but such an idea seems out of harmony in the present context.)

[6] Sanday, *Romans*, p.154. One might compare what Paul writes at Romans 1:11.

[7] Arndt-Gingrich, *Lexicon*, p.546.

[8] Cranfield, *Romans*, p.753.

[9] Note the bearing this passage has on the emphasis among some church people on what is called a 'mutual ministry.' Such a mutual ministry does not preclude the function of teachers and evangelists who through their special gifts may serve the whole body (Romans 12:4-8). Today, the word 'counseling' is commonly used. Members of the Roman church were competent to counsel, competent to admonish one another.

[10] The KJV reads "brethren" before "I have written to you," but it is against the better textual evidence to include "brethren" again in this verse, after we just had it in verse 14. (The location of the word varies even in the manuscripts in which it does occur.)

device whereby a 1st century writer observes the courtesy of putting himself at the view-point of the recipient of the letter. It views the letter which is just now being penned from the standpoint of the readers; in the reader's case, the actual writing will be a past event when they receive the letter.[11] The comparative adverb ("boldly") is slightly apologetic, and could be translated "somewhat boldly" or "rather boldly" or "more daringly." It acknowledges that some at first might think it presumptuous of Paul, who has never personally been to Rome, to write to the Romans. But his writing is not presumptuous; the commission given to an apostle is not limited to one community, or one country. Since Paul is the apostle to the Gentiles, the congregation in Rome is legitimately within his area of interest and concern.

On some points. Literally, it reads "in parts," that is, in parts of this letter.[12] In certain places, Paul's writing was intended to be a reminder of what they already knew.[13]

So as to remind you again. Paul has not been teaching something new, or writing anything which any properly instructed convert would not already know. He has simply been 'reminding them again'[14] of the principles and commands of the gospel that were universally presented as the gospel was preached.[15]

Because of the grace that was given me from God. The first clause of verse 16 shows Paul uses "grace" here with reference to his apostolic commission, a use of "grace" that has been seen before at Romans 1:5 and 12:3. It was "because" of his apostolic office, bestowed as an act of God's favor, that Paul had authority to write to Rome.

---

[11] Not only is there a usage called the "epistolary aorist," there is a usage called the "historical aorist." In the latter, the time of writing is looked at from the standpoint of the penman, rather than the standpoint of the recipient of the letter. If this were an "historical aorist," it would refer to some letter Paul had written to the Romans on a previous occasion. (The same verb form appears at 1 Corinthians 5:9, and has resulted in a whole body of literature debating whether it is an epistolary or an historical aorist at that place.) Dana and Mantey, *Grammar*, p.198, have a good introduction to the "epistolary aorist."

[12] This phrase has been variously interpreted. "In parts" follows immediately after "you" in the Greek. So some have supposed that the letter has been 'too bold for parts of you' (part of the Roman congregation). Others have taken "in parts" with the adverb "boldly," as though Paul realizes that his "more daring" writing is true only of certain parts of the letter, not all of it. Our comments suppose that "in parts" is to be construed with the verb "I have written," so that he says, "I have written parts of this letter as a reminder."

[13] In Special Study #9 on "Faith, Opinion, and Love," the point has been made that part of what Paul has written in the early chapters of Romans is his own exposition of the great gospel themes. It is therefore of interest that Paul here says that parts of what he has written they already knew, as indeed anyone who has become a Christian would know.

[14] This is a compound verb: *epi + ana + mimneskō*. The *epi* seems to soften the expression, so that it means something like "suggesting it to your memory." Sanday and Headlam, *Romans*, p.404. This is another delicate expression in this section of apology and explanation. Compare 2 Peter 1:12,13 and 3:1. Christian preachers often have to put the brethren in remembrance of things they already know.

[15] Once more it seems appropriate to emphasize the bearing this verse has on the content of the early apostolic preaching, a content that all the converts the world over could be expected to have received. It says that what we have read in Romans 1-11 is standard Christian gospel preaching, and Paul knew it to be so even in those communities where he himself had not personally evangelized.

15:16 – *to be a minister of Christ Jesus to the Gentiles, ministering as a priest the gospel of God, that* my *offering of the Gentiles might become acceptable, sanctified by the Holy Spirit.*

To be a minister of Christ Jesus to the Gentiles.   "To be" expresses the purpose[16] of the grace given to Paul.   It was in order that he might be a minister to the Gentiles.   "Minister" here translates the word *leitourgos*, a word regularly used in the LXX for priestly service; the word already was used in Romans 13:6, where it was applied to government officials "by whom God administers his affairs and executes his decrees."[17]   The word conveys the idea of generous "service," but regularly with religious connotations; it is a service for Christ that Paul is doing.[18]   "Minister" here is equivalent to apostle.   "To the Gentiles" emphasizes the distinctive difference between Paul and the rest of the apostles of Jesus. To go to Gentile peoples, and preach to them, was his vast and peculiar work (cp. what was written at Romans 1:5).

Ministering as a priest the gospel of God.   This is the activity of which Paul's service consists.   "Ministering as a priest" translates *hierougeō*, another word with priestly connotations.[19]   Paul pictures himself standing at the altar as a priest, but it is not a Jewish altar.[20]   The altar he pictures himself connected with is related to the gospel, not the Law. The offering which he offers up to God is the Gentile church, as the next phrase indicates.

That my **offering of the Gentiles.**   "The sacrifices (*prosphora*, 'offering') offered by the priest of the New Covenant were not the dumb animals as the old law commanded, but human beings, the great body of the Gentile churches."[21]   The NASB translators have added

---

[16] In the Greek, the construction is *eis* and an infinitive, which expresses purpose.   Dana and Mantey, *Grammar*, p.104.

[17] Thayer, *Lexicon*, p.376.

[18] George Mark Elliott commented on this passage (with its "priestly" language) that it was "a Messianic idea in Mosaic terminology."   He suggested that Paul's way of describing his ministry may throw some light on the interpretation of the closing words of Isaiah 66 (see verse 21 which speaks of a 'priesthood' that includes both Jews and Gentiles in the church).   Since Jesus is also pictured as a *leitourgos* at Hebrews 8:2, not a few writers make it a special point to emphasize the truth that Paul's priestly "service" is subordinate and auxiliary to that of Christ's priestly service.

[19] *Hierougeō* (from the Greek word *hierus*, "priest," and *ergō*, "to work") means "to be busied with sacred things; to perform sacred rites; used especially of persons sacrificing."   Thayer, *Lexicon*, p.300.

[20] The word in the accusative case ("gospel" in this verse) following *hierougeō* indicates that with regard to which the service is performed.   Arndt-Gingrich, *Lexicon*, p.374.   Cranfield, *Romans*, p.756, cites a passage from 4 Maccabees 7:8, where "law" is in the accusative case following this verb, and it also denotes the religion with regard to which the "sacrifices" are offered.

Surely it cannot be right from this passage to assert that the New Testament teaches that the ministry of the church is to be a special priesthood, such as one finds in several denominations.   Even the trappings of a priesthood (borrowed from the Old Testament) are worn, and the communion table is treated as the altar, and in one large religious group, the priest is thought of as offering sacrifice for the sins of the worshipers as he officiates at the altar.   But this is too much to find in this passage where Paul borrows priestly language to explain how he pictures his evangelistic work in relation to his commission from God.

[21] Sanday and Headlam, *Romans*, p.405.

the word "my" lest the reader get the idea that Paul is offering some sacrifice the Gentiles have brought to the "priest" for his priestly help. The Gentiles themselves constituted the offering Paul was making to God. Denny explains, "The offering which Paul conceives himself as presenting to God is the Gentile Church, and the priestly function in the exercise of which this offering is made is the preaching of the Gospel."[22]

Might become acceptable, sanctified by the Holy Spirit. The old Mosaic sacrifices were no longer pleasing to God (Hebrews 10:6,9); those Gentiles that the apostle was offering were approved and acceptable to Him. Just like the Mosaic sacrifices had to be without spot or blemish, so the Gentiles are "set apart" as a sacrifice suitable to offer to God by the work of the Holy Spirit.[23] The verb tenses indicate the sanctifying work preceded Paul's offering of them as a "sacrifice."[24] If this work of the Spirit is in leading people to conversion, what Paul writes here is similar to 1 Peter 1:2. These passages, among others, refer to the Spirit's work as He leads a man to become a Christian.[25]

15:17 – *Therefore in Christ Jesus I have found reason for boasting in things pertaining to God.*

Therefore. "Therefore" points back to what was said in the previous verses. In spite of the apologetic tone in verses 14-16, Paul is not without confidence in writing to the Romans. His confidence is justified by two things: it is "in Christ Jesus," and it is "in things pertaining to God."

In Christ Jesus I have found reason for boasting. "In Christ Jesus" seems to be a limitation of the authority that Paul assumes. There has been no personal assumption of authority; he has exercised authority only as Christ gave it to him. Paul's confidence arose

---

[22] Denny, *Romans*, p.712. In technical language, the genitive here is a genitive of apposition; thus, it is not an offering which the Gentiles bring, but which the Gentiles themselves are.

[23] "Here is a good place to pause and examine the offering we preachers are bringing to God. What are these members like that we are offering to God? Woe to him who thinks and says, 'God, these are a good enough offering for Thee!' Lowering the confessional standards, gathering great numbers at the price of truth, leaving unholy bonds unsevered, yielding contrary to God's plain injunctions, will bring about a frightful reckoning for many a public servant who failed to keep the holiness of his gospel work before his eyes, whose offering to God is a herd of sheep that are tainted and unclean in God's eyes." Lenski, *Romans*, p.881.

[24] "Sanctified" is a perfect tense participle. A perfect tense participle indicates a state simultaneous with the main verb, but which has resulted from an action prior to the action of the main verb. If it were not for this grammatical note, it would be possible to make reference to what Paul has written in Romans 8 (the help the indwelling Spirit gives to the Christian to live the Christian life) as an explanation of this phrase "sanctified by the Holy Spirit." And indeed, Christ will present the church to Himself in all her glory, having no spot or wrinkle or any such thing; she will be holy and blameless (Ephesians 5:27). We have no doubt that the Holy Spirit has had a part in preparing the bride for that glorious day.

[25] 1 Corinthians 12:13 ("by one Spirit we were all baptized into one body"), we have suggested, means that the Spirit is the agent who leads the man to the place where he wants to be baptized. Now, in Romans 15:16, "*by* the Holy Spirit" is not *hupo* and the genitive, the usual way to express agent; it is *en* and the dative. Yet this is probably a case where the dative of agent follows the passive verb form. (It is exactly the same construction as is found in 1 Corinthians 12:13, and we have explained them both the same way.)

from the fact that he was not serving and suffering as he did just to make a name for himself; he had a much higher purpose in mind. He was serving Christ, trying to bring glory to Him. That is why he could "more daringly" presume to write to the Romans.

In things pertaining to God. This expression is explained in the following verse to have reference to "the obedience of the Gentiles." "Things pertaining to God" is Jewish language to denote the functions of worship (cp. Hebrews 2:17, 5:1). Ever since the Gentiles exchanged the glory of the Creator for the image of the creature (see Romans 1:23), their worship has been wrong. Paul has been engaged in the restoration of the true worship of God among the Gentiles by leading them to be obedient to the gospel. This wonderful task in which he is engaged is the second reason he has confidence to write to the Romans. He only exercises authority in connection with helping men to worship their Creator properly.

15:18 – *For I will not presume to speak of anything except what Christ has accomplished through me, resulting in the obedience of the Gentiles by word and deed,*

For I will not presume to speak of anything. "For" with which this verse opens shows it is intended to explain something just said, likely the expression "things pertaining to God."[26] In writing to the Romans, it would be presumptuous of Paul to write about anything other than how Jesus has worked through him resulting in the conversion of many Gentiles. So he writes, 'I will not dare to speak of any mere activities of my own.'

Except what Christ has accomplished through me. "Paul saw himself, in the scheme of things, as an instrument in the hands of Christ. He did not talk of what he had done, but of what Christ had done with him.[27] He never said of anything, I did it. He always said, 'Christ used me to do it.'"[28] Paul is still giving his reason for being bold enough to write as he did to the Romans, and in these verses he is emphasizing his past ministry. Paul had to commit himself in order to be the servant Christ wanted him to be, but anything that was accomplished is attributed to the power of the message he preached, and to the power of the Holy Spirit.

Resulting in the obedience of the Gentiles. One should not miss the emphasis on *obedience* that is found in this letter on justification by faith. The "obedience" Paul has in view is the initial obedience to the gospel, the obedience that is one of the elements of the

---

[26] Some have supposed that two things in the previous context are explained by verse 18. First, his "boast in Christ Jesus" of verse 17 is explained by the first part of verse 18, "what Christ has accomplished through me." The "things pertaining to God" of verse 17 is then explained by the latter part of verse 18.

[27] There seems to be a touch of irony here when Paul says, 'I will not presume to speak more about my own work.' Lipscomb and Shepherd (*Romans*, p.263) suggest that "the others of whose work he would not boast are thought to be his converts, who had gone out and done much work in which he might have claimed a part, but he would not." However, this does not seem to do justice to the touch of irony that seems to be in the words. Perhaps we should look rather to Paul's enemies, who were claiming for themselves more than they should, as being the ones at whom this barb is aimed.

[28] Barclay, *Romans*, p.222.

condition of justification called "faith." Such obedience (i.e., their conversion) was the beginning of the restoration of true worship, a worship offered to God by these Gentiles ("things pertaining to God," verse 17). "This is the proximate earthly end for which the apostle toiled, the end for which the Holy Spirit exerted His power, the end of the word and deed, sign and wonder. The ultimate end, of course, was the final salvation of those obeying, to the glory of God."[29] The things which Christ did work through Paul, He wrought with a view of winning Gentiles to obedience. This combination – Christ working through Paul, to win the obedience of the Gentiles to the gospel – is the vindication of Paul's action in writing to Rome.

By word and deed. These words, along with the phrases in verse 19, cover Paul's apostolic work. "Word" stands for the message preached, the gospel; "deed" has a reference to miracles, as the next verse explains. The "word and deed" are attributed to Christ working through him. We should not fail to note that Paul's statement about Christ working through him assumes that He has risen from the dead, has been glorified, and continues to have a hand in the affairs of men.

15:19 – *in the power of signs and wonders, in the power of the Spirit; so that from Jerusalem and round about as far as Illyricum I have fully preached the gospel of Christ.*

In the power of signs and wonders. Paul here alludes to the credentials any genuine apostle could point to, namely, the miracles that regularly accompanied their ministries.[30] The combination "signs and wonders" is commonly found throughout the New Testament to designate genuine miracles.[31] The two words look at miracle from different standpoints. "Wonders" (*teras*) describes the effect of the miracle upon the imagination of the observer. The miracle excited wonder and awe; it was something exceptional that caused the beholder to marvel. "Signs" (*sēmeion*) describes the effect the miracle is intended to have on the observer's understanding. It calls to his attention the purpose which lay behind the working of the miracle.[32] "It is noteworthy how Paul alludes inciden-

---

[29] Lard, *Romans*, p.442.

[30] Compare 2 Corinthians 12:12, "The signs of a true apostle were performed among you with all perseverance, by signs and wonders and miracles." See also Hebrews 2:4, "God also bearing witness with them, both by signs and wonders and various miracles and by gifts of the Holy Spirit." The latter expression, as the margin shows, actually reads "by distributions of the Spirit," and it points to the apostles' ability to pass on spiritual gifts by the laying on of their hands.

[31] Note, in the Bible, when they are of God, miracles are always called "signs and wonders." "'Wonders' is never used alone as a designation for God's miracles. Pagan religions also had *tērata*, or 'wonders;' namely, the portents that astonished and made men gape and wonder. Their spuriousness lay in this, that they were not 'signs,' signified no great or blessed realities!" Lenski, *Romans*, p.883.

[32] See Reese, *New Testament History: Acts*, at Acts 2:22, for further explanation of the terms used in Scripture to designate miracle. "The evidence for the existence of miracles in the Apostolic Church is twofold. On the one hand, the apparently natural and unobtrusive claim made by the apostles on behalf of themselves or others to the power of working miracles. On the other, the definite historical narrative of the book of Acts. These two witnesses corroborate one another. Against them it has been argued that the standard of evidence was lax, and that the miraculous and non-miraculous were not sufficiently distinguished. But will the first argument hold against a personal assertion? And does not the narrative

tally in his letters to such 'signs and wonders' having accompanied his ministry, as to something familiar and acknowledged, so as to suggest the idea of their having been more frequent than we might think from the record in Acts."[33]

In the power of the Spirit. Having explained what he meant by "deed," Paul now turns to further explanation of "word" (verse 18).[34] The "word" (message) he preached was inspired by the Holy Spirit. This is not the only place where Paul claims inspiration for his message. See also 1 Corinthians 2:13 and 7:40 for two other affirmations of inspiration. That Paul's ministry was effective depended, then, not on Paul's own powers, but upon Christ, and the Holy Spirit whom He sent to inspire the message and credential the messengers.

So that from Jerusalem and round about as far as Illyricum. "So that" expresses result,[35] whether it be the result of grace given to him from God (verse 15), or the result of Christ working through him (verse 18). Both geographic terms have caused some problems for the commentators. Since the accounts of Paul's life (Acts 26:19,20; Galatians 1:17) show that he began his career as a preacher of the gospel in Damascus three years before his first visit to Jerusalem after his conversion, some have been puzzled why he names Jerusalem first here in Romans. Two perfectly reasonable solutions suggest themselves: (1) Paul is emphasizing his ministry to Gentiles; what he did in Damascus was among Jewish people, and it was not until years later, at Jerusalem, that Paul first began to work among Gentiles.[36] (2) "Jerusalem" is simply a geographical expression to define the eastern limits of the area in which he had preached the gospel.[37] "Round about"

---

of Acts make it clear that miracles in a perfectly correct sense of the word were definitely intended?" Sanday and Headlam, *Romans*, p.406.

[33] Barmby, *Romans*, p.420.

[34] This comment supposes that verse 19 is worded in reverse order from what was said in verse 18 about "word and deed." Another explanation offered for "in the power of the Spirit" is that the "signs and wonders" he has just referred to were done by the power of the Spirit. Still a third suggestion is that he refers everything (word, deed, signs, wonders) to the work of the Holy Spirit.

[35] The construction is *hōste* followed by an infinitive, and refers to the result that is tended to be produced. See this grammar explained in footnote #31 on Romans 7.

[36] Acts 9:28,29 tell about his first visit to Jerusalem, after his conversion about three years prior. Acts 22:17-21 show us that during this first visit to Jerusalem after his conversion, Jesus appeared to Paul and again (recall that Paul's first commission to go to the Gentiles was given on the Damascus' Road, Acts 26:16,17) told him to "Go! For I will send you far away to the Gentiles." Acts 13:1,2 record a third time that Paul's mission to the Gentiles was divinely stated. This time, with Antioch of Syria as the starting point, he began in earnest his evangelization of the Gentiles.

[37] We pause to point out these possible solutions because this "discrepancy" has been used by the critics as one of the building blocks of their theory about how the Biblical books came to be constructed. Some critics have argued that Paul never did preach in Jerusalem, nor would Paul have ever mentioned that place as the starting point of his missionary work, and that these words were included in the record as a concession made to the Jewish Christians, and hence that Romans 15 is a result of the same conciliation tendency which produced Acts. (Bauer's old theory of a tension between Pauline and Petrine elements in the early church, with some books reflecting one pole, and some reflecting the other, and some as

should likely be understood as describing the area between Jerusalem and Illyricum.[38]   It covers his evangelistic tours of Asia Minor, Macedonia, and Greece.   "A perfectly tenable explanation of the words would be that if Jerusalem were taken as one limit and the Eastern boundaries of Illyria as the other, St. Paul had traveled over the whole of the intervening district, and not merely confined himself to the direct route between the two places."[39] "Illyricum," the Roman province[40] which was located between Macedonia on the east and the Adriatic Sea on its west, has also been the occasion of numerous comments because there is no mention in the book of Acts of Paul's ever visiting this province.   It has also been debated whether the words "as far as" are inclusive or exclusive.[41]   As he traveled the Egnatian Way in a westerly direction between Thessalonica and Berea on any of his journeys through Macedonia, he would have come within about 100 miles of the border between the provinces of Macedonia and Illyria.   Perhaps that is close enough that he can say without exaggerating that he has evangelized to the border of Illyricum.[42]   The distance between Jerusalem and Illyricum was over 1000 miles.   The region "round about" would average 300 miles wide.   The area which Paul has evangelized is huge!

"peace-makers" trying to show a harmony between the two, should long ago have been abandoned. It resulted from an attempt to make the Bible fit Hegel's philosophy of thesis, synthesis, and antithesis, rather than from the facts of the Scripture themselves.)

[38] Many commentators explain "round about" as though it referred to the country around Jerusalem. Sanday and Headlam, *Romans*, p.407, argue that though the majority of commentators so explain it, it is probably not the proper Greek expression (there is no article in the genitive case in this phrase) to express that idea.

[39] Sanday and Headlam, *Romans*, p.407.

[40] "The word Illyria might apparently be used at this period in two senses: (1) As the designation of a Roman province it might be used for what was otherwise called Dalmatia, the province on the Adriatic seacoast north of Macedonia and west of Thrace.   (2) Ethnically it would mean the country inhabited by Illyrians, a portion of which was included in the Roman province of Macedonia.   In this sense it is used in Appian, *Illyrica* 1,7; Josephus, *Wars*, II.xvi.4; and Strabo VII.vii.4."   Sanday and Headlam, *Romans*, p.408.

[41] "The Greek is ambiguous; certainly it admits the exclusive use. *Mechri thalasses* ["as far as the sea"] can be used clearly as excluding the sea."   Sanday and Headlam, *Romans*, p.407.

[42] Those interpreters who opt for an inclusive sense, and try to find a place to insert this ministry in Illyricum in the accounts of his missionary journeys in Acts, usually opt for the third missionary journey, between the time Paul left Ephesus to go to Macedonia (Acts 20:1) and the time he left Macedonia to go into Greece (Acts 20:3).   The chronology of the apostolic age (see the author's commentary on *Acts*, p.x-xxi) we have adopted has Paul leaving Ephesus after Pentecost in AD 57, going to Troas and Macedonia, and then to Corinth for the winter of AD 58.   It is possible to fit a tour, say a three-month tour, of Illyricum between Pentecost of 57 and December of 57, and still have Paul in Greece during the three winter months of 58 (Acts 20:3).   (Some, opting for a different calendar, have Paul leaving Ephesus in AD 56, thus allowing a longer time for the tour of Illyricum, which they believe this passage in Romans indicates.)   Some even appeal to the expression "those districts" in Acts 20:2 to show that Paul visited the Illryian district of the province of Macedonia.

I have fully preached the gospel of Christ.   Though some have so understood it, this phrase[43] probably does *not* mean, "In my proclamation of the gospel, I did not leave out any important doctrine."   We have no doubt that this is true, but this is not the passage to prove it.[44]   Nor does the expression mean that he had preached in every town and village in that 300,000 square-mile area, or that every individual person in that area had heard the gospel at least once.   Paul pictured himself as a pioneer, a trailblazer who opened up new areas, anticipating that others would follow.   "His conception of the duties of an apostle was that he should found churches and leave to others to build on the foundation thus laid (1 Corinthians 3:7,10)."[45]   Indeed, the historical record in Acts of Paul's missionary journeys shows that he had opened up many new areas of evangelism in those regions between Jerusalem and Illyricum.

> As a matter of fact, within the limits laid down, Christianity had been very widely preached.   There were churches throughout all Cilicia (Acts 15:42), Galatia, and Phrygia (Galatians 1:1; Acts 18:23).   The three years' residence in Ephesus implied that that city had been the center of missionary activity extending throughout all the province of Asia (Acts 19:10), even to places not visited by Paul himself (Colossians 2:1).   Thessalonica was early a center of Christian propagation (1 Thessalonians 1:7,8, 4:10), and later Paul again spent some time there (Acts 20:2).   The Second Epistle to the Corinthians contains in the greeting the words, "with all the saints who are in the whole of Achaia," showing that the long residence at Corinth had again produced a wide extension of the Gospel.[46]

15:20 – *And thus I aspired to preach the gospel, not where Christ was* already *named, that I might not build upon another man's foundation;*

And thus I aspired to preach the gospel.   These words introduce a limitation on the statement in the previous verse.   Within that vast area, there were some places where he

---

[43] In the Greek, literally, it reads, "I have fulfilled the gospel of Christ."   "Gospel" has a broad sense in this passage, including the preaching of it and its effect in the lives of men, and his own commission to serve as an ambassador of Christ.   'I have accomplished what Christ sent me to do,' is Paul's claim.

[44] A better passage would be Acts 20:27, "I did not shrink from declaring to you the whole purpose of God."

[45] Sanday and Headlam, *Romans*, p.409.

[46] Sanday and Headlam, *Romans*, p.409.   Paul's language here might have some bearing on the discussion in the study of missions as to when a land or a people is evangelized.   The Roman Catholic Church considers a land evangelized when there is a bishop in the land, even though thousands have not yet heard any sermon.   The Lutheran Church considers an area evangelized when everyone in the area has heard the gospel (whether or not everyone responds).   At the other extreme, one missionary did not consider a certain city evangelized until he had immersed the last unconverted person in the whole city.   Though this generation has been evangelized, the area will quickly revert to paganism if the next generation is not evangelized too; indeed, this is exactly what happened within a century or two in each of the areas between Jerusalem and Illyricum in which Paul had "fully preached the gospel."   They are in need of the gospel again.

did not need to go, for others had already taken the gospel to them.[47]   "Aspired" (*philotimoumenon*) could be translated "eagerly striving."   To make it a point of honor is the idea.   For Paul, it was a point of personal honor to plant churches in unevangelized places, rather than to preach where Christ was already worshiped.[48]

Not where Christ was *already* named.   "Named" seems to have the sense of "worshiped," i.e., to be named with approval.[49]   No doubt, Paul's aspiration was related to his realization of the tremendous needs of peoples unreached by the gospel.   Some preachers in those early days boasted in other men's labors (cf. 2 Corinthians 10:13-18); perhaps it was also to avoid a temptation to so boast that Paul made it his eager desire to go to unreached peoples.   Though there already was a church there, and though Christ already had some worshipers there, Paul's anticipated visit to Rome would not violate his point of honor.   He was coming only for the purpose of a visit, in the interest of getting help and support for his hoped-for opportunity to open up a new territory (Spain) to the gospel.

That I might not build upon another man's foundation.   "Foundation" in this verse equals the first preaching of the gospel in a place.[50]   While "man" need not be limited to the apostles, it likely has reference especially to them.   Paul did not follow other apostles around, working to build up a congregation numerically[51] after others had started it by intro-

---

[47] In certain areas of Asia Minor, Luke had done some preaching before he ever joined up with Paul to travel with him; it is regularly explained that Luke is the one designated as "famous for his work in spreading the good news" at 2 Corinthians 8:18 (Goodspeed).   Someone, too, preached in the provinces of Pontus, Cappadocia, and Bithynia (1 Peter 1:1), though at one time the Spirit had hindered Paul from going to at least one of these provinces (Acts 16:7).

[48] We say a point of "personal honor" with Paul, though we admit it is difficult to decide whether or not all the apostles were expected to regularly work only in virgin territories.   To substantiate the statement that it was the function of an apostle to preach the gospel in places where Christ was unknown, one could point to the Great Commission, spoken originally to the apostles, which rather envisions those missionaries going to an ever-enlarging circle of nations.   On the other hand, the record seems to show that for some of the apostles, not all of one's apostolic work was among the unevangelized.   The visit of Peter to Antioch (Galatians 2), to Corinth (1 Corinthians 1:10, 9:5), and perhaps his epistles addressed (in part) to areas which Paul had evangelized, but which evidently Peter had also visited before writing to them, suggests that Peter certainly did not limit himself to unevangelized areas.   Then, too, there is the case of the apostle John, who settled in Ephesus after AD 70, and stayed there for over a quarter century.   Unless he simply made Ephesus the home base from which he went on evangelistic tours to other areas (do 2 John 12 and 3 John 10 imply such evangelistic crusades?), then we have another example of an apostle working in a place where Christ is already known (since both Paul and Timothy had fruitful ministries in Ephesus in the AD 50's and 60's).   Furthermore, appeal could be made to the apostle James (Galatians 1:19), who stayed at Jerusalem (Acts 15:13-21, 21:18) to work with the church there for his whole life.

[49] It is probably better to explain the passive verb "named" as having "some such solemn sense as 'be named in worship' or 'be acknowledged and confessed' or 'be proclaimed (as Lord),' than to understand it as signifying merely 'be known'." Cranfield, *Romans*, p.764.

[50] See notes at footnote #22 in the Introductory Studies for the possible meanings of "foundation."

[51] 1 Corinthians 3:10 is another verse where the idea of "building on a foundation that has been laid by another" is found.   "Building" evidently has the meaning of enlarging the congregation numerically (cp. "God giveth the increase," verse 7, KJV), and the verses following warn those teachers and preachers who

ducing the gospel to the area.[52]   Such numerical growth could be entrusted to "evangelists" like Timothy (2 Timothy 4:5) or any concerned Christian (Jude 23).   Paul's endowments from the Lord required that he give his time to new church planting.   Though he hoped to impart some spiritual gift to the Roman church members (Romans 1:11), that is not the kind of "building" that it was his point of honor not to do.[53]

15:21 – *but as it is written, "THEY WHO HAD NO NEWS OF HIM SHALL SEE, AND THEY WHO HAVE NOT HEARD SHALL UNDERSTAND."*

But as it is written.   The verse about to be quoted is taken from the LXX of Isaiah 52:15, a portion of one of the Suffering Servant Poems.   This most famous Suffering Servant poem includes Isaiah 52:13-53:12.   The Servant is none other than Jesus (cp. Acts 8:32-35, where this very same poem is used by Philip as a text to preach Jesus).[54]   Paul sees the

---

work with the church about the methods used to win men to the Lord.   Poor methods (wood, hay, straw) may result in the converts not lasting, and so the teacher suffers loss, missing some of the reward he might have had if he had used better methods.

[52] In the Introductory Studies, the use that has been made of this verse to cast doubt on Peter's alleged 25-year episcopate in Rome has already been noted.   There were Christians in Rome before Paul arrived there.   Some "man" had to have laid the foundation.   Unless Paul's anticipated visit to Rome is going to be a violation of his aspiration not to build on another man's foundation, "man" must have reference to other apostles.   This commentator doubts that Peter has already planted the church at Rome.

(Another topic is worth noting when evaluating the arguments made for and against the possibility of Peter's episcopate in Rome.   A writer's preconceived ideas about church polity, in particular the doctrine of apostolic succession, likely influence his interpretation of this passage in Romans.   Some writers will make a claim that the church at Rome is unorganized – i.e., no elders or deacons have been appointed – and then suggest this is evidence that no apostle or other high dignitary has been to Rome in order to install the elders or deacons into office.   This commentator does not subscribe to the idea of apostolic succession; thus, in his judgement, that whole line of thinking cannot be used either for or against a possible ministry of Peter in Rome before or during Paul's coming visit.)

[53] Apostles were not limited in authority to the churches in a certain province, or to churches they themselves planted.   Jesus, it will be recalled, had called Paul to be a minister to the Gentiles, and in harmony with this, at the Jerusalem Conference (Galatians 2:7), it was recognized by Peter and the others that he should confine his apostolic ministry to the Gentiles.   Consequently, we find him selecting as centers of his evangelistic work the principal cities of the Gentile world.   But Paul was further careful to avoid places, wherever they might be, in which churches were already founded.   Those founded by Paul himself (e.g., the Corinthian church and the churches of Galatia) were his special responsibility to shepherd and care for (2 Corinthians 11:28; cp. 10:8, 13:10); these he visited as need arose, and addressed letters of instruction to them, or sent other men to them to instruct and correct.   But his role in this respect did not preclude his also writing letters of general encouragement and admonition to any whom his peculiar commission as apostle of the Gentiles gave him a claim to be heard by.   Thus, he wrote to the Colossians, though he had never personally evangelized in their town (Colossians 1:4, 2:1), and also to the Romans.   Since all these return visits and letters were intended to strengthen those who were already converted, such strengthening must be a different activity from what is alluded to in the word "build" in this passage.

[54] See further comments about this same Suffering Servant Poem at Romans 10:15,16.   It is only by misinterpreting this passage that James D.G. Dunn, *Jesus and the Spirit* (Philadelphia: Westminster Press, 1975), p.113, can offer the suggestion that Paul thought of himself as the "suffering servant" that Isaiah predicted.   Rather, it is because of Paul (among others) that people who have not heard get news of "Him" (the Servant) – not that Paul himself claims to be "Him" (the Servant).   "There can be no question about the fact that, according to the New Testament, this prophecy refers directly to Jesus.   See John 12:37; Acts 8:26-35; Romans 10:16; 1 Peter 1:11, 2:24.   In fact, Jesus Himself so regarded it (Luke

words of the prophet about the spread of the knowledge about Jesus as being fulfilled in his own ministry to unevangelized areas.

"THEY WHO HAD NO NEWS OF HIM SHALL SEE, AND THEY WHO HAVE NOT HEARD SHALL UNDERSTAND."   In the opening verses of this Suffering Servant Poem, we have the Gentile world pictured as hearing things they have never heard before.   In harmony with God's intent for the gospel, Paul has made it his aim to go to Gentiles who have not had opportunity to hear the gospel.

B. Announcement of Paul's Future Plans and Request for Their Prayers. 15:22-33

> *Summary:*   His plans are to go to Jerusalem with the offering for the saints, then to visit Rome, and from thence go on to Spain.   His request for their prayers has particular reference to his coming visit to Jerusalem.

15:22 – *For this reason I have often been hindered from coming to you;*

For this reason.   At Romans 1:13, Paul told his readers he had been prevented from coming to Rome before now, but he did not say what had prevented his desired trip.   Now he fills in the gap of information.   It had to do with fully preaching the gospel where it had not been preached by others in the region between Jerusalem and Illyricum (verse 19).

I have often been hindered from coming to you.   "Often" could be rendered "these many times."   "Hindered" is *egkoptō*, "to cut into, to impede one's course by cutting off his way, to hinder."[55]   The imperfect tense implies a succession of hindrances: 'Because I found so many places to preach the gospel where other apostles had not been.'

15:23 – *but now, with no further place for me in these regions, and since I have had for many years a longing to come to you*

But now, having no further place for me in these regions.[56]   As far as Paul was concerned, his "new church evangelism" work was finished as far as the regions of Asia Minor, Macedonia, and Greece were concerned.   His pioneering work, his trailblazing in those regions, was sufficiently accomplished that he could look to new areas to evangelize.   "No further place" means no more opportunity, no further scope for action, no occasion to

---

22:37)." Hendriksen, *Romans*, p.490.

[55] Thayer, *Lexicon*, p.166.

[56] The sentence that begins in this verse is broken off.   There is no main verb (in the Greek text behind the NASB) expressing what Paul is about to do.   The NASB indicates the broken thought by the use of dashes in verse 24.   (The Textus Receptus does have a main verb, "I shall come to you," which also appears in verse 24 of the KJV.)

evangelize according to Paul's usual aspirations. In those regions where he has planted churches, the task of taking the gospel to those still unreached in the region could be left to the converts, and to the young helpers who trained under Paul and then went out to serve.

And since I have had for many years a longing to come to you. "Many" translates *hikanos*, "sufficient, several." He had desired[57] to come long enough. "You" has reference to the church in Rome, not just to the city of Rome. The fact that Paul can say there has been a church in Rome for "many years" has some bearing on the date of the beginning of the church there.[58]

15:24 – *whenever I go to Spain – for I hope to see you in passing, and to be helped on my way there by you, when I have first enjoyed your company for a while* –

Whenever I go to Spain – The broken sentence is so worded (including the particle *an*) that it expresses some uncertainty as to the time or the event.[59] In Paul's time, Spain included both the modern countries of Spain and Portugal, and was a Roman province.[60] Whether or not Paul ever visited Spain is discussed below at verse 28. Several ideas have been suggested to answer the question, Why would Paul wish to go to Spain?

> (1) It was the very western end of the Roman empire. He would characteristically wish to take the good news of God so far that he could not take it farther. It was told that when Livingstone volunteered as a missionary with the London Missionary Society they asked him where he would like to go. "Anywhere," he said, "so long as it is forward." And when he reached Africa he was haunted by the smoke of a thousand villages which he saw in the distance. It was Paul's one ambition to carry the good news of God to men who had never heard it. (2) At this time Spain was experiencing a kind of blaze of genius. Many of the greatest men in the empire were Spaniards. Lucian, the epic poet; Martial, the master of the epigram; Quintillian, the greatest teacher of oratory of his day, were all Spaniards. And above all, Seneca, the great Stoic philosopher, and first, the guardian, then, afterwards,

---

[57] "Longing" is *epipothian*, "a longing desire." See notes at Romans 1:11 on this word.

[58] See the Introductory Studies for a discussion of the origin of the church in Rome. "It is likely enough that Paul's special interest in the church at Rome ... dates from his acquaintance with Aquila and Priscilla at Corinth (Acts 18:18-21). This was about [five or] six years before the writing of this epistle to the Romans, and the interval would be sufficient to justify his language about having desired to visit them 'for many years'." Sanday and Headlam, *Romans*, p.411.

[59] Broken sentences are not unusual in Paul's writings. "Paul does not finish the sentence because he feels that he must explain what is the connection between his visit to Spain and his desire to visit Rome. So he begins the parenthesis, "for I hope ...." Then he feels he must explain the reason why he does not start at once; he mentions his contemplated visit to Jerusalem and the purpose of it. This leads him so far away from the original sentence that he is not able to complete it; but in verse 28 he resumes the main argument, and gives what is the logical, but not the grammatical, apodosis." Sanday and Headlam, *Romans*, p.411.

[60] "Spain passed under Roman rule in 133 BC, and became a 'Province,' though conquest of the whole country was not complete till 19 BC." Vine, *Romans*, p.212.

the prime minister of Nero, the Roman Emperor, was a Spaniard. It may well be that Paul was saying to himself that if only he could touch this land of Spain for Christ, tremendous things might happen. (3) And the presence of Jews and Jewish synagogues in Spain gave some of the conditions of missionary work that Paul followed – to the Jew first, then to the Greek.[61]

For I hope to see you in passing. Paul wants to see with his own eyes (*theaomai*) the brethren at Rome. Here Paul begins his explanation of the connection between his proposed evangelization of Spain and his desire to visit Rome. He wants the Roman church to have a part in that evangelistic effort.

And to be helped on my way there by you. "Helped on my way" may not mean more than to be sent forward on a journey with prayers and good wishes, of which a graphic example would be found in Acts 21:5. But it can also speak of financial help,[62] for Paul may be looking for financial help from the Roman church for his planned missionary travels. He wants them to take an interest in the work in Spain, to equip him for the journey, send men along to escort him, and offer prayers on his behalf.

When I have first enjoyed your company for a while – This clause expresses his wish to enjoy, before being sent along by them, some measure of fellowship with them. Literally the clause reads, "If first I may be partly filled with you."[63] By "partly filled with you" Paul shows that he expected to see them, talk with them, preach to them, and enjoy their company – but that he did not expect to be completely satisfied, for he could not stay that long. In some measure, partly, satisfied he would be, though.

15:25 – *but now, I am going to Jerusalem serving the saints.*

But now, I am going to Jerusalem. There will be a delay before he can actually begin his journey to Spain, for there remains one more task that must be done first. The offering that has been collected must be delivered to Jerusalem. His hopes were that this would be the last of the many things (verse 22) that would hinder a visit to Rome and a missionary journey to Spain. Putting all these travel plans together, Paul's proposed itinerary was from Corinth (where he was when he wrote) to Jerusalem, to Rome, to Spain.

Serving the saints. The ministry Paul was performing, as the next verse will explain, was to deliver the offering to the saints in Jerusalem. This is not the first time Paul has been involved in carrying an offering to Jerusalem. Over a dozen years earlier, when a famine had been predicted by Agabus, the church at Antioch had prepared an offering to relieve

---

[61] The quote is based on Barclay, *Romans*, p.222,223, with some additions, deletions, and rearrangement.

[62] The verb is *propempō*, and means "to send forward, bring on the way, escort, ... to set one forward, to fit him out with the requisites for his journey, Acts 15:3." Thayer, *Lexicon*, p.541.

[63] "The expression 'to be filled' with one (as the Greek reads), in the sense of being gratified, is sometimes used in the classic writers. See Clarke on this verse." Barnes, *Romans*, p.324.

the saints at Jerusalem. Paul and Barnabas had delivered that offering (Acts 11:28-30, 12:25).

15:26 – *For Macedonia and Achaia have been pleased to make a contribution for the poor among the saints in Jerusalem.*

For Macedonia and Achaia have been pleased to make a contribution. Here we have Paul's explanation of the phrase "serving the saints." Other provinces and churches were involved in this offering, as shown by the references in Acts 24:17; 1 Corinthians 16:1-4; 2 Corinthians 8-9; Galatians 6:6-10; and Acts 20:4 (which likely names the men who carried the offerings from the respective churches). Perhaps Paul mentions only Macedonia and Achaia here because he has for the past several months been in closest touch with them. "The fact that it was collected from so extensive a tract of country, and that it was more than a year in being taken up, would justify the conclusion that it must have been a very great offering."[64] The Greek reads *koinōnian tina*, a "certain collection," and this has led some to suppose that an assessment or levy or prescribed amount has been assigned to each church, or to each individual. However, the word "pleased" (*eudokeō*), in this verse and the next, implies that the contribution was a voluntary gesture on the part of the Gentile churches, made freely, generously, and with good will.[65] *Koinōnia* (here translated "contribution") is also regularly translated "fellowship, participation in a common cause" (e.g., Acts 2:42).[66] One practical way to demonstrate the unity of believers, their participation in a common cause, is to get involved in each other's lives, meeting needs, doing things together for Christ.

> There was no better way of demonstrating in the most practical way the unity of the Church. This was a way of teaching the young Churches that they were not isolated units, but members of a great Church throughout all the world. The great value of giving to others is that it makes us remember that we are not members of a congregation but of a Church which is as wide as the world.[67]

For the poor among the saints in Jerusalem. James 2:2 shows there were poor Christians at Jerusalem, even after the offering was received.[68] But both this passage and

---

[64] Lard, *Romans*, p.446.

[65] In spite of the fact that Paul insists that Macedonia and Achaia have been pleased to make the contribution, it did not prevent him from using well-calculated fund-raising techniques as he encouraged them in their resolve to share in this offering (2 Corinthians 8,9; 1 Corinthians 16:1-4).

[66] See comments on the verb *koinōneō* at Romans 12:13. A very rewarding exercise (one that will contribute to spiritual growth) is to do a word study of the different Greek words used by Paul to describe the offering, both here in Romans and in 2 Corinthians 8,9.

[67] Barclay, *Romans*, p.224.

[68] The date of the book of James is debated. These comments assume a late date (c. AD 62) rather than the early date (c. AD 45) that is sometimes posited for the writing of the book of James.

James also show that not all were poor; it says, "the poor among the saints."[69]   From the very beginning of the church in Jerusalem, there was a body of poor people included in their numbers (Acts 6:1-4).   That early congregation had been dispersed (Acts 8:4), yet the new congregation that grew up after the persecution and dispersion there were hurt by the famine so there was need to help, which the church at Antioch did (Acts 11:29).   Just what contributed to the poverty of some of the Jerusalem saints in the late AD 50's that this offering was intended to help alleviate we do not know.[70]   The statement about the offering here in Romans 15 plays an important part in enabling us to date the Roman letter, as has been shown in the Introductory Studies.[71]

15:27 – *Yes, they were pleased* to do so, *and they are indebted to them.   For if the Gentiles have shared in their spiritual things, they are indebted to minister to them also in material things.*

Yes, they were pleased *to do so.*   Here we have further explanation of the word "pleased" in the previous verse.[72]   There was a special reason why they were delighted to share in this offering.

And they are indebted to them.   Not just to the poor among them, but to the Jerusalem saints in general.   The Gentile churches were, in a sense, simply repaying a debt[73] they owed to their Jewish brethren.   How it is they have come to have this "obligation" is stated in the rest of the verse.

For if the Gentiles have shared in their spiritual things.   It was from Jerusalem that the gospel had spread.   It was still true that Gentiles were wild olive branches being grafted in among the genuine branches (Romans 11:17-24).   But there is this added thought: the Jewish believers (the genuine branches) have had a considerable part[74] in making known

---

[69] "Saints" was explained at Romans 1:7.

[70] This much is obvious: one should be very hesitant to affirm that the community of goods referred to in Acts 2:45 and 4:34,35 is the cause that had left an aftermath of poverty.   Acts 2 and 4 refer to something that happened a quarter of a century earlier, and to a congregation long since scattered, and whose place had been taken by a new group of converts.

[71] William Paley, *Horae Paulinae*, ch.II, No.1, long ago called attention to the evidence for the genuineness of Romans, and in particular for chapter 15 (which some critics are wont to doubt), that can be derived from the mention of the offering for Jerusalem.   "Without being in any way indebted to one another, and each contributing some new element, all the different accounts fit and dovetail into one another, and thus imply they all are historical."   Sanday and Headlam, *Romans*, p.413.

[72] While the voluntary nature of the contribution must be emphasized, it is also true that there is the connotation of "resolve" in the word.   Once the Gentile brethren were aware of the need, delighted that they had the opportunity, with resolve they determined to help.

[73] On the meaning of the word "debt," see notes on "obligation" at Romans 1:14.   It was a moral debt, not a legal one.

[74] The verb "shared" is *koinōneō*, again.   Now we see how Paul is saying that we are all in this together; we are sharing in a common task.   The Jewish believers have shared the gospel; now the Gentile believers

to others the opportunity to be grafted in. This language is tacit praise and acknowledgment of Jewish believers' persistent efforts and cheerful sacrifices, all of which were done in order that "their spiritual things" (the blessings of the gospel[75] that they have come to know about) might be shared and enjoyed by as many other people as possible. There is a sense in which the Jerusalem church could be called the mother-church, and the Gentile churches are the children, who are now, by means of this offering, expressing their gratitude for what Jerusalem did for them.

They are indebted to minister to them also in material things. Paul regularly taught that the people who receive teaching have a responsibility to support the teacher (see Galatians 6:6; 1 Corinthians 9:3-14). "Minister" is *leitourgeō*, a cognate form of the word translated "minister" at 13:6 and 15:16, and of the word translated "service" at 2 Corinthians 9:12, where it is one of the terms applied to the offering itself. It is part of one's priestly service offered to God to take care of the "material things"[76] of a brother who is in need.[77] It may be that part of the debt the Gentiles owe stems from the fact that the spiritual benefits they have received far outweigh the material benefits they are going to share (1 Corinthians 9:11).

15:28 – *Therefore, when I have finished this, and have put my seal on this fruit of theirs, I will go on by way of you to Spain.*

Therefore, when I have finished this. Paul here resumes the statement (begun in verses 23,24) of his future plans, a statement interrupted by several digressions. "Finished" translates *epiteleō*, a word which sometimes has religious or priestly overtones.[78] Perhaps Paul is still (cp. verse 16) depicting himself as fulfilling priestly duties as he delivers this offering;[79] perhaps "this phraseology indicates the sacredness in God's sight of ministering material assistance to the saints;"[80] perhaps it simply means "completed," with no religious

---

are sharing (making a contribution) financial assistance in return.

[75] The words *ta pneumatika* ("spiritual *gifts*") at 1 Corinthians 14:1 have a much more limited sense than does the expression here in Romans 15:27. Yet Cranfield, *Romans*, p.773,774, may well be right in calling our attention to the idea that the "spiritual things" just might have reference to the fact that the Holy Spirit has something to do with the preaching of the gospel, leading men to accept it, and then helping those who obey to live the Christian life thereafter. But the work of the Spirit, though foundational, is not the whole of the gospel blessings (i.e., things which are spiritual as opposed to things which are "material").

[76] The ASV reads "carnal things," and the word is *sarx* ("flesh"), about which notes have been given at several places in our study of Romans (e.g., Romans 1, footnote #12; Romans 4, footnote #3; Romans 11, footnote #61). There is hardly an ethical connotation here. "By 'fleshly things' are meant things pertaining to the flesh, or beneficial to it, such as food and clothing." Lard, *Romans*, p.447.

[77] "Who, then, cannot be Christ's priest, so long as we have Christ's poor with us?" Riddle, in Lange, *Romans*, p.442.

[78] Arndt-Gingrich, *Lexicon*, p.302.

[79] Sanday and Headlam, *Romans*, p.413.

[80] Vine, *Romans*, p.213.

overtones intended.[81]

And have put my seal on this fruit of theirs. "Fruit" is an unexpected term to characterize the offering. Perhaps Paul looks on the offering as the fruit produced by his ministry among the Gentiles. Perhaps Paul looks on the offering as the natural product of the Gentiles' walk with God. Perhaps he thinks of the offering as being the natural product resulting from the spiritual blessings the Jerusalem brethren had shared. Also, just what is intended by his use of the word "seal" is puzzling. One suggestion is that this is a formal business expression denoting final deliverance into safe custody. Another suggestion is that Paul was personally guaranteeing that the whole offering sent by the brethren was intact.[82] The most appealing of the suggestions is that by sealing this fruit Paul means that he will personally explain to the Jewish recipients how this offering is a guarantee of the genuineness of the Gentiles' faith and obedience to Jesus.[83]

I will go on by way of you to Spain. Paul's plans are these: as soon as he has seen the offering safely to Jerusalem, he will set out for Spain, by way of Rome. As will be demonstrated in comments on verse 32, Paul did get to Rome (though not in the way he expected). But the evidence that he ever got to Spain is not so clear.[84]

---

[81] Cranfield, *Romans*, p.774.

[82] This suggestion appears somewhat doubtful. Paul has given instructions that each church is to pick its own couriers (1 Corinthians 16:3), likely with the very purpose of guarding him from insinuations or suspicions that he helped himself to part of the offering.

[83] From a number of passages we perceive that there was not always harmony and unity between the brethren of differing ethnic backgrounds. We have intimated from time to time in our comments on Romans that Christians converted from Jewish backgrounds were having trouble accepting the Gentiles Christians, because the Gentiles failed to observe the Mosaic rituals and rules to which the Jews had so long been accustomed. Although Paul and the other apostles have been teaching that the Law of Moses was temporary, and its precepts and prohibitions about worship, dietary laws, and Levitical priesthood had all been abrogated at the cross, somehow the Jewish believers could not help but wonder if Gentile Christianity was the real thing, since in many ways their lifestyle was so different. The offering to Jerusalem, Paul believed, would be the very thing needed to demonstrate to the Jerusalem church that their Gentile brothers' conversion was real, that their religion was genuine. Those congregations who had made these contributions were all planted by Paul. He was the one who needed to be present when the delivery of the offering was made, so the intended effect (not merely to feed the poor among the saints) would be felt.

[84] Whether or not Paul ever carried out his planned journey to Spain is of little import, unless the evidence for his travels (or absence of such travels) is used by critics to question or deny the possibility of the Pauline authorship of several of the New Testament books that bear his name. In fact, because it has become fashionable in some liberal circles to deny the Pauline authorship of the Pastoral Epistles, we will pause to consider the question of a journey to Spain in some detail.

In brief, the relationship between a possible journey to Spain and the authorship of the Pastorals is this: the historical allusions in the Pastoral Epistles cannot be matched to Paul's life and ministry before the Roman imprisonment described in Acts 28. If Paul was executed at the end of that Acts 28 imprisonment, or even early in the Neronian persecution that began in AD 64, then it is almost impossible to believe that Paul wrote the Pastorals. On the other hand, if there is evidence of a trip to Spain, then it could be affirmed that Paul did survive long enough after that Roman imprisonment to have had time to do what the historical allusions in the Pastorals have the writer doing. In other words, there would be no persuasive reason (historically) why he could not be the author, just as the signature in those letters claim.

15:29 – *And I know that when I come to you, I will come in the fulness of the blessing of Christ.*

And I know that when I come to you. How soon Paul thought he would be in Rome can only be guessed. If he traveled by ship toward Jerusalem and then later to Rome, he could be there before the year is over. If he planned to make the trip from Jerusalem to Rome overland, the interval would be longer. How different from his anticipations were the cir-

---

What evidence, then, is there – both Biblical and traditional – concerning what happened at the close of the Roman imprisonment described in Acts 28? The Prison Epistles (Ephesians, Philippians, Colossians, and Philemon) show that Paul planned to visit the churches in Asia Minor as soon as he was released from prison (e.g., Philippians 1:26, 2:24; Philemon 22). (Does this imply that, before the end of his nearly five years in custody since he wrote the letter to the Romans, Paul has given up any intention of going to Spain?) If it could be assumed for the moment that Paul did write the Pastorals, these letters talk of travels through Crete (Titus 1:5), Asia Minor and Macedonia (1 Timothy 1:3, 3:14,15; 2 Timothy 4:20), and plans to visit Nicopolis (Titus 3:12). Early Christian literature has Paul released from his first Roman imprisonment, visiting the churches he had earlier established, and then coming to Rome a second time, and there being executed in the 14th year of Nero (i.e., AD 68). (Documentation of these points can be found in "The Last Labors and Letters of Paul," an epilogue to the author's commentary on *Acts*, p.951ff. See also Eusebius, *Church History*, II.xxii.1,2; and Jerome, *Lives*, ch.5.) If, in addition to this, it could be shown that Paul did go to Spain, so much the better as far as giving him time to write the Pastorals.

From early Christian literature come two references to a possible trip to Spain. (1) Clement of Rome, writing in about AD 96, has, "Let us set before our eyes the illustrious apostles ... After preaching both in the east and west, [Paul] gained the illustrious reputation due to his faith, having taught righteousness to the whole world, and having come to *the extreme limits of the west*, suffered martyrdom under the prefects. Thus he was removed from the world, and went into the holy place, having proved himself a striking example of patience" (I Clement 5:7). COMMENTS: The "prefects" would be Tigellinus and Sabinus, in the last year of the emperor Nero, i.e., AD 68. Many writers would affirm that "the extreme limits of the west," in a letter written to Rome, must be a reference to Spain. Still others are not so sure. One writer has proposed a different punctuation, so that the passage reads "having taught righteousness to the whole world even to the extreme limits of the west, came and suffered martyrdom under the prefects." So punctuated, it would not be impossible to interpret it to mean that Rome (not Spain) was the western limits of Paul's teaching. (2) The Muratorian Canon. The Latin is very corrupt. Hendriksen (*Romans*, p.492) suggests that the autograph likely read, "Luke relates them for the most excellent Theophilus because in his presence the individual events transpired, as he clearly declares by omitting the passion of Peter as well as the departure of Paul when the latter proceeded from the city [Rome] to Spain." COMMENTS: The Muratorian Canon was written about 100 years after Paul's death, and the writer may have had no independent knowledge. It is certainly more probable (say Sanday and Headlam, *Romans*, p.414) that he is merely drawing a conclusion, and not a correct one, from Romans 15:28.

This little bit of evidence from Scripture and Early Christian Literature has allowed scholars to draw different conclusions about a trip to Spain. (1) Some suggest Paul went to Spain after his release from the first Roman imprisonment, and then came to Crete and Ephesus and Macedonia (as the historical allusions in the Pastorals teach). Leaving Rome in AD 63, he could have spent upward of two years in Spain. (Some even posit a trip to Britain during this period.) Then in AD 65, he returned to the scene of his earlier labors, Macedonia and Asia Minor. (2) Thiessen (*Introduction to the New Testament* [Grand Rapids: Wm. B. Eerdmans Publishing Co., 1954], p.261) suggested that Paul went to Crete, Ephesus, and Macedonia first after his release, and then went to Spain, and from thence returned to Asia Minor and Macedonia before being arrested and returned to Rome for his second imprisonment and martyrdom. (3) The third conclusion drawn from the above evidence is that Paul went to Crete, Ephesus, and Macedonia after his release from the first Roman imprisonment, and DID NOT GO TO SPAIN as he had once planned. There are no records of churches in Spain at this early period (from AD 60-100), but that might only prove the fragmentary character of the records, rather than that Paul did not go to Spain and plant churches there. The somewhat doubtful nature of the tradition of a trip to Spain, plus the clearly stated plans in the Prison Epistles, lead this writer to doubt that Paul ever made his trip to Spain. Paul's own words in the Pastoral Epistles have him in the east, not the west, in the interval between imprisonments.

cumstances of Paul's first visit to Rome.   Acts 21-28 tell us what actually happened.[85]

I will come in the fulness of the blessing of Christ.[86]   Paul is confident both he and the Christians at Rome will be recipients of Christ's blessings.   He will be able to bestow "some spiritual gift" (1:11); each will be encouraged by the other's faith (1:12); they will refresh him and help him on his way (15:24,32).   Though probably not as he envisioned it when he wrote, even this confident expectation was realized during the two years of Paul's first Roman imprisonment.   They will come out to meet him as he was ending his voyage to Rome; and when he saw the brethren, he thanked God and took courage (Acts 28:15).   Philippians 1:12-18 shows several ways his imprisonment in Rome proved to be the occasion of "the blessing of Christ" being experienced in Rome.   Also, the writing of the Prison Epistles is one of the unexpected blessings that came out of Paul's stay in Rome.[87]

15:30 – *Now I urge you, brethren, by our Lord Jesus Christ and by the love of the Spirit, to strive together with me in your prayers to God for me,*

Now I urge you, brethren.[88]   Having unfolded his future plans, Paul now asks[89] for their prayers in his behalf.   The reference to his pending visit to Jerusalem reminds him of the dangers he knows he faces and the misgivings he harbors about how the offering will be received by the brethren there.   Paul's request for prayer is so urgent that he holds up two motives to underscore that urgency.

By our Lord Jesus Christ.   Motive number one is this: If you have any regard for Jesus Christ (perhaps also including His cause in the world), please spend time in prayer!

And by the love of the Spirit.   Motive number two: If the Holy Spirit has produced any love (probably love for the brethren, like Paul; perhaps, since it is *agapē*, love for the lost) in your hearts,[90] please be in prayer!   Alford reminds us that this is a "love which teaches

---

[85] "Would a forger, writing under the apostle's name in the second century, have made him pen a plan of the future so different from the way in which things really [came to pass]?" Godet, *Romans*, p.485.

[86] The additional words found in the KJV, "the fulness of the blessing *of the gospel* of Christ," do not rest on good manuscript authority.

[87] "The fact that, in our path of service for the Lord, circumstances take place very differently from our expectations and desires, affords no necessary indication that we are not being guided of God.   On the contrary, our very disappointments issue in the accomplishment of far greater things than we anticipate, and always in the fulfillment of God's all wise purpose."   Vine, *Romans*, p.213.

[88] Though "brethren" is omitted in P[46] and Codex Vaticanus, Cranfield (*Romans*, p.775,776) argues for its retention in the text.

[89] "Whether *parakalein* has its special sense of 'exhort' (see on 12:1) here or its more ordinary sense of 'ask,' 'request,' is not clear, though perhaps, on the whole, it is rather more naturally understood here as simply meaning 'ask,' ...."   Cranfield, *Romans*, p.776.

[90] Romans 5:8 has spoken about how the Holy Spirit makes men aware God loves them.   Galatians 5:22 shows that one of the fruits of the Spirit is "love," i.e., the Christian is helped to love others.

us to look not only on our own things but on the things of others."[91]

To strive together with me in your prayers to God for me. "To strive with one in prayer means to join him in a deeply earnest effort at prayer."[92] This is intercessory prayer. By this request,

> Paul expresses his confidence in the efficacy of the prayers of the brethren.
> He continually, in labors and dangers in which he was exposed, felt the need
> of and asked the prayers of the brethren on his behalf ... If Paul, the inspired
> apostle, felt the need of prayers of the brethren in his behalf and for the
> furtherance of his work, how much more should Christians feel the need of
> receiving and offering prayers one for another![93]

Two specific requests he wanted them to make in his behalf are indicated in the next verse.

15:31 – *that I may be delivered from those who are disobedient in Judea, and* that *my service for Jerusalem may prove acceptable to the saints;*

That I may be delivered from those who are disobedient in Judea. Years of past experience with the unbelieving Jews[94] has taught him that he has become the object of fierce hostility on their part.[95] Not long after the actual journey to Jerusalem had begun,

---

[91] Alford, *Romans*, p.464.

[92] Lard, *Romans*, p.448. *Sunagōnizomai*, in classical Greek, is an athletic term, describing the concerted action of a team of athletes, as they "agonized together" against another team. In Koine Greek, it means "to fight or contend along with someone," then, also generally, "to help, assist someone." Arndt-Gingrich, *Lexicon*, p.791. Paul is asking for team action (he and the Roman readers will make up the prayer team) in this matter of prayer, but it is highly questionable that God is conceived as being the opponent who is being struggled against, in some similar way as when Jacob wrestled with God (Genesis 32:24-32). No "opponent" is named (either here or in Colossians 4:12, where the same word is used). While some have suggested that in prayer Christians are "wrestling against the world rulers of darkness" (cp. Ephesians 6:12; Daniel 10:12,13; Colossians 2:1), or against temptations or distractions which hinder prayer, it may be that all Paul means is that their prayers are to be earnest (as opposed to half-hearted or casual), urgent, and persistent.

[93] Lipscomb and Shepherd, *Romans*, p.268. "The [word] order in the original is 'on my behalf toward God,' which throws emphasis upon the latter words. Paul's personal trust in God, and the Divine assurance given to him, did not make him independent of the prayers of the saints. Prayer is never regarded superfluous by any circumstances, not even by the knowledge of God's will and purpose. On the contrary, the revelation of that will is an incentive to prayer. See Ezekiel 36:37." Vine, *Romans*, p.214.

[94] The word *apeithō* can be translated either "disobedient" or "unbelieving." See notes at 10:16 and 11:30, 31. It describes the Jews who still persisted in rejecting Christ as being stiff-necked, obstinate, and as having a stubborn refusal to be persuaded.

[95] Shortly after his conversion, unbelieving Jews tried to kill him (Acts 9:29,30). But it was not just in Judea that the disobedient Jews were determined in their efforts to get rid of Paul. On his first missionary journey, unbelieving Jews had agitated against him so as to have him stoned to death (Acts 14:19). On the second journey, they succeeded in harassing him at Thessalonica and at Berea (Acts 17:5-15), and accused him of a crime before Gallio in Corinth, that, had he been found guilty, would have meant execution (Acts 18:12-17).

Paul is speaking to the elders from Ephesus, and he says, "I am on my way to Jerusalem, not knowing what will happen to me there, except that the Holy Spirit solemnly testifies to me in every city, saying that bonds and afflictions await me" (Acts 20:22,23). Perhaps his request for prayer indicates that the Holy Spirit had already given Paul warning while he was still at Corinth, before he wrote Romans.[96] Whether or not Paul was "delivered" depends on how this verb is interpreted.[97] If it be conceived as asking for protection from them, then we may say the petition was rejected by God, for the unbelieving Jews did beset Paul and create numerous problems (imprisonment, trials, false accusations) for him when he got to Jerusalem (Acts 21:27-36). If it be conceived as asking for rescue from their hands, then we may say the petition was answered in a positive way, for (while it resulted in his being held in protective custody and then in multiple years in prison) he was rescued from the mob that was set on killing him (Acts 21:31-36).

And *that* my service for Jerusalem may prove acceptable to the saints. This is the second specific request he wants them to make in their prayers on his behalf to God. There is a grace of receiving as well as the grace of giving. Some people are too proud to accept "charity." Paul did not know for sure that the Jewish Christians ("the saints," cp. verse 26) would receive the offering.[98] If they did, it would serve to improve attitudes and relations between the Jewish and Gentile brethren. If they did not, the Gentiles might well look on it as a serious rebuff, and it could have disastrous consequences on the unity of the church for years to come.[99] This request was answered positively: in Luke's own words

---

[96] Before he ever gets to Judea, in fact on the eve of his departure, how bitterly even the local unconverted Jews opposed him was made very clear. The plot they had made against him was discovered, and caused a change to be made in the route to be taken toward Jerusalem (Acts 20:3).

[97] The verb *rhuomai* can mean "preserve, deliver, rescue, set free" (Arndt-Gingrich, *Lexicon*, p.744,745). We have had the verb before at Romans 7:24 ("set free") and 11:26 ("remove"). It is the verb in the petition "Deliver us from the evil one" in the Model Prayer.

[98] Paul has used the verb "serving" (*diakoneō*) at verse 25 to express how he pictured his own part in this offering; now he uses the noun "service" (*diakonia*) to refer again to his "ministration in bringing the money collected ... [and] intended for Jerusalem." Thayer, *Lexicon*, p.138. (There is a manuscript variation at this place. "The variant reading (*dōrophoria*) 'bringing a gift' instead of 'ministration' (*diakonia*), though found in the Vatican and a few other MSS, is probably an explanatory gloss." Gifford, *Romans*, p.230.)

[99] Earlier in our comments (e.g., footnote #83 above) we have alluded to certain tensions between believers of differing ethnic backgrounds. Just how much those tensions are reflected in Paul's request for prayer that the offering be accepted by the saints in Judea is difficult to decide. After the offering was received, James will suggest to Paul another gesture that might help remove the suspicions that many Jewish Christians still harbored about Paul (Acts 21:20-26). While the Tubingen School's interpretation of this request for prayer has gone too far in finding evidence of serious tension between the Jewish (Petrine) and Gentile (Pauline) churches, some suspicions there certainly were. It was possible that Christian Jews who (after so many years!) were still "zealous for the Law" just might look on money from a Gentile's hands as tainted (unclean). So Lipscomb and Shepherd's comment may not be far from the truth as they explain why Paul was so exceedingly anxious that it be accepted: "[Paul] was fearful that the strong Jewish feeling existing among the Christians of Judea (Acts 21:20) might lead them to reject the offering of the Gentile Christians that he and his companions brought. This would have been disappointing, and he was anxious to perfect the bond of fraternal brotherhood between the Jewish and Gentile Christians. The cheerful sending of this offering (2 Corinthians 8:1-24) was the seal of the brotherly love on the part of the Gentiles. The acceptance of it would be the seal of the bond of

we read, "And when we had come to Jerusalem, the brethren received us gladly" (Acts 21:17). The following verses give Paul's brief explanation of what God had been doing among the Gentiles through his ministry (is it too much to suppose that at this time he presented the offering as evidence?); then we read, "And when they heard it they began glorifying God" (Acts 21:20). James and the elders praised God for their Gentile brethren's efforts at fellowship.

15:32 – *so that I may come to you in joy by the will of God and find* **refreshing** *rest in your* **company.**

So that. This verse evidently is intended to express a more remote purpose for their two requests to God (verse 31).[100] If he were delivered from the disobedient Jews in Judea, and if the offering is graciously welcomed, then he can come to Rome with a stronger and deeper Christian joy.

I may come to you in joy. Especially if the offering were refused, his disappointment would have been almost overwhelming. Even the time it would take to journey from Jerusalem to Rome would hardly be enough for the wounds to heal and for his spirits to revive.

By the will of God. All along, as Paul has been asking for their prayers, it has been tacitly assumed that God is active in His world, and that He controls and guides and arranges (to a certain extent) what men do.[101] Paul's deliverance and the Christians' acceptance of the offering were things that the people offering the prayers expected God Himself to have a hand in causing to happen. Their prayers were for God to actively intervene: to turn evil into good if need be (in the matter of deliverance), and to so work on the hearts of the Christians that they will be gracious and appreciative of what the Gentiles have done. Even then, after God's intervention at Jerusalem, the anticipated trip to Rome and Spain could be overruled by the providence of God (see Romans 1:10).

And find *refreshing* **rest in your company.**[102] 'I may rest and refresh my spirit with you'

---

brotherhood on the part of the Jews." *Romans*, p.269.

[100] Those reading the Greek text will have observed that both verses 31 and 32 begin with *hina*. In the NASB, the first one is translated "that" and the second is translated "so that." What the translators have done is treat the first as though it introduced an example of indirect discourse after the verb "strive together in prayer," and the second as a purpose clause depending on verse 31. With this we agree, but it should be noted that some would treat verse 32 as if it were another item to be included in the requests the Roman readers make of God.

[101] Consult the Special Studies on "The Providence of God" and "The Doctrine of Predestination" where God's involvement in His world was covered in detail.

[102] Those who treat verse 32 as listing more requests to be included in the Romans' prayers find this statement to be a fourth request. Not a few would write comments about prayers and their answers in the following vein: There were four requests Paul asked for, and see how they were answered. He prayed for deliverance. Answer: he wasn't protected from them completely, but was rescued from their murderous intent. He prayed that his mission might be welcomed. Answer: it was received gladly. He

is the sense of *sunanapauomai*.[103]   After the personal danger he faced whenever he was in the presence of unbelieving Jews, and after the anxiety about how the Christian Jews would accept a Gentile offering, he looked forward to his visit to Rome as a time of rest, rather than as another field of labor.   While there, he hoped to gather strength for his planned evangelistic tour of Spain.   Not that he will do nothing but relax while he is there (see 1:11,13 and 15:29); rather, their affection for him means their community is one where he is likely to be untroubled by the strife and distraction he faced in many other places.

15:33 – *Now the God of peace be with you all.   Amen.*

Now the God of peace be with you all.[104]   His request for their prayers for him leads him to offer a prayer for them.   "He prays that God, who dwells in peace and who bestows His peace upon His servants, might be with them."[105]   The title "God of peace" is frequent in Paul's writings.[106]   Perhaps the idea that God can bring about "peace" is suggested to Paul's mind as he thinks about the circumstances of danger about which he just wrote.   Perhaps "peace" is used in its Jewish connotation of all the blessings that accompany salvation (cp. Romans 1:7).   "The song of angels over the birth of Christ was 'peace on earth;' and the benediction for the church in Rome is 'the God of peace be with you.'"[107]

Amen.[108]   The meaning of the word "amen" has been explained at Romans 11:36.

---

prayed that he might be permitted to come to Rome.   Answer: He got to Rome, but not the way he anticipated in this prayer.   He prayed for a restful stay.   Answer: God had other ideas than a restful visit.

[103] Literally, the word means to lie down together, to sleep with someone else. In its metaphorical sense, the verb means "to rest with, or find rest in someone's company." Arndt-Gingrich, *Lexicon*, p.792. The only other place in the Greek Bible where the term is found is Isaiah 11:6, where the leopard lies down with the kid.

[104] See the Introductory Studies for a discussion of whether or not there was an early edition of the epistle to the Romans that came to an end with this benediction.   "That this verse is rather to be compared with such prayer-wishes as 15:13 and 1 Thessalonians 3:11-13 and the promise in Philippians 4:9 than with the concluding greetings of Paul's letters is indicated by the fact that all the concluding greetings of the whole Pauline corpus include the word *charis* ['grace']."   Cranfield, *Romans*, p.780.

[105] Lipscomb and Shepherd, *Romans*, p.179.

[106] It is used again at Romans 16:20.   See also 2 Corinthians 13:11; Philippians 4:9; 1 Thessalonians 5:23; and Hebrews 13:20.   The context in which the expression is found often gives it a special meaning. For example, "peace" would have been a contrast with the troubles among his readers in 1 Thessalonians 5:23.   Or "peace" might be the opposite of the distractions caused by the Judaizers which the readers were experiencing, as in 2 Corinthians 13:11.   In Hebrews 13:20, "peace" seems to be in contrast to the sufferings the readers were experiencing.

[107] Lard, *Romans*, p.449.

[108] "The weight of manuscript authority is decidedly in favor of retaining this word, though it is omitted by three manuscripts of some importance (P^{46}, A, G).   It does not, however, follow that the benediction was intended, as some have thought, to close the epistle.   Intercalated benedictions and doxologies are frequent in the writings of Paul.   (Comp. chs. 9:5, 11:36; Gal. 1:5; Eph. 3:20,21, *et al.*)."   Sanday, *Romans*, p.120,121.

C. Commendation of Phoebe, the Bearer of This Letter to Rome. 16:1,2

16:1 – *I commend to you our sister Phoebe, who is a servant of the church which is at Cenchrea;*

I commend to you our sister Phoebe. "Commend" is a good choice for an English word to represent *sunhistēmi*, for the Greek word is more than a mere introduction; there is also a connotation of praise included as Paul introduces and recommends Phoebe to the brethren at Rome.[1] While these words of commendation simply form part of the whole epistle to Rome,[2] verses 1 and 2 are worded in the familiar 1st century form found regularly in such "letters of commendation."[3] "Our sister" is likely to be taken in its spiritual sense, i.e., a fellow Christian.[4] All that is certainly known of Phoebe is what can be ascertained from this brief commendation of her. From her name it has often been deduced that she was of Gentile background, since it is thought that a Jewess would not likely have had a name derived from pagan mythology.[5] It is inferred from her commendation here that she served as the carrier of this letter from Paul to the brethren at Rome. It is supposed that she was about to set out on a journey to Rome on some business purpose (see verse 2), and this gave Paul the opportunity to send this epistle to the brethren there; this supposition is much more likely than that she set out only for the purpose of carrying the letter.[6]

---

[1] Arndt-Gingrich, *Lexicon*, p.798. The same word was translated "demonstrates" at Romans 3:5 and 5:8, which is the other of its two conspicuous meanings in the New Testament. See Sanday and Headlam, *Romans*, p.72.

[2] The presence of *de* in the better manuscripts of this epistle indicates that these two verses formed part of the letter as a whole, rather than being a "self-contained and independent letter of commendation" that somehow came to be included in what we now call Romans. See the Introductory Studies where this whole matter of the integrity of chapters 15 and 16 is discussed.

[3] 2 Corinthians 3:1 makes reference to such "letters of commendation." Barclay, after observing that "we still possess many of these letters written on papyrus, and recovered from the rubbish heaps ... of Egypt," gives an example of one such letter that introduced a certain servant who had been sent on an errand by his master to another businessman, and (here it differs from Paul's introduction of Phoebe) it even states the specific nature of the errand the servant has been sent to carry out.

[4] Such letters soon came to serve another purpose in the churches. Because of the generous practice of hospitality by the brethren, charlatans and parasites began to take advantage of the proffered hospitality. Soon such letters were written to introduce believers to each other, and such letters helped prevent the impostors from taking advantage of the Christian generosity.

[5] *Phoibos* is transliterated "Phoebus" and is another name for Apollo, the messenger of the gods in pagan mythology. The word has the connotation "prophetic," as well as "bright, clear, pure," and is related to the word *phoibas*, which was the term for "priestess of Phoebus," an "inspired female," a "prophetess." James Donnegan, *A New Greek and English Lexicon* (Boston: Hilliard, Gray and Co., 1833), p.1347. On the other hand, Greek influence after Alexander the Great led to Jewish children having Greek names, as, for example, did several of Jesus' apostles. Thus, no absolute conclusion about her ethnic background can be drawn from her name.

[6] Conybeare assumes Phoebe was a widow on the ground that she could not, according to Greek manners, have been mentioned as acting in the independent manner described, either if her husband had been living or if she had been unmarried. *Life and Epistles of St. Paul*, p.542.

Who is a servant of the church which is at Cenchrea. This is the first time in the New Testament that we learn there was a congregation of Christians in the seaport town of Cenchrea, which was about nine miles east of Corinth on the Saronic Gulf. 2 Corinthians 1:1 tells us there were saints throughout Achaia, and one might suppose that the church at Cenchrea was a mission church started by converts who went there from Corinth. Phoebe is characterized as being a "servant" of the congregation at Cenchrea; it is the only place in the New Testament where the word "servant" is used in its feminine form. Since the word in its masculine form is often translated "deacon," it is not surprising to find some modern translations using "deaconess" to render the feminine form.[7] While many pages have been

---

[7] The most difficult thing for present-day readers to do is to use the word "servant" or "deaconess" without automatically reading back into the verse in Romans the modern connotation given to these words. In addition, comments on this passage have surely been influenced by church polity considerations. In arriving at an understanding of this matter, the following items have bearing: 1) The word *diakonos* ("servant, minister") can have both a general meaning (e.g., Romans 15:8, where Christ is styled a "servant," that is, He ministered to the Jewish people), and a technical sense (e.g., "deacons" in Philippians 1:1 and 1 Timothy 3:8). By what criteria can it be decided absolutely in which sense Paul uses the word here? 2) In the *Epistles* (X.96.8) of Pliny the Younger, about AD 110, there is reference to deaconesses, or female ministers (*ministrae*, Lat.); however, such female "servants" are not referred to in any other 2nd century writing. Is there any way to demonstrate that Pliny's *ministrae* and Paul's *diakonon* refer to the same office or function? 3) It is also a fact that by the 4th century there was an ecclesiastical office of deaconess, as attested to by the instructions concerning this office (ordination, duties, authority over the order of widows, etc.) found in the *Apostolic Constitutions* (II.26.57; III.7.15). Is there any way to know whether or not a practice 300 years later is in any way related to Phoebe's position in 1st century Cenchrea? 4) There is very strong probability that no other New Testament passage has any specific mention of an office of deaconess. It is not legitimate to affirm that either 1 Timothy 3:11 or 1 Timothy 5:3-16 has any specific reference to an office of deaconess. 1 Timothy 3:11 (we believe) requires that a prospective deacon's wife must also meet certain high qualifications before the man himself is qualified for the special job of deacon. Likewise, it is difficult to show that "put on the list" (1 Timothy 5:9) has reference to selecting widows to an official church office. It could just as well be an official list of those widows whom the church had assumed the responsibility to care for. 5) One thing that would seem to show that there was no permanent office of deaconess is that there are no qualifications given (as there are for elder and deacon) by which they are to be selected by each individual congregation.

Sanday and Headlam (*Romans*, p.417) give what might be the most convincing argument of any that there must have been an order of deaconess in the early church. "From the very beginning of Christianity – more particularly in fact at the beginning – there must have been a want felt for women to perform for women the function which the deacons performed for men." It is not difficult to give some specific examples of the kind of thing for which women helpers would be needed: teaching prospective female converts in the privacy of their own homes, and baptizing the female converts are two that immediately come to mind. While women helpers would be needed, it is another thing entirely to affirm that there was an office of deaconess in the church to which only certain women were appointed. Hendriksen (*Romans*, p.500) has fairly summarized the evidence: "B.H. Beyer in his article on this word (*TDNT* Vol.2, p.93) states that it is an open question whether Paul is referring to a fixed office or simply to Phoebe's service on behalf of the community. James Denny, p.717, regards the rendering 'deaconess' as being 'too technical.' ... H. Ridderbos points out that if Phoebe ministers to the saints, as is clear from verse 2, she would be a *servant* of the church. What Paul stresses is Phoebe's importance for the church. That the word *diakonos*, as here used, refers to an ecclesiastical office of deaconess cannot be proved."

It is certainly not to be inferred that Phoebe's "service" was menial or unimportant, or that women were considered second-class citizens in the kingdom. Let it be considered that she is entrusted with carrying this letter – one of the inspired books of the New Testament. This is a notable and responsible task. Still, Hendriksen's "two extremes to be avoided" should be given weighty consideration. The two he calls to his reader's attention are: "a) that of ordaining women to an ecclesiastical office when there is no warrant for doing so in Scripture; b) that of ignoring the very important and valuable services devout and alert women are able to render to the church of our Lord and Savior Jesus Christ" (*Romans*, p.501).

written about what her position or duties likely were, we think Paul himself designates in what sense she had been a "servant" as he describes her as a "helper of many" in verse 2.

16:2 – *that you receive her in the Lord in a manner worthy of the saints, and that you help her in whatever matter she may have need of you; for she herself has also been a helper of many, and of myself as well.*

That you receive her in the Lord in a manner worthy of the saints.   One thing Paul wants the Christians in Rome to do is to heartily welcome Phoebe as a fellow Christian.[8] "In the Lord" could carry the idea of treating her just like you would treat the Lord if He were visiting.   Wuest observes that "worthy" (*axiōs*) means "weighing, having the weight of another thing, of like value, worth as much."   "Paul uses it in Philippians 1:27 when he urges the saints in that church to see to it that their manner of life as citizens of heaven weighs as much as the gospel they preach, that is, worthy of their gospel."[9]   Thus, what Paul asks is that the Romans give Phoebe a welcome that weighs as much as the position she holds as a saint, a member of the family of God.[10]

And that you help her in whatever matter she may have need of you.   The verb "help" is frequently used as a legal term; "matter" is also a legal term (cp. 1 Corinthians 6:1). "From the use of the legal terms here, it would seem that the business on which Phoebe was visiting Rome was connected with some trial at law."[11]   However, Cranfield is not at all convinced by the presence of the "legal terms" that her business was legal business. "In view of the indefinite 'in whatever matter she may have need of you,' it is unlikely that 'matter' carries here its special sense of 'law-business', 'law-suit'."[12]   Perhaps the language implies that Phoebe was in Rome on a business trip of some sort, and a woman in a strange city, even if she were a woman of means,[13] would need all kinds of assistance which the local people, familiar with the city and its people, could provide.

For she herself has also been a helper of many.   Here Paul gives a reason why the Chris-

---

[8] "Receive" is the same word used in 14:1 ("accept") and 15:7, and certainly implies no less than what was asked of the brethren in those verses.   In other words, there is more than simple hospitality being requested on Phoebe's behalf.   "No mere reception of Phoebe into their houses satisfies this – their Christian life was to be open for her to share in it; she was no alien to be debarred from spiritual intimacy." James Denny, *Romans*, p.718.

[9] Wuest, *Romans*, p.258.

[10] On the meaning of "saint," see notes at Romans 1:7.

[11] Conybeare and Howson, *Life and Epistles of St. Paul*, p.581.

[12] Cranfield, *Romans*, p.782.

[13] The next phrase, which characterizes Phoebe as a "helper of many" would imply that she was a woman of some means.   We think of another woman in similar circumstances at Philippi, Lydia the seller of purple.   Even though accompanied by servants on such a trip from Cenchrea to Rome, Phoebe could still use the assistance of local people.

tians at Rome should help her in her affairs at Rome: she has helped others, and Paul in particular. Not a few writers suppose that "helper" is the third in a series of legal terms in this verse, and indeed the masculine form of the word does at times have the meaning of "patron," that is, the legal representative of a foreigner. "In Jewish communities it meant the legal representative or wealthy patron."[14] Cranfield doubts that the feminine form here has its technical meaning, for he thinks it improbable that Phoebe, a woman, would have been in a position to fulfill the formal legal functions involved.[15] In any case, the expression suggests that Phoebe was a person of some wealth and social position, who was thus able to act as benefactor to many Christians who passed through the port of Cenchrea, showing hospitality and generosity where needed. In fact, we are inclined to find in these words Paul's own explanation of his language of verse 1, where he noted that Phoebe was a "servant of the church at Cenchrea." Is it not just possible that Phoebe has been 'ministering' by acting as patroness of a small and struggling congregation?

And of myself as well. What kind of help she gave Paul, and when, we can only surmise. The only time we are specifically told that Paul was in Cenchrea before the writing of 1 Corinthians is the mention in Acts 18:18, at the close of the second missionary journey. Perhaps something happened to Paul at that time and place that gave Phoebe an opportunity to help him.[16] There is another possibility for a visit to Cenchrea, and that is when Paul made the hurried intermediate trip from Ephesus to Corinth between the writing of 1 and 2 Corinthians.[17] A rejection from the Corinthian church such as Paul experienced on the occasion of his intermediate trip to Corinth would make the warm hospitality at Phoebe's home all the more memorable.

D. Greetings Addressed to Personal Friends in Rome. 16:3-16

16:3 – Greet Prisca and Aquila, my fellow workers in Christ Jesus,

Greet Prisca and Aquila. "Greet" has the meaning of "I send my greetings to (someone)."[18] The term expresses a fondness for someone. In the next fourteen verses,

---

[14] Sanday and Headlam, *Romans*, p.417. Arndt-Gingrich, *Lexicon*, under *prostatis*, p.726, give references in both Jewish and pagan religious literature where the masculine form has the technical sense of "patron."

[15] Cranfield, *Romans*, p.783.

[16] Sanday, *Romans*, p.163, and Barmby, *Romans*, p.454, suggest that Paul fell sick at Cenchrea, and that it was Phoebe who nursed him and gave him a place to stay until he recovered. Barmby even suggests that the vow that Paul finished at Cenchrea was related somehow to the illness and recovery.

[17] For the intimations in Scripture that such an "intermediate trip" was made, but not recorded in the book of Acts, see H.C. Thiessen, *New Testament Introduction*, p.207,208, and G.L. Reese, *New Testament History: Acts*, p.685,686, and 726,728.

[18] Arndt-Gingrich, *Lexicon*, p.116. In the KJV we find the word *aspazomai* translated variously as "greet" or "salute;" the two English words were used by the KJV translators simply to vary the diction.

Paul sends his personal greetings to twenty-six individuals, two households, and probably three congregations which met in various individual's homes.[19]   It is probably safe to say that Paul was personally acquainted with each of the people named, and indeed with many of them he had been associated in evangelistic work elsewhere in the empire before they moved to Rome.   Before Phoebe ever got to Rome, she would know the names of a large number of individuals in the church at Rome; these greetings would serve as an introduction of them to her, much as Paul's commendation served to introduce her to them.

"Priscilla," the diminutive form of Prisca, is found in some older manuscripts, but "Prisca" is the original reading.[20]   When this husband and wife team are introduced in Scripture, sometimes his name is given first (e.g., Acts 18:2; 1 Corinthians 16:19), and sometimes her name is given first (e.g., Acts 18:18; 2 Timothy 4:19).   The most plausible explanation for her name being given first in four out of the six places where their names occur is that she is of noble Roman ancestry, while Aquila was perhaps at one time a Jewish slave who had come to marry into this distinguished family.[21]   This seems more likely than the suggestion of some moderns that her name is first because she was the more distinguished in Christian service, or was the more prominent Christian worker.   That this greeting from Paul to them represents this couple as living once again in Rome[22] has raised

---

[19] "Ford: 'Some persons, regarding this chapter as containing little more than a register of *names*, treat it with comparative indifference, thereby defrauding their souls of much good. St. Chrysostom, in his day, had cause to complain of the same neglect shown by many to the conclusion of this Epistle. Hence, he bestows special pains in explaining it. 'It is possible,' he writes, 'even from bare *names* to find a treasure;' and then he at once proceeds to disclose what the treasure is.' The list of names shows: (1) Paul's personal regard. (2) The high place he accords to women. (3) The constitution of the Roman Church. (4) The great influence he exerted, if so many friends could be found in a church he had never visited. (5) The undying name received from his friendly mention, is a type of the eternal blessing which belongs to those whose names are written in the Lamb's Book of Life. Evidently there are not many rich or great in this list – few of whom we know any thing save what is here hinted; yet these names abide, while those of the wealthy and honored have been forgotten. Even Horace and Livy give no such extended fame as Paul has done to his friends and acquaintances at Rome." Riddle, *Lange's Commentary on Romans*, p.446.

[20] Bible readers have sometimes wondered why we find different forms or spelling for people's names in Acts and in the epistles of Paul. "Luke regularly uses the language of conversation, in which the diminutive forms were usual; and so he speaks of Priscilla, Sopatros, and Silas always; though Paul speaks of Prisca, Sosipatros, and Silvanus." Wm. Ramsay, *St. Paul the Traveler and Roman Citizen*, p.268.

[21] See the author's commentary on *Acts*, p.638ff, for information about the background of this family. Sanday and Headlam, *Romans*, p.418-420, have even more detailed allusions. Barclay, *Romans*, p.231, suggests a romantic scenario, something on this order: There is just the possibility that Priscilla is named first most of the time because she herself was not a freedwoman at all, but a great lady, actually a member of the Acilian family. And she fell in love and married the slave Aquila, embraced the Jewish religion and later the two embraced the Christian religion. And then these two, the Roman aristocrat and the Jewish tentmaker, were joined forever in Christian love and Christian service.

[22] From the references made, these are the travels of Aquila and Priscilla: Aquila had been born in Pontus in Asia Minor (Acts 18:1,2). He and his wife had been residents of Rome in the late AD 40's, until an edict by Claudius had compelled all Jews to leave Rome in AD 52. Because of this edict, they were living in Corinth when we first meet them (Acts 18:1-3). When Paul left Corinth at the close of the second missionary journey, the couple moved to Ephesus (Acts 18:18,19), where they still lived when 1 Corinthians was written from there in AD 57 (1 Corinthians 16:19). About 12 months later, as indicated by this greeting in Romans 16, they are back in Rome. About 8 years later, they are again in Ephesus (2 Timothy 4:19).

questions in some readers' minds about the integrity of chapter 16.[23]   But the travels of
Aquila and Priscilla (as alluded to in Acts and Paul's epistles) were not greatly different
from the lives many tradespeople lived in those days as they carried on their commerce.[24]
There is nothing unusual or atypical about their moving back and forth between Rome,
Corinth, and Ephesus.

My fellow workers in Christ Jesus.   "'In Christ Jesus' clearly serves to indicate that it is
in relation to Christ and in the work of the gospel of Christ rather than in any other sphere
or matter [e.g., tentmaking] that they are Paul's fellow workers."[25]   Ever since Paul joined
this husband and wife team at Corinth some six years before Romans was written, they
together have worked in missionary activity, making known the gospel of Christ.[26]

16:4 – *who for my life risked their own necks, to whom not only do I give thanks, but also all
the churches of the Gentiles;*

Who for my life risked their own necks.   The word picture in "risked their neck" is
'placed their neck under the executioner's axe.'   Whether this expression is to be taken literally or figuratively[27] (exposed themselves to great danger), we do not know.   Neither can

---

[23] It has been widely held, especially in theologically liberal circles, that this final chapter of Romans
was originally directed not to Rome but to Ephesus – that it was for Ephesus that Phoebe was bound and
that the friends to whom Paul sends greetings lived in Ephesus.   It is urged that the movements of Aquila
and Priscilla would fit an Ephesian destination better than a Roman one.   Of course, just how a separate
letter to the church at Ephesus lost its original signature, address and greeting, and then came to be tacked
on to a letter addressed to Rome, has never been satisfactorily explained, nor does the manuscript
evidence support such a suggestion.   The argument for an Ephesian destination of chapter 16 is
presented most cogently by T.W. Manson, *Studies in the Gospels and Epistles* (Philadelphia: The
Westminster Press, 1962), p.234ff.   The argument for a Roman destination is presented by C.H. Dodd,
The Epistle to the Romans (New York: Harper and Row, 1932), p.xvii ff.   F.F. Bruce, *Romans*, p.266-270,
briefly summarizes the arguments pro and con for an Ephesian vs. Roman destination for this chapter, and
finally concludes that the arguments for Rome are the more persuasive.   "It is, as Gifford points out, a very
strong, indeed a conclusive argument for the Roman destination of the letter, that of the twenty-two persons
named in verses 6-15, not one can be shown to have been at Ephesus; while (1) Urbanus, Rufus,
Ampliatus, Julia and Junia are specifically Roman names, and (2) besides the first four of these names,
ten others, Stachys, Apelles, Tryphaena, Tryphosa, Hermes, Hermas, Patrobas (or Patribius), Philologus,
Julia, Nereus are found in the sepulchral inscriptions on the Appian Way as the names of persons
connected with 'Caesar's household' (Philippians 4:22), and contemporary with St. Paul."   Denney,
Romans, p.581.

[24] J.B. Lightfoot, *Biblical Essays* (London: Macmillan Co., 1893), p.299, shows that such a nomadic
life was characteristic of Jews of the 1st century.

[25] Cranfield, *Romans*, p.785.

[26] Paul describes several persons who are not apostles as fellow workers in the task of spreading the
gospel (Romans 16:9,21; 2 Corinthians 8:23; Philippians 2:25, 4:3; Colossians 4:11; Philemon 1,24).
Whether a man be an apostle, or an evangelist, or a Christian with no special function or office, each has
the delightful opportunity to be a fellow worker with all the other brothers when it comes to responsibility of
spreading the gospel.   Part of being a Christian, a facet of one's obedient faith, is to share the good news.

[27] Vine, *Romans*, p.216, noting that the Greek word "neck" is singular, argues that this indicates the
phrase is to be taken figuratively.

we do more than guess at the event to which it refers. Some have supposed it has something to do with the tumult of Demetrius and the silversmiths at Ephesus (Acts 19:24-41). Some have thought a connection should be made to the event Paul refers to in 1 Corinthians 15:32 when he "fought with wild beasts at Ephesus." Still others have supposed the place was Corinth, and the event was when Paul was on trial before Gallio (Acts 18:12-17). It may have been at none of these known times when Paul's life was in danger that Aquila and Priscilla risked their own lives to help him, for Paul was frequently in peril of one sort or another (2 Corinthians 11:23-28).

To whom not only do I give thanks. After giving testimony that they had risked their lives for his sake, he expresses again (as he has on many occasions[28]) his heartfelt thanks to them for their heroic action.

But also all the churches of the Gentiles. Whatever the danger was, and whatever their heroic action was, this phrase suggests that knowledge of what Prisca and Aquila had done was widespread among the churches Paul had established. Sufficient time had elapsed since that notable occasion that news about it had spread among the churches, and made them aware of their deep indebtedness to Aquila and Priscilla for their help to Paul, and this in turn led the churches also to give thanks to God for them. It should not be missed that implied in this expression is Paul's own awareness of the deep-rooted affection the churches entertain for him, and that those Gentile people whom he has converted and gathered into congregations are appreciative of the valuable thing he has done for them as he introduced them to the gospel of Christ. That is why they give thanks to God for what Aquila and Priscilla did for him.[29]

16:5 – *also* greet *the church that is in their house.* *Greet Epaenetus, my beloved, who is the first convert to Christ from Asia.*

Also *greet* **the church that is in their house.** Of the two possible interpretations of this phrase, either the Christian members of their own household or the congregation that habitually assembled in their house, the latter one is the more probable one. 1 Corinthians 16:19 shows that a congregation of Christians met in their home for worship on the Lord's Day when they lived in Ephesus. Either it was so characteristic of this family generously to open their home to provide a meeting place[30] for the brethren that Paul simply assumes

---

[28] The verb "give thanks" is in the present tense, indicating continual, habitual, repeated action.

[29] Lipscomb and Shepherd, *Romans*, p.272, do not limit the cause for the churches' gratitude to the heroic help rendered to Paul. "Their services in building up the churches among the Gentiles had been such that all the churches of the Gentiles felt grateful to them."

[30] While there is some evidence of the existence of special buildings used as meeting places for the congregation in Syria in the 2nd century, there is no decisive evidence until the 3rd century of the existence of such buildings in Rome. Until that time, church members who had homes with large rooms in which a crowd could gather, opened those rooms to the congregation for the worship services (Acts 12:12; Colossians 4:15; Philemon 2).

they have done it in Rome too, or this greeting to the church indicates that Paul has had news from Rome about the situation of the church there, news that included the fact that several house-churches were meeting at various places in the city.[31]

Greet Epaenetus my beloved. This is the only mention of Epaenetus in the New Testament.[32] "The description of Epaenetus as Paul's 'beloved' is not to be taken to imply that he was more beloved than those who are not so described. Paul seems to have tried to attach some expression of kindly commendation to all the individuals he mentions."[33] In addition, it is not unusual to have a special memory associated with the first convert to respond to the gospel in any new work.

Who is the first convert to Christ from Asia.[34] Epaenetus was the first convert to respond to Paul's preaching in the Roman province of Asia,[35] an area he evangelized during the third missionary journey (Acts 18:23-29).[36]

16:6 – *Greet Mary, who has worked hard for you.*

Greet Mary. Two different spellings for this name are found in the Greek text: Mariam, which is a Greek transliteration of the Hebrew Miriam; and Maria(n), which is a Roman

---

[31] The phraseology implies that Paul knew there were house-churches meeting elsewhere in Rome besides the one in Aquila and Priscilla's house. Verses 14 and 15 imply similar bodies meeting elsewhere. "Zahn suggested that the church which met in the house of Prisca and Aquila included all the persons mentioned in verses 5b-13, but it seems more natural to understand the following greetings as fresh greetings rather than as a singling out of individuals already included in the general greeting of verse 5a." Cranfield, *Romans*, p.786.

[32] It is a Greek name, and was evidently a common name, for occurrences of it are found all over the Roman Empire. Documentation of this can be found in Arndt-Gingrich, *Lexicon*, p.281, and in Sanday and Headlam, *Romans*, p.421.

[33] Cranfield, *Romans*, p.786,787.

[34] The KJV, following the reading of the Textus Receptus, reads "Achaia" rather than Asia. However, "Asia" is the better supported reading, being the reading found in Sinaiticus, A, B, C, D, F, G, Vilg., Boh., Arm., Aeth., Origen, etc. "The Received Text has been influenced here by 1 Corinthians 16:15 where, however, it is 'the household of Stephanas' – a Corinthian family – that is 'the firstfruits of Achaia'." Bruce, *Romans*, p.271.

[35] "Asia" was "that strip of territory including the whole western end of the peninsula we now call Turkey, stretching from Propontis in the north to Lycia in the south. Ephesus was the capital, and the seven 'churches of Revelation' were the most central and important of its cities." Sanday, *Romans*, p.163.

[36] The name "Epaenetus from Asia" has "caused difficulty for the critic Renan, who has said, 'What! Had all the Church of Ephesus assembled at Rome?'" And he thus tried to cast doubt on the authenticity of chapter 16 of Romans. But Renan's "'all' when analyzed is found to mean three persons of whom two [Aquila and Priscilla] had been residents at Rome, and the third [Epaenetus] may have been a native of Ephesus but is only said to have belonged to the province of Asia. (Cf. Lightfoot, *Biblical Essays*, p.301)." Sanday ands Headlam, *Romans*, p.421. When Paul's helpers were traveling far and wide on missionary tours, is it improbable that three who were once members of the congregation in Ephesus should end up in Rome at the same time?

name, the feminine form of Marius. Whether the woman referred to was of Jewish or Gentile background is uncertain.[37] Of course, the reference is not to Mary the mother of Jesus, nor is it likely this Mary is to be identified with Mary of Bethany (John 11:1).

Who has worked hard for you. We wonder how Paul had learned of her outstanding service for the sake of the Roman church.[38] As did the note about the church that meets in Aquila and Priscilla's house (verse 5), this commendation implies that some intelligence concerning the progress of the gospel in the capital city has come to Paul.[39] These words about Mary's activities on behalf of the Christians at Rome are not for the sake of the Roman church, for they would already know about the work to which the apostle referred. Instead, these words are intended as words of praise for Mary herself. Here is a Christian woman being honored for the Christian work that she did. She is described in the Greek text (in the word "worked hard," *kopian*) as a person who had worked until she was utterly weary. The word "work" is not followed by "in Word;" it refers to practical activity, not to preaching and teaching. Acts of kindness are intended.

16:7 – *Greet Andronicus and Junias, my kinsmen, and my fellow prisoners, who are outstanding among the apostles, who also were in Christ before me.*

Greet Andronicus and Junias. "Andronicus" is a Greek name, found among names of members of the imperial household.[40] This is the only mention of this man in the New Testament. Since the way the name "Junias" is accented in the Greek determines whether it is masculine or feminine,[41] it is not possible with certainty to determine the gender of this

---

[37] In favor of her being of Gentile background, it may be noted that apparently in other cases (with the exception of Aquila) where Paul refers to Jewish people in this list, he distinguishes them as such by calling them his "kinsmen" (cp. verse 7). Too, if it is a Hebrew name, it is the only Hebrew name in the chapter. But neither of these is conclusive on the matter, as is shown in footnote #4 on page 787 in Cranfield on *Romans*.

[38] The true reading seems to be "for you" rather than as the KJV has it, "on us."

[39] Such a knowledge of what is happening in the city to which these greetings are addressed has been thought by some critics to point to an Ephesian destination, rather than to Rome; after all, Paul would know who did outstanding service in the church at Ephesus, but how could he know who had "worked hard for you" in Rome where he had never been? "We reply that Paul certainly had some sources of information about the Roman church (cf. 1:8-15); and if Mary's association with that church went back to its earliest days, Priscilla and Aquila would have known her. But we can only speculate; this is the only reference we have to this Mary (one of the six bearers of that name in the New Testament)." Bruce, *Romans*, p.271.

[40] Sanday and Headlam, *Romans*, p.422. Cranfield, *Romans*, p.788, has shown the name was common to both freedmen and to slaves, and that it was not an unusual name for a Jew to have, since it was of non-mythological derivation, and would therefore not be offensive to Jews.

[41] Greek manuscripts were not accented at first; the accents have been added later by men, so the accents found in our present Greek texts have no real authority. *Iounian* with a circumflex accent on the ultima (see Nestle's text) would be the masculine accusative form; such a man's name is unknown elsewhere in Greek, though an uncontracted form, Junianus, is known. If it is accented with an acute on the penult (see P46), it is the feminine accusative form of the common Roman female name Junia.

person.[42]   All we know about this person is what is here told us by Paul, for this is the only mention of "Junias" in the New Testament.

My kinsmen.   The word *sungenes* can denote physical relatives, so some have understood that Andronicus and Junias were relatives (cousins?) of Paul.[43]   But "from the number of persons (six in all, and those not only in Rome but also in Greece and Macedonia) to whom the title [kinsman] is given in this chapter, it would seem as if the word 'kinsmen' was to be taken in its wider sense ... meaning 'members of the same nation, Jews like myself'."[44]

And my fellow prisoners.   "We have no knowledge of a time when Paul and Andronicus and Junias were prisoners together, though it is not impossible that there was such an occasion (Paul had already been 'in prisons' more abundantly than his adversaries, according to 2 Corinthians 11:23; ...)."[45]   In fact, the three need not have been imprisoned at the same time and place; Paul might call them "fellow prisoners" if they at some time, like himself, had been imprisoned for Christ's sake.

Who are outstanding among the apostles.   These words may mean either (1) outstanding in the eyes of the apostles, or (2) outstanding apostles themselves.   The second option needs further elaboration, especially in light of the fact that this is how the passage was understood by all of the patristic commentators.   "Apostles" here seems to have the specific meaning 'apostles of Jesus,' rather than the more general meaning 'apostles of churches.'[46]   There is little evidence that the apostles of Jesus were ever limited in num-

---

[42] "Junia is of course a common Roman name, and in that case the two would probably be husband and wife [or brother and sister].   Junias, on the other hand, is less usual as a man's name, but seems to represent a form of contraction common in this list, as Patrobas, Hermas, Olympas."   Sanday and Headlam, *Romans*, p.422.   P. Lampe, "Iunia/Iunias ... (Rom. 16:7)," in *ZeitNTWiss* 76 (1-2, 1985), p.132-134, has shown that whether the early Christian greeted by Paul in Romans 16:7 was a female or a male, both names show some connection with past or present slave status.   Arndt-Gingrich, *Lexicon*, p.381, note that while most ancient commentators took Andronicus and Junia as a married couple, they believe the context rules out the idea that "Junia(s)" is a woman's name.

[43] Lard, *Romans*, p.456; Lipscomb and Shepherd, *Romans*, p.273.   One would expect "kinsman" to be used here in the same sense it had in Romans 9:3.

[44] Sanday, *Romans*, p.163,164.   Cranfield, *Romans*, p.788, observes that a recent suggestion that the word means "fellow-tribesmen, i.e., fellow-Benjamites" is not very convincing.

[45] Cranfield, *Romans*, p.789.   "The only imprisonment that Paul suffered, recorded in Acts, before the time he wrote this letter, was the one at Philippi (Acts 16).   However, he alludes to imprisonments about which we know no details (2 Corinthians 6:5, 11:23)."   Sanday, *Romans*, p.164.   I Clement 5:7, likely taking into account his whole life, records "seven times thrown into captivity."

[46] At Romans 1:1 we noted that Paul and the twelve were "apostles of Jesus," that is, they had been called and commissioned by Jesus Himself.   There were a number of men who were appointed by some local church to do a special task (like carry an offering to Jerusalem), who were designated as "apostles (messengers) of churches" (e.g., 2 Corinthians 8:23).

ber but to the original twelve.   In addition to the eleven who remained after Judas Iscariot defected, there are several men who are called apostles: Matthias (Acts 1:26), Paul (Romans 1:1, 11:13, et al.), James the brother of the Lord (Galatians 1:19), and Barnabas (Acts 14:14).   So the use of the term "apostles" here would not of itself be an argument against Andronicus and Junias being called 'outstanding apostles.'[47]   Nor is it proper to use 15:20 as proof that Andronicus and Junias cannot be apostles of Jesus.[48]   Still, in modern times, it has become popular to adopt the first of the two possible meanings (outstanding in the eyes of the apostles) as being what Paul has in mind in this word of commendation.

Who also were in Christ before me.   That is, they were converted to Christ at an earlier time than was Paul himself.   The date we assign to Paul's conversion is AD 34,[49] so these two people became Christians[50] sometime between AD 30 when the church began, and AD 34 when Paul was converted.[51]   Some have ventured the guess that these two belonged to the Hellenistic Jewish portion of the Christian church about which we read in Acts 6. Some have suggested that Andronicus and Junias may have been among those who, during the dispersion after the death of Stephen, began to spread the Word (cp. Acts 8:4 and 11:19).   Some have suggested they were among the 3000 converted on the first Pentecost after the resurrection of Jesus, and this is how they were so well known by the original apostles.

16:8 – *Greet Ampliatus, my beloved in the Lord.*

Greet Ampliatus my beloved in the Lord.   "Ampliatus" was a common slave name in

---

[47] "If, as is a possibility, Andronicus and Junias are included among the apostles ... then it is more probable that the name [Junias] is masculine, although Chrysostom does not appear to consider the idea of a female apostle impossible.   [Chrysostom, commenting on this passage, has] 'Oh! how great is the devotion of this woman, that she should be even counted worthy of the appelation apostle!'"   Sanday and Headlam, *Romans*, p.423.

[48] See comments at 15:20, especially footnote #50.   If Junia is a woman's name, and indeed there is no compelling proof that it cannot be, then the following note is worthy of special attention.   "That Paul should not only include a woman ... among the apostles but actually describe her, together with Andronicus, as outstanding among them, is highly significant evidence (along with the importance he accords in this chapter to Phoebe, Prisca, Mary, Tryphaena, Tryphosa, Persis, the mother of Rufus, Julia, and the sister of Nereus) of the falsity of the widespread and stubbornly persistent notion that Paul had a low view of women, and something to which the Church as a whole has not yet paid sufficient attention."   Cranfield, *Romans*, p.789.

[49] Reese, *New Testament History: Acts*, p.xix-xxi.

[50] The better attested Greek text reads "They became in Christ before me."   Some few manuscripts read in such a way that the phrase means "they became apostles in Christ before me."   The verb tense is a perfect tense, implying the idea that not only had they come into Christ in the past, but they still are in Christ when Paul writes this commendation of them.

[51] If the word "kinsmen" is taken to mean they were Paul's physical relatives, then he had family members who were Christians at the time he himself was persecuting the church.

the Roman world, and several different people who bore this name, and who were somehow connected to the imperial household, have been found in the inscriptions from the 1ˢᵗ century.[52] In fact, many of Paul's friends in this list have slave names. When it is remembered what Paul did for the run-away slave Onesimus (cf. Philemon), one begins to ponder whether or not Paul was one of those individuals about whom the slaves knew, a benefactor who would help them if he could, and to whom therefore they came when they needed help. Further, if this is the same Ampliatus who is a slave in the imperial household, where and under what circumstances had Paul met him (and associated with him long enough that a bond of affection had been forged), and what led to his becoming a slave, and how did he come to be a slave in the imperial household?

16:9 – *Greet Urbanus, our fellow worker in Christ, and Stachys my beloved.*

Greet Urbanus our fellow worker in Christ. "Urbanus" (which means "citybred") was a common Roman slave name, and is a name found in the inscriptions naming members of the imperial household who had become freedmen. If this is the Urbanus whom Paul greets, one is led to wonder if this man went right back to the place where he had once been a slave in order to share the gospel with those who were still slaves of sin. Perhaps the reason Paul calls him "our" fellow worker is that he has never personally worked with Urbanus, though since both are workers for Christ they were therefore "fellow workers." Or, perhaps, Urbanus has worked as a colleague with more than just Paul (see the partial listing of those fellow workers who are with Paul as he writes this letter, verses 21-23 below), so Paul can speak of him as "our" (rather than "my") fellow worker.[53]

And Stachys my beloved. "Stachys" (meaning "ear" [of grain]) is a Greek name, and comparatively rare in the inscriptions from the 1ˢᵗ century. There was a court physician in the imperial household by the name of Stachys (so we learn from the inscriptions), and we wonder if we may identify the Stachys in Romans with the one in the inscriptions. How we wish we knew more about these people whom Paul has immortalized in Scripture. Were Luke the physician, Stachys the physician, and Paul the apostle one-time school-mates at the University of Tarsus? Has Stachys been taken to Rome as a slave because of his profession? Before his enslavement, had he been led to Christ by Paul (his old schoolmate), after Paul himself had met the risen Lord and become a messenger for Him?

---

[52] "The name is common in Roman inscriptions of the period, and is found repeatedly as borne by members of the imperial household. A branch of the *gens Aurelia* bore this cognomen. Christian members of this branch of the family are buried in one of the oldest Christian burying-places in Rome, the Cemetery of Domitilla, the beginnings of which go back to the end of the first century. One tomb in that cemetery, decorated with paintings in a very early style, bears the inscription AMPLIAT in uncials of the first or early second century." Bruce, *Romans*, p.272. "Its character suggests that it is the tomb of someone who was specially esteemed. There seems to be a real possibility – we cannot put it more strongly – that this Ampliatus is the person greeted by Paul, and that it may have been through him – probably a slave – that the gospel first penetrated into the noble household to which Flavia Domitilla, the Emperor Domitian's niece and wife of Flavius Clemens, belonged." Cranfield, *Romans*, p.790.

[53] This commentator has been unable to ascertain why Sanday, *Romans*, p.164, speaks of Urbanus as being a *woman* who has helped Paul and others in the Roman church. The Greek in this place is masculine.

16:10 – *Greet Apelles, the approved in Christ.   Greet those who are of the* household *of Aristobulus.*

Greet Apelles, the approved in Christ.   "Apelles"[54] is a name so common to the Jews of Rome that Horace (in his *Satire* I.5.100) uses it as a typical Jewish name.   Again we have a name borne by members of the imperial household, as the inscriptions testify.[55] "Approved" may imply that at some time, and under very trying circumstances, Apelles' faith had been tested, and he had stood the test.   Or it may be that Paul simply wished to vary the word he used as he commended his friends, and there is a sense in which any true Christian could be described as "approved" (see Romans 12:2, 14:18).

Greet those who are of the *household* **of Aristobulus.**   The explanation of this name given by Lightfoot bears all the marks of probability.[56]   It includes the following information: There was an Aristobulus who was the grandson of Herod the Great[57] and a brother of Herod Agrippa I.   Caesar often carried off members of families granted rule in the provinces, and held them as hostages in Rome, to ensure compliance with the wishes of Rome.   So, in Rome, Aristobulus was educated and lived and died as a private citizen,[58] never having sought public office.   He and the future emperor Claudius became fast friends, and he supported Claudius when the latter became emperor.   From the friendly terms on which he stood with the Emperor Claudius, it seems not unlikely that, by a somewhat common custom, upon his death somewhere between AD 45 and 48, his household was united with the imperial household.   From the time the two households were united, the slaves who used to belong to Aristobulus would have been designated as *Aristobuliani*, the Latin equivalent of Paul's "those who are of the *household* of Aristobulus."[59]   Such names were given to each of the households united with the imperial one, in order to distinguish them from the other similar groups in the imperial household.[60] Paul's greeting is addressed not to the whole household, but to the Christians among them. We could wish we knew how the gospel was introduced to this household.   In Acts 13:1

---

[54] "Apelles" should not be confused with "Apollos," though this is something Origen did.

[55] Sanday and Headlam, *Romans*, p.418ff, quote many of the inscriptions at length, while giving brief information where they are located, and also direct attention to Lightfoot, *Philippians*, p.169ff, where more information may be found, especially about those who may have been a part of Caesar's household.

[56] J.B. Lightfoot, *Philippians*, p.174,175.

[57] There were several generations in the Herod family who bore the name Aristobulus, including the son of Herod of Chalcis, and also the third son of this second Aristobulus.   Cranfield, *Romans*, p.792, rejects either of these latter two as being very good attempts to identify the Aristobulus of Romans 16:10.

[58] Josephus, *Wars*, II.11.6; *Antiquities*, XX.1.2.

[59] "Household" is in italics because there is no corresponding word in the Greek; the translators have supplied the correct word if by "household" is meant the slaves that once belonged to Aristobulus.

[60] Even after the transferal to the imperial household at Aristobulus' death, his slaves would continue to bear his name – just as we find servants of Livia's household who had come from that of Maecenas called Maecenatiani, and those from the household of Amyntas called Amyntiani, so also Agrippiani, and Germaniciani.   See Sanday and Headlam, *op. cit.*, p.425.

we are introduced to a Christian leader named Manaen who was intimately connected with the house of Herod. Did he have something to do with the fact that some of his "relatives" and their households have been won to Christ? Or was it the next named person who had the privilege of sharing the gospel with these household members?

16:11 – *Greet Herodion, my kinsman.   Greet those of the* **household** *of Narcissus, who are in the Lord.*

Greet Herodion, my kinsman. This Jewish man[61] has a name that suggests either descent from Herod, or belonging to Herod (he could still be a slave or he could now be a freedman). The fact that Paul names "Aristobulus" and "Herodion" so closely together in this list has lent support to the suggestion that the Aristobulus intended did in fact belong to the Herod family.

Greet those of the *household* **of Narcissus, who are in the Lord.** Again, we follow Lightfoot's suggestion as to the identification of Narcissus.[62] There was a Narcissus, a freedman, a well-known and powerful favorite of Claudius. His wealth was proverbial,[63] and his influence with Claudius was practically unlimited. Narcissus was responsible for having Messalina, the beautiful and profligate wife of Claudius, put to death. Nero's mother, Agrippina, had forced Narcissus to commit suicide[64] shortly after her son had become emperor; this was two or three years before Paul wrote this letter to the Romans. Upon his death, all his fortune and all the slaves in Narcissus' household would become the property of the Emperor.[65] The slaves would help in the imperial household, though they would still keep the name *Narcissiani* to distinguish them from other such groups in the imperial household. "Those ... who are in the Lord" indicates that not all the slaves had become Christians, but many had, and it is to these Christians that Paul sends his greetings. How he would know any of them, or know of them, we have no means of ascertaining. In Philippians 4:22, Paul writes of saints in Caesar's household, and these names in Romans help explain that expression.

16:12 – *Greet Tryphaena and Tryphosa, workers in the Lord.   Greet Persis the beloved, who has worked hard in the Lord.*

---

[61] See notes at Romans 16:7 on "kinsman."

[62] J.B. Lightfoot, *Philippians*, p.175.

[63] Juvenal, 14.329. He was "Secretary of Letters" in Claudius' administration, and his power had lain in the fact that all correspondence addressed to the emperor had to pass through his hands to reach the emperor. He made much of his fortune from the bribes that people paid him to ensure that their petitions and requests did reach the emperor.

[64] Tacitus, *Annals*, XIII.1, XI.29, XII.57;   Suetonius, *Claudius* 28;   Dio Cassius, LX.34.

[65] "In the case of Aristobulus, the transference [to being a part of the imperial household] would be effected by bequest, in that of Narcissus by confiscation. Many instances of both methods occur in the history and records of the time. The interpretation here given, and the identification of Aristobulus and Narcissus with the historical bearers of those names, is some way short of certain, but may be said to have a high degree of probability." Sanday, *Romans*, p.164.

Greet Tryphaena and Tryphosa, workers in the Lord.   These women may have been sisters, perhaps twins, since parents often give twins similar sounding names.   Tryphaena means "delicate" and Tryphosa means "dainty," and both names are found in inscriptions from the imperial household.[66]   Many writers have called attention to the contrast (was it conscious on Paul's part?) between the meaning of their names and the fact they were "workers" for Jesus.[67]   The present participle translated "workers" implies they are continually engaged in their special work even as Paul writes.

Greet Persis the beloved, who has worked hard in the Lord.   The name "Persis" means "the Persian woman."   The name, a typical slave name, has also been found in the Greek and Latin inscriptions of the time, but not among those connected with the imperial household.   Her service is spoken of as in the past (contrast what is said of Tryphaena and Tryphosa in the preceding clause); perhaps we may infer that she was an elderly woman at the time Paul wrote, and because of her advanced years, not able to do all the work she once did.[68]   Whether her service was done in Rome or elsewhere before she moved to Rome, we cannot tell.   "It is also to be observed how, in calling her 'the beloved,' Paul avoids, with delicate propriety, adding 'my,' as he does in speaking of his male friends."[69]

16:13 – *Greet Rufus, a choice man in the Lord, also his mother and mine.*

Greet Rufus, a choice man in the Lord.   "Rufus" is a Latin name, a common slave name, meaning "red-haired."   The possibility is very real that the person referred to in Romans 16 is the same as the one named as the son of Simon of Cyrene, who helped bear the cross for Jesus (Mark 15:21).   There is a substantial tradition that Mark's Gospel was written at Rome, and addressed to the Romans.   In such a case, Mark 15:21 would be saying that the Simon who bore the cross part way to Calvary was the father of the Alexander and Rufus with whom the Romans are acquainted, since they were members of the congregation at Rome.   "Choice man"[70] likely means that Rufus is recognized as a prominent member or

---

[66] The name "Tryphaena" also appears in the 2nd century AD.   In the fictitious 2nd century *Acts of Paul and Thecla*, a queen named Tryphaena shows kindness to Thecla at Pisidian Antioch.   There really was a queen by that name, a grandniece of the Emperor Claudius; Thecla is a real person too, but the story about these two is likely fiction.   Nor is the Tryphaena of Romans to be identified with the later queen at Antioch.

[67] "Workers" is the same word used in verse 6; it denotes toiling until one is weary and exhausted. Before one could say that in no case could a woman teach (in the light of 1 Timothy 2:12), it should be explained just what the labors of these two women included and excluded.   And as long as this verse stands in Romans (along with those others which name women as fellow workers with the apostles), it behooves us not to be abrasively dogmatic about the application of 1 Timothy 2:12.

[68] "Does this say that the frailties connected with old age have caught up with Persis, so that she no longer is able to labor as diligently as was once the case?   If so, Paul takes care that her past labors are not forgotten.   A lesson for us all to remember!"   Hendriksen, *Romans*, p.507.

[69] Barmby, *Romans*, p.456.

[70] "Choice" is the word elsewhere translated "elect."   Some have supposed it should be given its technical sense here in Romans 16:13, and have even tried to explain the absence of Alexander's name in Romans by alluding to the fact that he was not a Christian (i.e., not one of the elect), while Rufus was.

leader in the church at Rome.   Barclay's reconstruction of Simon's impress into service for Rome, and its eventual results, is worthy of consideration:

> That must have been a terrible day for Simon.   He was a Jew; he came from far off Cyrene in North Africa. No doubt he had scraped and saved for half a lifetime to celebrate one Passover in Jerusalem.   He came and as he entered the city on that day with his heart full of the greatness of the Feast which he was going to attend, suddenly the flat of a Roman spear touched him on the shoulder; he was impressed into the Roman service; he found himself carrying a criminal's cross.   How the resentment must have blazed in his heart!   How angry and bitter he must have been at this terrible indignity!   All the way from Cyrene for this!   To have come so far to sit at the glory of the Passover and for this dreadful and shameful thing to have happened!   No doubt he meant, as soon as he reached Calvary, to fling the cross down and stride away with a loathing in his heart.   But something happened.   On the way to Calvary the spell of this broken figure must have laid its tendrils round his heart.   He must have stayed to watch, and that figure on the Cross drew Simon to Himself forever and forever.   The chance encounter on the road to Calvary changed Simon's life forever.   He came to sit at the Jewish Passover and he went away the slave of Christ.   He must have gone home and must have brought his wife and sons into the same experience as he had himself. We can weave all kinds of speculations about this.   It was men from Cyprus and Cyrene who came to Antioch and who first preached the gospel to the Gentile world (Acts 11:20).   Was Simon one of the men from Cyrene?   Was Rufus with him?   Was it they who helped the church to burst the bonds of Judaism in which it might have been fettered?   Can it be that in some sense we today owe the fact that we are Christians to the strange episode when a man from Cyrene was compelled to carry a cross on the road to Calvary?[71]

Also his mother and mine. Rufus' mother was now living at Rome. Has Simon since died, and has mother come to live with her son?   And where and when had this woman befriended Paul and treated him in a motherly way,[72] so that he gratefully acknowledges the

---

(We have already covered this Calvinistic doctrine of election earlier in Romans, and rejected such a "predestinated" meaning for the word.) Even if we were to take *eklektos* in its proper technical sense of "chosen" here, it would not be a feature that would distinguish Rufus from any other Christian.   So we have opted instead to explain it to mean that Rufus is eminent and distinguished.

[71] Barclay, *Romans*, p.235,236. Barclay's closing comment must not be taken in a simply naturalistic way. God had always intended that Gentiles be included in the salvation available in Christ, as Romans 9:24ff and 15:9ff have clearly demonstrated. So it was not just a human innovation and development, prompted by an unaided Simon or Rufus, that led to the gospel being offered to the Gentiles.   The opening of the door for the Gentiles was all along something God promoted (cf. Acts 10,11, and the calling of Paul to go to the Gentiles, etc.).

[72] We doubt that Paul and Rufus were physical brothers, so we treat "mother" in its literal sense in the case of Rufus, but in a figurative sense in the case of Paul.

fact and expresses his affection for her in this way?   Bruce offers this answer:

> We cannot be sure, but one might hazard the guess that it was at the time when Barnabas fetched Paul from Tarsus to become his colleague in ministry at Syrian Antioch (Acts 11:25ff).   Simeon surnamed Niger ("the dark skinned"), one of the other teachers of the church there (Acts 13:1), has been identified with Simon of Cyrene; if Paul lodged with him we can well envisage the wife of Simeon (or Simon) playing the part of a mother to their disinherited guest.   (Would a dark-skinned father have a red-haired son?   It is not impossible.)[73]

16:14 – *Greet Asyncritus, Phlegon, Hermes, Patrobas, Hermas and the brethren with them.*

Greet Asyncritus.   There is an inscription in which a freedman of Augustus bore this name.   But there is a name "Flavia" connected with Asyncritus in that same inscription, and that may indicate that the inscription comes from a time somewhat later than Paul's time.   Still the inscription suggests the possibility that here we have another slave (or ex-slave) greeted as a Christian leader in Rome.

Phlegon.   The inscriptions give us little help identifying this man.   "Phlegon" is the name of a dog in Xenophon (*Cyropaedia*, 7.5), and also is a slave name.   "Phlegon, by the merest tradition, is handed down to us as one of the seventy [Luke 10:1,17], and also as being at one time bishop of Marathon.   He is said to have suffered martyrdom."[74]

Hermes.   This is one of the commonest of slave names, and is borne by a number of members of the imperial household.   Hermes was the name of the god of good luck.   "Hermes, too, has been represented as one of the seventy, as has also Patrobas.   To each of these, as a matter of course, has been assigned some imaginary bishopric, of which, most likely, neither ever heard the name."[75]

Patrobas.   This is an abbreviated form of the name Patrobius, and Patrobius was the name of a well-known freedman of Nero, who was later put to death by Galba who ruled for about one year after the death of Nero.[76]   Lightfoot quotes instances from the inscriptions of other freedmen who bore this same name, so we cannot be sure if Paul's Patrobas is identical with any of these.

---

[73] Bruce, *Romans*, p.274,275.   Even if we do not agree with Bruce when it comes to identifying Simon of Cyrene with Simeon called Niger, it could still have been at Antioch where Paul was treated as her own son by Rufus' mother.

[74] Lard, *Romans*, p.459.

[75] Lard, *Romans*, p.459.

[76] Tacitus, *History*, I.49, II.95.

Hermas. This spelling is likewise an abbreviated form of several names that begin with "Herm-" – for example, Hermagoras, Hermerus, Hermodorus, Hermogenes. Like Hermes, Hermas was a name common among slaves, though not quite so often found in the inscriptions as Hermes. In early Christian literature, there is a work called *The Shepherd of Hermas*. (Christ, the Shepherd, allegedly appeared to Hermas, and gave him the apocalyptic visions, parables and "mandates" recorded in this 2nd century work.) Some in the early church,[77] and some modern writers, have supposed that Paul's Hermas and the writer of the *Shepherd* are to be identified, an identification which is almost certainly wrong.[78]

And the brethren with them. The five persons just named seem to have been a part of a house-church (compare verse 5); the "brethren with them" seem to have made up a (small?) congregation of Christians who regularly worshiped together in someone's home. The brethren assembling together in Priscilla and Aquila's home formed one house-church. This group of brethren formed another. Still another group identified in verse 15 "indicates that the Christians in Rome were separated into different bands, probably laboring in different points of the city to build up the Lord's work."[79]

16:15 – *Greet Philologus and Julia, Nereus and his sister, and Olympas, and all the saints who are with them.*

Greet Philologus and Julia. Philologus (which means "fond of learning") was a common slave name. Numerous instances are quoted from inscriptions of the imperial household. "A Caius Julias Philologus is mentioned in an inscription as a freedman of Caius. Thus both names point to a connection with the 'household of Caesar'."[80] Julia is generally supposed to be either the sister of Philologus, or more probably his wife. Those who think she is the wife also tend to identify the following two names as being the children of Philologus and Julia. Julia is "probably the commonest of all Roman female names, certainly the commonest among slaves in the imperial household."[81]

Nereus and his sister. In the legendary *Acts of Nereus and Achilleus*, a Nereus is a chamberlain of Flavia Domitilla, but whether there is any connection between that Nereus

---

[77] Origen, Irenaeus, and Tertullian, are named by Lard, *Romans*, p.459, as so identifying Hermas as the author of *The Shepherd*.

[78] The *Shepherd of Hermas* is said in the Muratorian Canon to have been written by a brother of Pius I, and therefore cannot have been written earlier than the 2nd century. It is hardly likely that a "Hermas" alive in the mid-60's AD, would still be living in the mid-2nd century. What is more likely is that the Hermas who wrote the *Shepherd* lived a couple of generations later than the Hermas to whom Paul sends greetings in Romans.

[79] Lipscomb and Shepherd, *Romans*, p.274.

[80] Gifford, *Romans*, p.234.

[81] Sanday and Headlam, *Romans*, p.427.

and the one greeted by Paul is at best speculation.[82]   The sister is not named in Romans, but the name Nereus is found on an inscription of this date containing the names of the emperor's servants.[83]   Barclay's reconstruction from the names and legends is at best a possibility:

> In the year AD 95 there happened an event which shocked Rome. Two of the most distinguished people in Rome were condemned for being Christians. They were husband and wife. The husband was Flavius Clemens. He had been consul of Rome. The wife was Domitilla and she was of royal blood. She was the granddaughter of Vespasian, a former Emperor, and the niece of Domitian the reigning Emperor. In fact the two sons of Flavius Clemens and Domitilla had been designated Domitian's successors in the imperial power. Flavius was executed and Domitilla was banished to the island of Pontia ... And now the point – the name of the chamberlain of Flavius and Domitilla was Nereus. Is it possible that Nereus the slave had something to do with the making into Christians of Flavius Clemens the ex-consul and Domitilla the princess of the royal blood? Again, maybe it is idle speculation, for Nereus is a common name, but again, maybe it is true. There is one other fact of interest to add to the story. Flavius Clemens was the son of Flavius Sabinus. Now Flavius Sabinus, the father, had been Nero's city prefect in the days when Nero had sadistically persecuted the Christians after he had charged them with being responsible for the appalling fire which had devastated Rome in AD 64. As city prefect, Flavius Sabinus must have been Nero's executive officer in that persecution. It was then that Nero ordered the Christians to be rolled in pitch and to be set alight to form living torches for his gardens, to be sewed up into the skins of wild beasts and to be flung to savage hunting dogs, to be shut up in ships which were sunk in the Tiber. Is it possible that 30 years before he died for Christ, the young Flavius Clemens, as he must then have been, had seen the dauntless courage and the heroism of the martyrs, and wondered what made men able to die like that?[84]

And Olympas. Olympas is another abbreviated form, like several in this list; the spelling in full would have been Olympiodorus. Was Olympas one of the members of the house-

---

[82] "Roman ecclesiastical tradition, as far back as the fourth century, associates Nereus (and his companion Achilleus) with Flavia Domitilla, a Christian lady of the imperial household who was banished to the island of Pandateria, off the Campanian coast, by her uncle Domitian in AD 95, but who was released after his death in the following year, and whose name is perpetuated in the 'Cemetery of Domitilla'."   Bruce, *Romans*, p.275.

[83] Lightfoot, *Philippians*, p.176.

[84] Barclay, *Romans*, p.237,238. Sanday and Headlam, *Romans*, p.428, give sources where one can read the legends and inscriptions from which Barclay has reconstructed the possible connection between the Nereus of Romans and the one named in the inscriptions. (At footnote #52 above, we have noted Cranfield's opinion, in contrast to that of Barclay, about who was the messenger who brought the gospel into the imperial household.)

hold of Philologus and Julia? "As to Olympas, he too has been set down as one of the seventy; and it is related of him that he suffered martyrdom at Rome in [AD] 69."[85]

---

[85] Lard, *Romans*, p.459. Allusion has been made earlier in our study of chapter 16 (see footnotes 23 and 39) to the fact that some critics doubt the integrity of chapter 16, and others doubt its Roman destination. Because of the pervasive influence of such critics, it seems well at this point to pause to quote at length from two different writers, who address themselves to this very problem.

"It has been observed as strange that of all the epistles of Paul, this to the Romans and the one to the Colossians contain the greatest number of personal salutations, though these were precisely the two churches that he had never seen up to the date of his writing to them. A few critics, headed by Baur, have used this as an argument against the genuineness of this portion of the epistles in question. But reasoning like this may safely be dismissed, as these very portions are just those which it would be most senseless and aimless to forge, even if it were possible on other grounds to think of them as a forgery. On the other hand, there is some truth in the suggestion that the apostle might think it invidious to single out individuals for special mention in the churches where he was known, while he would have no hesitation in naming those with whom he happened to be personally acquainted in churches where he was not known. Besides this, it should be remembered that the Christians at Rome had been recently in a state of dispersion. All Jews by birth had been expelled from Rome by Claudius. It was this fact which had brought Aquila and Priscilla to Corinth and Ephesus, where Paul fell in with them; and he would naturally meet with other members of the dispersed church in the same way. We are apt to underrate the amount of rapid circulation which went on in these early Christian communities. We know from pagan writers that there was a great tendency all along the shores of the Mediterranean to gravitate towards Rome, and the population thus formed would naturally be a shifting and changing one, loosely attached to their temporary dwelling-place, and with many ties elsewhere. It will be noticed how many of the persons mentioned in the list had some prior connection with Paul – quite apart from their relation to the church at Rome. Andronicus, Junias, and Herodion are described as his 'kinsmen'. Aquila and Priscilla, and Epaenetus, he had worked with in Corinth and Asia. Of Amplias, Urbanus, Stachys, Persis, and Rufus he speaks as if with personal knowledge. [These are the people he knows in Rome, for they have moved there after crossing Paul's path elsewhere in the empire.] Analyzing these lists of names from another point of view, two further general conclusions appear to be borne out. (1) The church at Rome did not consist to any great extent of native Romans – at least these named members were not natives ... (2) The names seem to belong in the main to the middle or lower classes of society. Many are such as are usually assigned to slaves or freedmen. This fact, taken along with the mention in Philippians 4:22 of saints in Caesar's household, may show that Christianity had at this early date established itself in the palace of the emperor, though only among the lower order of servants." Sanday, *Romans*, p.161,162.

On the basis of the content, some have argued that this section of chapter 16 is not Holy Spirit inspired: 'God would not inspire such incidentals as this!' But this seems to be an objection based on a misunderstanding of the nature and process of inspiration. (See 1 Corinthians 2:6-14, and the comments offered on these verses in this commentator's Special Study on "The Doctrine of Inspiration" included in his *New Testament History: Acts*, p.127-129.)

On the basis of these names, it has been widely held that this final chapter was addressed not to Rome but to Ephesus. There is even a footnote in *Diaglott*, p.553, to this effect: "Sharpe in his Notes on this passage says – 'This is an important change as helping to prove that the persons here greeted dwelt in Ephesus, where the apostle had numerous friends, and not in Rome, where he was unknown. Thus Prisca and Aquilas in particular dwelt in Ephesus; and it seems not improbable that this chapter, together, perhaps with 12:1 to 15:7, formed part of an epistle to the Ephesians; which by a mistake of the editor has been added on at the end of the epistle to the Romans. This remark is not a little supported by those MSS. which say that the epistle now titled as to the Ephesians was written not to that church, but to the Laodiceans'." We shall permit F.F. Bruce to reply to this allegation.

"That a separate letter to the church in Ephesus has somehow been tacked on to a letter addressed to Rome is highly improbable; in any case, 'a letter consisting almost entirely of greetings may be intelligible in the age of the picture-postcard; for any earlier period it is a monstrosity' (Hans Leitzmann). What then are the principal arguments for postulating an Ephesian destination for chapter 16?

And all the saints who are with them.   In notes on the previous verse, it was suggested that this speaks of a "house-church."   "Saints" has been explained in notes at Romans 16:2; it speaks of living Christians.

---

(1) In this chapter Paul sends personal greetings to twenty-six individuals and five households or 'house churches'. Is it probable that he knew so many people in a city which he had never visited? We think rather of one of the cities with which he was well acquainted. Corinth does not come into the picture, because this letter was written from Corinth; but Ephesus (where he had recently spent two and a half years) is clearly indicated especially for the two following reasons.

(2) The first persons to whom Paul sends greetings here are his friends, Priscilla and Aquila. When we last heard of them, either in Acts (18:26) or in Paul's correspondence (1 Corinthians 16:19), they were resident in Ephesus, where they had a church in their house, as they have here. In the absence of any hint to the contrary, we may presume they were still in Ephesus.

(3) The next person to be greeted by name is Epaenetus, 'the first fruits of Asia (not "Achaia," as in the KJV) unto Christ.' Paul's first convert in the province of Asia would naturally be looked for in Ephesus, not in Rome.

(4) Another argument, based on the admonition in verses 17-20, is considered below ...

What can now be said in favor of the Roman destination of this chapter, over and above the initial presumption that it was sent to the same people as the rest of the letter to which it is appended?

(1) Such a list of greetings would be exceptional in a letter written to a church with which Paul was well acquainted. If this chapter was intended for Ephesus, we can envisage the occasion when it was read aloud at a meeting of the church. Those present would hear Paul's greetings read out to twenty-six of their number. But Paul certainly knew more than twenty-six members of a church in whose midst he had spent such a long time. What would the others think? Each of them would surely ask: 'Why leave *me* out?' But in a letter written to a church in which he was personally unknown Paul might well send greetings to friends whom he had met elsewhere in the course of his apostolic service, and who were now resident in Rome. If he mentioned them by name, the other members of the church would not feel aggrieved at being omitted, because they would not expect to be included. In the epistle to the Colossians, which was also written to a church which Paul had never visited, similar greetings are sent to a few individuals – only a few, because Colossae was off the beaten track and not nearly such an important place as Rome. But Rome was the capital of the world; all roads led to Rome, and it is not surprising that many people whom Paul had come to know in other places should in the meantime have made their way to Rome. In particular, the death of the Emperor Claudius in October, AD 54, probably meant for all practical purposes the lapse of his edict of five years earlier, expelling the Jews from Rome. If there was a general return of Jews to Rome about this time, Jewish Christians would certainly be among them. Priscilla and Aquila, who had been compelled to leave Rome because of the edict of AD 49 (Acts 18:2), may well have gone back in AD 54 or shortly afterwards, leaving caretakers, perhaps, in charge of the Corinthian and Ephesian branches of their tentmaking business (as they may have left one in charge of their Roman branch when they had to leave the capital). Tradespeople like Priscilla and Aquila led very mobile lives in those days, and there is nothing improbable or unnatural about their moving back and forth in this way between Rome, Corinth, and Ephesus.

It is highly probable that some of these beloved brethren to whom Paul sends greetings formed a part of the two bands who, some three years later, went out on the Appian Way – the one thirty miles to The Three Taverns, and the other forty miles to the Market of Appius – to meet the beloved apostle, now coming to them as Christ's "ambassador in chains." It was natural that when he saw the little throng of Christians he should thank God and take courage from this proof of their affection and devotion, and that here at length his soul was filled with joy and his tired spirit found rest.[86]

16:16 – *Greet one another with a holy kiss.   All the churches of Christ greet you.*

Greet one another with a holy kiss. Implicit in this exhortation is the assumption on Paul's part that this letter will be read out loud in the public worship services at Rome.[87] Having completed his own greetings to the individuals and house-churches he knew about in Rome, Paul now makes a request that, as the public reading of the epistle comes to a close, the Christians in Rome greet one another with a holy kiss.[88] While it was but a few to whom Paul could express a greeting, this command would omit no one. Every member of every Roman congregation where this letter was read would thus bestow and receive a greeting. Just as Paul (in the special word of commendation that he has for each of the recipients whom he greets) expressed his affection to the brethren, he encourages them to

---

(2) A number of the names in verses 7-15 are better attested at Rome than at Ephesus. (The evidence is presented conveniently by J.B. Lightfoot in *The Epistle to the Philippians* [1868], pp.171ff, in his excursus on "Caesar's Household." Accepting the Roman provenience of Philippians, Bishop Lightfoot collected such evidence as he could find, from Romans 16:8-15 and extra-biblical literary and epigraphic material, with a possible bearing on the identity of some of the 'saints ... of Caesar's household' mentioned in Philippians 4:22 ....) This is due in large measure to the much larger number of inscriptions available from Rome than from Ephesus; and in any case it is, for the most part, the names and not the persons that are well attested. Details are given in the notes ....

(3) 'The churches of Christ' who send their greetings to the readers in verse 16 would be the Gentile churches whose delegates were joining Paul at this very time to convey their churches' contributions to Jerusalem. (The churches mentioned in Acts 20:4 are Berea, Thessalonica, Derbe ... and the churches of Asia. Philippi was probably represented by Luke, and Corinth was the church with which Paul was staying at the time of writing.) It would be a particularly happy thought to send these churches' greetings to Rome. Of course it might be said that it was an equally happy thought to send the churches' greetings to Ephesus, but since Ephesus was one of the churches represented – by Trophimus and possibly Tychicus (Acts 20:4) – there would not be the same point in sending their greetings there." Bruce, *Romans*, p.267-270.

[86] Lipscomb and Shepherd, *Romans*, p.274,275.

[87] Implicit also is an awareness that what he is writing is of such authority and importance as to have a rightful place in an assembly of Christians where the purpose of assembling was to offer worship to Christ.

[88] The men who listened should embrace each other and kiss each other's cheeks, in token that all offenses were forgotten and forgiven, and that there was nothing but peace and goodwill between them. The women should do likewise. The kiss was to be a sign of their perfect unity and mutual forgiveness.

express their affection to each other in such a way that there could be no room for feelings of condescension or disrespect or harbored animosity.   "Not only should there be a kiss and not only should it be a symbol of genuine affection but it should also be *holy*.   In other words, it should never imply less than three parties: God and the two who kiss each other. The holy kiss symbolizes Christ's love mutually shared."[89]   Though the exhortation "Greet one another with a holy kiss" or an equivalent expression occurs four times in the epistles of Paul,[90] and once in the writings of Peter,[91] it is doubtful that any of these were intended to create a church ordinance or ceremony that was to be repeated down through the ages.[92]

---

[89] Hendriksen, *Romans*, p.508.

[90] Romans 16:16;   1 Corinthians 16:20;   2 Corinthians 13:12;   1 Thessalonians 5:26.

[91] 1 Peter 5:14.

[92] There are not many verses in the epistles where one can find specific instructions about what actions or ceremonies should be included in a worship service conducted by the early church (though one does find directives intended as regulations of already existing services, e.g., 1 Corinthians 11:17-34, 14:26-40, and perhaps 1 Timothy 2:1-15).   Furthermore, the tense (it is aorist) of the Greek verb "greet," in "greet one another with a holy kiss," indicates that Paul is encouraging something (a holy kiss) that is to be done once, rather than something that is to become a repeated or habitual practice.

If we admit the suggestion that neither Paul's nor Peter's exhortation at the close of their letters was intended to introduce the ordinance of the "holy kiss" into the worship service of the church, how can we account for the fact that such a practice seems to have been customary in the apostolic churches, as well as in the Eastern and Western churches after the deaths of the apostles?   While there is a lack of any hard evidence that will help us with this question, there are some very live possibilities as to the origin of the practice.   Many of the practices in the worship services of the early church were carried over into Christianity from the synagogue, and there seems to be some evidence of the practice of a "kiss of peace" in the synagogue worship (see Conybeare, *The Expositor*, 9 [1894], p.461).   Or again, it has been suggested that each worshiper was given a visible opportunity to demonstrate compliance with Jesus' directive to "first be reconciled to your brother, and then come and present your offering" (Matthew 5:24) as he bestowed and received a kiss of peace before participating in the celebration of the Lord's Supper. Or, once more, in those Eastern lands where the usual greeting was an embrace and a kiss upon the cheek, it is easy to see how such a practice (after it was purified by Paul's directive that it should be a "holy" kiss) would become part of their public services, especially after such exhortations as are found in five of the New Testament epistles.

A brief overview of the history of the "kiss" in its actual usage in the church (when it is seen that there is very little uniformity in practice) tends to confirm that it was never actually intended to be an ordinance to be observed by all.

(1) The things that are recognized by all as ordinances were instituted and observed by Jesus and recorded in His life and teachings as part of His work.   Note, for example, how baptism and the Lord's Supper were (a) ordained by Jesus, (b) practiced by the apostles and churches as set forth in the Acts of the Apostles, and (c) then urged in the epistles by specific direction for observing them.   None of these can be clearly shown for the "kiss."   So far as we are told, Jesus never said anything about a "holy kiss," never kissed, nor was kissed – save by Judas Iscariot as he was betraying Him (Luke 22:47), and by the penitent woman who repeatedly kissed His feet (Luke 7:45).   There is no account in Acts of any such custom by the apostles or churches (save when people were separating for a time, as in Acts 20:37).   The five statements in the epistles enjoin a one-time act, rather than a regular, repeated action.   Institutions and practices ordained by God, to be observed by all His people, are treated in a different way than is the "holy kiss."

(2) The earliest reference to "kiss of peace" as a regular part of the Sunday worship service is in Justin Martyr, *Apology* I.65.   "Prayers being ended, we salute one another with a holy kiss; and then the bread and wine [of the Lord's Supper] are brought to president [i.e., the one presiding over the service]."

(3) Origen, commenting on Romans 16:16, wrote, "From this injunction and several similar ones the custom

All the churches of Christ greet you. About the time this letter to Rome was being dictated by Paul, there had already begun to gather with Paul in Corinth all the messengers of the churches who were to carry their congregations' offering to Jerusalem (Acts 20:3,4). It is those different congregations who are here stylized as "churches of Christ." We suppose something like the following happened. When the different offering bearers became aware that Paul was writing this letter, they would say, "Send them greetings from Berea!" or "Send them greetings from the church in Thessalonica!" etc. Paul simply sums

---

has been handed down to the churches, that after the prayers the brethren shall greet one another in turn" (Cranfield's translation, *Romans*, p.796).

(4) Tertullian, *De Oratione* 18 [14], refers to "the kiss of peace."

(5) Cyril of Jerusalem says of the holy kiss, "Think not that this kiss ranks with those given in public by common friends. It is not such: this kiss blends souls one with another, and solicits from them entire forgiveness. Therefore, this kiss is the sign that our souls are mingled together and have banished all remembrance of injury.   The kiss therefore is reconciliation, and for this reason is holy." *Catachumens* 23.3.

(6) In the 4th century *Apostolic Constitutions* (2.57, 8.11) we find this command concerning the worship service: "Let the deacons say to all, 'Salute ye one another with a holy kiss'; and let the clergy salute the bishop, the men of the laity salute the men, the women the women." Further, the deacons were to watch that there was no disorder during the act, and there was express prohibition of the sexes kissing one another in the public worship.

(7) The use of the holy kiss as a regular part of the Sunday service was abandoned by the Eastern church earlier than it was in the Western church, though in the former, it is still part of Easter Sunday services.

(8) By the time of the Middle Ages, "there was substituted in the place of the holy kiss the practice of kissing the altar, the sacred elements, or the stole by the clergy, and kissing the hand by both clergy and laity." (Victor Schultze, "Kiss of Peace," *The New Schaff-Herzog Encyclopedia of Religious Knowledge* [Grand Rapids: Baker, 1956], Vol.6, p.347.)

(9) In the 13th century, the practice of the holy kiss was suppressed in England by the archbishop of York, and was replaced by the act of kissing the "*pax* board," a metal or, in some cases, marble disc exhibiting the cross or sacred figures. Relics or even the book of the Gospels were sometimes employed in the practice. The *pax* board was first kissed by the clergy, and then passed around to the congregation. Because of confusion, the kissing of the board was later withheld from the people, and limited to the clergy. Disputes about Biblical precedents caused the congregational use of these tablets to be abandoned.

(10) It became the custom, by the 3rd century, to bestow a kiss on the new convert just after his baptism. First the one who did the baptizing kissed the new Christian, then all the other members of the congregation did likewise. Cyprian, *Epistle to Fidus, on the Baptism of Infants*, 4 (*Ante-Nicene Fathers*, Vol. 5, p.354).

(11) Another occasion on which it became customary to kiss was the reinstatement of repentant members to full communion, apparently after the example of what the father did to the returning prodigal son.

(12) Perhaps the kiss of homage (where the person who would acknowledge devotion or submission to another by kissing the right hand, or a ring on it) is related to an old Greek and Roman act of worship (where the worshipers kissed an effigy of the "god" to whom they professed allegiance as a token of their devotion and homage). (See A.E. Crawley, "Kissing," in *Hastings' Encyclopedia of Religion and Ethics*, Vol.7, p.742, where the last two practices are documented.)

In an earlier century, another Restoration Movement leader struggled with the question of whether or not the five exhortations in the New Testament make the practice of the holy kiss binding on Christians of the present day. He concludes his own study with these words: "Upon the whole, the view I prefer to take of the case is this: The Apostle, by his injunction, did not create the custom; for it was prevalent at the time. He meant merely to *purify* it. He hence says, 'Greet one another with a *holy* kiss'. Only therefore where the custom exists, is his injunction applicable. Where the custom does not exist, his injunction is not designed to create it. It hence does not bind it upon us. If we do kiss, it must be a *holy* kiss; but we are not compelled to kiss." Lard, *Romans*, p.460.

up all these hearty good wishes from each of the messengers in this one sentence.[93]   The phrase "churches of Christ" occurs only here in the New Testament; the expression denotes possession, and marks the congregations as belonging to Jesus.[94]

E. A Warning to be on Guard so as to Avoid any Damage that False Teachers Might Otherwise Cause.   16:17-20

16:17 – *Now I urge you, brethren, keep your eye on those who cause dissensions and hindrances contrary to the teaching which you learned, and turn away from them.*

Now I urge you, brethren.   We might have expected the letter to end with the greetings Paul has just written (verses 3-16).   Instead, he interrupts the flow of greetings (see them continued in verses 21-23) and inserts this warning.[95]   While, on first sight, it might seem unexpected to have such a warning inserted, further reflection suggests it is not at all out of place, or incongruous.   Paul's recent experiences with the churches in Galatia (Galatians 1:6ff), and perhaps even the divisive spirit manifested in the church at Corinth,[96] would certainly weigh heavily on his mind.   It is perfectly natural that he should warn the Romans to be on their guard, lest a similar divisiveness and defection from the faith mar their fellowship.[97]

---

[93] This proposed scenario is to be preferred, we think, to the one sometimes offered in the commentaries, that Paul simply assumes the different congregations would want to express their greeting, because, after all, he has founded those churches, and therefore was fully justified in speaking for them.

[94] The Greek genitive case could just as well be translated "Christ's churches" or "the Christian churches" since these two English forms likewise express possession, i.e., that the congregations (churches) belong to Christ.   See the author's *New Testament History: Acts*, p.420-422, where the sad struggle of churches over the proper, Biblical name to be worn, has been documented.   Readers are reminded (a) to beware of making the nomenclature found in any single English version the standard of orthodoxy, and (b) that there are other very acceptable Biblical names for congregations of believers, in addition to the one found in Romans 16:16.

[95] For the verb "urge," see notes at Romans 12:1,8 and 15:30.   For the word "brethren," see notes at 1:13.

[96] It was Judaizers who disturbed the churches in Galatia.   It is also possible that it was Judaizers who had been part of the cause of the party spirit in Corinth (2 Corinthians 11:13-15).   With all the instruction on the place of the Law that we have seen emphasized in this letter to the Romans, which implies that some at Rome were still not clear in their minds about the abrogation of the Law in favor of the gospel, it is conceivable that Judaizers would have little trouble convincing some at Rome that their peculiar devotion to the Law was, after all, the only right path for a true believer.

[97] Critics who have doubted the integrity and genuineness of chapter 16 have emphasized (1) the abruptness of the introduction of this warning, (2) its alleged sharpness in tone as compared with the rest of Romans, and (3) the fact that nothing in the context has prepared us for this unexpected warning. Perhaps if the last of the allegations is answered, the others too will be seen to carry less conviction than they might seem to on first sight.   The statement about "all the churches" at the end of verse 16 would remind Paul of the recent reception of the heartbreaking news about Galatia, and his hurried letter to the churches there.   His indignation is perfectly proper when it is recognized that the Judaizers who disturbed some of these very congregations who were sending greetings to Rome are not genuine Christians, but rather "false brethren" who, under false pretenses, "sneaked in[to the churches] to spy out our liberty which

Keep your eye on those who cause dissensions and hindrances. The language suggests that these divisive teachers have not yet disturbed the church at Rome; rather, it warns the Roman brethren to be on the lookout[98] for them, as without doubt they soon will get there.[99] "Dissensions" is a word which occurs in the list of the works of the flesh in Galatians 5:20. Worse than the dissension they cause is the fact that their activities prove to be a "hindrance;"[100] either they are an occasion of stumbling that encourages Christians to fall into sin (a potentially fatal step), or they cause unconverted people to stumble by rejecting the gospel, which is the way of salvation.[101]

Contrary to the teaching which you learned. The "teaching" which the Roman Christians have learned is not some peculiar Pauline teaching. Though it is true that some of the believers in Rome have had the personal experience of hearing Paul teach, it is but a small minority of whom this is true. Therefore, "teaching" is a word that presupposes a common body of doctrine[102] that Paul knew all Christians ("you" is plural; it is something all learned) have heard, and which also was incompatible with what the Judaizers taught, and which therefore made the Judaizers' teaching to be in error.[103]

---

we have in Christ, in order to bring us into bondage" (Galatians 2:4). Romans has certainly had something to say about liberty in Christ (chapters 14,15), as well as the Law being but temporary (Romans 10:4). Paul's implied delight in the Roman church's present situation (Romans 1:8-12) would quickly be turned to grief if that congregation's victories for Christ were to be slowed or stopped altogether by inroads made there by such "false brethren." Indeed, if Judaizers were to win the hearts of the Romans away from the gospel to which they had been won, then the chances of that congregation's participating in Paul's proposed mission to carry the gospel to Spain would be greatly diminished, too. In light of these facts, instead of saying this warning is out of place, it is rather exactly the kind of closing (and therefore most likely to be remembered) statement its author would want to leave in his readers' minds.

[98] The verb is *skopeō* in the Greek, and the translation "mark them" (KJV) can give a faulty idea, for the English can easily imply that the people to be marked are already present in Rome. Instead, what the verb asks the Romans to do is to direct their attention to, to watch out for, to keep their eyes open for these false teachers, who are likely to arrive any day now.

[99] "Cause" is a present tense participle; right now they are causing dissensions. They are engaged in producing splits (standing apart) among the brethren – among the churches of Galatia, for instance, rather than already in Rome.

[100] See the word "hindrances" ("stumbling-block") explained at 9:33, 11:9, and 14:13-16.

[101] Paul does not specifically state who it is that he contemplates as stumbling. That Christians who fall from grace to return to Law-keeping might be in his mind surely must be granted. But it can just as easily be affirmed that the dissensions (strife, fights between people who are allegedly members of the same faith) have proven to be an effective hindrance that many unconverted people have pointed to as an excuse to postpone any personal response to the gospel. The net result of the work of the Judaizers is that a prejudice against the gospel is effectively created in many unbelievers' minds. After all, who wants to become part of a church that is all the time fighting amongst themselves?

[102] We have identified this "body of doctrine" as being synonymous with *gospel* in Special Study #9 on "Faith, Opinion, and Love." Because "doctrine" (ASV), to some readers, is interpreted as dogmatic theology, some have preferred "teaching" as the English word to translate the Greek word here.

[103] It must be observed that it is teachers who cause "dissensions and hindrances *contrary to the teaching"* (i.e., the truth of the gospel) about whom Paul warns. Sometimes divisions have to be caused *for* the truth of the gospel. These are honorable and true divisions. Jesus came to bring a sword

And turn away from them. The teachers (not just their teaching) who would be divisive are not only to be carefully watched for, but they are also to be avoided.[104] They are not to be given a hearing; they are not to be opposed in a debate hosted by the local church, for in a debate some members might be lost to them; they are not to be associated with, lest some impressionable members be misled into thinking these people are not so dangerous after all. Compliance with this directive is imperative and necessary in order to preserve the harmony and unity of the churches of Christ.[105] To implement this command in contemporary situations requires several things: (1) to know and understand the gospel as presented by the apostles; (2) to judge the teachings of those who come to visit our congregation in the light of the apostolic gospel; and (3) for those whose teachings are incompatible with the gospel, to refuse them a platform or an opportunity to spread their erroneous doctrines.[106]

(Matthew 10:34-39 and Luke 12:49-53).

[104] Though there is a textual variation here, with some manuscripts reading a present imperative, the better attested reading is an aorist imperative. This aorist tense would imply a definite breaking off of relations; definitely, decisively, once for all, incline away from them. It is to be doubted that Paul is urging some formal break in relations, such as would be involved in a case of church discipline (he did counsel the Corinthian church to discipline an erring member, 1 Corinthians 5:1-8); it is more likely that he is encouraging personal dissociation from the offenders, shunning and avoiding them so their doctrines can get no foothold in Rome.

[105] "Note well that apostolic doctrine never causes either inward or outward rents in the church ... When those who hold this doctrine firmly reject those who refuse to hold it or some part of it, they cause no division but prevent division by not giving room to those who divide and disunite." Lenski, *Romans*, p.916,917.

[106] Among commentators on Romans, there surely has been a wide degree of difference in attitudes and actions when it comes to implementing what Paul here enjoins.

(1) Lipscomb and Shepherd, *Romans*, p.276, give what has come to be a standard church of Christ application of the passage to the question of the use or non-use of musical instruments (or other "innovations") in the worship service. "No greater evil, according to the Scriptures, could befall the churches than the divisions arising from the introduction of teachings and practices not required by God. The fundamental truth of the Bible is that God alone has the right to direct and guide the faith and service of His children. Everything added to the work or worship of God by man is a usurpation in the sight of God, and ought to be resisted. Things that enter into the worship of God ought to be distinguished from the things indifferent and from mere expedients used to help men in performing the service of God that render them comfortable while doing the worship. These constitute no part of the service, but are helps to man while doing that service, not additions to it. All additions to the service of God are sinful and cause divisions. God has forbidden anything to be added to what he has required. There cannot be a doubt but that the use of instrumental music in connection with the worship of God, whether used as a part of the worship or as an attractive accompaniment, is unauthorized by God and violates the oft-repeated prohibition to add nothing to, take nothing from, the commandments of the Lord. It destroys the difference between the holy and the unholy, counts the blood of the Son of God unclean, and tramples underfoot the authority of the Son of God. It has not been authorized by God or sanctioned by the blood of the Son." (In this commentator's view, while the main thrust of what is here said, about respect for the authority of God, is right, the way that matters of faith and matters of expedience are defined has led to an erroneous application of submission to God's authority.) Ketcherside, *The Twisted Scriptures*, p.86ff, appeals to his fellow-brethren not to use this passage in Romans as a proof text for withdrawing fellowship from every brother who does not agree with you in every point of doctrine.

(2) Wilson, *Romans*, p.248, thinks there is an application of this passage to be made when it comes to cooperation with the ecumenical movement. "The leaders of the anti-scriptural ecumenical movement

16:18 – *For such men are slaves, not of our Lord Christ but of their own appetites; and by their smooth and flattering speech they deceive the hearts of the unsuspecting.*

For. With "for" Paul introduces two reasons (in this verse) why he has warned the Romans to be on the lookout for the divisive teachers. First, he characterizes such teachers in their relationship to the Lord; then he characterizes them as far as innocent Christians are concerned.

Such men are slaves, not of our Lord Christ but of their own appetites. Although these false teachers profess to be servants of Jesus, they really serve "their own belly."[107] Their 'service' is inspired by self-interest and has self-satisfaction as its goal, rather than obedience to the Lord.[108]

> Had Paul thought of these people as sincere though mistaken, he doubtless would have treated them with the tenderness he shows towards weak brethren.

... betray the cause of Christ in the name of Christian 'love' and for the sake of Christian 'unity' ... It should be carefully noted that a 'love' which is indifferent to truth, and a 'unity' which is tolerant of error cannot be found within the pages of the New Testament, which urges Christians to 'earnestly contend for the faith which was once delivered unto the saints' (Jude 3)." He then writes, "For a penetrating discussion of ecumenism in the light of Scripture, see *The Basis of Christian Unity*, by D. Martyn Lloyd-Jones [Grand Rapids: Wm. B. Eerdmans, 1963]."

(3) Does Paul's injunctive to avoid teachers of contrary doctrine have any application to the debate raging in Christian Church circles about the validity and advisability of inviting denominational preachers and scholars to speak at conventions, on college campuses, etc.? The answer would seem to be "Yes" if the speaker is known to deny one of the points of the *gospel*.

(4) All conscientious readers of this imperative about avoiding the divisive teachers ponder what it means when it comes to actual personal behavior toward the divisive person. Is he to be avoided no matter what? Surely Paul does not mean that even in times of distress, when that teacher needs kindly help, he is still to be shunned. Surely Paul is not prohibiting any attempt to meet the man's spiritual needs by attempting to correct his views in the areas where his doctrine is not in harmony with the gospel. Is there not a vast difference between such kindly help, such an attempt at correction during a one-on-one study of the Word, and giving the divisive teacher a public platform and a ready-made audience to listen to his errors? It seems to us that what is prohibited is not an attempt to lead the man to repentance if the opportunity presents itself.

[107] "Their own belly" is the way the Greek reads literally, as the marginal note in the NASB indicates. Some have appealed to the more remote context (6:1ff) to suggest that this is Paul's way of speaking with disdain about those people whose habits are morally lax, sensually indulgent, and Epicurean. Some have appealed to the nearer context (chapters 14-15) to find an explanation, and think this expression is a rather ironic way of denoting preoccupation with food laws. Those who think that Judaizers in particular are in Paul's view appeal to the immediate context (see comments on verses 16 and 17) and to Philippians 3:2,19 for corroboration of their interpretation, for in that passage Paul warns about some persons (i.e., Judaizers, "false circumcision") "whose god is their appetite (belly)." As has been shown in the Introductory Studies, the identification of the divisive persons about whom Paul warns is not an easy matter.

[108] The verb *douleuō* ("are slaves") is placed at the end of the clause, so there is a certain emphasis on it. It is their own appetites, not the Lord, for whom they are slaving. The use of the verb *douleuō* (rather than *diakoneō*, which would put emphasis on the service itself) puts emphasis on the unquestioning obedience expected of a slave. Along with the negative particle, *douleuō* suggests that the divisive ones are not acting the part of "slaves" who obey without question every word of their master (Jesus).

But he regards them as self-interested, and of the flesh; and against such disturbers of the church's peace he is, here as elsewhere, indignant (compare Galatians 1:7,8, 2:4, 3:1, 5:11,12).[109]

And by their smooth and flattering speech they deceive the hearts of the unsuspecting. After describing the divisive teachers as servants of the wrong master, Paul now describes what makes them so dangerous as far as innocent Christians are concerned. The great danger lies in the fact that their false teaching sounds so beneficial and so pious. "Smooth speech" translates *chrēstologia*; it is a speech that is hypocritically made by a speaker who is pretending goodness.[110] "Flattering" translates *eulogias*, a word that often means "praise, laudation, or blessing," when used in its good sense; but which means "plausible, it sounds reasonable" when used in its bad sense.[111] "Deceive the hearts of the unsuspecting" reminds us of Satan in the Garden of Eden. "Unsuspecting" translates *akakos*, which literally means "not evil." The word speaks of the absence of any dishonest motives, which in turn makes a man an unsuspecting and easy prey for designing persons. "Those who have no evil intentions themselves do not readily suspect others of them."[112]

Jesus once warned his followers to be "wise as serpents and harmless as doves" (Matthew 10:16, ASV). Just as on other occasions Paul reflects this or that familiar saying of Jesus, so it is very likely that verses 18 and 19 are a deliberate reference to the Master's teaching which has been recorded in Matthew 10:16.[113] To those who are not careful to beware of possible danger, and "to those who are not instructed in the ways of God as revealed in Scripture, the smooth and fair speech of those who propagate false teaching is especially dangerous. Safety lies in a knowledge of, and adherence to, the Word of God."[114]

---

[109] Barmby, *Romans*, p.456.

[110] "The Greeks themselves defined a *chrēstologos* as a 'man who speaks well and who acts ill'. He is the kind of man who, behind a facade of pious and religious words, is a bad influence, the man who leads astray, not by direct attack, but by subtlety, the man who pretends to serve Christ, but who in reality is destroying the faith." Barclay, *Romans*, p.239.

[111] Who has not heard the gospel doctrine of eternal punishment for the wicked denied by the question about how could a loving God create a terrible place like hell? Who has not heard Bible terms (e.g., "resurrection" means the memory of Him or His teaching lives on) used with completely different meanings, so that Christianity is actually denied? These are modern examples of "smooth and flattering speech."

[112] Sanday, *Romans*, p.166.

[113] In the Greek of verse 19, Paul uses the same two adjectives ("wise" [= "shrewd"] and "innocent") as did Jesus in Matthew 10:16.

[114] Vine, *Romans*, p.220.

16:19 – *For the report of your obedience has reached to all; therefore I am rejoicing over you, but I want you to be wise in what is good, and innocent in what is evil.*

For. It seems likely that verse 19 is a further reason for the exhortation given in verse 17. Their example was a source of inspiration to others; if they continue in the gospel, well; but if they should fail because of what the false teachers will try to do, the harm would be great.

The report of your obedience has reached to all. Paul here repeats what he has said earlier (Romans 1:8) about the reputation of the Roman church. Among the churches, at least among those with whom Paul was acquainted, a report telling the progress of the gospel[115] in Rome had circulated, and was a topic of joy and satisfaction. Should they depart from the path of obedient faith, news of that would just as quickly spread among the churches, and how deep would be the disappointment and grief; how very likely it was that others would follow their example and defect from the gospel, too.

Therefore I am rejoicing over you. Paul rejoiced because they had such a splendid reputation as the first clause of this verse indicates.

But I want you to be wise in what is good. It would seem that the false teachers had not yet done any harm at Rome, but Paul wants them to be on their guard. If they wisely accept only what is good, as far as teaching is concerned, then their continued obedience will be assured. He wants them to be discreet and wary, so that they may continue to be blameless. It takes a lot of wisdom to discriminate between transparent truth and plausible error.

And innocent in what is evil. "Innocent" translates *akeraios*, a word which means "pure, untainted, unalloyed, unmixed."[116] It is used of metals (e.g., "*pure* gold") to which no foreign substance has been added, and of wine or milk that has not been mixed (adulterated) with water. The obedience of the Roman brethren is now "innocent (pure);" Paul issues this warning about the false teachers so that their beliefs and habits may remain untainted or uncorrupted by anything evil. He wanted them to remain uninfluenced by the evil teachers and the dissensions and hindrances (stumbling-blocks) they caused (verse 17).

---

[115] "Obedience" was explained in notes at Romans 1:5. The people who heard the gospel have obeyed; they have pledged their allegiance to Jesus as Lord, and have obeyed His will carefully. Up to this point, the slaves of Jesus have not listened to those who would try to make them into rebellious slaves. There seems to be implied also (in the words "your obedience") the idea that the Roman church is relatively free from doctrinal and ethical aberrations at the moment in history when Paul writes to them. A review of subsequent history is all that is needed to show that Paul was not wrong in his estimate of the influence of the church in Rome. Would that she had stayed as pure and free as she was in her early days.

[116] Arndt-Gingrich, *Lexicon*, p.29. Thayer, *Lexicon*, p.22. The KJV uses "simple" to translate both the last word of verse 18 and this word in verse 19. This could cause some confusion unless it is known that different Greek words are underneath the English rendering.

16:20 – *And the God of peace will soon crush Satan under your feet.   The grace of our Lord Jesus be with you.*

And the God of peace will soon crush Satan under your feet.   This promise would seem to have immediate reference to the efforts of those false teachers about whom Paul has just warned his Roman readers.[117]   God, who has a providential control over His creatures,[118] would soon put an end to those who would disturb the church by introducing discord and

---

[117] This briefly worded promise raises many questions in the mind of a student who has paused to meditate on it.

(1) Does it help us identify the false teachers about whom Paul warns?

Some have supposed the false teachers are antinomians, but they were not 'crushed' in the sense of being completely stopped; they continued to flourish for years.   Others have supposed the false teachers are Gnostics, but it was 200 years before they were 'crushed.' The Judaizers would fit this promise better than any other errorists we know about in the 1st century.   In just a few years, by the time 1 Timothy is written (c.AD 65), we are hearing the last of the Judaizers.   2 Timothy, like Colossians before it, is beginning to warn about a new divisive doctrine, Gnosticism; but the Judaizers are no longer a potent force to be reckoned with.   Did the Roman church, by her decisive stand against the Judaizers when they came there, help to cause their decline?

(2) How did Paul know what God would do in this matter?

Several suggestions may be considered: (a) Perhaps the thing promised is the result of a revelation just made to Paul, as he writes by revelation and inspiration.   (b) Perhaps the thing promised is also bound up with a prediction Jesus made earlier concerning the desolation of Jerusalem by the Romans (Matthew 24:3-28), an event that is now but a dozen years in the future as Paul writes, an event which (Paul anticipates) would remove much of the plausibility in the Judaizers' arguments for the permanent validity of the Mosaic system.   (c) Perhaps Paul's promise about Satan's being 'crushed' is contained in the same passage of Scripture where we read about "wise as serpents and harmless as doves," for Jesus did on that same occasion promise that faithfulness to the gospel would result in victory for His followers ("it is the one who has endured to the end who will be saved," Matthew 10:22).   (d) Perhaps Paul had in mind another of Jesus' sayings, where the language "tread upon serpents ... and over all the power of the enemy" occurs (Luke 10:18-20).

(3) Is this another of the verses which reflect an alleged mistaken notion about the time of the second advent of Messiah?

Sanday is typical of many who think Paul is looking forward to the soon return of the Messiah, and to that final victory for the faithful.   He comments, "The Romans have not begun to feel the bitterness of divisions as yet; he foresees a time when they will do so, but beyond that he foresees a further time when all will be hushed and quelled, and the Great Adversary himself shall be forever overthrown." *Romans*, p.167.   A.T. Robertson explains, "'shortly' (*en tachei*) as God counts time.   Meanwhile, patient loyalty from us." *Romans*, p.429.   In refutation of all these suggestions that an inspired writer included errors about the time of the second advent in his writings, see the comments offered earlier, at footnote #71 in chapter 13.

(4) Is there any reflection of the language of Genesis 3:16?

The language of Romans 16:20 does remind us of what God said to Eve in the garden (Genesis 3:16).   Christians participate in Christ's victory (there promised) by resistance to doctrines contrary to the gospel, and by divine aid.   Paul has already explained how the saints who are fellow-heirs with Christ (Romans 8:17) are also co-conquerors (Romans 8:37).

[118] This whole matter of God's providence has been referred to in detail in Special Study #2, "The Providence of God."

stumbling-blocks. He Himself would bring about peace.[119] Satan! Like a flash, the word "Satan" illumines all Paul has written about those who would cause dissension and erect stumbling-blocks in men's paths, by means of doctrines contrary to the gospel. The author of the discord and the cause of the divisions which break up the peace of the church is the old adversary, the devil. Those teachers whose doctrines oppose the gospel and disrupt the life of the church are actually servants of Satan.[120] However, Satan's servants could have no victory, they could gain no followers, and Satan would be "crushed under your feet," if Paul's injunction of verse 17 were heeded.[121] Satan may unremittingly continue to send his servants to attack the obedient believers, but God will oversee and interpose so that their attacks are repulsed and certainly crushed.[122]

The grace of our Lord Jesus be with you.[123] Paul closes this warning with a prayer that

---

[119] For the expression "God of peace," see notes at Romans 15:33.

[120] In 2 Corinthians 11:13-15, Paul seems to have Judaizers in mind when he calls such men false apostles, deceitful workers, and then illustrates his teaching about their pretense or disguise by reminding that "even Satan disguises himself as an angel of light. Therefore, it is not surprising if his servants also disguise themselves as servants of righteousness." This is the first time the adversary has been referred to by name in Romans (though his activities have been implied, and he has been referred to in the expression "the sin" in Romans 5-8). Satan is a defeated adversary (Revelation 12:7-9; Colossians 2:15; Luke 10:18). Still, he is permitted to carry on his activities in the world until the end of time, when he will be cast into the lake of fire (Revelation 20:10). He uses men as his instruments of unrighteousness, just as God uses men as instruments of righteousness (Romans 6:13).

[121] Note how the promise of verse 20 is worded in such a way that it depends on what has gone before in verse 17ff. If the Romans are faithful, God will see to it that the devil is unsuccessful in his attempts to disrupt and ruin the work of the church. "Crush" comes from *suntribō*, a word that means to "annihilate, or crush" one's enemies (Arndt-Gingrich, *Lexicon*, p.801). The promised victory is something the readers themselves will enjoy, but it does not necessarily promise world-wide annihilation of the devil and his influence. That ultimate victory over the devil awaits the end of the age. The meaning of the promise is – avoid the bad men, give no ear to their smooth and plausible speech, keep out of their way and their power, and so God shall destroy the work of the devil among you.

[122] The phrase translated "soon" is *en tachei*. It sometimes means "quickly, at once, without delay;" it sometimes means "soon, in a short time, shortly." Arndt-Gingrich, *Lexicon*, p.814. There are times it also seems to have the connotation "certainly," as for example, Luke 18:8 (where the NASB has "speedily"), and Revelation 1:1 (where the NASB has "shortly"). The latter example may be one where the Greek represents a Hebraism; if John's mind is steeped in Hebrew ideas (and many of Revelation's symbols are explained by an appeal to the Hebrew Scriptures), then "certainly" may just be the right idea for Revelation 1:1. Lipscomb and Shepherd do not believe that "soon" refers to any special time (say the second advent of Christ), but to "a general truth that if a congregation of Christians would avoid the teachers that are not faithful to God and will be wise and faithful to his service, then God will *quickly* enable them to triumph over the evil one." *Romans*, p.278.

[123] There is considerable variation in the manuscripts and versions and early church fathers concerning the location of this prayer-wish. Some manuscripts (e.g., P[46], Sinaiticus, Alexandrinus, Vaticanus, Ephraemi) have it only at verse 20, as does the ASV and NASB (note that these versions do not have a verse numbered "24"). Some manuscripts (e.g., D, E, F, G) have it only at verse 24 (in fact, F, G, L omit verses 25-27, so that the words of this prayer-wish form the end of the epistle). Some manuscripts and versions (e.g., Vulgate, Chrysostom, Textus Receptus) carry the prayer-wish at both verses 20 and 24, as does the KJV. Some manuscripts (e.g., P, 33) carry the verse after our verse 27 (P has the prayer-wish both at verse 20 and after verse 27). The weight of present evidence leads to the conclusion that the correct text has this prayer-wish at verse 20, and there only.

the grace of Jesus will be with them to aid in the crushing of Satan.[124]

After the secretary who did the actual penning of a letter as it was dictated had finished, it was customary for the man who dictated the letter to take up the pen and add a personal postscript in his own handwriting. Such a postscript often included just such a prayer-wish as this one (cp. verse 23 in the midst of such a personally written note at 1 Corinthians 16:21-24). If our text of Romans has this prayer-wish of verse 20 in the right place, then this prayer-wish is likely *not* part of what was added in Paul's own handwriting; it should rather be construed as the close of the warning that began in verse 17. Given the way Romans 16:21-23 are worded, we suppose Paul's postscript included just the doxology (verses 25-27). While the manuscript evidence shows considerable divergence, also, with reference to the doxology (a matter already dealt with in the Introductory Studies), there is no real evidence that Paul originally intended the epistle to end here at verse 20.

F. Greetings from Paul's Fellow workers to the Christians at Rome. 16:21-23

16:21 – *Timothy my fellow worker greets you, and* so do *Lucius and Jason and Sosipater, my kinsmen.*

Timothy my fellow worker greets you. After the warning of verses 17-20, the sending of personal greetings is resumed at this point. The senders of these greetings form a different group from the senders of the previous greetings. Earlier the greetings were Paul's own personal greetings, and those of all the churches of Christ. Now the greetings come from those men who, in one way or another, are regularly associated with Paul during this part of his third missionary journey. Timothy has been a long-time companion of Paul. He was converted during Paul's first missionary journey, and he began traveling with the apostle early on his second missionary journey. He has earned the title "fellow worker" during the latter portion of that second tour, as well as during this third tour. On the second tour, Timothy worked for a while in Berea (Acts 17:14), was sent by Paul to Thessalonica (1 Thessalonians 3:2), and then rejoined Paul after the latter began his evangelistic work in Corinth (Acts 18:5). He continued to be with Paul at the time both letters to the Thessalonians were written (1 Thessalonians 1:1; 2 Thessalonians 1:1). The next time we meet Timothy is during Paul's third missionary journey, when he sends him from Ephesus into Macedonia and Greece (Acts 19:21,22; 1 Corinthians 16:10). Upon Timothy's return from those two provinces, and after Paul's intermediate trip to Corinth, Timothy will accompany Paul as he leaves Ephesus and goes toward Macedonia, all the time awaiting word from Titus concerning affairs at Corinth (2 Corinthians 2:12,13). Timothy is with Paul in Macedonia when Paul writes 2 Corinthians (2 Corinthians 1:1). In due time, on this third tour, Paul will come to Corinth (Acts 20:2), from which he will

---

[124] On "grace," see notes at Romans 1:7, and Special Study #1 following comments on chapter 1. On such a prayer (or 'prayer-wish') as is offered in these words, see notes at Romans 15:13,33.

write this epistle to the Romans. This greeting from Timothy to the Romans is one evidence that the much-traveled Timothy is with Paul in Corinth during the winter of AD 58.[125]

And *so do* Lucius. This man may be none other than Lucius of Cyrene, who is named as one of the prophets and teachers at Antioch (Acts 13:1). However, the name Lucius is a rather common one, so the identification cannot be asserted positively.[126] If we make the identification, the association of Paul and Lucius together in advancing the gospel of Christ now spans nearly fifteen years.

And Jason. A man named Jason opened his home to Paul and his fellow workers on their initial visit to Thessalonica, and got himself into trouble in consequence (Acts 17:5-9). The Jason named here in Romans may be the same man.[127]

And Sosipater. This may be the man called "Sopater" in Acts 20:4.[128] It has earlier (verse 16) been observed that as Paul writes this letter to Rome, the couriers who are going to carry each church's portion of the benevolent offering to Jerusalem are already beginning

---

[125] One problem that has perplexed commentators is this: In the other epistles (2 Corinthians, Philippians, Colossians, 1 and 2 Thessalonians, and Philemon), when Timothy was present with Paul at the time of his writing those letters, his name is joined with Paul's in the signature and address at the very beginning of the letter. Why is Timothy's name not at the heading of this letter to Rome? Possible answers to this question include: (1) In those other letters, Timothy acts as Paul's secretary, whereas Tertius is the secretary for Romans (Romans 16:22). (2) Paul is seeking "living-link" mission support for himself in particular in this letter to Rome, so it would not be wise to include Timothy in the opening words of the letter. (3) Timothy is absent from Corinth at the time Paul began to dictate the letter, but has returned before he has finished it. (4) Timothy was unknown by the majority of brethren at Rome (though one might suppose that many of those greeted in Romans 16:3-15 would have known Paul's fellow-worker).

[126] Since Origen's time, some have supposed that Lucius (*Loukios*) of Romans 16 is Luke (*Loukas*), the physician and companion of Paul (Colossians 4:14; Philemon 24; 2 Timothy 4:11). Although Arndt-Gingrich, *Lexicon*, p.481, suggest that Lucius and Luke may be possible alternate spellings for the same name, Luke's name in Latin would be Lucas or Lucanus, and not Lucius (as would be the Latin spelling of the name here in Romans). In fact, Arndt-Gingrich give a separate entry for "Lucius" and for "Luke," even after admitting the words may be equivalent in one or two old inscriptions. If "my kinsmen" at the end of this verse refers to all three names which precede (and we are inclined to so take it), then Lucius would be a Jewish Christian, a fact that would rule out any identification with Luke the physician since the physician was a Gentile Christian. (It would be possible to punctuate after Lucius, so as to leave only the last two named [Jason and Sosipater] to be designated "my kinsmen." But even this leaves the identification of Lucius and Luke doubtful, for not a few scholars deny that Lucius and Luke are but two forms of the same name.)

[127] Some have urged that if we were to take "kinsmen" in its more limited sense of "physical relative," it might suggest a reason why Paul would have found a welcome and lodging in Jason's home. (On the contrary, if Paul were disinherited by his family [cp. Philippians 3:8] as a consequence of having accepted Christ, to take "kinsmen" in its limited sense would give a reason why he should *not* have found lodging there.) If we were to take "kinsmen" in its broader sense meaning "Jew," it still gives a reason for the hospitality.

[128] In earlier comments on Paul's use of names (cf. Prisca, verse 3, note #20), it has been observed that Paul regularly uses the more formal spelling, while Luke uses the conversational form.

to gather at Corinth. (Each courier is a trusted man chosen by his own church.) From Corinth, they will shortly embark together for the trip to Jerusalem. If the identification of Sosipater and Sopater is made, then it is possible that two of the chosen couriers (Timothy and Sosipater) were not at home at the time they were chosen, but rather were away working with Paul, wherever he was. All the church at Berea and the one at Lystra needed to do was to deliver their portion of the offering to their chosen messenger – Berea's to Sosipater, Lystra's to Timothy – and entrust him to see it safely the rest of the way.

My kinsmen.[129] At the time these last three men send their greetings to Rome, all those one-time Jews have become Christians.

16:22 – *I, Tertius, who write this letter, greet you in the Lord.*

I, Tertius, who write this letter. Paul generally seems to have dictated his letters;[130] here the man who took the dictation and actually penned the letter adds his greeting.[131] This is the only mention of the man in the New Testament. "That the Apostle's amanuensis should insert this salutation is, firstly, a mark of the genuineness of the epistle, as no forger would have mentioned his doing so."[132] This greeting in which the secretary is named is the only one like it in the New Testament. While it is likely that Timothy was the penman for many of Paul's letters, his name is usually included along with Paul's in the opening salutation of the letters, so that both Paul and he together pray for "grace and peace from the Lord" to be upon the readers. It would be an instance of Paul's characteristic courtesy to permit Tertius to add his own greeting. As will be indicated in comments on the next phrase, Tertius very well may have had some intimation of the importance of what he was doing for Paul, as he took this dictation from the apostle.

Greet you in the Lord. If "in the Lord" is taken with the verb "greet," then the implication is that Tertius too was a Christian.[133] If "in the Lord" is taken with "you," then only

---

[129] For the meaning of "kinsmen" see notes at Romans 9:3 and 16:7. See also footnotes #126 and #127 for some of the ramifications involved after one decides on the narrower or broader meaning, and after one decides if two or three of the men named here are characterized as "kinsmen."

[130] Galatians may be an exception to Paul's usual practice. See Galatians 6:11, which suggests the whole letter was written heatedly by Paul himself. Lest the use of a secretary be thought to impinge somehow on the doctrine of verbal inspiration, hear Sanday's comment. "We have observed in the course of this commentary how frequently the involved and broken style is to be accounted for by this habit of dictation, and, as it would seem, not very punctilious revision. We have the very thoughts and words of the apostle as they came warm from his own mind as directed by the Spirit." *Romans*, p.168.

[131] "Write" is another example of the Greek verb tense called "epistolary aorist." See the explanation of this usage in notes at 15:15 under "I have written."

[132] Vine, *Romans*, p.221,222.

[133] A study of the phrase "in the Lord" as used earlier in chapter 16 shows that it commonly is construed with the person being greeted, rather than the one doing the greeting. In harmony with this fact, most writers translate as does the NASB, putting "in the Lord" with "greet."

those who were Christians in Rome were greeted by Tertius.   It is just possible that "in the Lord" should be construed with the verb "write."   In this case, it is implied that Tertius was aware of the vital part he was playing in the cause of Christ while acting as Paul's secretary.   He was offering his whole-hearted cooperation to the apostle because both were deeply involved in the work of the Lord.

16:23 – *Gaius, host to me and to the whole church, greets you.   Erastus, the city treasurer greets you, and Quartus, the brother.*

Gaius, host to me and to the whole church, greets you.   At least three different persons with the name "Gaius" are found in the New Testament.   There was Gaius of Corinth (1 Corinthians 1:14), one of the few people there whom Paul personally immersed.   There is a Macedonian named Gaius (Acts 19:29), and a Gaius of Derbe (Acts 20:4).   The Gaius with whom Paul is staying as he writes this letter is probably identical with the first of these three.[134]   For some years now, New Testament scholars have also proposed the thesis that Gaius of Corinth is to be identified as being the same man who is named "Titius Justus" in Acts 18:7, who extended the hospitality of his house to Paul and the infant congregation at Corinth when they no longer found it feasible to assemble in the synagogue next door.   His whole Roman name would have been Gaius Titius Justus.[135]   It is not clear what Paul means in Romans when he characterizes Gaius as being "host to ... the whole church." Perhaps it means the church meets regularly in his home (as at Acts 18:7), or perhaps it means that Gaius regularly extended hospitality to any traveling Christian from abroad who happened to stop in Corinth.   Think of all the people who would come to visit Paul, of all the young evangelists who regularly accompanied him, and of their need for lodging, and the readiness of Gaius to open another room, so that the people would have easy access to the apostle, is all the more praiseworthy.

Erastus, the city treasurer greets you.   The name "Erastus," a rather common name in the 1st century, occurs in two other New Testament passages: (1) At a time previous to the writing of Romans, a man named Erastus was with Paul in Ephesus, from whence he had been sent (along with Timothy) into Macedonia on a mission of some kind, perhaps to arrange the details for the offering for the saints in Jerusalem (Acts 19:22).   (2) At a time nearly ten years subsequent to the writing of Romans, a man named Erastus had remained at Corinth while Paul himself had passed through the city on his way perhaps to Nicopolis (Titus 3:12) and eventually to Rome, from which 2 Timothy was written (2 Timothy 4:20). It is a matter of conjecture whether or not the Erastus in Romans is to be identified with

---

[134] In this commentator's opinion, the Gaius named in 3 John 1 is also to be identified with Gaius of Corinth.

[135] See F.F. Bruce, *Romans*, p.280; William M. Ramsay, *Pictures of the Apostolic Church* (Grand Rapids: Baker Book House, 1959), p.205; Edgar J. Goodspeed, "Gaius Titius Justus," in *Journal of Biblical Literature*, 69 (1950), p.382ff.   Gaius would have been his praenomen; Titius would have been his Roman *gens* name; Justus would have been his cognomen.

either or both of these other two men.[136]   Nor is it possible to say with certainty that Erastus of Romans is the Erastus whose name appears on a pavement near the theater northwest of downtown Corinth.

> This Erastus has been identified with the civic official of that name mentioned in a Latin inscription on a marble paving-block discovered at Corinth in 1929 by members of the American School of Classical Studies at Athens: [it reads] ERASTVS PRO: AED: S: P: STRAVIT ("Erastus, commissioner for public works, laid this pavement at his own expense"). The pavement belongs to the first century AD, and may well have been laid by Paul's friend. The public offices, however, are not the same: in Greek, the commissioner for public works, or 'aedile', is called *agoranomos*, whereas the city treasurer (as here) is *oikonomos tes poleos*. If we have to do with the same Erastus, he had presumably been promoted to the city treasurership from the lower office of 'aedile' by the time Paul wrote this epistle. (If anyone prefers to suppose, on the contrary, that he had been demoted from the higher to the lower office on account of his Christian profession, there is no evidence against this supposition.)[137]

In light of the fact that "not many mighty, not many noble" (1 Corinthians 1:26) were members of church at Corinth, it is of interest to find Erastus, who held a government position of considerable importance[138] in one of the great cities in the ancient world, a member of the Christian church.

And Quartus, the brother.   This is the only mention of this man in the New Testament. Paul has given a commendatory description about those to whom he sent greetings in verses 3-16; he has used a briefer commendation for those with him as he writes (verses 21-23). Is "brother" such a commendation, equivalent of saying that Quartus is a brother in the Lord? But if "brother" means "fellow Christian," why is he singled out to receive a designation which was common to all? Bruce has suggested that Quartus was the physical brother of either Erastus or of Tertius. "Is he Erastus' brother, since his name immediately precedes?   Or, since Quartus is Latin for 'fourth,' and Tertius is Latin for 'third,' would it

---

[136] Arndt-Gingrich, *Lexicon*, p.306, call the Erastus in Romans "Erastus 1" and the Erastus of the other two passages "Erastus 2."   Since both Romans and 2 Timothy connect that Erastus with Corinth, not many objections are raised against identifying those two as the same.   It is the one in Acts who creates the greater difficulty.   Those who reject making this identification urge that a man who was "treasurer of the city" would not be free to travel at Paul's behest as Acts 19:22 has that Erastus doing.   Those who favor the identification answer that any absence from the city was not that prolonged, for according to Acts 19:22 (when compared with 1 Corinthians 16:10) Timothy and Erastus were sent by way of Macedonia *to Corinth*, the very place where, according to Romans 16:23, Erastus was treasurer.   Or, they propose that for a while Erastus has stopped traveling with Paul in order to serve as treasurer of the city, but was free before and after his service in that office to serve with Paul as Acts and 2 Timothy suggest he did.

[137] Bruce, *Romans*, p.280,281.   See also H.J. Cadbury, "Erastus of Corinth," *Journal of Biblical Literature*, 50 (1931), p.42-58; and W. Miller, "Who was Erastus?" *Bibliotheca Sacra*, 88 (1931), p.342-346.

[138] The KJV translates *oikonomos* as "chamberlain," and this word in the 20th century could give a wrong impression of his position.   "Steward" is a common translation of *oikonomos*; city manager, city treasurer, and city administrator have all been suggested to translate the whole phrase *oikonomos tés poleōs*.

be excessively farfetched to think of him as Tertius' brother, born next after him?"[139] Barclay comments on Paul's ability in a single sentence, or a single word, to sum up the characteristics of the people about whom he is writing. "Here are two great summaries. Gaius is the man of hospitality. Quartus in one word is the brother. It is a great thing to go down in history as the man with the open house or the man with the brotherly heart. Some day people will sum us up in one sentence. What will that sentence be?"[140]

[16:24 – *The grace of our Lord Jesus Christ be with you all. Amen.*]

(The marginal note informs us that "Some ancient manuscripts add verse 24, *The grace of our Lord Jesus Christ be with you all. Amen.*" The evidence for and against the inclusion of these words as verse 24 has been examined as comment was made on Romans 16:20, where the phrase does belong.)

G. Concluding Doxology. 16:25-27

16:25 – *Now to Him who is able to establish you according to my gospel and the preaching of Jesus Christ, according to the revelation of the mystery which has been kept secret for long ages past,*

Now. The epistle concludes in a manner usual with Paul – with a doxology, or ascription of praise, to God.[141] The thing that is unusual about this one is its length, and the fact that it neatly sums up all the great thoughts of the epistle.[142] Paul regularly took up the pen at the close of his dictation to the scribe, and added a postscript to his letters.[143] It certainly is a possibility that verses 25-27 were in Paul's own handwriting in the autograph copy, added after Tertius had read back to Paul what he had just dictated.[144]

---

[139] Bruce, *Romans*, p.281. Cranfield, *Romans*, p.808, objects to all of Bruce's material on the word "brother" as highly improbable.

[140] Barclay, *Romans*, p.241. We would modify Barclay's note about "brotherly heart" to make it read "Quartus, my fellow-Christian," if we were to understand "the brother" in its metaphorical sense.

[141] While not all these doxologies come at the close of their respective letters, compare Ephesians 3:21; Philippians 4:20; 1 Timothy 1:17; and Hebrews 13:20,21.

[142] Critics of the New Testament often express doubts about whether verses 25-27 are original and genuine. Cranfield, a typical example of much modern scholarship, expresses almost total doubt that this doxology is as old as Paul, or that Paul had anything to do with its composition (*Romans*, p.808,809). The various questions bearing on the genuineness and integrity of these verses, and their different locations in the various manuscripts, have been sufficiently discussed in the Introductory Studies. In harmony with the conclusions there reached, the verses are here commented upon as the genuine and original conclusion to the epistle, exactly harmonizing with and summarizing its contents.

[143] See 1 Corinthians 16:21; Colossians 4:18; 2 Thessalonians 3:17.

[144] Moule, *Romans*, p.435ff.

To Him who is able. This word of praise is addressed to God the Father.[145] "Able" is a translation of the same root word translated "power" in Romans 1:16; the use of the synonym "able" includes the connotation of "natural ability, general and inherent."[146] That is the kind of ability God has.

To establish you. We are inclined to believe that "establish" is rather synonymous with 'right standing before God.' God is able to make such a standing possible, even for fallen man. Romans has shown some of what is included in God's way of saving man. Included is remission of sins and justification by faith (chapters 3-5), a new life in Christ which is helped by the power of the indwelling Spirit (chapters 6-8), and the corresponding right relationships to God and to one's fellow man (chapters 12-15).

According to my gospel. That God is able to "establish" men, and the way He does it, is the heart and soul of the gospel message Paul has been preaching.[147] The expression "my gospel" means 'the gospel committed to me and preached by me,' just as it did in Romans 2:16.

And the preaching of Jesus Christ. "And" (*kai*) here seems to be epexegetic; thus, the phrase is an explanation of the content of Paul's gospel. Romans 1:1-3 has introduced the whole book by telling us that the "gospel of God" that Paul was set apart to preach is "concerning His Son." He has been preaching about Jesus Christ.[148] One is reminded of Romans 10:8-17, which has clearly set forth the value of preaching.

> The establishment of the Roman Christians was to take place through those appointed ways and means that are laid down in the gospel, and form the main topic of Christian preaching. All means of grace center in Christ, and it is only in accordance with the due proclamation of Christ that the Christian can hope to become confirmed and strengthened.[149]

According to the revelation of the mystery. This phrase seems to be connected with

---

[145] "To Him who is able" is in the dative case. To this initial dative case, the one in verse 27 ("to the only wise God") corresponds. All that lies in between is dependent in some way upon "Him who is able."

[146] Thayer, *Lexicon*, p.160.

[147] The exact idea expressed by the preposition translated "according to" is not easy to explain at this place. One of its possible meanings is "through," as though the establishing would take place by means of the gospel. Another of its possible meanings is "in harmony with, in conformity with," so that the establishing takes place in conformity with the way Paul has been preaching that God does it. Arndt-Gingrich, *Lexicon*, p.408, opts for the latter meaning here.

[148] This last comment has treated the genitive "of Jesus Christ" as an objective genitive. Barclay, *Romans*, p.242, treats it as a genitive of originating source; thus, it means that the gospel which Paul preached was the same offered by Jesus. Barclay writes, "That is to say, the gospel which takes its source in Christ, and is transmitted by men."

[149] Sanday, *Romans*, p.170.

"preaching," and thus tells us that the present proclamation of the gospel is in harmony with God's plans to reserve the unfolding of His whole scheme of redemption until these latter days.[150]   The word "mystery" is used here precisely as it was at Romans 11:25 and elsewhere in the New Testament, "of something which up to the time of the apostles had remained secret, but had then been made known by divine intervention."[151]   A "mystery" is something which was not clearly revealed in Old Testament times, but now is.[152] "Revelation" has to do with uncovering something so that it can be clearly seen.[153]

Which has been kept secret for long ages past.   In the past ages[154] when God's way of saving man was a mystery, God had made few pronouncements on the subject.   There were, to be sure, His providential dealings with men; there were also those prophecies of coming redemptive events in which His plans would eventually be completely unfolded. But, looking back at the few revelations He granted to men before the incarnation of Jesus, it can be said that his plans were "hidden in silence."[155]   The preaching about Jesus was an

---

[150] We are in the midst of an involved and difficult sentence.   It has seemed best to take the first two phrases ("according to my gospel" and "according to the preaching of Jesus") as connected with "establish;" they thus tell that the "establish(ing)" is done in harmony with the way gospel preaching says God does it.   It also seems best to take all the words from "according to the revelation ... " down to the end of verse 26 as connected with "preaching;" they thus tell us that the present gospel preaching is in harmony with the way God all along planned to do things.   The "preaching," we shall be told, is something whose introduction was deliberately delayed until these latter days; the content of the message is not only preached but also is published in the prophetic writings; it is preached and published at God's express command; this gospel is the great instrument for bringing all nations to the obedience of faith.

[151] Sanday, *Romans*, p.170.

[152] A partial listing of some of the things that were once hidden but are revealed now in the Gospel Age has been provided in footnote #118 on chapter 11.   It is not easy to decide in this place whether the contents of the mystery here alluded to are the same as just set forth in the previous clauses of this doxology ('God is able to establish men in harmony with the gospel about Jesus Christ'), or whether there is a backward glance at the word "mystery" in Romans 11:25.   If taken the first way, then "all through the Old Testament dispensation, the Christian scheme, which was then future, had remained hidden; now, with Christ's coming, the veil has been taken away." Sanday, *Romans*, p.170.   If taken the second way, it gives "the conclusion to which the apostle has arrived in musing over the difficulties which the problems of human history as he knew them had suggested.   God who rules over all the aeons or periods of time, which have passed and which are to come, is working out an eternal purpose in the world.   For ages it was a mystery, now in these last days it has been revealed: and this revelation explains the meaning of God's working in the past."   Sanday and Headlam, *Romans*, p.434.

[153] Concerning the revelations that God made to the New Testament apostles and prophets, so they could know the right message to preach, compare what Paul wrote at 1 Corinthians 2:6-14.

[154] Literally, the Greek reads "eternal times" where the NASB has "long ages past."   The divine plan of redemption originated (2 Timothy 1:9) in God's mind before time began (Titus 1:2; Romans 8:28,29), and had been kept secret during the numerous times that have elapsed between the creation of man and the birth of Jesus in Bethlehem.   There was no public proclamation of it in all those ages, as there is now in the Gospel Age.   The silence is ended.   Heralds are heralding it!

[155] "Kept secret" is an attempt to translate the Greek verb *sigaō*.   It means to "be silent, keep still, say nothing, keep something secret, to conceal."   Arndt-Gingrich, *Lexicon*, p.757.   In the earlier expression "revelation," it was implied the mystery was something hidden to *sight*.   This word emphasizes *hearing*, and suggests that the mystery was hidden as far as hearing about it was concerned.

uncovering of the mystery which had never before been so clearly revealed, and it explained God's purpose in the world with a clarity which had never before been granted.

16:26 – *but now is manifested, and by the Scriptures of the prophets, according to the commandment of the eternal God, has been made known to all the nations,* leading *to obedience of faith;*

But now is manifested. The first clause of verse 26 concludes the thought begun in the last part of verse 25; it describes the mystery at first as having been kept secret, but now as made plainly visible or known.[156] The 'long ages of silence that stretched back into eternity' had lasted until the mystery was clearly revealed in the incarnation and the subsequent preaching of the gospel. Men could see with their eyes what God had done to establish men (verse 25) by looking at Jesus – His incarnation, ministry, death, burial, resurrection, ascension.[157]

And by the Scriptures of the prophets. The relationship of this phrase to its context,[158] and its meaning,[159] have been matters of serious dispute.[160] It, of course, is possible that

---

[156] "Manifested" translates the Greek *phaneroō*, which means "to make visible, to make known." Wuest, *Romans*, p.266. Thayer suggests a possible distinction between the synonyms "revelation" and "manifested" in his *Lexicon*, p.62. "*Phaneroō* [manifest] is thought to describe an external manifestation, to the senses and hence open to all ... *apokaluptō* [revelation] an internal disclosure ... The *apokalupsis* or *unveiling* precedes and produces the *phanerōsis* or *manifestation* ...."

[157] The aorist tense participle looks back to completed action in the past time. Jesus' visit to earth in human form was already a thing of the past when Paul wrote.

[158] The Greek word translated "and" is *te*, a particle denoting emphasis, but which is seldom translated. Some explanations offered for this phrase treat it as though there were no *te* present; others have translated it; some manuscripts even omit the word *te* (though neither the Nestle text nor the UBS Greek text mention this possible variant). "The *te* is undoubtedly genuine, and connects the two participles *gnōristhentos* ['made known'] and *phanerothentos* ['manifested']. The mystery or secret was not only brought to light and manifested (*phanerōthentos*) '*by the appearing of our Saviour Jesus Christ*' (2 Timothy 1:10), but it was also made generally known and published abroad (*gnōristhentos*), and St. Paul goes on to tell us (1) by what means, (2) at whose command, (3) for what purpose, and (4) to what extent this publication was made." Gifford, *Romans*, p.237.

[159] Are "prophets" the Old Testament prophets or the New Testament prophets? Cranfield, *Romans*, p.811, writes, "The suggestion that the prophetic writings referred to are Christian, not Old Testament, we regard as a counsel of desperation." Exactly the opposite of this is Vine, *Romans*, p.223, "He is pointing, therefore, not to Old Testament Scriptures, for this revelation [of the mystery] had not been given through them, but to those parts of the New Testament which had already been, and were in the process of being, written."

[160] Harnack, who denied the genuineness of the whole doxology, attributed a shorter form of it to Marcion, and suggested that certain additions (e.g., "the Scriptures of the prophets") were orthodox additions, and awkwardly added at that. How inept, he thought, to have a verse that says the mystery was kept secret for (through) long ages past" and then in the next breath to say "it was made clear by the Scriptures of the prophets." (There is no independent evidence for a shorter text of the doxology; Marcion's mutilated copy of Romans that he included in his canon had no doxology at all, having been truncated so that all after 14:23 is omitted; it is hard to believe Marcion himself thus wrote the alleged shorter doxology.) Bruce, *Romans*, p.281,282, presents Harnack's version of the supposed Marcionite doxology, along with further refutation of this hypothesis.

the whole phrase tells of an attendant circumstance,[161] that the present-time full manifestation of the mystery has this attendant circumstance: it was dimly foreshadowed in the Old Testament prophets.[162]   In other words, perhaps Paul has something in mind similar to what he wrote at Romans 1:2 (that God's way of saving man had been "promised beforehand through His prophets in the holy Scriptures") and at 3:21 ("being witnessed by the Law and the Prophets").[163]   On the other hand, it is also possible that the whole phrase tells one means or one instrument[164] by which the manifestation is made known.[165]   If this latter is the correct idea, then the prophets almost surely must be the New Testament prophets, and Paul would be saying that both the apostolic preaching and the New Testament prophetic writings are helping to make known the mystery.[166]

---

[161] That *dia* and the genitive ("by the Scriptures" is *dia* followed by a word in the genitive case) sometimes denotes "attendant circumstance" see Arndt-Gingrich, *Lexicon*, p.179.

[162] Calvin wrote, "Although the prophets had formerly taught all that Christ and the apostles have explained, yet they taught with so much obscurity, when compared with the shining clarity of the gospel, that we need not be surprised if these things which are now revealed are said to have been hidden."   Cited by Bruce, *Romans*, p.283.

[163] Those who think Old Testament prophets are intended have also recalled the constant allusion to the Old Testament Scriptures in chapters 9-11 of Romans.

[164] This is but another possible connotation of *dia* followed by a genitive case.   Arndt-Gingrich, *Lexicon*, p.179.

[165] Greek word order permits the location of subjects, verbs, objects, and prepositional phrases in almost any order the speaker wishes, whereas English usually expects the order to be subject, verb, and object (each, of course, with such desired adjectives and adverbs as needed to express the idea). This note on grammar is given to introduce the fact that the verb translated "made known" (*gnōristhentos*) does not occur until the very last word in the long series of words that make up verse 26.   However, when it comes to translation into English, the translator will follow the English order, and insert the verb where it usually would be found.   But where shall he put it?   Shall he read it with "to all the nations" as the NASB does ("has been made known to all the nations")?   Or shall he construe it with "by the Scriptures of the prophets" so that it reads "and has been made known by the Scriptures of the prophets"?   In our comments we have opted for the latter, since the former would require "all nations" to be in the dative case (as a study of the New Testament occurrences of *gnōrizō* makes clear) instead of the accusative case that Paul used here.

[166] "Prophetic" is used in the sense of speak by inspiration, its primary meaning, rather than predict the future, which is a secondary meaning.   All the books included in the New Testament were written either by an apostle or a prophet – such supernatural endowment being a necessary prerequisite to inspiration.

Since, if our dating of the New Testament books is correct, only Matthew, 1 and 2 Thessalonians, 1 and 2 Corinthians, and Galatians have been written, not a few find it difficult to accept the explanation that "Scriptures of the prophets" refers to New Testament writings.   These writers have offered an alternative explanation: the "Scriptures of the prophets" are the Old Testament writings, and Paul is referencing the way gospel preachers made use of the Messianic passages in those Old Testament writings as the "text" for their gospel preaching (e.g., Luke 24:27; Acts 2:17-21, 3:22-26, 4:11, 7:1-50, 8:32-35, 13:23-41,47, 17:2,11, 26:22,27; 1 Peter 1:10-12).   Lange, *Romans*, p.453, explains that "*through the Scriptures of the prophets* means that their sense has now become fully clear."   Only interpreted Christologically do the passages make any sense.

The apostles are here called "prophets," in as much as they are bearers of a new revelation. Their writings, then, certainly are prophetical; for a prophet is not primarily, but only accidentally, one who foretells the future, being rather one who, having been taught of God, speaks out His will ... Paul feels that the letter he has just written has this character, and that it ranks among the means which God is using to carry out the publication of the new revelation. It is therefore of this very letter, as well as others, which had proceeded from his pen, that he is speaking of in this passage.[167]

According to the commandment of the eternal God. It is according to the commandment or the appointment of God that the mystery, so long hidden, should thus now at last be made known. If the mystery had been kept silent (secret) through the ages past because God wanted it that way, it would require an express arrangement or command[168] from the eternal God[169] to go counter to what had been the prior order. Evidence of such a deliberate change (no longer is it to be kept silent!) is not difficult to find. The Great Commission spoke of making disciples of all the nations, preaching the gospel to the whole creation, and about repentance and remission of sins being proclaimed in His name to all the nations.[170] We are reminded of the words of Acts 13:1,2, how the apostle began his missionary tours among the Gentiles because he and Barnabas were specially "set apart" for that work by the Holy Spirit. All that has taken place since then was because the eternal God wanted the gospel to be made known so that all men could be "established" (verse 25).

To all the nations, *leading* to obedience of faith. The word order in the original is slightly different: it is "unto obedience of faith unto all the nations." That is, the eternal

---

[167] Lipscomb and Shepherd, *Romans*, p.281,282. Paul is so familiarly known as "Paul the *apostle*" that any suggestion that he calls himself a "prophet" falls on skeptical ears. Lest the idea be summarily rejected that Paul should call himself a prophet, when his actual function was apostle, it should be remembered that two men (Barnabas and Paul) later specifically styled "apostles" (Acts 14:14) are listed among the "prophets and teachers" at Acts 13:1. One further thought: if Vine and Lipscomb-Shepherd are correct (and there is a 50% chance they are) that the reference is to New Testament prophetic writings, then a statement often voiced about the consciousness of inspired men as they wrote ("No New Testament writer was aware he was writing a book or letter that would later be included in a collection of such called the Bible") may have to be revised, or at least spoken with less assurance. If verse 26 is affirmation that God's mystery is being manifested to men through the letters of New Testament like he himself is writing, Paul certainly was conscious of the importance of his letter, to say nothing of its lasting value.

[168] "Commandment" translates *epitagē*, a word that means "command, order, injunction, mandate." Arndt-Gingrich, *Lexicon*, p.302; Thayer, *Lexicon*, p.244.

[169] This is the only instance in the New Testament where "eternal" (*aiōnios*) is used to qualify "God." We have had *aidios* translated "eternal" at Romans 1:20; also, God has been designated as "incorruptible" (*aphthartos*) at 1:23. The Holy Spirit is identified as the "eternal (*aiōniou*) Spirit" in Hebrews 9:14. It is likely that the more common expression "the living God" is intended to convey the same idea, namely, that the true God has no beginning and no ending. Furthermore, we have just had (verse 25) the expression "*eternal* ages" ("long ages past," NASB). God is called "eternal" to remind us that He was there, that He is the one who formulated the plan, and that ever since, He is the one who has been implementing the plan of redemption by which men are "established."

[170] Matthew 28:19; Mark 16:15; Luke 24:47.

God had this purpose in mind when He ordered that the "mystery" which is now manifested also be made known: that all of mankind will have opportunity to become obedient believers ("faith comes from hearing," Romans 10:17).   It was God's purpose that "obedience of faith"[171] – the condition on which he reckons justification – be extended to include all nations (not just one nation).[172]

16:27 – *to the only wise God, through Jesus Christ, to whom be the glory forever.   Amen.*

To the only wise God.   By starting this verse with "to," our translators have tried to show that verse 27 picks up the thread of thought begun in verse 25.   Omitting some of the subordinate ideas, Paul wrote, "To Him who is able ... the only wise God, ... to Him (I say) be glory forever!"   The two adjectives used in this phrase to describe God pick up one of the chief ideas of the epistle.   God is *one* (cp. Romans 3:30); therefore, He is God of both Jews and Gentiles.   God is *wise*; His wisdom (seen in the planning, and the carrying out of the plan to create and to redeem man should he sin) has an unfathomable depth to it (cp. Romans 11:33).

Through Jesus Christ.   How are we to understand these words?   Taking it in the order it appears in the Greek, where it is joined to "the only wise God," it might mean that it is through Jesus that God is seen to be wise.   Or, if we were to connect this phrase to the word "establish" in verse 25, then the doxology's main idea is that God establishes men through Jesus Christ.   A third suggestion is that "through Jesus Christ" is somehow related to the ascription of praise that follows, so that the doxology is addressed to God through Jesus Christ who is the mediator of such praise.[173]   Either of the first two interpretations is probably to be preferred over the third one, especially if the word translated "to whom" (with which the last clause of the verse begins) enjoys integrity.[174]

---

[171] See comments at Romans 1:5 for the meaning of the expression "obedience of faith."   The faith that is the condition of salvation is an obedient faith.

[172] The Greek word *ethnos* here translated "nations" is the same word translated "Gentiles" at Romans 1:5.   All "ethnic groups" might catch the real import of the word here, for as Romans has so amply indicated, there is but one way of salvation for Jew and non-Jew alike; only those among all the "nations" who are obedient believers are the ones who have right standing in God's eyes.

[173] The KJV translators chose this last option, but to do so they were forced to leave untranslated some of what appears in the Greek.   Just as does the Nestle text and the UBS Greek text, the Textus Receptus reads literally, "To the only wise God, through Jesus Christ, *to whom* be glory forever."   "To whom" is left out of the KJV, which reads "to God only wise, be glory through Jesus Christ forever."

[174] The word translated "to whom" is omitted from Vaticanus, from Origen (Latin), and from the Peshitto Syriac version.   Vaticanus is one of the better manuscripts, and usually is free of suspicion of having words deliberately left out because of their difficulty of the resulting reading.   If the word indeed was not included in the original text, how did it come to be inserted into the present text?   Sanday, *Romans*, p.171,172, urges that doxologies so customarily begin with "to whom" that some copyist, early in the course of the transmission of the text, inserted it where it did not belong, and it was his exemplar that came to be the ancestor of all those manuscripts which include it.

On the other hand, a few of the manuscripts and versions which include the word in the text (even though it makes the reading more difficult) are P[46], Sinaiticus, Alexandrinus, Ephraemi, the whole Byzantine text family, the Latin Vulgate, etc.   This weighty evidence for the integrity of the word "to whom," though it

To whom be the glory forever. There are two ways the relative pronoun "to whom" has been explained. One is to find its antecedent in "Jesus Christ." The sudden shift of the focus from the Father (verse 25) to offering praise to Jesus (verse 27) is explained on the supposition that the author either lost his train of thought over the course of this long sentence,[175] or else he wanted praise to be offered to both the Father and the Son (and expressed this by deliberately writing a broken sentence).[176] The other way of explaining the relative pronoun is to find its antecedent in "God" (or even in "to Him who is able," verse 25), which effectively treats the relative pronoun as if it were a demonstrative pronoun.[177] This latter is what we have done above when we offered the translation "to Him (I say) be glory!" The Greek reads "*the* glory;" that is, all the glorification, honor, and praise that men are able to offer to God. It is the praise and adoration that a glad heart offers after it has contemplated all that Romans has said about God and His way of saving man. "Forever" is literally "unto the ages of the ages;" that is, through all the ages of eternity to come,[178] the goal toward which history is being conducted by the wise God Himself.

Amen.[179] The doxology has summed up all the great ideas of the epistle: in Jesus Christ is God manifested to human view; God as essentially gracious, attempting all along to help the man He has created to come to repentance and thus to proper relationship with Him; the gospel about Jesus (preached and written) as the power of God unto salvation; the eternal purpose of God; His wisdom displayed in His choice of ways and means to carry out His purpose; the fact that justification before God has always been on the condition of

---

disturbs the flow of the sentence, and though it is the more difficult reading, leads to the conclusion that it surely should be retained as being part of the original text.

[175] "The apostle's mind is so full of the thoughts of the epistle, that they come crowding out, and have produced the heavily loaded phrases of the doxology; the structure of the sentence is thus lost, and he concludes with a well-known formula of praise (compare Galatians 1:15; 2 Timothy 4:18; Hebrews 13: 21)." Sanday and Headlam, *Romans*, p.435. (The suggestion of some, that it was Paul's amanuensis, Tertius, who made a blunder and out of habit slipped this relative pronoun into the original letter, when Paul had not dictated it that way, would create real problems for the doctrine of plenary, verbal inspiration. Besides, we have earlier indicated our opinion that these words were penned by Paul himself.)

[176] To follow the old solution and insist that we have either an accidental or deliberately broken sentence here, leaves one with an impression that this is a poor way to end such a magnificent epistle.

[177] "A not dissimilar use of the relative pronoun is quite probably to be recognized in 1 Peter 4:11, and perhaps also in Hebrews 13:21." Cranfield, *Romans*, p.813.

[178] The doxology in 11:36 is worded simply "unto the ages," a phrase that differs slightly in meaning from the language here in 16:27, "unto the ages of the ages."

[179] See "Amen" explained in comments at Romans 11:36. The subscription (see some editions of the KJV), "Written to the Romans from Corinth, and sent by Phoebe, servant of the church at Cenchrea," has been commented upon in the Introductory Studies. In its present form, it hardly dates back beyond the 9th century. The earlier form of the subscription, up to the 6th century, was simply "To the Romans."

faithfulness; His interest in all the nations of the earth; the ultimate reason behind all He has done – that He wants men (of their own volition) to praise Him; and His moving of all history toward a goal.

Once more, the two destinies possible to each man, outlined in Romans 2:6-10, are recalled to mind.   God will render to every man according to his deeds.   To those who are selfishly ambitious and do not obey the truth, but obey unrighteousness, He will render wrath and indignation and tribulation and distress for every soul of man who does evil, to the Jew first and also to the Greek.   To those who by perseverance in doing good seek for glory and honor and immortality, He will render eternal life and glory and honor and peace to every man who does good, to the Jew first and also to the Greek.

"Oh the depth of the riches both of the wisdom and knowledge of God!   How unsearchable are His judgments and unfathomable His ways!   For from Him and through Him and to Him are all things.   To Him be the glory forever!"

SELECTED BIBLIOGRAPHY

As the student works through Romans again and again, it becomes evident that certain topics and certain passages have proven particularly difficult to explain. It is therefore of special interest to see how each new commentary or article handles these problem areas. While most students will have access to the more familiar commentaries in which these matters are addressed, and in which can be found bibliographies of older works on Romans, not all students will have access to the current periodical literature or monographs or collections in which continuing debate is carried on. It seems appropriate, therefore, in this bibliography, to pay particular attention to such literature from the late 20th century, and to offer a brief abstract of the main thrust of the articles referenced. By paying thoughtful attention to the abstracts, the student will have more opportunity to become acquainted with those areas of continuing concern involving the explanation and interpretation of Romans. In addition to this bibliography, the bibliographies included at the close of each of the Special Studies should also be consulted for further references to ongoing research on Romans.

INTRODUCTORY STUDIES

Influence of the Epistle

Godsey, John D., "The Interpretation of Romans in the History of the Christian Faith," *Interpretation* 34:1 (January 1980), p.3-16.

> Identifies several historical occasions when a theologian on whom Romans had a profound influence in turn dramatically and significantly influenced the history of the Christian faith. Examines and evaluates the views on Romans developed by Marcion, Augustine, Luther, Calvin, J. Wesley, and K. Barth.

Purpose and Occasion of Writing

Donfried, Karl P., ed., *The Romans Debate: Essays on the Origin and Purpose of the Epistle.* Minneapolis: Augsburg Publishing House, 1977.

> After an introduction in which Donfried presents a brief history of the interpretation of Romans, he outlines the present controversy by summarizing each of the nine previously-published articles included, and by means of incisive questions sketches the work still to be done. Donfried is a good introduction to the present beliefs about the purpose of Romans, now that historical-critical methods are being applied to the study. The articles included are by Catholic, Protestant, and Jewish scholars, and were written between 1938 and 1977.

Bruce, F.F., "The Romans Debate – Continued," *Bulletin of the John Rylands University Library* 64:2 (1982), p.334-359.

> While dictating his letter to Rome, Paul had three places in mind: Rome, the destination of the letter; Spain, where he wished to go shortly to evangelize that land; and Jerusalem, to which he was about to deliver a generous offering. Paul wished to involve the Roman saints in the impending visit to Jerusalem, and in the subsequent project in Spain. Each section of the letter is specially relevant to the situation in Rome in AD 57.

Drane, John W., "Why Did Paul Write Romans?" in *Pauline Studies: Essays Presented to Professor F.F. Bruce on his 70th Birthday*, edited by Donald A. Hagner and Murray J. Harris. Grand Rapids: Wm. B. Eerdmans Publishing Co., 1980.

After briefly weighing the arguments often advanced by proponents of both views, Drane concludes that Romans was written more to satisfy Paul than to deal directly with the situation in Rome. In part two of the paper, Drane summarizes what probably can be known (from other New Testament references, and from non-Biblical sources) about the Jewish community at Rome, and the nature of Roman Christianity at the time Paul writes. Drane's own hypothesis regarding the purpose of Romans is that it reflects events in Paul's own ministry, more in the recent past (e.g., rejection and persecution because of his message, and especially the troubles at Corinth) than in his dreams or hopes for the future. "As Paul reviewed his own position at this stage of his ministry, he must have asked himself what had gone wrong. Perhaps he even wondered if he had any kind of workable theology at all ... so the question became not just a matter of what he could say in Jerusalem to justify his anti-legalism ... but what he could say on a practical level ... to defend his own position ... [and] ... to preserve his own theological integrity. ... What we have in this, his *magnum opus*, is therefore a conscious effort to convince himself as well as his opponents that it is possible to articulate a theology which is at once anti-legalistic without also being intrinsically antinomian."

Haacker, Klaus, "Exegetische Probleme des Romerbriefs (Exegetical Problems of Romans)," *Novum Testamentum* 20:1 (1978), p.1-21.
> Alleges that the fact Romans was written on the eve of Paul's journey to Jerusalem with the offering for the saints sheds light on the composition and intention of the letter. He supposes Paul's letter is of a testamentary nature, or might even be called a "memorandum" (Romans 15:14-16) which summarizes Paul's teaching for the church. Judaizers are seen to be the opponents uppermost in Paul's mind. Considers several verses in chapters 1 to 6 to be interpolations.

Minear, Paul S., *The Obedience of Faith: The Purpose of Paul in the Epistle to the Romans.* Studies in Biblical Theology, Second Series, 19. London: SCM, 1971.
> According to Minear the purpose of Romans is Paul's effort to unite the "weak" and the "strong" communities in Rome. In his efforts at reconciliation in 14:1-12, Paul employs twelve axioms. It is the purpose of the rest of Romans to explain, support, and defend these twelve axioms, as Paul addresses in the various chapters of Romans one or more of the five separate communities that Minear believes he can identify.

Pedersen, Sigfred, "Theologische Uberlegungen Zur Isagogik Des Romerbriefes," *Zeitschrift fur die Neutestamentliche Wissenschaft* 76:1/2 (1985), p.47-67.
> Affirms that Romans 1:14 is the key to the letter itself and of Paul's view of his own apostolic commission. Alleges that Paul's commission to preach the gospel where it has not yet been heard (Romans 15:20,21) includes three main ethnic groups – to the Jew first, then to the Gentile, and then to the "barbarian" – and that Jerusalem, Rome, and Spain are geographical representations of these three groups.

Stulmacher, P., "Paul's Understanding of the Law in the Letter to the Romans," *Svensk Exegetisk Arsbok* 50 (1985), p.87-104.
> In response to objections from Jewish Christians at Rome against his gospel, Paul's purpose in writing was his wish to introduce a correct understanding of the Law and to make Christians into doers of the Law. Stulmacher asserts that Paul understood the Law of Moses as being: (1) the criterion by which men will be judged in the final judgment; and (2) a witness to the redemption and justification found in Christ. Although Paul honored the Scriptures and the Mosaic Law, he nevertheless evaluated them in light of the reality of Jesus Christ. Stulmacher also concludes that Paul considered the Decalogue to be the heart of the Law.

Wedderburn, A.J.M., "The Purpose and Occasion of Romans Again," *Expository Times* 90:5 (February 1979), p.137-141.
> Suggests that Paul's main purpose was to gain support for the collection for Jerusalem and for the coming mission to Gentiles in Spain. Causing problems for Paul was the extremely diverse audience

to which this letter is addressed. One group included Judaizing Gentiles and a few ethnic Jews who had been converted to Christianity and who still attended the synagogue and clung to its ways. A second group was comprised of Gentile Christians who had flung off whatever ties to Judaism they had before and had severed all connections with Judaism. The presence of these two groups is why Paul fails to call his readers a "church." Wedderburn is interacting with W. Schmithals' *Der Romerbrief als historisches Problem* (1975), in which it is posited that Paul wrote two letters (now combined in our "Romans") from Ephesus: one to group one urging law-free grace; the other to group two urging tolerance toward group one.

Textual Problems

Gamble, Harry, *The Textual History of the Letter to the Romans*. Studies and Documents 42. Grand Rapids: Wm. B. Eerdmans Publishing Co., 1977.
> The argument that Romans 16 is a later addition to Romans 1-15 on the basis of textual evidence alone has steadily weakened in recent years. Gamble persuasively defends the unity of Romans by showing that the textual evidence is inconclusive, and by bringing new evidence to the literary criticism of the letter from the developing field of ancient epistolography. This new evidence, which compares Paul's writings to other Hellenistic writings, tends to show from epistolary considerations that chapter 16 was originally part of the letter.

Kaye, B.N., "'To the Romans and Others' Revisited," *Novum Testamentum* 18:1 (1976), p.37-77.
> In 1948 T.W. Manson argued that Paul had sent from Corinth to Rome a letter comprising Romans 1-15, and to Ephesus a copy of his letter to Rome together with chapter 16. Kaye examines the hypothesis from internal probabilities and rejects Manson's theory.

Lampe, Peter, "Zur Textgeschichte Des Romerbriefes," *Novum Testamentum* 27:3 (1985), p.273-277.
> Textual critics have attempted to reconstruct the original text of Romans from the extant manuscript evidence. K. Aland's hypothesis was to arrange the 14 textual forms of Romans (combinations of 1-14, 15, 16:1-23, 16:24, and 16:26-27) into an original which included 1:1-16:23, of which no manuscript witness still exists. Textual critical rules have long suggested that the reading which is most likely original is the one from which all the known manuscript variations could be derived. Against Aland's hypothesis, Lampe instead urges that the original was 1:1-16:24; that it still survives in Codex D; and that all other variant forms of the text can be reconstructed from that original.

Lindemann, Andreas, "Die Gerechtigkeit aus dem Gesetz Erwagungen zur Aluslegung und zur Textgeschichte von Romer 10:5," *Zeitschrift fur die Newtestamentliche Wissenschaft* 73:3-4 (1982), p.231-250.
> Affirms that Romans 10:5, as a careful study of the textual options and history shows, must be read as Nestle[26] reads it, as over against previous editions. This in turn is thought to lead to an interpretation of the verse which has Paul never (neither in 10:5 nor in Romans 2:13) asserting that one may be righteous through Law.

Battle, John A., "Paul's Use of the Old Testament in Romans 9:25,26," *Grace Theological Journal* 2:1 (1981), p.115-129.
> Instead of connecting the Hosea 2:21 and 1:10 passages with the conversion of the Gentiles (Romans 9:24), the passages should be connected with 9:22, and be understood to refer to Israel's present-day separation from the Lord. In this way Paul is supposedly freed from the charge of interpreting Old Testament prophecies in a spiritualized way, since Hosea's words can be interpreted the same way in both original settings and in Paul's quotation.

Hermeneutics, Interpretation

Brinsmead, Robert N., "Justification by Faith Re-Examined," *The Christian Verdict*, Special Issue 1 (1983), p.1-22.
> Seventh-day Adventists claim to be the only true children of the Reformation when it comes to properly expounding the doctrine of justification by faith. One of their scholars who earlier chided the Adventists for having abandoned the classic Reformation position on justification by faith has himself come to question his own interpretation of that ancient doctrine. Brinsmead's thesis in this article is that the 16th century understanding of Paul left the Protestant movement with several serious weaknesses. (1) One of these he calls "the legacy of Christian nomism." He illustrates by calling attention to Lutheranism's Law/gospel dialectic. The Law must first be preached to bring a man to despair and so to prepare him for hearing the gospel. Melanchthon called this the second (or pedagogical) use of the Law. Then came a third use of the Law, wherein the Law became the Christian's rule of life after he had been justified by faith. In orthodox Protestantism, the "Law" came to refer to the Ten Commandments (i.e., the Mosaic Law minus its Jewish religious ceremonies). Scholars' use of the historical method has led them to question, "Where does the Protestant doctrine of the third use of the Law come from?" It is from the 16th century, not from Paul's 1st century writings. (2) Another weakness is in the legacy of Protestant individualism. The emphasis was on the individual and his relationship to God; the individual's personal assurance of salvation is of supreme importance. Brinsmead urges in his critique of individualism that such an idea is opposite of what Paul wrote in Romans, as he expounded the doctrine of justification and its concomitant requirement that all justified men embrace each other as brothers. Protestant individualism caused interpreters to fail to appreciate Paul's emphasis on community of believers, nor did it do justice to the social character of justification.

Campbell, W.S., "Romans III as a Key to the Structure and Thought of the Letter," *Novum Testamentum* 23:1 (January 1981), p.22-40.
> Campbell suggests that Romans 3:21-26 form the theological center of Paul's argument in Romans 1-11. Two themes are emphasized: God's own self-consistency, and His justification of those who have faith in Christ. Romans 3:1-8 poses real questions asked by his Roman readers, questions which are answered in chapters 6-7, and 9-12.

Greene, John T., "Paul's Hermeneutic Versus Its Competitors," *Journal of Religious Thought* 42:1 (1985), p.7-21.
> Greene attempts to demonstrate Paul did not teach that the validity of the Mosaic Law was ended now that Christ has come. Instead, Greene affirms, Paul interpreted Jewish law by Jewish hermeneutics in an attempt to arrive at a defensible Jewish position with respect to non-Jews. The solution of what to do with Gentile converts could be found in the Law by appealing to the example of Abraham.

Jewett, Robert, "Major Impulses in the Theological Interpretation of Romans Since Barth," *Interpretation* 34:1 (January 1980), p.17-31.
> A survey of research on Romans since World War II, with emphasis on the influence of K. Barth, R. Bultmann, and E. Kasemann, shows a slight shift toward orthodoxy, an emphasis on eschatology, and a concern for improvement in relations between Jews and Christians (including a review of the work of Wilkens, Davies, Schoeps, and Sanders).

Kourie, C., "The Historical Critical Method in Roman Catholic Biblical Scholarship," *Theologia Evangelica* 18:3 (1985), p.42-49.
> The history of Catholic scholarship since Vatican I (1870) is traced by making reference to Pope Leo XIII's *Providentissmus Deus* (1893), the Modernist crisis, Pope Pius XII's *Divino afflante Spiritu* (1943), Vatican II, and current trends in Catholic scholarship, and shows that acceptance of the Historical-critical method is now part of mainstream of Catholic methodology, though not without some opposition.

Paul and Judaism

Hagner, Donald A., "Paul in Modern Jewish Thought," in *Pauline Studies: Essays Presented to Professor F.F. Bruce on his 70th Birthday.* Grand Rapids: Wm. B. Eerdmans Publishing Co., 1980. p.143-165.
> An excellent introduction to and overview of the whole question of how contemporary Jewish writers attempt to explain Paul. (Is he the founder of a new religion? Did he depart from the teaching of Jesus? Did he depict the mainstream of Judaism in the 1st century, or do his writings reflect some heretical Jewish off-shoot to which he and all right-thinking Jews would be opposed?) Sets forth the possibility that some long-used Christian presentations of rabbinic Judaism are in error.

Dunn, James D.G., "The New Perspective on Paul," *Bulletin of the John Rylands University Library* 65/2 (Spring 1983), p.95-122.
> Dunn credits E.P. Sanders' *Paul and Palestinian Judaism* with breaking the mold in which Pauline studies had languished for decades. Sanders showed that the traditional picture of Judaism as allegedly drawn from Paul's writings was a false representation. The "legal (meritorious works) righteousness" often attributed to Judaism was actually a legacy of Reformation dogmatic theology, rather than a true reading of Paul. Dunn holds that Paul rejected "works of the Law" that involved characteristic national Jewish works such as circumcision and Sabbath. Instead, he sees Paul as making faith in Jesus as Messiah the only identifying mark of God's people. Dunn concludes that, for Paul, God's purposes and God's people have expanded beyond physical Israel. One serious weakness of Dunn's presentation is his suggestion that the seemingly contradictory verses in Paul are to be explained by the supposition that Paul's views on the topic actually change as he is writing. This suggestion by Dunn impinges on the doctrine of inspiration.

-----, "Works of the Law and the Curse of the Law (Galatians 3:10-14)," *New Testament Studies* 31:4 (1985), p.523-542.
> Argues (vs. E.P. Sanders and H. Raisanen) that Paul does not hold inconsistent and self-contradictory notions about the Law. Tries to show that "works of the Law" were "boundary markers" that Jews commonly used as outward evidence that a man was maintaining his Jewishness, as contrasted to giving up a claim to Jewishness because he had accepted too many Gentile practices and ideas.

Fischer, John, "Paul in His Jewish Context," *Evangelical Quarterly* 51/3 (July 1985), p.211-236.
> It is not necessary to appeal to Gnostic-Hellenistic materials in order to understand and explain Paul. He can be completely understood in the terms of the Judaism of his own time, though like many of his contemporary Jewish sectarians (i.e., Essenes or Sadducees), he differed in some respects from what developed into normative Judaism.

Campbell, W.S., "Christianity and Judaism: Continuity and Discontinuity," *International Bulletin for Missionary Research* 8/2 (April 1984), p.54-58.
> Relationships between Jews and Christians have often been strained at best, and seldom have been conducive to evangelistic work among the Jews. Campbell's attempts to explain away some of the New Testament passages (i.e., "new covenant," Paul's conversion-call, the use of the title "Israel" for Christians of any nationality, and Paul's treatment of national Israel in Romans 9-11) that Christians have appealed to in order to show that Judaism is no longer a valid religion, fail to carry conviction. Yet his call for Christians to carefully rethink their attitudes toward Israel, and to end all anti-Judaism based on racial prejudices, is certainly valid.

Jewett, Robert, "The Law and the Coexistence of Jews and Gentiles in Romans," *Interpretation* 39:4 (1985), p.341-356.
> Suggests that Paul's theme is the respectful coexistence of Jews and Gentiles as part of God's plan of

the unification of all peoples through the gospel. This is Jewett's contribution to the current scholarly discussion about the alleged role of Pauline theology in the rise of anti-Semitism. He examines the hypotheses set forth about Paul's attitude toward Israel as found in Stendahl, Lapide, Sanders, and others. He also enters the debate about the meaning of Romans 10:4, whether Christ is the "end" or "goal" of the Law, and opts for the latter.

Raisanen, H., *Paul and the Law*. Tubingen: Mohr-Siebeck, 1983.
> Raisanen has done the theological world a service by subjecting Paul's arguments about the Law to sustained scrutiny. Not all his conclusions are satisfactory, however. He affirms contradiction and logical inconsistencies are a regular feature of Paul's theology about the Law, and that one must study these indications of an ongoing conflict in Paul's mind if one would arrive at the proper historical and psychological explanation. He proposes to do this study under five headings: (1) The oscillating concept of Law. (2) Is the Law still in force? (3) Can the Law be fulfilled? (4) The origin and purpose of the Law. (5) The antithesis between works of Law and faith in Christ. He concludes that Paul wanted to think that the Law had been abolished in Christ's redemptive work, that Paul's description of Judaism was wrong, and that is a most unfortunate legacy to later generations of Christians, a legacy which has negatively influenced their dealings with Judaism.

Sanders, E.P., *Paul and Palestinian Judaism: A Comparison of Patterns of Religion*. Philadelphia: Fortress Press, 1977.
> After a study of Palestinian Judaism (as found in Tannaitic literature, the Dead Sea Scrolls, the Apocrypha and Pseudepigrapha), Sanders then tries to survey and outline Paul's "pattern of religion." One valuable point made early in the book is that Christian writers have not always represented normative Judaism in terms that a Jew familiar with the original sources would recognize. After studying such topics as the gospel, soteriology, the Law, covenantal nomism, judgment by works, and salvation by grace, Sanders concludes that Paul reflects and opposes a different type of religiousness than normative Judaism as found in Palestinian Jewish literature. Sanders studies but dismisses two other possible ways to take Paul's polemic statements against Judaism: (1) that they do not represent Paul's fundamental view, but should be discounted as the polemics of the moment (cp. W.D. Davies, *Paul and Rabbinic Judaism* [New York: Harper and Row, 1948]); (2) they are the point and represent the basic antithesis between Paul (i.e., Christianity) and normative Judaism.

-----, *Paul, the Law, and the Jewish People*. Philadelphia: Fortress Press, 1983.
> Sanders tries to prove (by appeal to Galatians 3:10, Philippians 3:6, Romans 3:23, 5:12, and 7:1ff, Galatians 5:3, and Romans 1:18-2:29) that Paul thought it was possible to obey the Law perfectly, but that in order to defend this thesis, Paul's thinking became so tortuous and contradictory that no coherent theology of the Law can be inferred. In treating Paul's attitude toward the Law, Sanders discusses (1) the Law as not an entrance requirement, (2) the purpose of the Law, (3) the obligation to fulfill the Law, and (4) the old dispensation and the new. Sanders' writings at times are likely flawed because of his attempt to make Paul's theology harmonize with Lutheran theological presuppositions.

Outline

Grumm, M.H., "The Gospel Call: Imperatives in Romans," *Expository Times* 93:8 (1982), p.239-242.
> Emphasis on Paul's use of imperative and indicative mood verbs challenges the theological adequacy and correctness of dividing Romans into doctrinal and practical sections.

Boers, H., "The Problem of Jews and Gentiles in the Macro-Structure of Romans," *Neotestamentica* 15 (1981), p.111.
> Boers' hypothesis is that an important clue to the macrostructure of Romans 3-11 can be found by

paying careful attention to Paul's use of rhetorical questions (3:2,3b,5c,9,27a,31; 4:1,9; 6:1,15; 7:7,13; 8:31; 9:14,19,30; 11:1,7,11,19). These highlight Paul's concern with the Jews and the Law, and the cutting edge of the whole letter is the argument that Israel, too, was saved by faith.

COMMENTARIES

Barclay, William, *The Letter to the Romans*, in the Daily Study Bible Series. Philadelphia: Westminster Press, 1958.
> Barclay is Neo-liberal in theology, and his comments reflect this bias frequently. His Greek word studies and his command of classical history are valuable, and his works may be used by students who recognize "liberal theology" when they see it. A more recent imprint is revised to reflect American terminology, whereas the original edition used English terms.

Barnes, Albert, *Notes on the New Testament*. Grand Rapids: Baker Book House, 1953. Reprinted many times.
> A verse-by-verse coverage of the text, with practical applications of the chapters given at the close of each. Barnes (1798-1870) was an American Presbyterian preacher. In the division between strict Calvinists and New School Presbyterians, he sided with the latter. He preached total abstinence from alcohol, the abolition of slavery, and an unlimited atonement. His notes tend to be faith-only, and he holds to unconditional election and to the Calvinistic doctrine of the perseverance of the saints. His doctrine of "imputation of righteousness" differs some from other Protestant theologians, and footnotes by the American editor point out such places of difference.

Barrett, Charles K., *A Commentary on the Epistle to the Romans*, in the Harper New Testament Commentary Series. New York: Harper and Brothers, 1957.
> Tends to be liberal. Expresses a Pelagian view of sin (he rejects the doctrine of inherited sin). Fails to handle the epistle as part of inspired Scripture. Has an inadequate view of the deity of Christ.

Barth, Karl, *Christ and Adam: Man and Humanity in Romans 5*. New York: Harper and Row, 1956.
> A serious objection is raised about this work for it makes universalism implicit in the atonement. It falls short of a thorough presentation of Paul's theology, especially justification by faith.

-----, *The Epistle to the Romans*. London: Oxford Press, 1933.
> This landmark book first appeared in German after World War I. In it, Barth showed the failure of religious liberalism, and used "Romans" as a platform from which to launch his "new orthodoxy." It is not a good exposition, but it has an historical interest when one studies the influence of Paul's epistle to the Romans.

Batey, Richard A., *The Letter of Paul to the Romans*, in Sweet's Living Word Commentary series. Austin, TX: Sweet Publishing Co., 1969.
> This is one of a series of commentaries based on the text of the Revised Standard Version, produced by Church of Christ writers.

Beet, Joseph A., *Commentary on St. Paul's Epistle to the Romans*. London: Hodder and Stoughton, 1902.
> This may be described as the leading Wesleyan or Arminian commentary. It is weak when handling the doctrine of the deity of Christ.

Bruce, F.F., *The Epistle of Paul to the Romans*, in the Tyndale New Testament Commentary

series.   Grand Rapids: Wm. B. Eerdmans Publishing Co., 1963.
> Draws upon a wide knowledge of literature, frequently cites theological writers, and provides an understandable exposition of the epistle.   At times his one-sentence explanation of certain phrases are the best summary of what can be found in much lengthier form in older commentaries.

Brunner, Emil (Heinrich E.), *The Letter to the Romans*.   Philadelphia: Westminster Press, 1959.   English translation of *Der Romerbrief*.
> A treatment of Romans by a Neo-orthodox scholar.   It minimizes the deity of Christ, but tends to reject the doctrine of original sin (inherited sinful nature).

Coffman, James B., *Commentary on Romans*.   Austin, TX: Firm Foundation Publishing House, 1973.
> A Church of Christ teacher who weaves together the comments by various commentators who have written some of the classical works on Romans.   A good source to get a quick awareness of some of the problem passages in Romans, as well as some of the suggested explanations.

Cranfield, C.E.B., *A Critical and Exegetical Commentary on the Epistle to the Romans*, 2 volumes, in the International Critical Commentary Series.   Edinburgh: T&T Clark, 1975-1979.
> These volumes are intended to replace the old ICC commentary on Romans written by Sanday and Headlam, which has long been recognized as one of the outstanding books on Romans.   Cranfield does well handling grammar and syntax, thus making the book a helpful tool for the Greek student. Bibliographical references to contemporary studies are helpful for those wishing to do more thorough research into the various themes and issues raised in Romans.   Essay I at the close of volume 2 is entitled "Paul's Purpose or Purposes in Writing Romans."   While interacting with both Minear and Kasemann, Cranfield insists on the unity of 1:16-15:13, on the integrity of Romans 16, and then urges that the purposes for writing Romans can be found both in the needs of the church at Rome and in Paul's own special interests as apostle to the Gentiles.

-----, *Romans.   A Shorter Commentary*.   Grand Rapids: Wm. B. Eerdmans Publishing House, 1985.   Edinburgh: T&T Clark, 1985.
> Cranfield abridged and adapted for a general audience his two-volume *Critical and Exegetical Commentary*.

Crouch, Owen W., *Not Guilty!*   2 Volumes.   Johnson City, TN: Published by the author, 1986.
> Volume 1 includes a translation, outlines, and exposition of the letter.   Volume 2 contains diagrams of each sentence in Romans, both in English and in Greek.

Denney, James, *St. Paul's Epistle to the Romans*, in The Expositor's Greek Testament. Grand Rapids: Wm. B. Eerdmans Publishing Co., 1967.   Volume 2.
> The Expositor's Greek Testament at times is theologically liberal, though this volume by Denney will give insights into the thread of Paul's argument.   Based on the Greek text, it will help the student who has learned Greek to refresh and renew his acquaintance with the language.

DeWelt, Don, *Romans Realized*, in the Bible Study Textbook series.   Joplin, MO: College Press, 1959.
> This workbook and teaching manual include a paraphrase of the epistle by James MacKnight, summaries of each paragraph by Moses Lard, and questions to guide the student's thinking.

Dodd, C.H., *The Epistle of Paul to the Romans*, in the Moffatt New Testament Commentary series. New York: Harper and Brothers, 1932.

> Dodd tends to espouse Neo-liberal theology, not hesitating to take issue with Paul when he feels Paul's logic is faulty. Not recommended. It was reissued with revisions in London: Wm. Collins & Son, Ltd., 1959.

Ellison, Henry L., *The Mystery of Israel – An Exposition of Romans 9-11*. Grand Rapids: Wm. B. Eerdmans Publishing Co., 1966.

> Amillennial handling of the subject of Israel, as well as insights from a scholar versed in the Hebrew and Rabbinic sources.

Gifford, E.H., "The Epistle of Paul to the Romans," in the *Bible Commentary*, edited by F.C. Cook. New York: Charles Scribner's Sons, 1886. Reprinted Grand Rapids: Wm. B. Eerdmans Publishing Co., 1978.

> This whole set is excellent, and should be in every serious Bible student's library. The commentary on Romans is a very thorough, amillennial exposition based on the Greek text. Anglican. Sanday believes this is the best of all the commentaries in English.

Godet, Frederic L., *Commentary on St. Paul's Epistle to the Romans*. Edinburgh: T&T Clark, 1881. Reprinted Grand Rapids: Zondervan Publishing House, nd.

> A French theologian with German training. A good treatment of the argument of the epistle. He gives a full discussion of divergent interpretations, refutes theological liberals who differ with him on important points, and is strong in exegesis but weak in textual criticism.

Hamilton, Floyd E., *The Epistle to the Romans*. Grand Rapids: Baker Book House, 1958.

> A strongly conservative exposition with a strong advocacy of the views of reformed theology.

Harrison, Everett F., "Romans," in *Expositor's Bible Commentary*, edited by Frank E. Gaebelein. Grand Rapids: Zondervan Publishing House, 1976. Volume 10.

> The volume that includes "Romans" was the first of a new and comprehensive commentary on the books of the Old and New Testaments, written from an evangelical viewpoint, "committed to the divine inspiration, complete trustworthiness, and full authority of the Bible." The chief principle of interpretation followed is the grammatical-historical one, namely, that the exegete's primary aim is to make clear the meaning of the text at the time and in the circumstance of its writing. There are introductory studies, followed by comments on the NIV text.

Hendriksen, William, *Exposition of Paul's Epistle to the Romans*. 2 Volumes. (New Testament Commentary series.) Grand Rapids: Baker Book House, 1980.

> A masterful commentary which will take its place among the leading Calvinistic expositions of this Pauline epistle. This is flawed, in this commentator's opinion, since included in these volumes is the strongest defense of Calvinistic dogma found anywhere in Hendriksen's writings. For example, chapters 9 to 11 are explained as being the result of God's unconditional election of some for salvation in eternity before creation. Also reflects one-covenant (a covenant of grace) theology.

Hodge, Charles, *Commentary on the Epistle to the Romans*. Grand Rapids: Wm. B. Eerdmans Publishing Co., 1950. Originally published in 1835, and rewritten in 1864.

> A weighty and learned doctrinal exposition, strongly Calvinistic, based on the principles of the Westminster Confession of Faith.

Kasemann, Ernst, *Commentary on Romans*. Grand Rapids: Wm. B. Eerdmans Publishing Co., 1980.

Clearly outlined and well documented.   Reflects Neo-liberal theological viewpoint and an individualism which necessitates reading with discernment.   Doubts the integrity of chapter 16; sees a number of "paradoxes" in Romans; Romans 7 is the position of a man under the Law (a view almost universal in Germany since Kummel's work).   Before attempting to read this book, the student needs some background in Bultmannian and post-Bultmannian language and theology in order to understand what he reads.   The Tubingen School recently has been searching in apocalyptic materials for the sources of Paul's ideas, and the resulting 'commentary' has left Kasemann open to the charge of letting Paul say only what the exegete wishes to hear.   (See this apocalyptic emphasis of Tubingen explained in T.N. Wright, "A New Tubingen School?   Ernst Kasemann and his Commentary on Romans," *Themelios* 7:3 (1982), p.6-16.)

Lard, Moses E., *Commentary on Paul's Letter to Romans*.   St. Louis: Christian Board of Publication, 1914.   Reprinted numerous times.
Before his 17th birthday, because he had little schooling, Lard was unable to write his own name. But he taught himself to read and write.   He went on to college after he was married and had his own family, and became a powerful preacher and writer for the Restoration Movement.   Born into a Baptist family, and indoctrinated in Calvinism, he strongly refutes the Calvinistic interpretation of various key passages in the letter.   (However, Lard's comments on chapters 9-11, in particular, at times are confusing, especially in those places where he tends to hold on too much to the old Calvinism he had learned.)   While at times he tends to be wordy, still many think this is the best commentary written by a member of the Christian church on the book of Romans.   A knowledge of Greek is helpful to one who would understand Lard.

Lenski, R.C.H., *The Interpretation of St. Paul's Epistle to the Romans*.   Minneapolis: Augsburg Publishing House, 1936.   Reprinted many times.
A conservative Lutheran exposition based on the Greek text.   Amillennial in its handling of Israel. His rigid handling of the Greek at times tends to mar his treatment of what Paul is saying.

Luther, Martin, *Lectures on Romans*.   Translated by Wilhelm Pauck.   Philadelphia: Westminster Press, 1961.
Luther's lectures to his students, delivered in 1515-1516, shows the process through which he went as he grappled with the problems of the Roman Catholic doctrine of justification by works versus his own insight into the doctrine of justification by faith.

Mills, Sanford C., *A Hebrew Christian Looks at Romans*.   Grand Rapids: Dunham Publishing Co., 1968.
Mill's thesis is that the questions which would naturally be asked of a gospel preacher by a Jew living at Rome during the 1st century regarding the gospel are exactly the same questions which a concerned religious Jew asks in the 20th century.   Doctrines emphasized include the sinful condition of the world, the doctrine of justification, and sanctification (intertwined with an emphasis on dedication), believer's baptism, the two-fold nature of the Christian (chapter 7?), the indwelling of the Holy Spirit, the sovereignty of God, and the vital relation of chapters 9-11 to the whole (from a pretribulation, premillennial viewpoint.)

Murray, John, *The Epistle to the Romans* in the New International Commentary on the New Testament.   2 Volumes.   Grand Rapids: Wm. B. Eerdmans Publishing Co., 1959-1965.
Strongly Reformed in doctrine, and advocates a postmillennial interpretation of chapters 9-11.

Nygren, Anders, *Commentary on Romans*.   Philadelphia: Muhlenberg Press, 1949.
A Neo-liberal theologian's commentary from the Lutheran perspective.   Sees the purpose of Romans as being a "compendium of the Christian religion."

Paisley, Ian R.K., *An Exposition of the Epistle to the Romans*. London: Marshall, Morgan & Scott, 1968.

> Written while this militant Irish preacher was imprisoned for political agitation, it is strong in Calvinistic theology, especially the sovereignty of God. (Paisley saw himself in prison because God willed it.) He settles the differences between foreknowledge and predestination by stating that God's foreknowledge rests on his foreordination; i.e., God knows what will happen because he foreordained it to happen.

Sanday, William, *The Epistle to the Romans* in the Layman's Handy Commentary Series, edited by Charles J. Ellicott. Grand Rapids: Zondervan Publishing House, 1957. Reprint of a portion of the 1903 edition of Ellicott's *Commentary on the Whole Bible*.

> Most students familiar with the Greek will appreciate the comments based on the nuances of the Greek language. Ellicott's Commentary is always a good place to look for explanatory comments on the Bible books.

Sanday, W., and Headlam, A.C., *A Critical and Exegetical Commentary on the Epistle to the Romans* in the International Critical Commentary series. Edinburgh: T&T Clark, 1895.

> A thorough commentary based on the Greek text, indispensable to the serious student of Romans. Arminian in doctrine. Helpful to understand the continuing thread of Paul's ideas.

Vine, W.E., *The Epistle to the Romans*. Grand Rapids: Zondervan Publishing House, 1965.

> Puts many of the nuances of the Greek text into understandable English, thus opening up the thread of Paul's argument.

INDIVIDUAL PASSAGES

Several issues of certain theological journals have been dedicated to a study of Romans, and so it is not unusual to find the latest historical-critical thinking about the epistle reflected in many of the individual articles in these studies. Among such journals are the following:

Expository Times, Volume 92:7 (April 1981), Volume 93:8 (May 1982), Volume 93:9 (June 1982), Volume 93:12 (December 1982).

Neotestamentica, Volume 15, 1981.

Review and Expositor, Volume 73:4 (Fall 1976).

The following articles are arranged by chapter and verse, rather than alphabetically by author. The listing of the scholarly articles that have recently appeared is not exhaustive, but is representative of the types of subject matter in Romans that are still being carefully scrutinized.

Chapter One

Moody, R.M., "The Habakkuk Quotation in Romans 1:17," *Expository Times* 92:7 (April 1981), p.205-208.

> Examines the possible translations, "those who are justified by faith shall live" and "the just shall live

by faith," and determines that the second is the correct option. Concludes that the original passage from Habakkuk and the context of Romans as a whole require the second option.

Williams, S.K., "The 'Righteousness of God' in Romans," *Journal of Biblical Literature* 99:2 (1980), p.241-290.
>Paul's thesis underlying the whole epistle is that the gospel he preached was in harmony with the divine plan and nature (the righteousness of God). The promise made to Abraham about being the "father of us all" (Romans 4:16), so forcefully restated by Habakkuk (Romans 1:17), is being fulfilled in the inclusion of the nations/Gentiles on the basis of faith (chapters 3, 9-11), and will be finally realized in the inclusion of "all Israel" (11:25-32) and the redemption of the cosmos (chapter 8).

Brinsmead, Robert D., "Notes on Justification in the Book of Romans," *Verdict* 9 (1983), p.1-6.
>Affirms that the word "justification" is related theologically and linguistically to the word "justice," and therefore we cannot understand Romans unless we interpret it in the light of what the Old Testament says about the justice of God. Laments the fact that most modern commentaries are dominated by the studies on justification that resulted from the 16th century debate between Catholics and Protestants, and calls for going back to 1st century issues in order to interpret "justification" in the sense originally intended and understood by the readers of this letter. God's justice for Jew and Gentile through the gospel has profound ethical ramifications requiring Christians to actively be involved in "justice" to the oppressed.

Clifford, Alan C., "The Gospel and Justification," *Evangelical Quarterly* 52/3 (July 1985), p.247-267.
>Examines the relationship between justification by faith and the message of the gospel ("the doctrine of justification by faith presupposes a message to be proclaimed, a gospel to be believed"), including the extent of the atonement, the role of works, and other soteriological details. (1) What is the gospel? In Calvin's view, Christ died for *all*: therefore, the gospel is to be preached to all. It was Theodore Beza, not Calvin himself, who taught a limited atonement. Reformation Anglicanism preserved Calvin's universal atonement; election is the result of believing, not vice-versa. (2) What is justification? The theological controversy about the nature of justification at the time of the Reformation still has residual effects on present-day discussion. "Justification" is a forensic term: based on substitutionary atonement, God is free to offer pardon and acquittal to the guilty. "The Greek *dikaiōsis* ('declaring righteous') is not therefore to be equated with the Latin *justificatio* ('making righteous')." Contrary to most Protestant presentations, Clifford proposes that justification is identical with forgiveness or pardon (and it is based on Christ's passive obedience [his death], not His active obedience [his obedience to the Law]); it is a life-long continuum (not a single occasion) which will be terminated at the proceedings on the day of final judgment; and the "faith" on which it is conditioned *must* involve obedience (albeit, obedience to the gospel, not to the Law). (3) What is faith? Clifford says, assent to the truth of the gospel, trust in the merits of Christ alone, and obedience to Christ as Lord. Each of the three parts (assent, trust, obedience) of faith correspond to Christ's offices of prophet, priest, and king. In order to be justified, the *whole* man (mind, heart, and will) must embrace the whole *Christ* (prophet, priest and king) with a *whole* faith (assent to his prophetic teaching, trust in His priestly mediation, and obedience to his kingly authority).

Watson, Nigel M., "Justification – A New Look," *Australian Bible Review* 18:1 (October 1970), p.31-44.
>Kasemann has seen righteousness as a power which seeks to master the men's hearts, take them into His service, and thereby establish God's dominion over the world. Watson suggests that Kasemann's view, which seems to confound justification and sanctification, while not wholly acceptable, has pointed Bible students to the truth that "justification" is more dynamic than the "forensic view" which has God doing no more than pinning a label onto a sinner. Watson insists that any explanation of the New Testament word (*dikaiosunē*) should include the dynamic connotations found in the corresponding Old Testament word (*tsaddik*).

Turner, D.L., "Cornelius van Til and Romans 1:18-21: A Study in the Epistemology of Presuppositional Apologetics," *Grace Theological Journal* 2:1 (1981), p.45-58.

> Reformed theology, with its view of the havoc wrought on man's mind and nature by the Fall of Adam, downplays any attempt at using theistic arguments to demonstrate the probable existence of God. Van Til, attempting to harmonize Romans 1:18-21 with Reformed theology, urged that the metaphysical common ground between believers and unbelievers lies in their bearing of God's image; human beings are accessible to the gospel because they bear God's image and live in God's universe.

Chapter Two

Watson, Nigel M., "Justified by Faith: Judged by Works – An Antinomy?" *New Testament Studies* 29:2 (April 1983), p.209-211.

> Not a few Bible students are of the opinion that "faith" and "works" are so opposite in meaning that what Paul writes on the two topics cannot be harmonized. So, for example, Watson suggests that Paul's word on justification is addressed to one audience (i.e., those who like the Galatians were overscrupulous, fearfully and meticulously keeping the Law hoping thereby to earn salvation), while his word about judgment was addressed to a different audience (i.e., those who like the Corinthians thought they were free to do whatever they wished).

Snodgrass, Kline R., "Justification by Grace – to the Doers: An Analysis of the Place of Romans 2 in the Theology of Paul," *News Testament Studies* 32:1 (1986), p.72-93.

> Many proposed ways of explaining Romans have ignored what is written in chapter 2 about the standards by which God will judge men in the final judgment. Snodgrass affirms that we will not understand Paul's doctrine of "justification by faith" unless we give serious attention to his presentation of judgment according to works. Rather than being contradictory statements, the two expressions are complementary. Taking Romans 2 seriously helps the commentator to make comments that are in harmony with what the Bible everywhere teaches – namely, "judgment according to works." "Any attempt to do justice to Romans 2 will have to show how this chapter fits with the purpose of the epistle, how it is related to current Jewish thought (and indeed the rest of the New Testament), how the thought of Romans 2-3 develops, and how this thought fits with what Paul says elsewhere, particularly in Romans."

Chapter Three

Hall, David R., "Romans 3:1-8 Reconsidered," *New Testament Studies* 29:2 (April 1983), p.183-197.

> The theory that Romans 3:1-8 is a series of objections which Paul answers one by one has many drawbacks. Romans 3:1-8 should be understood instead as Paul's own presentation of the implications of Psalm 51:4, and intended to answer the problem created by chapter 2. By an exposition of Psalm 51 Paul is showing that it is not his position about the salvation of the Gentiles by grace that leads to antinomianism, but the position of those Jews who deny that God's judgment could come upon His covenant people that has that consequence.

Stowers, Stanley K., "Paul's Dialogue with a Fellow Jew in Romans 3:1-9," *Catholic Biblical Quarterly* 46:4 (1984), p.707-722.

> Affirms that the prevailing explanations of 3:1-9 are unsatisfactory. Stevens offers the hypothesis that Paul employs the model of a dialogue from the Jewish diatribe form, in which two Jews are having a discussion about the fate of Israel now that Messiah has come in such an unexpected form. Paul's Gentile readers are allowed to overhear what is said.

Hays, Richard B., "Psalm 143 and the Logic of Romans 3," *Journal of Biblical Literature* 90:1 (March 1980), p.107-115.
> The major structural or paragraph break which commentators usually posit between Romans 3:20 and 3:21 has nothing to justify it in the text. In fact, Paul's continuing use of terminology from Psalm 143 (*dikaiosunē*) shows such a break is unwarranted. Romans 3:21 (Hays suggests) continues the theme introduced in 3:5, namely God's integrity, God's justice.

Canales, Isaac J., "Paul's Accusers in Romans 3:8 and 6:1," *Evangelical Quarterly* 57:3 (1985), p.237-245.
> Infers from the context of both passages (the Old Testament terminology in Romans 3:8-31, and the absence of Old Testament terms in 6:1-11) that Paul, while defending his doctrine of grace, contradicts a Jewish accusation in 3:8 and a Gentile antinomian misinterpretation in 6:1. This approach opposes W.S. Campbell's view that both passages are intended to reply to Gentile antinomian objections.

Roberts, J.H., "Righteousness in Romans with Special Reference to Romans 3:19-31," *Neotestimentica* 15 (1981), p.12-33.
> Roberts finds four different meanings for the word "righteousness" in the book of Romans.

Donfried, Karl P., "Romans 3:21-28," *Interpretation* 34:1 (January 1980), p.59-64.
> The word "righteousness" sometimes refers to God's acquittal of the believer, and sometimes refers to one of God's own attributes. Donfried calls for a careful exegetical study of this passage before one would preach from it. Donfried holds that Paul wrote to settle a specific problem within the church at Rome (the relationship of Jewish and Gentile Christians to each other), and then offers the results of his own study of the key words and phrases in the passage. Concludes that the "righteousness of God" is God's activity, and that "justify" refers to His acquittal of the believer.

Hultgren, Arland J., "The *pistis christou* Formulation in Paul," *Novum Testamentum* 22:3 (July 1980), p.248-263.
> On seven occasions in Romans, Galatians, and Philippians, Paul used the word "faith" followed by the genitive case. This construction could be a subjective genitive (i.e., faith that Jesus Himself had), or an objective genitive (i.e., our faith in Jesus, Jesus being the object of our faith). Hultgren concludes that every time Paul used this construction it is to be taken as an objective genitive.

Johnson, L.T., "Romans 3:21-26 and the Faith of Jesus," *Catholic Biblical Quarterly* 44:1 (1982), p.77-90.
> Affirms that the three occasions in chapter 3 when "faith of Jesus" occurs it should be understood as a subjective genitive. Jesus' own faith, understood as obedience, was soteriologically significant and provided the model for the obedient faith of others.

Meyer, B.F., "The Pre-Pauline Formula in Rom. 3:25-26a," *New Testament Studies* 29:2 (1983), p.198-208.
> The suggestion that some uninspired materials form the heart and source of certain of Paul's key doctrinal statements certainly causes readers of Paul to doubt the verity and abiding value of what Paul has written. Argues that Paul has adapted a hymnic fragment whose original life-setting was a baptismal liturgy used in Hellenistic churches, to which he has inserted a couple of his own original additions.

Raisanen, Heikki, "Das 'Gesetz des Glaubens' (Romans 3:27) und das 'Gesetz des Geistes' (Romans 8:2) (The 'Law of Faith' [Romans 3:27] and the 'Law of the Spirit' [Romans 8:2]")," *New Testament Studies* 26:1 (1979), p.101-117.

Raises the question as to how Paul uses the word "law" – literally or figuratively – in these two passages. Examines some of the newer interpretations, and concludes that the traditional one (*nomos* is used in a figurative sense, with a meaning close to "order") is correct.

Hannah, John D., "The Meaning of Saving Faith: Luther's Interpretation of Romans 3:28," *Bibliotheca Sacra* 140:560 (October-December, 1983), p.322-334.

Luther's theses indicate that he believed that the faith which is the condition on which God justifies a man is not merely intellectual, but personal. He insisted that an accurate, biblically warranted definition of faith is imperative if the heart is ever to be cleansed by the Redeemer.

Beasley-Murray, George R., "Faith in the New Testament: A Baptist Perspective," *American Baptist Quarterly* 1:2 (1982), p.137-143.

This issue of ABQ contains part of a symposium on Lutheran-Baptist dialogue. Beasley-Murray urged that while "faith" in the New Testament has several emphases, Paul's use of faith includes believing the truth of the gospel, obeying it, and believing in God. Faith, he insists, reaches its climax in baptism. Baptism marks the passage of the one who confesses Christ from alienation from Christ to existence in Christ.

Chapter Four

Hays, Richard B., "Have We Found Abraham to be our Forefather According to the Flesh?" *Novum Testamentum* 27:1 (1985), p.76-98.

Examination of linguistic evidence and alternative translations leads the author to opt for "What shall we say then? Have we found Abraham (to be) our forefather according to the flesh?" as the most probable translation. He urges that the verse thus yields an intelligible inference from the foregoing discussion (3:27-31), and offers an appropriate introduction to the discussion of Abraham as the father of the faithful (4:2-15), whether they are of Jewish or Gentile backgrounds.

Robertson, O. Palmer, "Genesis 15:6: New Covenant Expositions of an Old Covenant Text," *Westminster Theological Journal* 42:2 (Spring 1980), p.259-289.

Examines Paul's and James' use of this passage in the New Testament Scriptures in an effort to understand how New Testament writers interpreted Old Testament passages, and how the Old Testament affected their theological orientation.

Chapter Five

Fryer, N.S.L., "Reconciliation in Paul's Epistle to the Romans," *Neotestimentica* 15 (1981), p.34-68.

After a brief introduction to the controversy surrounding the Pauline terms pertaining to Christ's atoning work, four distinct facets in the process of restoration of a lost relationship of friendship with God are distinguished.

Wedderburn, A.J.M., "The Theological Structure of Romans 5:12," *New Testament Studies* 19:3 (1973), p.339-354.

Alleges that the source of 5:12 is not Gnostic, but that 5:12a-c is based on a 1st century Jewish apocalyptic tradition which blamed Adam for bringing death on his descendants, while holding that these descendants merited that fate. 5:12d then refers to the individual, who himself is responsible for actively sinning in the manner of all men. Wedderburn holds there is found in Paul's writing a tension or balance between the social and cosmic and the individual.

Caragounis, C.C., "Romans 5:15-16 in the Context of 5:12-21:   Contrast or Comparison?" *New Testament Studies* 31:1 (1985), p.142-148.
> Because of a puzzling and unusual grammatical structure at Romans 5:15a and 5:16a, the versions and commentaries have understood these verses to state a contrast between the effect of Adam's sin and Christ's obedience, though not without some confusion.   Caragounis suggests that both phrases be understood as questions expecting affirmative answers.   ("Does not the free gift operate just like the trespass did?"   "And is not the free gift transmitted in the same way as sin was transmitted by the one who sinned?")   Thus, the essential similarity between Adam and Christ is retained, the argument flows naturally, and the confusion disappears.

Zeisler, John A., "Anthropology of Hope (Romans 5:12-21)," *Expository Times* 90:4 (January 1979), p.104-108.
> The Augustinian doctrine of the Fall of Adam, inherited sinful nature, and eventual restoration, is shown to be but one of several theories held in the early church.   Zeisler questions whether or not the natural world was affected as a result of Adam's sin.   Suggests that while Jewish thinking looked forward to a simple "restoration," the word Paul used means "made new" and Paul looks forward to man becoming what he was originally meant to be, not just a restoration to what he was.

Chapter Six

Moo, J. Douglas, "Romans 6:1-14," *Trinity Journal* 3:2 (Fall 1982), p.215-220.
> There is a fundamental inconsistency in the life of a person who has "died to sin" should he fail to carry out in actual living the implications of the new status in Christ.

Price, James L., "Romans 6:1-14," *Interpretation* 34:1 (January 1980), p.65-69.
> Another attempt to explain Paul as interacting with Jewish apocalyptic ideas.   Rather than suggesting that 6:1 is a standard Jewish objection to Paul's message, which Paul then answers, Price supposes some reader has a serious misunderstanding of the gospel because of his reading of apocalyptic/rabbinic ideas of the two ages and the contrasting states of human existence in each, and this is what Paul attempts to correct.   Also, Price explores Paul's presentation of sin as an alien, enslaving power, and the meaning of the "transfer terminology" as Paul explains about believers having died with Christ to the power of sin.

Chapter Seven

Raisanen, Heikki, "Zum Gerbrauch von *epithumia* und *epithumein* bei Paulus (Concerning Paul's usage of *epithumia* and *epithumein*)," *Studia Theologica* 33:2 (1979), p.85-99.
> Bultmann's suggestion that *epithumia* in Romans 7:7,8 is a reference to "overzealousness for the Law" (rather than the traditional interpretation, namely, "desires" that would lead to lawless behavior) cannot be sustained by the context.   Raisanen suggests that the real source of Bultmann's suggestion is not exegesis but Lutheran-existentialist dogma.

Mile, D.J.W., "Paul's Pre-Conversion Experience," *Reformed Theological Review* 43:1 (1984), p. 9-17.
> Sees Romans 7:7-12 as foundational for understanding Romans 7, as well as Paul's theology, Paul's soteriology, and for present-day evangelistic and pastoral practice as well.   The sometimes-defended attempt to understand this passage as referring to Paul's Christian experience, or as an impersonal portrait of people under the Law, are both incorrect.   Only understanding this passage as referring to Paul's pre-Christian experience (and which is typical of all men's pre-conversion experience) adequately deals with the text.

Moo, J. Douglas, "Israel and Paul in Romans 7:7-12," *New Testament Studies* 32:1 (1986), p.122-135.
> Alleges that the main theme in Romans 7:7-12 is Israel's experience with the Law of Moses, though the use of the first-person style implies some degree of autobiographical reference also.

Nickle, Keith F., "Romans 7:7-25," *Interpretation* 33:2 (April 1979), p.181-187.
> Considers that Romans 7 describes the inner conflict between what we want to be and what we are. A man's religious heritage sets the standards of what he wants to be. Paul's religious heritage was the Mosaic Law; our religious heritage (Judeo-Christian, or whatever) is our contemporary equivalent, and reliance on it rather than upon God is the essence of sin in our lives.

Dockery, D.S., "Romans 7:14-25: Pauline Tension in the Christian Life," *Grace Theological Journal* 2:2 (1981), p.239-257.
> Defends the view that Romans 7:14-25 pictures the continuing tension between life in the Spirit and in the flesh, even after one has become a Christian.

Gundry, Robert H., "The Moral Frustration of Paul Before His Conversion: Sexual Lust in Romans 7:7-25," in *Pauline Studies: Essays Presented to Professor F.F. Bruce on his 70th Birthday*, edited by Donald A. Hagner and Murray J. Harris (Grand Rapids: Wm. B. Eerdmans Publishing Co., 1980), p.228-245.
> Gundry notes that his view, that Paul describes his own experience before converting to Christianity, has few advocates nowadays. What might be added is that even fewer try to limit Paul's use of "desire" in Romans 7:7 to sexual lust (viz., adolescent life when sexual passions begin to assert themselves), for such a view certainly ignores much of the context. The article succinctly explains the likely meaning of the relevant passages in Paul's writings which tend to describe the life and thoughts of the Jew under the Law. [GLR: Alongside Gundry, the student might wish to compare chapters on "Saul and the Law," "Legality and Law," and "The end of Nomism" in Richard N. Longnecker, *Paul, Apostle of Liberty* (Grand Rapids: Baker Book House, 1964).]

Newman, B.M., "Once Again – The Question of 'I' in Romans 7:7-25," *Bible Translator* 34:1 (1983), p.124-135.
> Newman suggests that Paul's primary goal in this section is to define the role of the Law in the history of salvation. The "I" references in the passage are best understood as describing how any man (whether Paul himself in the first instance, or others – whether Christians or non-Christians) were wrenched apart under the rule of the Law.

Martin, B.L., "Some Reflections on the Identity of *ego* in Rom. 7:14-24," *Scottish Journal of Theology* 34:1 (1981), p.39-47.
> Rejects the view that Romans 7:14-25 in some way refers to the Christian. Instead, the arguments for the view that the "I" in the passage refers to the "pre-Christian" are convincing. Proposes the suggestion that Paul was thinking of his own history in Adam in 7:7-13, and of his own past while under Moses in 7:14-25.

Chapter Eight

Comfort, Philip W., "Light from the New Testament Papyri Concerning the Translation of *pneuma*," *Bible Translator* 35:1 (1984), p.130-133.
> Translators and interpreters have been perplexed about how to render the word *pneuma* ("Spirit" or "spirit"?) in many verses in the New Testament, including Romans 8:1-9. Many New Testament papyrus manuscripts use the abbreviation *pna* to denote the Holy Spirit and the full word *pneuma* to

designate the human spirit or another spirit. The perceptions of the early scribes regarding the meaning of *pneuma* may be helpful to present-day translators or interpreters.

Meyer, Paul W., "The Holy Spirit in the Pauline Letters: A Contextual Exploration," *Interpretation* 33:1 (January 1979), p.3-18.
> Examines the context and content of several references to the Holy Spirit in "Paul's undisputed letters" (Romans, 1 and 2 Corinthians). Alleges that the problem of understanding the Holy Spirit in the New Testament involves exploring how New Testament writers use the "language of the world" when relating to God, His transcendence, His presence, and His power in men's experience. Concludes that it is not Paul's terminology describing the Holy Spirit that is so distinctively Christian, but his way of relating the Spirit to Jesus Christ.

Branick, V.P., "The Sinful Flesh of the Son of God (Romans 8:3): A Key Image of Pauline Theology," *Catholic Biblical Quarterly* 47:2 (1985), p.246-262.
> Affirms that Paul believed the earthly Jesus inherited a sinful body (flesh) that was no different in this respect than any other human body; the description of Christ in 2 Corinthians 5:21 as "not knowing sin" refers to Christ's pre-existence, not his earthly career.

Mitchell, Curtis C., "The Holy Spirit's Intercessory Ministry," *Bibliotheca Sacra* 139:555 (July-September 1982), p.230-242.
> Christians are inadequate when it comes to knowing what to pray. The promise that the indwelling Spirit helps believers in their prayers (Romans 8:26,27) is explored under three headings: the need for the Spirit's intercession, the nature of the Spirit's intercession, and the efficacy of the Spirit's intercession.

Rickards, Raymond R., "The Translation of *te astheneia hemon* ('in our weakness') in Romans 8:26," *The Bible Translator* 28:2 (April 1977), p.247, 248.
> Urges that the Arndt-Gingrich Lexicon is correct when it lists "weakness" in Romans 8:26 as an example of "lack of spiritual insight," and offers "our present limitations" or "our limited spiritual understanding" as viable translations. Thus, "The Spirit also helps us in our limited spiritual understanding ... by praying for us in those agonizing longings which cannot be put into words."

Vallauri, E., "I gemiti dello Spirito Santo (Romans 8:26)," *Revista Biblica* 27:12 (1979), p. 95-113.
> Urges that the several difficulties that face E. Kasemann's interpretation of "inexpressible groans" as describing speaking in tongues, make such an understanding extremely doubtful.

Osburn, Carroll D., "The Interpretation of Romans 8:28," *Westminster Theological Journal* 44:1 (Spring 1982), p.99-109.
> Suggests three possible subjects for the verb "works together" – all things, God, and the Spirit. While the insertion of "God" in certain manuscripts has no clear claim to authenticity, the writer believes that "God" is the implied subject, being found in the previous phrase. Osburn gives his imprimatur to C.H. Dodd's suggested translation, "God works in all things for good."

Pack, Frank, "A Study of Romans 8:28," *Restoration Quarterly* 22:1-2 (1979), p.44-53.
> Interacts with Cranfield who has listed 8 and possibly 9 options for *panta sunergei*. The arguments of Matthew Black and C.K. Barrett are brought to bear upon the passage. Concludes that Paul is expressing the view that God's active working in all things, even the calamities and persecutions Christians may suffer, is for the good of His people.

Chapter Nine

Burchard, Christoph, "Romer 9:25 *en to Hosee*," *Zeitschrift Newtestamentliche Wissenschaft* 76:1-2 (1985), p.131.
> Urges that just as "*en Elia*" in Romans 11:2 means in the Elijah-portion (of the Book of Kings), "*en to Hosee*" in Romans 9:25 means in the Hosea-section of the twelve minor prophets. [GLR: While it is true that there were no chapter and book divisions in Paul's time, so he like his contemporaries had to cite passages by name of author or by section title, it is hardly true, as Burchard thinks, that Paul did not even know there was a book of Hosea, as such.]

Piper, John, "Prolegomena to Understanding Romans 9:14,15: An Interpretation of Exodus 33:19," *Journal of the Evangelical Theological Society* 22:3 (September 1979), p.203-216.
> In order to appreciate Paul's use of the Exodus passage, a thorough study of the meaning of the Old Testament passage in its context is undertaken. Piper concludes that the point of Paul's quotation (in harmony with its original use in its Old Testament context) is not to demonstrate how God acted in any one particular instance, or how He acts in principle in certain situations, but rather is a declaration of the nature of God which underlies His decrees and His acts.

Hanson, A.T., "Vessels of Wrath or Instruments of Wrath?: Romans 9:22,23," *Journal of Theological Studies* 32:2 (October 1982), p.433-443.
> Urges that "instruments" would be a better translation in this place, since the use of that word would better guard against the idea that it is some preordained final destiny of either saved or lost that is the topic of this passage. The hypothesis is supported by appeal to rabbinic interpretations of Isaiah 13:5 and Jeremiah 27:50, modern commentaries on Romans, and the theological argument of the epistle itself.

Cranfield, C.E.B., "Romans 9:30-10:4," *Interpretation* 34:1 (January 1980), p.70-74.
> Holds that the Jews were right in pursuing the Law (9:32a), but that they erred in emphasizing the works of the Law while failing to see that the Law was pointing them to Christ (9:32b). Understands *telos* at Romans 10:4 to mean "goal," rather than "fulfillment" or "termination." Discusses the church's duty to unbelieving Jews.

Chapter Ten

Refoule, Francois, "Romains 10:4: Encore Une Fois," *Review Biblique* 91:3 (1984), p.321-350.
> Reviewed first are the interpretations of "Christ is the end of the law" (Romans 10:4) offered by others: (1) the end of its impossibility to give life; (2) the end of its curses; (3) the end of its misuse; and (4) the goal of the law. Refoule offers a fifth interpretation – Christ is the termination of Jewish exclusivism when it comes to salvation. Now that Christ has come, salvation is available to non-Jews as well.

-----, "Note sur Romains 9:30-33," *Review Biblique* 92:2 (1985), p.161-186.
> Urges that 9:30-33 is an exact parallel to Romans 10:1-6, and thus is further evidence to corroborate the author's interpretation of 10:4, that what is new about "faith" now that Christ has come is that it is no longer restricted just to Israel. Israel's mistake was to go on thinking salvation was something exclusively Jewish, now that Christ has come.

Rhyne, C. Thomas, "*Nomos Dikaiosynes* and the Meaning of Romans 10:4," *Catholic Bib-*

lical Quarterly 47:3 (1985), p.486-499.

> Rhyne's thesis is that the key to the meaning of 10:4 is to be discovered by examining the entire section of Romans (9:30 to 10:21). He interprets "law of righteousness" in 9:31 as having reference to the Law of Moses, and then affirms that the whole passage deals with Israel's disobedience to that Law. Such disobedience, of course, is incompatible with righteousness by faith. Still, the Law promised righteousness to all, and it is Christ who brings that promise to its goal.

Seifrid, Mark A., "Paul's Approach to the Old Testament in Romans 10:6-8," *Trinity Journal*, 6:1 (1985), p.3-37.

> Denies that Paul is using the *pesher* technique of Qumran as he makes his bold connection between Deuteronomy 30:11-14 and the advent, resurrection, and apostolic preaching of Christ. Paul's use of Deuteronomy 30 is not out of harmony with the book of Deuteronomy as a whole, and his insertion of the phrase "that is" before his Christological interpretation shows his explanation is completely unrelated to the Qumran *pesher* technique.

Rickards, R.R., "The translation of *dia rhematos Christou* ('through the word of Christ') in Romans 10:17," *Bible Translator* 27:4 (1976), p.447,448.

> Most translations render *rhēma* at Romans 10:17 as "word, saying." Rickards proposes that *rhēma* can also mean "a thing, a matter, an event, a happening," and that the whole phrase means "the happening of Christ, the fact of Christ," i.e., His whole life, death, and resurrection. Thus he defends a modern expression "the Christ-event" and supposes that faith is the response made to the preaching of the Christ-event.

Chapter Eleven

Baxter, A.G., and Zeisler, J.A., "Paul and Aboriculture: Romans 11:17-24," *Journal for the Study of the New Testament* 24 (1985), p.25-32.

> Paul's illustration of grafting wild branches onto cultivated stock has received varied reactions. Some have claimed it is impossible; others have claimed it was "against nature" but deliberately used to stress the miraculous nature of the operation. The writers show the practice was not only possible but successful, widespread, and well-known in the Greco-Roman world. It rejuvenated an aging or diseased cultivated tree – the exact point Paul wants as he would explain God's desires with reference to Israel as a nation.

Aus, Roger D., "Paul's Travel Plans to Spain and the 'Full Number of the Gentiles' of Romans 11:25," *Novum Testamentum* 21:3 (July 1979), p.232-262.

> Isaiah 66:19 (where Tarshish, a city in Spain, is named as the first place where the "redeemed" would go to proclaim the Lord's glory among the nations) and Jewish traditions looked forward to the time when Gentiles from all nations would come to Jerusalem with their gifts. The Gentile churches east of Italy are already going with their gifts (Romans 15:16). All that remains is for Paul to go to Spain, win some to Christ, and then have them also take their offerings to Jerusalem. Thus, the commission to take the gospel "to the ends of the earth" will be fulfilled, and the full number of the Gentiles would come in.

De Villiers, J.L., "The Salvation of Israel According to Romans 9-11," *Neotestamentica* 15 (1981), p.199-221.

> Divides Romans 9-11 into seven sections, which are then examined. Concludes that Paul is demonstrating that the church of the Gentiles has come to occupy the place of unbelieving Israel as God's instrument of evangelism, while at the same time insisting that God's interest in the redemption of Israel has not diminished.

Cooper, Craig, "Romans 11:25,26," *Restoration Quarterly* 21:2 (1978), p.84-94.
> Because fleshly Israel had rejected Christ by their own free choice, God had judicially hardened all who rejected His gracious gift. Romans 11:11-32 provides the context for an interpretation of 11:25,26. Proposes that Paul uses parallelism here: verse 25 is parallel to 11:11,12; verse 26 is parallel to 11:17-24, and both verses serve as a summary statement of what went before. Now the mystery is clearer: God's mercy is for everyone, but He has asked of men one thing – that all put their trust in the Messiah, the Lord and Savior Jesus Christ.

Guthrie, Shirley C., "Romans 11:25-32," *Interpretation* 38:3 (1984), p.286-291.
> Paul is said to give us guidelines for approaching Christian-Jewish issues (theological, moral, political, human) of today. Considers election or predestination the fundamental issue at stake in this passage. Paul is seen as emphasizing (1) the predestination of the community; (2) the unity of the church and Israel as the people of God; and (3) the large number of the elect. God can predestine the role reversals now seen by Gentiles and Jews, and the writer urges Christians to build hope for the coming kingdom of God.

Horne, Charles M., "The Meaning of the Phrase 'and thus all Israel will be Saved' (Romans 11:26)," *Journal of the Evangelical Theological Society* 21:4 (December 1978), p.329-334.
> When Paul uses the terminology "all Israel will be saved," he means to refer to the full number of elect Jews whom it pleases God to bring into His kingdom throughout the ages until the end of time. "All Israel" and the remnant according to the election of grace (Romans 11:5) should be seen as synonymous expressions. "All Israel" does not refer to the nation in its entirety.

Ponsot, H., "Et ainsi tout Israel sera sauve: Rom. 11:26a," *Revue Biblique* 89:3 (1982), p.406-417.
> The expression "all Israel" in 11:26 refers to spiritual Israel, not to Israel according to the flesh. Rejects the classic interpretation of the text (i.e., it refers to the conversion [or return] of Israel) in favor of the interpretation advanced by Augustine.

Chapter Twelve

Sauer, Jurgen, "Traditionsgeschichtliche Erwagungen zu den Synoptischen und Paulinischen Wiedervergeltungsverzicht," *Zeitschrift fur die New Testamentliche Wissenschaft* 76:1-2 (1985), p.1-28.
> In the debate about the sources of the New Testament writings, Sauer affirms that Paul preserves the older and more authentic sayings of Jesus in Romans 12:14-21 than does Luke 6:27-28. He also supposes that the material in chapter 12 that did not come from Jesus is to be traced to Old Testament wisdom literature, to Hellenistic popular philosophy, and to Hellenistic Judaism. He also affirms that the material was not originally circulated with reference to Jesus, but was later put into His mouth by a people looking for standards of conduct befitting the end-time.

Chapter Thirteen

Bruce, F.F., "Paul and the Powers that Be," *Bulletin of the John Rylands Library* 66:2 (1984), p.78-96.
> Examines Romans 13:1-7. Argues, contrary to J. Kallas and W. Munro, for the authenticity of Romans 13:1-7. In "the powers that be," understands Paul (contrary to O. Cullmann) to have reference to human rulers appointed by God. Holds that in Romans 13, Paul is teaching Christians to respect their government, to yield to its authority, and to give it what is due it.

Chapters Fourteen and Fifteen

Omanson, Roger L., "The 'Weak' and the 'Strong' and Paul's Letter to the Roman Christians," *Bible Translator* 33:1 (January 1982), p.106-114.
> Urges that the weak are Jewish Christians, and the strong are Gentile Christians. Also affirms that the translation of several passages (outside of chapter 14 and 15) which also address the same two groups, are so translated as to obscure or change the meaning.

Rauer, M., "Die 'Schwachen' in Korinth und Rom nach den Paulusbriefen," *Biblische Studien* 21:2-3 (1923). Frieburg im Breisgau: Herder, 1923.
> Rauer urges that the strong and weak brothers are individuals, rather than whole house-churches or parties. He identified the weak as being *Gentile* Christians whose practice of abstinence from meat stemmed from their prior religious background in the Gnostic, Hellenistic mystery religions. Their weakness in faith consisted in the fact that they were not convinced, now that they were Christians, that they could continue to be pleasing to God without abstinence from all meat. Other helpful matters found in Rauer include: (1) his summary of patristic, medieval, and modern research on the identification of the "weak"; (2) his arguments against identifying the "weak" as being exclusively Jews, Essenes, Pythagorians, or antinomians; (3) his emphasis on the mildness of tone that Paul employs in Romans 14:1ff; (4) his identification of the "days" as fast days rather than Sabbaths or ceremonial holy days. Of less permanent value is his discussion of whether the "weak" abstained from wine, for the arguments (i.e., if the weak abstained from wine, there could be no celebration of the Lord's Supper) advanced are less than convincing.

Chapter Sixteen

Fabrega, V., "War Junia(s), der hervorragende Apostel (Rom.16:7), eine Frau?" *Jahrbuch fur Antike und Christentum* 27-28 (1984-1985), p.47-64.
> Discusses the derivation of this Latin name in the Hellenistic world of the Roman empire, and also the meaning of "fellow prisoner." It is not certain that Junia(s) was Jewish or had been imprisoned for the gospel. Concludes that Andronicus and Junia(s) were themselves distinguished apostles. This article also includes a review of how this verse was treated in Greek and Latin church fathers.

Lampe, Peter, "Iunia/Iunias: Sklavenherkunft im Kreise der vorpaulinischen Apostel (Rom. 16:7)," *Zeitschrift fur die New Testamentliche Wissenschaft* 76:1-2 (1985), p.132-134.
> Suggests that the *Iounian* (whether male or female) whom Paul greets is a freed slave or slave of Caesar's household who formerly belonged to the household of Junias. This slave of Jewish ancestry was "outstanding" among the apostles who preceded Paul in the Syro-Palestinian area. Also offers the opinion that this man or woman was imprisoned with Paul at Ephesus before Romans was written.

Elliott, J.K., "The Language and Style of the Concluding Doxology to the Epistle to the Romans," *Zeitschrift fur die New Testamentliche Wissenschaft* 72:1-2 (1981), p.124-130.
> Alleges that while a study of the 50+ word vocabulary of Romans 16:25-27 reveals some vocabulary regularly found in Paul, the doxology is not likely to have been written by Paul himself since too many of the terms are unusual or unique. Suggests some editor of Romans used a late 1st century or early 2nd century liturgy, itself influenced by the "post-Pauline pastorals," as a suitable climax to either a 14-chapter or a 16-chapter version of Romans.

ACKNOWLEDGMENTS

Permission has been sought and granted to quote excerpts from the following publications:

The Scripture quotations contained herein, unless otherwise noted, are from the *New American Standard Bible*, copyrighted 1960, 1962, 1963, 1968, 1971, 1972, 1973, 1975, 1977 by the Lockman Foundation.

ACU PRESS, Abilene, Texas
The Letter of Paul to the Romans, by Richard A. Batey. Volume 7, Living Word Commentary. Published by ACU Press, Abilene, Texas. Used by permission.

AUGSBURG PUBLISHING / WARTBURG PRESS, Minneapolis, Minnesota
Excerpts reprinted by permission from *The Interpretation of St. Paul's Epistle to the Romans*, by R.C.H. Lenski. Copyrighted 1945 Wartburg Press. Copyright Augsburg Publishing House.

BAKER BOOK HOUSE, Grand Rapids, Michigan
Evangelical Dictionary of Theology, edited by Walter A. Elwell. c.1984.
Baker's Dictionary of Theology, edited by E.F. Harrison. c.1960.

BANNER OF TRUTH TRUST, Carlisle, Pennsylvania
Romans: A Digest of Reformed Comment, by Geoffrey B. Wilson. c.1969.

BEACON HILL PRESS OF KANSAS CITY
Beacon Dictionary of Theology, edited by Richard S. Taylor. c.1983.

BETHANY HOUSE PUBLISHERS, Minneapolis, Minnesota
Excerpts reprinted by permission from *If Ye Continue*, by Guy F. Duty. Published and copyright 1966 and 1987, Bethany House Publishers, Minneapolis, Minnesota, 55438.

BROADMAN PRESS, Nashville, Tennessee
Ray Summers, "Contemporary Approaches to New Testament Study," in *The Broadman Bible Commentary*, edited by Cliffton J. Allen. Copyright 1969 by Broadman Press, Nashville, Tennessee. Volume 8, p.55,56. All rights reserved. Used by permission.

CBS EDUCATIONAL AND PROFESSIONAL PUBLISHING / HOLT, RINEHART & WINSTON, New York, New York
Excerpts from *Basic Christian Doctrines*, edited by Carl F. H. Henry. Copyrighted 1962 by Carl F. H. Henry. Reprinted by permission of Henry Holt and Company, Inc.

JOHN KNOX PRESS, Atlanta, Georgia
Handbook of Biblical Criticism. Second Edition, p.87,88 by R.N. Soulen. Copyright 1976 and 1981 John Knox Press. Used by Permission.

SERVANT BOOKS, Ann Arbor, Michigan
Excerpts from *The New Bible Theorists*, copyrighted 1983 by George A. Kelly. Published by Servant Publications, P.O. Box 8617, Ann Arbor, Michigan, 48107. Used by permission.

ZONDERVAN PUBLISHING HOUSE / ASBURY PRESS, Grand Rapids, Michigan

Commentary on the St. Paul's Epistle to the Romans, by F. L. Godet. c.1956.

Excerpts taken from *The Zondervan Pictorial Encyclopedia of the Bible*, edited by Merrill C. Tenney.   Copyright 1975 by The Zondervan Corporation.   Used by permission.

Excerpts taken from *Expositor's Bible Commentary*, edited by Frank E. Gaebelein. Copyright 1979 by The Zondervan Corporation.   Used by permission.

Excerpts taken from *The New International Dictionary of the Christian Church*, General Editor, James D. Douglas.   Copyright 1974 and 1978 by The Zondervan Corporation.   Used by permission.

Excerpts taken from *The Zondervan Pictorial Dictionary of the Bible*, edited by Merrill C. Tenney.   Copyright 1963, 1964, and 1967 by The Zondervan Publishing House. Used by permission.

Excerpts taken from *The Epistle to the Romans*, by W.E. Vine.   c.1965.   Used by permission of Zondervan Publishing House.

The Epistle to the Romans, by William Sanday.   c.1957.

Excerpts taken from *A Contemporary Wesleyan Theology*, edited by Charles W. Carter. Copyright 1983 by The Zondervan Corporation.   Used by permission.

The author has sought to locate and secure permission to reprint copyrighted material in this book. If any such acknowledgements have been inadvertently omitted, the author would appreciate receiving information so that proper credit may be given in future printings.

INDEX OF AUTHORS, IDEAS AND TOPICS IN ROMANS

(Roman numerals refer to materials found in the Introductory Studies.   Arabic numbers refer to comments on the text.   Arabic numbers followed by ff. refer to the pages following.   Arabic numbers followed by n refer to footnotes found on that page.)

INDEX OF GREEK SYNONYMS

OTHER BOOKS BY GARETH L. REESE

New Testament History: *Acts* (097-176-5235)

New Testament Epistles: *1 Corinthians* (097-176-5251)

New Testament Epistles: *2 Corinthians and Galatians* (097-176-5278)

New Testament Epistles: *Paul's Prison Epistles* (099-845-1800)

New Testament Epistles: *1 & 2 Thessalonians* (099-845-186X)

New Testament Epistles: *1 & 2 Timothy and Titus* (097-176-5227)

New Testament Epistles: *Hebrews* (097-176-5219)

New Testament Epistles: *1 & 2 Peter and Jude* (097-176-5243)

New Testament Epistles: *James & 1,2,3 John* (097-176-526X)

Order from:
Scripture Exposition Books
803 McKinsey Place
Moberly, MO, 65270
www.glreese@cccb.edu

www.ingramcontent.com/pod-product-compliance
Lightning Source LLC
Chambersburg PA
CBHW061956090426
42811CB00006B/962